Pulpit Publications 1660–1782

being a new edition of

"THE PREACHER'S ASSISTANT"

VOLUME I

THE INDEX VOLUME

Pulpit Publications 1660–1782

being a new edition of

"THE PREACHER'S ASSISTANT"

A Bibliography
With Introductory Matter,
Indexes, Statistical Tables,
and other Interpretive Apparatus

by

John Gordon Spaulding

from Records Compiled by
John Cooke (1783), Sampson Letsome (1753), William Crowe (1668)
and some Anonymous others (1734 and 1751)
in consequence of an example set by the earliest Keepers
of Bodley's Library at Oxford:
Jean Vernevil (1637) and Thomas James (1635)

VOLUME I

THE INDEX VOLUME

Norman Ross Publishing Inc.
New York, New York

Library of Congress Cataloging-in-Publication Data

Pulpit publications, 1660-1782 : being a new edition of "The preacher's assistant" / now edited, with introductory matter, indexes, statistical tables, and other interpretive apparatus, by John Gordon Spaulding.
532, 462, 524, 482, 562, 470 p. cm.
"From records compiled by John Cooke (1783), Sampson Letsome (1753), William Crowe (1668), and some anonymous others (1734 and 1751) in consequence of an example set by the earliest keepers of Bodley's Library at Oxford: Jean Vernevil (1637) and Thomas James (1635)."
Contents: v. 1. Index vol. -- v. 2. John Cooke's books -- v. 3. Biblical books -- v. 4 Authors of sermons -- v. 5. Publication dates -- v. 6. Chronological list of sermons.
ISBN 0-88354-126-2
1. Preaching--Great Britain--History--17th century--Sources. 2. Preaching--Great Britain--History--18th century--Sources. 3. Sermons. English--Abstracts. I. Spaulding, John Gordon.
BV4208.G7P85 1996
016.251'00941--dc20

NORMAN ROSS PUBLISHING INC.
330 West 58th Street, New York, NY 10019
Printed in the United States of America

TABLE OF CONTENTS

Volume I

AUTHOR'S PREFACE

John Cooke's "The Preacher's Assistant" is of peculiar interest for several reasons:

(1) Pulpit literature was of seminal importance for the literature and thought (including scientific thought) of the times, and played a major role in politics throughout the period.

(2) Cooke's catalogue of this literature is remarkably complete, and each record is densely packed with informative data.

(3) The tradition in which Cooke's work lies formed the backbone out of which great research libraries have grown and from which union catalogues stem.

By translating the data from Cooke's two volumes into six volumes, the data are laid out in ways that make them accessible for purposes that Cooke did not have in view. His catalogue of sermons is herein transformed from a *Preacher's Assistant* to an *Historian's Assistant*. These volumes are for those who wish to search out the vital relations between religion and literature, philosophy, science, and politics in the seventeenth and eighteenth centuries or, more generally, are making bibliographical, philological, and economic studies concerning the period.

The usefulness of the sermon catalogue in historical studies is enhanced by the fact that the data within the catalogue come close to being exhaustive in regard to certain aspects of the period; in the form presented within the present edition, novel statistical studies of the data are quite possible. Transformation of Cooke's "The Preacher's Assistant" into a source-work for historical studies should not, of course, diminish its usefulness for students of theology.

The tradition within which Cooke's work has a place is outlined on the title page of the present volume. Study of relations between his work and antecedent works in the tradition is fascinating, and a curious reader may wish to pursue further historical details. The relevant names listed are those of Thomas James, William Crowe, and Sampson Letsome.

The compilation and analysis of indexes to Cooke's work relied heavily on the use of modern computers. From my experience, however, I judge that a computer, used for scholarly purposes, saves time for no one! It does make possible things which have never before been possible, and which may contribute to the Humanities, but its product does not satisfy the soul.

I wish to express my thanks to the Canada Council for its grants-in-aid of this work in its early states, and the Committee on Research at the University of British Columbia for grants in the early and middle states of my work. Much thanks goes to student research assistants who interpreted with great skill the directions I gave them, and who implemented them excellently in computer programming and in other ways. My appreciation goes to the University of British Columbia Computing Center for much, much computer time, and to its staff for their frequent help. Particularly, I want to thank three past directors: Vern Dettwiler, James Kennedy and A. G. Fowler, and a member of the staff, Frank Flynn.

The great libraries which have given me cooperation, access and valued assistance include the Huntington Library, the William Andrews Clark Library, the British Museum Library (now the British Library), the Dr. Williams's Library and the New College Library (now the Divinity School Library of the University of London). My special thanks go to my family for their patience and appreciation of my responsibilities during the years I was deeply involved in this major undertaking.

John Gordon Spaulding
Vancouver, British Columbia, August 1989

Posthumous Addendum by Spaulding's Literary Executor:

Names of people who helped Dr. Spaulding in many essential ways are listed herewith, but no acknowledgment on paper can adequately express the appreciation due to these individuals, whose help was crucial to the fulfillment of this project: Hilde Colinbrander, Peter Madderon, Linda Ruus, Pamela Brown, Mrs. Epp, Miss Matheson, Linda Lowe, Tony Buckland and Alan Lamb.

Alan C. James, Facilitator
Vancouver, British Columbia
January 1995

PUBLISHER'S PREFACE

In the late 1960s, Jeffrey Norton, then president of CCM Information Systems, a division of MacMillan Publishing, met Dr. John Gordon Spaulding for the first time and was informed about his attempt to computerize John Cooke's 18th-Century work, "The Preacher's Assistant." Norton was an innovator and leader in the burgeoning field of database publishing, which was then in relative infancy. He was, in fact, one of the founders of the Information Industry Association (IIA) and its first president. Norton immediately felt that Spaulding's work needed and deserved to be published and he offered him a contract, but Spaulding wasn't quite finished with his work. In fact, he was never quite ready to say he was finished because he always felt that the work was less than perfect, and he maintained this attitude until his death in 1993.

In 1971 Norton was invited to join Holt, Rinehart & Winston, where I was his "right hand." We offered Spaulding a contract with Holt, but he deferred. In 1972 Norton left Holt to form Jeffrey Norton Publishers and a third offer was sent. In 1973 I formed Clearwater Publishing, which, in 1987, became Norman Ross Publishing (NRP). In these years Norton made several invitations to Spaulding to publish the work, but as the direction of Norton's activities turned more toward audio and video, he suggested that I might want to pursue the matter. We offered Spaulding a Clearwater contract and then an NRP contract.

In a sense, Spaulding never did finish what was essentially his life's work. Although we met several times over a period of 20 years, he didn't feel it was morally correct to sign a contract until he was completely satisfied with his work. The last time I met him was just after his brother's funeral in Washington, D.C. The last time I spoke with him was shortly before his own. He no longer could climb steps, but he seemed still to be working on this project. And he still wasn't ready to sign the contract. However, he introduced me to his daughter, Amy Spaulding, whom he named his literary executor. He left instructions with her, and with Alan James (a family friend and computer expert who had helped him considerably in the last several years of the project, and who "finished" it after his death), to sign the contract if he did not live to complete the work himself.

Cooke was clearly a seminal work in historical and theological scholarship, worthy of devoting a life to increasing its usefulness. Spaulding tried not only to expand Cooke's data, but also to dot every "i" and cross every "t" that Cooke left undone. He analyzed not only Cooke's methodology, but also the practices of his typesetters and proofreaders, although some of Spaulding's description of these details have been omitted from the present edition. Now it remains for future scholars to utilize and judge Spaulding's work.

We believe that Spaulding has indeed changed Cooke's work into "The Historian's Assistant" and that his perseverance--and ours--will be justified. Our thanks to Jeffrey Norton for his vision and foresight when he met Spaulding a quarter of a century ago; to the Spaulding children, Amy and Stephen, for entrusting us with their father's lifetime work; to Alan James for answering our every question, though he came into this story late in the day; and to my father, Robert E. Ross, who edited all of the prefatory materials and prepared the six volumes for publication. We also wish to express our appreciation to The British Library for granting permission to publish Mr. Cooke's work from the microfilm Prof. Spaulding had made there in 1963 (the present Volume II).

Certainly it is sad that neither Gordon nor his wife Hildegarde lived to see the printed edition. We thank him for his dedication and devotion to this worthy purpose.

Norman A. Ross
New York, NY
March 1996

A BIOGRAPHICAL NOTE ON JOHN GORDON SPAULDING

J. Gordon Spaulding was born in Springfield, Illinois, in 1908 to a family with New England Puritan roots. My father was an earnest child, often chided by his easygoing father for being too serious. When the family moved to Pasadena, California, he became involved with the Pasadena Playhouse, where he fell in love with literature in the form of drama, and where he played Malvolio in *Twelfth Night*, having learned to balance his seriousness with a sense of humor.

Gordon's scholarly bent was recognized by prosperous family friends, who helped pay for his education at Pomona College in Claremont, California. He reveled in the philosophical and literary debate he encountered in college, and he continued in the academic world, earning his doctorate in 1945 from the University of California at Berkeley with his dissertation, "The Problems of Poetic Truth: Poetry and the Myth of the Greek Philosophers." In 1946 he accepted a position at the University of British Columbia in Vancouver, Canada, where he remained for the rest of his professional life, retiring as Professor Emeritus in 1973.

His wife provided a psychiatrist's broad outlook on culture and religion, and brought him to see how traditional rituals, while they may seem intellectually empty to some, can provide assurance to those who wish to counteract a seemingly careless, imprecise world. He conveyed to his children a profound respect for people who try to lead a Christian life without self-righteousness, and in later life he even came to rejoin the church.

Gordon devoted much time to the study of Milton and the Romantic Poets, particularly their intellectual debt to the religious ferment of their time. While on sabbatical he discovered in the British Museum a compilation of all of the sermons that had been printed in England between 1660 and 1782. The two volumes --Cooke's "The Preacher's Assistant"--provided a catalog of the changing religious concerns and interpretations of timeless Judeo-Christian themes, and a record of influences on contemporary thought in literature and philosophy. He devoted the last quarter century of his life to making the information in these rare volumes more accessible to other scholars.

The subject of access to information had always engaged his interest, as evidenced by an international symposium on "Man's Right to Knowledge" that he helped organize at Columbia University as part of its 1954 bicentennial celebration. In the 1960s he chaired a committee of the American Documentation Association (soon to become the American Society for Information Science) to help open to many the intellectual material previously available to only a few. He foresaw the promise that new techniques in information processing held for the Humanities and he believed the material in Cooke would provide an excellent prototype.

My father set rigid and extremely high standards for himself, and felt it important to assess every discrepancy in the original entries before "Pulpit Publications" could be published. He died in 1993, still engaged in this aspect of the project. With the help of a longstanding family friend, Alan James, Norman Ross Publishing is issuing this work--perhaps in a form less than its Platonic ideal--but confident of its utility to other scholars in many fields.

Amy E. Spaulding
New York, NY
1995

METHODOLOGY

Dr. John Gordon Spaulding began this work in 1961 after a visit to the British Museum Library where he rediscovered a 1783 copy of "The Preacher's Assistant" by John Cooke. Seeing the possibility of gaining new information about the history of that period, Dr. Spaulding correlated the 25,000 entries in Cooke's Volume I with the 9,000 entries in Volume II, using computer technology. By 1966 he had both volumes encoded and began the laborious process of matching the two sets of records. He found many discrepancies between the two and, using constantly upgraded computer systems, proceeded to match as many records as possible.

To determine the completeness of Cooke's coverage of sermons, Spaulding made comparisons between Cooke's listings and those of other sermon literature now held by four research libraries, selected because those four have large holdings of the literature in editions of that period. The four libraries were the Huntington and the William Andrews Clark libraries in southern California, and the Dr. Williams's and New College libraries in London, England.

For comparisons of completeness, twelve sample years were chosen, a decade apart throughout the period, representing 120 years. All sermons published in those sample years that were held by one or more of those libraries were compared with Cooke's listings in regard to the details by which Cooke had identified sermons. The comparisons involved a total of 857 different sermons preached by a total of 283 authors. These were contained in 357 different publications, of which 324 were single-sermon (s.s.) editions, and 30 were collective (coll.) editions. The use of Dr. Williams's Library for comparison purposes is not a duplication of the work Cooke had done there; that library has since greatly enlarged its holdings of 17th- and 18th-century imprints, so Dr. Spaulding's investigations there resulted in meaningful figures.

In a few issues of periodicals of Cooke's period, comparisons were made between Cooke's listings and those of then newly published works under the heading, "Divinity," and these figures support those in the library listings.

The contributions which the present edition makes to the tradition of Cooke's listings were made possible by the invention of computers. In addition to the now obvious methods of exhaustive indexing and statistical analyses, the computer used for this edition in production of editorial apparatus may be of special interest to librarians and other bibliographers, for it may prove innovative. The methods are described in Dr. Spaulding's paper, "The Sameness of Meaning and Where and How to Find it in Some Data," delivered at a conference in May 1976 at Laval University, Quebec, Canada, a copy of which was deposited at the Huntington Library.

This computer theory led to a program to compare all records in Cooke's Volume I with all records in his Volume II to determine which should and did refer to the same thing, and which did not and/or should not do so. Where differences were found, the program composed other records containing all non-redundant data from both sources. The first step produced the information conveyed by the symbols in the column headed "Sources Compared" in Volumes III, IV and VI. The last step produced Volume V.

Enlarged photocopies of Cooke's two volumes were made from different copies of the original edition, one in the British Museum Library and the other in the Yale University Library. Two operators, working independently, transcribed this data into machine-readable form, and a computer was programmed to show where a difference occurred between the two transcripts. Each difference was examined by a graduate student and, where an error was found, it was corrected. The data now represents Cooke's volumes correctly.

The author, of course, intervened between the computer and the source data at several points: in defining fields of information and in decisions regarding errors of transcription. He also examined all dubious matchings of records between Cooke's two volumes, and decided which should be allowed. Where the author's reasons are not obvious, they are indicated in footnotes of Volume V.

Concerning historical matters, some possible uses of statistical analysis of an index may be found in Volume I, illustrated in the Appendix to Index C to Volume III. For special examples, see those concerning sermons preached before a king, before a queen, or before king and queen, preached at a hospital or infirmary, or before governors thereof. Other illustrations may be found in the Appendix to Index D.

Concerning the great amount of time and effort Dr. Spaulding expended in this project, and his extreme care in establishing accuracy, it is hoped and expected that many academic specialists will find his innovative work of genuine value.

Locating the Texts of the Sermons

Although this present bibliographic edition does not contain the sermons themselves, it can be used to identify, through the British Library catalogue, the copies that the Library holds of those listed by Cooke. Although Cooke does not always give titles, and the British Library catalogue does not always give the texts, there is sufficient information to guide a reader to the correct publication, using author's name, format of publication, etc. To establish this as a viable method, Dr. Spaulding traced back a sample of 120 entries from Cooke.

Using entries in his Volume V, Spaulding referred to Donald Wing's "Short-title catalog of books printed in England, Scotland, Ireland, Wales and British America, and of English books printed in other countries, 1641-1700," which is, in effect, the union catalogue of British and American library holdings of such publications. From the listings which Wing indicated could be found at the British Museum, Spaulding then examined the British Museum catalogue, which then led to the book itself. For items not in the British Museum (now the British Library), he proceeded similarly at the Bodleian and Cambridge University libraries.

Dr. Spaulding's results indicated that at least four out of five of the entries he searched for in the years 1660, 1661, 1680, and hence, presumably for 1660-1700, can be identified; the relevant books can be located by proceeding through *Wing* to other catalogues. To determine if this ratio of success applies to the years 1701-1782, where Wing is not pertinent, Spaulding traced twelve entries from his Volume V, which occupied one hour of intensive investigation. He found that he could, with certainty, specify the shelf-mark (call number) for eight of the twelve works he traced during the hour. Two of the twelve were not to be found anywhere; for another, he found a probable shelf-mark; and he determined that the twelfth was not in the British Museum.

This method is a simple modification of typical methods of proceeding from a bibliography through a library catalog to the book on the shelf. However, if the proper entry does not easily spring into view, the researcher must give attention to the book format and date of publication. Under the name of the author, or likely variants, he scans the catalogue entries for a publication of the format and date given by Cooke. For these entries he consider the brief titles given by Wing, or the abbreviated titles given by the British Museum catalogue, in relation to Cooke's listings regarding occasion, audience and subject matter. If Cooke's data are insufficient, he then considers the titles in relation to the biblical text of the sermon, although this would not be necessary in most instances.

One of the values of Cooke's works is that he is not redundant among bibliographers; he gives information which no other bibliographer does. He gives biblical text; he shows that a publication was a sermon; and he often indicates the subject mater of the sermon better than does Wing. It must be clarified that this present six-volume work stands on its own merits as an immediate source of information, absent the need for consulting original sermon texts.

GUIDE TO THE SIX VOLUMES

The "Pulpit Publications," based on John Cooke's listings of sermons published during the years 1660 through 1782, will serve as a key to social, economic, political and historical circumstances at that time in the British Isles. Sermons of that era were replete with statements concerning prevailing conditions, and can now serve researchers who are investigating vital relations between religion and the fields of literature, philosophy, science, philology, etc., and especially the field of historical theology.

John Cooke's work, published in 1783 by Clarendon Press, consists of two volumes. The first, consisting of 487 numbered pages, contains a listing of preachers, categorized by Book, Chapter and Verse of the Old and New Testaments. Volume II, with 425 pages, contains a brief identification of each preacher, a title for each sermon he delivered (with its biblical reference), and the library where a copy of the printed sermon reposed during that period. Cooke's work was titled, "The Preacher's Assistant," and was intended as a theological source and a guide for preachers who followed.

Volume II contains self-explanatory listings and is now published as Volume II of this six-volume set. On the other hand, Cooke's Volume I contains a wealth of reference data, primarily in obscure alphabetical and numerical abbreviations and codes. This material in Cooke's Volume I, compared with and combined with the voluminous data in Volume II, has been expatiated and clarified in the other five volumes of the present publication by Dr. John Gordon Spaulding. Therefore, the original version of Volume I has not been reprinted.

Cooke did not attempt to list every edition in which a specific sermon was printed, but in relation to the total number of sermons delivered and published in England during that period of 122 years, his listing is nearly complete. His listings included 92% of all sermons given in England, and many from Ireland and Scotland, as well as some from the colonies. Of those sermons given in England, his listings include 99% of those by Anglican preachers; about 82% of those by Nonconformist preachers; and about 10% of the Roman Catholic sermons during the reign of James II (1685-1688). Cooke's coverage of Quaker sermons, in relation to their total number, is difficult to estimate as they were seldom printed. His listing of those in Ireland appears to be quite comprehensive, while the list from Scotland is less so. However, for the latter two countries it is not possible to assign percentages.

John Cooke's remarkable book was based on previous publications of this nature by other authors and on intensive work he did himself in university and private libraries of his time. He had been Chaplain of Christ-Church, Oxford, and in his elevated standing had access to, and comprehensively recorded, the broadest existing sources of published sermons at various locations, including:

Oxford University, 21 libraries
Cambridge University, 10 libraries
Libraries of the British Museum, Doctor Williams, Eton College,
Sion College, St. Paul's Church.

Cooke's data are now available in this new edition for the benefit of present and future generations.

VOLUME I: The index. This volume serves as the index to Volumes III and V, with seven indexes to Volume III, and five indexes to Volume V. Each of the seven indexes leads to a single series of code numbers in Volume III, arranged in numerical order. The five indexes for Volume V provide varieties of access to the straight chronological listing in that book of sermons by date of publication and by alphabetical listing of authors within each year.

VOLUME II: The Life and Work of John Cooke. This is a reprint of Volume II of John Cooke's "The Preacher's Assistant" (1783), which contains an alphabetical listing by author, together with the listing of sermons given by each, and data concerning subject and location. (Cooke's Volume I is not being reprinted because all of the data in it have been thoroughly cross-indexed and cross-referenced in the five volumes of Spaulding's work.)

VOLUME III: Sermons arranged in sequence by biblical book, with the codes from the indexes in Volume I provided in straight numerical order throughout. This listing details the following: Chapter and Verse; Author; Date; Format of Publication; Subject or Occasion; Comparison of Source Records.

VOLUME IV: Alphabetical listing of authors, with data in columnar form paralleling that in Volume III.

VOLUME V: Year of publication of printed sermons, listed chronologically, with the specific year shown at the head of each page. For each such year the authors are listed alphabetically, with subsequent years in which that author is also listed. Original library location is also shown.

VOLUME VI: Chronological listing, with an individual line item for each sermon by each author.

ARBITRARY SYMBOLS USED IN VOLUMES III AND/OR IV AND VI

SYMBOLS THAT OCCUR IN, OR THAT REPRESENT SYMBOLS THAT OCCUR IN, THE FIRST VOLUME OF COOKE'S OWN WORK

*Author's Name: A single asterisk before an author's name is Cooke's symbol that the record in which it occurs did not appear within the set of records that was compiled and published thirty years earlier, in 1753, by Sampson Letsome, who gave his antecedent work the same title as John Cooke adopted in 1783 for his later work: The Preacher's Assistant.

Author's Name: Underscoring of an author's name represents the italic lettering which Cooke used to indicate that the author was a Nonconformist: i.e., a Dissenter from the Church of England.

<Author's Name>: Pointed brackets around an author's name represent square brackets which Cooke used in the same positions to indicate that he might be wrong about authorship.

Abbreviations: All abbreviations are copied from the source records. Cooke's "List of Abbreviations" is reproduced in the present volume on the pages indicated by the "Table of Contents". Aids to interpretation of Cooke's abbreviations will be found after the list.

SYMBOLS THAT DO NOT REPLICATE OR REPRESENT ANY OF COOKE'S ARBITRARY SYMBOLS

** Footnote Double asterisks occur before some footnotes. They indicate that the footnote is the present editor's. All footnotes that do not begin with double asterisks are Cooke's own.

Coded Text: The eight digits enclosed within pointed brackets in the column headed Coded Text within Volume III of the present edition designate the biblical text of the sermon, as follows: The first two digits designate a book within the Bible; the succeeding three digits, a chapter within that biblical book; and the final three digits, the verse at which the text begins within that chapter. An example follows:

<06005010> This code specifies (by its first two digits, 06) the sixth book of the Bible (which for Cooke's listings of sermons includes some of the Apocrypha), the fifth chapter of that book (by the succeeding three digits, 005), and the tenth verse of that chapter (by the final three digits, 010). Thus it designates any biblical text that begins with the verse 10 in Chapter V of the book of Joshua within the Bible.

The Index Volume of the present edition uses these code numbers to specify the biblical texts of the sermons to which the index refers. The last six digits within a coded text are easily interpreted by a reader: three for chapter, three for beginning verse. The first two digits, not so immmediately interpretable, are listed, each with the name of the biblical book to which it refers, within the front cover of each volume of the present edition.

SYMBOLS USED IN THE COLUMN "Sources Compared" WITHIN THIS VOLUME

Superscript numbers on this page and the next refer to Notes. These begin at the bottom of the next page, immediately below the list entitled Source Symbols.

The Notes define what is meant by the statement that two sources of a record agree or disagree about author's Name, biblical Text, printing Format, or publication Date. Note 13 states Causes of disagreement.

The Notes also explain how the symbols of comparison may assist readers in cross reference[1] from this volume to Volumes II and V in the present edition of Cooke's work. Volumes II and V are useful for readers who wish to proceed from listings in this work to cognate listings in library and other catalogues.

Wherever Sources Compared shows two sources of information concerning a sermon, information from both sources will be found within a composite record in Volume V, sometimes with an accompanying footnote by the present editor. Within the composite record readers will often find that Cooke's abbreviations which appear under Occasion or Subject in the present volume are expanded and clarified.

Following the Notes is a two-page description of the evolution of Volumes III, IV, V, and VI of this edition from comparison of source records. Users will understand the symbols better if they read it first.

Symbols of Comparison

Sources Compared	Explanation
<1C ---- 2C >	In their separate records of what the present editor has judged[2] to be the same sermon,[3] Cooke's Vol.I <1C> and his Vol.II <2C> agree[4] on four points: (1) its biblical text, (2) its author's name and conformity or nonconformity to Church of England, (3) format and (4) date of printing.
<1C T--- 2C >	The source records 1C and 2C disagree about biblical Text[5] of sermon; agree on other three points.
<1C -N-- 2C >	The source records 1C and 2C may not fully agree about Name[6] of author, or they disagree about the author's conformity or nonconformity to the Church of England. (Underscoring or italicization of author's name indicates author's nonconformity.) They do agree on the other three points.
<1C --F- 2C >	The source records 1C and 2C do not give same Format[7] of printing; agree on other three points.
<1C ---D 2C >	The source records 1C and 2C do not give same Date[8] of a printing; agree on other three points.
<1C ---I 2C >	The source records 1C and 2C do not give same date of printing, and the 1C record indicates, by giving a page and/or volume number, that the sermon was printed as an Item[9] in a collective edition.
<1C >	Cooke I records the sermon as published in a collective edition.[11] Cooke II does not itemize the contents of this collective edition.
<1C NULL>	Cooke I records the sermon as published in a single-sermon edition or other edition the contents of which Cooke II would normally itemize, but Cooke II does not itemize the sermon.
<NULL 2C >	Cooke II itemizes the sermon, but Cooke I does not list it.
<NAME N 2C >	Cooke II records the sermon as anonymous, but gives author's name or initials parenthetically. Cooke I lists the sermon only with author's name or initials, not as anonymous.
<NAME ? 2C >	Cooke II records the sermon as anonymous, without parenthetic inclusion of an author's name. In Vol. V the present editor points out similarity between the record for Anonymous and some record for a named author.

Source Symbols

Primary sources of the present volume

Symbol	Significance
<1C	Record in Cooke's Vol.I as published in 1783
<1CAP	Record in Cooke's APPENDIX to his Vol.I
<1CAD	1C, with data added from Cooke's list of ADDENDA
<1CER	1C, corrected in accordance with Cooke's ERRATA
<1CST	1C, with obvious misprint[12] re biblical Text corrected by present editor, Spaulding
<1CSY	1C, with obvious misprint[12] re Year corrected by S.
<1CSC	1C, with one or more Characters corrected by S.
<1CCC	1C, corrected in present edition to agree with Correlative records elsewhere in 1783 edition.
<1CIC	1C, faultily transcribed for present edition; resultant record later corrected to agree with 1C

Secondary sources of the present volume

Symbol	Significance
2C >	Record in Cooke's Volume II
2CAP>	Record in Cooke's APPENDIX to his Volume II
2CAD>	2C, with data added from Cooke's ADDENDA to II
2CER>	2C, corrected in accordance with Cooke's ERRATA
2CST>	2C, with obvious misprint[12] re biblical Text corrected by present editor, Spaulding
2CSY>	2C, with obvious misprint[12] re Year corrected by S.
2CSR	2C, with its information about biblical text Rewritten (but not altered in substance) by S. to permit data processing by computer.
2CSW	2C, with its items of information rearranged or otherwise reWritten by S. to facilitate computer-processing of its data regarding (1) alternative editions, or (2) a collective edition published in volumes of different dates, or (3) sermons itemized as contents of an edition that is identified in 2C.

<1LS A record in Letsome's Part One: *i.e.*, Part One of the edition of *The Preacher's Assistant* that was printed in 1753 for its editor, Sampson Letsome, Cooke's predecessor by thirty years.

(In initial preparation of copy for the present edition of Cooke's work, Letsome's Part One was used to fill, so far as it would serve to do so, a gap in Cooke's records of sermons on Ecclesiastes vii, verses 2 to 14, that were published in collective editions. [See page 125 in our Volume III.] Records of sermons published in single-sermon editions on these texts are supplied by Cooke's second volume. A similar gap in regard to sermons on texts in II Kings between chapter iv verse 1, author TRIMNEL, and chapter v verse 18 is filled from the same source by a list in the Appendix to our Volume III. Evidently Cooke or his printer lost two separate manuscript pages of Cooke's copy for his first volume. Each manuscript page probably held twenty-five records or a few more.)

Notes

1. Cross-reference to Vols. II and V. To identify a publication specified by date and format in the column headed Edition within the present volume, consult Volume II. This replicates a copy of Volume II of Cooke's work in its original 1783 edition. In it authors are listed with their titles, degrees, and clerical appointments so far as Cooke was able to learn these matters. Below each author's name therein, relevant publications that are specified in the present volume by date and format are listed in chronological order, often with further information about them. The arrangement of authors' names in Volume II is alphabetical in the eighteenth-century fashion: J's and I's are intermingled, and so are U's and V's. In Volume V of the present edition all publications that are listed in Volume II are relisted in chronological order, with editorial apparatus appended to each listing. For more information about cross-reference to Volume V, see Note 10.

Notes (continued)

2. Editor's judgment: The present editor's judgment about whether or not two source records concern the same sermon is based upon his estimate of the probabilities, and this estimate is based on his experience with Cooke's data. Some of his judgments may be wrong. The present edition lays his evidence open to examination by the reader.

3. Same sermon: The term "same sermon" is used loosely. A printed sermon may differ substantially from the "same" sermon as spoken. One copy of a sermon may differ in significant detail (because of damage to a title-page, a type-face, a signature, or an assembly of signatures in binding) from another copy of the same edition or issue. One edition of a sermon may differ from another in substance.

4. - = agree. A hyphen "-" indicates agreement between primary and secondary sources as follows:

   - biblical text of a sermon if one source shows the biblical passage chosen for text as beginning with the same verse of the same chapter of the same biblical book as the other does;

   - name of author if source data concerning name fulfill three conditions simultaneously:
     (a) identical indications of conformity or nonconformity to Church of England [italic or underscored letters in name indicate nonconformity],
     (b) identical spelling of surname,
     (c) identical spelling of first name[s] or standard abbreviation or initial in one record of first name more fully represented in the other,

     (N.B. If author's first name[s] or initial[s] is preceded by "Bp." or "Abp." in one record and not in the other, the records are not judged to be in agreement in regard to author's name because agreement about first name has not been checked by computer. Hence in such cases "N" appears in the place of "-" in respect to name under Sources Compared even though disagreement has not been found and is highly unlikely),

   - format of printing if both source records indicate same format;

   - date of edition if both source records indicate same year.

5. T = disagreement about biblical Text. In our Vol. V the differing textual citations are both shown within one record. If the difference is greater than a single verse in regard to where the text begins, the sermon is listed for both texts in our Vol. III Sermons Listed by Biblical Text. The secondary listing there bears the parenthesis "<See Fifth Vol. of Present Biblio.>".

6. N = disagreement about author's Name or about his conformity or nonconformity to Church of England. In our Vol. V the discrepant information that the two sources offer regarding these matters is presented within a single record. If the discrepancy is substantial, the sermon is listed for both names (or spellings of the same name) in our Vol. IV Sermons Listed by Authors' Names. (The secondary listing there contains the parenthesis "<See Fifth Vol. of Present Biblio.>".)

   All disagreements, or uncertainties about agreement, that produce the letter "N" in place of a hyphen "-" under Sources Compared are treated as substantial and hence result in secondary records as well as primary within Vol. IV except as follows:

   (a) Church of England: Disagreement in regard to whether an author is a Nonconformist, as indicated by underscoring (italicization) of his name, is not treated as substantial.

   (b) Surname: Disagreement about whether or not the final letter of an author's surname should be doubled (e.g., Burnett vs. Burnet) is not treated as substantial.

Notes (continued)

(c) Given name: Uncertain agreement about given name of Bp. or Abp. (as described in the parenthetic N.B. that closes discussion of name of author in note 3, above) is not disagreement of any kind, substantial or otherwise. It is merely uncertainty.

7. F = disagreement about Format of printing. In our Vol. V the differing statements of format are shown within a single record.

8. D = disagreement about date of publication. In our Vol. V the differing dates are shown within a single record. To find it, use either of the two methods of cross-reference -- Direct or Indirect -- that are described in Note 10.

9. I = disagreement about date of publication of a sermon that was printed as an Item within a collective edition. To find a composite record that shows the differing dates, use the method of Indirect cross-reference that is described in the first paragraph within Note 10, below.

10. To find a composite record in Vol. V: If Sources Compared shows the two sources of information in agreement about date, the composite record will be found in Vol. V under the same date as is shown in the present volume, which gives the 1C date. But if disagreement about date is indicated, the composite record will be found in Vol. V under the 2C date. To learn that date, a reader should turn to Vol. II, where the relevant 2C record may be recognized under author's name by the biblical text cited within it. After noting the date given within this record, he may proceed to Vol. V. This is the method of Indirect cross-reference from the present volume through Vol. II to Vol. V.

If "I" is the symbol of disagreement, the reader should adopt the method of Indirect cross-reference. ("I" records are infrequent in the present volume: there are only 151 of them.)

If "D" is the symbol of disagreement about Date, a reader may, if he wishes, choose another method: Direct cross-reference from the present volume to Volume V. This method is somewhat hazardous. In about half the cases where the symbol is "D", a reader will find under the 1C date in Vol. V an entry directing him to the composite entry under the 2C date in the same volume. In the remaining cases he will find no such directive entry there under the 1C date, but will find the composite record itself under a date exactly one year earlier or one year later than the 1C date. Thus if a reader chooses the method of Direct cross-reference, he may need to look for a relevant entry not only within the set of records listed in Vol. V as publications of the year specified within the present volume but also within one or even two sets of records for immediately adjacent years.

11. <1C > Cooke I records the sermon as published in a collective edition of date and format as shown in the record. Presumably, a publication of the same date and format may be found listed under author's name in Cooke II with further information about it, such as abbreviated or full title and the names of those libraries, if within the universities at Oxford and Cambridge, or in the College at Eton, or among a certain three in London, that in Cooke's day contained a copy. The information in Cooke II, however, seldom includes an itemization of sermons contained in a collective edition. Since in Volume I Cooke lists most sermons as published in collective editions, the set of symbols <1C > occurs in more than half the records within the present volume. Correpondence between records in Volume I concerning sermons printed in collective editions and records in Volume II concerning the editions which contain them sometimes fails. It has not been possible for the present editor to search out these failures of correspondence between records in Cooke II and Cooke I regarding collective editions and the sermons printed within them.

Notes (continued)

12. Misprints and non-standard spellings: As users of these volumes will know, spelling was often erratic in eighteenth century documents. In principle, all erratic spellings and also all obvious misprints within Cooke's records have been preserved during transcription of them into machine-readable form in preparation of the present edition of his work except where alteration seemed required by common sense in editing or was needed for proper sorting, comparing, and other processing of the transcribed records by computer. To ensure accuracy in transcription, two distinct transcriptions were made by two different key-punch operators reading independently from two different enlarged Xerox copies of two different printed copies (one in the British Museum, the other in the Yale University Library) of the original edition. The two transcriptions were then compared by computer, differences discovered, and operators' errors corrected.

In regard to obvious misprints in Cooke's work, it should be remarked that, as the imprint upon title pages in the 1783 edition shows, Cooke's work was privately printed for him as editor. Probably he lacked financial resources for extensive resetting of type. He had received a stipend of only four pounds annually during the years 1765-1780 that he was a Chaplain at Christ Church in Oxford, where he had entered his College as a Sizar (a servitor). Appointment to a "good living" -- that of Rector of Wentnor, in Shropshire -- must have improved his financial situtation after 1780, but perhaps hurried him to get his work into print. There are signs of haste in his Volume II. It appears to have been set into type by at least two, more probably three, and perhaps four different compositors working under different conditions, but probably not always at different times. These facts are indicated by diversities between sets of gatherings of sheets in respect to such things as pagination, catchword usage, and frequency of certain types of phonetic confusion in regard to numerals. But Cooke's own work is not careless.

13. Causes of disagreement: By no means all disagreements between the primary and the secondary sources of this volume are due to error upon the part of Cooke or his printer. Many of them of them are due to differences between the sources of information that Cooke himself used in compiling his two volumes. Some of these differences are bibliographically significant.

Cooke's sources were of two kinds: (1) library catalogues and other lists, some of them in print and some in manuscript; and (2) books and pamphlets that he found on the shelves to which the catalogues of libraries public and private led him. In general, so the present editor has concluded, Cooke used library catalogues and other lists in compiling his Volume II and the books and pamphlets which he found in libraries (and perhaps sometimes in booksellers' shops) in compiling his Volume I. His readers would similarly proceed from catalogues to shelves.

Disagreement between sources of the two kinds arose in various ways. An author's name might be presented in standardized form throughout a library catalogue, in several forms upon the title pages of the books or pamphlets that bore it. Date of publication might be stated in New Style within a catalogue, in Old Style on a title page; or it might appear in a catalogue as announced by publisher to subscriber and might stand on the relevant title page as later set thereon by the printer. The date of the first volume of an edition might be left in a catalogue as the date of the entire edition, and succeeding volumes of the edition might stand on the shelves with different dates. Scribal errors might occur in manuscript lists; printers' errors in printed catalogues and on title pages.

Although Cooke attempted to reconcile data that he obtained from library catalogues and other lists with what he found in the books and pamphlets themselves, he could not always do so; and on occasion he purposely let disagreement stand for reasons that will become apparent to a reflective reader.

Some types of error that occurred in the listing of biblical texts within Cooke's first volume are described in Appendix A to Volume III of the present edition.

The symbols of agreement and disagreement between source records show the results of a comparison between Cooke's list of sermons printed in the years 1660-1782 and his listings of the publications in which these sermons had been printed. The list of sermons constitutes Volume I of Cooke's work in his own 1783 edition. The listings of publications occur in his Volume II, where they appear under the relevant authors' names. In his Volume I, the sermons within these publications are listed in the order in which their biblical texts occur in the bible. (As readers must know, in Cooke's day every sermon began with a biblical text.)

The comparison was made by the present editor with the aid of a computer. One purpose was to discover and resolve problems of cross reference from Cooke's first volume to his second. Another was to enable the present editor to produce by computer a set of composite records in which non-redundant information from the two source lists would be combined. Composite records of this kind are contained, along with others that are not composite, in Volume V of the present edition.

The comparison involved four points about each sermon that was recorded in both volumes: (1) biblical text, (2) name of author and the kind of type-face -- roman or italic -- in which the name was printed (indicating author's conformity or nonconformity to Church of England), (3) format of an edition in which the sermon was printed, and (4) date (year) of that edition. Symbols under Sources Compared indicate clearly the results of comparison in respect to these four points.

A fifth point was also involved in the comparison; but its results are not so directly indicated under Sources Compared. This point concerns the type or types of edition indicated in Cooke's record or records of a sermon: (a) collective edition of several works including one or more sermons by one or more authors, or (b) single-sermon edition or other edition containing sermons on a single text and by a single author.

In Cooke's Volume I the type of an edition in which a sermon may be found is indicated by information given in the column headed "Title, Page, &c.". In Volume II the type of the edition which is the subject of a record is indicated by the form of the record. The record of a single-sermon edition in Volume II begins with citation of the biblical text of the sermon contained in it. The record of a collective edition usually begins with title in brief or full followed by date and format of printing or else simply with a statement of the format and date. The sermons within a collective edition are seldom individually listed by biblical text in Volume II.

There were good reasons why Cooke treated single-sermon and collective editions in different ways within his second volume. Specification of the biblical text of the sermon contained in a single-sermon edition seldom required an extra line of print and was the best way to distinguish that publication from other single-sermon publications by the same author in the same year and the same format of printing. In the case of a collective edition, however, itemization of its contents would usually take many lines of print and was quite unnecessary for identification of the work. Very seldom was more than one collection of sermons by the same author printed in the same year and format. Hence author's name, date and format of printing, and an indication that the publication was a collective edition were usually sufficient to identify such a collection uniquely. Where these points of information were not sufficient in regard to a collective publication, Cooke almost invariably gave its title in full or brief form within his second volume and in highly abbreviated form within the related sermon records within his first volume.

(This discussion is continued on the next page.)

USE MADE OF SOURCE COMPARISONS IN DEVELOPMENT OF VOLUMES OF THIS EDITION OF COOKE'S WORK (continued)

Although Cooke in his second volume did not routinely itemize any of the sermons contained in a collective edition, he did so in the following circumstances: (1) often all, if they were few -- two or three or so -- and itemization of them was useful for identification of the publication; (2) sometimes some, if these had been printed in alternative editions of historical interest or of convenience to his readers; (3) usually as many as was proper, if a collective edition brought together sermons by several authors and he had not already recorded all of them as printed within editions of the individual authors' works. In this third case, after the name of every author whose work he would have omitted to list had he not found it in the collective edition of sermons by several authors, he itemized those sermons by this author that he would otherwise have omitted, added a "V." for "Vide", and then cited the collective edition by brief title, format, and date.

A copy of Cooke's second volume is reproduced, again as Volume II, in the present edition of his work.

Cooke's first volume is not similarly reproduced, but is represented in the present edition by Volume III _Sermons Listed by Biblical Text_. In it all records contained in Cooke's first volume are reproduced with editorial apparatus added, and note is made also of all sermons that Cooke recorded in his second volume and not in his first.

Volume IV lists the same sermons as Volume III but in the order described by its title: _Sermons Listed by Authors' Names_. There is no similar listing in Cooke's own edition of his work. Records in Volume IV were sorted by computer, and in consequence a reader must use his own intelligence to distinguish between the sermons of authors who bear the same name or to combine into a single set all records of sermons by an author whose name Cooke has represented variously. Similarities and differences in other items of information within records -- dates and formats of printing, volume and page numbers in collective editions, abbreviated titles -- will usually be sufficient guides.

Volume V lists by year of their printing all the publications that are recorded in Cooke's second volume. In addition, it lists all single-sermon publications that are recorded in Cooke's first volume but that, through oversight on the part of Cooke or his printer, were not included within the listings in Cooke's second volume. It also lists, so far as the present editor has found them, all those contributions made by individual authors to collective editions of sermons by several authors that were recorded in Cooke's first volume and that should have been recorded in Cooke's second volume but were not. It does not, however, list _per se_ any of the collective editions that Cooke or his printer neglected to record in Cooke's second volume even though reference was made to them within sermon-records in Cooke's first volume. Within every record in Volume V for which two sources are shown, there is printed all non-redundant information (including all discrepant information) from both source records.

Volume VI lists the same sermons as do Volumes III and IV but differs from them in arrangement. In it the sermons are recorded in the order of the publication dates given for them in Cooke's first volume.

The purpose of the chronological arrangement of records in Volumes V and VI will be obvious to students who recognize the data within them as a register of the conditions of life and of developments in literature, politics, religious thought, printing and publication, economics, and public attitudes in England from the Restoration into the period of the American colonial rebellion.

JOHN COOKE'S LIST OF ABBREVIATIONS

Acad.	Academica
Acc.s.	Accession-sermon
Act s.	Act-sermon
Admis.	Admission
Adv.s.	Advent-sermon
Ag. Pop.	Against Popery
All S.	All Souls-College
An.C. Meet.	Annual County Meeting
An.m.ch.sc.	Anniversary Meeting of the Charity Schools
An. of Cor.	Anniversary of Coronation
Anniv. of Ir. Reb.	Anniversary of Irish Rebellion
Annun.s.	Annunciation sermon
Anonym.	Anonymous
Antigallic.	Antigallicans
Apoth. F.	Apothecaries Feast
App.	Appendix
Archd.	Archdeacon
Art. Co.	Artillery Company
Artill. Co.	Artillery Company
Asc.s.	Ascension sermon
Ash. W. S.	Ash Wednesday sermon
Ass. and Acc.	Assize and Accession
Ass. and Ch.	Assize and Charity
Ass.s.	Assize sermon
Assoc.s.	Association sermon
b.	Before
B. A.	Bachelor of Arts
B. Ch.	Beautifying a Chapel or Church
B. D.	Bachelor of Divinity
B. D.	Body of Divinity
B. F. Pr.	Bellamy's Family Preacher
B. L.	Boyle's Lecture
B. S. s.	Berry-Street Sermons
Bal.	Baliol College
Bamp. L.	Bampton's Lecture
Bedf.	Bedford *or* Bedfordshire
Berks.	Berkshire
Bod.	Bodleian Library
Bp. W. L.	Bishop Warburton's Lecture
Brit. M.	British Museum
Bucks.	Buckingham *or* Buckinghamshire
Burg.	Burgesses
C.	Commons
C. C. C.	Corpus Christi College
C. *or* Camb.	Cambridge *or* Cambridgshire
C.m.e.	Casuistical Morning Exercise
c.m.e.	Continuation of Morning Exercise
c.m.e. C.	Continuation of Morning Exercise at Cripplegate
Can.	Canon
Cant.	Canterbury
Carl.	Carlisle
Carm.	Carmarthen *or* Carmarthenshire
Cat.	Catechism
Cathe. W.	Cathedral Worship
Ch.s.	Charity sermon
Ch. Ch.	Christ Church
Ch.sch.s.	Charity-school sermon
Chap.	Chaplain
Chart. H. sch. F.	Charterhouse school Feast
Chest.	Chester *or* Cheshire
Circumc.	Circumcision
Cl.s.	Before the sons of the clergy
Co. F.	Company, or County Feast
Co. *or* Corp. Trin. H.	Corporation of Trinity house
Co. Revell.	Country Revel
Co. S.	Surgeons Company
Col. Georg.	Before Trustees of the Colony of Georgia
Coll.	College
Collec.for Mini.	Collection for Ministers
Com.	Commentary
Com. Foun.	Commemoration of Founders
Com. *or* Commem.	Commemoration
Commence.	Commencement
Comp. F.	Company Feast
Con. *or* Conv.	Convocation

JOHN COOKE'S LIST OF ABBREVIATIONS

Conc. Acad.	Concio Academica
Conc. Lat.	Concio Latina
Conc.ad Aul.	Concio ad Aulam
Conc.ad Cl.	Concio ad Clerum
Conc.ad Mag.	Concio ad Magistratum
Conc.ad Pop.	Concio ad Populum
Conc.ad Syn.	Concio ad Synodum
Cond.	Condemned
Conf.s.	Confirmation sermon
Cons. Bp.	Consecration of a Bishop
Cons. Ch.	Consecration of a Church or Chapel
Cor.s. *or* Coron.s.	Coronation sermon
Cornw.	Cornwal
Corp.s.	Corporation sermon
Cov. *or* Covts.	On the Covenants
Covent.	Coventry
Cow. L.	Coward's Lecture
Cumb.	Cumberland
Cur.	Curate
D. B.rep.	Deathbed Repentance
D. C. L.	Doctor of Civil Law
D. Cov.	Doctrine of Covenants
D. D.	Doctor of Divinity
D. Dis. *or* Dth. D.	Death disarmed
D. P.	Death of Prince
D. P.	Doctor of Philosophy
Denb.	Denby *or* Denbyshire
Derb.	Derby *or* Derbyshire
Dis. *or* Disc.	Discourse
Dis.of P.	Discourse of Peace
Diss.	Dissertation(s)
Dist. Cattle.	Distemper among the Cattle
Dorset.	Dorsetshire
Dr. Ws's L.	Doctor Williams's Library, London
Dut. Serv.	Duty of Servants
E. A. P.	Ecclesiae Anglicanae Presbyter
E. S.	Easter sermon
E.and G.	Epistles and Gospels
East. C. L.	Eastcheap Lectures
El.	Election
El. M. Parl.	Election of Member of Parliament
El.and sw. M.	Election and swearing of Mayor
Eman.	Emanuel College
Emb. W.	Ember Week
En.af. Ha.	Enquiry after Happiness
Enq. *or* Enqui.	Enquiry into difficult Texts
Epiph.	Epiphany sermon
Erect. Organ.	Erecting an Organ
Erect.sch.	Erecting a school
Eton.	Eton Library
Ex. C.	Exeter College
Exerc.	Exercitations
Ext.sev.s.	Extract of several sermons
F. Plague.	Fast for the Plague
F. R. S.	Fellow of the Royal Society
F.and Ass.s.	Fast and Assize sermon
Fairch. L.	Fairchild's Lecture
Fam. In. *or* Inst.	Family Instructor
Farew.s.	Farewell sermon
Fire of L.	Fire of London
Fr. Mas.	Freemasons
Fst Ubiqua.	Feast before Ubiquarians
Fun.s.	Funeral sermon
Gard. F.	Gardiner's Feast
Glam.	Glamorgan *or* Glamorganshire
Glouc.	Gloucester *or* Gloucestershire
Goldsm.	Goldsmiths
Gov.	Governors
Gra. Doct.	Gradus Doctoratus
H. L.	Hutchin's Lecture
H. P.	Hyde Park
Hants.	Hampshire
Heref.	Hereford *or* Herefordshire
Herts.	Hertfordshire
Hex. Jac.	Hexapla Jacobaea
Hom.	Homilies

JOHN COOKE'S LIST OF ABBREVIATIONS

Hos. *or* Hosp.	Hospital
Ht's Ease.	Heart's Ease
Hum. Soc.	Humane Society
Huntingd.	Huntingdon *or* Huntingdonshire
Hutc.	Hutchin's Lecture
Inaug.s.	Inauguration sermon
Inf.s.	Infirmary sermon
Instal.of M.	Instalment of a Mayor
Ir. Mass.	Irish Massacre
Ir. Prot.	Irish Protestant
Ir.sch.	Irish schools
Jes.	Jesus College
K.	King *or* King's College
L L B.	Bachelor of Laws
L L D.	Doctor of Laws
L.	Library or Lords
L. C. S.	Student of Civil Law
L. M.	Lord Mayor
L. S.s.	Lime-Street sermons
L.s.	Lent sermon
Lanc.	Lancaster *or* Lancashire
Last Th.	Last Thoughts
Lect.	Lecture *or* Lecturer
Lev. Co.	Levant Company
Lieut.	Lieutenancy
Linc.	Lincoln College *or* Lincolnshire
Lit.	Liturgy
Lond.	London
Lond. Infirm.	London Infirmary
Loyal Soc. F.	Loyal Society Feast
M. A.	Master of Arts
M. L.	Moyer's Lecture
M. Parl.	Member of Parliament
m.ch.sch.	Meeting of charity schools
m.e. C.	Morning Exercise at Cripplegate
m.e. G.	Morning Exercise at St. Giles's
m.e. P.	Morning Exercise against Popery
Mag. H.	Magdalene Hospital
Magd.	Magdalene College
Mar. Soc.	Marine Society
Merch.	Merchant
Merion.	Merionetshire
Mert.	Merton College
Middles.	Middlesex
Mil. *or* Milit.	Military *or* Militia
Mir.	Miracles
Mis. T.	Miscellaneous Tracts
Mon. Fast s.	Monthly Fast sermon
Monm.	Monmouth *or* Monmouthshire
Montgom.	Montgomery *or* Montgomeryshire
Mus.s.	Music sermon
Norf.	Norfolk
Northampt.	Northampton *or* Northamptonshire
Northum.	Northumberland
Nottings.	Nottingham *or* Nottinghamshire
O. T.	Old, or Psalter Translation
Oc.s.	Occasional sermon
Occ. Commun.	Occasional Communion
Op. Ch.	Opening church or chapel
Op. Ch. Sch.	Opening charity school
Op. Fair.	Opening a fair
Op. Lect.	Opening a Lecture
Op. Organ.	Opening an Organ
Op. Workh.	Opening a workhouse
Or.	Oriel College
Ord.	Ordinary
Ord.s.	Ordination sermon
Orig.	Original
Ox. *or* Oxon.	Oxford or Oxfordshire
P. D.	Practical Discourses
P. S.	Passion sermon
P.of R.	Prince of Orange
Par.	Parables
Par. Cl.	Parish Clerks
Pemb.	Pembroke College, Hall, *or* Pembrokeshire

JOHN COOKE'S LIST OF ABBREVIATIONS

Po.st.	Popery stated
Pop.	Pope or Popery
Posth.	Posthumous
Pr. Den.	Prince of Denmark
Pr. Ir. Sch.	Protestant Irish Schools
Pr. Wal. Bth. D.	Prince of Wales's birth day
Pract. Dis.ap.	Practical Discourses. Appendix
Preb.	Prebendary
Pres.	Preservative
Presb.of the Ch.of Eng.	Presbyter of the Church of England
Prop. G.	Propagation of the Gospel
Pt.	Part
Pub. L.	Public Library, at Cambridge
Pur.	Purification
Q.	Quaere or Queen
Queen.	Queen's College
R.	Rector
R. Fun.s.	Royal Funeral sermon
R. P. Th.	Regius Professor Theologiae
Radnor.	Radnorshire
Reb. *or* Rebell.	Rebellion
Recant.	Recantation
Ref. M.	Reformation of Manners
Rel. Soc.	Religious Society
Reliq.	Reliquiae
Rem.	Remains
Rep. Ch.	Repairing a Church or Chapel
Rest.	Restoration
S. S.	Scriptures
S.af. Asc.	Sunday after Ascension
s.m.e.	Supplement to Morning Exercise
s.m.e. C.	Supplement to Morning Exercise at Cripplegate
s.s.	Single sermon
S.to Ass.	Sermon to Asses
S.to Cond.	to the condemned
S.to D D.	to Doctors in Divinity
S.to Min. St.	to Ministers of State
S.to R.& Stud.	to the Rich and Studious
S.to Trad.	to Tradesmen
S.to Y. M.	to young Men
S.to Y. W.	to young Women
Sacra.	On the Sacrament
Sacra.	Sacrament or Sacramental
Salop.	Shropshire
Sarum.	Salisbury
Sc. Pr.	Scotch Preacher
Sch. F.	School Feast
Sch.and Coll. F.	School and College Feast
Sel. Disc.	Select Discourses
Sel.s.	Select sermons
Sev.di.	Several discourses
Sev.serm.	Several sermons
Sion.	Sion College Library
Soc. Batch.	Society of Bachelors
Soc.s.	Society sermon
Somers.	Somersetshire
Southw.	Southwark
Spitt. M.	Spittal Monday
Spitt. T.	Spittal Tuesday
Spitt. W.	Spittal Wednesday
Staff.	Stafford *or* Staffordshire
Strict. Lu.	Stricturae Lucis
Stud.	Student
Sub.sev.s.	Substance of several sermons
Suff.	Suffolk
Suss.	Sussex
Syn.	Synod
T. Ac.	Terms of Acceptance
Th. Th.	Thesaurus Theologicus
Th.aft. Reb.	Thanksgiving after the Rebellion
Th.disc.	Theological discourses
Th.s.	Thanksgiving sermon
Theo. *or* Theol.	Theologia reformata
Tra.	Tracts
Treat.	Treatise
Trin.	Trinity College or Trinity Sunday

Trin. Corp.	Corporation of Trinity house
Un.	Union
Univ.	Universal *or* University College
V.	Vicar
V.	Vide
V. D. M.	Verbi Divini Minister
V.s.	Visitation sermon
W. F.	Welch Feast
W.s.	Whitsunday sermon
Wadh.	Wadham College
Warw.	Warwick *or* Warwickshire
Wedd.s.	Wedding sermon
Westm.	Westminster *or* Westmoreland
Winch.	Winchester
Wor.	Works
Worc.	Worcester College, Worcester, *or* Worcestershire
Xn. L.	Christian Life
Xrter.	Character
Xt.	Christ
Xtmas.s.	Christmas sermon

JOHN COOKE'S LIST OF ABBREVIATIONS

AIDS TO INTERPRETATION

In the column headed "Title, Page, &c.":
The abbreviation "ss." means that the sermon will be found in a single-sermon edition. A page number, on the other hand, indicates that it will be found in a collective edition of sermons or miscellaneous works by one or several authors. The number is the page on which the sermon begins in that collective edition.

An "&c." following a page number indicates that a series of sermons, all on the same biblical text and by the same given author, begins on the page so numbered within a collective edition. The number of sermons on that text, if greater than one, is usually (but not always) indicated by an arabic numeral preceding the "s." that stands before the page number: *e.g.*, "10 s. 189&c."

If no "&c." follows the page number, or there is no page number at all after the "10 s." or similar expression, the expression is usually an abbreviation of the title or description by means of which (along with date and format of printing) the publication is identified under author's name in Cooke's (and the present) Volume II. (The practice of naming a volume of sermons by the number of sermons contained in it was common in the 18th century.)

In case reference to Volume II does not resolve a reader's doubt about how such an expression as "10 s." is being used in a particular case, the reader should consult Volume IV. If the expression recurs there in several records of sermons by the same author and published in an edition of the same date and format, then it represents a title, not the number of sermons on a text.

In the column headed "Occasion or Subject":

(1) A single small "s." always stands for "sermon."

(2) Any other small letter or distinct pair of small letters usually stands for a preposition: *e.g.*, "b." for "before"; "a." or "ag." for "against."

(3) A capital letter following such an abbreviation stands for the grammatical object of the preposition, that object often denoting the audience of the sermon: *e.g.*, "b.K." stands for "before King"; "b.Q." for "before Queen"; "b.K. & Q." for "before King & Queen"; "b.C." for "before (House of) Commons"; "b.L." for "before (House of) Lords"; "b.L.M." for "before Lord Mayor."

(4) A capital letter before a small "s." or before an abbreviated preposition usually denotes the occasion for which the sermon was preached. Thus "F.s.b.C." stands for "Fast sermon before Commons"; "Th.b.M." for "Thanksgiving sermon before Mayor."

(5) Unfortunately, "F." can mean "Feast" as well as "Fast," but does so only after a designation of the feasters: *e.g.*, "Gard.F." stands for "Gardeners' Feast"; "Sch.F." for "School Feast."

(6) "Fun.s." always means "Funeral sermon."

If a reader finds that an abbreviation within the column "Occasion or Subject" remains unintelligible without further aid, he may usually obtain help in one of the ways listed below:

(1) from Volume II (or perhaps more conveniently Volume V) if the source symbol "2C" occurs in the column "Sources Compared" within the present volume, indicating that a relevant entry is contained therein; (In Volume II, Cooke often spelled out in full, or almost in full, the occasion and/or subject of a sermon if he had reason to include a record of it there.)

(2) from Volume I (Index Volume), where various abbreviations relevant to each index heading are displayed;

(3) from the biblical text of the sermon; (A reading of the biblical text will often make clear what the sermon is about and to what occasion or audience it might be suitable.)

(4) from the work of Cooke's predecessor Sampson Letsome; (Cooke says in his "Preface" that he is leaving to the "Dexterity of the Compositor" the abbreviations which are to be used in the column "Occasion or Subject." It is clear that the compositor formed most of them by replicating or, more commonly, compressing the abbreviations which Cooke's predecessor, Sampson Letsome, had used for similar matter. Readers who have access to a copy of Letsome's 1753 edition of *The Preacher's Assistant* will find therein (with few exceptions) a record of any sermon that Cooke has not listed with a prefixed asterisk, and in Letsome's record they will usually find a fuller and more easily interpreted abbreviation of occasion or subject.)

INDEXES IN VOLUME I TO VOLUME III

Note: Volumes IV and VI differ from Volume III only in arrangement of the data, not in the content of the data. They do not have, or need, separate indexes. Volume V does need, and has, its own indexes.

INDEXES IN VOLUME I TO VOLUME V

INDEX A: SOME NOTABLE SERIES OF LECTURES

(SEE ALSO INDEX B: COLLECTIONS)

<u>How to Read This Index</u>:

Under each heading in this index, the items should be read in line from left to right across the page. Double brackets precede all references to sermons published in the year named after those brackets. Within the set of items for that year, a two-letter combination identifies, by the first two letters of his surname, every author who, according to John Cooke's first volume, published a sermon relevant to the heading. The numbers following the two letters identify the biblical texts of the sermons by the author or authors who bear a surname that begins with the two letters. These numbers are correlated to the texts by a simple code: serial number of biblical book (two digits), of chapter (three digits), and of verse (three digits). Biblical books are listed by serial code numbers on endpapers inside the covers of the present volume.

For example, items on the first line under the first heading of this index show that in the year 1780 Bampton Lectures were published by one or more authors whose surname(s) began with the two letters BA and that the biblical texts chosen for these lectures were Isaiah lxi. 1; Romans x. 14; I Corinthians xi. 19; Ephesians i. 3; Philippians iv. 8; II Peter i. 19; and I John i. 3.

Since entries in Vol.III of the present edition of Cooke's work are arranged in the order of biblical text and the code number is printed at the beginning of each entry, reference from this index to that volume is easy. Within any set of entries there concerning the same text, the first two letters of an author's surname are in most cases sufficient to identify an entry uniquely.

The author of the sermons in the example given above was James Bandinel, as the reader will discover if he consults our Vol. III. He will find the sermons listed as a group, with date 1780, beside Bandinel's name in our Vol. IV <u>Sermons Listed by Authors' Names</u>. He will find the publication that contains them identified under the name BANDINELL James in Vol.II and under PUBLICATIONS OF THE YEAR 1780 in Vol. V.

A chronological ordering of items has been chosen for this index, because it has been assumed that most readers are primarily interested in publications of certain periods.

Users will find a ruler helpful in reading across lines.

Bampton's Lecture <"Bamp.L.">
<<YEAR 1780: BA 23061001, 48010014, 49011019, 52001003, 53004008, 64001019, 65001003>>
<<YEAR 1781: NE 45002011, 46005023, 46005039, 46017003, 48010010, 49001021, 51003021, 61004002>> <<YEAR 1782: HO 43003005, 44001007, 45003003, 46001006, 46001007, 46013019>>

INDEXES TO THIRD VOLUME: A: SOME NOTABLE SERIES OF LECTURES

Boyle's Lecture <"B.L.">
<<YEAR 1719: CL 23045007>> <<YEAR 1730: LE 48001020>> <<YEAR 1732: ST 48003031>> <<YEAR 1733: BE 66000010>>
<<YEAR 1739: BE 19014001, 43001001, 43011014, 43024015, 45001032, 45024025, 46001017,
47014015, 47017027, 48007024, 51003016, 61001001 BL 45016029 BR 46003016, 46006045,
57001015 BU 48010011 GA 61011006 GU 23005020, 46015024, 47017028, 48001022, 49001021,
55005021, 57004007, 64001016 HA 19010004, 24009024, 46004024, 47017023 IB 55005021
LE 23002003, 45007023, 46003002, 48001019, 61002003, 61003012, 61011006 ST 49001022,
49001025, 49002012, 58001010, 64001019, 65005003 WH 64001019 WI 45016031, 46005039,
47017011, 51001008, 61001001 WO 46001001, 46006068, 48001028, 49001021, 59001002,
64003014>> <<YEAR 1742: BI 63001008>> <<YEAR 1743: TW 01022018, 05018015, 05018018, 19016008,
23007014, 23053007, 27009024, 32005002, 38003001, 38004005, 46004048, 46005039,
46010024, 46020031, 64001016, 64001019, 64001021>> <<YEAR 1748: WA 48006023>> <<YEAR 1763:
HE 48001020>> <<YEAR 1769: WO 26030013, 27007019, 27011028, 43016018, 43028020, 45022042,
46008003, 57004001, 61013008, 65001003, 69011003, 69012001, 69013001, 69013011,
69013014>> <<YEAR 1773: OW 01006003, 01011004, 01012001, 01018014, 05032009, 19044003,
19078012, 19078056, 19078070, 24024005, 28005005, 43009002, 44016020, 46003002,
48007022, 48012002, 50004002, 58001010, 63003015, 68000007, 68000014>>

Coward's Lecture : See among collections listed in Index B

Croonian Lecture, Sermons At : See "Physicians or Surgeons Company" among the audiences listed in Index C

Fairchild's Lecture <"Fairch.L">
<<YEAR 1730: DE 43006028>> <<YEAR 1745: DE 19008004>> <<YEAR 1760: ST 01001011>> <<YEAR 1763: ST 01001011>>

Hutchin's Lecture <"Hutch.L.">
<<YEAR 1729: MA 19029002>> <<YEAR 1731: WA 45011002>> <<YEAR 1732: ST 05004008>> <<YEAR 1745: NE 45011001
SN 43004010>> <<YEAR 1752: SH 21005001>> <<YEAR 1755: RI 45011001>> <<YEAR 1757: CO 19080008>> <<YEAR 1760:
ST 43006009>> <<YEAR 1763: BU 19029002>> <<YEAR 1769: PE 49014040>> <<YEAR 1770: AS 59001009>> <<YEAR 1778:
AP 19095006>>

Morning Exercises (at Cripplegate, St. Paul's, etc.) : See among the collections listed in Index B

Moyer's Lecture <"M.L.">
<<YEAR 1720: BR 53002006 WA 43028019, 44012029, 46001001, 46001003, 53002005>> <<YEAR 1721:
KN 18033004, 45024027>> <<YEAR 1725: BE 05032007>> <<YEAR 1726: BI 23044008, 43004010, 68000003>>
<<YEAR 1730: TR 45016019, 45016023, 45016029, 65005007>> <<YEAR 1731: WH 57006020>> <<YEAR 1732:
BR 44016015, 48009005 FE 18011007, 49002011, 49002013, 49002014>> <<YEAR 1738: WH 23006001,
43028019, 44016015, 46001014, 65005007>> <<YEAR 1741: BE 57003016, 65005007>> <<YEAR 1742:
RI 47019001, 47019002, 59003003, 59003004, 59003005>> <<YEAR 1743: SE 18014003, 43028019,
46003002, 63003018 TW 44013032, 46001014, 46014028, 47005003, 49008005, 49015028,
61001002, 69003014>> <<YEAR 1774: MO 43018007>>

Warburton's (Bishop Warburton's) Lecture <"Bp.W.L.">
<<YEAR 1769: WO 01009025, 01016012>> <<YEAR 1776: HA 27002044, 27012008, 27012010, 47026002,
56002003, 57004001, 69001003, 69001019, 69003022, 69017018, 69018004, 69022006
HU 23043009, 26020049, 45012056, 46013019, 64001021, 65002018, 69019010, 69022007>>
<<YEAR 1780: BA 23010006, 27007014, 32005002, 34002003, 37004013, 43013031, 45002010,
45024027, 46014029, 46018036, 69003022, 69004001>>

INDEX B : SOME COLLECTIONS OF SERMONS BY ANONYMOUS OR SEVERAL AUTHORS

How to Read This Index:

Under the name of the sermon collection are listed, in a vertical row, the dates of publication that Cooke, in his first volume, gives for the sermons that he indicates to be contained in it. Under each date the names of authors are given in alphabetical order from left to right, and after each name the code numbers of the biblical texts of the relevant sermons as given in Volume Three of the present edition. (See directions for reading the preceding Index A.)

Bibliographical Note:

The present Index B contains all references that Cooke, in his first volume, makes to the collections named. His references sometimes occur in footnotes (q.v. in Volume Three of the present edition) and sometimes in the column headed "Title, Page, &c." (q.v. in the present edition). In his references, Cooke seems to have attempted a distinction between those sermons that, according to his evidence, had been published by his terminal date 1782 only in the collection named and those that had been published in some other way also. If according to his evidence a sermon had been published in an alternative way, he seems to have entered the alternative form in his main list and to have referred to the collection in a footnote. Thus if the main entry shows a year of publication different from the year of the collection, Cooke presumably believed that the sermon had been published in both years, and if the main entry describes the sermon as "ss." (Cooke's abbreviation for "single sermon") of the same date as the collection, presumably he thought that the sermon had been available to purchasers both unbound as a single sermon in pamphlet form and also bound into the collection with other sermons.

Underlining:

In this and the other indexes, as in the lists to which they refer, the underlining of an author's name represents the italic type which Cooke used to indicate that an author was a Nonconformist rather than an Anglican.

INDEXES TO THIRD VOLUME: B: COLLECTIONS OF SEVERAL AUTHORSHIP

Bellamy's Family Preacher <"B.F.Pr.">

1750

CARRINGTON : 49015023

1753

WEBSTER : 45010042,61010025

1754

ANONYMOUS : 01006009,06024024,13022009,18014001,18031003,18036011,20003017,20023020,43025031,45023034, 46005039,46006014,47002001,49002009,49010031,49013012,52006002,52006004,54004001,62001026,62004003,69014002, 69022013 BRAY : 20031010 CARRINGTON : 19112006,19119071,20018014 HALES : 23056012

1756

ANONYMOUS : 47002032,69022012

1776

ANONYM. : 21002013,43001021,48015002 ANONYMOUS : 02020007,04023010,06024024,11004025,18011007, 18014001,18036011,19015001,20003017,20023020,21007016,21012013,43005003,43005016,43005022,43006010,43006031, 43007012,43007014,43011016,43013054,43026074,44012030,45002030,45013008,45015018,45016025,45024034,46003001, 47001009,47016029,47017031,49011024,52005033,52005033,54004005,61010025,61010031,62005016,63002018,63002021, 69007014,69014013,69020011 CARRINGTON : 02020008,19112006,19119071,20018021,20027004,21011003,23002007, 52005015,52006004,62004003

Berry - Street (variantly spelled Bury or Bery - Street) Sermons <"B.S.s.","Berry-s.",etc.>

1753

WATTS : 01002003,20013004,20013004,43028019,47002033,47014015,48003025,48006023,48015006,52001003, 61008006,65003004 (Date 1753 is that of publication in vols. 1-2 of Watts' "Works", 6 vols.,1753.)

1757

GUYSE : 19025021,21007029,21012007,43015008,46001018,46004024,52004030,65005003 HUBBARD : 02020007,20018024,48005012,48008034,52001011,52006013,54001009,58002010,65002006 JENNINGS : 19103019, 43028019,47001002,47010002,48001018,50005014,52006018,57004007 NEAL : 19031019,27004035,46013034, 47003019,48007022,49009023,49011023,51004004,58001009,58003016 PRICE : 43005048,45001072,47002046, 48013007,48015013,51005005,59002011,61006002,63003018

Collection of Farewell Sermons <"Coll.Far.s.","Col.Farw.s",etc.>

1663

ANONYMOUS : 61012001 CRADACOT : 53004009 G. : 48008038 HORTON : 50004007 BATES : 61013020 BEERMAN : 47020017 BULL : 46014016,47020032 CALAMY : 09004013, 10024014,23057001 COLLINS : 68005003 COOPER : 53004009 EVANK : 43026039 GASPINE : 45012032 GREW : 47020032 JACOMB : 46008028 JENKINS : 02003002,61011038 LAMB : 46014023,46015023 LYE : 46013017,53004001 MANTON : 61012001 MEAD : 49001003 NEWCOME : 69003003 PLEDGER : 69002009 SCLATER : 65005001 SEAMAN : 61013020 THORN : 19037034 VENNING : 61010023 WADSWORTH : 69002005 WATSON : 23002010,46013034, 49010014,50007001

1707

BAXTER : 54002006 (Date 1707 is that of publication in Baxter's "Discourses in 4 vols.")

Conjugal Duty, Discourses on <"D.on Conj.D.","Disc.on Conj.D",etc.,etc.>

1681

GRANTHAM : 01029025

1682

WILKINSON : 20031014

17--

WHATLEY : 61013004

1708

MOXON : 43005028

1709

CORNWALLIS : 52005033

1710

MASTER : 45001026

1732

ANONYM. : 54003019 COLBY : 20031010 CROMPTON : 20031029 KING : 19128003
LATIMER : 46002001 PARSONS : 08004011 MEAD : 45001026

1740

BRADSHAW : 46002001 F.THO. : 45001006 GATAKER : 20018022,20019014 HACKET : 01002021
HARDY : 52005031 MEGOTT : 01002018 SNAWSEL : 20011029,20012004 W.L. : 20031010
SECKER : 01002018

Coward's Lecture <"Cow.L.">
1729

GIBBS : 65002001 GODWIN : 46001014 GUYSE : 47009020 HALL : 57002005
HUBBARD : 63001008 WOOD : 46007037

Discourses on Conjugal Duty : See "Conjugal Duty, Discourses on"

Discourses against Popery (In Cooke's second volume this work is called Sermons against Popery, or, simply, Against Popery.) <"Dis.ag.Popery","Ag.Popery", etc., etc.>
1735

BARKER : 50011003 BAYES : 49014009 BURROUGHS : 46020021 CHANDLER : 57003014
EARLE : 65001007 GROSVENOR : 46016002 HARRIS : 45022019,46006053 HUGHES : 23042008
HUNT : 44006012 LEAVESLY : 61011008 LOWMAN : 48011022 NEAL : 43016018
NEWMAN : 48003024,48004004 SMYTH : 50001024 WRIGHT : 52002020

Farewell Sermons, Collection of : See "Collection of Farewell Sermons"

House of Mourning <"H.M.">
1660

ANONYMOUS : 01003019,01015001,01015015,01023004,01035019,01050010,10012022,18014014,19090012,19116015,
21007002,21007015,21011009,28013014,43016026,45002029,45016002,46014001,48005012,48006011,48006023,48013011,
48014007,49007029,49010029,49015016,49015055,50005002,51006010,53003020,55005003,58004007,59002013,61002015,
61011001,61012010,62001004,69014007,69022012

1661

ANONYMOUS : 21012005,21012014,23026008,23057001,45008051,45010002,46011025,47013036,49015019,62002012,
62004014,63003007,69022019

Lime Street Sermons <"L.S.s.">
1732

BRADBURY : 48008032 BRAGGE : 23059019,51002016 GILL : 47026008 GOODWIN : 19051005,
48005019 HALL : 53001006 HURRION : 59002014 SLADEN : 56002013 TAYLOR : 48001022,
48005020,49011014,69003001 WILSON : 53002013

Morning Exercise : The titles of nine collections of Morning Exercises are listed below in a logical rather than an alphabetical order.

Morning Exercise <"m.e.">
16--

ALSOP : 43007001,43010016

1660

ANONYMOUS : 21007029,23053010

1661

ANONYMOUS : 26018023,43007012,57006017

1684

CHARNOCK : 01006005

INDEXES TO THIRD VOLUME: B: COLLECTIONS OF SEVERAL AUTHORSHIP

Morning Exercise, Supplement to <"s.m.e.">

1676

WADSWORTH : 49011024 DOOLITTLE : 06024015 HOOK : 43025010 JACOMB : 53004011
JANEWAY : 52006005 JENKYN : 50006001 LEE : 43006006 OWEN : 19141005
SEIGNIOR : 62001021 VINCENT : 19032001 WELLS : 52005019 WILKINSON : 54003017

Morning Exercise, Continuation of <"c.m.e.">

1683

ANONYMOUS : 19042011,63003015 ADAMS : 57002015 ALSOP : 35001008 BARKER : 46017020
BAXTER : 50002007 COLE : 14015002,19027014 COLLINGES : 23006013 COOPER : 68005021
CRAIL : 57004016 DOOLITTLE : 50004018 HOWE : 54002002 HUST : 20026028
JACOMB : 48008014 JENKINS : 64002007 LOBB : 48011033 LYE : 52006004
MAYO : 50012007 MILWARD : 48012021 OWEN : 63002003 SINGLETON : 46012028
STEELE : 49015002 SYLVESTER : 65001007 VEALE : 63003015 VINCENT : 64003018
VINK : 43016026

1690

ADAMS : 45016031 ALSOP : 52003019 BURGESS : 21012001 COLE : 52001019
HAMOND : 54004005 HURST : 47017021 MAYO : 61002015 SLATER : 48013003,48013005
STEEL : 51005015 SYLVESTER : 61010024 VEAL : 45023042 VINCENT : 63002021
VINK : 58002019 WILLIAMS : 28010012 WOODCOCK : 48014001

Morning Exercise at St. Giles <"m.e.G.">

1660

FAROM : 58003016 JACOMB : 58003016 NEEDLER : 65005007

1666

CRAFTON : 47015031

1676

ADAMS : 43025041 ANNESLEY : 61008006 CALAMY : 47026008 CASE : 58001013
COOPER : 01002016 CRAFTON : 47005031 DRAKE : 46001012 GIBBON : 48005001
HOWE : 21007029 JACOMB : 23053010,65005007 LYE : 49006017 MANTON : 48005006
MERITON : 53002008 PARSON : 47016031 POOL : 54001020 SHEFFIELD : 61012014
TAYLOR : 53002009 VINK : 48006006 WATKINS : 52002003 WATSON : 47017031
WELLS : 48005012 WHITAKER : 57002005 WHITE : 48008028 WOODCOCK : 43025034

1700

BATES : 61011006

Morning Exercise at Cripplegate <"m.e.C.">

1667

ANNESLEY : 47024016 WHITAKER : 54003011

1670

KITCHEN : 57005022 (Year "1670", given in Cooke I, probably misprint of "1677", given in Cooke II.)

1674

FOWLER : 63001008

1676

CASE : 23058013 LYE : 20022006 POOLE : 19015003 WATSON : 05017019

1677

TILLOTSON : 43007012 BRUMHALL : 45012001 CLARKSON : 13029018 COOPER : 55005018
DOOLITTLE : 65005013 DRAKE : 48007023 GIBBON : 51005016 GREENHILL : 26018032
HILL : 53004005 HURST : 19116012 JACKSON : 19120005 LEE : 48010001
LYE : 19062008 MALLERY : 01018027 MANTON : 43015007 NEEDLER : 43005029
NEST : 52006024 PLEDGER : 01042021 POLE : 18033023 SHEFFIELD : 61006004
SIMMONS : 19119037 WATSON : 45002049 WHITE : 62001006 WILKINSON : 45017027

1707

BAXTER : 43005016

Morning Exercise at Cripplegate, Supplement to <"s.m.e.C.">
1676
ADAMS : 54003020 | ANNESLEY : 43022037 | BARKER : 44002020 | COLE : 45003004
GALE : 65002015 | MANTON : 47002038 | MILWARD : 43022039 | STEELE : 52005033
SYLVESTER : 47020024 | VEAL : 23027011 | WEST : 52004029

Morning Exercise at Cripplegate, Continuation of <"c.m.e.C.">
1683
COLE : 09017034

Morning Exercise against Popery <"m.e.P.">
1675
ANNESLEY : 61010014 | BAXTER : 49012027 | CLARKSON : 48003024 | DOLITTLE : 24006016
FAIRECLOUGH : 64001007 | FOWLER : 55005027 | HURST : 47026002 | JENKINS : 48006023
LAWRENCE : 49011023 | LEE : 43016018 | LYE : 45017010 | MANTON : 56002015
MAYO : 48010014 | NEEDLER : 43004010 | OWEN : 45016029 | POOLE : 43023008
SILVESTER : 20030006 | STEEL : 43026027 | VEALE : 19062012 | VINCENT : 49014015,57004001
VINK : 45006022 | WADSWORTH : 61010012 | WEST : 49003015 | WILKINSON : 56002003

Morning Exercise, Casuistical <"C.m.e.">
1683
ANNESLEY : 21006011 | COLE : 20010029 | LYE : 38004006 | OAKEY : 20030008
SLATER : 19097001 | WATSON : 01015001 | WOODCOCK : 16008006
1690
ANNESLEY : 43011009,43012019 | BARKER : 43011024 | BATES : 01039009

Popery, against : For Discourses against Popery, see " Discourses"; for Sermons against Popery, likewise see "Discourses"; for Morning Exercise against Popery, see the heading under "Morning Exercise".

Protestant System <"Prot.Syst.">
17--
CLARK : 19036006 | MASON : 43004011
1748
BARKER : 23047008
1754
FORDYCE : 69018023 | PRIOR : 43011030
1758
KIPPIS : 49011029
177-
GRIGG : 47017031
1775
ROBERTSON : 54001026

Scotch Preacher <"Sc.P" or "Scot.Pr.">
1775
ROBERTSON : 54001026
1776
CARLYLE : 19048012 | LOTHIAN : 09016007
1779
CAMPBELL : 49001025 | GRAY : 19085006 | HUNTER : 06024015 | LECHMAN : 58001007
M'FARLAND : 48012010 | MACGILL : 46017020 | MAKENZIE : 18003017 | OGILVIE : 25001012
PETRIE : 61013015 | SOMERVILLE : 43027054
1780
BLAIR : 23011009 | GERARD : 05016020

INDEXES TO THIRD VOLUME: B: COLLECTIONS OF SEVERAL AUTHORSHIP

(I N D E X E S T O T H I R D V O L U M E)

I N D E X C : S O M E S P E C I A L A U D I E N C E S T O W H O M S E R M O N S W E R E A D D R E S S E D

<u>How</u> <u>to</u> <u>Read</u> <u>This</u> <u>Index</u>: See Directions for Reading Index A.

Antigallicans <"b. Antigallic.", "Antigal.", <u>etc</u>.>
<<YEAR 1748: BU 61013001 <<YEAR 1751: KI 19122006 <<YEAR 1752: AU 23031001 <<YEAR 1753: FR 24002018
<<YEAR 1754: BU 42004005 <<YEAR 1756: FR 63003008 PR 19133001 RO 04025017 <<YEAR 1758: PR 20014034
<<YEAR 1763: JO 06023011 <<YEAR 1781: PR 19122006

Apothecaries <"b.Apoth.", "Apoth.Co.", "Apoth.F."., "b.Apoth.Co.">
<<YEAR 1682: WA 21010001 <<YEAR 1704: RE 21003021 <<YEAR 1706: BR 19133001, 20017022 RE 48001019
<<YEAR 1731: CU 48001020 <<YEAR 1759: DO 19104024 <<YEAR 1760: DO 49015036 <<YEAR 1761: DO 10023004

Artillery Company <"b.Art.Co.", "Artill.Co.">
<<YEAR 1671: DU 49016013 <<YEAR 1673: MA 58002002 ME 06001007 <<YEAR 1677: PI 45003014 <<YEAR 1679:
PE 45003014 <<YEAR 1680: CR 12011008 <<YEAR 1696: ME 47010001 <<YEAR 1704: SC 20028001, 52006011
<<YEAR 1710: SP 45022036 <<YEAR 1713: HI 48013004 <<YEAR 1716: BE 51004017 <<YEAR 1740: BY 09017045

Artists <"b.Artists">
<<YEAR 1767: WI 18037014

Assize : See the heading in Index D

Association or Meeting of Dissenting Clergy <"Assoc.", "Assoc.s.","Gen.Assem.","Op.Gen.Ass.","Op.G.Asse.">
<<YEAR 1696: PE 10020001 <<YEAR 1706: SP 27012003 <<YEAR 1708: GI 54004017 <<YEAR 1713: CA 43010016
<<YEAR 1714: CU 19012001 <<YEAR 1718: HO 57004012 HU 68000003 <<YEAR 1719: GI 43007001 <<YEAR 1720:
DO 58002024 <<YEAR 1722: DO 63003015 <<YEAR 1731: NA 59002011 <<YEAR 1735: AM 46008011 <<YEAR 1738:
BO 53001027 <<YEAR 1739: PI 61004014 <<YEAR 1742: LA 27004026 <<YEAR 1743: LA 43010016 <<YEAR 1747:
GI 27002044 KI 50006003 <<YEAR 1749: BR 61012014 <<YEAR 1752: BO 44004030 <<YEAR 1753: PI 53001027
ST 23053001 <<YEAR 1754: JO 28004001 <<YEAR 1760: HO 47007032 <<YEAR 1764: PR 48014007 ST 46005041
<<YEAR 1766: OS 19016006 <<YEAR 1768: PO 19132016 <<YEAR 1769: SC 11022014 ST 45005005 <<YEAR 1770:
WA 57002008 <<YEAR 1771: GR 43004017 <<YEAR 1773: EV 37001003 GI 26010013 HU 50013008 <<YEAR 1775:
BE 48010002 TO 23049004 <<YEAR 1776: WA 49010033 <<YEAR 1779: EV 48003031 WA 50013011 <<YEAR 1780:
CA 46015012 GE 46008014 TU 54003014 <<YEAR 1781: HO 45017020 <<YEAR 1782: WO 50004007

Asylum <"Asyl.s.","Lun.Asy."> [Usually b. Gov.of "the" Asylum -- for orphans? but sometimes otherwise specified in Vol.V.]
<<YEAR 1670: SH 52006004 <<YEAR 1761: HA 52005016 <<YEAR 1763: MA 48012015 <<YEAR 1765: BR 19144012
<<YEAR 1766: HA 20029015 <<YEAR 1768: FR 28014003 <<YEAR 1770: AS 45016025 <<YEAR 1773: NE 46008012
PO 45006030 <<YEAR 1774: HO 47020035 WO 45015010 <<YEAR 1779: MA 43018014 <<YEAR 1780: SC 44005015
<<YEAR 1781: GL 43025035 TI 01001026

Bible Society : See, within the present Index C, the heading "Society, Bible."

Charity School : See the heading in Index D

Clergy, Sons of <"Cl.s">
<<YEAR 16--: HO 18011012 <<YEAR 1683: BU 48010015 RU 63003015 <<YEAR 1685: SC 45019046 TU 01018019
<<YEAR 1686: DO 68000003 <<YEAR 1688: MA 19100003 <<YEAR 1691: TE 57005021 <<YEAR 1692: FO 46013034
<<YEAR 1693: LA 61013007 <<YEAR 1695: WH 59003008 <<YEAR 1696: IS 45010037 <<YEAR 1697: EN 44010021
<<YEAR 1700: AS 21009010 WE 19122008 <<YEAR 1701: BY 57004006 <<YEAR 1702: KE 20017006 <<YEAR 1703:
RE 69002001 <<YEAR 1704: BU 62001027 <<YEAR 1705: SP 64001007 <<YEAR 1706: AL 51006010 <<YEAR 1708:
BI 16013013 WI 55002013 <<YEAR 1710: SP 51006010 <<YEAR 1711: BE 43004016 MA 51006010, 52006010
<<YEAR 1712: SM 02020012 <<YEAR 1713: BE 48001016 CO 18029012 SA 57005008 <<YEAR 1714: CH 12004001
<<YEAR 1715: SA 49009013 <<YEAR 1716: BI 23051001 <<YEAR 1717: SM 20022001 <<YEAR 1719: EA 50005014
SM 49004002 <<YEAR 1720: BE 43005016 <<YEAR 1721: WA 43005016 <<YEAR 1724: ED 19122006 <<YEAR 1725:
RO 49009011 <<YEAR 1726: DO 61013001 <<YEAR 1727: HU 44014006 ST 59001005 <<YEAR 1728: DE 19033012
<<YEAR 1729: KI 49009005 LU 49013013 <<YEAR 1730: AT 48011016 SP 61013007 <<YEAR 1731: TU 62001027
<<YEAR 1732: WA 63002012 <<YEAR 1733: ST 50003009 <<YEAR 1734: LA 55005013 MA 38002007 <<YEAR 1736:
BA 49013013 RO 18029011 <<YEAR 1737: BE 05014029 ST 19122008 TE 48016001 <<YEAR 1738: MA 61010024
<<YEAR 1739: BA 04011029 <<YEAR 1740: BA 12004001 <<YEAR 1741: YA 18031016 <<YEAR 1742: MA 08002020
<<YEAR 1744: TR 51006010 <<YEAR 1745: AS 61013016 <<YEAR 1746: NI 46019026 <<YEAR 1748: KE 48014016
<<YEAR 1750: HU 12004001 <<YEAR 1751: CL 05012012 KI 12004001 <<YEAR 1752: CO 62001027 <<YEAR 1754:
BU 49009011 <<YEAR 1755: SA 26037003 WO 51006009 <<YEAR 1756: CH 62001027 <<YEAR 1757: CO 43005007
RI 21009016 <<YEAR 1758: IB 51006010 <<YEAR 1759: AB 25003041 <<YEAR 1760: DO 24049011 <<YEAR 1761:
BU 19122008 <<YEAR 1762: HO 25005003 <<YEAR 1763: FR 24049011 SH 05014028, 12004001 <<YEAR 1764:
HI 48014016 <<YEAR 1765: HA 01047022 <<YEAR 1766: DA 62001027 <<YEAR 1767: EY 06013033 <<YEAR 1768:
FI 47004035 <<YEAR 1769: PE 46013035 SM 18029011, 24049011, 62001027 <<YEAR 1770: AS 61006010
WH 49009014 <<YEAR 1771: PA 50008003 <<YEAR 1772: MO 08002020 <<YEAR 1773: GL 28014003 <<YEAR 1774:
SH 43010041 <<YEAR 1776: PO 12004001 <<YEAR 1777: BU 49009013 CO 57006018 <<YEAR 1778: WA 62001027
<<YEAR 1779: RI 19122008 <<YEAR 1780: LA 19068005

Colony of Georgia : See the heading in Index D

Conciones Academicae <"Con.Acad.">
<<YEAR 1660: WI 49007029 <<YEAR 1664: MA 51005001 <<YEAR 1679: RE 49002014 <<YEAR 1688: CU 43006023
<<YEAR 1707: MI 68000003 <<YEAR 1712: BL 46009041 <<YEAR 1724: MA 43013058 <<YEAR 1729: BU 09002017,
09003012 <<YEAR 1737: ST 64001005 <<YEAR 1747: HU 46006053 <<YEAR 1748: BE 58002002 IB 45017020
<<YEAR 1749: MO 43005013 <<YEAR 1759: BU 11012002, 11019020 HE 54002008 TU 43013054 <<YEAR 1760:
BU 49003012 <<YEAR 1763: SH 46007017 <<YEAR 1773: CH 10001019 <<YEAR 1775: GO 23044028

Conciones ad Cleros <"Conc.ad Cl.">
<<YEAR 1663: BR 69002001 MA 50002016 <<YEAR 1666: OW 49009022 <<YEAR 1670: GL 48012001 <<YEAR 1671:
PI 47015028 <<YEAR 1672: ME 03019030 <<YEAR 1675: SM 48014019 <<YEAR 1677: MA 54001018 <<YEAR 1686:
YO 46013034 <<YEAR 1687: BA 29002012 BR 48010015 <<YEAR 1691: AN 50006003 <<YEAR 1696: SA 53002021
<<YEAR 1698: BE 58001013 <<YEAR 1700: ED 44005012 GA 48008014 <<YEAR 1701: MA 48005001, 49002006
SH 68000003 <<YEAR 1705: AL 58002015 LA 46020022 <<YEAR 1707: RO 24007012 <<YEAR 1708: RA 20006019
<<YEAR 1713: GA 50002016 <<YEAR 1714: BL 59001005 <<YEAR 1715: MI 50001012 <<YEAR 1724: DR 47017022
ES 52005016 RE 43011002 <<YEAR 1726: BI 49015028 <<YEAR 1727: TR 43010016 <<YEAR 1730: AT 48013001
<<YEAR 1732: GR 02033023 <<YEAR 1737: RO 49009016 <<YEAR 1739: WA 53002005, 57001018 <<YEAR 1742:
BE 57004016 <<YEAR 1743: TR 43010016 <<YEAR 1745: DE 64001016 <<YEAR 1746: HA 59002008 <<YEAR 1754:

HE 43006019	NO 19112009	SE 19122006	SH 45010036	WA 49012025	<<YEAR 1764:	AS 19103007	CU 45015010
NE 51006010	RI 19127003	YO 19041001	<<YEAR 1765:	EY 19106030	OW 09026010	SQ 45010027	WI 50009002
<<YEAR 1766:	CA 43014007	D' 21010020	DE 51006010	EW 61013016	OG 46008010	SE 48012008	<<YEAR 1767:
DO 20014028	GO 43018033	GR 13029014	NI 55004009	SE 45015018	WA 49013013	<<YEAR 1768:	DO 20019017
HA 24003001	MA 23053004	<<YEAR 1769:	BR 53001011	HA 05015011	MO 55004009	ST 09002007	TO 20018014
<<YEAR 1770:	BR 18029013	HA 43025040	MO 43005048	OG 45010035	RA 43014014	<<YEAR 1771:	GR 44001034
HU 45021003	LO 51006010	NO 20029008	RU 46005007	YO 43010010	<<YEAR 1772:	RO 19139014	SH 46013017,
48013008	YO 20022002	<<YEAR 1773:	HU 45015010	MA 49003009	<<YEAR 1774:	BR 41004010	
	DO 37003007	NO 24003013,	24031013,	57006018	SH 45010036	ST 47020035	<<YEAR 1775:
AU 50009012	SK 43025036	YO 48008013	<<YEAR 1776:	DO 46013035	MA 62005020	TU 49009022	
<<YEAR 1777:	BR 54003014	GL 46008011	HA 07016020	HE 52004028	MA 50007009	SC 46005006	WA 45014018
YO 44014007	<<YEAR 1779:	BA 43009004	WA 20016006	<<YEAR 1780:	HI 51004018	MA 45010037	<<YEAR 1781:
CH 20022002	HU 44016009	RU 20014031	<<YEAR 1782:	MI 43022037	RO 45015007		

ADDENDA under above heading ("Hospital or Infirmary, at, or before Governors of")

<<YEAR 1745:	HO 45016009	<<YEAR 1749:	YA 45010037	<<YEAR 1752:	BR 45010037	<<YEAR 1758:	FR 45010037
<<YEAR 1770:	AS 58003004	<<YEAR 1778:	BU 05015011				

House of Commons (or, in three instances, Parliament) <"b.C.", "F.s.b.C.", "Th.s.b.C.", etc.;"Conv.o.Parl.", etc.>

Note 1: The three instances are the items YEAR 1679 RE 53002012 & 57004007; YEAR 1746 LE 46021022.

Note 2: Occasions or subjects -- The occasions or subjects noted by Cooke in his first volume as those of sermons delivered before the House of Commons are indicated within the set of index items below by small letters following commas after the biblical-text code numbers of the relevant items: a = Accession, f = Fast, j = January 30, m =May 29, n = November 5, t = Thanksgiving, u = occasion or subject unstated in Cooke's first volume.

<<YEAR 1660:	GA 32006008,f	PR 09002009,t	<<YEAR 1661:	GR 23058005,f	<<YEAR 1662:	HA 37012011,j	<<YEAR 1666:
PE 03026018,f	<<YEAR 1671:	PI 05006012,m	<<YEAR 1677:	BR 20028013,u	<<YEAR 1679:	JA 28007009,f	RE 38004002,u
53002012	57004007	<<YEAR 1680:	DO 19064009,n	OU 25004005,j	<<YEAR 1681:	BU 69003002,f	<<YEAR 1685:
SH 21010017,m	<<YEAR 1689:	BI 46016003,n	BU 19144015,j	TE 58003001,f	<<YEAR 1690:	FR 19089021,n	HI 23060010,t
<<YEAR 1691:	JA 19096010,t	<<YEAR 1692:	MA 47017022,n	SH 19090015,j	<<YEAR 1693:	BY 23057001,j	<<YEAR 1694:
BI 10001021,j	<<YEAR 1695:	HA 15008021,f	19090015,j	WI 09002030,f	<<YEAR 1696:	AD 27003028,n	HA 32007002,j
LA 25005016,j	<<YEAR 1697:	LA 23053007,j	<<YEAR 1699:	SM 19080019,f	<<YEAR 1700:	ST 59003001,j	<<YEAR 1701:
FI 23001026,m	HO 53003020,f	IS 09004013,f	<<YEAR 1702:	BI 45023034,j	DE 43027025,j	ST 09012024,f	WH 24006008,f
<<YEAR 1704:	BI 19124006,n	GA 19046001,f	WY 52004003,j	<<YEAR 1705:	ST 19094020,j	WI 01049007,n	<<YEAR 1707:
BA 26036031,f	TR 20021030,f	<<YEAR 1708:	PE 02020005,j	<<YEAR 171-:	BR 21008014,j	<<YEAR 1710:	BI 23062006,f
BL 59003001,a	SP 43005010,j	WE 24031029,j	<<YEAR 1711:	FR 24003025,j	TO 19085001,m	TR 20017014,j	<<YEAR 1712:
AL 63003010,f	GO 19011003,j	NE 63002017,a	PH 19075007,m	<<YEAR 1713:	HO 19122007,t	SA 63002016,m	<<YEAR 1714:
BI 19071020,m	<<YEAR 1715:	AW 23028029,m	LI 10022051,a	PO 63002017,a	WR 47023014,n	<<YEAR 1716:	BL 23049020,j
WA 29002012,f	<<YEAR 1718:	HO 49010011,j	<<YEAR 1719:	SY 19118023,a	WA 21008014,j	<<YEAR 1720:	BA 46005014,j
MA 23057001,j	WI 01018032,f	<<YEAR 1721:	HA 23041017,m	MA 02020005,j	<<YEAR 1722:	BU 63002016,n	<<YEAR 1723:
AL 02033019,t	ST 21008014,j	<<YEAR 1724:	SM 01049006,j	<<YEAR 1725:	KN 12011019,m	LO 25005007,j	<<YEAR 1726:
BA 68000011,j	CA 18027005,u	LO 24005007,j	<<YEAR 1729:	LU 09012025,j	SH 05005029,f	69002005,f	YO 63002017,j
<<YEAR 1730:	AT 26037003,m	57002001,a	CR 20025005,j	LI 63002016,j	<<YEAR 1732:	GE 19097001,m	MA 48013001,j
<<YEAR 1733:	RY 64002019,m	<<YEAR 1734:	CL 19050023,t	<<YEAR 1735:	DE 14009008,a	TI 21009011,f	45009055,n
<<YEAR 1736:	AY 48012003,j	<<YEAR 1737:	FL 12008013,j	46016002,n	<<YEAR 1738:	MO 25005007,j	WI 20024021,j
<<YEAR 1739:	GA 57002001,a	TH 19077009,m	<<YEAR 1740:	BA 14020003,f	WH 61011004,j	<<YEAR 1741:	CL 11008044,f
HU 63002017,j	<<YEAR 1742:	ST 25002006,j	TE 57002001,a	<<YEAR 1743:	CH 63002016,j	NE 20017014,j	<<YEAR 1744:
CR 20017014,j	<<YEAR 1745:	AS 43007015,n	NE 69002005,f	SN 19076010,m	30004010,f	TH 49010011,j	<<YEAR 1746:
BE 59003001,f	HA 19071017,t	19089020,a	LE 46021022,u	RU 23058004,j	TU 19126003,m	<<YEAR 1747:	HU 24031013,m
NI 19057001,f	PE 19020006,a	<<YEAR 1748:	DR 23019002,j		<<YEAR 1749:	CO 19122006,t	EL 43022021,j
FU 05009006,m	WA 61004012,f	<<YEAR 1750:	BE 57002001,j	<<YEAR 1751:	AL 12008011,j	SQ 63002013,j	<<YEAR 1752:
CR 63002016,j	<<YEAR 1753:	BL 12008011,j	HO 23032001,j	<<YEAR 1754:	WI 49012021,j	<<YEAR 1755:	FR 63002016,j
<<YEAR 1756:	MO 23026009,f	TE 24018007,f	<<YEAR 1757:	PA 20017014,j	<<YEAR 1758:	BU 45019041,f	FO 19122006,m
TH 48012003,j	48013003,j	<<YEAR 1759:	DA 19095001,t	RO 28013009,j	<<YEAR 1760:	BU 49010011,j	HA 18001005,f

<<YEAR 1761:	SQ 19018003,f	<<YEAR 1762:	BA 23005003,f	SA 20017014,j	<<YEAR 1763:	BR 63002016,j	<<YEAR 1764:
RI 43022021,j	<<YEAR 1765:	HI 50003017,j	<<YEAR 1766:	BA 43022021,j	<<YEAR 1767:	PO 43006033,j	<<YEAR 1768:
ST 59003001,j	<<YEAR 1769:	HA 51005013,j	YO 55004011,j	<<YEAR 1770:	AS 43010034,j	45012051,j	BA 19076010,j
<<YEAR 1771:	BU 46009001,j	KI 48013005,j	<<YEAR 1774:	SH 10023003,a	19122006,t	<<YEAR 1778:	PA 09004013,f
<<YEAR 1779:	PO 24018011,f	ST 63002017,f	<<YEAR 1780:	HO 05023009,f	<<YEAR 1781:	HO 23026009,f	<<YEAR 1782:
DA 26018030,f							

House of Lords <"b.L.", "F.s.b.L.", "Th.s.b.L.", etc., etc.>

<<YEAR 1660:	BU 48007025,	62003015	HA 23057019	<<YEAR 1663:	PA 10019014	<<YEAR 1666:	HA 19007009
<<YEAR 1673:	PE 19111004	<<YEAR 1674:	CR 23057021	WA 12006033	<<YEAR 1678:	TH 45013005	<<YEAR 1679:
RE 53002012,	53004005,	57004007	<<YEAR 1680:	FE 43012025	<<YEAR 1689:	BU 32006005	<<YEAR 1691:
PA 05004009	<<YEAR 1692:	KI 43023035	<<YEAR 1694:	SA 19057001	<<YEAR 1695:	GA 19079009	<<YEAR 1696:
HU 28010003	PA 27004035	<<YEAR 1697:	ES 62001021	LL 37007005	<<YEAR 1701:	HO 19127001	<<YEAR 1702:
TR 06023008	WI 47007059	<<YEAR 1703:	NI 58002011	<<YEAR 1704:	BR 17009020	CL 45009055	HO 50010003
WI 19145004	<<YEAR 1707:	TY 21008014	<<YEAR 1708:	TR 19020006	<<YEAR 1709:	HO 19031023	<<YEAR 1711:
BI 37008010	<<YEAR 1713:	HO 19122007	<<YEAR 1715:	MO 57002001	WI 20024021	WY 19147001	<<YEAR 1716:
RA 19066012	SY 23001026	<<YEAR 1717:	CH 07017006	<<YEAR 1719:	BR 43012025	KE 44014019	<<YEAR 1720:
BE 17009027	BO 23055006	<<YEAR 1721:	GR 23026009	RE 11012019	<<YEAR 1722:	BO 20024021	WA 43007015,
43026051	<<YEAR 1723:	BA 57002001	BL 25005007	<<YEAR 1724:	SM 19115001	<<YEAR 1725:	WH 23054017
<<YEAR 1726:	LE 62004001	<<YEAR 1727:	EG 20024021	ST 46016002	<<YEAR 1728:	SM 09026009	<<YEAR 1729:
SH 48010002,	59003001	WA 24026014	<<YEAR 1730:	BR 48013005	CL 09012025	<<YEAR 1731:	TA 23058003
<<YEAR 1732:	PE 43010034	<<YEAR 1733:	DA 19021007,	43021038	<<YEAR 1734:	HA 28010006	<<YEAR 1735:
CL 57002001	TI 24006008,	37007005	<<YEAR 1737:	BU 19122006	<<YEAR 1738:	BE 19078005	<<YEAR 1739:
MA 19111004	<<YEAR 1740:	GO 14020015	MA 09007006	<<YEAR 1742:	CL 19092001	GI 52004026	MA 15009009
<<YEAR 1743:	HU 43012025	<<YEAR 1744:	LI 23005004	<<YEAR 1745:	LI 69002005	TH 64002019	TR 23005020
<<YEAR 1746:	GI 20024021	HA 20024021	HU 06001007	LA 19047007	LE 46021022	MA 62003016	<<YEAR 1747:
TR 49010011	<<YEAR 1748:	KI 45009054	OS 04021005	TH 31001007	<<YEAR 1749:	BU 57002001,	63002016
CR 19066007	DR 19144010	PE 47023005	<<YEAR 1750:	HA 63002017	<<YEAR 1751:	CO 12019003,	19078072
<<YEAR 1752:	BE 09015023	<<YEAR 1753:	JO 19111004	KE 49010011	PO 19020005	<<YEAR 1754:	EL 63002016
HO 49010011	<<YEAR 1756:	GR 23026009	NE 61012005	SQ 69002005	TH 23026009	<<YEAR 1757:	EG 14022007
HU 06024015	<<YEAR 1758:	EL 23001026	HU 45008024	TE 62004001	TH 45008024	<<YEAR 1759:	AS 09012024
JO 27002010	<<YEAR 1760:	PE 19020007	<<YEAR 1761:	EG 28003004	YO 20021030	<<YEAR 1762:	EW 20021031
<<YEAR 1763:	GR 48013007	HE 63002013	<<YEAR 1764:	NE 53004005	<<YEAR 1765:	LY 45002014	<<YEAR 1766:
KE 62003017	SE 19106012	<<YEAR 1767:	LO 20024021	WA 23019013	<<YEAR 1768:	LA 62003016	<<YEAR 1769:
MO 62004001	NE 46008047	WO 45021023	<<YEAR 1770:	SH 23033006	<<YEAR 1771:	LA 27002020	<<YEAR 1772:
BA 20001032	<<YEAR 1773:	HI 53004005	<<YEAR 1774:	MA 23003003	SH 44003024,	45009054	<<YEAR 1776:
TH 45009054	YO 43005009	<<YEAR 1777:	HU 19119059	MO 63002017	<<YEAR 1778:	BU 21007014	PO 19022028
<<YEAR 1779:	RO 20024021	<<YEAR 1780:	TH 63002017	WA 29001014			

Humane Society <"b.Hum.Soc.", etc.>

<<YEAR 1775:	HA 51006010	<<YEAR 1778:	MA 19103004	MI 48014007	<<YEAR 1779:	FR 09020003	<<YEAR 1780:
NE 19124004	<<YEAR 1781:	DU 31002005	<<YEAR 1782:	BR 45008052			

King, or both King and Queen <"b.K.","Rest.s.b.K.","Th.s.b.K.", etc.; "Th.s.b.K.& Q." etc.>

Note 1: Ampersand "&": Sermons before both King and Queen: An ampersand "&" has been inserted immediately before the biblical-text code numbers of all items concerning sermons that Cooke in his first volume recorded as delivered before King and Queen together.

Note 2: Occasions or Subjects: The occasions or subjects recorded by Cooke in his first volume as those of sermons delivered before King or King and Queen are indicated within the set of index items below by small letters following commas after the biblical-text code numbers of the relevant items: a = accession, f = fast, j = January 30, m = May 29, n = November 5, t = thanksgiving, u = occasion or subject unstated in Cooke's first volume; o = observance of religious holy day or season, r = some other religious or theological subject, x = some occasion or subject other than those named above.

INDEXES TO THIRD VOLUME: C: SPECIAL AUDIENCES

Note 3: It is worth notice that the proportion of items concerning sermons occasioned by the remembrance days January 30 (execution of Charles I), May 29 (Restoration of Charles II), and November 5 (Guy Fawkes Day) in this set regarding sermons delivered before King or King and Queen appears significantly lower than in the sets regarding sermons before the House of Commons, the House of Lords, or the Lord Mayor.

Note 4: It is also interesting that many of the sermons delivered before King (as also of those before Queen) were occasioned by religious holy days or seasons, whereas few or none of those delivered before House of Commons, House of Lords, or Lord Mayor had such occasions or subjects.

Note 5: Number of items regarding religious observances o or religious subjects r:
31 o = 1 Advent + 1 Ash-Wednesday + 3 Easter + 5 Christmas + 15 Lent + 6 Passion;
9 r = 1 Purification + 2 Religion + 1 Christian Union + 1 Mutual Charity + 1 Sacred Love + 1 Blessing God + 1 Censure + 1 Fear of God. (Relevant items within the Addenda at bottom of this list are included in these counts.)

<<YEAR 1660:
<<YEAR 1666:
BA 65005004,u
<<YEAR 1674:
30009002,n
68000022,u
SU 43028020,m
<<YEAR 1682:
AL 28003005,m
GO 51003021,o
<<YEAR 1690:
RO 61011033,u
<<YEAR 1694:
<<YEAR 1696:
52005002,o
ST&09002030,x
FI 52002018,o
LY 27012003,u
WA 16004011,n
WA&45016025,u
TA 50001010,t
21007014,x
<<YEAR 1740:
51002018,u
45016002,u
<<YEAR 1772:
48002014,u
43009013,u
<<YEAR 1782:
HA 47015039,o
DO 19018001,t
<<YEAR 1671:
JA 45001074,u
47028005,n
CR 53001021,o
WI 21012013,r
CR 49001010,u
HE 43005017,u
KI 19002006,m
BU&19144010,t
&65005003,u
CL&21005001,u
HA 47016030,u
KI 10024014,n
<<YEAR 1709:
<<YEAR 1713:
WI 23033006,t
<<YEAR 1718:
61010031,o
65004001,n
TI 06024015,u
BU 05004006,u
<<YEAR 1757:
49011001,u
SH 19075007,u
50005017,u
43011006,u
YO 24005025,f
SH 19018049,x
<<YEAR 1667:
NO 19001001,u
LL 48008013,o
LA 51006007,u
HA 38003014,u
21012014,o
FU 43006023,u
IR 63004015,u
<<YEAR 1686:
GR&65002015,u
<<YEAR 1692:
HO&46007017,u
LA 20003006,u
<<YEAR 1699:
BA 51005012,u
BU&14015002,x
<<YEAR 1716:
BR 46017020,r
<<YEAR 1729:
<<YEAR 1733:
&45010042,u
<<YEAR 1741:
CO 43005003,u
<<YEAR 1767:
20015024,u
53002012,u
45016008,u
SW 19082006,u
MO 49014033,n
PI 32006009,f
VI 19008005,u
ME 59001016,u
PA 47007059,u
<<YEAR 1678:
43022021,u
MA 28003005,m
LA 20022004,u
PE&45001071,u
WA 05010012,t
ST&21005001,o
ME&48012005,u
HE 24005005,u
<<YEAR 1710:
<<YEAR 1714:
BR 45012051,u
CH 46001014,o
SH&19097001,t
DA 18005012,n
53003020,u
JO 20028001,u
43005004,u
WA 20014009,o
24010023,u
58003004,u
46010025,u
TO 46014002,o
<<YEAR 1668:
45002022,r
<<YEAR 1675:
ST 50005020,u
SC 18028028,u
LA 45009055,n
<<YEAR 1683:
TU 28006002,o
<<YEAR 1688:
WI&54003001,u
<<YEAR 1693:
<<YEAR 1695:
&62002026,u
<<YEAR 1706:
LU 48006021,o
BU 19002010,u
HA 43015009,u
HA 54003014,r
46020029,o
<<YEAR 1734:
&59003002,o
50001003,r
43005005,u
49009024,o
45015031,u
<<YEAR 1779:
59003010,u
<<YEAR 1665:
LA 44004024,o
<<YEAR 1673:
BA 64003016,t
SU 53004022,u
SU 57003015,u
<<YEAR 1679:
ST 48008003,o
<<YEAR 1685:
SC&20008015,j
<<YEAR 1691:
FR 65005004,u
BU 50006001,o
<<YEAR 1697:
YO 46015022,o
SP&43007021,o
<<YEAR 1715:
<<YEAR 1717:
<<YEAR 1721:
51005013,u
SH 43018007,u
<<YEAR 1737:
<<YEAR 1754:
43005006,u
<<YEAR 1770:
46003018,u
GL 19044006,u
61003013,u
DO 19054006,t
LI 14029020,u
HA 56002010,u
HA 16001004,f
<<YEAR 1676:
<<YEAR 1677:
PI 65004001,u
TU 19144009,t
CA 19004007,u
<<YEAR 1689:
LL&19075006,u
LA 23057021,u
PE 19109027,u
BU 14009008,t
<<YEAR 1707:
51004018,r
BR 48002028,u
BE 48014007,u
PE&20014034,f
<<YEAR 1731:
<<YEAR 1735:
FL 21007004,o
HO 19126003,m
43005008,u
SE 50005021,o
46012024,u
LO 45013001,o
<<YEAR 1780:
46019019,o
<<YEAR 1670:
JA 24026019,u
19041009,u
CA 50002011,u
ME 43003008,u
RE 61013020,o
<<YEAR 1684:
DO 47016004,u
LL&19057006,n
PE&47024016,u
WI&43006034,u
SM 45022036,u
51004004,o
KI 21008011,u
<<YEAR 1712:
BU 19147001,m
LA 48006023,u
<<YEAR 1722:
MA 45011035,n
LI 19019011,r
43023015,n
48014004,r
&43005010,u
53002021,o
48002007,u
PE 19119071,u
LA 43016026,u

ADDENDA under above heading ("King, or both King and Queen")

<<YEAR 1667: LL 46006014,o <<YEAR 1686: EL&43012041,o <<YEAR 1690: LL&64003009,f <<YEAR 1691: BU&19012001,f
<<YEAR 1707: ST 18023015,r <<YEAR 1722: WA 43012025,j <<YEAR 1726: CA 20001010,u <<YEAR 1752: HA 40007031,u
<<YEAR 1754: HO 49007031,u

Levant - Company <"Lev.Co.">
<<YEAR 1664: LU 49015029 <<YEAR 1668: SM 63003019 <<YEAR 1681: HI 46004021 <<YEAR 1683: HU 19107023
<<YEAR 1689: SM 23026009 <<YEAR 1690: MA 21007016 <<YEAR 1698: CH 19107023 <<YEAR 1701: BR 43013045
TI 43016026 <<YEAR 1702: TI 43026006 <<YEAR 1706: OW 19119059 <<YEAR 1707: HA 32006008 <<YEAR 1713:
CR 61001014 <<YEAR 1717: MO 23034016 <<YEAR 1718: PA 21008002 <<YEAR 1719: SO 21007001 <<YEAR 1724:
BU 20003017

Lord Mayor <"b.L.M.", "F.s.b.L.M.", "Th.s.b.L.M.", etc.> (Also see "Mayor, Admission of," in following Index D.)
<<YEAR 1660: PO 46004023 TE 68000003 <<YEAR 1661: BE 19127001 HI 19118024 <<YEAR 1662: ST 20014008
<<YEAR 1669: BA 36001009 <<YEAR 1671: PI 48013012 <<YEAR 1673: CA 59003008 GR 05023009 LA 56003002
<<YEAR 1675: DU 20029001 <<YEAR 1676: CO 46008034 <<YEAR 1677: HE 10001017 PI 20017027 <<YEAR 1678:
BA 63002015 <<YEAR 1679: LY 14020017 NE 61009027 RE 14007013, 32006006, 37002005, 37003001
SE 62003013 WI 52004016 WO 19011003 <<YEAR 1680: CA 47017006 HA 45019042 HI 11018021 HO 19074020
LI 19037005, 19122008 PA 52006010 RO 20011011 SH 19097001 SM 37014007 <<YEAR 1681: BU 37008019
HO 51005022 JE 24005029 <<YEAR 1682: CA 46005014 EV 53004005 FR 19034012 HO 46001047 KI 63003011
LA 19119165 MA 45019041 PA 55004006 RI 20014034 TU 57002001 WE 20011019 <<YEAR 1683: CO 48012018
JA 65003008 LA 10001018 PE 45019042, 55004011 TU 49014040 <<YEAR 1684: BR 19058010 HE 63002015
LI 69021002 PE 55004013 WA 49008012 <<YEAR 1686: BE 68000003 FE 65005004 HI 20030008 ST 48013005
WE 26021025 <<YEAR 1688: TA 45010021 <<YEAR 1689: BA 53002002 LY 19127001 MA 46020009 TU 53004005
<<YEAR 1690: BU 45019041 FO 28011008 MA 53004005 <<YEAR 1692: BO 51005025 <<YEAR 1693: KN 19064009
WA 43024003 <<YEAR 1696: BR 48003008 BU 16009026 FO 19086012 ME 19011003 ST 54003015 <<YEAR 1697:
BU 62004009 GO 32004005, 43019016, 47017031 HI 61011006 PR 23001005 WO 26016049 <<YEAR 1698:
BR 52004003 ED 44003024 MI 49013003 <<YEAR 1699: MO 23001026, 45001074 <<YEAR 1700: BR 19011003
LA 68000003 <<YEAR 1701: BU 28010012 HO 65005007 NO 20027001 <<YEAR 1702: AL 27009007 KN 20023017
<<YEAR 1703: NE 10019030 ST 03019017 <<YEAR 1704: EL 57002001 PR 37001016 SC 10018028, 20024021,
45009056 WH 65003020 <<YEAR 1705: FO 19097001 KE 19144010 PO 46013035 <<YEAR 1708: MO 10019009
ZI 55005021 <<YEAR 1709: AD 19005011 GO 19119059 HI 45016029 <<YEAR 1710: BR 20004025 CO 24007023
LU 50005014 <<YEAR 1711: ST 45017016 <<YEAR 1713: BR 20029025, 51005001 HI 47017007 JO 43015014
<<YEAR 1714: BR 50001009 <<YEAR 1715: KE 20001012 MO 57006003 SK 48013001 TO 46013035 <<YEAR 1716:
AS 49004007 HI 07005023 ST 19129001 TU 43022021 <<YEAR 1717: SM 55002004 <<YEAR 1719: SH 54002008
SP 20021021 <<YEAR 172-: ME 19004004 <<YEAR 1720: EV 14015002 HA 37007005 <<YEAR 1721: BE 04023023
<<YEAR 1722: CA 19129001 WA 19144009 <<YEAR 1723: LA 48010002 MA 32006004 <<YEAR 1725: WA 43022021
<<YEAR 1726: PA 21009002 <<YEAR 1727: BR 11003009 <<YEAR 1728: BE 23001026 <<YEAR 1729: SH 48014019,
57004007 SY 19072006 TR 45023028 <<YEAR 1730: AT 19030006 BA 23009012 FR 57002001 <<YEAR 1731:
TH 62003017 WA 69003021 <<YEAR 1732: FE 63003008 SI 19044007 <<YEAR 1733: GO 43007020 MO 19035011
<<YEAR 1734: AT 43014001 <<YEAR 1736: MY 55005021 <<YEAR 1737: AR 48014019 FL 09026010, 21006011
<<YEAR 1738: BR 19118023 SH 58002023 WI 53001021 <<YEAR 1740: MO 48013001 VE 40003004 <<YEAR 1741:
FO 15007025 TO 19050014 <<YEAR 1742: KI 45013007 <<YEAR 1743: CO 48011033 <<YEAR 1744: CR 15009013
HA 57002002 PE 37003006 <<YEAR 1745: ME 23007005 PE 48003016 <<YEAR 1746: ME 14020027 SA 27004027
<<YEAR 1747: BA 30003002 GI 19115001 <<YEAR 1748: PI 19083018 WA 52005007 <<YEAR 1749: BR 49010031
WA 31003008 WI 27002004, 48013007 <<YEAR 1750: CO 47017022 MA 19002011 ME 49010017 PI 10001027
SA 19118024, 57002001 <<YEAR 1751: KI 19144010 WI 47024005 <<YEAR 1752: MU 20014034 <<YEAR 1753:
CO 23026009 <<YEAR 1759: TO 19122006 <<YEAR 1776: IB 43022021 <<YEAR 1782: WH 68000008

Lying - In Hospitals, at, about, or before Governors of <"Ly-Hosp.s.", "Ly-in.Hosp.", etc.>
<<YEAR 1750: TH 44012042 <<YEAR 1752: DO 51006002 TH 47010004 <<YEAR 1753: CH 12019003 <<YEAR 1754:
CH 51006009 DO 01003016 <<YEAR 1755: HA 02001019 <<YEAR 1757: DA 43005016 <<YEAR 1763: NO 19112009
<<YEAR 1764: RI 19127003 <<YEAR 1767: NI 55004009 <<YEAR 1771: NO 20029008 <<YEAR 1772: SH 48013008
<<YEAR 1782: MI 43022037

Marine - Society <"Mar.soc.", "Mar.Soc.">

<<YEAR 1774: GL 18030025 <<YEAR 1778: GL 48012008 <<YEAR 1779: MA 20019017

Masons : See "Free - Masons"

Military Company <"b.Milit.Co.","In a Siege","b.Garrison","b.Army","After Siege","Militar.s.","b.Malitia","F.s.b.Mil.">
(Also see Artillery Company in present Index C and Military Sermons in following Index D.)

<<YEAR 1671:	SC 69002010	<<YEAR 1673:	SC 51006011	<<YEAR 1690:	WH 24001018	<<YEAR 1692:	FA 45003014
<<YEAR 1694:	PE 09004009	<<YEAR 1715:	KE 19077019	<<YEAR 1744:	TA 52005013	<<YEAR 1759:	CA 45012004
PE 05023009	<<YEAR 1778:	BA 14015001	<<YEAR 1781:	HA 47010007			

Physicians or Surgeons Company <"Surg.Co.","b.Coll. Phys.", etc.>

<<YEAR 1708:	MO 19144003,	21003019	<<YEAR 1749:	BI 19139014	<<YEAR 1750:	ST 43011005	<<YEAR 1751:
HA 18010011	<<YEAR 1752:	CH 19103002	<<YEAR 1753:	VE 19119073	<<YEAR 1754:	BA 19104024	

Queen <"b.Q.", "F.s.b.Q.", "Th.s.b.Q.", *etc.*, *etc.*>

Note 1: The following set of index items does not include any that refer to sermons which Cooke described in his first volume as delivered before King and Queen together. Regarding such items, see the heading, *supra* within the present Index C, "King, or both King and Queen."

Note 2: *Occasions or Subjects*: The occasions or subjects recorded by Cooke in his first volume as those of sermons delivered before Queen are indicated within the set of index items below by small letters following commas after the biblical-text code numbers of the relevant items: a=accession, f = fast, j = January 30, m = May 29, n= November 5, t = thanksgiving, u = occasion or subject unstated in Cooke's first volume; o = observance of some holy day or holy season, r = some other religious or theological subject, x = some occasion or subject other than those named above.

Note 3: For comment upon the comparatively small proportion of items concerning January 30, May 29, and November 5 and the comparatively large number concerning religious matters, see Notes 3 and 4 under the heading, *supra* in the present Index C, "King, or both King and Queen."

Note 4: *Number of items regarding religious observances o or religious subjects r*:
17 o = 1 Ash-Wednesday + 2 Christmas + 2 Easter + 1 Good Friday + 10 Lent + 1 Passion;
7 r = 1 Temptation + 1 Christian Simplicity + 1 Mystery of Godliness + 1 Censure + 2 Humility + 1 Future State [of Soul & Body].

<<YEAR 1689:	PA 54003015,o	<<YEAR 1690:	DO 19018023,u	HI 19004004,u	<<YEAR 1691:	FO 62002010,u	HO 45016031,u
LA 59002010,u	LY 43006006,u	RE 18036028,u	<<YEAR 1692:	HI 05030015,u	LA 64001004,o	MA 23056007,u	PA 04010009,f
PE 54001012,u	RE 18033022,u	<<YEAR 1694:	BU 19105005,m	49001026,o	CO 19122006,f	KI 37007005,f	MA 19139023,u
20008012,u	TY 65003003,u	WY 06024015,u	<<YEAR 1695:	TE 19014001,u	<<YEAR 1696:	ME 10024014,f	43003008,o
65003020,u	<<YEAR 1702:	TA 65003008,o	<<YEAR 1703:	PE 48015005,u	ST 43004001,r	<<YEAR 1704:	CL 50001012,r
DU 19025014,u	LU 48012010,u	SH 19058011,t	ST 43008002,o	<<YEAR 1705:	AD 47028005,u	BL 57003016,r	RO 20016032,u
ST 43018035,u	VE 18002010,u	WI 23011013,t	<<YEAR 1706:	KE 21007014,u	MA 48008006,u	ST 05033029,t	43011028,u
<<YEAR 1707:	AD 28011009,u	46006067,o	BR 21008011,u	45010041,u	BU 19072004,t	CA 47011018,u	PA 48014010,r
<<YEAR 1708:	BR 47007060,j	MA 19046010,u	RA 19037037,u	<<YEAR 1709:	MA 21007014,t	49015028,u	WI 19090012,x
<<YEAR 1710:	BA 49015019,u	LU 19112007,f	SP 44010015,u	WI 20011020,u	<<YEAR 1711:	HI 45023028,j	<<YEAR 1712:
CH 48012019,x	GA 48014018,u	SP 54001026,o	<<YEAR 1713:	BU 23049023,a	NE 48010002,n	ST 46015005,u	<<YEAR 1714:
RE 54004005,u	<<YEAR 1715:	MO 18021015,u	43022021,a	<<YEAR 1719:	SH 19077010,f	<<YEAR 1722:	WA 57005022,o
61004001,u	<<YEAR 1723:	BL 43005003,r	48013004,a	<<YEAR 1724:	SM 43010016,n	<<YEAR 1727:	ST 05004007,n
45024025,u	50001009,t	<<YEAR 1729:	SH 47010040,o	53003010,o	61002003,o	65003008,o	<<YEAR 1730:
AT 18022021,u	43007012,n	<<YEAR 1731:	TA 05032029,o	19016008,u	19133001,t	<<YEAR 1733:	DA 05023009,f
49007031,o	<<YEAR 1734:	AT 51006014,o	CL 14031021,a	SH 20024021,j	31003005,f	58001010,r	<<YEAR 1735:
TI 43005044,o	<<YEAR 1737:	FL 05020001,f	43027024,u	MO 53002003,r	ST 43022021,j	<<YEAR 1738:	MO 21008011,f
<<YEAR 1774:	SH 20024021,j						

Schools : See following Index D under "School - Feasts" for sermons delivered at School Feasts, under "Charity Schools" for sermons concerning Charity Schools, and under "Irish Protestant Schools" for sermons concerning Irish Protestant Schools.

Smallpox Hospitals, at, about, or before Governors of <"Sm.Pox.H.", "Sm.Pox H.", "Smallpox H.", etc.>
<<YEAR 1752: MA 23058007 <<YEAR 1755: WA 19091001 <<YEAR 1758: BA 43025035 <<YEAR 1760: SQ 19041001
<<YEAR 1763: GR 45016019 <<YEAR 1764: YO 19041001 <<YEAR 1765: EY 19106030 <<YEAR 1766: D' 21010020
<<YEAR 1767: DO 20014028 <<YEAR 1769: HA 05015011 <<YEAR 1771: YO 43010010

Society, Bible, <"Bible soc.">
<<YEAR 1782: RO 58003015

Society for the Propagation of the Gospel or of Religion: See "Gospel Or Religion" in Index D.

Society for the Reformation of Manners : See the topic Reformation of Manners in the following Index D.

Society, Marine : See "Marine Society."
Society - Sermons, Batchelors <"Soc.Batch.">
<<YEAR 1707: HU 49006018

Society - Sermons, Charity <"Char.soc."> (Also see "Charity School" in Index D)
<<YEAR 1752: GI 43013045

Society - Sermons, Cole-Abby-Society <"Soc.s."> Note: The corresponding record in our Volume V under YEAR 17-- for an ss. by author HOWSON gives name of society.
<<YEAR 17--: HO 46013034

Society - Sermons, Education <Educ.Soc.">
<<YEAR 1773: EV 50003006

Society - Sermons, Female <"b.Fem.Soc.">
<<YEAR 1776: YO 54002002

Society - Sermons, Friendly <"Soc.s", "b.Frien.Soc.", "b.Friend.Soc.">
<<YEAR 1754: DA 62001027 <<YEAR 1765: PR 61013001 <<YEAR 1779: GI 52004025

Society - Sermons, Grateful <"Grat.Soc.">
<<YEAR 1772: LO 18029011

Society - Sermons, Lincoln's Inn, a Society at <"b.Soc.Linc.">
<<YEAR 1732: AN 18034013

Society - Sermons, Loving <"Lov. Society">
<<YEAR 1685: AS 23057021

Society - Sermons, Loyal <"Loy.Soc."> Note: In Cooke's "Index of Occasions, &c. &c." the following item appears indexed among "Society - Sermons, Relig."
<<YEAR 1687: LO 20024021

Society - Sermons, Religious
<<YEAR 1698: PO 03019017 <<YEAR 1710: LU 20013020 <<YEAR 1714: CA 38003016
<<YEAR 1721: TR 23058013 <<YEAR 1732: H. 19119136 <<YEAR 1739: BE 44009050 WH 21004009
<<YEAR 1743: TW 55005008 <<YEAR 1752: BA 38003017 <<YEAR 1766: SE 38003016
<<YEAR 1780: CA 13020020

Society - Sermons, Saltburgers <"b.Society"> Note: The corresponding record in our Volume V under YEAR 1733 for an ss. by author BURROUGHS gives name of society.
<<YEAR 1733: BU 68000003

Society - Sermons, Virtuous <"Virt.Soc.">
<<YEAR 1725: SH 20014034

Society - Sermons, Young Men <"Soc.Y.M."> Note: In Cooke's "Index of Occasional Sermons, &c. &ec." this heading appears as "Society - Sermons, Young Women."
<<YEAR 1714: WR 61010025 <<YEAR 1719: CU 68000003

Society - Sermons, society not specified by any further name within Cooke's records
<<YEAR 1754: DA 62001027 <<YEAR 1777: AD 51006002 <<YEAR 1778: AD 46015017

Spittal - Sermons : See the heading in Index D

Trinity House Corporation
<<YEAR 1665: FO 19107024 <<YEAR 1680: HO 27012004 <<YEAR 1695: FI 23043002 <<YEAR 1701: BA 21003012
<<YEAR 1710: WE 26027033 <<YEAR 1715: ST 43005016 <<YEAR 1724: WE 19107030 <<YEAR 1727: ST 19107023

Ubiquarians
<<YEAR 1738: BA 12010015 <<YEAR 1739: AU 09020019 <<YEAR 1746: BA 46008036, 47007017

Weaver's Company
<<YEAR 1742: EM 20022029 <<YEAR 1751: JE 02035035 <<YEAR 1753: WH 56002010

(INDEXES TO THIRD VOLUME)

APPENDIX TO INDEX C: SOME SETS OF AUDIENCE INDEX ITEMS SORTED AND ANALYZED IN RESPECT TO THE BIBLICAL TEXTS TO WHICH THE ITEMS REFER

APPENDIX TO INDEX C TO THIRD VOLUME: SOME SETS OF AUDIENCE INDEX ITEMS SORTED AND ANALYZED FOR BIBLICAL TEXT REFERENCE
(b. Commons)

HOUSE OF COMMONS: SERMONS BEFORE (Read columns downward in succession. Biblical text omitted if same as preceding text.)
(For a list of biblical books by code no. see end papers inside covers of this volume.)

Bib.Text BkChpVrs	Sermons printed
01018032	YEAR 1720
01049006	YEAR 1724
01049007	YEAR 1705
02020005	YEAR 1708
	YEAR 1721
02033019	YEAR 1723
03026018	YEAR 1666
05005029	YEAR 1729
05006012	YEAR 1671
05009006	YEAR 1749
05023009	YEAR 1780
09002009	YEAR 1660
09002030	YEAR 1695
09004013	YEAR 1701
	YEAR 1778
09012024	YEAR 1702
09012025	YEAR 1729
10001021	YEAR 1694
10022051	YEAR 1715
10023003	YEAR 1774
11008044	YEAR 1741
12008011	YEAR 1751
	YEAR 1753
12008013	YEAR 1737
12011019	YEAR 1725
14009008	YEAR 1735
14020003	YEAR 1740
15008021	YEAR 1695
18001005	YEAR 1760
18027005	YEAR 1726
19011003	YEAR 1712
19018003	YEAR 1761
19020006	YEAR 1747
19046001	YEAR 1704
19050023	YEAR 1734
19057001	YEAR 1747
19064009	YEAR 1680
19071017	YEAR 1746
19071020	YEAR 1714
19075007	YEAR 1712
19076010	YEAR 1745
	YEAR 1770
19077009	YEAR 1739
19080019	YEAR 1699
19085001	YEAR 1711
19089020	YEAR 1746
19089021	YEAR 1690

Bib.Text BkChpVrs	Sermons printed
19090015	YEAR 1692
	YEAR 1695
19094020	YEAR 1705
19095001	YEAR 1759
19096010	YEAR 1691
19097001	YEAR 1732
19118023	YEAR 1719
19122006	YEAR 1749
	YEAR 1758
	YEAR 1774
19122007	YEAR 1713
19124006	YEAR 1704
19126003	YEAR 1746
19144015	YEAR 1689
20017014	YEAR 1711
	YEAR 1743
	YEAR 1744
	YEAR 1757
	YEAR 1762
20021030	YEAR 1707
20024021	YEAR 1738
20025005	YEAR 1730
20028013	YEAR 1677
21008014	YEAR 171-
	YEAR 1719
	YEAR 1723
21009011	YEAR 1735
21010017	YEAR 1685
23001026	YEAR 1701
23005003	YEAR 1762
23019002	YEAR 1748
23026009	YEAR 1756
	YEAR 1781
23028029	YEAR 1715
23032001	YEAR 1753
23041017	YEAR 1721
23049020	YEAR 1716
23053007	YEAR 1697
23057001	YEAR 1693
	YEAR 1720
23058004	YEAR 1746
23058005	YEAR 1661
23060010	YEAR 1690
23062006	YEAR 1710
24003025	YEAR 1711
24005007	YEAR 1726
24006008	YEAR 1702

Bib.Text BkChpVrs	Sermons printed
24018007	YEAR 1756
24018011	YEAR 1779
24031013	YEAR 1747
24031029	YEAR 1710
25002006	YEAR 1742
25004005	YEAR 1680
25005007	YEAR 1725
	YEAR 1738
25005016	YEAR 1696
26018030	YEAR 1782
26036031	YEAR 1707
26037003	YEAR 1730
27003028	YEAR 1696
28007009	YEAR 1679
28013009	YEAR 1759
29002012	YEAR 1716
30004010	YEAR 1745
32006008	YEAR 1660
32007002	YEAR 1696
37012011	YEAR 1662
38004002	YEAR 1679
43005010	YEAR 1710
43006033	YEAR 1767
43007015	YEAR 1745
43010034	YEAR 1770
43022021	YEAR 1749
	YEAR 1764
	YEAR 1766
43027025	YEAR 1702
45009055	YEAR 1735
45012051	YEAR 1770
45019041	YEAR 1758
45023034	YEAR 1702
46005014	YEAR 1720
46007046	YEAR 1749
46009001	YEAR 1771
46016002	YEAR 1737
46016003	YEAR 1689
46021022	YEAR 1746
47017022	YEAR 1692
47023014	YEAR 1715
48012003	YEAR 1736
	YEAR 1758
48013001	YEAR 1732
48013003	YEAR 1758
48013005	YEAR 1771
49010011	YEAR 1718
	YEAR 1745
	YEAR 1760

Bib.Text BkChpVrs	Sermons printed
49012021	YEAR 1754
50003017	YEAR 1765
51005013	YEAR 1769
52004003	YEAR 1704
53002012	YEAR 1679
53003020	YEAR 1701
55004011	YEAR 1769
57002001	YEAR 1730
	YEAR 1739
	YEAR 1742
	YEAR 1750
57004007	YEAR 1679
58003001	YEAR 1689
59003001	YEAR 1700
	YEAR 1710
	YEAR 1746
	YEAR 1768
61004012	YEAR 1749
61011004	YEAR 1740
63002013	YEAR 1751
63002016	YEAR 1713
	YEAR 1722
	YEAR 1730
	YEAR 1743
	YEAR 1752
	YEAR 1755
	YEAR 1763
63002017	YEAR 1712
	YEAR 1715
	YEAR 1729
	YEAR 1741
	YEAR 1779
63003010	YEAR 1712
64002019	YEAR 1733
68000011	YEAR 1726
69002005	YEAR 1729
	YEAR 1745
69003002	YEAR 1681

House of Commons: Statistical Analysis of Set of Index Items Regarding Texts Used for Sermons before This Audience

a. Frequency (Number of records of a text)	b. Number of texts with that frequency of record	c. Number of records of those texts (c = a X b)	d. Cumulative percentage of the texts	e. Cumulative percentage of records	f. Percentage of all the records in this set (c/ Total c)
1	124	124	86.71	68.51	68.51
2	10	20	93.71	79.56	11.05
3	4	12	96.50	86.19	6.63
4	2	8	97.90	90.61	4.42
5	2	10	99.30	96.13	5.52
7	1	7	100.00	100.00	3.87
Totals	143	181			100.00

Average no. of records per text within this set: M = 1.2657 Standard deviation from average: SD = .8442
Type/token ratio = 1/M = 0.7901 Coefficient of variation = SD/M = .6669
Yule's K = 45.7861 (A measure of the concentration of records upon a relatively few texts)

APPENDIX TO INDEX C TO THIRD VOLUME: SOME SETS OF AUDIENCE INDEX ITEMS SORTED AND ANALYZED FOR BIBLICAL TEXT REFERENCE
(b. Lords)

HOUSE OF LORDS: SERMONS BEFORE (Read columns downward in succession. Biblical text omitted if same as preceding text.)
(For a list of biblical books by code no. see end papers inside covers of this volume.)

Bib.Text BkChpVrs	Sermons printed
04021005	YEAR 1748
05004009	YEAR 1691
06001007	YEAR 1746
06023008	YEAR 1702
06024015	YEAR 1757
07017006	YEAR 1717
09007006	YEAR 1740
09012024	YEAR 1759
09012025	YEAR 1730
09015023	YEAR 1752
09026009	YEAR 1728
10019014	YEAR 1663
11012019	YEAR 1721
12006033	YEAR 1674
12019003	YEAR 1751
14020015	YEAR 1740
14022007	YEAR 1757
15009009	YEAR 1742
17009020	YEAR 1704
17009027	YEAR 1720
19007009	YEAR 1666
19020005	YEAR 1753
19020006	YEAR 1708
19020007	YEAR 1760
19021007	YEAR 1733
19022028	YEAR 1778
19031023	YEAR 1709
19047007	YEAR 1746
19057001	YEAR 1694
19066007	YEAR 1749
19066012	YEAR 1716
19078005	YEAR 1738
19078072	YEAR 1751
19079009	YEAR 1695
19092001	YEAR 1742
19106012	YEAR 1766
19111004	YEAR 1673
	YEAR 1739
	YEAR 1753
19115001	YEAR 1724
19119059	YEAR 1777
19122006	YEAR 1737
19122007	YEAR 1713
19127001	YEAR 1701
19144010	YEAR 1749
19145004	YEAR 1704
19147001	YEAR 1715

Bib.Text BkChpVrs	Sermons printed
20001032	YEAR 1772
20021030	YEAR 1761
20021031	YEAR 1762
20024021	YEAR 1715
	YEAR 1722
	YEAR 1727
	YEAR 1746
	YEAR 1746
	YEAR 1767
	YEAR 1779
21007014	YEAR 1778
21008014	YEAR 1707
23001026	YEAR 1716
	YEAR 1758
23003003	YEAR 1774
23005004	YEAR 1744
23005020	YEAR 1745
23019013	YEAR 1767
23026009	YEAR 1721
	YEAR 1756
	YEAR 1756
23033006	YEAR 1770
23054017	YEAR 1725
23055006	YEAR 1720
23057019	YEAR 1660
23057021	YEAR 1674
23058003	YEAR 1731
24006008	YEAR 1735
24026014	YEAR 1729
25005007	YEAR 1723
27002010	YEAR 1759
27002020	YEAR 1771
27004035	YEAR 1696
28003004	YEAR 1761
28010003	YEAR 1696
28010006	YEAR 1734
29001014	YEAR 1780
31001007	YEAR 1748
32006005	YEAR 1689
37007005	YEAR 1697
	YEAR 1735
37008010	YEAR 1711
43005009	YEAR 1776
43007015	YEAR 1722
43010034	YEAR 1732
43012025	YEAR 1680
	YEAR 1719
	YEAR 1743

Bib.Text BkChpVrs	Sermons printed
43021038	YEAR 1733
43023035	YEAR 1692
43026051	YEAR 1722
44003024	YEAR 1774
44014019	YEAR 1719
45002014	YEAR 1765
45008024	YEAR 1758
	YEAR 1758
45009054	YEAR 1748
	YEAR 1774
	YEAR 1776
45009055	YEAR 1704
45013005	YEAR 1678
45021023	YEAR 1769
46008047	YEAR 1769
46016002	YEAR 1727
46021022	YEAR 1746
47007059	YEAR 1702
47023005	YEAR 1749
48007025	YEAR 1660
48010002	YEAR 1729
48013005	YEAR 1730
48013007	YEAR 1763
49010011	YEAR 1747
	YEAR 1753
	YEAR 1754
50010003	YEAR 1704
52004026	YEAR 1742
53002012	YEAR 1679
53004005	YEAR 1679
	YEAR 1764
	YEAR 1773
57002001	YEAR 1715
	YEAR 1723
	YEAR 1735
	YEAR 1749
57004007	YEAR 1679
58002011	YEAR 1703
59003001	YEAR 1729
61012005	YEAR 1756
62001021	YEAR 1697
62003015	YEAR 1660
62003016	YEAR 1746
	YEAR 1768
62003017	YEAR 1766
62004001	YEAR 1726
	YEAR 1758
	YEAR 1769

Bib.Text BkChpVrs	Sermons printed
63002013	YEAR 1763
63002016	YEAR 1749
	YEAR 1754
63002017	YEAR 1750
	YEAR 1777
	YEAR 1780
64002019	YEAR 1745
69002005	YEAR 1745
	YEAR 1756

House of Lords: Statistical Analysis of the Set of Index Items Regarding Texts Used for Sermons before This Audience

a. Frequency (Number of records of a text)	b. Number of texts with that frequency of record	c. Number of records of those texts (c = a X b)	d. Cumulative percentage of the texts	e. Cumulative percentage of records	f. Percentage of all the records in this set (c/ Total c)
1	105	105	86.78	69.08	69.08
2	6	12	91.74	76.97	7.89
3	8	24	98.35	92.76	15.79
4	1	4	99.17	95.39	2.63
7	1	7	100.00	100.00	4.61
Totals	121	152			100.00

Average no. of records per text within this set: M = 1.2562 Standard deviation from average: SD = .7876
Type/token ratio = 1/M = 0.7961 Coefficient of variation = SD/M = .6270
Yule's K = 49.3421 (A measure of the concentration of records upon a relatively few texts)

APPENDIX TO INDEX C TO THIRD VOLUME: SOME SETS OF AUDIENCE INDEX ITEMS SORTED AND ANALYZED FOR BIBLICAL TEXT REFERENCE
(b.King or K.& Q.)

KING OR K. & QUEEN: SERMONS BEFORE (Read columns downward in succession. Biblical text omitted if same as preceding text.)
(For a list of biblical books by code no. see end papers inside covers of this volume.)

Symbols under "Use" below: &=preached before King & Queen together; a=Accession sermon(s), f=Fast, j=Jan. 30 (ann. beheading Chas. I), m=May 29 (ann. Restoration Chas. II), n=Nov. 5 (Guy Fawkes' day), o=Observance of holy day or season, r=some other Religious or theological topic, t=day of Thanksgiving, u=occasion or subject Unstated within indexed record, x=some secular occasion or topic not named above.

Bib.Text BkChpVrs	Use	Sermons printed	By
05004006	u	YEAR 1740	BU
05010012	t	YEAR 1692	WA
06024015	u	YEAR 1735	TI
09002030	&x	YEAR 1707	ST
10024014	n	YEAR 1697	KI
14009008	t	YEAR 1697	BU
14015002	&x	YEAR 1713	BU
14029020	u	YEAR 1668	LI
16001004	f	YEAR 1675	HA
16004011	n	YEAR 1717	WA
18005012	n	YEAR 1733	DA
18023015	r	YEAR 1707	ST
18028028	u	YEAR 1676	SC
19001001	u	YEAR 1671	NO
19002006	m	YEAR 1685	KI
19002010	u	YEAR 1714	BU
19004007	u	YEAR 1685	CA
19008005	u	YEAR 1674	VI
19012001	&f	YEAR 1691	BU
19018001	t	YEAR 1666	DO
19018049	x	YEAR 1660	SH
19019011	r	YEAR 1735	LI
19041009	u	YEAR 1675	HA
19044006	u	YEAR 1779	GL
19054006	t	YEAR 1665	DO
19057006	&n	YEAR 1689	LL
19075006	&u	YEAR 1691	LL
19075007	u	YEAR 1772	SH
19082006	u	YEAR 1660	SW
19097001	&t	YEAR 1729	SH
19109027	u	YEAR 1695	PE
19119071	u	YEAR 1779	PE
19126003	m	YEAR 1754	HO
19144009	t	YEAR 1683	TU
19144010	&t	YEAR 1690	BU
19147001	m	YEAR 1715	BU
20001010	u	YEAR 1726	CA
20003006	u	YEAR 1696	LA
20008015	&j	YEAR 1688	SC
20014009	o	YEAR 1767	WA
20014034	&f	YEAR 1721	PE
20015024	u	YEAR 1772	SH
20022004	u	YEAR 1686	LA
20028001	u	YEAR 1741	JO
21005001	&u	YEAR 1694	CL

Bib.Text BkChpVrs	Use	Sermons printed	By
	&o	YEAR 1694	ST
21007004	o	YEAR 1737	FL
21007014	x	YEAR 1735	LI
21008011	u	YEAR 1707	KI
21012013	r	YEAR 1677	WI
21012014	o	YEAR 1677	WI
23033006	t	YEAR 1715	WI
23057021	u	YEAR 1693	LA
24005005	u	YEAR 1699	HE
24005025	f	YEAR 1782	YO
24010023	u	YEAR 1772	SH
24026019	u	YEAR 1673	JA
27012003	u	YEAR 1715	LY
28003005	m	YEAR 1684	AL
	m	YEAR 1684	MA
28006002	o	YEAR 1684	TU
30009002	n	YEAR 1675	HA
32006009	f	YEAR 1671	PI
38003014	u	YEAR 1676	HA
40007031	u	YEAR 1752	HA
43003008	u	YEAR 1677	ME
43005003	u	YEAR 1757	CO
43005004	u	YEAR 1757	CO
43005005	u	YEAR 1757	CO
43005006	u	YEAR 1757	CO
43005008	u	YEAR 1757	CO
43005010	&u	YEAR 1757	CO
43005017	u	YEAR 1684	HE
43006023	u	YEAR 1682	FU
43006034	&u	YEAR 1693	WI
43007021	&o	YEAR 1710	SP
43009013	u	YEAR 1779	PE
43011006	u	YEAR 1779	PE
43012025	j	YEAR 1722	WA
43012041	&o	YEAR 1686	EL
43015009	u	YEAR 1716	HA
43016026	u	YEAR 1780	LA
43018007	u	YEAR 1734	SH
43022021	u	YEAR 1682	FU
43023015	n	YEAR 1737	FL
43028020	m	YEAR 1677	SU
44004024	o	YEAR 1668	LA
45001071	&u	YEAR 1690	PE
45001074	u	YEAR 1674	JA
45002022	r	YEAR 1671	PI

Bib.Text BkChpVrs	Use	Sermons printed	By
45009055	n	YEAR 1678	LA
45010042	&u	YEAR 1735	TI
45011035	n	YEAR 1731	MA
45012051	u	YEAR 1716	BR
45013001	o	YEAR 1779	LO
45015031	u	YEAR 1772	SH
45016002	u	YEAR 1757	CO
45016008	u	YEAR 1779	PE
45016025	&u	YEAR 1722	WA
45022036	u	YEAR 1695	SM
46001014	o	YEAR 1718	CH
46003018	u	YEAR 1772	SH
46006014	o	YEAR 1667	LL
46007017	&u	YEAR 1694	HO
46010025	u	YEAR 1779	PE
46012024	u	YEAR 1772	SH
46014002	o	YEAR 1660	TO
46015022	o	YEAR 1706	YO
46017020	r	YEAR 1718	BR
46019019	o	YEAR 1665	DO
46020029	o	YEAR 1729	SH
47007059	u	YEAR 1676	PA
47015039	o	YEAR 1660	HA
47016004	u	YEAR 1685	DO
47016030	u	YEAR 1696	HA
47024016	&u	YEAR 1691	PE
47028005	n	YEAR 1675	HA
48002007	u	YEAR 1772	SH
48002014	u	YEAR 1772	SH
48002028	u	YEAR 1715	BR
48006021	o	YEAR 1710	LU
48006023	u	YEAR 1717	LA
48008003	o	YEAR 1683	ST
48008013	o	YEAR 1674	LL
48012005	&u	YEAR 1696	ME
48014004	r	YEAR 1754	HO
48014007	u	YEAR 1717	BE
49001010	u	YEAR 1682	CR
49007031	u	YEAR 1754	HO
49009024	o	YEAR 1767	WA
49011001	u	YEAR 1757	CO
49014033	n	YEAR 1667	MO
50001003	r	YEAR 1741	JO
50001010	t	YEAR 1731	TA
50002011	u	YEAR 1676	CA

Bib.Text BkChpVrs	Use	Sermons printed	By
50005017	u	YEAR 1772	SH
50005020	u	YEAR 1675	ST
50005021	o	YEAR 1770	SE
50006001	o	YEAR 1695	BU
51002018	u	YEAR 1754	HO
51003021	o	YEAR 1685	GO
51004004	o	YEAR 1697	BU
51004018	r	YEAR 1710	SP
51005012	u	YEAR 1709	BA
51005013	u	YEAR 1729	SH
51006007	u	YEAR 1675	LA
52002018	o	YEAR 1712	FI
52005002	o	YEAR 1697	BU
53001021	o	YEAR 1676	CR
53002012	u	YEAR 1772	SH
53002021	o	YEAR 1770	SE
53003020	u	YEAR 1735	TI
53004022	u	YEAR 1675	SU
54003001	&u	YEAR 1690	WI
54003014	r	YEAR 1718	HA
56002010	u	YEAR 1673	HA
57003015	u	YEAR 1676	SU
58003004	u	YEAR 1772	SH
59001016	u	YEAR 1675	ME
59003002	&o	YEAR 1735	TI
59003010	u	YEAR 1779	PE
61003013	u	YEAR 1779	PE
61010031	o	YEAR 1722	WA
61011033	u	YEAR 1691	RO
61013020	o	YEAR 1679	RE
62002026	&u	YEAR 1696	ME
63004015	u	YEAR 1684	IR
64003009	&f	YEAR 1690	LL
64003016	t	YEAR 1675	BA
65002015	&u	YEAR 1690	GR
65004001	u	YEAR 1679	PI
	n	YEAR 1731	TA
65005003	&u	YEAR 1691	RO
65005004	u	YEAR 1670	BA
	u	YEAR 1693	FR
68000022	u	YEAR 1676	CA

KING OR KING & QUEEN: SERMONS BEFORE: STATISTICS AND NOTES ABOUT THIS SET OF INDEX ITEMS

Biblical Texts: Statistical Analysis of Frequencies of Occurrence in This Set

a. Frequency (Number of records of a text)	b. Number of texts with that frequency of record	c. Number of records of those texts (c = a X b)	d. Cumulative percentage of the texts	e. Cumulative percentage of records	f. Percentage of all the records in this set (c/ Total c)
1	168	168	97.67	95.45	95.45
2	4	8	100.00	100.00	4.55
Totals	172	176			100.00

Average no. of records per text within this set: M = 1.0233 Standard deviation from average: SD = .1507
Type/token ratio = 1/M = 0.9773 Coefficient of variation = SD/M = .1473
Yule's K = 2.5826 (Here a measure of the concentration of records upon relatively few of the biblical texts)

Occasions or Subjects ("Use"): Statistics about Frequencies of Various Kinds of "Use"

N.B.: The u items (Unstated occasion|subject) are not included in the table below. They form 97/176 of the entire set.

"Use" (occasion or subject)	Its frequency	Percentage of the occasions or subjects in this set
j	2	2.53
x	4	5.06
f	6	7.59
m	6	7.59
r	9	11.39
t	10	12.66
n	11	13.92
o	31	39.24

Total records of occasion or subject (except the u's) in this set: 79

Statistics overall in respect to "Use" within this set (exclusive of the u items in it)

Average no. of records per kind of "Use":	9.8750
Std. deviation from that average:	8.4770
Coef. of variation:	.8584
Type/token ratio:	.1013
Yules's K:	2044.5441

The Most Frequently Cited Biblical Texts within This Set

Freq. in this set	Code no.	Denotation	Some Keywords of Biblical Text	No. of records in Cooke I	No. of sermons noted in them	No. texts that have higher no. of records
2	21005001	Eccles. v. 1	when thou goest to the house of God, be ready to hear	9	15	485
2	28003005	Hosea iii. 5	Afterward the children of Israel return to God and king	3	3	1769
2	65004001	I John iv. 1	Believe not every spirit, but try whether of God	10	10	421
2	65005004	I John v. 4	whatsoever is born of God [faith] overcometh the worl	23	24	77

APPENDIX TO INDEX C TO THIRD VOLUME: SOME SETS OF AUDIENCE INDEX ITEMS SORTED AND ANALYZED FOR BIBLICAL TEXT REFERENCE (b.King or K.& Q.)

KING OR KING & QUEEN: SERMONS BEFORE: STATISTICS AND NOTES ABOUT THIS SET OF INDEX ITEMS

Notes and Comments Concerning Set Named Above

1. A reader may conjecture, perhaps wrongly, that in two of the four cases where frequency=2, the sermons involved were designed to supplement, or to offset, one the other: in each case, they were published in the same year (1694 in one case, 1684 in the other) but were by different clergymen, as a glance at the set of index items shows.

2. For a sermon before King a clergyman seldom chose the same text as had been chosen by some predecessor -- or, at least, his sermon was seldom printed if he did so. This fact, which is obvious to the eye as a reader scans the set of index items, is given quantitative statement by the extremely low value (2.5826) of Yule's K in regard to the distribution of the biblical text references within the set. It suggests that before composing a sermon to preach before the King, a clergyman looked through records in the King's Library.

3. It is worth remark also that in preaching to King, clerymen seem to have avoided the texts most commonly used in other circumstances; for the figures in the three columns concerning frequencies in Cooke I appear abnormal. No text with frequency greater than 1 in the above set ranks among the 50 most popular texts overall in Cooke I. These 50 account for about 8% of the 23532 records in Cooke I, but for only 4% of the items in the present set.

4. The high percentage of religious topics (39.24% are of type o, 11.39% are of type r: a total of 50.63%) among the occasions or subjects recorded by Cooke for sermons delivered before King or King and Queen is worth attention. See notes 3 - 5 under the heading "King, or both King and Queen" in Index C, where further details are given. Some of the topics and texts there identified in note 5 suggest that sometimes a sermon addressed reproof to the King. It is worth remark also that the concentration of occasion or subject upon one or two kinds in this set of items contrasts sharply with the wide dispersal of biblical texts that has already been noted. In regard to occasion or subject, Yule's K has an extremely high value: 2044.5441.

5. In the above set is a group of six items with consecutive (or nearly consecutive) code numbers 43005003,4,5,6,8,10 (Matthew v 3,4,5,6,8,10: the Beatitudes), all with the same date (1757) and same two initial letters of author surname (CO). The author is COBDEN Edward, Chaplain in Ordinary, who published the six sermons among others in a collective edition, "28 Discourses". For some purposes the items might be considered as six records of sermons on a single text.

6. The reasons for a clergyman's choice of biblical text for a special occasion before a specific audience at a particular time is of historical interest. So are reasons for publication of his sermon. Speculation now and then on these matters may relieve a reader's tedium in perusal of undecorated data. Examples follow below.

   Sometimes the reasons seem obvious: e.g., in the cases of two sermons, mentioned in note 1 above, delivered before Charles II on an anniversary (May 29) of his Restoration and printed in the year just before his brother, James II, succeeded to his throne. Here religious reasons are clear for choice of a biblical text with keywords "Afterward the the children of Israel return to God and king," and political reasons are clear for publication in single-sermon [pamphlet] form. It is doubtful that many copies were bought. (Were some distributed free?) The biblical text appears to have been unpopular outside courtier and recusant circles (Cooke I records it as used for only three published sermons in 123 years), and the Bloodless Revolution soon deposed the openly Roman Catholic James II from the throne.

   In the other cases mentioned in note 1 above, reasons are not so obvious, but might prove amusing. The text is Ecclesisastes v. 1: "...when thou goest to the house of God, be more ready to hear ...." The special audience is King and Queen, who in the year of publication, 1794, were William and Mary. That year was the year of Mary's death

   In all cases so far mentioned the year of publication was probably (but not necessarily) also the year of delivery or the year immediately following delivery; for the form of publication was single-sermon.

   In the case of another interesting text for which freq = 2 in the set named above, the year of publication is unlikely

KING OR KING & QUEEN: SERMONS BEFORE: STATISTICS AND NOTES ABOUT THIS SET OF INDEX ITEMS

Notes and Comments Concerning Set Named Above

to have been the year of delivery; for, as our Vol. III shows, the two sermons involved were published in collective editions. The text which elicits interest is I John iv.1: "Beloved, believe not every spirit, but try the spirits whether they are of God: because many false prophets are gone out into the world." One of the sermons, published in 1731 by William Talbot, Bp. of Durham from 1721 to 1730 (Cooke in our Vol. II, pp. 397-406, lists bishops by their sees and dates) was preached on Nov. 5 (Guy Fawkes' Day), and we may therefore conjecture that it warned the king against religious zealots turned political activists. The other was published in 1679. The type of occasion is not stated in Cooke's record; but we may assume that, in preaching it, Thomas Pierce, President of Magdalen College, Oxford, was not advising Charles I against Royal attendance at Quaker meetings.

APPENDIX TO INDEX C TO THIRD VOLUME: SOME SETS OF AUDIENCE INDEX ITEMS SORTED AND ANALYZED FOR BIBLICAL TEXT REFERENCE (b.L.Mayor)

LORD MAYOR: SERMONS BEFORE (Read columns downward in succession. Biblical text omitted if same as preceding text.)
(For a list of biblical books by code no. see end papers inside covers of this volume.)

Bib.Text BkChpVrs	Sermons printed
03019017	YEAR 1703
04023023	YEAR 1721
05023009	YEAR 1673
07005023	YEAR 1716
09026010	YEAR 1737
10001017	YEAR 1677
10001018	YEAR 1683
10001027	YEAR 1750
10018028	YEAR 1704
10019009	YEAR 1708
10019030	YEAR 1703
11003009	YEAR 1727
11018021	YEAR 1680
14007013	YEAR 1679
14015002	YEAR 1720
14020017	YEAR 1679
14020027	YEAR 1746
15007025	YEAR 1741
15009013	YEAR 1744
16009026	YEAR 1696
19002011	YEAR 1750
19004004	YEAR 172-
19005011	YEAR 1709
19011003	YEAR 1679
	YEAR 1696
	YEAR 1700
19030006	YEAR 1730
19034012	YEAR 1682
19035011	YEAR 1733
19037005	YEAR 1680
19044007	YEAR 1732
19050014	YEAR 1741
19058010	YEAR 1684
19064009	YEAR 1693
19072006	YEAR 1729
19074020	YEAR 1680
19083018	YEAR 1748
19086012	YEAR 1696
19097001	YEAR 1680
	YEAR 1705
19115001	YEAR 1747
19118023	YEAR 1738
19118024	YEAR 1661
	YEAR 1750
19119059	YEAR 1709
19119165	YEAR 1682
19122006	YEAR 1759

Bib.Text BkChpVrs	Sermons printed
19122008	YEAR 1680
19127001	YEAR 1661
	YEAR 1689
19129001	YEAR 1716
	YEAR 1722
19144009	YEAR 1722
19144010	YEAR 1705
	YEAR 1751
20001012	YEAR 1715
20004025	YEAR 1710
20011011	YEAR 1680
20011019	YEAR 1682
20014008	YEAR 1662
20014034	YEAR 1682
	YEAR 1752
20017027	YEAR 1677
20021021	YEAR 1719
20023017	YEAR 1702
20024021	YEAR 1704
20027001	YEAR 1701
20029001	YEAR 1675
20029025	YEAR 1713
20030008	YEAR 1686
21006011	YEAR 1737
21009002	YEAR 1726
23001005	YEAR 1697
23001026	YEAR 1699
	YEAR 1728
23007005	YEAR 1745
23009012	YEAR 1730
23026009	YEAR 1753
24005029	YEAR 1681
24007023	YEAR 1710
26016049	YEAR 1697
26021025	YEAR 1686
27002004	YEAR 1749
27004027	YEAR 1746
27009007	YEAR 1702
28010012	YEAR 1701
28011008	YEAR 1690
30003002	YEAR 1747
31003008	YEAR 1749
32004005	YEAR 1697
32006004	YEAR 1723
32006006	YEAR 1679
36001009	YEAR 1669
37001016	YEAR 1704

Bib.Text BkChpVrs	Sermons printed
37002005	YEAR 1679
37003001	YEAR 1679
37003006	YEAR 1744
37007005	YEAR 1720
37008019	YEAR 1681
37014007	YEAR 1680
40003004	YEAR 1740
43007020	YEAR 1733
43014001	YEAR 1734
43015014	YEAR 1713
43019016	YEAR 1697
43022021	YEAR 1716
	YEAR 1725
	YEAR 1776
43024003	YEAR 1693
44003024	YEAR 1698
45001074	YEAR 1699
45009056	YEAR 1704
45010021	YEAR 1688
45013007	YEAR 1742
45016029	YEAR 1709
45017016	YEAR 1711
45019041	YEAR 1682
	YEAR 1690
45019042	YEAR 1680
	YEAR 1683
45023028	YEAR 1729
46001047	YEAR 1682
46004023	YEAR 1660
46005014	YEAR 1682
46008034	YEAR 1676
46013035	YEAR 1705
	YEAR 1715
46020009	YEAR 1689
47017006	YEAR 1680
47017007	YEAR 1713
47017022	YEAR 1750
47017031	YEAR 1697
47024005	YEAR 1751
48003008	YEAR 1696
48003016	YEAR 1745
48010002	YEAR 1723
48011033	YEAR 1743
48012018	YEAR 1683
48013001	YEAR 1715
	YEAR 1740
48013005	YEAR 1686

Bib.Text BkChpVrs	Sermons printed
48013007	YEAR 1749
48013012	YEAR 1671
48014019	YEAR 1729
	YEAR 1737
49004007	YEAR 1716
49008012	YEAR 1684
49010017	YEAR 1750
49010031	YEAR 1749
49013003	YEAR 1698
49014040	YEAR 1683
50001009	YEAR 1714
50005014	YEAR 1710
51005001	YEAR 1713
51005022	YEAR 1681
51005025	YEAR 1692
52004003	YEAR 1698
52004016	YEAR 1679
52005007	YEAR 1748
52006010	YEAR 1680
53001021	YEAR 1738
53002002	YEAR 1689
53004005	YEAR 1682
	YEAR 1689
	YEAR 1690
54002008	YEAR 1719
54003015	YEAR 1696
55002004	YEAR 1717
55004006	YEAR 1682
55004011	YEAR 1683
55004013	YEAR 1684
55005021	YEAR 1708
	YEAR 1736
56003002	YEAR 1673
57002001	YEAR 1682
	YEAR 1704
	YEAR 1730
	YEAR 1750
57002002	YEAR 1744
57004007	YEAR 1729
57006003	YEAR 1715
58002023	YEAR 1738
59003008	YEAR 1673
61009027	YEAR 1679
61011006	YEAR 1697
62003013	YEAR 1679
62003017	YEAR 1731
62004009	YEAR 1697

Bib.Text BkChpVrs	Sermons printed
63002015	YEAR 1678
	YEAR 1684
63003008	YEAR 1732
63003011	YEAR 1682
65003008	YEAR 1683
65003020	YEAR 1704
65005004	YEAR 1686
65005007	YEAR 1701
68000003	YEAR 1660
	YEAR 1686
	YEAR 1700
68000008	YEAR 1782
69003021	YEAR 1731
69021002	YEAR 1684

APPENDIX TO INDEX C TO THIRD VOLUME: SOME SETS OF AUDIENCE INDEX ITEMS SORTED AND ANALYZED FOR BIBLICAL TEXT REFERENCE
(Lord Mayor)

Lord Mayor: Statistical Analysis of the Set of Index Items Regarding Texts Used for Sermons before This Audience

a. Frequency (Number of records of a text)	b. Number of texts with that frequency of record	c. Number of records of those texts (c = a X b)	d. Cumulative percentage of the texts	e. Cumulative percentage of records	f. Percentage of all the records in this set (c/ Total c)
1	158	158	89.27	78.22	78.22
2	14	28	97.18	92.08	13.86
3	4	12	99.43	98.02	5.94
4	1	4	100.00	100.00	1.98
Totals	177	202			100.00

Average no. of records per text within this set: M = 1.1412 Standard deviation from average: SD = .4476
Type/token ratio = 1/M = 0.8762 Coefficient of variation = SD/M = .3922
Yule's K = 15.6847 (A measure of the concentration of records upon a relatively few texts)

APPENDIX TO INDEX C TO THIRD VOLUME: SOME SETS OF AUDIENCE INDEX ITEMS SORTED AND ANALYZED FOR BIBLICAL TEXT REFERENCE
(b. Queen)

QUEEN: SERMONS BEFORE (Read columns downward in succession. Biblical text omitted if same as preceding text.)
(For a list of biblical books by code no. see end papers inside covers of this volume.)

Symbols under "Use" below: a=Accession sermon(s), f=Fast, j=Jan. 30 (ann. beheading Chas. I), m=May 29 (ann. Restoration Chas. II), n=Nov. 5 (Guy Fawkes' Day) o=Observance of some holy day or season, r=some other Religious or theological topic, t=a day proclaimed for public Thanksgiving, x=some secular occasion or topic not named above.

N.B.: Index items that refer to sermons delivered before both King & Queen are excluded from this set.

Bib.Text BkChpVrs	Use	Sermons printed	By
04010009	f	YEAR 1692	PA
05004007	n	YEAR 1727	ST
05020001	f	YEAR 1737	FL
05023009	f	YEAR 1733	DA
05030015	u	YEAR 1692	HI
05032029	o	YEAR 1731	TA
05033029	t	YEAR 1706	ST
06024015	u	YEAR 1694	WY
10024014	f	YEAR 1696	ME
14031021	a	YEAR 1734	CL
18002010	u	YEAR 1705	VE
18021015	u	YEAR 1715	MO
18022021	u	YEAR 1730	AT
18033022	u	YEAR 1692	RE
18036028	u	YEAR 1691	RE
19004004	u	YEAR 1690	HI
19014001	u	YEAR 1695	TE
19016008	u	YEAR 1731	TA
19018023	u	YEAR 1690	DO
19025014	u	YEAR 1704	DU
19037037	u	YEAR 1708	RA
19046010	u	YEAR 1708	MA
19058011	t	YEAR 1704	SH
19072004	t	YEAR 1707	BU
19077010	f	YEAR 1719	SH
19090012	x	YEAR 1709	WI
19105005	m	YEAR 1694	BU
19112007	f	YEAR 1710	LU
19122006	f	YEAR 1694	CO
19133001	t	YEAR 1731	TA
19139023	u	YEAR 1694	MA
20008012	u	YEAR 1694	MA
20011020	u	YEAR 1710	WI
20016032	u	YEAR 1705	RO
20024021	j	YEAR 1734	SH
	j	YEAR 1774	SH
21007014	u	YEAR 1706	KE
	t	YEAR 1709	MA
21008011	u	YEAR 1707	BR
	f	YEAR 1738	MO
23011013	t	YEAR 1705	WI
23049023	a	YEAR 1713	BU
23056007	u	YEAR 1692	MA
28011009	u	YEAR 1707	AD
31003005	f	YEAR 1734	SH
37007005	f	YEAR 1694	KI
43003008	o	YEAR 1696	ME
43004001	r	YEAR 1703	ST
43005003	r	YEAR 1723	BL
43005044	o	YEAR 1735	TI
43006006	u	YEAR 1691	LY
43007012	n	YEAR 1730	AT
43008002	o	YEAR 1704	ST
43010016	n	YEAR 1724	SM
43011028	u	YEAR 1706	ST
43018035	u	YEAR 1705	ST
43022021	a	YEAR 1715	MO
	j	YEAR 1737	ST
43027024	u	YEAR 1737	FL
44010015	u	YEAR 1710	SP
45010041	u	YEAR 1707	BR
45016031	u	YEAR 1691	HO
45023028	j	YEAR 1711	HI
45024025	u	YEAR 1727	ST
46006067	o	YEAR 1707	AD
46015005	u	YEAR 1713	ST
47007060	j	YEAR 1708	BR
47010040	o	YEAR 1729	SH
47011018	u	YEAR 1707	CA
47028005	u	YEAR 1705	AD
48008006	u	YEAR 1706	MA
48010002	n	YEAR 1713	NE
48012010	u	YEAR 1704	LU
48012019	x	YEAR 1712	CH
48013004	a	YEAR 1723	BL
48014010	r	YEAR 1707	PA
48014018	u	YEAR 1712	GA
48015005	u	YEAR 1703	PE
49001026	o	YEAR 1694	BU
49007031	o	YEAR 1733	DA
49015019	u	YEAR 1710	BA
49015028	u	YEAR 1709	MA
50001009	t	YEAR 1727	ST
50001012	r	YEAR 1704	CL
51006014	o	YEAR 1734	AT
53002003	r	YEAR 1737	MO
53003010	o	YEAR 1729	SH
54001012	u	YEAR 1692	PE
54001026	o	YEAR 1712	SP
54003015	o	YEAR 1689	PA
54004005	u	YEAR 1714	RE
57003016	r	YEAR 1705	BL
57005022	o	YEAR 1722	WA
58001010	r	YEAR 1734	SH
59002010	u	YEAR 1691	LA
61002003	o	YEAR 1729	SH
61004001	u	YEAR 1722	WA
62002010	u	YEAR 1691	FO
64001004	o	YEAR 1692	LA
65003003	u	YEAR 1694	TY
65003008	o	YEAR 1702	TA
	o	YEAR 1729	SH
65003020	u	YEAR 1696	ME

QUEEN: SERMONS BEFORE: STATISTICS AND NOTES ABOUT THIS SET OF INDEX ITEMS

Biblical Texts: Statistical Analysis of Frequencies of Occurrence in This Set

a. Frequency (Number of records of a text)	b. Number of texts with that frequency of record	c. Number of records of those texts (c = a X b)	d. Cumulative percentage of the texts	e. Cumulative percentage of records	f. Percentage of all the records in this set (c/ Total c)
1	93	93	94.90	90.29	90.29
2	5	10	100.00	100.00	9.71
Totals	98	103			100.00

Average no. of records per text within this set: M = 1.0510 Standard deviation from average: SD = .2200
Type/token ratio = 1/M = 0.9515 Coefficient of variation = SD/M = .2094
Yule's K = 9.4260 (Here a measure of the concentration of records upon relatively few of the biblical texts)

Occasions or Subjects ("Use"): Statistics about Frequencies of Various Kinds of "Use"

N.B.: The u items (Unstated occasion|subject) are not included in the table below. They form 46/103 of the entire set.

"Use" (occasion or subject)	Its frequency	Percentage of the occasions or subjects in this set
m	1	1.75
x	2	3.51
a	4	7.02
n	4	7.02
j	5	8.77
r	7	12.28
t	7	12.28
f	10	17.54
o	17	29.82

Statistics overall in respect to "Use" within this set (exclusive of the u items in it)

Average no. of records per kind of "Use":	6.3333
Std. deviation from that average:	4.5704
Coef. of variation:	.7216
Type/token ratio:	.1579
Yule's K:	1514.3121

Total records of occasions and subjects (except the u's) in this set: 57

The Most Frequently Cited Biblical Texts within This Set

Freq. in this set	Code no.	Denotation	Some Keywords of Biblical Text	No. of records in Cooke I	No. of sermons noted in them	No. texts that have higher no. of records
2	20024021	Proverbs xxiv.21	My son, fear Lord and king & meddle not with change	68	68	1
2	21007014	Eccles. vii.14	prosperity & adversity: God hath set one against other	16	16	202
2	21008011	Eccles. viii.11	Because sentence against evil work not executed speedily	20	21	130
2	43022021	Matth.xxii.21	he saith, Render unto Caesar, Caesar's; to God, God's	30	30	30
2	65003008	I John iii. 8	He that committeth sin is of the devil [but the Son]	19	21	146

APPENDIX TO INDEX C TO THIRD VOLUME: SOME SETS OF AUDIENCE INDEX ITEMS SORTED AND ANALYZED FOR BIBLICAL TEXT REFERENCE
(b.queen)

QUEEN: SERMONS BEFORE: STATISTICS AND NOTES ABOUT THIS SET OF INDEX ITEMS

Notes and Comments Concerning Above Set

1. It is of interest that in the Queen set there are four items referring to Accession sermons, none in the King set.

2. Regarding the high proportion (30%) of, and for details about, items o concerning holy days or seasons and (12%) items r related to other religious topics, see notes 3 and 4 under the heading "Queen" within Index C.

3. The high concentration of items upon relatively few types of occasion or subject in this set is measured by the value (1514.3) of Yule's K in respect to this matter. The contrasting wide dispersal of items over many biblical texts is indicated by the low value (9.426) of Yule's K in respect to this other matter. Compare the corresponding values for the set concerning sermons before King; these are even more extreme.

4. Readers may welcome some comments and questions to turn index items into points of curiosity or information regarding social forces which bring together biblical text, author, occasion, and publication of a sermon. Some follow.

As the first item under The Most Frequently Cited Biblical Texts within This Set brings to attention, there are two records of sermons delivered before Queen on Proverbs xxiv.21: "My son, fear thou the Lord and king: and meddle not with them that are given to change." The occasion stated in both records is Jan.30, an anniversary of the beheading of Charles I. There is no question about why the text was chosen for this type of occasion: its suitability is self-evident -- perhaps partly because the text is so familiar to us. As is shown in the three columns following those keywords of the text that are set out in the item, this text is cited in 68 of the records in Cooke's first volume (his list of sermons 1660-1782 by biblical text); those records note a total of 68 sermons upon it; and in all of that volume there is only one text in regard to which there are more records. Furthermore, a glance at the set of index items under "January 30 Sermons" within the present APPENDIX TO INDEXES TO THE THIRD VOLUME and a quick count of the items there for text-code number 20024021 will show that the text was used at least 20 times for sermons on January 30. It is the most frequent of all texts recorded in Cooke for that occasion -- twice as frequent as any other.

There may be some question, however, about why the text was chosen for delivery before a Queen, whom preachers would not often think in need of such advice as is conveyed by it. No sermon on this text was ever delivered before a King, so far as records in Cooke I show. Perhaps the Queen to whom the sermon was preached had been meddling in affairs of Church or had given ear to enemies of a minister of state; or perhaps there were reasons for concern about welfare of church and state that should be set forth for a Queen to hear. To determine who the Queen(s) might be, we look at the dates of publication and also at the relevant records in our Volume III. We observe that one sermon upon the text was published in a single-sermon edition in 1734 and that the author was Shuckford, S., DD., who (we learn from Vol. II) was Prebendary of Canterbury and Chaplain in Ordinary and for whom sermon publications are listed with years 1723-1752. Most likely the Queen was George II's: Caroline of Brandenburg. The sermon (as we also learn from Vol. II) was delivered in Norwich. Was there some special reason for the Queen to be in Norwich, for a sermon to be preached there before her on this text, and for the sermon to be published in single-sermon form, easily purchasable by the public? Or, less likely, did the King's Chaplain in Ordinary take January 30 and the Queen's absence from her usual environment as an opportunity to remind her of the dangers of lending support to unorthdox theologians? Or is there some error in Cooke's records? The problem would be interesting to pursue.

The other sermon recorded in Cooke I for Proverbs xxiv. 21 was preached by Thomas Sherlock, Bishop of London from 1748 to 1761. (See Cooke's list of Bishops, pp. 397-406 in Volume II.) Hence most likely the Queen before whom it was preached was George III's: Charlotte of Mecklenburg. But the date of delivery is quite uncertain so far as Cooke's records show; for his only record of it specifies it as on page 1 of Volume V ("Occasional Serm.") of a collective edition dated 1772, 1774 of the Bishop's preachings.

In regard to other items listed under The Most Frequently Cited Biblical Texts comment and question may be avoided or made brief. Two sermons delivered before Queen are recorded for the text Ecclesiastes vii.14. Its keywords are "prosperity and adversity: God hath set one against the other." Clearly, the one published in 1709 (ss. edition) was delivered (probably before Queen Anne) on a day of rejoicing; for the occasion was a day of publicly proclaimed Thanks-

QUEEN: SERMONS BEFORE: STATISTICS AND NOTES ABOUT THIS SET OF INDEX ITEMS

Notes and Comments Concerning Above Set

giving. (Was it for a temporary prospect of peace?). The one published in 1706, on the other hand, may have been delivered (probably also before Queen Anne) in a day of adversity: Cooke does not record the type of occasion, and the text was used both on days of Thanksgiving and on days of Fast.

Comment upon the items which concern Eccles. viii.11 (evil work and speedy sentence) or Matthew xxii. 21 (Caesar's and God's) would be superfluous: questions regarding the nexus of biblical text, audience, occasion, and date and form of publication are obvious, and answers may be pursued by readers who wish to find them. A comment upon the item concerning I John iii. 8 may be in order, however; for the keywords which have been taken from the text may mislead the reader about uses to which the text was put. In preaching upon the text before the Queen (and elsewhere also) clergymen placed their emphasis not upon the devil, but upon the Son of God as Redeemer. It was used as text for Christmas sermons before the Queen, and often elsewhere. The full text reads: "He that committeth sin is of the devil; for the devil sinneth from the beginning. For this purpose was the Son of God manifested, that he might destroy the works of the devil."

Hospital or Infirmary, at, or before Governors of, <"Hosp.s.","Hos.s.","Inf.s.","Lond.Inf.s.","b.Gov....Hos.", etc.>

Note 1: Spittal sermons. Spittal sermons are not indexed here. They are indexed under their own special heading within the following Index D.

Note 2: Special symbols p, y, g. Because smallpox hospitals, lying-in hospitals, and a Magdalen Hospital of the eighteenth century have much interest for many readers of the late twentieth century, index items referring to them receive special treatment here. A comma followed by a small letter has been placed after each item that refers to such an institution: p = a smallpox hospital, y = a lying-in hospital, g = Magdalen Hospital. More is said about these institutions in the explanatory note that is mentioned in Note 3, below.

Note 3: Cooke's records of particular hospitals and infirmaries. A table summarizing data compiled from Cooke's records of individual hospitals and infirmaries follows the set of index items and their addenda immediately below this note. An explanatory note precedes the table.

<<YEAR 17--:	NE 45010037	<<YEAR 1730:	TR 20014034	<<YEAR 1737:	CL 45009002	<<YEAR 1738:	RE 43025040
<<YEAR 1739:	MA 43025036	<<YEAR 1740:	SM 46013035			<<YEAR 1742:	AU 43004024
<<YEAR 1743:	DO 19041001	MA 19041001	SL 45010036	<<YEAR 1744:	GR 43025037	JO 45010036	MA 45011002
<<YEAR 1745:	GI 43007012	<<YEAR 1746:	HU 45016020	LA 63004008	<<YEAR 1747:	BI 23029019	HO 49012031
<<YEAR 1748:	MA 51006009	MI 45005031	TH 46005006	<<YEAR 1749:	AD 51006009	BA 45016009	BU 63004008
NI 19090016	TH 45019041	<<YEAR 1750:	HA 49012031	MA 20019006	TH 44012042,y	<<YEAR 1751:	BI 61010024
TO 48012015	TR 43026011	<<YEAR 1752:	BR 54003014	CO 55003013	DO 51006002,y	JE 50009012	MA 23058007,p
TH 47010004,y	WA 43004023	<<YEAR 1753:	CH 12019003,y	LE 20003009	MA 19027012	ME 61013003	WA 43005016
<<YEAR 1754:	BU 43011004	CH 51006009,y	DA 43025035	DO 01003016,y	43022037	<<YEAR 1755:	HA 02001019,y
LA 47003006	TA 19041001	WA 19091001,p	<<YEAR 1756:	TE 46006012	WI 43025004	<<YEAR 1757:	AU 45016027
	CO 43025019	DA 43005016,y	46005014	LO 55004009	<<YEAR 1758:	BA 43025035,p	CA 46013035
RE 45015020,g	<<YEAR 1759:	DO 43009012,g	HA 45009011	OL 23055001	RE 49013001	SE 55004009	WE 46013034
<<YEAR 1760:	BL 46013034	DO 45019010,g	SQ 19041001,p	YO 65003017	<<YEAR 1761:	DO 48012015	PO 61013016,g
TE 05015011	<<YEAR 1762:	DO 18029011,g	HU 20003027	MA 45010027	<<YEAR 1763:	DE 43005027,g	GR 45016019,p
HE 43006019	NO 19112009,y	SE 19122006	SH 45010036	WA 49012025	<<YEAR 1764:	AS 19103007	CU 45015010,g
NE 51006010	RI 19127003,y	YO 19041001,p	<<YEAR 1765:	EY 19106030,p	OW 09026010	SQ 45010027	WI 50009002
<<YEAR 1766:	CA 43014007	D' 21010020,p	DE 51006010	EW 61013016	OG 46008010,g	SE 48012008	<<YEAR 1767:
DO 20014028,p	GO 43018033	GR 13029014	NI 55004009,y	SE 45015018,g	WA 49013013	<<YEAR 1768:	DO 20019017
HA 24003001,g	MA 23053004	<<YEAR 1769:	BR 53001011	HA 05015011,p	MO 55004009	ST 09002007	TO 20018014,g
<<YEAR 1770:	BR 18029013	HA 43025040	MO 43005048	OG 45010035	RA 43014014	<<YEAR 1771:	GR 44001034
HU 45021003	LO 51006010	NO 20029008,y	RU 46005007	YO 43010010,p	<<YEAR 1772:	RO 19139014	SH 46013017
48013008,y	YO 20022002	<<YEAR 1773:	HU 45015010,g	MA 49003009	<<YEAR 1774:	BR 41004010	
	DO 37003007,g	NO 24003013,g	24031013,g	57006018	SH 45010036	ST 47020035	<<YEAR 1775:
AU 50009012	SK 43025036	YO 48008013,g	<<YEAR 1776:	DO 46013035	MA 62005020,g	TU 49009022	
<<YEAR 1777:	BR 54003014	GL 46008011,g	HA 07016020,g	HE 52004028	MA 50007009	SC 46005006	WA 45014018
YO 44014007	<<YEAR 1779:	BA 43009004	WA 20016006	<<YEAR 1780:	HI 51004018	MA 45010037	<<YEAR 1781:
CH 20022002	HU 44016009,g	RU 20014031	<<YEAR 1782:	MI 43022037,y	RO 45015007,g		

ADDENDA under above heading ("Hospital or Infirmary, at, or before Governors of")

<<YEAR 1745:	HO 45016009	<<YEAR 1749:	YA 45010037	<<YEAR 1752:	BR 45010037	<<YEAR 1758:	FR 45010037
<<YEAR 1770:	AS 58003004	<<YEAR 1778:	BU 05015011				

Explanatory Note in Regard to Following Table: Most of the records indexed above concern sermons that Cooke found printed in single-sermon editions. He was able to describe these more fully in his second volume than in his first. His more complete descriptions are repeated in our Vol.V; his abbreviated and often less complete descriptions in our Vol.III. The present editor has looked through all records to which this set of items and addenda has led him in both Volumes III and V and has prepared a summary of his findings. This is presented below in tabular form.

The primary purpose of the summary table is to outline the development of medical-related philanthropy in the eighteenth century in so far as this is reflected in Cooke's records. A secondary purpose is to assist a reader in finding records of hospitals and infirmaries that are of particular interest to him.

The table presents seven columns of data: (1) the name of a hospital or infirmary, (2) the number of sermons that Cooke records as preached at, or on behalf of, the institution so named, (3) the number of these that he records in his first volume as printed in single-sermon editions, (4) the earliest date of publication recorded by him for one of these sermons, (5) the latest date, (6) any discrepancy between Cooke's first volume and his second volume in regard to edition in which a relevant sermon was printed, and (7) notes regarding Cooke's records or sermons for the institution.

To serve the primary purpose of the table, institutions named in it are divided into three groups: those presumably in the London area, those elsewhere, and those of uncertain region, type, and name. Within each group, institutional names are arranged in chronological order of the earliest date of publication recorded by Cooke for sermons at or on behalf of institutions of the type or name specified in the table. Hence the table enables a reader to observe the emergence of clerical attention to first one and then another hospital or infirmary in or outside the London area. It also measures the amount and persistence of the attention given to each, so far Cooke's records accurately reflect these matters. Readers may wish to draw histograms of some of the data.

A reader who wishes to find Cooke's records concerning a particular hospital or infirmary need not look through all the records to which the set of index items and addenda immediately above this note refer, but only those to which reference is made by items within the chronological range defined by earliest and latest date of publication as given for the institution in the table below. How many of the items within this range concern it is stated by the number in the first column after the institutional name, and the succeeding column indicates how many of the relevant items concern sermons in single-sermon editions that he will find listed under the same date in our Volume V as is recorded for them in our Volume III. All exceptions to this rule about correspondence in regard to date he will find noted in the final two columns after the institutional name.

The names of hospitals and infirmaries as listed in the table and the way in which records are credited to them require explanation. The name to which a sermon is credited is the most specific name that can be found in Cooke's records of the sermon. For example, if "Inf.s." is used in the record of a sermon in Cooke's first volume and the same sermon is described more fully in his second volume as "b. Gov. of London-Infirmary," the sermon is credited to "London Infirmary" within section A. Hospitals and Infirmaries Presumably in the London Area. It is not credited to C. Hospitals and Infirmaries Not Specified by Type, Name, or Region in Cooke's Records.

In consequence of the rule stated above, there are some tabulations which should perhaps be combined. Thus in section A of the table there are two listings "Small pox-Hospital" and "London Smallpox Hospital," as if in Cooke's period there were two hospitals, presumably both in London, set aside for treatment of smallpox patients. In the present editor's inexpert opinion, there was probably only one smallpox hospital in all England, but a possibly real semantic distinction between the two names should not be inexpertly obliterated. Specialists in medical history may easily merge the two entries into one set of data if they know it proper to do so. A similar problem exists in regard to three distinct entries "Middlesex Lying-in Hospital or, simply, Middlesex Hospital," "Lying-in Hospital," and "London Lying-in Hospital."

Medical historians may also be interested in a further note about Cooke's listings. Throughout his records, Cooke seems to have followed his sources scrupulously in his use of the words "Hospital" and "Infirmary." In only three cases does he use the term "Hospital" in one of his volumes and "Infirmary" in the other in his descriptions of a sermon. Two of the cases concern sermons for the Lincoln "Infirmary" (2C) or "Hosp." (1C); the third case concerns a sermon at Devon and Exon. "Hosp." (2C) or "Inf." (1C).

Table Summarizing Cooke's Records of Sermons Preached on Behalf of Hospitals and Infirmaries

A. Hospitals and Infirmaries Presumably in the London Area	Rcds. in 1C	Rcds. ss. in 1C	First date	Last date	Discrepant dates or eds. 1C / 2C	Notes
Name Recorded in 1C or 2C						
London Hospital	15	14	1730	1775	None	Of the 15 sermons, 11 are by Bishops or an Abp. The sermon not in ss. ed. is in a 1766 coll. ed. Were ss. printed annually for a time? 1757-1767?
Westminster Infirmary	3	3	1739	1754	None	Of the 3 sermons, 1 is by a Bishop (Bp. Maddox).
London Infirmary	9	8	1743	1752	None	Of the 9 sermons, all are by Bishops or Archbishop. The sermon not in ss. ed. is in a 1749 coll. ed.
Middlesex Lying-in Hospital or, simply, Middlesex Hospital	7	5	1749	1770	1759/NULL	A sermon, dated 1759 in 1C, is not recorded in 2C. Two sermons are in collective eds.: 1757, 1770. Of the 7 sermons, the last 5 are recorded in both 1C and 2C simply for Middlesex Hospital; the first two, simply for Middlesex Hospital in 2C, simply for Lying-in Hospital in 1C.
Lying-in Hospital	4	3	1752	1782	1782/NULL	A sermon, dated 1782 in 1C, is not recorded in 2C. One sermon is in a collective ed. dated 1757.
London Lying-in Hospital	8	7	1753	1772	1755/NULL	A sermon, dated 1755 in 1C, is not recorded in 2C. The sermon of last date, 1772, is in a coll. ed.
Small pox-Hospital	7	7	1752	1771	None	Of the 7 sermons, 4 are by Bishops.
London Small-pox Hospital	4	4	1755	1766	None	Of the 4 sermons, 1 is by a Bishop (Bp. North).
Magdalen Hospital	21	20	1758	1782	1767/NULL 1773/NULL 1774/NULL	No record in 2C of any eds. that would contain any of the three Magd. Hosp. sermons that 1C lists as in ss. eds. dated 1767, 73, 74. The first ss. is described, "Op.Magd.Hosp." Annual ss. recorded 1758-77 except 1765, 70-72. Three ss. dated 1774; two, 1777. One sermon in collective edition dated 1781. Of the 21 sermons, 4 are by Bps.
Misericordia Hospital	2	2	1744?	1776	1744/1774	Is the 1C date "1744" a misprint of "1774"?

Table Summarizing Cooke's Records of Sermons Preached on Behalf of Hospitals and Infirmaries (continued)

	Rcds. in 1C	Rcds. ss. in 1C	First date	Last date	Discrepant dates or eds. 1C / 2C	Notes
Foundling Hospital	3	3	1763	1774	1763/NULL	The sermon of earliest date, 1763, is described in 1C: "Op.Found.H." No record of it in 2C.
Lock Hospital	1	1	1777	1777	None	A hospital for treatment of venereal diseases.

B. Hospitals and Infirmaries in Other Areas

Name Recorded in 1C or 2C	Rcds. in 1C	Rcds. ss. in 1C	First date	Last date	Discrepant dates or eds. 1C / 2C	Notes
Winchester Hospital	1	1	1737 or 1736	1737 or 1736	1737/1736	In 2C yr. 1736: "Opening an Hosp. at Winchester"
Bristol Infirmary	4	4	1738	1766	17--/176-	In 2C yr. 1738: "On Erect.... Infirm.... Bristol"
Worcester Infirmary	8	8	1740?	1770	1740/1749	If 1740 a misprint, 1748 ss. by Bp.Maddox is 1st.
Bath Infirmary	3	2	1742	1759	1753/1742	In 2C an ss. yr. 1742: "Opening ... Bath." Same sermon listed in 1C in coll. ed. of 1753.
Northampton Infirmary	8	8	1743	1750	None	
Devon and Exon. Hospital(s)	8	8	1743 or 1739?	1781	1759/1739	In 2C record for 1743 plural "Hospitals" used. If "1739" not a misprint in 2C, 1739 is first date.
Salop Infirmary	8	8	1747	1780	None	
Newcastle Infirmary	6	6	1754	1777	1777/1771	
Gloucester Infirmary	1	1	1755	1755	None	In 2C: "Open. Gloucester-Infirmary."
Liverpool Infirmary	2	2	1765	1769	None	
Sarum Infirmary	2	2	1767	1774	1774/1771	Sarum Infirmary same as Salisbury Infirmary?
Salisbury Infirmary	3	3	1767	1770	None	Salisbury Infirmary same as Sarum Infirmary?
Cambridge: Addenbrook Hospital	6	6	1767	1777	None	Of the 6 sermons, 2 are by Bishops.
Lincoln Infirmary (or Hosp.)	3	3	1769	1777	None	The ss. dated 1777 is by Bp. Yorke.
Oxford: Radcliffe Infirmary	4	4	1771	1779	1779/1776	Of the 4 sermons, 3 are by Bps., 1 by an Abp.
Norfolk Hospital	1	1	1772	1772	None	Sermon is by Bp. Yonge. Perhaps opening hosp.?
Hereford Infirmary	1	1	1781	1781	None	2C: "The Advantages of general Infirmaries ..."

	Rcds. in 1C	Rcds. ss. in 1C	First date	Last date	Discrepant dates or eds. 1C / 2C	Notes
C. Hospitals and Infirmaries Not Specified by Type, Name, or Region in Cooke's Records	15	7	1753	1777	1754/NULL	In 1C is included in coll ed. of 18 sermons by Wm. Davies, who is not listed in 2c.
					1758/NULL	2C does not record any ed. that would contain this sermon that is listed in 1C as 1758 ss.
					1775/1776	Perhaps different eds.: 12° 1775, 8° 1776.
					1777/NULL	A single-sermon by Brereton, who is not in 2C.

Review by Regions

	Rcds. in 1C	Rcds. ss. in 1C	First date	Last date
A. London Region Overall	84	77	1730	1782
B. Other Specific Regions	69	68	1737 or 1736	1781
C. Quite Uncertain Regions	15	7	1753	1781
England Overall: A + B + C:	168	152	1730	1782

(INDEXES TO THIRD VOLUME)

INDEX D: OCCASIONS OR CAUSES FOR WHICH SOME OF THE SERMONS WERE DELIVERED, AND A FEW TOPICS RELATED TO THESE OCCASIONS OR CAUSES

<u>How to Read This Index</u>: See Directions for Reading Index A.

```
Accession - Sermon    <"Acc.s.","Access.s.","Ass.& Acc.s.","Th.& Acc.s.","Acc.s.b.C.","Acc.s.b.L.","Acc.s.b.L.M.", etc.>
   <<YEAR 1660:   HU 19021001>>  <<YEAR 1661:   BR 10006012    WH 19126003>>  <<YEAR 1685:   NI 20024021    WA 20024021
   WY 63002017>>  <<YEAR 1686:   CA 11008066    ST 20024021,      48013005    WE 19046010>>  <<YEAR 1696:   JO 04023023>>
   <<YEAR 1702:   BR 57006006    SH 27010021>>  <<YEAR 1703:   BR 20016012>>  <<YEAR 1704:   EL 57002001    JO 45011002
   LL 19060011    TA 07005007    WI 19145004    WR 20029002>>  <<YEAR 1705:   HO 04014024,      20029002    KE 19144010
   TA 20029002    TR 20028002>>  <<YEAR 1706:   LE 43022021>>  <<YEAR 1707:   NI 03025020    TH 48013007>>  <<YEAR 1709:
   LA 19045017    RE 57002001    SH 21010017>>  <<YEAR 1710:   BL 59003001    JE 19132017    RO 19021001>>  <<YEAR 1711:
   AD 23049023    BI 19144015    CO 10006012    WI 17004014>>  <<YEAR 1712:   DI 19037006    HO 23049023    NE 63002017>>
   <<YEAR 1713:   BU 23049023    TI 11010009>>  <<YEAR 1714:   AR 11002015    BI 11010009    BO 19122007    ED 21007010
   FA 57002001    GO 23049023    HA 11008066    LE 19133001    SM 01012001    SU 53003016    SY 09012023    WR 19072001>>
   <<YEAR 1715:   AB 19020006    AC 19111004    AN 02012051,      47013022    BR 19136023,      21010017    EN 57002001
   FO 07012023,      09012023,      57002001    HA 20025005    HO 09015028    JE 59003001    LI 10022051    LO 20024021
   MO 43022021    PE 10005001    PO 63002017    SM 55005012,      55005013,      57002001    SY 21003001    T. 45017017
   WA 57002001    WH 20024021    WI 20024021>>  <<YEAR 1716:   BO 05033029    LE 19092001,      19097001    LL 43022021
   LO 48013003    TU 43022021    WA 05004007    WR 20016012>>  <<YEAR 1717:   AN 63002017    GI 07017006    GO 09024017
   LO 14009008    RU 63002017>>  <<YEAR 1718:   BA 19132018    ST 43022021>>  <<YEAR 1719:   BU 48013004    SY 19118023>>
   <<YEAR 1720:   CO 19045008    SY 20008015>>  <<YEAR 1722:   WA 19021001>>  <<YEAR 1723:   BL 20024021,      48013004
   JA 48013001>>  <<YEAR 1724:   WH 51005001>>  <<YEAR 1725:   BU 05004006    HU 11010009    MA 19082006>>  <<YEAR 1727:
   HU 19055003    TI 15006010>>  <<YEAR 1728:   BO 19122006    NE 20016012    OL 19085008    WI 19097001>>  <<YEAR 1729:
   KI 19122006    MA 19118024    SH 57002001    WI 10023003>>  <<YEAR 1730:   AT 57002001    BR 19072001    FE 20029002
   FR 57002001>>  <<YEAR 1732:   AN 59003001>>  <<YEAR 1733:   DA 19021007>>  <<YEAR 1734:   CL 14031021>>  <<YEAR 1735:
   AR 48013001    DE 14009008>>  <<YEAR 1737:   BU 19122006    FL 14009008>>  <<YEAR 1738:   KN 48013005    WI 48013001>>
   <<YEAR 1739:   GA 57002001    MA 19111004>>  <<YEAR 1740:   MO 48013001>>  <<YEAR 1741:   FO 15007025>>  <<YEAR 1742:
   CL 19092001    TE 57002001>>  <<YEAR 1743:   CO 48011033>>  <<YEAR 1744:   PA 07009008>>  <<YEAR 1745:   SN 48013007>>
   <<YEAR 1746:   HA 19089020,      48013004    HU 06001007>>  <<YEAR 1747:   PE 19020006>>  <<YEAR 1749:   BU 57002001
   WI 27002004>>  <<YEAR 1750:   SA 57002001>>  <<YEAR 1751:   CO 19078072>>  <<YEAR 1752:   PA 23044028>>  <<YEAR 1753:
   PO 19020005>>  <<YEAR 1754:   HO 19095002>>  <<YEAR 1755:   SH 19072001>>  <<YEAR 1756:   GR 48013005,      48013007>>
   <<YEAR 1758:   OG 05004006>>  <<YEAR 1759:   ED 19122008>>  <<YEAR 1760:   LO 19133001    PE 59003001    SA 63002017>>
   <<YEAR 1761:   CO 20020028    HO 10023003    NE 64002017    PE 23049023>>  <<YEAR 1766:   SE 59003001>>  <<YEAR 1770:
   SE 55005021>>  <<YEAR 1772:   SC 57002001    SI 21010020>>  <<YEAR 1774:   SH 10023003>>  <<YEAR 1776:   IB 14002011,
      43022021,      57002001>>  <<YEAR 1778:   TO 69017005>>  <<YEAR 1779:   WI 57002001>>
```

INDEXES TO THIRD VOLUME: D: OCCASIONS OR SUBJECTS

Act - Sermon <"Act.s.","Act s.">
<<YEAR 1660: WI 50005020>> <<YEAR 1689: JO 51002020>> <<YEAR 17--: BE 49011019 CO 04014011>> <<YEAR 1710:
LE 20001010>> <<YEAR 1712: SA 43005013>> <<YEAR 1713: BI 49003010 HI 49012004>> <<YEAR 1716: HO 19102013>>
<<YEAR 1717: HI 46001014>> <<YEAR 1722: BE 43007006>> <<YEAR 1724: BR 50005007>> <<YEAR 1730: CO 04024011>>
<<YEAR 1731: BU 06005013>> <<YEAR 1733: CO 48012002>> <<YEAR 1737: TI 50004001>> <<YEAR 1740: SM 47002004>>
<<YEAR 1745: GA 09002035>> <<YEAR 1746: WH 30007014>> <<YEAR 1750: FR 19058011>> <<YEAR 1754: SH 48014016>>
<<YEAR 1755: PA 53004008>> <<YEAR 1756: BL 43006033>> <<YEAR 1757: CO 50013012>> <<YEAR 1759: NE 52005008>>
<<YEAR 1761: HI 64001005 SI 20003013>> <<YEAR 1762: FO 27012010>> <<YEAR 1765: FO 24045005>> <<YEAR 1766:
SE 05032046>> <<YEAR 1769: FR 64003018>> <<YEAR 1773: GR 20004014 WH 18028012>> <<YEAR 1775: NI 20019027>>

Advent - Sermon <"Adv.s.","Adv.S.","Sund.Adv.","Adv.s.","S.Adv.">
<u>Note</u>: For five items referring to sermons about Advent in the sense (probably) of Christ's Second-Coming as Judge, see the keyword "ADVENT" within Index E.
<<YEAR 1663: EL 48013008 GO 45021034>> <<YEAR 1666: KI 43021009 MA 43021009>> <<YEAR 1667: LL 46006014>>
<<YEAR 1672: FR 43021009, 44001003, 45021027, 53004005>> <<YEAR 1674: FA 45021028>> <<YEAR 1678:
PA 48015004>> <<YEAR 1684: HA 23002004 WA 57001015>> <<YEAR 1686: GR 48013011>> <<YEAR 1697: BL 46003016>>
<<YEAR 1700: WI 49011001>> <<YEAR 1703: DO 46005028>> <<YEAR 1713: HI 19034011>> <<YEAR 1715: KE 46003017
ST 43011002, 43021001, 45021025, 46001019, 48013008, 48015004, 49004001, 53004004>>
<<YEAR 1716: HO 43011002, 43021001, 45021025, 46001019, 48013008, 48015004, 49004001,
53004004 WH 45022019>> <<YEAR 1725: SH 23040003>> <<YEAR 1728: RE 23001011, 23005001, 23025001,
23030007>> <<YEAR 1730: RE 23002019, 23024001, 23026001, 23032001>> <<YEAR 1731: CA 38003001
MA 23052003>> <<YEAR 1732: AL 45021028, 46006014>> <<YEAR 1733: MO 24007004>> <<YEAR 1734: AT 43011003
ST 45007019>> <<YEAR 1738: HO 36002007>> <<YEAR 1745: SN 43025031, 47013048>> <<YEAR 1746: WH 45024027,
46001041, 46001045, 47003022, 61009007>> <<YEAR 1747: WE 38003001>> <<YEAR 1748: WA 46005036,
48015012, 50005010>> <<YEAR 1751: BE 46005027>> <<YEAR 1757: PE 43003002 WA 43011003>> <<YEAR 1772:
FL 51004004>> <<YEAR 1774: CL 45007020>>

All Saints Day <"All Saints","All.Saints","All Saint's","All Saints-d.","All Saints d.">
<<YEAR 1672: FR 19149009, 61012001>> <<YEAR 1675: HA 69006009, 69006010>> <<YEAR 1685: EL 43005012>>
<<YEAR 1689: FE 19016011>> <<YEAR 1692: ST 54001012>> <<YEAR 1704: GA 52002019, 54002018, 69022009>>
<<YEAR 1710: LU 61012002>> <<YEAR 1713: HI 52004011, 52004013>> <<YEAR 1715: ST 43005001, 69007002>>
<<YEAR 1716: HO 43005001, 69007002 ST 61006012>> <<YEAR 1731: MA 19149009>> <<YEAR 1735: TI 45011049,
58002011, 61013007, 69014013>> <<YEAR 1740: BU 62005010>> <<YEAR 1746: WH 61012001>> <<YEAR 1750:
BA 61012002>>

Ascension Sermon <"Asc.s.","Ascen.s.","Ascension","Xt's.Ascension","Asc.s.& Wh.","Sund.af.Asc.","S.af."Ascen.", <u>etc</u>.>
<<YEAR 1661: BR 46020017 MA 46020017 NI 45024050>> <<YEAR 1672: FA 47001010 FR 19024003>> <<YEAR 1679:
HO 46014003>> <<YEAR 1702: PI 44016019>> <<YEAR 1703: DO 44016019>> <<YEAR 1706: BR 45024050 FO 46016028>>
<<YEAR 1708: GR 52004008>> <<YEAR 1709: GO 46020017>> <<YEAR 1713: HI 61004014>> <<YEAR 1714: ST 44016014,
46015026, 47001001, 63004007>> <<YEAR 1716: BA 44016019 HO 44016014, 46015026, 47001001,
63004007>> <<YEAR 1717: WI 52004008>> <<YEAR 1719: SH 46016023>> <<YEAR 1723: SC 61004014>> <<YEAR 1728:
RE 05012032 WH 44016019>> <<YEAR 1729: WI 52004008>> <<YEAR 1730: BR 52004008 RE 05013001 TR 47003021>>
<<YEAR 1732: AL 46016007>> <<YEAR 1735: CL 53003020, 61008001 TI 44016019>> <<YEAR 1736: NE 47001009>>
<<YEAR 1737: NA 19068018>> <<YEAR 1739: BA 61009024>> <<YEAR 1740: JO 45024050 SM 46016028>> <<YEAR 1743:
DE 52004008>> <<YEAR 1744: SO 52004010>> <<YEAR 1745: SN 46006062>> <<YEAR 1747: WE 47001011>> <<YEAR 1748:
WA 44016019>> <<YEAR 1757: MO 47001009, 47005032 WA 46020017 WI 45024050>> <<YEAR 1760: ST 52004008,
61001003>> <<YEAR 1771: BU 47001011>> <<YEAR 1775: AM 47001009>> <<YEAR 1776: AN 47001009>> <<YEAR 1777:
CA 47001009 OG 61002010 PY 19068018, 19068018>> <<YEAR 1780: HU 47001011>>

Ash Wednesday <"Ash W.S.","Ashwedn.","Ashwedn.d.","Ash-W.b.K.","Ash W.b.Q.", <u>etc</u>.>
<<YEAR 1663: EL 19095007>> <<YEAR 1682: MA 43004002>> <<YEAR 1707: HI 69003002>> <<YEAR 1715: ST 43006016>>
<<YEAR 1716: HO 29002012, 43006016>> <<YEAR 1720: CO 45007036>> <<YEAR 1726: CA 44006012 IB 19038018>>
<<YEAR 1729: SH 43003008, 61002003>> <<YEAR 1731: MA 43009014 TA 43016026>> <<YEAR 1765: DU 43006013>>
<<YEAR 1770: SE 51005024>> <<YEAR 1776: AN 61010031>> <<YEAR 1779: LO 45013001>>

Assize Sermon <"Ass.s.","Ass.s","Ass.& Acc.S.","Ass.& Ch.s.","Month& Ass.s.">

<<YEAR ----:
NI 10012014>>
HE 48015005
<<YEAR 1663:
SC 02018021>>
HA 48013004
<<YEAR 1670:
FU 49011022
FA 48013004
PI 47017006
<<YEAR 1679:
BE 05001016
AL 02020012,
IN 20014034
BA 47019038
VE 19122006
CA 10015003
64003013,
ST 57002001
GO 43013029
19106030,
DR 32006006
<<YEAR 1693:
CA 19127001>>
FO 20019014,
02018025
MA 52002019
EY 09012025
20024023>>
AY 63002007
RO 43005005
PL 47007026
YO 14019006,
HA 05001016,
CA 24023010,
RA 14019009
BA 20014034
47024016
<<YEAR 1711:
CA 21003007,
48012019
RE 20024021
MA 43007012
CO 23057020
SW 45010042>>
LE 48013003
52004025
CA 51005013,
54003015,
WH 05004007>>
TA 55005021
PE 11018021
PE 47024016
ST 09007016>>
LA 50001012
<<YEAR 1660:
ST 09007015,
BR 18029014,
<<YEAR 1666:
ST 63002013
DR 48013006
HA 20014034,
LO 19082006
ST 04016015
CA 32004005
BI 53001029
03019012
KN 28010004
CL 55004011
WI 19082001>>
FO 20017026
65005016,
WY 07017006>>
HE 19015004
20019021,
FR 19082006>>
EY 47024016
<<YEAR 1695:
48013004
EC 20011001
OL 20010009>>
GI 19002012
<<YEAR 1702:
CL 03019012,
SA 05004006,
TI 20024010>>
18028028,
10015004
47024016
WE 19147020
BE 48014019
MU 68000003
BI 14019006
59003001
WO 62002024,
SL 20029002
RA 20014034
DU 21007010
<<YEAR 1716:
LU 03019012
TH 61013009
57002002
62003017
<<YEAR 1718:
WH 37008016>>
PR 21012014>>
SH 20014034
<<YEAR 1722:
RO 24017009
CR 23001025
23033001,
43022021
BO 45019042>>
WE 24015010>>
HO 14019005
30005023
SM 63002021,
TU 23032001>>
RE 19047009
BY 48013001
AS 07017006
OL 50005010
CO 20025005
<<YEAR 1684:
LI 07020027,
69020004
<<YEAR 1686:
KE 48013004>>
20024010,
<<YEAR 1691:
HI 10021016
DR 43028015
KN 47024016
ED 19082006
<<YEAR 17--:
OL 20008015>>
CL 10001027
43005034,
57005021
<<YEAR 1706:
57002002,
HI 32006008
CO 07005001
WI 19078037>>
BY 47024016
OL 19014001,
CO 48008033>>
CH 19029010,
62003017>>
TR 14019007>>
TR 48013003>>
FE 46006026
BO 21008002
PE 09012007
WH 07009015>>
DE 19122006
NE 47007039
CH 47017031,
<<YEAR 1719:
<<YEAR 1720:
WR 63002017>>
BE 43007012
SM 11008039
HO 47024016,
58003005>>
GL 19122006
<<YEAR 1667:
<<YEAR 1669:
JO 30006012
HO 14019006>>
65004008>>
<<YEAR 1677:
WA 10014012>>
FO 57001018
CH 21012013
PO 48013005
GI 48013001,
AT 20024021
46008009,
VE 19082006>>
BE 43007012
<<YEAR 1689:
23001026
EL 20024021
HO 20014034
MA 19082001>>
LE 14019006
FA 19002012
CO 23033015
<<YEAR 1701:
PU 50010005>>
43005038
SC 48013001>>
BR 05001017
61004013>>
HO 53004005
DO 05005029,
<<YEAR 1709:
CO 51004018
19037037
<<YEAR 1712:
53004005
<<YEAR 1713:
<<YEAR 1714:
<<YEAR 1715:
FU 43005033
CA 21008002
PY 04016041
<<YEAR 1717:
DO 43007012
OF 20017013
65005020
BO 64002010
BR 57002002
<<YEAR 1721:
BO 05001016
WH 48013001>>
55004018
<<YEAR 1662:
RI 69020012>>
BR 48005019
JO 05016018
ME 48013005
<<YEAR 1673:
<<YEAR 1675:
TA 20008012>>
<<YEAR 1680:
NI 09012014
CO 61006016
SH 55004010
59003001
BA 43007012
46014002,
<<YEAR 1685:
CR 43024012
CA 23001026
ST 09012007,
TH 30005015
PE 23059011
<<YEAR 1696:
WA 49013013
SK 19126003>>
HO 09001008
HE 20020001,
<<YEAR 1703:
DU 46018036
<<YEAR 1705:
SA 47023001
<<YEAR 1707:
HU 07018007
57001008
DA 19127001
FO 43005033
RI 20001022,
BR 57002001
DU 19122006
AL 10018003
BU 19112007
BE 49010010
GO 19122006
CO 48014019
RA 59003001
BA 05006011
HA 48013007
SK 05032029,
DE 20029002
GI 24007003,
IB 53004005
BA 46015024
CO 48013010
<<YEAR 16--:
ST 04017008>>
CA 23001026
<<YEAR 1664:
ST 18029015>>
WI 09002025>>
ST 13002007
HO 59003001
AL 15007027>>
<<YEAR 1678:
HI 47024025
OK 44012017
CU 02020007
SM 68000003
JE 14019006
BE 48012018
46018031,
BA 50007002
TU 46003035,
NE 63003013
10012007
WA 20014034>>
RU 49010010
HE 59003001
WY 49006001>>
<<YEAR 1699:
JA 19097002
48013003
TR 19037016
JO 06024014
BL 10020019
SM 19127001
AL 48015005
JA 20008015
HO 27004037
IL 07002016
GR 14019005
20029001
BU 47024016,
LE 45016008
AN 19073009
DU 09004013
BO 63002013
OL 19072001
CR 62004001
SA 19033012
BE 19122008,
LA 48012018,
62003017
LO 57002001
47023005
JO 65004007
CO 19047009
HA 26017019
BE 37007009
<<YEAR 1661:
RI 23001026
AN 19094020
<<YEAR 1668:
<<YEAR 167-:
WE 57004007>>
SA 48013005>>
<<YEAR 1676:
BA 19101001
LI 09007015>>
ST 47024025>>
FO 62003017
WE 61012014>>
KI 48013005
BI 04026009,
47017031,
HO 02014013
46013035>>
SA 02023001,
WI 32006008>>
<<YEAR 1692:
WA 20012026>>
ME 62001025>>
<<YEAR 1698:
GI 48013007
WH 48012018>>
KN 61004013
WH 51005001>>
KE 55004006
JO 06024015
WA 20024029
BA 19127001
WE 45012051>>
JO 19094016
SA 57005022>>
HA 09002030
TH 20024021
64002010
PA 19119138
HO 20014034
LO 18028028,
BU 17010003,
SH 37008017
CU 19107043
SK 48014019,
20014034,
48013004,
SO 50005010
SQ 04030002,
HA 11003009
LE 54003015
SA 19058011
IB 48013004
FO 20022006
BO 19072004
ST 23001026>>
MA 05017012
BR 27006021
DU 62005009>>
<<YEAR 1672:
<<YEAR 1674:
CA 07017006
LL 48003031>>
<<YEAR 1681:
<<YEAR 1682:
HI 20020008
<<YEAR 1683:
ST 20024021
07017006
62005009,
KE 09002025
<<YEAR 1688:
09012003,
<<YEAR 1690:
WA 01018025>>
<<YEAR 1694:
<<YEAR 1697:
BE 01018025,
HE 57001009
<<YEAR 1700:
ST 02023001,
<<YEAR 1704:
NE 03019012
LL 24030010
WH 05005029
GL 48006021
<<YEAR 1708:
MI 62005009
<<YEAR 1710:
LU 47023003,
TR 58002019>>
BY 49015033
PO 48012018,
MA 51004018
43011019
59003001
SM 58001007
JO 20029002
51005001,
63002013
49015058,
WA 48012019
09012025
ME 37008017
NE 05001017
SL 47018014
LU 63004007

INDEXES TO THIRD VOLUME: D: OCCASIONS OR SUBJECTS

MA 37008016
MA 05001016
DI 26017018
SA 68000014>>
CO 15007026,
SO 43010033>>
43022037
CO 19082001
CO 20029002
TA 47002047>>
BA 05004006
FO 43007012
CL 48013004
BR 19122006
MO 43007012
MU 19097002
TR 14019007,
HO 18029014,
AL 02020016
<<YEAR 1745:
BR 19133001,
SM 46008032>>
<<YEAR 1749:
TE 14009008
WI 63002013>>
47022025
HE 32006008
BA 48013003
FO 48013005
ST 61013018>>
AL 46013034
AB 02018019
KE 32006008>>
PR 32001008,
MA 48012019
TR 23005020
OS 62002008
PA 58003016
<<YEAR 1726:
23049023
<<YEAR 1728:
WH 48012019>>
FE 43005039
LE 09002030
<<YEAR 1732:
DO 19144010
HA 48013004
MO 23032017
MA 43018007,
PE 11022043
TR 51004018>>
24022015>>
47024016
ED 24029007
BA 15007025
46008032
<<YEAR 1747:
AS 18029014
WI 19082001>>
<<YEAR 1753:
TU 05006013>>
PR 20014034>>
SE 05004008>>
LO 05004007
<<YEAR 1768:
FR 48013003>>
CO 48012019
<<YEAR 1776:
43016027>>
TO 23059014>>
WY 18005012>>
WA 49001020>>
SM 53002004,
CA 48002014
DI 51005013
GA 51005015
<<YEAR 1729:
GI 28007009
OS 48013003
BR 47024025
EN 42004050
MO 48012018
NE 20014012,
46020029,
SL 23057020
<<YEAR 1740:
<<YEAR 1741:
MA 19101001
LA 43005040>>
GR 02020007
BU 01039009
BR 63002013
BE 19085010
<<YEAR 1751:
HU 14019006
<<YEAR 1755:
<<YEAR 1757:
<<YEAR 1761:
PU 48013014>>
CO 48012017>>
<<YEAR 1771:
HE 61008013
BE 48013001
<<YEAR 1779:
<<YEAR 1781:
<<YEAR 1723:
<<YEAR 1724:
57001009
CO 10023003
FO 43023023
NE 02023001
BA 20014034
NE 09003012
WA 62003017>>
GR 50005010
MY 51005013
OS 59003001
20014025,
47004012
WE 20014034>>
BR 20021003
BO 48013001
PE 07018007,
<<YEAR 1744:
HO 47022028
DA 19057007
BU 20030008
WA 19029011>>
JE 14019005
RI 19147019>>
CA 52004031
CO 19058011
BR 48003016>>
<<YEAR 1765:
<<YEAR 1769:
CO 50003017
HO 59002011
WA 46005044>>
CL 14019006
HA 23033006
AT 43007012
BR 19001002,
ST 43007012>>
GA 63002017
HO 63002013
PE 48012003,
BO 13005006,
PE 14019005
<<YEAR 1731:
OS 20014034>>
SI 02020016>>
TI 61006016>>
20020012,
TI 20016010
<<YEAR 1739:
LE 05004008
GA 10020019>>
46020022
BE 48001028
HU 48013003
IB 01049004,
EU 20024021
<<YEAR 1750:
WA 05014008>>
<<YEAR 1754:
NE 15007026
FO 48013008>>
<<YEAR 1763:
FO 01020011>>
CO 20014026
MA 05005029
WH 48001016>>
<<YEAR 1777:
MO 53004005>>
HO 20014034>>
CO 63002013
21007010,
<<YEAR 1725:
LA 63002017
LO 46001047
48013003
14019005
RA 15007026
CL 55004011
<<YEAR 1733:
<<YEAR 1735:
<<YEAR 1736:
44007037
WE 44008038>>
AL 19032009
PA 48013003
<<YEAR 1742:
WA 48012018
CR 47024002
WE 61011026>>
03025005
WA 54003014>>
DO 48013003
<<YEAR 1752:
AL 57001008,
PE 43005039>>
<<YEAR 1758:
RO 01009006>>
<<YEAR 1766:
VE 37009012
PU 43007013
<<YEAR 1775:
BU 20016006
<<YEAR 1780:
<<YEAR 1782:
DE 57002001
48006021
AL 19133001
PE 52004025>>
SC 63002013
ST 20014034
BR 20014034
SL 18027006>>
CO 20029002,
OS 15007026>>
CL 03019012
CA 19082006,
PI 02020016>>
<<YEAR 1738:
BR 63002016
SH 57001009
BL 57001005
WE 43007029>>
SI 20012026
<<YEAR 1746:
LO 43005044
<<YEAR 1748:
PI 20029002
CO 68000022
61006016
<<YEAR 1756:
DO 02023001>>
<<YEAR 1764:
HO 48013004
WA 49006007>>
ST 30005024>>
BE 05007013
CH 57001008>>
GE 05016020
HU 01009006>>
HA 05006013
CL 20014034
BU 32006006
<<YEAR 1727:
SN 47024002
SY 09002025,
BU 19085010
<<YEAR 1730:
32006006
<<YEAR 1734:
DO 20017015
48013005
<<YEAR 1737:
BR 48005013
CL 45012005
SM 48005007
ED 23005020
<<YEAR 1743:
WI 48002014>>
BA 59003001
OW 02020016
BA 48012010>>
SE 19133001
HU 62003018
HO 09008009,
CR 19101004
<<YEAR 1759:
BU 57002002
RA 05004008
<<YEAR 1770:
<<YEAR 1773:
HO 09002030
<<YEAR 1778:
GW 48003016

Calendar Change : See "Style, New."

Charity Sermons <"Ch.s.","Charity">

<u>Note</u>: Under the present heading are indexed only those sermons that are described in Cooke's Vol. I and hence in our Vol. III either by the simple abbreviation "Ch.s" or by the single word "Charity" within the column headed "Occasion or Subject."

The records in which occasion or subject is named by the single word "Charity" are few: thirty-four in all. A percentage sign "%" has been prefixed to the biblical text code number in each item below that refers to a record belonging to this group.

The great majority (about 77%) of the sermons in the much larger group -- the "Ch.s" sermons -- were published in <u>single-sermon</u> editions shortly after delivery and presumably were delivered in support of specific charitable causes. In some instances the cause for which such a sermon was delivered is stated in the record in our Vol. V which corresponds to the record in our Vol. III that is indexed below. To find that record, a reader should proceed first to the record in our Vol. III; and then, if the symbols there within the column "Sources Compared" reveal that a corresponding (and probably more complete) record exists in our Vol. V, he may go on to the record in Vol. V.

Most of the sermons in the "Charity" group, on the other hand, are recorded by Cooke as published in collective editions of their authors' works. Indeed, thirty of the thirty-four sermons in this group are so recorded in our Vol. III, and hence are not to be found individually listed in our Vol. V (because not recorded within Cooke's Vol. II as distinct editions).

The biblical texts of sermons in the "Charity" group suggest that in general the sermons in this group were not directed toward support of specific charitable institutions but toward promotion of the charitable spirit among people. Twelve of these thirty-four sermons have for biblical text some verse or verses in the passage I Corinthians x111 1 - 13. Five of the sermons have I Peter iv. 8 as text: a fact which suggests that at least five were intended to promote help for the poor within the preacher's own congregation or parish. However directed, many or most of the sermons were of course occasioned by some event or need of which the speaker was aware.

Sermons on Charity as qualified by some other word or phrase -- for example, "Xn. Charity", "Of Charity", "Durat. of Char." -- or on Love or some other related topic may be found by searching through the permuted keywords and abbreviations within Index E to our Third Volume.

Many sermons in support of certain kinds of charitable causes are indexed under their own proper headings within the present Index D or the preceding Index C: for example, within the present index, "Charity Schools", "Irish Protestant Schools", "Colony of Georgia", "Spittal Sermons"; within the preceding Index C, "Hospital or Infirmary, at, or before Governors of." As implied by the first paragraph of this note, items referring to these sermons are not included among those below.

<<YEAR 1678:
BO 48008018>>
FR 49015058
HO 45010037
%49013001>>
SW 62001027
ST 52006004>>
HO 20029015
WI 47020035>>
AC 20031013
NI 52002008>>
<<YEAR 1719:
<<YEAR 1722:
AL 61006010
CH 47010038
<<YEAR 1729:
47010038
<<YEAR 1734:
CL 43005048>>
<<YEAR 1738:
AL 46012008
SI 57006018
KE 61013003>>
<<YEAR 1752:
HG%01042018
LO 62001027>>
<<YEAR 1769:
FR%49013001
<<YEAR 1776:
HU 43006011>>
TA 45012021>>
<<YEAR 1694:
WO 20023005>>
WO 20005022,
<<YEAR 1705:
WE 20022015>>
<<YEAR 1709:
NE 43025035
<<YEAR 1713:
MI 43025046>>
<<YEAR 1717:
BE 26036034
CR%49013005,
BL 45006030>>
GR 61013016
CO 20022006
WI 57001005>>
BE 47011029
<<YEAR 1736:
MA 20003009
DE 51006009
TW 44010013>>
<<YEAR 1748:
BA%65003017
KE%44012041,
<<YEAR 1763:
CH%57001005>>
HE 61013016>>
PE%63004008
<<YEAR 1680:
HA 18031019>>
<<YEAR 1699:
57006017>>
BU 49012026>>
<<YEAR 1707:
WH 58003015>>
NI 18031015
CU 09002018
<<YEAR 1716:
BI 53001018
CO 08002019
%49013006,
<<YEAR 1724:
LE 45016009>>
EV 45016002>>
<<YEAR 1732:
CL 43005016,
CH 62001027>>
MI 61013016>>
FI 20003027>>
<<YEAR 1744:
BE 43012007>>
BU%63004008
%47010038>>
SH 47020035>>
<<YEAR 1770:
<<YEAR 1772:
WA 63004008>>
LI 45019008
<<YEAR 1695:
BA 51006010
<<YEAR 1702:
<<YEAR 1706:
WE 51006009>>
<<YEAR 1710:
ST 51006010>>
WA 19027010>>
BA%61010024
DA 45016009
IN 43026041
63004008
GO 61013016>>
<<YEAR 1728:
<<YEAR 1730:
EL 57006017>>
%49013003
<<YEAR 1737:
<<YEAR 1739:
<<YEAR 1742:
CA 45016009>>
<<YEAR 1749:
WI 05015011>>
<<YEAR 1760:
<<YEAR 1764:
BR%45011024
SH%63004008>>
<<YEAR 1777:
RO 61013016>>
WH%63004008>>
ST 19145009>>
BA 43009009>>
BR 46021015
<<YEAR 1708:
KI 45014014>>
<<YEAR 1712:
<<YEAR 1714:
BE 65004011
WI%65004007>>
SY 62005019>>
DY%20031006
<<YEAR 1725:
AL 65004020
AT 63004008
<<YEAR 1733:
WI 46013038>>
FL 51006010
MU%61013016
CA 65004016
<<YEAR 1746:
BR 44012043
<<YEAR 1754:
ST 11017016,
LA 02002006
SE%51006011,
<<YEAR 1773:
CA%43005007
<<YEAR 1682:
<<YEAR 1697:
<<YEAR 17--:
<<YEAR 1703:
KI 20022006
CL 61013016
<<YEAR 1711:
AR 50008009
DU 21011001
FR%44008001
<<YEAR 1718:
<<YEAR 1721:
SU 43006019
HA 19071005
BE%49013001,
PR 65003017>>
DA 47020035
<<YEAR 1735:
HA 57006017
OR 49013013
TE%49013002
TE 61010024
MI 48013008>>
HO%49013001>>
%44012014>>
RI 43025040>>
%63004008>>
LA 43025045>>
IB 47020035
BO 51004029>>
DO 19112009>>
DA 52004006>>
CH 61013016
LO 20003009
KE 20031029
BO%50009015
MA 23032008
SM 19008002>>
MA 45016009
HE 69019006
DO 21011010
WA 57006018>>
HO%49013002>>
%49013004,
<<YEAR 1731:
TR 20003027
BA 48006004
TO 19132018
WI 47020035>>
WA%48012021>>
WA 44014007>>
<<YEAR 1750:
<<YEAR 1757:
<<YEAR 1761:
<<YEAR 1765:
<<YEAR 1771:
<<YEAR 1775:
WE 43025034>>
<<YEAR 1689:
<<YEAR 1698:
<<YEAR 1700:
CO 46012003,
PR 19133001
PE 45016009
BR 53004017
WA 49013013
<<YEAR 1715:
MO 51006010
PE 49013005>>
YA 27004027>>
<<YEAR 1723:
<<YEAR 1727:
%49013013>>
MA 19036004,
WA 45012021>>
BO 49016002
WR 23032008>>
<<YEAR 1741:
<<YEAR 1743:
<<YEAR 1747:
CO 12004001>>
CO%49013001
DO 43018014
WE%21011001>>
AD 49013013
HA 59003008>>
<<YEAR 1781:

INDEXES TO THIRD VOLUME: D: OCCASIONS OR SUBJECTS

Charity School <"Ch.Sch.s.","An.m.ch.sc.","A.m.ch.sch.", "Ch.Sc.Com.","Op.Ch.Sch.","Use of Ch.Sc.", etc.>

Note: Within Index E, after the keyword "SCH", are four additional items about schools -- presumably, but not certainly, Charity Schools.

<<YEAR 1698:	JE 59003008>>	<<YEAR 17--:	HO 47026022>>	<<YEAR 1704:	WI 01018019>>	<<YEAR 1705:	ST 45016025>>
<<YEAR 1706:	KE 19144012>>	<<YEAR 1707:	GA 19147012>>	<<YEAR 1708:	TR 48012013>>	<<YEAR 1709:	BR 47004032>>
<<YEAR 1710:	BE 48012013	EL 44014007	JA 61013016>>	<<YEAR 1712:	DA 51006009	VE 47020035>>	<<YEAR 1713:
OA 05006006>>	<<YEAR 1714:	RO 43019014>>	<<YEAR 1715:	FA 12002023>>	<<YEAR 1716:	GI 27012003>>	<<YEAR 1717:
ST 20030009	TA 46013034>>	<<YEAR 1719:	HO 57006017>>	<<YEAR 1720:	KN 19072004>>	<<YEAR 1721:	MA 23054013>>
<<YEAR 1722:	BO 01018019	WA 23054013	WO 43025040>>	<<YEAR 1723:	WA 20022006>>	<<YEAR 1724:	SM 02002009>>
<<YEAR 1725:	BE 19112009	BI 19144012	NE 21012011	SH 57006017>>	<<YEAR 1726:	MA 43011005>>	<<YEAR 1727:
CL 01012002	WA 20003028>>	<<YEAR 1728:	YA 23058010>>	<<YEAR 1729:	LU 59002014>>	<<YEAR 1730:	CO 44012041
HO 20022002	PE 43025040>>	<<YEAR 1731:	CL 21002001	WI 63004010>>	<<YEAR 1732:	ST 65003017>>	<<YEAR 1733:
CL 21010018	DA 52006004,	57006018>>	<<YEAR 1735:	PE 49010024>>	<<YEAR 1736:	DE 05006006	RO 51006009>>
<<YEAR 1737:	ST 47010038	TH 43018014>>	<<YEAR 1738:	CO 51006009	MO 20022002	SA 05008010>>	<<YEAR 1739:
BA 43025040	CL 61013016	MU 62005020>>	<<YEAR 1740:	TH 43025040>>	<<YEAR 1741:	CL 48013010	MA 18029016>>
<<YEAR 1742:	TR 51006009>>	<<YEAR 1744:	HU 50008021>>	<<YEAR 1745:	SN 25003027,	43011025>>	<<YEAR 1746:
FA 20022006	LA 24005004>>	<<YEAR 1747:	TR 27012003>>	<<YEAR 1748:	BE 19034014	LA 05008002>>	<<YEAR 1749:
BU 20022006	HE 45016019	SQ 43006019>>	<<YEAR 1750:	NE 57006019	YA 47020035>>	<<YEAR 1751:	BA 51006010
CH 20030009	MO 45002052>>	<<YEAR 1752:	BA 59003008	CH 43010042	CO 20028027	FL 01018019	GE 05015011>>
<<YEAR 1753:	DR 18029016	HU 20022006>>	<<YEAR 1754:	SH 44010013>>	<<YEAR 1755:	FU 20022006	HA 43018010>>
<<YEAR 1756:	NI 19078005>>	<<YEAR 1757:	CO 52006004	NO 52006004	RI 20022006>>	<<YEAR 1758:	DO 19034011>>
<<YEAR 1759:	BU 58003015>>	<<YEAR 1760:	PI 20022006>>	<<YEAR 1761:	NE 57001005	TO 49010024>>	<<YEAR 1762:
CO 61010024>>	<<YEAR 1763:	DE 57006018	SA 18028028>>	<<YEAR 1764:	NE 52004020	RI 52006004>>	<<YEAR 1765:
NE 43011005>>	<<YEAR 1766:	DE 69014013	SE 48014016>>	<<YEAR 1767:	KE 43011005	NI 21012001>>	<<YEAR 1768:
WO 04011029>>	<<YEAR 1769:	PA 20013020	YO 46013035>>	<<YEAR 1770:	AS 45007022	EY 43010008	WI 47009006>>
<<YEAR 1771:	HA 05006006>>	<<YEAR 1772:	BE 20022002	CA 51006010	CO 43025040	KN 48014016>>	<<YEAR 1773:
GR 62003017>>	<<YEAR 1774:	FI 44010014	PA 02002006	SH 50009012>>	<<YEAR 1775:	AM 19065011	OG 43011005
WI 43025019>>	<<YEAR 1776:	KA 46021015>>	<<YEAR 1777:	FI 43023037	SH 20022006	TO 43005047>>	<<YEAR 1778:
BE 05010008	HA 55004009	MO 19116012>>	<<YEAR 1779:	MA 45010024>>	<<YEAR 1780:	CA 43005048	KI 45002051>>
<<YEAR 1781:	PA 20011025	WI 47013048>>	<<YEAR 1782:	PO 45007002>>			

Christmas Day, Sunday or Season <"Xmas.s.","Xtmas.s.","Xmas.& Epi.","Xmas.or East.","Xmas.s.b.K.", etc.>

Note 1: For items referring to sermons on Advent, see "Advent" within present Index D.

Note 2: For seventy-two further items referring to Christmas sermons, see the keyword abbreviation "XTMAS" within Index E to our Third Volume.

<<YEAR 16--:	GO 45002015>>	<<YEAR 1661:	BR 43003007,	65003008,	65004010>>	<<YEAR 1664:	BR 51004004>>
<<YEAR 1672:	FA 61002017	FR 45001068,	45002007,	45002030,	57001015>>	<<YEAR 1675:	HA 43002001,
43002002,	45001068,	45001069,	45002007,	45002008,	45002009,	45002010,	45002011,
45002014,	45002029>>	<<YEAR 1679:	RA 45002010,	51004004>>	<<YEAR 1680:	LI 45002014,	57003016>>
<<YEAR 1683:	ST 48008003>>	<<YEAR 1684:	AL 45002034	HA 43001023>>	<<YEAR 1685:	GO 51003021	KI 65003005>>
<<YEAR 1687:	GI 45002014>>	<<YEAR 1689:	BU 57003016>>	<<YEAR 1697:	BU 51004004	CO 53002006,	53002008
FA 45002011>>	<<YEAR 17--:	RA 58002019>>	<<YEAR 1702:	NE 43001020	TA 65003008	WA 43001021>>	<<YEAR 1703:
DO 57001015>>	<<YEAR 1704:	GA 45002010>>	<<YEAR 1706:	YO 46015022>>	<<YEAR 1707:	ST 46003017>>	<<YEAR 1708:
GR 45002011>>	<<YEAR 1712:	BI 11008018	GL 61001005>>	<<YEAR 1713:	BR 57003016	ED 45002011	HI 05018018>>
<<YEAR 1714:	DU 61002016>>	<<YEAR 1715:	ST 43001018,	45002041,	46001001,	51004001,	61001001>>
<<YEAR 1716:	BA 43001030,	45002010,	46001014	HO 43001018,	45002014,	45002041,	46001001,
51004001,	61001001>>	<<YEAR 1719:	MA 43001023>>	<<YEAR 1720:	BE 46001014	SH 45002010>>	<<YEAR 1721:
CO 57003016>>	<<YEAR 1723:	SC 51004004>>	<<YEAR 1724:	SM 46001011>>	<<YEAR 1726:	CA 43001021	SC 19002011>>
<<YEAR 1727:	RI 45002010	SO 46001011>>	<<YEAR 1728:	BO 61001001	WH 45002014,	49001023>>	<<YEAR 1729:
JO 43002001	SH 65003008	UP 45002011	WI 65004009>>	<<YEAR 1730:	RE 23037031,	23038001,	23043001>>
<<YEAR 1731:	AN 46001014	MA 51004004>>	<<YEAR 1732:	AL 46001014>>	<<YEAR 1733:	MO 51004004>>	<<YEAR 1734:
RI 45002010>>	<<YEAR 1735:	CL 43001022	TI 65004009>>	<<YEAR 1736:	NE 23040001>>	<<YEAR 1737:	NA 45002012>>
<<YEAR 1740:	BU 57003016	JO 65004009>>	<<YEAR 1741:	GA 45002010>>	<<YEAR 1742:	DE 65004009>>	<<YEAR 1744:
SO 65003008>>	<<YEAR 1745:	SN 51004004>>	<<YEAR 1746:	TE 51004004>>	<<YEAR 1747:	BU 45002013>>	<<YEAR 1748:

Consecration, Opening, Beautification of Church or Chapel <"Cons.Ch.","Cons.ch.","Op.Ch.","Rep.Ch.","Open Ch.","Beaut.Ch.">

Note 1: For six further items regarding sermons on beautification of churches, see within Index E the keyword "B" followed by the expression "B.Ch."

Note 2: Also consider items under the heading "Meeting - House, Opening of," within the present Index E.

<<YEAR 1675: KE 11009003>> <<YEAR 1680: LI 52002021>> <<YEAR 1683: ST 46010022>> <<YEAR 1684: RO 14007016>>
<<YEAR 1692: WH 19026008>> <<YEAR 1694: SY 11008018>> <<YEAR 1697: WI 13022005>> <<YEAR 1698: AD 43021013>>
<<YEAR 1699: WA 59002014>> <<YEAR 1702: BU 14006041>> <<YEAR 1704: LE 03026002 WO 19122001>> <<YEAR 1705:
GA 23060013 ST 49014040>> <<YEAR 1706: WI 03019030>> <<YEAR 1707: GE 19096009>> <<YEAR 1708: MO 19022009>>
<<YEAR 1710: BI 45007004>> <<YEAR 1712: HI 19122001 SM 43021009>> <<YEAR 1713: NE 19096009 PE 16013014
WA 19084010>> <<YEAR 1714: BR 44011017>> <<YEAR 1715: KE 19122001 LA 19084001 LY 45007004>> <<YEAR 1716:
NE 19026008>> <<YEAR 1719: GI 19084010 MA 19093005 SH 19096009 TO 19055001>> <<YEAR 1720: BE 19122001,
49014026>> <<YEAR 1721: ST 61013016>> <<YEAR 1723: BU 19005007 TR 11009003>> <<YEAR 1726: IN 19122001>>
<<YEAR 1727: MA 45007005 PE 01028018 SO 19087002 ST 01028016>> <<YEAR 1728: AL 19096009 GR 03019030
ST 46004022 WA 61010025>> <<YEAR 1730: RE 20003009 TR 19096009>> <<YEAR 1732: PA 01028020>> <<YEAR 1733:
BA 49011022>> <<YEAR 1735: PI 20003009>> <<YEAR 1736: DE 21005001 WA 47017024>> <<YEAR 1740: DO 14007015>>
<<YEAR 1743: AT 02020024 HO 36001008>> <<YEAR 1745: SN 02025002>> <<YEAR 1746: GO 02003005>> <<YEAR 1747:
BU 11008030>> <<YEAR 1749: CO 23056007 HE 57006017>> <<YEAR 1750: CO 14006019>> <<YEAR 1751: MU 50009005>>
<<YEAR 1752: GR 19093005>> <<YEAR 1753: WA 46004023>> <<YEAR 1754: AS 45007004 BA 45007005 DO 19002011>>
<<YEAR 1756: FO 01004026 TA 36002008>> <<YEAR 1757: CO 19093005>> <<YEAR 1762: SM 11008013, 11008057>>
<<YEAR 1763: BI 46010022 JO 19048009 SH 21005001>> <<YEAR 1764: BR 46004023 MA 46008007>> <<YEAR 1766:
BU 02029044>> <<YEAR 1767: AL 44004009>> <<YEAR 1768: FA 52002021>> <<YEAR 1771: BL 46004021>> <<YEAR 1773:
DI 19096009>> <<YEAR 1774: CL 01028016 DU 14006040 LI 52004003>> <<YEAR 1775: GR 19084010>> <<YEAR 1776:
GL 02020024 WI 61010025>> <<YEAR 1777: JO 01028019 WE 04023023>> <<YEAR 1778: LI 46004023>> <<YEAR 1781:
WI 02020024, 14006040>>

Coronation <"Cor.s.","Coron.s.">

Note: For an item referring to a sermon on the anniversary of a coronation, see the keyword "COR" followed by the expression "Ann.of Cor." within the following Index E.

<<YEAR 1661: BR 04023023 CA 19021003 HE 12011012 LI 19018050 MO 20028002>> <<YEAR 1662: AY 12002012
WI 63002017>> <<YEAR 1673: FL 22003011>> <<YEAR 1675: HA 09002030, 09009013>> <<YEAR 1677: BR 19126007>>
<<YEAR 1685: TU 13029023>> <<YEAR 1686: WE 57002001>> <<YEAR 1689: BU 10023003>> <<YEAR 1696: ME 09010024>>
<<YEAR 17--: BR 57002001>> <<YEAR 1702: BE 23049023 MI 23049023>> <<YEAR 1714: CR 19072001 HO 19132018
RO 19132017 SA 19132018 SH 19132018>> <<YEAR 1715: DU 14009008>> <<YEAR 1716: GR 19132018>> <<YEAR 1717:
BE 43022021>> <<YEAR 1718: BA 48013001>> <<YEAR 1721: EV 10024014 HA 19097001>> <<YEAR 1724: GU 19132018
KN 59003001 WR 27002021>> <<YEAR 1727: CU 19097007 EV 19063011 SM 20008015 WR 69021024>> <<YEAR 1728:
CO 57002001 DO 13028010>> <<YEAR 1729: SH 23049023>> <<YEAR 1731: TA 19118024>> <<YEAR 1733: DA 20014034>>
<<YEAR 1735: HU 19132018>> <<YEAR 1753: PO 14009008>> <<YEAR 1755: HU 19097001>> <<YEAR 1761: BU 11008066
DR 11010009 FA 43025031 JO 20008015 KI 19021003 RI 19021003 TO 69002010>>

Duelling <"Of Duel.","Duell.b.Q.","Ag.Duelling","Ag.Duell.","Duelling">

<<YEAR 1673: HA 04035033>> <<YEAR 1712: CH 48012019>> <<YEAR 1720: FI 45006037>> <<YEAR 1727: HO 09017048>>
<<YEAR 1754: DE 02020013>> <<YEAR 1772: DO 43005038>>

Earthquake <"Earthq.","Af.Earthq.","Earthquake", etc.>

<<YEAR 1692: AN 24018007>> <<YEAR 1727: FO 19095004>> <<YEAR 1749: CH 18009005>> <<YEAR 1750: AL 20029001
BR 19106017 CO 11009003 MA 30004012 MI 23026020 PO 47016029 RI 24018006>> <<YEAR 1751: PI 19139007>>
<<YEAR 1755: FL 23026009 GI 34003002 PE 69011013>> <<YEAR 1756: AN 25003022, 45013004 BA 23026009,
27004035 BY 45013001 CR 24006008 GI 21007014 HA 24018007 HO 45013002 JO 62004009 KI 43010029
LE 30004012 NO 19018003 RI 24017006 SE 45013035 ST 19018007, 31003009 TO 63005006 WA 30004011,
30004012 WI 45013003>> <<YEAR 1757: PE 48011022>> <<YEAR 1760: ST 45013035>> <<YEAR 1766: SE 19002011>>
<<YEAR 1767: TO 28011009>> <<YEAR 1770: AS 64002009>> <<YEAR 1777: PO 43027051>>

Easter - Day <"E.S.","Easter s.","E.S.b.K.", *etc.*,*etc.*>

Note: The following items do not include references to sermons for the first, second, ..., fifth Sunday after Easter, for the Sunday before Easter, or for Easter Monday, Tuesday, etc. There are fifty-four such items within Index E following the keywords "EAST" and "EASTER". There is also one item which reads "Shro.& East." following the keyword "EAST".

<<YEAR 1661: BR 44016007, 46002019, 46012024, 49015058, 61013020 HA 49005007 MA 44016007,
46002019, 46012024 NI 48004025>> <<YEAR 1664: BR 18019025, 48008011>> <<YEAR 1672: FA 54003001,
69001018 FR 19118024, 43027052, 43028005, 45024004, 49015019>> <<YEAR 1673: SH 47026008>>
<<YEAR 1675: HA 43028002, 43028003, 43028009, 43028013, 44016009, 46011043, 46011044,
46020001, 47002024>> <<YEAR 1679: RE 61013020 WA 49015020>> <<YEAR 1680: LI 45024034>> <<YEAR 1684:
AL 46020028, 49015057 HA 47003026 TU 28006002>> <<YEAR 1685: KI 48008011>> <<YEAR 1687: HO 48008018>>
<<YEAR 1689: MA 46020009>> <<YEAR 1692: ST 47002024>> <<YEAR 1694: TE 49015053>> <<YEAR 1697: AL 47002027
BE 46005028 CO 49015019, 63001003, 65005012>> <<YEAR 1698: PA 47026008 ST 47018017>> <<YEAR 1699:
ST 54003001>> <<YEAR 1703: DO 58002007>> <<YEAR 1704: GA 48008029>> <<YEAR 1706: HI 64003011 YO 55004018>>
<<YEAR 1707: BO 47002024 PE 54003001>> <<YEAR 1708: GR 47026008 NO 58002008>> <<YEAR 1709: BR 46020020
LY 47002042>> <<YEAR 1710: HO 47002024>> <<YEAR 1712: FI 52002018>> <<YEAR 1713: BR 49015019 HI 45016031
WY 45024036>> <<YEAR 1714: DU 45024034>> <<YEAR 1715: ST 46020001, 54003001, 63003017>> <<YEAR 1716:
AD 49015055 BA 47001003 HO 46020001, 48006009, 49005007, 49015020, 54003001, 63003017
LU 49015058 ST 49015020, 69001018>> <<YEAR 1717: KI 49015015 WI 47024015>> <<YEAR 1718: TI 53003010>>
<<YEAR 1719: HO 46005028>> <<YEAR 1720: BE 19118024, 48004025, 49015020 CL 47010040 FI 19118024
NE 63001003>> <<YEAR 1721: CO 43028005>> <<YEAR 1722: MA 46005028>> <<YEAR 1723: SC 49015020>> <<YEAR 1724:
LA 49005007 SM 63001003 SO 46020029>> <<YEAR 1725: SH 47026008>> <<YEAR 1726: CA 49015035 RE 47010040>>
<<YEAR 1727: SO 47002024, 47024015>> <<YEAR 1728: NE 69001017 RE 02012021 WH 47002024, 47010040,
54003001>> <<YEAR 1729: LU 43022031 SH 47010040, 53003010 WA 49015020 WI 45024046>> <<YEAR 1730:
BR 63001003 HO 49015020 RE 02014030 TR 46005028>> <<YEAR 1731: FR 46011021>> <<YEAR 1732: AN 46011025>>
<<YEAR 1734: AT 47001003>> <<YEAR 1735: CL 19016009, 49001022, 49015014, 49015056 RO 49015023
TI 47001003, 47026008>> <<YEAR 1736: NE 46002018, 49015042, 49015056>> <<YEAR 1740: JO 47001003,
61013020 SM 49006014>> <<YEAR 1741: LU 43028013>> <<YEAR 1742: HO 69020006>> <<YEAR 1744: SO 48001003>>
<<YEAR 1746: TE 58002008 WH 49015020>> <<YEAR 1747: GR 45024034 WE 46006057, 46020029, 47017030>>
<<YEAR 1748: WA 48004025, 48006009>> <<YEAR 1749: OR 46020029>> <<YEAR 1750: BU 49015017 FR 47001003>>
<<YEAR 1752: AL 49015020 BA 49015020>> <<YEAR 1753: PR 26037003>> <<YEAR 1755: RE 48001004>> <<YEAR 1757:
MO 47003021>> <<YEAR 1758: HO 47002024>> <<YEAR 1763: BE 69001018>> <<YEAR 1766: RO 49015020>> <<YEAR 1770:
DI 49015017 SE 46020029, 47010040, 48014009, 49015019, 54003001>> <<YEAR 1772: OR 58001010,
69001018>> <<YEAR 1773: FR 61004015>> <<YEAR 1774: CL 46020029>> <<YEAR 1775: SA 52006011>> <<YEAR 1776:
AN 45024034>> <<YEAR 1777: PY 61002003, 64001004>> <<YEAR 1778: EV 49015021>> <<YEAR 1780: HU 47026009>>

Elections : Parliament, Burgesses, Magistrates <"El.Burg.",El.M.Parl.","El.of Mag.","El.M.Coun.", *etc.*>

Note: For Admission or Election of Lord Mayor, see "Mayor" below within present Index D; and for at least two further items referring to sermons about election of officials, see the keyword "ELECTION" and abbreviation "ELECT" within Index E to our Third Volume. Other items there refer to sermons about Election in the theological sense of the word.

<<YEAR ----: SC 24008009>> <<YEAR 1661: WI 21010017>> <<YEAR 1670: ST 47013036>> <<YEAR 1693: MA 47013036>>
<<YEAR 1698: ED 02018025>> <<YEAR 1705: CA 20003007>> <<YEAR 1709: PE 02018021>> <<YEAR 1722: DO 02018021>>
<<YEAR 1727: PE 19082006>> <<YEAR 1734: VA 50013011>> <<YEAR 1745: CA 18029014>> <<YEAR 1746: ME 02018021>>
<<YEAR 1749: KI 02018021>> <<YEAR 1754: BE 02018021>> <<YEAR 1765: EL 13012032>> <<YEAR 1774: WA 23001026>>
<<YEAR 1779: ER 06001017>>

Epiphany <"Epiph.","Epiph.s.","Epiphany","Xmas& Epi.","S.af.Epiph.">

Note: Regarding first, second, ... , sixth Sunday of Epiphany, see keyword abbreviation "EPIPH" in Index E.

<<YEAR 1663: SP 43002010>> <<YEAR 1664: CH 51005005>> <<YEAR 1672: BE 43002010 FR 43002010>> <<YEAR 1680:
GR 43002002>> <<YEAR 1684: GR 46001029>> <<YEAR 1689: HO 45002014>> <<YEAR 1712: IB 57003016>> <<YEAR 1715:
ST 43002001, 52003001, 54003012, 65003001>> <<YEAR 1716: HO 43002001, 52003001, 65003001>>
<<YEAR 1717: BO 43002001>> <<YEAR 1722: CA 45002032>> <<YEAR 1729: JO 43002001>> <<YEAR 1730: BR 45002032>>
<<YEAR 1735: CL 38001011>> <<YEAR 1739: WA 45002032>> <<YEAR 1742: MO 43002001>> <<YEAR 1745: SN 49007008>>
<<YEAR 1746: HA 45002032>> <<YEAR 1747: BU 45002032>> <<YEAR 1748: WA 45002032>> <<YEAR 1749: BI 23049006
HE 57004010>> <<YEAR 1752: BA 43002001>> <<YEAR 1778: HO 43011001>>

Fairs, Opening of, etc. <"Op.Fair","Fair time","Op. new fair">
Note: Also see the keyword "FAIR" followed by "S.b.Fair" within Index E.

<<YEAR 1698: ED 26027027>> <<YEAR 1710: HO 20023023>> <<YEAR 1723: BU 32006006>>

Farewell Sermons <"Far.s.","Farw.s.","Farew.s.","Xt's.H.Far.s.">
Note: Also see "Collection of Farewell Sermons" within the preceding Index B.

<<YEAR ----:
GR 47020032
<<YEAR 1694:
SC 61013014>>
WI 45006027>>
<<YEAR 1712:
<<YEAR 1715:
GI 56003003
LO 63001008
MA 53001027>>
CA 62001022
AT 48012018>>
BE 61010023>>
JO 50013011>>
<<YEAR 1745:
<<YEAR 1753:
<<YEAR 1769:
69022021>>
JE 61010026>>
ME 49001003>>
OL 64001002>>
<<YEAR 1702:
<<YEAR 1708:
MO 50013011
AT 50013011
MO 53001009>>
WA 50013011>>
<<YEAR 1727:
LU 53001027
<<YEAR 1735:
<<YEAR 1739:
<<YEAR 1742:
WA 50013011>>
WA 49015058>>
SC 50001012>>
<<YEAR 1773:
<<YEAR 1662:
<<YEAR 1685:
<<YEAR 1696:
HE 47020026>>
TR 54002006>>
SW 30003003>>
MO 51006007>>
<<YEAR 1719:
<<YEAR 1723:
CO 50013011
SH 53004008>>
WO 61012014>>
WH 19107030,
PI 19027013>>
<<YEAR 1746:
<<YEAR 1755:
<<YEAR 1770:
CO 43005048
BA 50013011
HO 48015005>>
BR 47020032>>
<<YEAR 1704:
<<YEAR 1710:
<<YEAR 1713:
<<YEAR 1716:
RO 19037031>>
GR 53001027>>
KE 01028020>>
<<YEAR 1730:
<<YEAR 1736:
50013011>>
<<YEAR 1743:
MA 50013011>>
CO 47020032>>
HO 46014027
MA 61013014>>
CA 69002005
<<YEAR 1692:
<<YEAR 1697:
RA 50013011
TR 05008001>>
MA 54001011>>
AN 48014023
<<YEAR 1721:
<<YEAR 1724:
<<YEAR 1728:
PA 26018024>>
RO 43025019>>
<<YEAR 1740:
SC 53002015
<<YEAR 1748:
<<YEAR 1764:
WI 50013011>>
<<YEAR 1774:
SW 47020032>>
JO 51004016>>
WI 61013020>>
RO 44011024>>
<<YEAR 1711:
<<YEAR 1714:
EV 47020032>>
HE 21012013>>
PE 47020032
CO 55004001
<<YEAR 1731:
<<YEAR 1737:
DO 50001012,
SE 57001018>>
KI 50013011>>
JO 50013011>>
<<YEAR 1771:
WA 50013011>>
<<YEAR 1663:
<<YEAR 1693:
<<YEAR 1699:
<<YEAR 1707:
AS 50004005
FY 49015058
<<YEAR 1717:
<<YEAR 1722:
ST 53004008>>
MO 50013011>>
MA 53002005>>
PE 48012021>>
55005023>>
<<YEAR 1744:
<<YEAR 1750:
<<YEAR 1766:
WH 02028012,
BU 47020032
PR 61013014>>
MI 53004009
MA 47020032
GA 48008014>>
WH 19107043>>
CO 47002032
BO 50013011
<<YEAR 1726:
<<YEAR 1729:
<<YEAR 1734:
<<YEAR 1738:
<<YEAR 1741:
BE 49015028>>
NI 68000020>>
SE 50013011>>
46010027,

Fast - Sermons <"F.s.","F.s.b.L.M.", etc.; "F.s.Earthq.","F.s.Fire Lond.","F.s.F.L.","F.s.Storm.","F.s.Plague", etc.; "F.s.Plag.b.K.", etc.>
Note 1: Regarding Lenten sermons, including most Lenten fast sermons, see the heading "Lent Sermons." within the present Index D.
Note 2: For one more item referring to a Fast sermon on the Fire of London, see within Index E the keyword "F" followed by "F.F.Lond."

<<YEAR ----:
GA 32006008
BU 06007016
WI 30005006>>
AL 10019009>>
57004016>>
CA 19018002
JA 28007009
AN 29002013
FU 47005038
HO 46005014>>
MA 23042022,
AN 19062001
BU 19012001,
<<YEAR 1694:
GA 19079009
<<YEAR 1697:
SM 19080019>>
BU 28010012
KI 29002018
PO 14020012>>
28008007
WA 24008020>>
SA 14006034>>
TH 23058003
HA 23057019
KI 14007013>>
<<YEAR 1667:
<<YEAR 1671:
<<YEAR 1674:
CR 63005006
RE 14007013,
FE 43012025
GL 31003005
<<YEAR 1684:
30004012,
BA 30004012
23057021
CO 19122006
HA 15008021
BU 62004009
<<YEAR 17--:
HA 23001016
PA 23059008
<<YEAR 1704:
HA 23029006
<<YEAR 1705:
<<YEAR 1707:
WI 19089003>>
WI 23062006,
<<YEAR 1666:
GE 18009012
PI 30004012,
CR 23057021
LA 45013005
15009015,
JE 56002007
GO 35002001
AL 45016030
38003007>>
BU 19085008,
IR 19012001
KI 37007005
PE 23030001
PR 23001005>>
BR 29003019
HO 19127001,
ST 09012024
AN 43006016
HO 29002012
CO 17001008
BA 26036031
<<YEAR 16--:
30005015>>
EL 26020047
ST 11017015>>
32006009>>
WA 21011009>>
PA 23005025,
16014031,
LI 43004017,
PA 69002016,
CA 23057021>>
<<YEAR 1689:
45019041
TA 30004012>>
SA 19057001,
WO 05009026>>
<<YEAR 1698:
DA 02023009
53003020
WH 24006008>>
C. 10024014
LE 19018007
WO 14015002>>
BR 05023009
CR 23027015
<<YEAR 1661:
HA 19007009,
<<YEAR 1669:
<<YEAR 1672:
<<YEAR 1675:
24014009
28011012,
43006034>>
69003003>>
<<YEAR 1685:
LE 14014011
LL 64003009
<<YEAR 1692:
23026009
<<YEAR 1696:
ED 06007012
EA 24009023
IS 09004013
<<YEAR 1703:
CL 45013005
OF 19148008
<<YEAR 1706:
ED 25001008
DI 14020012
GR 23058005
45019041
DA 37001003
FA 46005014>>
HA 16001004>>
TH 45013005>>
28014001,
<<YEAR 1681:
<<YEAR 1682:
CR 19108010>>
SA 19119075
PA 20014034
PA 04010009>>
SH 12009022,
BU 16009026
HO 17006013>>
GR 21007010>>
KN 01018032>>
CO 19148008
CO 45013005
PE 23026016
BR 46005014
LO 24005003
WI 19089003>>
RE 10019012>>
HU 04016046
FL 38004005>>
<<YEAR 1673:
<<YEAR 1678:
<<YEAR 1679:
53004005>>
BU 30004011,
WR 15004015>>
<<YEAR 1688:
TE 58003001>>
WI 06005013>>
<<YEAR 1693:
31003008>>
ME 10024014
<<YEAR 1699:
<<YEAR 1701:
<<YEAR 1702:
HA 24018011
GA 19046001
PR 33001003
GA 19021001
TR 20021030>>
<<YEAR 1660:
<<YEAR 1665:
PE 03026018
<<YEAR 167-:
GR 05023009,
BR 30008011
BR 23022012
<<YEAR 1680:
69003002
<<YEAR 1683:
GE 23024015
<<YEAR 1690:
<<YEAR 1691:
BO 10022004>>
<<YEAR 1695:
TO 19051009>>
LI 63004010
BA 46005014
CO 26018030
P. 19148008
GR 19089032,
SC 46005014
PA 05023009
<<YEAR 1708:

Funeral Sermons

<"Fun.s.","Fun.Czar","Roy.Fun.","R.Fun.","Univ.Fun.s.","F.Day Lab.", etc.>

Note: An alphabetical list of the proper names that appear in Cooke's descriptions of authors' publications is provided by Index C to our Fifth Volume. The names of some (630 or so) of the people about whom funeral sermons were preached may be found in that list.

<<YEAR ----:
WO 43024036>>
AN 01003019,
28013014,
48014007,
53003020,
69014007,
HA 48005005,
PH 21003020
23057001,
CA 19119092
RE 37011002
RO 49003021
<<YEAR 1664:
<<YEAR 1665:
RI 18030023
HE 53003021
50005009
PI 18014001>>
PA 43024046
46019040
BR 43009038
JE 64001015,
LA 49015057
R. 21012007
LL 10003033
48008010
BA 46012026
PO 19112006
LY 46011011
CA 61012009
<<YEAR 1683:
CA 69014013
<<YEAR 1685:
SM 53001023>>
MA 19015001
TU 69014013
LA 49006013
ME 18033023
EA 19103015
49007031
69014013
69014013
WH 19112006
FI 23040006
PA 19072006,
TE 21007014
PR 21002016
ME 48008011
CR 01049008
SH 21009010,
<<YEAR 17--:

BO 19018046
<<YEAR 16--:
01015001,
43016026,
49007029,
55005003,
69022012
48006005
SM 48005002
45008051,
CO 23057001
SM 20011018
SP 69002010>>
BO 61013014
A. 01048021
VI 23057001>>
JA 69014013
WA 49015057>>
<<YEAR 1672:
WA 10012015>>
JE 43024046
TA 49015010
64001015
LO 18030023>>
RA 20014001
TA 10014014,
RE 23026018,
BU 61013007
PY 49015031
ME 19090012
FR 46001047,
AN 04016001
FO 47013036
CA 49007030
<<YEAR 1686:
PE 21012001>>
WO 46011011>>
ME 18014013
QU 37001003
FL 21007001
SO 05032029
CR 18019025
CA 46009004
WR 21011003>>
GO 19073024
19082006
TH 37011002
SE 23060001
MI 69014013
GI 55004013
46011004,
DO 69002010

GA 21007002
AL 53001021
01050010,
45002029,
49010029,
58004007,
BA 55004014,
KI 61009027
TO 69014013
45010002,
EV 32007009
SW 69014013
<<YEAR 1663:
BR 11019004
FO 47021014
<<YEAR 1668:
WO 21012007>>
<<YEAR 1671:
DU 53001021
<<YEAR 1673:
KI 19039005
VI 49015055
SM 46009004>>
<<YEAR 1677:
VI 09025001>>
49015023
47007017,
GR 23057001
RE 23003001>>
MO 69014013
55004014
GA 19082006
HA 61002015
CU 48013001
BO 69014005
<<YEAR 1688:
<<YEAR 1689:
SM 19039006,
WR 61007025,
MI 37001005
SP 55004013
HA 58002015
CL 47009036
<<YEAR 1695:
HO 61012023,
PE 43026013,
WE 69014013>>
ST 48008017
PR 19037037
GO 61002014
50005004,
GA 53001021

KE 46005024
MA 53001021
10012022,
45016002,
49015016,
59002013,
58004007,
L. 10003038
TR 46011025>>
47013036,
EW 18003017
WA 46011011>>
CA 23057001
HA 26024016
SH 23038001
BR 63001004
<<YEAR 1670:
BU 52005015
EL 61009027
AN 37001005
NE 45023028
WA 45010042>>
<<YEAR 1676:
CL 10003032
<<YEAR 1678:
WA 20031029>>
53001021
JO 43013043
<<YEAR 1681:
PL 69014013
KE 20011016
HE 21011010
PA 49015058
FR 19082005
KI 61013014
CR 21003002
AN 10012005
21004002
61009027>>
PA 46011011,
WH 62001012
LA 26024015
CU 06024014
BO 14034027
69020006
45023028
<<YEAR 1696:
WI 04023010>>
SK 55004017
HA 19090012
61013007
HA 69010005

LA 23060001
RE 19116015
19090012,
48005012,
49015026,
61002015,
61012011
LI 10003038
<<YEAR 1661:
49015019,
HE 19039005
<<YEAR 1662:
HO 47007056,
PE 61011005
WI 50005001>>
HA 47013036>>
AN 45023003
JA 69014015
FA 19119019
BA 61011004
PA 12002012
<<YEAR 1675:
B. 19037037
DI 58004007
AN 50005001
<<YEAR 1679:
SL 61013007
LI 20031030,
GR 61011010
QU 05032029
LA 55004013
HI 69004004
PE 50005001
GO 12002011,
N. 46005024>>
HI 23057001
BU 58001006
TE 54003001>>
<<YEAR 1692:
69014013
WO 37001003
MO 46011025,
DO 50005001
CH 45008052
HU 62004014
PO 14035024
JO 09004022
<<YEAR 1698:
WI 61004001
HO 20031031,
SP 46011004
IN 53003020

LE 47009036
SM 01005024
19116015,
48006011,
49015055,
61011001,
BR 19039009
LY 55004013
AN 21012005,
62004014,
HI 01025008
BO 43025021
50004007
RU 58001010
<<YEAR 1666:
<<YEAR 1669:
CA 19002010
LA 69002010
FU 48008002
BU 69014013
WA 10003038>>
BY 21012007,
CL 53001023
GR 23057001
BE 47024016,
JO 49015024
SP 01023002
47013039
HI 53003020
RE 23057001>>
WA 45012040,
NI 21012005
SC 43025046
46011021
<<YEAR 1687:
K. 26024016
HU 47013036>>
<<YEAR 1691:
BU 21002026
PO 45002029
WR 48002007>>
49015012>>
MA 30008009
DA 14035024
IS 53003020
SH 10001019,
ME 18014014
AN 45010036
WR 47008002>>
46011016
ST 20014032
LE 45013005

RI 46012026
TU 49015055>>
21007002,
48006023,
50005002,
61012010,
EE 10003033
MO 26017022
21012014,
63003007
HO 45016009
CA 55004014
OL 28006002
WA 18014001,
HA 53001023>>
BO 53003020
DO 55004013
LL 19037037
GU 49015058
FL 10023005,
<<YEAR 1674:
45018013
HO 18014012,
HO 48008020
52005015
LA 19037037
WI 45020036>>
OW 10012021
HO 50005008
<<YEAR 1682:
46009004,
WE 61009027>>
TH 69014013
HA 46005035
AT 19090012
SH 49015055
<<YEAR 1690:
BU 20031030
CA 04023010
PR 61009027
<<YEAR 1693:
<<YEAR 1694:
MO 23040006
DE 27004018
KE 23057001
53001023
OF 18001021>>
BE 34003002
<<YEAR 1699:
KN 04023010
TA 18021026
MO 12002012,

WI 20010007
<<YEAR 1660:
21007015,
48013011,
51006010,
62001004,
GA 12002012
PA 19090012
23026008,
BA 19090012
NA 50004017
KI 19116015
SW 19073026>>
45007012>>
<<YEAR 1667:
DU 27012002
PA 50005001,
MA 61009027
LL 61013007
14035024,
AL 54003004
GA 09001016
21007001
OL 61011017
BU 50005002
RA 19142009,
<<YEAR 1680:
PA 45015007
JO 58004007
BU 19037037
61013014>>
<<YEAR 1684:
WR 19112006>>
HI 01035019
BO 21012005
SY 55004017
HO 45013016
CR 19119137
DE 69014013
RO 01045024,
BR 69014013,
BU 58004007,
SE 69014013
EV 20031031
MA 19082006
TA 04023010
<<YEAR 1697:
KI 41016022
AD 50005001
OL 69014013
WE 61012023>>
19112006>>

INDEXES TO THIRD VOLUME: D: OCCASIONS OR SUBJECTS

Funerals of Royalty <"Roy.Fun.","R.Fun.s.","R.Fun.","R.F.","Fun.Czar">

<u>Note</u>: The following items are included among the items above under the heading "Funeral Sermons."

WR 21012005>> <<YEAR 1728: BO 14035024>> <<YEAR 1737: BY 19082006 CR 19146003 DI 19082006 FL 10002007,
14035024 MO 19119096>> <<YEAR 1760: CH 13029028 CO 11003009 FA 13029028 FO 13029026 FR 14032033
JO 18038017 NO 27006021 PA 13029027 ST 13029027>> <<YEAR 1761: BE 13029027 BU 14035024>> <<YEAR 1765:
CO 10003038 TO 10003038 WA 10001027>> <<YEAR 1767: BU 13029027>> <<YEAR 1768: PR 21007001>> <<YEAR 1771:
DA 10001019>> <<YEAR 1772: BR 13017011 WE 19049010>>

Gaming <"Ag.Gaming">
<<YEAR 1706: DO 20010023>> <<YEAR 1720: AN 33003001>> <<YEAR 1754: DE 48012002>> <<YEAR 1764: BR 20003017>>
<<YEAR 1772: DO 45016003>>

Georgia : See Colony Of Georgia

Good - Friday <"Good Friday","Good-Friday","East.or G.F.","G.Frid.b.Q.">
<<YEAR 1712: SP 54001026>> <<YEAR 1736: NE 61010010>> <<YEAR 1752: BA 23053005>> <<YEAR 1757: CO 63003018>>
<<YEAR 1762: SH 46019030>> <<YEAR 1763: BE 46003014>> <<YEAR 1765: WA 61004006>> <<YEAR 1768: WE 46012027>>
<<YEAR 1771: DI 46019030>> <<YEAR 1772: FA 46019030 OR 51003001, 61009026>> <<YEAR 1776: AN 63002021>>
<<YEAR 1777: PY 64001004>> <<YEAR 1778: HO 43016021>>

Gospel Or Religion, Propagation Of <"Prop.Gosp.","Prop.G.","Ch s.Pro.G."; "Prop.Xn.Kn.","Pro.Xn.Kn.";"Prop.of Rel.">
Note: For one more item that probably should have been included under this heading, see "Mir.Prop.G." following keyword "PROP" within Index E.
<<YEAR 17--: FL 50009002 SM 65003008>> <<YEAR 1700: ST 43009037>> <<YEAR 1702: WI 53001027>> <<YEAR 1704:
BU 38001011 CO 48006018>> <<YEAR 1705: HO 47017030>> <<YEAR 1706: WI 47016009>> <<YEAR 1707: BE 50009002>>
<<YEAR 1709: TR 43011005>> <<YEAR 1711: ST 43028019 WA 43028019>> <<YEAR 1712: KE 49009012>> <<YEAR 1713:
BU 58004013>> <<YEAR 1714: FO 45014021 ST 23060001>> <<YEAR 1715: AS 19067002 MO 47026028>> <<YEAR 1716:
HA 51005001>> <<YEAR 1718: BI 43005016 CH 43013031>> <<YEAR 1719: BR 43028019>> <<YEAR 1720: WA 45022032>>
<<YEAR 1722: BO 45024047 WA 63003019>> <<YEAR 1723: GR 45002032>> <<YEAR 1724: WY 43006010>> <<YEAR 1726:
LE 52003005 WI 19067005>> <<YEAR 1727: RE 65003008>> <<YEAR 1729: EG 27012003>> <<YEAR 1730: DE 44016015
PE 23049006>> <<YEAR 1732: BE 46017003 SM 19002007>> <<YEAR 1733: DA 47022021 MA 59002011>> <<YEAR 1735:
RU 23066005>> <<YEAR 1736: CL 47011018 LY 47005038>> <<YEAR 1737: FL 47026018>> <<YEAR 1740: BE 38001011>>
<<YEAR 1743: MA 48010014>> <<YEAR 1744: BE 51006009 GI 48001016>> <<YEAR 1745: SN 45006035>> <<YEAR 1746:
HA 48010013 HU 46008032 TH 43006010>> <<YEAR 1748: BA 51006010 LI 23049006 WA 43006010>> <<YEAR 1749:
BU 43024014 GE 46010016>> <<YEAR 1750: TR 45002032>> <<YEAR 1751: TH 48002011>> <<YEAR 1752: OS 43008011
RU 21011001>> <<YEAR 1753: CR 58002009, 58003009>> <<YEAR 1754: DR 05029029>> <<YEAR 1755: HA 69014006>>
<<YEAR 1756: CO 47026018 ER 23055013>> <<YEAR 1757: KE 43024012>> <<YEAR 1758: HO 50011014 JO 19144010>>
<<YEAR 1759: EL 46015008 SM 19002006>> <<YEAR 1760: AS 48001016 CU 43011005>> <<YEAR 1761: NE 48009026>>
<<YEAR 1762: HU 43009036>> <<YEAR 1763: EG 43022009>> <<YEAR 1764: TE 23011009>> <<YEAR 1765: YO 43028018>>
<<YEAR 1766: BU 01018019 MU 43008011 SE 44006034>> <<YEAR 1767: EL 44016020 EW 48010014 WA 69011011>>
<<YEAR 1768: GR 48001016>> <<YEAR 1769: NE 46010016>> <<YEAR 1770: KE 43028019>> <<YEAR 1771: LO 47002039>>
<<YEAR 1772: MO 48011025>> <<YEAR 1773: SH 45002014>> <<YEAR 1774: LA 38001011 SH 43004017>> <<YEAR 1775:
BA 19002008 RO 54001026>> <<YEAR 1776: HI 47010034 PO 43013032>> <<YEAR 1777: KI 43011005 MA 27007014>>
<<YEAR 1778: NO 51003014>> <<YEAR 1779: BU 43009036 TO 43006010 WH 44015016 YO 44015016>>

Inauguration Sermon <"Inaug s.","Inaug.">
Note: Also consider the items under the headings "Induction" and "Lecturer."
<<YEAR 1661: BR 36002023 MA 10006012, 36002023>> <<YEAR 1720: PE 20029002>> <<YEAR 1735: CL 20013021>>
<<YEAR 1742: CO 48013006>> <<YEAR 1760: ST 19147012>> <<YEAR 1762: RO 27002020>> <<YEAR 1764: BU 13028009>>
<<YEAR 1766: ST 05016020>> <<YEAR 1773: LA 20014034>>

Induction <"Induct.s.","Induction.s.">
Note 1: For another item see, within Index E, the keyword "INDUCT" followed by "S. af Induct."
Note 2: Also consider the items under the headings "Inauguration Sermon" and "Lecturer."
<<YEAR 1708: SC 48001016>> <<YEAR 1714: WH 61013018>> <<YEAR 1747: CO 50002004>>

Inoculation, and Remedies for the Smallpox <"Inoculation","Ag.Inoculation","For Inoculation","Rem.sm.pox">
Note 1: For another possible item, see "Small-Pox" following keyword "SMALL" within Index E.
Note 2: Regarding smallpox hospitals, see the heading "Smallpox Hospitals" within Index C.
<<YEAR 1712: FR 19116011>> <<YEAR 1722: MA 18002007>> <<YEAR 1753: DE 48003008>> <<YEAR 1755: HO 46011004>>
<<YEAR 1782: GR 44005010>>

Invasion <"Invasion","F.s.Invas.","Intend.Inv.", etc.>
Note: For one further item, see "French Inv." following keyword "INV" within Index E.
<<YEAR 1708: CA 11001005>> <<YEAR 1744: LE 23007005 WH 23037033>> <<YEAR 1745: CH 23008012 HO 12019032>>
<<YEAR 1746: FI 23005030>> <<YEAR 1756: GR 02034024>>

Irish Massacre, Irish Rebellion, or Irish Protestant Thanksgiving <"Ir.Mass.","Com.Ir.Mas.","Co.Ir.Mas.",
"Th.s.Ir.Mas.", etc.; "Ir.Rebell."; ""Th.s.Ir.Prot." etc.>

<<YEAR 1689: VE 19102013>> <<YEAR 1690: TE 14028009>> <<YEAR 1692: WE 50001009>> <<YEAR 1708: LA 23059007>>
<<YEAR 1709: PA 19037012>> <<YEAR 1710: DA 50001010>> <<YEAR 1712: ST 57004001>> <<YEAR 1714: RA 46016002
ST 24007004>> <<YEAR 1715: SM 05030015>> <<YEAR 1717: ST 19014005>> <<YEAR 1721: BO 59003001>> <<YEAR 1725:
SY 45014023>> <<YEAR 1728: BO 43023029, 51001008, 54001018>> <<YEAR 1735: RU 37012005>> <<YEAR 1751:
AB 43005044>> <<YEAR 1763: YO 43010034>> <<YEAR 1767: NE 59003001>>

Irish Protestant Schools <"Ir.Prot.Sch.","Prot.Ir.Sch.", etc.; "Irish Sch.","I.Sch.", etc.;"A.m.Pr.Ir.S.">
Note: For another item see "A.m. Pr. Ir. S" following keyword "IR" within Index E.
<<YEAR 1736: RU 69003015>> <<YEAR 1738: HO 01003019>> <<YEAR 1739: WI 21007010>> <<YEAR 1740: CL 56003010
MA 23011013>> <<YEAR 1742: BE 25003027 ST 21011001>> <<YEAR 1743: CA 62001027 TH 59003014>> <<YEAR 1744:
DE 46013034>> <<YEAR 1745: HU 57004007>> <<YEAR 1746: FL 20013023>> <<YEAR 1747: TH 43020003>> <<YEAR 1748:
CO 19112009>> <<YEAR 1749: NI 23060022>> <<YEAR 1750: DO 19008002>> <<YEAR 1752: BA 43003009 CO 43018010>>
<<YEAR 1753: HA 19122008>> <<YEAR 1755: KE 24029007>> <<YEAR 1756: GA 45015007>> <<YEAR 1758: JO 58001005
ST 57001005>> <<YEAR 1759: FL 19072003>> <<YEAR 1760: HU 51006009>> <<YEAR 1762: PO 55002019, 56002019>>
<<YEAR 1763: HE 45010036 YO 06024013>> <<YEAR 1764: WO 20003016>> <<YEAR 1766: YO 20019027>> <<YEAR 1767:
GR 59003008>> <<YEAR 1768: DO 23058006>> <<YEAR 1770: MA 51006009 NE 52006004>> <<YEAR 1773: LO 48012011>>
<<YEAR 1774: RI 19068028 SH 05032045>> <<YEAR 1776: BO 56001003>>

January 30 <"Jan.30.","J.30","Jan 30 b.L.","Jan.30 b.C.","Jan.30 b.L.M.","Jan.30 b.K.","Jan.30 b.Q" etc.;Jan.b C.", etc.>
<<YEAR 1660: PA 10024005>> <<YEAR 1661: FO 10001014 HA 14035024 ME 21010020 PA 09024005 RE 61011004
SW 09001010, 09010027, 11021019, 47014028>> <<YEAR 1662: BU 10001018 DO 19022012 HA 37012011
ST 25004020 WI 47007032>> <<YEAR 1664: GL 01004010 KI 14035024>> <<YEAR 1665: GR 09026009 TW 25004020
WI 14024025>> <<YEAR 1666: FL 46018040>> <<YEAR 1667: AN 48013002>> <<YEAR 1669: LA 47002037>> <<YEAR 1670:
OV 14035024>> <<YEAR 1672: AL 47008001>> <<YEAR 1674: ST 46019015 WA 12006033>> <<YEAR 1675: BU 10002012
CO 56003002 JE 65004020>> <<YEAR 1676: BA 19037037 DU 47007060 MA 07019030>> <<YEAR 1677: HE 10001017>>
<<YEAR 1678: RO 09024005>> <<YEAR 1679: CA 57002001 PE 20008015>> <<YEAR 1680: JE 01004015 LI 46019015
OU 25004005>> <<YEAR 1681: BU 37008019 CR 25004020 GL 48013002 HO 19099001 MA 23037003 TU 25004019
WI 48013001>> <<YEAR 1682: CA 47007060 MI 47025008 PE 25005016>> <<YEAR 1683: BU 69002009 LA 10001018,
10015006 LO 05034005 MA 43007015 PA 09026009 PE 10001014>> <<YEAR 1684: BU 45021025 EL 20030031
HI 20030031 PE 48013002 TU 47005028 WA 29002015 WO 24003008>> <<YEAR 1685: GR 20028002 KI 09012025
MA 19079008 PE 19137001>> <<YEAR 1686: HA 20008018>> <<YEAR 1687: BO 23054008>> <<YEAR 1688: SC 20008015,
45017012>> <<YEAR 1689: BU 19144015 PA 19075001 ST 14035024>> <<YEAR 1691: BU 24005029 LL 14035024>>
<<YEAR 1692: KI 43023035 SH 19090015>> <<YEAR 1693: BY 23057001 HO 43019018>> <<YEAR 1694: BI 10001021
NE 10001014 SN 19146003 ST 25005016>> <<YEAR 1695: HA 19090015 HO 65003020>> <<YEAR 1696: HA 32007002
HU 28010003 LA 25005016 ME 19011003 WI 43023034>> <<YEAR 1697: ES 62001021 LA 23053007 LL 37007005>>
<<YEAR 1698: BR 20024021>> <<YEAR 1699: GI 10021001>> <<YEAR 17--: BR 37012011 BU 29003019 FL 47022020>>
<<YEAR 1700: ST 59003001>> <<YEAR 1701: HA 12009031 MI 63003014>> <<YEAR 1702: AL 27009007 BI 45023034
DE 43027025 MI 10001014 PL 43023035 WI 47007059>> <<YEAR 1703: BU 19051017 GO 20024021 NI 58002011>>
<<YEAR 1704: BU 09026011 CL 45009055 GR 25004020 HO 50010003 KE 24044023 WY 52004003>> <<YEAR 1705:
DO 63002017 ST 19094020>> <<YEAR 1706: KE 01042021 SY 20024021 VA 62001012>> <<YEAR 1707: MI 48013001
TY 21008014>> <<YEAR 1708: AN 07019030 BR 47007060 CO 20028002 MI 23014020 PE 02020005 ST 09012024>>
<<YEAR 1709: MI 47025010>> <<YEAR 171-: BR 21008014>> <<YEAR 1710: BR 20004025 BU 10002010 FL 59003001

HO 18005012,
WH 12008013>>
TR 20017014>>
AN 21008004
MI 48013003>>
AS 19005006
ST 43021033
EN 47015007
KN 10018003
KE 44014019
FI 21007015,
MA 02020005
43026051>>
CR 19122006
SO 07019030
BA 68000011
<<YEAR 1728:
SH 57004007,
CL 09012025
AL 05021008,
<<YEAR 1733:
SH 20024021>>
FL 09026010,
FE 02020005,
JO 69002010
<<YEAR 1743:
SO 34002012>>
11021009
TE 20024021
<<YEAR 1748:
PE 47023005
PI 10001027>>
WI 47024005>>
FO 14035025
53004005
CO 06024015
48013003>>
EG 28003004
<<YEAR 1764:
BA 43022021
LA 62003016
AS 43010034,
ST 43007012>>
44003024>>
PO 19022028>>
25005016,
<<YEAR 1711:
<<YEAR 1712:
BR 20029025
<<YEAR 1714:
CA 20024021
WI 20024021>>
MI 46018036
LE 10001014
MI 63002015
21009002
RE 11012019>>
<<YEAR 1723:
FE 23037003
WA 14035025>>
BE 57002001
NE 69002010
59003001
CR 20025005
43022021,
BE 21005008
<<YEAR 1735:
12008013
25003040
VE 40003004
BU 20024021
<<YEAR 1745:
TH 49010011,
TR 10001014>>
DR 23019002
WI 48013007>>
<<YEAR 1751:
<<YEAR 1752:
FR 02031018
WA 48013004
HU 06024015
<<YEAR 1759:
HO 63002021>>
NE 53004005
KE 62003017
ST 59003001>>
45012051
<<YEAR 1772:
<<YEAR 1776:
<<YEAR 1779:
63002013
AR 37007004
CO 23057001
CO 01049005,
AN 09026009,
GO 09024010
<<YEAR 1716:
PO 19109002
MI 48003008>>
WA 21008014>>
HA 37007005
<<YEAR 1722:
BA 57002001
GA 14035025
<<YEAR 1725:
LE 62004001
PE 23011013
TR 45023028
LI 63002016>>
48013002
DA 43021038
CL 57002001>>
ST 43022021,
MO 25005007
WH 61011004>>
CH 63002016
BR 46018038
64002019>>
<<YEAR 1747:
OS 04021005
<<YEAR 1750:
AL 12008011
BE 09015023
HO 23032001
WI 49012021>>
PA 20017014
RO 28013009
<<YEAR 1762:
RI 43022021>>
SE 23026009>>
<<YEAR 1769:
BA 19076010
BA 20001032>>
PO 25004013
RO 20024021>>
LL 45013002
CR 09026011
GA 25005016
45023028
15004015
LO 01049006
AN 46011049
RU 45019041
<<YEAR 1718:
<<YEAR 1720:
MA 23057001
BO 20024021
BL 25005007
HO 23058006
BL 37007005
LO 24005007
PI 20026002
WA 24026014
<<YEAR 1731:
BU 43012025
MO 19035011>>
<<YEAR 1736:
64003016
WI 20024021>>
<<YEAR 1741:
HU 43012025
CL 09024017
<<YEAR 1746:
BA 30003002
WA 52005007>>
BE 57002001
CO 12019003
CR 63002016
KE 49010011>>
<<YEAR 1755:
PE 63002017>>
SM 43007012
SA 20017014>>
<<YEAR 1765:
<<YEAR 1767:
HA 51005013
SH 23033006>>
<<YEAR 1773:
TU 63002017
<<YEAR 1780:
MI 48013002
FR 24003025
GO 19011003
EC 43005010
MI 10001016,
MO 57002001
BL 21008002,
TA 20024021>>
HO 49010011
BA 46005014
MI 16009033
CO 09024004
FO 59003001
LI 48013001
LO 25005007
PA 21009002>>
SM 09026009>>
YO 63002017>>
CL 19078008
GO 18034030
<<YEAR 1734:
AY 48012003
TI 46016002>>
<<YEAR 1739:
HU 63002017>>
NE 20017014>>
DE 48013001
BR 09012023
BR 49011001
<<YEAR 1749:
CO 01040020,
HO 68000008
HA 24012001
<<YEAR 1754:
FR 63002016>>
<<YEAR 1758:
YO 20004023>>
<<YEAR 1763:
FO 63002016
LO 20024021
MO 62004001
<<YEAR 1771:
HI 53004005>>
YO 43005009>>
RO 48013001
OL 19051003
HI 45023028
LL 45013003
FO 43021038
20024021
NE 47023005
23049020
<<YEAR 1717:
MA 50011026>>
BE 47022020,
SH 07009019>>
DI 20024021
HU 19133001
SH 05029024
OR 20028002
<<YEAR 1727:
<<YEAR 1729:
<<YEAR 1730:
MA 12008013
HO 19122006
AT 45023028
ST 63004017>>
<<YEAR 1738:
LE 48013001
<<YEAR 1742:
<<YEAR 1744:
JO 31001014
HA 20024021
BU 48013001
BR 46007046
01042021,
JE 21008002
MU 20014034>>
EC 47026011
<<YEAR 1756:
NE 58003001
<<YEAR 1760:
BR 63002016
HI 50003017
PO 43006033
ST 15009006
BU 46009001
<<YEAR 1774:
<<YEAR 1777:
TH 63002017>>
SP 43005010
JE 47024016
WI 19122006>>
HI 47017007
RE 09024005>>
SK 48013001
BR 20024021
BE 43005004
<<YEAR 1719:
63001008,
<<YEAR 1721:
MA 20024021
ST 21008014>>
SM 01049006,
WA 43022021>>
EG 20024021
LU 09012025
BR 43022021,
WA 69003021>>
MA 48013001
FE 43022021
<<YEAR 1737:
BE 19078005
SP 43012025>>
GI 52004026
CR 20017014
PE 48003016
MA 62003016
DE 20025004
BU 63002016
23037003
SQ 63002013
<<YEAR 1753:
EL 63002016
NE 61012005>>
TE 62004001
BU 49010011>>
GR 48013007
LY 45002014>>
WA 23019013>>
YO 55004011>>
KI 48013005
MA 23003003
MO 63002017>>
<<YEAR 1781:
WE 24031029
MI 09024013
<<YEAR 1713:
HU 21010020
<<YEAR 1715:
SM 09012025
CA 43012025
CH 07017006
BR 43012025
63002013
BE 11021012
WA 43012025,
<<YEAR 1724:
07019030
<<YEAR 1726:
PO 07019030>>
RE 57002001
48013005
<<YEAR 1732:
PE 43010034>>
HA 28010006
AR 48014019
BO 43007012
<<YEAR 1740:
ST 25002006>>
GI 48013001
SN 01020011,
RU 23058004
TR 49010011>>
EL 43022021
HA 63002017
WA 48013007
BL 12008011
HO 49010011,
<<YEAR 1757:
TH 48012003,
<<YEAR 1761:
HE 63002013>>
<<YEAR 1766:
<<YEAR 1768:
<<YEAR 1770:
LA 27002020
SH 20024021,
<<YEAR 1778:
CO 05028049>>

Lecturer, Election of a Lecturer, Opening of a Lecture, etc. <"El.Lecturer","Op.Lecture","El.Lecturer">
<<YEAR 1697: BA 47024014>> <<YEAR 1727: MA 48010014>> <<YEAR 1738: SH 47001024>>

Lent Sermons <"L.s.","L.S.","L.s.b.K.","L.s.b.K.","L.S.b.K.","Lent b. K.","L.s.b.Q.", etc.>
Note: For another forty-eight items in addition to those below, see the keyword "LENT" within Index E. They were missed during preparation of present Index D because of technical error.
<<YEAR ----: OV 43017021>> <<YEAR 1660: HA 47015039>> <<YEAR 1661: BR 47002037 MA 47002037>> <<YEAR 1663: LA 61013015>> <<YEAR 1668: LA 44004024>> <<YEAR 1671: PI 48013012>> <<YEAR 1672: FR 48006021, 48008021, 49009024, 49009025, 49009027>> <<YEAR 1674: LL 48008013>> <<YEAR 1676: CR 53001021>> <<YEAR 1677:

Mayor, Admission or Election of, etc. <"Elect.L.M.","El.L.Ma.","El.s.b.L.M.","El.& Sw.L.M.", etc.; "El.Mayor","Elect.Ma.","El.M.", etc.; "Adm.L.M.","Adm. Mayor",etc.; "Install of M.">

<<YEAR 1673: BA 23001026>> <<YEAR 1679: RI 48013004 >> <<YEAR 1680: HA 68000008>> <<YEAR 1681: BU 43012025>>
<<YEAR 1682: DO 59003001>> <<YEAR 1685: WH 48013001 WI 20024021>> <<YEAR 1688: WA 18034029>> <<YEAR 1689:
MA 45011017>> <<YEAR 1692: SM 19094016 20029002>> <<YEAR 1693: GR 55004011 ST 43020022>> <<YEAR 1696:
BU 20029002>> <<YEAR 1698: BA 20021015>> <<YEAR 1700: BR 23001026 EL 21008011>> <<YEAR 1701: WO 47008008>>
<<YEAR 1702: AL 30005024>> <<YEAR 1705: HA 48014022>> <<YEAR 1706: SM 19094016>> <<YEAR 1707: SA 20029002>>
<<YEAR 1710: LU 19094016>> <<YEAR 1711: CO 14019006 KE 45010029 WO 63002013>> <<YEAR 1712: CA 54003014
<<YEAR 1713: BE 63001022 ED 10023003>> <<YEAR 1714: BU 19122008>> <<YEAR 1715: WA 48012017>> <<YEAR 1716:
SK 48013004>> <<YEAR 1717: AN 48014019>> <<YEAR 1718: BR 02018021>> <<YEAR 1722: BE 18031028 BU 57002001>>
<<YEAR 1723: BU 14019005>> <<YEAR 1724: BU 16005019 DI 10023003>> <<YEAR 1725: MA 45013024>> <<YEAR 1726:
BI 48013003 CA 24006008 OL 48013003>> <<YEAR 1727: PA 49004005>> <<YEAR 1728: NI 63002013>> <<YEAR 1729:
BU 02018021>> <<YEAR 1730: AT 18029014>> KN 05016018>> <<YEAR 1731: HA 21012013>> <<YEAR 1732: MI 20029002>>
<<YEAR 1733: PI 10023003 TR 09002030>> <<YEAR 1736: NE 10023003 44009035>> <<YEAR 1737: ST 23049023>>
<<YEAR 1738: GO 20029002>> <<YEAR 1741: TO 20016012>> <<YEAR 1742: CO 20029002 SM 63002014>> <<YEAR 1743:
GI 10023003>> <<YEAR 1746: WH 05001011>> <<YEAR 1747: SA 19122006>> <<YEAR 1750: CO 09012003 SA 10023003>>
<<YEAR 1752: RO 43005016>> <<YEAR 1754: BA 43012025 DE 57002002 HO 48013001 TA 05004008>> <<YEAR 1757:
HA 10023003>> <<YEAR 1764: GR 57002002>> <<YEAR 1771: EV 20004025>> <<YEAR 1775: WI 63003008>> <<YEAR 1776:
IB 47018014 SA 20011003>>

Meeting - House, Opening of, etc. <"Op. Meet. H.", etc.>
Note: Also see the separate heading "Consecration, Opening, Beautification of Church or Chapel" within the present Index D.

<<YEAR 1722: NO 52001022>> <<YEAR 1730: RE 63001024>> <<YEAR 1769: BE 43018020, 47005042>> <<YEAR 1771:
PA 36002009>> <<YEAR 1773: GI 02020024>>

Military Sermons <"Xtian Warfare"%, "Sold.wages","Sold.duty","Roy.Sold.","b.Army","Milit.Song">

Notes: Related topics (1) Within present Index D, see "Invasion", "Irish Massacre", "Naval Sermons", "Peace", "Rebellion","Siege","Victory", and "War."
(2) Within preceding Index C, see "Military Company" and Artillery Company."
(3) Within following Index E, see "VOLUNTEERS","VOLUNT","SOLDIER", and "SOLD."

"Xtian Warfare"% The six items with the symbol "%" prefixed to the biblical code numbers within them refer to sermons on Christian Warfare and probably should not have been included under "Military Sermons". Another sermon on the same topic is identified after the keyword abbreviation "WARF" within Index E.

<<YEAR 1660: ST%50009004>> <<YEAR 1662: HA 45003014>> <<YEAR 1694: PE 09004009>> <<YEAR 1698: WH%62004007>>
<<YEAR 1713: BU 14015002>> <<YEAR 1720: NE%45012035>> <<YEAR 1727: PE 45003014>> <<YEAR 1746: BE 53002025>>
<<YEAR 1748: HO%52006011, %52006014>> <<YEAR 1752: WE%52006010>> <<YEAR 1759: AG 45003014 SM 45003014>>
<<YEAR 1764: ER 19111001>> <<YEAR 1769: SW 45003014>>

Music - Meeting <"Mus.meet.","Mus.s.","Ch. Mus.">
Note: Also see the separate heading "Organ, Opening of" within the present Index D.

<<YEAR 1663: RE 12003015>> <<YEAR 1693: BA 19100001>> <<YEAR 1696: ES 54003016 HI 19100001 TO 52005018>>
<<YEAR 17--: SA 09016023>> <<YEAR 1700: NA 69019001>> <<YEAR 1706: BR 14005013>> <<YEAR 1711: BE 19150005>>
<<YEAR 1713: DI 19104033>> <<YEAR 1719: SH 19081001>> <<YEAR 1723: AN 19057009>> <<YEAR 1724: AB 19081001>>
<<YEAR 1725: LA 52005018>> <<YEAR 1726: BI 21002008 NA 69019003>> <<YEAR 1727: NA 43006010 SE 01027004>>
<<YEAR 1728: BR 54003016>> <<YEAR 1729: BI 37004010>> <<YEAR 1730: HA 12003015>> <<YEAR 1731: PH 19084004>>
<<YEAR 1732: CO 19047007>> <<YEAR 1734: AT 19057007>> <<YEAR 1737: BA 62005013>> <<YEAR 1738: PA 19066001
SH 09016023>> <<YEAR 1741: CR 19087007>> <<YEAR 1742: TA 13016039>> <<YEAR 1743: BR 19033001>> <<YEAR 1746:
MO 19107031>> <<YEAR 1748: NE 09008005>> <<YEAR 1749: HU 09018006>> <<YEAR 1753: PA 19147001>> <<YEAR 1755:
ED 19137005>> <<YEAR 1756: CO 19068004>> <<YEAR 1758: DA 24048010>> <<YEAR 1760: NE 19096009>> <<YEAR 1762:
BA 02015020>> <<YEAR 1766: BI 19068004>> <<YEAR 1773: RA 19057007>> <<YEAR 1778: GL 45002013>>

Naval Sermons <"The Navy">
Note: Also see the works of three authors to whom a footnote in Cooke's second volume refers the reader for sermons concerning the Navy.
These authors are named Philips, Ramsey, and Stockdale. The relevant works as listed in Cooke's volume appear to be Michael PHILIPS, "Occasional Serm. in 12° 1775. For the Royal Navy"; James RAMSEY [or RAMSAY], "12 Serm. in 8° 1782. For the Use of the Royal Navy"; and Percival STOCKDALE, "6 Disc. in 8° 1777." Single sermons published by Ramsey [or Ramsay] in 1778 and by Nicholas (not Michael) Philips in 1681 may also have been addresed to Naval audiences.
<<YEAR 1735: BA 19107023>>

New Year's Day <"New Year's Day","N Year's D.","New Year", etc.; "Ch.&n.Y's d.">
<<YEAR 1720: NE 21001004>> <<YEAR 1726: HE 23063004 IB 21007010>> <<YEAR 1739: AN 50005017>> <<YEAR 1740:
BU 48002029>> <<YEAR 1741: HU 01047009>> <<YEAR 1742: GR 27005023 HU 21012001>> <<YEAR 1743: JE 06024015,
60000010>> <<YEAR 1745: AN 20009006>> <<YEAR 1747: GR 19090004>> <<YEAR 1751: BE 21001004 MI 21003002>>
<<YEAR 1756: GU 21009010>> <<YEAR 1766: DA 24028016 RO 45013008>> <<YEAR 1771: SE 51006015>> <<YEAR 1780:
GE 52005016>>

November 5 <"Nov.5","Nov 5.";"Th.s.Nov.5","Th.Nov.5";"No.5.b.L.M.","No.5.b.LM.">
<<YEAR ----: BR 48010002>> <<YEAR 1661: BR 27003028, 27010021, 32006005 MA 32006005>> <<YEAR 1663:
CA 43007016>> <<YEAR 1667: MO 49014033>> <<YEAR 1673: PE 19111004>> <<YEAR 1674: WA 48013002>> <<YEAR 1675:
HA 24035006, 30009002, 47028005>> <<YEAR 1676: DU 19124007>> <<YEAR 1678: BA 10015031 LA 45009055
TA 45009054 WI 19083003>> <<YEAR 1679: BE 19007015 GR 46016002 HA 19124007 HO 05004020 LL 46016002
RA 20014025 RE 37003001 WI 19124001>> <<YEAR 1680: BA 19122006 DO 19064009 GR 10019003 LI 48013001
LL 19124001>> <<YEAR 1681: CA 48001015>> <<YEAR 1682: CH 09007012 HO 43022021 WR 01049006>> <<YEAR 1684:
AL 45009055 BU 19022021 CH 02015009, 02015011 LI 27010021, 47013009, 58003008, 64002015,
69013002, 69020007 WH 45001074>> <<YEAR 1685: KI 19011003 PE 48001008>> <<YEAR 1687: BO 19124001>>
<<YEAR 1689: AN 32006005 BI 46016003 BU 32006005 JE 19034003>> <<YEAR 1690: FR 19089021>> <<YEAR 1691:
KN 19068028>> <<YEAR 1692: MA 47017022 ST 43007016, 46016002>> <<YEAR 1693: KN 19064009 MA 01003015,
32006005>> <<YEAR 1694: PU 19118024 W. 04023023>> <<YEAR 1696: AD 27003028 GR 19118024 PA 27004035>>
<<YEAR 1697: KI 10024014 KN 21010020>> <<YEAR 1698: HA 50001010>> <<YEAR 17--: BU 19076010 RO 20003015>>
<<YEAR 1702: KI 02015002 WH 18005012>> <<YEAR 1704: BI 19124006 BR 17009020 GA 46016002>> <<YEAR 1705:
DO 19107001 ST 48009004 WI 01049007>> <<YEAR 1706: HO 19124002 RO 20013006>> <<YEAR 1707: ST 43007015>>
<<YEAR 1708: GR 23043011>> <<YEAR 1709: SA 50011026>> <<YEAR 1710: BU 09012023, 19144015 ED 19126003
GA 48013002 GR 19048003 ST 46016002 WA 19124006>> <<YEAR 1711: DE 19124001 LL 19124007>> <<YEAR 1712:
AT 19076010 LL 23008010 RE 19106021 TI 23054017>> <<YEAR 1713: AV 32006005 DE 19036007 HA 43016018
LO 69017006 NE 48010002>> <<YEAR 1714: CH 46018036>> <<YEAR 1715: AN 45009055 BE 50002017 BR 48010002
BU 19078042, 69018004 FO 04023023 HA 19122006 HO 19086010 KE 20001012 LE 57002001 LO 51005001
SM 45009055 ST 45009051, 48013001 SY 47015010 WH 43023007 WR 47023014>> <<YEAR 1716: BA 19064009
BR 20012022 GA 30004011 HA 23005020 HO 48013001 KN 17005013 NE 23032001 ST 46016002 WI 19124006>>
<<YEAR 1717: BR 07008034 CU 19021011 LO 19126003 RU 47010034 WA 16004011>> <<YEAR 1718: BR 46016002
LU 45014023 WR 19009004>> <<YEAR 1719: PO 47026009 WR 19009014>> <<YEAR 1720: BE 17009027 CL 46018036
DI 47023012 EV 07010011 HA 23001026 KN 19124005>> <<YEAR 1721: BE 04023023 IM 19122006 KE 19118008
NE 45009055 PE 25003039 WR 45009054>> <<YEAR 1722: BA 04023023 BU 63002016 NE 50001010 SY 19035020
WA 43007015 WI 19111004>> <<YEAR 1724: MA 45009054 NA 45009055 SI 45014023 SM 43010016 SO 23005004,
48013005>> <<YEAR 1725: SU 19050015 WH 23054017>> <<YEAR 1726: GA 19105001 GO 50001010 HE 23051023
ME 20024021>> <<YEAR 1727: SO 19144010 ST 05004007, 46016002 WA 45009055>> <<YEAR 1728: KE 19075001
MO 43016018>> <<YEAR 1729: AN 21010020 LU 51003028 NO 56002008 RE 19118024 SH 48010002>> <<YEAR 1730:
AT 43007012 BR 19124006 PA 48010002 TA 27002044>> <<YEAR 1731: MA 45011035 TA 65004001>> <<YEAR 1732:
AN 20024021 MA 49013003 SI 05023032>> <<YEAR 1733: DA 18005012 TE 20024021>> <<YEAR 1735: AN 47019025
BO 47019025 CL 19033010, 27007023 SO 59003001 TI 45009055, 46016002, 48010002 WA 46013035>>
<<YEAR 1737: EN 47027012 FL 43023015, 46016002 ST 47023012 TI 23044017>> <<YEAR 1738: SH 21005008>>
<<YEAR 1739: AT 23033022 CO 52005008 ME 19106034 MU 48013001>> <<YEAR 1740: AD 45009055 BU 51004017
ST 07008034>> <<YEAR 1741: JO 23005003 MA 48013001>> <<YEAR 1743: ST 32006009>> <<YEAR 1744: HO 06024020>>
<<YEAR 1745: AS 43007015 TR 23005020>> <<YEAR 1746: FO 44007013 HU 19107002 WA 19124001>> <<YEAR 1747:
DA 51002018 GR 02012014>> <<YEAR 1748: KI 45009054>> <<YEAR 1749: BI 05032010>> <<YEAR 1750: FR 03024020>>

INDEXES TO THIRD VOLUME: D: OCCASIONS OR SUBJECTS

<<YEAR 1751: KI 19144010>> <<YEAR 1753: NE 19106010>> <<YEAR 1754: HO 56002011>> <<YEAR 1755: BO 47019028>>
<<YEAR 1756: DE 49013001>> <<YEAR 1757: WA 58002024>> <<YEAR 1758: CO 09012024>> <<YEAR 1763: BA 18005012>>
<<YEAR 1764: BR 46008032>> <<YEAR 1766: SE 46016002>> <<YEAR 1769: NE 46008047>> <<YEAR 1772: BR 01049014,
07002018, 07006012, 11002046, 13012016, 13012023, 16002010, 19053006, 19063011,
20008015, 23009027, 47007017, 48013002, 57006015, 61011013, 68000005, 68000011,
69011018>> <<YEAR 1774: HE 63002016 SH 45009054>> <<YEAR 1775: EV 51005013>> <<YEAR 1776: PO 63002017
TH 45009054>> <<YEAR 1778: EV 61010032 WO 43011030>> <<YEAR 1779: RE 46005039>> <<YEAR 1781: CR 02012024>>

Ordination - Sermon <"Ord.s.","Ord.& V.s.","Or.s.b.L.M." etc.>
<<YEAR 1679: RE 50004005>> <<YEAR 1681: CL 59001005>> <<YEAR 1699: JO 43009036>> <<YEAR 1700: BR 27012003
LA 68000003>> <<YEAR 1707: ST 57005022>> <<YEAR 1711: RI 61005004>> <<YEAR 1712: SM 52004011>> <<YEAR 1713:
GO 59001009>> <<YEAR 1714: RA 43028020>> <<YEAR 1715: KE 09015023 MA 49004001>> <<YEAR 1716: CA 47020028
LU 47020028>> <<YEAR 1717: BI 50005001 WR 43010016>> <<YEAR 1719: NE 55005021 RU 57004016>> <<YEAR 1720:
BE 47001026, 47013003, 50004001>> <<YEAR 1721: WR 58001013>> <<YEAR 1722: LA 50004005>> <<YEAR 1725:
DE 44004030 EA 43023009 EN 53001001 HA 63005001>> <<YEAR 1726: HI 58002002 ST 57004016 WY 49001010>>
<<YEAR 1727: CL 49003006, 58002015>> <<YEAR 1728: BO 46005035, 57003001 WI 47013002>> <<YEAR 1729:
HA 49004002>> <<YEAR 1730: BU 57003013 CO 45006026 HA 57004012>> <<YEAR 1731: CL 43016018 HU 55005012>>
<<YEAR 1732: ST 20014034, 59001006 WA 52004011>> <<YEAR 1734: FA 49001021 GI 57004016>> <<YEAR 1735:
FO 57004014 GO 57004016>> <<YEAR 1736: NE 55004008>> <<YEAR 1737: DO 50004005 HA 47014023 TO 57003001>>
<<YEAR 1739: MI 50001024>> <<YEAR 1740: GO 63005002>> <<YEAR 1741: AM 59002001 BI 50004005>> <<YEAR 1742:
HO 46005035 JE 50004005>> <<YEAR 1745: FR 50002016 MO 46003002>> <<YEAR 1746: HE 57004016 HU 43028018
MI 53002020 PA 43009038 WH 48010014>> <<YEAR 1747: GR 53001021 PE 48010016 ST 50011023>> <<YEAR 1749:
LA 50005018>> <<YEAR 1750: FR 50005019 WI 50002016, 54004017>> <<YEAR 1751: AM 50001024>> <<YEAR 1753:
BL 58003016>> <<YEAR 1754: FA 37011004>> <<YEAR 1755: FO 49014026 MI 57004016 WA 55005012>> <<YEAR 1756:
GU 53001009>> <<YEAR 1757: FO 57002012>> <<YEAR 1758: CO 55005012 FO 57001011 GR 43010034 LO 47002029>>
<<YEAR 1759: AM 49001021 BA 61006001 CH 49001021 CO 24023028 OL 57003015>> <<YEAR 1760: WI 54001018>>
<<YEAR 1764: GI 26010020, 51005013>> <<YEAR 1765: AM 58002015 BU 56003001>> <<YEAR 1766: FU 49004001
GI 49012025 WR 43016026>> <<YEAR 1767: TO 49016014>> <<YEAR 1769: FU 46007046 KI 46007046>> <<YEAR 1770:
EN 61013022 LA 47023011 TO 53001009>> <<YEAR 1773: EV 53002029, 54004017, 58004005, 67000011
GE 68000001 GI 58001013, 58002007, 58004016>> <<YEAR 1774: FA 50004005>> <<YEAR 1775: WH 62001021>>
<<YEAR 1776: TO 55005012 TU 61001001>> <<YEAR 1777: AS 56003001 EN 48011013>> <<YEAR 1778: WR 55005012>>
<<YEAR 1779: RA 49012031>> <<YEAR 1780: LA 59002015 TO 43009036>>

Organ, opening of, etc. <"Op.Organ","Op.Org.","Erect. Org.">
Note: Also see the separate heading "Music - Meeting" within present Index D.
<<YEAR 1696: NE 19150004>> <<YEAR 1700: SH 52005019>> <<YEAR 1718: WA 19150004>> <<YEAR 1727: BO 19150004
ST 19093005>> <<YEAR 1734: MA 52005019>> <<YEAR 1738: CO 19150003>> <<YEAR 1747: BU 19148013>> <<YEAR 1749:
OW 19150005>> <<YEAR 1766: BR 18021012>> <<YEAR 1771: BR 19122001>>

Parliament, Election of : See Elections

Passion Sermon <"P.S.">
Note: In our Third Volume there are six records of sermons which Cooke did not describe with the abbreviation "P.S." that he defined for Passion Sermon but with the undefined abbreviation "P.s." (in five cases) or "P.s.E.s.A.s." (in one case). These are not indexed below, but are identified at their proper places within Index E among other items with the keyword "P". All but one of the sermons so indexed are Passion Sermons, as we may judge from their biblical texts and from correponding records in the work of Cooke's predecessor Letsome. The exception is the sermon by the author LITTLETON.
<<YEAR 1661: NI 23053010, 45024046, 46019005>> <<YEAR 1665: DO 46019019>> <<YEAR 1666: FL 46019040
PA 45023027>> <<YEAR 1670: HO 47002023>> <<YEAR 1672: FA 48008032 FR 43021008, 49002002 GO 43021013>>
<<YEAR 1675: HA 01022013, 43027024, 46003014, 46019034, 47002023>> <<YEAR 1680: LI 46019005>>
<<YEAR 1681: SI 61002014>> <<YEAR 1692: ST 46019037>> <<YEAR 1693: MO 46018011 PE 52001007>> <<YEAR 1697:
CO 45023027>> <<YEAR 1701: MA 46019034>> <<YEAR 1702: NE 47003018>> <<YEAR 1703: DO 53002008>> <<YEAR 1708:
NO 49002002>> <<YEAR 1710: SP 63002021>> <<YEAR 1713: HI 51006014>> <<YEAR 1715: ST 46019001, 61010001>>

<<YEAR 1716: AD 49001023 BA 47003018, 49001023, 53002008 HO 46019001, 61010001>> <<YEAR 1718:
SU 45022044>> <<YEAR 1720: BE 46001029, 46019030, 53002008 DA 46010018>> <<YEAR 1721: BA 61002010
CR 51006014>> <<YEAR 1722: WA 61010031>> <<YEAR 1723: SC 46011035>> <<YEAR 1726: IN 63002021>> <<YEAR 1727:
SO 23053008>> <<YEAR 1729: SH 46020029 WI 49005007>> <<YEAR 1732: AL 63001019>> <<YEAR 1733: DA 61009026>>
<<YEAR 1734: AT 43027025, 51006014>> <<YEAR 1735: CL 43012039, 43012039 TI 49001023>> <<YEAR 1736:
MA 49005007 NE 46011047, 46019037>> <<YEAR 1740: JO 50005021 SM 46019018>> <<YEAR 1741: HA 61010014>>
<<YEAR 1747: BU 23053005>> <<YEAR 1748: WA 47002037, 48005008>> <<YEAR 1749: HE 61002010>> <<YEAR 1750:
FR 48011022, 65002001>> <<YEAR 1763: PE 48008018>> <<YEAR 1770: SE 49001022, 51006014>>

Peace <"Th.s.f.Pea.">
Note: Besides the two sermons indexed below as having for their occasion a public Thanksgiving for Peace, our Third Volume lists many other sermons with Peace as their subject. These are indexed by keyword "PEACE" or keyword abbreviation "PEA" or "PE" within the following Index E. The items following these keywords there may be searched for those which are likely to concern sermons about peace after war.
<<YEAR 1697: WA 19107008>> <<YEAR 1713: BU 19046010>>

Plague <"Plague","Af.Plague", etc.; "F.s.Plague", etc.; "Th.s.Plague", etc.; "F.s.Plague b.K.", etc.>
<<YEAR 1665: KI 14007013>> <<YEAR 1666: HU 04016046>> <<YEAR 1671: PI 32006009>> <<YEAR 1674: WA 05032006>>
<<YEAR 1679: RE 53004005>> <<YEAR 1684: AL 45016030>> <<YEAR 1715: CA 10024016>> <<YEAR 1716: HO 19106030>>
<<YEAR 1720: BA 30004012 BO 23055006 SH 45021036>> <<YEAR 1721: FO 43003009 GR 45012047 JE 19046008,
27009009 LE 19119123 MA 24005029 NE 19078050, 26009004 NO 29002012 PA 01006003 SA 23005004
WI 32006009>> <<YEAR 1722: HO 23045007 HU 23026020 PR 19127001>> <<YEAR 1723: PE 19130004 TO 19116007>>
<<YEAR 1725: MO 10024025 SH 23026009>> <<YEAR 1728: NE 31003005>> <<YEAR 1729: LU 05028021>> <<YEAR 1734:
CL 23026009, 43024007, 45013002>> <<YEAR 1738: SH 19107043>> <<YEAR 1772: GO 23026009>>

Plays or Playhouses <"Of Plays","Ag.Playhou.">
Note 1: Also consider sermons delivered to the Society for the Reformation of Manners. These are indexed within the present Index D under the heading "Reformation of Manners."
Note 2: Within Index E the keyword "THEATRE" points to an interesting record.
<<YEAR 1730: BE 58002016>> <<YEAR 1757: PE 52005006>> <<YEAR 1776: OR 58002016>>

Popery <"Popery","Pop.","On Pop.","Ag.Pop.","Ag.D.& Pop.", etc.; "Popish Mira.","Pope's supre.","Cruel.o.Pop.", etc.>
<<YEAR 1674: GR 55005021>> <<YEAR 1675: DO 24006016 VI 57004001 WI 56002003>> <<YEAR 1678: CA 43016018
LL 47002042>> <<YEAR 1679: PE 56002011 TH 26021024>> <<YEAR 1680: BA 51003001>> <<YEAR 1686: CA 51005006>>
<<YEAR 1690: BA 48008034>> <<YEAR 1691: AT 69018002>> <<YEAR 1697: OU 53001027>> <<YEAR 17--: CO 43005048
PA 65004020>> <<YEAR 1702: WH 62003017>> <<YEAR 1703: WH 46007047>> <<YEAR 1712: AT 45018008, 69018004
LO 62001027>> <<YEAR 1713: BU 52001003>> <<YEAR 1715: GO 51005001>> <<YEAR 1716: BA 43010002>> <<YEAR 1717:
LA 19124006>> <<YEAR 1721: KE 46004022>> <<YEAR 1723: BI 48013001, 56002015>> <<YEAR 1724: RY 45017010,
46006053>> <<YEAR 1735: GR 46016002 HA 45022019, 46006053 HU 23042008, 44006012 LO 48011022
NE 43016018>> <<YEAR 1746: SM 55005021>> <<YEAR 1757: CO 43010034>> <<YEAR 1761: BU 24006016 PE 43015009>>
<<YEAR 1768: DO 62003015>> <<YEAR 1771: BU 58003008 SE 63005012>> <<YEAR 1772: BR 48010014>>

Propagation of the Gospel or Religion: See the heading "Gospel or Religion, Propagation of" within the present Index D.

Rebellion <"Rebellion","Rebell.","Rebel.s.", etc.; "F.s.Rebel.","Th.s.Rebel." etc.; "Th.Ir.Reb.","Th.s.Pr.Reb.", etc.>
Note: For two items in addition to those below, see keyword "REB" followed by "Flight Reb." and "On late Reb." within Index E.
<<YEAR 1661: BR 48013002>> <<YEAR 1674: AN 15006010>> <<YEAR 1685: GR 59003001 WI 31003004>> <<YEAR 1686:
WE 63003011>> <<YEAR 1696: HE 19107043>> [Item deleted by the editor] <<YEAR 17--: DA 20009001>> <<YEAR 1710:
SH 12019028>> <<YEAR 1715: CA 19118006 CO 24028016 GR 43005033 HA 46016002 SK 19009010 SO 45018008>>
<<YEAR 1716: AD 48013001, 49013001 CR 19053005 GO 19132018 PO 19147001 SA 05023009 SH 18012016
TO 47017006>> <<YEAR 1717: LA 19118006, 20024021>> <<YEAR 1719: GI 19106043 SM 05006006>> <<YEAR 1728:
BO 43023029>> <<YEAR 1737: FL 19107002>> <<YEAR 1738: HO 51004018>> <<YEAR 1743: GO 19120005>> <<YEAR 1745:
AN 47024002 AR 20024021, 23026009 AS 59003001 BA 06024015, 44007013 BR 43007020 BU 19035020
CO 09012024 DA 52005006 DE 51005001, 63002013 DO 11012014 DR 19122006 DU 10015021, 23037034

Sessions <"Sessions","Quarter-sess.">
<<YEAR 1689: SA 18029014>> <<YEAR 1713: JE 19011003>> <<YEAR 1728: FA 20024021>> <<YEAR 1743: SI 57001009>>
<<YEAR 1754: SK 45006036>>

Siege <"In a Siege","After siege">
<<YEAR 1690: WH 24001018>> <<YEAR 1715: KE 19077019>>

Spittal - Sermons <"Spitt.","Spittal", etc.; "Spitt.M.","Spitt.T.",Spitt.W.>
Note: Oxford English Dictionary: "Spittle sermon, one of the sermons preached on Easter Monday, and Tuesday from a special pulpit at St. Mary Spital ... (afterwards at St. Bride's and finally at Christ Church in the City)."
<<YEAR 1672: HA 43006019>> <<YEAR 1679: RE 57006017>> <<YEAR 1681: TE 19112005>> <<YEAR 1682: WI 23032008>>
<<YEAR 1684: PI 21011006 TU 45014013>> <<YEAR 1685: HA 52004032>> <<YEAR 1687: CL 48012013>> <<YEAR 1688:
FO 45016009>> <<YEAR 1690: KI 57006017>> <<YEAR 1692: FO 49006014>> <<YEAR 1694: FR 43025046 KI 63001003>>
<<YEAR 1695: GR 49013003 MA 45012021>> <<YEAR 1696: PA 58002008>> <<YEAR 1697: JE 43005016 WI 47010040>>
<<YEAR 1698: BU 51006010 LY 57006017>> <<YEAR 1700: HA 43025034 IS 47020035>> <<YEAR 1701: GA 47010031
LA 54003001 WH 65003018>> <<YEAR 1702: HO 54003001 SH 50008012 ST 45016009 WI 51006010>> <<YEAR 1705:
BA 45016009>> <<YEAR 1706: BU 43024012>> <<YEAR 1708: CH 45010028>> <<YEAR 1710: KE 46006010 LA 54002006
LU 09025010, 47010004>> <<YEAR 1711: BU 19122006 WE 19041001 WI 43019023>> <<YEAR 1712: HO 45016025
KE 43019016 LY 46015008>> <<YEAR 1713: HI 61013016>> <<YEAR 1714: BU 27004027 WA 50009006>> <<YEAR 1715:
BL 43005003 TR 61010024>> <<YEAR 1716: BA 19112009 BO 61010024 KE 45016001 NI 17002008>> <<YEAR 1717:
BE 43025040 WI 50008009>> <<YEAR 1719: KE 45019008 SH 45006035>> <<YEAR 1720: BE 57006017>> <<YEAR 1722:
MA 47020035 WA 51006010>> <<YEAR 1723: SK 49013003 WI 49014012>> <<YEAR 1724: BR 50005010 LE 51006010
SM 45014014, 61013016>> <<YEAR 1726: IB 45016009 LA 43019023 SM 43025034>> <<YEAR 1727: WA 45006035>>
<<YEAR 1729: CL 43025023, 65004021 KN 61006010 LU 45016009 SH 57006017>> <<YEAR 1730: AT 43025040,
45010032 BE 21011002>> <<YEAR 1731: MA 21011001 PI 47016028 TA 46015022>> <<YEAR 1733: AS 20003027
CL 49010023 DA 45014012, 46020020>> <<YEAR 1734: RO 20011025>> <<YEAR 1735: NE 51006010 RE 50009008
TI 51006009>> <<YEAR 1736: BE 21007002>> <<YEAR 1737: MO 50004018>> <<YEAR 1738: BA 65004007 MO 45012021>>
<<YEAR 1739: BO 51006010>> <<YEAR 1740: DE 43007012>> <<YEAR 1741: MA 49007017>> <<YEAR 1743: GI 51006010
PE 43018033>> <<YEAR 1744: HU 43007012>> <<YEAR 1745: SN 18029015, 51006002, 58003002 SQ 46013035>>
<<YEAR 1748: TH 18029011>> <<YEAR 1749: BU 20022002 YA 47010040>> <<YEAR 1750: MA 18005016 MO 43025040>>
<<YEAR 1751: CO 20011017 GO 57006017>> <<YEAR 1753: CO 47020035 MO 23035005>> <<YEAR 1758: CH 47010038>>
<<YEAR 1759: IB 46005006>> <<YEAR 1762: BR 48013008>> <<YEAR 1763: HE 43005007>> <<YEAR 1766: SE 63004010>>
<<YEAR 1770: AS 63004010>> <<YEAR 1774: SH 43018029, 47020035>> <<YEAR 1780: AP 43025040>>

Storm <"Storm","On Storm", etc.:"Seam. Storm","Com. Storm","F.s.Storm","F.Storm b.L.", etc.>
<<YEAR 1673: FL 19107023>> <<YEAR 1703: CO 19148008 P. 19148008>> <<YEAR 1704: FI 19139007 GR 19089032,
28008007 HA 23029006 HO 29002012 HU 46003008 LE 19018007 MA 23026009 OF 19148008 PA 69016009
ST 19118023>> <<YEAR 1714: DE 33001003 SM 46005014 ST 24051015>> <<YEAR 1723: BL 45013004>> <<YEAR 1731:
TA 23058003>> <<YEAR 1732: MO 45013005>> <<YEAR 1733: GI 46003008>> <<YEAR 1737: ST 30004012>>

Style, New <"New Style">
Note: For an item in addition to the one below, see keyword "STYLE" within Index E.
<<YEAR 1753: GR 53002002>>

Suicide <"Self Murder","Self-Murder","Ag. Suiscide" [sic.]>
Note: Also consider sermons referred to under the heading "Humane Society" within Index C.
<<YEAR 1695: WH 43005021>> <<YEAR 1708: KN 11019004>> <<YEAR 1725: SH 18014014>> <<YEAR 1736: PE 18002010>>
<<YEAR 1737: FL 10017023>> <<YEAR 1751: JE 18002009>> <<YEAR 1755: AY 18014014>> <<YEAR 1773: FR 18002010>>
<<YEAR 1774: HE 18014014>> <<YEAR 1777: RI 02020013>>

INDEXES TO THIRD VOLUME: D: OCCASIONS OR SUBJECTS

59003001
SK 19105045
DE 45013005
GI 19106043
SY 45009055>>
MO 31003010
<<YEAR 1728:
<<YEAR 1731:
07005031>>
ST 57002001
<<YEAR 1738:
HU 19124001>>
<<YEAR 1745:
BE 07009015,
19107002,
FR 45019027
HO 07005002
MI 45017017
RE 05033046
WH 19105045
BE 19106012
FO 33001015
<<YEAR 1750:
<<YEAR 1757:
CL 19050023
HO 23025009
RA 02015002
WY 19124002>>
MA 23052013>>
DA 14015002
<<YEAR 1764:
<<YEAR 1769:
50001009,
SI 19050014>>
TO 19009016>>
KE 19033001
SM 10018032
LA 19118006
MO 19126003>>
<<YEAR 1722:
PE 19130004
BO 43023029,
SY 01049005
<<YEAR 1733:
TI 15009013,
CL 48014019
<<YEAR 1741:
HU 19050015
09012024,
45017017
GI 11008066,
LA 07005009,
MO 19018050
ST 19147001
WI 10018032,
WA 19018047,
HA 47007026
AN 02015009
FR 19022023>>
DA 19095001
JO 27002010
RI 19027003
<<YEAR 1760:
<<YEAR 1762:
DE 19122006
RI 23045006>>
ST 14015014>>
52005020>>
<<YEAR 1774:
<<YEAR 1777:
LU 05033029,
WA 04023023,
LO 23008009
<<YEAR 1720:
HO 19100005
SC 46005014
46018036,
TA 19133001,
MA 19124005>>
24009023>>
HO 51004018
FA 19147001>>
PR 19118023>>
14016009,
CH 23025009
19126003,
26036032
NE 19066013
SY 19116007
46005014
19116012>>
HE 19147012
PR 19107033
<<YEAR 1758:
DU 06001004
KI 19126003,
SC 19108013
FA 19027006
DO 69006002
FO 19107001
<<YEAR 1765:
<<YEAR 1770:
<<YEAR 1772:
JO 52005020
DE 19034001>>
19122006,
10020001,
OW 68000011>>
BE 19095001
WA 19144009>>
WR 25002022>>
51001008,
50001010>>
<<YEAR 1734:
<<YEAR 1737:
WI 09017037,
<<YEAR 1743:
<<YEAR 1746:
19075001
CL 46005014
20024021
MA 07005002,
NI 23007005
TO 23027008
YA 10022048>>
<<YEAR 1749:
KE 24033010
SE 63002017>>
CA 19118015
GE 26036032
24009024
SM 19097001
FO 19018047
ST 01014018>>
JE 20016007
WA 06023011>>
AS 19065007
BR 16005018,
SH 19122006>>
54004002
19028007
<<YEAR 1718:
FI 19065007,
<<YEAR 1723:
<<YEAR 1724:
52001022,
<<YEAR 1732:
CL 19050023,
FL 11020011,
14020026,
KI 19107039
AL 19002011
BL 19129005
DO 14020027
GR 23005011
10022038,
PE 14020027
TU 23012002
<<YEAR 1747:
BE 56003016
KI 19122007
<<YEAR 1751:
SA 19126003
GI 19034003
LA 19044003
ST 19047007
WA 19118027>>
<<YEAR 1763:
PA 19097001
<<YEAR 1766:
SE 43005006>>
19122006,
<<YEAR 1775:
PE 19068019
WI 26017015
WA 52005020>>
19118008
AL 02033019
SM 19122006>>
54001018>>
MO 53004006
19145002>>
19107002,
23012007,
ST 19144009>>
AR 12014008
BR 19021011,
DU 05033029,
H. 09012024
10022048,
PI 19097001,
WA 09012024,
DO 54003015
BL 19033010
ST 19085008
DU 19147013>>
TO 19118027>>
GO 05033029
MA 19007014
TO 19122006
<<YEAR 1761:
BO 19029010
PO 19076010
WA 26036022>>
<<YEAR 1771:
23024016,
GO 25003022
PO 19107002,
WR 09007012>>
<<YEAR 1719:
SY 10022044>>
CO 19034003
<<YEAR 1727:
<<YEAR 1729:
ST 05033009,
<<YEAR 1735:
26036032
23026015>>
<<YEAR 1744:
BA 19002011,
19107043
19132018
HA 06001009,
19052001
19107002
50003017
PR 02014013>>
CO 19122006
TH 19144010
<<YEAR 1754:
<<YEAR 1759:
HA 05033029
OB 19126004
WI 09007012,
AN 19126003
BR 43005009
ST 19085008
<<YEAR 1767:
SA 19144010
69018020
PH 07005002>>
19147001
<<YEAR 1717:
DO 19076010
<<YEAR 1721:
CR 23038018
ST 50001009>>
SH 19097001>>
07005015,
BE 19116012
PA 54003015>>
<<YEAR 1739:
HO 19067002>>
19107001
BU 09012007,
FI 19124001
19071017
ME 14020027
RA 07006014
WE 17008017
<<YEAR 1748:
DR 19144010
WR 46005014>>
HA 19098001>>
BA 19096008
HI 52005020
PR 19147020
14020027
EY 45013001
CR 19029011
WH 10002026>>
WA 45013001>>
SE 46005014,
GO 23026009
<<YEAR 1776:

Trinity Sunday <"Trin.S.","S.Trin.">

Note: In our Third Volume there are 125 records of sermons described by Cooke as delivered on one or another of the 1, 2, 3, ..., 26 Sundays of Trinity. These are all indexed by number of Sunday after the keyword "SUND" within our Index E. In the same index are 31 items referring to sermons which Cooke described not with the abbreviation "Trin.S." but with "Trin.s." These sermons may have been delivered on Trinity Sunday, or they may be about the Trinity but have been delivered on other days. After the keyword "TRINITY" within Index E there are 27 items about sermons on the subject of the Trinity but presumably not delivered on Trinity Sunday. After the keyword "TRIN" there are five items about sermons described with "Trin.b. L.M.", one with "Bapt.Trin.", and one with "On the Trin."

<<YEAR 171-: BU 61001006>> <<YEAR 1714: ST 69004001>> <<YEAR 1716: HO 69004001>> <<YEAR 1722: ST 61001006>>
<<YEAR 1728: RE 01001026>> <<YEAR 1730: RE 01018001>>

Union <"Th.for Un.","Th.on Un.","Th.Un.">

Note: Also consider several items with keyword "UNION" or "UNI" within Index E.

<<YEAR 1707: WI 23049023>> <<YEAR 1731: TA 19133001>> <<YEAR 1732: ST 07005015>>

Victory <"Th.for V.">
<<YEAR 1732: ST 07005031>> <<YEAR 1762: ST 01014018>>

INDEXES TO THIRD VOLUME: D: OCCASIONS OR SUBJECTS

Visitation - Sermons <"V.s.","V.s.Confi.","Visit.of "Fal.">
Note: Within Index E following the keyword "V" there are two items "V. Sch." and "V.sch.& H." that should be added to those below.

<<YEAR ----:
<<YEAR 1663:
WE 11018021>>
SH 47020028
<<YEAR 1673:
WA 52003008>>
RO 49011016
48014019>>
BR 48013001
BR 47020016
BA 49004021
48003008,
SP 49001010
<<YEAR 1694:
WH 19050023,
TA 49004001>>
BU 27012003
<<YEAR 1705:
SA 54004017>>
LI 47020028>>
SC 61013017
OL 59002015
CH 57004016
TA 52004014
BO 45012042,
HA 47016017>>
ST 61013017
W. 48010015
RA 59002015>>
<<YEAR 1720:
GI 63003015
<<YEAR 1723:
HA 19072010
RE 59002015
NE 27005017
WA 58003017>>
CU 49009016>>
<<YEAR 1735:
<<YEAR 1737:
68000003
DO 59002015
PO 09003013
ST 48002004>>
WA 57004016>>
LE 47010004
QU 45011035,
VI 46021017>>
WA 64001005>>
<<YEAR 1757:
CO 43010016
<<YEAR 1763:
NI 16005012

BE 38002007
BI 50005020
<<YEAR 1664:
SP 55003008>>
BU 55005014
<<YEAR 1675:
TE 47015036>>
<<YEAR 1680:
WI 59002015>>
FA 50005018
BI 49011034
48014003,
TA 19122006>>
MA 57004016>>
65004001>>
<<YEAR 1700:
FU 53001027>>
CO 50006003,
<<YEAR 1706:
<<YEAR 1708:
SY 48010015
RO 61005004
JA 43013057
WE 19119158>>
49001010
<<YEAR 1716:
SY 46018036,
WI 48012001,
<<YEAR 1719:
BR 45010025
HA 62001008
BL 46006066
ST 54002008>>
SE 45024027
NO 48003031
<<YEAR 1730:
<<YEAR 1732:
EY 44016016
AR 05033008
WA 43005014
JO 46015008
SH 58002019>>
<<YEAR 1745:
<<YEAR 1747:
MU 50010008
50004002
<<YEAR 1753:
<<YEAR 1755:
CO 10012007>>
GO 68000003
BA 11013001
RI 50006006

MI 61013017>>
BO 53002005
HO 23060013>>
<<YEAR 1671:
NE 59003010>>
BO 69001016
<<YEAR 1677:
FY 43006009
<<YEAR 1683:
HA 50012014
CL 57004015
48014023,
<<YEAR 1692:
<<YEAR 1697:
<<YEAR 1699:
FA 47018003
<<YEAR 1704:
57004016,
TE 59003001
AD 20010009
TA 43018017
TU 45010016>>
RI 43010034>>
<<YEAR 1713:
BU 47020032
AW 43022021
50004005>>
49004002>>
KE 43022021,
HI 58002024
RE 57003016>>
BU 02020007
<<YEAR 1725:
WI 50006003>>
ST 51004018>>
BL 46012037
AY 69003017>>
HA 50006003
MA 43005010,
WH 19051012>>
SY 53002021
<<YEAR 1743:
HO 58003016
BU 44016020
PE 43005016>>
SE 61010023>>
EL 49012011
BA 58003016
<<YEAR 1758:
MU 46012046
JO 47020026
TA 46004023

<<YEAR 1660:
BR 47015028
<<YEAR 1666:
DU 57004012>>
<<YEAR 1674:
BY 44009050
AR 58004005>>
HO 47002017>>
BA 53001015
LE 19118024
CR 11018021
49012007>>
GO 19122006
BA 38002007>>
MO 55005017>>
NY 49015010>>
BU 53002001
61012014
TO 49015058
HO 64001011
WH 46018036>>
<<YEAR 1710:
<<YEAR 1712:
BU 62003001
CH 46020021
BE 59003001
<<YEAR 1717:
<<YEAR 1718:
49014012
OL 47004029
<<YEAR 1722:
DE 23049001
CO 57006003
<<YEAR 1727:
<<YEAR 1729:
BO 53001010
<<YEAR 1733:
LI 46001046>>
64003003
<<YEAR 1740:
UP 55005021>>
TW 43010016>>
MO 19101002
CA 48010017
<<YEAR 1749:
<<YEAR 1751:
HE 51006014
PI 46005039>>
LO 43006010>>
SC 49008001
SH 57003014>>
WH 54002008>>

ST 19076011>>
HI 28009007
LA 47026009>>
<<YEAR 1672:
GO 49014040
HO 54004017>>
<<YEAR 1678:
<<YEAR 1681:
FO 57004016
LO 49001023>>
GA 47011024
<<YEAR 1690:
HU 50005019
<<YEAR 1698:
<<YEAR 17--:
<<YEAR 1701:
SA 54001018
DA 45011001
WO 57002002>>
JO 54002008
<<YEAR 1709:
BU 49001010
CO 19122006
HA 19133001
ST 61013017>>
BI 57006003
CO 61013007
BE 43003009
KN 05017012
WA 62003017>>
CO 50005001
SH 19133001
HO 49012031
CU 63002015
DU 53003016
GR 43010016
CL 52002012
<<YEAR 1736:
ST 43028020,
BU 43028020
<<YEAR 1742:
<<YEAR 1744:
WE 43010016>>
HA 46004023
AS 59002015
HE 43005048
LE 05031024>>
<<YEAR 1756:
<<YEAR 1759:
VE 54004017
<<YEAR 1764:
<<YEAR 1765:

<<YEAR 1662:
KI 59002001
<<YEAR 1669:
GA 50005020
JA 68000003
<<YEAR 1676:
JA 49004001>>
EL 57004015
RO 47002042>>
<<YEAR 1685:
TH 61013017>>
TO 45012001>>
RA 52004012>>
CL 50004007
BR 52004003
AL 52004011
SM 51004018
HA 47015041
<<YEAR 1707:
LI 57004016
HA 57003009
WE 21008002
DI 50004002
HO 19133001
<<YEAR 1715:
GR 51006006
EY 54001028
BU 51004018
MA 52004011,
<<YEAR 1721:
JE 57002001
WA 59002007>>
SH 19014001>>
GA 02020005>>
JO 53002006,
LE 53003015>>
MO 46004048>>
FE 50002016
55005021>>
CO 59003001>>
PE 26033032,
AN 63004011
<<YEAR 1746:
HU 46001001
WH 05032029>>
JE 50004005
<<YEAR 1754:
BU 53002006
SM 58001010
WA 46007017>>
CO 46016008
HE 57004016

OL 50007001
RI 19001003
BE 49014040
IG 44009050
LO 50005020
AL 46004023
<<YEAR 1679:
GL 19123003>>
<<YEAR 1684:
AD 45020014>>
<<YEAR 1689:
<<YEAR 1691:
<<YEAR 1693:
ED 49014012
CA 44004024
BY 49004001>>
WA 57004016
IS 47008017
BA 51001010
NO 49004001
LA 49013013
WH 49004013>>
JE 58001005
LA 48010015>>
BR 19073013
HO 68000003
KI 49004002
CO 48013005
61013008
CL 51004018
SA 64003018
<<YEAR 1724:
<<YEAR 1726:
<<YEAR 1728:
69005013
<<YEAR 1731:
<<YEAR 1734:
HO 49011023
<<YEAR 1738:
<<YEAR 1741:
46006014
DO 63001008
HA 61013017
NE 43007028>>
<<YEAR 1750:
LE 01003006
ED 52004014
LE 57001015
TU 49004002>>
<<YEAR 1761:
HO 48010003
HI 47005042

SH 49011034>>
ST 61013017
CO 43005016
SM 49004001>>
PR 57004016
PA 43005016
RE 37011007,
<<YEAR 1682:
AN 49014040
<<YEAR 1686:
SA 43015009,
NO 46021015
PE 57004016>>
HO 52005016
CO 64003003
<<YEAR 1703:
WE 03026002>>
OV 43007022
JE 59002015
SA 43010016
NE 49003004
<<YEAR 1711:
NE 59002015
<<YEAR 1714:
BU 53004005
LY 50006001
ST 49015010
CR 49003010
ST 46001014>>
CO 49012004
WH 58003016>>
BR 48010015
CL 49014026
JO 45022029
TI 45014033
BO 43015006
AL 18027005>>
NE 46015016>>
SY 58002023,
BO 45006026
PI 49004001
SI 53002005
TO 45012057
<<YEAR 1748:
CO 64001019
TO 46020029
KE 52004011
PE 57004016>>
<<YEAR 1760:
BR 63005001>>
NE 57004016
SH 20008012

VI 47005042>> <<YEAR 1766: CO 44016015, 47020024 MU 59003001 WA 61010023>> <<YEAR 1767: FO 46010025>>
<<YEAR 1768: FI 43010016>> <<YEAR 1769: CR 46002016 DU 43005010 SC 43021021>> <<YEAR 1770: CL 46006044
FO 49014033>> <<YEAR 1771: DI 48014005 SA 45022035>> <<YEAR 1772: OR 50006003 PE 48009028 TO 43004023>>
<<YEAR 1773: CA 48014001 SA 20014024>> <<YEAR 1774: BE 20024021>> <<YEAR 1775: DU 43018007 FO 49009016>>
<<YEAR 1776: AN 43011016 HA 62005004 LA 05028002 WA 57004006>> <<YEAR 1777: AD 48002014 BU 55005021
DA 19101002 HU 48002014 PA 64003015>> <<YEAR 1778: HO 43005014 LA 47005038 TO 45004032 WA 11003009>>
<<YEAR 1779: FU 46007017>> <<YEAR 1780: HA 58004002 HU 50004005 MA 44009050>> <<YEAR 1781: PY 43013034,
44004034>> <<YEAR 1782: BA 46007017 CA 43005013 NI 57004015>>

War <"F.s.War.","F.s.last war."; "Procl.War","Declar.War.";"War Wn. Jus.";"Amer.War.","War w. Am.>
Note: For cross-references to related topics, see the note below the heading "Military Sermons" within the present Index D.
<<YEAR 1698: ED 01014014>> <<YEAR 1756: GI 24004019>> <<YEAR 1758: DA 31004010 FR 31004007>>
<<YEAR 1769: ER 07020028>> <<YEAR 1775: PH 48012018>> <<YEAR 1776: TO 24004019>> <<YEAR 1778: AN 45009056>>

Wedding - Sermon <"Wed.s.","Wedd.s.">
Note: Also see the separate heading "Matrimony" within the present Index D.
<<YEAR 1681: GR 01029025>> <<YEAR 1682: WI 20031014>> <<YEAR 1699: SP 49007034>> <<YEAR 17--: WH 61013004>>
<<YEAR 1708: MA 01002021 MU 54003018>> <<YEAR 1709: AN 52005003 CO 52005033>> <<YEAR 1711: SH 01002021>>
<<YEAR 1713: SH 01002018>> <<YEAR 1715: AY 49007033>> <<YEAR 1716: LE 01002020>> <<YEAR 1717: CR 20018022>>
<<YEAR 1732: AN 54003019 CO 20031010 CR 20031029, 57002008 KI 19128003 LA 46002001 PA 08004011>>
<<YEAR 1734: WR 45020034>> <<YEAR 1735: FO 01002018>> <<YEAR 1740: BR 46002001 GA 20018022, 20019014
HA 01002021, 52005031 ME 01002018 SE 01002018 SN 20011029, 20012004 W. 20031010>> <<YEAR 1742:
HU 61013004>> <<YEAR 1775: EL 52005031>> <<YEAR 1776: BE 52005031>>

Whitsunday <"W.S.","W.s.","Asc.s.& Wh.","Asc.& Wh.">
<<YEAR 1660: HA 48008014, 65001005>> <<YEAR 1661: BR 45011013, 46014015, 47002038 MA 45011013,
46014015, 47002038 NI 47002001, 47002001, 47002002, 47002003, 47002004>> <<YEAR 1663:
SP 47002001>> <<YEAR 1664: BR 12011009>> <<YEAR 1671: PI 47002004>> <<YEAR 1672: FA 46016013, 47002013
FR 46016013, 47002001>> <<YEAR 1675: HA 47002001, 47002002, 47002003, 47002004, 47002012>>
<<YEAR 1676: GE 43012031, 47002004>> <<YEAR 1680: LI 46015026>> <<YEAR 1685: KI 46016008>> <<YEAR 1692:
ST 46016007>> <<YEAR 1693: MO 47002001>> <<YEAR 17--: ST 47002011>> <<YEAR 1701: JE 49002012>> <<YEAR 1703:
DO 50013014>> <<YEAR 1704: GA 23049006, 46014016, 46014026>> <<YEAR 1705: MA 65003024>> <<YEAR 1706:
PA 46014016>> <<YEAR 1707: ST 46007039, 49002004>> <<YEAR 1708: GR 49012007 NO 46016007>> <<YEAR 1712:
BI 55005019>> <<YEAR 1713: BR 55005019 HI 45011013, 55005019>> <<YEAR 1714: DU 47019002 ST 46003016,
46014015, 47002001>> <<YEAR 1715: EY 46016012 HO 47002004>> <<YEAR 1716: AD 46014025 BA 47002038
HO 46003016, 46014015, 47002001>> <<YEAR 1717: MO 47002004 WI 64003018>> <<YEAR 1718: WA 69003020>>
<<YEAR 1720: BE 47002001 CL 46014016 NE 46014016>> <<YEAR 1721: KE 46016013>> <<YEAR 1722: CO 46014025>>
<<YEAR 1723: SC 51004006>> <<YEAR 1724: SM 49012004>> <<YEAR 1725: CO 46014016>> <<YEAR 1727: SO 49012004>>
<<YEAR 1728: RE 05016010 WH 46014025, 46016008>> <<YEAR 1729: HI 47002001 SH 49014015 WI 47002004>>
<<YEAR 1730: BR 46014016 RE 23011001 TR 45011013>> <<YEAR 1734: AT 44016020 SH 46014016>> <<YEAR 1735:
CL 43012031, 47019002, 50003017, 61002003 TI 46007039, 46016007, 46016012, 47002001,
52005009>> <<YEAR 1736: NE 49012004>> <<YEAR 1737: ST 65004001 TI 52004003>> <<YEAR 1739: MU 46014016
SK 46003005 WH 46007037>> <<YEAR 1740: BU 47002039 JO 47002038 SK 65004004 VE 44003028>> <<YEAR 1743:
AT 46014026 DO 46003008, 47002004>> <<YEAR 1745: SN 45024049>> <<YEAR 1747: WE 46014023>> <<YEAR 1749:
GA 18042010 HE 47002002>> <<YEAR 1750: BA 53002013 BU 49012011 QU 46003005>> <<YEAR 1752: BA 46016007>>
<<YEAR 1753: PR 65004001>> <<YEAR 1754: AN 47002001>> <<YEAR 1756: AN 47002032 MU 47002001>> <<YEAR 1757:
WA 49012004>> <<YEAR 1758: FR 65004001>> <<YEAR 1760: ST 45024049>> <<YEAR 1761: DO 47002001>> <<YEAR 1766:
DE 47002001 HA 46016013 RO 49011007>> <<YEAR 1769: CH 47002001>> <<YEAR 1770: AS 46008032>> <<YEAR 1771:
BU 47002001 DI 46016007 SP 47002004>> <<YEAR 1772: OR 45011013, 65003009>> <<YEAR 1774: CL 48008014>>
<<YEAR 1776: BO 47002004 PO 46015026, 52005018, 64003015, 65003015 WA 46014012>> <<YEAR 1777:
BA 47001008 PY 19068018>>

Workhouse <"Op.Work-H.","Work-house", etc.; "G.Work-h">
<<YEAR 1728: AC 43025035>> <<YEAR 1729: CH 19090017>> <<YEAR 1730: TR 56003010>> <<YEAR 1751: MI 56003010>>
<<YEAR 1780: SM 49013013>>

(INDEXES TO THIRD VOLUME)

APPENDIX TO INDEX D: SOME SETS OF OCCASION OR SUBJECT INDEX ITEMS SORTED AND ANALYZED IN RESPECT TO THE BIBLICAL TEXTS TO WHICH THE ITEMS REFER

APPENDIX TO INDEX D TO THIRD VOLUME: SOME SETS OF OCCASION INDEX ITEMS SORTED AND ANALYZED FOR BIBLICAL TEXT REFERENCE
(Accession)

Accession Sermons (In present index read columns downward.)

Bib.Text BkChpVrs	Sermons printed
01012001	YEAR 1714
02012051	YEAR 1715
03025020	YEAR 1707
04014024	YEAR 1705
04023023	YEAR 1696
05004006	YEAR 1725
	YEAR 1758
05004007	YEAR 1716
05033029	YEAR 1716
06001007	YEAR 1746
07005007	YEAR 1704
07009008	YEAR 1744
07012023	YEAR 1715
07017006	YEAR 1717
09012023	YEAR 1714
	YEAR 1715
09015028	YEAR 1715
09024017	YEAR 1717
10005001	YEAR 1715
10006012	YEAR 1661
	YEAR 1711
10022051	YEAR 1715
10023003	YEAR 1729
	YEAR 1761
	YEAR 1774
11002015	YEAR 1714
11008066	YEAR 1686
	YEAR 1714
11010009	YEAR 1713
	YEAR 1714
	YEAR 1725
14002011	YEAR 1776
14009008	YEAR 1717
	YEAR 1735
	YEAR 1737
14031021	YEAR 1734
15006010	YEAR 1727
15007025	YEAR 1741
17004014	YEAR 1711
19020005	YEAR 1753
19020006	YEAR 1715
	YEAR 1747
19021001	YEAR 1660
	YEAR 1710
	YEAR 1722
19021007	YEAR 1733
19037006	YEAR 1712

Bib.Text BkChpVrs	Sermons printed
19045008	YEAR 1720
19045017	YEAR 1709
19046010	YEAR 1686
19055003	YEAR 1727
19060011	YEAR 1704
19072001	YEAR 1714
	YEAR 1730
	YEAR 1755
19078072	YEAR 1751
19082006	YEAR 1725
19085008	YEAR 1728
19089020	YEAR 1746
19092001	YEAR 1716
	YEAR 1742
19095002	YEAR 1754
19097001	YEAR 1716
	YEAR 1728
19111004	YEAR 1715
	YEAR 1739
19118023	YEAR 1719
19118024	YEAR 1729
19122006	YEAR 1728
	YEAR 1729
	YEAR 1737
19122007	YEAR 1714
19122008	YEAR 1759
19126003	YEAR 1661
19132017	YEAR 1710
19132018	YEAR 1718
19133001	YEAR 1714
	YEAR 1760
19136023	YEAR 1715
19144010	YEAR 1705
19144015	YEAR 1711
19145004	YEAR 1704
20008015	YEAR 1720
20016012	YEAR 1703
	YEAR 1716
	YEAR 1728
20020028	YEAR 1761
20024021	YEAR 1685
	YEAR 1685
	YEAR 1686
	YEAR 1715
	YEAR 1715
	YEAR 1715
	YEAR 1723

Bib.Text BkChpVrs	Sermons printed
20025005	YEAR 1715
20028002	YEAR 1705
20029002	YEAR 1704
	YEAR 1705
	YEAR 1705
	YEAR 1730
21003001	YEAR 1715
21007010	YEAR 1714
21010017	YEAR 1709
	YEAR 1715
21010020	YEAR 1772
23044028	YEAR 1752
23049023	YEAR 1711
	YEAR 1712
	YEAR 1713
	YEAR 1714
	YEAR 1761
27002004	YEAR 1749
27010021	YEAR 1702
43022021	YEAR 1706
	YEAR 1715
	YEAR 1716
	YEAR 1716
	YEAR 1718
	YEAR 1776
45011002	YEAR 1704
45017017	YEAR 1715
47013022	YEAR 1715
48011033	YEAR 1743
48013001	YEAR 1723
	YEAR 1735
	YEAR 1738
	YEAR 1740
48013003	YEAR 1716
48013004	YEAR 1719
	YEAR 1723
	YEAR 1746
48013005	YEAR 1686
	YEAR 1738
	YEAR 1756
48013007	YEAR 1707
	YEAR 1745
	YEAR 1756
51005001	YEAR 1724
53003016	YEAR 1714
55005012	YEAR 1715
55005013	YEAR 1715

Bib.Text BkChpVrs	Sermons printed
55005021	YEAR 1770
57002001	YEAR 1704
	YEAR 1709
	YEAR 1714
	YEAR 1715
	YEAR 1715
	YEAR 1715
	YEAR 1715
	YEAR 1729
	YEAR 1730
	YEAR 1730
	YEAR 1739
	YEAR 1742
	YEAR 1749
	YEAR 1750
	YEAR 1772
	YEAR 1776
	YEAR 1779
57006006	YEAR 1702
59003001	YEAR 1710
	YEAR 1715
	YEAR 1732
	YEAR 1760
	YEAR 1766
63002017	YEAR 1685
	YEAR 1712
	YEAR 1715
	YEAR 1717
	YEAR 1717
	YEAR 1760
64002017	YEAR 1761
69017005	YEAR 1778

Accession: Statistical Analysis of the Set of Index Items Regarding Texts Used for This Subject or Occasion

a. Frequency (Number of records of a text)	b. Number of texts with that frequency of record	c. Number of records of those texts (c = a X b)	d. Cumulative percentage of the texts	e. Cumulative percentage of records	f. Percentage of all the records in this set (c/ Total c)
1	69	69	71.13	39.88	39.88
2	10	20	81.44	51.45	11.56
3	10	30	91.75	68.79	17.34
4	2	8	93.81	73.41	4.62
5	2	10	95.88	79.19	5.78
6	2	12	97.94	86.13	6.94
7	1	7	98.97	90.17	4.05
17	1	17	100.00	100.00	9.83
Totals	97	173			100.00

Average no. of records per text within this set: M = 1.7835 Standard deviation from average: SD = 1.9857
Type/token ratio = 1/M = 0.5607 Coefficient of variation = SD/M = 1.1133
Yule's K = 173.0763 (A measure of the concentration of records upon a relatively few texts)

APPENDIX TO INDEX D TO THIRD VOLUME: SOME SETS OF OCCASION INDEX ITEMS SORTED AND ANALYZED FOR BIBLICAL TEXT REFERENCE
(Assize)

Assize Sermons (In present index, read columns downward.)

Bib.Text BkChpVrs	Sermons printed
01009006	YEAR 1763
	YEAR 1782
01018025	YEAR 1692
	YEAR 1698
01020011	YEAR 1765
01039009	YEAR 1746
01049004	YEAR 1746
02014013	YEAR 1685
02018019	YEAR 1773
02018021	YEAR 1664
02018025	YEAR 1698
02020007	YEAR 1682
	YEAR 1745
02020012	YEAR 1682
02020016	YEAR 1734
	YEAR 1736
	YEAR 1743
	YEAR 1746
02023001	YEAR 1689
	YEAR 1701
	YEAR 1728
	YEAR 1758
03019012	YEAR 1682
	YEAR 1704
	YEAR 1704
	YEAR 1716
	YEAR 1735
03025005	YEAR 1746
04016015	YEAR 1676
04016041	YEAR 1716
04017008	YEAR 1660
04026009	YEAR 1684
04030002	YEAR 1718
05001016	YEAR 1681
	YEAR 1707
	YEAR 1722
	YEAR 1723
05001017	YEAR 1706
	YEAR 1720
05004006	YEAR 1704
	YEAR 1734
05004007	YEAR 1717
	YEAR 1764
05004008	YEAR 1740
	YEAR 1759
	YEAR 1766
05005029	YEAR 1706
	YEAR 1708
	YEAR 1771

Bib.Text BkChpVrs	Sermons printed
05006011	YEAR 1717
05006013	YEAR 1723
	YEAR 1754
05007013	YEAR 1775
05014008	YEAR 1751
05016018	YEAR 1669
05016020	YEAR 1780
05017012	YEAR 1664
05032029	YEAR 1717
06024014	YEAR 1704
06024015	YEAR 1705
07002016	YEAR 1709
07005001	YEAR 1708
07009015	YEAR 1716
07017006	YEAR 1676
	YEAR 1682
	YEAR 1684
	YEAR 1685
07018007	YEAR 1707
	YEAR 1742
07020027	YEAR 1684
09001008	YEAR 17--
09002025	YEAR 1669
	YEAR 1685
	YEAR 1728
09002030	YEAR 1710
	YEAR 1730
	YEAR 1775
09003012	YEAR 1729
09004013	YEAR 1714
09007015	YEAR 1661
	YEAR 1680
09007016	YEAR 1721
09008009	YEAR 1754
09012003	YEAR 1689
09012007	YEAR 1689
	YEAR 1716
09012014	YEAR 1681
09012025	YEAR 1700
	YEAR 1718
10001027	YEAR 1702
10012007	YEAR 1689
10012014	YEAR 16--
10014012	YEAR 1679
10015003	YEAR 1684
10015004	YEAR 1707
10018003	YEAR 1713

Bib.Text BkChpVrs	Sermons printed
10020019	YEAR 1705
	YEAR 1741
10021016	YEAR 1693
10023003	YEAR 1726
11003009	YEAR 1719
11008039	YEAR ----
11018021	YEAR 1719
11022043	YEAR 1738
13002007	YEAR 1670
13005006	YEAR 1729
14009008	YEAR 1750
14019005	YEAR 1670
	YEAR 1710
	YEAR 1729
	YEAR 1729
	YEAR 1751
14019006	YEAR 1672
	YEAR 1683
	YEAR 1697
	YEAR 1706
	YEAR 1711
	YEAR 1753
	YEAR 1779
14019007	YEAR 1713
	YEAR 1740
14019009	YEAR 1708
15007025	YEAR 1745
15007026	YEAR 1727
	YEAR 1729
	YEAR 1733
	YEAR 1755
15007027	YEAR 1675
17010003	YEAR 1715
18005012	YEAR 1722
18027006	YEAR 1729
18028028	YEAR 1706
	YEAR 1714
18029014	YEAR 1663
	YEAR 1742
	YEAR 1749
18029015	YEAR 1667
19001002	YEAR 1724
19002012	YEAR 1698
	YEAR 1700
19014001	YEAR 1710
19015004	YEAR 1688
19029010	YEAR 1712

Bib.Text BkChpVrs	Sermons printed
19029011	YEAR 1749
19032009	YEAR 1739
19033012	YEAR 1716
19037016	YEAR 1703
19037037	YEAR 1710
19047009	YEAR 1679
	YEAR 1721
19057007	YEAR 1746
19058011	YEAR 1721
	YEAR 1757
19072001	YEAR 1715
19072004	YEAR 1661
19073009	YEAR 1713
19078037	YEAR 1708
19082001	YEAR 1683
	YEAR 1695
	YEAR 1729
	YEAR 1750
19082006	YEAR 1674
	YEAR 1684
	YEAR 1690
	YEAR 1698
	YEAR 1736
19085010	YEAR 1729
	YEAR 1749
19094016	YEAR 1708
19094020	YEAR 1664
19097002	YEAR 17--
	YEAR 1739
19101001	YEAR 1678
	YEAR 1742
19101004	YEAR 1756
19106030	YEAR 1689
19107043	YEAR 1716
19112007	YEAR 1714
19119138	YEAR 1712
19122006	YEAR 1663
	YEAR 1683
	YEAR 1712
	YEAR 1715
	YEAR 1717
	YEAR 1737
19122008	YEAR 1717
19126003	YEAR 1698
19127001	YEAR 1694
	YEAR 1706
	YEAR 1707
	YEAR 1709

Bib.Text BkChpVrs	Sermons printed
19133001	YEAR 1725
	YEAR 1746
	YEAR 1750
19144010	YEAR 1734
19147019	YEAR 1753
19147020	YEAR 1708
20001022	YEAR 1710
20008012	YEAR 1677
20008015	YEAR 1700
	YEAR 1707
20010009	YEAR 1699
20011001	YEAR 1698
20012026	YEAR 1693
	YEAR 1744
20014012	YEAR 1736
20014025	YEAR 1736
20014026	YEAR 1769
20014034	YEAR 1672
	YEAR 1682
	YEAR 1691
	YEAR 1693
	YEAR 1710
	YEAR 1713
	YEAR 1714
	YEAR 1717
	YEAR 1720
	YEAR 1724
	YEAR 1728
	YEAR 1729
	YEAR 1729
	YEAR 1732
	YEAR 1738
	YEAR 1756
	YEAR 1781
20016006	YEAR 1777
20016010	YEAR 1737
20017013	YEAR 1717
20017015	YEAR 1735
20017026	YEAR 1684
20019014	YEAR 1697
20019021	YEAR 1689
20020001	YEAR 1701
20020008	YEAR 1682
20020012	YEAR 1736
20021003	YEAR 1740
20022006	YEAR 16--
20024010	YEAR 1689
	YEAR 1705

APPENDIX TO INDEX D TO THIRD VOLUME: SOME SETS OF OCCASION INDEX ITEMS SORTED AND ANALYZED FOR BIBLICAL TEXT REFERENCE
(Assize)

Assize Sermons (In present index, read columns downward.)

Bib.Text BkChpVrs	Sermons printed
20024021	YEAR 1683
	YEAR 1684
	YEAR 1691
	YEAR 1710
	YEAR 1713
	YEAR 1747
20024023	YEAR 1701
20024029	YEAR 1706
20025005	YEAR 1683
20029001	YEAR 1710
20029002	YEAR 1713
	YEAR 1716
	YEAR 1718
	YEAR 1730
	YEAR 1731
	YEAR 1750
20030008	YEAR 1747
21003007	YEAR 1712
21007010	YEAR 1715
	YEAR 1724
21008002	YEAR 1716
	YEAR 1716
21012013	YEAR 1682
21012014	YEAR 1719
23001025	YEAR 1660
23001026	YEAR 1662
	YEAR 1662
	YEAR 1662
	YEAR 1689
	YEAR 1689
23005020	YEAR 1722
	YEAR 1742
23032001	YEAR 1676
23032017	YEAR 1736
23033001	YEAR 1661
23033006	YEAR 1781
23033015	YEAR 17--
23049023	YEAR 1727
23057020	YEAR 1715
	YEAR 1738
23059011	YEAR 1693
23059014	YEAR 1780
24007003	YEAR 1719
24015010	YEAR 1668
24017009	YEAR ----
24022015	YEAR 1740
24023010	YEAR 1708

Bib.Text BkChpVrs	Sermons printed
24029007	YEAR 1743
24030010	YEAR 1705
26017018	YEAR 1724
26017019	YEAR 1722
27004037	YEAR 1708
27006021	YEAR 1668
28007009	YEAR 1729
28010004	YEAR 1682
30005015	YEAR 1691
30005023	YEAR 1672
30005024	YEAR 1771
30006012	YEAR 1670
32001008	YEAR 1778
32004005	YEAR 1679
32006006	YEAR 1690
	YEAR 1725
	YEAR 1731
32006008	YEAR 1689
	YEAR 1707
	YEAR 1756
	YEAR 1775
37007009	YEAR 16--
37008016	YEAR 1718
	YEAR 1722
37008017	YEAR 1715
	YEAR 1719
37009012	YEAR 1769
42004050	YEAR 1734
43005005	YEAR 1704
43005033	YEAR 1710
	YEAR 1715
43005034	YEAR 1704
43005038	YEAR 1704
43005039	YEAR 1729
	YEAR 1755
43005040	YEAR 1743
43005044	YEAR 1746
43007012	YEAR 1684
	YEAR 1686
	YEAR 1714
	YEAR 1717
	YEAR 1722
	YEAR 1723
	YEAR 1724
	YEAR 1735
	YEAR 1738
43007013	YEAR 1771

Bib.Text BkChpVrs	Sermons printed
43007029	YEAR 1742
43010033	YEAR 1727
43011019	YEAR 1714
43013029	YEAR 1688
43016027	YEAR 1778
43018007	YEAR 1737
43022021	YEAR 1663
43022037	YEAR 1728
43023023	YEAR 1727
43024012	YEAR 1686
43028015	YEAR 1695
44007037	YEAR 1736
44008038	YEAR 1737
44012017	YEAR 1681
45010042	YEAR 1715
45012005	YEAR 1739
45012051	YEAR 1707
45016008	YEAR 1712
45019042	YEAR 1666
46001047	YEAR 1727
46003035	YEAR 1686
46005044	YEAR 1776
46006026	YEAR 1715
46008009	YEAR 1684
46008032	YEAR 1746
	YEAR 1746
46013034	YEAR 1770
46013035	YEAR 1686
46014002	YEAR 1684
46015024	YEAR 1721
46018031	YEAR 1684
46018036	YEAR 1704
46020022	YEAR 1742
46020029	YEAR 1737
47002047	YEAR 1731
47004012	YEAR 1737
47007026	YEAR 1705
47007039	YEAR 1717
47017006	YEAR 1676
47017031	YEAR 1684
	YEAR 1718
47018014	YEAR 1721
47019038	YEAR 1683
47022025	YEAR 1754
47022028	YEAR 1745
47023001	YEAR 1706
47023003	YEAR 1710

Bib.Text BkChpVrs	Sermons printed
47023005	YEAR 1719
47024002	YEAR 1727
	YEAR 1744
47024016	YEAR 1660
	YEAR 1693
	YEAR 1697
	YEAR 1708
	YEAR 1710
	YEAR 1710
	YEAR 1712
	YEAR 1720
	YEAR 1742
47024025	YEAR 1680
	YEAR 1681
	YEAR 1732
48001016	YEAR 1773
48001028	YEAR 1744
48002014	YEAR 1726
	YEAR 1744
48003016	YEAR 1761
	YEAR 1780
48003031	YEAR 1678
48005007	YEAR 1740
48005013	YEAR 1738
48005019	YEAR 1667
48006021	YEAR 1707
	YEAR 1724
48008033	YEAR 1711
48012003	YEAR 1728
48012010	YEAR 1748
48012017	YEAR 1768
48012018	YEAR 1684
	YEAR 17--
	YEAR 1712
	YEAR 1717
	YEAR 1735
	YEAR 1742
48012019	YEAR 1712
	YEAR 1717
	YEAR 1728
	YEAR 1773
	YEAR 1780
48013001	YEAR ----
	YEAR 1681
	YEAR 1683
	YEAR 1704
	YEAR 1741
	YEAR 1776

Bib.Text BkChpVrs	Sermons printed
48013003	YEAR 1701
	YEAR 1714
	YEAR 1716
	YEAR 1728
	YEAR 1730
	YEAR 1740
	YEAR 1745
	YEAR 1750
	YEAR 1759
	YEAR 1770
48013004	YEAR 1668
	YEAR 1674
	YEAR 1688
	YEAR 1697
	YEAR 1717
	YEAR 1722
	YEAR 1735
	YEAR 1736
	YEAR 1766
48013005	YEAR 1670
	YEAR 1673
	YEAR 1682
	YEAR 1683
	YEAR 1736
	YEAR 1764
48013006	YEAR 1670
48013007	YEAR 1699
	YEAR 1717
48013008	YEAR 1757
48013010	YEAR 1722
48013014	YEAR 1764
48014019	YEAR 1710
	YEAR 1716
	YEAR 1716
48015005	YEAR 1661
	YEAR 1707
49001020	YEAR 1723
49006001	YEAR 1697
49006007	YEAR 1769
49010010	YEAR 1693
	YEAR 1715
49011022	YEAR 1672
49013013	YEAR 1697
49015033	YEAR 1712
49015058	YEAR 1717
50001012	YEAR ----
50003017	YEAR 1771

APPENDIX TO INDEX D TO THIRD VOLUME: SOME SETS OF OCCASION INDEX ITEMS SORTED AND ANALYZED FOR BIBLICAL TEXT REFERENCE
(Assize)

Assize Sermons (In present index, read columns downward.)

Bib.Text BkChpVrs	Sermons printed
50005010	YEAR 1682
	YEAR 1717
	YEAR 1732
50007002	YEAR 1685
50010005	YEAR 1702
51004018	YEAR 1710
	YEAR 1713
	YEAR 1739
51005001	YEAR 1703
	YEAR 1716
51005013	YEAR 1717
	YEAR 1727
	YEAR 1734
51005015	YEAR 1728
52002019	YEAR 1699
52004025	YEAR 1716
	YEAR 1726
52004031	YEAR 1755
53001029	YEAR 1681
53002004	YEAR 1724
53004005	YEAR 1707
	YEAR 1712
	YEAR 1720
	YEAR 1779
54003014	YEAR 1747
54003015	YEAR 1717
	YEAR 1720
55004006	YEAR 1704
55004010	YEAR 1682
55004011	YEAR 1683
	YEAR 1731
55004018	YEAR 1660
55005021	YEAR 1718
57001005	YEAR 1742
57001008	YEAR 1708
	YEAR 1754
	YEAR 1777
57001009	YEAR 1699
	YEAR 1724
	YEAR 1740
57001018	YEAR 1681
57002001	YEAR 1685
	YEAR 1712
	YEAR 1718
	YEAR 1723
57002002	YEAR 1706
	YEAR 1717
	YEAR 1720
	YEAR 1764

Bib.Text BkChpVrs	Sermons printed
57004007	YEAR 1670
57005021	YEAR 1704
57005022	YEAR 1709
58001007	YEAR 1715
58002019	YEAR 1710
58003005	YEAR 1661
58003016	YEAR 1724
59002011	YEAR 1773
59003001	YEAR 1673
	YEAR 1683
	YEAR 1696
	YEAR 1712
	YEAR 1715
	YEAR 1716
	YEAR 1735
	YEAR 1746
61004013	YEAR 1701
	YEAR 1706
61006016	YEAR 1682
	YEAR 1735
	YEAR 1754
61008013	YEAR 1773
61011026	YEAR 1745
61012014	YEAR 1682
61013009	YEAR 1716
61013018	YEAR 1766
62001025	YEAR 1696
62002008	YEAR 1723
62002024	YEAR 1712
62003017	YEAR 1682
	YEAR 1712
	YEAR 1717
	YEAR 1717
	YEAR 1730
62003018	YEAR 1752
62004001	YEAR 1716
62005009	YEAR 167-
	YEAR 1684
	YEAR 1708
63002007	YEAR 1704
63002013	YEAR 1668
	YEAR 1715
	YEAR 1717
	YEAR 1723
	YEAR 1727
	YEAR 1727
	YEAR 1747
	YEAR 1752

Bib.Text BkChpVrs	Sermons printed
63002016	YEAR 1739
63002017	YEAR 1720
	YEAR 1726
	YEAR 1726
63002021	YEAR 1674
63003013	YEAR 1689
63004007	YEAR 1722
64002010	YEAR 1712
	YEAR 1719
64003013	YEAR 1684
65004007	YEAR 1720
65004008	YEAR 1674
65005016	YEAR 1684
65005020	YEAR 1718
68000003	YEAR 1682
	YEAR 1710
68000014	YEAR 1725
68000022	YEAR 1752
69020004	YEAR 1684
69020012	YEAR 1663

Assize: Statistical Analysis of the Set of Index Items Regarding Texts Used for This Subject or Occasion

a. Frequency (Number of records of a text)	b. Number of texts with that frequency of record	c. Number of records of those texts (c = a X b)	d. Cumulative percentage of the texts	e. Cumulative percentage of records	f. Percentage of all the records in this set (c/ Total c)
1	260	260	73.24	43.92	43.92
2	47	94	86.48	59.80	15.88
3	17	51	91.27	68.41	8.61
4	11	44	94.37	75.84	7.43
5	6	30	96.06	80.91	5.07
6	6	36	97.75	86.99	6.08
7	1	7	98.03	88.18	1.18
8	2	16	98.59	90.88	2.70
9	3	27	99.44	95.44	4.56
10	1	10	99.72	97.13	1.69
17	1	17	100.00	100.00	2.87
Totals	355	592			100.00

Average no. of records per text within this set: M = 1.6676 Standard deviation from average: SD = 1.6485
Type/token ratio = 1/M = 0.5997 Coefficient of variation = SD/M = .9886
Yule's K = 38.8057 (A measure of the concentration of records upon a relatively few texts)

APPENDIX TO INDEX D TO THIRD VOLUME: SOME SETS OF OCCASION INDEX ITEMS SORTED AND ANALYZED FOR BIBLICAL TEXT REFERENCE (Fast)

Fast Sermons (In present index read columns downward.)

Bib.Text BkChpVrs	Sermons printed
01018032	YEAR 1701
	YEAR 1720
	YEAR 1740
	YEAR 1756
	YEAR 1779
01019027	YEAR 1753
02008020	YEAR 1781
02014015	YEAR 1757
02023009	YEAR 17--
03026018	YEAR 1666
04010009	YEAR 1692
	YEAR 1740
04011033	YEAR 1736
04016034	YEAR 1756
04016046	YEAR 1666
05005029	YEAR 1729
05009026	YEAR 1695
05010016	YEAR 1756
05020001	YEAR 1710
	YEAR 1737
05023009	YEAR 1673
	YEAR 1706
	YEAR 1707
	YEAR 1733
	YEAR 1740
	YEAR 1741
	YEAR 1758
	YEAR 1759
	YEAR 1761
	YEAR 1780
	YEAR 1780
05028021	YEAR 1729
05029009	YEAR 1780
05031016	YEAR 1710
05032020	YEAR 1773
05032028	YEAR 1758
05032029	YEAR 1754
06005013	YEAR 1690
06007008	YEAR 1758
06007012	YEAR 1698
06007016	YEAR 1665
06009014	YEAR 1773
06023009	YEAR 1778
07012007	YEAR 1773
07016020	YEAR 1758
07020023	YEAR 1757
07020026	YEAR 1782

Bib.Text BkChpVrs	Sermons printed
07021002	YEAR 1777
	YEAR 1778
09002030	YEAR 1757
09004013	YEAR 1701
	YEAR 1778
09007006	YEAR 1740
09012003	YEAR 1745
09012024	YEAR 1702
	YEAR 1745
	YEAR 1745
09012025	YEAR 1742
09017026	YEAR 1748
09017044	YEAR 1760
10010012	YEAR 1737
	YEAR 1744
	YEAR 1745
10019009	YEAR 167-
10019012	YEAR 1661
10022004	YEAR 1693
10024014	YEAR 1696
	YEAR 1704
	YEAR 1777
10024016	YEAR 1715
11008044	YEAR 1739
	YEAR 1740
	YEAR 1741
11012010	YEAR 1746
11017015	YEAR 1667
11020011	YEAR 1744
11021029	YEAR 1717
12009022	YEAR 1694
12019019	YEAR 1760
14006034	YEAR 1706
	YEAR 1757
14007013	YEAR 1665
	YEAR 1679
	YEAR 1721
14007014	YEAR 1757
	YEAR 1779
14012007	YEAR 1779
14013005	YEAR 1757
14014011	YEAR 1689
	YEAR 1758
14015002	YEAR 1705
	YEAR 1756
	YEAR 1759
	YEAR 1771

Bib.Text BkChpVrs	Sermons printed
14020003	YEAR 1740
	YEAR 1745
	YEAR 1758
	YEAR 1777
14020004	YEAR 1781
14020005	YEAR 1745
	YEAR 1761
14020009	YEAR 1711
14020012	YEAR 16--
	YEAR 1703
14020015	YEAR 1740
14022007	YEAR 1757
14028010	YEAR 1749
14032007	YEAR 1744
15004015	YEAR 1682
15008021	YEAR 1695
15009015	YEAR 1679
16001004	YEAR 1675
16005019	YEAR 1780
16009026	YEAR 1696
16009028	YEAR 1757
16014031	YEAR 1679
17001008	YEAR 1705
17003015	YEAR 1712
17006013	YEAR 1698
18001005	YEAR 1749
	YEAR 1760
18009012	YEAR 1667
18012023	YEAR 1780
	YEAR 1782
18037014	YEAR 1756
19002011	YEAR 1766
19004005	YEAR 1761
19007009	YEAR 1666
	YEAR 1777
19010001	YEAR 1745
19012001	YEAR 1691
	YEAR 1691
19018002	YEAR 1678
19018003	YEAR 1736
	YEAR 1756
	YEAR 1756
	YEAR 1761
19018007	YEAR 1704
	YEAR 1756
19020007	YEAR 1760
	YEAR 1770

Bib.Text BkChpVrs	Sermons printed
19020009	YEAR 1761
19021001	YEAR 1706
19024014	YEAR 1777
19026008	YEAR 1748
19030006	YEAR 1730
19033020	YEAR 1740
19035012	YEAR 1745
19044004	YEAR 1739
	YEAR 1757
19046001	YEAR 1704
19046008	YEAR 1750
	YEAR 1756
19046009	YEAR 1749
19046010	YEAR 1756
19050016	YEAR 1745
19050021	YEAR 1745
19051009	YEAR 1696
19056007	YEAR 1777
19057001	YEAR 1694
	YEAR 1747
19060010	YEAR 1740
19060012	YEAR 1741
19062001	YEAR 1690
19068030	YEAR 1711
	YEAR 1737
19076010	YEAR 1775
19077010	YEAR 1719
19078034	YEAR 1758
19078050	YEAR 1721
19079009	YEAR 1695
19080019	YEAR 1699
19081013	YEAR 1712
	YEAR 1742
	YEAR 1744
19085008	YEAR 1690
19089003	YEAR ----
	YEAR 16--
19089031	YEAR 1776
19089032	YEAR 1704
19094022	YEAR 1767
19103009	YEAR 1770
19108010	YEAR 1685
19108012	YEAR 1762
19112007	YEAR 1710
19114007	YEAR 1756
19119059	YEAR 1777
19119075	YEAR 1689

Bib.Text BkChpVrs	Sermons printed
19119123	YEAR 1721
	YEAR 1722
19120005	YEAR 1711
19122006	YEAR 1694
	YEAR 1712
	YEAR 1712
	YEAR 1716
	YEAR 1742
	YEAR 1745
	YEAR 1749
	YEAR 1759
	YEAR 1771
19122008	YEAR 1757
19122009	YEAR 1780
19124008	YEAR 1716
19127001	YEAR 1701
19132018	YEAR 1746
19145018	YEAR 1746
19145019	YEAR 1758
19147012	YEAR 1763
19148008	YEAR 1703
	YEAR 1703
	YEAR 1704
19149006	YEAR 1758
20003005	YEAR 1709
20011011	YEAR 1740
20014034	YEAR 1690
	YEAR 1721
	YEAR 1740
	YEAR 1745
	YEAR 1746
	YEAR 1747
	YEAR 1759
	YEAR 1770
	YEAR 1778
20015008	YEAR 1760
20021030	YEAR 1707
	YEAR 1712
	YEAR 1761
20021031	YEAR 1762
20024021	YEAR 1746
	YEAR 1776
	YEAR 1778
	YEAR 1780
20028001	YEAR 1758
20030004	YEAR 1772
21007010	YEAR 17--

APPENDIX TO INDEX D TO THIRD VOLUME: SOME SETS OF OCCASION INDEX ITEMS SORTED AND ANALYZED FOR BIBLICAL TEXT REFERENCE (Fast)

Fast Sermons (In present index read columns downward.)

Bib.Text BkChpVrs	Sermons printed
21007014	YEAR 1778
21008011	YEAR 1738
	YEAR 1761
21009011	YEAR 1735
	YEAR 1735
21011009	YEAR 1674
21012001	YEAR 1776
23001002	YEAR 1776
23001004	YEAR 1720
23001005	YEAR 1697
23001016	YEAR 1701
23001019	YEAR 1760
	YEAR 1779
23002004	YEAR 1780
23003004	YEAR 1757
23003010	YEAR 1778
23005003	YEAR 1762
23005004	YEAR 1721
	YEAR 1740
	YEAR 1744
23005007	YEAR 1748
23005025	YEAR 1678
	YEAR 1778
23007005	YEAR 1744
23008012	YEAR 1746
23009012	YEAR 1730
23009013	YEAR 1747
23022012	YEAR 1679
	YEAR 1757
23024015	YEAR 1688
23026004	YEAR 1756
23026009	YEAR 1694
	YEAR 1720
	YEAR 1721
	YEAR 1721
	YEAR 1725
	YEAR 1734
	YEAR 1748
	YEAR 1753
	YEAR 1755
	YEAR 1755
	YEAR 1756
	YEAR 1756
	YEAR 1756
	YEAR 1756
	YEAR 1756
	YEAR 1756
	YEAR 1758
	YEAR 1777

Bib.Text BkChpVrs	Sermons printed
	YEAR 1777
	YEAR 1781
23026012	YEAR 1712
23026016	YEAR 1704
23026020	YEAR 1756
23027015	YEAR 16--
23029006	YEAR 1704
	YEAR 1756
23030001	YEAR 1695
23033001	YEAR 1779
23042022	YEAR 1688
23042024	YEAR 1765
23044023	YEAR 1759
23045007	YEAR 1722
23049004	YEAR 1758
23051009	YEAR 1758
23057019	YEAR 1660
23057021	YEAR 1674
	YEAR 1684
	YEAR 1691
23058003	YEAR ----
	YEAR 1717
	YEAR 1745
	YEAR 1781
23058005	YEAR 1661
	YEAR 1762
	YEAR 1779
23058006	YEAR 1748
23059001	YEAR 1708
23059002	YEAR 1781
23059003	YEAR 1778
23059008	YEAR 1702
23062006	YEAR 1660
	YEAR 1710
24003021	YEAR 1762
24004014	YEAR 1711
	YEAR 1759
24004019	YEAR 1756
	YEAR 1759
24004021	YEAR 1762
24005003	YEAR 1707
	YEAR 1779
24005009	YEAR 1782
24005010	YEAR 1744
24005025	YEAR 1782
24005029	YEAR 1709
	YEAR 1721
	YEAR 1781

Bib.Text BkChpVrs	Sermons printed
24006008	YEAR 1702
	YEAR 1735
	YEAR 1745
	YEAR 1756
24006029	YEAR 1778
24007010	YEAR 1721
24007012	YEAR 1720
24007023	YEAR 1710
24008007	YEAR 1762
24008015	YEAR 1712
24008020	YEAR 1704
24009023	YEAR 17--
	YEAR 1744
24014008	YEAR 1714
24014009	YEAR 1678
24014012	YEAR 1761
24017006	YEAR 1756
24017007	YEAR 1776
24018007	YEAR 1756
	YEAR 1756
	YEAR 1777
24018008	YEAR 1779
24018011	YEAR 1703
	YEAR 1779
24036007	YEAR 1740
24045005	YEAR 1773
24047006	YEAR 1777
	YEAR 1778
24047007	YEAR 1773
25001008	YEAR 1707
25003039	YEAR 1759
26007014	YEAR 1758
26009004	YEAR 1721
26011004	YEAR 1773
26012023	YEAR 1773
26014012	YEAR 1748
26018027	YEAR 1759
26018030	YEAR 1702
	YEAR 1782
26018031	YEAR 1782
26018033	YEAR 1747
26020037	YEAR 1773
26020047	YEAR 1666
26026017	YEAR 1756
26027027	YEAR 1779
26033011	YEAR 1710
26035006	YEAR 1778

Bib.Text BkChpVrs	Sermons printed
26036031	YEAR 1707
27004035	YEAR 1756
27009003	YEAR 1757
27009009	YEAR 1721
27009012	YEAR 1777
27009016	YEAR 1749
27009018	YEAR 1727
28002006	YEAR 1717
28002008	YEAR 1773
28005015	YEAR 1766
28007009	YEAR 1679
28008003	YEAR 1745
28008007	YEAR 1704
28009012	YEAR 1776
28010012	YEAR 1701
	YEAR 1762
28011008	YEAR 1773
28011012	YEAR 1679
28013009	YEAR 1779
28014001	YEAR 1679
29001014	YEAR 1780
29002012	YEAR 1704
	YEAR 1716
	YEAR 1740
	YEAR 1742
	YEAR 1744
	YEAR 1747
	YEAR 1757
	YEAR 1758
	YEAR 1759
	YEAR 1777
	YEAR 1778
29002013	YEAR 1680
29002015	YEAR 1746
	YEAR 1776
	YEAR 1777
	YEAR 1778
29002016	YEAR 1745
29002018	YEAR 1702
	YEAR 1744
29002020	YEAR 1754
29003019	YEAR 17--
30003006	YEAR 1781
30004010	YEAR 1745
30004011	YEAR 1681
	YEAR 1756
30004012	YEAR 1671
	YEAR 1688
	YEAR 1690

Bib.Text BkChpVrs	Sermons printed
	YEAR 1691
	YEAR 1720
	YEAR 1720
	YEAR 1755
	YEAR 1756
	YEAR 1756
	YEAR 1756
30005006	YEAR 1666
	YEAR 1757
30005015	YEAR 1660
30008011	YEAR 1678
31001006	YEAR 1716
	YEAR 1772
31001007	YEAR 1748
31003004	YEAR 1757
31003005	YEAR 1681
	YEAR 1728
	YEAR 1734
31003008	YEAR 1694
	YEAR 1744
31003009	YEAR 1756
31003010	YEAR 1747
31004007	YEAR 1758
31004010	YEAR 1758
32006008	YEAR 1660
32006009	YEAR 1671
	YEAR 1719
33001003	YEAR 1704
35002001	YEAR 1681
	YEAR 1781
36001005	YEAR 1744
	YEAR 1778
37001003	YEAR 1669
37007005	YEAR 1694
	YEAR 1735
37014007	YEAR 1745
38001003	YEAR 1745
38003001	YEAR 1772
38003007	YEAR 1688
38004005	YEAR 1669
41036026	YEAR 1756
43003008	YEAR 1780
43003009	YEAR 1721
43004017	YEAR 1680
43005025	YEAR 1763
43006016	YEAR 1704
	YEAR 1778

APPENDIX TO INDEX D TO THIRD VOLUME: SOME SETS OF OCCASION INDEX ITEMS SORTED AND ANALYZED FOR BIBLICAL TEXT REFERENCE
(Fast)

Fast Sermons (In present index read columns downward.)

Bib.Text BkChpVrs	Sermons printed
43006034	YEAR 1680
	YEAR 1712
43010036	YEAR 1758
43012003	YEAR 1759
43012025	YEAR 1680
43016003	YEAR 1757
	YEAR 1759
43022021	YEAR 1781
43024007	YEAR 1756
45008024	YEAR 1758
	YEAR 1758
45009055	YEAR 1778
45009056	YEAR 1778
45012004	YEAR 1756
45013001	YEAR 1756
	YEAR 1779
45013002	YEAR 1721
	YEAR 1721
	YEAR 1734
	YEAR 1755
	YEAR 1756
	YEAR 1781
45013003	YEAR 1744
	YEAR 1756
45013004	YEAR 1723
	YEAR 1756
45013005	YEAR 1678
	YEAR 1678
	YEAR 1704
	YEAR 1704
	YEAR 1732
	YEAR 1774
45013007	YEAR 1742
45013034	YEAR 1746
45013035	YEAR 1756
	YEAR 1760
45016030	YEAR 1684
45019041	YEAR 1666
	YEAR 1690
	YEAR 1754
	YEAR 1758
45019044	YEAR 1761
45021036	YEAR 1720
45022036	YEAR 1758
46005014	YEAR 1672
	YEAR 1683
	YEAR 1701
	YEAR 1704
	YEAR 1706

Bib.Text BkChpVrs	Sermons printed
	YEAR 1717
	YEAR 1720
47002040	YEAR 1773
47005038	YEAR 1681
47007026	YEAR 1754
	YEAR 1777
47011023	YEAR 1773
48001028	YEAR 1777
48001032	YEAR 1763
48002014	YEAR 1741
48010001	YEAR 1758
48011012	YEAR 1760
48011022	YEAR 1757
	YEAR 1760
	YEAR 1761
48013001	YEAR 1776
	YEAR 1777
49003002	YEAR 1761
49006020	YEAR 1757
49010009	YEAR 1746
49010011	YEAR 1740
49011031	YEAR 1782
50007009	YEAR 1721
52005016	YEAR 1773
53003020	YEAR 1701
53004005	YEAR 1679
	YEAR 1776
56002007	YEAR 1680
57004016	YEAR 1673
57005022	YEAR 1746
57006017	YEAR 1766
58001010	YEAR 1761
58003001	YEAR 1689
59003001	YEAR 1746
	YEAR 1777
61003018	YEAR 1748
61004012	YEAR 1749
61011007	YEAR 1756
61011028	YEAR 1759
61012006	YEAR 1781
62004009	YEAR 1697
	YEAR 1756
62004010	YEAR 1777
63001011	YEAR 1781
63002016	YEAR 1778
63002017	YEAR 1779
63003010	YEAR 1712

Bib.Text BkChpVrs	Sermons printed
63004010	YEAR 1699
63004017	YEAR 1776
63005006	YEAR 1678
	YEAR 1720
	YEAR 1756
	YEAR 1771
	YEAR 1778
64003009	YEAR 1690
64003011	YEAR 1776
64003013	YEAR 1781
64003015	YEAR 1720
65002015	YEAR 1757
69001010	YEAR 1777
69002004	YEAR 1711
	YEAR 1745
69002005	YEAR 1729
	YEAR 1744
	YEAR 1745
	YEAR 1745
	YEAR 1756
69002016	YEAR 1681
69003002	YEAR 1681
69003003	YEAR 1681
69003019	YEAR 1758
	YEAR 1779
69011013	YEAR 1756
69018023	YEAR 1754
69019006	YEAR 1769

APPENDIX TO INDEX D TO THIRD VOLUME: SOME SETS OF OCCASION INDEX ITEMS SORTED AND ANALYZED FOR BIBLICAL TEXT REFERENCE (Fast)

Fast: Statistical Analysis of the Set of Index Items Regarding Texts Used for This Subject or Occasion

a. Frequency (Number of records of a text)	b. Number of texts with that frequency of record	c. Number of records of those texts (c = a X b)	d. Cumulative percentage of the texts	e. Cumulative percentage of records	f. Percentage of all the records in this set (c/ Total c)
1	298	298	75.83	49.75	49.75
2	60	120	91.09	69.78	20.03
3	15	45	94.91	77.30	7.51
4	8	32	96.95	82.64	5.34
5	3	15	97.71	85.14	2.50
6	2	12	98.22	87.15	2.00
7	1	7	98.47	88.31	1.17
9	2	18	98.98	91.32	3.01
10	1	10	99.24	92.99	1.67
11	2	22	99.75	96.66	3.67
20	1	20	100.00	100.00	3.34
Totals	393	599			100.00

Average no. of records per text within this set: M = 1.5242 Standard deviation from average: SD = 1.5856
Type/token ratio = 1/M = 0.6561 Coefficient of variation = SD/M = 1.0403
Yule's K = 36.2875 (A measure of the concentration of records upon a relatively few texts)

APPENDIX TO INDEX D TO THIRD VOLUME: SOME SETS OF OCCASION INDEX ITEMS SORTED AND ANALYZED FOR BIBLICAL TEXT REFERENCE (Funeral)

Funeral Sermons (In present index, read columns downward.)

Bib.Text BkChpVrs	Sermons printed
01003015	YEAR 1773
01003019	YEAR 1660
	YEAR 1702
01005024	YEAR 16--
	YEAR 1703
	YEAR 1707
01006009	YEAR 1753
01009006	YEAR 1714
01015001	YEAR 1660
01018030	YEAR 1779
01018032	YEAR 1721
01023002	YEAR 1679
01025008	YEAR 1661
01035019	YEAR 1685
01045024	YEAR 1692
01048021	YEAR 1665
01049008	YEAR 1699
01050010	YEAR 1660
02015016	YEAR 1773
03024021	YEAR 1768
04016001	YEAR 1683
04023010	YEAR 1692
	YEAR 1695
	YEAR 1697
	YEAR 1699
	YEAR 1764
	YEAR 1771
05021001	YEAR 1763
05032029	YEAR 1681
	YEAR 1692
	YEAR 1704
	YEAR 1708
	YEAR 1728
	YEAR 1739
05034005	YEAR 1702
06024014	YEAR 1694
07008034	YEAR 1727
09001016	YEAR 1675
09004022	YEAR 1696
09020003	YEAR 1753
	YEAR 1777
09025001	YEAR 1677
	YEAR 1779
10001019	YEAR 1695
	YEAR 1771
10001023	YEAR 1715
10001026	YEAR 1740

Bib.Text BkChpVrs	Sermons printed
10001027	YEAR 1715
	YEAR 1765
10002007	YEAR 1737
10003031	YEAR 1708
10003032	YEAR 1677
10003033	YEAR 1660
	YEAR 1678
10003038	YEAR 1660
	YEAR 1660
	YEAR 1673
	YEAR 1712
	YEAR 1749
	YEAR 1765
	YEAR 1765
	YEAR 1776
10012005	YEAR 1689
	YEAR 1737
10012015	YEAR 1672
10012021	YEAR 1680
10012022	YEAR 1660
	YEAR 1744
10012023	YEAR 1720
	YEAR 1756
10013033	YEAR 1736
10014014	YEAR 1678
10018033	YEAR 1743
	YEAR 1767
10023002	YEAR 1748
10023005	YEAR 1673
11002010	YEAR 1724
11003009	YEAR 1760
11016030	YEAR 1714
11019004	YEAR 1664
12002003	YEAR 1721
12002009	YEAR 1704
12002011	YEAR 1685
12002012	YEAR 1660
	YEAR 1673
	YEAR 17--
	YEAR 1781
12020001	YEAR 1777
12022019	YEAR 1715
12023025	YEAR 1714
13015013	YEAR 1757
13017011	YEAR 1772
13029015	YEAR 1759
13029026	YEAR 1760

Bib.Text BkChpVrs	Sermons printed
13029027	YEAR 1760
	YEAR 1760
	YEAR 1761
	YEAR 1767
13029028	YEAR 1760
	YEAR 1760
14032033	YEAR 1760
14034003	YEAR 1751
14034027	YEAR 1695
14035024	YEAR 1673
	YEAR 1695
	YEAR 1695
	YEAR 1728
	YEAR 1737
	YEAR 1761
17009021	YEAR 1711
18001020	YEAR 1739
18001021	YEAR 1696
	YEAR 1736
	YEAR 1749
	YEAR 1771
18003017	YEAR 1661
	YEAR 1732
	YEAR 1738
18005026	YEAR 1726
	YEAR 1727
	YEAR 1736
	YEAR 1773
	YEAR 1779
18007001	YEAR 1738
18007016	YEAR 1747
18009023	YEAR 1724
18014001	YEAR 1664
	YEAR 1671
	YEAR 1772
18014002	YEAR 1740
	YEAR 1749
18014010	YEAR 1778
18014012	YEAR 1676
	YEAR 1730
18014013	YEAR 1690
	YEAR 1773
18014014	YEAR 1696
	YEAR 1704
	YEAR 1705
	YEAR 1707
	YEAR 1708
	YEAR 1708
	YEAR 1714

Bib.Text BkChpVrs	Sermons printed
	YEAR 1728
18014020	YEAR 1717
18017011	YEAR 1758
18018014	YEAR 1747
18019025	YEAR 1693
	YEAR 1702
	YEAR 1713
	YEAR 1714
	YEAR 1755
	YEAR 1773
18021026	YEAR 1699
18028028	YEAR 1747
18030023	YEAR 1667
	YEAR 1676
18033023	YEAR 1691
18033024	YEAR 1773
18038017	YEAR 1760
19001003	YEAR 1703
19002010	YEAR 1670
19004004	YEAR 1768
19008002	YEAR 1764
19009012	YEAR 1757
19010016	YEAR 1714
19012001	YEAR 1712
19015001	YEAR 1687
19016011	YEAR 1773
19016012	YEAR 1710
19017015	YEAR 1758
	YEAR 1767
19018046	YEAR ----
19023001	YEAR 1756
	YEAR 1758
19023004	YEAR 1713
	YEAR 1728
	YEAR 1762
	YEAR 1769
19027013	YEAR 1702
	YEAR 1771
19027015	YEAR 1717
19031005	YEAR 1733
	YEAR 1763
19033004	YEAR 1758
19034019	YEAR 1728
19034022	YEAR 1728
19035014	YEAR 1718
19037011	YEAR 1723
19037037	YEAR 1671
	YEAR 1676
	YEAR 1679

Bib.Text BkChpVrs	Sermons printed
	YEAR 1682
	YEAR 1698
	YEAR 1703
	YEAR 1705
	YEAR 1707
	YEAR 1709
	YEAR 1713
	YEAR 1718
	YEAR 1748
	YEAR 1762
	YEAR 1770
	YEAR 1773
	YEAR 1778
19039004	YEAR 1706
	YEAR 1708
19039005	YEAR 1661
	YEAR 1673
	YEAR 1737
	YEAR 1756
19039006	YEAR 1690
	YEAR 1718
	YEAR 1728
19039008	YEAR 1751
19039009	YEAR 1660
	YEAR 1719
19042011	YEAR 1702
	YEAR 1706
19043005	YEAR 1714
19046001	YEAR 1771
19046006	YEAR 1732
19048014	YEAR 1705
	YEAR 1774
19049010	YEAR 1772
19049015	YEAR 1781
19050023	YEAR 1728
19071005	YEAR 1713
19072006	YEAR 1695
19073004	YEAR 1727
19073024	YEAR 1695
19073025	YEAR 1744
19073026	YEAR 1663
	YEAR 1776
19075007	YEAR 1714
19077003	YEAR 1743
19082005	YEAR 1685
19082006	YEAR 1683
	YEAR 1695
	YEAR 1695
	YEAR 1714

Funeral Sermons (In present index, read columns downward.)

Bib.Text BkChpVrs	Sermons printed	Bib.Text BkChpVrs	Sermons printed	Bib.Text BkChpVrs	Sermons printed	Bib.Text BkChpVrs	Sermons printed	Bib.Text BkChpVrs	Sermons printed
	YEAR 1714	19119092	YEAR 1661	21007001	YEAR 1676	21012014	YEAR 1661	24012001	YEAR 1733
	YEAR 1724	19119096	YEAR 1735		YEAR 1692	23002022	YEAR 1724	25005016	YEAR 1702
	YEAR 1737		YEAR 1737		YEAR 1704		YEAR 1778		YEAR 1702
	YEAR 1737	19119137	YEAR 1691		YEAR 1705	23003001	YEAR 1680		YEAR 1702
19089047	YEAR 1708	19119165	YEAR 1720		YEAR 1706	23003010	YEAR 1772	26017022	YEAR 1660
19090012	YEAR 1660	19142009	YEAR 1679		YEAR 1708	23008018	YEAR 1770	26024015	YEAR 1693
	YEAR 1660	19146001	YEAR 1708		YEAR 1715	23012001	YEAR 1765	26024016	YEAR 1664
	YEAR 1661	19146003	YEAR 1715		YEAR 1717	23026003	YEAR 1736		YEAR 1688
	YEAR 1681		YEAR 1722		YEAR 1754		YEAR 1771		YEAR 1738
	YEAR 1687		YEAR 1737		YEAR 1763	23026008	YEAR 1661	26037003	YEAR 1722
	YEAR 1699		YEAR 1737		YEAR 1764	23026018	YEAR 1679	27004018	YEAR 1695
	YEAR 1705	20003016	YEAR 1716		YEAR 1768	23030021	YEAR 1773	27006021	YEAR 1760
	YEAR 1728	20010007	YEAR ----		YEAR 1773	23032008	YEAR 1741	27012002	YEAR 1669
	YEAR 1735		YEAR 1706	21007002	YEAR ----	23038001	YEAR 1665	27012003	YEAR 1770
19092014	YEAR 1720		YEAR 1743		YEAR 1660	23038003	YEAR 1747	27012013	YEAR 1744
19097001	YEAR 1714		YEAR 1759		YEAR 1706	23040006	YEAR 1694	28006002	YEAR 1663
19097002	YEAR 1778		YEAR 1769		YEAR 1716		YEAR 1695	28013014	YEAR 1660
19102023	YEAR 1736	20011004	YEAR 1713		YEAR 1730		YEAR 1712	30008009	YEAR 1694
19102026	YEAR 1700	20011016	YEAR 1682		YEAR 1732		YEAR 1742	32007009	YEAR 1661
19102027	YEAR 1740	20011018	YEAR 1661		YEAR 1743	23048010	YEAR 1771	34003002	YEAR 1698
19103013	YEAR 1746	20012026	YEAR 1729	21007014	YEAR 1695	23054010	YEAR 1756	36001005	YEAR 1704
19103015	YEAR 1692	20014001	YEAR 1677		YEAR 1725	23055006	YEAR 1775	37001003	YEAR 1691
	YEAR 1724	20014032	YEAR 1699	21007015	YEAR 1660	23057001	YEAR 1661		YEAR 1692
19106030	YEAR 1702		YEAR 1717	21007029	YEAR 1765		YEAR 1661		YEAR 1704
19107007	YEAR 1758		YEAR 1717	21009005	YEAR 1710		YEAR 1663		YEAR 1704
19107029	YEAR 1734		YEAR 1719		YEAR 1715		YEAR 1667		YEAR 1738
19107030	YEAR 1724		YEAR 1729		YEAR 1733		YEAR 1677		YEAR 1759
19112002	YEAR 1734		YEAR 1743	21009010	YEAR 1699		YEAR 1680	37001005	YEAR 1673
19112004	YEAR 1753	20014034	YEAR 1779	21011001	YEAR 1717		YEAR 1681		YEAR 1692
19112006	YEAR 1680	20016031	YEAR 1728	21011003	YEAR 1694		YEAR 1688		YEAR 1706
	YEAR 1684		YEAR 1754		YEAR 1727		YEAR 1695	37003002	YEAR 1781
	YEAR 1694	20018001	YEAR 1765	21011008	YEAR 1704		YEAR 1701	37011002	YEAR 1661
	YEAR 17--	20022001	YEAR 1708	21011009	YEAR 1714		YEAR 1706		YEAR 1695
	YEAR 1704	20022006	YEAR 1702		YEAR 1714		YEAR 1710		YEAR 1700
	YEAR 1713	20030007	YEAR 1768	21011010	YEAR 1683		YEAR 1711	38004002	YEAR 1715
	YEAR 1714	20031028	YEAR 1726	21012001	YEAR 1687		YEAR 1714	41016022	YEAR 1698
	YEAR 1729	20031029	YEAR 1678		YEAR 1708		YEAR 1730	43002018	YEAR 1736
19112009	YEAR 1721	20031030	YEAR 1680		YEAR 1724		YEAR 1750	43005004	YEAR 1751
19116015	YEAR 16--		YEAR 1691	21012005	YEAR 1661		YEAR 1760	43005008	YEAR 1714
	YEAR 1660	20031031	YEAR 1695		YEAR 1683		YEAR 1761	43009038	YEAR 1674
	YEAR 1662		YEAR 1699		YEAR 1687		YEAR 1770	43013043	YEAR 1680
	YEAR 1705	21002016	YEAR 1697		YEAR 1700		YEAR 1778		YEAR 1727
	YEAR 1723	21002026	YEAR 1692	21012007	YEAR 1669	23057002	YEAR 1762		YEAR 1761
19118008	YEAR 1702	21003002	YEAR 1688		YEAR 1675	23060001	YEAR ----	43016026	YEAR 1660
19119019	YEAR 1672	21003020	YEAR 1660		YEAR 1677		YEAR 1697	43017005	YEAR 1727
19119071	YEAR 1714	21004002	YEAR 1690		YEAR 1705	23060019	YEAR 1769	43021015	YEAR 1770
19119081	YEAR 1728		YEAR 1773		YEAR 1709	24009023	YEAR 1726	43022032	YEAR 1754

APPENDIX TO INDEX D TO THIRD VOLUME: SOME SETS OF OCCASION INDEX ITEMS SORTED AND ANALYZED FOR BIBLICAL TEXT REFERENCE
(Funeral)

Funeral Sermons (In present index, read columns downward.)

Bib.Text BkChpVrs	Sermons printed
43024036	YEAR ----
43024044	YEAR 1709
	YEAR 1714
	YEAR 1727
	YEAR 1736
43024045	YEAR 1709
	YEAR 1719
	YEAR 1727
43024046	YEAR 1672
	YEAR 1673
	YEAR 1703
43025008	YEAR 1714
43025020	YEAR 1740
43025021	YEAR 1662
	YEAR 1705
	YEAR 1707
	YEAR 1714
	YEAR 1717
	YEAR 1726
	YEAR 1750
	YEAR 1762
43025034	YEAR 1721
43025046	YEAR 1684
	YEAR 1703
	YEAR 1729
43026013	YEAR 1695
43026039	YEAR 1707
44006016	YEAR 1714
44013035	YEAR 1728
44016015	YEAR 1771
45002029	YEAR 1660
	YEAR 1692
	YEAR 1746
	YEAR 1753
	YEAR 1762
45007012	YEAR 1664
45008051	YEAR 1661
45008052	YEAR 1695
45010002	YEAR 1661
	YEAR 1775
45010036	YEAR 1698
45010037	YEAR 1778
45010042	YEAR 1674
45012040	YEAR 1682
	YEAR 1769
	YEAR 1778
45012042	YEAR 1728

Bib.Text BkChpVrs	Sermons printed
45013005	YEAR 17--
45013016	YEAR 1690
45014013	YEAR 1750
45015007	YEAR 1680
45016002	YEAR 1660
	YEAR 1762
45016009	YEAR 1661
45018013	YEAR 1675
45020036	YEAR 1679
45020037	YEAR 1735
45023003	YEAR 1670
45023028	YEAR 1673
	YEAR 1695
	YEAR 1769
45023046	YEAR 1700
46001047	YEAR 1682
	YEAR 1753
46003001	YEAR 1706
46005024	YEAR ----
	YEAR 1686
46005028	YEAR 1741
46005035	YEAR 1685
	YEAR 1745
	YEAR 1750
46008032	YEAR 1767
46009002	YEAR 1744
46009004	YEAR 1675
	YEAR 1682
	YEAR 1694
	YEAR 1705
	YEAR 1707
	YEAR 1760
46011004	YEAR 1699
	YEAR 1699
46011011	YEAR 1661
	YEAR 1681
	YEAR 1688
	YEAR 1692
46011016	YEAR 1699
	YEAR 1712
46011021	YEAR 1685
	YEAR 1708
46011025	YEAR 1660
	YEAR 1693
	YEAR 1705
	YEAR 1730
46011026	YEAR 1712
	YEAR 1750

Bib.Text BkChpVrs	Sermons printed
46011035	YEAR 1761
	YEAR 1764
46012026	YEAR ----
	YEAR 1680
	YEAR 1700
	YEAR 1764
46012035	YEAR 1735
46013007	YEAR 1746
46013017	YEAR 1726
46013036	YEAR 1714
46014001	YEAR 1700
	YEAR 1761
46014002	YEAR 1712
	YEAR 1742
	YEAR 1744
46014028	YEAR 1714
	YEAR 1742
	YEAR 1751
46016002	YEAR 1748
46017004	YEAR 1710
	YEAR 1752
46017024	YEAR 1751
	YEAR 1753
46018011	YEAR 1741
46019030	YEAR 1727
46019040	YEAR 1673
47001018	YEAR 1703
47005020	YEAR 1702
47007017	YEAR 1679
47007056	YEAR 1663
47007057	YEAR 1736
47008002	YEAR 1698
	YEAR 1711
47009006	YEAR 1770
47009036	YEAR ----
	YEAR 1694
47010038	YEAR 1725
47011023	YEAR 1753
47013026	YEAR 1736
47013036	YEAR 1661
	YEAR 1668
	YEAR 1684
	YEAR 1689
	YEAR 1702
	YEAR 1702
	YEAR 1702
	YEAR 1702
	YEAR 1722
	YEAR 1727

Bib.Text BkChpVrs	Sermons printed
	YEAR 1738
	YEAR 1739
	YEAR 1744
	YEAR 1749
47013039	YEAR 1680
47020024	YEAR 1736
47020025	YEAR 1720
	YEAR 1746
47020031	YEAR 1722
47020032	YEAR 1720
47020037	YEAR 1711
	YEAR 1726
	YEAR 1772
	YEAR 1779
47020038	YEAR 1773
47021014	YEAR 1665
	YEAR 1768
47021026	YEAR 1779
47024016	YEAR 1678
47026017	YEAR 1709
48002007	YEAR 1692
48005002	YEAR 1660
48005005	YEAR 1660
48005007	YEAR 1731
48005012	YEAR 1660
48005020	YEAR 1773
48006005	YEAR 1660
48006008	YEAR 1719
48006011	YEAR 1660
48006023	YEAR 1660
	YEAR 1707
	YEAR 1741
	YEAR 1767
48008002	YEAR 1672
48008010	YEAR 1679
48008011	YEAR 1698
48008017	YEAR 1697
48008018	YEAR 1714
48008020	YEAR 1677
48008033	YEAR 1773
48008034	YEAR 1770
48008038	YEAR 1758
48013001	YEAR 1685
48013011	YEAR 1660
48014007	YEAR 1660
	YEAR 1761
48014008	YEAR 1738

Bib.Text BkChpVrs	Sermons printed
49001030	YEAR 1763
49002009	YEAR 1703
49003021	YEAR 1662
49004001	YEAR 1726
49004007	YEAR 1702
49006013	YEAR 1690
49007029	YEAR 1660
49007030	YEAR 1685
	YEAR 1700
49007031	YEAR 1692
49009025	YEAR 1700
49010029	YEAR 1660
49011001	YEAR 1780
49015010	YEAR 1674
	YEAR 1736
49015012	YEAR 1693
49015016	YEAR 1660
49015019	YEAR 1661
	YEAR 1701
	YEAR 1704
	YEAR 1730
49015022	YEAR 1743
49015023	YEAR 1678
49015024	YEAR 1679
49015026	YEAR 1660
	YEAR 1716
	YEAR 1750
	YEAR 1753
49015031	YEAR 1680
49015041	YEAR 1721
49015052	YEAR 1711
49015054	YEAR 1772
49015055	YEAR 16--
	YEAR 1660
	YEAR 1674
	YEAR 1688
	YEAR 1713
	YEAR 1715
	YEAR 1733
	YEAR 1768
	YEAR 1773
49015056	YEAR 1731
49015057	YEAR 1670
	YEAR 1676
	YEAR 1752
	YEAR 1766
49015058	YEAR 1672
	YEAR 1684

APPENDIX TO INDEX D TO THIRD VOLUME: SOME SETS OF OCCASION INDEX ITEMS SORTED AND ANALYZED FOR BIBLICAL TEXT REFERENCE
(Funeral)

Funeral Sermons (In present index, read columns downward.)

Bib.Text BkChpVrs	Sermons printed
50001006	YEAR 1752
50001012	YEAR 1738
	YEAR 1779
50004007	YEAR 1663
	YEAR 1716
	YEAR 1726
	YEAR 1732
50004017	YEAR 1661
50005001	YEAR 1665
	YEAR 1670
	YEAR 1678
	YEAR 1684
	YEAR 1694
	YEAR 1699
	YEAR 1706
	YEAR 1708
	YEAR 1740
	YEAR 1759
	YEAR 1769
50005002	YEAR 1660
	YEAR 1678
50005004	YEAR 1699
	YEAR 1729
	YEAR 1732
	YEAR 1755
50005006	YEAR 1722
	YEAR 1735
50005008	YEAR 1681
	YEAR 1734
	YEAR 1773
50005009	YEAR 1670
	YEAR 1702
	YEAR 1716
50005010	YEAR 1713
50006010	YEAR 1707
50006011	YEAR 1767
50008016	YEAR 1726
50010017	YEAR 1707
50013005	YEAR 1707
51006010	YEAR 1660
52001011	YEAR 1761
52002008	YEAR 1775
52005015	YEAR 1671
	YEAR 1678
53001021	YEAR 16--
	YEAR 16--
	YEAR 1672
	YEAR 1679
	YEAR 17--

Bib.Text BkChpVrs	Sermons printed
	YEAR 1702
	YEAR 1702
	YEAR 1705
	YEAR 1715
	YEAR 1726
	YEAR 1728
	YEAR 1731
	YEAR 1738
	YEAR 1756
	YEAR 1763
	YEAR 1763
	YEAR 1770
	YEAR 1773
	YEAR 1775
53001022	YEAR 1736
53001023	YEAR 1666
	YEAR 1676
	YEAR 1685
	YEAR 1695
	YEAR 1702
	YEAR 1702
	YEAR 1703
	YEAR 1704
	YEAR 1714
	YEAR 1728
	YEAR 1729
	YEAR 1749
	YEAR 1757
	YEAR 1758
	YEAR 1773
53002020	YEAR 1704
53002021	YEAR 1723
	YEAR 1758
53002027	YEAR 1726
53003008	YEAR 1738
	YEAR 1746
53003020	YEAR 1660
	YEAR 1669
	YEAR 1681
	YEAR 1695
	YEAR 17--
53003021	YEAR 1669
	YEAR 1746
53004001	YEAR 1759
53004009	YEAR 1757
54001012	YEAR 1745
54003001	YEAR 1690
	YEAR 1737

Bib.Text BkChpVrs	Sermons printed
54003003	YEAR 1717
	YEAR 1717
	YEAR 1728
54003004	YEAR 1674
55002016	YEAR 1730
55004013	YEAR 1660
	YEAR 1670
	YEAR 1682
	YEAR 1692
	YEAR 1699
	YEAR 1702
	YEAR 1711
	YEAR 1712
	YEAR 1714
	YEAR 1714
	YEAR 1722
	YEAR 1726
	YEAR 1727
	YEAR 1728
	YEAR 1755
	YEAR 1758
	YEAR 1759
	YEAR 1773
55004014	YEAR 1660
	YEAR 1662
	YEAR 1682
	YEAR 1708
	YEAR 1719
	YEAR 1755
55004016	YEAR 1777
55004017	YEAR 1688
	YEAR 1698
	YEAR 1700
	YEAR 1767
55004018	YEAR 1711
	YEAR 1736
55005003	YEAR 1660
56001010	YEAR 1740
56002016	YEAR 1730
	YEAR 1773
56002019	YEAR 1781
57001015	YEAR 1714
57003001	YEAR 1713
57006012	YEAR 1709
58001006	YEAR 1689
58001010	YEAR 1664
	YEAR 1727
	YEAR 1738
	YEAR 1775

Bib.Text BkChpVrs	Sermons printed
58001012	YEAR 1729
	YEAR 1758
	YEAR 1766
	YEAR 1769
	YEAR 1778
58002015	YEAR 1693
58003015	YEAR 1705
58004006	YEAR 1749
58004007	YEAR 1660
	YEAR 1660
	YEAR 1677
	YEAR 1681
	YEAR 1694
	YEAR 1709
	YEAR 1713
	YEAR 1714
	YEAR 1726
	YEAR 1728
	YEAR 1729
	YEAR 1734
	YEAR 1736
	YEAR 1741
	YEAR 1750
	YEAR 1754
	YEAR 1760
	YEAR 1763
	YEAR 1768
	YEAR 1771
	YEAR 1771
	YEAR 1773
58004008	YEAR 1736
	YEAR 1749
59001001	YEAR 1760
59002006	YEAR 1760
59002013	YEAR 1660
61002014	YEAR 1699
	YEAR 1750
61002015	YEAR 1660
	YEAR 1684
	YEAR 1736
61003007	YEAR 1729
61003017	YEAR 1716
61004001	YEAR 1698
61004009	YEAR 1705
	YEAR 1714
61005009	YEAR 1732
61006011	YEAR 1755

Bib.Text BkChpVrs	Sermons printed
61006012	YEAR 1719
	YEAR 1723
	YEAR 1741
	YEAR 1769
61007025	YEAR 1691
61009027	YEAR 1660
	YEAR 1671
	YEAR 1672
	YEAR 1683
	YEAR 1691
	YEAR 1692
61011001	YEAR 1660
61011004	YEAR 1673
	YEAR 1710
	YEAR 1725
	YEAR 1749
	YEAR 1749
	YEAR 1770
61011005	YEAR 1664
61011010	YEAR 1681
61011013	YEAR 1707
	YEAR 1712
	YEAR 1747
	YEAR 1766
	YEAR 1769
61011014	YEAR 1749
61011016	YEAR 1773
61011017	YEAR 1677
61011026	YEAR 1770
61011038	YEAR 1714
61012002	YEAR 1708
61012007	YEAR 1709
61012009	YEAR 1682
	YEAR 1728
61012010	YEAR 1660
61012011	YEAR 1660
	YEAR 1714
61012023	YEAR 1695
	YEAR 1699
	YEAR 1753
61013007	YEAR 1672
	YEAR 1679
	YEAR 1680
	YEAR 1699
	YEAR 1714
	YEAR 1714
	YEAR 1716
	YEAR 1718
	YEAR 1719

APPENDIX TO INDEX D TO THIRD VOLUME: SOME SETS OF OCCASION INDEX ITEMS SORTED AND ANALYZED FOR BIBLICAL TEXT REFERENCE
(Funeral)

Funeral Sermons (In present index, read columns downward.)

Bib.Text BkChpVrs	Sermons printed
	YEAR 1728
	YEAR 1728
	YEAR 1737
	YEAR 1762
	YEAR 1768
	YEAR 1770
61013014	YEAR 1664
	YEAR 1682
	YEAR 1686
	YEAR 1708
	YEAR 1731
61013017	YEAR 1762
62001002	YEAR 1706
62001004	YEAR 1660
62001012	YEAR 1692
62001027	YEAR 1724
	YEAR 1728
62004014	YEAR 1661
	YEAR 1695
	YEAR 1711
63001003	YEAR 1703
63001004	YEAR 1668
	YEAR 1770
63001022	YEAR 1761
63001024	YEAR 1728
	YEAR 1736
	YEAR 1754
63003004	YEAR 1712
63003007	YEAR 1661
63003014	YEAR 1736
63004018	YEAR 1759
63005004	YEAR 1727
	YEAR 1752
	YEAR 1766
64001012	YEAR 1731
64001013	YEAR 1733
	YEAR 1759
64001015	YEAR 1675
	YEAR 1675
64003014	YEAR 1733
65003002	YEAR 1710
65003020	YEAR 1730
68000021	YEAR 1729
69002001	YEAR 1752
69002005	YEAR 1748
69002010	YEAR 1662
	YEAR 1671
	YEAR 17--
	YEAR 1708

Bib.Text BkChpVrs	Sermons printed
	YEAR 1773
	YEAR 1774
	YEAR 1774
69003001	YEAR 1752
69004004	YEAR 1683
69007014	YEAR 1780
69010005	YEAR 17--
69014005	YEAR 1686
69014006	YEAR 1760
69014007	YEAR 1660
69014013	YEAR 1660
	YEAR 1661
	YEAR 1669
	YEAR 1673
	YEAR 1681
	YEAR 1681
	YEAR 1684
	YEAR 1684
	YEAR 1688
	YEAR 1692
	YEAR 1692
	YEAR 1693
	YEAR 1693
	YEAR 1694
	YEAR 1694
	YEAR 1695
	YEAR 1698
	YEAR 1699
	YEAR 1700
	YEAR 1704
	YEAR 1706
	YEAR 1707
	YEAR 1709
	YEAR 1711
	YEAR 1713
	YEAR 1713
	YEAR 1715
	YEAR 1715
	YEAR 1716
	YEAR 1716
	YEAR 1718
	YEAR 1720
	YEAR 1721
	YEAR 1723
	YEAR 1723
	YEAR 1725
	YEAR 1727
	YEAR 1727
	YEAR 1727

Bib.Text BkChpVrs	Sermons printed
	YEAR 1728
	YEAR 1728
	YEAR 1731
	YEAR 1732
	YEAR 1732
	YEAR 1741
	YEAR 1749
	YEAR 1754
	YEAR 1756
	YEAR 1763
	YEAR 1764
	YEAR 1774
	YEAR 1775
	YEAR 1776
	YEAR 1776
	YEAR 1780
69014015	YEAR 1671
69015003	YEAR 1774
69020006	YEAR 1695
69020013	YEAR 1709
69021004	YEAR 1760
69022003	YEAR 1767
69022012	YEAR 1660
	YEAR 1700
	YEAR 1738
69022014	YEAR 1720
69022017	YEAR 1774

Funeral: Statistical Analysis of the Set of Index Items Regarding Texts Used for This Subject or Occasion

a. Frequency (Number of records of a text)	b. Number of texts with that frequency of record	c. Number of records of those texts (c = a X b)	d. Cumulative percentage of the texts	e. Cumulative percentage of records	f. Percentage of all the records in this set (c/ Total c)
1	365	365	69.00	33.73	33.73
2	75	150	83.18	47.60	13.86
3	28	84	88.47	55.36	7.76
4	22	88	92.63	63.49	8.13
5	9	45	94.33	67.65	4.16
6	10	60	96.22	73.20	5.55
7	2	14	96.60	74.49	1.29
8	5	40	97.54	78.19	3.70
9	2	18	97.92	79.85	1.66
11	1	11	98.11	80.87	1.02
13	1	13	98.30	82.07	1.20
14	1	14	98.49	83.36	1.29
15	2	30	98.87	86.14	2.77
16	1	16	99.05	87.62	1.48
18	1	18	99.24	89.28	1.66
19	1	19	99.43	91.03	1.76
20	1	20	99.62	92.88	1.85
22	1	22	99.81	94.92	2.03
55	1	55	100.00	100.00	5.08
Totals	529	1082			100.00

Average no. of records per text within this set: M = 2.0454 Standard deviation from average: SD = 3.3698
Type/token ratio = 1/M = 0.4889 Coefficient of variation = SD/M = 1.6475
Yule's K = 60.9708 (A measure of the concentration of records upon a relatively few texts)

APPENDIX TO INDEX D TO THIRD VOLUME: SOME SETS OF OCCASION INDEX ITEMS SORTED AND ANALYZED FOR BIBLICAL TEXT REFERENCE
(Jan. 30)

January 30 Sermons (In present index, read columns downward.)

Bib. Text BkChpVrs	Sermons printed
01004010	YEAR 1664
01004015	YEAR 1680
01020011	YEAR 1745
01040020	YEAR 1750
01042021	YEAR 1706
	YEAR 1750
01049005	YEAR 1713
01049006	YEAR 1715
	YEAR 1724
02020005	YEAR 1708
	YEAR 1721
	YEAR 1738
02031018	YEAR 1753
04021005	YEAR 1748
05021008	YEAR 1732
05028049	YEAR 1781
05029024	YEAR 1724
05034005	YEAR 1683
06024015	YEAR 1757
	YEAR 1757
07009019	YEAR 1720
07017006	YEAR 1717
07019030	YEAR 1676
	YEAR 1708
	YEAR 1724
	YEAR 1724
	YEAR 1727
09001010	YEAR 1661
09010027	YEAR 1661
09012023	YEAR 1746
09012024	YEAR 1708
09012025	YEAR 1685
	YEAR 1715
	YEAR 1729
	YEAR 1730
09015023	YEAR 1752
09024004	YEAR 1722
09024005	YEAR 1661
	YEAR 1678
	YEAR 1714
09024010	YEAR 1715
09024013	YEAR 1711
09024017	YEAR 1745
09026009	YEAR 1665
	YEAR 1683
	YEAR 1714
	YEAR 1728

Bib. Text BkChpVrs	Sermons printed
09026010	YEAR 1737
09026011	YEAR 1704
	YEAR 1711
10001014	YEAR 1661
	YEAR 1683
	YEAR 1694
	YEAR 1702
	YEAR 1717
	YEAR 1746
10001016	YEAR 1714
10001017	YEAR 1677
10001018	YEAR 1662
	YEAR 1683
10001021	YEAR 1694
10001027	YEAR 1750
10002010	YEAR 1710
10002012	YEAR 1675
10015006	YEAR 1683
10018003	YEAR 1717
10021001	YEAR 1699
10024005	YEAR 1660
11012019	YEAR 1721
11021009	YEAR 1745
11021012	YEAR 1721
11021019	YEAR 1661
12006033	YEAR 1674
12008011	YEAR 1751
	YEAR 1753
12008013	YEAR 1710
	YEAR 1731
	YEAR 1737
12009031	YEAR 1701
12019003	YEAR 1751
14024025	YEAR 1665
14035024	YEAR 1661
	YEAR 1664
	YEAR 1670
	YEAR 1689
	YEAR 1691
14035025	YEAR 1724
	YEAR 1724
	YEAR 1753
15004015	YEAR 1714
15009006	YEAR 1769
16009033	YEAR 1720
18005012	YEAR 1710
18034030	YEAR 1732

Bib. Text BkChpVrs	Sermons printed
19005006	YEAR 1715
19011003	YEAR 1696
	YEAR 1712
19022012	YEAR 1662
19022028	YEAR 1778
19035011	YEAR 1733
19037037	YEAR 1676
19051003	YEAR 1710
19051017	YEAR 1703
19075001	YEAR 1689
19076010	YEAR 1770
19078005	YEAR 1738
19078008	YEAR 1731
19079008	YEAR 1685
19090015	YEAR 1692
	YEAR 1695
19094020	YEAR 1705
19099001	YEAR 1681
19109002	YEAR 1716
19122006	YEAR 1712
	YEAR 1724
	YEAR 1732
19133001	YEAR 1723
19137001	YEAR 1685
19144015	YEAR 1689
19146003	YEAR 1694
20001032	YEAR 1772
20004023	YEAR 1759
20004025	YEAR 1710
20008015	YEAR 1679
	YEAR 1688
20008018	YEAR 1686
20014034	YEAR 1752
20017014	YEAR 1711
	YEAR 1743
	YEAR 1744
	YEAR 1757
	YEAR 1762
20024021	YEAR 1698
	YEAR 1703
	YEAR 1706
	YEAR 1714
	YEAR 1715
	YEAR 1715
	YEAR 1716
	YEAR 1716
	YEAR 1722
	YEAR 1722
	YEAR 1722

Bib. Text BkChpVrs	Sermons printed
	YEAR 1727
	YEAR 1734
	YEAR 1738
	YEAR 1743
	YEAR 1746
	YEAR 1746
	YEAR 1767
	YEAR 1774
	YEAR 1779
20025004	YEAR 1747
20025005	YEAR 1730
20026002	YEAR 1728
20028002	YEAR 1685
	YEAR 1708
	YEAR 1725
20029025	YEAR 1713
20030031	YEAR 1684
	YEAR 1684
21005008	YEAR 1733
21007015	YEAR 1720
21008002	YEAR 1716
	YEAR 1751
21008004	YEAR 1713
21008014	YEAR 1707
	YEAR 171-
	YEAR 1719
	YEAR 1723
21009002	YEAR 1720
	YEAR 1726
21010020	YEAR 1661
	YEAR 1713
23003003	YEAR 1774
23011013	YEAR 1728
23014020	YEAR 1708
23019002	YEAR 1748
23019013	YEAR 1767
23026009	YEAR 1766
23032001	YEAR 1753
23033006	YEAR 1770
23037003	YEAR 1681
	YEAR 1724
	YEAR 1750
23049020	YEAR 1716
23053007	YEAR 1697
23054008	YEAR 1687
23057001	YEAR 1693
	YEAR 1712
	YEAR 1720

Bib. Text BkChpVrs	Sermons printed
23058004	YEAR 1746
23058006	YEAR 1724
24003008	YEAR 1684
24003025	YEAR 1711
24005007	YEAR 1726
24005029	YEAR 1691
24012001	YEAR 1752
24026014	YEAR 1729
24031029	YEAR 1710
24044023	YEAR 1704
25002006	YEAR 1742
25003040	YEAR 1738
25004005	YEAR 1680
25004013	YEAR 1776
25004019	YEAR 1681
25004020	YEAR 1662
	YEAR 1665
	YEAR 1681
	YEAR 1704
25005007	YEAR 1723
	YEAR 1725
	YEAR 1738
25005016	YEAR 1682
	YEAR 1694
	YEAR 1696
	YEAR 1710
	YEAR 1712
27002020	YEAR 1771
27009007	YEAR 1702
28003004	YEAR 1761
28010003	YEAR 1696
28010006	YEAR 1734
28013009	YEAR 1759
29002015	YEAR 1684
29003019	YEAR 17--
30003002	YEAR 1747
31001014	YEAR 1745
32007002	YEAR 1696
34002012	YEAR 1744
37007004	YEAR 1711
37007005	YEAR 1697
	YEAR 1720
	YEAR 1725
37008019	YEAR 1681
37012011	YEAR 1662
	YEAR 17--
40003004	YEAR 1740

January 30 Sermons (In present index, read columns downward.)

Bib.Text BkChpVrs	Sermons printed
43005004	YEAR 1717
43005009	YEAR 1776
43005010	YEAR 1710
	YEAR 1713
43006033	YEAR 1767
43007012	YEAR 1738
	YEAR 1759
	YEAR 1771
43007015	YEAR 1683
43010034	YEAR 1732
	YEAR 1770
43012025	YEAR 1716
	YEAR 1719
	YEAR 1722
	YEAR 1732
	YEAR 1739
	YEAR 1743
43019018	YEAR 1693
43021033	YEAR 1715
43021038	YEAR 1713
	YEAR 1733
43022021	YEAR 1725
	YEAR 1730
	YEAR 1732
	YEAR 1734
	YEAR 1737
	YEAR 1749
	YEAR 1764
	YEAR 1766
43023034	YEAR 1696
43023035	YEAR 1692
	YEAR 1702
43026051	YEAR 1722
43027025	YEAR 1702
44003024	YEAR 1774
44014019	YEAR 1719
45002014	YEAR 1765
45009055	YEAR 1704
45012051	YEAR 1770
45013002	YEAR 1710
45013003	YEAR 1712
45017012	YEAR 1688
45019041	YEAR 1716
45021025	YEAR 1684
45023028	YEAR 1711
	YEAR 1713
	YEAR 1729
	YEAR 1734

Bib.Text BkChpVrs	Sermons printed
45023034	YEAR 1702
46005014	YEAR 1720
46007046	YEAR 1749
46009001	YEAR 1771
46011049	YEAR 1716
46016002	YEAR 1737
46018036	YEAR 1716
46018038	YEAR 1745
46018040	YEAR 1666
46019015	YEAR 1674
	YEAR 1680
47002037	YEAR 1669
47005028	YEAR 1684
47007032	YEAR 1662
47007059	YEAR 1702
47007060	YEAR 1676
	YEAR 1682
	YEAR 1708
47008001	YEAR 1672
47014028	YEAR 1661
47015007	YEAR 1716
47017007	YEAR 1713
47022020	YEAR 17--
	YEAR 1720
47023005	YEAR 1715
	YEAR 1749
47024005	YEAR 1751
47024016	YEAR 1711
47025008	YEAR 1682
47025010	YEAR 1709
47026011	YEAR 1754
48003008	YEAR 1717
48003016	YEAR 1745
48012003	YEAR 1736
	YEAR 1758
48013001	YEAR 1681
	YEAR 1707
	YEAR 1715
	YEAR 1724
	YEAR 1732
	YEAR 1739
	YEAR 1744
	YEAR 1745
	YEAR 1747
	YEAR 1780
48013002	YEAR 1667
	YEAR 1681
	YEAR 1684
	YEAR 1710

Bib.Text BkChpVrs	Sermons printed
	YEAR 1732
48013003	YEAR 1713
	YEAR 1758
48013004	YEAR 1754
48013005	YEAR 1730
	YEAR 1771
48013007	YEAR 1749
	YEAR 1751
	YEAR 1763
48014019	YEAR 1737
49010011	YEAR 1718
	YEAR 1745
	YEAR 1747
	YEAR 1753
	YEAR 1754
	YEAR 1760
49011001	YEAR 1747
49012021	YEAR 1754
50003017	YEAR 1765
50010003	YEAR 1704
50011026	YEAR 1718
51005013	YEAR 1769
52004003	YEAR 1704
52004026	YEAR 1742
52005007	YEAR 1748
53004005	YEAR 1754
	YEAR 1764
	YEAR 1773
55004011	YEAR 1769
56003002	YEAR 1675
57002001	YEAR 1679
	YEAR 1715
	YEAR 1723
	YEAR 1726
	YEAR 1729
	YEAR 1735
	YEAR 1750
57004007	YEAR 1729
58002011	YEAR 1703
58003001	YEAR 1758
59003001	YEAR 1700
	YEAR 1710
	YEAR 1723
	YEAR 1729
	YEAR 1768
61011004	YEAR 1661
	YEAR 1740

Bib.Text BkChpVrs	Sermons printed
61012005	YEAR 1756
62001012	YEAR 1706
62001021	YEAR 1697
62003016	YEAR 1746
	YEAR 1768
62003017	YEAR 1766
62004001	YEAR 1726
	YEAR 1758
	YEAR 1769
63001008	YEAR 1720
63002013	YEAR 1710
	YEAR 1720
	YEAR 1751
	YEAR 1763
63002015	YEAR 1719
63002016	YEAR 1730
	YEAR 1743
	YEAR 1749
	YEAR 1752
	YEAR 1754
	YEAR 1755
	YEAR 1763
	YEAR 1765
63002017	YEAR 1705
	YEAR 1729
	YEAR 1741
	YEAR 1750
	YEAR 1757
	YEAR 1776
	YEAR 1777
	YEAR 1780
63002021	YEAR 1761
63003014	YEAR 1701
63004017	YEAR 1736
64002019	YEAR 1745
64003016	YEAR 1737
65003020	YEAR 1695
65004020	YEAR 1675
68000008	YEAR 1751
68000011	YEAR 1726
69002009	YEAR 1683
69002010	YEAR 1728
	YEAR 1740
69003021	YEAR 1731

January 30: Statistical Analysis of the Set of Index Items Regarding Texts Used for This Subject or Occasion

a. Frequency (Number of records of a text)	b. Number of texts with that frequency of record	c. Number of records of those texts (c = a X b)	d. Cumulative percentage of the texts	e. Cumulative percentage of records	f. Percentage of all the records in this set (c/ Total c)
1	194	194	75.49	45.54	45.54
2	27	54	85.99	58.22	12.68
3	15	45	91.83	68.78	10.56
4	6	24	94.16	74.41	5.63
5	6	30	96.50	81.46	7.04
6	3	18	97.67	85.68	4.23
7	1	7	98.05	87.32	1.64
8	3	24	99.22	92.96	5.63
10	1	10	99.61	95.31	2.35
20	1	20	100.00	100.00	4.69
Totals	257	426			100.00

Average no. of records per text within this set: M = 1.6576 Standard deviation from average: SD = 1.7926
Type/token ratio = 1/M = 0.6033 Coefficient of variation = SD/M = 1.0815
Yule's K = 60.9447 (A measure of the concentration of records upon a relatively few texts)

APPENDIX TO INDEX D TO THIRD VOLUME: SOME SETS OF OCCASION INDEX ITEMS SORTED AND ANALYZED FOR BIBLICAL TEXT REFERENCE (May 29)

May 29 Sermons (In present index, read columns downward.)

Bib.Text BkChpVrs	Sermons printed
02020005	YEAR 1732
05003007	YEAR 1681
05006012	YEAR 1671
05009006	YEAR 1749
06003007	YEAR 1684
06023011	YEAR 1764
07017006	YEAR 1662
09012022	YEAR 1733
09012024	YEAR 1759
09019014	YEAR 1715
10019009	YEAR 1708
10019014	YEAR ----
	YEAR 1661
	YEAR 1663
	YEAR 1676
	YEAR 1715
	YEAR 1729
10019030	YEAR 1703
10022002	YEAR 1698
12011019	YEAR 1725
15009009	YEAR 1742
15009013	YEAR 1717
16006016	YEAR 1727
19002001	YEAR 1685
19002006	YEAR 1670
	YEAR 1677
	YEAR 1685
19014007	YEAR 1713
19016007	YEAR 1730
19021001	YEAR 1661
19022028	YEAR 1715
19031021	YEAR 1661
19047007	YEAR 1697
19050014	YEAR 1730
	YEAR 1741
19066007	YEAR 1749
19066012	YEAR 1716
19068034	YEAR 1715
19071020	YEAR 1714
19073025	YEAR 1685
19075007	YEAR 1712
19076010	YEAR 1745
19077009	YEAR 1739
19077020	YEAR 1661
	YEAR 1662
19078070	YEAR 1721
19085001	YEAR 1711
	YEAR 1780

Bib.Text BkChpVrs	Sermons printed
19091001	YEAR 1718
19097001	YEAR 1705
	YEAR 1718
	YEAR 1733
19105005	YEAR 1694
19106007	YEAR 1744
19106012	YEAR 1766
19106048	YEAR 1730
19107002	YEAR 1747
19107039	YEAR 1755
19107043	YEAR 1725
	YEAR 1744
19111004	YEAR 1722
	YEAR 1753
19116012	YEAR 1665
19117001	YEAR 1754
19118022	YEAR 1661
	YEAR 1694
19118023	YEAR 1745
19118024	YEAR 1702
	YEAR 1729
19122006	YEAR 1728
	YEAR 1758
	YEAR 1782
19126003	YEAR 1685
	YEAR 1724
	YEAR 1746
	YEAR 1754
19130004	YEAR 1710
19147001	YEAR 1715
	YEAR 1715
20021031	YEAR 1714
20024021	YEAR 1680
	YEAR 1682
	YEAR 1746
20028002	YEAR 1685
21007010	YEAR 1680
21007016	YEAR 1743
21010017	YEAR 1660
	YEAR 1685
23001025	YEAR 1736
23001026	YEAR 1685
	YEAR 1701
	YEAR 1709
	YEAR 1711
	YEAR 1716
	YEAR 1716
	YEAR 1758

Bib.Text BkChpVrs	Sermons printed
23041017	YEAR 1721
23044024	YEAR 1757
23049023	YEAR 1680
23058012	YEAR 1661
24031013	YEAR 1747
26021027	YEAR 1661
26037003	YEAR 1730
28003005	YEAR 1684
	YEAR 1684
28007007	YEAR 1772
31001006	YEAR 1721
37008010	YEAR 1711
37012005	YEAR 16--
37012008	YEAR 1685
43005044	YEAR 1727
43008025	YEAR 1661
43021042	YEAR 1684
43022016	YEAR 1715
43022021	YEAR 1710
	YEAR 1712
43028020	YEAR 1677
46005014	YEAR 1662
	YEAR 1705
	YEAR 1736
47001009	YEAR 1735
48011033	YEAR 1724
48013001	YEAR 1684
	YEAR 1713
	YEAR 1766
48013002	YEAR 1685
48013003	YEAR 1776
48013006	YEAR 1721
48013007	YEAR 1717
48014019	YEAR 16--
	YEAR 1730
49010010	YEAR 1684
52005020	YEAR 1716
55005013	YEAR 1758
55005021	YEAR 1782
57002001	YEAR 1692
	YEAR 1716
	YEAR 1735
58003001	YEAR 1725
59003001	YEAR 1705
63002013	YEAR 1720
63002016	YEAR 1713
63002017	YEAR 1676

Bib.Text BkChpVrs	Sermons printed
64002019	YEAR 1733

APPENDIX TO INDEX D TO THIRD VOLUME: SOME SETS OF OCCASION INDEX ITEMS SORTED AND ANALYZED FOR BIBLICAL TEXT REFERENCE (May 29)

May 29: Statistical Analysis of the Set of Index Items Regarding Texts Used for This Subject or Occasion

a. Frequency (Number of records of a text)	b. Number of texts with that frequency of record	c. Number of records of those texts (c = a X b)	d. Cumulative percentage of the texts	e. Cumulative percentage of records	f. Percentage of all the records in this set (c/ Total c)
1	82	82	78.85	56.94	56.94
2	12	24	90.38	73.61	16.67
3	7	21	97.12	88.19	14.58
4	1	4	98.08	90.97	2.78
6	1	6	99.04	95.14	4.17
7	1	7	100.00	100.00	4.86
Totals	104	144			100.00

Average no. of records per text within this set: M = 1.3846 Standard deviation from average: SD = .9538
Type/token ratio = 1/M = 0.7222 Coefficient of variation = SD/M = .6889
Yule's K = 72.3380 (A measure of the concentration of records upon a relatively few texts)

Mayor Admission or Election of etc. (In present index read columns downward.)

Bib.Text BkChpVrs	Sermons printed	Bib.Text BkChpVrs	Sermons printed	Bib.Text BkChpVrs	Sermons printed	Bib.Text BkChpVrs	Sermons printed
02018021	YEAR 1718	19094016	YEAR 1692	23049023	YEAR 1737	48014019	YEAR 1717
	YEAR 1729		YEAR 1706	24006008	YEAR 1726	48014022	YEAR 1705
05001011	YEAR 1746		YEAR 1710	30005024	YEAR 1702	49004005	YEAR 1727
05004008	YEAR 1754	19122006	YEAR 1747	43005016	YEAR 1752	54003014	YEAR 1712
05016018	YEAR 1730	19122008	YEAR 1714	43012025	YEAR 1681	55004011	YEAR 1693
09002030	YEAR 1733	20004025	YEAR 1771		YEAR 1754	57002001	YEAR 1722
09012003	YEAR 1750	20011003	YEAR 1776	43020022	YEAR 1693	57002002	YEAR 1754
10023003	YEAR 1713	20016012	YEAR 1741	44009035	YEAR 1736		YEAR 1764
	YEAR 1724	20021015	YEAR 1698	45010029	YEAR 1711	59003001	YEAR 1682
	YEAR 1733	20024021	YEAR 1685	45011017	YEAR 1689	63001022	YEAR 1713
	YEAR 1736	20029002	YEAR 1692	45013024	YEAR 1725	63002013	YEAR 1711
	YEAR 1743		YEAR 1696	47008008	YEAR 1701		YEAR 1728
	YEAR 1750		YEAR 1707	47018014	YEAR 1776	63002014	YEAR 1742
	YEAR 1757		YEAR 1732	48012017	YEAR 1715	63003008	YEAR 1775
14019005	YEAR 1723		YEAR 1738	48013001	YEAR 1685	68000008	YEAR 1680
14019006	YEAR 1711		YEAR 1742		YEAR 1754		
16005019	YEAR 1724	21008011	YEAR 1700	48013003	YEAR 1726		
18029014	YEAR 1730	21012013	YEAR 1731		YEAR 1726		
18031028	YEAR 1722	23001026	YEAR 1673	48013004	YEAR 1679		
18034029	YEAR 1688		YEAR 1700		YEAR 1716		

APPENDIX TO INDEX D TO THIRD VOLUME: SOME SETS OF OCCASION INDEX ITEMS SORTED AND ANALYZED FOR BIBLICAL TEXT REFERENCE (Mayor, Adm. or El. of)

Mayor: Admission or Election of: Statistical Analysis of the Set of Index Items Regarding Texts Used for This Subject

a. Frequency (Number of records of a text)	b. Number of texts with that frequency of record	c. Number of records of those texts (c = a X b)	d. Cumulative percentage of the texts	e. Cumulative percentage of records	f. Percentage of all the records in this set (c/ Total c)
1	43	43	79.63	57.33	57.33
2	8	16	94.44	78.67	21.33
3	1	3	96.30	82.67	4.00
6	1	6	98.15	90.67	8.00
7	1	7	100.00	100.00	9.33
Totals	54	75			100.00

Average no. of records per text within this set: M = 1.3889 Standard deviation from average: SD = 1.0957
Type/token ratio = 1/M = 0.7200 Coefficient of variation = SD/M = .7889
Yule's K = 167.1111 (A measure of the concentration of records upon a relatively few texts)

November 5 Sermons (In present index, read columns downward.)

Bib.Text BkChpVrs	Sermons printed
01003015	YEAR 1693
01049006	YEAR 1682
01049007	YEAR 1705
01049014	YEAR 1772
02012014	YEAR 1747
02012024	YEAR 1781
02015002	YEAR 1702
02015009	YEAR 1684
02015011	YEAR 1684
03024020	YEAR 1750
04023023	YEAR 1694
	YEAR 1715
	YEAR 1721
	YEAR 1722
05004007	YEAR 1727
05004020	YEAR 1679
05023032	YEAR 1732
05032010	YEAR 1749
06024020	YEAR 1744
07002018	YEAR 1772
07006012	YEAR 1772
07008034	YEAR 1717
	YEAR 1740
07010011	YEAR 1720
09007012	YEAR 1682
09012023	YEAR 1710
09012024	YEAR 1758
10015031	YEAR 1678
10019003	YEAR 1680
10024014	YEAR 1697
11002046	YEAR 1772
13012016	YEAR 1772
13012023	YEAR 1772
16002010	YEAR 1772
16004011	YEAR 1717
17005013	YEAR 1716
17009020	YEAR 1704
17009027	YEAR 1720
18005012	YEAR 1702
	YEAR 1733
	YEAR 1763
19007015	YEAR 1679
19009004	YEAR 1718
19009014	YEAR 1719
19011003	YEAR 1685
19021011	YEAR 1717
19022021	YEAR 1684

Bib.Text BkChpVrs	Sermons printed
19033010	YEAR 1735
19034003	YEAR 1689
19035020	YEAR 1722
19036007	YEAR 1713
19048003	YEAR 1710
19050015	YEAR 1725
19053006	YEAR 1772
19063011	YEAR 1772
19064009	YEAR 1680
	YEAR 1693
	YEAR 1716
19068028	YEAR 1691
19075001	YEAR 1728
19076010	YEAR 17--
	YEAR 1712
19078042	YEAR 1715
19083003	YEAR 1678
19086010	YEAR 1715
19089021	YEAR 1690
19105001	YEAR 1726
19106010	YEAR 1753
19106021	YEAR 1712
19106034	YEAR 1739
19107001	YEAR 1705
19107002	YEAR 1746
19111004	YEAR 1673
	YEAR 1722
19118008	YEAR 1721
19118024	YEAR 1694
	YEAR 1696
	YEAR 1729
19122006	YEAR 1680
	YEAR 1715
	YEAR 1721
19124001	YEAR 1679
	YEAR 1680
	YEAR 1687
	YEAR 1711
	YEAR 1746
19124002	YEAR 1706
19124005	YEAR 1720
19124006	YEAR 1704
	YEAR 1710
	YEAR 1716
	YEAR 1730
19124007	YEAR 1676
	YEAR 1679
	YEAR 1711

Bib.Text BkChpVrs	Sermons printed
19126003	YEAR 1710
	YEAR 1717
19144010	YEAR 1727
	YEAR 1751
19144015	YEAR 1710
20001012	YEAR 1715
20003015	YEAR 17--
20008015	YEAR 1772
20012022	YEAR 1716
20013006	YEAR 1706
20014025	YEAR 1679
20024021	YEAR 1726
	YEAR 1732
	YEAR 1733
21005008	YEAR 1738
21010020	YEAR 1697
	YEAR 1729
23001026	YEAR 1720
23005003	YEAR 1741
23005004	YEAR 1724
23005020	YEAR 1716
	YEAR 1745
23008010	YEAR 1712
23009027	YEAR 1772
23032001	YEAR 1716
23033022	YEAR 1739
23043011	YEAR 1708
23044017	YEAR 1737
23051023	YEAR 1726
23054017	YEAR 1712
	YEAR 1725
24035006	YEAR 1675
25003039	YEAR 1721
27002044	YEAR 1730
27003028	YEAR 1661
	YEAR 1696
27004035	YEAR 1696
27007023	YEAR 1735
27010021	YEAR 1661
	YEAR 1684
30004011	YEAR 1716
30009002	YEAR 1675
32006005	YEAR 1661
	YEAR 1661
	YEAR 1689
	YEAR 1689
	YEAR 1693
	YEAR 1713

Bib.Text BkChpVrs	Sermons printed
32006009	YEAR 1743
37003001	YEAR 1679
43007012	YEAR 1730
43007015	YEAR 1707
	YEAR 1722
	YEAR 1745
43007016	YEAR 1663
	YEAR 1692
43010016	YEAR 1724
43011030	YEAR 1778
43016018	YEAR 1713
	YEAR 1728
43022021	YEAR 1682
43023007	YEAR 1715
43023015	YEAR 1737
44007013	YEAR 1746
45001074	YEAR 1684
45009051	YEAR 1715
45009054	YEAR 1678
	YEAR 1721
	YEAR 1724
	YEAR 1748
	YEAR 1774
	YEAR 1776
45009055	YEAR 1678
	YEAR 1684
	YEAR 1715
	YEAR 1715
	YEAR 1721
	YEAR 1724
	YEAR 1727
	YEAR 1735
	YEAR 1740
45011035	YEAR 1731
45014023	YEAR 1718
	YEAR 1724
46005039	YEAR 1779
46008032	YEAR 1764
46008047	YEAR 1769
46013035	YEAR 1735
46016002	YEAR 1679
	YEAR 1679
	YEAR 1692
	YEAR 1704
	YEAR 1710
	YEAR 1716
	YEAR 1718
	YEAR 1727
	YEAR 1735

Bib.Text BkChpVrs	Sermons printed
	YEAR 1737
	YEAR 1766
46016003	YEAR 1689
46018036	YEAR 1714
	YEAR 1720
47007017	YEAR 1772
47010034	YEAR 1717
47013009	YEAR 1684
47015010	YEAR 1715
47017022	YEAR 1692
47019025	YEAR 1735
	YEAR 1735
47019028	YEAR 1755
47023012	YEAR 1720
	YEAR 1737
47023014	YEAR 1715
47026009	YEAR 1719
47027012	YEAR 1737
47028005	YEAR 1675
48001008	YEAR 1685
48001015	YEAR 1681
48009004	YEAR 1705
48010002	YEAR ----
	YEAR 1713
	YEAR 1715
	YEAR 1729
	YEAR 1730
	YEAR 1735
48013001	YEAR 1680
	YEAR 1715
	YEAR 1716
	YEAR 1739
	YEAR 1741
48013002	YEAR 1674
	YEAR 1710
	YEAR 1772
48013005	YEAR 1724
49013001	YEAR 1756
49013003	YEAR 1732
49014033	YEAR 1667
50001010	YEAR 1698
	YEAR 1722
	YEAR 1726
50002017	YEAR 1715
50011026	YEAR 1709
51002018	YEAR 1747
51003028	YEAR 1729

APPENDIX TO INDEX D TO THIRD VOLUME: SOME SETS OF OCCASION INDEX ITEMS SORTED AND ANALYZED FOR BIBLICAL TEXT REFERENCE

November 5 Sermons (In present index, read columns downward.)

Bib.Text BkChpVrs	Sermons printed
51004017	YEAR 1740
51005001	YEAR 1715
51005013	YEAR 1775
52005008	YEAR 1739
56002008	YEAR 1729
56002011	YEAR 1754
57002001	YEAR 1715
57006015	YEAR 1772
58002024	YEAR 1757
58003008	YEAR 1684
59003001	YEAR 1735
61010032	YEAR 1778
61011013	YEAR 1772
63002016	YEAR 1722
	YEAR 1774
63002017	YEAR 1776
64002015	YEAR 1684
65004001	YEAR 1731
68000005	YEAR 1772
68000011	YEAR 1772
69011018	YEAR 1772
69013002	YEAR 1684
69017006	YEAR 1713
69018004	YEAR 1715
69020007	YEAR 1684

November 5: Statistical Analysis of the Set of Index Items Regarding Texts Used for This Subject or Occasion

a. Frequency (Number of records of a text)	b. Number of texts with that frequency of record	c. Number of records of those texts (c = a X b)	d. Cumulative percentage of the texts	e. Cumulative percentage of records	f. Percentage of all the records in this set (c/ Total c)
1	147	147	80.77	55.68	55.68
2	17	34	90.11	68.56	12.88
3	9	27	95.05	78.79	10.23
4	2	8	96.15	81.82	3.03
5	2	10	97.25	85.61	3.79
6	3	18	98.90	92.42	6.82
9	1	9	99.45	95.83	3.41
11	1	11	100.00	100.00	4.17
Totals	182	264			100.00

Average no. of records per text within this set: M = 1.4505 Standard deviation from average: SD = 1.2947
Type/token ratio = 1/M = 0.6894 Coefficient of variation = SD/M = .8925
Yule's K = 60.8356 (A measure of the concentration of records upon a relatively few texts)

Ordination Sermons (In present index, read columns downward.)

Bib.Text BkChpVrs	Sermons printed
09015023	YEAR 1715
20014034	YEAR 1732
24023028	YEAR 1759
26010020	YEAR 1764
27012003	YEAR 1700
37011004	YEAR 1754
43009036	YEAR 1699
	YEAR 1780
43009038	YEAR 1746
43010016	YEAR 1717
43010034	YEAR 1758
43016018	YEAR 1731
43016026	YEAR 1766
43023009	YEAR 1725
43028018	YEAR 1746
43028020	YEAR 1714
44004030	YEAR 1725
45006026	YEAR 1730
46003002	YEAR 1745
46005035	YEAR 1728
	YEAR 1742
46007046	YEAR 1769
	YEAR 1769
47001026	YEAR 1720
47002029	YEAR 1758
47013002	YEAR 1728
47013003	YEAR 1720
47014023	YEAR 1737
47020028	YEAR 1716
	YEAR 1716
47023011	YEAR 1770
48010014	YEAR 1746
48010016	YEAR 1747
48011013	YEAR 1777
49001010	YEAR 1726
49001021	YEAR 1734
	YEAR 1759
	YEAR 1759
49003006	YEAR 1727
49004001	YEAR 1715
	YEAR 1766
49004002	YEAR 1729
49012025	YEAR 1766
49012031	YEAR 1779
49014026	YEAR 1755
49016014	YEAR 1767
50001024	YEAR 1739
	YEAR 1751

Bib.Text BkChpVrs	Sermons printed
50002016	YEAR 1745
	YEAR 1750
50004001	YEAR 1720
50004005	YEAR 1679
	YEAR 1722
	YEAR 1737
	YEAR 1741
	YEAR 1742
	YEAR 1774
50005001	YEAR 1717
50005018	YEAR 1749
50005019	YEAR 1750
50011023	YEAR 1747
51005013	YEAR 1764
52004011	YEAR 1712
	YEAR 1732
53001001	YEAR 1725
53001009	YEAR 1756
	YEAR 1770
53001021	YEAR 1747
53002020	YEAR 1746
53002029	YEAR 1773
54001018	YEAR 1760
54004017	YEAR 1750
	YEAR 1773
55004008	YEAR 1736
55005012	YEAR 1731
	YEAR 1755
	YEAR 1758
	YEAR 1776
	YEAR 1778
55005021	YEAR 1719
56003001	YEAR 1765
	YEAR 1777
57001011	YEAR 1758
57002012	YEAR 1757
57003001	YEAR 1728
	YEAR 1737
57003013	YEAR 1730
57003015	YEAR 1759
57004012	YEAR 1730
57004014	YEAR 1735
57004016	YEAR 1719
	YEAR 1726
	YEAR 1734
	YEAR 1735
	YEAR 1746
	YEAR 1755

Bib.Text BkChpVrs	Sermons printed
57005022	YEAR 1707
58001013	YEAR 1721
	YEAR 1773
58002002	YEAR 1726
58002007	YEAR 1773
58002015	YEAR 1727
	YEAR 1765
58003016	YEAR 1753
58004005	YEAR 1773
58004016	YEAR 1773
59001005	YEAR 1681
59001006	YEAR 1732
59001009	YEAR 1713
59002001	YEAR 1741
59002015	YEAR 1780
61001001	YEAR 1776
61005004	YEAR 1711
61006001	YEAR 1759
61013022	YEAR 1770
62001021	YEAR 1775
63005001	YEAR 1725
63005002	YEAR 1740
67000011	YEAR 1773
68000001	YEAR 1773
68000003	YEAR 1700

APPENDIX TO INDEX D TO THIRD VOLUME: SOME SETS OF OCCASION INDEX ITEMS SORTED AND ANALYZED FOR BIBLICAL TEXT REFERENCE
(Ordination)

Ordination: Statistical Analysis of the Set of Index Items Regarding Texts Used for This Subject or Occasion

a. Frequency (Number of records of a text)	b. Number of texts with that frequency of record	c. Number of records of those texts (c = a X b)	d. Cumulative percentage of the texts	e. Cumulative percentage of records	f. Percentage of all the records in this set (c/ Total c)
1	73	73	80.22	60.33	60.33
2	14	28	95.60	83.47	23.14
3	1	3	96.70	85.95	2.48
5	1	5	97.80	90.08	4.13
6	2	12	100.00	100.00	9.92
Totals	91	121			100.00

Average no. of records per text within this set: M = 1.3279 Standard deviation from average: SD = .9024
Type/token ratio = 1/M = 0.7521 Coefficient of variation = SD/M = .6787
Yule's K = 77.8635 (A measure of the concentration of records upon a relatively few texts)

APPENDIX TO INDEX D TO THIRD VOLUME: SOME SETS OF OCCASION INDEX ITEMS SORTED AND ANALYZED FOR BIBLICAL TEXT REFERENCE (Ref.of Manners)

Reformation of Manners (In present index, read columns downward.)

Bib.Text BkChpVrs	Sermons printed
01004009	YEAR 1699
	YEAR 1724
01018019	YEAR 1732
02017011	YEAR 1753
02032026	YEAR 1699
	YEAR 1702
02037023	YEAR 1697
03005001	YEAR 1734
03019017	YEAR 1696
	YEAR 1702
04025011	YEAR 1698
05008011	YEAR 1725
05032029	YEAR 1716
06022020	YEAR 1699
06024014	YEAR 1700
07005008	YEAR 1706
09002003	YEAR 1760
09002030	YEAR 1700
	YEAR 1742
09003013	YEAR 1708
09012023	YEAR 1702
09017029	YEAR 1706
11003013	YEAR 17--
15005002	YEAR 1706
15006014	YEAR 1708
15010003	YEAR 1697
15010004	YEAR 1701
16002020	YEAR 1697
16004010	YEAR 1754
16011002	YEAR 1719
16013015	YEAR 1728
17004010	YEAR 1765
18022010	YEAR 1721
18022030	YEAR 1721
19007009	YEAR 1712
19094015	YEAR 1704
19094016	YEAR 1698
	YEAR 1716
	YEAR 1716
	YEAR 1722
	YEAR 1771
19106030	YEAR 1701
	YEAR 1727
19119053	YEAR 1711
19119059	YEAR 1697
19119136	YEAR 1700
	YEAR 1701
	YEAR 1723
19119158	YEAR 1718
19126006	YEAR 1737
19144015	YEAR 1698
20008015	YEAR 1699
20009007	YEAR 1699
20011011	YEAR 1705
20014009	YEAR 1704
20014034	YEAR 1699
	YEAR 1704
	YEAR 1731
	YEAR 1746
20016007	YEAR 1698
20021011	YEAR 1716
	YEAR 1723
20024025	YEAR 1713
20027005	YEAR 1700
20028004	YEAR 1698
	YEAR 1738
20029001	YEAR 1700
	YEAR 1700
20029024	YEAR 1704
21008011	YEAR 1707
23001006	YEAR 1698
23005020	YEAR 1738
	YEAR 1753
23049004	YEAR 1736
23051007	YEAR 1721
23059004	YEAR 1698
23059019	YEAR 1733
24005029	YEAR 1699
24018007	YEAR 1699
27012003	YEAR 1757
28002019	YEAR 1761
30005015	YEAR 1699
30005025	YEAR 1699
36002004	YEAR 1697
37003006	YEAR 1703
37003008	YEAR 1727
38003016	YEAR 1709
43005016	YEAR 1698
	YEAR 1719
	YEAR 1737
43007005	YEAR 1699
43009013	YEAR 1738
43012030	YEAR 1738
43018032	YEAR 1733
43024006	YEAR 1737
43024012	YEAR 1709
	YEAR 1737
44008034	YEAR 1760
44008038	YEAR 1710
	YEAR 1726
44010022	YEAR 1700
45009062	YEAR 1697
45015007	YEAR 1704
45020025	YEAR 1720
46003008	YEAR 1705
47010038	YEAR 1704
47026029	YEAR 1706
48002028	YEAR 1704
48013004	YEAR 1698
	YEAR 1728
48014016	YEAR 1727
48014017	YEAR 1704
49010031	YEAR 1729
49016008	YEAR 1701
50004018	YEAR 1722
51004018	YEAR 1697
	YEAR 1702
	YEAR 1713
51005007	YEAR 1709
52005011	YEAR 1699
	YEAR 1711
	YEAR 1722
	YEAR 1726
52006007	YEAR 1699
55005014	YEAR 1734
57004010	YEAR 1722
58002007	YEAR 1700
61010023	YEAR 1736
61011007	YEAR 1701
61011008	YEAR 1735
61012003	YEAR 1704
62005019	YEAR 1714
63004014	YEAR 1726
64002008	YEAR 1702
65003008	YEAR 1702
	YEAR 1705
	YEAR 1708
	YEAR 1768
68000022	YEAR 1700
	YEAR 1713
69002012	YEAR 1704
69018004	YEAR 1718

Reformation of Manners: Statistical Analysis of the Set of Index Items Regarding Texts Used for This Subject or Society

a. Frequency (Number of records of a text)	b. Number of texts with that frequency of record	c. Number of records of those texts (c = a X b)	d. Cumulative percentage of the texts	e. Cumulative percentage of records	f. Percentage of all the records in this set (c/ Total c)
1	90	90	81.82	63.38	63.38
2	13	26	93.64	81.69	18.31
3	3	9	96.36	88.03	6.34
4	3	12	99.09	96.48	8.45
5	1	5	100.00	100.00	3.52
Totals	110	142			100.00

Average no. of records per text within this set: M = 1.2909   Standard deviation from average: SD = .7304
Type/token ratio = 1/M = 0.7746   Coefficient of variation = SD/M = .5658
Yule's K = 49.5933   (A measure of the concentration of records upon a relatively few texts)

APPENDIX TO INDEX D TO THIRD VOLUME: SOME SETS OF OCCASION INDEX ITEMS SORTED AND ANALYZED FOR BIBLICAL TEXT REFERENCE
(Thanks.)

Thanksgiving Sermons (In present index, read columns downward.)

Bib.Text BkChpVrs	Sermons printed
01014018	YEAR 1762
01049005	YEAR 1731
02009016	YEAR 1707
02014013	YEAR 1713
	YEAR 1747
02015002	YEAR 1706
	YEAR 1759
02015009	YEAR 1750
02017013	YEAR 1706
02017015	YEAR 1704
02023029	YEAR 1710
02029030	YEAR 1709
02033019	YEAR 1723
04016026	YEAR 1683
04023023	YEAR 1689
	YEAR 1698
	YEAR 1702
	YEAR 1716
05003024	YEAR 1673
05004006	YEAR 1706
05004007	YEAR 1707
05004009	YEAR 1691
05010012	YEAR 1692
05011026	YEAR 1716
05012010	YEAR 1713
05017015	YEAR 1715
05028007	YEAR 1710
05030015	YEAR 1715
05032006	YEAR 1674
	YEAR 1716
05032035	YEAR 1706
05033009	YEAR 1732
05033029	YEAR 1706
	YEAR 1706
	YEAR 1715
	YEAR 1716
	YEAR 1746
	YEAR 1759
	YEAR 1759
05033046	YEAR 1746
06001004	YEAR 1759
06001009	YEAR 1746
06006026	YEAR 1689
06022022	YEAR 1686
06023008	YEAR 1702
06023011	YEAR 1765
07005001	YEAR 1703

Bib.Text BkChpVrs	Sermons printed
07005002	YEAR 1702
	YEAR 1746
	YEAR 1746
	YEAR 1775
07005003	YEAR 1705
07005009	YEAR 1746
07005012	YEAR 1704
	YEAR 1704
	YEAR 1704
	YEAR 1705
07005013	YEAR 1706
07005015	YEAR 1732
07005021	YEAR 1704
07005031	YEAR 1685
	YEAR 1732
07006014	YEAR 1746
07009015	YEAR 1746
09002009	YEAR 1660
09007012	YEAR 1716
	YEAR 1759
09010024	YEAR 1660
	YEAR 1660
	YEAR 1715
09012007	YEAR 1746
09012023	YEAR 1705
09012024	YEAR 1703
	YEAR 1710
	YEAR 1715
	YEAR 1746
	YEAR 1746
	YEAR 1746
09017037	YEAR 1738
10002026	YEAR 1763
10003001	YEAR 1695
10005003	YEAR 1707
10010012	YEAR 1715
10015011	YEAR 1682
	YEAR 1685
10015012	YEAR 1683
10018028	YEAR 1683
	YEAR 1685
	YEAR 1704
	YEAR 1716
10018032	YEAR 1716
	YEAR 1746
10019014	YEAR 1660
	YEAR 1660
	YEAR 1660

Bib.Text BkChpVrs	Sermons printed
10019015	YEAR 1660
10019030	YEAR 1660
	YEAR 1660
10020001	YEAR 1716
10022024	YEAR 1683
10022038	YEAR 1696
	YEAR 1746
10022044	YEAR 1716
	YEAR 1720
10022047	YEAR 1696
10022048	YEAR 1746
	YEAR 1746
10022051	YEAR 1684
10023010	YEAR 1704
11001005	YEAR 1685
11001039	YEAR 1714
11008066	YEAR 1746
11010009	YEAR 1715
11020011	YEAR 1737
12011012	YEAR 1660
12013025	YEAR 1715
12014008	YEAR 1746
12020019	YEAR 1713
13016008	YEAR 1706
13016034	YEAR 1707
13029011	YEAR 1708
13029022	YEAR 1715
14009008	YEAR 1689
	YEAR 1697
14015002	YEAR 1763
14015014	YEAR 1769
14016009	YEAR 1746
14020026	YEAR 1738
14020027	YEAR 1709
	YEAR 1746
	YEAR 1746
	YEAR 1746
	YEAR 1759
14020028	YEAR 1706
14028009	YEAR 1690
14032007	YEAR 1704
15003011	YEAR 1695
15004001	YEAR 1683
15009013	YEAR 1735
16005013	YEAR 1715
16005018	YEAR 1772
16009017	YEAR 1696

Bib.Text BkChpVrs	Sermons printed
17004014	YEAR 1704
17008017	YEAR 1746
19002001	YEAR 1685
	YEAR 1696
19002003	YEAR 1694
19002004	YEAR 1706
19002011	YEAR 1710
	YEAR 1716
	YEAR 1746
	YEAR 1746
19004004	YEAR 1716
19005011	YEAR 1709
19007014	YEAR 1759
19009016	YEAR 1696
	YEAR 1776
19010002	YEAR 1709
19010010	YEAR 1683
19010014	YEAR 1716
19018001	YEAR 1666
19018047	YEAR 1696
	YEAR 1716
	YEAR 1748
	YEAR 1760
19018048	YEAR 1683
19018049	YEAR 1683
	YEAR 1703
	YEAR 1716
19018050	YEAR 1668
	YEAR 1683
	YEAR 1696
	YEAR 1706
	YEAR 1716
	YEAR 1746
19018051	YEAR 1706
19020005	YEAR 1696
19020006	YEAR 1706
	YEAR 1708
	YEAR 1708
19020007	YEAR 1706
	YEAR 1709
19021001	YEAR 1660
	YEAR 1684
19021003	YEAR 1706
	YEAR 1715
19021011	YEAR 1716
	YEAR 1746
19022023	YEAR 1757

Bib.Text BkChpVrs	Sermons printed
19025002	YEAR 1697
19027003	YEAR 1759
19027006	YEAR 1702
	YEAR 1760
19028007	YEAR 1716
19029010	YEAR 1763
19029011	YEAR 1697
	YEAR 1713
	YEAR 1763
19030003	YEAR 1699
19031023	YEAR 1709
19033001	YEAR 1695
	YEAR 1716
	YEAR 1716
19033010	YEAR 1749
19034001	YEAR 1777
19034003	YEAR 1723
	YEAR 1759
19034019	YEAR 1683
19044003	YEAR 1759
19046007	YEAR 1704
19046010	YEAR 1685
	YEAR 1713
19047006	YEAR 1713
19047007	YEAR 1704
	YEAR 1759
19050014	YEAR 1704
	YEAR 1772
19050015	YEAR 1715
	YEAR 1745
19050023	YEAR 1715
	YEAR 1734
	YEAR 1759
19052001	YEAR 1703
	YEAR 1746
19054006	YEAR 1665
19055019	YEAR 1716
19058011	YEAR 1704
19064005	YEAR 1683
19064009	YEAR 1683
	YEAR 1703
	YEAR 1706
19065001	YEAR 1716
19065007	YEAR 1716
	YEAR 1720
	YEAR 1770
19065011	YEAR 1706

APPENDIX TO INDEX D TO THIRD VOLUME: SOME SETS OF OCCASION INDEX ITEMS SORTED AND ANALYZED FOR BIBLICAL TEXT REFERENCE
(Thanks.)

Thanksgiving Sermons (In present index, read columns downward.)

Bib.Text BkChpVrs	Sermons printed
19066013	YEAR 1746
19067002	YEAR 1744
19068001	YEAR 1704
	YEAR 1706
19068019	YEAR 1716
19068020	YEAR 1716
19068028	YEAR 17--
	YEAR 1704
19068030	YEAR 1712
19071017	YEAR 1746
19072004	YEAR 1707
19072018	YEAR 1715
19073001	YEAR 1684
19075001	YEAR 1660
	YEAR 1696
	YEAR 17--
	YEAR 1746
19076010	YEAR ----
	YEAR 1684
	YEAR 1699
	YEAR 1706
	YEAR 1719
	YEAR 1763
19076011	YEAR 1702
19077014	YEAR 1689
	YEAR 1710
19085001	YEAR 1689
19085008	YEAR 1713
	YEAR 1713
	YEAR 1713
	YEAR 1749
	YEAR 1763
19086012	YEAR 1696
19091015	YEAR 1664
19092004	YEAR 1714
19095001	YEAR 1720
	YEAR 1759
19096008	YEAR 1759
19096010	YEAR 1691
19097001	YEAR 1703
	YEAR 1707
	YEAR 1729
	YEAR 1746
	YEAR 1759
	YEAR 1763
19098001	YEAR 1704
	YEAR 1708
	YEAR 1716
	YEAR 1754

Bib.Text BkChpVrs	Sermons printed
19100005	YEAR 1722
19102013	YEAR 1689
19103010	YEAR 1704
19103013	YEAR 1689
19105004	YEAR 1702
19105045	YEAR 1716
	YEAR 1746
19106007	YEAR 1704
19106012	YEAR 1748
19106021	YEAR 1708
19106043	YEAR 1719
19107001	YEAR 1746
	YEAR 1763
19107002	YEAR 1689
	YEAR 1691
	YEAR 1716
	YEAR 1737
	YEAR 1746
	YEAR 1746
19107008	YEAR 1683
	YEAR 1697
	YEAR 1707
19107021	YEAR 1706
19107033	YEAR 1750
19107039	YEAR 1743
19107042	YEAR 1710
19107043	YEAR 1707
	YEAR 1746
19108013	YEAR 1759
19111004	YEAR 1709
19115001	YEAR 1702
19115017	YEAR 1716
19116001	YEAR 1697
19116007	YEAR 1746
19116011	YEAR 1698
19116012	YEAR 1735
	YEAR 1748
19118001	YEAR 1703
19118006	YEAR 1717
19118008	YEAR 1720
19118015	YEAR 1758
19118022	YEAR 1660
	YEAR 167-
19118023	YEAR 1689
	YEAR 1745
19118024	YEAR 1704
	YEAR 1707

Bib.Text BkChpVrs	Sermons printed
19118027	YEAR 1758
	YEAR 1760
19119078	YEAR 1696
19122006	YEAR 1696
	YEAR 1710
	YEAR 1716
	YEAR 1724
	YEAR 1749
	YEAR 1759
	YEAR 1763
	YEAR 1772
	YEAR 1774
19122007	YEAR 1697
	YEAR 1713
	YEAR 1749
19124001	YEAR 1689
	YEAR 1739
	YEAR 1746
19124002	YEAR 1759
19124005	YEAR 1733
19124006	YEAR 1685
	YEAR 1696
19126001	YEAR 1660
19126002	YEAR 1710
19126003	YEAR 1660
	YEAR 1698
	YEAR 1704
	YEAR 1719
	YEAR 1746
	YEAR 1758
	YEAR 1759
	YEAR 1761
19126004	YEAR 1759
19126005	YEAR 1715
19129005	YEAR 1746
19130004	YEAR 1723
19132007	YEAR 1697
19132017	YEAR 1696
19132018	YEAR 1716
	YEAR 1746
19133001	YEAR 1689
	YEAR 1707
	YEAR 1707
	YEAR 1707
	YEAR 1707
	YEAR 1715
	YEAR 1731

Bib.Text BkChpVrs	Sermons printed
19135019	YEAR 1683
19144009	YEAR 1683
	YEAR 1693
	YEAR 1722
	YEAR 1743
19144010	YEAR 1690
	YEAR 1692
	YEAR 1697
	YEAR 17--
	YEAR 1704
	YEAR 1706
	YEAR 1707
	YEAR 1709
	YEAR 1713
	YEAR 1714
	YEAR 1749
	YEAR 1749
	YEAR 1771
19144015	YEAR 1704
	YEAR 1710
19145002	YEAR 1734
19145016	YEAR 1716
19146001	YEAR 1661
	YEAR 1702
19147001	YEAR 1716
	YEAR 1741
	YEAR 1746
19147006	YEAR 1713
19147012	YEAR 1679
	YEAR 1703
	YEAR 1749
19147013	YEAR 1751
19147020	YEAR 1674
	YEAR 1759
19149006	YEAR 1707
19150002	YEAR 1714
20001010	YEAR 1683
20011021	YEAR 1685
20016007	YEAR 1708
	YEAR 1709
	YEAR 1713
	YEAR 1763
20016020	YEAR 1698
20020028	YEAR 1691
20021030	YEAR 1697
20024021	YEAR 1683
	YEAR 1685
	YEAR 1746

Bib.Text BkChpVrs	Sermons printed
20029002	YEAR 1660
	YEAR 1691
21007014	YEAR 1709
21009011	YEAR 17--
21010017	YEAR 1660
21010020	YEAR 1683
	YEAR 1683
	YEAR 1696
23005001	YEAR ----
23005011	YEAR 1746
23007005	YEAR 1746
23008009	YEAR 1717
23011013	YEAR 1705
	YEAR 1710
23012002	YEAR 1746
23012007	YEAR 1738
23014016	YEAR 1697
	YEAR 1709
23024016	YEAR 1712
	YEAR 1772
23025009	YEAR 1746
	YEAR 1759
23026004	YEAR 1692
23026009	YEAR 1772
23026015	YEAR 1738
23027008	YEAR 1746
23033006	YEAR 1715
23033022	YEAR 1706
23038018	YEAR 1723
23038019	YEAR 1696
23043003	YEAR 1715
23045006	YEAR 1764
23045007	YEAR 1713
23049023	YEAR 1707
	YEAR 1716
23052007	YEAR 1697
23052010	YEAR 1703
23052013	YEAR 1761
23054008	YEAR 1715
23057019	YEAR 1706
	YEAR 1713
23059007	YEAR 1708
23060010	YEAR 1690
23066010	YEAR 1696
24007004	YEAR 1714
24008011	YEAR 1660
24009023	YEAR 1735

APPENDIX TO INDEX D TO THIRD VOLUME: SOME SETS OF OCCASION INDEX ITEMS SORTED AND ANALYZED FOR BIBLICAL TEXT REFERENCE (Thanks.)

Thanksgiving Sermons (In present index, read columns downward.)

Bib.Text BkChpVrs	Sermons printed
24009024	YEAR 1759
24016014	YEAR 1712
24024016	YEAR 1710
24033010	YEAR 1749
24050022	YEAR 1704
25002022	YEAR 1723
25003022	YEAR 1775
26017015	YEAR 1716
26020044	YEAR 1694
26021027	YEAR 1705
26036022	YEAR 1766
26036032	YEAR 1737
	YEAR 1746
	YEAR 1759
26037022	YEAR 1707
	YEAR 1707
	YEAR 1707
	YEAR 1707
	YEAR 1707
	YEAR 1707
	YEAR 1707
	YEAR 1707
	YEAR 1707
	YEAR 1707
27002010	YEAR 1759
27004009	YEAR 1698
27006010	YEAR 1660
29002023	YEAR 1716
31003010	YEAR 1723
31004004	YEAR ----
	YEAR 17--
33001015	YEAR 1713
	YEAR 1749
37002005	YEAR 1679
37003006	YEAR 1679
43005006	YEAR 1770
43005009	YEAR 1713
	YEAR 1763
43007015	YEAR 1707
43008026	YEAR 1688
43021031	YEAR 1685
43023029	YEAR 1728
43026052	YEAR 1686
45002014	YEAR 1698
45005026	YEAR 1689
45009055	YEAR 1721
45013001	YEAR 1761
	YEAR 1767

Bib.Text BkChpVrs	Sermons printed
45013005	YEAR 1717
45017015	YEAR 1709
45017017	YEAR 1705
	YEAR 1709
	YEAR 1746
	YEAR 1746
45019014	YEAR 1683
45019027	YEAR 1746
46005014	YEAR 1713
	YEAR 1713
	YEAR 1723
	YEAR 1746
	YEAR 1746
	YEAR 1749
	YEAR 1771
46010016	YEAR 1707
46016002	YEAR 1714
46018036	YEAR 1728
47007026	YEAR 1707
	YEAR 1749
47024002	YEAR 1713
48001020	YEAR 1697
48003007	YEAR 1685
48007025	YEAR 1660
48013001	YEAR 1706
48013002	YEAR 1683
48013004	YEAR 1713
48014019	YEAR 1707
	YEAR 1716
	YEAR 1738
49010010	YEAR 1683
49013006	YEAR 1716
50001009	YEAR 1727
	YEAR 1771
50001010	YEAR 1731
50003017	YEAR 1746
50011026	YEAR 1716
51001008	YEAR 1728
51004018	YEAR 1738
52001022	YEAR 1728
52005020	YEAR 1716
	YEAR 1716
	YEAR 1718
	YEAR 1759
	YEAR 1771
	YEAR 1774
53004006	YEAR 1732

Bib.Text BkChpVrs	Sermons printed
54001018	YEAR 1728
54003015	YEAR 1696
	YEAR 1737
	YEAR 1747
54004002	YEAR 1716
55005012	YEAR 1715
55005013	YEAR 1696
55005018	YEAR 1714
56003016	YEAR 1749
57002001	YEAR 1706
	YEAR 1715
	YEAR 1735
58003001	YEAR 1696
59001016	YEAR 1695
59003001	YEAR 1684
	YEAR 1713
	YEAR 1716
63002013	YEAR 1685
63002015	YEAR 1684
63002017	YEAR 1715
	YEAR 1750
63002020	YEAR 1683
63003013	YEAR 1706
64003016	YEAR 1675
68000011	YEAR 1717
69006002	YEAR 1762
69015003	YEAR 1699
69018020	YEAR 1772
69019003	YEAR 1706

Thanksgiving: Statistical Analysis of the Set of Index Items Regarding Texts Used for This Subject or Occasion

a. Frequency (Number of records of a text)	b. Number of texts with that frequency of record	c. Number of records of those texts (c = a X b)	d. Cumulative percentage of the texts	e. Cumulative percentage of records	f. Percentage of all the records in this set (c/ Total c)
1	272	272	72.53	45.48	45.48
2	56	112	87.47	64.21	18.73
3	21	63	93.07	74.75	10.54
4	11	44	96.00	82.11	7.36
5	2	10	96.53	83.78	1.67
6	6	36	98.13	89.80	6.02
7	3	21	98.93	93.31	3.51
8	1	8	99.20	94.65	1.34
9	1	9	99.47	96.15	1.51
10	1	10	99.73	97.83	1.67
13	1	13	100.00	100.00	2.17
Totals	375	598			100.00

Average no. of records per text within this set: M = 1.5947 Standard deviation from average: SD = 1.3994
Type/token ratio = 1/M = 0..6271 Coefficient of variation = SD/M = .8776
Yule's K = 30.4806 (A measure of the concentration of records upon a relatively few texts)

APPENDIX TO INDEX D TO THIRD VOLUME: SOME SETS OF OCCASION INDEX ITEMS SORTED AND ANALYZED FOR BIBLICAL TEXT REFERENCE (Visit.)

Visitation Sermons (In present index, read columns downward.)

Bib.Text BkChpVrs	Sermons printed
01003006	YEAR 1751
02020005	YEAR 1727
02020007	YEAR 1723
03026002	YEAR 1704
05017012	YEAR 1719
05028002	YEAR 1776
05031024	YEAR 1753
05032029	YEAR 1749
05033008	YEAR 1737
09003013	YEAR 1742
10012007	YEAR 1757
11003009	YEAR 1778
11013001	YEAR 1763
11018021	YEAR 1663
	YEAR 1686
16005012	YEAR 1764
18027005	YEAR 1734
19001003	YEAR 1663
19014001	YEAR 1725
19050023	YEAR 1698
19051012	YEAR 1738
19072010	YEAR 1724
19073013	YEAR 1715
19076011	YEAR 1660
19101002	YEAR 1745
	YEAR 1777
19118024	YEAR 1684
19119158	YEAR 1712
19122006	YEAR 1691
	YEAR 1692
	YEAR 1712
19123003	YEAR 1681
19133001	YEAR 1713
	YEAR 1713
	YEAR 1723
20008012	YEAR 1765
20010009	YEAR 1708
20014024	YEAR 1773
20024021	YEAR 1774
21008002	YEAR 1710
23049001	YEAR 1723
23060013	YEAR 1664
26033032	YEAR 1742
27005017	YEAR 1728
27012003	YEAR 1703
28009007	YEAR 1663
37011007	YEAR 1679

Bib.Text BkChpVrs	Sermons printed
38002007	YEAR ----
	YEAR 1697
43003009	YEAR 1718
43004023	YEAR 1772
43005010	YEAR 1737
	YEAR 1769
43005013	YEAR 1782
43005014	YEAR 1738
	YEAR 1778
43005016	YEAR 1669
	YEAR 1676
	YEAR 1748
43005048	YEAR 1751
43006009	YEAR 1680
43006010	YEAR 1758
43007022	YEAR 1705
43007028	YEAR 1747
43010016	YEAR 1708
	YEAR 1730
	YEAR 1743
	YEAR 1745
	YEAR 1760
	YEAR 1768
43010034	YEAR 1711
43011016	YEAR 1776
43013034	YEAR 1781
43013057	YEAR 1711
43015006	YEAR 1731
43015009	YEAR 1689
43018007	YEAR 1775
43018017	YEAR 1708
43021021	YEAR 1769
43022021	YEAR 1716
	YEAR 1719
43028020	YEAR 1737
	YEAR 1740
44004024	YEAR 17--
44004034	YEAR 1781
44009050	YEAR 1672
	YEAR 1675
	YEAR 1780
44016015	YEAR 1766
44016016	YEAR 1735
44016020	YEAR 1747
45004032	YEAR 1778
45006026	YEAR 1741
45010016	YEAR 1709

Bib.Text BkChpVrs	Sermons printed
45010025	YEAR 1720
45011001	YEAR 1705
45011035	YEAR 1750
45012001	YEAR 1690
45012042	YEAR 1714
45012057	YEAR 1746
45014033	YEAR 1729
45020014	YEAR 1685
45022029	YEAR 1728
45022035	YEAR 1771
45024027	YEAR 1726
46001001	YEAR 1747
46001014	YEAR 1719
46001046	YEAR 1735
46002016	YEAR 1769
46004023	YEAR 1676
	YEAR 1747
	YEAR 1764
46004048	YEAR 1733
46005039	YEAR 1755
46006014	YEAR 1742
46006044	YEAR 1770
46006066	YEAR 1723
46007017	YEAR 1760
	YEAR 1779
	YEAR 1782
46010025	YEAR 1767
46012037	YEAR 1730
46012046	YEAR 1760
46015008	YEAR 1741
46015016	YEAR 1736
46016008	YEAR 1764
46018036	YEAR 1708
	YEAR 1716
46020021	YEAR 1714
46020029	YEAR 1751
46021015	YEAR 1691
46021017	YEAR 1751
47002017	YEAR 1680
47002042	YEAR 1683
47004029	YEAR 1720
47005038	YEAR 1778
47005042	YEAR 1765
	YEAR 1765
47008017	YEAR 1705
47010004	YEAR 1748
47011024	YEAR 1686

Bib.Text BkChpVrs	Sermons printed
47015028	YEAR 1663
47015036	YEAR 1676
47015041	YEAR 1705
47016017	YEAR 1715
47018003	YEAR 1700
47020016	YEAR 1684
47020024	YEAR 1766
47020026	YEAR 1763
47020028	YEAR 1669
	YEAR 1707
47020032	YEAR 1714
47026009	YEAR 1666
48002004	YEAR 1744
48002014	YEAR 1777
	YEAR 1777
48003008	YEAR 1689
48003031	YEAR 1728
48009028	YEAR 1772
48010003	YEAR 1764
48010015	YEAR 1708
	YEAR 1713
	YEAR 1717
	YEAR 1724
48010017	YEAR 1747
48012001	YEAR 1717
48013001	YEAR 1682
48013005	YEAR 1718
48014001	YEAR 1773
48014003	YEAR 1689
48014005	YEAR 1771
48014019	YEAR 1679
48014023	YEAR 1689
49001010	YEAR 1691
	YEAR 1710
	YEAR 1714
49001023	YEAR 1684
49003004	YEAR 1709
49003010	YEAR 1718
49004001	YEAR 1672
	YEAR 1678
	YEAR 17--
	YEAR 1701
	YEAR 1708
	YEAR 1742
49004002	YEAR 1717
	YEAR 1717
	YEAR 1759

Bib.Text BkChpVrs	Sermons printed
49004013	YEAR 1710
49004021	YEAR 1686
49008001	YEAR 1760
49009016	YEAR 1731
	YEAR 1775
49011016	YEAR 1676
49011023	YEAR 1736
49011034	YEAR 1662
	YEAR 1686
49012004	YEAR 1721
49012007	YEAR 1689
49012011	YEAR 1753
49012031	YEAR 1725
49013013	YEAR 1709
49014012	YEAR 1698
	YEAR 1719
49014026	YEAR 1726
49014033	YEAR 1770
49014040	YEAR 1669
	YEAR 1674
	YEAR 1684
49015010	YEAR 1700
	YEAR 1717
49015058	YEAR 1706
50002016	YEAR 1736
50004002	YEAR 1712
	YEAR 1750
50004005	YEAR 1716
	YEAR 1751
	YEAR 1780
50004007	YEAR 1698
50005001	YEAR 1722
50005018	YEAR 1684
50005019	YEAR 1692
50005020	YEAR 1663
	YEAR 1672
	YEAR 1674
50006001	YEAR 1716
50006003	YEAR 1705
	YEAR 1726
	YEAR 1735
	YEAR 1772
50006006	YEAR 1764
50007001	YEAR 1662
50010008	YEAR 1748
50012014	YEAR 1684
51001010	YEAR 1707

APPENDIX TO INDEX D TO THIRD VOLUME: SOME SETS OF OCCASION INDEX ITEMS SORTED AND ANALYZED FOR BIBLICAL TEXT REFERENCE (Visit.)

Visitation Sermons (In present index, read columns downward.)

Bib.Text BkChpVrs	Sermons printed
51004018	YEAR 1704
	YEAR 1718
	YEAR 1721
	YEAR 1728
51006006	YEAR 1716
51006014	YEAR 1753
52002012	YEAR 1733
52003008	YEAR 1674
52004003	YEAR 17--
52004011	YEAR 1701
	YEAR 1719
	YEAR 1754
52004012	YEAR 1692
52004014	YEAR 1712
	YEAR 1754
52005016	YEAR 1698
53001010	YEAR 1730
53001015	YEAR 1683
53001027	YEAR 1703
53002001	YEAR 1704
53002005	YEAR 1663
	YEAR 1744
53002006	YEAR 1729
	YEAR 1756
53002021	YEAR 1741
53003015	YEAR 1730
53003016	YEAR 1729
53004005	YEAR 1715
54001018	YEAR 1704
54001028	YEAR 1717
54002008	YEAR 1708
	YEAR 1724
	YEAR 1764
54004017	YEAR 1675
	YEAR 1705
	YEAR 1760
55003008	YEAR 1669
55005014	YEAR 1673
55005017	YEAR 1699
55005021	YEAR 1737
	YEAR 1741
	YEAR 1777
57001015	YEAR 1756
57002001	YEAR 1722
57002002	YEAR 1706
57003009	YEAR 1709
57003014	YEAR 1763

Bib.Text BkChpVrs	Sermons printed
57003016	YEAR 1721
57004006	YEAR 1776
57004012	YEAR 1671
57004015	YEAR 1681
	YEAR 1686
	YEAR 1782
57004016	YEAR 1674
	YEAR 1683
	YEAR 1693
	YEAR 1694
	YEAR 1704
	YEAR 1705
	YEAR 1708
	YEAR 1711
	YEAR 1746
	YEAR 1756
	YEAR 1764
	YEAR 1765
57006003	YEAR 1716
	YEAR 1725
58001005	YEAR 1712
58001010	YEAR 1759
58002019	YEAR 1742
58002023	YEAR 1738
58002024	YEAR 1720
58003016	YEAR 1722
	YEAR 1745
	YEAR 1755
58003017	YEAR 1729
58004002	YEAR 1780
58004005	YEAR 1677
59002001	YEAR 1663
59002007	YEAR 1723
59002015	YEAR 1682
	YEAR 1707
	YEAR 1709
	YEAR 1712
	YEAR 1718
	YEAR 1726
	YEAR 1741
	YEAR 1749
59003001	YEAR 1706
	YEAR 1716
	YEAR 1740
	YEAR 1766
59003010	YEAR 1673
61005004	YEAR 1709

Bib.Text BkChpVrs	Sermons printed
61010023	YEAR 1750
	YEAR 1766
61012014	YEAR 1705
61013007	YEAR 1717
61013008	YEAR 1719
61013017	YEAR ----
	YEAR 1663
	YEAR 1686
	YEAR 1708
	YEAR 1714
	YEAR 1716
	YEAR 1746
62001008	YEAR 1721
62003001	YEAR 1713
62003017	YEAR 1720
62005004	YEAR 1776
63001008	YEAR 1744
63002015	YEAR 1727
63003015	YEAR 1721
63004011	YEAR 1744
63005001	YEAR 1761
64001005	YEAR 1754
64001011	YEAR 1708
64001019	YEAR 1750
64003003	YEAR 17--
	YEAR 1737
64003015	YEAR 1777
64003018	YEAR 1722
65004001	YEAR 1698
68000003	YEAR 1674
	YEAR 1716
	YEAR 1738
	YEAR 1760
69001016	YEAR 1675
69003017	YEAR 1732
69005013	YEAR 1729

APPENDIX TO INDEX D TO THIRD VOLUME: SOME SETS OF OCCASION INDEX ITEMS SORTED AND ANALYZED FOR BIBLICAL TEXT REFERENCE (Visitation)

Visitation: Statistical Analysis of the Set of Index Items Regarding Texts Used for This Subject or Occasion

a. Frequency (Number of records of a text)	b. Number of texts with that frequency of record	c. Number of records of those texts (c = a X b)	d. Cumulative percentage of the texts	e. Cumulative percentage of records	f. Percentage of all the records in this set (c/ Total c)
1	211	211	81.15	57.81	57.81
2	22	44	89.62	69.86	12.05
3	17	51	96.15	83.84	13.97
4	5	20	98.08	89.32	5.48
6	2	12	98.85	92.60	3.29
7	1	7	99.23	94.52	1.92
8	1	8	99.62	96.71	2.19
12	1	12	100.00	100.00	3.29
Totals	260	365			100.00

Average no. of records per text within this set: M = 1.4038   Standard deviation from average: SD = 1.1579
Type/token ratio = 1/M = 0.7123   Coefficient of variation = SD/M = .8248
Yule's K = 37.2302   (A measure of the concentration of records upon a relatively few texts)

(INDEXES TO THIRD VOLUME)

INDEX E: SUBJECTS OR OCCASIONS OF SERMONS THAT ARE NOT ENTERED IN THE PRECEDING INDEXES A, B, C, OR D

Contents of This Index:

The following list gives John Cooke's abbreviated descriptions of the subjects or occasions of sermons not classified by means of the preceding indexes. In effect, it lets the remaining entries find their own classifications by means of the principle of key-word-in-context indexing, which is sometimes known by the acronym K W I C indexing. In its application here, this principle results in an alphabetically ordered listing of all words and abbreviations that John Cooke used in describing these sermons in the "Occasion or Subject" segment of the entries that are printed in the Third Volume of the present edition. Within the index below, every key word or abbreviation is followed by the context in which it appears in that segment of Cooke's entry,then by the name of the author and the date of the publication that the entry concerns, and finally by the code number of the biblical text associated with it.

Three limitations of this index should be noted: (1) No entry that is indexed in the preceding indexes A, C, or D is listed in it, and from Index B only a very few are included. (2) The index gives no more than fifteen characters from John Cooke's abbreviated description of the occasion or subject of a sermon, and key words that occur after the fifteenth character are likewise excluded. This limitation affects less than a half of one per cent of the entries, and so does not greatly falsify the statement that every word or abbreviation from Cooke's "Occasion or Subject" segment of these entries is listed in the index. (3) The prepositions "in", "on", and "of", the article "the", and the abbreviations "&c.", "o.", and "s." have also been deleted from the key word list except in the few cases where these words begin John Cooke's descriptions of the occasions or subjects.

Underlining and Abbreviations:

In this as in the other indexes and the lists to which they refer, the underlining of an author's name represents the italic type which Cooke used to indicate that an author was a Nonconformist rather than an Anglican.

Cooke's Table of Abbreviations is printed in the prefatory matter to the Third Volume of the present edition. However, Cooke's Table is not at all complete. Fortunately, the significance of most of his abbreviations is unfolded by the contexts within which they appear in this index. The reader will usually be able to verify his own interpretation of an abbreviation by proceeding from a single-sermon entry ("ss." entry) containing it in the Third Volume to the more complete entry in the Fifth Volume. Reference to the biblical text of a sermon will likewise serve to verify a reader's interpretation of an abbreviated title.

INDEXES TO THIRD VOLUME: E: KEYWORD-IN-CONTEXT INDEX OF OTHER SUBJECTS OR OCCASIONS

Keyword	In its Context	Author	Year	BkChpVrs
A	A bleed. Sav.	DYER	1676	49005007
A	A reckoning.	ELLIS	1704	45016002
A	A sign Wisd.	HORTON	1679	49001022
A	A wor.mind.	DORRINGTON	1705	53003019
A	A.& P.o. S. S.	NEAL	1757	58003016
A	A. Excise.	WYNER	1733	45002001
A	A. Gen. Sick.	ANONYMOUS	1712	19091005
A	A. O.& N. T.	GILL	1773	47026022
A	A.d. A.a. Xt.	DOUGHTY	1761	49015022
A	A.d.t.s. X's.d	ORTON	1776	46008056
A	A.f.m.f. G.a.	PARSONS	1774	50003006
A	A.m. Pr. Ir. S	SECKER	1766	20009006
A	A.s.	SOUTH	1724	45021015
A	A King.	BRAGGE	1702	45014018
A	A Priest.	HARRIS	1724	19110004
A	A Prophet.	HARRIS	1724	05018015
A	Ab.f.a.ev. A.	PIERCE	1679	55005022
A	Ab.f.a.ev. A.	ATTERBURY	1699	55005022
A	Ab.f.a.ev. A.	HOPKINS	1700	55005022
A	Ab.f.a.ev. A.	SMALRIDGE	1727	55005022
A	Ab.f.a.ev. A.	TUNSTALL	1759	55005022
A	Ab.f.a.ev. A.	WOOD	1775	55005022
A	Ans.a Fool.	WARBURTON	1767	20026004
A	Bear one a B.	STRAIGHT	1741	62005011
A	Conv. H. A.	SMITH	1763	19002008
A	Dea.a. Comf.	BURNET	1747	49015055
A	Del.d. Y& A.	BENSON	1725	21012001
A	Den. S.a Dec.	NICOLSON	1661	65001008
A	Enq.a.truth.	SCOTT	1743	20002003
A	Enq.a Happ.	WEBB	1765	18028012
A	Fas. W.pas.a.	DUNLOP	1722	49007031
A	Forg.t. Xt.a.	WHICHCOTE	1698	47013038
A	Forg.t. Xt.a.	HOOLE	1748	47013038
A	G. A.of o. R.	BEVERIDGE	1720	50005018
A	G. Judge o.a.	HILL	1755	61012023
A	G. Un.a Pro.	CHANDLER	1691	55005013
A	G.gov.m. A.	LELAND	1769	43010029
A	G.not A.of S.	STEPHENS	1737	23045007
A	God a Spirit.	HAVETT	1703	46004024
A	Gosp. Ob. A.	BOURN	1760	46018036
A	Ki.o. Xt.& A.	K.	1667	69016001
A	L. G.f.a. Xn.	ANONYMOUS	1770	47026023
A	Life a Pilgr.	CONYBEARE	1759	61011013
A	Meth.do. A.	BLACKALL	1723	43006002
A	Meth.do. A.	BLAIR	1740	43006002
A	Mic.&all- A.	MARSHALL	1731	61002005
A	N.&off.o. A.	TILLOTSON	1735	61001014
A	N.&off.o. A.	WHEATLY	1746	61001014
A	No Pain a bl.	WATTS	1753	69021004
A	Ob. Xt's m.a.	CHANDLER	1769	47010040
A	Ob.of C.& A.	KENNICOTT	1747	01004001
A	Obj.to Pr.a.	NEWMAN	1711	18021015
A	Of a King.	BRAGGE	1702	43022002
A	On a Murd.	FAWCETT	1764	10003034
A	On S.a. D. S.	HOLE	1713	24026014
A	One just o. A.	DORRINGTON	1683	49007031
A	Pr. Xn.k.a.p.	JONES	1761	50005014
A	Pro. M.to A.	GERARD	1780	01022018
A	R. U.& A. W.	PEARSON	1718	49007031
A	R. U.& A. W.	NORRIS	1728	49007031
A	R. U.& A. W.	MILLER	1749	49007031
A	R. U.& A. W.	ORR	1749	49007031
A	Rep. Stam.a.	MAYHEW	1767	19124007
A	Rep.stam. A.	CHAUNCY	1767	20025025
A	S.a.ador.ma.	PARRY	1666	43002009
A	Seek.a.m's S.	WALLIS	1740	49010032
A	Sin dou.b.a.	ORTON	1776	48014023
A	Sp. Bon.& A.	WESTLEY	1746	48008015
A	Sub.to A.&c.	SHEPHEARD	1771	51005001
A	T.a. T.b. S. S	GOAD	1664	55005021
A	U.& Ab.o.a.	EDWARDS	1698	57002008
A	U.& Ab.o.a.	NOURSE	1708	57002009
A	Use& A. W.	ANONYMOUS	1772	20031006
A	W. Xns.n. Ar.a	CLARKE	1736	51002017
A	W. Xns.n. Ar.a	GROVE	1741	51002017
A	W.a. Salt.of t	GARDINER	1720	43005013
A	W.a. Salt.of t	BLAIR	1740	43005013
A	W.a. Salt.of t	WESTLEY	1748	43005013
A	Watchm's a.	GILL	1773	23021011
A	Well-do.a. S.	TILLOTSON	1735	63003013
A	Xn.a. Jew. L.	WESTON	1747	43005020
A	Xn.comp. A.	GURNALL	1662	52006017
A	Xn.pos.a.th.	IBBBOT	1726	50006010
A	Xt.a Gift.	WILLISON	1761	50009015
A	Xt.a Proph.	DODSON	1728	61001001
A	Xt.a Saviour.	BEVERIDGE	1720	46006037
A	Xt.a Saviour.	BEVERIDGE	1729	46005017
A	Xt.red.n. A.	COLMAN	1728	61002016
A	Xt's. A.expl.	WATERLAND	1742	45020037
A	Xt's. D. A.r.	HOADLY	1754	43020026
A	Xt's. D.pr. A.	WITHERSPOON	1768	65002002
A	Xty a Myst.	BENSON	1748	52006019
A	Youth& A.	DUCHAL	1765	18032006
AAR	Mos.& Aar.	WOMOCK	1675	09024005
AARON	Aaron& Kor.	WATSON	1756	04016047
AB	Ab.&c.o. St.	BEDFORD	1705	58002016
AB	Ab. G's. G.	HORTON	1679	48002004
AB	Ab. Xn. Lib.	LUCE	1672	63002016
AB	Ab.f.a.ev. A.	PIERCE	1679	55005022
AB	Ab.f.a.ev. A.	ATTERBURY	1699	55005022
AB	Ab.f.a.ev. A.	HOPKINS	1700	55005022
AB	Ab.f.a.ev. A.	SMALRIDGE	1727	55005022
AB	Ab.f.a.ev. A.	TUNSTALL	1759	55005022
AB	Ab.f.a.ev. A.	WOOD	1775	55005022
AB	Ab.free-th.	FOSTER	1732	51005013
AB	Ab.h. G's w.	PIDDLE	1777	26033030
AB	Ab.no Happ.	NEWMAN	1760	45012015
AB	Ab.not nec.	ROE	1766	45012015
AB	Ab.of mi. G.	BULKLEY	1771	49011017
AB	Faith ab W.	JOHNSON	1740	43008010
AB	G.w.ab.our.	BARKER	1763	23055008
AB	G's.lo.of ab.	TOWGOOD	1676	47007008

Keyword	In its Context	Author	Year	BkChpVrs
AB	Mor. D.ab. P.	EMLYN	1742	43023023
AB	R.ab. Busin.	BATTY	1739	45010041
AB	T.ab.ob.&c.	MUNTON	1756	54003002
AB	U.& Ab.o.a.	EDWARDS	1698	57002008
AB	U.& Ab.o.a.	NOURSE	1708	57002009
AB	Us.& Ab. Pas.	HICKMAN	1706	47014015
AB	Us.& Ab. Pas.	BATTY	1739	47014015
AB	Us.& Ab. Sp.	SHARP	1734	52004029
AB	Us.& Ab. Sp.	ROGERS	1735	52004029
AB	Us.& Ab. Sp.	TILLOTSON	1735	52004029
AB	Us.& Ab. Sp.	BATTY	1739	52004029
AB	Us.& Ab. Sp.	PEARCE	1779	52004029
AB	Use& Ab. W.	CARTER	1729	49007031
AB	Xn.ab. Mos.	MICHELL	1737	61008006
AB	Xt.ab.to save	HOPKINS	1710	61007025
ABEL	Cain& Abel.	JENKINS	1779	01004006
ABID	Abid.in Xt.	PEARSON	1718	65002028
ABID	Abid.in Xt.	BEVERIDGE	1720	46015007
ABID	Abid.w. G.	CHANDLER	1769	49007024
ABID	Relig. Abid.	STENNETT	1769	53001006
ABIJ	Case of Abij.	EVANS	1725	11014013
ABIJ	Case of Abij.	JENKINS	1779	11014013
ABIL	Abil.of Faith	REEVES	1729	65005004
ABIM	Abim. P.sus.	ORTON	1776	01020011
ABJUR	Abjur.s.	LUZANCY	1676	46008032
ABO	Seek.th.abo.	SCATTERGOOD	1723	54003001
ABO	Seek.th.abo.	SNAPE	1745	54003001
ABO	Sett.aff.abo.	LLOYD	1765	54003002
ABOUN	Aboun. Iniq.	CLARKE	1736	43024012
ABP	Enthr. Abp.	BLOMER	1716	47009015
ABR	Abr. Faith.	CONYBEARE	1757	61011017
ABR	Abr. Faith.	WILSON	1781	61011008
ABR	Abr. Sacrif.	MACE	1751	61011017
ABR	Abr.off. Isaac	JENKINS	1779	01022012
ABR	Abr.off. Son.	SCOTT	1743	01022002
ABR	Abr.off. Son.	JORTIN	1774	01022001
ABR	Case of Abr.	STONE	1733	61011017
ABR	Case of Abr.	SCOTT	1743	01022015
ABR	Case of Abr.	STEBBING	1760	01022001
ABR	Ex Abr. Fai.	TILLOTSON	1735	61011017
ABR	Ex Abr. Fai.	FRANCIS	1773	61011017
ABR	Ex Abr. Fai.	BROUGHTON	1778	61011017
ABR	Seed of Abr.	HARRIS	1724	01022018
ABR'S	Abr's Fam.	MURRAY	1777	01025001
ABR'S	Abr's Xrter.	MURRAY	1777	01025019
ABRAH	Abrah.&c.	MURRAY	1777	01020001
ABRAH	Abrah.&c.	MURRAY	1777	01022001
ABRAH	Call Abrah.	MURRAY	1777	01012010
ABRAH	Faith Abrah.	CLARKE	1734	01015006
ABRAM	Xr.of Abram	ENFIELD	1777	62002023
ABRAM'S	Abram's Fai.	DUNCOMB	1697	62002023
ABRAM'S	Abram's Fai.	EVANSON	1773	48004022
ABS	Conf.& Abs.	SPARROW	1704	65001009
ABS	Conf.& Abs.	BAYLY	1721	50002007
ABS	Conf.& Abs.	WARREN	1739	65001009
ABS	Nat.& N.of Abs	HOLE	1716	46020023

Keyword	In its Context	Author	Year	BkChpVrs
ABS	Nat.& N.of Abs	BINGHAM	1726	46020023
ABS	Sen.af. Abs.	HOLE	1717	65002001
ABSO	Abso. Obed.	EMLYN	1742	19118009
ABSOL	Absol. Elect.	NEVILLE	1682	52001004
ABST	Abst.fm.flesh.	MONRO	1693	63002011
ABST	Abst.fm.flesh.	HOLE	1715	63002011
ABST	Abst.fm.flesh.	IBBOT	1726	63002011
ABSTAIN	Abstain&c.	NEWTON	1782	55005022
ABSTIN	Xn. Abstin.	BRADY	1713	49009025
ABU	Abu. G's Pat.	HOLLAND	1753	21008011
ABUS	Abus. Feast.	RIDGLEY	1718	02032006
ABUS	Abus. Prosp.	TREBECK	1730	20001032
ABUS	Abus.of Kn.	NEWSON	1781	43001020
ABUS	Abus.of Pray.	CARRINGTON	1776	62004003
ABUS	Abus.of Xty.	FISHER	1741	43010034
ABUSE	Abuse mercy	WILSON	1741	23005003
ABUSE	Abuse Rich.	LANGHORNE	1773	21004006
AC	Alm.how ac.	GOUGE	1677	57006017
AC	Ea. Tr.su.ac.	BLAIR	1740	43006019
AC	Rea.jud.r.ac.	CLARKE	1735	65003020
AC	The ac.time	RUSSEL	1746	50006002
AC	Vic.of Ac. E.	POWELL	1776	61012001
ACC	Acc.with G.	BOSTON	1775	50008012
ACC	Bold.of Acc.	CLARKSON	1696	61004016
ACC	G's.acc.pen.	BURNET	1747	65001009
ACC	Man acc. Cr.	FARRINGTON	1769	48014012
ACC	No acc.by F.	ALLEN	1761	62002014
ACC	Sinc.acc.f. P.	SIMONS	1743	50008012
ACC	T.false Acc.	ANONYMOUS	1753	45016002
ACC	Terms Acc.	HOADLY	1727	45010025
ACC	Will.m.acc.	HICKES	1726	50008012
ACCOUNT	Fin.account.	MAY	1757	48014012
ACCOUNT	Sin.account.	GLASSE	1781	48006021
ACKNOW	Acknow. G,	ABERNETHY	1748	20003006
ACT	Hum. Act.	CLARKE	1734	45011035
ACT	Hum. Act.	TRAPP	1751	09002003
ACT	Rule m.act.	CLARKE	1734	45006044
ACT	Xn's.sh.act.f.	CONANT	1699	67000005
ACTS	Romish Acts.	BENNETT	1714	69017004
ACTUAL	Actual Hol.	FORSTER	1759	65003002
AD	Ad.& Ev. Xr.	MURRAY	1777	01002015
AD	Ad.to Debt.	DREW	1725	05006012
AD	Cl. Ad.t. Par.	STEDMAN	1776	58002006
AD	Con.ad Con.	LISLE	1735	49001021
AD	Conc.ad cl.	WALL	1660	22003009
AD	Conc.ad. Cl.	WILLIS	1702	47020028
AD	Conc.ad. Cl.	DRAKE	1719	43026029
AD	Conc.ad. Cl.	RODERICK	1723	44013013
AD	Conc.ad. Cl.	BATEMAN	1746	48001020
AD	Conc.ad. Cl.	ASHTON	1770	45010034
AD	Conc.ad. Cl.	BUTLER	1775	47005038
AD	Conc.ad. M.	FULLWOOD	1673	20014034
AD	Conc.ad Sy.	PIERCE	1661	47011028
AD	Dea.b. Ad. F.	LAWSON	1764	48005012
AD	Dea.b. Ad. F.	BOSTON	1773	48005012
AD	G's S.on Ad.	PYLE	1777	01003019

INDEXES TO THIRD VOLUME: E: KEYWORD-IN-CONTEXT INDEX OF OTHER SUBJECTS OR OCCASIONS

Keyword	In its Context	Author	Year	BkChpVrs
AD	Inf. R.in Ad.	BLAIR	1777	19027005
AD	Rich M's Ad.	WELCHMAN	1704	45016024
AD	Tem. Ad. R.	TAYLOR	1719	20003017
AD	Tem. Ad. R.	STERNE	1769	20003017
AD'S	Ad's L.b. Xt.	MASON	1758	48005015
AD'S	Imp. Ad's. S.	TAYLOR	1725	48005019
ADAM	Fall in Adam	BOSTON	1773	48005019
ADAM	Xt.2 Adam.	PENTYCROSS	1781	48005014
ADAM'S	Adam's in. S.	GREEN	1758	19008003
ADAM'S	Adam's Fall.	GREEN	1758	01003010
ADD	Add.to reg.	DODDERIDGE	1742	62001018
ADD	S.add to Gos.	TILLOTSON	1735	51001008
ADDIT	Xt's.addit.	MOSS	1737	43005021
ADE	Ade. R.of C.	SANDERSON	1722	62004012
ADM	Adm. Ch. E.	WATSON	1755	68000005
ADM	Adm.to Att.	HORTON	1679	61002001
ADM	Adm.to You.	EDWARDS	1775	58002022
ADM	Broth. Adm.	HOPKINS	1716	03019017
ADM	Xt's. Adm.u.	CLARKE	1734	45017037
ADMISS	Admiss.s.	BAINE	1778	48010015
ADOP	Adop.& Reg.	DRAKE	1676	46001012
ADOP	Glor. Adop.	SPOONER	1771	65003001
ADOPT	Seal Adopt.	USHER	1678	48008015
ADOPTION	Adoption.	COLE	1692	51004005
ADOPTION	Adoption.	ALLEN	1758	48008016
ADOPTION	Adoption.	BAINE	1778	51003026
ADOR	S.a.ador.ma.	PARRY	1666	43002009
ADUL	Bapt.of adul.	SOUTHCOMB	1701	58002019
ADUL	Bpt.of Adul.	PILKINGTON	1760	01017010
ADULT	Ag. Adult.	S.	1672	43005028
ADULT	Ag. Adult.	WHALEY	1698	01039009
ADULT	Ag. Adult.	MOXON	1708	43005028
ADULTE	The Adulte.	BRAGGE	1706	46008003
ADULTERY	Adultery.	HOPKINS	1692	02020014
ADULTERY	Adultery.	COBDEN	1757	01039009
ADULTERY	Adultery.	PRESTON	1771	10012007
ADULTERY	Adultery.	ANONYMOUS	1777	02020014
ADV	Adv.& Pl. R.	STOCKDALE	1777	55005016
ADV	Adv.& Prosp.	BOURDALOUE	1776	43008023
ADV	Adv.& Rep.	HOLLAND	1753	20015032
ADV	Adv.& Repr.	HOLLAND	1753	54003016
ADV	Adv. Afflict.	BRODBURST	1733	18034031
ADV	Adv. Peace.	REGIS	1718	43005009
ADV	Adv. Xt's.as.	BEVERIDGE	1720	46014002
ADV	Adv. Xt's.as.	WARREN	1748	46014002
ADV	Adv.of Hol.	BEVERIDGE	1720	57004007
ADV	Adv.of Piety	BAINE	1778	69003004
ADV	Adv.of Rel.	EDWARDS	1726	57004007
ADV	Adv.of Rel.	DAVIES	1754	57004007
ADV	Adv.of Rel.	FOTHERGILL	1765	57004007
ADV	Adv.of Rel.	DELANY	1766	59002011
ADV	Adv.of Rev.	SAURIN	1775	49001021
ADV	Adv.of Tru.	TILLOTSON	1735	65004004
ADV	Adv.of Xns.	HODGE	1758	43005047
ADV	Adv.of Xty.	BURTON	1685	52003006
ADV	Adv.of Xty.	STERNE	1766	48001022

Keyword	In its Context	Author	Year	BkChpVrs
ADV	Adv.to appr.	DODD	1772	52006006
ADV	Adv.to Prot.	WILCOCKS	1709	55004001
ADV	Adv.to Sail.	HAYWARD	1746	19107031
ADV	Adv.to Son.	PEMBERTON	1727	13020010
ADV	Adv.to You.	ENFIELD	1772	11020011
ADV	Agr.w. Adv.	HORNECK	1706	43005025
ADV	Agr.w. Adv.	BLAIR	1740	43005025
ADV	Death Adv.	DAVIS	1756	55004014
ADV	Faithf. Adv.	GOSWELL	1715	21012001
ADV	Good Adv.	BOURN	1777	61003013
ADV	Gosp. Adv.	STANHOPE	1705	43020009
ADV	Gosp. Adv.	DODD	1757	43020016
ADV	Jes.our Adv.	SUTTON	1718	65002001
ADV	Pastor. Adv.	SMITH	1775	51004016
ADVANT	Advant. Rel.	STERNE	1769	21012013
ADVANT	Advant.virt.	GERARD	1780	19037016
ADVENT	Advent.	TAYLOR	1668	50005010
ADVENT	Advent.	BARNES	1752	43016027
ADVENT	Advent.	ANONYMOUS	1776	43013054
ADVENT	Advent.	CLEMENT	1774	53004005
ADVENT	Xt's. Advent.	BURNET	1747	48015008
ADVER	Prosp Adver.	BULL	1713	21007014
ADVERS	Spir. Advers.	ANONYMOUS	1731	63005008
ADVERS	Spir. Advers.	ATTERBURY	1743	63005008
ADVERSITY	Adversity.	BERRIMAN	1751	20024016
ADVICE	Advice to Y.	SHOWER	1699	19119009
ADVICE	Tak. Advice	MILNER	1751	20019020
AECON	Dom. Aecon	DYKES	1722	20031015
AF	Af. Child.ex.	COOKE	1752	05006007
AF	Af.high. W.	MARKLAND	1729	46002011
AF	Life af. Flesh	CLARKE	1735	48008013
AF	M.af. G.o. H.	EVANSON	1773	47013022
AF	Obj.o.our af.	MILLER	1749	54003002
AF	S.af. Induct.	BERRIMAN	1763	38002007
AF	Sen.af. Abs.	HOLE	1717	65002001
AF	Xt's.pr.af. R.	DELANY	1766	49015006
AF	1 S.af. East.	STANHOPE	1714	65005004
AF	1 S.af. East.	HOLE	1716	65005004
AF	1 S.af. Trin.	STANHOPE	1714	65004007
AF	2 S.af. East.	STANHOPE	1714	63002019
AF	2 S.af. East.	HOLE	1716	63002019
AF	2 S.af. Trin.	STANHOPE	1714	65003013
AF	2 S.af. Trin.	HOLE	1716	65003013
AF	3 S.af. East.	STANHOPE	1714	63002011
AF	3 S.af. East.	HOLE	1716	63002011
AF	3 S.af. Trin.	STANHOPE	1714	63005005
AF	3 S.af. Trin.	HOLE	1716	63005005
AF	5 S.af. East.	STANHOPE	1714	62001022
AF	5 S.af. East.	HOLE	1716	62001022
AFER	Afer baptiz.	HILL	1702	48006018
AFF	Aff. C.& Civ.	LANGHORNE	1773	63003008
AFF	Aff.m.o.joy.	HOWE	1744	62001002
AFF	Amer. Aff.	SMITH	1775	06022022
AFF	Bear. Aff.	QUINCY	1750	18002010
AFF	Faith Aff.	DUBOURDIEU	1712	19039009
AFF	Hap.o. G.aff.	NEWMAN	1760	65004016

Keyword	In its Context	Author	Year	BkChpVrs
AFF	Ill-disp. Aff.	SOUTH	1727	56002011
AFF	Misp.our aff.	REEVES	1713	58003004
AFF	Prosp.& Aff.	DORRINGTON	1705	20013021
AFF	Prov. G.aff.	LAWSON	1764	27004025
AFF	Rel.ser.aff.	DYER	1758	50005010
AFF	Sett.aff.abo.	LLOYD	1765	54003002
AFF	Subm.to Aff.	D'COETLOGAN	1778	18001020
AFF	Undisc. Aff.	MARSHALL	1731	62004001
AFFEC	Heav. Affec.	GREGORY	1696	54003002
AFFEC	Heav. Affec.	SHARP	1734	54003002
AFFEC	Relig. Affec.	EDWARDS	1762	63001008
AFFECT	Good affect.	BULKLEY	1752	43012033
AFFECT	Kind Affect.	M'FARLAND	1779	48012010
AFFL	Affl.of Rig.	HUNTER	1774	07006012
AFFL	Ben.of affl.	BERRIMAN	1751	62001009
AFFL	Benef.of affl.	STEWARD	1734	61012010
AFFL	Benef.of affl.	HOADLY	1754	61012011
AFFL	Bless.of affl.	COCK	1710	62001012
AFFL	Choi affl. Pi.	TILLOTSON	1735	61011024
AFFL	G's end affl.	CLARKSON	1696	23027009
AFFL	Happy Affl.	SPOONER	1771	50004017
AFFL	Prosp.& Affl.	REYNER	1745	24049011
AFFL	Relig.in Affl.	STENNETT	1769	19046010
AFFLIC	Afflic. Good.	MEDE	1672	69003019
AFFLIC	Benef. Afflic.	NEWTON	1736	19094012
AFFLIC	Hap.of afflic.	HOWARD	1710	62005011
AFFLICT	Adv. Afflict.	BRODBURST	1733	18034031
AFFLICT	Fam. Afflict.	TAYLOR	1703	10023005
AFFLICT	Good afflict.	FIDDES	1720	48008028
AFFLICT	Good afflict.	CLARKE	1727	48008028
AFFLICTION	Affliction.	CONANT	1699	25003039
AFFLICTION	Affliction.	COTES	1721	19119071
AFFLICTION	Affliction.	CAMELL	1726	19137001
AFFLICTION	Affliction.	BUNDY	1740	19119071
AFFLICTION	Affliction.	CARRINGTON	1754	19119071
AFFLICTION	Affliction.	WHITFIELD	1771	23024015
AFFLICTION	Affliction.	ATKINSON	1775	19119071
AFFLICTION	Affliction.	CARRINGTON	1776	19119071
AFFLICTION	Affliction.	CARR	1777	18005006
AFFLICTION	Affliction.	MILNE	1780	19055022
AFFLICTIONS	Afflictions.	MANNINGHAM	1680	19119067
AFFLICTIONS	Afflictions.	CHARNOCK	1684	61012005
AFFLICTIONS	Afflictions.	WAKE	1701	19030005
AFFLICTIONS	Afflictions.	BATES	1700	61012005
AFFLICTIONS	Afflictions.	DUKE	1714	20012021
AFFLICTIONS	Afflictions.	MOORE	1716	19025007
AFFLICTIONS	Afflictions.	WAPLE	1720	19119071
AFFLICTIONS	Afflictions.	PIERCE	1731	50004017
AFFLICTIONS	Afflictions.	ST.	1737	61012005
AFFLICTIONS	Afflictions.	FARRINGTON	1741	19119071
AFFLICTIONS	Afflictions.	WARREN	1748	19119071
AFFLICTIONS	Afflictions.	SMITH	1758	19119071
AFFLICTIONS	Afflictions.	SMITH	1762	19042006
AFFLICTIONS	Afflictions.	HALES	1766	19119072
AFFLICTIONS	Afflictions.	EATON	1764	48005003
AFFLICTIONS	Afflictions.	JORTIN	1774	19119071

Keyword	In its Context	Author	Year	BkChpVrs
AFTER	After Death.	ELLIS	1704	45016023
AG	Ag. Adult.	S.	1672	43005028
AG	Ag. Adult.	WHALEY	1698	01039009
AG	Ag. Adult.	MOXON	1708	43005028
AG	Ag. Anger.	BLACKBURNE	1694	52004031
AG	Ag. Anger.	HOLLAND	1753	52004031
AG	Ag. Antiser.	WARD	1674	58003016
AG	Ag. Aposta.	SCOTT	1700	57001018
AG	Ag. Atha. C.	CARTER	1752	43023008
AG	Ag. Atheism.	SMITH	1673	18021014
AG	Ag. Atheism.	LIDGOULD	1699	24007017
AG	Ag. Atheism.	BALGUY	1748	19014001
AG	Ag. Atheism.	PIERS	1748	52002012
AG	Ag. Bowman	SMITH	17--	48012003
AG	Ag. Bowman	SMITH	1731	43015006
AG	Ag. Bribery.	KELSALL	1712	05016019
AG	Ag. Bribery.	REEVES	1729	43027003
AG	Ag. Censure.	LITTLETON	1735	45013002
AG	Ag. Ch.of R.	HILL	1680	69018004
AG	Ag. Clipp.	FLEETWOOD	1737	01023016
AG	Ag. Compre.	SOUTH	1724	51002005
AG	Ag. Covet.	FREEMAN	1722	45014013
AG	Ag. Coveto.	FREEMAN	1722	45012015
AG	Ag. Coveto.	BLAIR	1740	43006019
AG	Ag. Coveto.	ENFIELD	1772	45012015
AG	Ag. Decept.	SHERIDAN	1720	51006007
AG	Ag. Disaffec.	SYNGE	1720	19095008
AG	Ag. Distract.	STEEL	1667	49007035
AG	Ag. Enthus.	HAWKINS	1769	58002015
AG	Ag. Envy.	LAMBE	1695	18005002
AG	Ag. Envy.	DELANY	1747	20014030
AG	Ag. F.of M.	WOOD	1775	20029025
AG	Ag. Fear o D.	TATNAL	1665	61002015
AG	Ag. Fear. D.	BOOKEY	1739	55004013
AG	Ag. Fear Fire	ANONYMOUS	1710	19004008
AG	Ag. Fraud.	FIDDES	1720	55004006
AG	Ag. Fraud.	ENFIELD	1772	03019013
AG	Ag. Fren. K.	KNAGGS	1705	50013011
AG	Ag. Heresy.	SHARP	1734	49011019
AG	Ag. Infallab.	SHARP	1735	63003015
AG	Ag. Infidel.	DAVIES	1754	45016031
AG	Ag. Infideli.	WATTS	1753	58002005
AG	Ag. Lying.	DRAKE	1760	52004025
AG	Ag. Method.	WILDER	1739	65004001
AG	Ag. Method.	BROWNSWORD	1749	43019020
AG	Ag. Method.	WHITE	1748	49014033
AG	Ag. Method.	POTTER	1758	46003005
AG	Ag. Method.	DODD	1759	52004003
AG	Ag. Method.	HELME	1762	61002003
AG	Ag. Middl.	PARKER	1749	44016017
AG	Ag. Middl.	JEPHSON	1750	44016017
AG	Ag. Middlet.	BAYLY	1751	61011004
AG	Ag. Observ.	SMYTHIES	1684	51006002
AG	Ag. Papists.	BAGSHAW	1680	48001018
AG	Ag. Perjury.	ROWLAND	1755	38003003
AG	Ag. Persecut.	BOURN	1777	43018007

Keyword	In its Context	Author	Year	BkChpVrs
AG	Ag. Persecut.	ROTHERAM	1780	45009055
AG	Ag. Phil.&c.	CASE	1774	54002008
AG	Ag. Polig.	SHORTHOSE	1738	43019008
AG	Ag. Pride.	DELANY	1747	20026012
AG	Ag. Profus.	BOURN	1777	45016009
AG	Ag. Purgat.	WEST	1675	49003015
AG	Ag. Quak.	KEITH	1707	61011006
AG	Ag. Quakeri.	ANONYMOUS	1710	47002024
AG	Ag. Revenge	STRATFORD	1684	48012017
AG	Ag. Revenge	HORNECK	1697	43005021
AG	Ag. Revenge.	LAMONT	1780	48012017
AG	Ag. Revolt.	HAMMOND	1684	23001005
AG	Ag. Riots.	KAGGS	1704	52005007
AG	Ag. Seducers	HILLIARD	1717	54002004
AG	Ag. Self-dec.	BOURN	1777	49003018
AG	Ag. Self-love	BUTLER	1716	53002021
AG	Ag. Sl's.slee.	WHISTON	1709	53003008
AG	Ag. Slander.	WEALES	1768	46008007
AG	Ag. Socin.	SMITH	1696	65005007
AG	Ag. Sodomy.	RUMLEY	1732	02023002
AG	Ag. Sodomy.	LEWIS	1772	48001018
AG	Ag. Spi. Liq.	HALES	1754	23056012
AG	Ag. Stealing.	WHITE	1747	52004028
AG	Ag. Strife.	NOURSE	1708	58002024
AG	Ag. Superst.	DODWELL	1754	19031007
AG	Ag. Swear.	BOREMAN	1662	43005034
AG	Ag. Swear.	NOURSE	1708	02020007
AG	Ag. Swear.	PIERCE	1731	19111009
AG	Ag. Swear.	SECKER	1770	62005012
AG	Ag. Taleb.	FROST	17--	03019016
AG	Ag. Tempta.	KILLINBECK	1717	18002009
AG	Ag. Transub.	LE FRANK	1662	43026026
AG	Ag. Transub.	FOWLER	1699	45022019
AG	Ag. Transub.	DELANY	1766	43026026
AG	Ag. Trouble.	PATRICK	1707	46014001
AG	Ag.b.run. G.	UNWIN	1773	48013007
AG	Ag.conf. W.	LARDNER	1739	48012002
AG	Ag.cursing.	DORRINGTON	1703	02023002
AG	Ag.cursing.	FOSTER	1737	02023002
AG	Ag.cursing.	DUNCOMB	1738	02023002
AG	Ag.ev. Tid.	ANONYMOUS	1710	19112007
AG	Ag.fr. Proph.	CHISHULL	1707	62005008
AG	Ag.m. Philo.	CRADDOCK	1739	49001023
AG	Ag.n. Proph.	CALAMY	1708	24014004
AG	Ag.prof.sw.	WRIGHT	1723	62005012
AG	Ag.reviling.	SOUTH	1744	63002023
AG	Ag.sen. Lusts	WISE	1717	63002011
AG	Ag.sen. Lusts	WESTON	1747	63002011
AG	Ag.whoring	ANONYMOUS	1743	50007009
AG	Ag F.of Dea.	ANONYMOUS	1710	49015055
AG	Ag Method.	LAND	1771	51005005
AG	Ag Presum.	ROGERS	1736	45017010
AG	Ag Quakers.	KEITH	1700	50005014
AG	Ant.ag. Pap.	OWEN	1683	63002003
AG	Cav.ag. Sed.	STANFAST	1660	43024004
AG	Cl.ag. J.ind.	PECKARD	1753	49009020
AG	Consp.ag. Xt	SHERIDAN	1720	44012014
AG	D. G.ag.evil.	QUINCY	1750	48012021
AG	Div.&h. Ag.	BOURN	1777	53002012
AG	Lib.mor. Ag.	CLARKE	1734	46008032
AG	Mo. Ag.o. G.	ABERNETHY	1743	69015004
AG	Obj.ag. Rev.	SEED	1750	49001025
AG	Of ag. Piety.	PEIRCE	1728	20016031
AG	Off.ag. Gosp.	CLARKE	1735	45017001
AG	Off.ag. Gosp.	HODGE	1758	43011006
AG	Off.ag. Gosp.	SHERLOCK	1772	43011006
AG	Off.ag. Xty.	ELSMERE	1767	43011006
AG	Prej.ag. Xt.	TILLOTSON	1735	43011006
AG	Reb.ag. G.	DUNLOP	1722	26016063
AG	Rem.ag.+sin.	DORRINGTON	1703	19119106
AG	Rem.ag. An.	HOWE	1683	54002002
AG	Sin ag. H. G.	HARRIS	1718	43012031
AG	Sin ag. H. G.	SHARP	1729	43012031
AG	Sin ag. H. G.	MARSHALL	1731	43012031
AG	Sin ag. H. G.	TILLOTSON	1735	43012031
AG	Sin ag. H. G.	STEPHENS	1737	43012031
AG	Sin ag. H. G.	WATERLAND	1742	43012031
AG	Sin ag. H. G.	GREEN	1747	43012031
AG	Sin ag. H. G.	HOOLE	1748	43012031
AG	Sin ag. H. G.	SECKER	1770	43012031
AG	Sin ag. H. G.	JORTIN	1774	43012031
AG	Sin ag. H. G.	PEARCE	1779	43012031
AG	Sin.ag. H. G.	ANONYMOUS	1740	44003028
AG	Test ag. Con.	SMITH	1719	50001012
AG	Well-do. S.ag.	CLAGETT	1720	63003013
AG	Well-do. S.ag.	CLARKE	1736	63003013
AG	Xt. Sign.s.ag.	BRACKENRIDGE	1764	45002034
AG	Zeal ag. En.	STELLING	1755	51004018
AGE	Infid.of age.	NEWTON	1782	61003012
AGE	Meth. Age.	PIGOTT	1762	01005027
AGE	Old age.	EATON	1764	19071017
AGE	Old Age.	SMITH	1676	21012001
AGE	R.of Age H.	GERARD	1780	20016031
AGED	Dut.of aged.	SECKER	1770	20016031
AGED	Dut.of aged.	BLAIR	1777	20016031
AGED	Supp. Aged.	FARMER	1756	23044004
AGED	To aged.	STRYPE	1699	59002002
AGGR	Aggr. Guilt.	BOURN	1777	45012047
AGGR	Aggr.of Sin.	CONYBEARE	1757	61010029
AGITATIONS	Agitations.	MORER	1708	09019024
AGONY	Agony of Xt.	BROWNE	1749	43026038
AGONY	Xt's. Agony.	WILLISON	1761	45022044
AGR	Agr.alm. Xn.	BREKELL	1765	47026028
AGR	Agr.w. Adv.	HORNECK	1706	43005025
AGR	Agr.w. Adv.	BLAIR	1740	43005025
AGREE	Broth.agree.	REYNOLDS	1679	53002001
AGRIPP	Agripp. Ans.	HORBERY	1774	47026028
AGUR'S	Agur's wish.	NEWTON	1759	20030007
AGUR'S	Agur's Pray.	BROWNRIG	1661	20030007
AGUR'S	Agur's Pray.	MEDE	1672	20030008
AGUR'S	Agur's Pray.	KIDDER	1697	20030007
AGUR'S	Agur's Pray.	FOSTER	1732	20030008

Keyword	In its Context	Author	Year	BkChpVrs
AGUR'S	Agur's Pray.	HORT	1738	20030007
AGUR'S	Agur's Pray.	HOADLY	1755	20030008
AGUR'S	Agur's Pray.	STEBBING	1760	20030008
AGUR'S	Agur's Pray.	SMITH	1777	20030008
AGUR'S	Agur's Req.	AGAR	1759	20030007
AGUR'S	Agur's Req.	JORTIN	1774	20030007
AL	Ben. Fear.al.	LARDNER	1751	20028014
AL	Dis.al.prov.	NEWMAN	1750	23005012
AL	Forg.t. Xt.al.	SHERLOCK	1719	47013038
AL	G. Fath. Al.	BARROW	1716	69011017
AL	Salv b. Xt.al.	BEVERIDGE	1720	47004012
AL	Salv.b. Xt.al.	STAYNOE	1700	47004012
AL	Salv.faith al.	WARBURTON	1767	43022012
ALL	All f. Good.	FARMER	1756	48008028
ALL	All und. Sin.	WITHERSPOON	1768	48003023
ALL	All N.wine.	SPOONER	1771	43009017
ALL	Cup to all.	STEEL	1675	43026027
ALL	D.all Xt's. N.	WILKINSON	1676	54003017
ALL	Des.all Nat.	HARRIS	1724	36002006
ALL	Do all in Na.o	BARROW	1716	54003017
ALL	Do all in Na.o	BEVERIDGE	1720	54003017
ALL	Do all Gl. G.	BEVERIDGE	1720	49010031
ALL	Do all Gl. G.	BERRIMAN	1751	49010031
ALL	Do go.to all.	BURTON	1685	51006010
ALL	Do go.to all.	BILLINGSLEY	1712	51006010
ALL	G.disp.all.	CLARKE	1735	20016004
ALL	G's. King.all	BEVERLEY	1698	49015024
ALL	Hea.n.in all.	BAINE	1778	49006009
ALL	Hon.all men	TRAPP	1752	63002017
ALL	Ld own.all.	CLARKSON	1696	13029011
ALL	Ld rules all.	CLARKSON	1696	19103019
ALL	Mic.&all- A.	MARSHALL	1731	61002005
ALL	Time f.all.	HALL	1660	21003004
ALL	Wait.all T.	GREENHILL	1773	63004007
ALL	Xns fors.all.	SUTTON	1754	45014033
ALL	Xt.all in all.	ROWLAND	1774	61001009
ALL	Xt.all in all.	JOHNSON	1776	49001030
ALL	Xt.do all t.w.	ORTON	1776	44007037
ALLEG	Alleg. Jewels	SPOONER	1771	43013044
ALLEGIANCE	Allegiance.	MAYNWARING	1709	21008002
ALM	Agr.alm. Xn.	BREKELL	1765	47026028
ALM	Alm.g.& M.	HOLE	1725	49013003
ALM	Alm.how ac.	GOUGE	1677	57006017
ALMIGH	The Almigh.	HOLE	1715	69001008
ALMO	Sacr. Almo.	FAWCETT	1757	49016002
ALMON	Sacr. Almon.	FAWCETT	1757	23032008
ALMOST	Almost. Xn.	WHITFIELD	1739	47026028
ALMOST	Almost Xn.	MEAD	1666	47026028
ALMOST	Almost Xn.	HOPKINS	1710	47026028
ALMOST	Almost Xn.	WESTLEY	1746	47026028
ALMS	Alms&c.	ANONYMOUS	1661	57006017
ALMS	Alms-deeds.	NOURSE	1705	61013016
ALMS	Alms-giving	GARDINER	1720	43006001
ALMSG	Pr.& Almsg.	BEVERIDGE	1720	47010004
ALMSGIVING	Almsgiving.	SMEDLEY	1719	65003017
ALTAR	Xn. Altar&c.	BRETT	1713	61013010

Keyword	In its Context	Author	Year	BkChpVrs
ALTER	Alter. Pray.	HOLE	1716	19051015
AM	For Am. Col.	WATSON	1763	23049006
AMB	World Amb.	BAYLY	1721	46005044
AMB	World Amb.	STRAIGHT	1741	46005044
AMBITION	Ambition.	WEBB	1772	17005013
AMEN	Amen.	WOODCOCK	1683	16008006
AMER	Amer. Aff.	SMITH	1775	06022022
AN	An.&m. Id.	ANONYMOUS	1716	26008014
AN	An. Co.m.	LANGHORNE	1777	47007026
AN	An. Conv. Cl.	BEACH	1760	46003009
AN	An. F.perm.	JENKINS	1779	01009003
AN	An.m. Cl.	THANE	1706	51006009
AN	An.m. Qua.	ANONYMOUS	1767	45016005
AN	Angel's. An.	HARWOOD	1662	45002014
AN	Gosp. Ob.an.	BOURN	1760	49001022
AN	Jes.an. H. Pr.	WHEATLY	1746	61005009
AN	Not ans.an.	SEATON	1720	59002009
AN	On an Exec.	ROSEWELL	1716	04026010
AN	On an Exec.	DENHAM	1745	61008012
AN	Rem.ag. An.	HOWE	1683	54002002
AN	Sal.in an. W.	SMITH	1696	47016030
AN	Sin Apo. An.	WHEATLY	1746	68000006
AN	States of An.	STURMY	1716	68000006
AN	Watch-an.i.	GILL	1773	14020020
AN	b.an Execut.	ANONYMOUS	1720	50007009
ANAL	Anal. D.wis.	BARTON	1737	45006038
ANALOGY	Analogy.	BARTON	1737	48001020
ANALOGY	Analogy.	HARVEST	1753	46003001
ANALY	Analy.of M.	FREE	1764	01001026
ANARCHY	Anarchy.	MUDGE	1739	07021002
ANC	Anc. Xn R.	REGIS	1753	01003015
AND	Debt.and Cred.	MILBOURNE	1709	62002013
AND	St. And. Day	FRANK	1672	43004020
AND	St. And. Day	LITTLETON	1680	43004018
AND	St. And. Day	STANHOPE	1715	43004018
AND	St. And. Day	HOLE	1716	43004018
AND	St. And.d.	HUNTER	1778	05015017
AND	Stars and C.	ANONYMOUS	1670	43002009
ANDR	St. Andr.d.	STRIPLING	1691	58002012
ANDR	St. Andr.day	STANHOPE	1715	48010009
ANDR	St. Andr.day	HOLE	1716	48010009
ANG	Ang.&office	BULL	1713	61001014
ANG	Ang.&office	BOYSE	1728	61001014
ANG	Ang.&office	HORT	1738	61001013
ANG	Ang.&office.	WHEATLY	1746	61001007
ANG	Ang.illegal.	ANONYMOUS	1776	43005022
ANG	Ang.life.	SHAW	1753	43022030
ANG	Ang.of Cain.	FELTON	1748	01004005
ANG	Ang.wo. Xt.	BRETT	1720	61001006
ANG	Fall of Ang.	MEDE	1672	64002004
ANG	Fall of Ang.	DAVISON	1684	64002004
ANG	Fall of Ang.	BOYSE	1728	64002004
ANG	Fall of Ang.	WHEATLY	1746	64002004
ANG	Joy Ang.&c.	ORTON	1776	18038007
ANG	Mich.d. Ang.	LITTLETON	1680	43018010
ANG	Mich.d. Ang.	PATRICK	1719	43018010

INDEXES TO THIRD VOLUME: E: KEYWORD-IN-CONTEXT INDEX OF OTHER SUBJECTS OR OCCASIONS

Keyword	In its Context	Author	Year	BkChpVrs
ANG	Min.of Ang.	WILKINSON	1660	61001014
ANG	Pride& Ang.	DEVEREL	1777	41010018
ANGEL	Angel of Co.	PEARSON	1718	38003001
ANGEL	Angel.wors.	SCATTERGOOD	1723	54002018
ANGEL	The Angel.	HARRIS	1724	02023020
ANGEL'S	Angel's. An.	HARWOOD	1662	45002014
ANGELS	Angels.	JOHNSON	1728	19103020
ANGELS	Angels.	WILLISON	1761	64002004
ANGELS	Angels Emp.	WHITE	1757	19104004
ANGELS	Good angels.	CONYBEARE	1757	61001014
ANGELS	Min. Angels.	WHEATLEY	1746	19091010
ANGELS	Of Angels.	SHEPHERD	1702	61001004
ANGELS	of Angels.	HUTCHINSON	1720	19148002
ANGER	Ag. Anger.	BLACKBURNE	1694	52004031
ANGER	Ag. Anger.	HOLLAND	1753	52004031
ANGER	Anger.	HORNECK	1706	43005021
ANGER	Anger.	BLACKALL	1723	43005021
ANGER	Anger.	COLLIER	1725	52004026
ANGER	Anger.	GALE	1726	52004026
ANGER	Anger.	TREBECK	1730	52004026
ANGER	Anger.	MOSS	1732	52004026
ANGER	Anger.	UPTON	1736	52004026
ANGER	Anger.	FOSTER	1737	52004026
ANGER	Anger.	SMITH	1740	62001019
ANGER	Anger.	WILDER	1741	52004026
ANGER	Anger.	SEED	1750	52004026
ANGER	Anger.	WHITTY	1768	54003011
ANGER	Anger.	SECKER	1771	52004026
ANGER	Anger.	JORTIN	1774	54003008
ANGER	Anger.	NEWTON	1782	43005022
ANGER	Caus. Anger.	GARDINER	1720	43005021
ANGER	G's Anger.	DUNLOP	1722	19090011
ANGER	G's Anger.	SOUTH	1744	19090011
ANGER	Imm. Anger	DAVIES	1720	31004004
ANGER	Sin of Anger	STANHOPE	1714	43005020
ANGER	Sin of Anger	HOLE	1716	43005020
ANGER	Sin of Anger	FELTON	1748	01004005
ANN	Ann.of Cor.	PYLE	1706	11003009
ANN	Ann.s.	D'COETLOGAN	1780	49015010
ANN	Ann& Saph.	BULKLEY	1771	47005003
ANNEX	Pun.annex.	SKELTON	1754	50005010
ANNEX	Rew.annex.	SKELTON	1754	54003002
ANNIV	Anniv.s.	PIERS	1761	43017011
ANNIV	Anniv.s.	FREE	1769	01014014
ANNIV	Anniv.s.	HENLEY	1774	24014003
ANNIV	Anniv.s.	MONTGOMERY	1780	26033011
ANNUN	Annun.s.	STRADLING	1692	45011027
ANNUNC	Annunc.	STANHOPE	1715	23007010
ANNUNC	Annunc.	HOLE	1716	23007010
ANNUNCIAT	Annunciat.	FRANK	1672	45001028
ANNUNCIAT	Annunciat.	MILL	1676	45001028
ANNUNCIAT	Annunciat.	LITTLETON	1680	45001028
ANNUNCIAT	Annunciat.	BETHAM	1686	45001031
ANNUNCIAT	Annunciat.	HICKES	1713	45001028
ANNUNCIAT	Annunciat.	BULL	1713	45001048
ANNUNCIAT	Annunciat.	STANHOPE	1715	45001026

Keyword	In its Context	Author	Year	BkChpVrs
ANNUNCIAT	Annunciat.	HOLE	1716	45001026
ANNUNCIAT	Annunciat.	WAKE	1716	45001048
ANNUNCIAT	Annunciat.	MARSHALL	1731	45001046
ANNUNCIAT	Annunciat.	BARNES	1752	45011027
ANOIN	Wo.anoin. J.	LARDNER	1760	43026013
ANS	Agripp. Ans.	HORBERY	1774	47026028
ANS	Ans.a Fool.	WARBURTON	1767	20026004
ANS	Not ans.an.	SEATON	1720	59002009
ANS	W's Ans.im.	GILL	1752	13012032
ANT	Ant.ag. Pap.	OWEN	1683	63002003
ANT	b.ant. Brit.	PRICE	1754	19118024
ANTICHRIST	Antichrist.	JONES	1676	56002003
ANTICHRIST	Antichrist.	HILDROP	1711	37011016
ANTICHRIST	Antichrist.	WARBURTON	1767	64001016
ANTIQ	Antiq.of Fai.	GLANVIL	1681	68000003
ANTIQ	Antiq.of S.	CATCOTT	1753	01002003
ANTISER	Ag. Antiser.	WARD	1674	58003016
ANX	Anx.& Pray.	SHARP	1729	53004006
ANX	Anx.f.raim.	BLAIR	1740	43006028
ANX	Anx.hurtf.	BLAIR	1740	43006027
ANX	M. Anx.f.p.	DAVIES	1771	51004019
ANX	Unrea. Anx.	FOORD	1719	43006034
ANX	Unrea. Anx.	BLACKALL	1723	43006034
ANX	Unrea. Anx.	BLAIR	1740	43006034
ANX	Unrea. Anx.	BUNDY	1740	43006034
ANXIETY	Anxiety.	CONANT	1688	53004006
ANXIETY	Anxiety.	CLARKSON	1696	53004006
ANXIETY	Anxiety.	BEVERIDGE	1720	53004006
ANXIETY	Anxiety.	COLLIER	1725	53004006
ANXIETY	Anxiety.	ATTERBURY	1734	43006034
ANXIETY	Anxiety.	CLARKE	1736	43006031
ANXIETY	Anxiety.	CONEY	1730	53004006
ANXIETY	Anxiety.	BLAIR	1740	43006025
ANXIETY	Anxiety.	BLAIR	1740	43006031
ANXIETY	Anxiety.	GROVE	1742	43006034
ANXIETY	Anxiety.	COBDEN	1757	43006034
ANXIETY	Anxiety.	CARMICHAEL	1757	53004006
AP	Ap. S.p.o. Xy	LANGHORNE	1773	49015019
AP	Ap.f. Ch. En.	PARSONS	1767	55005021
AP	Ap.rul.o.pr.	WILLIAMS	1770	50004005
AP	Bles.ap.b. G.	WATTS	1753	19042002
AP	Bles.ap.b. G.	PEARSE	1763	19042002
AP	Ch. Eng. Ap.	LOWTH	1722	47002042
AP	Fals.ap. Sac.	WILLIAMS	1774	49011027
AP	On ap. Creed	BENNETT	1775	46020031
APO	Apo. Decree.	GALE	1726	47015028
APO	Sin Apo. An.	WHEATLY	1746	68000006
APOL	Apol.f. Gos.	SMITH	1709	49015001
APOL	Apol.f. Rel.	POOL	1673	43011019
APOL	Xt's apol.f.d.	ORTON	1776	43026004
APOS	Apos. Bened.	BARKER	1763	52006024
APOS	Apos. Creed.	BENNETT	1775	47003018
APOS	Apos. Creed.	BENNETT	1775	47010042
APOS	Apos. Creed.	BENNETT	1775	52001007
APOS	Call.of Apos.	HOLE	1716	45005001
APOST	Apost. Auth.	JORTIN	1774	43023009

Keyword	In its Context	Author	Year	BkChpVrs
APOST	Apost. Auth.	JORTIN	1774	45016013
APOST	Apost. Caut.	CARRINGTON	1776	52005015
APOST	Apost. Creed	NEWCOME	1702	61011006
APOST	Apost. Creed	BENNETT	1775	44016019
APOST	Apost. Creed	BENNETT	1775	47026008
APOST	Apost. Creed	BENNETT	1775	61011006
APOST	Apost. Creed.	BENNETT	1775	47002031
APOST	Apost. Creed.	BENNETT	1775	52002019
APOST	Apost. Deb.	DUCHAL	1753	47001008
APOST	Apost. Doctr.	CASE	1774	47002042
APOST	Apost.bene.	LARDNER	1760	50013014
APOST	Apost.creed.	BENNETT	1775	47019003
APOST	Cat. Apost.	WENSLEY	1679	58001013
APOST	Cred. Apost.	HODGE	1758	65004014
APOST	Pun.o. Apost.	BRETT	1720	61010028
APOST	Sanct. Apost.	STERNE	1769	43011006
APOST	Xt.co. Apost.	SECKER	1771	43028019
APOSTA	Ag. Aposta.	SCOTT	1700	57001018
APOSTACY	Apostacy.	CRUSO	1699	19080017
APOSTACY	Apostacy.	SUTTON	1718	61010026
APOSTACY	Apostacy.	LESTLEY	1720	61010028
APOSTACY	Apostacy.	CLAGETT	1720	64002021
APOSTACY	Apostacy.	WELTON	1724	58002012
APOSTACY	Apostacy.	SHARP	1729	61010026
APOSTACY	Apostacy.	SHARP	1729	65005016
APOSTACY	Apostacy.	TILLOTSON	1735	61006004
APOSTACY	Apostacy.	TILLOTSON	1735	61010038
APOSTACY	Apostacy.	TRAPP	1752	46006066
APOSTACY	Apostacy.	WILCOX	1757	46006067
APOSTOL	Apostol. Off.	ST.	1757	43005013
APP	App.of Mess.	LAWSON	1764	45001078
APP	Xt's.app.&c.	CATCOTT	1753	53002006
APP	Xt's.app.b. I.	CATCOTT	1753	53002006
APP	Xt's.fin.app.	WHITAKER	1773	43025044
APPAR	Prud.appar.	DYKES	1722	20031021
APPAR	Stra. Appar.	ALSOP	1683	35001008
APPEAR	Sav. Appear.	ERSKINE	1664	22002008
APPEAR	Xt's appear.	FIDDES	1720	23053002
APPEAR	Xt's. Appear.	ERSKINE	1764	19040007
APPR	Adv.to appr.	DODD	1772	52006006
APPR	Appr. Faith.	WILLISON	1761	51002020
APPRO	Appro.to G.	WATTS	1753	19065004
APPROB	Approb.	ELY	1720	49004005
APRIL	April 21.	SCLATER	1681	19106016
AR	Ar.f. Xn. Rel.	KNOX	1768	63003015
AR	W. Xns.n. Ar.a	CLARKE	1736	51002017
AR	W. Xns.n. Ar.a	GROVE	1741	51002017
AR	Xy.fo.on Ar.	COOKSEY	1743	63003015
AR	Zeal f. Ar. F.	OGDEN	1777	68000003
ARBITRA	G.n.arbitra.	FOSTER	1732	48009020
ARCHANG	7 Archang.	MEDE	1672	37004010
ARG	Arg.f. Provi.	HUNTER	1774	18007020
ARG	Arg.f. Xnity.	POWELL	1776	46005037
ARG	Arg.fm. Mir.	JORTIN	1774	46011047
ARG	2 Arg.f. C. P.	BROOKS	1665	43006006
ARIANISM	Arianism.	SMALBROKE	1719	43004010

Keyword	In its Context	Author	Year	BkChpVrs
ARITHM	Div. Arithm.	WHEATLAND	1739	19090012
ARK	Noah's Ark.	WILLISON	1761	61011007
ARK	Noah's Ark.	JENKINS	1779	01007016
ARK	Xt.our Ark.	WILLISON	1761	01007001
ARM	Build. Arm.	ERSKINE	1674	16004018
ARM	Xn's. Arm.	WILSON	1781	52006010
ARM	Xn's.sp.arm.	ANONYMOUS	1685	52006011
ARRAIG	Sinn. Arraig.	ANONYMOUS	1668	61010027
ART	Art.2 Creed.	EDWARDS	1713	46001014
ART	Art.5th.	NEWCOME	1702	44016019
ART	Art.5th.	EDWARDS	1713	44016019
ART	Art.5th.	HOLE	1715	44016019
ART	Art.6.	CARRINGTON	1750	63003022
ART	W.art thou	JENKINS	1779	01003009
ART	1 Art. Creed.	CARRINGTON	1750	46014026
ART	1 Art. Creed.	CARRINGTON	1750	49008006
ART	10 Art. Creed	EDWARDS	1713	47010043
ART	10 Art. Creed	CARRINGTON	1750	47010043
ART	11 Art. Creed	CARRINGTON	1750	49015023
ART	11 Art Creed.	NEWCOME	1702	47024015
ART	11 Art Creed.	EDWARDS	1713	47024015
ART	2 Art. Creed.	HOLE	1715	47008037
ART	2 Art. Creed.	CARRINGTON	1750	47008037
ART	5 Art. Creed.	HOLE	1715	49015003
ART	5 Art. Creed.	CARRINGTON	1750	49015003
ART	8 Art. Creed.	EDWARDS	1713	48008009
ART	9 Art. Creed.	CARRINGTON	1750	43016018
ARTICLE	12 Article.	CARRINGTON	1750	43025046
ARTICLE	4 Article.	CARRINGTON	1750	43027026
ARTIF	Artif. Ref.	MARRIOTT	1774	34002016
ARTS	Arts diabol.	EDWARDS	1702	05018010
AS	Adv. Xt's.as.	BEVERIDGE	1720	46014002
AS	Adv. Xt's.as.	WARREN	1748	46014002
AS	Beh.at rel.as.	ROBINSON	1776	58003014
AS	D.as done to.	BENNETT	1728	43007012
AS	M.reap.as s.	BOURN	1777	51006007
AS	Not as.o. G.	HARTLEY	1754	48001016
AS	Not as.o. G.	SHIRLEY	1762	48001016
AS	P.s. E.s. As.s	BERRIMAN	1751	48008033
AS	Wlk.as Xt.d.	BARROW	1716	65002006
ASA'S	Asa's Pray.	CUMMING	1739	14014011
ASCENS	Souls ascens.	LOEFFS	1670	53001023
ASH	Xn.n.ash. G.	ENFIELD	1772	48002016
ASHA	Asha.of Xt.	WEST	1762	44008038
ASHA	Asha.of Xt.	SHERLOCK	1772	44008038
ASHA	Xn.not asha.	MOIR	1759	63004016
ASHER	Tribe Asher.	BEVERLEY	1693	05033025
ASS	Ass.o. H. Gh.	OGDEN	1777	65003024
ASS	Ass.of G's.sp.	HUSSEY	1758	46006045
ASS	Div.ass.	LYNFORD	16--	19012007
ASS'	Ass' Repr.	JENKINS	1779	04022028
ASSE	Duty of asse.	ANONYMOUS	1776	61010025
ASSEM	b.gen.assem.	STITH	1746	44012017
ASSEMB	Pub.assemb.	BRIGGS	1675	61010025
ASSERT	Xn. Assert.	ECCLES	1755	43010034
ASSES	To Asses.	MURRAY	1772	07003022

INDEXES TO THIRD VOLUME: E: KEYWORD-IN-CONTEXT INDEX OF OTHER SUBJECTS OR OCCASIONS

Keyword	In its Context	Author	Year	BkChpVrs
ASSID	Wid's. Assid.	BOURN	1763	45018001
ASSIST	Assist.in Du.	HUBBARD	1757	54001009
ASSIST	Assist.o. H. S	BENNETT	1728	53001019
ASSIST	Ch.of Assist.	MACRO	1732	51005014
ASSIST	Div. Assist.	ALTHAM	1732	45018042
ASSIST	Div.assist.	KELSEY	1721	45011013
ASSIZE	Gre. Assize.	SMITH	1665	69020011
ASSIZE	Gre. Assize.	VENN	1759	69020011
ASSIZE	Great Assize.	JEPHSON	1742	47017031
ASSIZE	Great Assize.	KIMBER	1756	47017031
ASSIZE	Great Assize.	HORNE	1778	47017031
ASSOCIATION	Association.	BROAD	1696	19009016
ASSU	Assu.of faith	CENNICK	1762	23038017
ASSU	Assu.of Salv.	SCOTT	1700	65003002
ASSUR	Assur. Grace.	MATHER	1701	65005013
ASSUR	Assur.of Fai.	NEWTON	1767	65005019
ASSUR	Assur.of Sal.	HAVETT	1703	63001009
ASSUR	Assur.of Sal.	HOPKINS	1710	61012028
ASSUR	Assur.of Sal.	KNIGHT	1728	61012028
ASSUR	Assur.possi.	DOOLITTLE	1677	65005013
ASSURAN	Assuran.&c.	FAIRECLOUGH	1675	64001007
ASSURANCE	Assurance.	MATHER	1701	65003014
ASSURANCE	Assurance.	MATHER	1701	65003012
ASSURANCE	Assurance.	BEDFORD	1738	48014001
ASSURANCE	Assurance.	LEIGHTON	1746	48008035
ASSURANCE	Assurance.	SAURIN	1777	48008038
AST	C. Hear.ast.	BOURN	1777	43007028
ASTRON	Rel. Astron.	FAWCETT	1749	19008003
AT	At Camp.	WILLIAMS	1696	19060012
AT	At Court.	BLAGRAVE	1691	45012004
AT	At Court.	BRADY	1706	49002014
AT	At Hanover.	LOMBARD	1714	48012018
AT	At Law Lect.	LITTLETON	1680	45007033
AT	At N.mark.	ANONYMOUS	1774	19045005
AT	At Newg.ch.	FORSTER	1777	47009011
AT	At Quak.m.	ANONYMOUS	1771	49013014
AT	At Serj. Inn.	PARKER	1750	45016031
AT	At Spithead.	HOULTON	1740	09017037
AT	At Whiteh.	HACKET	1675	46006011
AT	Beh.at rel.as.	ROBINSON	1776	58003014
AT	Behav.at Ch.	LANGHORNE	1773	21005001
AT	Bir.at Beth.	DOWNES	1761	43002003
AT	Fol mock.at Si	STILLINGFLEET	1707	20014009
AT	Fol mock.at Si	ROGERS	1730	20014009
AT	Fol mock.at Si	TRAPP	1752	20014009
AT	Fol.mock.at Si	DAVIES	1720	20014009
AT	Fol.mock.at Si	CLARKE	1734	20014009
AT	Ho.o.r.at D.	STEPHENS	1699	53003013
AT	Mock.at Rel.	WARREN	1730	68000017
AT	Scoff.at Rel.	SUTTON	1754	64003003
AT	St. P.at Meli.	NEWTON	1782	47028001
AT	U.of R.at D.	STENNETT	1769	19023004
AT	Xt.at G's.r.h.	HURRION	1719	61012001
AT	at Camp.	RAWLINS	1713	14009007
AT	at Whiteh.	HACKET	1675	46004013
AT	at Whiteh.	HACKET	1675	46004014

Keyword	In its Context	Author	Year	BkChpVrs
ATH	Ath.& Deism	STEPHENS	1737	46005039
ATH	Caus.of Ath.	HUNT	1748	05032003
ATH	Specul. Ath.	BATE	1748	48001020
ATH	Sup.w. Ath.	WESTON	1739	53003006
ATHA	Ag. Atha. C.	CARTER	1752	43023008
ATHA	Atha. Creed.	HOLE	1716	44016016
ATHA	Atha. Creed.	PENN	1756	57003016
ATHAL	Athal. Treas.	L.	1660	12011014
ATHE	Pract. Athe.	OAKES	1747	52002012
ATHEISM	Ag. Atheism.	SMITH	1673	18021014
ATHEISM	Ag. Atheism.	LIDGOULD	1699	24007017
ATHEISM	Ag. Atheism.	BALGUY	1748	19014001
ATHEISM	Ag. Atheism.	PIERS	1748	52002012
ATHEISM	Atheism.	KNAGGS	1701	20014009
ATHEISM	Atheism.	LESTLEY	1720	19014001
ATHEISM	Atheism.	BAYLY	1721	19139013
ATHEISM	Atheism.	TALBOT	1731	19014001
ATHEISM	Atheism.	SOUTH	1744	19014001
ATHEISM	Atheism.	ORR	1749	19014001
ATHEISM	Atheism&c.	SWORDER	1714	11018021
ATHEISM	Pr. Atheism.	BRAGGE	1713	59001016
ATHEISM	Pr. Atheism.	NORRIS	1728	59001016
ATHEISM	Pr. Atheism.	MILLER	1749	59001016
ATHEIST	Prac. Atheist.	BATE	1748	48001020
ATONE	Xt's. Atone.	WATTS	1753	69013008
ATT	Adm.to Att.	HORTON	1679	61002001
ATT	B.& Att.o. G.	HUSSEY	1755	48001019
ATT	L.es.t.att. G.	HUNTER	1774	65004016
ATT	Salv.how att.	PAYNE	1698	47016030
ATT	Salv.how att.	HOPKINS	1708	47016030
ATT	Salv.how att.	JORTIN	1774	47016030
ATTAIN	Wisd.attain.	LARDNER	1751	20008017
ATTE	Nat.of Atte.	SMITH	1740	61002001
ATTENTION	Attention.	MUNTON	1756	45008018
ATTENTION	Attention.	MUNTON	1756	61003001
ATTER	Bp Atter. Im.	CHAMBRES	1722	47012005
ATTRIB	Attrib. God.	HOOLE	1748	18021015
ATTRIB	D. Attrib.	EDWARDS	1715	19008009
ATTRIB	Div. Attrib.	ERSKINE	1764	19085010
ATTRIB	G's attrib.&c	HUNTER	1774	19145017
AU	Au.1.b. R. S.	ANDERSON	1720	68000003
AU	Di.au.o. S. S.	FAROM	1660	58003016
AU	Di.au.o. S. S.	JACOMB	1660	58003016
AU	Div. Au. S. S.	HUMPHREYS	1712	55004008
AU	Div. Au. S. S.	BELLAMY	1744	64002021
AU	b. Great Au.	FULLER	1672	57006003
AUDIT	St. P's. Audit	SHERIDAN	1720	47017032
AUDIT	Year Audit.	ANONYMOUS	1735	19090009
AUG	Aug. Ch.	BOWYER	1734	16013014
AUG	Aug. Vicar.	COOKE	1723	45001046
AUG	Aug.1.	BOLDE	1715	19136023
AUG	Aug.1.	ANONYMOUS	1726	27004017
AUG	Aug.1.	BENSON	1758	19044001
AUG	Aug.1.	LANGFORD	1759	04023023
AUG	Aug.1.	PRIOR	1750	69018004
AUG	Aug.1.	HODGE	1751	19078003

Keyword	In its Context	Author	Year	BkChpVrs
AUG	Aug.1.	PICKARD	1761	19147001
AUG	Aug.19.	STANLEY	1662	19014007
AUG	Aug.8.	SMITH	1714	14009008
AURIC	Auric.conf.	BURROUGHS	1735	46020021
AUTH	Apost. Auth.	JORTIN	1774	43023009
AUTH	Apost. Auth.	JORTIN	1774	45016013
AUTH	Auth.mat. F.	ANONYMOUS	1774	43023008
AUTH	Auth.of Ch.	MASON	1705	49014040
AUTH	Auth.of Ch.	HOARD	1709	49014040
AUTH	Auth.of S. S.	SCOTT	1700	46005039
AUTH	Auth.of S. S.	GUYSE	1724	54003016
AUTH	G.auth.pea.	COTES	1721	49014033
AUTH	Mag. Auth.	PASTON	1673	48013005
AUTH	Or.civ. Auth.	PEARSON	1718	48013005
AUTH	S. S.on Auth.	GALE	1726	43023008
AUTH	Sub to Auth.	MOORE	1715	61010036
AUTH	Xt.auth. Ob.	HORT	1738	61005009
AUTH	Xt's.auth. M.	FLAVEL	1673	46006027
AUTH	Xt's.auth. T.	LELAND	1769	43007028
AUTHOR	Author. Ch.	BAKER	1716	47001008
AUTHOR	Author. S. S.	OWEN	1675	45016029
AUTHOR	Ch. Author.	LESTLIE	1709	43018017
AUTHOR	Ch. Author.	INNES	1717	43018017
AUTHOR	Ch. Author.	HOLBROOK	1722	43016019
AUTHOR	Ch. Author.	MICHELL	1737	43023002
AUTHOR	Ch. Author.	WARBURTON	1754	43023002
AUTHOR	Ch. Author.	WARBURTON	1754	43023009
AUTHOR	Xt's. Author.	GARDINER	1720	43007028
AUTHOR	Xt's. Author.	CLARKE	1735	43028018
AUTHOR	Xt's. Author.	TILLOTSON	1735	43028018
AV	Av.to Truth.	STRAIGHT	1741	46008045
AVAR	Avar.& Lux.	CONEY	1750	45012020
AVARICE	Avarice.	DELANY	1747	19010003
AVOID	Avoid. Off.	DAVIES	1754	44009047
AVOID	Avoid Divis.	COCK	1707	48016017
AVOID	Avoid Extre.	ENFIELD	1772	20004027
AW	Tak.aw. Sin.	SUTTON	1718	46001029
AXE	Axe laid t. R.	KEACH	1692	43003010
B	Ad's L.b. Xt.	MASON	1758	48005015
B	Ag.b.run. G.	UNWIN	1773	48013007
B	Au.1.b. R. S.	ANDERSON	1720	68000003
B	B.& Att.o. G.	HUSSEY	1755	48001019
B	B. Ch.	ATTERBURY	1699	19096009
B	B. Ch.	MORER	1708	02035035
B	B. Ch.	HOLE	1713	19029002
B	B. Ch.	WELTON	1724	01028017
B	B. Ch.	WELTON	1724	11006028
B	B. Ch.	ATTERBURY	1743	43005016
B	B. Pe.mak.	HORNECK	1706	43005009
B	B. Pe.mak.	NORRIS	1728	43005009
B	B. Pe.mak.	GROVE	1742	43005009
B	B. Pe.mak.	HALES	1766	43005009
B	B. Pe.mak.	ORR	1772	43005009
B	B. R.n. M. S.	ANONYMOUS	1735	56002001
B	B. Un.w. Xt.	FLAVEL	1673	46017023
B	B.o. R. M.o. S	BENSON	17--	56002001

Keyword	In its Context	Author	Year	BkChpVrs
B	B.of Pers.for	FARINDON	1672	43005010
B	B.of Pers.for	HORNECK	1706	43005010
B	B.of Pers.for	GROVE	1742	43005010
B	Bear one a B.	STRAIGHT	1741	62005011
B	Bles.ap.b. G.	WATTS	1753	19042002
B	Bles.ap.b. G.	PEARSE	1763	19042002
B	Bless.of b. Pe	COLLINGES	1684	43005010
B	Bless.of b. Pe	BLACKBURNE	1708	43005010
B	Bless.of b. Pe	BRAGGE	1713	43005010
B	Bless.of b. Pe	GARDINER	1720	43005010
B	Bless.of b. Pe	BLACKALL	1723	43005010
B	Bless.of b. Pe	EDWARDS	1726	43005010
B	Bless.of b. Pe	NORRIS	1728	43005010
B	Bless.of b. Pe	BLAIR	1740	43005010
B	Bless.of b. Pe	ORR	1772	43005010
B	C.b. F.&f. G.	PIKE	1748	48004016
B	Ch.g.&b. M.	TILLOTSON	1735	65003010
B	Co. Child-b.	CHARNOCK	1684	57002015
B	Com. Xt's.b.	JONES	1756	49010016
B	D. B. Rep.	DORRINGTON	1703	04023010
B	Dea.b. Ad. F.	LAWSON	1764	48005012
B	Dea.b. Ad. F.	BOSTON	1773	48005012
B	Dea.b. Rep.	BEVERLEY	1670	45023039
B	Dea.b. Rep.	VEAL	1690	45023042
B	Dea.b. Rep.	MARCH	1699	45023039
B	Dea.b. Rep.	LAKE	1705	45023043
B	Dea.b. Rep.	FIDDES	1720	47026020
B	Dea.b. Rep.	BURNET	1747	45023043
B	Death b. R.	WHALEY	1695	43020009
B	Death b.rep.	SCOTT	1700	43025010
B	Death b.rep.	SHERLOCK	1772	43027038
B	Death-b. R.	SCAMLER	1685	19095008
B	Death-b. R.	WARREN	1748	47017030
B	Dis b. P.& B.	CONYBEARE	1757	47015039
B	Duty b. Dan.	ERSKINE	1764	24013016
B	E.dr. X. F. B.	SUTTON	1754	46006053
B	En.g.&b.m.	LUCAS	1722	20014032
B	En.g.&b.m.	TILLOTSON	1735	20014032
B	Ev.co.&b. B.	WHITE	1757	49015033
B	F.f.b. L.& G.	WILSON	1781	52005003
B	Fai b.on Kn.	WATTS	1753	58001012
B	Fai.w.b. L.	GROVE	1742	51005006
B	Fear of God b.	STILLINGFLEET	1707	18023015
B	Fool.&w. B.	SOUTH	1727	43007026
B	Fool.&w. B.	BLAIR	1740	43007026
B	Fth&w.b. L.	TAYLOR	1678	62002024
B	G.&.b. Com.	TRAPP	1752	20018014
B	G.&b. Princ.	IBBOT	1726	43006022
B	G.&b. Spir.	WILSON	1781	44005013
B	G. Xrter.b. F.	WORTHINGTON	1775	20022001
B	G.l.b.or. Xn.	WILKINS	1682	59002010
B	G.l.b.or. Xn.	ROGERS	1735	59002010
B	G.only b.ser.	BEVERIDGE	1720	43004010
B	G's Pres.b. S.	BRADBURY	1772	19046005
B	Good&b. C.	CONEY	1750	20013020
B	Good&b. C.	ABERNETHY	1751	20013020

INDEXES TO THIRD VOLUME: E: KEYWORD-IN-CONTEXT INDEX OF OTHER SUBJECTS OR OCCASIONS

Keyword	In its Context	Author	Year	BkChpVrs
B	Good&b. C.	PETERS	1776	65003020
B	Good&b. E.	MOORE	1716	49010011
B	Good&b. Z.	SEIGNIOR	1670	51004017
B	Good&b.co.	WILKINS	1682	20013020
B	Gr.b. Gift.	NALSON	1737	45011011
B	Heath.b. Xt.	SHERLOCK	1719	52002012
B	Inno.b. Rep.	FIDDES	1720	45015007
B	Int.b.r.&w.	BOURDALOUE	1776	43013025
B	Just.b. Faith.	COYTE	1761	51005006
B	K's b. Day.	WALKER	1738	43007012
B	King's b. D.	WRIGHT	1718	01040023
B	King's b. D.	ROBINSON	1719	19118022
B	Kn. Sin b. L.	CLARKE	1735	48007007
B	Kn. Sin b. L.	VENN	1759	48007009
B	Law est.b. F.	WESTLEY	1750	48003031
B	Law est.b. G.	TAYLOR	1704	48003031
B	Ma.b. Cr.&c.	ERSKINE	1764	23054005
B	Man b.blind.	BRAGGE	1702	46009001
B	Man b.blind.	DODD	1757	46009030
B	Marks n.b.	WHITFIELD	1739	47019005
B	Mon.b. East.	STANHOPE	1715	44014001
B	Mond.b. E.	STANHOPE	1715	23063001
B	Mond.b. E.	WARREN	1748	43011030
B	Mor.b. P. L.	HICKES	1726	45011042
B	Mor.b. Rit.	MANTON	1708	43009013
B	N.5.b.	VENN	1778	62003017
B	Nat.dis.b. Goo	STRADLING	1692	23005020
B	Nat.dis.b. Goo	SOUTH	1727	23005020
B	Nat.dis.b. Goo	MOSS	1732	23005020
B	Nat.dis.b. Goo	STEPHENS	1737	23005020
B	Nat.dis.b. Goo	ORR	1749	23005020
B	New Cr.or b.	HAMMOND	1684	51006015
B	New Cr.or b.	IBBOT	1726	51006015
B	New Cr.or b.	STEBBING	1739	51006015
B	Not.t.b. Off.	HEYLYN	1749	43011004
B	Obed.b. Rep.	PAYNE	1698	45015031
B	Pr.&fut.st. B.	COLLIER	1686	49015029
B	Pr.b.hinde.	PARKHURST	1707	63003007
B	Proof.b. Mir.	BULLOCK	1726	46015024
B	Pub. W.b. P.	CLARKSON	1696	19087002
B	Queen's b.d.	MORER	1708	47010038
B	Red.b. Xt.	FLAVEL	1673	49001030
B	Red.b. Xt.	USHER	1678	69021008
B	Red.b. Xt.	ERSKINE	1764	49001030
B	Red.b. Xt.	HALL	1777	48008003
B	Redem.b. Xt	DORRINGTON	1705	49006020
B	Res.of B.&c.	PRICE	1757	61006002
B	Res.same B.	FELTON	1725	49015023
B	Res.same B.	JOHNSON	1733	49015036
B	Res.same B.	WHITFIELD	1751	49015035
B	Rest.t.b.obt.	ALLESTREE	1684	43011028
B	S. S.t.b.read.	FOWLER	1675	55005027
B	S.b. Easter.	STANHOPE	1715	43027001
B	S.b. Easter.	HOLE	1716	43027001
B	S.b. Easter.	ANONYMOUS	1776	69007014
B	S.b. Fair.	KEMP	1668	50002017

Keyword	In its Context	Author	Year	BkChpVrs
B	S.b. Xtmas.	WADE	1729	43011002
B	Sac.of our B.	HUSSEY	1758	48012001
B	Salv b. Faith	WESTLEY	1746	52002008
B	Salv b. Xt.al.	BEVERIDGE	1720	47004012
B	Salv.b. Faith.	ANONYMOUS	1768	52002008
B	Salv.b. Gra.	ACTON	1714	52002005
B	Salv.b. Gra.	DUNLOP	1722	52002008
B	Salv.b. Gra.	SUTTON	1754	52002008
B	Salv.b. Gra.	HAWEIS	1762	52002008
B	Salv.b. Xt.al.	STAYNOE	1700	47004012
B	Salv.b Faith	STRAIGHT	1741	52002008
B	Salv.b Grace	TAYLOR	1719	52002008
B	Sat. Pow.b.	ERSKINE	1764	45022031
B	Self-lo.& B.	WEBSTER	1748	58003001
B	Si.& M.b. N.	ENGLAND	1700	52002001
B	Sin dou.b.a.	ORTON	1776	48014023
B	Soul dis.f. B.	HOLDEN	1755	45022043
B	St. P.b. Felix	NEWTON	1782	47024010
B	Sub.to S. B.	LANGHORNE	1773	62004007
B	Sund.b. East.	KILLIGREW	1689	19110007
B	Sund.b. East.	STANHOPE	1715	53002005
B	Sund.b. East.	HOLE	1716	53002005
B	Sund.b. L.	HOWARD	1742	43012041
B	T. Shep.b. K.	LANEY	1662	63002025
B	T. T. Xt's. B.	CATCOTT	1753	46001014
B	T.a. T.b. S. S	GOAD	1664	55005021
B	Thur.b. East.	STANHOPE	1715	45023001
B	Thurs.b. E.	STANHOPE	1715	49011017
B	Tr. Xn.b. Xr.	GODDARD	1781	47026029
B	Trin.b.	JACOMB	1676	65005007
B	Trin.b.	LITTLETON	1680	65005007
B	Trin.b.	HOWELL	1711	65005007
B	Trin.b.	LESTLEY	1720	65005007
B	Trin.b.	MARSHALL	1731	65005007
B	Trth.b. Em.	PRICE	1661	51004016
B	Tues.b. East.	STANHOPE	1715	44015001
B	Wal.b. Rule.	HORTON	1679	51006016
B	Walk.b. Fai.	NORRIS	1728	50005007
B	Walk.b. Fai.	MILLER	1749	50005007
B	Walk.b. Fai.	ABERNETHY	1751	50005007
B	Wed.b. East.	STANHOPE	1715	61009016
B	Wis.b.reiig.	BARNES	1752	18028028
B	Wis.b.relig.	BATTY	1739	18028028
B	Wis.b.relig.	CARR	1777	18028028
B	Wisd.b. R.	CARR	1777	18027006
B	Wisd.b. Rel.	DAVIES	1771	19111010
B	Wisd.b. Rel.	HUNTER	1774	19111010
B	Wisd.b. Rel.	ORTON	1776	19111010
B	X's.d.b.cup.	BRINSLEY	1660	46018011
B	Xn. Z.b. L.j.	SYNGE	1716	51004018
B	Xt b.of virg.	KENNICOTT	1765	23007013
B	Xt's.app.b. I.	CATCOTT	1753	53002006
B	Xty.b. Juda.	ROBOTHAM	1756	51003021
B	Xy.j.b. O. T.	BULLOCK	1726	61008007
B	b. Blacks.	BACON	1749	52006008
B	b. Bp.	COCK	1707	62001027

Keyword	In its Context	Author	Year	BkChpVrs
B	b. Brit. Mer.	GOLDWIN	1715	69018023
B	b. Candid.	BROWNSWORD	1704	54003002
B	b. Chels. Ho.	SHORTHOSE	1738	58002002
B	b. Co.merch.	RAINSTORP	1684	10015021
B	b. Convoc.	KENNET	1710	45014027
B	b. Corp.	COLEIRE	1721	49013004
B	b. Corpor.	COLIERE	1726	10023003
B	b. Corpor.	DUBOIS	1742	19039004
B	b. Crim.	DE GOLS	1711	19023004
B	b. Crim.con.	CROOKE	1695	47003019
B	b. Crim.con.	DYCHE	1723	47003019
B	b. Criminals.	CROOKE	1695	32003004
B	b. Criminals.	FIDDES	1720	20018014
B	b. Criminals.	ALLEN	1744	48010009
B	b. Cromwell.	THOMSON	1665	20029002
B	b. D. Marlb.	RICH	1685	48013002
B	b. Freehold.	OWEN	1713	10019027
B	b. Goldsm.	DELL	1711	20003013
B	b. Gov. Disp.	DODD	1773	02002006
B	b. Gov. Disp.	YORKE	1776	19127005
B	b. Great Au.	FULLER	1672	57006003
B	b. Gregor.	GREGORY	1673	44013037
B	b. Incorp.s.	TRAIL	1779	27012003
B	b. K's forces.	WHITTEL	1692	04014014
B	b. King.	CALAMY	1726	20001010
B	b. L. Just.	GOODWIN	1716	26017019
B	b. L. Justices.	WILLIS	1701	20012026
B	b. L. Justices.	FORSTER	1716	49001010
B	b. L. Mayor.	STANDISH	1684	05006011
B	b. Ld. L.	VESEY	1692	07017006
B	b. Ld Just.	KING	1685	23059006
B	b. Lords.	SMITH	1703	23066025
B	b. Loyalists	BAXTER	1782	07015011
B	b. Merchant.	BRENT	1708	20003009
B	b. Officers.	KENNET	1715	49014008
B	b. Par. Cl.	MILBOURNE	1713	14029030
B	b. Par. Clerks	HILLIARD	1714	43006013
B	b. Pr. Or.	PATRICK	1689	23011006
B	b. Pr. Orange	BURNET	1668	27012003
B	b. Prin.of W.	HOWARD	1742	49013005
B	b. Soc. Linc.	ANONYMOUS	1732	18034013
B	b. Society.	BURROUGHS	1733	68000003
B	b. Univ.	LIGHTFOOT	1684	49014026
B	b. Univ.	LIGHTFOOT	1684	63005013
B	b. Univ.	STUBBS	1722	20003005
B	b. Univ.	HOLE	1720	47014017
B	b. Univ.	WYNNE	1724	55004011
B	b. Univer.	BELLAS	1779	10024011
B	b. University	LIGHTFOOT	1684	45011002
B	b. University	LIGHTFOOT	1684	48008023
B	b. Volunt.	CHAMBRE	1759	52006010
B	b. Volunt.	ROBERTSON	1780	13019013
B	b.an Execut.	ANONYMOUS	1720	50007009
B	b.ant. Brit.	PRICE	1754	19118024
B	b.gen.assem.	STITH	1746	44012017
B	b.the Duke.	LITTLETON	1735	45010041

Keyword	In its Context	Author	Year	BkChpVrs
B	b Criminals.	TUTTY	1747	49015033
B	b University	WESTLEY	1742	52005014
BAAL	Baal Peor.	MORE	1692	19106028
BAB	Bab.& Suc.	COLMAN	1728	19008002
BAB	Dan.in Bab.	HORNE	1778	27006010
BABEL	Babel&c.	MURRAY	1777	01011001
BABY	Rome, Baby.	BARNARD	1759	69018004
BACKSL	Call backsl.	WESTLEY	1771	19077007
BAD	Bad books.	DODD	1772	47019019
BAD	Bad m's Imp.	FALLE	1694	21008011
BAD	Bad. Comp.	DODDERIDGE	1743	20004014
BAD	Bad. Comp.	FARMER	1756	20013020
BAD	Bad Comp.	BRIGHT	1695	49015033
BAD	Bad Comp.	ALLEN	1712	49015033
BAD	Bad Comp.	WAKE	1722	49005009
BAD	Bad Comp.	DODD	1772	49015033
BAD	Bad Comp.	ENFIELD	1772	49015033
BAD	Bad Comp.	BOURN	1777	49015033
BAD	Bad Hab.	JORTIN	1774	24013023
BAD	Bad Habits.	SHOREY	1725	24013023
BAD	Bad Habits.	MASON	1758	48014022
BAD	Bad M.rep.g.	SNAPE	1745	63004004
BAD	Dan.bad Co.	PRIEST	1710	19119115
BAD	Good&bad.	JORTIN	1774	43013030
BALAAM	Of Balaam.	THEED	1712	04023010
BALAAM	Of Balaam.	WATERLAND	1742	04022010
BALAAM'S	Balaam's W.	PYLE	1777	04023010
BALAAM'S	Balaam's Xr.	JORTIN	1755	04022012
BALM	Balm.of Gil.	ROMAINE	1760	24008022
BANKRUP	On Bankrup.	CALAMY	1709	57006009
BANQ	Spir.banq.	LAMBERT	1779	22002004
BAP	Bap. Ld. Has.	JONES	1668	45003021
BAP	Bel.n.to Bap.	CLARKE	1734	44016016
BAP	Faith& Bap.	REAY	1755	44016016
BAP	Herod& Bap.	CONYBEARE	1757	43014006
BAP	St. John Bap.	STANHOPE	1715	45001057
BAP	St. John Bap.	HOLE	1716	45001057
BAP	St. John Bap.	NEWLIN	1720	44006020
BAP	St. John Bap.	NEWLIN	1728	23057020
BAP	St. John Bap.	MARSHALL	1731	43014008
BAPT	Bapt. Mess.	STENNETT	1734	43011011
BAPT	Bapt. Mess.	ECCLES	1755	43011002
BAPT	Bapt. Minist.	HUNT	1748	43003001
BAPT	Bapt.behead.	HALL	1660	43014006
BAPT	Bapt.f.dead.	EDWARDS	1692	49015029
BAPT	Bapt.f.dead.	FORD	1692	49015029
BAPT	Bapt.in Trin.	ANONYMOUS	1720	43028019
BAPT	Bapt.into N.o.	PIERCE	1718	49001013
BAPT	Bapt.into N.o.	CLARKE	1734	49001013
BAPT	Bapt.necess.	BEVERIDGE	1720	46003005
BAPT	Bapt.o. H. G.	JOHNSON	1776	47011016
BAPT	Bapt.of adul.	SOUTHCOMB	1701	58002019
BAPT	Bapt.office.	PIERS	1758	45001017
BAPT	Bapt.or Reg.	ANONYMOUS	1708	59003004
BAPT	Bapt.s.	TOWERS	1660	43019014
BAPT	Com.to bapt.	BRETT	1712	43028019

INDEXES TO THIRD VOLUME: E: KEYWORD-IN-CONTEXT INDEX OF OTHER SUBJECTS OR OCCASIONS

Keyword	In its Context	Author	Year	BkChpVrs
BAPT	End of Bapt.	CLARKE	1734	48006003
BAPT	Episc. Bapt.	SUTTON	1718	46003005
BAPT	H. Gh.bapt.	JOHNSON	1776	47002016
BAPT	Inf. Bapt.	BOSTWICK	1765	47002039
BAPT	Inf. Bapt.	LAKE	1781	47002039
BAPT	Infant. Bapt.	HOLLAND	1700	47002038
BAPT	Infant Bapt.	SALMON	1701	44010014
BAPT	Infant Bapt.	NEWCOME	1702	44010014
BAPT	Infant Bapt.	ANONYMOUS	1715	45018015
BAPT	Infant Bapt.	HENRY	1726	44010016
BAPT	Infant Bapt.	TRAPP	1737	44010014
BAPT	John Bapt.	WESTON	1747	44001003
BAPT	Necess. Bapt.	UMFREVILLE	1739	44016016
BAPT	Obl.of Bapt.	ALLESTREE	1684	48006003
BAPT	Spir. Bapt.	WHITFIELD	1771	48006003
BAPT	St. J. Bapt.	LITTLETON	1680	43003002
BAPT	St.john bapt.	STANHOPE	1715	23040001
BAPT	St.john bapt.	HOLE	1716	23040001
BAPT	Tr. Xn. Bapt.	RELLY	1762	52004005
BAPT	Water Bapt.	COLLINGES	1680	48006003
BAPT	Water-bapt.	ANONYMOUS	1715	43028019
BAPT	Xt.& Bapt.	CONEY	1730	45007033
BAPT	Xt.& Bapt.	HOADLY	1754	45007033
BAPTISM	Baptism.	MEDE	1672	59003005
BAPTISM	Baptism.	MANTON	1676	47002038
BAPTISM	Baptism.	STUBBS	1693	43028019
BAPTISM	Baptism.	WELCHMAN	1706	43028019
BAPTISM	Baptism.	MAYO	1713	43028019
BAPTISM	Baptism.	HOLE	1715	43028019
BAPTISM	Baptism.	WILLIAMS	1714	63003021
BAPTISM	Baptism.	HOLE	1715	47002038
BAPTISM	Baptism.	HOLE	1715	48006004
BAPTISM	Baptism.	HOLE	1716	48006003
BAPTISM	Baptism.	BOYS	1716	63003021
BAPTISM	Baptism.	HOLE	1717	63003020
BAPTISM	Baptism.	HOLE	1717	63003021
BAPTISM	Baptism.	HOLE	1719	47002038
BAPTISM	Baptism.	HOLE	1719	48006004
BAPTISM	Baptism.	HOLE	1719	52005020
BAPTISM	Baptism.	LESTLEY	1720	43028019
BAPTISM	Baptism.	BAYLY	1721	48006004
BAPTISM	Baptism.	STEPHENS	1737	43028019
BAPTISM	Baptism.	RUDD	1740	43028019
BAPTISM	Baptism.	BRADBURY	1749	43028019
BAPTISM	Baptism.	BRADBURY	1749	61010022
BAPTISM	Baptism.	BRADBURY	1749	63003021
BAPTISM	Baptism.	BROWN	1764	47008036
BAPTISM	Baptism.	GILL	1765	65005003
BAPTISM	Baptism.	CASE	1774	47002038
BAPTISM	Baptism.	PENTYCROSS	1781	43028019
BAPTISM	Inf. Baptism.	ROSSINGTON	1700	54002012
BAPTISM	Inf. Baptism.	CRAGGE	1741	44016015
BAPTISM	On Baptism.	BROWNRIG	1661	47016033
BAPTISM	On Baptism.	MARTYN	1661	47016033
BAPTISM	On Baptism.	PATRICK	1670	47016033
BAPTISM	On Baptism.	HOLE	1715	47016033

Keyword	In its Context	Author	Year	BkChpVrs
BAPTISM	Xn. Baptism.	WATTS	1753	43028019
BAPTISM	Xn. Baptism.	FLEMING	1771	63003015
BAPTISM	Xt's Baptism	HALL	1661	43003015
BAPTISM	Xt's Baptism	HACKET	1675	43003013
BAPTISM	Xt's Baptism	HACKET	1675	43003014
BAPTISM	Xt's Baptism	HACKET	1675	43003015
BAPTISM	Xt's Baptism	HACKET	1675	43003016
BAPTISM	Xt's Baptism	HACKET	1675	43003017
BAPTISM	on Baptism.	HOLE	1719	43007007
BAPTIZ	Afer baptiz.	HILL	1702	48006018
BAR	Bar. Fig-tree	DODD	1757	43021018
BAR	Bar. Fig-tree.	BYRDALL	1667	45013006
BAR	Bar. Fig-tree.	BRAGGE	1702	45013006
BAR	Bar. Fig-tree.	BULKLEY	1771	45013007
BAR	Bar. H.& C.	WILKINSON	1660	24045005
BARABB	Barabb.rel.	ANONYMOUS	1711	46018020
BARABB	Rel. Barabb.	ANONYMOUS	1771	46018040
BARN	St. Barn.day.	CRADOCK	1713	55005001
BARN	St. Barn.day.	STANHOPE	1715	47011023
BARN	St. Barn.day.	HOLE	1716	47011023
BARNA	Barna. Xrter.	BARTLETT	1716	47011024
BARNAB	St. Barnab.d.	STANHOPE	1715	46015012
BARNAB	St. Barnab.d.	HOLE	1716	46015012
BARR	Barr. Fig- T.	LUCAS	1717	44011013
BARR	Barr. Fig- T.	BULKLEY	1771	44011021
BARR	Barr. Fig- T.	JORTIN	1774	44011021
BARTH	St. Barth.day	SEIGNIOR	1670	47005012
BARTH	St. Barth.day	EDWARDS	1702	45022021
BARTH	St. Barth.day	COCK	1705	45022024
BARTH	St. Barth.day	BAXTER	1707	47020024
BARTH	St. Barth.day	STANHOPE	1715	45022023
BARTH	St. Barth.day	HOLE	1716	46001047
BARTH	St. Barth.day	STANHOPE	1715	47005012
BARTH	St. Barth.day	HOLE	1716	47005012
BARTH	St. Barth.day	MARSHALL	1731	46001047
BARTH	St. Barth.day	BARON	1742	47020023
BARTI	Blind Barti.	MARKLAND	1729	45018042
BARTI	Blind Barti.	DODD	1757	45018042
BATH	Bath Waters.	JACKSON	1707	19103003
BE	Be.& Fear G.	LITTLETON	1680	62002010
BE	Be.&c.o. G.	CONANT	1722	46017003
BE	Be.&g.of G.	JONES	1741	47014017
BE	Co. Ch.be.w.	ADAMS	1683	57002015
BE	G.to be fear.	SMALRIDGE	1724	23051012
BE	Min.be.est.	HICKES	1726	50003001
BEAR	Bear one a B.	STRAIGHT	1741	62005011
BEAR	Bear. Aff.	QUINCY	1750	18002010
BEAR	Bear. Fruit.	BEVERIDGE	1720	46015008
BEAT	Beat.& Con.	BLACKALL	1723	43005001
BEAT	Beat.& Con.	EDWARDS	1726	43005001
BEAT	Beat.& Con.	JOHNSON	1740	43005001
BEAT	Beat. Spirits.	ROE	1766	65003002
BEAT	Beat. Vision.	REEVES	1729	65003002
BEAT	Beat. Vision.	CENNICK	1762	46001029
BEATIF	Beatif. Spir.	BOURN	1722	65003002
BEATITUDES	Beatitudes.	CENNICK	1762	43005003

Keyword	In its Context	Author	Year	BkChpVrs
BEATITUDES	Beatitudes.	JORTIN	1774	43005003
BEAU	Beau. Creat.	BOURN	1760	19111002
BEAUT	Beaut. Mag.	HALL	1660	19082001
BEAUT	Beaut. Sprin.	JONES	1763	22002010
BEAUT	Beaut.of Ho.	GREGORY	1708	19084001
BEAUT	G's w.beaut.	HUSSEY	1755	21003011
BEELZ	Beelz.d. H.	BURGESS	1770	44005011
BEF	bef. K.	HAYTER	1752	49007031
BEF	bef. K.	HOADLY	1754	49007031
BEG	Beg.& E.o. Y.	CLEMENT	1774	61009027
BEH	Beh. Husb.	BARKSDALE	1677	62005007
BEH	Beh.at rel.as.	ROBINSON	1776	58003014
BEH	Hezek's beh.	GODDARD	1781	23038001
BEHAV	Behav.at Ch.	LANGHORNE	1773	21005001
BEHAV	Faelix Behav.	STERNE	1766	47024026
BEHAV	Rule Behav.	MOGRIDGE	1766	43023001
BEHEAD	Bapt.behead.	HALL	1660	43014006
BEI	Bei.& P.o. G.	HOPKINS	1708	61011006
BEI	Bei.foll.o. G.	LELAND	1762	52005001
BEI	Bei.o. H. Gh.	OGDEN	1777	48015013
BEING	Being in G.	SCOTT	1743	47017028
BEING	Being in G.	HUSSEY	1755	47017028
BEING	Being of G.	NICOLSON	1661	01001001
BEING	Being of G.	ATTERBURY	1703	19014001
BEING	Being of G.	BARROW	1716	01001027
BEING	Being of G.	BARROW	1716	19019003
BEING	Being of G.	EDWARDS	1713	61001006
BEING	Being of G.	WISHEART	1716	61011006
BEING	Being of G.	LESTLEY	1720	02003014
BEING	Being of G.	PARSONS	1721	01002005
BEING	Being of G.	WAPLE	1729	61011006
BEING	Being of G.	ADAMS	1736	61011006
BEING	Being of G.	WILDER	1741	61011006
BEING	Being of G.	ABERNETHY	1743	48001019
BEING	Being of G.	DORMAN	1743	61011006
BEING	Being of G.	LELAND	1769	48001020
BEING	Being of G.	OGDEN	1777	61002006
BEING	Being G.pro.	BARROW	1716	46005017
BEING	Being God.	BARROW	1716	24051015
BEING	Da.being overr	STILLINGFLEET	1707	21007016
BEING	Da.being overr	TRAPP	1739	21007016
BEL	Bel.& Unb.	IBBOT	1726	44016016
BEL	Bel. Burden.	ERSKINE	1757	50005004
BEL	Bel. D.to L.	HALL	1777	51002019
BEL	Bel. H.in G.	WILCOX	1757	25003024
BEL	Bel. Triump.	WILCOX	1757	18019025
BEL	Bel. U.w. Xt.	LYE	1676	49006017
BEL	Bel. Xt's. Fr.	BOSTON	1773	46015014
BEL	Bel.n.to Bap.	CLARKE	1734	44016016
BEL	Bel.necess.	SNAPE	1745	46020031
BEL	Bel.of Fut. S.	ANONYMOUS	1776	45016025
BEL	Bel.of Xnty.	HAWKINS	1756	45012057
BEL	Bel.sealed.	WILSON	1735	50001022
BEL	Bel.unw. W.	ERSKINE	1764	65005010
BEL	Bless.of Bel.	IBBOT	1726	46020029
BEL	Bless.of Bel.	PEARSE	1763	19002012

Keyword	In its Context	Author	Year	BkChpVrs
BEL	Effic.of Bel.	SHARP	1734	44016016
BEL	Joy in bel.	DODSON	1728	48015013
BEL	Reas.bel. Xt.	HARRIS	1728	46011045
BEL	Rest.of Bel.	SHEPHEARD	1748	61004003
BEL	Sin in Bel.	WESTLEY	1771	50005017
BEL	Tempt. Bel.	FARMER	1756	56003005
BEL	Virt.& Bel.	BEVERIDGE	1720	46020029
BEL	Virt.& Bel.	BATTY	1739	46020029
BEL	Virt.& Bel.	BERRIMAN	1751	46020029
BEL	Xt.pr.to Bel.	DAVIES	1766	63002007
BELIE	Belie.sealed.	WILSON	1735	52001013
BELIE	Lib.of Belie.	FLAVEL	1673	46008036
BELIEF	Belief in G.	CLARKE	1732	48004003
BELIEF	Belief in Xt.	OUTRAM	1697	46014001
BELIEF	Belief in Xt.	CRAIG	1775	46006019
BELIEF	Belief o. Gos.	OUTRAM	1697	46007017
BELIEF	Belief. Gosp.	CASE	1774	44016006
BELIEF	Belief. Pray.	WATTS	1753	18023003
BELIEF	Belief.in G.	PARKHURST	1707	46005024
BELIEF	Belief.of Xy.	GOUGH	1751	65001004
BELIEF	Xn. Belief.	CLELAND	1660	43010011
BELIEV	Believ. Glo.	WHITFIELD	1771	23060019
BELIEV	Believ. Hope	BOURN	1722	65003003
BELIEV	Believ. J. Xt.	ABERNETHY	1751	65003023
BELIEV	Believ. Priv.	CENNICK	1762	46001012
BELIEV	Believ. Saf.	GIBBES	1677	19004008
BELIEV	Believ. Sec.	WELCH	1752	46010027
BELIEV	Believ.pard.	HILL	1755	19098008
BELIEV	Believ.str.h.	WALKER	1764	37009012
BELIEV	Believ.supp.	BROUSTON	1699	23041014
BELIEV	C.of Believ.	BRODHURST	1733	46011026
BELIEV	Low.believ.	WILLISON	1761	43008008
BELIEV	Qual. Believ.	CLAGETT	1720	46006044
BELIEV	Wisd.believ.	YOUNG	1706	48001022
BELIEV	X's.1.believ.	FARMER	1756	23040011
BELIEV	Xt.& Believ.	M'GEORGE	1729	19045011
BELOV	Belov. Disc.	GOUGH	1751	46013023
BELOV	Belov.of G.	WHITFIELD	1771	05032012
BELOV	Xt.belov.&c.	BOSTON	1775	52001006
BEN	Ben.& Edif.	WOOD	1775	61010024
BEN	Ben. Fear.al.	LARDNER	1751	20028014
BEN	Ben.f. Pray.	OGDEN	1770	43007007
BEN	Ben.of affl.	BERRIMAN	1751	62001009
BEN	Ben.of Sch.	ANONYMOUS	1780	45014014
BEN	Ben.preach.	SHERLOCK	1772	49001021
BEN	Sacerd. Ben.	GIBSON	1709	14030018
BEN	Vain Gl. Ben.o	CARLETON	1736	51005026
BEN	Vain Gl. Ben.o	MILLER	1749	51005026
BENE	Apost.bene.	LARDNER	1760	50013014
BENED	Apos. Bened.	BARKER	1763	52006024
BENEF	Benef. Afflic.	NEWTON	1736	19094012
BENEF	Benef.of affl.	STEWARD	1734	61012010
BENEF	Benef.of affl.	HOADLY	1754	61012011
BENEF	Benef.of Pr.	IBBOT	1726	18021015
BENEF	Benef.of Pr.	LANGHORNE	1773	18021015
BENEF	Benef.of Xt.	STAFFORD	1699	61002015

INDEXES TO THIRD VOLUME: E: KEYWORD-IN-CONTEXT INDEX OF OTHER SUBJECTS OR OCCASIONS

Keyword	In its Context	Author	Year	BkChpVrs
BENEFIC	Xn. Benefic.	FIDDES	1720	61013016
BENEFIC	Xn. Benefic.	HUTCHINS	1782	20003009
BENEFICENCE	Beneficence.	LANGHORNE	1773	51006010
BENEV	Div. Benev.	FARMER	1756	52002005
BENEV	Div. Benev.	AMORY	1766	52002005
BENEV	Div. Benev.	AMORY	1766	61013010
BENEV	Univ. Benev.	TUTTY	1741	45010037
BENEV	Univ. Benev.	STONE	1771	49013003
BENEV	Univ. Benev.	ORR	1772	49013013
BENEV	Univ. Benev.	STOCKDALE	1773	49013013
BENEVOL	Benevol.	CARRINGTON	1754	19112006
BENEVOL	L's. Benevol.	WHITE	1757	46013034
BENEVOL	Xn. Benevol.	MOSS	1737	48012009
BENEVOL	Xn. Benevol.	STRAIGHT	1741	48012009
BENEVOL	Xn. Benevol.	HEYLYN	1749	48012009
BENEVOL	Xn. Benevol.	COCKMAN	1750	61013016
BENEVOLENCE	Benevolence	SILVESTER	1734	46013034
BENEVOLENCE	Benevolence	HUNT	1748	48013009
BENEVOLENCE	Benevolence	LAWSON	1764	48012006
BENEVOLENCE	Benevolence	ENFIELD	1772	49010024
BENEVOLENCE	Benevolence	JEBB	1773	47020035
BENEVOLENCE	Benevolence	BOURN	1777	51006009
BEREA	Cond. Berea.	BALGUY	1750	47017011
BEST	Best. Wisd.	BRUNNING	1660	62003017
BEST	Best.bond.	ERSKINE	1764	24030021
BEST	Best G.et.life	AMORY	1766	46006068
BEST	C.best Gifts.	HORTON	1679	49012031
BEST	G.best. Go.	BEVERIDGE	1720	19073025
BEST	Pl.best Rel.	DODSLEY	1745	20007017
BEST	Rel.& Vir.best	ROGERS	1730	63003013
BEST	Rel.& Vir.best	WARREN	1739	63003013
BEST	Rel.best ch.	NICOLSON	1661	45010041
BET	H.bet.hearts	ANGIER	1662	23029013
BET	Str.bet.two.	WILLISON	1761	53001023
BETH	Bir.at Beth.	DOWNES	1761	43002003
BETHES	Cure Bethes.	HALL	1661	46005002
BETHES	Cure Bethes.	BRAGGE	1702	46005001
BETHES	Pool Bethes.	DODD	1757	46005004
BETHES	Pool Bethes.	BULKLEY	1771	46005002
BETHL	of Bethl.	HARRIS	1724	32005011
BIB	Bib.wd.o. G.	SKELTON	1754	58003014
BIB	Excel.o. Bib.	SIMPSON	1774	48001016
BIBLE	Bible soc.	ROBINSON	1782	58003015
BIGOTRY	Bigotry.	CHANDLER	1699	48014017
BIGOTRY	Bigotry.	WESTLEY	1750	44009038
BIGOTRY	On Bigotry.	ENFIELD	1772	46004009
BILL	Jews. Bill.	WINSTANLEY	1753	49009022
BIR	Bir.at Beth.	DOWNES	1761	43002003
BIR	Bir.of Pr.&c.	TURNER	1688	07017006
BIR	P. Fr. Bir.d.	SHAW	1729	13028009
BIRTH	Birth day.	HUTCHINSON	1717	10010012
BIRTH	Birth of Xt.	COLMAN	1728	19022009
BIRTH	Birth of Xt.	SAURIN	1775	23010006
BIRTH	Birth of Xt.	BOURDALOUE	1776	45002010
BIRTH	Birth Prince.	CAESAR	1717	19127003
BIRTH	Birth-day.	MACQUEENE	1687	19002006
BIRTH	K.birth d.	PATRICK	1686	19072015
BIRTH	K.birth day.	WETENHALL	1686	21010017
BIRTH	K's birth d.	GROSVENOR	1720	05033016
BIRTH	New Birth or R	BYAM	1675	46003005
BIRTH	New Birth or R	HOPKINS	1710	46003005
BIRTH	New Birth or R	HOLE	1715	46003005
BIRTH	New Birth or R	LAMBE	1717	46003005
BIRTH	New Birth or R	HOLE	1719	46003005
BIRTH	New Birth or R	FARINGTON	1741	46003005
BIRTH	New Birth or R	JONES	1756	46003005
BIRTH	New Birth.	BATTY	1739	46003008
BIRTH	New Birth.	STEPHENS	1737	65003009
BIRTH	New Birth.	SIMONS	1743	65003009
BIRTH	New Birth.	REAY	1755	46003007
BIRTH	New Birth.	WESTLEY	1771	46003007
BIRTH	New Birth.	WILSON	1781	46003007
BIRTH	Second birth	STANHOPE	1705	46001012
BITT	Heart-bitt.	SOMERVILLE	1776	20016010
BL	Bl.keep G. C.	GALLIMORE	1694	69022014
BL	Bl.pol.o. S.	FLAVEL	1673	50004003
BL	Cl V. Xt's bl.	CHARNOCK	1684	65001007
BL	Cr. Bl.& Glo.	COOKE	1739	49002009
BL	Nat. Xt's. Bl.	HOADLY	1754	47003026
BL	No Pain a bl.	WATTS	1753	69021004
BL	R. Sea, X's bl	WILLISON	1761	02014015
BL	Redeem Bl.	WILLISON	1761	52001007
BL	Tem. Bl.&c.	JENNINGS	1757	57004007
BL	Tem. Bl.&c.	LARDNER	1769	57004007
BL	Tem. Bl.&c.	JORTIN	1774	57004007
BL	The bl.choi.	HART	1702	61011025
BL	Zeb.& Iss.bl.	ORTON	1776	05033018
BLACKS	b. Blacks.	BACON	1749	52006008
BLAMELESSN	Blamelessn.	BRADY	1730	55005023
BLASP	Blasp. H. G.	BREKELL	1765	44003028
BLASPH	Blasph.&c.	NEWTON	1782	43012031
BLASPH	Of Blasph.	FORSTER	1744	02020007
BLASPHEMY	Blasphemy.	CONEY	1750	23037004
BLASPHEMY	Blasphemy.	PYLE	1777	57006001
BLAST	Blast. Men.	WHICHCOTE	1702	19039011
BLEED	A bleed. Sav.	DYER	1676	49005007
BLES	Bles.ap.b. G.	WATTS	1753	19042002
BLES	Bles.ap.b. G.	PEARSE	1763	19042002
BLES	Bles.dy.in L.	DURHAM	1681	69014013
BLES	Bles.dy.in L.	HOPKINS	1710	69014013
BLES	Bles.dy.in L.	HILL	1748	69014013
BLESS	Bless. Justif.	BAINE	1778	48008001
BLESS	Bless. Meek.	FARINDON	1674	43005005
BLESS	Bless. Meek.	LITTLETON	1680	43005005
BLESS	Bless. Meek.	HORNECK	1706	43005005
BLESS	Bless. Meek.	GARDINER	1720	43005005
BLESS	Bless. Meek.	BLACKALL	1723	43005004
BLESS	Bless. Meek.	EDWARDS	1726	43005005
BLESS	Bless. Meek.	COOKE	1739	43005005
BLESS	Bless. Meek.	BLAIR	1740	43005005
BLESS	Bless. Meek.	BUNDY	1740	43005005
BLESS	Bless. Meek.	GROVE	1742	43005005

Keyword	In its Context	Author	Year	BkChpVrs
BLESS	Bless. Meek.	WESTLEY	1748	43005005
BLESS	Bless. Meek.	COYTE	1761	43005005
BLESS	Bless. Meek.	ORR	1772	43005005
BLESS	Bless. Xt's. Y	PETERS	1776	43011028
BLESS	Bless.hear. G'	ALTHAM	1732	45011028
BLESS	Bless.hear. G'	BURNET	1747	45011028
BLESS	Bless.imp. F.	LAWSON	1764	46020029
BLESS	Bless.merc.	GARDINER	1720	43005007
BLESS	Bless.merc.	BLACKALL	1723	43005007
BLESS	Bless.merc.	EDWARDS	1726	43005007
BLESS	Bless.merc.	COOKE	1739	43005007
BLESS	Bless.merc.	BLAIR	1740	43005007
BLESS	Bless.merc.	GROVE	1742	43005007
BLESS	Bless.mourn.	FARINDON	1672	43005004
BLESS	Bless.mourn.	ALLESTRE	1684	43005004
BLESS	Bless.mourn.	HORNECK	1706	43005004
BLESS	Bless.mourn.	BRAGGE	1713	43005004
BLESS	Bless.mourn.	LUCAS	1717	43005004
BLESS	Bless.mourn.	GARDINER	1720	43005004
BLESS	Bless.mourn.	BLACKALL	1723	43005004
BLESS	Bless.mourn.	EDWARDS	1726	43005004
BLESS	Bless.mourn.	NORRIS	1728	43005004
BLESS	Bless.mourn.	COOKE	1739	43005004
BLESS	Bless.mourn.	BLAIR	1740	43005004
BLESS	Bless.mourn.	GROVE	1742	43005004
BLESS	Bless.mourn.	ORR	1772	43005004
BLESS	Bless.o. Faith	BROME	1711	47017034
BLESS	Bless.of affl.	COCK	1710	62001012
BLESS	Bless.of b. Pe	COLLINGES	1684	43005010
BLESS	Bless.of b. Pe	BLACKBURNE	1708	43005010
BLESS	Bless.of b. Pe	BRAGGE	1713	43005010
BLESS	Bless.of b. Pe	GARDINER	1720	43005010
BLESS	Bless.of b. Pe	BLACKALL	1723	43005010
BLESS	Bless.of b. Pe	EDWARDS	1726	43005010
BLESS	Bless.of b. Pe	NORRIS	1728	43005010
BLESS	Bless.of b. Pe	BLAIR	1740	43005010
BLESS	Bless.of b. Pe	ORR	1772	43005010
BLESS	Bless.of Bel.	IBBOT	1726	46020029
BLESS	Bless.of Bel.	PEARSE	1763	19002012
BLESS	Bless.of Xty.	CARMICHAEL	1757	54001012
BLESS	Bless.pur in H	BEVERIDGE	1720	43005008
BLESS	Bless.pur in H	BLACKALL	1723	43005008
BLESS	Bless.pur in H	ABERNETHY	1751	43005008
BLESS	Bless.right.	HAWEIS	1762	20012028
BLESS	Fath.l. Bless.	HART	1702	18030023
BLESS	Fount. Bless.	ERSKINE	1764	50005018
BLESS	Sav. Bless.	ERSKINE	1764	36002019
BLESSED	G's blessed.	WISHEART	1716	19119012
BLESSED	Hap.blessed.	DUNLOP	1722	23028005
BLIND	Blind Barti.	MARKLAND	1729	45018042
BLIND	Blind Barti.	DODD	1757	45018042
BLIND	Blind M.cur.	BRAGGE	1706	44008022
BLIND	Man b.blind.	BRAGGE	1702	46009001
BLIND	Man b.blind.	DODD	1757	46009030
BLINDN	Misl. Blindn.	JORTIN	1774	05027018
BLO	Wom.blo. Is.	DODD	1757	45009042

Keyword	In its Context	Author	Year	BkChpVrs
BLOOD	Eat. Blood.	SYNGE	1733	51005001
BLOOD	Xt's. Blood.	BROWNE	1749	61009014
BLOOD	Xt's.blood	ROMAINE	1760	37013001
BLOOD	Xt's.blood.	ERSKINE	1764	37013007
BO	Pe. Lo.g.bo.	BAYLY	1721	65004017
BOARD	On Board- S.	STOCKDALE	1777	63005008
BOAZ	Boaz& R.	TURNER	1685	05025005
BOAZ	Jach.& Boaz.	HUME	1676	61010023
BOD	Bod. Ex.i. R.	SCOTT	1700	57004006
BOD	Ill bod. Sym.	PEMBERTON	1727	28007009
BODIES	Busy bodies.	HOWE	1769	56003011
BODY	Ident. Body.	SKEELER	1740	49015035
BODY	Res. Body.	OGDEN	1777	49015035
BODY	Res. Body.	BATEMAN	1780	49015035
BODY	Res.of Body.	STILLINGFLEET	1707	47026008
BODY	Resur. Body.	HORNE	1778	53003020
BODY	Resurr.body	PIGGOTT	1702	46005028
BODY	Resurr.body	HORT	1738	46005028
BOLD	Bold.of Acc.	CLARKSON	1696	61004016
BON	Sp. Bon.& A.	WESTLEY	1746	48008015
BOND	Best.bond.	ERSKINE	1764	24030021
BOND	Sp.of Bond.	EVANS	1737	48008015
BONES	V.dry Bones.	CENNICK	1762	26037014
BOOKS	Bad books.	DODD	1772	47019019
BOSOM	Bosom S.	NEWCOMBE	1686	19018023
BOUNTY	Div. Bounty.	BAINE	1778	24005024
BOWMAN	Ag. Bowman	SMITH	17--	48012003
BOWMAN	Ag. Bowman	SMITH	1731	43015006
BP	Bp. G. L.	WORTHINGTON	1769	23023005
BP	Bp. G. L.	WORTHINGTON	1769	23023008
BP	Bp Atter. Im.	CHAMBRES	1722	47012005
BP	b. Bp.	COCK	1707	62001027
BP'S	Bp's Co.w. C.	LUZANEY	1697	58001013
BPS	Deac. P. Bps.	CRUCHY	1723	49012005
BPS	Office of Bps.	LAWSON	1764	43010046
BPT	Bpt. Cort.	DORRINGTON	1703	05004023
BPT	Bpt.of Adul.	PILKINGTON	1760	01017010
BPTISM	Bptism.	BROUGH	1660	51003029
BPTISM	Bptism.	BOOTH	1718	51003027
BPTISM	Bptism.	TATHAM	1780	51003027
BR	Br. Ki.& Ch.	ABERNETHY	1748	64001007
BR	Clem.to Br.	ANONYMOUS	1760	20012010
BR	Clem.to Br.	GRANGER	1772	20012010
BR	Dut. Br. Rep.	CHANDLER	1769	45017003
BR	L.of G.& Br.	SMALRIDGE	1724	65004021
BR	L.of G.& Br.	NEWTON	1736	65004021
BR	L.of G.& Br.	HOWE	1744	65004020
BR	Xt.br.of life.	WILLISON	1761	20009005
BRA	Trees& Bra.	HOW	1723	07009014
BREACH	Pub. Breach.	WEST	1716	19060002
BREAD	Daily Bread.	FARINDON	1674	43006011
BREAD	Daily Bread.	GELL	1676	43006011
BREAD	Daily Bread.	STEPHENS	1699	43006011
BREAD	Daily Bread.	NEWCOME	1702	43006011
BREAD	Daily Bread.	EDWARDS	1713	43006011
BREAD	Daily Bread.	MANGEY	1717	43006011

INDEXES TO THIRD VOLUME: E: KEYWORD-IN-CONTEXT INDEX OF OTHER SUBJECTS OR OCCASIONS

Keyword	In its Context	Author	Year	BkChpVrs
BREAD	Daily Bread.	CLAGETT	1720	43006011
BREAD	Daily Bread.	BLACKALL	1723	43006011
BREAD	Daily Bread.	MOSS	1732	43006011
BREAD	Daily Bread.	MOSS	1732	45011003
BREAD	Daily Bread.	LITTLETON	1735	43006011
BREAD	Daily Bread.	BISSE	1740	43006011
BREAD	Daily Bread.	BLAIR	1740	43006011
BREAD	Daily Bread.	JACKSON	1758	43006011
BREAD	Daily Bread.	CHURCHILL	1765	43006011
BREAD	Xt. Bread. L.	CLARKE	1734	46006035
BRIBERY	Ag. Bribery.	KELSALL	1712	05016019
BRIBERY	Ag. Bribery.	REEVES	1729	43027003
BRID	Brid.f. Ton.	HOOTTON	1709	62001026
BRIDEG	Brideg.com.	ELSMERE	1767	43025005
BRIT	Brit. Cause.	SMYTH	1745	09017029
BRIT	Brit. Mercies	WILLISON	1761	19147020
BRIT	Ins. Sit. Brit	BONAR	1773	33003008
BRIT	b. Brit. Mer.	GOLDWIN	1715	69018023
BRIT	b.ant. Brit.	PRICE	1754	19118024
BRITISH	British Vine.	BULKLEY	1764	19080008
BROTH	Broth. Adm.	HOPKINS	1716	03019017
BROTH	Broth. Love.	BRIDGE	1671	19133001
BROTH	Broth. Love.	BAYLY	1721	65003014
BROTH	Broth. Love.	WARREN	1748	65004011
BROTH	Broth. Love.	HUSSEY	1755	65004011
BROTH	Broth. Love.	DAVIS	1756	61013001
BROTH	Broth. Love.	MUSCOTT	1760	46013034
BROTH	Broth. Reco.	REYNOLDS	1679	53003015
BROTH	Broth. Repr.	BRADY	1713	55005014
BROTH	Broth.agree.	REYNOLDS	1679	53002001
BROTH	Broth.repr.	SMALRIDGE	1724	48010001
BROTH	Broth.repr.	ROWLAND	1774	43025018
BROTH	Broth Love.	SWIFT	1754	61013001
BRU	Saint or Bru.	BAXTER	1707	45010041
BTH	Pr. W. Bth-d.	SMEDLEY	1716	63002017
BUIL	W.&f. Buil.	BRAGGE	1704	43007024
BUILD	Build. Arm.	ERSKINE	1674	16004018
BUILDER	Builder.	BRAGGE	1704	45014028
BUILDER	Builder.	BULKLEY	1771	45014028
BURDEN	Bel. Burden.	ERSKINE	1757	50005004
BURIAL	Jes. Burial.	COLMAN	1728	43028006
BURN	Burn. Bush.	WHITFIELD	1771	02003002
BURN	Burn. World	JOHNSON	1740	64003011
BUS	Bus.of life.	DORRINGTON	1705	46009004
BUS	One's o. Bus.	ROSEWELL	1708	46021021
BUS	Rel.ch.bus.l.	BLACKALL	1723	43006033
BUS	Rel.ch.bus.l.	BEVERIDGE	1726	43006033
BUSH	Burn. Bush.	WHITFIELD	1771	02003002
BUSI	Rel.our Busi.	WATSON	1677	45002049
BUSIN	Busin.of life.	MAY	1757	21012013
BUSIN	R.ab. Busin.	BATTY	1739	45010041
BUSIN	Worl. Busin.	WHITFIELD	1739	43008022
BUSY	Busy bodies.	HOWE	1769	56003011
BUTCH	Butch. L.	HENLEY	1729	19008006
BUYERS	Buyers& S.	BRAGGE	1706	46002013
BUYERS	Buyers& S.	MARKLAND	1729	46002013
BUYERS	Buyers& S.	DODD	1757	43021012
BUYERS	Buyers& S.	BULKLEY	1771	46002013
BY	Ch.del.by Xt	ERSKINE	1764	21009014
BY	F. Gl.by Son.	JOHNSON	1776	46016025
BY	Judg.by Xt.	HURRION	1712	58004001
BY	Jus.by Faith.	USHER	1678	48005001
BY	Jus.by Faith.	SCOTT	1701	48003028
BY	Jus.by Faith.	WILLIAMS	1708	48005001
BY	Jus.by Faith.	BARROW	1716	48005001
BY	Jus.by Faith.	BILLINGSLEY	1723	48005001
BY	Jus.by Faith.	DODSON	1728	48005002
BY	Jus.by Faith.	BIRCH	1729	48005001
BY	Jus.by Faith.	STEPHENS	1737	48003028
BY	Jus.by Faith.	WESTLEY	1746	48004005
BY	Jus.by Faith.	HOOLE	1748	48003028
BY	Jus.by Faith.	ABERNETHY	1748	48004016
BY	Jus.by Faith.	SHEPHERD	1748	51002016
BY	Jus.by Faith.	SMITH	1752	48003028
BY	Jus.by Faith.	HAYWARD	1758	48005001
BY	Jus.by Faith.	HALLIFAX	1760	48003028
BY	Jus.by Faith.	RANDOLPH	1768	48003028
BY	Jus.by Faith.	JOHNSON	1776	48005001
BY	Jus.by Faith.	PETERS	1776	48005001
BY	Just by works	HOOKER	1705	34001004
BY	Just.by F.	BOWMAN	1764	46003014
BY	Just.by Wor.	GALE	1726	53003009
BY	Just.by Wor.	BRADBURY	1772	48004003
BY	Just.by Xt.	WHITFIELD	1739	49006011
BY	Led by Sp.	SOUTH	1724	48008014
BY	Liv.by Faith.	SUTTON	1754	51003011
BY	No acc.by F.	ALLEN	1761	62002014
BY	O. L.g.by Xt.	BRAILSFORD	1776	49015022
BY	Pray.by Sp.	OUTRAM	1697	49014015
BY	Prof.by Ser.	WILSON	1781	45008018
BY	Reco.by Xt.	SHEPHERD	1748	52002013
BY	Red.by Xt.	USHER	1678	46001012
BY	Red.by Xt.	USHER	1678	53002006
BY	Red.by Xt.	ERSKINE	1764	69002009
BY	Rede.by Xt.	USHER	1678	52001013
BY	Rede.by Xt.	LOVEDER	1756	54001014
BY	Sal.by gr. G.	KIMBER	1756	59002011
BY	Salv.by Fai.	BEVERIDGE	1720	47016031
BY	Salv.by Fai.	DUNLOP	1722	47016031
BY	Salv.by Fai.	BARKER	1748	47016031
BY	Salv.by Gra.	SPOONER	1771	59002011
BY	Salv.by Xt.	WHICHCOTE	1702	58001009
BY	Salv.by Xt.	SEAGRAVE	1737	46003016
BY	Salv.by Xt.	BUNDY	1740	46004022
BY	Salv.by Xt.	MALTUS	1762	43007021
BY	Salv.by Xt.	CHANDLER	1769	47004012
BY	Salv.by Xt.	WILSON	1781	57001015
BY	Salvat.by Xt.	SHERLOCK	1772	57001015
BY	Suff.by Fire.	MILLS	1781	43025040
C	Ade. R.of C.	SANDERSON	1722	62004012
C	Aff. C.& Civ.	LANGHORNE	1773	63003008
C	Ag. Atha. C.	CARTER	1752	43023008

Keyword	In its Context	Author	Year	BkChpVrs
C	Bar. H.& C.	WILKINSON	1660	24045005
C	Bl.keep G. C.	GALLIMORE	1694	69022014
C	Bp's Co.w. C.	LUZANEY	1697	58001013
C	C.& Redem.	EATON	1764	19071005
C	C. Hear.ast.	BOURN	1777	43007028
C	C.b. F.&f. G.	PIKE	1748	48004016
C	C.best Gifts.	HORTON	1679	49012031
C	C.o. O.&n.t.	KNOX	1768	46005039
C	C.of Believ.	BRODHURST	1733	46011026
C	C.of Tong.	JENKINS	1779	01011006
C	C.pro. G. D.	RAWSON	1708	47015039
C	C.to o.m's. S.	STOWE	1681	49003006
C	Ch.suf.f.p's c	BREKEL	1767	24031029
C	Distem.of C.	KING	1747	02009003
C	Distem.of C.	ANONYMOUS	1750	02009003
C	Doct.o. C. C.	ADAMS	1716	57001013
C	Engl. C.	PARKHURST	1706	30004011
C	Ephraim's C.	HAMMOND	1684	24031018
C	F. C.of H. L.	SANDERSON	1722	15010007
C	F.judg.c.& P.t	BRYAN	1685	50005010
C	F.judg.c.& P.t	BURNET	1747	50005010
C	Faith c. Salv.	CHARNOCK	1684	46003036
C	Faith c. Salv.	MORRIS	1743	46003036
C	Fear& C.&c.	WILSON	1781	63001017
C	Fin. C. H. L.	SANDERSON	1722	58002002
C	Fol. Hum. C.	LLOYD	1765	19118008
C	G's pres.in C.	WHITTY	1772	19132014
C	G's Gl.o.c.e.	WISHEART	1716	49010031
C	G's Gl.o.c.e.	TILLOTSON	1735	49010031
C	Gl.in C.o. Xt.	MACLAURIN	1772	51006014
C	Good& E. C.	SALMON	1753	18025005
C	Good&b. C.	CONEY	1750	20013020
C	Good&b. C.	ABERNETHY	1751	20013020
C	Good&b. C.	PETERS	1776	65003020
C	Happ.rel. C.	REYNER	1745	20010029
C	Haz. Self- C.	JENKINS	1779	12008013
C	Hum. Na. C.	WEBB	1772	05032005
C	Imp.or.in C.	BLAIR	1780	49014040
C	M.& Xs.c. S.	SLADEN	1733	45014034
C	M's. Sins n.c.	MACLAURIN	1772	62001013
C	Ma. C.& E. S.	SIMONS	1743	64001010
C	Ma. C.& E. S.	WARREN	1748	64001010
C	Ma, C.& El.s.	SHARP	1734	64001010
C	Martha's C.	CONEY	1730	45010041
C	Ob.of C.& A.	KENNICOTT	1747	01004001
C	Old w.e.n. C.	PITTIS	1682	65002024
C	On C.& Exc.	ANONYMOUS	1779	02020001
C	On Lib.o. C.	SALKELD	1673	46011044
C	Or.& C.o. S.	BATTY	1739	48005019
C	Party Zeal c.	RANDOLPH	1752	49003003
C	Pers.in m. C.	STOCKDALE	1777	01049004
C	Pr. Test. J. C	BRACKENRIDGE	1764	69019010
C	R.nec.to c. S.	SKELTON	1754	63002017
C	R.poor.p. C.	BRADY	1730	62002015
C	Rel.& Virt.c.	DOUGHTY	1761	20003007
C	Rel.chief. C.	TRAPP	1752	43006023

Keyword	In its Context	Author	Year	BkChpVrs
C	Ren. Gosp.c.	ERSKINE	1764	22002013
C	Ruler's S.c.	HALL	1661	46004046
C	Self-denial& C	HOWARD	1710	43016024
C	Sinn.und. C.	CLARKSON	1696	51003010
C	St. P's. C.i.	WILSON	1781	53001021
C	St. Pa.c.&m.	BROUGHTON	1778	47009015
C	Stars and C.	ANONYMOUS	1670	43002009
C	T. X's.c.fit.	FOSTER	1737	51004004
C	T. X's.c.fit.	CLEAVER	1743	51004004
C	Text c.&ex.	MEDE	1672	61010005
C	The Jailor c.	WEBB	1766	47016033
C	Time Xt's. C.	PYLE	1777	69022012
C	Un. C. Xn. C.	HOLBROOK	1727	55004007
C	Va.of C.& Y.	WILLIAMS	1750	21011010
C	W.w. F.c. J.	HORNE	1761	62002014
C	Xn's C.to L.	BULKLEY	1771	51005013
C	Xrter true C.	D'ASTOR	1700	04024005
C	Xt.c.charity	CONYBEARE	1757	49013013
C	Xt's. C. L. G.	CRAIG	1775	46011033
C	Xt's. D.on C.	FLAVEL	1673	47002023
C	Xt's.c.t. Xns.	MARTIN	1779	43005029
C	Xt's.c.to C.	WALLIN	1746	45023034
C	Xt's.myst.c.	DODDERIDGE	1761	46008007
C	Zacheus's C.	SHEPHERD	1703	45019001
C	Zacheus's C.	BRAGGE	1706	45019002
C	2 Arg.f. C. P.	BROOKS	1665	43006006
C	4 S. Xt.on C.	FLAVEL	1673	43027046
CA	Ca.of Child.	JENNINGS	1753	13029019
CA	G.1 Ca.l. E.	TILLOTSON	1735	48011036
CA	G's ten. Ca.	BRADY	1730	23005003
CA	Lust Ca.of S.	CLARKE	1735	62001014
CA	Lust Ca.of S.	SOUTH	1744	62001014
CA	Lust Ca.of S.	ABERNETHY	1751	62001014
CA	Vice ca. Inf.	PYLE	1777	46007017
CA	Worldly Ca.	MARSHALL	1731	58004013
CA	Xy.ca.rat. D.	ORR	1739	63003015
CAIN	Ang.of Cain.	FELTON	1748	01004005
CAIN	Cain& Abel.	JENKINS	1779	01004006
CAL	Cal.not Jud.	LLOYD	1765	46009001
CAL	G's.cal.t.ob.	WARREN	1748	61003015
CAL	South S. Cal.	SMITH	1721	50004018
CALAM	Pub. Calam.	BOURN	1760	45013001
CALL	Call backsl.	WESTLEY	1771	19077007
CALL	Call to unc.	BOURN	1754	26033002
CALL	Call to Rep.	CLARKE	1734	44002017
CALL	Call to Rep.	WARREN	1748	44002017
CALL	Call to Rep.	SUTTON	1754	61004007
CALL	Call to Shul.	TANNER	1674	22006013
CALL	Call to Sinn.	DYER	1666	69003020
CALL	Call.& El. Su.	BREKELL	1765	64001010
CALL	Call.& El. Su.	SANDERCOCK	1776	64001010
CALL	Call.of life.	SHARP	1734	49007017
CALL	Call.of Apos.	HOLE	1716	45005001
CALL	Call& Elect.	WHEATLAND	1739	43022014
CALL	Call Abrah.	MURRAY	1777	01012010
CALL	Differ. Call.	STEBBING	1760	49007024

INDEXES TO THIRD VOLUME: E: KEYWORD-IN-CONTEXT INDEX OF OTHER SUBJECTS OR OCCASIONS

Keyword	In its Context	Author	Year	BkChpVrs
CALL	Eff.call.&c.	GOUGH	1709	58001009
CALL	Eff.call.&c.	NEAL	1757	58001009
CALL	Effect.call.	WHITE	1676	48008028
CALL	N.call.unc.	ANONYMOUS	1756	26033011
CALL	Seam's call.	BARNETT	1712	19107023
CALL	Xn. Call.& E.	BERRIMAN	1751	64001010
CALL'D	Sinn.call'd.	HORNE	1778	52005014
CALLING	Eff. Calling.	ERSKINE	1764	45019005
CALLING	Xt's. Calling.	BENSON	1748	45005031
CALM	Calm Dispos.	M.	1733	43005005
CALUMNY	Calumny.	MEADOWCOURT	1722	47006009
CAM	Xt.cam.f. L.	BROWNE	1749	43005017
CAMP	At Camp.	WILLIAMS	1696	19060012
CAMP	at Camp.	RAWLINS	1713	14009007
CAN	Extirp. Can.	SCOTT	1743	03018025
CAN	Marr.in Can.	WHEATLY	1746	46002011
CAN	Marr.in Can.	DODD	1757	46002001
CAN	Marr.in Can.	BULKLEY	1771	46002001
CAN	P. Gosp.can.	FLEMING	1772	49002004
CAN	Woman Can.	GODDARD	1781	43005028
CANA	Faith Cana.	DODD	1757	43015022
CANA	Faith Cana.	WILLISON	1761	43015027
CAND	Cand.mind.	STURMY	1716	21007021
CAND	Xn.lig.cand.	HORNECK	1706	43005015
CAND	Xn.lig.cand.	BLAIR	1740	43005015
CANDID	b. Candid.	BROWNSWORD	1704	54003002
CANDOUR	Candour.	WALLIS	1748	51006001
CANDOUR	Candour.	BLAIR	1780	49013005
CAP	Cap. Punish.	DODD	1772	02020013
CAP	Doom Cap.	DODDRIDGE	1761	43011023
CAP	Paul cap. Xt.	BREKELL	1765	50011014
CAPTIVE	Red. Captive	BERRIMAN	1721	19102019
CAR	Car.ly-in W.	LAWSON	1764	23049022
CAR	Xt. Wor. Car.	ORTON	1776	44006003
CARE	Care of souls.	DODDERIDGE	1761	20024011
CARE	Care of H-k.	DYKES	1722	20031027
CARE	Care of Soul.	SUTTON	1754	05004009
CARE	Care on G.	KIDDER	1697	63005007
CARE	Excess. Care.	BLACKALL	1723	43006025
CARE	Heav.o.care.	BLAIR	1740	43006033
CARE	R. Care of F.	FORD	1770	01018019
CARE	Solic. Care.	SHERLOCK	1719	43006034
CARE	Solic. Care.	SMITH	1740	43006034
CARE	Solic. Care.	PRIEST	1753	43006034
CAREF	Caref. Sheph.	BOURN	1763	45015003
CAREFULNESS	Carefulness.	STANHOPE	1714	43006024
CAREFULNESS	Carefulness.	HOLE	1716	43006024
CAREL	Carel. Tem.	CARTER	1729	20021029
CARES	Cares of life.	DUCHAL	1765	21002023
CARES	World. Cares	BLACKALL	1723	43006025
CARN	Carn.&sp.m.	STILLINGFLEET	1707	48008006
CARN	Carn.&sp.m.	IBBOT	1726	48008006
CARN	Carn.&sp.m.	EVANS	1737	48008006
CARN	Carn. Cons.	ERSKINE	1764	51001016
CARN	Carn.mind.	LEIGHTON	1746	48008007
CAS	Cas. Events.	ADAMS	1736	21009011

Keyword	In its Context	Author	Year	BkChpVrs
CAS	Cas. Events.	DUCHAL	1765	21009010
CASE	Case of Abij.	EVANS	1725	11014013
CASE	Case of Abij.	JENKINS	1779	11014013
CASE	Case of Abr.	STONE	1733	61011017
CASE	Case of Abr.	SCOTT	1743	01022015
CASE	Case of Abr.	STEBBING	1760	01022001
CASE	Case of Hez.	STERNE	1766	12020015
CASE	Case of Jews.	HORNE	1778	46001011
CASE	Case Cornel.	SHERLOCK	1772	47010034
CASE	En. Case&c.	STEWARD	1687	12018022
CASE	Faelix Case.	WARNEFORD	1776	47024025
CAST	Cast. Devils.	WILLIAMS	1664	43017021
CAST	Cast Devil.	BRAGGE	1706	43015021
CAST	Cast Devil.	HOLE	1716	43015021
CAST	Usur.cast.	JELLINGER	1676	19015005
CAST	Usur.cast.	JELINGER	1676	43016026
CAT	Cat. Apost.	WENSLEY	1679	58001013
CAT	Quest. G.cat.	ERSKINE	1764	43022043
CATCH	Man.catch.	HICKERINGILL	1716	24005025
CATE	On the Cate.	WALKER	1763	47016030
CATE	On the Cate.	WALKER	1763	47016031
CATECHIS	On Catechis.	BASSET	1684	63002013
CATECHISING	Catechising.	LYE	1676	20022006
CATECHISM	Catechism.	JONES	1756	61008010
CATECHISM	Catechism.	WALKER	1763	51003024
CATH	Cath. Ch. Xt.	CLARKE	1734	61012022
CATH	Cath. Chur.	PIGOTT	1702	54001018
CATH	Cath. Comm.	BULKLEY	1754	46003005
CATH	Cath. Prot.	HARRISON	1781	43005022
CATH	Cath. Protes.	HARRISON	1781	45009056
CATH	Cath. Spirit.	WESTLEY	1771	12010015
CATH	Cath. Xrter.	GLANVILL	1681	63001022
CATHE	Cathe. Wor.	BISSE	1720	13016004
CATHO	Catho. Ch.	BAYLY	1721	46010016
CATTLE	Dis Cattle.	POWELL	1748	36001005
CATTLE	Dist. Cattle.	PARSONS	1746	19106030
CATTLE	Dist. Cattle.	ECCLES	1750	28004003
CATTLE	Mort. Cattle.	BATES	1714	31004011
CATTLE	Sick Cattle.	WIND	1748	19136001
CAU	Cau.of Infid.	SOUTH	1727	46007017
CAU	Vi. Cau. Evil.	QUINCY	1750	20019003
CAUS	Caus. Anger.	GARDINER	1720	43005021
CAUS	Caus.o. Infid.	DELAUNE	1728	56003001
CAUS	Caus.o. Unb.	TIDCOMBE	1757	46006066
CAUS	Caus.o Vices	CARR	1777	61012001
CAUS	Caus.of Ath.	HUNT	1748	05032003
CAUS	Caus.of Infi.	PENN	1757	58002025
CAUS	Caus.of R.	LONG	1684	62004001
CAUSA	Causa Dei.	GAUDEN	1661	19074022
CAUSE	Brit. Cause.	SMYTH	1745	09017029
CAUSE	Cause of Sin.	JEFFERY	1710	21007029
CAUSES	Causes Err.	CARR	1777	45011035
CAUT	Apost. Caut.	CARRINGTON	1776	52005015
CAUT	Caut. Livery	PENN	1767	20020001
CAUT	Caut.in Rep.	BLACKALL	1723	43007006
CAUT	Caut.in Rep.	BLAIR	1749	43007006

Keyword	In its Context	Author	Year	BkChpVrs
CAUTION	Caution to Y.	MUNTON	1756	21011009
CAUTION	Caution to Y.	STEBBING	1759	21011009
CAUTION	Xn. Caution.	SCATTERGOOD	1723	49010012
CAV	Cav.ag. Sed.	STANFAST	1660	43024004
CE	Fut Pun.ce.	PENTYCROSS	1781	19010013
CE	Sou. D.n.ce.	CASE	1774	58004003
CECIL	St. Cecil.day	BRADSHAW	1697	14005013
CELES	Celes.worsh.	FERNE	1721	23006003
CELEST	Celest. Race.	BUSH	1692	49009024
CEN	Cen.in.w. R.	STEEL	1776	43007003
CENS	Cens.& Rep.	GARDINER	1720	43007001
CENS	Cens. G's.m.	ALTHAM	1732	49004005
CENS	Ch. Cens. V.	NICOLSON	1661	49004021
CENS	Mistak. Cens.	DOUGHTY	1761	47028004
CENS	Mistak. Cens.	DOWNES	1761	47028004
CENS	Rash Cens.	MASON	1742	43007001
CENSORIOUSN	Censoriousn.	BARROW	1716	43007001
CENSORIOUSN	Censoriousn.	BAYLY	1721	43007001
CENSORIOUSN	Censoriousn.	EVANS	1737	43007001
CENSORIOUSN	Censoriousn.	BLAIR	1740	43007005
CENSORIOUSN	Censoriousn.	BALGUY	1750	43007001
CENSORIOUSN	Censoriousn.	FOTHERGILL	1765	59003002
CENSORIOUSN	Censoriousn.	CLEMENT	1774	43007001
CENSORIOUSN	Censoriousn.	BOURN	1777	45006037
CENSORIOUSN	Censoriousn.	JORTIN	1774	59003002
CENSUR	Censur.	PYLE	1777	48014010
CENSUR	Censur.&c.	BRADY	1730	48002001
CENSUR	Censur. Sin.	LUCAS	1710	46008007
CENSUR	Church. Censur	SMITH	1708	46020023
CENSUR	Church. Censur	REEVES	1729	46020023
CENSURE	Ag. Censure.	LITTLETON	1735	45013002
CENSURE	Censure.	GODDARD	1710	62003001
CENSURE	Censure.	CONEY	1730	43007003
CENSURING	Censuring.	PATRICK	1689	49004005
CENSURING	Censuring.	SMEDLEY	1719	62004012
CENSURING	Censuring.	MOSS	1732	62004012
CENSURING	Censuring.	WEBB	1772	62004012
CENT	Cent. Petit.	ECCLES	1755	43008008
CENT	Cent. Xrter.	WILKINS	1682	45007005
CENT	Good Cent.	BULKLEY	1771	45008005
CENTUR	G. Centur.	DODD	1757	43008013
CER	Cer.fu.judg.	HAWKINS	1725	49015019
CER	Fu. Rew.cer.	DORRINGTON	1705	57004007
CER	Rites& Cer.	JEACOCKE	1702	43015009
CEREM	Cerem. Law.	HEYLYN	1749	44002027
CEREM	Cerem. Law.	HUTCHINSON	1740	51003019
CEREM	Cerem. Law.	ROMAINE	1760	22004006
CEREMONIES	Ceremonies.	ROBINSON	1781	50004003
CERT	Cert. Death.	WHITAKER	1674	19039013
CERT	Cert. Rew.	MILLER	1749	49015058
CERT	Cert.of D.	JONES	1741	19089048
CERT	Cert.of Dea.	DICKSON	1731	61009027
CERT	Cert.of Dea.	DOUGHTY	1761	18030023
CERT	Judgm.cert.	BOURN	1755	47017031
CERT	Judgm.cert.	ANONYMOUS	1776	47017031
CERT	Mor. Cert.	SEED	1750	64001016

Keyword	In its Context	Author	Year	BkChpVrs
CERT	Resurr.cert.	IBBOT	1726	49015021
CERT	Resurr.cert.	IBBOT	1726	50011021
CH	Adm. Ch. E.	WATSON	1755	68000005
CH	Ag. Ch.of R.	HILL	1680	69018004
CH	Ap.f. Ch. En.	PARSONS	1767	55005021
CH	At Newg.ch.	FORSTER	1777	47009011
CH	Aug. Ch.	BOWYER	1734	16013014
CH	Auth.of Ch.	MASON	1705	49014040
CH	Auth.of Ch.	HOARD	1709	49014040
CH	Author. Ch.	BAKER	1716	47001008
CH	B. Ch.	ATTERBURY	1699	19096009
CH	B. Ch.	MORER	1708	02035035
CH	B. Ch.	HOLE	1713	19029002
CH	B. Ch.	WELTON	1724	01028017
CH	B. Ch.	WELTON	1724	11006028
CH	B. Ch.	ATTERBURY	1743	43005016
CH	Behav.at Ch.	LANGHORNE	1773	21005001
CH	Br. Ki.& Ch.	ABERNETHY	1748	64001007
CH	Cath. Ch. Xt.	CLARKE	1734	61012022
CH	Catho. Ch.	BAYLY	1721	46010016
CH	Ch p. F.& H.	HOLE	1725	49013013
CH	Ch.& Union.	WAKE	1716	48015005
CH	Ch.&just.	SOUTHCOMB	1714	43007012
CH	Ch.&just.	PYLE	1777	43007012
CH	Ch. Author.	LESTLIE	1709	43018017
CH	Ch. Author.	INNES	1717	43018017
CH	Ch. Author.	HOLBROOK	1722	43016019
CH	Ch. Author.	MICHELL	1737	43023002
CH	Ch. Author.	WARBURTON	1754	43023002
CH	Ch. Author.	WARBURTON	1754	43023009
CH	Ch. Cens. V.	NICOLSON	1661	49004021
CH	Ch. Ch.of R.	BAYLEY	1721	44007009
CH	Ch. Comm.	JEACOCKE	1702	52004004
CH	Ch. Comm.	WARBURTON	1754	52004003
CH	Ch. Confo.	SHERWILL	1704	43023023
CH	Ch. Distrib.	BROWN	1764	65003017
CH	Ch. Eng. Ap.	LOWTH	1722	47002042
CH	Ch. G's Port.	BLIGH	1765	05032009
CH	Ch. Ha.of G.	WALLIN	1774	52002022
CH	Ch. Priv.	DODSON	1728	24007004
CH	Ch. Reform.	THOMAS	1661	21005001
CH	Ch.commu.	BRIGGS	1675	49001010
CH	Ch.commu.	WARBURTON	1754	45009049
CH	Ch.d.to d. P.	BURNABY	1777	51006010
CH	Ch.del.by Xt	ERSKINE	1764	21009014
CH	Ch.e. F.& H.	MOSS	1732	49013013
CH	Ch.e. F.& H.	MORRIS	1743	49013013
CH	Ch.g.&b. M.	TILLOTSON	1735	65003010
CH	Ch.indefect.	HUTCHIN	1689	43016018
CH	Ch.indefect.	GOODMAN	1697	43016018
CH	Ch.indefect.	GREY	1730	43016018
CH	Ch.indefect.	CLARKE	1734	43016018
CH	Ch.of Assist.	MACRO	1732	51005014
CH	Ch.of Eng.v.	LE FRANK	1662	49011018
CH	Ch.of Engl.	STANHOPE	1716	48010015
CH	Ch.of Engl.	BAYLY	1721	45011002

Keyword	In its Context	Author	Year	BkChpVrs
CH	Ch.of R.im.	BENNETT	1714	43005019
CH	Ch.of Scorn.	STRAIGHT	1741	45006025
CH	Ch.of Scotl.	CARLYLE	1776	19048012
CH	Ch.of Xt.	MARCH	1689	69002005
CH	Ch.of Xt.	HILLIARD	1717	43006010
CH	Ch.request.	BULL	1695	19122006
CH	Ch.s. Fr. Pro.	HICKES	1713	50004009
CH	Ch.s. Frost.	TREBECK	1739	53004006
CH	Ch.s.f. Wid.	CHANDLER	1748	50009012
CH	Ch.stated.	SEED	1750	20003027
CH	Ch.suf.f.p's c	BREKEL	1767	24031029
CH	Ch.to poor.	DYKES	1722	20031020
CH	Ch.to poor.	STEBBING	1760	05015011
CH	Ch.to Clergy	POTTER	1753	51004018
CH	Ch.to Poor.	NORRIS	1728	65003017
CH	Claim Ch. R.	BULKLEY	1761	43016018
CH	Co. Ch.be.w.	ADAMS	1683	57002015
CH	Corr. Ch. R.	SKELTON	1754	65004001
CH	Cruel R. Ch.	STEPHENS	1728	43005007
CH	Def. Ch. En.	HARRISON	1729	53001020
CH	Def. Ch. En.	STOCKDALE	1777	19096009
CH	Design o. Ch.	CRADOCK	1706	57001005
CH	Diff.off. Ch.	ROGERS	1730	49012028
CH	Dut.o. Pa.& Ch	ADAMS	1676	54003020
CH	Dut.o. Pa.& Ch	NICHOLS	1701	54003020
CH	E.& N.o. Ch.	HOLE	1725	49013001
CH	Educ. Ch.	FLEETWOOD	1737	20013024
CH	Establ. Ch.	ALLEN	1773	23008009
CH	F.& Ch.s.	DELANY	1766	51005024
CH	Fallen Ch.	ENGLISH	1776	69002005
CH	G's.ch.mer.	MACLAURIN	1772	48008032
CH	Gov. Ch. Ch.	NICOLSON	1661	23002004
CH	Gov. Xt's.ch.	BAINE	1778	49005012
CH	Ign. Jew. Ch.	BILSTONE	1763	51004003
CH	Inf. Ch.of R.	SMYTH	1735	50001024
CH	Inst.of Ch.	WILSON	1781	05006006
CH	Invis. Ch.	LEE	1675	43016018
CH	Kn.& Ch.un.	WRIGHT	1732	49008001
CH	Know.& Ch.	HORNE	1778	49008001
CH	Lit. Ch. Eng.	DURELL	1688	49011016
CH	Lo.& Ch.enf.	HOLE	1716	65004007
CH	Love& Ch.	CLARKE	1734	65004021
CH	Meas.of Ch.	HORNECK	1706	43005042
CH	Meas.of Ch.	BLACKALL	1723	43005040
CH	Meas.of Ch.	BLAIR	1740	43005042
CH	Misap. P. Ch.	WILSON	1768	41004001
CH	Mort.of Ch.	EATON	1764	18001018
CH	N.& P.of Ch.	CONANT	1703	49013004
CH	N.& P.of Ch.	CROSSINGE	1722	49013004
CH	N.& P.of Ch.	HOLE	1725	49013004
CH	Notes tr. Ch.	KIDDER	1697	47002042
CH	Notes tr. Ch.	KEITH	1704	47002041
CH	Notes tr. Ch.	CHANDLER	1735	57003014
CH	Of the Ch.	SHARP	1735	49012013
CH	On rob. Ch.	GREEN	1737	52004028
CH	P's. Ch. Tim.	NEWLIN	1728	58004005

Keyword	In its Context	Author	Year	BkChpVrs
CH	Par D.to Ch.	EATON	1764	20022006
CH	Pea. Ch. Ch.	REYNOLDS	1679	48014009
CH	Persua.t. Ch.	DOUGHTY	1742	44012041
CH	Plea.f. Ch. E.	HOLLINGWORTH	1676	46006068
CH	Pros. Ch. Ch.	CLAGETT	1720	23011009
CH	Purity& Ch.	BURTON	1684	62001027
CH	R. Loy.& Ch.	STUBBS	1704	63002017
CH	Reb. Ch.	HOW	1731	45007005
CH	Reb. Ch.	CRANER	1749	16002020
CH	Rebuild. Ch.	CONANT	1699	36002006
CH	Rel.best ch.	NICOLSON	1661	45010041
CH	Rel.ch.bus.l.	BLACKALL	1723	43006033
CH	Rel.ch.bus.l.	BEVERIDGE	1726	43006033
CH	Rever.to Ch.	BERRIMAN	1763	01028017
CH	Saf.of Ch.	BAINE	1778	19087007
CH	Sal. Ch.only.	NEWCOME	1702	47002047
CH	Sal. Ch.only.	COCKBURN	1712	47002047
CH	Sal. Ch.only.	BOYS	1716	47002047
CH	Sal. Ch.only.	BEVERIDGE	1720	47002047
CH	Sta. F. Ch. S.	ERSKINE	1764	23030007
CH	Stab. Ch. Ch.	NICOLSON	1661	23002001
CH	Stabil.ch.ch.	NICOLSON	1661	23002003
CH	Sub t. D. Ch.	SAVAGE	1732	61012009
CH	Sub.in Ch. E.	POWELL.	1776	49001010
CH	Tr. Ch.of G.	CLARKE	1736	51004022
CH	Tr. Mot. Ch.	ANONYMOUS	1688	47002041
CH	Unity of Ch.	CLAGETT	1704	49012013
CH	Unity of Ch.	BARROW	1716	52004004
CH	Unity of Ch.	SHERIDAN	1720	46010016
CH	Unity of Ch.	BENNETT	1728	49012013
CH	X's. Ch.&c.	WHITTY	1772	52003014
CH	X's. Sov. Ch.	SAURIN	1777	48014007
CH	Xency of Ch.	ELSMERE	1767	45014014
CH	Xt's u.w. Ch.	NICOLSON	1661	50011002
CH	Xt's. Inv. Ch.	DAVIES	1758	44010014
CH	Xt's.dy. Ch.	WILLISON	1761	49002024
CH	Zeal f. Ch.	PRIEST	1753	19122006
CH'S	Ch's Peace.	ADDERLEY	1679	19122006
CHA	Cha.to poor.	WILLIAMS	1774	45014012
CHA	Cha.to rich.	BOYSE	1728	57006017
CHA	Faith& Cha.	LOVEDER	1756	56001003
CHA	Perf.of Cha.	JEFFERY	1710	45014015
CHA	Pow.of Cha.	HOADLY	1727	63004008
CHA	Truth& Cha.	MICHELL	1737	52004015
CHA	Wait f. Cha.	COBDEN	1757	18014014
CHALL	Lord's chall.	BRADBERRY	1766	30004012
CHANCE	T.& Chance.	STERNE	1760	21009011
CHANGE	Change of S.	UMFREVILLE	1739	02020008
CHANGELING	Changeling.	H.	1660	20024021
CHAPL	New Chapl.	KENNET	1715	49003006
CHAR	Char. Instit.	LANGHORNE	1764	20010015
CHAR	Durat.of Char.	CONANT	1703	49013008
CHAR	Durat.of Char.	BAYLY	1721	49013008
CHAR	Durat.of Char.	HOLE	1725	49013008
CHAR	Durat.of Char.	BENNETT	1728	49013008
CHAR	Exc.of Char.	HAWKINS	1755	49013013

Keyword	In its Context	Author	Year	BkChpVrs
CHAR	Excell.of Char	GROVE	1742	49013008
CHAR	F. H.& Char.	CLAGETT	1720	49013013
CHAR	Grand Char.	LAWSON	1686	43028018
CHAR	Hum. Char.	WHICHCOTE	1702	31004001
CHAR	Jehos's char.	LIVESEY	1660	14019006
CHAR	Just.& Char.	LUCAS	1716	48013008
CHAR	Perf.of Char.	HOLE	1725	49013009
CHAR	Pray.&char.	HARTLEY	1737	13004010
CHAR	Pro.of Char.	FARINDON	1674	49013007
CHAR	Pro.of Char.	HOWE	1681	49013006
CHAR	Pro.of Char.	CONANT	1703	49013006
CHAR	Pro.of Char.	CROSSINGE	1722	49013007
CHAR	Pro.of Char.	HOLE	1725	49013005
CHAR	Pro.of Char.	HOLE	1725	49013006
CHAR	Pro.of Char.	HOLE	1725	49013007
CHAR	Prot. Char.	STILLINGFLEET	1707	51006009
CHAR	Rev.& Char.	BIRCH	1720	48012021
CHAR	Univ. Char.	FOSTER	1737	49013003
CHARGE	G's.charge.	HILL	1755	38003007
CHARITY	Of Charity.	BARROW	1716	52005002
CHARITY	On Charity.	DODWELL	1749	49013013
CHARITY	Xn. Charity.	LLOYD	1705	61012014
CHARITY	Xn. Charity.	COTES	1721	46013034
CHARITY	Xn. Charity.	IBBOT	1726	49013013
CHARITY	Xn. Charity.	WESTON	1747	57001005
CHARITY	Xn. Charity.	COCKMAN	1750	57001005
CHARITY	Xn. Charity.	HOLDEN	1757	49016014
CHARITY	Xn. Charity.	MILNE	1780	54003014
CHARITY	Xn Charity.	ROLLS	1672	49001010
CHARITY	Xt.c.charity	CONYBEARE	1757	49013013
CHASTIS	Div. Chastis.	STENNETT	1732	20003011
CHASTITY	Chastity.	JENKS	17--	01039009
CHASTITY	Chastity.	GARDINER	1720	43005027
CHASTITY	Chastity.	DYKES	1722	20031003
CHASTITY	Chastity.	DODWELL	1748	55004003
CHEAR	Chear.&w. S.	NEWTON	1759	20018014
CHECK	Check. Sin.	GIBBON	1677	51005016
CHELS	b. Chels. Ho.	SHORTHOSE	1738	58002002
CHG	Chg.t. Suret.	HOLE	1719	52006004
CHI	Chi.of Prom.	ERSKINE	1764	51004028
CHIEF	Chief. Good.	SOUTH	1727	43006021
CHIEF	Chief Sinn.	CHARNOCK	1699	57001015
CHIEF	Rel.chief. C.	TRAPP	1752	43006023
CHILD	Af. Child.ex.	COOKE	1752	05006007
CHILD	Ca.of Child.	JENNINGS	1753	13029019
CHILD	Child of G.	CLARKE	1732	48008016
CHILD	Child.g. M.	ROSEWELL	1720	19116016
CHILD	Child.of G.	HORNECK	1706	43005045
CHILD	Co. Child-b.	CHARNOCK	1684	57002015
CHILD	Dut. Child.	FLEETWOOD	1737	02020012
CHILD	Educ. Child.	HOLLAND	1753	54003020
CHILD	Educ. Child.	TROUTBECK	1778	20029015
CHILD	Fath. Child.	ASHWOOD	1707	28014003
CHILD	Little Child.	ALLESTRE	1684	44010015
CHILD	Little Child.	HICKES	1726	44010014
CHILD	Little Child.	LARDNER	1751	43019013

Keyword	In its Context	Author	Year	BkChpVrs
CHILD	R. Ed. Child.	DODDERIDGE	1743	20022006
CHILD	Virt. Child.	TAYLOR	----	20010001
CHILD'S	Child's ret.	CULVERWELL	1661	20023026
CHILDREN	To children.	PALMER	1777	46021015
CHO	David's cho.	MACHIN	1740	10024014
CHOI	Choi affl. Pi.	TILLOTSON	1735	61011024
CHOI	St. P's.choi.	ROGERS	1730	53001022
CHOI	The bl.choi.	HART	1702	61011025
CHOICE	Choice of L.	DOWNES	1761	49011018
CHOICE	Holy Choice	PHILIPS	1679	61011015
CHOS	G.chos. Inh.	ORTON	1776	19047004
CHRIST	Christ. L.	BUNDY	1740	19019007
CHUR	Cath. Chur.	PIGOTT	1702	54001018
CHUR	Glory of Chur.	CALAMY	1715	43016018
CHURCH	Church mil.	NICOLSON	1661	22001005
CHURCH	Church.	BEVERIDGE	1720	43016018
CHURCH	Church. Censur	SMITH	1708	46020023
CHURCH	Church. Censur	REEVES	1729	46020023
CHURCH	Church Un.	SHERLOCK	1719	19122006
CHURCH	Xn. Church.	KEDDINGTON	1757	61013008
CHURCH'S	Church's Gl.	HARTLEY	1754	19045014
CHURCHES	Of Churches	MEDE	1672	49011022
CHUS	Chus. Relig.	WATERLAND	1742	55005021
CIRC	Circ.of H.	BRAGGE	1713	48002029
CIRC	Circ.of H.	SHARP	1734	48002028
CIRC	Circ.of H.	WESTLEY	1748	48002029
CIRC	Cov.of Circ.	WHISTON	17--	01017007
CIRC	True Circ.	MANTON	1685	53003003
CIRC	True Circ.	TILLY	1737	53003002
CIRCU	Circu.of Xt.	WARREN	1748	61002016
CIRCUM	Circum.s.	BURY	1692	02004024
CIRCUMC	Circumc.	READING	1728	01017011
CIRCUMCIS	Circumcis.	NICOLSON	1661	45002021
CIRCUMCIS	Circumcis.	PARRY	1666	45002021
CIRCUMCIS	Circumcis.	FRANK	1672	45002021
CIRCUMCIS	Circumcis.	FRANK	1672	50005017
CIRCUMCIS	Circumcis.	STANHOPE	1715	45002015
CIRCUMCIS	Circumcis.	HOLE	1716	45002015
CIRCUMCIS	Circumcis.	STANHOPE	1715	48004008
CIRCUMCIS	Circumcis.	HOLE	1716	48004008
CIRCUMCIS	Circumcis.	READING	1730	05010016
CIRCUMCIS	Circumcis.	WESTON	1747	45002021
CIRCUMCIS	Circumcis.	HORNE	1778	45011021
CIRCUMCIS	Circumcis.d.	TILLY	1737	61008008
CIRCUMS	Xn. Circums.	ALTHAM	1732	52005015
CIRCUMS	Xn. Circums.	OGILVIE	1766	52005015
CIRCUMS	Xn. Circums.	ORR	1772	52005015
CIRCUMSPEC	Circumspec.	MEAD	1660	52005015
CIRCUMSPEC	Circumspec.	PIERCE	1679	43024004
CIRCUMSPEC	Circumspec.	PIERCE	1679	52005015
CIRCUMSPEC	Circumspec.	CONANT	1699	52005015
CIRCUMSPEC	Circumspec.	LUCAS	1710	52005015
CIRCUMSPEC	Circumspec.	EDWARDS	1726	52005015
CIRCUMSPEC	Circumspec.	SHARP	1734	52005015
CIRCUMSPEC	Circumspec.	ATTERBURY	1743	52005015
CIT	Cit.of Zion.	BOSTON	1773	19015001

INDEXES TO THIRD VOLUME: E: KEYWORD-IN-CONTEXT INDEX OF OTHER SUBJECTS OR OCCASIONS

Keyword	In its Context	Author	Year	BkChpVrs
CITSHIP	Citship.o. Xt.	WHICHCOTE	1702	53003020
CITY	Holy City.	SPARKES	1663	69019002
CITY	No con.city.	STEBBING	1760	61013014
CIV	Aff. C.& Civ.	LANGHORNE	1773	63003008
CIV	Civ.&rel. G.	MURRAY	1777	01003001
CIV	Civ.&rel. L.	PECKARD	1754	63002016
CIV	Or. Civ. Gov.	HORNE	1778	48013004
CIV	Or.civ. Auth.	PEARSON	1718	48013005
CIV	Rig.civ. Go.	HOLE	1716	43022015
CIV	Zeal civ.& R.	WEBSTER	1776	19137005
CL	An. Conv. Cl.	BEACH	1760	46003009
CL	An.m. Cl.	THANE	1706	51006009
CL	Cl. Ad.t. Par.	STEDMAN	1776	58002006
CL	Cl.ag. J.ind.	PECKARD	1753	49009020
CL	Cl V. Xt's bl.	CHARNOCK	1684	65001007
CL	Conc.ad cl.	WALL	1660	22003009
CL	Conc.ad. Cl.	WILLIS	1702	47020028
CL	Conc.ad. Cl.	DRAKE	1719	43026029
CL	Conc.ad. Cl.	RODERICK	1723	44013013
CL	Conc.ad. Cl.	BATEMAN	1746	48001020
CL	Conc.ad. Cl.	ASHTON	1770	45010034
CL	Conc.ad. Cl.	BUTLER	1775	47005038
CL	Hards.o. Cl.	PRESTON	1767	58002002
CL	M.d.o. Cl. L.	HARRISON	1730	48015029
CL	Privi.of Cl.	DUDLEY	1731	64003016
CL	b. Par. Cl.	MILBOURNE	1713	14029030
CLAIM	Claim Ch. R.	BULKLEY	1761	43016018
CLAUSE	Dam. Clause	SEED	1750	44016016
CLEAN	Clean Water.	ERSKINE	1764	26036025
CLEANNESS	Cleanness.	COOKE	1739	20016002
CLEAR	Clear&st. Ju.	OUTRAM	1697	53001010
CLEM	Clem.to Br.	ANONYMOUS	1760	20012010
CLEM	Clem.to Br.	GRANGER	1772	20012010
CLER	Cont.o. Cler.	DOWNES	1761	59002015
CLERGY	Ch.to Clergy	POTTER	1753	51004018
CLERGY	Clergy vind.	LEWIS	1710	49004013
CLERGY	To Clergy.	BROWNRIG	1664	49014001
CLERGY	Use o. Clergy	ROBINSON	1735	57006020
CLERKS	b. Par. Clerks	HILLIARD	1714	43006013
CLIPP	Ag. Clipp.	FLEETWOOD	1737	01023016
CLOSET	Closet Pray.	SLATER	1691	43006006
CLOSET	Closet Pray.	RESBURY	1693	43006006
CO	An. Co.m.	LANGHORNE	1777	47007026
CO	Angel of Co.	PEARSON	1718	38003001
CO	Bp's Co.w. C.	LUZANEY	1697	58001013
CO	Co. Ch.be.w.	ADAMS	1683	57002015
CO	Co. Child-b.	CHARNOCK	1684	57002015
CO	Co. Founders	COLBATCH	1718	20010007
CO	Co. G's.will.	NALSON	1737	61010006
CO	Co. G's.will.	NALSON	1737	61010009
CO	Co. King. W.	EARL	1725	20010007
CO	Co. Skinners	CAWTHORNE	1748	23058012
CO	Co.of Grace.	TAYLOR	1725	10022005
CO	Co.of Grace.	SHEPHERD	1748	10023005
CO	Co.s.& W. S.	BERRIMAN	1751	47008014
CO	Dan.bad Co.	PRIEST	1710	19119115

Keyword	In its Context	Author	Year	BkChpVrs
CO	Des. Xt's.co.	PAYNE	1763	69022020
CO	Ev.co.&b. B.	WHITE	1757	49015033
CO	Evil life co.	GLANVIL	1681	43022032
CO	Evil Co mp.	LAWSON	1764	20001015
CO	Fth&go. Co.	BRAGGE	1713	57001018
CO	Fth&go. Co.	WELTON	1724	57001018
CO	Fth&go. Co.	MACE	1751	57001018
CO	G's. Co.n.gr.	DUNLOP	1722	65005003
CO	G's. Co.n.gr.	BRADY	1730	65005003
CO	Good&b.co.	WILKINS	1682	20013020
CO	L. G.& W.co.	DAWES	1733	62004004
CO	Love of Co.	WOODWARD	1693	19122008
CO	Love of Co.	STEPHENS	1721	19122006
CO	Love of Co.	JORTIN	1774	16005018
CO	M's co.w. G.	WILSON	1676	19073023
CO	St. Paul's co.	STANHOPE	1715	43019027
CO	St. Paul's co.	HOLE	1716	43019027
CO	St. Paul's.co.	HOLE	1716	47009001
CO	St. Paul's.co.	SHERIDAN	1720	47009003
CO	St. Paul's.co.	WATERLAND	1742	47009004
CO	St. Paul's Co.	WILDER	1729	57001013
CO	St. Paul's Co.	FARMER	1756	57001013
CO	St Paul's Co.	LUCAS	1717	49015009
CO	Tr.& F. Co.	AGAR	1759	06023006
CO	Ver.&tr. Co.	MICHELL	1737	57006004
CO	Worth. Co.	DYKE	1667	13015013
CO	Xn. Co.&lo.	SMITH	1673	62004007
CO	Xt.co. Apost.	SECKER	1771	43028019
CO	Xt.co.t.jud.	FLAVEL	1673	47010042
CO	Xt.co.t.jud.	CARRINGTON	1750	47010042
CO	Xt's. Co.&c.	HORTON	1679	69022017
CO	b. Co.merch.	RAINSTORP	1684	10015021
COESIDERAT	Coesiderat.	WROUGHTON	1728	19119059
COESIDERAT	Coesiderat.	TILLOTSON	1735	19119059
COESIDERAT	Coesiderat.	WESCOTT	1762	19119059
COIN	Restor. Coin.	ANONYMOUS	1697	24006030
COL	For Am. Col.	WATSON	1763	23049006
COLD	Cold Weath.	STEWARD	1734	19147015
COLL	Coll.f. Min.	TRIMNELL	1711	48015013
COLL	Coll.f.poor.	SELLON	1763	20030008
COLL	Coll.poor M.	MAULDEN	1738	20003006
COM	Brideg.com.	ELSMERE	1767	43025005
COM	Com. Pray.	BISSE	1717	13016029
COM	Com. Xt's.b.	JONES	1756	49010016
COM	Com. Xt's.w.	DAVIS	1756	46017004
COM	Com.m.suff.	BRADY	1730	45016031
COM	Com.of Men	ROGERS	1736	43015009
COM	Com.of Sts.	BEVERIDGE	1720	52002019
COM	Com.of Xt.	MANTON	1679	56002001
COM	Com.of Xt.	LEIGHTON	1746	23060001
COM	Com.to bapt.	BRETT	1712	43028019
COM	Com.to Xt.	HORTON	1679	46006037
COM	Com.to Xt.	CLARKSON	1696	46005040
COM	Com.to Xt.	BEVERIDGE	1720	46005040
COM	Com.to Xt.	COOKE	1739	46005040
COM	Com.to Xt.	HUNT	1748	46005040

Keyword	In its Context	Author	Year	BkChpVrs
COM	Com.to Xt.	NEWTON	1767	43011028
COM	Com.to Xt.	BARCLAY	1763	61007025
COM	Com.w. G.	HENRY	1713	19025005
COM	Com.with G.	SYLVESTER	1683	65001007
COM	Com.with G.	HUNT	1748	65001006
COM	Daily Com.	HENRY	1731	19004008
COM	Daily Com.	HENRY	1731	19005003
COM	Early Com.	DODDERIDGE	1743	23044003
COM	F.&com. Sw.	SMALWOOD	1666	43005034
COM	F.&com. Sw.	WILSON	1700	43005034
COM	F.&com. Sw.	KINSMAN	1700	43005034
COM	F.&com. Sw.	HORNECK	1706	43005034
COM	F.&com. Sw.	GREGORY	1708	43005034
COM	F.&com. Sw.	CALAMY	1726	43005034
COM	F.&com. Sw.	LITTLETON	1735	43005034
COM	F.&com. Sw.	WHITFIELD	1739	43005034
COM	F.&com. Sw.	BOURN	1777	43005034
COM	Freq. Com.	BEVERIDGE	1708	49011026
COM	G.&.b. Com.	TRAPP	1752	20018014
COM	G's. Com.ea.	SCOTT	1701	65005003
COM	G's. Com.ea.	SHARP	1729	65005003
COM	G's. K.com.	MANGEY	1717	43006010
COM	G's. K.com.	MOSS	1732	43006010
COM	Great Com.	ANONYMOUS	1776	44012030
COM	Hum. Com.	BENNETT	1714	43015009
COM	Me.7 Com.	HORNECK	1706	43005027
COM	Me.7 Com.	BLACKALL	1723	43005027
COM	Me.7 Com.	BLAIR	1740	43005027
COM	No ne. Com.	SECKER	1770	65002007
COM	Paroch.com.	GRIFFITH	1711	49003005
COM	Saint's com.	HAYDON	1770	48007024
COM	Sinful Com.	BACON	1760	02023002
COM	Spec. Com.	SHAW	1723	20028007
COM	Succes. Com.	DYKES	1722	20031018
COM	Terms Com,	LORTIE	1720	43018007
COM	Worth.com.	BEVERIDGE	1720	49011029
COM	Xt.com. Jud.	MALBON	1673	43016027
COM	Xt.com. Jud.	RALEIGH	1679	43016027
COM	Xt.our Com.	MOIR	1759	23032002
COM	Xt's.2 Com.	WILSON	1781	69022012
COM	Xt's.2d.com.	NEWMAN	1760	61009028
COM	Xt's.2d.com.	TOTTIE	1775	43024037
COM	Xt's Com.	ROMAINE	1759	22008014
COM	Xty. Com. L.	OUTRAM	1697	43005017
COM	Xty. Com. L.	MUDGE	1739	43005017
COMF	Comf. Faith.	FOWLER	1674	63001008
COMF	Comf. Piety.	SHERLOCK	1772	19119165
COMF	Comf.in D.	LANGHORNE	1773	04023010
COMF	Dea.a. Comf.	BURNET	1747	49015055
COMF	Div. Comf.	REYNER	1745	19094019
COMF	Div. Comf.	STEBBING	1759	19094019
COMF	Div. Comf.	SHERLOCK	1772	19094019
COMF	G's. Comf.	CREYGHTON	1720	50001004
COMF	G's Pr.comf.	BAINE	1778	02033014
COMF	Rachel comf.	HORNE	1778	24031015
COMF	Relig. Comf.	CARMICHAEL	1757	19094019

Keyword	In its Context	Author	Year	BkChpVrs
COMF	Xt's. Comf.	HORTON	1679	46014018
COMFORT	Comfort.	MYNORS	1716	19073012
COMFORT	Comfort.	TREBECK	1730	19042011
COMING	Xt's.coming	MEDE	1672	44001014
COMING	Xt's.coming.	WARREN	1748	64001016
COMING	Xt's.coming.	CHANDLER	1769	57001015
COMM	Cath. Comm.	BULKLEY	1754	46003005
COMM	Ch. Comm.	JEACOCKE	1702	52004004
COMM	Ch. Comm.	WARBURTON	1754	52004003
COMM	Comm. Pray.	HEWERDINE	1717	47024014
COMM	Comm.o. Sts.	NICOLSON	1661	52004016
COMM	Comm.of G.	BAYLEY	1778	19119048
COMM	Comm.vind.	CAMFIELD	1680	05027015
COMM	Comm.vind.	CLARKE	1736	05027026
COMM	Comm Pray.	JONES	1750	57002001
COMM	Corr.comm.	DAVIES	1754	52004029
COMM	Corr.comm.	DODD	1772	52004029
COMM	Corr.comm.	JORTIN	1774	52004029
COMM	G. Comm.	NEWTON	1782	43022040
COMM	G's. Comm.	DAVIS	1756	47007053
COMM	Jon. Comm.	POTTS	1758	31003002
COMM	Occ. Comm.	STUBBS	1702	11018021
COMM	Rat. Comm.	YARDLEY	1728	49014016
COMM	Rel. Comm.	BRUCE	1725	48015007
COMM	St. P's comm.	WATTS	1753	47025018
COMMAND	Command.	PIGOTT	1702	02020003
COMMU	Ch.commu.	BRIGGS	1675	49001010
COMMU	Ch.commu.	WARBURTON	1754	45009049
COMMUN	Commun.d.	LITTLETON	1680	57001015
COMMUN	Commun.s.	GRIFFITH	1662	65001007
COMMUNIC	Communic.	WILLISON	1761	11019009
COMMUNION	Communion	BOURDALOUE	1776	43008007
COMP	Bad. Comp.	DODDERIDGE	1743	20004014
COMP	Bad. Comp.	FARMER	1756	20013020
COMP	Bad Comp.	BRIGHT	1695	49015033
COMP	Bad Comp,	ALLEN	1712	49015033
COMP	Bad Comp.	WAKE	1722	49005009
COMP	Bad Comp.	DODD	1772	49015033
COMP	Bad Comp.	ENFIELD	1772	49015033
COMP	Bad Comp.	BOURN	1777	49015033
COMP	Comp. F.	MORER	1708	17009019
COMP	Comp. F.	NICHOLSON	1707	69002017
COMP	Comp. F.	MARSHALL	1731	18010011
COMP	Comp. Paint.	MORER	1708	50008018
COMP	Comp.i. Xt.	WHITAKER	1667	54003011
COMP	Comp.of G.	ERSKINE	1764	45014023
COMP	Comp.of Xt.	BLAIR	1780	61004015
COMP	Comp.our P.	SNAPE	1745	45018011
COMP	Good Comp.	JENNINGS	1743	19119063
COMP	Gosp. Comp.	BATES	1700	45014023
COMP	Gosp. Comp.	ACTON	1714	45014023
COMP	Gosp. Comp.	CLARKE	1727	45014023
COMP	Gosp. Comp.	BOSTON	1753	45014023
COMP	Scept. Comp.	COLE	1761	20019027
COMP	Scept. Comp.	SHERLOCK	1772	20019027
COMP	Xn.comp. A.	GURNALL	1662	52006017

Keyword	In its Context	Author	Year	BkChpVrs
COMP	Xt's.comp. S.	DAVIES	1771	43023037
COMPAS	G's Compas.	SAURIN	1775	19103013
COMPAS	Xt's.compas.	MUNTON	1756	45019041
COMPAS	Xt's.compas.	DAVIES	1766	43012020
COMPASSION	Compassion.	BUTLER	1749	48012015
COMPASSION	Compassion.	HOLLAND	1753	63003008
COMPASSION	Compassion.	ENFIELD	1772	18019023
COMPL	Sinf. Compl.	GODDARD	1781	45009026
COMPRE	Ag. Compre.	SOUTH	1724	51002005
COMPREHEN	Comprehen.	ANONYMOUS	1716	51002005
CON	Beat.& Con.	BLACKALL	1723	43005001
CON	Beat.& Con.	EDWARDS	1726	43005001
CON	Beat.& Con.	JOHNSON	1740	43005001
CON	Con. Minist.	MAURICE	1719	59002015
CON	Con.ad Con.	LISLE	1735	49001021
CON	Con.fut.jud.	STILLINGFLEET	1707	21011009
CON	Con.fut.jud.	SUTTON	1754	21011009
CON	Con.in w.d.	DUCHAL	1765	48002007
CON	Con.in w.d.	CHANDLER	1769	48002007
CON	Con.in w.d.	PYLE	1777	48002007
CON	Con.is Hap.	STILLINGFLEET	1707	23057021
CON	Con.lat end.	HOLLAND	1753	05032029
CON	Con.of Salv.	TILLOTSON	1735	61005009
CON	Con.ov. Evil.	ALTHAM	1732	48012021
CON	Cornel. Con.	MEDE	1672	47010004
CON	Cornel. Con.	SHARP	1734	47010004
CON	Cornel. Con.	JORTIN	1774	47010022
CON	Du.low con.	MARSHALL	1750	53004012
CON	Err. M's.con.	GROVE	1747	48014016
CON	Force o. Con.	MAYNARD	1722	47024025
CON	G.&ev. Con.	SMITH	1740	46020019
CON	Good con.its H	FIDDES	1720	47024016
CON	Good con.its H	FISHER	1741	47024016
CON	M's.con.&c.	TOULMIN	1770	51006007
CON	Martyr.con.	NICHOLS	1746	43005010
CON	N.& D. Con.	CRAIG	1775	10012017
CON	No con.city.	STEBBING	1760	61013014
CON	Obj.to S.con.	AMORY	1775	49001025
CON	Pea. Con.&c.	PRICE	1757	48015013
CON	R.con.w. L.	GERARD	1780	19116009
CON	Rel.first.con.	WILLIAMS	1665	43006033
CON	Rel.first.con.	TILLOTSON	1735	43006033
CON	Sea.del.con.	BRADBURY	1772	05032036
CON	Ser.con.o. D.	LOCKIER	1671	23057001
CON	Sin Self-con.	DODD	1755	45019022
CON	Test ag. Con.	SMITH	1719	50001012
CON	Uubec. Con.	SMITH	1740	53001027
CON	Xn. Con.&c.	WALLIN	1764	49009027
CON	Xn. Sch.con.	BOURN	1760	47010042
CON	b. Crim.con.	CROOKE	1695	47003019
CON	b. Crim.con.	DYCHE	1723	47003019
CONC	Conc. En. Pr.	BROUGHTON	1778	46011047
CONC	Conc. En. Pr.	MILNE	1780	46011047
CONC	Conc. Lat.	FOWNES	1660	56002003
CONC	Conc. Lat.	FELL	1667	54002008
CONC	Conc. Lat.	TURNER	1681	69019010
CONC	Conc. Lat.	BARROW	1687	43016019
CONC	Conc. Lat.	SHEPHEARD	1776	21007030
CONC	Conc. Si.im.	HOLLAND	1753	18034022
CONC	Conc.ad cl.	WALL	1660	22003009
CONC	Conc.ad. Cl.	WILLIS	1702	47020028
CONC	Conc.ad. Cl.	DRAKE	1719	43026029
CONC	Conc.ad. Cl.	RODERICK	1723	44013013
CONC	Conc.ad. Cl.	BATEMAN	1746	48001020
CONC	Conc.ad. Cl.	ASHTON	1770	45010034
CONC	Conc.ad. Cl.	BUTLER	1775	47005038
CONC	Conc.ad. M.	FULLWOOD	1673	20014034
CONC	Conc.ad Sy.	PIERCE	1661	47011028
CONC	Conc.lat.	BARTON	1756	64001019
CONC	Lev.& Conc.	STERNE	1766	07019003
CONC	Sup.conc. Xt.	FLEMING	1772	23007013
CONCEIT	Conceit.	ANONYMOUS	1777	20026005
CONCEIT	Self conceit.	ABERNETHY	1748	43006022
CONCEIT	Self conceit.	BOURN	1777	20026012
CONCEIT	Self-conceit.	CALAMY	1726	48012016
CONCEIT	Self-conceit.	NEWTON	1736	48012016
CONCEIT	Self-conceit.	ERSKINE	1764	20030012
CONCL	J's h. Concl.	JENKINS	1779	01042036
CONCRUCIFIX	Concrucifix.	WILLAN	1661	51002020
CONCUPISC	Concupisc.	JENKINS	1779	04011033
COND	Cond. Berea.	BALGUY	1750	47017011
COND	Cond. L.o. Dar	SUTTON	1754	46003019
COND	Cond. Unb.	MORRIS	1743	46008024
COND	Cond.o.unb.	FLAVEL	1673	46003018
COND	Cond.of Dis.	WRIGHT	1718	01042020
COND	Cond.wick.	WELCH	1752	46003018
COND	Desp.cond.	ELLIS	1704	45016026
COND	Diff.o. Cond.	WHITE	1757	45016008
COND	Inoff. Cond.	MASON	1758	49010032
COND	Judas cond.	NEWLIN	1728	43027003
COND	Midd. Cond.	OAKEY	1683	20030008
COND	Prud. Cond.	ROGERS	1735	48012017
CONDES	Div. Condes.	TIDCOMBE	1757	19008003
CONDES	Div. Condes.	SHERLOCK	1772	19008004
CONDIT	Ineq. Condit.	LAWSON	1764	20022002
CONF	Ag.conf. W.	LARDNER	1739	48012002
CONF	Auric.conf.	BURROUGHS	1735	46020021
CONF	Conf.& Abs.	SPARROW	1704	65001009
CONF	Conf.& Abs.	BAYLY	1721	50002007
CONF	Conf.& Abs.	WARREN	1739	65001009
CONF	Conf.& Pray.	CONANT	1698	62005016
CONF	Conf. Sins.	WADE	1697	65001009
CONF	Conf.div. W.	AICKIN	1705	47009006
CONF	Conf.fash. N.	CARR	1777	48012002
CONF	Conf.in Rel.	LANGHORNE	1773	49010012
CONF	Conf.of Sin.	NEAL	1757	47003019
CONF	Conf.of Sins.	BULKLEY	1752	65001009
CONF	Conf.pu.&p.	NICOLSON	1661	65001009
CONF	Conf.s.	PRIAULX	1662	47008017
CONF	Conf.s.	CAMFIELD	1682	47011023
CONF	Conf.s.	CAMFIELD	1682	61006002
CONF	Conf.s.	SAVAGE	1683	47008017

Keyword	In its Context	Author	Year	BkChpVrs
CONF	Conf.s.	STUBBS	1693	61006002
CONF	Conf.s.	PROWDE	1694	47008017
CONF	Conf.s.	PENN	17--	47008017
CONF	Conf.s.	ELLISON	1700	47008014
CONF	Conf.s.	SAYWELL	1701	47008014
CONF	Conf.s.	NEWCOME	1702	61006002
CONF	Conf.s.	BRADY	1708	47008014
CONF	Conf.s.	HOLE	1712	47008014
CONF	Conf.s.	BETTESWORTH	1712	47008017
CONF	Conf.s.	BRADY	1715	47015041
CONF	Conf.s.	HOLE	1716	47008014
CONF	Conf.s.	LEWIS	1717	47008017
CONF	Conf.s.	HOLE	1719	47008015
CONF	Conf.s.	BAYLY	1721	47008014
CONF	Conf.s.	WHITE	1723	47008017
CONF	Conf.s.	BRADFORD	1724	61006001
CONF	Conf.s.	HICKES	1726	61006002
CONF	Conf.s.	STEBBING	1729	47008017
CONF	Conf.s.	STEPHENS	1737	47008017
CONF	Conf.s.	DENNE	1737	47019005
CONF	Conf.s.	BELBIN	1741	47014015
CONF	Conf.s.	WHEATLY	1746	47008014
CONF	Conf.s.	BUNDY	1750	61006002
CONF	Conf.s.	PARSONS	1761	47008014
CONF	Conf.s.	BUCKRIDGE	1767	47008017
CONF	Conf.s.	SECKER	1771	47008017
CONF	Conf.s.	IBBETSON	1774	47008017
CONF	Conf.to W.	SHARP	1734	48012002
CONF	Conf.to W.	ROGER	1735	48012002
CONF	Conf.to W.	NEWMAN	1760	48012002
CONF	Conf.to W.	WEST	1762	48012002
CONF	Conf.to W.	STENNETT	1771	48012002
CONF	Conf.tow. G.	ABERNETHY	1751	65003012
CONF	Conf.w.ser.	MAY	1757	44012034
CONF	Loy.& Conf.	PLEYDELL	1682	48013004
CONF	N.conf.t. W.	S.	1695	48012002
CONF	N.conf.t. W.	ERSKINE	1764	48012002
CONF	Paul's Conf.	HAMMOND	1684	57001015
CONF	Peter's Conf.	ADAM	1776	43016016
CONF	Prin.o. Conf.	HAWKINS	1773	49001010
CONF	St. P's. Conf.	LEWIS	1729	47026026
CONFESSION	Confession.	LITTLETON	1680	19051003
CONFESSION	Confession.	BRIGHT	1695	19032005
CONFESSION	Confession.	WAPLE	1718	20028013
CONFESSION	Confession.	SHERLOCK	1719	19038018
CONFESSION	Confession.	SHERIDAN	1720	20028013
CONFESSION	Confession.	SHARP	1734	20028013
CONFESSION	Confession.	TILLOTSON	1735	19038018
CONFID	Of Confid.	SOUTH	1744	52003012
CONFID	Rel. Confid.	PYLE	1777	43003008
CONFID	Self-confid.	HENRY	1726	20015032
CONFID	Self-confid.	MARTIN	1760	20028026
CONFID	Self-confid.	ADEY	1760	49010012
CONFID	Xn. Confid.	LEIGHTON	1746	19042008
CONFIRMAT	Confirmat.	KING	1725	52006004
CONFIRMAT	Confirmat.	BURTON	1764	19119009

Keyword	In its Context	Author	Year	BkChpVrs
CONFIRMAT	Confirmat.	ELSMERE	1767	52005013
CONFL	Souls Confl.	STURMY	1716	21008008
CONFLA	Gen. Confla.	LELAND	1769	64003010
CONFLAGRAT	Conflagrat.	KNIGHT	1736	64003010
CONFO	Ch. Confo.	SHERWILL	1704	43023023
CONFOR	Confor.to O.	SMITH	1777	20029025
CONGR	Hap. Congr.	ERSKINE	1764	01049010
CONGRESS	Congress.	AYERST	1712	19122006
CONIF	Conif. Xnity	MOSS	1737	43011028
CONJ	Conj. Fidel.	DYKES	1722	20031011
CONJ	Conj. Love.	BRETT	1757	61013004
CONJ	Hon.conj. F.	DYKES	1722	20031023
CONQ	Grad. Conq.	ERSKINE	1764	05007022
CONQ	Wor. Conq.	ALLEINE	1676	65005004
CONQ	Xn. Conq.	MOSS	1738	48012021
CONQ	Xn's. Conq.	TAYLOR	1678	48007019
CONS	Carn. Cons.	ERSKINE	1764	51001016
CONS	Cons.o. Med.	FLAVEL	1673	46017019
CONS	Cons.of Sin.	EVANS	1725	01039009
CONS	Cons.of Sin.	MUSCOTT	1760	48006021
CONS	Force Cons.	SHERLOCK	1772	43014001
CONS	Good Cons.	KEITH	1709	63003016
CONS	Good Cons.	DAWES	1733	65003012
CONS	Good Cons.	WATERLAND	1742	65003021
CONS	Guilty Cons.	FISHER	1741	47024025
CONS	Late Cons.	ANONYMOUS	1723	19118001
CONS	Lib.of Cons.	HART	1726	48014010
CONS	Relig.cons.	PYLE	1777	20004026
CONS	Woun. Cons.	DAWES	1733	20018010
CONS	Woun. Cons.	WILCOX	1757	20018014
CONS	Woun. Cons.	ELSMERE	1767	20018014
CONS	Woun. Cons.	PYLE	1777	20018014
CONS	Wrong Cons.	BOURDALOUE	1776	46001022
CONSC	Consc.scrup.	CALAMY	1683	45011041
CONSC	Consc.scrup.	SOUTH	1727	45011035
CONSC	Good Consc.	COCK	1710	50001012
CONSC	Good Consc.	SUTTON	1718	47024016
CONSC	Good Consc.	DODSON	1728	50001012
CONSC	Good Consc.	FARRINGTON	1741	50001012
CONSC	Good Consc.	NEWMAN	1760	50001012
CONSC	Inoff. Consc.	ALLESTREE	1684	47024016
CONSC	Inoff. Consc.	BEVERIDGE	1720	47024016
CONSC	Inoff. Consc.	EDWARDS	1726	47024016
CONSC	Inoff. Consc.	TILLOTSON	1735	47024016
CONSC	Inoff. Consc.	ATTERBURY	1743	47024016
CONSC	Inoff. Consc.	ABERNETHY	1748	47024016
CONSC	Pow. Consc.	BLAIR	1777	01042021
CONSC	Rem. Consc.	BOURDALOUE	1776	45019041
CONSC	Weak consc.	SOUTH	1727	49008012
CONSCIENCE	Conscience.	CADE	1661	48002015
CONSCIENCE	Conscience.	ANNESLEY	1667	47024016
CONSCIENCE	Conscience.	HOPKINS	1710	47024016
CONSCIENCE	Conscience.	WAPLE	1720	48002015
CONSCIENCE	Conscience.	READING	1724	47024016
CONSCIENCE	Conscience.	SOUTH	1727	65003021
CONSCIENCE	Conscience.	WALKER	1729	47024016

INDEXES TO THIRD VOLUME: E: KEYWORD-IN-CONTEXT INDEX OF OTHER SUBJECTS OR OCCASIONS

Keyword	In its Context	Author	Year	BkChpVrs
CONSCIENCE	Conscience.	SHARP	1729	61013018
CONSCIENCE	Conscience.	CARLETON	1736	47024016
CONSCIENCE	Conscience.	FOSTER	1737	47023001
CONSCIENCE	Conscience.	HOOLE	1748	19037038
CONSCIENCE	Conscience.	SWIFT	1744	50001012
CONSCIENCE	Conscience.	HOOLE	1748	47024016
CONSCIENCE	Conscience.	HEYLYN	1749	48002014
CONSCIENCE	Conscience.	VENN	1759	47024016
CONSCIENCE	Conscience.	STEBBING	1760	47024016
CONSCIENCE	Conscience.	STERNE	1769	48002014
CONSCIENCE	Conscience.	FRANCIS	1773	32006006
CONSCIENCE	Conscience.	STONE	1771	47024016
CONSCIENCE	Conscience.	SHEPHEARD	1776	48002014
CONSID	Mir.consid.	MARKLAND	1729	43008027
CONSIDERAT	Considerat.	COLLIER	1695	21007014
CONSIDERAT	Considerat.	ATTERBURY	1699	19119059
CONSIDERAT	Considerat.	BRADY	1704	36001007
CONSIDERAT	Considerat.	HARRIS	1716	58002006
CONSIDERAT	Considerat.	EDWARDS	1726	36001005
CONSIDERAT	Considerat.	GALE	1726	36001005
CONSIDERAT	Considerat.	EDWARDS	1726	57004015
CONSIDERAT	Considerat.	TILLOTSON	1735	05032029
CONSIDERAT	Considerat.	SMITH	1740	36001001
CONSIDERAT	Considerat.	FOSTER	1744	36001001
CONSIDERAT	Considerat.	FAWCETT	1749	19119059
CONSIDERAT	Considerat.	LARDNER	1751	19119059
CONSIDERAT	Considerat.	BOURN	1777	19119059
CONSIDERAT	Considerat.	CARR	1777	19119059
CONSIST	Rel.consist.	FOSTER	1744	43006024
CONSOL	Div. Consol.	WILCOX	1757	18015011
CONSOLATION	Consolation.	CRUSO	1698	43028005
CONSP	Consp.ag. Xt	SHERIDAN	1720	44012014
CONSP	Disc. Consp.	SMALWOOD	1696	43013013
CONSPIC	Xns.conspic.	BLAIR	1740	43005014
CONST	Const.& Pers.	CREYGHTON	1720	49015058
CONST	Const.& Pers.	EVANS	1737	49015058
CONST	Const. Relig.	GERARD	1780	49010013
CONST	Const. Th.	BURROUGHS	1733	55005018
CONST	Const.in Fth.	BEVERIDGE	1720	61010023
CONST	Const.in Rel.	COOKE	1689	44008038
CONSTANCY	Constancy.	WELTON	1724	18027005
CONSUM	Fin. Consum.	DUCHAL	1765	19102025
CONT	Cont.f. Faith	MARSH	1737	68000003
CONT	Cont.f. Faith	MARSHALL	1750	68000003
CONT	Cont.f. Faith	HOADLEY	1754	68000003
CONT	Cont.f. Faith	TOULMIN	1771	68000003
CONT	Cont.o. Cler.	DOWNES	1761	59002015
CONT	Cont.of Gos.	DAVIS	1756	48001016
CONT	Cont.watch.	LITTLETON	1735	44013037
CONT	Holy Cont.	YOUNG	1706	45002019
CONT	Relig. Cont.	HOWE	1693	51005016
CONT	Unch Cont.	STEEL	1690	51005015
CONTEM	Contem. Sin.	YOUNG	1706	45022048
CONTENTM	Contentm.	KNAGGS	1700	61012005
CONTENTM	Contentm.	PATRICK	1719	57006008
CONTENTM	Contentm.	PATRICK	1719	61013005

Keyword	In its Context	Author	Year	BkChpVrs
CONTENTM	Contentm.	DODWELL	1748	57006006
CONTENTM	Contentm.	MILLER	1749	53004006
CONTENTM	Contentm.	MILLER	1749	57006008
CONTENTM	Contentm.	STEBBING	1760	57006008
CONTENTM	Contentm.	SIMS	1772	61013005
CONTENTM	Contentm.	ATKINSON	1775	61013005
CONTENTM	Contentm.	CARR	1777	57006006
CONTENTME	Contentme.	JACOMB	1676	53004011
CONTENTME	Contentme.	HICKMAN	1693	53004011
CONTENTME	Contentme.	STAFFORD	1699	53004011
CONTENTME	Contentme.	PULLEYN	1700	53004011
CONTENTME	Contentme.	BARROW	1716	53004011
CONTENTME	Contentme.	BENNETT	1728	53004011
CONTENTME	Contentme.	WEDDESPOON	1733	53004011
CONTENTME	Contentme.	EVANS	1737	53004011
CONTENTME	Contentme.	ST.	1737	53004011
CONTENTME	Contentme.	FARINGTON	1741	53004012
CONTENTME	Contentme.	MASON	1742	53004011
CONTENTME	Contentme.	REYNER	1745	53004011
CONTENTME	Contentme.	BURNET	1747	53004011
CONTENTME	Contentme.	HUNT	1748	53004011
CONTENTME	Contentme.	BERRIMAN	1751	53004011
CONTENTME	Contentme.	AMORY	1753	53004011
CONTENTME	Contentme.	DELANY	1754	53004011
CONTENTME	Contentme.	SMITH	1758	53004012
CONTENTME	Contentme.	LAWSON	1764	53004011
CONTENTME	Contentme.	SECKER	1771	53004011
CONTENTME	Contentme.	JORTIN	1774	53004011
CONTENTME	Contentme.	PYLE	1777	53004012
CONTRITION	Contrition.	WALSALL	1661	19051017
CONTRITION	Contrition.	LEE	1663	19051017
CONTRITION	Contrition.	WILLINGTON	1670	19051017
CONTRITION	Contrition.	MOSS	1732	19051017
CONV	An. Conv. Cl.	BEACH	1760	46003009
CONV	Conv. H. A.	SMITH	1763	19002008
CONV	Conv. Hyp.	CLARKSON	1696	43007022
CONV	Conv. Sinn.	LITTLETON	1680	26018027
CONV	Conv. Sinn.	WHICHCOTE	1702	26018027
CONV	Conv. Sinner	MEDE	1672	23055007
CONV	Conv.of P.	MARSHALL	1731	47017022
CONV	Conv.of Sin.	CHARNOCK	1684	46016008
CONV	Conv.w. G.	CRUSO	1698	24003032
CONV	Good conv.	BARROW	1716	48012017
CONV	Good Conv.	ROGERS	1735	19119063
CONV	Good Conv.	QUINCY	1750	62003013
CONV	Heav. Conv.	CLAGETT	1720	53003020
CONV	Heav. Conv.	KELSEY	1721	53003020
CONV	Heav. Conv.	BRADY	1730	53003020
CONV	Heav. Conv.	ALTHAM	1732	53003020
CONV	Heav. Conv.	BUNDY	1740	53003020
CONV	Heav. Conv.	FOSTER	1744	53003020
CONV	Heav. Conv.	STERNE	1769	53003020
CONV	Holy Conv.	STANHOPE	1705	52005011
CONV	Joy in Conv.	WILCOX	1757	55002019
CONV	Noble Conv.	HORNE	1778	47008024
CONV	Paul's Conv.	GROVE	1741	51001015

Keyword	In its Context	Author	Year	BkChpVrs
CONV	Paul's Conv.	WHITTY	1766	51001013
CONV	Relig. Conv.	WARNEFORD	1776	52004029
CONV	Spir. Conv.	WAPLE	1729	52004030
CONVER	Conver. Y. P.	BURGESS	1690	21012001
CONVER	Rel. Conver.	NEWMAN	1760	20010021
CONVERS	Convers.	TREBECK	1730	19016003
CONVERS	On Convers.	STEVENS	1760	50005021
CONVERS	Rel.convers.	ABERNETHY	1748	38003016
CONVERS	Rel.convers.	WOOD	1775	38003016
CONVERS	Xn. Convers.	CHAMBRE	1711	53001027
CONVERS	Xn. Convers.	KELSEY	1721	53001027
CONVERS	Xn. Convers.	DAWES	1733	53001027
CONVERS	Xn. Convers.	HOLLAND	1753	52004001
CONVERS	Xn. Convers.	BRACKENRIDGE	1764	53001027
CONVERS	Xn. Convers.	ELSMERE	1767	53001027
CONVERSAT	Conversat.	DALTON	1773	54004006
CONVERSAT	Conversat.	NEWTON	1782	54004006
CONVERSION	Conversion.	MATHER	1674	01006003
CONVERSION	Conversion.	MATHER	1674	43007014
CONVERSION	Conversion.	MATHER	1674	43018003
CONVERSION	Conversion.	GREENHILL	1677	26018032
CONVERSION	Conversion.	MATHER	1674	53002012
CONVERSION	Conversion.	MATHER	1674	54004005
CONVERSION	Conversion.	MATHER	1674	61006007
CONVERSION	Conversion.	MATHER	1674	69003020
CONVERSION	Conversion.	LEE	1677	48010001
CONVERSION	Conversion.	USHER	1678	51006003
CONVERSION	Conversion.	BRAGGE	1713	43018002
CONVERSION	Conversion.	BARKER	1723	46015016
CONVERSION	Conversion.	HARTLEY	1748	47002037
CONVERSION	Conversion.	BARNES	1752	43018003
CONVERT	Pris.convert.	WEBB	1765	47026033
CONVICT	On Convict.	CASE	1774	47002037
CONVICT	Self-convict.	BURNET	1747	01042021
CONVOC	Convoc.s.	HACKET	1662	49014016
CONVOC	b. Convoc.	KENNET	1710	45014027
COR	Ann.of Cor.	PYLE	1706	11003009
COR	Cor.of Wor.	MONRO	1693	64001004
COR	G.cor.&par.	HOWE	1771	19099008
COR	G.m.lia.cor.	HICKMAN	1706	49015033
COR	G.m.lia.cor.	TREBECK	1730	49015033
COR	Monop. Cor.	DOWNES	1761	20011026
COR	Monop. Cor.	SAMPSON	1771	20011026
COR	Po.cor.o. Xy.	BARKER	1735	50011003
COR	Rainb. Cor.	ERSKINE	1757	69004003
CORNEL	Case Cornel.	SHERLOCK	1772	47010034
CORNEL	Cornel. Con.	MEDE	1672	47010004
CORNEL	Cornel. Con.	SHARP	1734	47010004
CORNEL	Cornel. Con.	JORTIN	1774	47010022
CORP	b. Corp.	COLEIRE	1721	49013004
CORPOR	b. Corpor.	COLIERE	1726	10023003
CORPOR	b. Corpor.	DUBOIS	1742	19039004
CORR	Corr. Ch. R.	SKELTON	1754	65004001
CORR	Corr.comm.	DAVIES	1754	52004029
CORR	Corr.comm.	DODD	1772	52004029
CORR	Corr.comm.	JORTIN	1774	52004029
CORR	Corr.o. H. N.	HAWEIS	1762	48005018
CORR	Corr.of Fai.	MEDE	1672	64002001
CORRP	Corrp. G.w.	GIPPS	1697	20030006
CORT	Bpt. Cort.	DORRINGTON	1703	05004023
CORVI	Vox Corvi.	CLOGIE	1694	54003008
COU	Gamal. Cou.	DICK	1776	47005034
COU	Love of Cou.	BULKLEY	1761	19137005
COU	Pray.f. Cou.	BARKER	1763	19122006
COUNCILS	Councils fal.	POOLE	1675	43023008
COUNSEL	Of Counsel.	BALGUY	1748	20012015
COUNSIL	Par. Counsil.	MAY	1744	20006020
COUNT	Count. Loy.	HUTCHINSON	1717	43023029
COUNTRY	Country life.	STURMY	1712	23007011
COUR	Cour. Faith.	ERSKINE	1757	19023004
COUR	Pity& Cour.	MAINWARING	1760	64003008
COURAGE	Xn. Courage.	LLOYD	1765	20028001
COURSE	Course Nat.	OGDEN	1770	47017027
COURSE	Fin. Course.	STAPLETON	1736	47020024
COURSE	Xn. Course.	OLDISWORTH	1666	49009024
COURSE	Xn. Course.	LUCAS	1710	49009024
COURSE	Xn. Course.	EVANS	1725	45014028
COURSE	Xn. Course.	WALKER	1765	49009024
COURSE	Xn. Course.	WEBB	1765	49009024
COURSE	Xn. Course.	NEWTON	1767	49009024
COURT	At Court.	BLAGRAVE	1691	45012004
COURT	At Court.	BRADY	1706	49002014
COURT	Court. Lieut.	WELTON	1710	21008002
COURT	Pity& Court.	MAINWARING	1780	63003008
COURTEOUSY	Courteousy.	WARREN	1739	63003008
COV	Cov. Grace.	ERSKINE	1764	05026017
COV	Cov. Idolat.	GODDARD	1781	52005005
COV	Cov. S.h. Ha.	PEAD	1701	52002001
COV	Cov. S.h. Ha.	WARREN	1748	52002001
COV	Cov.o. Grace	BRINSLEY	1667	61012024
COV	Cov.o. Grace	ANNESLEY	1676	61008006
COV	Cov.o. Grace	BOSTON	1773	49015025
COV	Cov.o. Grace	BOSTON	1773	49015042
COV	Cov.o. Grace	BAINE	1778	61009016
COV	Cov.o. Peace.	SKELTON	1754	54001021
COV	Cov.of Circ.	WHISTON	17--	01017007
COV	Cov.of Gr.	CROSS	1693	10023005
COV	Cov.of Gr.	TAYLOR	1725	19089003
COV	Cov.of Gr.	BOSTON	1773	19089003
COV	Cov.of Red.	FLAVEL	1673	23053012
COV	Cov.of W.	BOSTON	1773	01002016
COV	Cov.of Wor.	TATHAM	1780	48005012
COV	Cov.renew.	SKELTON	1754	49011028
COV	Gosp. Cov.	FAWCET	1749	01017001
COV	L's. S.n. Cov.	CHANDLER	1769	49011025
COV	Mess.of Cov.	HARRIS	1724	38003001
COV	Scotch. Cov.	WREN	1662	19044018
COV	Xt.our Cov.	ERSKINE	1764	23042006
COVEN	Two Coven.	HARTLEY	1754	24031033
COVEN	Two Coven.	TURNER	1771	24031033
COVEN	Xn. Coven.	WHISTON	1709	61008006
COVET	Ag. Covet.	FREEMAN	1722	45014013

Keyword	In its Context	Author	Year	BkChpVrs
COVETING	Coveting.	BURTON	1685	48013009
COVETO	Ag. Coveto.	FREEMAN	1722	45012015
COVETO	Ag. Coveto.	BLAIR	1740	43006019
COVETO	Ag. Coveto.	ENFIELD	1772	45012015
COVETOUSN	Covetousn.	HOPKINS	1692	02020017
COVETOUSN	Covetousn.	DORRINGTON	1703	61013005
COVETOUSN	Covetousn.	SOUTH	1727	45012015
COVETOUSN	Covetousn.	NORRIS	1728	45012020
COVETOUSN	Covetousn.	SHERIDAN	1720	57006010
COVETOUSN	Covetousn.	ABERNETHY	1731	45012015
COVETOUSN	Covetousn.	TILLOTSON	1735	45012015
COVETOUSN	Covetousn.	WHEATLAND	1739	57006009
COVETOUSN	Covetousn.	FOSTER	1744	02020017
COVETOUSN	Covetousn.	SMITH	1740	52005005
COVETOUSN	Covetousn.	SUTTON	1754	45012015
COVETOUSN	Covetousn.	STEBBING	1760	45012015
COVETOUSN	Covetousn.	SECKER	1761	53004006
COVETOUSN	Covetousn.	DOWNES	1761	54003008
COVETOUSN	Covetousn.	ANONYMOUS	1770	43019024
COVETOUSN	Covetousn.	LAMONT	1780	61013004
COWARDICE	Cowardice.	FOSTER	1732	20029025
CR	Cr. Bl.& Glo.	COOKE	1739	49002009
CR	Cr. Sacr. His.	POWELL	1776	46015021
CR	Di. W.in Cr.	DAVIS	1756	19104015
CR	Div. Wis. Cr.	TILLOTSON	1735	19104024
CR	Div. Wis. Cr.	BOURN	1760	19104024
CR	Div. Wis. Cr.	WEST	1762	19104024
CR	Div. Wis. Cr.	STONE	1771	19104024
CR	Introd.to Cr.	CARRINGTON	1750	50013005
CR	Ma.b. Cr.&c.	ERSKINE	1764	23054005
CR	Man acc. Cr.	FARRINGTON	1769	48014012
CR	New Cr.or b.	HAMMOND	1684	51006015
CR	New Cr.or b.	IBBOT	1726	51006015
CR	New Cr.or b.	STEBBING	1739	51006015
CR	Title on Cr.	FLAVEL	1673	45023038
CRAFT	Craft Policy.	ELLIS	1704	45016003
CRE	Cre.of N. T.	LARDNER	1769	64001015
CRE	Gosp.n. Cre.	PALMER	1674	19025011
CRE	Gosp.n. Cre.	STRONG	1678	19025011
CRE	Wisd.in Cre.	BOURN	1760	18035010
CREA	Why n. Crea.	BARNES	1752	50005017
CREAT	Beau. Creat.	BOURN	1760	19111002
CREAT	Creat. God.	FISHER	1741	19104024
CREAT	Creat.man.	HOWE	1676	21007029
CREAT	Creat.of M.	BOSTON	1773	01001027
CREAT	Creat.of M.	HORNE	1778	01001026
CREAT	Creat.ruins.	MARRIOTT	1774	48008022
CREAT	G. Creat.&c.	HUNT	1748	48011036
CREAT	New Creat.	FLAVEL	1673	50005017
CREAT	New Creat.	CLARKSON	1696	51006015
CREAT	New Creat.	BEVERIDGE	1720	52002010
CREAT	New Creat.	GARNET	1739	51006015
CREAT	New Creat.	SMITH	1753	51006015
CREAT	New Creat.	STANTON	1758	50005017
CREAT	Rem. Creat.	HORNECK	1686	21012001
CREAT	Rem. Creat.	HICKMAN	1708	21012001
CREAT	Rem. Creat.	DUNLOP	1722	21012001
CREAT	Van. Creat.	REYNOLDS	1679	21001014
CREAT	Van. Creat.	PIERCE	1731	19119096
CREAT	Wisd. Creat.	BOURN	1760	47017026
CREATION	Creation.	BOSTON	1773	61011003
CREATOR	G. Creator.	MARSHAL	1731	19071006
CRED	Cred.& Deb.	BRAGGE	1704	45007041
CRED	Cred.& Deb.	ANONYMOUS	1743	45007041
CRED	Cred. Apost.	HODGE	1758	65004014
CRED	Cred.of Gos.	LELAND	1769	46020032
CRED	Debt.and Cred.	MILBOURNE	1709	62002013
CRED	Gosp.cred.	HALL	1756	43028020
CRED	Myst.cred.	SMITH	1675	57003016
CRED	Myst.cred.	WHEATLY	1746	57003016
CREDIB	Credib. Mir.	RUTHERFORTH	1751	46020030
CREED	Apos. Creed.	BENNETT	1775	47003018
CREED	Apos. Creed.	BENNETT	1775	47010042
CREED	Apos. Creed.	BENNETT	1775	52001007
CREED	Apost.,Creed	NEWCOME	1702	61011006
CREED	Apost. Creed	BENNETT	1775	44016019
CREED	Apost. Creed	BENNETT	1775	47026008
CREED	Apost. Creed	BENNETT	1775	61011006
CREED	Apost. Creed.	BENNETT	1775	47002031
CREED	Apost. Creed.	BENNETT	1775	52002019
CREED	Apost.creed.	BENNETT	1775	47019003
CREED	Art.2 Creed.	EDWARDS	1713	46001014
CREED	Atha. Creed.	HOLE	1716	44016016
CREED	Atha. Creed.	PENN	1756	57003016
CREED	Creed Devils	TOPLADY	1775	62002010
CREED	Exp o. Creed	LEIGHTON	1746	57003009
CREED	On ap. Creed	BENNETT	1775	46020031
CREED	On Creed.	BYFIELD	1662	65005007
CREED	The Creed.	WILSON	1781	46017003
CREED	The Creed.	WILSON	1781	47002032
CREED	The Creed.	WILSON	1781	59001016
CREED	Use.o. Creed	BAYLY	1721	58001013
CREED	1 Art. Creed.	CARRINGTON	1750	46014026
CREED	1 Art. Creed.	CARRINGTON	1750	49008006
CREED	10 Art. Creed	EDWARDS	1713	47010043
CREED	10 Art. Creed	CARRINGTON	1750	47010043
CREED	11 Art. Creed	CARRINGTON	1750	49015023
CREED	11 Art Creed.	NEWCOME	1702	47024015
CREED	11 Art Creed.	EDWARDS	1713	47024015
CREED	2 Art. Creed.	HOLE	1715	47008037
CREED	2 Art. Creed.	CARRINGTON	1750	47008037
CREED	5 Art. Creed.	HOLE	1715	49015003
CREED	5 Art. Creed.	CARRINGTON	1750	49015003
CREED	8 Art. Creed.	EDWARDS	1713	48008009
CREED	9 Art. Creed.	CARRINGTON	1750	43016018
CRI	M.pl.w.cri.	FARINDON	1672	51001010
CRIES	Cries sons G.	CENNICK	1762	44015037
CRIM	b. Crim.	DE GOLS	1711	19023004
CRIM	b. Crim.con.	CROOKE	1695	47003019
CRIM	b. Crim.con.	DYCHE	1723	47003019
CRIMINALS	Criminals.	HALLEY	1691	05032029
CRIMINALS	b. Criminals.	CROOKE	1695	32003004

Keyword	In its Context	Author	Year	BkChpVrs
CRIMINALS	b. Criminals.	FIDDES	1720	20018014
CRIMINALS	b. Criminals.	ALLEN	1744	48010009
CRIMINALS	b Criminals.	TUTTY	1747	49015033
CROMWELL	b. Cromwell.	THOMSON	1665	20029002
CROSS	Cross of Xt.	BEVERIDGE	1720	51006014
CROSS	Cross of Xt.	MOIR	1759	51004014
CROSS	Doc.o. Cross.	HOPKINS	1708	45014027
CROSS	Ene.o. Cross.	COCK	1705	53003018
CROSS	Ta.up Cross.	CLARKSON	1696	45014027
CROSS	Xt.on Cross.	WILLISON	1761	46003014
CROWN	Crown.o. Ri.	HAYWARD	1758	58004007
CROWN	Supr. Crown.	RYE	1713	45020025
CROWN	Xn. Crown.	HAYWARD	1758	58004008
CRU	Xt.cru. G. S.	WADSWORTH	1675	61010012
CRU	Xt.cru.daily.	SKELTON	1754	44015021
CRUC	Cruc. Malef.	KEELING	1767	45023039
CRUC	Cruc.t. Lusts.	SOUTH	1744	51005024
CRUC	Cruc.t. Lusts.	BROWNE	1749	51005024
CRUC	Kn. Xt.cruc.	CHARNOCK	1684	49002002
CRUC	Kn. Xt.cruc.	BEVERIDGE	1720	49002002
CRUC	Kn. Xt.cruc.	FIDDES	1720	49002002
CRUC	Kn. Xt.cruc.	WHITFIELD	1739	49002002
CRUC	Kn. Xt.cruc.	SHEPHEARD	1748	49002002
CRUC	Kn. Xt.cruc.	BUNDY	1750	49002002
CRUCIF	Crucif. Xt.	WILKINSON	1660	51005024
CRUCIF	Xt's. Crucif.	BRINSLEY	1667	49001023
CRUCIF	Xt's. Crucif.	HORTON	1679	49001023
CRUCIF	Xt's. Crucif.	COLE	1692	49001023
CRUCIF	Xt's. Crucif.	HUSSEY	1753	49001002
CRUCIF	Xt's. Crucif.	LOVEDER	1756	49001023
CRUCIF	Xt's. Crucif.	VENN	1759	49001023
CRUCIF	Xt's.crucif.	HURRION	1727	49002002
CRUCIF	Xt's.crucif.	ATKINSON	1775	49002002
CRUCIFIED	Jes.crucified.	DAVIS	1756	43021043
CRUCIFIED	Xt. Crucified	KELSEY	1691	49001023
CRUCIFIED	Xt.crucified.	LATHOM	1666	52004014
CRUCIFIED	Xt.crucified.	LATHOM	1666	62003017
CRUCIFIED	Xt.crucified.	COLMAN	1728	51003001
CRUCIFIX	Xt's.crucifix.	HUSSEY	1753	47002023
CRUEL	Cruel R. Ch.	STEPHENS	1728	43005007
CRUELTY	Hd's Cruelty	HALL	1661	43002016
CRUELTY	Hd's Cruelty	STERNE	1760	43002017
CRUELTY	Hd's Cruelty	STERNE	1760	43011017
CULT	Cult.o.mind	HUNT	1748	59002012
CUNN	Cunn. Hunt.	SUTTON	1754	61012016
CUNNING	Cunning M.	SKELTON	1754	24009005
CUP	Cup to all.	STEEL	1675	43026027
CUP	X's.d.b.cup.	BRINSLEY	1660	46018011
CUR	Blind M.cur.	BRAGGE	1706	44008022
CUR	Cur.&swear.	READING	1731	45016024
CUR	Elij. Cur.	MORRIS	1743	12002023
CUR	Elij. Cur.	GOUGH	1751	12002023
CUR	Intemp. Cur.	LLOYD	1765	05029029
CUR	Misapp. Cur.	GRIFFITH	1760	47017021
CUR	Needl. Cur.	GODDARD	1781	46021022
CURE	Cure l. Man.	BULKLEY	1771	47004008

Keyword	In its Context	Author	Year	BkChpVrs
CURE	Cure of mel.	BAXTER	1683	50002007
CURE	Cure of Lep.	DODD	1757	43008001
CURE	Cure of Lep.	BULKLEY	1771	43008001
CURE	Cure Bethes.	HALL	1661	46005002
CURE	Cure Bethes.	BRAGGE	1702	46005001
CURE	Cure Paralyt.	BRAGGE	1702	45007001
CURES	Mir. Cures.	STANHOPE	1715	43008001
CURES	Mir. Cures.	HOLE	1716	43008001
CURIOS	Curios.in Rel.	STANHOPE	1705	46021022
CURIOS	Curios.in Rel.	SEED	1750	46021022
CURSE	Curse cut off.	TAYLOR	1679	01020005
CURSE	Jes.m. Curse.	HURST	1678	51003010
CURSE	Jes.m. Curse.	LARDNER	1769	51003013
CURSING	Ag.cursing.	DORRINGTON	1703	02023002
CURSING	Ag.cursing.	FOSTER	1737	02023002
CURSING	Ag.cursing.	DUNCOMB	1738	02023002
CUT	Curse cut off.	TAYLOR	1679	01020005
CUT	Cut.off M. E.	BULKLEY	1771	46018010
D	A.d. A.a. Xt.	DOUGHTY	1761	49015022
D	A.d.t.s. X's.d	ORTON	1776	46008056
D	Ag. Fear o D.	TATNAL	1665	61002015
D	Ag. Fear. D.	BOOKEY	1739	55004013
D	Anal. D.wis.	BARTON	1737	45006038
D	Beelz.d. H.	BURGESS	1770	44005011
D	Bel. D.to L.	HALL	1777	51002019
D	C.pro. G. D.	RAWSON	1708	47015039
D	Cert.of D.	JONES	1741	19089048
D	Ch.d.to d. P.	BURNABY	1777	51006010
D	Circumcis.d.	TILLY	1737	61008008
D	Comf.in D.	LANGHORNE	1773	04023010
D	Commun.d.	LITTLETON	1680	57001015
D	Con.in w.d.	DUCHAL	1765	48002007
D	Con.in w.d.	CHANDLER	1769	48002007
D	Con.in w.d.	PYLE	1777	48002007
D.	D.& D.o. Sin	PAYNE	1698	61003013
D	D.& D.o. Sin	WHICHCOTE	1702	61003013
D	D.& D.o. Sin	STILLINGFLEET	1707	61003013
D	D.& D.o. Sin	TILLOTSON	1735	61003013
D	D.& H. Mer.	BRAILSFORD	1776	10024014
D	D. Attrib.	EDWARDS	1715	19008009
D	D. B. Rep.	DORRINGTON	1703	04023010
D	D. G.ag.evil.	QUINCY	1750	48012021
D	D. Inst.of M.	BETTY	1729	51001001
D	D. M.to pen.	DAVIES	1766	24031018
D	D. P. Wales.	ATWOOD	1751	19146002
D	D. Perf.in.	COYTE	1761	18011007
D	D. Prov.mys.	HOWE	1771	46013007
D	D. Recon.& Rep	BLACKALL	1723	43005023
D	D. Recon.& Rep	BLAIR	1740	43005023
D	D. Rememb.	GATAKER	1737	19013001
D	D. Virt.m. H.	WILLIAMS	1770	43005006
D	D.all Xt's. N.	WILKINSON	1676	54003017
D	D.as done to.	BENNETT	1728	43007012
D	D.in G's L.	LELAND	1769	19119047
D	D.o. G's wra.	GODDARD	1781	45019041
D	D.of Friend.	CLEMENT	1774	19090012

INDEXES TO THIRD VOLUME: E: KEYWORD-IN-CONTEXT INDEX OF OTHER SUBJECTS OR OCCASIONS

Keyword	In its Context	Author	Year	BkChpVrs
D	D.of Manna.	JENKINS	1779	02016018
D	D.of P.& M.	SKELTON	1754	06024015
D	D.of R. R. In.	HORNECK	1706	43005023
D	D.rel.t. H. S.	GUYSE	1757	52004030
D	D.son&h.sp.	EVANS	1766	47005004
D	Dan.o.d. Re.	LANGHORNE	1773	46009004
D	Del.d. Y& A.	BENSON	1725	21012001
D	Diff. R.d. W.	SMALRIDGE	1724	49003008
D	Diff. R.d. W.	BOYSE	1728	49003008
D	Dumb&d. S.	BRAGGE	1702	44009014
D	End& D. M.	SHERIDAN	1720	47017027
D	Ex. D.re. W.	ORR	1739	61010025
D	F. Sp. X's. D.	PEARSE	1763	48012011
D	F.of d. Good.	SCOTLAND	1776	28003005
D	Fear of D.	ENFIELD	1772	19023004
D	G.short d.	ANONYMOUS	1745	19089045
D	G's w.in D.	HOWE	1771	19107023
D	G's. D.of Pu.	CONYBEARE	1757	64003008
D	G's. J.in d. S	EDWARDS	1774	48003019
D	Gosp. Min.d.	HARRIS	1710	45010016
D	Hap. D.t. Xn.	LANGHORNE	1773	69014013
D	Ho.o.r.at D.	STEPHENS	1699	53003013
D	Hum.&d. F.	OAKES	1747	45002052
D	Hum.&d. F.	TOULMIN	1770	45002052
D	Ig d.o. G's P.	RILAND	1764	28004006
D	Innocents-d.	NEVILLE	1687	63003013
D	Instr. Xt's. D	FLAVEL	1673	45023034
D	Joy D. Xns'.	BEVERIDGE	1720	53004004
D	K.birth d.	PATRICK	1686	19072015
D	K's birth d.	GROSVENOR	1720	05033016
D	King's b. D.	WRIGHT	1718	01040023
D	King's b. D.	ROBINSON	1719	19118022
D	L. D. G. Life.	ERSKINE	1764	51002019
D	Lesson on D.	CARRINGTON	1776	21011003
D	Life& D. R.	DUCHE	1779	19037037
D	Liv.& D. Fai.	NEWTON	1767	62002026
D	M.d.o. Cl. L.	HARRISON	1730	48015029
D	M's Temp.d.	GERARD	1780	20025008
D	Ma.d.sup.p.	SLATER	1690	48013005
D	Man. Xt's. D.	FLAVEL	1673	37013007
D	Man. Xt's D.	FLAVEL	1673	23053007
D	Mess.fm. D.	PAYNE	1698	45016031
D	Mi.f. D.o. G.	WILLIS	1720	53001017
D	Mich.d. Ang.	LITTLETON	1680	43018010
D	Mich.d. Ang.	PATRICK	1719	43018010
D	Michaelm.d.	STRADLING	1692	61001014
D	Mir. Pr.d. M.	SKELTON	1754	46005036
D	Mir. Pr.d. M.	POWELL	1776	46005036
D	Mo.&pos. D.	CLARKE	1735	43022040
D	Mor.&p. D.	WHITBY	1720	43011030
D	Mor.&p. D.	MORRIS	1743	43012007
D	Mor.&p. D.	WESTON	1747	43012007
D	Mor.&pos.d.	WESTON	1747	43009013
D	Mor.&pos.d.	HUNT	1748	43009013
D	Mor. D.ab. P.	EMLYN	1742	43023023
D	N.& D. Con.	CRAIG	1775	10012017

Keyword	In its Context	Author	Year	BkChpVrs
D	N's mes.to D.	DE COURCY	1773	10012007
D	Nec. Xt's. D.	DAVIS	1756	46011051
D	Nec.of D.t.	ROMAINE	1760	46006045
D	Necess.of D.	BLACKLOCK	1776	12020001
D	Num.of D.	CROWE	1744	19090012
D	Num.our D.	HAVETT	1703	19090012
D	Ob. Lord's d.	ORTON	1769	23058013
D	Ob. Lord's d.	D'COETLOGAN	1776	23058013
D	Ob.to D. W.	STEPHENS	1699	43006010
D	Ob.to D. W.	NEWCOME	1702	43006010
D	Ob.to D. W.	NORRIS	1728	43006010
D	Ob.to D. W.	ROGERS	1736	43006010
D	Obed. D. W.	SCATTERGOOD	1723	43007021
D	Obed. D. W.	SKEELER	1740	43007021
D	Obl.to L's d.	ORTON	1769	02020008
D	On S.a. D. S.	HOLE	1713	24026014
D	P.&c. X's. D.	LARDNER	1751	46015005
D	P. Fr. Bir.d.	SHAW	1729	13028009
D	P.ob.of D. F.	DAVIES	1766	23066002
D	Par D.to Ch.	EATON	1764	20022006
D	Pas.& Peo. D.	ROE	1766	57004016
D	Past.& De. D.	WILSON	1736	24003015
D	Pat.i.well-d.	MACE	1751	61010036
D	Pea wick. D.	HORTON	1679	55005003
D	Pow. Xt's D.	MAY	1757	46007046
D	Pr. M.p.d.m.	CONYBEARE	1757	46020031
D	Pr. W. Bth-d.	SMEDLEY	1716	63002017
D	Prea.& H. D.	GODDARD	1781	05022002
D	Pres. Joy D.	WILCOX	1757	19097011
D	Queen's b.d.	MORER	1708	47010038
D	R.&off.o. D.	COLMAN	1728	69022016
D	Reas.judg.d.	JOHNSON	1733	46011026
D	Ren.h.th. D.	RYVES	1715	50004002
D	S.c. G.f.d. J.	DAVIES	1771	49003007
D	Sea dan.& D.	RYTHER	1674	47027018
D	Seek. Xt. D.	GUYSE	1729	20008017
D	Ser. Refl.s. D	WHITTY	1772	24008006
D	Ser.con.o. D.	LOCKIER	1671	23057001
D	Sin. D.of S.	DUNLOP	1722	23001005
D	Sou. D.n.ce.	CASE	1774	58004003
D	Sp. Lig.& D.	SKELTON	1754	48013011
D	St. And.d.	HUNTER	1778	05015017
D	St. Andr.d.	STRIPLING	1691	58002012
D	St. Barnab.d.	STANHOPE	1715	46015012
D	St. Barnab.d.	HOLE	1716	46015012
D	St. David's d.	OWEN	1716	09012024
D	St. Jame's-d.	COOKE	1739	61010023
D	St. James d.	STANHOPE	1715	43020020
D	St. James d.	HOLE	1716	43020020
D	St. John's d.	PEGGE	1742	46001005
D	St. Luke's d.	HACKETT	1675	47011026
D	St. Luke's d.	JENNER	1676	58004011
D	St. Luke's d.	FRANCIS	1773	50005020
D	St. Luke's.d.	STANHOPE	1715	45010001
D	St. Luke's.d.	HOLE	1716	45010001
D	St. Luke's-d.	STANHOPE	1715	58004005

Keyword	In its Context	Author	Year	BkChpVrs
D	St. Luke's-d.	HOLE	1716	58004005
D	St. Mark's d.	LITTLETON	1680	47015037
D	St. Mark's d.	PATRICK	1686	52004014
D	St. Mark's d.	STANHOPE	1715	46015001
D	St. Mark's d.	HOLE	1716	46015001
D	St. Mark's d.	BERRIMAN	1763	52004014
D	St. Mark's-d.	HOLE	1716	52004007
D	St. Mark's-d.	STANHOPE	1718	52004007
D	St. Matth.d.	COCK	1705	50004001
D	St. Matth.d.	COCK	1705	50004005
D	St. Matth.d.	STANHOPE	1715	50004001
D	St. Matth.d.	HOLE	1716	50004001
D	St. Mich.d.	MARSHALL	1731	49011010
D	St. P's.d.to F	HOADLY	1754	47024024
D	St. P's.d.to F	CHANDLER	1769	47024025
D	St. P's.d.to F	HURD	1780	47024024
D	St. Patrick.d.	HENRY	1756	45024005
D	St. Paul's d.	NEEDHAM	1716	45014023
D	St. Paul's d.	COBDEN	1757	47020024
D	St. Paul's.d.	STANHOPE	1715	47009001
D	St. Pet.d. Xt.	GELL	1676	43010032
D	St. Pet.d. Xt.	COOKE	1739	43010032
D	St. Pet.d. Xt.	BUNDY	1740	43010033
D	St. Peter's d.	GODDEN	1686	43016018
D	St. Peter's d.	PATRICK	1687	43016018
D	St. Peter's d.	STANHOPE	1715	47012001
D	St. Peter's d.	HOLE	1716	47012001
D	St. Peter's d.	MARSHALL	1731	44014029
D	St. Peter's d.	BERRIMAN	1763	43016018
D	St. Peter's.d.	MARSHALL	1731	47010034
D	St. Peters d.	STANHOPE	1715	43016013
D	St. Peters d.	HOLE	1716	43016013
D	St. Step.d. P.	MAY	1757	47007058
D	St. Steph.d.	FRANK	1672	47007055
D	St. Steph.d.	LITTLETON	1680	47007060
D	St. Steph.d.	LIGHTFOOT	1684	47007053
D	St. Steph.d.	WISE	1717	43013021
D	St. Steph.d.	STANHOPE	1715	47007055
D	St. Steph.d.	HOLE	1716	47007055
D	St. Steph.d.	LEEKE	1727	47007037
D	St. Steph.d.	ROBINSON	1730	58002022
D	St. Steph.d.	SECKER	1771	47007059
D	St. Tho.d.	STANHOPE	1715	52002019
D	St. Tho.d.	HOLE	1716	52002019
D	St. Tho.d.	WILDER	1741	46020027
D	St. Thom.d.	HICKMAN	1713	50005007
D	St. Thom.d.	STANHOPE	1715	46020024
D	St. Thom.d.	HOLE	1716	46020024
D	St. Thom.d.	ADAMS	1716	46020027
D	St. Thom.d.	SCATTERGOOD	1723	46020027
D	St. Thom.d.	LEEKE	1730	46014001
D	St. Thom.d.	WHEATLY	1746	46020024
D	St. Thom.d.	LARDNER	1760	46020029
D	Sub t. D. Ch.	SAVAGE	1732	61012009
D	Sub. D. Will.	MEDE	1672	43007021
D	Suff.of d. Gr.	ATTERBURY	1699	50012009

Keyword	In its Context	Author	Year	BkChpVrs
D	Suff.of d. Gr.	BEVERIDGE	1720	50012009
D	Sure m.of D.	HEYWOOD	1672	23055005
D	Surp.in D.	WATTS	1753	44013035
D	Surp.in D.	ADEY	1755	44013037
D	T.o.tr.&f.d.	ADAMS	1777	65004001
D	Tr. D. Du. M.	BREVALL	1670	65005004
D	Tra. Xt's. D.	HORTON	1679	66000009
D	Tri.tr.&f. D.	TILLOTSON	1735	65004001
D	U.of R:at D.	STENNETT	1769	19023004
D	Unfr.wks. D.	MOORE	1716	52005011
D	Unj.m's.d.	SMITH	1670	49006009
D	View X's. D.	BOURN	1777	43007024
D	W.& D. Wis.	OUTRAM	1697	45016008
D	W.& D. Wis.	NORRIS	1728	45016008
D	W.& D. Wis.	SMITH	1740	45016008
D	Wh. D.of M.	HOOLE	1748	21012013
D	Whym.1. D.	MOSS	1732	46003019
D	Wic. M.o. D.	CLARKE	1735	46008044
D	Wiv.& H. D.	STEELE	1676	52005033
D	Wiv.& H. D.	HOLE	1719	52005033
D	Wiv.& H. D.	ANONYMOUS	1754	52006002
D	Wiv.& H. D.	ANONYMOUS	1754	52006004
D	Wiv.& H. D.	FRANKLIN	1765	52005033
D	Wiv. D.to H.	FLEETWOOD	1737	63003001
D	Wiv. D.to H.	FLEETWOOD	1737	63003003
D	Wiv. D.to H.	FLEETWOOD	1737	63003004
D	Wive's& Hus. D	ANONYMOUS	1776	52005033
D	Wlk.as Xt.d.	BARROW	1716	65002006
D	X's.d.b.cup.	BRINSLEY	1660	46018011
D	Xn. D.& Ho.	WEBB	1772	54001009
D	Xn. Supp. D.	COMBER	1691	19023004
D	Xn's. D.easy.	SMITH	1740	51004031
D	Xn's.des.t.d.	EDWARDS	1726	53001025
D	Xt.mind. D.	COLMAN	1728	46013001
D	Xt's apol.f.d.	ORTON	1776	43026004
D	Xt's. D.& M.	BURNET	1747	49001025
D	Xt's. D. A.r.	HOADLY	1754	43020026
D	Xt's. D. Hell.	ROBINSON	1660	47002027
D	Xt's. D. Hell.	PIGOTT	1702	47002026
D	Xt's. D. Hell.	HOLE	1715	47002027
D	Xt's. D. Hell.	BARROW	1716	47002027
D	Xt's. D. Hell.	BOYS	1716	47002027
D	Xt's. D. Hell.	FISHER	1741	47002027
D	Xt's. D. Hell.	TERRY	1746	47002027
D	Xt's. D. Wis.	PARKHURST	1707	65003008
D	Xt's. D.foret.	MEDE	1672	45024045
D	Xt's. D.in. H.	NICOLSON	1661	52004009
D	Xt's. D.in. H.	HURRION	1719	52004010
D	Xt's. D.on C.	FLAVEL	1673	47002023
D	Xt's. D.pr. A.	WITHERSPOON	1768	65002002
D	Xt's. S.& D.	COWPER	1773	49002002
D	Xt's.d.&res.	JOHNSON	1728	47002031
D	Xt's.p.rais.d.	MORRIS	1757	46005025
D	Xt's.tr.ov. D.	FANCH	1768	49015025
D	Xt's.2 p.f. D.	FLAVEL	1673	49011023
D	Xtmas d.	DELANY	1754	48013013

Keyword	In its Context	Author	Year	BkChpVrs
D	Xtmas d.	ORR	1772	46006045
D	Xy.ca.rat. D.	ORR	1739	63003015
D	b. D. Marlb.	RICH	1685	48013002
D	2 S.un. S. D.	LEAKE	1773	49015033
DA	Da. Repent.	SECKER	1770	10012013
DA	Da.being overr	STILLINGFLEET	1707	21007016
DA	Da.being overr	TRAPP	1739	21007016
DA	Negl. Sal.da.	CONANT	1698	61002003
DA	Unc. Sin Da.	CLARKSON	1696	52005008
DAI	Dai. Self-ex.	WARREN	1710	19004004
DAI	Dai.pub. Pr.	PEARSALL	1751	47002046
DAILY	Daily Bread.	FARINDON	1674	43006011
DAILY	Daily Bread.	GELL	1676	43006011
DAILY	Daily Bread.	STEPHENS	1699	43006011
DAILY	Daily Bread.	NEWCOME	1702	43006011
DAILY	Daily Bread.	EDWARDS	1713	43006011
DAILY	Daily Bread.	MANGEY	1717	43006011
DAILY	Daily Bread.	CLAGETT	1720	43006011
DAILY	Daily Bread.	BLACKALL	1723	43006011
DAILY	Daily Bread.	MOSS	1732	43006011
DAILY	Daily Bread.	MOSS	1732	45011003
DAILY	Daily Bread.	LITTLETON	1735	43006011
DAILY	Daily Bread.	BISSE	1740	43006011
DAILY	Daily Bread.	BLAIR	1740	43006011
DAILY	Daily Bread.	JACKSON	1758	43006011
DAILY	Daily Bread.	CHURCHILL	1765	43006011
DAILY	Daily Com.	HENRY	1731	19004008
DAILY	Daily Com.	HENRY	1731	19005003
DAILY	Daily Dev.	AMORY	1747	19002005
DAILY	Daily Devot.	AMORY	1747	19092001
DAILY	Daily Devot.	AMORY	1746	19003005
DAILY	Dy. Daily.	HILL	1755	49015031
DAILY	Xt.cru.daily.	SKELTON	1754	44015021
DAM	Dam. Clause	SEED	1750	44016016
DAN	Dan.bad Co.	PRIEST	1710	19119115
DAN	Dan.in Bab.	HORNE	1778	27006010
DAN	Dan.kn. Sin	TILLOTSON	1735	48001018
DAN	Dan.lit. Sins.	HOPKINS	1710	43005019
DAN	Dan.neg. Sa.	QUINCY	1750	61002003
DAN	Dan.neg.rel.	STILLINGFLEET	1707	61002003
DAN	Dan.o.d. Re.	LANGHORNE	1773	46009004
DAN	Dan.70 W.	MARKWICK	1728	27009024
DAN	Dan.70 W.	BLAYNEY	1775	27009020
DAN	Duty b. Dan.	ERSKINE	1764	24013016
DAN	Sea dan.& D.	RYTHER	1674	47027018
DAN'S	Dan's. Xter.	ENFIELD	1777	27006005
DANG	Dang. Hyp.	ASHETON	1673	43007021
DANG	Dang. Rep.	CARR	1777	23055007
DANG	Dang. Vice.	BAINE	1778	48001018
DANG	Dang.ev. H.	ABERNETHY	1751	24013023
DANG	Dang.liv.&c.	WILSON	1781	49013011
DANG	Dang.of fall.	HOLDSWORTH	1725	49010012
DANG	Dang.of fall.	NEWTON	1736	49010012
DANG	Dang.of fall.	HOOLE	1748	49010012
DANG	Dang.of fall.	HILL	1755	49010012
DANG	Dang.of Rel.	SMALRIDGE	1724	64002020

Keyword	In its Context	Author	Year	BkChpVrs
DANG	Dang.of Rel.	ADEY	1760	64002022
DANG	Dang.riches.	CARTWRIGHT	1662	43019024
DANG	Saf.in Dang.	ERSKINE	1764	23026020
DANG	Ti.of Dang.	HERVEY	1759	61011029
DANGER	Danger of Pros	BATES	1700	20001032
DANGER	Danger of Pros	SOUTH	1727	20001032
DAR	Cond. L.o. Dar	SUTTON	1754	46003019
DARK	Dark.& Lig.	TAYLOR	1719	52005018
DARK	Dark Script.	PARKHURST	1706	47013027
DARK	Intell. Dark.	BALGUY	1748	43006023
DARK	The dark vis.	WILKINSON	1660	34002003
DARK	Wks. Dark.	ALTHAM	1732	48013012
DARKN	Wilf. Darkn.	WEST	1762	46003019
DARKN	Wilf. Darkn.	SHERLOCK	1772	46003019
DARKN	Wor. Darkn.	SECKER	1770	52005011
DAUGH	Jair's Daugh.	BRAGGE	1702	44005021
DAV	Dav.& Sol.	HARRINGTON	1714	19072001
DAV	Dav. Xrter.	PEMBERTON	1727	47013036
DAV	Life of Dav.	CREYGHTON	1720	19119071
DAV'S	Dav's Guilt.	DOUGHTY	1761	19051003
DAVID	Offsp. David	HARRIS	1724	23009006
DAVID'S	David's cho.	MACHIN	1740	10024014
DAVID'S	David's p. Xr	HARRIS	1755	45024044
DAVID'S	David's Xr.	PORTEUS	1761	09013013
DAVID'S	David's Xr.	CLEAVER	1762	09013013
DAVID'S	David's Xr.	ENFIELD	1777	10007008
DAVID'S	St. David's d.	OWEN	1716	09012024
DAY	Birth day.	HUTCHINSON	1717	10010012
DAY	Birth-day.	MACQUEENE	1687	19002006
DAY	Day of Gra.	SHOWER	1694	19081011
DAY	Day Judgm.	TILLOTSON	1735	44013032
DAY	Day Judgm.	SHARP	1734	47017031
DAY	Day Judgm.	BROWNE	1749	69020012
DAY	Day Judgm.	ATKINSON	1775	50005010
DAY	Innoc. Day.	FRANK	1672	43002011
DAY	Innoc. Day.	FRANK	1672	43002016
DAY	Innoc. Day.	LITTLETON	1680	43002013
DAY	Innoc. Day.	STANHOPE	1715	43002013
DAY	Innoc. Day.	HOLE	1716	43002013
DAY	Innoc. Day.	STANHOPE	1715	69014001
DAY	Innoc. Day.	HOLE	1716	69014001
DAY	Innoc. Day.	WILDER	1729	43002016
DAY	Innoc. Day.	WESTON	1747	43016003
DAY	Innoc. Day.	BARNES	1752	43002016
DAY	Innoc. Day.	PYLE	1777	43002016
DAY	Jugdm.day.	WATSON	1676	47017031
DAY	K.birth day.	WETENHALL	1686	21010017
DAY	K's b. Day.	WALKER	1738	43007012
DAY	Lady-day.	GRIFFITH	1660	20024021
DAY	Lord's day.	BRYAN	1686	02020008
DAY	Lord's day.	BULKLY	1697	02020008
DAY	Lord's day.	VENN	1760	26020013
DAY	Lord's day.	ORTON	1769	03023003
DAY	Lord's Day.	ORTON	1769	01002003
DAY	Lord's-day.	WETENHALL	1697	69001003
DAY	Lord's-day.	ORTON	1769	23056002

Keyword	In its Context	Author	Year	BkChpVrs
DAY	St. And. Day	FRANK	1672	43004020
DAY	St. And. Day	LITTLETON	1680	43004018
DAY	St. And. Day	STANHOPE	1715	43004018
DAY	St. And. Day	HOLE	1716	43004018
DAY	St. Andr.day	STANHOPE	1715	48010009
DAY	St. Andr.day	HOLE	1716	48010009
DAY	St. Barn.day.	CRADOCK	1713	55005001
DAY	St. Barn.day.	STANHOPE	1715	47011023
DAY	St. Barn.day.	HOLE	1716	47011023
DAY	St. Barth.day	SEIGNIOR	1670	47005012
DAY	St. Barth.day	EDWARDS	1702	45022021
DAY	St. Barth.day	COCK	1705	45022024
DAY	St. Barth.day	BAXTER	1707	47020024
DAY	St. Barth.day	STANHOPE	1715	45022023
DAY	St. Barth.day	HOLE	1716	46001047
DAY	St. Barth.day	STANHOPE	1715	47005012
DAY	St. Barth.day	HOLE	1716	47005012
DAY	St. Barth.day	MARSHALL	1731	46001047
DAY	St. Barth.day	BARON	1742	47020023
DAY	St. Cecil.day	BRADSHAW	1697	14005013
DAY	St. Matt.day.	LITTLETON	1680	43009009
DAY	St. Matt.day.	STANHOPE	1715	43009009
DAY	St. Matt.day.	HOLE	1716	43009009
DAY	St. Matt.day.	COOKE	1739	45012015
DAY	St. Matt.day.	WHEATLY	1746	43009009
DAY	St. Mich.day	PHILPOT	1663	46005007
DAY	St. Mich.day	STANHOPE	1715	43018001
DAY	St. Mich.day	HOLE	1716	43018001
DAY	St. Mich.day	STANHOPE	1715	69012007
DAY	St. Mich.day	HOLE	1716	69012007
DAY	St. Mich.day	LESTLEY	1721	69012007
DAY	St. Steph.day	STANHOPE	1715	43023034
DAY	St. Steph.day	HOLE	1716	43023034
DAY	Xtmas-day.	PIETY	1737	52002004
DAY	Xtmas-day.	TOULMIN	1770	54002016
DAYS	Xr. L. Days.	FELL	1675	64003003
DE	De. S.& H. G.	EVANS	1766	65005020
DE	De.o. H. Gh.	BROME	1709	46016007
DE	Dif.de.f. Gl.	BULL	1713	64001011
DE	G's De.eter.	BRINE	1754	20022023
DE	Good m. De.	WILCOX	1757	19027004
DE	M's De.vain.	HORTON	1679	20019021
DE	Past.& De. D.	WILSON	1736	24003015
DE	Self.de.r.m.	BRAILSFORD	1776	51006007
DE	Self-de.t. G.	AMORY	1742	50004005
DE	Sp. Hous.de.	MASTERSON	1661	63002004
DE	St. P's de. Xy	NEWTON	1782	49013001
DE	Temp.o De.	WHARTON	1728	63005008
DE	Wick. M.de.	CLARKE	1736	56002011
DEA	Ag F.of Dea.	ANONYMOUS	1710	49015055
DEA	Cert.of Dea.	DICKSON	1731	61009027
DEA	Cert.of Dea.	DOUGHTY	1761	18030023
DEA	Dea.& Life.	MALBON	1715	48008013
DEA	Dea. Geor. I.	WATTS	1753	23005012
DEA	Dea.a. Comf.	BURNET	1747	49015055
DEA	Dea.b. Ad. F.	LAWSON	1764	48005012

Keyword	In its Context	Author	Year	BkChpVrs
DEA	Dea.b. Ad. F.	BOSTON	1773	48005012
DEA	Dea.b. Rep.	BEVERLEY	1670	45023039
DEA	Dea.b. Rep.	VEAL	1690	45023042
DEA	Dea.b. Rep.	MARCH	1699	45023039
DEA	Dea.b. Rep.	LAKE	1705	45023043
DEA	Dea.b. Rep.	FIDDES	1720	47026020
DEA	Dea.b. Rep.	BURNET	1747	45023043
DEA	Dea.wag. Sin	PEARSE	1763	48006023
DEA	Dec.of Dea.	WHARTON	1728	61009027
DEA	Dec.of Dea.	WHEATLY	1746	61009027
DEA	Del.fm Dea.	CENNICK	1762	46008051
DEA	Des.of Dea.	EDWARDS	1726	53001023
DEA	Fear of Dea.	MAYO	1690	61002015
DEA	Fear of Dea.	NOURSE	1701	61002015
DEA	Fear of Dea.	LAMBE	1717	61002015
DEA	Fear of Dea.	NORRIS	1728	61002015
DEA	Fear of Dea.	LATHAM	1774	61002015
DEA	G's.dea.w. S.	STEPHENS	1737	48009017
DEA	Sin un. Dea.	LAMBE	1717	65005016
DEA	Xt.dest. Dea.	BREKELL	1765	61011015
DEAC	Deac. P. Bps.	CRUCHY	1723	49012005
DEAD	Bapt.f.dead.	EDWARDS	1692	49015029
DEAD	Bapt.f.dead.	FORD	1692	49015029
DEAD	Dead in Sin.	WAPLE	1720	52002004
DEAD	Nat.m.dead.	USHER	1678	25005016
DEAD	Nat.m.dead.	USHER	1678	48006023
DEAD	Nat.m.dead.	USHER	1678	51003022
DEAF	Deaf& Dum.	DODD	1757	44007032
DEATH	After Death.	ELLIS	1704	45016023
DEATH	Cert. Death.	WHITAKER	1674	19039013
DEATH	Death b. R.	WHALEY	1695	43020009
DEATH	Death b.rep.	SCOTT	1700	43025010
DEATH	Death b.rep.	SHERLOCK	1772	43027038
DEATH	Death of rig.	CAWTON	1675	04023010
DEATH	Death of rig.	LACY	1720	04023010
DEATH	Death of rig.	BUNDY	1740	04023010
DEATH	Death of rig.	ECCLES	1755	04023010
DEATH	Death of rig.	FARMER	1756	04023010
DEATH	Death of rig.	AGAR	1759	04023010
DEATH	Death of rig.	BARCLAY	1777	04023010
DEATH	Death of Fr.	MOIR	1776	23057001
DEATH	Death of K.	PIGGOTT	1714	19146003
DEATH	Death of Xt.	BARROW	1716	49015003
DEATH	Death of Xt.	SOMERVILLE	1779	43027054
DEATH	Death of Xt.	LANGHORNE	1773	46019030
DEATH	Death of Xt.	BLAIR	1777	46017001
DEATH	Death of Xt.	SAURIN	1777	50005014
DEATH	Death uncer.	FOTHERGILL	1765	44013032
DEATH	Death.	ELLIS	1704	45016022
DEATH	Death.	BURNET	1713	21012007
DEATH	Death.	MAYNARD	1724	04023010
DEATH	Death.	LUCAS	1722	53001022
DEATH	Death.	PIERCE	1731	21009005
DEATH	Death.	BOURN	1755	61009027
DEATH	Death.	ELSMERE	1767	21009005
DEATH	Death.	BOURDALOUE	1776	01003019

Keyword	In its Context	Author	Year	BkChpVrs
DEATH	Death.	CARR	1777	61012027
DEATH	Death.	MILNE	1780	05032029
DEATH	Death Adv.	DAVIS	1756	55004014
DEATH	Death P. Or.	TRUSTLER	1759	20011016
DEATH	Death Pr. Or.	MACLAINE	1752	25003028
DEATH	Death Rig.	LUCAS	1722	21002015
DEATH	Death Youth	TOULMIN	1770	45007012
DEATH	Death-b. R.	SCAMLER	1685	19095008
DEATH	Death-b. R.	WARREN	1748	47017030
DEATH	F.of Death.	EATON	1764	19023004
DEATH	Fear o. Death	SYLVESTER	1676	47020024
DEATH	Of Death.	BATES	1700	61002015
DEATH	On Death.	WHALEY	1708	50005005
DEATH	On Death.	SMALRIDGE	1724	53001021
DEATH	Pre.f. Death.	HOOK	1676	43025010
DEATH	Pre.f. Death.	LUCAS	1722	23038001
DEATH	Pre.f. Death.	WHEATLAND	1739	12020001
DEATH	Pre.f. Death.	TIDCOMBE	1757	43024044
DEATH	Prep. Death.	BOURDALOUE	1776	45007012
DEATH	Relig. Death	DORRINGTON	1703	19037037
DEATH	Sin& Death.	SOUTH	1744	48006023
DEATH	Sin& Death.	CHANDLER	1769	48005012
DEATH	Spir. Death.	FLAVEL	1673	52005014
DEATH	Spir. Death.	DAVIES	1766	52002001
DEATH	Xt's. Death.	CHARNOCK	1684	52005002
DEATH	on Death.	BOYSE	1728	21007002
DEATH	on Death.	BLAIR	1780	19023004
DEB	Apost. Deb.	DUCHAL	1753	47001008
DEB	Cred.& Deb.	BRAGGE	1704	45007041
DEB	Cred.& Deb.	ANONYMOUS	1743	45007041
DEB	Deb. Heart.	LAMONT	1780	43005027
DEBT	Ad.to Debt.	DREW	1725	05006012
DEBT	Debt.and Cred.	MILBOURNE	1709	62002013
DEBT	Run.in debt.	NEWTON	1782	48013008
DEBT	Two Debt.	BULKLEY	1771	45007047
DEBTOR	Ev.m.debtor	HUTCHINS	1782	49004007
DEBTOR	Forg. Debtor	BULKLEY	1771	43018023
DEBTS	Pay. Debts.	DELANY	1747	48013008
DEBTS	Pay. Debts.	BERRIMAN	1763	48013008
DEC	Ag. Self-dec.	BOURN	1777	49003018
DEC	Dec.& Ord.	BISSE	1723	49014040
DEC	Dec.in Wor.	SUTTON	1717	49014040
DEC	Dec.o. G.&c.	WISHEART	1716	52001011
DEC	Dec.o. G.&c.	HUBBARD	1757	52001011
DEC	Dec.of Dea.	WHARTON	1728	61009027
DEC	Dec.of Dea.	WHEATLY	1746	61009027
DEC	Dec.31.	STEPHENS	1707	46008032
DEC	Decei.&dec.	WATERLAND	1742	52004014
DEC	Den. S.a Dec.	NICOLSON	1661	65001008
DECALOGUE	Decalogue.	FIDDES	1720	02020001
DECALOGUE	Decalogue.	STACKHOUSE	1743	02020003
DECAY	Decay o. Rel.	ATKINSON	1737	38003018
DECAY	Decay of R.	ATKINSON	1737	38003016
DECAY	Decay of R.	ATKINSON	1737	38003017
DECEI	Decei.&dec.	WATERLAND	1742	52004014
DECEIT	Deceit. Sin.	LLOYD	1765	61003013

Keyword	In its Context	Author	Year	BkChpVrs
DECEIT	Deceit. Sin.	CRAIG	1775	19036002
DECEIT	Deceit.o. Sin	LUCAS	1716	52005006
DECEIT	Deceit.o. Sin.	CLARKE	1736	61003013
DECEIT	Heart deceit.	SHARP	1729	24017009
DECEIT	Heart deceit.	MAYHEW	1755	24017009
DECEIT	Heart deceit.	HAWEIS	1762	24017009
DECEIT	Meth.deceit	SMITH	1770	50004002
DECEIT	Self-deceit	BUTLER	1749	10012007
DECEIT	Self-deceit.	HORT	1738	62001022
DECEITF	Sin deceitf.	PRIEST	1753	20011018
DECENCY	Decency life	WHICHCOTE	1703	48013013
DECEPT	Ag. Decept.	SHERIDAN	1720	51006007
DECL	Decl.in Rel.	BARKER	1748	69002004
DECL	Decl.in Rel.	HOGG	1775	69002005
DECR	Decr. Xn. F.	GREENHILL	1756	45018008
DECREE	Apo. Decree.	GALE	1726	47015028
DECREES	G's Decrees.	BOSTON	1773	52001011
DECTRACTION	Dectraction.	H.	1707	62001019
DED	Self-ded. G.	CHANDLER	1769	48012001
DEDIC	Dedic.to G.	DAVIES	1766	49006019
DEEDS	Alms-deeds.	NOURSE	1705	61013016
DEF	Def. Ch. En.	HARRISON	1729	53001020
DEF	Def. Ch. En.	STOCKDALE	1777	19096009
DEF	Def. H. Reas.	BURNET	1747	49013012
DEF	Def. H.wisd.	FIDDES	1720	21001018
DEF	Def. H.wisd.	MARKLAND	1729	21001018
DEF	Def. Litur.	ATTERBURY	1734	25003041
DEF	Def. Liturgy.	ANNAND	1661	28014002
DEF	Def. Pr. Rel.	ATKINSON	1737	24006029
DEF	Def. R. R.	HALLYWELL	1694	48001016
DEF	Def. Wisd.	BOURN	1777	18028028
DEF	Def.of Gosp.	WATTS	1753	48001016
DEF	Def.of Lit.	WARREN	1686	57002001
DEF	Def.of Litur.	PRIEST	1750	19096009
DEF	Def.of Reb.	BULKLEY	1761	19107001
DEF	Def.of Rev.	SCOTT	1743	47002036
DEF	Def.of Rev.	SCOTT.	1743	47015018
DEF	Def.of Xnity	SCOTT	1743	46014001
DEF	Def.of Xty.	SHARPE	1755	47002022
DEF	Right. Def.	MOSS	1737	43005020
DEF	St. P's. Def.	ATTERBURY	1734	47024025
DEF	St. P's. Def.	MOSS	1737	47024025
DEFAMATION	Defamation.	STRAIGHT	1741	63003008
DEFECT	Peter's Defect	LOVEDER	1756	44014071
DEFEN	Episc.defen.	D'ANVERS	1712	43005014
DEFEND	Defend. Rel.	DOUGHTY	1761	19139021
DEFIN	Defin.of Sin.	PYLE	1777	65003004
DEG	Deg.of Men.	WHICHCOTE	1703	48001021
DEG	Dif. Deg. Gl.	CONYBEARE	1757	65003002
DEGENER	Degener.of Men	WHICHCOTE	1698	48001029
DEGENER	Degener.of Men	WHICHCOTE	1703	48001028
DEGR	Degr. Glory.	FRANK	1716	43020023
DEI	Causa Dei.	GAUDEN	1661	19074022
DEI	Pecul.dei.	HICKES	1713	48009004
DEISM	Ath.& Deism	STEPHENS	1737	46005039
DEISM	Deism.	SCOTT	1743	46006029

Keyword	In its Context	Author	Year	BkChpVrs
DEISM	Folly. Deism	SHERLOCK	1702	46014001
DEITY	Deity of Xt.	RUSSEL	1719	59002013
DEITY	Ex.of Deity.	COCKRANE	1780	48001020
DEJE	Soul's Deje.	WHITFIELD	1771	19042005
DEJEC	Dejec.mind.	WATERLAND	1742	20018014
DEL	Ch.del.by Xt	ERSKINE	1764	21009014
DEL	Del.& Judg.	HORNE	1684	21011009
DEL	Del. Repent.	BARROW	1716	19119060
DEL	Del. Repent.	MARKLAND	1729	21012001
DEL	Del. Repent.	SHARP	1734	19119059
DEL	Del. Repent.	BURNET	1747	19119060
DEL	Del. Repent.	WESTON	1747	19119060
DEL	Del. Repent.	CLEMENT	1774	19119060
DEL	Del.d. Y& A.	BENSON	1725	21012001
DEL	Del.fm Dea.	CENNICK	1762	46008051
DEL	Del.thro' Xt.	CLARKE	1735	48007024
DEL	Del.unreas.	LARDNER	1751	19119060
DEL	G.m's Del.	LELAND	1769	19037004
DEL	Sea.del.con.	BRADBURY	1772	05032036
DELAY	Delay. Rep.	BLACKALL	1723	43005025
DELAY	Delay Rep.	SCOTT	1700	69002021
DELAY	Delay Rep.	LUCAS	1717	61003007
DELAY	Delay Rep.	CREYGHTON	1720	43024046
DELAY	Delay Sent.	LENG	1699	21008011
DELAY	G's delay.	WARREN	1739	21008011
DELIG	Delig. G's w.	LELAND	1769	19111002
DELIG	Delig. Rev.	WILCOX	1757	19119092
DELIGHT	Delight in oth	SWADLIN	1661	48001032
DELIGHT	Delight in oth	SOUTH	1727	48001032
DELIGHT	Xt's Delight.	COLMAN	1728	20008031
DELIV	Deliv.fm. T.	FARINDON	1674	43006013
DELIV	Deliv.fm. T.	EDWARDS	1713	43006013
DELIV	Deliv.fm. Tem.	STEPHENS	1699	43006013
DELIV	Deliv.fm. Tem.	BUCK	17--	43006013
DELIV	Deliv.fm. Tem.	NEWCOME	1702	43006013
DELIV	Deliv.fm. Tem.	HOLE	1715	43006013
DELIV	Deliv.fm. Tem.	MANGEY	1717	43006013
DELIV	Deliv.fm. Tem.	BLACKALL	1723	43006013
DELIV	Deliv.fm. Tem.	JACKSON	1728	43006013
DELIV	Deliv.fm. Tem.	MOSS	1732	43006013
DELIV	Deliv.fm. Tem.	LITTLETON	1735	43006013
DELIV	Deliv.fm. Tem.	BISSE	1740	43006013
DELIV	Deliv.fm. Tem.	BLAIR	1740	43006013
DELIV	God's Deliv.	ALLESTREE	1684	19102013
DELIV	Nat. Deliv.	BULKLEY	1761	19044001
DELIV	Right.deliv.	HORNE	1778	01019029
DELIVER	G's. Deliver.	HORTON	1679	50001010
DELIVER	G's. Deliver.	WALLIS	1692	50001010
DELIVER	Isra Deliver.	CLARKE	1727	02015009
DELUGE	Deluge.	LELAND	1769	64002005
DELUGE	Deluge&c.	MURRAY	1777	01008009
DELUGE	on Deluge.	GROVE	1742	01008021
DELUS	Delus.o. Sin.	SMITH	1769	51006007
DEM	Heart dem.	DUCHAL	1765	20023026
DEM	Xn. R.dem.	HUTCHINSON	1720	46015024
DEMONIACS	Demoniacs.	MEDE	1672	46010020

Keyword	In its Context	Author	Year	BkChpVrs
DEMONIACS	Demoniacs.	HUTCHINSON	1738	45013032
DEMONIACS	Demoniacs.	SKEELER	1740	43012026
DEMONIACS	Demoniacs.	LARDNER	1758	44005019
DEMONIACS	Demoniacs.	BULKLEY	1771	43008031
DEMONS	Xty.demons.	BELLAMY	1744	47026026
DEMONS	Xy.demons.	BREKELL	1765	49002004
DEN	Den. S.a Dec.	NICOLSON	1661	65001008
DEN	Self. Den.& Mo	HORNECK	1706	43005029
DEN	Self. Den.& Mo	BLACKALL	1723	43005029
DEN	Self. Den.& Mo	BLAIR	1740	43005029
DEN	Self-den. M.	NEEDLER	1677	43005029
DEN	Self-den. M.	MOSS	1732	43005029
DEN	Self-den. M.	WESTON	1747	43005029
DENI	Peter's deni.	ABERNETHY	1748	43026074
DENIAL	Self Denial.	SMITH	1675	19131002
DENIAL	Self- Denial.	HAVETT	1703	43016024
DENIAL	Self- Denial.	WHITBY	1703	43016024
DENIAL	Self- Denial.	BRADY	1704	43016021
DENIAL	Self- Denial.	YOUNG	1706	43016024
DENIAL	Self- Denial.	EDWARDS	1726	43016024
DENIAL	Self- Denial.	TILLOTSON	1735	43016024
DENIAL	Self- Denial.	CARLETON	1736	43016026
DENIAL	Self- Denial.	STRAIGHT	1741	43016024
DENIAL	Self- Denial.	ABERNETHY	1748	43016021
DENIAL	Self- Denial.	WEST	1762	43016024
DENIAL	Self- Denial.	YOUNG	1764	43016024
DENIAL	Self- Denial.	WILLIAMS	1770	43016024
DENIAL	Self-denial	REYNOLDS	1679	43016024
DENIAL	Self-denial	MANTON	1689	43016024
DENIAL	Self-denial	SCOTT	1700	43016024
DENIAL	Self-denial	LACY	1720	43016024
DENIAL	Self-denial	JEPHSON	1742	43016024
DENIAL	Self-denial	SNAPE	1745	43016024
DENIAL	Self-denial	POTTER	1753	43016024
DENIAL	Self-denial	JORTIN	1774	43016024
DENIAL	Self-denial.	CHILLINGWORTH	1664	45009023
DENIAL	Self-denial.	GELL	1676	45009023
DENIAL	Self-denial.	BAXTER	1707	45009023
DENIAL	Self-denial.	COCK	1710	44008034
DENIAL	Self-denial.	WHITFIELD	1739	45009023
DENIAL	Self-denial.	ATTERBURY	1743	45009023
DENIAL	Self-denial.	HEYLYN	1749	45009023
DENIAL	Self-denial.	BOSTON	1753	45009023
DENIAL	Self-denial.	SECKER	1770	44008034
DENIAL	Self-denial.	WESTLEY	1771	45009023
DENIAL	Self-denial.	WILSON	1781	49015032
DENIAL	Self-denial& C	HOWARD	1710	43016024
DENY	Deny Prov.	BERRIMAN	1751	35001012
DEP	Dep. St.&c.	SCOTT	1764	10011020
DEP	Dep.fm. Ini.	FOORD	1719	58002019
DEP	Dep.fm. Ini.	DUNLOP	1722	58002019
DEPART	Sim. Depart.	MOIR	1759	45002029
DEPRAV	Deprav.man	FELTON	1748	21007029
DEPRAV	H. N.deprav.	MARRIOTT	1774	19051005
DEPRECATION	Deprecation	HOLE	1716	29002017
DES	Des.& H. Xty	WILSON	1781	57004015

INDEXES TO THIRD VOLUME: E: KEYWORD-IN-CONTEXT INDEX OF OTHER SUBJECTS OR OCCASIONS

Keyword	In its Context	Author	Year	BkChpVrs
DES	Des.& H. Xy.	WILSON	1781	57004001
DES	Des. Xt's.co.	PAYNE	1763	69022020
DES	Des.all Nat.	HARRIS	1724	36002006
DES	Des.o. Dissol.	SNAPE	1745	53001023
DES	Des.o. Parac.	FALLE	1695	46016007
DES	Des.of Dea.	EDWARDS	1726	53001023
DES	Des.of Gos.	CLARKE	1735	43003012
DES	Des.of Gosp.	MICHELL	1731	59002011
DES	Des.of Gosp.	MORRIS	1743	59002011
DES	Des.see. Xt.	WILCOX	1757	46012020
DES	Ho.des. Gos.	HOLE	1715	59002014
DES	Ho.des. Gos.	BEVERIDGE	1720	59002011
DES	Ho.des. Gos.	BEVERIDGE	1720	59002013
DES	Ho.des. Gos.	BEVERIDGE	1720	59002014
DES	Ho.des. Gos.	RINGER	1734	59002013
DES	Hyp.des. Pr.	ORTON	1776	24042020
DES	Templ. Des.	ERSKINE	1764	46002019
DES	Van. Di. Des.	HODGES	1676	45016030
DES	Xn's.des.t.d.	EDWARDS	1726	53001025
DES	Xt.the Des.	NICOLSON	1661	22001001
DESC	Desc.o. Wor.	STERNE	1769	64003011
DESC	Relig. Desc.	EVANS	1728	58001005
DESERT	Div. Desert.	WHITAKER	1674	23008017
DESERT	Div. Desert.	CRUSO	1699	07016020
DESERT	Div. Desert.	HILL	1755	19051011
DESERTION	Desertion.	RAMSEY	1781	16006011
DESI	N. Desi.of L.	SMITH	1777	18042016
DESIGN	Design o. Ch.	CRADOCK	1706	57001005
DESIGN	Design of Xy	ANONYMOUS	1739	48008006
DESIGN	Design of Xy	HUNT	1748	48008005
DESIRE	Desire of L.	WILCOX	1757	19039013
DESIRES	Desires to S.	MOORE	1716	62001015
DESIRES	Irreg.desires	BALGUY	1748	21006009
DESP	Desp. L.nat.	HAMMOND	1684	48001026
DESP	Desp. Relig.	SMITH	1777	55004008
DESP	Desp.cond.	ELLIS	1704	45016026
DESP	Presu.&desp.	COLE	1676	45003004
DEST	Xt.dest. Dea.	BREKELL	1765	61011015
DESTR	Destr. Sinn.	SOUTH	1766	19095011
DESTR	Lot's Destr.	ORTON	1776	45017032
DESTR	Vice destr. S.	BUTLER	1719	43008022
DETRACTION	Detraction.	POOLE	1676	19015003
DETRACTION	Detraction.	BARROW	1716	62004010
DETRACTION	Detraction.	HOLTON	1765	20015002
DETRACTION	Detraction.	ANONYMOUS	1770	43007001
DEV	Daily Dev.	AMORY	1747	19002005
DEV	Dev. Medit.	WARNEFORD	1776	19004004
DEV	Dev. Patriot.	BULKLEY	1761	19018009
DEV	Dev. Patriot.	BULKLEY	1761	19028009
DEV	Dev. Tempt.	STAFFORD	1699	50002011
DEV	Dev. Tempt.	WAKE	1716	50002011
DEV	Dev. Tempt.	SHARP	1729	50002011
DEV	Dev. Tempt.	WHITFIELD	1739	50002011
DEV	Dev. Tempt.	WESTLEY	1750	50002011
DEV	Dev. Votar.	CORNWALLIS	1705	19116009
DEV	Dev. Worsh.	BAINE	1778	19005007

Keyword	In its Context	Author	Year	BkChpVrs
DEV	Devil's Dev.	BRADY	1704	50002011
DEV	Imm. Dev.	BALL	1756	20007014
DEV	Insinc. Dev.	WARNEFORD	1776	19066016
DEV	Leg.of Dev.	BRAGGE	1702	45008026
DEV	Leg.of Dev.	DODD	1757	45008027
DEV	Res.the Dev.	COOKE	1739	63005008
DEVIL	Cast Devil.	BRAGGE	1706	43015021
DEVIL	Cast Devil.	HOLE	1716	43015021
DEVIL	Resist. Devil.	ST.	1737	62004007
DEVIL	Resist Devil.	ALLESTREE	1684	62004007
DEVIL'S	Devil's Dev.	BRADY	1704	50002011
DEVILS	Cast. Devils.	WILLIAMS	1664	43017021
DEVILS	Creed Devils	TOPLADY	1775	62002010
DEVOT	Daily Devot.	AMORY	1747	19092001
DEVOT	Daily Devot.	AMORY	1746	19003005
DEVOT	Devot. Rel.	STEBBING	1760	45010039
DEVOT	Hab. Devot.	PRIESTLEY	1782	19010004
DEVOT	True Devot.	BRAGGE	1713	45002025
DEVOTION	Devotion.	TRAPP	1721	06024015
DEVOTION	Devotion.	BATTY	1739	19027004
DEVOTION	Devotion.	GROVE	1742	19073028
DEVOTION	Devotion.	WELCH	1752	19088001
DEVOTION	Devotion.	SHERLOCK	1772	19019014
DEVOTION	Devotion.	WARNEFORD	1776	19037004
DEVOTION	Devotion.	BLAIR	1777	47010002
DEW	Dew Div.gr.	STEFFE	1743	28014005
DI	Di.&inc. Xt.	WISE	1717	51004004
DI	Di. Truth ev.&	WHICHCOTE	1698	46007046
DI	Di. W.in Cr.	DAVIS	1756	19104015
DI	Di.au.o. S. S.	FAROM	1660	58003016
DI	Di.au.o. S. S.	JACOMB	1660	58003016
DI	Di Or.o. S. S.	SMITH	1769	51001011
DI	Sub.t. Di. W.	JONES	1741	46018011
DI	Van. Di. Des.	HODGES	1676	45016030
DI	Wisd.di.pro.	LELAND	1769	23028029
DIAB	Diab. Poss.	WHEATLY	1746	43017014
DIABOL	Arts diabol.	EDWARDS	1702	05018010
DIATRIBAE	Diatribae.	BAGSHAW	1680	46006068
DIF	Dif. Deg. Gl.	CONYBEARE	1757	65003002
DIF	Dif. Gifts sp.	CLARKE	1735	49012004
DIF	Dif. Talents.	SHERLOCK	1772	45012048
DIF	Dif.de.f. Gl.	BULL	1713	64001011
DIFF	Diff. Dispen.	MOSS	1737	43011021
DIFF	Diff. Duties.	JORTIN	1774	43022035
DIFF	Diff. R.d. W.	SMALRIDGE	1724	49003008
DIFF	Diff. R.d. W.	BOYSE	1728	49003008
DIFF	Diff. Rel.sur.	STENNETT	1769	43011030
DIFF	Diff. Sinn.	CLARKE	1736	68000022
DIFF	Diff. Talents	MARKLAND	1729	43025014
DIFF	Diff. Times.	WHICHCOTE	1702	19095007
DIFF	Diff. Truth.	CLARKE	1735	46004011
DIFF	Diff. Xn.life.	CROFTON	1662	43007014
DIFF	Diff. Xn.life.	BARKER	1697	43007014
DIFF	Diff. Xn.life.	PARSONS	1711	43007013
DIFF	Diff. Xn.life.	GARDINER	1720	43007013
DIFF	Diff. Xn.life.	STEPHENS	1737	43007014

Keyword	In its Context	Author	Year	BkChpVrs
DIFF	Diff. Xn.life.	BUNDY	1740	43007014
DIFF	Diff. Xn.life.	WESTLEY	1750	43007013
DIFF	Diff.o. Cond.	WHITE	1757	45016008
DIFF	Diff.of Rel.	BALGUY	1748	46004009
DIFF	Diff.of Rel.	STENNETT	1769	43016024
DIFF	Diff.of S. S.	ATTERBURY	1734	64003016
DIFF	Diff.of Salv.	COOKE	1739	63004018
DIFF	Diff.of Salv.	DAVIES	1766	63004018
DIFF	Diff.of Scrip.	NEWTON	1782	63003016
DIFF	Diff.off. Ch.	ROGERS	1730	49012028
DIFF	Diff.rewards	MEDE	1672	43010041
DIFF	Diff.st.tr. R.	JEFFERY	1751	58003015
DIFF	Eas.& Diff. R.	BRINGHURST	1689	43011030
DIFF	Sav. Fai.diff.	COLE	1690	52001019
DIFF	Script. Diff.	SHERLOCK	1772	47015001
DIFFER	Differ. Call.	STEBBING	1760	49007024
DIFFI	Paul's Diffi.	CONYBEARE	1757	50011023
DIFFIC	Diffic. Salv.	STILLINGFLEET	1707	63004018
DIFFIC	Diffic. Salv.	SCATTERGOOD	1723	63004018
DIFFIC	Diffic. Salv.	WHARTON	1728	63004018
DIFFIC	Diffic. Salv.	ROGERS	1735	63004018
DIFFIC	Diffic. Salv.	WILCOX	1757	63004018
DIG	Dig.& H. Xt.	CLARKE	1727	65004009
DIG	Dig. Minist.	SKELTON	1754	44010043
DIG	Dig.of Min.	WALROND	1707	48011013
DIGN	Dign. H.nat.	BOURN	1777	19008005
DIGN	Dign.of Soul	WILKINSON	1660	44008036
DILIG	Rew. Dilig.	SHARP	1674	43025029
DILIG	Spir. Dilig.	BALGUY	1750	21009010
DILIGEN	Xn. Diligen.	GROVE	1741	46009004
DILIGEN	Xn. Diligen.	WATTS	1753	20013004
DILIGENCE	Diligence or I	BARROW	1716	48012011
DILIGENCE	Diligence or I	BALGUY	1750	48012011
DILIGENCE	Diligence.	GREGORY	1696	21009010
DILIGENCE	Diligence.	WAPLE	1720	21009010
DILIGENCE	Diligence.	SEATON	1720	43008009
DILIGENCE	Diligence.	TILLOTSON	1735	21009010
DILIGENCE	Diligence.	HOLLAND	1753	48012011
DIR	Dir.to Sinn.	DODDERIDGE	1742	47009006
DIR	Dir.to Y.	NESBIT	1713	19119009
DIR	Dir.to Y.	MAY	1744	19119009
DIRECT	Direct.to pr.	HORTON	1679	13004010
DIS	Cond.of Dis.	WRIGHT	1718	01042020
DIS	Dis b. P.& B.	CONYBEARE	1757	47015039
DIS	Dis.al.prov.	NEWMAN	1750	23005012
DIS	Dis.of Saints	WHITAKER	1674	09023005
DIS	Dis Cattle.	POWELL	1748	36001005
DIS	Ineq.rel.dis.	MAINWARING	1780	47010034
DIS	Nat.dis.b. Goo	STRADLING	1692	23005020
DIS	Nat.dis.b. Goo	SOUTH	1727	23005020
DIS	Nat.dis.b. Goo	MOSS	1732	23005020
DIS	Nat.dis.b. Goo	STEPHENS	1737	23005020
DIS	Nat.dis.b. Goo	ORR	1749	23005020
DIS	Soul dis.f. B.	HOLDEN	1755	45022043
DIS	Xr. Xt's. Dis.	MAY	1757	47004013
DIS	Xt.leav. Dis.	WILLISON	1761	46016007

Keyword	In its Context	Author	Year	BkChpVrs
DIS	Xt's. F.t. Dis	LARDNER	1760	46014027
DIS	Xt's.last Dis.	DUCHAL	1753	46014001
DISAFFEC	Ag. Disaffec.	SYNGE	1720	19095008
DISAP	Disap. Seam.	FLAVEL	1673	45005005
DISC	Belov. Disc.	GOUGH	1751	46013023
DISC	Disc. Consp.	SMALWOOD	1696	43013013
DISC	Disc. Plot.	LITTLETON	1680	19036005
DISC	Disc. Plot.	LATHOM	1683	20008015
DISC	Disc.f. Prop.	BLACKALL	1723	43007016
DISC	Disc.of Plot.	BRADY	1706	02014013
DISC	Fruits& Disc.o	STANHOPE	1714	43007015
DISC	Fruits& Disc.o	HOLE	1716	43007015
DISC	Fruits& Disc.o	GARDINER	1720	43007015
DISC	Fruits& Disc.o	BLAIR	1740	43007015
DISC	Fruits& Disc.o	WESTLEY	1750	43007015
DISC	Introd. Disc.	ANONYMOUS	1776	45013008
DISC	Relig. Disc.	NORRIS	1728	19037030
DISC	Savr's Disc.	NEWTON	1782	46004007
DISCIP	Early Discip.	SUTTON	1754	25003027
DISCIP	True Discip.	VEAL	1703	46008031
DISCONTENT	Discontent.	LANGHORNE	1764	25003039
DISCOV	Discov. Plot.	ANONYMOUS	1683	28010002
DISCRET	Priv. Discret.	KIDDER	1697	55005021
DISCRETION	Discretion.	CLAGETT	1720	21007015
DISEASE	Disease.	MARRIOTT	1774	18007003
DISO	Punish.of Diso	WHICHCOTE	1698	48001018
DISOB	Disob.& Un.	SMALRIDGE	1724	65002004
DISOB	Disob. G. In.	WILSON	1781	46015022
DISORD	Pass.disord.	BLAIR	1777	17005013
DISP	G.disp. Ev.	LELAND	1769	43010030
DISP	G.disp.all.	CLARKE	1735	20016004
DISP	Good Disp.	BAYLY	1721	46008047
DISP	Good Disp.	NALSON	1737	45008015
DISP	Good Disp.	HODGE	1758	46007016
DISP	Ill-disp. Aff.	SOUTH	1727	56002011
DISP	Inquis. Disp.	ORR	1739	47017011
DISP	Lond. Disp.	FRANKLIN	1774	44010014
DISP	Relig. Disp.	IBBOT	1726	58002019
DISP	V.disp. Gos.	PRICE	1757	45001072
DISP	Westm. Disp.	SOWDEN	1766	63003008
DISP	b. Gov. Disp.	DODD	1773	02002006
DISP	b. Gov. Disp.	YORKE	1776	19127005
DISPEN	Diff. Dispen.	MOSS	1737	43011021
DISPEN	Div. Dispen.	MAINWARING	1780	61001002
DISPEN	Jew. Dispen.	SWANNE	1760	48003001
DISPEN	Sev Dispen.	JEFFERY	1710	43008011
DISPENS	Xn. Dispens.	FIDDES	1720	57001015
DISPENS	Xn. Dispens.	WATTS	1753	61008006
DISPOS	Calm Dispos.	M.	1733	43005005
DISPOS	Gen. Dispos.	MOIR	1776	47020035
DISPOSI	Gen. Disposi.	SKELTON	1754	47020035
DISQ	Sinn.disq.	WAPLE	1729	32006006
DISS	Diss.	EDWARDS	1692	49011014
DISS	Diss.of Wor.	DAVIES	1720	64003011
DISS	Diss.of Wor.	WEBB	1772	64003011
DISS	Diss.sm. Err.	BENTHAM	1669	62001016

INDEXES TO THIRD VOLUME: E: KEYWORD-IN-CONTEXT INDEX OF OTHER SUBJECTS OR OCCASIONS

Keyword	In its Context	Author	Year	BkChpVrs
DISS	Diss.187	WARD	1761	48001011
DISS	Duty of Diss.	WILLIAMS	1712	44010029
DISS	Protest. Diss.	WILLIAMS	1738	44011029
DISS	Reduc. Diss.	NADEN	1712	49012025
DISS	Truth diss.	SMITH	1777	43002005
DISS	Xrter of Diss.	WRIGHT	1712	47028022
DISSENT	Dissent.imp.	BOWTELL	1711	48016017
DISSOL	Des.o. Dissol.	SNAPE	1745	53001023
DISSR	Neb.'s Dissr.	ORTON	1776	27004033
DISSRS	Dissrs. Jub.	NICHOLETS	1687	19126003
DIST	Dist. Cattle.	PARSONS	1746	19106030
DIST	Dist. Cattle.	ECCLES	1750	28004003
DIST	G. Ref. Dist.	DUCHE	1779	19042011
DIST	Treat. Dist.	CLARKE	1727	19031011
DISTEM	Distem.of C.	KING	1747	02009003
DISTEM	Distem.of C.	ANONYMOUS	1750	02009003
DISTR	Distr. Hon.	WELTON	1724	50007004
DISTR	Distr.in Dut.	MANTON	1677	43015007
DISTR	Fin. Distr.eq.	CLARKE	1735	63004017
DISTRACT	Ag. Distract.	STEEL	1667	49007035
DISTRIB	Ch. Distrib.	BROWN	1764	65003017
DISTRIB	Une.distrib.	FRANCIS	1771	21008014
DIV	Conf.div. W.	AICKIN	1705	47009006
DIV	Dew Div.gr.	STEFFE	1743	28014005
DIV	Div theatre.	WALL	1662	45003006
DIV	Div.& H. H.	SHERLOCK	1772	46005044
DIV	Div.&h. Ag.	BOURN	1777	53002012
DIV	Div. Arithm.	WHEATLAND	1739	19090012
DIV	Div. Assist.	ALTHAM	1732	45018042
DIV	Div. Attrib.	ERSKINE	1764	19085010
DIV	Div. Au. S. S.	HUMPHREYS	1712	55004008
DIV	Div. Au. S. S.	BELLAMY	1744	64002021
DIV	Div. Benev.	FARMER	1756	52002005
DIV	Div. Benev.	AMORY	1766	52002005
DIV	Div. Benev.	AMORY	1766	61013010
DIV	Div. Bounty.	BAINE	1778	24005024
DIV	Div. Chastis.	STENNETT	1732	20003011
DIV	Div. Comf.	REYNER	1745	19094019
DIV	Div. Comf.	STEBBING	1759	19094019
DIV	Div. Comf.	SHERLOCK	1772	19094019
DIV	Div. Condes.	TIDCOMBE	1757	19008003
DIV	Div. Condes.	SHERLOCK	1772	19008004
DIV	Div. Consol.	WILCOX	1757	18015011
DIV	Div. Desert.	WHITAKER	1674	23008017
DIV	Div. Desert.	CRUSO	1699	07016020
DIV	Div. Desert.	HILL	1755	19051011
DIV	Div. Dispen.	MAINWARING	1780	61001002
DIV	Div. Fa.imp.	WHARTON	1728	47010034
DIV	Div. Favor.	HOLDEN	1755	19063003
DIV	Div. Goodn.	STEFFE	1743	10007018
DIV	Div. Goodn.	CHANDLER	1769	19036007
DIV	Div. Govern.	OGDEN	1770	53004006
DIV	Div. Govern.	OGDEN	1770	62005016
DIV	Div. Grace.	CRUSO	1699	44010026
DIV	Div. Grace.	CRUSO	1699	52004007
DIV	Div. Grace.	JOHNSON	1740	63005010

Keyword	In its Context	Author	Year	BkChpVrs
DIV	Div. Grace.	SHEPHERD	1748	53002012
DIV	Div. Grace.	NEWTON	1767	43011026
DIV	Div. Grace.	BUCKRIDGE	1767	46014016
DIV	Div. Grace.	BOURDALOUE	1776	46004010
DIV	Div. H. Gh.	BARROW	1716	49003016
DIV	Div. H. Gh.	STEPHENS	1717	47005003
DIV	Div. Happi.	LELAND	1769	57006015
DIV	Div. Influ.	DODDERIDGE	1742	59003005
DIV	Div. Influ.	PRIESTLEY	1779	43013003
DIV	Div. Intent.	BOURN	1760	19089047
DIV	Div. Judgm.	WEDDERSPOON	1733	45013001
DIV	Div. Judgm.	FOTHERGILL	1765	23026009
DIV	Div. Knowl.	SMITH	1673	19003003
DIV	Div. Knowl.	SMITH	1673	46007017
DIV	Div. Lig.&c.	STEELE	1776	19043003
DIV	Div. Love.	WELCH	1752	19062001
DIV	Div. Love.	DAVIS	1756	43022036
DIV	Div. Love.	WILLISON	1761	65003001
DIV	Div. Love.	ELLIOTT	1764	65004010
DIV	Div. Medit.	BRINSLEY	1667	19104034
DIV	Div. Medit.	BATES	1700	19119097
DIV	Div. Medit.	STEWARD	1734	19104034
DIV	Div. Medit.	PEARSE	1763	19104034
DIV	Div. Medita.	LEE	1751	19077012
DIV	Div. Mess.	DE COETLOGAN	1773	07003020
DIV	Div. Nature.	STURMY	1716	64001004
DIV	Div. Omnip.	CHARNOCK	1684	24023024
DIV	Div. Omnip.	LUPTON	1726	24023024
DIV	Div. Omnip.	MOSS	1737	24023024
DIV	Div. Omnip.	BRACKENRIDGE	1764	24023024
DIV	Div. Omnip.	WESTON	1766	24023023
DIV	Div. Omnip.	JORTIN	1774	24023023
DIV	Div. Omnip.	AMORY	1775	24023023
DIV	Div. Omnip.	PETERS	1776	24023024
DIV	Div. Operat.	DODDERIDGE	1742	49012006
DIV	Div. Or. Gos.	SWINDEN	1718	58003016
DIV	Div. Or.o. R.	STENNETT	1769	62003017
DIV	Div. Patien.	EMLYN	1742	69002021
DIV	Div. Perfect.	WEST	1762	46001005
DIV	Div. Philant.	SHERLOCK	1772	46003016
DIV	Div. Pres.	NORRIS	1728	19016009
DIV	Div. Preserv.	HORBERY	1774	47017028
DIV	Div. Prom.	CRUSO	1698	50001020
DIV	Div. Prov.	DEVEREL	1777	01045004
DIV	Div. Provid.	PINDAR	1679	19127001
DIV	Div. Provid.	HERNE	1679	61004013
DIV	Div. Provid.	OUTRAM	1680	43010029
DIV	Div. Provid.	GOODMAN	1683	19017001
DIV	Div. Provid.	DORRINGTON	1705	48011036
DIV	Div. Provid.	HOPKINS	1710	43010029
DIV	Div. Provid.	EDWARDS	1713	43010029
DIV	Div. Provid.	BARKER	1748	43010029
DIV	Div. Provid.	BOSTON	1753	23041014
DIV	Div. Provid.	BOURN	1760	19036006
DIV	Div. Provid.	DUCHAL	1765	23040015
DIV	Div. Provid.	DAVIES	1766	19097001

Keyword	In its Context	Author	Year	BkChpVrs
DIV	Div. Provid.	LELAND	1769	48011036
DIV	Div. Provid.	CARR	1777	19097001
DIV	Div. Redee.	DAWSON	1765	44001002
DIV	Div. Revel.	HENLEY	1729	54004014
DIV	Div. Revelat.	BULLOCK	1726	65004006
DIV	Div. T.to Jes.	LARDNER	1760	43027052
DIV	Div. Truth.	CROWE	1744	46003020
DIV	Div. Truth.	HUNTER	1774	46017017
DIV	Div. Wis. Cr.	TILLOTSON	1735	19104024
DIV	Div. Wis. Cr.	BOURN	1760	19104024
DIV	Div. Wis. Cr.	WEST	1762	19104024
DIV	Div. Wis. Cr.	STONE	1771	19104024
DIV	Div. Wisd.	BARTON	1737	46003012
DIV	Div. Worsh.	HALL	1661	46004024
DIV	Div. Worsh.	MUDGE	1739	19096009
DIV	Div.ass.	LYNFORD	16--	19012007
DIV	Div.assist.	KELSEY	1721	45011013
DIV	Div.gr.expl.	HORBERY	1774	46003008
DIV	Div.mer.ex.	CALAMY	1702	48009016
DIV	Div.of Sav.	SCOTT	1700	46001014
DIV	Div.of Scrip.	PINDAR	1728	58003016
DIV	Exc.div. M.	BEDFORD	1733	49014015
DIV	Exp.div. Rel.	CONYBEARE	1729	46006045
DIV	H. Gh. Div.	PIGOTT	1702	46016013
DIV	H. Gh.div. P.	LESTLEY	1720	46014016
DIV	Har. Div. Pe.	WEST	1762	65001005
DIV	Salv.f.div.m.	BOURN	1760	48007024
DIV	Sp. Div. Pers.	BRETT	1720	46014016
DIV	Und. Div.w.	BURTON	1685	52005017
DIV	World. Div.	BOURDALOUE	1776	46016020
DIV	Xt's. Div.&c.	TILLOTSON	1735	48001004
DIV	Xt's. Div.p.fm	JOHNSON	1713	48001004
DIV	Xt's. Div.p.fm	BEVERIDGE	1720	48001004
DIVERSIONS	Diversions.	SEED	1743	20017027
DIVES	Dives.& Laz.	TILLOTSON	1735	45016031
DIVES	Dives.& Laz.	STERNE	1766	45016031
DIVES	Dives.& Laz.	JORTIN	1774	45016031
DIVES	Dives& Laz.	STEVENS	1697	45016022
DIVES	Dives& Laz.	STEPHENS	1697	45016022
DIVES	Dives& Laz.	CRUSO	1697	45016027
DIVES	Dives& Laz.	STEVENT	1697	45016027
DIVES	Dives& Laz.	STEVENS	1697	45016030
DIVES	Dives& Laz.	CRUSO	1698	45016023
DIVES	Dives& Laz.	CRUSO	1698	45016030
DIVES	Dives& Laz.	WELCHMAN	1704	45016022
DIVES	Dives& Laz.	THEED	1710	45016027
DIVES	Dives& Laz.	BENNETT	1728	45016025
DIVES	Dives& Laz.	DODD	1757	45016025
DIVES	Dives& Laz.	BULKLEY	1771	45016031
DIVES	Dives& Laz.	BROUGHTON	1778	45016031
DIVIN	Divin.of Xt.	WHITAKER	1674	59002010
DIVIN	Divin.of Xt.	SKELTON	1692	46014009
DIVIN	Divin.of Xt.	PAYNE	1697	46010036
DIVIN	Divin.of Xt.	LA MOTHE	1693	53002006
DIVIN	Divin.of Xt.	JEFFERY	1726	46001001
DIVIN	Divin.of Xt.	HURRION	1734	49003016

Keyword	In its Context	Author	Year	BkChpVrs
DIVIN	Divin.of Xt.	SCOTT	1743	23043010
DIVIN	Divin.of Xt.	RANDOLPH	1753	44013023
DIVIN	Divin.of Xt.	REGIS	1753	46001001
DIVIN	Divin.of Xt.	HAYWARD	1758	48009005
DIVIN	Divin.of Xt.	WHITTY	1766	69022002
DIVIN	Xt'. Divin.	SMITH	1777	46001001
DIVIN	Xt's. Divin.	BUERDSELL	1700	46001001
DIVIN	Xt's. Divin.	PALKE	1719	46020028
DIVIN	Xt's. Divin.	CONANT	1722	48009005
DIVIN	Xt's. Divin.	SKELTON	1754	46005022
DIVIN	Xt's. Divin.	SKELTON	1754	53003008
DIVIN	Xt's. Divin.	SAURIN	1777	69005011
DIVINE	Divine life.	DAVIES	1771	51003020
DIVINE	Divine Love.	ELLIOTT	1764	65005016
DIVINE	Divine Wisl.	CREYGHTON	1720	43006010
DIVIS	Avoid Divis.	COCK	1707	48016017
DIVIS	Nat. Divis.	PORTER	1768	44003024
DIVISIONS	Divisions.	PEIRCE	1719	49001003
DIVORCE	of Divorce.	HORNECK	1706	43005031
DIVORCE	of Divorce.	BLACKALL	1723	43005031
DIVORCE	of Divorce.	BLAIR	1740	43005031
DIVORCES	Divorces.	DOWNES	1761	49007016
DO	Do all in Na.o	BARROW	1716	54003017
DO	Do all in Na.o	BEVERIDGE	1720	54003017
DO	Do all Gl. G.	BEVERIDGE	1720	49010031
DO	Do all Gl. G.	BERRIMAN	1751	49010031
DO	Do go.to all.	BURTON	1685	51006010
DO	Do go.to all.	BILLINGSLEY	1712	51006010
DO	Do justly&c.	BOURN	1777	32006006
DO	Do&h. G's w.	DORMAN	1743	62001022
DO	Do&h. W.	BROWNRIG	1664	62001022
DO	Do&h. W.	BEVERIDGE	1720	62001022
DO	Do&h. W.	ALTHAM	1732	62001022
DO	Do&h. W.	ATTERBURY	1743	62001022
DO	H.&do word	FIDDES	1720	62001022
DO	H.&do word	SNAPE	1745	62001023
DO	H&do word	MORE	1692	62001022
DO	Meth.do. A.	BLACKALL	1723	43006002
DO	Meth.do. A.	BLAIR	1740	43006002
DO	Per.well-do.	DORMAN	1743	51006009
DO	Quiet do.our o	FARINDON	1672	55004011
DO	Quiet do.our o	BURTON	1685	55004011
DO	Quiet do.our o	DUKE	1714	55004011
DO	Quiet do.our o	BARROW	1716	55004011
DO	To do good.	GALE	1726	57006018
DO	To do o.duty	MILWARD	1683	48012021
DO	Well-do. S.ag.	CLAGETT	1720	63003013
DO	Well-do. S.ag.	CLARKE	1736	63003013
DO	Well-do.a. S.	TILLOTSON	1735	63003013
DO	Xt.do all t.w.	ORTON	1776	44007037
DOC	Doc.o. Cross.	HOPKINS	1708	45014027
DOCT	Doct.o. C. C.	ADAMS	1716	57001013
DOCT	Doct.of Gra.	GILL	1773	57006003
DOCT	Pro.gr. Doct.	PALMER	1726	20014034
DOCT	Sound Doct.	TAYLOR	1719	58004003
DOCTR	Apost. Doctr.	CASE	1774	47002042

Keyword	In its Context	Author	Year	BkChpVrs
DOCTR	Sav.'s Doctr.	ORR	1739	46007046
DOING	Doing good.	WHEATLAND	1739	21003012
DOING	Doing good.	MILLER	1749	21003012
DOING	Doing good.	MILLER	1749	43019016
DOING	Doing Good	TENISON	1690	19078005
DOING	Doing Good.	MORE	1692	61013016
DOING	Doing Good.	GREGORY	1708	61013016
DOING	Well-doing.	DAVIES	1754	51006009
DOING	Well-doing.	SHERLOCK	1772	51006009
DOM	Dom. Aecon	DYKES	1722	20031015
DOM	Dom. Happ.	FRANKLIN	1765	20015017
DOM	Dom. Happ.	ENFIELD	1772	01045024
DOM	Dom- Love.	HOLLAND	1753	19133001
DOMIN	Domin. G.	WHITBY	1710	19103019
DOMIN	Domin.of G.	CHURCHILL	1765	43006013
DONE	D.as done to.	BENNETT	1728	43007012
DOOM	Doom Cap.	DODDRIDGE	1761	43011023
DOOM	Fi.doom.im.	WARREN	1748	69021008
DOOM	Plott. Doom.	ANONYMOUS	1680	19037012
DOOM	Sinn's doom.	DAVIES	1771	20029001
DOOR	Door of H.o.	WILCOX	1757	45014022
DOOR	Door of Ho.	FARMER	1756	23055007
DOOR	Door Sal.op.	F.	1667	69003020
DOU	Sin dou.b.a.	ORTON	1776	48014023
DOUB	Doub.mind.	SCOTT	1700	62001008
DOUB	Doub.mind.	SMALRIDGE	1724	62004008
DOUBT	Doubt. Xns.	FARMER	1756	43014031
DR	E.dr. X. F. B.	SUTTON	1754	46006053
DR	G's wrth.dr.	HOPKINS	1710	61010030
DRAU	Drau of Fish.	BRAGGE	1702	45005004
DRAU	Drau.of Fish.	FRANK	1672	45005005
DRAU	Drau.of Fish.	FRANK	1672	45005008
DRAU	Drau.of Fish.	MARKLAND	1729	45005008
DRAU	Drau.of Fish.	BULKLEY	1771	45005009
DRAW	Draw.n. G.	EATON	1764	19073028
DRAW	Xt.draw. M.	WILLISON	1761	46012032
DREAMS	Of Dreams.	ATTERBURY	1703	18033014
DRESS	Dress.	HALL	1660	49011010
DRI	Laws of Dri.	CORNWALLIS	1705	52005019
DRINK	Intem.drink.	ANONYMOUS	1754	20023020
DRUKENNESS	Drukenness.	FROST	1729	20023029
DRUKENNESS	Drukenness.	RAMSEY	1781	20023029
DRUNK	Hab. Drunk.	CARTER	1729	51005021
DRUNKEN	Drunken.	SKELTON	1754	23005022
DRUNKENN	Drunkenn.	LAMONT	1780	20020001
DRUNKENNESS	Drunkenness	WHITFIELD	1739	52005006
DRUNKENNESS	Drunkenness.	PHELPES	1676	52005018
DRUNKENNESS	Drunkenness.	NOURSE	1705	52005018
DRUNKENNESS	Drunkenness.	EDWARDS	1726	52005018
DRY	V.dry Bones.	CENNICK	1762	26037014
DTH	Dth.& Judg.	FOORD	1719	61009027
DU	Assist.in Du.	HUBBARD	1757	54001009
DU	Du. Xs.& M.	WILSON	1781	46017004
DU	Du.low con.	MARSHALL	1750	53004012
DU	Du.marr.st.	COCKBURN	1708	61013004
DU	Du.of Preac.	MEADOWCOURT	1721	57001005

Keyword	In its Context	Author	Year	BkChpVrs
DU	Du.of Quiet.	DAVIS	1756	55004011
DU	Du.to Equals	HUBBARD	1757	20018024
DU	Good m. Du.	BURNETT	1774	09030006
DU	Th. Du. Xn's	GROVE	1741	55005018
DU	Th. Du. Xn's.	COOPER	1677	55005018
DU	Th. Du. Xn's.	DORRINGTON	1703	55005018
DU	Th. Du. Xn's.	BEVERIDGE	1720	55005018
DU	Tr. D. Du. M.	BREVALL	1670	65005004
DU	Who. Du. M.	BALL	1756	59002011
DUE	Ho.due t. G.	NORRIS	1728	58003003
DUE	R.due G's N.	SMALBROKE	1722	03019030
DUKE	b.the Duke.	LITTLETON	1735	45010041
DUM	Deaf& Dum.	DODD	1757	44007032
DUMB	Dumb&d. S.	BRAGGE	1702	44009014
DURAT	Durat.of Char.	CONANT	1703	49013008
DURAT	Durat.of Char.	BAYLY	1721	49013008
DURAT	Durat.of Char.	HOLE	1725	49013008
DURAT	Durat.of Char.	BENNETT	1728	49013008
DUT	Distr.in Dut.	MANTON	1677	43015007
DUT	Dut. Br. Rep.	CHANDLER	1769	45017003
DUT	Dut. Child.	FLEETWOOD	1737	02020012
DUT	Dut. G.& K.	BALL	1682	43022021
DUT	Dut. G.& K.	ROSEWELL	1716	20024021
DUT	Dut. G.& K.	TOPPING	1716	63002017
DUT	Dut. H.& W.	NICHOLS	1701	54003018
DUT	Dut. H.& W.	FLEETWOOD	1737	54003019
DUT	Dut. M.& P.	WILSON	1781	49004001
DUT	Dut. Minist.	HODGES	1685	43005013
DUT	Dut. Pas.& P.	HOWARD	1728	59002015
DUT	Dut. Poor.	SECKER	1770	43011005
DUT	Dut. Subj.	NICHOLS	1701	48013005
DUT	Dut. Subject	BURNET	1674	48013005
DUT	Dut.mar. St.	DELANY	1747	52005033
DUT	Dut.o. Pa.& Ch	ADAMS	1676	54003020
DUT	Dut.o. Pa.& Ch	NICHOLS	1701	54003020
DUT	Dut.of aged.	SECKER	1770	20016031
DUT	Dut.of aged.	BLAIR	1777	20016031
DUT	Dut.of Mag.	WILSON	1781	05001017
DUT	Dut.of Min.	HURRION	1721	61013017
DUT	Dut.of Pare.	LYE	1683	52006004
DUT	Dut.of Pray.	CLARKE	1736	48012012
DUT	Dut.of Prea.	LORTIE	1720	59002015
DUT	Dut.sick.	SECKER	1779	23038001
DUT	Dut.to infer.	JENNINGS	1757	47010002
DUT	Dut.to Neig.	BLAIR	1740	43007012
DUT	Dut.to Par.	HOLLAND	1753	02020012
DUT	Dut.to Sup.	PRICE	1757	48013007
DUT	Eas. Xn. Dut.	STILEMAN	1733	43011030
DUT	Ev.dut.same	CLAGETT	1704	21003015
DUT	Mor. P. Dut.	ROGERS	1736	43023023
DUT	N. Eng. Dut.	NOYES	1698	24031023
DUT	Negl. R. Dut.	NEWCOME	1702	45014018
DUT	Negl. R. Dut.	MARSH	1737	45014018
DUT	Negl. R Dut.	DAVIES	1720	45014018
DUT	Order Dut.	SLADE	1727	43023023
DUT	Order Dut.	TRAPP	1752	43023023

Keyword	In its Context	Author	Year	BkChpVrs
DUT	Pos.&m. Dut.	CARR	1777	43023009
DUT	Rel.m's Dut.	HOLDEN	1755	20009012
DUT	W. Dut man.	WAPLE	1729	32006008
DUT	Xn's.dut.pr.	FIDDES	1720	65005003
DUTIES	Diff. Duties.	JORTIN	1774	43022035
DUTIES	Fam. Duties.	JONES	1692	06024015
DUTIES	Mor. Duties.	BURNET	1747	20015008
DUTIES	Relat. Duties	CLARKE	1734	54003020
DUTY	Duty b. Dan.	ERSKINE	1764	24013016
DUTY	Duty hear.	MOSS	1732	44004024
DUTY	Duty o. Mast.	FLEETWOOD	1737	54004001
DUTY	Duty o. Mast.	BACON	1750	54004001
DUTY	Duty o. Mast.	FRANKLIN	1765	54004001
DUTY	Duty o. Mast.	ANONYMOUS	1776	54004005
DUTY	Duty o. Min.	SCATTERGOOD	1723	57004016
DUTY	Duty o. Pea.	GARDINER	1713	48014019
DUTY	Duty o. Prea.	LORTIE	1720	58004002
DUTY	Duty of asse.	ANONYMOUS	1776	61010025
DUTY	Duty of life.	MARRIOTT	1774	32006006
DUTY	Duty of rej.	SCATTERGOOD	1723	21011009
DUTY	Duty of rich.	SECKER	1770	57006017
DUTY	Duty of rich.	ENFIELD	1772	53004012
DUTY	Duty of Diss.	WILLIAMS	1712	44010029
DUTY	Duty of Fai.	SUTTON	1718	47016031
DUTY	Duty of M.	RALEIGH	1679	21012013
DUTY	Duty of Man.	ANONYMOUS	1776	21012013
DUTY	Duty of Min.	GOODALL	1748	50006003
DUTY	Duty of Min.	STUART	1753	50006003
DUTY	Duty of Min.	WILSON	1781	50005010
DUTY	Duty of Par.	FLEETWOOD	1737	52006004
DUTY	Duty of Par.	FLEETWOOD	1737	57005008
DUTY	Duty of Par.	DELANY	1747	20022006
DUTY	Duty of Rep.	HORTON	1679	51006004
DUTY	Duty of Serv.	FLEETWOOD	1737	54003022
DUTY	Duty of Serv.	DELANY	1747	52006005
DUTY	Duty of Serv.	ANONYMOUS	1776	63002018
DUTY	Duty of Xty.	HORT	1738	59002011
DUTY	Duty of Xty.	KIMBER	1756	68000020
DUTY	Duty of Y.	SECKER	1770	59002006
DUTY	Duty of Yo.	BLAIR	1777	58002006
DUTY	Duty to G.	HUNT	1748	18022021
DUTY	Duty to G.	JORTIN	1774	59002011
DUTY	Duty to Mast.	NICHOLS	1701	54003022
DUTY	Duty to Mast.	FRANKLIN	1765	54003022
DUTY	Duty to Par.	DAVIES	1754	02002002
DUTY	Duty& Hap.	TENNISON	1695	48012002
DUTY	Duty& Hap.	BALGUY	1748	46013017
DUTY	Duty Mast.	DELANY	1747	52006009
DUTY	Duty Neigh.	ADEY	1760	43022039
DUTY	Duty Neigh.	SHERLOCK	1772	43022040
DUTY	Duty Parish.	NICHOLS	1701	55005013
DUTY	Duty Rulers.	DELANY	1747	48013003
DUTY	Engl. Duty.	FLAVEL	1673	48001018
DUTY	Engl. Duty.	FLAVEL	1673	69003020
DUTY	Husb. Duty.	ANONYMOUS	1698	54003019
DUTY	Mag. Duty.	SLATER	1690	48013003

Keyword	In its Context	Author	Year	BkChpVrs
DUTY	Min. Duty.	TAYLOR	1678	59002007
DUTY	Min. Duty.	LOB.	1708	58002002
DUTY	Minist. Duty	FULLWOOD	1673	57005017
DUTY	Minist.duty.	NEWTON	1740	58002024
DUTY	P.& M. Duty.	WOOD	1773	49011001
DUTY	Paren. Duty.	FRANKLIN	1765	52006004
DUTY	Pastor's Duty	HENDLEY	1716	57006020
DUTY	Pastor's Duty	HENDLEY	1716	58004002
DUTY	Pers. Duty.	CLARKE	1735	46021022
DUTY	Subj. Duty.	CLEAVER	1676	59003001
DUTY	Subj. Duty.	CHISHULL	1716	59003001
DUTY	To do o.duty	MILWARD	1683	48012021
DUTY	Xn's Duty.	WALLIN	1756	19046008
DUTY	Xn's Duty.	BAINES	1778	47011023
DW	G.dw.w. M.	FLEMING	1701	14006018
DY	Bles.dy.in L.	DURHAM	1681	69014013
DY	Bles.dy.in L.	HOPKINS	1710	69014013
DY	Bles.dy.in L.	HILL	1748	69014013
DY	Dy. Daily.	HILL	1755	49015031
DY	Dy.in Faith.	CLARKSON	1696	61011013
DY	Dy.in Faith.	PARKHURST	1707	61011013
DY	Xt.dy.f. Sin.	CLARKSON	1696	48005008
DY	Xt's.dy. Ch.	WILLISON	1761	49002024
DY	Xt's.dy. Pr.	NEWMAN	1760	45023024
E	Adm. Ch. E.	WATSON	1755	68000005
E	Beg.& E.o. Y.	CLEMENT	1774	61009027
E	Ch.e. F.& H.	MOSS	1732	49013013
E	Ch.e. F.& H.	MORRIS	1743	49013013
E	Cut.off M. E.	BULKLEY	1771	46018010
E	E.& N.o. Ch.	HOLE	1725	49013001
E	E. Tra. O. T.	WHITE	1778	16008007
E	E.dr. X. F. B.	SUTTON	1754	46006053
E	E.f. Xn.w. T.	HORNE	1671	68000020
E	E.walk.w. G	MACE	1751	01005024
E	E.walk.w. G.	FANCH	1768	01005024
E	E.walk.w. G.	BRACKENRIDGE	1775	01005024
E	Ex.& E.of G.	KNOWLES	1750	48001020
E	G.& E.fm. G.	LEIGHTONHOUSE	1697	23045007
E	G. E. Neigh.	ANONYMOUS	1776	43005016
E	G.1 Ca.l. E.	TILLOTSON	1735	48011036
E	G's Gl.o.c.e.	WISHEART	1716	49010031
E	G's Gl.o.c.e.	TILLOTSON	1735	49010031
E	Good& E. C.	SALMON	1753	18025005
E	Good&b. E.	MOORE	1716	49010011
E	Happ. E. Int.	HOLDEN	1755	19037037
E	Ig.good&e.	BLAIR	1777	21006012
E	M's. L.on E.	COLLETT	1774	01047009
E	Ma. C.& E. S.	SIMONS	1743	64001010
E	Ma. C.& E. S.	WARREN	1748	64001010
E	Man his o. E.	SKELTON	1754	51005017
E	Mer.f. X's E.	DEVEREL	1777	46008011
E	Mond.b. E.	STANHOPE	1715	23063001
E	Mond.b. E.	WARREN	1748	43011030
E	N. E.mor. G.	STEELE	1776	19126005
E	Old w.e.n. C.	PITTIS	1682	65002024
E	P.s. E.s. As.s	BERRIMAN	1751	48008033

INDEXES TO THIRD VOLUME: E: KEYWORD-IN-CONTEXT INDEX OF OTHER SUBJECTS OR OCCASIONS

Keyword	In its Context	Author	Year	BkChpVrs
E	Plea.f. Ch. E.	HOLLINGWORTH	1676	46006068
E	Sub.in Ch. E.	POWELL.	1776	49001010
E	Thurs.b. E.	STANHOPE	1715	49011017
E	True nat. E.	DOWNES	1761	06007012
E	Vic.of Ac. E.	POWELL	1776	61012001
E	Xn. Call.& E.	BERRIMAN	1751	64001010
E	Xns. Salt. E.	HORNECK	1706	43005013
E	Xns. Salt. E.	ORR	1772	43005013
E	Xt.e. Spouse.	WHITLOCK	1698	28002015
EA	Ea. Tr.su.ac.	BLAIR	1740	43006019
EA	G.s. H.& Ea.	ORTON	1776	19113005
EA	G's. Com.ea.	SCOTT	1701	65005003
EA	G's. Com.ea.	SHARP	1729	65005003
EA	Go.str.on Ea.	TILLOTSON	1735	61011013
EAR	Ear. Educat.	CLEAVER	1750	58003015
EARL	Good earl. O.	MEAD	1683	25003027
EARLY	Early Com.	DODDERIDGE	1743	23044003
EARLY	Early Discip.	SUTTON	1754	25003027
EARLY	Early Indust.	DELANY	1747	20006006
EARLY	Early Piety.	BUCK	1704	11018012
EARLY	Early Piety.	PARKHURST	1706	11018012
EARLY	Early Piety.	GOUGE	1706	21012001
EARLY	Early Piety.	BRAY	1714	21012001
EARLY	Early Piety.	SMYTHIES	1723	25003027
EARLY	Early Piety.	EVANS	1725	21012001
EARLY	Early Piety.	BRADY	1730	21012001
EARLY	Early Piety.	DICKSON	1731	21012001
EARLY	Early Piety.	JENNINGS	1743	24002002
EARLY	Early Piety.	ANONYMOUS	1745	11018001
EARLY	Early Piety.	LARDNER	1751	11018012
EARLY	Early Piety.	WILCOX	1757	48015007
EARLY	Early Piety.	GIBBONS	1763	11018012
EARLY	Early Piety.	BADDELLEY	1766	21012001
EARLY	Early Piety.	CHANDLER	1769	20008017
EARLY	Early Piety.	ROBINSON	1772	19144011
EARLY	Early Piety.	DODD	1772	20008017
EARLY	Early Piety.	WARNEFORD	1776	21012005
EARLY	Early Piety.	DEVERELL	1777	21012001
EARLY	Early R.	BOYSE	1728	13028009
EARLY	Early R.	BOURN	1755	13028009
EARLY	Early Relig.	ROGERS	1683	21012001
EARLY	Early Relig.	DORRINGTON	1703	21012001
EARLY	Early Relig.	WALKER	1720	21012001
EARLY	Early Relig.	SCATTERGOOD	1723	21012001
EARLY	Early Relig.	EDWARDS	1726	21012001
EARLY	Early Relig.	TILLOTSON	1735	21012001
EARLY	Early Relig.	WHITFIELD	1739	21012001
EARLY	Early Relig.	TRAPP	1752	21012001
EARLY	Early Relig.	WESTCOTT	1762	21012001
EARLY	Early Relig.	WESTON	1768	21012001
EARLY	Hap.early P.	GALLIMORE	1694	21012001
EARN	Earn. Pray.	BAINE	1778	01032026
EARS	Itching Ears.	DOWNES	1761	58004003
EART	Witn.& Eart.	C.	1692	69011013
EARTH	Earth. Trea.	ADEY	1760	43006019
EARTH	Earth Enj.	EMLYN	1742	21002020

Keyword	In its Context	Author	Year	BkChpVrs
EARTH	Soj.on Earth.	HOADLY	1754	61013014
EARTH	Soj.on Earth.	CARR	1777	61013014
EARTHLY	Earthly Th.	SMITH	1740	45008014
EAS	Eas.& Diff. R.	BRINGHURST	1689	43011030
EAS	Eas. Xn. Dut.	STILEMAN	1733	43011030
EAS	Eas. Xt's. Y.	DODD	1757	43011028
EAS	Eas. Xts. Y.	COCKBURN	1697	43011028
EAS	Eas. Xts. Y.	CLAGETT	1704	43011028
EAS	Eas. Xts. Y.	BEVERIDGE	1720	43011028
EAST	East. Eve.	STANHOPE	1715	43027057
EAST	East. Eve.	HOLE	1716	43027057
EAST	East. Mond.	STANHOPE	1715	45024013
EAST	East. Mond.	HOLE	1716	45024013
EAST	East. Mond.	STANHOPE	1715	47010034
EAST	East. Mond.	HOLE	1716	47010034
EAST	East. Tuesd.	STANHOPE	1715	45024036
EAST	East. Tuesd.	HOLE	1716	45024036
EAST	East. Tuesd.	STANHOPE	1715	47013026
EAST	East. Tuesd.	HOLE	1716	47013026
EAST	East. Tuesd.	TRAPP	1730	62001021
EAST	Mon.b. East.	STANHOPE	1715	44014001
EAST	Shro.& East.	HALES	1673	45016025
EAST	Star in East.	DOWNES	1761	43002001
EAST	Sund.b. East.	KILLIGREW	1689	19110007
EAST	Sund.b. East.	STANHOPE	1715	53002005
EAST	Sund.b. East.	HOLE	1716	53002005
EAST	Thur.b. East.	STANHOPE	1715	45023001
EAST	Tues.b. East.	STANHOPE	1715	44015001
EAST	Wed.b. East.	STANHOPE	1715	61009016
EAST	1 S. East.	STANHOPE	1714	46020019
EAST	1 S. East.	HOLE	1716	46020019
EAST	1 S.af. East.	STANHOPE	1714	65005004
EAST	1 S.af. East.	HOLE	1716	65005004
EAST	2 S. East.	STANHOPE	1714	46010011
EAST	2 S. East.	HOLE	1716	46010011
EAST	2 S.af. East.	STANHOPE	1714	63002019
EAST	2 S.af. East.	HOLE	1716	63002019
EAST	3 S.af. East.	STANHOPE	1714	63002011
EAST	3 S.af. East.	HOLE	1716	63002011
EAST	4 S. East.	STANHOPE	1714	62001017
EAST	4 S. East.	HOLE	1716	62001017
EAST	5 S.af. East.	STANHOPE	1714	62001022
EAST	5 S.af. East.	HOLE	1716	62001022
EASTER	S.b. Easter.	STANHOPE	1715	43027001
EASTER	S.b. Easter.	HOLE	1716	43027001
EASTER	S.b. Easter.	ANONYMOUS	1776	69007014
EASTER	1 S. Easter.	READING	1728	04016007
EASTER	1 S. Easter.	READING	1730	04022018
EASTER	2 S. Easter.	H.	1686	26009005
EASTER	2 S. Easter.	READING	1728	04023007
EASTER	2 S. Easter.	READING	1730	04025010
EASTER	3 S. Easter.	STANHOPE	1714	46016016
EASTER	3 S. Easter.	HOLE	1716	46016016
EASTER	3 S. Easter.	READING	1728	05004001
EASTER	3 S. Easter.	READING	1730	05005002
EASTER	4 S. Easter.	STANHOPE	1714	46016005

Keyword	In its Context	Author	Year	BkChpVrs
EASTER	4 S. Easter.	READING	1728	05006006
EASTER	4 S. Easter.	READING	1730	05007012
EASTER	5 S. Easter.	STANHOPE	1714	46016023
EASTER	5 S. Easter.	HOLE	1716	46016023
EASTER	5 S. Easter.	READING	1728	05008003
EASTER	5 S. Easter.	READING	1730	05009006
EASY	Rel.easy.	LAMBE	1717	43011030
EASY	Rel.easy.	NEWTON	1767	43011030
EASY	Relig.easy.	HAMMON	1684	43011030
EASY	Relig.easy.	DORRINGTOU	1703	43011029
EASY	Relig.easy.	EDWARDS	1726	43011030
EASY	Xn's. D.easy.	SMITH	1740	51004031
EASY	Xt's.easy Y.	HOADLEY	1754	43011030
EASY	Xt's.easy Y.	JORTIN	1774	43011030
EASY	Xty.easy Y.	BRAGGE	1713	43011030
EASY	Xty.easy Y.	BEVERIDGE	1720	43011030
EASY	Xty.easy Y.	BARNES	1752	43011030
EAT	Eat. Blood.	SYNGE	1733	51005001
EAT	Temper.eat.	ANONYMOUS	1772	20023001
EBAL	Mount Ebal.	CULVERWELL	1661	07005023
ECCL	Eccl. Gover.	LORTIE	1720	49014032
ECCLES	Eccles. Ord.	WAKEMAN	1664	47013004
ECCLES	Eccles. Polic.	SOUTH	1727	11013033
ECLIPSE	Eclipse.	BURROUGHS	1715	24010002
ED	Gard.of Ed.	HORNE	1778	01002008
ED	R. Ed. Child.	DODDERIDGE	1743	20022006
EDIF	Ben.& Edif.	WOOD	1775	61010024
EDIFIC	Mut. Edific.	ABERNETHY	1748	48015002
EDIFICATION	Edification.	WHITEHALL	1694	49014026
EDIFICATION	Edification.	RENNELL	1705	49003003
EDIFICATION	Edification.	MOSS	1737	49014026
EDU	Edu.poor G.	WILSON	1781	58001004
EDUC	Educ. Ch.	FLEETWOOD	1737	20013024
EDUC	Educ. Child.	HOLLAND	1753	54003020
EDUC	Educ. Child.	TROUTBECK	1778	20029015
EDUC	Educ.of Y.	KIDDER	17--	52006004
EDUC	Educ.s.	RYLAND	1780	57004015
EDUC	Relig. Educ.	WROUGHTON	1728	01018019
EDUCAT	Ear. Educat.	CLEAVER	1750	58003015
EDUCAT	Educat.s.	NEWTON	1776	45016002
EDUCAT	Rel. Educat.	HOPKINS	1708	20022006
EDUCAT	Rel. Educat.	HOLLAND	1753	20022006
EDUCAT	Xn. Educat.	HARRIS	1715	20022006
EDUCAT	Xn. Educat.	BUNDY	1740	52006004
EDUCAT	Xn. Educat.	ANONYMOUS	1742	52006004
EDUCATION	Education.	BURTON	1685	20022006
EDUCATION	Education.	SOUTH	1724	20022006
EDUCATION	Education.	WOODS	1747	20022006
EDUCATION	Education.	BALGUY	1748	20022006
EDUCATION	Education.	HUNT	1748	20022006
EDUCATION	Education.	SPRY	1744	58003014
EDUCATION	Education.	DAVIES	1754	20022006
EDUCATION	Education.	WHISHAW	1755	20022006
EDUCATION	Education.	DAWSON	1759	20022006
EDUCATION	Education.	FREE	1750	52006004
EDUCATION	Education.	MUSCOTT	1760	20022006

Keyword	In its Context	Author	Year	BkChpVrs
EDUCATION	Education.	BROWN	1764	20022006
EDUCATION	Education.	CRAIG	1775	20022006
EDUCATION	Education.	TOMMAS	1774	57004012
EDUCATION	Education.	DAY	1779	58002006
EFF	Eff. Calling.	ERSKINE	1764	45019005
EFF	Eff.call.&c.	GOUGH	1709	58001009
EFF	Eff.call.&c.	NEAL	1757	58001009
EFF	Eff.fm. Min.	ST.	1757	43005015
EFF	Eff.of prea.	FLEMING	1701	50003005
EFF	Eff.of Faith.	BEVERIDGE	1720	55002013
EFF	Eff.of H. Gh.	BROWNE	1722	47002032
EFF	Eff.of H. Sp.	SAURIN	1775	47002037
EFF	Eff.of Pray.	STRAIGHT	1741	53004006
EFF	Eff.of Prea.	STEWARD	1734	50002015
EFF	G. Eff. Gos.	SECKER	1770	43010034
EFF	Man.&eff. X's	BLACKALL	1723	43007028
EFF	Man.&eff. X's	BLAIR	1740	43007028
EFFECT	Effect.call.	WHITE	1676	48008028
EFFIC	Effic. Grace.	WILSON	1732	53002013
EFFIC	Effic.o. Pray.	SCOTT	1711	45011013
EFFIC	Effic.o. Pray.	TILLOTSON	1735	45011013
EFFIC	Effic.o. Pray.	MOSS	1737	45011013
EFFIC	Effic.of Bel.	SHARP	1734	44016016
EJAC	Ejac. Pra.	BENNETT	1735	16002010
EJAC	Ejac. Pra.	OLDING	1767	16001004
EL	Call.& El. Su.	BREKELL	1765	64001010
EL	Call.& El. Su.	SANDERCOCK	1776	64001010
EL	El.& Repro.	CLARKE	1734	48009023
EL	Ma, C.& El.s.	SHARP	1734	64001010
ELEC	G's Elec.&c.	WATTS	1753	52001003
ELECT	Absol. Elect.	NEVILLE	1682	52001004
ELECT	Call& Elect.	WHEATLAND	1739	43022014
ELECT	Elect.& Rep.	SCOTT	1743	48010019
ELECT	Elect. Eton.	GOLDWIN	1741	19072017
ELECT	Elect. Xn.	STANHOPE	1705	43022014
ELECT	Elect.s.	MAYHEW	1754	43025021
ELECT	God's Elect.	LEIGHTON	1746	48008034
ELECT	Part. Elect.	SLADEN	1732	56002013
ELECTION	Election.	BUNDY	1740	43022014
ELECTION	Election.	BREKELL	1765	48009011
ELECTION	Election.	ALLEN	1769	49009027
ELECTION	Election.	BOSTON	1773	52001003
ELECTION	Election&c.	RALEIGH	1679	28013009
ELIJ	Elij. Cur.	MORRIS	1743	12002023
ELIJ	Elij. Cur.	GOUGH	1751	12002023
ELIJ	Elij. Epitap.	BRADLEY	1670	11019004
ELIJ	Elij. Fire.	MORRIS	1743	12001011
ELIJ	Elij. Sup.	THEAD	1712	11019004
ELIJ	Elij. Transl.	FARMER	1756	12002011
ELIJAH'S	Elijah's Pr.	MORRIS	1743	11017001
ELOHIM	Elohim.	HOWE	1663	19082006
ELOQU	Xt's. Eloqu.	BROUGHTON	1778	46007046
ELOQUE	Sav. Eloque.	NEWTON	1782	45002046
ELYMAS	Elymas.	BULKLEY	1771	47013010
EM	Hus.m. Em.	CORNWALLIS	1706	01026012
EM	Rel. Em.o. T.	CARR	1777	52005015

INDEXES TO THIRD VOLUME: E: KEYWORD-IN-CONTEXT INDEX OF OTHER SUBJECTS OR OCCASIONS

Keyword	In its Context	Author	Year	BkChpVrs
EM	Trth.b. Em.	PRICE	1661	51004016
EMB	Emb. Week.	HOLE	1716	52004011
EMBER	Ember W.	HOLE	1716	48010014
EMIN	Hol.emin.	BEVERIDGE	1720	43005020
EMP	Angels Emp.	WHITE	1757	19104004
EMP	Emp. Poor.	JOHNSTON	1726	20013023
EMPL	Empl. Time.	DODD	1772	20006006
EN	Ap.f. Ch. En.	PARSONS	1767	55005021
EN	Conc. En. Pr.	BROUGHTON	1778	46011047
EN	Conc. En. Pr.	MILNE	1780	46011047
EN	Def. Ch. En.	HARRISON	1729	53001020
EN	Def. Ch. En.	STOCKDALE	1777	19096009
EN	En. Case&c.	STEWARD	1687	12018022
EN	En.g.&b.m.	LUCAS	1722	20014032
EN	En.g.&b.m.	TILLOTSON	1735	20014032
EN	Mar's En. Xt.	HORTON	1679	45010038
EN	Xt's. En.ill.t	FLAVEL	1673	45023023
EN	Zeal ag. En.	STELLING	1755	51004018
ENC	Enc.f. Sinn.	ELLIOTT	1759	51002021
END	Con.lat end.	HOLLAND	1753	05032029
END	End of Bapt.	CLARKE	1734	48006003
END	End of Sabb.	ORR	1777	44002027
END	End of Sacra.	TATHAM	1780	47017030
END	End of Time	RUSSELL	1746	69010005
END	End of Time	WATTS	1753	69010005
END	End of Xty.	BOURN	1755	49001030
END	End& D. M.	SHERIDAN	1720	47017027
END	End&c. Rel.	TATHAM	1780	48006023
END	End Jew. L.	CLARKE	1736	51002015
END	End Xt's.g.h.	JOHNSON	1740	59002014
END	G's end affl.	CLARKSON	1696	23027009
END	Latter End.	BARROW	1716	19090012
END	Latter End.	DUNLOP	1722	19090012
END	Latter End.	TILLOTSON.	1735	19090012
END	M's End&c.	BOSTON	1773	49010031
END	Man's End.	BOSTON	1773	19073024
END	Use& End L.	MAYHEW	1755	19034012
END	latter End	LUCAS	1722	21007002
ENE	Ene.o. Cross.	COCK	1705	53003018
ENEM	Forg. Enem.	NEWLIN	1728	45011004
ENEM	Love Enem.	NEEDHAM	1679	43005044
ENEM	Love Enem.	ALLESTREE	1684	43005044
ENEM	Love Enem.	BURTON	1685	43005044
ENEM	Love Enem.	KIDDER	1697	43005043
ENEM	Love Enem.	HORNECK	1706	43005043
ENEM	Love Enem.	HORNECK	1706	43005044
ENEM	Love Enem.	HORNECK	1706	43005046
ENEM	Love Enem.	ANDERSON	1708	43005044
ENEM	Love Enem.	GARDINER	1720	43005043
ENEM	Love Enem.	KELSEY	1721	43005044
ENEM	Love Enem.	HAILES	1722	43005044
ENEM	Love Enem.	BLACKALL	1723	43005045
ENEM	Love Enem.	GALE	1726	43005048
ENEM	Love Enem.	SCOUGAL	1726	45006027
ENEM	Love Enem.	CARLETON	1736	43005044
ENEM	Love Enem.	PELIER	1737	43005044

Keyword	In its Context	Author	Year	BkChpVrs
ENEM	Love Enem.	BLAIR	1740	43005043
ENEM	Love Enem.	SMITH	1740	43005044
ENEM	Love Enem.	BLAIR	1740	43005045
ENEM	Love Enem.	BLAIR	1740	43005046
ENEM	Love Enem.	SEED	1743	43005044
ENEM	Love Enem.	EDWARDS	1745	43005044
ENEM	Love Enem.	BALGUY	1748	43005044
ENEM	Love Enem.	MACE	1751	43005043
ENEM	Love Enem.	WHITTY	1772	43005044
ENEM	Love Enem.	JORTIN	1774	43005044
ENEM	Love Enem.	PYLE	1777	45006027
ENEM	Love Enem.	BROUGHTON	1778	43005043
ENEM	Love Enem.	JORTIN	1774	48012020
ENERGY	Grace Energy	SKEPP	1752	52001019
ENF	Lo.& Ch.enf.	HOLE	1716	65004007
ENG	Ch. Eng. Ap.	LOWTH	1722	47002042
ENG	Ch.of Eng.v.	LE FRANK	1662	49011018
ENG	Eng.to Hol.	WILKINSON	1660	64003011
ENG	Lit. Ch. Eng.	DURELL	1688	49011016
ENG	N. Eng. Dut.	NOYES	1698	24031023
ENGL	Ch.of Engl.	STANHOPE	1716	48010015
ENGL	Ch.of Engl.	BAYLY	1721	45011002
ENGL	Engl. C.	PARKHURST	1706	30004011
ENGL	Engl. Duty.	FLAVEL	1673	48001018
ENGL	Engl. Duty.	FLAVEL	1673	69003020
ENGL	Engl. Litur.	SNAPE	1745	48012012
ENGL	Engl.restit.	REEVE	1661	20028002
ENGL	Engl.warn.	OWEN	1694	26005008
ENGL	Isr.& Engl.	KNELL	1681	30003002
ENGL	Isr.& Engl.	REGIS	1753	05011026
ENJ	Earth Enj.	EMLYN	1742	21002020
ENJ	Fr.wor. Enj.	KIMBER	1756	65002017
ENJ	Sublun. Enj.	DAVIS	1756	21008008
ENJ	Van.hu. Enj.	OGILVIE	1766	49007031
ENL	Enl. Heart.	BURROUGHS	1733	19119032
ENM	M's. Enm. G.	CHARNOCK	1699	48008007
ENMITY	Enmity to T.	TILLOTSON	1735	46003020
ENOCH	of Enoch.	HACKET	1675	01005024
ENOCH	of Enoch.	ORR	1772	01005024
ENOCH'S	Enoch's Fai.	DODSON	1728	61011005
ENOCH'S	Enoch's Tr.	DODDERIDGE	1761	01005024
ENOCH'S	Enoch's Tr.	BOSTON	1764	01005024
ENOCH'S	Enoch's Tr.	MURRAY	1777	01005024
ENOCH'S	Enoch's Tra.	BOYSE	1728	61011005
ENQ	Enq.a.truth.	SCOTT	1743	20002003
ENQ	Enq.a Happ.	WEBB	1765	18028012
ENQ	Enq.in Rel.	HOADLY	1754	55005021
ENQ	Enq.into Xy.	DUCHAL	1753	50004002
ENQ	Futil.enq. F.	WHELDON	1772	46021022
ENQ	Self- Enq.	WHITFIELD	1771	04023023
ENQUI	Free Enqui.	BENSON	1748	55005021
ENSL	Sin.ensl.&c.	NEWLIN	1718	64002019
ENT	Ent.into rest.	BOSTON	1773	61004003
ENT	Xt's.ent.i. H.	EMLYN	1742	61006020
ENTHR	Enthr. Abp.	BLOMER	1716	47009015
ENTHUS	Ag. Enthus.	HAWKINS	1769	58002015

Keyword	In its Context	Author	Year	BkChpVrs
ENTHUS	Enthus.hope	DAVIS	1756	45009055
ENTHUSIASM	Enthusiasm.	BAYLY	1721	49014037
ENTHUSIASM	Enthusiasm.	WESTLEY	1750	47026024
ENTHUSIASM	Enthusiasm.	HAWKINS	1769	18036026
ENTHUSIASM	Enthusiasm.	STERNE	1769	46015005
ENTHUSIASM	Enthusiasm.	DUCHAL	1765	50005013
ENTR	King's Entr.	DUBOURDIEU	1714	09010024
ENTRY	Kings Entry.	WALKER	1660	14023011
ENVY	Ag. Envy.	LAMBE	1695	18005002
ENVY	Ag. Envy.	DELANY	1747	20014030
ENVY	Envy.	ASPIN	1684	21004004
ENVY	Envy.	WISE	1717	21004004
ENVY	Envy.	SOUTH	1724	62003016
ENVY	Envy.	BENNETT	1728	63002001
ENVY	Envy.	MOSS	1732	20027004
ENVY	Envy.	WHEATLAND	1739	62003016
ENVY	Envy.	JONES	1741	01037011
ENVY	Envy.	LLOYD	1765	62003016
ENVY	Envy.	CARRINGTON	1776	20027004
ENVY	Envy.	JORTIN	1774	49013004
EOVE	Eove of G.	WESTON	1747	49013003
EPHRAIM'S	Ephraim's C.	HAMMOND	1684	24031018
EPIPH	Epiph. S.	SNAPE	1745	49002007
EPIPH	1 S. Epiph.	STANHOPE	1715	48012001
EPIPH	1 S. Epiph.	STANHOPE	1715	48013001
EPIPH	1 S. Epiph.	HOLE	1716	48012001
EPIPH	1 S. Epiph.	READING	1728	23044006
EPIPH	1 S. Epiph.	READING	1730	23046001
EPIPH	2 S. Epiph.	STANHOPE	1715	46002001
EPIPH	2 S. Epiph.	HOLE	1716	46002001
EPIPH	2 S. Epiph.	STANHOPE	1715	48012006
EPIPH	2 S. Epiph.	HOLE	1716	48012006
EPIPH	2 S. Epiph.	READING	1728	23051012
EPIPH	2 S. Epiph.	READING	1730	23053001
EPIPH	3 S. Epiph.	STANHOPE	1715	48012016
EPIPH	3 S. Epiph.	HOLE	1716	48012016
EPIPH	3 S. Epiph.	READING	1728	23055003
EPIPH	3 S. Epiph.	READING	1730	23056010
EPIPH	4 S. Epiph.	LITTLETON	1680	46003016
EPIPH	4 S. Epiph.	READING	1730	23057015
EPIPH	4 S. Epiph.	READING	1730	23058003
EPIPH	5 S. Epiph.	HOLE	1716	54003012
EPIPH	5 S. Epiph.	READING	1730	23059001
EPIPH	5 S. Epiph.	READING	1730	23064001
EPIPH	6 S. Epiph.	STANHOPE	1715	43024023
EPIPH	6 S. Epiph.	HOLE	1716	43024023
EPIPH	6 S. Epiph.	READING	1730	23065001
EPIPH	6 S. Epiph.	READING	1730	23066001
EPIS	The Epis.expla	SMALRIDGE	1724	60000010
EPIS	The Epis.expla	MARSHALL	1731	60000010
EPISC	Episc.& Pres.	HICKES	1726	69013011
EPISC	Episc. Bapt.	SUTTON	1718	46003005
EPISC	Episc. Vind.	NICOLSON	1661	61013017
EPISC	Episc.defen.	D'ANVERS	1712	43005014
EPISC	Rest. Episc.	LEIGHTON	1746	23028005
EPITAP	Elij. Epitap.	BRADLEY	1670	11019004

Keyword	In its Context	Author	Year	BkChpVrs
EQ	Fin. Distr.eq.	CLARKE	1735	63004017
EQ	Mut. Eq.&h.	BOURN	1777	43007012
EQ	Xt.eq.w. G.	LESTLEY	1720	53002006
EQ	Xt.eq.w. G.	SHERLOCK	1772	53002006
EQUAL	Equal mank.	SAURIN	1777	20022001
EQUALS	Du.to Equals	HUBBARD	1757	20018024
EQUITY	Equity expl.	GOODMAN	1697	43007012
EQUITY	Equity expl.	HOLE	1717	43007012
EQUITY	Equity expl.	GROVE	1741	43007012
EQUITY	Equity.	JACKSON	1673	43007012
EQUITY	Equity.	TILLOTSON	1677	43007012
EQUITY	Equity.	BEVERIDGE	1720	43007012
EQUITY	Equity.	BLACKALL	1720	43007012
EQUITY	Equity.	IBBOT	1726	43007012
EQUITY	Equity.	MILLER	1749	43007012
EQUITY	Equity.	ORR	1749	43007012
EQUITY	Equity.	HUNT	1748	53004005
EQUITY	Equity.	TRAPP	1752	43007012
EQUITY	Equity.	ANONYMOUS	1777	43007012
EQUITY	L.& Equity.	PIERCE	1686	46013013
EQUITY	Rule Equity.	ATTERBURY	1699	43007012
EQUITY	Xn. Equity.	TALBOT	1706	43007012
EQUITY	Xn. Equity.	EVANS	1737	43007012
EQUITY	Xn. Equity.	WATTS	1753	43007012
ER	Go.lif.st. Er.	PEARSON	1718	46007017
ERECT	Erect. Sch.	MARCH	1682	19034011
ERR	Causes Err.	CARR	1777	45011035
ERR	Diss.sm. Err.	BENTHAM	1669	62001016
ERR	Err. M's.con.	GROVE	1747	48014016
ERRORS	Errors of Po.	TOWGOOD	1746	57004001
ES	L.es.t.att. G.	HUNTER	1774	65004016
ES	Law.es. Gos.	LITTLETON	1680	43005017
ES	Law.es. Gos.	HORNECK	1706	43005017
ES	Law.es. Gos.	HOLE	1715	43005017
ES	Law.es. Gos.	MOSS	1737	43005017
ESSAYED	Mon.essayed	BRENT	1728	21010019
ESSEN	Essen.of Rel.	WHICHCOTE	1703	52002022
EST	Law est.b. F.	WESTLEY	1750	48003031
EST	Law est.b. G.	TAYLOR	1704	48003031
EST	Min.be.est.	HICKES	1726	50003001
ESTA	Gosp.esta. L.	FISHER	1741	48003031
ESTA	Gosp.esta. L.	GILL	1773	48003031
ESTAB	Estab. Min.	BRADY	1713	48010014
ESTABL	Establ. Ch.	ALLEN	1773	23008009
ESTABLISH	Of Establish.	CRUSO	1698	47011023
ESTEEM	Self-esteem.	STRAIGHT	1741	48012003
ESTIM	Estim.of life.	BLAIR	1780	21012008
ESTIM	Estim.of L.	WILLIAMS	1774	19039004
ET	Best G.et.life	AMORY	1766	46006068
ET	Hell Tor.et.	MOSS	1732	43025046
ET	Hell Tor.et.	TILLOTSON	1735	43025046
ET	Hell Tor.et.	WARREN	1739	43025046
ET	Hell Tor.et.	WHITFIELD	1739	43025046
ET	Hell Tor.et.	VENN	1740	43025046
ET	Hell Tor.et.	WATERHOUSE	1753	43025046
ET	Th.tem.&et.	BADLAND	1676	50004018

INDEXES TO THIRD VOLUME: E: KEYWORD-IN-CONTEXT INDEX OF OTHER SUBJECTS OR OCCASIONS

Keyword	In its Context	Author	Year	BkChpVrs
ET	Th.tem.&et.	BEVERIDGE	1720	50004018
ET	Way to et. S.	SYNGE	1734	55005021
ETE	Ete. Pr.o. Xt.	KELSEY	1691	61006020
ETE	Ete. Pr.o. Xt.	STILLINGFLEET	1707	61006020
ETE	Hell tor.ete.	JENKS	1707	48006023
ETER	Eter. Hell T.	KILLINBECK	1717	45016023
ETER	Eter. Judgm.	BATES	1700	47017031
ETER	Eter. Salvat.	SYNGE	1714	43019016
ETER	Eter. Salvat.	STEWARD	1734	57001015
ETER	Eter. Salvat.	HOLDEN	1755	57001015
ETER	Eter. Salvat.	LOVEDER	1756	57001016
ETER	Eter. Salvat.	PEARSE	1763	57001016
ETER	Eter.life.	WILDER	1729	46017003
ETER	Eter.life.	SHIRLEY	1762	46017003
ETER	Eter.life&c.	GODDARD	1781	46006068
ETER	G's De.eter.	BRINE	1754	20022023
ETER	God's Eter.	WISHEART	1716	18036026
ETER	Saint's Eter.	RUSSEL	1746	55005017
ETER	T.&eter.m.	FOTHERGILL	1765	43006033
ETER	Time& Eter.	MANTON	1693	50004018
ETER	Time& Eter.	HOPKINS	1712	50004018
ETER	Time& Eter.	HORT	1738	50004018
ETER	Time& Eter.	JOHNSON	1740	50004018
ETER	Time& Eter.	HARWOOD	1767	50004018
ETERN	Etern. Hell.	BOURDALOUE	1776	43022013
ETERN	Etern. Inher.	MORE	1692	48008017
ETERN	Etern. Life.	WILKINSON	1660	44010017
ETERN	Etern. Life.	STRAIGHT	1741	46006068
ETERN	Etern. Miser.	WISHEART	1716	19062012
ETERN	Etern.life.	REAY	1755	48006023
ETERN	Etern.of G.	CHARNOCK	1684	19090002
ETERN	Etern.of G.	WHITBY	1710	57001017
ETERN	Etern.of G.	TILLOTSON	1735	19090002
ETERN	Etern.of G.	CLARKE	1732	69001008
ETERN	Etern.of G.	ABERNETHY	1743	19090002
ETERN	Etern.of G.	ATTERBURY	1743	19090002
ETERN	Etern.of G.	DAVIS	1756	19102026
ETERN	Etern.of G.	BRACKENRIDGE	1764	19090002
ETERN	Etern.of G.	LELAND	1769	19090002
ETERN	Etern.of G.	SAURIN	1775	64003008
ETERN	God's Etern.	HUNT	1748	48016026
ETERNAL	Eternal.life.	TILLOTSON	1735	43016026
ETERNITY	Eternity.	C.	1667	50003017
ETERNITY	Eternity.	DOOLITTLE	1683	50004018
ETERNITY	Eternity.	PEARSE	1763	50004018
ETERNITY	Eternity.	ORTON	1764	50004018
ETERNITY	On Eternity.	HEYLYN	1761	05032029
ETON	Elect. Eton.	GOLDWIN	1741	19072017
EUCHARIST	Eucharist.	LORTIE	1720	38001011
EUCHARIST	Eucharist.	HOLLOWAY	1739	47002038
EUCHARIST	Eucharist.	HEYLIN	1761	49011028
EV	Ab.f.a.ev. A.	PIERCE	1679	55005022
EV	Ab.f.a.ev. A.	ATTERBURY	1699	55005022
EV	Ab.f.a.ev. A.	HOPKINS	1700	55005022
EV	Ab.f.a.ev. A.	SMALRIDGE	1727	55005022
EV	Ab.f.a.ev. A.	TUNSTALL	1759	55005022
EV	Ab.f.a.ev. A.	WOOD	1775	55005022
EV	Ad.& Ev. Xr.	MURRAY	1777	01002015
EV	Ag.ev. Tid.	ANONYMOUS	1710	19112007
EV	Dang.ev. H.	ABERNETHY	1751	24013023
EV	Di. Truth ev.&	WHICHCOTE	1698	46007046
EV	Ev. K.of Xt.	BOURN	1777	49015021
EV	Ev. Xt's. Res.	STEBBING	1760	47005032
EV	Ev.co.&b. B.	WHITE	1757	49015033
EV	Ev.dut.same	CLAGETT	1704	21003015
EV	Ev.m.debtor	HUTCHINS	1782	49004007
EV	Ev.o. T.n.sc.	SMYTH	1717	58001010
EV	Ev.o. Xn.rel.	TATHAM	1780	61002003
EV	Ev.th.not s.	SMITH	1717	45016019
EV	Fut.st.its Ev.	FOSTER	1732	58001010
EV	G.&ev. Con.	SMITH	1740	46020019
EV	G.disp. Ev.	LELAND	1769	43010030
EV	Gos. Ev.suff.	WHARTON	1728	45016031
EV	Gos. Ev.suff.	WESTON	1747	45016031
EV	Int. Ev.of G.	CARR	1777	53003008
EV	Leg.& Ev. R.	SMITH	1673	48009031
EV	Mor.&n. Ev.	FOSTER	1737	62001017
EV	S.&ev. Eye.	BLAIR	1740	43006022
EV	St. John Ev.	STANHOPE	1715	65001001
EV	St. John Ev.	HOLE	1716	65001001
EV	St. John's Ev.	STANHOPE	1715	46021019
EV	St. John's Ev.	HOLE	1716	46021019
EV	Temp. Ev.not G	BROWN	1722	45013004
EV	Temp. Ev.not G	HOLLAND	1753	45013004
EV	Turn f.ev.w.	FOORD	1719	26033011
EV	Word ev. G.	BRETT	1720	46001001
EV	Word ev. G.	LESTLEY	1720	46001001
EV	Xn. Ev.o.f.st.	BOURN	1760	49015012
EV	3 Ev.last.t.	HILDROP	1711	43024021
EVAN	Evan. Right.	TAYLOR	1673	43005020
EVANG	Evang. Gra.	BEVERIDGE	1720	64001005
EVANG	Evang. Past.	FLAVEL	1673	43024045
EVANG	Evang. Poli.	DUPORT	1661	53001027
EVANG	Evang. Rep.	HILL	1755	24031019
EVANG	Evang. Rep.	JOHNSON	1776	45024047
EVE	East. Eve.	STANHOPE	1715	43027057
EVE	East. Eve.	HOLE	1716	43027057
EVEN	Even. Lect.	BAINE	1758	48004006
EVENTS	Cas. Events.	ADAMS	1736	21009011
EVENTS	Cas. Events.	DUCHAL	1765	21009010
EVENTS	Extr. Events.	MEADOWCOURT	1723	19077020
EVERL	Everl. Life.	BULL	1713	19103015
EVERL	Life everl.	NICOLSON	1661	43025046
EVERL	Life everl.	NEWCOME	1702	43025046
EVERL	Life everl.	OGDEN	1777	43025046
EVERL	Live everl.	EDWARDS	1713	43025046
EVERLAST	Life everlast.	PIGOTT	1702	65005011
EVERM	Rej.everm.	BARROW	1716	55005016
EVID	Evid. O. T. P.	POWELL	1776	45024025
EVID	Evid.fut.st.	AMORY	1766	43007011
EVID	Evid.of Fai.	ALLESTREE	1684	58001012
EVID	Evid.of Gos.	CENNICK	1762	45016031

Keyword	In its Context	Author	Year	BkChpVrs
EVID	Evid.of Gos.	BADDELLEY	1766	45016031
EVID	Evid.of Gos.	SHERLOCK	1772	45016031
EVID	Evid.of Gos.	CARR	1777	45016031
EVID	Evid.of Xy.	DODDERIDGE	1736	64001016
EVID	Evid.of Xy.	CAMPLIN	1777	50004007
EVID	Exter. Evid.	SCOTT	1743	46010024
EVID	Exter. Evid.	SCOTT	1743	63001011
EVID	Scrip. Evid.	CLARKE	1735	45016031
EVIL	Con.ov. Evil.	ALTHAM	1732	48012021
EVIL	D. G.ag.evil.	QUINCY	1750	48012021
EVIL	Evil life co.	GLANVIL	1681	43022032
EVIL	Evil of Sin.	HORTON	1679	48006021
EVIL	Evil of Sin.	CARLETON	1736	48006023
EVIL	Evil speak.	GORDON	1771	47023005
EVIL	Evil.speak.	FIDDES	1720	19039001
EVIL	Evil.thhugh.	STEBBING	1760	43015019
EVIL	Evil.though.	CALAMY	1726	43015019
EVIL	Evil.though.	CHILCOT	1734	43015019
EVIL	Evil Co mp.	LAWSON	1764	20001015
EVIL	Evil Examp.	STENNET	1732	02023002
EVIL	Evil Govern.	HAYWOOD	1663	47023005
EVIL	Evil Habits.	TILLOTSON	1735	24013023
EVIL	Evil Habits.	UPTON	1735	47024025
EVIL	Evil Spirits.	GREGORY	1696	63005008
EVIL	Evil Spirits.	SEED	1750	63005008
EVIL	Evil Thoug.	FIDDES	1720	20024009
EVIL	Evil-sp.in g.	BARROW	1716	59003002
EVIL	Evil-sp.in g.	SCURLOCK	1733	59003002
EVIL	Evil-sp.in g.	SIMS	1772	59003002
EVIL	Evil-speak.	LAMONT	1710	62001026
EVIL	Evil-speak.	PEARSON	1718	62004010
EVIL	Evil-speak.	SEED	1743	62004010
EVIL	Evil-speak.	ADEY	1755	62004010
EVIL	Evil-speak.	STERNE	1760	62001026
EVIL	Evil-speak.	CARR	1777	62004010
EVIL	Good& Evil.	SHERLOCK	1719	23005020
EVIL	Good& Evil.	CLARKE	1735	23005020
EVIL	Good& Evil.	FORSTER	1732	47024025
EVIL	Good& Evil.	BENSON	1748	23005020
EVIL	Good& Evil.	HUSSEY	1755	23005020
EVIL	Mor. Evil.	AMORY	1766	19136001
EVIL	Nat. Evil.	AMORY	1766	62001013
EVIL	Orig.of Evil.	HENLEY	1731	23047007
EVIL	Resist.of Evil	PAYNE	1763	62004007
EVIL	Vi. Cau. Evil.	QUINCY	1750	20019003
EVIL	3 Evil last T.	HILDROP	1711	44013019
EX	Af. Child.ex.	COOKE	1752	05006007
EX	Bod. Ex.i. R.	SCOTT	1700	57004006
EX	Dai. Self-ex.	WARREN	1710	19004004
EX	Div.mer.ex.	CALAMY	1702	48009016
EX	Ex.& E.of G.	KNOWLES	1750	48001020
EX	Ex. D.re. W.	ORR	1739	61010025
EX	Ex. Xn. Prin.	CHANDLER	1769	46015005
EX	Ex.fut. Rew.	DORRINGTON	1705	54003001
EX	Ex.of Deity.	COCKRANE	1780	48001020
EX	Ex.of Pray.	GROSVENOR	1711	19073028

Keyword	In its Context	Author	Year	BkChpVrs
EX	Ex Abr. Fai.	TILLOTSON	1735	61011017
EX	Ex Abr. Fai.	FRANCIS	1773	61011017
EX	Ex Abr. Fai.	BROUGHTON	1778	61011017
EX	G's H.in Ex.	BRODHURST	1733	01022014
EX	Int.ex.o. Xy.	BULLOCK	1726	46008046
EX	Integ. Ex. Jos	ANONYMOUS	1776	43007012
EX	Jes.our Ex.	VINCENT	1690	63002021
EX	Jes.our Ex.	TILLOTSON	1735	63002021
EX	No Ex.f.fall.	ROGERS	1735	49010012
EX	Saints o. Ex.	BERRIMAN	1751	61006012
EX	Sav.ex.teac.	LELAND	1769	46007046
EX	Seas. Xn. Ex.	NICOLSON	1661	61003013
EX	Self ex.of G.	WHITAKER	1674	19018046
EX	Text c.&ex.	MEDE	1672	61010005
EX	Use o. Sc. Ex.	LLOYD	1765	53003017
EXA	Saint's Exa.	ROE	1766	61012001
EXALT	Exalt. Savr.	MARRYATT	1719	46020028
EXALT	L's. Exalt.	ELSMERE	1767	63003022
EXALT	Walk.exalt.	BURTON	1685	52005015
EXALT	Xt's. Exalt.	TAYLOR	1676	53002009
EXALT	Xt's. Exalt.	LITTLETON	1680	53002009
EXALT	Xt's. Exalt.	CLARKE	1727	47002033
EXALT	Xt's. Exalt.	BENNETT	1735	53002009
EXALT	Xt's. Exalt.	TERRY	1746	53002009
EXALT	Xt's. Exalt.	WATTS	1753	47002033
EXALT	Xt's. Exalt.	CATCOTT	1753	53002009
EXALT	Xt's. Exalt.	WARNEFORD	1757	53002009
EXALTED	Xt.exalted.	TREBELL	1703	23045004
EXALTED	Xt.exalted.	TREBELL	1703	23055004
EXAM	Exam.of Xt.	MOSS	1732	49011001
EXAM	Exam.of Xt.	MILLER	1749	43011029
EXAM	Good Exam.	BROGRAVE	1689	43005016
EXAM	Good Exam.	BRADY	1713	43005016
EXAM	Good Exam.	BOYS	1716	43005016
EXAM	Good Exam.	BLACKALL	1723	43005016
EXAM	Good Exam.	CARLETON	1736	43005016
EXAM	Good Exam.	BLAIR	1740	43005016
EXAM	Good Exam.	GROVE	1747	61013007
EXAM	Good Exam.	BUNDY	1750	61013007
EXAM	Good Exam.	WELD	1766	61013007
EXAM	Good Exam.	BRAILSFORD	1776	09002023
EXAM	Good Exam.	ANONYMOUS	1776	48015002
EXAM	Self-exam.	LITTLETON	1680	49011028
EXAM	Self-exam.	CHARNOCK	1684	50013005
EXAM	Self-exam.	MATHER	1701	50013005
EXAM	Self-exam.	HOLE	1717	50013005
EXAM	Self-exam.	WAPLE	1718	50013005
EXAM	Self-exam.	NEWLIN	1728	49011028
EXAM	Self-exam.	M'GEORGE	1729	49011028
EXAM	Self-exam.	WARREN	1748	50013005
EXAM	Self-exam.	BALGUY	1750	50013005
EXAM	Self-exam.	STERNE	1760	23001003
EXAM	Self-exam.	BARKER	1763	50013005
EXAM	Self-exam.	SECKER	1770	25003040
EXAM	Self-exam.	ATKINSON	1775	51006004
EXAM	Self-exam.	NEWSON	1781	25003040

INDEXES TO THIRD VOLUME: E: KEYWORD-IN-CONTEXT INDEX OF OTHER SUBJECTS OR OCCASIONS

Keyword	In its Context	Author	Year	BkChpVrs
EXAM	Ser.exam.	BOURN	1764	43025014
EXAM	Xt's. Exam.	JOHNSON	1740	43011029
EXAM	Xt's Exam.	STEBBING	1760	63002021
EXAMINING	Examining.	MICHELL	1737	55005021
EXAMP	Evil Examp.	STENNET	1732	02023002
EXAMP	Infl. Examp.	BRERETON	1721	20001010
EXAMP	Xt's. Examp.	CALAMY	1726	47010038
EXAMP	Xt's. Examp.	TILLOTSON	1735	47010038
EXAMP	Xt's. Examp.	WILDER	1741	47010038
EXAMP	Xt's. Examp.	SCOTT	1743	64001021
EXAMP	Xt's. Examp.	LELAND	1769	46013015
EXAMP	Xt's. Examp.	LELAND	1769	46018029
EXAMP	Xt's. Examp.	LELAND	1769	52005002
EXAMP	Xt's. Examp.	LELAND	1769	53002005
EXC	Exc. Xn. Rel.	TILLOTSON	1735	46003019
EXC	Exc.div. M.	BEDFORD	1733	49014015
EXC	Exc.o. Gosp.	SECKER	1770	53004008
EXC	Exc.o. Gosp.	TOTTIE	1775	53004008
EXC	Exc.o. Xt'.o.	FLAVEL	1673	61010014
EXC	Exc.of Char.	HAWKINS	1755	49013013
EXC	Exc.of J. L.	RANDOLPH	1773	05004005
EXC	Exc.of Soul.	DORRINGTON	1703	37012001
EXC	Exc.of Soul.	QUINCY	1750	43016026
EXC	Good m.exc.	BARKER	1763	19016003
EXC	More exc.w.	HUSSEY	1758	49012031
EXC	On C.& Exc.	ANONYMOUS	1779	02020001
EXC	Sin exc.sinf.	DUNLOP	1722	48008013
EXC	Sin.exc.sinf.	DUNLOP	1722	48007013
EXC	Things exc.	HUSSEY	1753	53001010
EXC	Things exc.	WEBB	1772	53001010
EXC	W.exc. Folly	ANONYMOUS	1776	21002013
EXC	Xn. Rel.exc.	MOORE	1716	48015013
EXCEL	Excel. Men.	ROGERS	1735	20012026
EXCEL	Excel. Men.	ORR	1739	20012026
EXCEL	Excel. Xn. R.	WHICHCOTE	1698	48001016
EXCEL	Excel. Xnity	WILDER	1741	49001018
EXCEL	Excel.o. Bib.	SIMPSON	1774	48001016
EXCEL	Excel.of S. S.	SEED	1743	63003015
EXCEL	Excel.of S. S.	DAVIS	1756	19119092
EXCEL	Xns.excel.	PRICE	1661	43005047
EXCELL	Excell. Pray.	OGDEN	1770	45011008
EXCELL	Excell. Rel.	CORNWALL	1701	20008009
EXCELL	Excell. Rel.	ABERNETHY	1751	20008006
EXCELL	Excell. S. S.	ANONYMOUS	1780	06001008
EXCELL	Excell. Xty.	WHISTON	1709	53001023
EXCELL	Excell. Xty.	BARROW	1716	49002006
EXCELL	Excell.in Xt.	FLAVEL	1673	49002008
EXCELL	Excell.of Char	GROVE	1742	49013008
EXCELL	Excell.of S.	ZAMBRANA	1685	41010031
EXCELL	Rel.excell.	SCOUGAL	1726	20012026
EXCESS	Excess. Care.	BLACKALL	1723	43006025
EXCESS	Excess. Zeal.	JORTIN	1774	21007016
EXCESS	Excess. Zeal.	ANONYMOUS	1776	21007016
EXCH	Exch.of Soul	JORTIN	1774	44008036
EXCISE	A. Excise.	WYNER	1733	45002001
EXEC	On an Exec.	ROSEWELL	1716	04026010

Keyword	In its Context	Author	Year	BkChpVrs
EXEC	On an Exec.	DENHAM	1745	61008012
EXECU	On Execu.	BROUGHTON	1713	10012005
EXECUT	b.an Execut.	ANONYMOUS	1720	50007009
EXEM	Exem.holin.	BEVERIDGE	1720	47002042
EXEM	Exem.life Xt	BAYLY	1721	46013015
EXEM	Exem.right.	REEVES	1729	48012017
EXEM	Xt. G. Exem.	BUNDY	1740	63002021
EXEM	Xt. G. Exem.	FOSTER	1744	63002021
EXEM	Xt. G. Exem.	COCKMAN	1750	63002021
EXEM	Xt. G. Exem.	HOLLAND	1753	63002021
EXEMP	Exemp.man.	CARR	1777	55005022
EXEMPLARIN	Exemplarin.	ALLESTREE	1684	43005016
EXEMPLARIN	Exemplarin.	WAKE	1701	43005016
EXEMPLARIN	Exemplarin.	HAVETT	1703	43005016
EXEMPLARIN	Exemplarin.	HORNECK	1706	43005014
EXEMPLARIN	Exemplarin.	HORNECK	1706	43005016
EXEMPLARIN	Exemplarin.	WHARTON	1728	43005016
EXEMPLARIN	Exemplarin.	FOSTER	1744	43005016
EXEMPLARIN	Exemplarin.	ST.	1757	43005016
EXER	Exer. Health	DYKES	1722	20031017
EXER	Exer.of Fai.	LARDNER	1751	57006012
EXER	Exer.of Xn.	WHICHCOTE	1702	53003012
EXERCISE	On Exercise.	ANONYMOUS	1772	20006009
EXH	Exh.pr. Lib.	SQUIRE	1716	51005001
EXH	Exh.repent.	MASON	1742	28010012
EXH	Exh.to Lib.	SQUIRE	1714	51006010
EXHOR	Min. Exhor.	GUYSE	1756	57004016
EXHOR	Mut. Exhor.	WAPLE	1718	61010025
EXHORTATION	Exhortation.	FANCH	1768	53001027
EXILE	Volun.exile.	FREE	1763	49009013
EXIS	Xt's.self.exis	ROMAINE	1755	46001014
EXIST	Exist.of G.	KNOWLES	1750	18011007
EXIST	Exist.of God	HOOLE	1748	61011006
EXIST	G's. Exist.	BATES	1700	61011006
EXP	Exp o. Creed	LEIGHTON	1746	57003009
EXP	Exp. Ld's. Pr.	MANTON	1684	43006009
EXP	Exp. Proph.	GARDINER	17--	23007014
EXP	Exp.div. Rel.	CONYBEARE	1729	46006045
EXP	Exp.fit.of th.	DOWARS	1775	21003002
EXP	P's.wish exp.	WATERLAND	1742	48009003
EXP	P's.wish exp.	DODWELL	1752	48009003
EXP	P's.wish exp.	KEELING	1766	48009003
EXP	Pan.exp. Pe.	HENLEY	1729	61012007
EXPED	Exped. Lit.	HOLE	1725	19089007
EXPEDIT	On Expedit.	PHILIPS	1725	05004007
EXPERIENCE	Experience.	SNAPE	1745	48005004
EXPL	Div.gr.expl.	HORBERY	1774	46003008
EXPL	Equity expl.	GOODMAN	1697	43007012
EXPL	Equity expl.	HOLE	1717	43007012
EXPL	Equity expl.	GROVE	1741	43007012
EXPL	Jud. S.expl.	WILSON	1781	45022021
EXPL	Media.expl.	DUCHAL	1765	57002005
EXPL	Ps.expl.	PETERS	1776	19109016
EXPL	Resur.expl.	WILSON	1781	43028011
EXPL	Text expl.	HORTON	1679	66000008
EXPL	Text expl.	ALLESTREE	1684	50006002

Keyword	In its Context	Author	Year	BkChpVrs
EXPL	Text expl.	ALLESTREE	1684	63004001
EXPL	Text expl.	MORE	1692	51006014
EXPL	Text expl.	CLAGETT	1704	48008028
EXPL	Text expl.	BULL	1713	50012007
EXPL	Text expl.	WAKE	1716	68000003
EXPL	Text expl.	DUNLOP	1722	56001001
EXPL	Text expl.	DUNLOP	1722	56001007
EXPL	Text expl.	SCATTERGOOD	1723	48013014
EXPL	Text expl.	SHARP	1734	43020016
EXPL	Text expl.	TILLOTSON	1734	45016008
EXPL	Text expl.	STEPHENS	1737	44013032
EXPL	Text expl.	ALTHAM	1732	65005011
EXPL	Text expl.	STEPHENS	1737	63003018
EXPL	Text expl.	STEPHENS	1737	63004007
EXPL	Text expl.	COOKE	1739	47024025
EXPL	Text expl.	GROVE	1741	43027046
EXPL	Text expl.	JOHNSON	1740	69014013
EXPL	Text expl.	GROVE	1741	49015019
EXPL	Text expl.	LEIGHTON	1746	48013011
EXPL	Text expl.	LEIGHTON	1746	49001030
EXPL	Text expl.	WESTLEY	1748	65003009
EXPL	Text expl.	WESTLEY	1771	52005014
EXPL	Text.expl.	HORTON	1679	50013008
EXPL	Text.expl.	MORE	1692	46004031
EXPL	Text Expl.	KIDDER	1697	55005012
EXPL	Truth expl.	BRADY	1730	52004025
EXPL	Truth expl.	BERRIMAN	1751	52004025
EXPL	Xt's. A.expl.	WATERLAND	1742	45020037
EXPLA	Res.expla.	CHANDLER	1769	49015035
EXPLA	Text expla.	LEIGHTON	1746	45013001
EXPLA	The Epis.expla	SMALRIDGE	1724	60000010
EXPLA	The Epis.expla	MARSHALL	1731	60000010
EXPLAI	Text explai.	SHARP	1734	47013048
EXPLAIN	Par.explain.	CLARKE	1735	45016025
EXPLANATION	Explanation	NEWTON	1782	44009049
EXPOST	G's Expost.	ORTON	1776	24022015
EXPOST	Job's Expost.	STERNE	1760	18002010
EXTEMP	Extemp. Pr.	SOUTH	1727	21005002
EXTENT	Extent.of R.	MARSHALL	1731	19119096
EXTENT	Extent.of R.	LEIGHTON	1746	19119096
EXTER	Exter. Evid.	SCOTT	1743	46010024
EXTER	Exter. Evid.	SCOTT	1743	63001011
EXTER	Exter. Perf.	HOADLY	1727	48010013
EXTERN	Extern. Prof.	LAWSON	1764	43007021
EXTIRP	Extirp. Can.	SCOTT	1743	03018025
EXTR	Extr. Events.	MEADOWCOURT	1723	19077020
EXTR	Extr. Worsh.	ATTERBURY	1734	19095006
EXTR	Saints extr.	WILSON	1735	43008025
EXTRE	Avoid Extre.	ENFIELD	1772	20004027
EXTRE	Extre. Unct.	KILLINBECK	1717	62005014
EYE	Pluck Eye.	BROWNE	1749	44009047
EYE	S.&ev. Eye.	BLAIR	1740	43006022
EYE	Single Eye.	MORE	1692	43006022
F	A.f.m.f. G.a.	PARSONS	1774	50003006
F	Ab.f.a.ev. A.	PIERCE	1679	55005022
F	Ab.f.a.ev. A.	ATTERBURY	1699	55005022

Keyword	In its Context	Author	Year	BkChpVrs
F	Ab.f.a.ev. A.	HOPKINS	1700	55005022
F	Ab.f.a.ev. A.	SMALRIDGE	1727	55005022
F	Ab.f.a.ev. A.	TUNSTALL	1759	55005022
F	Ab.f.a.ev. A.	WOOD	1775	55005022
F	Ag. F.of M.	WOOD	1775	20029025
F	Ag F.of Dea.	ANONYMOUS	1710	49015055
F	All f. Good.	FARMER	1756	48008028
F	An. F.perm.	JENKINS	1779	01009003
F	Anx.f.raim.	BLAIR	1740	43006028
F	Ap.f. Ch. En.	PARSONS	1767	55005021
F	Apol.f. Gos.	SMITH	1709	49015001
F	Apol.f. Rel.	POOL	1673	43011019
F	Ar.f. Xn. Rel.	KNOX	1768	63003015
F	Arg.f. Provi.	HUNTER	1774	18007020
F	Arg.f. Xnity.	POWELL	1776	46005037
F	Auth.mat. F.	ANONYMOUS	1774	43023008
F	Bapt.f.dead.	EDWARDS	1692	49015029
F	Bapt.f.dead.	FORD	1692	49015029
F	Ben.f. Pray.	OGDEN	1770	43007007
F	Bless.imp. F.	LAWSON	1764	46020029
F	Brid.f. Ton.	HOOTTON	1709	62001026
F	C.b F.&f. G.	PIKE	1748	48004016
F	Ch p. F.& H.	HOLE	1725	49013013
F	Ch.e. F.& H.	MOSS	1732	49013013
F	Ch.e. F.& H.	MORRIS	1743	49013013
F	Ch.s.f. Wid.	CHANDLER	1748	50009012
F	Ch.suf.f.p's c	BREKEL	1767	24031029
F	Coll.f. Min.	TRIMNELL	1711	48015013
F	Coll.f.poor.	SELLON	1763	20030008
F	Comp. F.	MORER	1708	17009019
F	Comp. F.	NICHOLSON	1707	69002017
F	Comp. F.	MARSHALL	1731	18010011
F	Cont.f. Faith	MARSH	1737	68000003
F	Cont.f. Faith	MARSHALL	1750	68000003
F	Cont.f. Faith	HOADLEY	1754	68000003
F	Cont.f. Faith	TOULMIN	1771	68000003
F	Dea.b. Ad. F.	LAWSON	1764	48005012
F	Dea.b. Ad. F.	BOSTON	1773	48005012
F	Decr. Xn. F.	GREENHILL	1756	45018008
F	Dif.de.f. Gl.	BULL	1713	64001011
F	Disc.f. Prop.	BLACKALL	1723	43007016
F	E.dr. X. F. B.	SUTTON	1754	46006053
F	E.f. Xn.w. T.	HORNE	1671	68000020
F	Enc.f. Sinn.	ELLIOTT	1759	51002021
F	F.& Ch.s.	DELANY	1766	51005024
F	F.& Po.o. G.	ATTERBURY	1699	58003005
F	F.& Po.o. G.	BULL	1713	58003005
F	F.&com. Sw.	SMALWOOD	1666	43005034
F	F.&com. Sw.	WILSON	1700	43005034
F	F.&com. Sw.	KINSMAN	1700	43005034
F	F.&com. Sw.	HORNECK	1706	43005034
F	F.&com. Sw.	GREGORY	1708	43005034
F	F.&com. Sw.	CALAMY	1726	43005034
F	F.&com. Sw.	LITTLETON	1735	43005034
F	F.&com. Sw.	WHITFIELD	1739	43005034
F	F.&com. Sw.	BOURN	1777	43005034

INDEXES TO THIRD VOLUME: E: KEYWORD-IN-CONTEXT INDEX OF OTHER SUBJECTS OR OCCASIONS

Keyword	In its Context	Author	Year	BkChpVrs
F	F.&good W.	DUKE	1714	52002008
F	F. C.of H. L.	SANDERSON	1722	15010007
F	F. F. Lond.	WOODWARD	1706	28006001
F	F. Gl.by Son.	JOHNSON	1776	46016025
F	F. Gr.mag.	LAMBERT	1779	24032008
F	F. H.& Char.	CLAGETT	1720	49013013
F	F. Hap.or M.	BUNDY	1740	45016025
F	F. Rew.& P.	CONANT	1708	48006023
F	F. Rew.& P.	CLARKE	1735	43025046
F	F. Sp. X's. D.	PEARSE	1763	48012011
F	F. St.of R.	DUCHE	1779	19001003
F	F.f.b. L.& G.	WILSON	1781	52005003
F	F.in.j.tr.w.	BREVALL	1670	69002010
F	F.judg.c.& P.t	BRYAN	1685	50005010
F	F.judg.c.& P.t	BURNET	1747	50005010
F	F.o. G.&c. O.	JONES	1778	63002017
F	F.of d. Good.	SCOTLAND	1776	28003005
F	F.of Death.	EATON	1764	19023004
F	Futil.enq. F.	WHELDON	1772	46021022
F	G. News f. H	TOPLADY	1774	19089012
F	G. Xrter.b. F.	WORTHINGTON	1775	20022001
F	G.o. Obj. F.	NEWLIN	1720	45012004
F	G.o. Obj. F.	TILLOTSON	1735	45012004
F	G.p. M's. F.	ANONYMOUS	1776	43006031
F	Goldsmi. F.	LUCAS	1699	59003014
F	Good f.	CLEMENT	1774	18002010
F	Gosp h.f w.	BARKER	1763	43011025
F	Hap.f.mind.	NEWMAN	1760	20014014
F	Hon.conj. F.	DYKES	1722	20031023
F	Hum.&d. F.	OAKES	1747	45002052
F	Hum.&d. F.	TOULMIN	1770	45002052
F	Inf.f.	HOLME	1745	45016009
F	Inf.f.	BUTLER	1778	05015011
F	John's P.f. G.	ORTON	1776	67000002
F	Joy& F.in R.	BLAIR	1777	19002011
F	Just.by F.	BOWMAN	1764	46003014
F	Kno.in F. S.	DODD	1767	10012023
F	L. G.f.a. Xn.	ANONYMOUS	1770	47026023
F	Law est.b. F.	WESTLEY	1750	48003031
F	Lent. F.	GUNNING	1662	45005035
F	Lent. F.	SYDALL	1713	45005034
F	Lent. F.	BAYLEY	1721	43009015
F	Loaves& F.	HEYLIN	1761	43015036
F	M. Anx.f.p.	DAVIES	1771	51004019
F	Man f. Virt.	GOUGH	1751	21012013
F	Mer.f. X's E.	DEVEREL	1777	46008011
F	Mi.f. D.o. G.	WILLIS	1720	53001017
F	Min.pray.f.	EVANS	1723	55005025
F	Nec.of S.f. S.	GILL	1773	61002010
F	Neg.of F. W.	ORTON	1769	24010025
F	No acc.by F.	ALLEN	1761	62002014
F	No Ex.f.fall.	ROGERS	1735	49010012
F	O. G.f.& M.	FROST	1741	21005003
F	One F.& F.	ROMAINE	1759	21001008
F	Opp. Prot. F.	GIBBONS	1755	30006006
F	Orig. St.& F.	CHANDLER	1769	01002017

Keyword	In its Context	Author	Year	BkChpVrs
F	Our Sins f.our	TILLOTSON	1735	62001013
F	Our Sins f.our	MOSS	1737	62001013
F	P.ob.of D. F.	DAVIES	1766	23066002
F	P's Pr.f. Ones	ORTON	1776	58001018
F	Per.& F. R.	SAUNDERS	1701	06024014
F	Per.& F. R.	READER	1765	06024014
F	Plea.f. Ch. E.	HOLLINGWORTH	1676	46006068
F	Plea.f.godly.	WATSON	1672	20012026
F	Pr.& F.ineff.	WILLIAMS	1774	49015014
F	Pr.&f. State.	DUCHAL	1765	50004018
F	Pr.&f. State.	ELSMERE	1767	50004018
F	Pr.f. G's. M.	SMALRIDGE	1724	50001011
F	Pr.f. Kings.	MOSS	1733	57002001
F	Pr.f. Mercy.	ERSKINE	1764	34003002
F	Praise f. Rec,	LITTLETON	1680	23038017
F	Pray.f. Cou.	BARKER	1763	19122006
F	Pre.f. Death.	HOOK	1676	43025010
F	Pre.f. Death.	LUCAS	1722	23038001
F	Pre.f. Death.	WHEATLAND	1739	12020001
F	Pre.f. Death.	TIDCOMBE	1757	43024044
F	Prep.f. Sacra.	SMITH	1740	63004007
F	Pres.&f. Ha.	ROBINSON	1736	62004017
F	Prog. Hell-f.	HENLEY	1730	11018024
F	Pub. P.of F.	BEVERIDGE	1720	43010032
F	Qual.f fu. H.	CLARKE	1734	69003004
F	Qual.f.fu. H.	BULL	1713	69003004
F	R. Care of F.	FORD	1770	01018019
F	R. Gov.of F.	PICKARD	1762	01018019
F	Rea.f. Xn's.r.	GALE	1726	55005016
F	Rea.f. Xn's.r.	MORRIS	1743	55005016
F	Rec.f. Sick.	PETERS	1776	46005014
F	Recant.f.	DANVERS	1736	61009022
F	Rej.f. Peace.	PHILIPS	1775	23066010
F	Rel.sec.f.w.	ROE	1766	43006033
F	Rem.f. Grie.	BURROUGHS	1662	19032009
F	Rep.for.of F.	HORNE	1756	23040003
F	Rid.no f. Tr.	GODDARD	1781	21002002
F	Rules f.judg.	BLACKALL	1723	43007003
F	Rules f.judg.	BLAIR	1740	43007003
F	S. S. G.f. Y.	BERRIMAN	1763	19119008
F	S. S. Rul. F.	MARSH	1737	45016031
F	S.o. G.f.d. J.	DAVIES	1771	49003007
F	Salv.f. J.& G.	SHIRLEY	1762	47010034
F	Salv.f.div.m.	BOURN	1760	48007024
F	Salv.thro' F.	BEVERIDGE	1720	53002012
F	Sinc.acc.f. P.	SIMONS	1743	50008012
F	Sorrow f. Sin	WARBURTON	1754	43026026
F	Sorrow f. Sin	WILLISON	1761	43026026
F	Sorrow f. Sin	CORNWALL	1773	43026026
F	Soul dis.f. B.	HOLDEN	1755	45022043
F	Soul pre.f. H.	WATTS	1753	50005005
F	St. P's.d.to F	HOADLY	1754	47024024
F	St. P's.d.to F	CHANDLER	1769	47024025
F	St. P's.d.to F	HURD	1780	47024024
F	Sta. F. Ch. S.	ERSKINE	1764	23030007
F	Stated F. Pr.	SMALRIDGE	1724	45011001

Keyword	In its Context	Author	Year	BkChpVrs
F	Stated F. Pr.	MOSS	1732	45011001
F	Ste.in Xn. F.	STEVENS	1771	49016013
F	Su.f.we&c.	ALTHAM	1732	63002020
F	Suff.f. Relig.	CLARKE	1735	54001024
F	Sup.f.our N.	WILLISON	1761	53004019
F	T.o.tr.&f.d.	ADAMS	1777	65004001
F	T.t. S.n.f. G.	SHARP	1734	62001013
F	T.t. S.n.f. G.	BURNET	1747	62001013
F	T.t. S.n.f. G.	ABERNETHY	1751	62001013
F	Test.ne.f. M.	SKELTON	1754	58001013
F	Time f.all.	HALL	1660	21003004
F	Tok.f.mour.	FLAVEL	1673	45007008
F	Tr.& F. Co.	AGAR	1759	06023006
F	Tr.&f.wisd.	CARMICHAEL	1757	62003013
F	Tri.tr.&f. D.	TILLOTSON	1735	65004001
F	Turn f.ev.w.	FOORD	1719	26033011
F	Un.of Xn. F.	SMITH	1682	52004005
F	W.&f. Buil.	BRAGGE	1704	43007024
F	W.w. F.c. J.	HORNE	1761	62002014
F	Wait f. Cha.	COBDEN	1757	18014014
F	Weak.of F.	PAYNE	1763	23042003
F	Welch. F.	WILLIAMS	1731	19033012
F	Welch F.	SCURLOCK	1736	19118024
F	Wick. M. F.	HORTON	1679	45012020
F	Wis.prov.f.	BOURN	1777	43006019
F	Witnes.f. G.	ERSKINE	1764	23043012
F	Xn. Ev.o.f.st.	BOURN	1760	49015012
F	Xn. Life o. F.	TILLOTSON	1735	50005007
F	Xn. Rule F.	MICHELL	1737	46005039
F	Xn's.sh.act.f.	CONANT	1699	67000005
F	Xt. Sac.f.us.	CHARNOCK	1684	49005007
F	Xt.cam.f. L.	BROWNE	1749	43005017
F	Xt.dy.f. Sin.	CLARKSON	1696	48005008
F	Xt.first F.&c.	BREKELL	1765	49015020
F	Xt.hon.to F.	WILLIAMS	1770	63002007
F	Xt's apol.f.d.	ORTON	1776	43026004
F	Xt's. F.t. Dis	LARDNER	1760	46014027
F	Xt's.2 p.f. D.	FLAVEL	1673	49011023
F	Youth f. G.	POWELL	1676	21012001
F	Zeal f. Ar. F.	OGDEN	1777	68000003
F	Zeal f. Ch.	PRIEST	1753	19122006
F	Zeal f. Faith.	REEVES	1729	68000003
F	Zeal f. G's H.	CLARKE	1727	16010039
F	Zeal f. Xty.	THEED	1712	68000003
F	Zeal f. Xty.	TILLY	1729	68000003
F	2 Arg.f. C. P.	BROOKS	1665	43006006
FA	Div. Fa.imp.	WHARTON	1728	47010034
FA	Fa.& Virtue.	MOSS	1732	64001005
FA	Fa.&sec. W.	JENNINGS	1757	52006018
FA	Fa.&sec. W.	LANGHORNE	1773	52006018
FA	Fa. Gift o. G.	SHERLOCK	1772	52002008
FA	Incred.& Fa.	FOSTER	1744	46020029
FA	St. Paul's Fa.	SHERIDAN	1720	47024014
FACTION	Faction.	WALLIS	1748	51005015
FAELIX	Faelix Behav.	STERNE	1766	47024026
FAELIX	Faelix Case.	WARNEFORD	1776	47024025

Keyword	In its Context	Author	Year	BkChpVrs
FAI	Abram's Fai.	DUNCOMB	1697	62002023
FAI	Abram's Fai.	EVANSON	1773	48004022
FAI	Antiq.of Fai.	GLANVIL	1681	68000003
FAI	Assur.of Fai.	NEWTON	1767	65005019
FAI	Corr.of Fai.	MEDE	1672	64002001
FAI	Duty of Fai.	SUTTON	1718	47016031
FAI	Enoch's Fai.	DODSON	1728	61011005
FAI	Evid.of Fai.	ALLESTREE	1684	58001012
FAI	Ex Abr. Fai.	TILLOTSON	1735	61011017
FAI	Ex Abr. Fai.	FRANCIS	1773	61011017
FAI	Ex Abr. Fai.	BROUGHTON	1778	61011017
FAI	Exer.of Fai.	LARDNER	1751	57006012
FAI	Fai b.on Kn.	WATTS	1753	58001012
FAI	Fai.& Hum.	NEWLIN	1720	43008008
FAI	Fai.& Light.	BOSTON	1753	50005007
FAI	Fai.& Pract.	WALKER	1763	65002003
FAI	Fai.& Virt.	MARSHALL	1750	57001018
FAI	Fai.&it's N.	FEUILLERADE	1717	51005006
FAI	Fai. Xt's. Re.	SKELTON	1754	47010040
FAI	Fai.in the R.	HILL	1755	61011013
FAI	Fai.n.to Sal.	CLAGETT	1704	61011006
FAI	Fai.n.to Sal.	HOPKINS	1708	47016031
FAI	Fai.p. Xn. L.	BOYSE	1728	51002020
FAI	Fai.triumph.	DAVIES	1754	65005004
FAI	Fai.w.b. L.	GROVE	1742	51005006
FAI	Fai& H.in J.	PRICE	1757	51005005
FAI	Fear n.to Fai.	PIERCE	1679	49010012
FAI	God our Fai.	JONES	1741	23064008
FAI	Life of Fai.	MANTON	1689	62001006
FAI	Life of Fai.	TOULMIN	1770	50005007
FAI	Liv.& D. Fai.	NEWTON	1767	62002026
FAI	Nec.of Fai.	DELAUNE	1728	52004005
FAI	Obed.of Fai.	ROBOTHAM	1680	48016026
FAI	Pray.in Fai.	WHITE	1677	62001006
FAI	Reas.of Fai.	WHARTON	1728	63003015
FAI	Rely.on Fai.	HOADLY	1727	52002008
FAI	Right.of Fai.	WESTLEY	1746	48010005
FAI	Salv.by Fai.	BEVERIDGE	1720	47016031
FAI	Salv.by Fai.	DUNLOP	1722	47016031
FAI	Salv.by Fai.	BARKER	1748	47016031
FAI	Sav. Fai.diff.	COLE	1690	52001019
FAI	Stedf.in Fai.	BRADBURY	1749	61010023
FAI	Tr. Xn. Fai.	CLARKE	1727	65005004
FAI	Walk.b. Fai.	NORRIS	1728	50005007
FAI	Walk.b. Fai.	MILLER	1749	50005007
FAI	Walk.b. Fai.	ABERNETHY	1751	50005007
FAI	Xt.obj.o. Fai.	GOODWIN	16--	48008038
FAIR	Fair Sex.	FOURDYCE	1776	46011005
FAIR	S.b. Fair.	KEMP	1668	50002017
FAIRH	Tri.of Fairh.	WILCOX	1757	43015021
FAITH	Abil.of Faith	REEVES	1729	65005004
FAITH	Abr. Faith.	CONYBEARE	1757	61011017
FAITH	Abr. Faith.	WILSON	1781	61011008
FAITH	Appr. Faith.	WILLISON	1761	51002020
FAITH	Assu.of faith	CENNICK	1762	23038017
FAITH	Bless.o. Faith	BROME	1711	47017034

INDEXES TO THIRD VOLUME: E: KEYWORD-IN-CONTEXT INDEX OF OTHER SUBJECTS OR OCCASIONS

Keyword	In its Context	Author	Year	BkChpVrs
FAITH	Comf. Faith.	FOWLER	1674	63001008
FAITH	Cont.f. Faith	MARSH	1737	68000003
FAITH	Cont.f. Faith	MARSHALL	1750	68000003
FAITH	Cont.f. Faith	HOADLEY	1754	68000003
FAITH	Cont.f. Faith	TOULMIN	1771	68000003
FAITH	Cour. Faith.	ERSKINE	1757	19023004
FAITH	Dy.in Faith.	CLARKSON	1696	61011013
FAITH	Dy.in Faith.	PARKHURST	1707	61011013
FAITH	Eff.of Faith.	BEVERIDGE	1720	55002013
FAITH	Faith ab W.	JOHNSON	1740	43008010
FAITH	Faith c. Salv.	CHARNOCK	1684	46003036
FAITH	Faith c. Salv.	MORRIS	1743	46003036
FAITH	Faith in G.	BEVERIDGE	1720	46014001
FAITH	Faith in G.	CLARKE	1732	61011006
FAITH	Faith in G.	ATTERBURY	1743	46014001
FAITH	Faith in G.	KNOWLES	1750	34003017
FAITH	Faith in Pr.	CLARKSON	1696	62001006
FAITH	Faith in Pr.	MATHER	1710	19072019
FAITH	Faith in Pr.	STUART	1753	03002013
FAITH	Faith in Xt.	BEVERIDGE	1720	46001012
FAITH	Faith in Xt.	SCATTERGOOD	1723	43009021
FAITH	Faith in Xt.	EVANS	1737	63001008
FAITH	Faith in Xt.	JOHNSON	1740	47010043
FAITH	Faith in Xt.	WALKER	1755	46006037
FAITH	Faith in Xt.	WILLIAMS	1770	46003036
FAITH	Faith in Xt.	SHERLOCK	1772	46006067
FAITH	Faith our S.	WILCOX	1757	19027014
FAITH	Faith pr. Pie.	BEVERIDGE	1720	47015009
FAITH	Faith w. S.	PEARSON	1718	46020029
FAITH	Faith w. S.	SHERLOCK	1719	46020029
FAITH	Faith.	USHER	1678	48005002
FAITH	Faith.	CLARKSON	1696	61010038
FAITH	Faith.	BARROW	1716	64001001
FAITH	Faith.	CREYGHTON	1720	43015025
FAITH	Faith.	IBBOT	1726	61011001
FAITH	Faith.	BRADY	1730	43015028
FAITH	Faith.	MARSHALL	1731	61011006
FAITH	Faith.	TILLOTSON	1735	61011006
FAITH	Faith.	SOUTH	1744	50001024
FAITH	Faith.	MARSHALL	1750	61011001
FAITH	Faith.	WELCH	1752	48001017
FAITH	Faith.	SMITH	1769	44011022
FAITH	Faith.	FARRINGTON	1769	50004018
FAITH	Faith.	BOURDALOUE	1776	43008013
FAITH	Faith.	JORTIN	1774	47017011
FAITH	Faith. Influ.	BEVERIDGE	1711	50005007
FAITH	Faith.ins.w. W	BEVERIDGE	1720	43007021
FAITH	Faith.ins.w. W	BLACKALL	1723	43007021
FAITH	Faith& Bap.	REAY	1755	44016016
FAITH	Faith& Cha.	LOVEDER	1756	56001003
FAITH	Faith& Pati.	EMLYN	1742	61006012
FAITH	Faith& Pati.	HARTLEY	1754	61006012
FAITH	Faith& Unb.	BURNET	1747	46020029
FAITH	Faith&c.	ERSKINE	1764	23055011
FAITH	Faith Abrah.	CLARKE	1734	01015006
FAITH	Faith Aff.	DUBOURDIEU	1712	19039009
FAITH	Faith Cana.	DODD	1757	43015022
FAITH	Faith Cana.	WILLISON	1761	43015027
FAITH	Gosp. Faith.	BEVERLEY	1695	46017007
FAITH	Heal. Faith.	WILLISON	1761	46005006
FAITH	Implic. Faith	ANONYMOUS	1764	46010029
FAITH	Inf.& Faith.	RAWLINS	1768	48011020
FAITH	Infl.of Faith.	HOLDEN	1755	44016015
FAITH	Infl.of Faith.	VENN	1759	44016015
FAITH	Jus.by Faith.	USHER	1678	48005001
FAITH	Jus.by Faith.	SCOTT	1701	48003028
FAITH	Jus.by Faith.	WILLIAMS	1708	48005001
FAITH	Jus.by Faith.	BARROW	1716	48005001
FAITH	Jus.by Faith.	BILLINGSLEY	1723	48005001
FAITH	Jus.by Faith.	DODSON	1728	48005002
FAITH	Jus.by Faith.	BIRCH	1729	48005001
FAITH	Jus.by Faith.	STEPHENS	1737	48003028
FAITH	Jus.by Faith.	WESTLEY	1746	48004005
FAITH	Jus.by Faith.	HOOLE	1748	48003028
FAITH	Jus.by Faith.	ABERNETHY	1748	48004016
FAITH	Jus.by Faith.	SHEPHERD	1748	51002016
FAITH	Jus.by Faith.	SMITH	1752	48003028
FAITH	Jus.by Faith.	HAYWARD	1758	48005001
FAITH	Jus.by Faith.	HALLIFAX	1760	48003028
FAITH	Jus.by Faith.	RANDOLPH	1768	48003028
FAITH	Jus.by Faith.	JOHNSON	1776	48005001
FAITH	Jus.by Faith.	PETERS	1776	48005001
FAITH	Just.b. Faith.	COYTE	1761	51005006
FAITH	Justif. Faith.	E.	1679	65005012
FAITH	Late Faith.	KILLINBECK	1717	46016030
FAITH	Law of Faith	ROMAINE	1760	48003027
FAITH	Life of Faith	MANTON	1689	51002020
FAITH	Life of Faith	WELCH	1752	46005024
FAITH	Life of Faith.	BAXTER	1660	61011001
FAITH	Life of Faith.	WALLIS	1683	61010038
FAITH	Life of Faith.	MANTON	1689	61004002
FAITH	Life of Faith.	STUART	1753	61010038
FAITH	Life of Faith.	SAURIN	1777	34002014
FAITH	Liv.by Faith.	SUTTON	1754	51003011
FAITH	Nat.of Faith	CLARKE	1735	46020029
FAITH	Nat.of Faith.	TRAPP	1722	48004003
FAITH	Nat.of Faith.	HOLDEN	1755	43016015
FAITH	Nat.of Faith.	WITHERSPOON	1768	65003023
FAITH	Obj.of Faith	CHARNOCK	1684	46014001
FAITH	Of Faith.	ALLESTRE	1684	44009024
FAITH	Of Faith.	WHALEY	1695	61011017
FAITH	Of Faith.	HOLE	1715	44009024
FAITH	Of Faith.	COOKE	1739	44009024
FAITH	On Faith.	PARIS	1726	46014001
FAITH	On Faith.	BRACKENRIDGE	1764	47016031
FAITH	On Faith.	CARR	1777	61010038
FAITH	On Faith.	TATHAM	1780	46003036
FAITH	Orig.o. Faith	ROTHERAM	1761	46010037
FAITH	Pr. Faith&c.	BEVERLEY	1683	19079006
FAITH	Prim. Faith.	SOMMERS	1731	68000003
FAITH	Prom. Faith.	WELCH	1752	46010024
FAITH	Ration Faith	DODWELL	1745	63003015

Keyword	In its Context	Author	Year	BkChpVrs
FAITH	Reas.of Faith	SHERLOCK	1702	50004018
FAITH	Rel. Faith.	OUTRAM	1680	61010038
FAITH	Rel. Faith.	ORR	1749	61010038
FAITH	Rep.& Faith.	HOLE	1715	44001015
FAITH	Rep.& Faith.	BEVERIDGE	1720	44001015
FAITH	Rep.& Faith.	JONES	1756	44001015
FAITH	Rep.& Faith.	ELLIOTT	1764	47020021
FAITH	Rep.& Faith.	CASE	1774	47002038
FAITH	Repos. Faith.	ERSKINE	1764	22002003
FAITH	Rig.of Faith.	MILWAY	1751	53003009
FAITH	Salv b. Faith	WESTLEY	1746	52002008
FAITH	Salv.b. Faith.	ANONYMOUS	1768	52002008
FAITH	Salv.b Faith	STRAIGHT	1741	52002008
FAITH	Salv.faith al.	WARBURTON	1767	43022012
FAITH	Sav. Faith.	MANTON	1708	63001009
FAITH	Sav. Faith.	GROVE	1747	48001016
FAITH	Sav. Faith.	FAWCETT	1749	46020030
FAITH	Sav. Faith.	WELCH	1752	61011001
FAITH	Saving Faith	MANTON	1708	61010039
FAITH	Str.for Faith.	STENNETT	1738	53001027
FAITH	Suffer. Faith.	WILKINSON	1660	53001029
FAITH	Tri.of Faith.	FOORD	1719	65005004
FAITH	Tri.of Faith.	FIDDES	1720	65005004
FAITH	Unw. Faith.	SMITH	1751	62002018
FAITH	Vict.of Faith	ALLESTREE	1684	65005004
FAITH	Vict.of Faith	MONRO	1693	65005004
FAITH	Vict.of Faith	STRATFORD	1700	65005005
FAITH	Vict.of Faith	BEVERIDGE	1720	65005005
FAITH	Vict.of Faith	DAWES	1733	65005004
FAITH	Vict.of Faith	MOSS	1737	65005004
FAITH	Vict.of Faith	PEARCE	1770	65005005
FAITH	Want Faith.	CLAGETT	1704	45018008
FAITH	Weak. Faith.	STANHOPE	1705	44009024
FAITH	Xn. Faith.	TILLOTSON	1735	46020031
FAITH	Xn. Faith.	ROGERS	1736	48010010
FAITH	Xn. Faith.	EVANS	1737	50005007
FAITH	Xn. Faith.	BUNDY	1740	50005007
FAITH	Xn. Faith.	ALLEN	1751	65005004
FAITH	Xn. Faith.	BADDELLEY	1752	47016030
FAITH	Xn. Faith.	SECKER	1770	48010010
FAITH	Xn. Faith.	ATKINSON	1775	49013013
FAITH	Xt.faith. W.	HORTON	1679	69001005
FAITH	Zeal f. Faith.	REEVES	1729	68000003
FAITH	of Faith.	REGIS	1750	43017020
FAITH'S	Faith's Vict.	BATTELY	1694	65005004
FAITH'S	Faith's Vict.	BRADY	1730	65005004
FAITHF	Faithf. Adv.	GOSWELL	1715	21012001
FAITHF	Faithf. Xn.	ADEY	1755	69002010
FAITHFUL	On Faithful.	WHICHCOTE	1702	61003012
FAL	Councils fal.	POOLE	1675	43023008
FAL	Fal. Pre. Rel.	CLARKE	1735	43022011
FAL	Fal. Weights	DRAKE	1697	20016011
FAL	Fal. Weights	DICKINSON	1779	20020010
FAL	Fal. Witness.	CLARKE	1736	20024028
FAL	Fal.hop.hea.	BLAIR	1740	43007021
FAL	Fal.pret.sal.	BLACKALL	1723	43007022

Keyword	In its Context	Author	Year	BkChpVrs
FAL	Fal Id.o. Pr.	SMITH	1673	64001021
FAL	Truth& Fal.	REEVES	1712	52004025
FAL	Truth& Fal.	MAYHEW	1750	45012054
FALL	Adam's Fall.	GREEN	1758	01003010
FALL	Dang.of fall.	HOLDSWORTH	1725	49010012
FALL	Dang.of fall.	NEWTON	1736	49010012
FALL	Dang.of fall.	HOOLE	1748	49010012
FALL	Dang.of fall.	HILL	1755	49010012
FALL	Fall fm. G.	NOURSE	1708	24002019
FALL	Fall in Adam	BOSTON	1773	48005019
FALL	Fall of Ang.	MEDE	1672	64002004
FALL	Fall of Ang.	DAVISON	1684	64002004
FALL	Fall of Ang.	BOYSE	1728	64002004
FALL	Fall of Ang.	WHEATLY	1746	64002004
FALL	Fall of Man.	WELLS	1676	48005012
FALL	Fall of Man.	ADAMS	1716	21007029
FALL	Fall of Man.	KING	1731	01002016
FALL	Fall of Man.	HUBBARD	1757	48005012
FALL	Fall of Man.	BARRINGTON	1770	01003001
FALL	Fall. Satan.	WARBURTON	1767	43004024
FALL	Fall.of Pleas.	AGAR	1759	19001001
FALL	Fall&1st S.	BOSTON	1773	01003006
FALL	No Ex.f.fall.	ROGERS	1735	49010012
FALL	On the Fall.	PARKER	1750	50011003
FALL	Peter's Fall&r	STANHOPE	1705	44014072
FALL	The Fall.	CRAIG	1775	01003001
FALLEN	Fallen Ch.	ENGLISH	1776	69002005
FALS	Fals.ap. Sac.	WILLIAMS	1774	49011027
FALS	Lies& Fals.	SOUTH	1727	20012022
FALSE	False Piety.	WILLIAMS	1774	19050021
FALSE	False Princ.	OUTRAM	1697	43006023
FALSE	False Proph.	BLANCH	1708	51001007
FALSE	False Proph.	BLACKALL	1723	43007015
FALSE	False Proph.	ATTERBURY	1743	43007015
FALSE	False Shame.	LAWSON	1764	45009026
FALSE	T.false Acc.	ANONYMOUS	1753	45016002
FALSH	Tru.& Falsh.	MOSS	1732	52004025
FAM	Abr's Fam.	MURRAY	1777	01025001
FAM	Fam. Afflict.	TAYLOR	1703	10023005
FAM	Fam. Duties.	JONES	1692	06024015
FAM	Fam. Instr.	JACOMB.	1719	01018019
FAM	Fam. Pray.	DOOLITTLE	1676	06024015
FAM	Fam. Prayer	WAPLE	1718	01018019
FAM	Fam. Prayer.	MORRIS	1757	63003007
FAM	Fam. Prayer.	WARNEFORD	1776	43018020
FAM	Fam. Relig.	BELL	1672	06024015
FAM	Fam. Relig.	PAYNE	1691	06024015
FAM	Fam. Relig.	PARKHURST	1706	13016043
FAM	Fam. Relig.	GIFFARD	1713	24010025
FAM	Fam. Relig.	WHITFIELD	1739	06024015
FAM	Fam. Relig.	BERRIMAM	1763	06024015
FAM	Fam. Relig.	KNOX	1768	06024015
FAM	Fam. Relig.	DAVIES	1766	57005008
FAM	Fam. Relig.	SECKER	1770	06024015
FAM	Fam. Relig.	WALLIN	1771	01018019
FAM	Fam. Relig.	JORTIN	1774	06024015

Keyword	In its Context	Author	Year	BkChpVrs
FAM	Fam. Relig.	HUNTER	1779	06024015
FAM	Fam. Worsh.	SLATER	1694	06024015
FAM	Fam. Worsh.	YOUNG	1746	06024015
FAM	Fam. Worsh.	WESTON	1766	06024015
FAM	Fam. Worsh.	ORTON	1769	10006020
FAM	Fam. Worsh.	ORTON	1769	18021015
FAM	Fam. Worsh.	ORTON	1769	19101002
FAM	Fam. Worsh.	ORTON	1769	20003033
FAM	Fam. Worsh.	ORTON	1760	47010002
FAM	Gover. Fam.	ANONYMOUS	1722	06024015
FAM	X's fam.titles	DYER	1666	23005016
FAMINE	Famine.	HILDROP	1711	30004007
FAN	Godl.no fan.	ANONYMOUS	1683	63003015
FAN	Godl.no Fan.	VEALE	1683	63003015
FAR	Far.to life.	LAMBERT	1779	45002029
FARW	Farw.to life.	SHAW	1667	50005006
FARW	Seam.farw.	FLAVEL	1673	47021005
FAS	Fas. W.pas.a.	DUNLOP	1722	49007031
FASH	Conf.fash. N.	CARR	1777	48012002
FASHI	Fashi.of W.	BREKELL	1765	49007031
FAST	Fast.	USHER	1678	61004007
FAST	Fast.& Tem.	BURNET	1747	45004012
FAST	Fast.s.	CAPPE	1776	20029014
FAST	Lent. Fast.	MARSHAL	1706	43004002
FAST	Lent. Fast.	SMALRIDGE	1724	43004002
FAST	Prep.to.fast.	GREENHILL	1757	48010001
FAST	Rel. Fast.	BARKER	1676	44002020
FAST	Rel. Fast.	BROME	1711	44002020
FAST	Stand fast&c.	DUCHE	1775	51005001
FAST	Xt's Fast.	WILLIAMS	1667	43004002
FAST	Xt's Fast.	THEED	1712	43004002
FASTING	Fasting.	GARDINER	1720	43006016
FASTING	Fasting.	BEVERIDGE	1720	49009027
FASTING	Fasting.	BENNETT	1735	43006017
FASTING	Fasting.	SOUTH	1744	43017021
FASTING	Fasting.	DODD	1757	43006016
FASTING	Fasting.	KEDDINGTON	1757	47014023
FASTING	Xn. Fasting.	BROME	1711	43006016
FASTING	Xn. Fasting.	CLAGETT	1720	43006016
FASTING	of Fasting.	LITTLETON	1735	43009015
FAT	God our Fat.	WILLISON	1761	24003019
FATAL	Sin fatal.	DUNLOP	1722	26018031
FATH	Fath. Child.	ASHWOOD	1707	28014003
FATH	Fath.1. Bless.	HART	1702	18030023
FATH	G. Fath. Al.	BARROW	1716	69011017
FATH	Xt. Fath.ser.	BRODHURST	1733	43012018
FATHER	G. Father&c	ORR	1772	38001006
FATHER	G.o. Father.	MANGEY	1717	43006009
FATHER	G.o. Father.	LITTLETON	1735	43006009
FATHER	G.o. Father.	CHURCHILL	1765	43006009
FATHER	G.our father	NICOLSON	1661	48008015
FATHER	G.our Father	CLARKE	1732	43023009
FATHER	G.t. Father.	BARROW	1716	52004006
FATHER	Indul. Father	MASON	1742	45015011
FATHER	Rev. Father.	HORTON	1679	46001018
FAULTS	Secret Faults	SEDGEWICK	1660	19019012

Keyword	In its Context	Author	Year	BkChpVrs
FAULTS	Secret Faults	REYNER	1745	19019012
FAVOR	Div. Favor.	HOLDEN	1755	19063003
FE	Fe. G.&h. K.	SEABURY	17--	63002017
FEAR	Ag. Fear o D.	TATNAL	1665	61002015
FEAR	Ag. Fear. D.	BOOKEY	1739	55004013
FEAR	Ag. Fear Fire	ANONYMOUS	1710	19004008
FEAR	Be.& Fear G.	LITTLETON	1680	62002010
FEAR	Ben. Fear.al.	LARDNER	1751	20028014
FEAR	Fear n.to Fai.	PIERCE	1679	49010012
FEAR	Fear o. Death	SYLVESTER	1676	47020024
FEAR	Fear of D.	ENFIELD	1772	19023004
FEAR	Fear of Dea.	MAYO	1690	61002015
FEAR	Fear of Dea.	NOURSE	1701	61002015
FEAR	Fear of Dea.	LAMBE	1717	61002015
FEAR	Fear of Dea.	NORRIS	1728	61002015
FEAR	Fear of Dea.	LATHAM	1774	61002015
FEAR	Fear of G.	BRIDGE	1671	16005015
FEAR	Fear of G.	MORE	1692	20001007
FEAR	Fear of G.	MARCH	1699	19076007
FEAR	Fear of G.	HAVETT	1703	21012013
FEAR	Fear of G.	SKELTON	1754	20014026
FEAR	Fear of G.	KIMBER	1756	20014027
FEAR	Fear of God b.	STILLINGFLEET	1707	18023015
FEAR	Fear of God.	BATES	1700	18028028
FEAR	Fear of God.	SHERLOCK	1719	20009010
FEAR	Fear of God.	BENNETT	1728	20023017
FEAR	Fear of God.	CLARKE	1732	18023015
FEAR	Fear of God.	BURROUGHS	1733	18028023
FEAR	Fear of God.	ROGERS	1735	19033008
FEAR	Fear of God.	CARLETON	1736	19089007
FEAR	Fear of God.	UMFREVILLE	1739	21012013
FEAR	Fear of God.	ATTERBURY	1734	53002012
FEAR	Fear of God.	JOHNSON	1740	20016006
FEAR	Fear of God.	POTTER	1753	45012004
FEAR	Fear of God.	SHIRLEY	1762	45012004
FEAR	Fear of God.	SECKER	1770	20009010
FEAR	Fear of God.	WEBB	1772	18023015
FEAR	Fear of God.	SHERLOCK	1772	20009010
FEAR	Fear of God.	JORTIN	1774	45012015
FEAR	Fear of God.	PETERS	1776	18028026
FEAR	Fear of God.	CARR	1777	20016006
FEAR	Fear of M. S.	HUNT	1748	20029025
FEAR	Fear.wick.	DUKE	1714	20010024
FEAR	Fear& C.&c.	WILSON	1781	63001017
FEAR	Fear G.& M.	DUNLOP	1722	45012004
FEAR	Fear God.	MARTYN	1661	45012004
FEAR	Fear God.	NEAL	1757	19031019
FEAR	Fear God.	GRANT	1775	63002016
FEAR	G.to be fear.	SMALRIDGE	1724	23051012
FEAR	Godly Fear.	TAYLOR	1668	61012028
FEAR	Godly Fear.	COOKE	1739	21012013
FEAR	Gui.ob. Fear	BRYSON	1778	49015056
FEAR	H.& Fear G.	OUTRAM	1697	38001006
FEAR	Rel. Fear.	SHERLOCK	1772	19077009
FEAR	Relig. Fear.	BOURN	1760	45012004
FEAR	Relig. Fear.	LLOYD	1765	19002011

Keyword	In its Context	Author	Year	BkChpVrs
FEAR	Won.& Fear.	CREYGHTON	1720	44010032
FEAR	of Fear.	FLAVEL	1673	23008012
FEAST	Abus. Feast.	RIDGLEY	1718	02032006
FEASTING	Feasting.	TAYLOR	1668	49015032
FEASTING	Of Feasting.	SHERIDAN	1720	18001005
FEASTING	On Feasting.	WHEATLY	1746	18001004
FEET	Wash. Feet.	BRAGGE	1706	46013004
FELIC	Hol.& Felic	DAVIES	1766	61012014
FELIX	St. P.b. Felix	NEWTON	1782	47024010
FELL	Fell.with G.	CLARKSON	1696	65001003
FELL	Fell.with G.	MACE	1751	65001003
FELLOWS	Xn. Fellows.	WATTS	1753	48015006
FEM	Fem. Meek.	FORDYCE	1707	63003003
FEM	Fem. Piety.	FORDYCE	1767	20031030
FEM	Fem. Preach.	ERSKINE	1764	46004029
FEM	Fem. Vir.&c.	FORDYCE	1767	54004006
FEM	Fem. Virtue.	DYKES	1722	20031010
FEM	Fem. Virtue.	FORDYCE	1767	20031010
FESTIV	Jew. Festiv.	DAVIS	1756	46010022
FESTIV	Keep. Festiv.	SMITH	1740	49005008
FESTIVALS	Festivals.	HACKET	1675	19118024
FEW	Few saved.	SCOUGAL	1726	45013023
FEW	Tr. Xns.few.	CONEY	1730	69003004
FI	Fi.doom.im.	WARREN	1748	69021008
FIDEL	Conj. Fidel.	DYKES	1722	20031011
FIDEL	Rew. Fidel.	BOURN	1777	43025023
FIELD	Treas.field.	BULKLEY	1771	43013044
FIERY	Fiery Spirit.	HARRIS	1710	45009055
FIG	Bar. Fig-tree	DODD	1757	43021018
FIG	Bar. Fig-tree.	BYRDALL	1667	45013006
FIG	Bar. Fig-tree.	BRAGGE	1702	45013006
FIG	Bar. Fig-tree.	BULKLEY	1771	45013007
FIG	Barr. Fig- T.	LUCAS	1717	44011013
FIG	Barr. Fig- T.	BULKLEY	1771	44011021
FIG	Barr. Fig- T.	JORTIN	1774	44011021
FIG	Fig-tree.	BOURN	1764	45013006
FILIAL	Filial Love.	DODD	1772	46019026
FILL	Fill.w. Spir.	EVANS	1737	52005018
FIN	Fin. C. H. L.	SANDERSON	1722	58002002
FIN	Fin. Consum.	DUCHAL	1765	19102025
FIN	Fin. Course.	STAPLETON	1736	47020024
FIN	Fin. Distr.eq.	CLARKE	1735	63004017
FIN	Fin. Persev.	PENTYCROSS	1781	48008038
FIN	Fin. Punish.	LUCAS	1716	48002002
FIN	Fin. Retrib.	MACE	1751	43013043
FIN	Fin.account.	MAY	1757	48014012
FIN	Xt's.fin.app.	WHITAKER	1773	43025044
FINAL	Final Impen.	BOURDALOUE	1776	46008021
FIRE	Ag. Fear Fire	ANONYMOUS	1710	19004008
FIRE	Elij. Fire.	MORRIS	1743	12001011
FIRE	Fire Lond.	THORP	1677	43007012
FIRE	Fire Lond.	STILLINGFLEET	1707	30004011
FIRE	Fire Lond.	SALTER	1740	45013001
FIRE	Fire Lond.	DOUGHTY	1744	19107034
FIRE	Fire Lond.	HOWE	1744	27009025
FIRE	Fire Lond.	CHAUNCEY	1747	49010011
FIRE	Fire Lond.	APTHORPE	1770	34003002
FIRE	Suff.by Fire.	MILLS	1781	43025040
FIRST	First Fr. Sp.	WESTLEY	1746	48008001
FIRST	First Fr.o. G.	PARSONS	17--	43002001
FIRST	Rel.first.con.	WILLIAMS	1665	43006033
FIRST	Rel.first.con.	TILLOTSON	1735	43006033
FIRST	Xt.first F.&c.	BREKELL	1765	49015020
FISH	Drau of Fish.	BRAGGE	1702	45005004
FISH	Drau.of Fish.	FRANK	1672	45005005
FISH	Drau.of Fish.	FRANK	1672	45005008
FISH	Drau.of Fish.	MARKLAND	1729	45005008
FISH	Drau.of Fish.	BULKLEY	1771	45005009
FISH	Loav.& Fish.	DODD	1757	43014019
FISH	Loav.& Fish.	BULKLEY	1771	46006012
FIT	Exp.fit.of th.	DOWARS	1775	21003002
FIT	T. X's.c.fit.	FOSTER	1737	51004004
FIT	T. X's.c.fit.	CLEAVER	1743	51004004
FIVE	Five Thous.	BRAGGE	1702	46006005
FL	Works of Fl.	MOSS	1733	51005019
FLATTERY	Flattery.	HUST	1683	20026028
FLATTERY	Flattery.	PIERCE	1731	19005009
FLATTERY	Flattery.	SOUTH	1744	20029005
FLATTERY	Flattery.	CONEY	1750	19012003
FLATTERY	Flattery.	WEBB	1772	20026028
FLESH	Abst.fm.flesh.	MONRO	1693	63002011
FLESH	Abst.fm.flesh.	HOLE	1715	63002011
FLESH	Abst.fm.flesh.	IBBOT	1726	63002011
FLESH	Flesh. Lusts.	SHERLOCK	1772	63002011
FLESH	Flesh& Sp.	BROWNE	1749	51005017
FLESH	Flesh& Spir.	TAYLOR	1668	43026041
FLESH	Flesh& Spir.	WATTS	1753	48008001
FLESH	G.man.flesh.	WEBB	1765	57003016
FLESH	Life af. Flesh	CLARKE	1735	48008013
FLESH	Thorn flesh.	JORTIN	1774	50012007
FLESH	Wd.m.flesh.	BRETT	1720	46001014
FLIGHT	Flight Reb.	DODDRIDGE	1745	45001074
FLIGHT	Lot's Flight.	CENNICK	1762	01019017
FLOCK	Ret.flock Xt.	SPOONER	1751	63002015
FLOOD	Flood univ.	EDWARDS	1702	01007019
FLOODS	Viol. Floods.	FARRER	1768	19090004
FM	Abst.fm.flesh.	MONRO	1693	63002011
FM	Abst.fm.flesh.	HOLE	1715	63002011
FM	Abst.fm.flesh.	IBBOT	1726	63002011
FM	Arg.fm. Mir.	JORTIN	1774	46011047
FM	Del.fm Dea.	CENNICK	1762	46008051
FM	Deliv.fm. T.	FARINDON	1674	43006013
FM	Deliv.fm. T.	EDWARDS	1713	43006013
FM	Deliv.fm. Tem.	STEPHENS	1699	43006013
FM	Deliv.fm. Tem.	BUCK	17--	43006013
FM	Deliv.fm. Tem.	NEWCOME	1702	43006013
FM	Deliv.fm. Tem.	HOLE	1715	43006013
FM	Deliv.fm. Tem.	MANGEY	1717	43006013
FM	Deliv.fm. Tem.	BLACKALL	1723	43006013
FM	Deliv.fm. Tem.	JACKSON	1728	43006013
FM	Deliv.fm. Tem.	MOSS	1732	43006013
FM	Deliv.fm. Tem.	LITTLETON	1735	43006013

INDEXES TO THIRD VOLUME: E: KEYWORD-IN-CONTEXT INDEX OF OTHER SUBJECTS OR OCCASIONS

Keyword	In its Context	Author	Year	BkChpVrs
FM	Deliv.fm. Tem.	BISSE	1740	43006013
FM	Deliv.fm. Tem.	BLAIR	1740	43006013
FM	Dep.fm. Ini.	FOORD	1719	58002019
FM	Dep.fm. Ini.	DUNLOP	1722	58002019
FM	Eff.fm. Min.	ST.	1757	43005015
FM	Fall fm. G.	NOURSE	1708	24002019
FM	G.& E.fm. G.	LEIGHTONHOUSE	1697	23045007
FM	Life fm. Xt.	TAYLOR	1719	46010010
FM	Life fm. Xt.	SHEPHERD	1748	65005012
FM	Mess.fm. D.	PAYNE	1698	45016031
FM	Rem.fm.&c.	READING	1724	56003004
FM	Xt's. Div.p.fm	JOHNSON	1713	48001004
FM	Xt's. Div.p.fm	BEVERIDGE	1720	48001004
FM	Xy.pr.fm. Pr.	SKELTON	1754	69019010
FNT	Fnt. State.	CRAVEN	1775	61009027
FO	G. Fo.o. Go.	SCOTT	1743	62001017
FO	Seal Fo.o. G.	EVANSON	1773	58002019
FO	Xy.fo.on Ar.	COOKSEY	1743	63003015
FOL	Fol mock.at Si	STILLINGFLEET	1707	20014009
FOL	Fol mock.at Si	ROGERS	1730	20014009
FOL	Fol mock.at Si	TRAPP	1752	20014009
FOL	Fol. Hum. C.	LLOYD	1765	19118008
FOL	Fol.gain W.	PYLE	1777	45009025
FOL	Fol.mock.at Si	DAVIES	1720	20014009
FOL	Fol.mock.at Si	CLARKE	1734	20014009
FOLD	Fold Xt's Sh.	SMITH	1726	21001007
FOLL	Bei.foll.o. G.	LELAND	1762	52005001
FOLL	Foll. G.fully.	WALKER	1765	04014024
FOLL	Foll.of Sin.	WAPLE	1729	20014024
FOLLY	Folly o. Slan.	BARROW	1716	20010018
FOLLY	Folly of striv	BRAGGE	1713	23045009
FOLLY	Folly of striv	BALGUY	1750	23045009
FOLLY	Folly of wic.	LANGHORNE	1773	23057021
FOLLY	Folly of Sin.	BRADY	1730	20001010
FOLLY	Folly. Deism	SHERLOCK	1702	46014001
FOLLY	Folly Riches	MARKLAND	1729	21005010
FOLLY	Folly Sinn.	DUNLOP	1722	24002005
FOLLY	Folly Sinner.	HOPKINS	1710	20014009
FOLLY	Sin Folly.	MOORE	1716	23030010
FOLLY	W.exc. Folly	ANONYMOUS	1776	21002013
FOOD	Food of Soul.	DUCHAL	1765	46003034
FOOD	Sp.&n.food.	BEVERIDGE	1720	46006027
FOOL	Ans.a Fool.	WARBURTON	1767	20026004
FOOL	Fool.&w. B.	SOUTH	1727	43007026
FOOL	Fool.&w. B.	BLAIR	1740	43007026
FOOL	Fool. Virgins	FOORD	1719	43025010
FOOL	Fool.talk.	BARROW	1716	52005004
FOOL	Rich Fool.	BRAGGE	1702	45012016
FOOL	Rich Fool.	DODD	1757	45012021
FOOL	Rich Fool.	DODD	1757	45012025
FOOL	Rich Fool.	BULKLEY	1771	45012021
FOOL	Rich Fool.	SHERLOCK	1772	45012021
FOOL	Wor.w.fool.	SOUTH	1727	49003019
FOOT	Keep. Foot.	JORTIN	1774	21005001
FOR	B.of Pers.for	FARINDON	1672	43005010
FOR	B.of Pers.for	HORNECK	1706	43005010

Keyword	In its Context	Author	Year	BkChpVrs
FOR	B.of Pers.for	GROVE	1742	43005010
FOR	For sick.	BLADEN	1695	50005001
FOR	For.of Godl.	SECKER	1770	58003005
FOR	For Am. Col.	WATSON	1763	23049006
FOR	G's. For.& P.	MARSHALL	1731	64003009
FOR	G's. For.& P.	NEWSON	1781	64003009
FOR	Le. L.in for.	JONES	1775	03017008
FOR	Plea for Tr.	WALKER	1710	11018021
FOR	Pr.for You.	MAY	1753	13004010
FOR	Prep.for suff.	FLAVEL	1673	47021013
FOR	Reb.for Sin.	T.	1667	23066015
FOR	Rel.for Soc.	TILLOTSON	1735	20014034
FOR	Rep.for.of F.	HORNE	1756	23040003
FOR	Str.for Faith.	STENNETT	1738	53001027
FOR	Suff.for R.sa.	BRADBURY	1722	63003014
FORBEAR	G's Forbear.	HORTON	1679	45013008
FORBEAR	Xn. Forbear.	COCK	1710	52004002
FORBEARANCE	Forbearance	STRAIGHT	1741	51006002
FORCE	Force o. Con.	MAYNARD	1722	47024025
FORCE	Force words.	SOUTH	1727	23005020
FORCE	Force Cons.	SHERLOCK	1772	43014001
FORCES	b. K's forces.	WHITTEL	1692	04014014
FOREKN	G's. Forekn.	HUSSEY	1753	48004011
FORET	Foret.o. Hea.	WATTS	1753	48008023
FORET	Mess.foret.	BURTON	1764	23053001
FORET	Mess.foret.	FARQUAR	1772	23053003
FORET	Persecut.foret	HORNECK	1706	43005011
FORET	Persecut.foret	BLAIR	1740	43005010
FORET	Xt's. D.foret.	MEDE	1672	45024045
FORG	Forg. Debtor	BULKLEY	1771	43018023
FORG	Forg. Enem.	NEWLIN	1728	45011004
FORG	Forg. Injur.	GARDINER	1720	43005038
FORG	Forg. Injur.	BRADY	1730	43018035
FORG	Forg. Injur.	MOSS	1737	43006014
FORG	Forg. Injur.	BLAIR	1740	43005038
FORG	Forg. Injur.	BLAIR	1740	43006014
FORG	Forg. Injur.	WESTON	1747	45017004
FORG	Forg. Injur.	DODWELL	1749	54003012
FORG	Forg.of Inju.	CREYGHTON	1720	52004032
FORG	Forg.of Inju.	CLARKE	1736	52004032
FORG	Forg.of Sins.	KILLINBECK	1717	43009002
FORG	Forg.t. Xt.a.	WHICHCOTE	1698	47013038
FORG	Forg.t. Xt.a.	HOOLE	1748	47013038
FORG	Forg.t. Xt.al.	SHERLOCK	1719	47013038
FORGIV	Forgiv. Sins.	BATES	1700	19130004
FORGIV	Forgiv. Sins.	MARSHALL	1750	19130004
FORGIV	Forgiv. Sins.	OGDEN	1777	45005020
FORGIV	G's forgiv.	SOUTH	1744	19130004
FORGIV	Hope forgiv.	WITHERSPOON	1768	19130004
FORGIVEN	Xn. Forgiven.	TILLY	1737	45006037
FORGIVENESS	Forgiveness.	VINCENT	1676	19032001
FORGIVENESS	Forgiveness.	STEPHENS	1699	43006012
FORGIVENESS	Forgiveness.	NEWCOME	1702	43006012
FORGIVENESS	Forgiveness.	HOLE	1716	45006036
FORGIVENESS	Forgiveness.	BEVERIDGE	1720	19032001
FORGIVENESS	Forgiveness.	MOSS	1732	43006012

Keyword	In its Context	Author	Year	BkChpVrs
FORGIVENESS	Forgiveness.	STEPHEN	1770	43006012
FORGIVN	Forgivn.&c.	MATTHEWS	1706	45023034
FORGIVNESS	Forgivness.	FARINDON	1672	43006012
FORGIVNESS	Forgivness.	EDWARDS	1713	43006012
FORGIVNESS	Forgivness.	STANHOPE	1714	43018021
FORGIVNESS	Forgivness.	HOLE	1716	43018021
FORGIVNESS	Forgivness.	MANGEY	1717	43006012
FORGIVNESS	Forgivness.	CLAGETT	1720	43006012
FORGIVNESS	Forgivness.	HENRY	1726	43006012
FORGIVNESS	Forgivness.	JACKSON	1728	43006012
FORGIVNESS	Forgivness.	LITTLETON	1735	43006012
FORGIVNESS	Forgivness.	BISSE	1740	43006012
FORGIVNESS	Forgivness.	BLAIR	1740	43006012
FORGIVNESS	Forgivness.	BOURN	1764	43018021
FORGIVNESS	Forgivness.	CHURCHILL	1765	43006012
FORGIVNESS	Forgivness.	FRANCIS	1771	43018021
FORM	Form. Prof.	PORTER	1661	58003005
FORM	Form. Xt.	HORTON	1679	51004019
FORM	Form.in Rel.	LAKE	1705	58003005
FORM	Form.in Rel.	DORMAN	1743	58003005
FORMS	Forms of Pr.	PEARSON	1711	45011002
FORMS	Forms of Pr.	BULL	1713	57002001
FORMS	Forms of Pr.	CLAGETT	1720	43006009
FORNICATION	Fornication.	MOORE	1667	61013004
FORNICATION	Fornication.	BARLOW	1690	49006018
FORS	Xns fors.all.	SUTTON	1754	45014033
FORSAK	Forsak. God.	BOSTON	1753	24002013
FORT	Mod. Fort.	FIDDES	1720	20030008
FORTH	set forth S. S.	ROBINSON	1740	46006068
FORTIT	L's. Fortit.	WHITE	1757	61012001
FORTIT	Xn. Fortit.	EVANS	1737	64001005
FORTITU	Xn. Fortitu.	ABERNETHY	1748	64001005
FORTITU	Xn. Fortitu.	KENNICOTT	1757	48008035
FORTITU	Xn. Fortitu.	BADDELLEY	1766	27003016
FORTITUDE	Fortitude.	DODWELL	1749	45012004
FORTITUDE	Fortitude.	HUNT	1748	49016013
FORTITUDE	Fortitude.	DUCHAL	1765	49016002
FOU	Fou.life op.	FLAVEL	1673	49002002
FOUN	Foun.of Vir.	MOLE	1732	19011007
FOUN	T.sure Foun.	ROMAINE	1756	49003011
FOUND	Sure Found.	ROMAINE	1756	23028016
FOUND	Xt.only Found.	DAVIES	1766	23028016
FOUND	Xt Found Pr.	BEVERIDGE	1720	50001020
FOUNDERS	Co. Founders	COLBATCH	1718	20010007
FOUNT	Fount. Bless.	ERSKINE	1764	50005018
FR	Ag.fr. Proph.	CHISHULL	1707	62005008
FR	Bel. Xt's. Fr.	BOSTON	1773	46015014
FR	Ch.s. Fr. Pro.	HICKES	1713	50004009
FR	Death of Fr.	MOIR	1776	23057001
FR	First Fr. Sp.	WESTLEY	1746	48008001
FR	First Fr.o. G.	PARSONS	17--	43002001
FR	Fr.wor. Enj.	KIMBER	1756	65002017
FR	P. Fr. Bir.d.	SHAW	1729	13028009
FR	Rel.fr.mind.	MARSHALL	1731	48002028
FR	Xt.seek. Fr.	CLARKSON	1696	45013006
FRAIL	Frail. Man.	CROWE	1744	19039004

Keyword	In its Context	Author	Year	BkChpVrs
FRAILTY	Hum. Frailty	CREYTON	1720	49010012
FRAME	Frame Man.	DAVIES	1720	19139014
FRAME	Frame Man.	ATTERBURY	1743	19139014
FRAT	Frat. Love	DODD	1772	46011005
FRAUD	Ag. Fraud.	FIDDES	1720	55004006
FRAUD	Ag. Fraud.	ENFIELD	1772	03019013
FRAUD	Fraud.	STEBBING	1760	55004003
FRAUD	Fraud.	WILSON	1781	01043012
FRAUD	Sin of Fraud.	CLARKE	1736	47005003
FRE	Fre.of Will.	MARRIOTT	1774	19073011
FRE	M's. Fre.&c.	GODDARD	1781	62001014
FREE	Ab.free-th.	FOSTER	1732	51005013
FREE	Free gr.of G.	FELTON	1748	48003023
FREE	Free. Salvat.	PENTYCROSS	1781	48004005
FREE	Free Enqui.	BENSON	1748	55005021
FREE	Free Grace.	WILKINSON	1660	37013001
FREE	Free Grace.	BRIDGE	1671	52002008
FREE	Free Grace.	BRIDGE	1671	56002016
FREE	Free Grace.	FARMER	1756	45023042
FREE	Free Grace.	ROWLAND	1774	45023042
FREE	Free Judgm.	DUCHAL	1765	50003002
FREE	Free Know.	HEYLYN	1749	01002017
FREE	Free Will.	TOPLADY	1774	19115001
FREE	G's.ser. Free.	DAVIS	1756	45001074
FREED	Freed. Saints	WELCH	1752	45001074
FREED	Gosp. Freed.	CLAGETT	1720	46008036
FREED	Gosp. Freed.	EDWARDS	1726	46008036
FREED	Gosp. Freed.	BATTY	1739	46008036
FREED	True Freed.	ECCLES	1755	43002030
FREEHOLD	b. Freehold.	OWEN	1713	10019027
FREN	Ag. Fren. K.	KNAGGS	1705	50013011
FRENCH	French inv.	BRADBURY	1772	23007005
FREQ	Freq. Com.	BEVERIDGE	1708	49011026
FREQ	Freq. Prayer.	WAPLE	1718	45018001
FREQ	Freq. Worsh.	LOVELL	1774	23002002
FRI	Peace& Fri.	BRADY	1730	48012018
FRIEND	D.of Friend.	CLEMENT	1774	19090012
FRIEND	Friend w. G.	COOKE	1739	46015014
FRIEND	Friend. Rep.	ATTERBURY	1699	20019025
FRIEND	Friend. Rep.	FIDDES	1720	20019025
FRIEND	Friend. Visit.	HENRY	1704	47015036
FRIEND	G.our Friend	WALKER	1765	48008031
FRIEND	N.of Friend.	HORNE	1769	19055012
FRIEND	Sacr. Friend.	DEVEREL	1777	09018003
FRIEND	Xr.of Friend	LOCKIER	1761	20017017
FRIEND	Xt. Friend.	CASE	1774	20018024
FRIENDS	Xt's. Friends.	ALLESTREE	1684	46015014
FRIENDS	Xt's. Friends.	HAVETT	1703	46015014
FRIENDS	Xt's. Friends.	HICKES	1713	46015014
FRIENDS	Xt's. Friends.	BEESTON	1739	46015014
FRIENDSHIP	Friendship.	WILKINS	1682	21004009
FRIENDSHIP	Friendship.	SOUTH	1727	46015015
FRIENDSHIP	Friendship.	PIERCE	1731	20018024
FRIENDSHIP	Friendship.	DODWELL	1749	02033011
FRIENDSHIP	Friendship.	DODWELL	1749	05013006
FRIENDSHIP	Friendship.	DODWELL	1749	20018024

INDEXES TO THIRD VOLUME: E: KEYWORD-IN-CONTEXT INDEX OF OTHER SUBJECTS OR OCCASIONS

Keyword	In its Context	Author	Year	BkChpVrs
FRIENDSHIP	Friendship.	CONEY	1750	20017017
FRIENDSHIP	Friendship.	HOLLAND	1753	20017017
FRIENDSHIP	Friendship.	DUCHAL	1765	20018024
FRIENDSHIP	Friendship.	DODD	1772	46013023
FRM	Frm. Pow. G.	TILLOTSON	1735	58003005
FRM	Frm.sou. W.	BEVERIDGE	1720	58001013
FROST	Ch.s. Frost.	TREBECK	1739	53004006
FROST	Great Frost.	CAMFIELD	1684	19147015
FRUGALITY	Frugality.	SEATON	1720	01031017
FRUIT	Bear. Fruit.	BEVERIDGE	1720	46015008
FRUIT	Fruit of Sp.	HAWEIS	1762	52005009
FRUIT	Fruit of Sp.	COWPER	1773	52005009
FRUITS	Fruits o. Xty.	HORBERRY	1774	43007006
FRUITS	Fruits of Rel.	STENNETT	1769	48006022
FRUITS	Fruits of Sp.	ATTERBURY	1742	51005022
FRUITS	Fruits of Sp.	KIMBER	1756	51005022
FRUITS	Fruits of Sp.	SECKER	1771	51005022
FRUITS	Fruits& Disc.o	STANHOPE	1714	43007015
FRUITS	Fruits& Disc.o	HOLE	1716	43007015
FRUITS	Fruits& Disc.o	GARDINER	1720	43007015
FRUITS	Fruits& Disc.o	BLAIR	1740	43007015
FRUITS	Fruits& Disc.o	WESTLEY	1750	43007015
FRUITS	Fruits Rep.	BURTON	1684	43003008
FRUITS	Fruits Rep.	SCOTT	1700	43003008
FTH	Const.in Fth.	BEVERIDGE	1720	61010023
FTH	Fth.triump.	CONEY	1730	61011024
FTH	Fth&go. Co.	BRAGGE	1713	57001018
FTH	Fth&go. Co.	WELTON	1724	57001018
FTH	Fth&go. Co.	MACE	1751	57001018
FTH	Fth&w.b. L.	TAYLOR	1678	62002024
FTH	Fth&works.	MOORE	1716	62002022
FTH	Fth&works.	NEWLIN	1720	62002010
FTH	Fth&works.	WARREN	1748	62002010
FU	Cer.fu.judg.	HAWKINS	1725	49015019
FU	Fu. Rew.cer.	DORRINGTON	1705	57004007
FU	Fu. St.n.t. H.	CONYBEARE	1757	49015019
FU	H.own Fu.s.	ALEXANDER	1766	21009010
FU	Qual.f fu. H.	CLARKE	1734	69003004
FU	Qual.f.fu. H.	BULL	1713	69003004
FUL	L.& P.ful. Xt.	BLACKALL	1723	43005017
FULF	Love fulf. L.	QUINCY	1750	51005014
FULLY	Foll. G.fully.	WALKER	1765	04014024
FULN	Fuln. G.wh.	ALSOP	1690	52003019
FULN	Fuln.o Med.	GILL	1773	54001019
FULN	Fuln.of G.	DUCHAL	1765	52003019
FUNCT	Min. Funct.	SCOUGAL	1726	50002016
FUNCT	Min. Funct.	ATTERBURY	1743	50002016
FUND	Fund.of Xy.	SKELTON	1754	61010038
FUNDAMENT	Fundament.	CLARKE	1736	61006001
FUT	Bel.of Fut. S.	ANONYMOUS	1776	45016025
FUT	Con.fut.jud.	STILLINGFLEET	1707	21011009
FUT	Con.fut.jud.	SUTTON	1754	21011009
FUT	Evid.fut.st.	AMORY	1766	43007011
FUT	Ex.fut. Rew.	DORRINGTON	1705	54003001
FUT	Fut. Happ.	NEWMAN	1760	19036009
FUT	Fut. Happ.	DUCHAL	1765	19036008
FUT	Fut. Happ.g.	TILLOTSON	1735	65003002
FUT	Fut. Happin.	TRAILE	1705	46017024
FUT	Fut. Happin.	WILCOX	1757	46017024
FUT	Fut. Inherit.	WHITAKER	1674	54001012
FUT	Fut. Judg.	HAVETT	1703	21012014
FUT	Fut. Judg.	EVANS	1725	21011009
FUT	Fut. Judgm.	NEEDHAM	1679	50005010
FUT	Fut. Judgm.	GLANVIL	1681	47017031
FUT	Fut. Judgm.	MANTON	1693	47017031
FUT	Fut. Judgm.	SHERLOCK	1699	47017031
FUT	Fut. Judgm.	PIGOTT	1702	57004001
FUT	Fut. Judgm.	DORRINGTON	1703	50005010
FUT	Fut. Judgm.	BARROW	1716	21003017
FUT	Fut. Judgm.	HOPKINS	1712	50005010
FUT	Fut. Judgm.	BARROW	1716	47010042
FUT	Fut. Judgm.	MOORE	1716	47017031
FUT	Fut. Judgm.	WAKE	1716	47024025
FUT	Fut. Judgm.	KILLINBECK	1717	64003004
FUT	Fut. Judgm.	FIDDES	1720	47017031
FUT	Fut. Judgm.	FIDDES	1720	47024025
FUT	Fut. Judgm.	COLLIER	1725	50005010
FUT	Fut. Judgm.	CLARKE	1727	47017031
FUT	Fut. Judgm.	TILLOTSON	1735	50005010
FUT	Fut. Judgm.	ORR	1739	47017030
FUT	Fut. Judgm.	JEPHSON	1742	43025046
FUT	Fut. Judgm.	SEED	1743	43026024
FUT	Fut. Judgm.	STRAIGHT	1741	50005010
FUT	Fut. Judgm.	BURNET	1747	47017031
FUT	Fut. Judgm.	AMORY	1748	50005010
FUT	Fut. Judgm.	PRIEST	1753	64003003
FUT	Fut. Judgm.	ANONYMOUS	1756	69022012
FUT	Fut. Judgm.	TIDCOMBE	1757	50005010
FUT	Fut. Judgm.	MOIR	1759	50005010
FUT	Fut. Judgm.	FARRINGTON	1769	18019025
FUT	Fut. Judgm.	LELAND	1769	21003017
FUT	Fut. Judgm.	BRACKENRIDGE	1764	69022012
FUT	Fut. Judgm.	ELSMERE	1767	61009027
FUT	Fut. Judgm.	SMITH	1769	47017031
FUT	Fut. Judgm.	SIMS	1772	61009002
FUT	Fut. Judgm.	ORR	1772	63001017
FUT	Fut. Judgm.	JORTIN	1774	48002006
FUT	Fut. Judgm.	OGDEN	1777	55004014
FUT	Fut. Judgm.	SAURIN	1777	61009027
FUT	Fut. Judgm.	PYLE	1777	64003011
FUT	Fut. Know.	REAY	1755	49013012
FUT	Fut. Life.	REAY	1755	46006068
FUT	Fut. Life.	HODGE	1758	46006068
FUT	Fut. Punish.	FARRINGTON	1769	43025046
FUT	Fut. Punish.	BOURN	1760	56001009
FUT	Fut. R.& Pun.	ADEY	1755	46005028
FUT	Fut. Re.& P.	ROGERS	1736	51006007
FUT	Fut. Ret.just.	BARNES	1752	45016025
FUT	Fut. Rew.	CLARKE	1736	69022011
FUT	Fut. Rew..	BALGUY	1748	51006007
FUT	Fut. Rew.	FARRINGTON	1769	49002009
FUT	Fut. Sate.	RANDOLPH	1755	21012014

Keyword	In its Context	Author	Year	BkChpVrs
FUT	Fut. State.	HART	1702	46014002
FUT	Fut. State.	ROMAINE	1739	44012024
FUT	Fut. State.	FOSTER	1744	21009002
FUT	Fut. State.	BURNET	1747	20014032
FUT	Fut. State.	BALGUY	1748	21012007
FUT	Fut. State.	BELLAMY	1744	47023008
FUT	Fut. State.	LARDNER	1751	19084011
FUT	Fut. State.	BOURN	1760	46014001
FUT	Fut. State.	BOURN	1760	47026008
FUT	Fut. State.	BOURN	1760	48002016
FUT	Fut. State.	DAVIES	1766	50004018
FUT	Fut. State.	CRAVEN	1775	21009002
FUT	Fut. State.	JORTIN	1774	61011013
FUT	Fut. State.	CRAVEN	1775	51006009
FUT	Fut. State.	CRAVEN	1775	61013008
FUT	Fut. State.	CRAVEN	1775	64003012
FUT	Fut. State.	BRAILSFORD	1776	48015004
FUT	Fut. State.	BLAIR	1777	49013012
FUT	Fut. State.	LAMONT	1780	63001003
FUT	Fut.gen. J.	AMORY	1748	43025031
FUT	Fut.jud.&c.	HORTON	1679	50005010
FUT	Fut.life hap.	STRADLING	1692	49015019
FUT	Fut.life.	BRYSON	1778	65003002
FUT	Fut.rew. Xn.	WILLIAMS	1774	69014025
FUT	Fut.rew.un.	BULL	1713	61011026
FUT	Fut.rewards.	WHITBY	1720	48002006
FUT	Fut.st.its Ev.	FOSTER	1732	58001010
FUT	Fut.state.	CALAMY	1726	58001010
FUT	Fut.state.	BOURN	1760	58001010
FUT	Fut.state.	TOTTIE	1775	58001010
FUT	Fut Pun.ce.	PENTYCROSS	1781	19010013
FUT	Hap.o.fut.st.	BLAIR	1780	69007009
FUT	Happ.fut. St.	WELTON	1724	49002009
FUT	Happ.fut.st.	CARTER	1729	53003020
FUT	Happ.fut.st.	BROWNE	1749	53003020
FUT	Infl.fut. L.	BRYSON	1778	65003003
FUT	J.sp.&fut.st.	CARTER	1729	51006007
FUT	Pr.&fut.st. B.	COLLIER	1686	49015029
FUT	Uncert.of fut.	LEIGHTONHOUSE	1697	20027001
FUT	Uncert.of fut.	MOSS	1737	20027001
FUTIL	Futil.enq. F.	WHELDON	1772	46021022
G	A.f.m.f. G.a.	PARSONS	1774	50003006
G	Ab. G's. G.	HORTON	1679	48002004
G	Ab.of mi. G.	BULKLEY	1771	49011017
G	Abid.w. G.	CHANDLER	1769	49007024
G	Acc.with G.	BOSTON	1775	50008012
G	Acknow. G,	ABERNETHY	1748	20003006
G	Ag.b.run. G.	UNWIN	1773	48013007
G	Alm.g.& M.	HOLE	1725	49013003
G	Appro.to G.	WATTS	1753	19065004
G	B.& Att.o. G.	HUSSEY	1755	48001019
G	Bad M.rep.g.	SNAPE	1745	63004004
G	Bapt.o. H. G.	JOHNSON	1776	47011016
G	Be.& Fear G.	LITTLETON	1680	62002010
G	Be.&c.o. G.	CONANT	1722	46017003
G	Be.&g.of G.	JONES	1741	47014017

Keyword	In its Context	Author	Year	BkChpVrs
G	Bei.& P.o. G.	HOPKINS	1708	61011006
G	Bei.foll.o. G.	LELAND	1762	52005001
G	Being in G.	SCOTT	1743	47017028
G	Being in G.	HUSSEY	1755	47017028
G	Being of G.	NICOLSON	1661	01001001
G	Being of G.	ATTERBURY	1703	19014001
G	Being of G.	BARROW	1716	01001027
G	Being of G.	BARROW	1716	19019003
G	Being of G.	EDWARDS	1713	61001006
G	Being of G.	WISHEART	1716	61011006
G	Being of G.	LESTLEY	1720	02003014
G	Being of G.	PARSONS	1721	01002005
G	Being of G.	WAPLE	1729	61011006
G	Being of G.	ADAMS	1736	61011006
G	Being of G.	WILDER	1741	61011006
G	Being of G.	ABERNETHY	1743	48001019
G	Being of G.	DORMAN	1743	61011006
G	Being of G.	LELAND	1769	48001020
G	Being of G.	OGDEN	1777	61002006
G	Being G.pro.	BARROW	1716	46005017
G	Bel. H.in G.	WILCOX	1757	25003024
G	Belief in G.	CLARKE	1732	48004003
G	Belief.in G.	PARKHURST	1707	46005024
G	Belov.of G.	WHITFIELD	1771	05032012
G	Best G.et.life	AMORY	1766	46006068
G	Bib.wd.o. G.	SKELTON	1754	58003014
G	Bl.keep G. C.	GALLIMORE	1694	69022014
G	Blasp. H. G.	BREKELL	1765	44003028
G	Bles.ap.b. G.	WATTS	1753	19042002
G	Bles.ap.b. G.	PEARSE	1763	19042002
G	Bp. G. L.	WORTHINGTON	1769	23023005
G	Bp. G. L.	WORTHINGTON	1769	23023008
G	C.b. F.&f. G.	PIKE	1748	48004016
G	C.pro. G. D.	RAWSON	1708	47015039
G	Care on G.	KIDDER	1697	63005007
G	Ch. Ha.of G.	WALLIN	1774	52002022
G	Ch.g.&b. M.	TILLOTSON	1735	65003010
G	Child of G.	CLARKE	1732	48008016
G	Child.g. M.	ROSEWELL	1720	19116016
G	Child.of G.	HORNECK	1706	43005045
G	Civ.&rel. G.	MURRAY	1777	01003001
G	Com.w. G.	HENRY	1713	19025005
G	Com.with G.	SYLVESTER	1683	65001007
G	Com.with G.	HUNT	1748	65001006
G	Comm.of G.	BAYLEY	1778	19119048
G	Comp.of G.	ERSKINE	1764	45014023
G	Conf.tow. G.	ABERNETHY	1751	65003012
G	Conv.w. G.	CRUSO	1698	24003032
G	Corrp. G.w.	GIPPS	1697	20030006
G	Cries sons G.	CENNICK	1762	44015037
G	D. G.ag.evil.	QUINCY	1750	48012021
G	De. S.& H. G.	EVANS	1766	65005020
G	Dec.o. G.&c.	WISHEART	1716	52001011
G	Dec.o. G.&c.	HUBBARD	1757	52001011
G	Dedic.to G.	DAVIES	1766	49006019
G	Disob. G. In.	WILSON	1781	46015022

INDEXES TO THIRD VOLUME: E: KEYWORD-IN-CONTEXT INDEX OF OTHER SUBJECTS OR OCCASIONS

Keyword	In its Context	Author	Year	BkChpVrs
G	Do all Gl. G.	BEVERIDGE	1720	49010031
G	Do all Gl. G.	BERRIMAN	1751	49010031
G	Domin. G.	WHITBY	1710	19103019
G	Domin.of G.	CHURCHILL	1765	43006013
G	Draw.n. G.	EATON	1764	19073028
G	Dut. G.& K.	BALL	1682	43022021
G	Dut. G.& K.	ROSEWELL	1716	20024021
G	Dut. G.& K.	TOPPING	1716	63002017
G	Duty to G.	HUNT	1748	18022021
G	Duty to G.	JORTIN	1774	59002011
G	E.walk.w. G	MACE	1751	01005024
G	E.walk.w. G.	FANCH	1768	01005024
G	E.walk.w. G.	BRACKENRIDGE	1775	01005024
G	Edu.poor G.	WILSON	1781	58001004
G	En.g.&b.m.	LUCAS	1722	20014032
G	En.g.&b.m.	TILLOTSON	1735	20014032
G	End Xt's.g.h.	JOHNSON	1740	59002014
G	Eove of G.	WESTON	1747	49013003
G	Etern.of G.	CHARNOCK	1684	19090002
G	Etern.of G.	WHITBY	1710	57001017
G	Etern.of G.	TILLOTSON	1735	19090002
G	Etern.of G.	CLARKE	1732	69001008
G	Etern.of G.	ABERNETHY	1743	19090002
G	Etern.of G.	ATTERBURY	1743	19090002
G	Etern.of G.	DAVIS	1756	19102026
G	Etern.of G.	BRACKENRIDGE	1764	19090002
G	Etern.of G.	LELAND	1769	19090002
G	Etern.of G.	SAURIN	1775	64003008
G	Evil-sp.in g.	BARROW	1716	59003002
G	Evil-sp.in g.	SCURLOCK	1733	59003002
G	Evil-sp.in g.	SIMS	1772	59003002
G	Ex.& E.of G.	KNOWLES	1750	48001020
G	Exist.of G.	KNOWLES	1750	18011007
G	F.& Po.o. G.	ATTERBURY	1699	58003005
G	F.& Po.o. G.	BULL	1713	58003005
G	F.f.b. L.& G.	WILSON	1781	52005003
G	F.o. G.&c. O.	JONES	1778	63002017
G	Fa. Gift o. G.	SHERLOCK	1772	52002008
G	Faith in G.	BEVERIDGE	1720	46014001
G	Faith in G.	CLARKE	1732	61011006
G	Faith in G.	ATTERBURY	1743	46014001
G	Faith in G.	KNOWLES	1750	34003017
G	Fall fm. G.	NOURSE	1708	24002019
G	Fe. G.&h. K.	SEABURY	17--	63002017
G	Fear of G.	BRIDGE	1671	16005015
G	Fear of G.	MORE	1692	20001007
G	Fear of G.	MARCH	1699	19076007
G	Fear of G.	HAVETT	1703	21012013
G	Fear of G.	SKELTON	1754	20014026
G	Fear of G.	KIMBER	1756	20014027
G	Fear G.& M.	DUNLOP	1722	45012004
G	Fell.with G.	CLARKSON	1696	65001003
G	Fell.with G.	MACE	1751	65001003
G	First Fr.o. G.	PARSONS	17--	43002001
G	Foll. G.fully.	WALKER	1765	04014024
G	Free gr.of G.	FELTON	1748	48003023

Keyword	In its Context	Author	Year	BkChpVrs
G	Friend w. G.	COOKE	1739	46015014
G	Frm. Pow. G.	TILLOTSON	1735	58003005
G	Fuln. G.wh.	ALSOP	1690	52003019
G	Fuln.of G.	DUCHAL	1765	52003019
G	Fut. Happ.g.	TILLOTSON	1735	65003002
G	G.&.b. Com.	TRAPP	1752	20018014
G	G.& E.fm. G.	LEIGHTONHOUSE	1697	23045007
G	G.&b. Princ.	IBBOT	1726	43006022
G	G.&b. Spir.	WILSON	1781	44005013
G	G.&ev. Con.	SMITH	1740	46020019
G	G.&nat.per.	GUYSE	1757	46004024
G	G. A.of o. R.	BEVERIDGE	1720	50005018
G	G. Centur.	DODD	1757	43008013
G	G. Comm.	NEWTON	1782	43022040
G	G. Creat.&c.	HUNT	1748	48011036
G	G. Creator.	MARSHAL	1731	19071006
G	G. E. Neigh.	ANONYMOUS	1776	43005016
G	G. Eff. Gos.	SECKER	1770	43010034
G	G. Fath. Al.	BARROW	1716	69011017
G	G. Father&c	ORR	1772	38001006
G	G. Fo.o. Go.	SCOTT	1743	62001017
G	G. H. Men.	TILLOTSON	1735	19073025
G	G. Judge o.a.	HILL	1755	61012023
G	G. M's Hope.	LACY	1720	19039008
G	G. M's Xrter.	WILCOX	1757	19084011
G	G. News f. H	TOPLADY	1774	19089012
G	G. News G.	ROWLAND	1774	43002008
G	G. Obj. Tr.	HOLLAND	1753	19118008
G	G. Ref. Dist.	DUCHE	1779	19042011
G	G. Refuge.	FARMER	1756	19142004
G	G. Saviour.	KIMBER	1756	19050015
G	G. Shepherd	BRODHURST	1733	19023003
G	G. Support.	ADAMS	1736	19011003
G	G. Ten. Gos.	BOTT	1724	45009056
G	G. Ten. Gos.	ORR	1739	45009056
G	G. Un.a Pro.	CHANDLER	1691	55005013
G	G. Xrter.b. F.	WORTHINGTON	1775	20022001
G	G.auth.pea.	COTES	1721	49014033
G	G.best. Go.	BEVERIDGE	1720	19073025
G	G.chos. Inh.	ORTON	1776	19047004
G	G.cor.&par.	HOWE	1771	19099008
G	G.disp. Ev.	LELAND	1769	43010030
G	G.disp.all.	CLARKE	1735	20016004
G	G.dw.w. M.	FLEMING	1701	14006018
G	G.g. Hearts.	LELAND	1769	19033015
G	G.giv. Rain.	FOTHERGILL	1765	47014017
G	G.go.world.	HUNT	1748	19022028
G	G.go.world.	BRACKENRIDGE	1764	19022028
G	G.go.world.	LELAND	1769	19022028
G	G.gov. Pass.	BLAIR	1780	19076010
G	G.gov.m. A.	LELAND	1769	43010029
G	G.hates Sin.	DORRINGTON	1703	20015009
G	G.hear Pray.	BOSTON	1775	19065002
G	G.immutab.	ATTERBURY	1743	62001017
G	G.immutab.	BLAIR	1780	62001017
G	G.impartial.	LANGHORNE	1773	48002011

Keyword	In its Context	Author	Year	BkChpVrs
G	G.impartial.	JORTIN	1774	48002011
G	G.in Xt. Sav.	WATTS	1753	23045022
G	G.incomp.	HUNT	1748	18011007
G	G.incomp.	HUSSEY	1755	18011007
G	G.incomp.	ROE	1766	18011007
G	G.is Light.	COCK	1710	65001005
G	G.is Light.	STURMY	1716	65001005
G	G.know. H.	HORT	1738	24017009
G	G.l.b.or. Xn.	WILKINS	1682	59002010
G	G.l.b.or. Xn.	ROGERS	1735	59002010
G	G.m.lia.cor.	HICKMAN	1706	49015033
G	G.m.lia.cor.	TREBECK	1730	49015033
G	G.m's Del.	LELAND	1769	19037004
G	G.man.flesh.	WEBB	1765	57003016
G	G.n.arbitra.	FOSTER	1732	48009020
G	G.no res. P.	MOORE	1716	47010034
G	G.no res. P.	IBBOT	1726	47010034
G	G.no res. P.	MUNTON	1756	47010034
G	G.no res. P.	HUSSEY	1758	47010034
G	G.no resp.of P	BARROW	1716	48002011
G	G.no resp.of P	FOSTER	1744	48002011
G	G.no R.o. P.	PYLE	1777	63001017
G	G.not A.of S.	STEPHENS	1737	23045007
G	G.o. Father.	MANGEY	1717	43006009
G	G.o. Father.	LITTLETON	1735	43006009
G	G.o. Father.	CHURCHILL	1765	43006009
G	G.o. Obj. F.	NEWLIN	1720	45012004
G	G.o. Obj. F.	TILLOTSON	1735	45012004
G	G.on.o. Lwg.	MICHELL	1737	62004012
G	G.only b.ser.	BEVERIDGE	1720	43004010
G	G.our father	NICOLSON	1661	48008015
G	G.our Father	CLARKE	1732	43023009
G	G.our Friend	WALKER	1765	48008031
G	G.p. M's. F.	ANONYMOUS	1776	43006031
G	G.pres.of w.	LELAND	1769	16009006
G	G.prov'd.u.	SKELTON	1754	43011005
G	G.rev.mself.	CARR	1777	57002004
G	G.s. H.& Ea.	ORTON	1776	19113005
G	G.short d.	ANONYMOUS	1745	19089045
G	G.sp.&sp.w.	BAGSHAW	1662	46004024
G	G.sp.&sp.w.	CHARNOCK	1684	46004024
G	G.sp.&sp.w.	CLAGETT	1720	46004024
G	G.sp.&sp.w.	ATTERBURY	1743	46004024
G	G.sp.&sp.w.	BALGUY	1748	46004024
G	G.sup.u.suf.	TILLOTSON	1735	63004019
G	G.t. Father.	BARROW	1716	52004006
G	G.tempts n.	BERRIMAN	1763	62001013
G	G.terrible.	ATTERBURY	1743	33001003
G	G.to be fear.	SMALRIDGE	1724	23051012
G	G.unchang.	TILLOTSON	1735	62001017
G	G.w.ab.our.	BARKER	1763	23055008
G	G.w.incom.	SAURIN	1775	23055008
G	G.wond. W.	WILLISON	1761	18037014
G	G.1 Ca.l. E.	TILLOTSON	1735	48011036
G	G's g. Name.	ERSKINE	1764	19106008
G	G's Wk's g.	DUCHAL	1765	01001031

Keyword	In its Context	Author	Year	BkChpVrs
G	Gifts of G.	HAVETT	1703	62001017
G	Glor.of G.	TRAPP	1752	19092005
G	Glory of G.	WISHEART	1716	19148013
G	Glory of G.	WISHEART	1716	50003018
G	Glory of G.	BEVERIDGE	1720	20016004
G	Glory of G.	SMALRIDGE	1724	46008050
G	Glory of G.	BENNETT	1728	49010031
G	Glory of G.	SHARP	1729	49010031
G	Glory of G.	CLARKE	1732	49010031
G	Glory of G.	FOSTER	1737	49010031
G	Glory of G.	WILCOX	1757	02033018
G	Glory of G.	PEARSE	1763	49010031
G	Glory of G.	DUCHAL	1765	49010031
G	Glory of G.	LELAND	1769	49010031
G	Glory to G.	HOLE	1717	45002024
G	Good.of G.	CHARNOCK	1684	44010018
G	Good.of G.	ABERNETHY	1743	44010018
G	Good.of G.	WEST	1762	43019017
G	Good.of G.	HALES	1766	44010018
G	Goodn.of G.	REAY	1755	65004017
G	Gos. W.o G.	BAINE	1778	49002007
G	Gos.g.str.th.	WHITTY	1772	45005026
G	Gosp.of G.	CREYGHTON	1720	55002008
G	Grace of G.	MARSHALL	1731	50012009
G	Grace of G.	CLARKE	1732	53002012
G	Grace of G.	CLARKE	1732	59002011
G	Grace of G.	TILLY	1737	53002012
G	Grand.of G.	SAURIN	1775	23040012
G	Grat.to G.	MAYNARD	1722	45017017
G	Grat.to G.	BRADY	1730	45017017
G	Grat.to G.	WHITE	1757	19086012
G	Grat.to G.	EATON	1764	19116012
G	Grat.to G.	DEVEREL	1777	19116012
G	H.& Fear G.	OUTRAM	1697	38001006
G	H. G. Parac.	LESTLEY	1720	46016007
G	Hap.o. G.aff.	NEWMAN	1760	65004016
G	Happ.o.g. P.	ROWLAND	1775	48008028
G	Helps t.g. M.	STEELE	1683	49015002
G	Ho.due t. G.	NORRIS	1728	58003003
G	Holin.o. G.	HUNT	1748	69015004
G	Holin.of G.	WISHEART	1716	09002002
G	Holin.of G.	SAURIN	1775	03019001
G	Honor of G.	HUNT	1748	09002030
G	Hope& T. G.	MARSHAL	1750	19042005
G	Hu.tow. G.	WAPLE	1720	62004010
G	Ignor.of G.	FREKE	1716	18024013
G	Ignor.of G.	MASON	1758	18026014
G	Image of G.	ATTERBURY	1702	01001027
G	Image of G.	STURMY	1716	01001027
G	Image of G.	SOUTH	1727	01001027
G	Imitat.of G.	ENFIELD	1772	52005001
G	Immut.of G.	JORTIN	1774	62001017
G	In.to w.o. G.	SNAPE	1745	49007029
G	Incomp. G.	LUCAS	1710	18011007
G	Incomp. G.	WISHEART	1716	18011007
G	Infl.of H. G.	SIMS	1772	53004013

Keyword	In its Context	Author	Year	BkChpVrs
G	Ingrat.to G.	DAVIES	1766	14032008
G	Int. Ev.of G.	CARR	1777	53003008
G	Interc.w. G.	NALSON	1737	18022021
G	Interc.w. G.	REAY	1755	18022021
G	Interc.w. G.	RICHMOND	1764	18022021
G	Interc.w. G.	LANGHORNE	1773	18022021
G	J.& M.of G.	ABERNETHY	1743	19089014
G	J.& M.of G.	KNOWLES	1750	19089014
G	J. Xt. Im. G.	BRETT	1720	54001015
G	J. Xt. Im. G.	LESTLEY	1720	54001015
G	Jes. Son o. G.	LARDNER	1760	46020017
G	Jes. Xt. G.m.	GUYSE	1719	48009005
G	John's P.f. G.	ORTON	1776	67000002
G	Joy of g. Xn.	BATTY	1739	53004004
G	Jud. G.& M.	HUNTER	1774	09016007
G	Just.of G.	WILDER	1741	69015003
G	Just.of G.	BRACKENRIDGE	1764	69015003
G	Justice of G.	WISHEART	1716	05032004
G	K.& L.of G.	ROMAINE	1760	44012028
G	King of G.	CLARKE	1732	43006010
G	King. G.in P.	WILLIAMS	1738	49004020
G	King.of G.	JACKSON	1728	43006010
G	King.of G.	LIRTLETON	1735	43006010
G	King.of G.	EVANS	1775	43006010
G	Kingd.of G.	BULKLEY	1752	45017020
G	Kn. G.l.o. N.	WATTS	1753	47014015
G	Kn.o. X.in G.	COLE	1692	46008054
G	Kno. G.& Xt.	WOOD	1674	48001019
G	Know. G.&c.	CLARKE	1736	49001021
G	Know.of G.	CHARNOCK	1684	46017003
G	Know.of G.	DUCHE	1779	18013005
G	Knowl.of G.	HOWE	1744	59001016
G	L. D. G. Life.	ERSKINE	1764	51002019
G	L. G.& Man.	ECCLES	1755	43022037
G	L. G.& W.co.	DAWES	1733	62004004
G	L. G.& W.incon	GALE	1676	65002015
G	L. G.& W.incon	CLARKE	1734	65002015
G	L. G.& W.incon	DORMAN	1743	65002015
G	L. G.& W.incon	BALL	1756	65002015
G	L. G.& W.incon	CARR	1777	65002015
G	L. G.f.a. Xn.	ANONYMOUS	1770	47026023
G	L. G& W.incons	WAKE	1701	65002015
G	L. G& W.incons	ROGERS	1735	65002015
G	L. G& W.incons	SNAPE	1745	65002015
G	L.es.t.att. G.	HUNTER	1774	65004016
G	L.of G.& Br.	SMALRIDGE	1724	65004021
G	L.of G.& Br.	NEWTON	1736	65004021
G	L.of G.& Br.	HOWE	1744	65004020
G	L.of G.& M.	WARBURTON	1753	20017005
G	L.of G.& M.	WARBURTON	1753	65004020
G	L.of G.& N.	WILSON	1781	44012032
G	L.of G. Mot. O	PIERCE	1679	46014015
G	L.of G. Mot. O	READING	1724	46014015
G	Lamb of G.	WILLISON	1761	46001036
G	Law est.b. G.	TAYLOR	1704	48003031
G	Law pre. G.	TRAIL	1696	61004016

Keyword	In its Context	Author	Year	BkChpVrs
G	Li.o. G.in M.	MOIR	1759	52004018
G	Light G.rej.	CONANT	1699	46003019
G	Lo.o. G.& M.	FARRINGTON	1741	57001005
G	Lo.of G.& N.	HOLE	1716	43022034
G	Lo.of G.&c.	BRAILSFORD	1776	19033026
G	Lo.t. G.& Xt.	DAVIES	1766	46021017
G	Long suff. G.	TILLOTSON	1735	21008011
G	Love of G.	WHITAKER	1674	48008038
G	Love of G.	CRUSO	1699	19026003
G	Love of G.	DORRINGTON	1703	22001004
G	Love of G.	SCOTT	1701	65005003
G	Love of G.	COCK	1710	52003017
G	Love of G.	SHARP	1729	43022037
G	Love of G.	CROSSINGE	1732	19004006
G	Love of G.	STENNETT	1732	44012030
G	Love of G.	STENNETT	1732	65005003
G	Love of G.	ATTERBURY	1743	44012029
G	Love of G.	SEED	1743	44012030
G	Love of G.	HUNT	1748	44012030
G	Love of G.	WATTS	1753	44012030
G	Love of G.	ROMAINE	1759	22001004
G	Love of G.	WILLISON	1761	22001004
G	Love of G.	JORTIN	1774	44012030
G	Love tow. G.	SKELTON	1754	45010027
G	Love G.& N.	COCK	1710	43022035
G	Love G.& N.	CARLETON	1736	45010027
G	Love G.&c.	GUYSE	1757	65005003
G	Lovers of G.	ERSKINE	1764	48008028
G	Loving G.	BEVERIDGE	1720	48008028
G	M.af. G.o. H.	EVANSON	1773	47013022
G	M's co.w. G.	WILSON	1676	19073023
G	M's. Enm. G.	CHARNOCK	1699	48008007
G	M's.rel.to G.	FOSTER	1744	47017028
G	Men offs. G.	HOLLAND	1753	47017028
G	Merc.of G.	SMITH	1762	02015001
G	Mercy of G.	WHICHCOTE	1702	29002013
G	Mercy of G.	GREGORY	1708	26033011
G	Mercy of G.	WISHEART	1716	19062012
G	Mercy of G.	NEWLIN	1720	19103004
G	Mi.f. D.o. G.	WILLIS	1720	53001017
G	Min.n.g.off.	ERSKINE	1775	50006003
G	Min.t.pr. G.	ANONYMOUS	1679	48001014
G	Mir. Prop. G.	ATTERBURY	1730	23060022
G	Mo. Ag.o. G.	ABERNETHY	1743	69015004
G	Mor. Perf. G.	PRICE	1757	43005048
G	N. E.mor. G.	STEELE	1776	19126005
G	Name of G.	MEDE	1672	43006009
G	Name of G.	MEDE	1672	45011002
G	Name of G.	MOSS	1732	43006009
G	Nat.of G.	JOHNSON	1728	46004024
G	Nat.of G.	JORTIN	1774	46004024
G	Nature of G.	ANONYMOUS	1776	18011007
G	No s. G.& M.	HOADLY	1754	45016013
G	Not as.o. G.	HARTLEY	1754	48001016
G	Not as.o. G.	SHIRLEY	1762	48001016
G	O. G.f.& M.	FROST	1741	21005003

Keyword	In its Context	Author	Year	BkChpVrs
G	O. L.g.by Xt.	BRAILSFORD	1776	49015022
G	Ob to sp. G.	SMALRIDGE	1724	61013017
G	Ob.sign l. G.	SHERLOCK	1719	65005003
G	Ob.to sp. G.	BARROW	1716	61013017
G	Omnip.of G.	CHARNOCK	1684	18026014
G	Omnip.of G.	WHITBY	1710	01017001
G	Omnip.of G.	ABERNETHY	1743	01017001
G	Omnip.of G.	KNOWLES	1750	18026014
G	Oper. H. G.	BADDELLEY	1752	46016008
G	Oracles o. G.	BREKELL	1765	48003002
G	P.& G. H. G.	PAYNE	1763	46014015
G	P. Kno.of G.	SUTTON	1754	24009024
G	Pe. Lo.g.bo.	BAYLY	1721	65004017
G	Peace of G.	MOSS	1738	54003015
G	Pers.of H. G.	HARRISON	1734	46015026
G	Piety tow. G.	SEATON	1720	01024048
G	Pleas. G. M.	ANONYMOUS	1754	18036011
G	Pos.& Ne. G.	ELSMERE	1767	23001016
G	Power of G.	WISHEART	1716	19062011
G	Power of G.	TILLOTSON	1735	19062011
G	Power of G.	BRACKENRIDGE	1764	19062011
G	Prom.of G.	ROMAINE	1760	63003008
G	Proof of G.	LATHAM	1678	48001020
G	Prov. G.aff.	LAWSON	1764	27004025
G	Quest. G.cat.	ERSKINE	1764	43022043
G	R. N. G.& R.	COCKBURN	1708	61012012
G	R. Not.of G.	HUNT	1748	20009010
G	R.ins.g.m. R	RANDOLPH	1738	50003005
G	R.ins.g.m. R.	JOHNSON	1731	50003005
G	R.to G.in Xt.	BRIGHT	1695	50005019
G	Reas.ins. G.	EDGCUMBE	1736	50003005
G	Reas.ins. G.	AGAR	1759	49002005
G	Reb.ag. G.	DUNLOP	1722	26016063
G	Recon.w. G.	BRADY	1713	50005020
G	Recon.w. G.	DAVIES	1766	50005020
G	Recon.w. G.	BOURN	1777	50005020
G	Rem.love G.	HICKES	1726	69002004
G	Resign.to G.	CARR	1777	09003018
G	Return to G.	READER	1765	24050005
G	Rew. L.of G.	PYLE	1776	49002009
G	Rig.&g.man	HICKMAN	1706	48005007
G	Rig.&g.man	FOSTER	1732	48005007
G	Rig.&g.man	HORBERY	1774	48005007
G	Right of G.	CLAGETT	1704	48001017
G	S. S. G.f. Y.	BERRIMAN	1763	19119008
G	S. S.wo.of G.	LUCAS	1710	55002013
G	S.o. G.f.d. J.	DAVIES	1771	49003007
G	S.of G.pr. T.	CAMPBELL	1779	49001025
G	Sal.by gr. G.	KIMBER	1756	59002011
G	Salv.f. J.& G.	SHIRLEY	1762	47010034
G	Seal Fo.o. G.	EVANSON	1773	58002019
G	Seek. K.o. G.	FARINDON	1672	43006033
G	Seek. K.o. G.	BURTON	1684	43006033
G	Seek. K.o. G.	DUNLOP	1722	43006033
G	Seek. K.o. G.	CLARKE	1732	43006033
G	Seek. K.o. G.	JONES	1741	43006033

Keyword	In its Context	Author	Year	BkChpVrs
G	Self ex.of G.	WHITAKER	1674	19018046
G	Self-de.t. G.	AMORY	1742	50004005
G	Self-ded. G.	CHANDLER	1769	48012001
G	Serv. G.	ANONYMOUS	1754	06024024
G	Serv. G.& M.	BLACKALL	1723	43006024
G	Serv. G.& M.	BLAIR	1740	43006024
G	Sev.of G. L.	HOPKINS	1708	21008011
G	Sin ag. H. G.	HARRIS	1718	43012031
G	Sin ag. H. G.	SHARP	1729	43012031
G	Sin ag. H. G.	MARSHALL	1731	43012031
G	Sin ag. H. G.	TILLOTSON	1735	43012031
G	Sin ag. H. G.	STEPHENS	1737	43012031
G	Sin ag. H. G.	WATERLAND	1742	43012031
G	Sin ag. H. G.	GREEN	1747	43012031
G	Sin ag. H. G.	HOOLE	1748	43012031
G	Sin ag. H. G.	SECKER	1770	43012031
G	Sin ag. H. G.	JORTIN	1774	43012031
G	Sin ag. H. G.	PEARCE	1779	43012031
G	Sin hides G.	LEIGHTON	1746	23059001
G	Sin.ag. H. G.	ANONYMOUS	1740	44003028
G	Sin.gr. H. G.	WILSON	1781	52004030
G	Sin.temp. G.	ADAMS	1716	43004007
G	Sons G. Priv.	WHEATLAND	1739	65003001
G	Sonsh.w. G.	DAVIES	1766	65003001
G	Soul's rest. G	WILCOX	1757	19116007
G	Spe.t. Or. G.	FENTON	1720	63004011
G	Spirit of G.	WHITBY	1710	46004024
G	Spirit of G.	CLARKE	1732	46004024
G	Spirit of G.	TILLOTSON	1735	46004024
G	Spirit of G.	WILDER	1741	46004024
G	Spirit of G.	ABERNETHY	1743	46004024
G	Spirit of G.	KNOWLES	1750	46004024
G	State of G.	JORTIN	1774	43013043
G	Strait g.pass.	ANONYMOUS	1776	43007014
G	Subm.to G.	ATTERBURY	1703	18002010
G	Subm.to G.	JENKS	1700	48010003
G	Swift pro. G.	MOSS	1732	47019020
G	T. Hap.in G.	MASON	1758	24002013
G	T.t. S.n.f. G.	SHARP	1734	62001013
G	T.t. S.n.f. G.	BURNET	1747	62001013
G	T.t. S.n.f. G.	ABERNETHY	1751	62001013
G	Tea. G.&c.	FLAVEL	1673	46006045
G	Temp. Ev.not G	BROWN	1722	45013004
G	Temp. Ev.not G	HOLLAND	1753	45013004
G	Th.to G.&c.	PHILIPS	1775	19107043
G	Tim.in G.h.	AMORY	1775	19031015
G	To kee.l. G.	COOPER	1683	68000021
G	Tr. Ch.of G.	CLARKE	1736	51004022
G	Tr.of G.	WHITBY	1709	05032004
G	Tr.of G.	TILLOTSON	1735	05032004
G	True g. M.	ORR	1773	21002003
G	Trump.of G.	ERSKINE	1764	23027013
G	Trust in G.	CONANT	1703	23026004
G	Trust in G.	SPINCKES	1714	63003014
G	Trust in G.	NEWLIN	1720	19037005
G	Trust in G.	LUCAS	1722	19039007

INDEXES TO THIRD VOLUME: E: KEYWORD-IN-CONTEXT INDEX OF OTHER SUBJECTS OR OCCASIONS

Keyword	In its Context	Author	Year	BkChpVrs
G	Trust in G.	SCATTERGOOD	1723	19028007
G	Trust in G.	SMALRIDGE	1724	19042011
G	Trust in G.	CLARKE	1727	19071001
G	Trust in G.	WHARTON	1728	46014001
G	Trust in G.	REEVES	1729	19034008
G	Trust in G.	SHARP	1729	19042006
G	Trust in G.	ROGERS	1738	24017007
G	Trust in G.	SKEELER	1740	20016020
G	Trust in G.	ABERNETHY	1743	19062008
G	Trust in G.	ATTERBURY	1743	23049010
G	Trust in G.	LEIGHTON	1746	19112007
G	Trust in G.	LEIGHTON	1746	34003017
G	Trust in G.	GIBSON	1749	19112007
G	Trust in G.	CONEY	1750	20003005
G	Trust in G.	BADDELLY	1752	23026004
G	Trust in G.	WILCOX	1757	19083028
G	Trust in G.	MOIR	1759	34003017
G	Trust in G.	STEBBING	1760	20003005
G	Trust in G.	WEARE	1767	43006011
G	Trust in G.	STERNE	1769	19037003
G	Trust in G.	LANGHORNE	1773	19118008
G	Trust in G.	PHILIPS	1775	05004039
G	Trust in G.	CARR	1777	24017007
G	Truth of G.	WISHEART	1716	19108004
G	Truth of G.	HUNT	1748	69021015
G	Tust in G.	ADEY	1755	19084013
G	Un. G.& Tr.	TILLOTSON	1735	57002005
G	Union w. G.	BARKER	1683	46017020
G	Unity of G.	WHITBY	1710	44012029
G	Unity of G.	CLARKE	1732	43004010
G	Unity of G.	ABERNETHY	1743	05006004
G	Unity of G.	ATTERBURY	1743	23045005
G	Unity of G.	KNOWLES	1750	05006004
G	Unity of G.	SKELTON	1754	23045008
G	Unity of G.	COCKMAN	1750	49008004
G	Unity of G.	BOSTON	1773	05006004
G	Unity of G.	BOSTON	1773	49008004
G	Virt.g.m's S.	CONEY	1730	20014014
G	W.& G.o. G.	KNOWLES	1750	48011033
G	W.m pl. G.	WATERLAND	1742	20016004
G	W.to L.& G.	TALBOT	1674	05005029
G	Wait on G.	PEARSE	1763	23040031
G	Walk.w.o. G	GROVE	1741	55002012
G	Wick. Sec.g.	JORTIN	1774	45012020
G	Wisd. Gl. G.	TILLOTSON	1735	68000025
G	Wisd.of G.	HORTON	1679	49001021
G	Wisd.of G.	CHARNOCK	1684	48016027
G	Wisd.of G.	WHITBY	1710	48016027
G	Wisd.of G.	WISHEART	1716	68000025
G	Wisd.of G.	ABERNETHY	1743	57001017
G	Witnes.f. G.	ERSKINE	1764	23043012
G	Wor. G.only	GUYSE	1757	43015008
G	Wor.only G.	COLLIER	1725	45004008
G	Word ev. G.	BRETT	1720	46001001
G	Word ev. G.	LESTLEY	1720	46001001
G	Word of G.	SCATTERGOOD	1723	47017011

Keyword	In its Context	Author	Year	BkChpVrs
G	Word of G.	HART	1767	24002004
G	Word of G.	BOURDALOUE	1776	46008047
G	Word of G.	JOHNSON	1776	55002013
G	Worsh.of G.	CLARKE	1727	19096009
G	Worsh.of G.	BURNET	1747	19096008
G	Worsh.of G.	EMLYN	1742	47017025
G	Worsh.of G.	LANGHORNE	1773	46004024
G	Wosd.of G.	CLARKE	1732	54002003
G	Xn.n.ash. G.	ENFIELD	1772	48002016
G	Xns. Sons G.	WILCOX	1757	65003001
G	Xt. G.& M.	HORBERY	1774	61001001
G	Xt. G.& M.	MEAD	1780	53002006
G	Xt. G. Exem.	BUNDY	1740	63002021
G	Xt. G. Exem.	FOSTER	1744	63002021
G	Xt. G. Exem.	COCKMAN	1750	63002021
G	Xt. G. Exem.	HOLLAND	1753	63002021
G	Xt. G.of Isr.	BRADBURY	1752	01032030
G	Xt. Ima.o. G.	MASON	1758	50004006
G	Xt. Son of G.	GUYSE	1729	47009020
G	Xt.cru. G. S.	WADSWORTH	1675	61010012
G	Xt.eq.w. G.	LESTLEY	1720	53002006
G	Xt.eq.w. G.	SHERLOCK	1772	53002006
G	Xt.g. Sheph.	PYLE	1777	46010010
G	Xt.ma.of G.	STEVENS	1757	50005021
G	Xt.si.r.h. G.	FLAVEL	1673	61001003
G	Xt.to J.& G.	BROWNE	1722	45002032
G	Xt.very G.	HORNE	1775	48010013
G	Xt's. C. L. G.	CRAIG	1775	46011033
G	Youth f. G.	POWELL	1676	21012001
G	manif.of G.	WHICHCOTE	1703	48001019
G'	Bless.hear. G'	ALTHAM	1732	45011028
G'	Bless.hear. G'	BURNET	1747	45011028
G'S	Ab. G's. G.	HORTON	1679	48002004
G'S	Ab.h. G's w.	PIDDLE	1777	26033030
G'S	Abu. G's Pat.	HOLLAND	1753	21008011
G'S	Ass.of G's.sp.	HUSSEY	1758	46006045
G'S	Cens. G's.m.	ALTHAM	1732	49004005
G'S	Ch. G's Port.	BLIGH	1765	05032009
G'S	Co. G's.will.	NALSON	1737	61010006
G'S	Co. G's.will.	NALSON	1737	61010009
G'S	D.in G's L.	LELAND	1769	19119047
G'S	D.o. G's wra.	GODDARD	1781	45019041
G'S	Delig. G's w.	LELAND	1769	19111002
G'S	Do&h. G's w.	DORMAN	1743	62001022
G'S	G's attrib.&c	HUNTER	1774	19145017
G'S	G's blessed.	WISHEART	1716	19119012
G'S	G's delay.	WARREN	1739	21008011
G'S	G's end affl.	CLARKSON	1696	23027009
G'S	G's forgiv.	SOUTH	1744	19130004
G'S	G's g. Name.	ERSKINE	1764	19106008
G'S	G's go.worl.	LELAND	1769	19135006
G'S	G's just.& M.	ATTERBURY	1703	69004003
G'S	G's long suff.	SAURIN	1775	21008011
G'S	G's love to us	BLAIR	1740	43007009
G'S	G's mercy.	TAYLOR	1668	19086005
G'S	G's mercy.	LEIGHTON	1746	23030015

Keyword	In its Context	Author	Year	BkChpVrs
G'S	G's mo. Gov.	WARBURTON	1753	19144003
G'S	G's mor. Go.	BEARE	1710	19099001
G'S	G's mor. Go.	DUCHAL	1753	19098009
G'S	G's mor. Go.	DUCHAL	1765	19100003
G'S	G's pec. Peo.	WEBBER	1738	05014002
G'S	G's power.	HUNT	1748	19147005
G'S	G's pr. Mer.	HILL	1755	19059010
G'S	G's pres. Sts.	S.	1695	56003016
G'S	G's pres.in C.	WHITTY	1772	19132014
G'S	G's presence	BARRINGTON	1770	01004016
G'S	G's right.	HUNT	1748	19129004
G'S	G's right&c.	LELAND	1769	19145017
G'S	G's sever.&c.	S.	1695	26021013
G'S	G's ten. Ca.	BRADY	1730	23005003
G'S	G's veracity.	LOVEDER	1756	04023019
G'S	G's w.beaut.	HUSSEY	1755	21003011
G'S	G's w.hid. T.	TAYLOR	1776	19112011
G'S	G's w.in D.	HOWE	1771	19107023
G'S	G's wisd.&c.	SAURIN	1775	24032019
G'S	G's wor.&c.	JOHNSON	1776	58002009
G'S	G's wrth.dr.	HOPKINS	1710	61010030
G'S	G's. Co.n.gr.	DUNLOP	1722	65005003
G'S	G's. Co.n.gr.	BRADY	1730	65005003
G'S	G's. Com.ea.	SCOTT	1701	65005003
G'S	G's. Com.ea.	SHARP	1729	65005003
G'S	G's. Comf.	CREYGHTON	1720	50001004
G'S	G's. Comm.	DAVIS	1756	47007053
G'S	G's. D.of Pu.	CONYBEARE	1757	64003008
G'S	G's. Deliver.	HORTON	1679	50001010
G'S	G's. Deliver.	WALLIS	1692	50001010
G'S	G's. Exist.	BATES	1700	61011006
G'S	G's. For.& P.	MARSHALL	1731	64003009
G'S	G's. For.& P.	NEWSON	1781	64003009
G'S	G's. Forekn.	HUSSEY	1753	48004011
G'S	G's. Goodn.	SCOTT	1701	46003016
G'S	G's. Goodn.	WISHEART	1716	37009017
G'S	G's. Goodn.	WHARTON	1728	48002004
G'S	G's. Goodn.	ROGERS	1735	48002004
G'S	G's. Goodn.	WARREN	1748	37009017
G'S	G's. Goodn.	PENTYCROSS	1781	37009017
G'S	G's. Gov. W.	DUCHAL	1765	46014011
G'S	G's. Govern.	SAURIN	1777	61013008
G'S	G's. Grace.	HOADLY	1727	50003005
G'S	G's. Holin.	WHITBY	1709	63001015
G'S	G's. Holin.	DELAUNE	1728	63001015
G'S	G's. Holin.	TILLOTSON	1735	63001015
G'S	G's. Holin.	HUSSEY	1758	63001015
G'S	G's. J.in d. S	EDWARDS	1774	48003019
G'S	G's. J.sp.&t.	LOCKIER	1671	48007025
G'S	G's. Judgm.	SINGLETON	1683	46012028
G'S	G's. Judgm.	BARROW	1716	48011033
G'S	G's. Judgm.	SNAPE	1745	61010031
G'S	G's. Justice.	CLAGETT	1704	48008033
G'S	G's. K.com.	MANGEY	1717	43006010
G'S	G's. K.com.	MOSS	1732	43006010
G'S	G's. King.all	BEVERLEY	1698	49015024

Keyword	In its Context	Author	Year	BkChpVrs
G'S	G's. Kingd.	BOURN	1777	43006010
G'S	G's. L.in Xt.	WILKINSON	1660	48005008
G'S	G's. L.in Xt.	LELAND	1769	48005011
G'S	G's. L.in Xt.	WALKER	1775	48005010
G'S	G's. L.kept.	SHERIDAN	1720	45017010
G'S	G's. L.to M.	PELLING	1694	46003016
G'S	G's. L.to Sin.	CLARKE	1732	46003016
G'S	G's. Lo. Red.	CARMICHAEL	1757	65004011
G'S	G's. Love&c.	FLAVEL	1673	46003016
G'S	G's. Love M's.	BEVERIDGE	1711	46003016
G'S	G's. Majesty.	HUNT	1748	68000025
G'S	G's. Mercies	KIDDER	1697	47017028
G'S	G's. Mercy.	TAYLOR	1668	48002004
G'S	G's. Omnisc.	WHITBY	1710	65003020
G'S	G's. Omnisc.	CARTER	1729	61004013
G'S	G's. Omnisc.	BATTY	1739	61004013
G'S	G's. Omnisc.	WILDER	1741	61004013
G'S	G's. Omnisc.	SOUTH	1744	65003020
G'S	G's. Omnisc.	STEELE	1776	61004013
G'S	G's. Patience	WHITBY	1710	48002004
G'S	G's. Patience	WISHEART	1716	48002004
G'S	G's. Patience	HUNT	1748	48002004
G'S	G's. Perfect.	BOSTON	1773	46005024
G'S	G's. Provid.	EDWARDS	1713	63005007
G'S	G's. Provid.	ATKINSON	1775	48011036
G'S	G's. Remn.	ERSKINE	1741	69003004
G'S	G's. Right.	MATHER	1701	48010003
G'S	G's. Right.	SEAGRAVE	1737	48010003
G'S	G's. Servants	SHEPHEARD	1748	48006016
G'S	G's. Severity	SAURIN	1775	61012029
G'S	G's. Subjects	SHEPHEARD	1748	65003002
G'S	G's. W.in R.	HUSSEY	1758	49002007
G'S	G's. Wisd.	HUNT	1748	57001017
G'S	G's.acc.pen.	BURNET	1747	65001009
G'S	G's.cal.t.ob.	WARREN	1748	61003015
G'S	G's.ch.mer.	MACLAURIN	1772	48008032
G'S	G's.charge.	HILL	1755	38003007
G'S	G's.dea.w. S.	STEPHENS	1737	48009017
G'S	G's.good. M.	SKEELER	1740	61002006
G'S	G's.immut.	WHITBY	1710	38003006
G'S	G's.immut.	CLARKE	1732	38003006
G'S	G's.immut.	HUNT	1748	38003006
G'S	G's.immut.	WARREN	1748	38003006
G'S	G's.immut.	LAMBERT	1779	38003006
G'S	G's.judgm.	TREVOR	1722	34003005
G'S	G's.lo.of ab.	TOWGOOD	1676	47007008
G'S	G's.reg.to ri.	REYNER	1745	63003012
G'S	G's.reg.to P.	WILCOX	1757	38003017
G'S	G's.rel. Goo.	HUTCHINS	1771	65004016
G'S	G's.right.	PAYNE	1698	48009014
G'S	G's.right. R.	HUSSEY	1753	48003025
G'S	G's.ser. Free.	DAVIS	1756	45001074
G'S	G's.w.uns.	MOIR	1759	48011033
G'S	G's&our Th.	SHOWER	1699	23055007
G'S	G's Anger.	DUNLOP	1722	19090011
G'S	G's Anger.	SOUTH	1744	19090011

INDEXES TO THIRD VOLUME: E: KEYWORD-IN-CONTEXT INDEX OF OTHER SUBJECTS OR OCCASIONS

Keyword	In its Context	Author	Year	BkChpVrs
G'S	G's Compas.	SAURIN	1775	19103013
G'S	G's De.eter.	BRINE	1754	20022023
G'S	G's Decrees.	BOSTON	1773	52001011
G'S	G's Elec.&c.	WATTS	1753	52001003
G'S	G's Expost.	ORTON	1776	24022015
G'S	G's Forbear.	HORTON	1679	45013008
G'S	G's Gl.o.c.e.	WISHEART	1716	49010031
G'S	G's Gl.o.c.e.	TILLOTSON	1735	49010031
G'S	G's Glo.& R.	HUSSEY	1758	19008001
G'S	G's Glo.&c.	M'GEORGE	1729	19063002
G'S	G's Good.	ORR	1749	34001013
G'S	G's Good.	DOUGHTY	1761	18012007
G'S	G's Goodn.	SCOTT	1701	19119068
G'S	G's Goodn.	SCOTT	1701	19145008
G'S	G's Goodn.	SCOTT	1701	19145009
G'S	G's Goodn.	WHITBY	1710	19145009
G'S	G's Goodn.	BARROW	1716	19145009
G'S	G's Goodn.	CLARKE	1727	19119068
G'S	G's Goodn.	MARKLAND	1729	45013006
G'S	G's Goodn.	CLARKE	1732	19145009
G'S	G's Goodn.	TILLOTSON	1735	19145009
G'S	G's Goodn.	BEESTON	1739	19145009
G'S	G's Goodn.	WILDER	1741	19119068
G'S	G's Goodn.	ATTERBURY	1743	19119068
G'S	G's Goodn.	SOUTH	1744	19145009
G'S	G's Goodn.	HUNT	1748	19086005
G'S	G's Goodn.	HOLDEN	1755	19145009
G'S	G's Goodn.	DAVIS	1756	19145009
G'S	G's Goodn.	NEWTON	1759	19119069
G'S	G's Goodn.	AMORY	1766	19145009
G'S	G's Goodn.	LELAND	1769	19145009
G'S	G's Goodn.	LANGHORNE	1773	19145009
G'S	G's Goodn.	JORTIN	1774	19145009
G'S	G's Goodn.	CARR	1777	19107031
G'S	G's H.in Ex.	BRODHURST	1733	01022014
G'S	G's Holiness.	LELAND	1769	34001013
G'S	G's Im.in M.	FAWCETT	1749	01002026
G'S	G's Judg.	WARREN	1739	19119075
G'S	G's Judgm.	FORD	1678	19009016
G'S	G's Judgm.	WHICHCOTE	1702	23026009
G'S	G's Judgm.	DORRINGTON	1702	23045007
G'S	G's Judgm.	TILLOTSON	1735	45013005
G'S	G's Judgm.	HUNT	1748	19009008
G'S	G's Justice	HUTCHINS	1782	05022004
G'S	G's Justice.	WHITBY	1710	19145017
G'S	G's Kingd.	STAFFORD	1697	05008002
G'S	G's Know.	GROVE	1741	19103014
G'S	G's Knowl.	HUNT	1748	09002003
G'S	G's Knowl.	HUTCHINS	1771	24032019
G'S	G's Love&c.	KIMBER	1756	19146008
G'S	G's Omnip.	CLARKE	1732	11008027
G'S	G's Omnipre.	NEWTON	1759	19139007
G'S	G's Patience	CLARKE	1732	21008011
G'S	G's Power	LEIGHTON	1746	19076010
G'S	G's Power.	NICHOLSON	1661	19078020
G'S	G's Pr.comf.	BAINE	1778	02033014

Keyword	In its Context	Author	Year	BkChpVrs
G'S	G's Pr.perf.	ERSKINE	1764	01028015
G'S	G's Pres.	MEDE	1672	19132007
G'S	G's Pres.b. S.	BRADBURY	1772	19046005
G'S	G's Presence	WELCH	1752	05012018
G'S	G's Provid.	WILKINSON	1660	14016009
G'S	G's Return.	BRINSLEY	1667	19090013
G'S	G's Right.	HUSSEY	1753	27009007
G'S	G's S.on Ad.	PYLE	1777	01003019
G'S	G's Sover.	HUSSEY	1755	05009017
G'S	G's Tempt.	FROYSELL	1678	01022001
G'S	G's Truth.	LELAND	1769	19117002
G'S	G's Truth.	PENTYCROSS	1781	19031005
G'S	G's Wk's g.	DUCHAL	1765	01001031
G'S	H.to G's N.	SKELTON	1754	03019030
G'S	Hear G's.w.	DORRINGTON	1703	49001021
G'S	Hear G's.w.	WAKE	1716	45008008
G'S	Ig d.o. G's P.	RILAND	1764	28004006
G'S	Im.of G's. P.	HORNECK	1706	43005048
G'S	Im.of G's. P.	KELSEY	1721	43005048
G'S	Imit. G's. H.	CLARKE	1732	63001015
G'S	Kno. G's W.	NEEDHAM	1679	46007017
G'S	Law o. G's h.	ERSKINE	1764	26043002
G'S	Men G's.offs.	GOUGH	1751	47017028
G'S	Nat. G's. K.	CLARKE	1735	48014017
G'S	Nat. G's. K.	FOSTER	1737	48014017
G'S	Nat. G's. K.	ABERNETHY	1751	48014017
G'S	Neg. G's. Sal.	ROE	1766	61002003
G'S	Pr.f. G's. M.	SMALRIDGE	1724	50001011
G'S	Prof. G's N.	CARR	1777	03019012
G'S	R. G's.right.	DORRINGTON	1705	43005048
G'S	R.due G's N.	SMALBROKE	1722	03019030
G'S	Rev. G's h.	MEDE	1672	21005001
G'S	Sin. Obed. G's	CLAGETT	1704	46007017
G'S	Sin. Obed. G's	ABERNETHY	1748	46007017
G'S	Sp.of G's. L.	HAWEIS	1762	51003010
G'S	Sub. G's. W.	SCOTT	1700	45022042
G'S	Sub. G's. W.	BARROW	1716	45022042
G'S	Sub.t. G's w.	DU MOULIN	1684	43026039
G'S	Sub.t. G's w.	BATES	1700	43026039
G'S	Sub.t. G's w.	ATTERBURY	1743	43026039
G'S	Unw. G's M.	ORTON	1776	01032010
G'S	Xn's. G's. T.	BREKELL	1765	50006016
G'S	Xt. G's. Ima.	MASON	1758	50003006
G'S	Xt.at G's.r.h.	HURRION	1719	61012001
G'S	Zeal f. G's H.	CLARKE	1727	16010039
GAD	Gad.	ERSKINE	1764	01049019
GAIN	Fol.gain W.	PYLE	1777	45009025
GAIN	Gain&loss.	MOSS	1732	43016026
GAIN	True Gain.	REYNOLDS	1679	43016026
GAIN	Worl. Gain.	BYRDALL	1666	44008036
GAMAL	Gamal. Cou.	DICK	1776	47005034
GAR	Linsw. Gar.	CENNICK	1762	05022011
GARD	Gard.of Ed.	HORNE	1778	01002008
GARD	Xt.in Gard.	MAY	1757	46018001
GATE	Strait Gate.	IBBOT	1726	45013023
GATE	Strait Gate.	ATTERBURY	1743	44013021

Keyword	In its Context	Author	Year	BkChpVrs
GATE	Strait Gate.	ATTERBURY	1743	45013024
GATE	Strait Gate.	BOSTON	1753	43007013
GATE	Strait Gate.	SECKER	1770	45013023
GATE	Strait Gate.	SHERLOCK	1772	45013023
GD	Gd. Reward.	ATTERBURY	1743	61011006
GEN	A. Gen. Sick.	ANONYMOUS	1712	19091005
GEN	Fut.gen. J.	AMORY	1748	43025031
GEN	Gen.&m. Z.	BULKLEY	1761	43016021
GEN	Gen. Confla.	LELAND	1769	64003010
GEN	Gen. Dispos.	MOIR	1776	47020035
GEN	Gen. Disposi.	SKELTON	1754	47020035
GEN	Gen. Judgm.	EDWARDS	1713	47017031
GEN	Gen. Judgm.	SCATTERGOOD	1723	45018008
GEN	Gen. Judgm.	PEIRCE	1731	50005010
GEN	Gen. Judgm.	COCKMAN	1750	64003003
GEN	Gen. Judgm.	DAVIS	1756	47017031
GEN	Gen. Judgm.	CARR	1777	43024044
GEN	Gen. Obser.	BLAIR	1740	43007024
GEN	Gen. Observ.	BLAIR	1740	43006009
GEN	Gen. Patriot.	STEPHEN	1774	15009013
GEN	Gen. Provid.	ADAMS	1736	13029011
GEN	Gen. Resurr.	DAVIES	1766	46005028
GEN	Gen.judg.vi.	COCKMAN	1750	65003003
GEN	Gen.of Gosp.	MOIR	1776	45019041
GEN	b.gen.assem.	STITH	1746	44012017
GENER	Ris. Gener.	DODDERIDGE	1743	19022030
GENT	Heal. Gent.	WHEATLY	1746	43008013
GENTLENESS	Gentleness.	BLAIR	1777	62003017
GEOR	Dea. Geor. I.	WATTS	1753	23005012
GET	Get. Wealth.	BRADFORD	1720	20013011
GET	Get. Wealth.	HUTCHINS	1782	20013011
GH	Ass.o. H. Gh.	OGDEN	1777	65003024
GH	Bei.o. H. Gh.	OGDEN	1777	48015013
GH	De.o. H. Gh.	BROME	1709	46016007
GH	Div. H. Gh.	BARROW	1716	49003016
GH	Div. H. Gh.	STEPHENS	1717	47005003
GH	Eff.of H. Gh.	BROWNE	1722	47002032
GH	Gift o. H. Gh.	COWPER	1773	47002038
GH	Gifts H. Gh.	BATTY	1739	52004008
GH	H. Gh. Div.	PIGOTT	1702	46016013
GH	H. Gh. Parac.	BRETT	1720	46016007
GH	H. Gh.bapt.	JOHNSON	1776	47002016
GH	H. Gh.div. P.	LESTLEY	1720	46014016
GH	Joy in H. Gh.	DODSON	1728	48014017
GH	Ly.to H. Gh.	NEWLIN	1728	47005003
GH	Off.o. H. Gh.	CENNICK	1762	47002038
GH	Off.o. H. Gh.	ELLIOTT	1764	63001012
GHOST	H. Ghost&c.	DAWSON	1765	49012004
GIFT	Fa. Gift o. G.	SHERLOCK	1772	52002008
GIFT	Gift o. H. Gh.	COWPER	1773	47002038
GIFT	Gift of Spir.	JORTIN	1774	47001008
GIFT	Gift of Spirit	BENNETT	1728	45011013
GIFT	Gift.s.	ROMAINE	1755	26036025
GIFT	Gr.b. Gift.	NALSON	1737	45011011
GIFT	N. Yr's. Gift.	DAVIES	1771	48013012
GIFT	Unsp. Gift.	HORNE	1778	52004007

Keyword	In its Context	Author	Year	BkChpVrs
GIFT	Xt.a Gift.	WILLISON	1761	50009015
GIFTS	C.best Gifts.	HORTON	1679	49012031
GIFTS	Dif. Gifts sp.	CLARKE	1735	49012004
GIFTS	Gifts of G.	HAVETT	1703	62001017
GIFTS	Gifts of Spir.	BRADY	1713	51005022
GIFTS	Gifts H. Gh.	BATTY	1739	52004008
GIFTS	Gifts H. Sp.	TATHAM	1780	46014016
GIFTS	God's Gifts.	KENNET	1715	19104015
GIFTS	Spir. Gifts.	COTES	1721	49014012
GIL	Balm.of Gil.	ROMAINE	1760	24008022
GIV	G.giv. Rain.	FOTHERGILL	1765	47014017
GIV	Giv.&recei.	TILLOTSON	1735	47020035
GIV	Giv.&receiv.	COLLIER	1725	47020035
GIV	Giv. Offence	PYLE	1777	45017001
GIV	Giv. Scandal	WESTON	1747	44009042
GIV	Giv.no Off.	QUINCY	1750	49010032
GIV	Giv.offences	BUNDY	1740	43018007
GIV	Sinf.giv.off.	STEPHENS	1737	48014013
GIVING	Alms-giving	GARDINER	1720	43006001
GL	Church's Gl.	HARTLEY	1754	19045014
GL	Dif. Deg. Gl.	CONYBEARE	1757	65003002
GL	Dif.de.f. Gl.	BULL	1713	64001011
GL	Do all Gl. G.	BEVERIDGE	1720	49010031
GL	Do all Gl. G.	BERRIMAN	1751	49010031
GL	F. Gl.by Son.	JOHNSON	1776	46016025
GL	G's Gl.o.c.e.	WISHEART	1716	49010031
GL	G's Gl.o.c.e.	TILLOTSON	1735	49010031
GL	Gl.in C.o. Xt.	MACLAURIN	1772	51006014
GL	Suff.w.to Gl.	BRADY	1730	63007014
GL	Vain Gl. Ben.o	CARLETON	1736	51005026
GL	Vain Gl. Ben.o	MILLER	1749	51005026
GL	Wisd. Gl. G.	TILLOTSON	1735	68000025
GL	Xn's. Gl.& J.	BUNDY	1740	55002020
GL	Xt.ho.of Gl.	BALL	1692	54001027
GL	Xt's. Gl. H.	FANCH	1768	49015028
GLAST	Glast- Wat.	RAWLINS	1771	46005002
GLO	Believ. Glo.	WHITFIELD	1771	23060019
GLO	Cr. Bl.& Glo.	COOKE	1739	49002009
GLO	G's Glo.& R.	HUSSEY	1758	19008001
GLO	G's Glo.&c.	M'GEORGE	1729	19063002
GLO	Glo.& H. H.	SIMS	1772	54003001
GLO	King of Glo.	HORNE	1778	69001007
GLO	Way to Glo.	HILL	1755	19107007
GLOR	Glor. Adop.	SPOONER	1771	65003001
GLOR	Glor.o. God.	PARKHURST	1707	46021019
GLOR	Glor.of G.	TRAPP	1752	19092005
GLORIF	Glorif. God.	WISHEART	1716	49006019
GLORIFIED	Xt.glorified.	MAY	1757	56001010
GLORY	Degr. Glory.	FRANK	1716	43020023
GLORY	Glory in Rel.	WHICHCOTE	1707	24009023
GLORY	Glory in Rel.	WHICHCOTE	1707	24009024
GLORY	Glory in Xt.	WITHERSPOON	1768	51006014
GLORY	Glory of Chur.	CALAMY	1715	43016018
GLORY	Glory of G.	WISHEART	1716	19148013
GLORY	Glory of G.	WISHEART	1716	50003018
GLORY	Glory of G.	BEVERIDGE	1720	20016004

INDEXES TO THIRD VOLUME: E: KEYWORD-IN-CONTEXT INDEX OF OTHER SUBJECTS OR OCCASIONS

Keyword	In its Context	Author	Year	BkChpVrs
GLORY	Glory of G.	SMALRIDGE	1724	46008050
GLORY	Glory of G.	BENNETT	1728	49010031
GLORY	Glory of G.	SHARP	1729	49010031
GLORY	Glory of G.	CLARKE	1732	49010031
GLORY	Glory of G.	FOSTER	1737	49010031
GLORY	Glory of G.	WILCOX	1757	02033018
GLORY	Glory of G.	PEARSE	1763	49010031
GLORY	Glory of G.	DUCHAL	1765	49010031
GLORY	Glory of G.	LELAND	1769	49010031
GLORY	Glory to G.	HOLE	1717	45002024
GLORY	Glory. God.	LUCAS	1710	19034002
GLORY	Love Glory.	SOUTH	1744	43023005
GLORY	Of Glory.	BUNDY	1750	51006014
GLORY	Vain Glory.	BLACKALL	1723	43006001
GLORY	Vain Glory.	BLAIR	1740	43006001
GLORY	Xt. Ld Glory	RANDOLPH	1769	46012041
GLORY	Xt.in Glory.	FLAVEL	1673	20008030
GLORYING	No Glorying	BULL	1713	24009023
GLY	Gly.of Par.	BAYLYE	1710	49002009
GO	Do go.to all.	BURTON	1685	51006010
GO	Do go.to all.	BILLINGSLEY	1712	51006010
GO	Fth&go. Co.	BRAGGE	1713	57001018
GO	Fth&go. Co.	WELTON	1724	57001018
GO	Fth&go. Co.	MACE	1751	57001018
GO	G. Fo.o. Go.	SCOTT	1743	62001017
GO	G.best. Go.	BEVERIDGE	1720	19073025
GO	G.go.world.	HUNT	1748	19022028
GO	G.go.world.	BRACKENRIDGE	1764	19022028
GO	G.go.world.	LELAND	1769	19022028
GO	G's go.worl.	LELAND	1769	19135006
GO	G's mor. Go.	BEARE	1710	19099001
GO	G's mor. Go.	DUCHAL	1753	19098009
GO	G's mor. Go.	DUCHAL	1765	19100003
GO	Go. Tongue.	TAYLOR	1668	52004029
GO	Go.lif.st. Er.	PEARSON	1718	46007017
GO	Go.str.on Ea.	TILLOTSON	1735	61011013
GO	Go.to Law.	HORNECK	1706	43005040
GO	Go.wor.nec.	BULL	1713	28010012
GO	Pres.o.go.m.	WILCOX	1757	46017015
GO	Rig.civ. Go.	HOLE	1716	43022015
GO	Ser.m.to Go.	FOTHERGILL	1765	57004008
GOD	Attrib. God.	HOOLE	1748	18021015
GOD	Being God.	BARROW	1716	24051015
GOD	Creat. God.	FISHER	1741	19104024
GOD	Exist.of God	HOOLE	1748	61011006
GOD	Fear of God b.	STILLINGFLEET	1707	18023015
GOD	Fear of God.	BATES	1700	18028028
GOD	Fear of God.	SHERLOCK	1719	20009010
GOD	Fear of God.	BENNETT	1728	20023017
GOD	Fear of God.	CLARKE	1732	18023015
GOD	Fear of God.	BURROUGHS	1733	18028023
GOD	Fear of God.	ROGERS	1735	19033008
GOD	Fear of God.	CARLETON	1736	19089007
GOD	Fear of God.	UMFREVILLE	1739	21012013
GOD	Fear of God.	ATTERBURY	1734	53002012
GOD	Fear of God.	JOHNSON	1740	20016006
GOD	Fear of God.	POTTER	1753	45012004
GOD	Fear of God.	SHIRLEY	1762	45012004
GOD	Fear of God.	SECKER	1770	20009010
GOD	Fear of God.	WEBB	1772	18023015
GOD	Fear of God.	SHERLOCK	1772	20009010
GOD	Fear of God.	JORTIN	1774	45012015
GOD	Fear of God.	PETERS	1776	18028026
GOD	Fear of God.	CARR	1777	20016006
GOD	Fear God.	MARTYN	1661	45012004
GOD	Fear God.	NEAL	1757	19031019
GOD	Fear God.	GRANT	1775	63002016
GOD	Forsak. God.	BOSTON	1753	24002013
GOD	Glor.o. God.	PARKHURST	1707	46021019
GOD	Glorif. God.	WISHEART	1716	49006019
GOD	Glory. God.	LUCAS	1710	19034002
GOD	God a Spirit.	HAVETT	1703	46004024
GOD	God impart.	BRADY	1713	51005006
GOD	God in wild.	PEARSE	1763	28013005
GOD	God in Xt.	KIMBER	1756	49001030
GOD	God incarn.	WARREN	1739	57003016
GOD	God is Love.	RUST	1686	65004016
GOD	God is Love.	BRADY	1704	65004008
GOD	God is Love.	HUSSEY	1755	65004008
GOD	God is Love.	DAVIES	1766	65004008
GOD	God is Love.	LELAND	1769	65004008
GOD	God our Fai.	JONES	1741	23064008
GOD	God our Fat.	WILLISON	1761	24003019
GOD	God our Joy.	DUNLOP	1722	19043004
GOD	God w.us.	BRADBURY	1772	23008009
GOD	God.ov. Seas	STUBBS	1701	19135006
GOD	God& K.	STAFFORD	1697	13029018
GOD	God& King.	HARVEST	1754	63002017
GOD	God& King.	SMITH	1759	63002017
GOD	Good. God.	DORMAN	1743	19073001
GOD	Hon. God.	BARROW	1716	09002030
GOD	Imit.of God.	WHITBY	1710	43005048
GOD	Imit.of God.	TILLOTSON	1735	43005048
GOD	Imit.of God.	SHERLOCK	1772	43005048
GOD	Jes. God.	PEAD	1694	43013058
GOD	Kno.of God.	PIGGOTT	1702	46017003
GOD	Know. God.	WISHEART	1716	23011009
GOD	Love o. God.	DUCHAL	1765	56003005
GOD	Love o. God.	BOURDALOUE	1776	46007039
GOD	Love of God	GELL	1676	43022037
GOD	Love of God	ANNESLEY	1676	43022037
GOD	Love of God	ELLIS	1686	43022037
GOD	Love of God	NEWCOME	1702	43022037
GOD	Love of God	BURNET	1713	43022035
GOD	Love of God	EDWARDS	1713	43022037
GOD	Love of God	HOLE	1715	43022037
GOD	Love of God	BARROW	1716	43022037
GOD	Love of God	KILLINBECK	1717	43022036
GOD	Love of God	BEVERIDGE	1720	43022037
GOD	Love of God	CREYGHTON	1720	43022037
GOD	Love of God	BEVERIDGE	1720	43022037
GOD	Love of God	READING	1724	43022037

Keyword	In its Context	Author	Year	BkChpVrs
GOD	Love of God	BOYSE	1728	43022035
GOD	Love of God	NORRIS	1728	43022037
GOD	Love of God	SHARP	1729	43022035
GOD	Love of God	SHARP	1729	43022037
GOD	Love of God	ALTHAM	1732	43022037
GOD	Love of God	CLARKE	1732	43022037
GOD	Love of God	MUDGE	1739	43022037
GOD	Love of God	ABERNETHY	1743	43022037
GOD	Love of God	FOSTER	1744	43022037
GOD	Love of God	BUTLER	1749	43022037
GOD	Love of God	POTTER	1753	43022037
GOD	Love of God	HUSSEY	1758	43022037
GOD	Love of God	ADEY	1760	43022037
GOD	Love of God	MASON	1761	43022037
GOD	Love of God	SECKER	1770	43022037
GOD	Love of God	LANGHORNE	1773	43022037
GOD	Love of God	PETERS	1776	43022037
GOD	Love of God.	WILLIAMS	1662	65004019
GOD	Love of God.	SCOTT	1701	65004019
GOD	Love of God.	DUNLOP	1722	19031023
GOD	Love of God.	BOYSE	1728	65004010
GOD	Love of God.	DAVIS	1756	19031023
GOD	Mer.of God.	TILLOTSON	1735	04014018
GOD	Mer.of God.	HUNT	1748	04014019
GOD	Obed. God.	EMLYN	1742	44010022
GOD	Perfect. God.	ABERNETHY	1743	18011007
GOD	Pleas. God.	BEVERIDGE	1720	55004001
GOD	Prais. God.	BROWN	1722	55004001
GOD	Prais. God.	SAURIN	1775	19033001
GOD	Rej.in God.	SMALRIDGE	1724	19097012
GOD	Rev.to God.	CROWE	1744	24005024
GOD	Seek. God.	BEVERIDGE	1720	23055006
GOD	Suff.of God.	BUNDY	1740	50003005
GOD	Un.of God.	FORSTER	1744	02020001
GOD	Worsh. God.	PHILIPS	1717	21005001
GOD	Worsh. God.	WAPLE	1720	21005001
GOD	Worsh. God.	DORMAN	1743	19100002
GOD	Worsh. God.	ABERNETHY	1751	21005001
GOD	Worsh. God.	WILSON	1781	69005010
GOD	Wp.of God.	CLAGETT	1704	43004010
GOD	Wp.of God.	DORRINGTON	1712	43004010
GOD	Xt. God- M.	EDWARDS	1749	46001014
GOD'S	God's holin.	PENTYCROSS	1781	23006003
GOD'S	God's judg.	TILLOTSON	1735	23009012
GOD'S	God's king.	BEVERIDGE	1720	19097001
GOD'S	God's love.	HAMMOND	1684	26018031
GOD'S	God's love.	SOUTH	1744	23027011
GOD'S	God's name.	DAVIES	1766	02033018
GOD'S	God's Deliv.	ALLESTREE	1684	19102013
GOD'S	God's Elect.	LEIGHTON	1746	48008034
GOD'S	God's Eter.	WISHEART	1716	18036026
GOD'S	God's Etern.	HUNT	1748	48016026
GOD'S	God's Gifts.	KENNET	1715	19104015
GOD'S	God's Gov.	BUNDY	1750	19097001
GOD'S	God's Happ.	TILLOTSON	1735	57001011
GOD'S	God's Happ.	HUNT	1748	57001011
GOD'S	God's Imm.	HUNT	1748	11008027
GOD'S	God's Imm.	DUCHAL	1765	11008027
GOD'S	God's Judg.	WALLIS	1692	19058011
GOD'S	God's Love.	DUNLOP	1722	48005008
GOD'S	God's Mercy	HUSSEY	1758	45006036
GOD'S	God's Omni.	CLARKE	1732	18037016
GOD'S	God's Pat.	SAURIN	1775	01015016
GOD'S	God's Pr.	COTES	1721	34002020
GOD'S	God's Pres.	CARR	1777	20005021
GOD'S	God's Prov.	UMFREVILLE	1739	19058011
GOD'S	God's Sor.	STEWARD	1734	18033012
GOD'S	God's Spirit.	HUNT	1748	46004024
GOD'S	God's Unity	HUNT	1748	05004039
GODL	For.of Godl.	SECKER	1770	58003005
GODL	Godl.happy.	CLARKE	1736	57004007
GODL	Godl.no fan.	ANONYMOUS	1683	63003015
GODL	Godl.no Fan.	VEALE	1683	63003015
GODL	Godl.profit.	BARROW	1716	57004007
GODL	Godl.profit.	SCOTT	1718	57004007
GODL	Godl.profit.	ST.	1737	57004007
GODL	Godl.profit.	MILLER	1749	57004007
GODL	Mys o. Godl.	M'GEORGE	1727	57003016
GODL	Mys.o. Godl.	BRADBURY	1726	57003015
GODL	Mys.o. Godl.	LARDNER	1760	57003016
GODL	Oblig. Godl.	SHARP	1734	52004001
GODL	Pr.of Godl.	BYRDALL	1666	57004004
GODL	Prof.o. Godl.	HALES	1673	57004007
GODL	Prof.o. Godl.	SMITH	1740	57004007
GODL	Prof.o Godl.	BYRDALL	1666	57004007
GODLIN	Godlin. Hap.	CHANDLER	1769	57004007
GODLINESS	Godliness.	EVANS	1737	64001006
GODLINESS	Godliness.	TORRIANO	1767	57003016
GODLINESS	Godliness.	ORR	1772	64001006
GODLY	Godly life.	CAWTON	1662	53001027
GODLY	Godly Fear.	TAYLOR	1668	61012028
GODLY	Godly Fear.	COOKE	1739	21012013
GODLY	Godly Sorr.	LEIGHTON	1746	19119136
GODLY	Godly Sorr.	SHERLOCK	1772	50007010
GODLY	Godly Wisd.	LEIGHTON	1746	19107043
GODLY	Plea.f.godly.	WATSON	1672	20012026
GOLD	Gold Remai.	STUART	1661	61010001
GOLDSM	b. Goldsm.	DELL	1711	20003013
GOLDSMI	Goldsmi. F.	LUCAS	1699	59003014
GOO	G's.rel. Goo.	HUTCHINS	1771	65004016
GOO	Nat.dis.b. Goo	STRADLING	1692	23005020
GOO	Nat.dis.b. Goo	SOUTH	1727	23005020
GOO	Nat.dis.b. Goo	MOSS	1732	23005020
GOO	Nat.dis.b. Goo	STEPHENS	1737	23005020
GOO	Nat.dis.b. Goo	ORR	1749	23005020
GOOD	Afflic. Good.	MEDE	1672	69003019
GOOD	All f. Good.	FARMER	1756	48008028
GOOD	Chief. Good.	SOUTH	1727	43006021
GOOD	Doing good.	WHEATLAND	1739	21003012
GOOD	Doing good.	MILLER	1749	21003012
GOOD	Doing good.	MILLER	1749	43019016
GOOD	Doing Good	TENISON	1690	19078005

INDEXES TO THIRD VOLUME: E: KEYWORD-IN-CONTEXT INDEX OF OTHER SUBJECTS OR OCCASIONS

Keyword	In its Context	Author	Year	BkChpVrs
GOOD	Doing Good.	MORE	1692	61013016
GOOD	Doing Good.	GREGORY	1708	61013016
GOOD	F.&good W.	DUKE	1714	52002008
GOOD	F.of d. Good.	SCOTLAND	1776	28003005
GOOD	G's.good. M.	SKEELER	1740	61002006
GOOD	G's Good.	ORR	1749	34001013
GOOD	G's Good.	DOUGHTY	1761	18012007
GOOD	Good affect.	BULKLEY	1752	43012033
GOOD	Good afflict.	FIDDES	1720	48008028
GOOD	Good afflict.	CLARKE	1727	48008028
GOOD	Good angels.	CONYBEARE	1757	61001014
GOOD	Good con.its H	FIDDES	1720	47024016
GOOD	Good con.its H	FISHER	1741	47024016
GOOD	Good conv.	BARROW	1716	48012017
GOOD	Good earl. O.	MEAD	1683	25003027
GOOD	Good f.	CLEMENT	1774	18002010
GOOD	Good l. Hon.	FOTHERGILL	1765	20004008
GOOD	Good m. De.	WILCOX	1757	19027004
GOOD	Good m. Du.	BURNETT	1774	09030006
GOOD	Good m.exc.	BARKER	1763	19016003
GOOD	Good m's p.	DAVIES	1679	19119057
GOOD	Good m's Su.	HOLLAND	1753	19034019
GOOD	Good wks.n.	TILLOTSON	1735	59003008
GOOD	Good works.	EDWARDS	1726	52002010
GOOD	Good works.	JONES	1756	46014015
GOOD	Good works.	BALGUY	1750	49015058
GOOD	Good. God.	DORMAN	1743	19073001
GOOD	Good.ho. M.	MOSS	1737	20004025
GOOD	Good.of G.	CHARNOCK	1684	44010018
GOOD	Good.of G.	ABERNETHY	1743	44010018
GOOD	Good.of G.	WEST	1762	43019017
GOOD	Good.of G.	HALES	1766	44010018
GOOD	Good.sup. P.	BOURN	1777	45010017
GOOD	Good& E. C.	SALMON	1753	18025005
GOOD	Good& Evil.	SHERLOCK	1719	23005020
GOOD	Good& Evil.	CLARKE	1735	23005020
GOOD	Good& Evil.	FORSTER	1732	47024025
GOOD	Good& Evil.	BENSON	1748	23005020
GOOD	Good& Evil.	HUSSEY	1755	23005020
GOOD	Good&b. C.	CONEY	1750	20013020
GOOD	Good&b. C.	ABERNETHY	1751	20013020
GOOD	Good&b. C.	PETERS	1776	65003020
GOOD	Good&b. E.	MOORE	1716	49010011
GOOD	Good&b. Z.	SEIGNIOR	1670	51004017
GOOD	Good&b.co.	WILKINS	1682	20013020
GOOD	Good&bad.	JORTIN	1774	43013030
GOOD	Good Adv.	BOURN	1777	61003013
GOOD	Good Cent.	BULKLEY	1771	45008005
GOOD	Good Comp.	JENNINGS	1743	19119063
GOOD	Good Cons.	KEITH	1709	63003016
GOOD	Good Cons.	DAWES	1733	65003012
GOOD	Good Cons.	WATERLAND	1742	65003021
GOOD	Good Consc.	COCK	1710	50001012
GOOD	Good Consc.	SUTTON	1718	47024016
GOOD	Good Consc.	DODSON	1728	50001012
GOOD	Good Consc.	FARRINGTON	1741	50001012

Keyword	In its Context	Author	Year	BkChpVrs
GOOD	Good Consc.	NEWMAN	1760	50001012
GOOD	Good Conv.	ROGERS	1735	19119063
GOOD	Good Conv.	QUINCY	1750	62003013
GOOD	Good Disp.	BAYLY	1721	46008047
GOOD	Good Disp.	NALSON	1737	45008015
GOOD	Good Disp.	HODGE	1758	46007016
GOOD	Good Exam.	BROGRAVE	1689	43005016
GOOD	Good Exam.	BRADY	1713	43005016
GOOD	Good Exam.	BOYS	1716	43005016
GOOD	Good Exam.	BLACKALL	1723	43005016
GOOD	Good Exam.	CARLETON	1736	43005016
GOOD	Good Exam.	BLAIR	1740	43005016
GOOD	Good Exam.	GROVE	1747	61013007
GOOD	Good Exam.	BUNDY	1750	61013007
GOOD	Good Exam.	WELD	1766	61013007
GOOD	Good Exam.	BRAILSFORD	1776	09002023
GOOD	Good Exam.	ANONYMOUS	1776	48015002
GOOD	Good Gr.	BULKLEY	1771	45008022
GOOD	Good Intent.	ALLESTREE	1684	43006022
GOOD	Good Intent.	BLACKALL	1723	43006022
GOOD	Good Intent.	WESTLEY	1748	43006001
GOOD	Good King.	PRICE	1661	21010017
GOOD	Good Less.	STRYPE	1707	20014012
GOOD	Good Man.	CLARKE	1734	01018019
GOOD	Good Mas.	TERRY	1746	02018021
GOOD	Good Name.	MARKLAND	1729	21002016
GOOD	Good Name.	CONEY	1750	20022001
GOOD	Good P.t.m.	AMORY	1766	43005045
GOOD	Good Patr.	MACKQUEENE	1694	45007004
GOOD	Good Samar.	BRAGGE	1702	45010030
GOOD	Good Samar.	HOADLY	1755	45010037
GOOD	Good Samar.	DODD	1757	45010037
GOOD	Good Samar.	STEBBING	1760	45010037
GOOD	Good Samar.	BOURN	1764	45010025
GOOD	Good Samar.	BULKLEY	1771	45010036
GOOD	Good Samar.	SHERLOCK	1772	45010029
GOOD	Good Samar.	JORTIN	1774	45010030
GOOD	Good Samar.	SANDWICH	1774	45010037
GOOD	Good Samar.	PYLE	1777	45010029
GOOD	Good Samar.	SMITH	1777	45010036
GOOD	Good Samar.	BROUGHTON	1778	45010029
GOOD	Good Serv.	EDWARDS	1726	45012043
GOOD	Good Sold.	DAVIES	1758	01018019
GOOD	Good Stew.	WESTLEY	1771	45016002
GOOD	Good T.in l.	DUCHAL	1765	53001010
GOOD	Good Works	BEVERIDGE	1720	19037027
GOOD	Good Works	SMALRIDGE	1724	61006010
GOOD	Good Works	GALE	1726	57006019
GOOD	Good Works.	PENTYCROSS	1781	45017009
GOOD	Ig.good&e.	BLAIR	1777	21006012
GOOD	Love Good.	BOURN	1777	19119015
GOOD	Pract. Good.	WOODCOCK	1690	48014001
GOOD	Supre. Good.	FARRINGTON	1741	19016011
GOOD	The L.good.	BROWNE	1749	48007019
GOOD	To do good.	GALE	1726	57006018
GOOD	X's Good w.	HILL	1755	05033016

Keyword	In its Context	Author	Year	BkChpVrs
GOOD	Xr.good M.	HUNTER	1774	45023050
GOOD	Xt's.good W.	BOSTON	1773	45019005
GOODN	Div. Goodn.	STEFFE	1743	10007018
GOODN	Div. Goodn.	CHANDLER	1769	19036007
GOODN	G's. Goodn.	SCOTT	1701	46003016
GOODN	G's. Goodn.	WISHEART	1716	37009017
GOODN	G's. Goodn.	WHARTON	1728	48002004
GOODN	G's. Goodn.	ROGERS	1735	48002004
GOODN	G's. Goodn.	WARREN	1748	37009017
GOODN	G's. Goodn.	PENTYCROSS	1781	37009017
GOODN	G's Goodn.	SCOTT	1701	19119068
GOODN	G's Goodn.	SCOTT	1701	19145008
GOODN	G's Goodn.	SCOTT	1701	19145009
GOODN	G's Goodn.	WHITBY	1710	19145009
GOODN	G's Goodn.	BARROW	1716	19145009
GOODN	G's Goodn.	CLARKE	1727	19119068
GOODN	G's Goodn.	MARKLAND	1729	45013006
GOODN	G's Goodn.	CLARKE	1732	19145009
GOODN	G's Goodn.	TILLOTSON	1735	19145009
GOODN	G's Goodn.	BEESTON	1739	19145009
GOODN	G's Goodn.	WILDER	1741	19119068
GOODN	G's Goodn.	ATTERBURY	1743	19119068
GOODN	G's Goodn.	SOUTH	1744	19145009
GOODN	G's Goodn.	HUNT	1748	19086005
GOODN	G's Goodn.	HOLDEN	1755	19145009
GOODN	G's Goodn.	DAVIS	1756	19145009
GOODN	G's Goodn.	NEWTON	1759	19119069
GOODN	G's Goodn.	AMORY	1766	19145009
GOODN	G's Goodn.	LELAND	1769	19145009
GOODN	G's Goodn.	LANGHORNE	1773	19145009
GOODN	G's Goodn.	JORTIN	1774	19145009
GOODN	G's Goodn.	CARR	1777	19107031
GOODN	Goodn.of G.	REAY	1755	65004017
GOODN	Of Goodn.	SMITH	1740	48002004
GOODNESS	Goodness.	SCOTT	1701	19011007
GOODNESS	Goodness.	BROWN	1764	48005007
GORD	Ld Gord.rel.	CLARKE	1781	19050015
GOS	Apol.f. Gos.	SMITH	1709	49015001
GOS	Belief o. Gos.	OUTRAM	1697	46007017
GOS	Cont.of Gos.	DAVIS	1756	48001016
GOS	Cred.of Gos.	LELAND	1769	46020032
GOS	Des.of Gos.	CLARKE	1735	43003012
GOS	Div. Or. Gos.	SWINDEN	1718	58003016
GOS	Evid.of Gos.	CENNICK	1762	45016031
GOS	Evid.of Gos.	BADDELLEY	1766	45016031
GOS	Evid.of Gos.	SHERLOCK	1772	45016031
GOS	Evid.of Gos.	CARR	1777	45016031
GOS	G. Eff. Gos.	SECKER	1770	43010034
GOS	G. Ten. Gos.	BOTT	1724	45009056
GOS	G. Ten. Gos.	ORR	1739	45009056
GOS	Gos.& L. Li.	ABERNETHY	1748	62002012
GOS	Gos. Ev.suff.	WHARTON	1728	45016031
GOS	Gos. Ev.suff.	WESTON	1747	45016031
GOS	Gos. L.of L.	SUTTON	1718	62001025
GOS	Gos. La. Nat.	BULLOCK	1728	43021033
GOS	Gos. Mor.	JONES	1741	53004008

Keyword	In its Context	Author	Year	BkChpVrs
GOS	Gos. Mor.	LARDNER	1751	53004008
GOS	Gos. Repent.	CHANDLER	1769	47011018
GOS	Gos. W.o G.	BAINE	1778	49002007
GOS	Gos.g.str.th.	WHITTY	1772	45005026
GOS	Gos.how pr.	HAMOND	1690	54004005
GOS	Gos.un.th.u.	BEVERIDGE	1720	61004002
GOS	Gos.un.th.u.	CLARKE	1727	61004002
GOS	Gos.unf.&c.	ST.	1757	43005013
GOS	Gr.&m. Gos.	CLAGETT	1720	43005019
GOS	Gra.of Gos.	MACE	1751	63005010
GOS	Ho.des. Gos.	HOLE	1715	59002014
GOS	Ho.des. Gos.	BEVERIDGE	1720	59002011
GOS	Ho.des. Gos.	BEVERIDGE	1720	59002013
GOS	Ho.des. Gos.	BEVERIDGE	1720	59002014
GOS	Ho.des. Gos.	RINGER	1734	59002013
GOS	Law.es. Gos.	LITTLETON	1680	43005017
GOS	Law.es. Gos.	HORNECK	1706	43005017
GOS	Law.es. Gos.	HOLE	1715	43005017
GOS	Law.es. Gos.	MOSS	1737	43005017
GOS	Light o. Gos.	SHERLOCK	1722	55001009
GOS	Live of Gos.	MEDE	1672	49009014
GOS	Mor.of Gos.	REAY	1755	44009040
GOS	Myst.of Gos.	PACK	1691	48009005
GOS	Pow.of Gos.	MONRO	1693	49002003
GOS	Remov. Gos.	CHARNOCK	1684	69002005
GOS	S.add to Gos.	TILLOTSON	1735	51001008
GOS	Sanc.of Gos.	HORBERRY	1774	43010028
GOS	Succ.of Gos.	NEWTON	1767	43011025
GOS	Succ.of Gos.	DAVIES	1771	50010004
GOS	Un. Gos.tea.	FLEMING	1772	49001001
GOS	V.disp. Gos.	PRICE	1757	45001072
GOSP	Belief. Gosp.	CASE	1774	44016006
GOSP	Def.of Gosp.	WATTS	1753	48001016
GOSP	Des.of Gosp.	MICHELL	1731	59002011
GOSP	Des.of Gosp.	MORRIS	1743	59002011
GOSP	Exc.o. Gosp.	SECKER	1770	53004008
GOSP	Exc.o. Gosp.	TOTTIE	1775	53004008
GOSP	Gen.of Gosp.	MOIR	1776	45019041
GOSP	Gosp h.f w.	BARKER	1763	43011025
GOSP	Gosp. Adv.	STANHOPE	1705	43020009
GOSP	Gosp. Adv.	DODD	1757	43020016
GOSP	Gosp. Comp.	BATES	1700	45014023
GOSP	Gosp. Comp.	ACTON	1714	45014023
GOSP	Gosp. Comp.	CLARKE	1727	45014023
GOSP	Gosp. Comp.	BOSTON	1753	45014023
GOSP	Gosp. Cov.	FAWCET	1749	01017001
GOSP	Gosp. Faith.	BEVERLEY	1695	46017007
GOSP	Gosp. Freed.	CLAGETT	1720	46008036
GOSP	Gosp. Freed.	EDWARDS	1726	46008036
GOSP	Gosp. Freed.	BATTY	1739	46008036
GOSP	Gosp. Grace.	VINK	1690	58002019
GOSP	Gosp. Hum.	ERSKINE	1764	26016063
GOSP	Gosp. Invit.	DAVIES	1771	45014021
GOSP	Gosp. L.o. L.	BERRIMAN	1763	62001015
GOSP	Gosp. Mess.	WARBURTON	1753	43010005
GOSP	Gosp. Mess.	WARBURTON	1753	43010016

INDEXES TO THIRD VOLUME: E: KEYWORD-IN-CONTEXT INDEX OF OTHER SUBJECTS OR OCCASIONS

Keyword	In its Context	Author	Year	BkChpVrs
GOSP	Gosp. Min.	FLAVEL	1673	50005020
GOSP	Gosp. Min.	BEVERIDGE	1720	50005020
GOSP	Gosp. Min.	NEWTON	1780	52004015
GOSP	Gosp. Min.d.	HARRIS	1710	45010016
GOSP	Gosp. Minis.	DUCKINFIELD	1707	50002016
GOSP	Gosp. Minis.	KNOX	1768	48010005
GOSP	Gosp. Myst.	TAYLOR	1719	43013011
GOSP	Gosp. Ob. A.	BOURN	1760	46018036
GOSP	Gosp. Ob.an.	BOURN	1760	49001022
GOSP	Gosp. Obed.	HOPKINS	1708	43011025
GOSP	Gosp. Princ.	ERSKINE	1764	54002006
GOSP	Gosp. Prom.	TILLOTSON	1735	64001004
GOSP	Gosp. Publ.	ATTERBURY	1734	47026026
GOSP	Gosp. Rep	HAMMOND	1684	43003002
GOSP	Gosp. Rep	HOLE	1716	43003002
GOSP	Gosp. Rep	SHIRLEY	1762	43003001
GOSP	Gosp. Sacra.	EDWARDS	1702	22007002
GOSP	Gosp. Salv.	STILLINGFLEET	1707	48001016
GOSP	Gosp. Salvat.	PARSON	1676	47016031
GOSP	Gosp. Salvat.	PIERCE	1686	47016031
GOSP	Gosp. Salvat.	MARCH	1699	61002003
GOSP	Gosp. Salvat.	NEWCOME	1719	61002003
GOSP	Gosp. Salvat.	SHARP	1729	47016031
GOSP	Gosp. Salvat.	ROGERS	1735	61002003
GOSP	Gosp. Salvat.	DAVIES	1754	53002012
GOSP	Gosp. Salvat.	WALKER	1763	61002003
GOSP	Gosp. Sanct.	CARDALE	1740	02020024
GOSP	Gosp. Spirit.	HAMMOND	1684	45009055
GOSP	Gosp.cred.	HALL	1756	43028020
GOSP	Gosp.esta. L.	FISHER	1741	48003031
GOSP	Gosp.esta. L.	GILL	1773	48003031
GOSP	Gosp.n. Cre.	PALMER	1674	19025011
GOSP	Gosp.n. Cre.	STRONG	1678	19025011
GOSP	Gosp.of G.	CREYGHTON	1720	55002008
GOSP	Gosp.relief.	MASON	1758	46006035
GOSP	Gosp.remiss.	BURROUGHS	1668	19032001
GOSP	Gosp.revel.	LEECHMAN	1758	49001021
GOSP	Gosp.sin. O.	SUTTON	1718	43007021
GOSP	Gosp.sin. O.	ABERNETHY	1748	43007021
GOSP	Gosp.suff.	NARSHALL	1731	50004003
GOSP	Gosp.w.o. S.	LARDNER	1751	47016031
GOSP	Gosp.worth.	CARKEET	1719	43010011
GOSP	Infl.of Gosp.	HODGE	1758	54002013
GOSP	Law& Gosp.	SMALRIDGE	1724	50003011
GOSP	Law& Gosp.	ALTHAM	1732	50003009
GOSP	Law& Gosp.	WATTS	1753	51003021
GOSP	Law& Gosp.	BREKELL	1765	51003024
GOSP	Law& Gosp.	DAVIES	1771	51003023
GOSP	Len.o. Gosp.	TOTTIE	1775	46008010
GOSP	Min.o. Gosp.	CLAYTON	1776	49010033
GOSP	Negl. Gosp.	MARSH	1737	43022012
GOSP	Off.ag. Gosp.	CLARKE	1735	45017001
GOSP	Off.ag. Gosp.	HODGE	1758	43011006
GOSP	Off.ag. Gosp.	SHERLOCK	1772	43011006
GOSP	P. Gosp.can.	FLEMING	1772	49002004
GOSP	Perf. Gosp.	TRAPP	1752	58002011

Keyword	In its Context	Author	Year	BkChpVrs
GOSP	Pow. Gosp.	MARSH	1737	47019020
GOSP	Rec.of Gosp.	BADDELLEY	1752	46001012
GOSP	Rej.of Gosp.	DAVIES	1771	46003019
GOSP	Ren. Gosp.c.	ERSKINE	1764	22002013
GOSP	Succ. Gosp.	BOSTON	1753	23053001
GOSP	Temp. Gosp.	WEST	1762	45009055
GOSP	Temp. Gosp.	JORTIN	1774	45009056
GOSP	Trid. Gosp	RAMSAY	1672	51001008
GOSP	Xrter. Gosp.	ROBINSON	1738	43020026
GOSPEL	The Gospel.	TERRY	1746	49001021
GOV	G.gov. Pass.	BLAIR	1780	19076010
GOV	G.gov.m. A.	LELAND	1769	43010029
GOV	G's mo. Gov.	WARBURTON	1753	19144003
GOV	G's. Gov. W.	DUCHAL	1765	46014011
GOV	God's Gov.	BUNDY	1750	19097001
GOV	Gov. Ch. Ch.	NICOLSON	1661	23002004
GOV	Gov. Heart.	MEDE	1672	20004023
GOV	Gov. Heart.	DAWES	1687	20004024
GOV	Gov. Heart.	NEWLIN	1720	20004023
GOV	Gov. Heart.	SHARP	1729	20004023
GOV	Gov. Heart.	MOSS	1737	20004023
GOV	Gov. Heart.	ORR	1739	20004023
GOV	Gov. Heart.	SMITH	1740	20004023
GOV	Gov. Heart.	SEED	1743	20004023
GOV	Gov. Heart.	MARSHAL	1750	20004023
GOV	Gov. Heart.	MACE	1751	20004023
GOV	Gov. Heart.	TRAPP	1752	20004023
GOV	Gov. Heart.	HUSSEY	1755	20004023
GOV	Gov. Heart.	WEBBER	1758	20004023
GOV	Gov. Heart.	DUCHAL	1765	20004023
GOV	Gov. Heart.	LLOYD	1765	20004023
GOV	Gov. Heart.	LARDNER	1769	20004023
GOV	Gov. Heart.	LATHAM	1774	20004023
GOV	Gov. Heart.	STONE	1777	20004023
GOV	Gov. Pass.	CLAGETT	1720	20025028
GOV	Gov. Passion.	TRAPP	1751	45021019
GOV	Gov. Passions	CARR	1777	20004023
GOV	Gov. Tong.	BARROW	1716	62003002
GOV	Gov. Tong.	FIDDES	1720	53001027
GOV	Gov. Tong.	LARDNER	1751	62003002
GOV	Gov. Xt's.ch.	BAINE	1778	49005012
GOV	Gov.of Passi.	CLARKE	1734	52004026
GOV	Gov.of Spir.	BARKER	1748	20025028
GOV	Gov.of Spir.	BARKER	1748	20026028
GOV	Gov.of Ton.	WEST	1676	52004029
GOV	Gov.of Ton.	SHORTHOSE	1738	62001026
GOV	Gov.of Ton.	BUTLER	1749	62001026
GOV	M.& J. Gov.	BOURN	1760	19058010
GOV	Ob.to Gov.	WATSON	1763	59003001
GOV	Obed.t. Gov.	SHERLOCK	1772	48013001
GOV	Or. Civ. Gov.	HORNE	1778	48013004
GOV	R. Gov.of F.	PICKARD	1762	01018019
GOV	Rel.& Gov.	HENLEY	1772	44012017
GOV	Subj.to Gov.	BOURN	1777	59003001
GOV	b. Gov. Disp.	DODD	1773	02002006
GOV	b. Gov. Disp.	YORKE	1776	19127005

Keyword	In its Context	Author	Year	BkChpVrs
GOVER	Eccl. Gover.	LORTIE	1720	49014032
GOVER	Gover. Fam.	ANONYMOUS	1722	06024015
GOVERN	Div. Govern.	OGDEN	1770	53004006
GOVERN	Div. Govern.	OGDEN	1770	62005016
GOVERN	Evil Govern.	HAYWOOD	1663	47023005
GOVERN	G's. Govern.	SAURIN	1777	61013008
GOVERN	Govern. Pass.	HUSSEY	1755	47014015
GOVERN	On Govern.	READING	1739	45019027
GOVERN	Self. Govern.	IBBOT	1726	20016032
GOVERN	Self. Govern.	PIERCE	1731	20016032
GOVERN	Self Govern.	ABERNETHY	1751	20025028
GOVERN	Self-govern.	DUCHAL	1765	49006012
GOVERN	on Govern.	READING	1739	21008011
GR	Cov.of Gr.	CROSS	1693	10023005
GR	Cov.of Gr.	TAYLOR	1725	19089003
GR	Cov.of Gr.	BOSTON	1773	19089003
GR	Dew Div.gr.	STEFFE	1743	28014005
GR	Div.gr.expl.	HORBERY	1774	46003008
GR	F. Gr.mag.	LAMBERT	1779	24032008
GR	Free gr.of G.	FELTON	1748	48003023
GR	G's. Co.n.gr.	DUNLOP	1722	65005003
GR	G's. Co.n.gr.	BRADY	1730	65005003
GR	Good Gr.	BULKLEY	1771	45008022
GR	Gr.&m. Gos.	CLAGETT	1720	43005019
GR	Gr.b. Gift.	NALSON	1737	45011011
GR	Gr.of Jes.&c.	LARDNER	1760	46019030
GR	Gr.wick.&c.	STUART	1753	48003010
GR	Grow in Gr.	MARCH	1699	64003018
GR	Grow in Gr.	INNES	1726	64003018
GR	Grow in Gr.	MARSHALL	1731	64003018
GR	Grow.in Gr.	WHALEY	1695	64003018
GR	Grow.in Gr.	EDWARDS	1726	64003018
GR	Grow.in Gr.	BATTY	1739	64003018
GR	Means Gr.	WESTLEY	1749	38003007
GR	Ord.mea.gr.	ADAMS	1690	45016031
GR	Peace of Gr.	MAKENZIE	1779	18003017
GR	Pre. Xy.n.gr.	TILLOTSON	1735	65005003
GR	Pro.gr. Doct.	PALMER	1726	20014034
GR	Reign.of Gr.	BAINE	1778	48005021
GR	Req.of R.gr.	SPOONER	1771	19034015
GR	Sal.by gr. G.	KIMBER	1756	59002011
GR	Sec.of w. Gr.	TAYLOR	1719	23065008
GR	Sen. Rev.gr.	GREEN	1758	49010012
GR	Sens.gr. Sep.	LONG	1677	68000019
GR	Sin.gr. H. G.	WILSON	1781	52004030
GR	Suff.of d. Gr.	ATTERBURY	1699	50012009
GR	Suff.of d. Gr.	BEVERIDGE	1720	50012009
GR	Value of Gr.	WILCOX	1757	22001012
GR	World. Gr.	WEBB	1772	27004030
GR	Xt.gr. Prop.	WILSON	1746	65004010
GR	Xt.gr. Salv.	BURNET	1747	61002003
GR	Xt's. Inst.gr.	TOTTIE	1775	46016012
GR	Xt's.gr. Int.	PARR	1661	45019041
GRA	Day of Gra.	SHOWER	1694	19081011
GRA	Doct.of Gra.	GILL	1773	57006003
GRA	Evang. Gra.	BEVERIDGE	1720	64001005

Keyword	In its Context	Author	Year	BkChpVrs
GRA	Gra.of Gos.	MACE	1751	63005010
GRA	Persev. Gra.	FARMER	1756	53001006
GRA	Salv.b. Gra.	ACTON	1714	52002005
GRA	Salv.b. Gra.	DUNLOP	1722	52002008
GRA	Salv.b. Gra.	SUTTON	1754	52002008
GRA	Salv.b. Gra.	HAWEIS	1762	52002008
GRA	Salv.by Gra.	SPOONER	1771	59002011
GRA	Xt. Gra.& T.	BEVERIDGE	1720	46001017
GRACE	Assur. Grace.	MATHER	1701	65005013
GRACE	Co.of Grace.	TAYLOR	1725	10022005
GRACE	Co.of Grace.	SHEPHERD	1748	10023005
GRACE	Cov. Grace.	ERSKINE	1764	05026017
GRACE	Cov.o. Grace	BRINSLEY	1667	61012024
GRACE	Cov.o. Grace	ANNESLEY	1676	61008006
GRACE	Cov.o. Grace	BOSTON	1773	49015025
GRACE	Cov.o. Grace	BOSTON	1773	49015042
GRACE	Cov.o. Grace	BAINE	1778	61009016
GRACE	Div. Grace.	CRUSO	1699	44010026
GRACE	Div. Grace.	CRUSO	1699	52004007
GRACE	Div. Grace.	JOHNSON	1740	63005010
GRACE	Div. Grace.	SHEPHERD	1748	53002012
GRACE	Div. Grace.	NEWTON	1767	43011026
GRACE	Div. Grace.	BUCKRIDGE	1767	46014016
GRACE	Div. Grace.	BOURDALOUE	1776	46004010
GRACE	Effic. Grace.	WILSON	1732	53002013
GRACE	Free Grace.	WILKINSON	1660	37013001
GRACE	Free Grace.	BRIDGE	1671	52002008
GRACE	Free Grace.	BRIDGE	1671	56002016
GRACE	Free Grace.	FARMER	1756	45023042
GRACE	Free Grace.	ROWLAND	1774	45023042
GRACE	G's. Grace.	HOADLY	1727	50003005
GRACE	Gosp. Grace.	VINK	1690	58002019
GRACE	Grace of G.	MARSHALL	1731	50012009
GRACE	Grace of G.	CLARKE	1732	53002012
GRACE	Grace of G.	CLARKE	1732	59002011
GRACE	Grace of G.	TILLY	1737	53002012
GRACE	Grace of Xt.	DUNLOP	1722	50008009
GRACE	Grace.	TAYLOR	1668	48008009
GRACE	Grace.	BENNETT	1728	47026019
GRACE	Grace.	BENNETT	1728	49015010
GRACE	Grace.	BENNETT	1728	51001015
GRACE	Grace.	BENNETT	1728	57001014
GRACE	Grace.	BILSON	1756	49015010
GRACE	Grace&c.	FROYSELL	1676	19078056
GRACE	Grace Energy	SKEPP	1752	52001019
GRACE	Nat.& Grace	YOUNG	1706	43026035
GRACE	Nat.& Grace	ANONYMOUS	1711	50005017
GRACE	Nec. Grace.	TILLOTSON	1735	46015005
GRACE	Of Grace.	PELIERE	1737	40014003
GRACE	Salv.b Grace	TAYLOR	1719	52002008
GRACE	Sav. Grace.	LORTIE	1720	52002005
GRACE	Sav. Grace.	PIKE	1758	02033019
GRACE	Suff.o. Grace	WILCOX	1757	50012009
GRACE	Thr.o Grace	WALKER	1765	61004016
GRAD	Grad. Conq.	ERSKINE	1764	05007022
GRAD	Grad. Pr. R.	SECKER	1770	23001016

INDEXES TO THIRD VOLUME: E: KEYWORD-IN-CONTEXT INDEX OF OTHER SUBJECTS OR OCCASIONS

Keyword	In its Context	Author	Year	BkChpVrs
GRAD	Grad. Revel.	REAY	1755	61001001
GRAND	Grand.of G.	SAURIN	1775	23040012
GRAND	Grand Char.	LAWSON	1686	43028018
GRAT	Grat.to G.	MAYNARD	1722	45017017
GRAT	Grat.to G.	BRADY	1730	45017017
GRAT	Grat.to G.	WHITE	1757	19086012
GRAT	Grat.to G.	EATON	1764	19116012
GRAT	Grat.to G.	DEVEREL	1777	19116012
GRAT	Relig. Grat.	BOURN	1760	19103002
GRATITUDE	Gratitude.	DODWELL	1748	45006032
GRATITUDE	Gratitude.	WATKINSON	1763	45010021
GRAVE	Suf.in Grave	WATTS	1753	18014013
GRE	Gre. Assize.	SMITH	1665	69020011
GRE	Gre. Assize.	VENN	1759	69020011
GREAT	Great.loss.	LIVESEY	1660	43016026
GREAT	Great.of Sal.	GREGORY	1696	61002003
GREAT	Great Assize.	JEPHSON	1742	47017031
GREAT	Great Assize.	KIMBER	1756	47017031
GREAT	Great Assize.	HORNE	1778	47017031
GREAT	Great Com.	ANONYMOUS	1776	44012030
GREAT	Great Frost.	CAMFIELD	1684	19147015
GREAT	Great Ruin.	ERSKINE	1764	27012009
GREAT	Wor. Great.	REYNER	1745	27005027
GREAT	b. Great Au.	FULLER	1672	57006003
GREGOR	b. Gregor.	GREGORY	1673	44013037
GRI	Orig.of Gri.	BEDFORD	1770	62004001
GRIE	Rem.f. Grie.	BURROUGHS	1662	19032009
GRIEF	Grief. Sins.	DORRINGTON	1703	19119158
GRIEV	Griev. H. Sp.	MOORE	1716	52004030
GRIEV	Griev. H. Sp.	SCATTERGOOD	1723	52004030
GRIEV	Griev. H. Sp.	SHARP	1734	52004030
GRIEV	Griev. H. Sp.	TILLY	1737	52004030
GRIEV	Griev. H. Sp.	ATTERBURY	1743	52004030
GROUN	Si. H.groun.	ASHTON	1770	19119123
GROW	Grow in Gr.	MARCH	1699	64003018
GROW	Grow in Gr.	INNES	1726	64003018
GROW	Grow in Gr.	MARSHALL	1731	64003018
GROW	Grow. K. Xt.	VINCENT	1683	64003018
GROW	Grow.in Gr.	WHALEY	1695	64003018
GROW	Grow.in Gr.	EDWARDS	1726	64003018
GROW	Grow.in Gr.	BATTY	1739	64003018
GROWTH	Xn's.growth	GOODWIN	16--	46015002
GUESTS	King. Guests	BOURN	1764	43022008
GUI	Gui.ob. Fear	BRYSON	1778	49015056
GUID	Guid. Spirit.	HOLE	1716	46016005
GUIDE	Xn's Guide.	FULWOOD	1673	54001010
GUILT	Aggr. Guilt.	BOURN	1777	45012047
GUILT	Dav's Guilt.	DOUGHTY	1761	19051003
GUILT	Guilt of Sin.	PYLE	1777	18007020
GUILT	Orig. Guilt.	HAYWARD	1758	51003022
GUILT	Terr. Guilt.	CONEY	1730	47024025
GUILT	Univ. Guilt.	WALKER	1764	48003019
GUILTY	Guilty Cons.	FISHER	1741	47024025
H	Ab.h. G's w.	PIDDLE	1777	26033030
H	Ass.o. H. Gh.	OGDEN	1777	65003024
H	Assist.o. H. S	BENNETT	1728	53001019

Keyword	In its Context	Author	Year	BkChpVrs
H	Bapt.o. H. G.	JOHNSON	1776	47011016
H	Bar. H.& C.	WILKINSON	1660	24045005
H	Beelz.d. H.	BURGESS	1770	44005011
H	Bei.o. H. Gh.	OGDEN	1777	48015013
H	Bel. H.in G.	WILCOX	1757	25003024
H	Believ.str.h.	WALKER	1764	37009012
H	Blasp. H. G.	BREKELL	1765	44003028
H	Bless.pur in H	BEVERIDGE	1720	43005008
H	Bless.pur in H	BLACKALL	1723	43005008
H	Bless.pur in H	ABERNETHY	1751	43005008
H	Care of H-k.	DYKES	1722	20031027
H	Ch p. F.& H.	HOLE	1725	49013013
H	Ch.e. F.& H.	MOSS	1732	49013013
H	Ch.e. F.& H.	MORRIS	1743	49013013
H	Circ.of H.	BRAGGE	1713	48002029
H	Circ.of H.	SHARP	1734	48002028
H	Circ.of H.	WESTLEY	1748	48002029
H	Conv. H. A.	SMITH	1763	19002008
H	Corr.o. H. N.	HAWEIS	1762	48005018
H	Cov. S.h. Ha.	PEAD	1701	52002001
H	Cov. S.h. Ha.	WARREN	1748	52002001
H	D.& H. Mer.	BRAILSFORD	1776	10024014
H	D. Virt.m. H.	WILLIAMS	1770	43005006
H	D.rel.t. H. S.	GUYSE	1757	52004030
H	D.son&h.sp.	EVANS	1766	47005004
H	Dang.ev. H.	ABERNETHY	1751	24013023
H	De. S.& H. G.	EVANS	1766	65005020
H	De.o. H. Gh.	BROME	1709	46016007
H	Def. H. Reas.	BURNET	1747	49013012
H	Def. H.wisd.	FIDDES	1720	21001018
H	Def. H.wisd.	MARKLAND	1729	21001018
H	Des.& H. Xty	WILSON	1781	57004015
H	Des.& H. Xy.	WILSON	1781	57004001
H	Dig.& H. Xt.	CLARKE	1727	65004009
H	Dign. H.nat.	BOURN	1777	19008005
H	Div.& H. H.	SHERLOCK	1772	46005044
H	Div.&h. Ag.	BOURN	1777	53002012
H	Div. H. Gh.	BARROW	1716	49003016
H	Div. H. Gh.	STEPHENS	1717	47005003
H	Do&h. G's w.	DORMAN	1743	62001022
H	Do&h. W.	BROWNRIG	1664	62001022
H	Do&h. W.	BEVERIDGE	1720	62001022
H	Do&h. W.	ALTHAM	1732	62001022
H	Do&h. W.	ATTERBURY	1743	62001022
H	Door of H.o.	WILCOX	1757	45014022
H	Dut. H.& W.	NICHOLS	1701	54003018
H	Dut. H.& W.	FLEETWOOD	1737	54003019
H	Eff.of H. Gh.	BROWNE	1722	47002032
H	Eff.of H. Sp.	SAURIN	1775	47002037
H	End Xt's.g.h.	JOHNSON	1740	59002014
H	F. C.of H. L.	SANDERSON	1722	15010007
H	F. H.& Char.	CLAGETT	1720	49013013
H	Fai& H.in J.	PRICE	1757	51005005
H	Fe. G.&h. K.	SEABURY	17--	63002017
H	Fin. C. H. L.	SANDERSON	1722	58002002
H	Fu. St.n.t. H.	CONYBEARE	1757	49015019

Keyword	In its Context	Author	Year	BkChpVrs
H	G. H. Men.	TILLOTSON	1735	19073025
H	G. News f. H	TOPLADY	1774	19089012
H	G.know. H.	HORT	1738	24017009
H	G.s. H.& Ea.	ORTON	1776	19113005
H	G's H.in Ex.	BRODHURST	1733	01022014
H	Gift o. H. Gh.	COWPER	1773	47002038
H	Gifts H. Gh.	BATTY	1739	52004008
H	Gifts H. Sp.	TATHAM	1780	46014016
H	Glo.& H. H.	SIMS	1772	54003001
H	Good con.its H	FIDDES	1720	47024016
H	Good con.its H	FISHER	1741	47024016
H	Gosp h.f w.	BARKER	1763	43011025
H	Griev. H. Sp.	MOORE	1716	52004030
H	Griev. H. Sp.	SCATTERGOOD	1723	52004030
H	Griev. H. Sp.	SHARP	1734	52004030
H	Griev. H. Sp.	TILLY	1737	52004030
H	Griev. H. Sp.	ATTERBURY	1743	52004030
H	H.& Fear G.	OUTRAM	1697	38001006
H	H.& Meek.	ANONYMOUS	1776	43005003
H	H.& Mord.	THEED	1712	17005013
H	H.& Mord.	WHARTON	1728	17005013
H	H.&do word	FIDDES	1720	62001022
H	H.&do word	SNAPE	1745	62001023
H	H.&pr.word	STUART	1773	46010025
H	H. G. Parac.	LESTLEY	1720	46016007
H	H. Gh. Div.	PIGOTT	1702	46016013
H	H. Gh. Parac.	BRETT	1720	46016007
H	H. Gh.bapt.	JOHNSON	1776	47002016
H	H. Gh.div. P.	LESTLEY	1720	46014016
H	H. Ghost&c.	DAWSON	1765	49012004
H	H. Ign.& M.	BOURN	1777	18008009
H	H. N.deprav.	MARRIOTT	1774	19051005
H	H. Nat.vind.	STERNE	1760	48014007
H	H. S. S.	CROWNFIELD	1752	58003016
H	H. S. T.o. Xt.	JOHNSON	1776	46015026
H	H. Sp. Oper.	WATERLAND	1742	48008014
H	H. Sp. Sanct.	FARMER	1756	46014026
H	H. Spirit.	GUYSE	1721	49012011
H	H. W. Xr. Xs.	POWELL	1776	43005011
H	H. Y.sh.o. H.	WATTS	1753	44010021
H	H.bet.hearts	ANGIER	1662	23029013
H	H.own Fu.s.	ALEXANDER	1766	21009010
H	H.reas.insuf.	SHUCKBURGH	1721	21001015
H	H.to G's N.	SKELTON	1754	03019030
H	H&do word	MORE	1692	62001022
H	Imit. G's. H.	CLARKE	1732	63001015
H	Inf. H. Nat.	CONYBEARE	1757	43025005
H	Inf. H. Spir.	ATTERBURY	1743	55005019
H	Infl.of H. G.	SIMS	1772	53004013
H	Integ.h.nat.	HOLDEN	1755	21007029
H	J's h. Concl.	JENKINS	1779	01042036
H	Jes.an. H. Pr.	WHEATLY	1746	61005009
H	Joy in H.&c.	WATERLAND	1742	45015007
H	Joy in H.&c.	TOPLADY	1775	45015007
H	Joy in H.&c.	PETERS	1776	45015010
H	Joy in H.&c.	PYLE	1777	45015007
H	Joy in H. Gh.	DODSON	1728	48014017
H	Joy Pea.& H.	LUCAS	1710	48015013
H	Joys of H.	ADEY	1760	19016012
H	Law in X's h.	GILL	1773	05010005
H	Law o. G's h.	ERSKINE	1764	26043002
H	Ly.to H. Gh.	NEWLIN	1728	47005003
H	M.af. G.o. H.	EVANSON	1773	47013022
H	M's Inv.to H.	ORTON	1776	04010029
H	Mat.of H. L.	SANDERSON	1722	20008015
H	Mea. H. Nat.	BOURN	1777	19144003
H	Middles. H.	YARDLEY	1749	45010037
H	Middles. H.	FRANKLIN	1758	45010037
H	Middles. H.	ASHTON	1770	58003004
H	Mut. Eq.&h.	BOURN	1777	43007012
H	Names in H.	DAVIES	1771	45010020
H	No per. H.h.	JOHNSON	1740	61011039
H	No Happ.h.	MASON	1758	32002010
H	Off. Op. H. S.	WARBURTON	1753	46014016
H	Off.o. H. Gh.	CENNICK	1762	47002038
H	Off.o. H. Gh.	ELLIOTT	1764	63001012
H	Oper. H. G.	BADDELLEY	1752	46016008
H	Or. H. H.sp.	WATSON	1660	63001022
H	P.& G. H. G.	PAYNE	1763	46014015
H	Pe.&imp. H.	MOORE	1716	50007001
H	Pe.&imp. H.	LEIGHTON	1746	50007001
H	Pers.of H. G.	HARRISON	1734	46015026
H	Pleas.no H.	NEWMAN	1760	21002001
H	Prea.& H. D.	GODDARD	1781	05022002
H	Prog. V.& H.	ATTERBURY	1743	64003018
H	Prot. R.vi. H.	COYTE	1761	47024014
H	Pur.of H.	HILL	1755	20016001
H	Qual.f fu. H.	CLARKE	1734	69003004
H	Qual.f.fu. H.	BULL	1713	69003004
H	R.& Pr.im.h.	WHEATLY	1746	61011039
H	R.of Age H.	GERARD	1780	20016031
H	Read. H. S.	STRATFORD	1687	54003016
H	Rejoi.in H.	ANONYMOUS	1693	48012012
H	Ren.h.th. D.	RYVES	1715	50004002
H	Rev. G's h.	MEDE	1672	21005001
H	Road to H.	YOUNG	1706	09002030
H	Shor.of H. L.	TIDCOMBE	1757	10019034
H	Short.h. Life	WARREN	1748	64001014
H	Si. H.groun.	ASHTON	1770	19119123
H	Sin ag. H. G.	HARRIS	1718	43012031
H	Sin ag. H. G.	SHARP	1729	43012031
H	Sin ag. H. G.	MARSHALL	1731	43012031
H	Sin ag. H. G.	TILLOTSON	1735	43012031
H	Sin ag. H. G.	STEPHENS	1737	43012031
H	Sin ag. H. G.	WATERLAND	1742	43012031
H	Sin ag. H. G.	GREEN	1747	43012031
H	Sin ag. H. G.	HOOLE	1748	43012031
H	Sin ag. H. G.	SECKER	1770	43012031
H	Sin ag. H. G.	JORTIN	1774	43012031
H	Sin ag. H. G.	PEARCE	1779	43012031
H	Sin.ag. H. G.	ANONYMOUS	1740	44003028
H	Sin.gr. H. G.	WILSON	1781	52004030

INDEXES TO THIRD VOLUME: E: KEYWORD-IN-CONTEXT INDEX OF OTHER SUBJECTS OR OCCASIONS

Keyword	In its Context	Author	Year	BkChpVrs
H	Sin.sh.&h.l.	PIERCE	1679	48006021
H	Sin.sh.&h.l.	TILLOTSON	1735	48006021
H	So. H.or M.	SKELTON	1754	24013023
H	Soul pre.f. H.	WATTS	1753	50005005
H	Sup. K.in H.	PEARSE	1763	49013012
H	Tim.in G.h.	AMORY	1775	19031015
H	Use H. S. S.	HOPKINS	1710	54003016
H	V.sch.& H.	COMBE	1708	20014034
H	Van.h.judg.	ABERNETHY	1748	49004003
H	Van.of h. W.	DELAUNE	1728	48012016
H	Ven. H.life.	HOWE	1702	19089047
H	Vener. H. Sp.	BOURN	1777	52004030
H	W.of Sin h.	DAVIES	1771	47009006
H	Ways H.uns.	DAVIS	1756	19077019
H	Wiv.& H. D.	STEELE	1676	52005033
H	Wiv.& H. D.	HOLE	1719	52005033
H	Wiv.& H. D.	ANONYMOUS	1754	52006002
H	Wiv.& H. D.	ANONYMOUS	1754	52006004
H	Wiv.& H. D.	FRANKLIN	1765	52005033
H	Wiv. D.to H.	FLEETWOOD	1737	63003001
H	Wiv. D.to H.	FLEETWOOD	1737	63003003
H	Wiv. D.to H.	FLEETWOOD	1737	63003004
H	Wo.ins.t. H.	CARR	1777	54003002
H	Wor.in pr. H	H.	1693	01034022
H	Xn's.ob.t. H.	TILLOTSON	1735	58002019
H	Xn's& H. H.	BARNES	1752	20010028
H	Xns. H.& Sa.	WEBB	1765	63003005
H	Xns.wa.to H.	ANONYMOUS	1726	47016030
H	Xt.at G's.r.h.	HURRION	1719	61012001
H	Xt.sear. H.	NEWLIN	1728	46002024
H	Xt.si.r.h. G.	FLAVEL	1673	61001003
H	Xt's. D.in. H.	NICOLSON	1661	52004009
H	Xt's. D.in. H.	HURRION	1719	52004010
H	Xt's. Gl. H.	FANCH	1768	49015028
H	Xt's. H.to S.	GOODWIN	16--	46013001
H	Xt's.ent.i. H.	EMLYN	1742	61006020
H	Xt's.pow.h.	FOORD	1719	43008003
H	Zeal f. G's H.	CLARKE	1727	16010039
HA	Ch. Ha.of G.	WALLIN	1774	52002022
HA	Cov. S.h. Ha.	PEAD	1701	52002001
HA	Cov. S.h. Ha.	WARREN	1748	52002001
HA	Hol.w.t. Ha.	BROOKS	1662	61012014
HA	Pres.&f. Ha.	ROBINSON	1736	62004017
HAB	Bad Hab.	JORTIN	1774	24013023
HAB	Hab. Devot.	PRIESTLEY	1782	19010004
HAB	Hab. Drunk.	CARTER	1729	51005021
HAB	Hab. Piety.	TOULMIN	1770	20023017
HAB	Hab. Repen.	BENNETT	1728	23057015
HAB	Hab. Repr.	BENNETT	1723	19015002
HAB	Vicious Hab.	HORTON	1679	24013023
HAB	Vicious Hab.	CONANT	1699	24013023
HAB	Vicious Hab.	HAVETT	1703	24013023
HAB	Vicious Hab.	CARTER	1729	24013023
HAB	Vicious Hab.	CARR	1777	24013023
HABIT	Habit. Rel.	AMORY	1775	19016008
HABITS	Bad Habits.	SHOREY	1725	24013023

Keyword	In its Context	Author	Year	BkChpVrs
HABITS	Bad Habits.	MASON	1758	48014022
HABITS	Evil Habits.	TILLOTSON	1735	24013023
HABITS	Evil Habits.	UPTON	1735	47024025
HADES	Hades.	STURMY	1716	23038018
HAGAR'S	Hagar's mot.	JENKINS	1779	01016013
HAND	Sad hand wr.	WILKINSON	1660	18013026
HAND	W. Hand res.	BRAGGE	1706	45006006
HAND	With.hand.	DODD	1757	43012013
HANOVER	At Hanover.	LOMBARD	1714	48012018
HAP	Con.is Hap.	STILLINGFLEET	1707	23057021
HAP	Duty& Hap.	TENNISON	1695	48012002
HAP	Duty& Hap.	BALGUY	1748	46013017
HAP	F. Hap.or M.	BUNDY	1740	45016025
HAP	Fut.life hap.	STRADLING	1692	49015019
HAP	Godlin. Hap.	CHANDLER	1769	57004007
HAP	Hap. Congr.	ERSKINE	1764	01049010
HAP	Hap. D.t. Xn.	LANGHORNE	1773	69014013
HAP	Hap.blessed.	DUNLOP	1722	23028005
HAP	Hap.early P.	GALLIMORE	1694	21012001
HAP	Hap.f.mind.	NEWMAN	1760	20014014
HAP	Hap.hol. M.	PARKHURST	1706	43022030
HAP	Hap.o. G.aff.	NEWMAN	1760	65004016
HAP	Hap.o.fut.st.	BLAIR	1780	69007009
HAP	Hap.of afflic.	HOWARD	1710	62005011
HAP	Hap.of righ.	DUCHAL	1765	23060020
HAP	Hap.of Hea.	AMORY	1758	69014013
HAP	Hap.of Hea.	SKEELER	1772	69014013
HAP	Hap.of Piety	LANGHORNE	1773	19119001
HAP	Hap.of Rel.	ATTERBURY	1699	57004007
HAP	Hap.of Rel.	BEVERIDGE	1720	19144015
HAP	Hap.thr. Xt.	CLARKE	1736	59001002
HAP	T. Hap.in G.	MASON	1758	24002013
HAP	Way of Hap.	GLANVIL	1681	45013024
HAP	Way to Hap.	RALEIGH	1679	43006033
HAP	Way to Hap.	WHALEY	1695	61012013
HAP	Xty pr. Hap.	BADDELLEY	1766	20003017
HAPP	Ab.no Happ.	NEWMAN	1760	45012015
HAPP	Dom. Happ.	FRANKLIN	1765	20015017
HAPP	Dom. Happ.	ENFIELD	1772	01045024
HAPP	Enq.a Happ.	WEBB	1765	18028012
HAPP	Fut. Happ.	NEWMAN	1760	19036009
HAPP	Fut. Happ.	DUCHAL	1765	19036008
HAPP	Fut. Happ.g.	TILLOTSON	1735	65003002
HAPP	God's Happ.	TILLOTSON	1735	57001011
HAPP	God's Happ.	HUNT	1748	57001011
HAPP	Happ. E. Int.	HOLDEN	1755	19037037
HAPP	Happ. Pros.	NEWMAN	1760	48012012
HAPP	Happ. Relig.	FIDDES	1720	21012013
HAPP	Happ. Saints	WILLIAMS	16--	46020026
HAPP	Happ.fut. St.	WELTON	1724	49002009
HAPP	Happ.fut.st.	CARTER	1729	53003020
HAPP	Happ.fut.st.	BROWNE	1749	53003020
HAPP	Happ.here.	DICKSON	1731	45016025
HAPP	Happ.o.g. P.	ROWLAND	1775	48008028
HAPP	Happ.rel. C.	REYNER	1745	20010029
HAPP	Heav. Happ.	BEVERIDGE	1720	54001012

Keyword	In its Context	Author	Year	BkChpVrs
HAPP	Heav. Happ.	VENN	1759	69022003
HAPP	No Happ.h.	MASON	1758	32002010
HAPP	Right.happ.	ABERNETHY	1748	23003010
HAPP	Saints Happ.	BEVERIDGE	1720	45012032
HAPP	True happ.	ORR	1749	23003010
HAPP	True Happ.	DORRINGTON	1703	19004006
HAPP	True Happ.	STILLINGFLEET	1707	46006068
HAPP	True Happ.	HOPKINS	1710	69022014
HAPP	True Happ.	REYNER	1745	19004006
HAPP	World.happ.	SHARP	1734	21002011
HAPPI	Div. Happi.	LELAND	1769	57006015
HAPPIN	Fut. Happin.	TRAILE	1705	46017024
HAPPIN	Fut. Happin.	WILCOX	1757	46017024
HAPPIN	Xn. Happin.	VENN	1759	50013014
HAPPINESS	Happiness.	YOUNG	1706	19037004
HAPPINESS	Happiness.	READING	1724	19004006
HAPPINESS	Happiness.	PIERCE	1731	19004006
HAPPINESS	Happiness.	CLARKE	1736	19004006
HAPPINESS	Happiness.	SHORTHOSE	1738	21007001
HAPPINESS	Happiness.	COOKE	1739	45012015
HAPPINESS	Happiness.	SEED	1743	45012015
HAPPINESS	Happiness.	FOSTER	1744	19004006
HAPPINESS	Happiness.	HUSSEY	1755	21002003
HAPPINESS	Happiness.	HUSSEY	1758	19004006
HAPPINESS	Happiness.	NEWMAN	1760	01002008
HAPPINESS	Happiness.	NEWMAN	1760	19004006
HAPPINESS	Happiness.	STERNE	1760	19004006
HAPPINESS	Happiness.	NEWMAN	1760	19016008
HAPPINESS	Happiness.	NEWMAN	1760	19090012
HAPPINESS	Happiness.	ORR	1772	19004006
HAPPINESS	Happiness.	ENFIELD	1772	45010041
HAPPY	Godl.happy.	CLARKE	1736	57004007
HAPPY	Happy Affl.	SPOONER	1771	50004017
HAPPY	Happy Vict.	ERSKINE	1764	48008037
HAPPY	Live happy.	COTES	1721	21003012
HAPPY	Rel.l.happy.	KILLINBECK	1717	21008012
HAPPY	Sep.st.happy	MARCH	1699	45023043
HAR	Har. Div. Pe.	WEST	1762	65001005
HARD	Hard.o. Hea.	NEVILLE	1683	61003015
HARD	Hard Heart.	HOPKINS	1768	19095007
HARDS	Hards.o. Cl.	PRESTON	1767	58002002
HARVEST	Harvest.	BROWNE	1708	02023016
HARVEST	Harvest.	FROST	1729	08002004
HAS	Bap. Ld. Has.	JONES	1668	45003021
HASTY	Hasty Riches	BERRIMAN	1751	20028020
HATES	G.hates Sin.	DORRINGTON	1703	20015009
HAUGHTINESS	Haughtiness.	BRADY	1730	24013015
HAV	Hav. Son.	PARKHURST	1707	65005012
HAZ	Haz. Self- C.	JENKINS	1779	12008013
HAZ	Haz. Xrter.	BLAIR	1780	12008012
HAZ	Haz.of Salv.	TILLOTSON	1735	49003015
HD'S	Hd's. Xrter.	CRAIG	1775	44006020
HD'S	Hd's Cruelty	HALL	1661	43002016
HD'S	Hd's Cruelty	STERNE	1760	43002017
HD'S	Hd's Cruelty	STERNE	1760	43011017
HEA	Fal.hop.hea.	BLAIR	1740	43007021

Keyword	In its Context	Author	Year	BkChpVrs
HEA	Foret.o. Hea.	WATTS	1753	48008023
HEA	Hap.of Hea.	AMORY	1758	69014013-
HEA	Hap.of Hea.	SKEELER	1772	69014013
HEA	Hard.o. Hea.	NEVILLE	1683	61003015
HEA	Hea.n.in all.	BAINE	1778	49006009
HEA	Heav.o. Hea.	HENLEY	1729	69021010
HEA	Joys of Hea.	JOHNSON	1740	49002009
HEA	Kingd. Hea.	POPE	1675	43022001
HEA	Name in hea.	MANTON	1708	45009057
HEA	No Nig. Hea.	WATTS	1753	69021025
HEAD	Xt.t. Head.	BAXTER	1675	49012027
HEAL	Heal. Faith.	WILLISON	1761	46005006
HEAL	Heal. Gent.	WHEATLY	1746	43008013
HEALTH	Exer. Health	DYKES	1722	20031017
HEAR	Bless.hear. G'	ALTHAM	1732	45011028
HEAR	Bless.hear. G'	BURNET	1747	45011028
HEAR	C. Hear.ast.	BOURN	1777	43007028
HEAR	Duty hear.	MOSS	1732	44004024
HEAR	G.hear Pray.	BOSTON	1775	19065002
HEAR	Hear word.	BRADBURY	1713	23052007
HEAR	Hear word.	REYNOLDS	1713	61003007
HEAR	Hear.& Sight	MARKLAND	1729	44007037
HEAR	Hear. Serm.	SMALRIDGE	1724	45008018
HEAR	Hear. Serm.	WARREN	1739	45008018
HEAR	Hear. Serm.	WHITFIELD	1739	45008018
HEAR	Hear. Serm.	SECKER	1770	45008018
HEAR	Hear. Word.	NEWMAN	1713	20028009
HEAR	Hear.insuff.	READ	1728	62001027
HEAR	Hear.of S.	BLAIR	1740	43005001
HEAR	Hear.word.	CLARKSON	1696	45008018
HEAR	Hear.word.	HARRIS	1713	45008018
HEAR	Hear.word.	EARLE	1711	55005020
HEAR	Hear.word.	BROWN	1722	55002013
HEAR	Hear.word.	RICHMOND	1764	45008018
HEAR	Hear.word.	HURD	1780	45008018
HEAR	Hear.word.	NEWSON	1781	45008018
HEAR	Hear G's.w.	DORRINGTON	1703	49001021
HEAR	Hear G's.w.	WAKE	1716	45008008
HEAR	Hear Serm.	MOSS	1732	45008018
HEAR	Hear Serm.	MARSHALL	1750	45008018
HEAR	Perf.in hear.	WHITTY	1772	49015049
HEAR	Right hear.	SHIRLEY	1762	46008047
HEAR	Xn. Hear.	ELLIS	1694	49003007
HEARD	Heard word	SEIGNIOR	1676	62001021
HEART	Deb. Heart.	LAMONT	1780	43005027
HEART	Enl. Heart.	BURROUGHS	1733	19119032
HEART	Gov. Heart.	MEDE	1672	20004023
HEART	Gov. Heart.	DAWES	1687	20004024
HEART	Gov. Heart.	NEWLIN	1720	20004023
HEART	Gov. Heart.	SHARP	1729	20004023
HEART	Gov. Heart.	MOSS	1737	20004023
HEART	Gov. Heart.	ORR	1739	20004023
HEART	Gov. Heart.	SMITH	1740	20004023
HEART	Gov. Heart.	SEED	1743	20004023
HEART	Gov. Heart.	MARSHAL	1750	20004023
HEART	Gov. Heart.	MACE	1751	20004023

INDEXES TO THIRD VOLUME: E: KEYWORD-IN-CONTEXT INDEX OF OTHER SUBJECTS OR OCCASIONS

Keyword	In its Context	Author	Year	BkChpVrs
HEART	Gov. Heart.	TRAPP	1752	20004023
HEART	Gov. Heart.	HUSSEY	1755	20004023
HEART	Gov. Heart.	WEBBER	1758	20004023
HEART	Gov. Heart.	DUCHAL	1765	20004023
HEART	Gov. Heart.	LLOYD	1765	20004023
HEART	Gov. Heart.	LARDNER	1769	20004023
HEART	Gov. Heart.	LATHAM	1774	20004023
HEART	Gov. Heart.	STONE	1777	20004023
HEART	Hard Heart.	HOPKINS	1768	19095007
HEART	Heart deceit.	SHARP	1729	24017009
HEART	Heart deceit.	MAYHEW	1755	24017009
HEART	Heart deceit.	HAWEIS	1762	24017009
HEART	Heart dem.	DUCHAL	1765	20023026
HEART	Heart of Rel.	ACTON	1714	24030021
HEART	Heart of Un.	PYLE	1777	61003012
HEART	Heart word.	GROSVENOR	1713	62001019
HEART	Heart-bitt.	SOMERVILLE	1776	20016010
HEART	Keep. Heart.	ATTERBURY	1699	20004023
HEART	Keep. Heart.	BARROW	1716	20004023
HEART	Keep. Heart.	BEVERIDGE	1726	20004023
HEART	Keep. Heart.	CHANDLER	1769	20014023
HEART	Keep. Heart.	BLAIR	1780	20004023
HEART	Keep Heart.	NEWTON	1759	20004023
HEART	Law i. Heart	LEIGHTON	1746	61008010
HEART	Of the Heart.	JONES	1678	54003023
HEART	Plag. Heart.	EDWARDS	1665	11008038
HEART	Pur. Heart.	CHEESEMAN	1663	43005008
HEART	Pur. Heart.	HORNECK	1706	43005008
HEART	Pur. Heart.	PERKINS	1707	43005008
HEART	Pur. Heart.	HOLE	1716	19051010
HEART	Pur. Heart.	GARDINER	1720	43005008
HEART	Pur. Heart.	EDWARDS	1726	43005008
HEART	Pur. Heart.	GALE	1726	43005008
HEART	Pur. Heart.	NORRIS	1728	43005008
HEART	Pur. Heart.	COOKE	1739	43005008
HEART	Pur. Heart.	BLAIR	1740	43005008
HEART	Pur. Heart.	GROVE	1742	43005008
HEART	Pur. Heart.	SOUTH	1744	43005008
HEART	Pur. Heart.	ORR	1772	43005008
HEART	Sac.o.heart.	NALSON	1737	20023026
HEARTS	G.g. Hearts.	LELAND	1769	19033015
HEARTS	H.bet.hearts	ANGIER	1662	23029013
HEATH	Heath.b. Xt.	SHERLOCK	1719	52002012
HEAV	Heav.& Hell	BEVERIDGE	1720	43025046
HEAV	Heav. Affec.	GREGORY	1696	54003002
HEAV	Heav. Affec.	SHARP	1734	54003002
HEAV	Heav. Conv.	CLAGETT	1720	53003020
HEAV	Heav. Conv.	KELSEY	1721	53003020
HEAV	Heav. Conv.	BRADY	1730	53003020
HEAV	Heav. Conv.	ALTHAM	1732	53003020
HEAV	Heav. Conv.	BUNDY	1740	53003020
HEAV	Heav. Conv.	FOSTER	1744	53003020
HEAV	Heav. Conv.	STERNE	1769	53003020
HEAV	Heav. Happ.	BEVERIDGE	1720	54001012
HEAV	Heav. Happ.	VENN	1759	69022003
HEAV	Heav. Inher.	WILCOX	1754	63001003

Keyword	In its Context	Author	Year	BkChpVrs
HEAV	Heav. Patt.	YOUNG	1706	43006010
HEAV	Heav. Stud.	STEFFE	1743	63001012
HEAV	Heav. Treas.	OUTRAM	1697	43006021
HEAV	Heav. Treas.	PAYNE	1698	43006019
HEAV	Heav. Treas.	HOPKINS	1710	43006020
HEAV	Heav. Treas.	CREYGHTON	1720	43006020
HEAV	Heav. Treas.	BROWN	1722	43006020
HEAV	Heav. Treas.	ADEY	1760	43006020
HEAV	Heav. Wisd.	MOSS	1737	62003017
HEAV	Heav. Wisd.	LEIGHTON	1746	62003017
HEAV	Heav. Wisd.	SHERLOCK	1772	62003017
HEAV	Heav.mind.	FARINGDON	1672	54003002
HEAV	Heav.mind.	DORRINGTON	1703	54003002
HEAV	Heav.mind.	FOORD	1719	54003002
HEAV	Heav.mind.	BEVERIDGE	1720	54003002
HEAV	Heav.mind.	NORRIS	1728	53003020
HEAV	Heav.mind.	ALTHAM	1732	54003002
HEAV	Heav.mind.	DORMAN	1743	54003002
HEAV	Heav.mind.	FOTHERGILL	1765	54003002
HEAV	Heav.o. Hea.	HENLEY	1729	69021010
HEAV	Heav.o.care.	BLAIR	1740	43006033
HEAV	Joy of Heav.	LANGHORNE	1773	69022014
HEAV	Joys o. Heav.	SHARP	1729	61004011
HEAV	Mak. Heav.	BARROW	1716	47004024
HEAV	Rest.heav. S.	ELLIS	1685	43011028
HEAV	The 3 Heav.	STURMY	1716	50012002
HEAV	Way t. Heav.	PHILIPS	1681	47002047
HEAV	Way to Heav.	FERNE	1721	64001011
HEAVEN	Heaven.	WOODCOCK	1676	43025034
HEAVEN	Heaven.	BATES	1700	19016011
HEAVEN	Heaven.	DORRINGTON	1703	19016011
HEAVEN	Heaven.	HUBBARD	1757	58002010
HEAVEN	Heaven.	ERSKINE	1764	46003035
HEAVEN	Heaven.	BROUGHTON	1778	19016011
HEAVEN	Heaven.	SAURIN	1777	65003002
HEAVEN	Of Heaven.	BOYSE	1728	52003014
HELL	Eter. Hell T.	KILLINBECK	1717	45016023
HELL	Etern. Hell.	BOURDALOUE	1776	43022013
HELL	Heav.& Hell	BEVERIDGE	1720	43025046
HELL	Hell tor.ete.	JENKS	1707	48006023
HELL	Hell torm.	DAWES	1733	43025041
HELL	Hell torm.	DAVIS	1756	43025041
HELL	Hell.	ADAMS	1676	43025041
HELL	Hell.	BOND	1711	68000006
HELL	Hell.	JENNINGS	1757	48001018
HELL	Hell.	SAURIN	1777	69014011
HELL	Hell Tor.et.	MOSS	1732	43025046
HELL	Hell Tor.et.	TILLOTSON	1735	43025046
HELL	Hell Tor.et.	WARREN	1739	43025046
HELL	Hell Tor.et.	WHITFIELD	1739	43025046
HELL	Hell Tor.et.	VENN	1740	43025046
HELL	Hell Tor.et.	WATERHOUSE	1753	43025046
HELL	Hell Torm.	DODWELL	1743	56001007
HELL	Hell- Torm.	DUNLOP	1722	44009046
HELL	Hell- Torm.	SCOTT	1743	48013013
HELL	Hell- Torm.	WATTS	1753	44009046

Keyword	In its Context	Author	Year	BkChpVrs
HELL	Hell-torm.	LAKE	1703	69021008
HELL	Judg. Hell.	WILKINSON	1660	01006003
HELL	Na.of Hell.	MEDE	1672	20021016
HELL	Pains o. Hell.	BOURDALOUE	1776	45016022
HELL	Prog. Hell-f.	HENLEY	1730	11018024
HELL	Pun.of Hell.	LORTIE	1720	50005010
HELL	Xt.key Hell.	DUNLOP	1722	69001018
HELL	Xt's. D. Hell.	ROBINSON	1660	47002027
HELL	Xt's. D. Hell.	PIGOTT	1702	47002026
HELL	Xt's. D. Hell.	HOLE	1715	47002027
HELL	Xt's. D. Hell.	BARROW	1716	47002027
HELL	Xt's. D. Hell.	BOYS	1716	47002027
HELL	Xt's. D. Hell.	FISHER	1741	47002027
HELL	Xt's. D. Hell.	TERRY	1746	47002027
HELL	of Hell.	BATES	1700	44009048
HELP	Sp. Help Pr.	STEVENS	1755	48008026
HELP	Sp. Help Pr.	BOSTON	1775	48008026
HELPL	Helpl. Man.	WALKER	1755	23063005
HELPS	Helps t.g. M.	STEELE	1683	49015002
HER	Her.& S.una.	MOSSOM	1685	49011019
HER	Her.& S.una.	MARCH	1699	49011019
HER	Her.& S.una.	CLAGETT	1704	49011019
HER	Her.& S.una.	ROGERS	1736	49011019
HER	Nec.of Her.	ANONYMOUS	1688	49002009
HER	Nec.of Her.	TAYLOR	1719	49011019
HER	Nec.of Her.	WARREN	1739	49011019
HER	Nec.of Her.	WHEATLY	1746	49011019
HER	Nec.of Her.	TURTON	1749	49011019
HER	Nec.of Her.	STEBBING	1760	49011019
HER	Nec.of Her.	WARBURTON	1767	49011019
HERE	Happ.here.	DICKSON	1731	45016025
HERES	Heres.neces.	BALLARD	1733	49011019
HERESIES	Heresies&c.	NEWTON	1782	43018007
HERESY	Ag. Heresy.	SHARP	1734	49011019
HERESY	Heresy.	FOSTER	1732	59003010
HERESY	Heresy&c.	KEELING	1767	49003018
HERET	Heret.reject.	CONEY	1750	59003010
HEROD	Herod& Bap.	CONYBEARE	1757	43014006
HEROD	Sadd. Herod	STRAIGHT	1741	43022023
HEZ	Case of Hez.	STERNE	1766	12020015
HEZEK'S	Hezek's beh.	GODDARD	1781	23038001
HEZEK'S	Hezek's Pr.	ORTON	1776	14030018
HID	G's w.hid. T.	TAYLOR	1776	19112011
HID	Hid. Manna.	HOLLOWAY	1751	69002017
HID	Hid. Treas.	CENNICK	1762	43013044
HID	Hid.li.o. Xn.	WATTS	1753	54003003
HID	Hid.li.o. Xn.	ERSKINE	1764	54003003
HID	Xt.hid. Mys.	HARTLEY	1754	54001026
HIDES	Sin hides G.	LEIGHTON	1746	23059001
HIDING	Hiding place	ALLESTREE	1684	23026020
HIER	Hier.secul.	PIERCE	1671	63002013
HIGH	Af.high. W.	MARKLAND	1729	46002011
HIMS	Vin.o.hims.	JOHNSON	1730	46007024
HINDE	Pr.b.hinde.	PARKHURST	1707	63003007
HIS	Cr. Sacr. His.	POWELL	1776	46015021
HIS	Man his o. E.	SKELTON	1754	51005017

Keyword	In its Context	Author	Year	BkChpVrs
HIST	Hist.of Jacob	STERNE	1766	01047009
HIST	Hist.of Jos.	CONYBEARE	1757	01037036
HIST	Hist.of Jos.	CONYBEARE	1757	01039001
HIST	Hist.of Jos.	CONYBEARE	1757	01041046
HIST	Hist.of Jos.	HUNTER	1774	01039002
HIST	Scrip. Hist.	GIBSON	1761	64001016
HISTORY	Jon. History.	DOWNES	1761	31001017
HO	Beaut.of Ho.	GREGORY	1708	19084001
HO	Door of Ho.	FARMER	1756	23055007
HO	Good.ho. M.	MOSS	1737	20004025
HO	Ho.des. Gos.	HOLE	1715	59002014
HO	Ho.des. Gos.	BEVERIDGE	1720	59002011
HO	Ho.des. Gos.	BEVERIDGE	1720	59002013
HO	Ho.des. Gos.	BEVERIDGE	1720	59002014
HO	Ho.des. Gos.	RINGER	1734	59002013
HO	Ho.due t. G.	NORRIS	1728	58003003
HO	Ho.o.r.at D.	STEPHENS	1699	53003013
HO	Means o. Ho.	HAWEIS	1762	64001010
HO	Means o. Ho.	ELSMERE	1767	64001010
HO	Xn. D.& Ho.	WEBB	1772	54001009
HO	Xt.ho.of Gl.	BALL	1692	54001027
HO	Xy.ho. Prie.	BEVERIDGE	1720	63002005
HO	b. Chels. Ho.	SHORTHOSE	1738	58002002
HOL	Actual Hol.	FORSTER	1759	65003002
HOL	Adv.of Hol.	BEVERIDGE	1720	57004007
HOL	Eng.to Hol.	WILKINSON	1660	64003011
HOL	Hap.hol. M.	PARKHURST	1706	43022030
HOL	Hol.& Felic	DAVIES	1766	61012014
HOL	Hol.emin.	BEVERIDGE	1720	43005020
HOL	Hol.nec.to S.	BENSON	1748	61012014
HOL	Hol.of life.	CLARKE	1735	48012001
HOL	Hol.w.t. Ha.	BROOKS	1662	61012014
HOL	Nat.of Hol.	HAWEIS	1762	52002010
HOL	Nec.of Hol.	CLARKE	1735	61012014
HOL	Obl.to Hol.	WHITAKER	1674	58002019
HOL	Peace& Hol.	PIERCE	1679	61012014
HOL	Peace& Hol.	UMFREVILLE	1739	61012014
HOL	Pers.to Hol.	HARRISON	1710	50007001
HOLIN	Exem.holin.	BEVERIDGE	1720	47002042
HOLIN	G's. Holin.	WHITBY	1709	63001015
HOLIN	G's. Holin.	DELAUNE	1728	63001015
HOLIN	G's. Holin.	TILLOTSON	1735	63001015
HOLIN	G's. Holin.	HUSSEY	1758	63001015
HOLIN	God's holin.	PENTYCROSS	1781	23006003
HOLIN	Holin.o. G.	HUNT	1748	69015004
HOLIN	Holin.of G.	WISHEART	1716	09002002
HOLIN	Holin.of G.	SAURIN	1775	03019001
HOLIN	Holin.of L.	MARSHAL	1731	19026012
HOLIN	Pers. Holin.	HAWEIS	1762	61012014
HOLIN	Wisd. Holin.	BEVERIDGE	1720	19111010
HOLINESS	G's Holiness.	LELAND	1769	34001013
HOLINESS	Holiness.	BROOKS	1662	61013014
HOLINESS	Holiness.	SHEFFIELD	1676	61012014
HOLINESS	Holiness.	BENNETT	1728	19045013
HOLINESS	Holiness.	WILSON	1781	61012014
HOLINESS	Xn. Holiness	HAMMOND	1745	44005036

Keyword	In its Context	Author	Year	BkChpVrs
HOLINESS	Xn. Holiness	HAMMOND	1745	46001029
HOLINESS	Xn. Holiness	HAMMOND	1745	61013014
HOLL	Inund. Holl.	SPANHEIM	1676	69003020
HOLY	Holy Choice	PHILIPS	1679	61011015
HOLY	Holy City.	SPARKES	1663	69019002
HOLY	Holy Cont.	YOUNG	1706	45002019
HOLY	Holy Conv.	STANHOPE	1705	52005011
HOLY	Holy Life.	BOLDE	1675	63001015
HOLY	Holy Men.	EMLYN	1742	45013029
HOLY	Holy Resol.	TENISON	1695	19119106
HOLY	Holy Resol.	TILLOTSON	1735	18034031
HOLY	Holy Resol.	WARNEFORD	1776	19119106
HOM	Hom. Neigh.	BURNET	1713	43022039
HON	Distr. Hon.	WELTON	1724	50007004
HON	Good l. Hon.	FOTHERGILL	1765	20004008
HON	Hon.& Pleas.	DODD	1772	20003013
HON	Hon. God.	BARROW	1716	09002030
HON	Hon. Wisd.	BAYLY	1721	20014008
HON	Hon. Xn. Pr.	BRETT	1712	61005004
HON	Hon.all men	TRAPP	1752	63002017
HON	Hon.conj. F.	DYKES	1722	20031023
HON	Hon.mind.	WISHART	1733	46007017
HON	Hon.mind.	WISHART	1733	46007013
HON	Hon.of poor.	MILNER	1750	45007022
HON	Hon.prosec.	CONEY	1730	27006005
HON	Hon.stop. M.	TILLOTSON	1735	46007017
HON	Marr. Hon.	SIMPSON	1774	61013004
HON	Path to Hon.	WHEATLAND	1739	20003016
HON	Prov.th.hon.	BARROW	1716	50008021
HON	Xt.hon.to F.	WILLIAMS	1770	63002007
HONOR	Honor of G.	HUNT	1748	09002030
HONOR	On Honor.	MACQUEEN	1711	17006006
HONOUR	Honour.	MARKLAND	1729	21003016
HONOUR	Honour.	JORTIN	1774	09002030
HOP	Fal.hop.hea.	BLAIR	1740	43007021
HOPE	Believ. Hope	BOURN	1722	65003003
HOPE	Enthus.hope	DAVIS	1756	45009055
HOPE	G. M's Hope.	LACY	1720	19039008
HOPE	Hope forgiv.	WITHERSPOON	1768	19130004
HOPE	Hope in Xt.	BROUGHTON	1778	49015019
HOPE	Hope of Xn.	FARRINGTON	1741	65003003
HOPE	Hope.	ALLESTREE	1684	65003003
HOPE	Hope.	JORTIN	1774	48012012
HOPE	Hope& Pat.	STRAIGHT	1741	48012012
HOPE	Hope& T. G.	MARSHAL	1750	19042005
HOPE	Nat.o. Hope.	JOHNSON	1740	65003003
HOPE	Of Hope.	SIMONS	1743	18008013
HOPE	Orph. Hope.	DODDERIDGE	1743	19027010
HOPE	Rej.in Hope.	LELAND	1769	48005002
HOPE	Xn. Hope p.	OUTRAM	1697	65003003
HOPE	Xn. Hope.	NICOLSON	1661	53003020
HOPE	Xn. Hope.	MOSS	1737	48015013
HOPE	Xn. Hope.	TILLY	1737	61006019
HOPE	Xn. Hope.	SKEELER	1740	65003003
HOPE	Xn. Hope.	HOWE	1744	48005005
HOPE	Xn's. Hope.	WALKER	1765	48008032
HOPES	Hopes Hyp.	SOUTH	1744	18008013
HOSPITALITY	Hospitality.	BURTON	1685	48012013
HOSPITALITY	Hospitality.	PERRONET	1745	48012013
HOUS	Sp. Hous.de.	MASTERSON	1661	63002004
HOUSE	House Pray.	MEDE	1672	44011017
HOW	Alm.how ac.	GOUGE	1677	57006017
HOW	Gos.how pr.	HAMOND	1690	54004005
HOW	How. R. S. S.	FOSTER	1732	46005039
HOW	Salv.how att.	PAYNE	1698	47016030
HOW	Salv.how att.	HOPKINS	1708	47016030
HOW	Salv.how att.	JORTIN	1774	47016030
HU	Hu.nat. Xt.	DAWSON	1765	57002005
HU	Hu.tow. G.	WAPLE	1720	62004010
HU	Lib.hu.nat.	LAMBE	1681	49006012
HU	Pride& Hu.	BALGUY	1750	62004006
HU	Van.hu. Enj.	OGILVIE	1766	49007031
HU	Xn. Hu.	KING	1705	53002003
HUM	Fai.& Hum.	NEWLIN	1720	43008008
HUM	Fol. Hum. C.	LLOYD	1765	19118008
HUM	Gosp. Hum.	ERSKINE	1764	26016063
HUM	Hum.&d. F.	OAKES	1747	45002052
HUM	Hum.&d. F.	TOULMIN	1770	45002052
HUM	Hum. Act.	CLARKE	1734	45011035
HUM	Hum. Act.	TRAPP	1751	09002003
HUM	Hum. Char.	WHICHCOTE	1702	31004001
HUM	Hum. Com.	BENNETT	1714	43015009
HUM	Hum. Frailty	CREYTON	1720	49010012
HUM	Hum. Impot.	HORTON	1679	46015005
HUM	Hum. Indus.	DYKES	1722	20031019
HUM	Hum. Instit.	WEST	1762	43015009
HUM	Hum. Learn.	NEVILL	1681	20019002
HUM	Hum. Liber.	SKELTON	1754	46008031
HUM	Hum. Na. C.	WEBB	1772	05032005
HUM	Hum. Nat.	DORINGTON	1705	19100003
HUM	Hum. Natur.	DUCHAL	1765	19034015
HUM	Hum. Perf.	MANTON	1685	53003015
HUM	Hum. Prud.	CARLETON	1736	20003005
HUM	Hum. Reas.	NEWLIN	1720	27004031
HUM	Hum. Van.	BALGUY	1750	19094011
HUM	Hum.in Paul	WATTS	1753	52002018
HUM	Hum.life.	FOSTER	1737	21007001
HUM	Hum.nature	BUTLER	1749	48002014
HUM	Hum.st. Mes.	WEBB	1766	43002023
HUM	Obl. Hum. L.	THORP	1703	48013005
HUM	Obl. Hum. L.	SANDERSON	1722	48013005
HUM	Pre.hum.na.	SNAPE	1745	61002007
HUM	Xn. Hum.&c	EVANS	1737	54003012
HUMB	Pride Humb.	SKELTON	1754	20029023
HUMIL	L's. Humil.	WILDER	1741	43011029
HUMIL	L's. Humil.	WHITE	1757	43011029
HUMIL	Xn. Humil.	COCKMAN	1750	63005005
HUMIL	Xt's humil.	FLAVEL	1673	23053002
HUMIL	Xt's. Humil.	FLAVEL	1673	46017011
HUMIL	Xt's. Humil.	MERITON	1676	53002008
HUMIL	Xt's. Humil.	COLLIER	1725	50008009
HUMIL	Xt's. Humil.	M'GEORGE	1727	53002007

Keyword	In its Context	Author	Year	BkChpVrs
HUMIL	Xt's. Humil.	CLARKE	1735	43016021
HUMIL	Xt's. Humil.	MOSS	1738	53002005
HUMIL	Xt's. Humil.	COWPER	1773	53002005
HUMILI	Humili.&c.	PHILIPS	1775	62004010
HUMILIAT	Humiliat.	MUNTON	1756	11021029
HUMILIAT	Xt.humiliat.	WILLISON	1761	23055005
HUMILIAT	Xt.humiliat.	SHERLOCK	1772	23055003
HUMILITY	Humility.	HOLE	1716	45014001
HUMILITY	Humility.	WAPLE	1720	48012003
HUMILITY	Humility.	SCATTERGOOD	1723	63005005
HUMILITY	Humility.	BRADY	1730	43011029
HUMILITY	Humility.	ROGERS	1730	43011029
HUMILITY	Humility.	CLARKE	1734	45014011
HUMILITY	Humility.	NALSON	1737	19113005
HUMILITY	Humility.	MUDGE	1739	45018014
HUMILITY	Humility.	HEYLYN	1749	43011029
HUMILITY	Humility.	FARRINGTON	1741	62004006
HUMILITY	Humility.	DODWELL	1748	48012003
HUMILITY	Humility.	HARVEST	1751	45018014
HUMILITY	Humility.	DELANY	1754	43011028
HUMILITY	Humility.	HOLLAND	1753	63005005
HUMILITY	Humility.	JENNINGS	1757	63005005
HUMILITY	Humility.	COOPER	1766	43011029
HUMILITY	Humility.	STERNE	1766	43011029
HUMILITY	Humility.	MASON	1761	63005005
HUMILITY	Humility.	BRACKENRIDGE	1764	63005005
HUMILITY	Humility.	JORTIN	1774	63005005
HUMILITY	Humility.	CARR	1777	63005005
HUMILITY	Humility.	PEARCE	1779	63005005
HUMILITY	on Humility	WAPLE	1720	43018004
HUMILITY	on Humility	GALE	1726	43018003
HUNG	Hung.souls.	WILLISON	1761	45006021
HUNG	Sp. Hung.&c	HORNECK	1706	43005006
HUNG	Sp. Hung.&c	GARDINER	1720	43005006
HUNG	Sp. Hung.&c	BLACKALL	1723	43005006
HUNG	Sp. Hung.&c	EDWARDS	1726	43005006
HUNG	Sp. Hung.&c	INNES	1726	43005006
HUNG	Sp. Hung.&c	NORRIS	1728	43005006
HUNG	Sp. Hung.&c	BLAIR	1740	43005006
HUNG	Sp. Hung.&c	GROVE	1742	43005006
HUNT	Cunn. Hunt.	SUTTON	1754	61012016
HURTF	Anx.hurtf.	BLAIR	1740	43006027
HUS	Hus.m. Em.	CORNWALLIS	1706	01026012
HUS	Wive's& Hus. D	ANONYMOUS	1776	52005033
HUSB	Beh. Husb.	BARKSDALE	1677	62005007
HUSB	Husb. Duty.	ANONYMOUS	1698	54003019
HUSB	Husb.spirit.	FLAVEL	1673	49003009
HUSB	Wick.husb.	ANONYMOUS	1703	43021033
HUSB	Wick.husb.	BRAGGE	1704	43021033
HUSBAN	Husban time	LITTLETON	1735	19090012
HYP	Conv. Hyp.	CLARKSON	1696	43007022
HYP	Dang. Hyp.	ASHETON	1673	43007021
HYP	Hopes Hyp.	SOUTH	1744	18008013
HYP	Hyp.des. Pr.	ORTON	1776	24042020
HYP	Hyp.worsh.	BENNETT	1714	44007006
HYP	Jew. Hyp.	PATRICK	1670	32006008

Keyword	In its Context	Author	Year	BkChpVrs
HYPOC	Rel. Hypoc.	CHEYNEY	1677	18027008
HYPOC	Rel. Hypoc.	WELTON	1724	18027008
HYPOC	Rel. Hypoc.	LITTLETON	1735	18027008
HYPOC	Rel. Hypoc.	WILCOX	1751	18027008
HYPOC	Rel. Hypoc.	WEEDON	1777	18027008
HYPOCR	Hypocr.&c.	BRUMHALL	1677	45012001
HYPOCR	Hypocr.&c.	ANONYMOUS	1683	45012001
HYPOCR	Hypocr.&c.	OUTRAM	1697	45012001
HYPOCR	Hypocr.&c.	MOSS	1737	45012001
HYPOCR	Hypocr.&c.	STRAIGHT	1741	45012001
HYPOCR	Of Hypocr.	CLARKE	1736	18013016
HYPOCRISY	Hypocrisy.	WAKE	1701	43007005
HYPOCRITE	Hypocrite.	BLACKALL	1723	43007024
HYPOT	Hypot.in R.	SCOTT	1743	20030006
I	Bod. Ex.i. R.	SCOTT	1700	57004006
I	Comp.i. Xt.	WHITAKER	1667	54003011
I	Dea. Geor. I.	WATTS	1753	23005012
I	Diligence or I	BARROW	1716	48012011
I	Diligence or I	BALGUY	1750	48012011
I	Law i. Heart	LEIGHTON	1746	61008010
I	Pat.i.well-d.	MACE	1751	61010036
I	Renew.i. Sp.	HUSSEY	1758	52004023
I	St. P's. C.i.	WILSON	1781	53001021
I	Watch-an.i.	GILL	1773	14020020
I	Xn's. Joy i. S	BOURN	1777	63001008
I	Xt's.app.b. I.	CATCOTT	1753	53002006
I	Xt's.ent.i. H.	EMLYN	1742	61006020
ID	An.&m. Id.	ANONYMOUS	1716	26008014
ID	Fal Id.o. Pr.	SMITH	1673	64001021
IDENT	Ident. Body.	SKEELER	1740	49015035
IDLE	Idle words.	GALE	1726	43012036
IDLE	Idle words.	SECKER	1770	43012036
IDLE	Idle words.	SHERLOCK	1772	43012036
IDLEN	Idlen.in Rel.	BRAILSFORD	1776	43020006
IDLENESS	Idleness.	NOURSE	1705	56003010
IDLENESS	Idleness.	MARKLAND	1729	20024032
IDOL	Idol.&v.un.	BARKER	1763	23046008
IDOL	Idol. Worsh.	BENNETT	1714	47017016
IDOL	Idol.of Mass.	ANONYMOUS	1680	45022019
IDOL	Word Idol.	WALKER	1755	62004004
IDOLAT	Cov. Idolat.	GODDARD	1781	52005005
IDOLAT	Soul. Idolat.	CLARKSON	1696	52005009
IDOLATERS	Idolaters.	SKELTON	1754	43004010
IG	Ig d.o. G's P.	RILAND	1764	28004006
IG	Ig.good&e.	BLAIR	1777	21006012
IG	Sp.kno.&ig.	MEDE	1672	65002003
IGN	H. Ign.& M.	BOURN	1777	18008009
IGN	Ign. Jew. Ch.	BILSTONE	1763	51004003
IGNEA	Lex. Ignea.	SANCROFT	1666	24026009
IGNO	Igno.in Rel.	REYNER	1745	43015016
IGNO	Sins of Igno.	HOOLE	1748	19019012
IGNOR	Ignor.& Kn.	SKEELER	1740	46009041
IGNOR	Ignor. Man.	BUTLER	1749	21008016
IGNOR	Ignor.of G.	FREKE	1716	18024013
IGNOR	Ignor.of G.	MASON	1758	18026014
IGNOR	Ignor.wilf.	SECKER	1770	45012057

INDEXES TO THIRD VOLUME: E: KEYWORD-IN-CONTEXT INDEX OF OTHER SUBJECTS OR OCCASIONS

Keyword	In its Context	Author	Year	BkChpVrs
IGNOR	Inexc. Ignor.	WHICHCOTE	1703	48001020
IGNOR	Instr.ignor.	WILSON	1781	44004028
IGNOR	Pet. Ignor.	HORTON	1679	46013007
IGNOR	Wilf. Ignor.	SCOTT	1743	64003005
ILL	Ill bod. Sym.	PEMBERTON	1727	28007009
ILL	Ill-disp. Aff.	SOUTH	1727	56002011
ILL	Xt's. En.ill.t	FLAVEL	1673	45023023
ILLEGAL	Ang.illegal.	ANONYMOUS	1776	43005022
IM	Bp Atter. Im.	CHAMBRES	1722	47012005
IM	Ch.of R.im.	BENNETT	1714	43005019
IM	Conc. Si.im.	HOLLAND	1753	18034022
IM	Fi.doom.im.	WARREN	1748	69021008
IM	G's Im.in M.	FAWCETT	1749	01002026
IM	Im. Repent.	WROUGHTON	1728	19119060
IM	Im.of G's. P.	HORNECK	1706	43005048
IM	Im.of G's. P.	KELSEY	1721	43005048
IM	J. Xt. Im. G.	BRETT	1720	54001015
IM	J. Xt. Im. G.	LESTLEY	1720	54001015
IM	Lif.& Im.&c.	DAVIES	1766	58001010
IM	R.& Pr.im.h.	WHEATLY	1746	61011039
IM	W's Ans.im.	GILL	1752	13012032
IMA	Xt. G's. Ima.	MASON	1758	50003006
IMA	Xt. Ima.o. G.	MASON	1758	50004006
IMAG	Imag.worsh.	TULLIE	1686	02020004
IMAG	Imag.worsh.	WELCH	1752	02020004
IMAGE	Image of G.	ATTERBURY	1702	01001027
IMAGE	Image of G.	STURMY	1716	01001027
IMAGE	Image of G.	SOUTH	1727	01001027
IMAGE	Image wp.	NEEDLER	1675	43004010
IMIT	Imit. G's. H.	CLARKE	1732	63001015
IMIT	Imit.of God.	WHITBY	1710	43005048
IMIT	Imit.of God.	TILLOTSON	1735	43005048
IMIT	Imit.of God.	SHERLOCK	1772	43005048
IMIT	Imit.of Xt.	FLAVEL	1673	64002006
IMIT	Imit.of Xt.	DUKE	1703	65002006
IMIT	Imit.of Xt.	BARROW	1716	49004016
IMIT	Imit.of Xt.	EDWARDS	1726	46012015
IMIT	Imit.of Xt.	SHARP	1734	63002021
IMIT	Imit.of Xt.	HUBBARD	1757	65002006
IMIT	Imit.of Xt.	CARR	1777	63002021
IMITAT	Imitat.&c.	HUSSEY	1758	43005048
IMITAT	Imitat.of G.	ENFIELD	1772	52005001
IMM	God's Imm.	HUNT	1748	11008027
IMM	God's Imm.	DUCHAL	1765	11008027
IMM	Imm.& Prof.	THANE	1700	46012026
IMM	Imm. Anger	DAVIES	1720	31004004
IMM	Imm. Dev.	BALL	1756	20007014
IMM	Imm. L.o. Pl.	CHANDLER	1769	58003004
IMM	Imm. Soul.	BRYSON	1778	50005010
IMM	Imm.o. Soul.	SMITH	1673	61011006
IMM	Imm.o. Soul.	PARSONS	1721	58001010
IMM	Life& Imm.	MOSS	1737	58001010
IMM	Life& Imm.	KEDDINGTON	1757	58001010
IMM	Life& Imm.	TIDCOMBE	1757	58001010
IMM	Life& Imm.	LELAND	1769	58001010
IMM	Life& Imm.	JORTIN	1774	58001010
IMM	Life& Imm.	BRYSON	1778	58001010
IMMANUEL	Immanuel.	HARRIS	1724	23007014
IMMED	Immed. Rep.	STEWARD	1734	23055006
IMMED	Immed. Rep.	FARRINGTON	1769	26018027
IMMED	Immed. St.	JORTIN	1774	43022032
IMMOR	Immor. Not.	HOLDEN	1755	43015013
IMMOR	Immor. Soul.	MOORE	1715	43010028
IMMOR	Immor. Soul.	STEPHENS	1728	43010028
IMMOR	Immor. Soul.	WILDER	1729	43010028
IMMOR	Immor. Soul.	PILLOK	1734	49010015
IMMOR	Immor. Soul.	SOUTH	1744	43010028
IMMOR	Immor.of S.	GALE	1726	43010028
IMMOR	Soul immor.	TILLOTSON	1739	58001010
IMMOR	Soul immor.	HOOLE	1748	21012007
IMMOR	Soul immor.	WARREN	1748	57006012
IMMOR	Soul.immor.	DELANY	1754	43010028
IMMORALITY	Immorality.	TILLY	1712	46003019
IMMORALITY	Immorality.	HILDROP	1746	46003019
IMMORTALITY	Immortality.	EMLYN	1742	57005008
IMMUT	G's.immut.	WHITBY	1710	38003006
IMMUT	G's.immut.	CLARKE	1732	38003006
IMMUT	G's.immut.	HUNT	1748	38003006
IMMUT	G's.immut.	WARREN	1748	38003006
IMMUT	G's.immut.	LAMBERT	1779	38003006
IMMUT	Immut.of G.	JORTIN	1774	62001017
IMMUTAB	G.immutab.	ATTERBURY	1743	62001017
IMMUTAB	G.immutab.	BLAIR	1780	62001017
IMP	Bad m's Imp.	FALLE	1694	21008011
IMP	Bless.imp. F.	LAWSON	1764	46020029
IMP	Dissent.imp.	BOWTELL	1711	48016017
IMP	Div. Fa.imp.	WHARTON	1728	47010034
IMP	Imp. Ad's. S.	TAYLOR	1725	48005019
IMP	Imp. Prayer.	BLAIR	1740	43007007
IMP	Imp. Re.pr.l.	CRAIG	1775	52002012
IMP	Imp. Right.	VENN	1759	43019006
IMP	Imp. Right.	ROMAINE	1760	50005021
IMP	Imp. Sorrow	ABERNETHY	1748	21007002
IMP	Imp. Xn. Na.	CROWE	1744	58002019
IMP	Imp. Xn. R.	HOLDEN	1755	46007016
IMP	Imp.in Rel.	STENNETT	1760	64003018
IMP	Imp.of w.	LARDNER	1751	43012036
IMP	Imp.of w.&c	FOTHERGILL	1765	24005003
IMP	Imp.of Rel.	STENNETT	1769	45010042
IMP	Imp.of S.&c.	GAUNT	1769	62002024
IMP	Imp.of Sex.	FORDYCE	1767	57002008
IMP	Imp.of Souls	OAKES	1747	18032008
IMP	Imp.or.in C.	BLAIR	1780	49014040
IMP	Ld. Pres. Imp.	JAY	1682	61011033
IMP	Pe.&imp. H.	MOORE	1716	50007001
IMP	Pe.&imp. H.	LEIGHTON	1746	50007001
IMP	R.imp. Soc.	CRAIG	1775	14015002
IMP	Saints imp.	WILSON	1735	49013010
IMP	Wor.w.imp.	ELLIS	1704	45016008
IMP	Wor.w.imp.	KETTLEWELL	1719	45016008
IMP	Xt's.res.imp.	WILSON	1781	47001021
IMPART	God impart.	BRADY	1713	51005006

Keyword	In its Context	Author	Year	BkChpVrs
IMPARTIAL	G.impartial.	LANGHORNE	1773	48002011
IMPARTIAL	G.impartial.	JORTIN	1774	48002011
IMPEN	Final Impen.	BOURDALOUE	1776	46008021
IMPEN	Impen.inex.	SNAPE	1745	26018031
IMPENITENCE	Impenitence	WHALEY	1695	43011021
IMPENITENCE	Impenitence	TILLOTSON	1735	43011021
IMPENITENCE	Impenitence	JAGO	1755	45016031
IMPENITENCY	Impenitency	WARD	1674	69009020
IMPENITENCY	Impenitency	WEBSTER	1747	45012020
IMPLIC	Implic. Faith	ANONYMOUS	1764	46010029
IMPOR	Impor. Ques.	ANONYMOUS	1776	47016029
IMPORT	Import. Pr.	PENTYCROSS	1781	01032026
IMPORT	Import. Wid.	BRAGGE	1702	45018001
IMPORT	Import. Wid.	DODD	1757	45018001
IMPORT	Import. Wid.	BULKLEY	1771	45018006
IMPORT	Import.of R.	FOTHERGILL	1765	19037031
IMPOT	Hum. Impot.	HORTON	1679	46015005
IMPOT	M's. Impot.	MANTON	1676	48005006
IMPR	Impr. Time.	GEE	1692	52005016
IMPR	Impr. Time.	LARDNER	1769	52005016
IMPR	Impr.of life.	WATTS	1753	49003022
IMPRO	Impro.in R.	STENNETT	1769	28014005
IMPROV	Improv. Tal.	GOUGH	1751	43025021
IMPROV	Improv. Tal.	WILSON	1781	45012048
IMPROV	Improv.life.	BRODHURST	1733	19090012
IMPROV	Improv.life.	SHIRLEY	1762	19090012
IMPURITY	Impurity.	DODD	1772	20007024
IMPUT	Imput.right.	COLE	1755	48009032
IN	D.of R. R. In.	HORNECK	1706	43005023
IN	Disob. G. In.	WILSON	1781	46015022
IN	In th.&n. W.	LITTLETON	1735	54003002
IN	In. O.& N. T.	CALAMY	1710	64001021
IN	In.to w.o. G.	SNAPE	1745	49007029
IN	In.wit.o. Xy.	WATTS	1753	65005010
IN	In Xt.or not.	FAWCETT	1757	50005017
IN	Nat.& In. R.	LAW	1768	32006008
INA	M's.ina.k. S.	HURST	1660	48007007
INC	Di.&inc. Xt.	WISE	1717	51004004
INC	Inc. Superst.	CHANDLER	1749	32004005
INC	Inc.o. Xt.&c.	NEAL	1757	51004004
INC	Pers.inc. Xy.	BRACKENRIDGE	1764	45009056
INCAP	Pri.incap.of W	ATTERBURY	1730	20014006
INCAP	Pri.incap.of W	ABERNETHY	1751	20014006
INCARN	God incarn.	WARREN	1739	57003016
INCARN	Xt's. Incarn.	PIGOTT	1702	45001035
INCARN	Xt's. Incarn.	SOUTH	1744	61002016
INCARN	Xt's. Incarn.	HOOLE	1748	57003016
INCARN	Xt's. Incarn.	FAWCETT	1749	61002017
INCARN	Xt's. Incarn.	BOSTON	1773	45001035
INCARN	Xt's. Incarn.	OGDEN	1777	45001034
INCARN	Xt's. Incarn.	COWPER	1773	61002016
INCARNATION	Incarnation.	DORRINGTON	1703	46001014
INCARNATION	Incarnation.	NOURSE	1705	57003016
INCARNATION	Incarnation.	SHEPHERD	1748	46001014
INCARNATION	Incarnation.	SCOTT	1743	65004003
INCENDARIES	Incendaries.	CROXALL	1715	46013035

Keyword	In its Context	Author	Year	BkChpVrs
INCENSE	Xt's. Incense	ORTON	1776	69008003
INCOM	G.w.incom.	SAURIN	1775	23055008
INCOMP	G.incomp.	HUNT	1748	18011007
INCOMP	G.incomp.	HUSSEY	1755	18011007
INCOMP	G.incomp.	ROE	1766	18011007
INCOMP	Incomp.	GROVE	1741	18011007
INCOMP	Incomp. G.	LUCAS	1710	18011007
INCOMP	Incomp. G.	WISHEART	1716	18011007
INCON	Incon.in R.	TIDCOMBE	1757	28006004
INCON	Incon.in R.	MASON	1758	28006004
INCON	L. G.& W.incon	GALE	1676	65002015
INCON	L. G.& W.incon	CLARKE	1734	65002015
INCON	L. G.& W.incon	DORMAN	1743	65002015
INCON	L. G.& W.incon	BALL	1756	65002015
INCON	L. G.& W.incon	CARR	1777	65002015
INCONS	L. G& W.incons	WAKE	1701	65002015
INCONS	L. G& W.incons	ROGERS	1735	65002015
INCONS	L. G& W.incons	SNAPE	1745	65002015
INCONS	Pract.incons.	SEED	1743	48001018
INCONSIDER	Inconsider.	GROVE	1741	23001003
INCONSIDERA	Inconsidera.	BARNES	1752	19050022
INCONSTANCY	Inconstancy.	GROVE	1741	28006004
INCORP	b. Incorp.s.	TRAIL	1779	27012003
INCR	Xnty.n.incr.	SKELTON	1754	46017015
INCRED	Incred.& Fa.	FOSTER	1744	46020029
IND	Cl.ag. J.ind.	PECKARD	1753	49009020
INDEED	Xn. Indeed.	POWELL	1730	47011026
INDEF	Polyg.indef.	SMITH	1780	01002024
INDEFECT	Ch.indefect.	HUTCHIN	1689	43016018
INDEFECT	Ch.indefect.	GOODMAN	1697	43016018
INDEFECT	Ch.indefect.	GREY	1730	43016018
INDEFECT	Ch.indefect.	CLARKE	1734	43016018
INDIF	Indif.in Rel.	LITTLETON	1684	47018017
INDIFF	Indiff.in Rel.	WEBB	1765	69003017
INDIFF	Indiff.to life	MOSS	1732	49007029
INDIFF	Indiff.to life	DAVIES	1766	49007029
INDIFF	Indiff.to R.	GRAY	1779	19085006
INDIFFERENCE	Indifference.	YOUNG	1706	43006024
INDIS	King's Indis.	HEYWOOD	1756	27006021
INDISP	Rel.indisp.	BRADY	1730	24005004
INDUCT	S.af. Induct.	BERRIMAN	1763	38002007
INDUL	Indul. Father	MASON	1742	45015011
INDUL	Ment. Indul.	GERARD	1782	24009003
INDULGENC	Indulgenc.	ANNESLEY	1675	61010014
INDUS	Hum. Indus.	DYKES	1722	20031019
INDUST	Early Indust.	DELANY	1747	20006006
INDUST	Usef. Indust.	DYKES	1722	20031024
INDUSTRY	Industry.	BARROW	1716	21009010
INDUSTRY	Industry.	DYKES	1722	20031013
INDUSTRY	Industry.	PIERCE	1731	46009004
INDUSTRY	Industry.	BURNET	1747	53004008
INDUSTRY	Industry.	SHERLOCK	1772	52004028
INDUSTRY	Industry.	GRANGER	1773	48012011
INDUSTRY	Industry.	JORTIN	1774	56003008
INDUSTRY	Industry.	PYLE	1777	48012011
INDUSTRY	Rel. Industry	COLMAN	1727	46009004

INDEXES TO THIRD VOLUME: E: KEYWORD-IN-CONTEXT INDEX OF OTHER SUBJECTS OR OCCASIONS

Keyword	In its Context	Author	Year	BkChpVrs
INDUSTRY	Rel. Industry	FOTHERGILL	1757	46009004
INDUSTRY	Rel. Industry	BOURN	1760	46006027
INDUSTRY	Rel. Industry	FARRINGTON	1769	46006027
INDWELL	Indwell. Spi.	FLAVEL	1673	65003024
INEFF	Ineff.of pr.	MOIR	1776	48010021
INEFF	Pr.& F.ineff.	WILLIAMS	1774	49015014
INEQ	Ineq. Condit.	LAWSON	1764	20022002
INEQ	Ineq.rel.dis.	MAINWARING	1780	47010034
INEX	Impen.inex.	SNAPE	1745	26018031
INEXC	Inexc. Ignor.	WHICHCOTE	1703	48001020
INEXCUS	Sin.inexcus.	WITHERSPOON	1768	19130003
INF	Inf.& Faith.	RAWLINS	1768	48011020
INF	Inf. Bapt.	BOSTWICK	1765	47002039
INF	Inf. Bapt.	LAKE	1781	47002039
INF	Inf. Baptism.	ROSSINGTON	1700	54002012
INF	Inf. Baptism.	CRAGGE	1741	44016015
INF	Inf. Ch.of R.	SMYTH	1735	50001024
INF	Inf. H. Nat.	CONYBEARE	1757	43025005
INF	Inf. H. Spir.	ATTERBURY	1743	55005019
INF	Inf. L. Revel.	WARBURTON	1754	45018008
INF	Inf. R.in Ad.	BLAIR	1777	19027005
INF	Inf. R.on Pr.	BLAIR	1777	19001003
INF	Inf.f.	HOLME	1745	45016009
INF	Inf.f.	BUTLER	1778	05015011
INF	Learn.& Inf.	HAMMOND	1684	46007048
INF	Nat.&m. Inf.	SPARKE	1745	62001027
INF	Sins inf.&pr.	GODDARD	1781	19019012
INF	Vice ca. Inf.	PYLE	1777	46007017
INF	West. Inf.	BRUCE	1752	45010037
INFALLAB	Ag. Infallab.	SHARP	1735	63003015
INFANT	Infant. Bapt.	HOLLAND	1700	47002038
INFANT	Infant Bapt.	SALMON	1701	44010014
INFANT	Infant Bapt.	NEWCOME	1702	44010014
INFANT	Infant Bapt.	ANONYMOUS	1715	45018015
INFANT	Infant Bapt.	HENRY	1726	44010016
INFANT	Infant Bapt.	TRAPP	1737	44010014
INFAT	Infat.of Sin.	FIDDES	1720	61003013
INFER	Dut.to infer.	JENNINGS	1757	47010002
INFI	Caus.of Infi.	PENN	1757	58002025
INFID	Cau.of Infid.	SOUTH	1727	46007017
INFID	Caus.o. Infid.	DELAUNE	1728	56003001
INFID	Infid.of age.	NEWTON	1782	61003012
INFID	Prof.& Infid.	BRAILSFORD	1776	23058001
INFID	Sin.of infid.	HAMMOND	1684	43010015
INFIDEL	Ag. Infidel.	DAVIES	1754	45016031
INFIDEL	Infidel.	GALE	1672	45019041
INFIDELI	Ag. Infideli.	WATTS	1753	58002005
INFIDELITY	Infidelity.	WILKINSON	1660	46008024
INFIDELITY	Infidelity.	NICOLSON	1661	61003012
INFIDELITY	Infidelity.	WARD	1674	61003012
INFIDELITY	Infidelity.	DUKE	1714	61003012
INFIDELITY	Infidelity.	BARROW	1716	61003012
INFIDELITY	Infidelity.	ADAMS	1736	20015002
INFIDELITY	Infidelity.	MOSS	1732	61003012
INFIDELITY	Infidelity.	STEWARD	1734	61012025
INFIDELITY	Infidelity.	DAVIS	1756	02023002
INFIDELITY	Infidelity.	WELCH	1752	50004002
INFIDELITY	Infidelity.	COLE	1761	57003016
INFIDELITY	Infidelity.	SHERLOCK	1772	61003012
INFIRM	Sins Infirm.	WATERLAND	1742	43026041
INFIRM	Sins Infirm.	HOOLE	1748	43026041
INFL	Infl. Examp.	BRERETON	1721	20001010
INFL	Infl.fut. L.	BRYSON	1778	65003003
INFL	Infl.of Faith.	HOLDEN	1755	44016015
INFL	Infl.of Faith.	VENN	1759	44016015
INFL	Infl.of Gosp.	HODGE	1758	54002013
INFL	Infl.of H. G.	SIMS	1772	53004013
INFL	Infl.of Piety.	FOTHERGILL	1765	20003005
INFL	Infl.sp. Mor.	FOSTER	1737	52005009
INFL	Spirit's Infl.	ROMAINE	1759	22004016
INFLU	Div. Influ.	DODDERIDGE	1742	59003005
INFLU	Div. Influ.	PRIESTLEY	1779	43013003
INFLU	Faith. Influ.	BEVERIDGE	1711	50005007
INGRAT	Ingrat.of Irre	WHICHCOTE	1698	48001021
INGRAT	Ingrat.to G.	DAVIES	1766	14032008
INGRATITUDE	Ingratitude.	HOLE	1716	45017011
INGRATITUDE	Ingratitude.	STERNE	1769	12017007
INH	G.chos. Inh.	ORTON	1776	19047004
INH	Inh.rich Jew	BOURN	1763	45016019
INHE	Inhe. S.in L.	CAMPION	1700	54001012
INHER	Etern. Inher.	MORE	1692	48008017
INHER	Heav. Inher.	WILCOX	1754	63001003
INHERIT	Fut. Inherit.	WHITAKER	1674	54001012
INI	Dep.fm. Ini.	FOORD	1719	58002019
INI	Dep.fm. Ini.	DUNLOP	1722	58002019
INIQ	Aboun. Iniq.	CLARKE	1736	43024012
INIQ	Nat. Iniq.	BRODBURST	1733	23001004
INJ	Inj.to Souls.	CLAGETT	1720	20008036
INJU	Forg.of Inju.	CREYGHTON	1720	52004032
INJU	Forg.of Inju.	CLARKE	1736	52004032
INJUR	Forg. Injur.	GARDINER	1720	43005038
INJUR	Forg. Injur.	BRADY	1730	43018035
INJUR	Forg. Injur.	MOSS	1737	43006014
INJUR	Forg. Injur.	BLAIR	1740	43005038
INJUR	Forg. Injur.	BLAIR	1740	43006014
INJUR	Forg. Injur.	WESTON	1747	45017004
INJUR	Forg. Injur.	DODWELL	1749	54003012
INN	At Serj. Inn.	PARKER	1750	45016031
INN	State of Inn.	HAWEIS	1762	01001026
INN	Wisd.& Inn.	BAGNOLD	1709	43010016
INNO	Inno.b. Rep.	FIDDES	1720	45015007
INNOC	Innoc. Day.	FRANK	1672	43002011
INNOC	Innoc. Day.	FRANK	1672	43002016
INNOC	Innoc. Day.	LITTLETON	1680	43002013
INNOC	Innoc. Day.	STANHOPE	1715	43002013
INNOC	Innoc. Day.	HOLE	1716	43002013
INNOC	Innoc. Day.	STANHOPE	1715	69014001
INNOC	Innoc. Day.	HOLE	1716	69014001
INNOC	Innoc. Day.	WILDER	1729	43002016
INNOC	Innoc. Day.	WESTON	1747	43016003
INNOC	Innoc. Day.	BARNES	1752	43002016
INNOC	Innoc. Day.	PYLE	1777	43002016

Keyword	In its Context	Author	Year	BkChpVrs
INNOCENTS	Innocents-d.	NEVILLE	1687	63003013
INOFF	Inoff. Cond.	MASON	1758	49010032
INOFF	Inoff. Consc.	ALLESTREE	1684	47024016
INOFF	Inoff. Consc.	BEVERIDGE	1720	47024016
INOFF	Inoff. Consc.	EDWARDS	1726	47024016
INOFF	Inoff. Consc.	TILLOTSON	1735	47024016
INOFF	Inoff. Consc.	ATTERBURY	1743	47024016
INOFF	Inoff. Consc.	ABERNETHY	1748	47024016
INORD	Inord. L. W.	MASON	1758	46002015
INORD	Inord. Mort.	BARNES	1752	54003005
INORD	Inord. Passi.	DAVIS	1756	65002016
INQUIS	Inquis. Disp.	ORR	1739	47017011
INS	Faith.ins.w. W	BEVERIDGE	1720	43007021
INS	Faith.ins.w. W	BLACKALL	1723	43007021
INS	Ins. Sit. Brit	BONAR	1773	33003008
INS	Ins. Usurp.	T.	1669	11021019
INS	Ins. Usurper.	T.	1660	45004006
INS	Obj. Mir.ins.	POWELL	1776	47017032
INS	R.ins.g.m. R	RANDOLPH	1738	50003005
INS	R.ins.g.m. R.	JOHNSON	1731	50003005
INS	Reas.ins. G.	EDGCUMBE	1736	50003005
INS	Reas.ins. G.	AGAR	1759	49002005
INS	Wo.ins.t. H.	CARR	1777	54003002
INSINC	Insinc. Dev.	WARNEFORD	1776	19066016
INSINCERITY	Insincerity.	DOUGHTY	1761	19055012
INSP	Insp.of S. S.	HORBERY	1774	49007040
INSP	Insp.of S S.	SEED	1743	55002013
INSPI	Inspi.of. S. S	BATTY	1739	58003016
INSPI	Inspi.of S. S.	KIDDELL	1779	58003016
INSPIR	Inspir. S. S.	HORBERY	1774	55004008
INSPIR	Inspir.o. S. S	CALAMY	1710	48003002
INSPIRATION	Inspiration.	CALAMY	1710	45016031
INSPIRATION	Inspiration.	SHEPHEARD	1776	58003016
INST	D. Inst.of M.	BETTY	1729	51001001
INST	Inst.of Ch.	WILSON	1781	05006006
INST	Pos. Inst.&c.	HUTCHINS	1782	12005012
INST	Xt's. Inst.gr.	TOTTIE	1775	46016012
INSTIT	Char. Instit.	LANGHORNE	1764	20010015
INSTIT	Hum. Instit.	WEST	1762	43015009
INSTIT	Pos. Instit.	GERARD	1780	45001016
INSTITUT	Institut.	WILKINSON	1713	05001018
INSTR	Fam. Instr.	JACOMB.	1719	01018019
INSTR	Instr. Xt's. D	FLAVEL	1673	45023034
INSTR	Instr.ignor.	WILSON	1781	44004028
INSTR	Minist.instr.	LOBB	1712	47020026
INSTR	Poor instr.	GREEN	1750	19068010
INSTR	Scribe instr.	SOUTH	1727	43013052
INSTRUC	Pub. Instruc.	ABERNETHU	1751	20008034
INSTRUCT	Par. Instruct.	DYKES	1722	20031001
INSTRUCT	Rel. Instruct.	SECKER	1770	43013016
INSUF	H.reas.insuf.	SHUCKBURGH	1721	21001015
INSUF	Insuf.o. N. R.	TAYLOR	1732	49011014
INSUF	Insuf.of Rea.	ECCLES	1755	47017022
INSUF	Reas.insuf.	BUNDY	1750	19019007
INSUFF	Hear.insuff.	READ	1728	62001027
INSUFF	Reas.insuff.	JOHNSON	1740	46006066

Keyword	In its Context	Author	Year	BkChpVrs
INSUFFIC	M's. Insuffic.	CLARKSON	1696	46015005
INSURRECTION	Insurrection.	TOTTON	1761	48013001
INSURRECTION	Insurrection.	BROWN	1764	49012024
INT	Happ. E. Int.	HOLDEN	1755	19037037
INT	Int. Ev.of G.	CARR	1777	53003008
INT	Int. St. Soul.	BATEMAN	1780	45023042
INT	Int.b.r.&w.	BOURDALOUE	1776	43013025
INT	Int.ex.o. Xy.	BULLOCK	1726	46008046
INT	Int.op.of Sp.	SECKER	1771	46014015
INT	Int.prf o. Xy.	BOYSE	1728	65005010
INT	Pers. Int. Xt.	CASE	1774	51002020
INT	Rel.our Int.	HOLDEN	1755	20011012
INT	Use& Int. Pr.	SHERLOCK	1740	64001019
INT	Xt's.gr. Int.	PARR	1661	45019041
INTE	Love of Inte.	STENNETT	1732	53002021
INTEG	Integ. Ex. Jos	ANONYMOUS	1776	43007012
INTEG	Integ.h.nat.	HOLDEN	1755	21007029
INTEG	Integ.of Xte.	DUCHAL	1765	21010001
INTEGRITY	Integrity.	STEPHENS	1699	18027005
INTEGRITY	Integrity.	CREYGHTON	1720	46001047
INTEGRITY	Integrity.	ST JOHN	1737	18027005
INTEGRITY	Integrity.	WHEATLAND	1739	19037037
INTEGRITY	Integrity.	WARREN	1748	18027005
INTEGRITY	Integrity.	STEEL	1778	18027005
INTEGRITY	Integrity&c.	BRYSON	1778	01017001
INTELL	Intell. Dark.	BALGUY	1748	43006023
INTEM	Intem.drink.	ANONYMOUS	1754	20023020
INTEMP	Intemp. Cur.	LLOYD	1765	05029029
INTEMPE	Temp.& Intempe	SMITH	1740	49009025
INTEMPER	Intemper.	GIBSON	1743	49009025
INTEMPER	Intemper.	HOLLAND	1750	45021034
INTEMPER	Intemper.	DODD	1772	49009025
INTEMPERAN	Intemperan.	WROUGHTON	1728	48013013
INTENT	Div. Intent.	BOURN	1760	19089047
INTENT	Good Intent.	ALLESTREE	1684	43006022
INTENT	Good Intent.	BLACKALL	1723	43006022
INTENT	Good Intent.	WESTLEY	1748	43006001
INTENT	Pur. Intent.	WESTLEY	1748	43006019
INTENT	Rig. Intent.	CLAGETT	1720	43006022
INTER	Inter. Soul.	CARTER	1722	44008036
INTER	Inter. Soul.	WHARTON	1728	44008036
INTER	Inter. Soul.	DUPREE	1782	44008036
INTER	Self-inter.	STONE	1771	18001009
INTERC	Interc.of Xt.	BROWNE	1749	61009024
INTERC	Interc.w. G.	NALSON	1737	18022021
INTERC	Interc.w. G.	REAY	1755	18022021
INTERC	Interc.w. G.	RICHMOND	1764	18022021
INTERC	Interc.w. G.	LANGHORNE	1773	18022021
INTERC	Prev. Interc.	HORNE	1778	04016047
INTERC	Sav. Interc.	OGDEN	1770	23054007
INTERC	Xt's. Interc.	FLAVEL	1673	61006023
INTERC	Xt's. Interc.	CHARNOCK	1684	65002001
INTERC	Xt's. Interc.	CRUSO	1699	61007025
INTERC	Xt's. Interc.	HURRION	1719	61007025
INTERC	Xt's. Interc.	STENNETT	1732	61007025
INTERC	Xt's. Interc.	DODDERIDGE	1736	61007025

INDEXES TO THIRD VOLUME: E: KEYWORD-IN-CONTEXT INDEX OF OTHER SUBJECTS OR OCCASIONS

Keyword	In its Context	Author	Year	BkChpVrs
INTERC	Xt's. Interc.	HUBBARD	1757	48008034
INTERC	Xt's. Interc.	FANCH	1768	46017024
INTERCESSION	Intercession.	HOLE	1716	19067001
INTERCESSION	Intercession.	WHITFIELD	1739	55005025
INTERCESSION	Intercession.	FOSTER	1744	57002001
INTERCESSION	Intercession.	OGDEN	1770	18042010
INTERCESSION	Intercession.	OGDEN	1770	57002001
INTERM	Interm. St.	MARRIOTT	1775	49015014
INTERM	Interm. St.	MARRIOTT	1775	54003001
INTERM	Interm. State	SMALRIDGE	1724	23057002
INTERM	Interm. State	HOLDEN	1755	45023043
INTERM	Interm. State	GODDARD	1756	45023043
INTERM	Interm. State	REGIS	1751	64002009
INTERM	Interm. State	MARRIOTT	1775	46014001
INTERP	Interp.o. S. S	JAMES	1729	47008030
INTERP	Par.interp.	ROMAINE	1756	26037004
INTO	Bapt.into N.o.	PIERCE	1718	49001013
INTO	Bapt.into N.o.	CLARKE	1734	49001013
INTO	Enq.into Xy.	DUCHAL	1753	50004002
INTO	Ent.into rest.	BOSTON	1773	61004003
INTO	Wat.into W.	BRAGGE	1702	46002001
INTRO	Intro.to Ord.	HALL	1759	45010023
INTROD	Introd. Disc.	ANONYMOUS	1776	45013008
INTROD	Introd.to Cr.	CARRINGTON	1750	50013005
INTRODUCTION	Introduction	GARDINER	1720	43005001
INUND	Inund. Holl.	SPANHEIM	1676	69003020
INV	French inv.	BRADBURY	1772	23007005
INV	Inv o. Saints.	MAYO	1675	48010014
INV	Inv.t.thir. S.	DODDERIDGE	1761	46007037
INV	Inv.t.thir. S.	PEARSE	1763	46007037
INV	Inv.to Xt.	MAY	1757	69022003
INV	Inv.to Xt.	WHITTY	1766	69022017
INV	M's Inv.to H.	ORTON	1776	04010029
INV	Vis.&inv. W.	ORR	1772	50004018
INV	Xt's. Inv. Ch.	DAVIES	1758	44010014
INVEST	Invest. P. Or.	WILLEMSON	1747	37009016
INVI	Invi.refused.	BOURN	1764	45014016
INVIS	Invis. Ch.	LEE	1675	43016018
INVIT	Gosp. Invit.	DAVIES	1771	45014021
INVIT	Xt's. Invit.	GREGORY	1696	43011028
INVIT	Xt's. Invit.	SCATTERGOOD	1723	43011028
INVIT	Xt's. Invit.	NEWTON	1736	43011028
INVITAT	Xt's. Invitat.	CLARKSON	1696	69003020
INVOCATION	Invocation.	HOLE	1716	45018013
INVOCATION	Invocation.	BLAIR	1740	43006009
INVOLUN	Involun. Sin.	DORRINGTON	1703	48007019
INW	Inw. Peace.	TILLOTSON	1735	19119165
INW	Wp.inw.&o.	WAPLE	1720	48012001
IR	A.m. Pr. Ir. S	SECKER	1766	20009006
IRRE	Ingrat.of Irre	WHICHCOTE	1698	48001021
IRREG	Irreg.desires	BALGUY	1748	21006009
IRRELIGION	Irreligion.	WEATHERLEY	1750	69003002
IRRES	Irres.in Rel.	CLARK	1742	47026028
IRRESOLUTION	Irresolution.	TILLOTSON	1735	19119060
IRRESOLUTION	Irresolution.	COOKE	1739	47026028
IS	Con.is Hap.	STILLINGFLEET	1707	23057021

Keyword	In its Context	Author	Year	BkChpVrs
IS	G.is Light.	COCK	1710	65001005
IS	G.is Light.	STURMY	1716	65001005
IS	God is Love.	RUST	1686	65004016
IS	God is Love.	BRADY	1704	65004008
IS	God is Love.	HUSSEY	1755	65004008
IS	God is Love.	DAVIES	1766	65004008
IS	God is Love.	LELAND	1769	65004008
IS	Wom.blo. Is.	DODD	1757	45009042
ISAAC	Abr.off. Isaac	JENKINS	1779	01022012
ISAI'S	Isai's Vision.	JENKINS	1779	23006001
ISR	Isr.& Engl.	KNELL	1681	30003002
ISR	Isr.& Engl.	REGIS	1753	05011026
ISR	Word to Isr.	CHISHULL	1668	61003008
ISR	Xt. G.of Isr.	BRADBURY	1752	01032030
ISRA	Isra Deliver.	CLARKE	1727	02015009
ISS	Zeb.& Iss.bl.	ORTON	1776	05033018
IT'S	Fai.&it's N.	FEUILLERADE	1717	51005006
ITCHING	Itching Ears.	DOWNES	1761	58004003
ITS	Fut.st.its Ev.	FOSTER	1732	58001010
ITS	Good con.its H	FIDDES	1720	47024016
ITS	Good con.its H	FISHER	1741	47024016
ITS	Sin its Pun.	BOYSE	1728	24002019
ITSELF	Seedsp.itself.	DODD	1757	44004026
J	Believ. J. Xt.	ABERNETHY	1751	65003023
J	Cl.ag. J.ind.	PECKARD	1753	49009020
J	Exc.of J. L.	RANDOLPH	1773	05004005
J	F.in.j.tr.w.	BREVALL	1670	69002010
J	Fai& H.in J.	PRICE	1757	51005005
J	Fut.gen. J.	AMORY	1748	43025031
J	G's. J.in d. S	EDWARDS	1774	48003019
J	G's. J.sp.&t.	LOCKIER	1671	48007025
J	J.& M.of G.	ABERNETHY	1743	19089014
J	J.& M.of G.	KNOWLES	1750	19089014
J	J. Xt. Im. G.	BRETT	1720	54001015
J	J. Xt. Im. G.	LESTLEY	1720	54001015
J	J.sp.&fut.st.	CARTER	1729	51006007
J	Joy in Xt. J.	DODSON	1728	53003003
J	Know. J. Xt.	BOLDE	1697	53003008
J	Know. J. Xt.	NEWMAN	1728	49002002
J	Knowl. J. Xt.	STEBBING	1721	53003C07
J	M.& J. Gov.	BOURN	1760	19058010
J	O.30. J. Scot.	ANONYMOUS	1720	21003004
J	Pr. Test. J. C	BRACKENRIDGE	1764	69019010
J	R. Sold. J. R.	LARDNER	1760	43028012
J	S.o. G.f.d. J.	DAVIES	1771	49003007
J	Salv.f. J.& G.	SHIRLEY	1762	47010034
J	St. J. Bapt.	LITTLETON	1680	43003002
J	St. Ph.& St. J	STANHOPE	1715	62001001
J	St. Ph.& St. J	HOLE	1716	62001001
J	St. Phil.& J.	LITTLETON	1680	46001046
J	St. Phil.& J.	STANHOPE	1715	46014001
J	St. Phil.& J.	HOLE	1716	46014001
J	St. Sim.& J.	STANHOPE	1715	46015017
J	St. Sim.& J.	HOLE	1716	46015017
J	W.w. F.c. J.	HORNE	1761	62002014
J	Wo.anoin. J.	LARDNER	1760	43026013

Keyword	In its Context	Author	Year	BkChpVrs
J	Xn. Z.b. L.j.	SYNGE	1716	51004018
J	Xn's. Gl.& J.	BUNDY	1740	55002020
J	Xt.to J.& G.	BROWNE	1722	45002032
J	Xy.j.b. O. T.	BULLOCK	1726	61008007
J'S	J's h. Concl.	JENKINS	1779	01042036
JAC	Jac. Judgm.	FRANCIS	1773	01049005
JAC	Jac. Proph.	LAMBERT	1779	01032009
JACH	Jach.& Boaz.	HUME	1676	61010023
JACOB	Hist.of Jacob	STERNE	1766	01047009
JACOB	Jacob&c.	MURRAY	1777	01049008
JACOB'S	Jacob's Pro.	KEDDINGTON	1758	01050021
JACOB'S	Jacob's Vow.	HALES	1673	01028020
JACOB'S	Jacob's Xrter	ENFIELD	1777	01025027
JACOB'S	Jacob's Xrter.	MURRAY	1777	01028001
JAILOR	The Jailor c.	WEBB	1766	47016033
JAIR'S	Jair's Daugh.	BRAGGE	1702	44005021
JAME'S	St. Jame's-d.	COOKE	1739	61010023
JAMES	St. James d.	STANHOPE	1715	43020020
JAMES	St. James d.	HOLE	1716	43020020
JAMES	St. James.	HOLE	1716	43016024
JEHOS'S	Jehos's char.	LIVESEY	1660	14019006
JEPTH	Jepth. Vow.	HOLBROOK	1731	07011030
JEPTH	Jepth. Vow.	ROMAINE	1744	07011030
JEPTH	Jepth. Vow.	RANDOLPH	1766	07011030
JEPTH	Jepth. Vow.	SMITH	1777	07011030
JER	Jer. Obs.&c.	ORTON	1776	24005004
JER	Jer. Sins&c.	SMITH	1691	45019041
JER	Peace of Jer.	REYNOLDS	1679	19122006
JERUS	Jerus. Rise.	SHARP	1765	19028009
JES	Div. T.to Jes.	LARDNER	1760	43027052
JES	Gr.of Jes.&c.	LARDNER	1760	46019030
JES	Jes. Burial.	COLMAN	1728	43028006
JES	Jes. God.	PEAD	1694	43013058
JES	Jes. Mess.	TILLOTSON	1735	43011002
JES	Jes. Messiah.	BARROW	1716	46005037
JES	Jes. Messiah.	WEBB	1765	43027054
JES	Jes. Messias.	SHERLOCK	1719	45024025
JES	Jes. Messias.	BARROW	1716	47009022
JES	Jes. Propitia.	COCKMAN	1750	65004010
JES	Jes. Son o. G.	LARDNER	1760	46020017
JES	Jes. Son o. M.	LARDNER	1760	45017022
JES	Jes. Temper.	GROSVENOR	1724	45024047
JES	Jes. Xt. G.m.	GUYSE	1719	48009005
JES	Jes.an. H. Pr.	WHEATLY	1746	61005009
JES	Jes.crucified.	DAVIS	1756	43021043
JES	Jes.m. Curse.	HURST	1678	51003010
JES	Jes.m. Curse.	LARDNER	1769	51003013
JES	Jes.our Adv.	SUTTON	1718	65002001
JES	Jes.our Ex.	VINCENT	1690	63002021
JES	Jes.our Ex.	TILLOTSON	1735	63002021
JES	Jes.t. Proph.	BULLOCK	1724	47003022
JES	Jes.the Xt.	GROVE	1741	47004027
JES	Jes.weeping.	LOTHIAN	1776	46011035
JES	Na. Jes.& Xt.	NEWTON	1782	45002021
JES	Salv.th. Jes.	DAVIES	1766	46003026
JESUS	Jesus risen.	HORNE	1778	45024034

Keyword	In its Context	Author	Year	BkChpVrs
JESUS	Jesus Xt.	BARROW	1716	52001013
JESUS	Name Jesus.	GROSVENOR	1724	43001021
JESUS	Suffer. Jesus.	FARMER	1757	63003018
JEW	End Jew. L.	CLARKE	1736	51002015
JEW	Ign. Jew. Ch.	BILSTONE	1763	51004003
JEW	Inh.rich Jew	BOURN	1763	45016019
JEW	Jew.& Xn. P.	WESTON	1747	43023001
JEW	Jew. Dispen.	SWANNE	1760	48003001
JEW	Jew. Festiv.	DAVIS	1756	46010022
JEW	Jew. Hyp.	PATRICK	1670	32006008
JEW	Jew. Peo.&c.	LARDNER	1743	48011011
JEW	Jew. Proph.	SCOTT	1743	55005020
JEW	Jew. Sabbath.	MEDE	1672	26020030
JEW	Kind.to Jew.	STEPHENS	1735	58001016
JEW	Xn.a. Jew. L.	WESTON	1747	43005020
JEWELS	Alleg. Jewels	SPOONER	1771	43013044
JEWS	Case of Jews.	HORNE	1778	46001011
JEWS	Jews.	MUNTON	1756	05005029
JEWS	Jews. Bill.	WINSTANLEY	1753	49009022
JEWS	Unb.o Jews.	CLAGETT	1720	46012037
JOB'S	Job's Expost.	STERNE	1760	18002010
JOB'S	Job's Xrter.	ENFIELD	1777	18001001
JOH	Joh. Xr.& W.	DUCHAL	1753	46021024
JOHN	John Bapt.	WESTON	1747	44001003
JOHN	St. John Bap.	STANHOPE	1715	45001057
JOHN	St. John Bap.	HOLE	1716	45001057
JOHN	St. John Bap.	NEWLIN	1720	44006020
JOHN	St. John Bap.	NEWLIN	1728	23057020
JOHN	St. John Bap.	MARSHALL	1731	43014008
JOHN	St. John Ev.	STANHOPE	1715	65001001
JOHN	St. John Ev.	HOLE	1716	65001001
JOHN	St.john bapt.	STANHOPE	1715	23040001
JOHN	St.john bapt.	HOLE	1716	23040001
JOHN'S	John's l.life.	NEWTON	1782	46021022
JOHN'S	John's P.f. G.	ORTON	1776	67000002
JOHN'S	St. John's d.	PEGGE	1742	46001005
JOHN'S	St. John's Ev.	STANHOPE	1715	46021019
JOHN'S	St. John's Ev.	HOLE	1716	46021019
JON	Jon. Comm.	POTTS	1758	31003002
JON	Jon. History.	DOWNES	1761	31001017
JON	Jon. Xrter.	CRAIG	1775	31004004
JONAS	Sign of Jonas	JORTIN	1774	43012039
JOS	Hist.of Jos.	CONYBEARE	1757	01037036
JOS	Hist.of Jos.	CONYBEARE	1757	01039001
JOS	Hist.of Jos.	CONYBEARE	1757	01041046
JOS	Hist.of Jos.	HUNTER	1774	01039002
JOS	Integ. Ex. Jos	ANONYMOUS	1776	43007012
JOS	Jos. Minist.	HUNTER	1774	01041046
JOS	Jos. T.of Xt.	WILLISON	1761	01045004
JOS	Jos. T.of Xt.	BLISS	1769	01045004
JOS	Jos. Xrter.	ENFIELD	1777	01045004
JOS	Jos. Xrter.	MURRAY	1777	01037003
JOS	Story of Jos.	LANGHORNE	1773	01045004
JOSEP	Josep. Xrter.	ENFIELD	1777	01037034
JOSH	Josh. Res.	GOUGE	1663	06024015
JOSH	Josh.walk.	ORTON	1776	37003006

INDEXES TO THIRD VOLUME: E: KEYWORD-IN-CONTEXT INDEX OF OTHER SUBJECTS OR OCCASIONS

Keyword	In its Context	Author	Year	BkChpVrs
JOSI	Josi. Xrter.	CLARIDGE	1692	12023025
JOSI	Josi. Xrter.	MAY	1744	14034003
JOY	Aff.m.o.joy.	HOWE	1744	62001002
JOY	God our Joy.	DUNLOP	1722	19043004
JOY	Joy in bel.	DODSON	1728	48015013
JOY	Joy in the L.	WILKINSON	1660	34003018
JOY	Joy in Conv.	WILCOX	1757	55002019
JOY	Joy in H.&c.	WATERLAND	1742	45015007
JOY	Joy in H.&c.	TOPLADY	1775	45015007
JOY	Joy in H.&c.	PETERS	1776	45015010
JOY	Joy in H.&c.	PYLE	1777	45015007
JOY	Joy in H. Gh.	DODSON	1728	48014017
JOY	Joy in Lord.	REYNOLDS	1679	53004004
JOY	Joy in Xt. J.	DODSON	1728	53003003
JOY	Joy of g. Xn.	BATTY	1739	53004004
JOY	Joy of right.	WHICHCOTE	1702	19033001
JOY	Joy of Heav.	LANGHORNE	1773	69022014
JOY	Joy on Rep.	TILLOTSON	1735	45015007
JOY	Joy on Rep.	NALSON	1737	45015007
JOY	Joy& F.in R.	BLAIR	1777	19002011
JOY	Joy Ang.&c.	ORTON	1776	18038007
JOY	Joy D. Xns'.	BEVERIDGE	1720	53004004
JOY	Joy Pea.& H.	LUCAS	1710	48015013
JOY	Minist. Joy.	MAY	1753	66000004
JOY	Parental Joy.	HOLLAND	1753	20023024
JOY	Peace& Joy.	CROSSINGE	1718	23032017
JOY	Pres. Joy D.	WILCOX	1757	19097011
JOY	Relig. Joy.	GROVE	1741	19097012
JOY	Relig. Joy.	BOURN	1760	53004004
JOY	Rep. Sin. Joy	BROUGHTON	1778	45015007
JOY	Spir. Joy.	BRADY	1704	46016022
JOY	Sympa. Joy.	ENFIELD	1772	48012015
JOY	Sympa. Joy.	WOOD	1775	48012015
JOY	Xn. Joy.	BURROUGHS	1733	55005016
JOY	Xn. Joy.	COCKMAN	1750	53004004
JOY	Xn. Joy.	FARQUAR	1772	55005016
JOY	Xn's. Joy i. S	BOURN	1777	63001008
JOY	Xn's. Joy.	BRADBURY	1713	46020024
JOY	Xn's. Joy&c.	BRADBURY	1772	47020024
JOYS	Joys o. Heav.	SHARP	1729	61004011
JOYS	Joys of H.	ADEY	1760	19016012
JOYS	Joys of Hea.	JOHNSON	1740	49002009
JOYS	Joys& Sorr.	MARSHALL	1750	50004018
JU	Clear&st. Ju.	OUTRAM	1697	53001010
JU	Right.pr. Ju.	ANONYMOUS	1721	49010015
JU	St. Sim.& Ju.	JACKSON	1673	68000004
JU	St. Sim.& Ju.	TURNER	1678	58001007
JU	St. Sim.& Ju.	ATTERBURY	1730	45016031
JU	Su.sum.to ju.	VINCENT	1667	69022020
JUB	Dissrs. Jub.	NICHOLETS	1687	19126003
JUB	Westm. Jub.	PEARCE	1760	20031031
JUD	Cal.not Jud.	LLOYD	1765	46009001
JUD	Con.fut.jud.	STILLINGFLEET	1707	21011009
JUD	Con.fut.jud.	SUTTON	1754	21011009
JUD	Fut.jud.&c.	HORTON	1679	50005010
JUD	Jud. G.& M.	HUNTER	1774	09016007

Keyword	In its Context	Author	Year	BkChpVrs
JUD	Jud. Obdur.	WILCOX	1757	26047011
JUD	Jud. Pr. Rig.	SKELTON	1754	44014043
JUD	Jud. S.expl.	WILSON	1781	45022021
JUD	Pros.of Jud.	CONEY	1750	19090008
JUD	Rea.jud.r.ac.	CLARKE	1735	65003020
JUD	Xt.co.t.jud.	FLAVEL	1673	47010042
JUD	Xt.co.t.jud.	CARRINGTON	1750	47010042
JUD	Xt.com. Jud.	MALBON	1673	43016027
JUD	Xt.com. Jud.	RALEIGH	1679	43016027
JUDA	Xty.b. Juda.	ROBOTHAM	1756	51003021
JUDAS	Judas cond.	NEWLIN	1728	43027003
JUDAS	Judas Trea.	FLAVEL	1673	43026047
JUDAS	Judas Xrter.	CRAIG	1775	43026014
JUDG	Cer.fu.judg.	HAWKINS	1725	49015019
JUDG	Del.& Judg.	HORNE	1684	21011009
JUDG	Dth.& Judg.	FOORD	1719	61009027
JUDG	F.judg.c.& P.t	BRYAN	1685	50005010
JUDG	F.judg.c.& P.t	BURNET	1747	50005010
JUDG	Fut. Judg.	HAVETT	1703	21012014
JUDG	Fut. Judg.	EVANS	1725	21011009
JUDG	G's Judg.	WARREN	1739	19119075
JUDG	Gen.judg.vi.	COCKMAN	1750	65003003
JUDG	God's judg.	TILLOTSON	1735	23009012
JUDG	God's Judg.	WALLIS	1692	19058011
JUDG	Judg. Hell.	WILKINSON	1660	01006003
JUDG	Judg. Neigh.	PETERS	1776	62004012
JUDG	Judg.by Xt.	HURRION	1712	58004001
JUDG	Judg.of Xt.	NEWTON	1736	50005010
JUDG	Judg.others.	NEEDHAM	1679	49004005
JUDG	Judg.others.	SMEDLEY	1719	62005012
JUDG	Judg.others.	MAYNARD	1722	49004005
JUDG	Judg.right.	NORRIS	1728	46007024
JUDG	Judg.right.	WILDER	1729	46007024
JUDG	Rash.judg.	BLAIR	1740	43007004
JUDG	Rash Judg.	WATERLAND	1742	45013002
JUDG	Rash Judg.	HOOLE	1748	45006037
JUDG	Reas.judg.d.	JOHNSON	1733	46011026
JUDG	Rig.of Judg.	MICHELL	1737	45012057
JUDG	Rules f.judg.	BLACKALL	1723	43007003
JUDG	Rules f.judg.	BLAIR	1740	43007003
JUDG	Sin of judg.	SIMONS	1743	49004005
JUDG	Temp. Judg.	TREBECK	1730	45013001
JUDG	Univ. Judg.	SMALBROOKE	1706	46005028
JUDG	Univ. Judg.	BOURN	1764	43025031
JUDG	Univ. Judg.	DAVIES	1766	47017030
JUDG	Van.h.judg.	ABERNETHY	1748	49004003
JUDG	Words judg.	LITTLETON	1735	43012036
JUDG	Xt.on Judg.	JOHNSON	1776	43025031
JUDGE	G. Judge o.a.	HILL	1755	61012023
JUDGE	Judge not.	HEYLIN	1761	43007001
JUDGE	Son m.judge	MARSH	1699	43024030
JUDGE	Xt.the judge	DUNLOP	1722	48002016
JUDGING	Judging&c.	FIDDES	1720	43007001
JUDGING	Judging&c.	WESTLEY	1750	43007001
JUDGING	Judging&c.	MOTTERSHEAD	1759	43007001
JUDGING	of Judging.	BLACKALL	1723	43007001

Keyword	In its Context	Author	Year	BkChpVrs
JUDGING	of Judging.	GALE	1726	43007001
JUDGING	of Judging.	BLAIR	1740	43007001
JUDGM	Day Judgm.	TILLOTSON	1735	44013032
JUDGM	Day Judgm.	SHARP	1734	47017031
JUDGM	Day Judgm.	BROWNE	1749	69020012
JUDGM	Day Judgm.	ATKINSON	1775	50005010
JUDGM	Div. Judgm.	WEDDERSPOON	1733	45013001
JUDGM	Div. Judgm.	FOTHERGILL	1765	23026009
JUDGM	Eter. Judgm.	BATES	1700	47017031
JUDGM	Free Judgm.	DUCHAL	1765	50003002
JUDGM	Fut. Judgm.	NEEDHAM	1679	50005010
JUDGM	Fut. Judgm.	GLANVIL	1681	47017031
JUDGM	Fut. Judgm.	MANTON	1693	47017031
JUDGM	Fut. Judgm.	SHERLOCK	1699	47017031
JUDGM	Fut. Judgm.	PIGOTT	1702	57004001
JUDGM	Fut. Judgm.	DORRINGTON	1703	50005010
JUDGM	Fut. Judgm.	BARROW	1716	21003017
JUDGM	Fut. Judgm.	HOPKINS	1712	50005010
JUDGM	Fut. Judgm.	BARROW	1716	47010042
JUDGM	Fut. Judgm.	MOORE	1716	47017031
JUDGM	Fut. Judgm.	WAKE	1716	47024025
JUDGM	Fut. Judgm.	KILLINBECK	1717	64003004
JUDGM	Fut. Judgm.	FIDDES	1720	47017031
JUDGM	Fut. Judgm.	FIDDES	1720	47024025
JUDGM	Fut. Judgm.	COLLIER	1725	50005010
JUDGM	Fut. Judgm.	CLARKE	1727	47017031
JUDGM	Fut. Judgm.	TILLOTSON	1735	50005010
JUDGM	Fut. Judgm.	ORR	1739	47017030
JUDGM	Fut. Judgm.	JEPHSON	1742	43025046
JUDGM	Fut. Judgm.	SEED	1743	43026024
JUDGM	Fut. Judgm.	STRAIGHT	1741	50005010
JUDGM	Fut. Judgm.	BURNET	1747	47017031
JUDGM	Fut. Judgm.	AMORY	1748	50005010
JUDGM	Fut. Judgm.	PRIEST	1753	64003003
JUDGM	Fut. Judgm.	ANONYMOUS	1756	69022012
JUDGM	Fut. Judgm.	TIDCOMBE	1757	50005010
JUDGM	Fut. Judgm.	MOIR	1759	50005010
JUDGM	Fut. Judgm.	FARRINGTON	1769	18019025
JUDGM	Fut. Judgm.	LELAND	1769	21003017
JUDGM	Fut. Judgm.	BRACKENRIDGE	1764	69022012
JUDGM	Fut. Judgm.	ELSMERE	1767	61009027
JUDGM	Fut. Judgm.	SMITH	1769	47017031
JUDGM	Fut. Judgm.	SIMS	1772	61009002
JUDGM	Fut. Judgm.	ORR	1772	63001017
JUDGM	Fut. Judgm.	JORTIN	1774	48002006
JUDGM	Fut. Judgm.	OGDEN	1777	55004014
JUDGM	Fut. Judgm.	SAURIN	1777	61009027
JUDGM	Fut. Judgm.	PYLE	1777	64003011
JUDGM	G's. Judgm.	SINGLETON	1683	46012028
JUDGM	G's. Judgm.	BARROW	1716	48011033
JUDGM	G's. Judgm.	SNAPE	1745	61010031
JUDGM	G's.judgm.	TREVOR	1722	34003005
JUDGM	G's Judgm.	FORD	1678	19009016
JUDGM	G's Judgm.	WHICHCOTE	1702	23026009
JUDGM	G's Judgm.	DORRINGTON	1702	23045007
JUDGM	G's Judgm.	TILLOTSON	1735	45013005

Keyword	In its Context	Author	Year	BkChpVrs
JUDGM	G's Judgm.	HUNT	1748	19009008
JUDGM	Gen. Judgm.	EDWARDS	1713	47017031
JUDGM	Gen. Judgm.	SCATTERGOOD	1723	45018008
JUDGM	Gen. Judgm.	PEIRCE	1731	50005010
JUDGM	Gen. Judgm.	COCKMAN	1750	64003003
JUDGM	Gen. Judgm.	DAVIS	1756	47017031
JUDGM	Gen. Judgm.	CARR	1777	43024044
JUDGM	Jac. Judgm.	FRANCIS	1773	01049005
JUDGM	Judgm.cert.	BOURN	1755	47017031
JUDGM	Judgm.cert.	ANONYMOUS	1776	47017031
JUDGM	Last. Judgm.	SHERIDAN	1720	47017031
JUDGM	Last. Judgm.	SHERIDAN	1720	68000014
JUDGM	Last. Judgm.	BOURDALOUE	1776	45021025
JUDGM	Last Judgm.	PARKHURST	1704	69020011
JUDGM	Last Judgm.	HEBDEN	1738	61009027
JUDGM	Last Judgm.	HORT	1738	61009027
JUDGM	Last Judgm.	COCKMAN	1750	61009027
JUDGM	Last Judgm.	ELSMERE	1767	50005010
JUDGM	Nat. Judgm.	MOIR	1759	24009009
JUDGM	Priv. Judgm.	SYNGE	1737	45012057
JUDGM	Priv. Judgm.	FISHER	1741	47008031
JUDGM	Rash judgm.	SHOREY	1725	49004005
JUDGM	Sol's Judgm.	PENTYCROSS	1781	11003026
JUDGM	Vis. Judgm.	BRODBURST	1733	14028010
JUDGMENT	Judgment.	BOYSE	1728	47017030
JUDGMENT	Judgment.	BOYSE	1728	69020011
JUDGMENT	Judgment.	DODDRIDGE	1743	21011009
JUDGMENT	Judgment.	ANONYMOUS	1776	69020011
JUDGMENTS	Judgments.	BRIDGE	1671	32006009
JUGDM	Jugdm.day.	WATSON	1676	47017031
JUL	T. Jul. Ship.	RAMSAY	1681	47027015
JULY	July 2.	STERNE	1699	18036024
JUNE	June 10.	KNAGGS	1716	46005014
JUNE	June 11.	ERSKINE	1710	52004003
JUNE	June 12.	KNAGGS	1715	20013010
JUNE	June 21.	THOMPSON	1685	59003001
JUS	Jus.by Faith.	USHER	1678	48005001
JUS	Jus.by Faith.	SCOTT	1701	48003028
JUS	Jus.by Faith.	WILLIAMS	1708	48005001
JUS	Jus.by Faith.	BARROW	1716	48005001
JUS	Jus.by Faith.	BILLINGSLEY	1723	48005001
JUS	Jus.by Faith.	DODSON	1728	48005002
JUS	Jus.by Faith.	BIRCH	1729	48005001
JUS	Jus.by Faith.	STEPHENS	1737	48003028
JUS	Jus.by Faith.	WESTLEY	1746	48004005
JUS	Jus.by Faith.	HOOLE	1748	48003028
JUS	Jus.by Faith.	ABERNETHY	1748	48004016
JUS	Jus.by Faith.	SHEPHERD	1748	51002016
JUS	Jus.by Faith.	SMITH	1752	48003028
JUS	Jus.by Faith.	HAYWARD	1758	48005001
JUS	Jus.by Faith.	HALLIFAX	1760	48003028
JUS	Jus.by Faith.	RANDOLPH	1768	48003028
JUS	Jus.by Faith.	JOHNSON	1776	48005001
JUS	Jus.by Faith.	PETERS	1776	48005001
JUS	Merit& Jus.	NEWMAN	1735	48004004
JUST	Ch.&just.	SOUTHCOMB	1714	43007012

INDEXES TO THIRD VOLUME: E: KEYWORD-IN-CONTEXT INDEX OF OTHER SUBJECTS OR OCCASIONS

Keyword	In its Context	Author	Year	BkChpVrs
JUST	Ch.&just.	PYLE	1777	43007012
JUST	Fut. Ret.just.	BARNES	1752	45016025
JUST	G's just.& M.	ATTERBURY	1703	69004003
JUST	Just by works	HOOKER	1705	34001004
JUST	Just.& Char.	LUCAS	1716	48013008
JUST	Just.b. Faith.	COYTE	1761	51005006
JUST	Just.by F.	BOWMAN	1764	46003014
JUST	Just.by Wor.	GALE	1726	53003009
JUST	Just.by Wor.	BRADBURY	1772	48004003
JUST	Just.by Xt.	WHITFIELD	1739	49006011
JUST	Just.of G.	WILDER	1741	69015003
JUST	Just.of G.	BRACKENRIDGE	1764	69015003
JUST	Lawf.just w.	FOURESTIER	1758	43024006
JUST	Nat.of Just.	WEBSTER	1754	43005006
JUST	One just o. A.	DORRINGTON	1683	49007031
JUST	Path of Just.	ABERNETHY	1748	20004018
JUST	Reform.just.	STILLINGFLEET	1707	47024014
JUST	Rew.of Just.	CLARKE	1736	45014014
JUST	b. L. Just.	GOODWIN	1716	26017019
JUST	b. Ld Just.	KING	1685	23059006
JUSTICE	G's. Justice.	CLAGETT	1704	48008033
JUSTICE	G's Justice	HUTCHINS	1782	05022004
JUSTICE	G's Justice.	WHITBY	1710	19145017
JUSTICE	Justice of G.	WISHEART	1716	05032004
JUSTICE	Justice.	WHICHCOTE	1702	32006008
JUSTICE	Justice.	DYKES	1722	20031008
JUSTICE	Justice.	DYKES	1722	20031009
JUSTICE	Justice.	DODWELL	1749	48013007
JUSTICE	Justice.	MASON	1757	32006008
JUSTICE	Justice.	STEBBING	1760	63004014
JUSTICE	Justice.	SECKER	1771	43006012
JUSTICE	Justice.	WEBB	1772	48013007
JUSTICE	Justice&c.	SHERIDAN	1720	32006008
JUSTICES	b. L. Justices.	WILLIS	1701	20012026
JUSTICES	b. L. Justices.	FORSTER	1716	49001010
JUSTIF	Bless. Justif.	BAINE	1778	48008001
JUSTIF	Justif. Faith.	E.	1679	65005012
JUSTIF	Sinn. Justif.	BRAGGE	1732	51002016
JUSTIF	Wisd. Justif.	H.	1699	45007035
JUSTIF	Wisd.justif.	MANTON	1708	43011018
JUSTIF	Xnity.justif.	BULLOCK	1726	45024025
JUSTIF	Xnity.justif.	BULLOCK	1726	47003025
JUSTIFICAT	Of Justificat.	GIBBON	1676	48005001
JUSTIFICATIO	Justification.	CLARKSON	1675	48003024
JUSTIFICATIO	Justification.	TOMLYNS	1696	24023006
JUSTIFICATIO	Justification.	MARSHALL	1692	48003023
JUSTIFICATIO	Justification.	KEACH	1694	48003024
JUSTIFICATIO	Justification.	CLARKSON	1696	53003009
JUSTIFICATIO	Justification.	BOEHM	1717	45018014
JUSTIFICATIO	Justification.	HAYWARD	1718	51002016
JUSTIFICATIO	Justification.	NEWMAN	1735	48003024
JUSTIFICATIO	Justification.	SEAGRAVE	1737	48003024
JUSTIFICATIO	Justification.	SEAGRAVE	1737	51003024
JUSTIFICATIO	Justification.	WARREN	1748	34002004
JUSTIFICATIO	Justification.	FOSTER	1744	48010003
JUSTIFICATIO	Justification.	BENSON	1748	47013038

Keyword	In its Context	Author	Year	BkChpVrs
JUSTIFICATIO	Justification.	FAWCETT	1749	51001016
JUSTIFICATIO	Justification.	ALLEN	1751	24023006
JUSTIFICATIO	Justification.	STUART	1753	51003026
JUSTIFICATIO	Justification.	JONES	1756	62002024
JUSTIFICATIO	Justification.	GUYSE	1757	48003024
JUSTIFICATIO	Justification.	HAYWARD	1758	51001016
JUSTIFICATIO	Justification.	GREEN	1758	62002024
JUSTIFICATIO	Justification.	MARTIN	1760	48005001
JUSTIFICATIO	Justification.	MADAN	1761	62002024
JUSTIFICATIO	Justification.	SHIRLEY	1762	48003031
JUSTIFICATIO	Justification.	DAVIES	1771	48001016
JUSTIFICATIO	Justification.	WHITTY	1772	48003031
JUSTLY	Do justly&c.	BOURN	1777	32006006
K	Ag. Fren. K.	KNAGGS	1705	50013011
K	Care of H-k.	DYKES	1722	20031027
K	Death of K.	PIGGOTT	1714	19146003
K	Dut. G.& K.	BALL	1682	43022021
K	Dut. G.& K.	ROSEWELL	1716	20024021
K	Dut. G.& K.	TOPPING	1716	63002017
K	Ev. K.of Xt.	BOURN	1777	49015021
K	Fe. G.&h. K.	SEABURY	17--	63002017
K	G's. K.com.	MANGEY	1717	43006010
K	G's. K.com.	MOSS	1732	43006010
K	God& K.	STAFFORD	1697	13029018
K	Grow. K. Xt.	VINCENT	1683	64003018
K	K.& L.of G.	ROMAINE	1760	44012028
K	K.birth d.	PATRICK	1686	19072015
K	K.birth day.	WETENHALL	1686	21010017
K	M's.ina.k. S.	HURST	1660	48007007
K	Nat. G's. K.	CLARKE	1735	48014017
K	Nat. G's. K.	FOSTER	1737	48014017
K	Nat. G's. K.	ABERNETHY	1751	48014017
K	Obed.to K.	GODDARD	1715	20029004
K	Per.of Xn. K.	SAURIN	1775	61005012
K	Perp. Xt's. K.	HUSSEY	1753	45001033
K	Pr. Xn.k.a.p.	JONES	1761	50005014
K	Prof.in K.	TAYLOR	1719	28006003
K	Seek. K.o. G.	FARINDON	1672	43006033
K	Seek. K.o. G.	BURTON	1684	43006033
K	Seek. K.o. G.	DUNLOP	1722	43006033
K	Seek. K.o. G.	CLARKE	1732	43006033
K	Seek. K.o. G.	JONES	1741	43006033
K	Sup. K.in H.	PEARSE	1763	49013012
K	T. Shep.b. K.	LANEY	1662	63002025
K	Xn. K.m. St.	FOTHERGILL	1765	53004001
K	Xt's K.n.t.w.	GREENHILL	1768	46018036
K	bef. K.	HAYTER	1752	49007031
K	bef. K.	HOADLY	1754	49007031
K'S	K's b. Day.	WALKER	1738	43007012
K'S	K's birth d.	GROSVENOR	1720	05033016
K'S	b. K's forces.	WHITTEL	1692	04014014
KEE	To kee.l. G.	COOPER	1683	68000021
KEEP	Bl.keep G. C.	GALLIMORE	1694	69022014
KEEP	Keep. Festiv.	SMITH	1740	49005008
KEEP	Keep. Foot.	JORTIN	1774	21005001
KEEP	Keep. Heart.	ATTERBURY	1699	20004023

Keyword	In its Context	Author	Year	BkChpVrs
KEEP	Keep. Heart.	BARROW	1716	20004023
KEEP	Keep. Heart.	BEVERIDGE	1726	20004023
KEEP	Keep. Heart.	CHANDLER	1769	20014023
KEEP	Keep. Heart.	BLAIR	1780	20004023
KEEP	Keep. Sabb.	WROUGHTON	1716	02020008
KEEP	Keep.un.&c.	THORNBY	1742	52004003
KEEP	Keep Heart.	NEWTON	1759	20004023
KEEP	Keep Resol.	NEWSON	1781	43026035
KEPT	G's. L.kept.	SHERIDAN	1720	45017010
KEY	Xt.key Hell.	DUNLOP	1722	69001018
KGS	Kgs.no.s. P.	HURST	1675	47026002
KI	Br. Ki.& Ch.	ABERNETHY	1748	64001007
KI	Ki.o. Xt.& A.	K.	1667	69016001
KIND	Kind.to Jew.	STEPHENS	1735	58001016
KIND	Kind Affect.	M'FARLAND	1779	48012010
KIND	World.kind.	STANHOPE	1700	45014023
KING	A King.	BRAGGE	1702	45014018
KING	Co. King. W.	EARL	1725	20010007
KING	G's. King.all	BEVERLEY	1698	49015024
KING	God& King.	HARVEST	1754	63002017
KING	God& King.	SMITH	1759	63002017
KING	God's king.	BEVERIDGE	1720	19097001
KING	Good King.	PRICE	1661	21010017
KING	King of G.	CLARKE	1732	43006010
KING	King of Glo.	HORNE	1778	69001007
KING	King.	HARRIS	1724	19002006
KING	King.& Will of	BLACKALL	1723	43006010
KING	King.& Will of	BISSE	1740	43006010
KING	King.& Will of	BLAIR	1740	43006010
KING	King. G.in P.	WILLIAMS	1738	49004020
KING	King. Guests	BOURN	1764	43022008
KING	King.of G.	JACKSON	1728	43006010
KING	King.of G.	LIRTLETON	1735	43006010
KING	King.of G.	EVANS	1775	43006010
KING	King& Subj.	BOURN	1764	43022001
KING	Merc. King.	BRAGGE	1702	43018023
KING	Of a King.	BRAGGE	1702	43022002
KING	Procl. King.	WOMOCK	1660	19132018
KING	Procl. King.	HEYRICKE	1685	20021001
KING	Xt. King.of.	SAURIN	1775	46018036
KING	Xt's.king.sp.	BRADBURY	1772	69011017
KING	b. King.	CALAMY	1726	20001010
KING'S	King's b. D.	WRIGHT	1718	01040023
KING'S	King's b. D.	ROBINSON	1719	19118022
KING'S	King's Entr.	DUBOURDIEU	1714	09010024
KING'S	King's Indis.	HEYWOOD	1756	27006021
KING'S	King's Supr.	CRAGGE	1661	48013001
KINGD	G's. Kingd.	BOURN	1777	43006010
KINGD	G's Kingd.	STAFFORD	1697	05008002
KINGD	Kingd. Hea.	POPE	1675	43022001
KINGD	Kingd.of G.	BULKLEY	1752	45017020
KINGD	Xt's. Kingd.	HALES	1673	46018036
KINGD	Xt's. Kingd.	BARNE	1682	46018036
KINGD	Xt's. Kingd.	C.	1717	46018036
KINGD	Xt's. Kingd.	LOVELING	1717	46018036
KINGD	Xt's. Kingd.	TRAPP	1717	46018036

Keyword	In its Context	Author	Year	BkChpVrs
KINGD	Xt's. Kingd.	GROVE	1747	46018036
KINGD	Xt's. Kingd.	HUSSEY	1753	61001008
KINGD	Xt's. Kingd.	HOADLY	1754	46018036
KINGD	Xt's. Kingd.	RADCLIFF	1763	46018036
KINGD	Xt's. Kingd.	BREKELL	1765	46018036
KINGD	Xt's. Kingd.	DAVIES	1766	46018037
KINGD	Xt's. Kingd.	ANONYMOUS	1776	43006010
KINGD	Xt's. Kingd.	HARWOOD	1772	49015024
KINGD	Xt's. Kingd.	PYLE	1777	46018036
KINGD	Xt's Kingd.	REYNOLDS	1679	19110001
KINGD	Xt's Kingd.	GROVE	1735	46013016
KINGS	Kings Entry.	WALKER	1660	14023011
KINGS	Pr.f. Kings.	MOSS	1733	57002001
KINGS	Saints Kings.	DUNLOP	1722	69001006
KN	Abus.of Kn.	NEWSON	1781	48001020
KN	Dan.kn. Sin	TILLOTSON	1735	48001018
KN	Fai b.on Kn.	WATTS	1753	58001012
KN	Ignor.& Kn.	SKEELER	1740	46009041
KN	Kn.& Ch.un.	WRIGHT	1732	49008001
KN	Kn. G.l.o. N.	WATTS	1753	47014015
KN	Kn. Sin b. L.	CLARKE	1735	48007007
KN	Kn. Sin b. L.	VENN	1759	48007009
KN	Kn. Xt.cruc.	CHARNOCK	1684	49002002
KN	Kn. Xt.cruc.	BEVERIDGE	1720	49002002
KN	Kn. Xt.cruc.	FIDDES	1720	49002002
KN	Kn. Xt.cruc.	WHITFIELD	1739	49002002
KN	Kn. Xt.cruc.	SHEPHEARD	1748	49002002
KN	Kn. Xt.cruc.	BUNDY	1750	49002002
KN	Kn.o. X.in G.	COLE	1692	46008054
KN	Pr.in kn. T.	VINCENT	1675	49014015
KN	Relig. Kn.	WEARE	1763	28004006
KNO	Kno. G.& Xt.	WOOD	1674	48001019
KNO	Kno. G's W.	NEEDHAM	1679	46007017
KNO	Kno.in F. S.	DODD	1767	10012023
KNO	Kno.of God.	PIGGOTT	1702	46017003
KNO	Kno.ourselv.	NEWTON	1782	50013005
KNO	Kno.wout P.	PRICE	1770	46013017
KNO	P. Kno of G.	SUTTON	1754	24009024
KNO	Rel.& Kno.	ENFIELD	1780	43013033
KNO	Sp.kno.&ig.	MEDE	1672	65002003
KNO	Test.kno. Xt.	WHEATLY	1746	65002003
KNO	Way of Kno.	TAYLOR	1678	46007017
KNOCKING	Xt.knocking	WILLISON	1761	69003020
KNOW	Free Know.	HEYLYN	1749	01002017
KNOW	Fut. Know.	REAY	1755	49013012
KNOW	G.know. H.	HORT	1738	24017009
KNOW	G's Know.	GROVE	1741	19103014
KNOW	Know.& Ch.	HORNE	1778	49008001
KNOW	Know. G.&c.	CLARKE	1736	49001021
KNOW	Know. God.	WISHEART	1716	23011009
KNOW	Know. J. Xt.	BOLDE	1697	53003008
KNOW	Know. J. Xt.	NEWMAN	1728	49002002
KNOW	Know. Rel.	ORR	1739	48002014
KNOW	Know. Xn. P.	WAPLE	1718	46013015
KNOW	Know. Xn. P.	TILLOTSON	1735	46013015
KNOW	Know.o. S. S.	TILLOTSON	1735	43023013

INDEXES TO THIRD VOLUME: E: KEYWORD-IN-CONTEXT INDEX OF OTHER SUBJECTS OR OCCASIONS

Keyword	In its Context	Author	Year	BkChpVrs
KNOW	Know.o. Xt.	CLARKSON	1696	53003008
KNOW	Know.o. Xt.	FARRINGTON	1741	53003008
KNOW	Know.o. Xt.	HAYDON	1772	53003008
KNOW	Know.of G.	CHARNOCK	1684	46017003
KNOW	Know.of G.	DUCHE	1779	18013005
KNOW	Rel. Know.	TERRY	1746	23011009
KNOW	Rel. Know.	BLAIR	1780	23011009
KNOW	Rev. Know.	CRUSO	1699	43016017
KNOW	Sav. Know.	LEIGHTONHOUSE	1697	19086011
KNOW	Sav. Know.	MARSHAL	1750	19086011
KNOW	Self- Know.	LANGHORNE	1773	19004004
KNOW	Self-know.	SWIFTH	1745	12008013
KNOW	Self-know.	STERNE	1760	10012007
KNOW	Self-know.	WILLIAMS	1774	19019012
KNOWL	Div. Knowl.	SMITH	1673	19003003
KNOWL	Div. Knowl.	SMITH	1673	46007017
KNOWL	G's Knowl.	HUNT	1748	09002003
KNOWL	G's Knowl.	HUTCHINS	1771	24032019
KNOWL	Knowl.& Pr.	CHANDLER	1728	46013017
KNOWL	Knowl.& Pr.	CONEY	1750	46013017
KNOWL	Knowl.& Pr.	LANGHORNE	1773	46013017
KNOWL	Knowl. J. Xt.	STEBBING	1721	53003007
KNOWL	Knowl.o. Xt.	CHANDLER	1753	53003007
KNOWL	Knowl.of G.	HOWE	1744	59001016
KNOWL	Rel. Knowl.	BULKLEY	1752	46013017
KNOWL	Sav. Knowl.	WARREN	1739	46017003
KNOWL	Sav. Knowl.	SNAPE	1745	46017003
KNOWL	Self-knowl.	WHARTON	1728	48012003
KNOWL	Spir. Knowl.	TILLY	1737	49008002
KNOWL	Xn. Knowl.	REYNOLDS	1679	53003008
KNOWL	Xn. Knowl.	TILLOTSON	1735	53003008
KNOWL	Xn. Knowl.	SMITH	1740	45018040
KNOWL	Xn. Knowl.	JORTIN	1774	20015014
KNOWLEDGE	Knowledge.	ABERNETHY	1748	64001005
KOR	Aaron& Kor.	WATSON	1756	04016047
L	Ad's L.b. Xt.	MASON	1758	48005015
L	Bel. D.to L.	HALL	1777	51002019
L	Bles.dy.in L.	DURHAM	1681	69014013
L	Bles.dy.in L.	HOPKINS	1710	69014013
L	Bles.dy.in L.	HILL	1748	69014013
L	Bp. G. L.	WORTHINGTON	1769	23023005
L	Bp. G. L.	WORTHINGTON	1769	23023008
L	Butch. L.	HENLEY	1729	19008006
L	Choice of L.	DOWNES	1761	49011018
L	Christ. L.	BUNDY	1740	19019007
L	Civ.&rel. L.	PECKARD	1754	63002016
L	Cond. L.o. Dar	SUTTON	1754	46003019
L	Cure l. Man.	BULKLEY	1771	47004008
L	D.in G's L.	LELAND	1769	19119047
L	Desire of L.	WILCOX	1757	19039013
L	Desp. L.nat.	HAMMOND	1684	48001026
L	End Jew. L.	CLARKE	1736	51002015
L	Estim.of L.	WILLIAMS	1774	19039004
L	Exc.of J. L.	RANDOLPH	1773	05004005
L	F. C.of H. L.	SANDERSON	1722	15010007
L	F.f.b. L.& G.	WILSON	1781	52005003

Keyword	In its Context	Author	Year	BkChpVrs
L	Fai.p. Xn. L.	BOYSE	1728	51002020
L	Fai.w.b. L.	GROVE	1742	51005006
L	Fath.l. Bless.	HART	1702	18030023
L	Fin. C. H. L.	SANDERSON	1722	58002002
L	Fth&w.b. L.	TAYLOR	1678	62002024
L	G.l.b.or. Xn.	WILKINS	1682	59002010
L	G.l.b.or. Xn.	ROGERS	1735	59002010
L	G.1 Ca.l. E.	TILLOTSON	1735	48011036
L	G's. L.in Xt.	WILKINSON	1660	48005008
L	G's. L.in Xt.	LELAND	1769	48005011
L	G's. L.in Xt.	WALKER	1775	48005010
L	G's. L.kept.	SHERIDAN	1720	45017010
L	G's. L.to M.	PELLING	1694	46003016
L	G's. L.to Sin.	CLARKE	1732	46003016
L	Good l. Hon.	FOTHERGILL	1765	20004008
L	Good T.in l.	DUCHAL	1765	53001010
L	Gos.& L. Li.	ABERNETHY	1748	62002012
L	Gos. L.of L.	SUTTON	1718	62001025
L	Gosp. L.o. L.	BERRIMAN	1763	62001015
L	Gosp.esta. L.	FISHER	1741	48003031
L	Gosp.esta. L.	GILL	1773	48003031
L	Holin.of L.	MARSHAL	1731	19026012
L	Imm. L.o. Pl.	CHANDLER	1769	58003004
L	Imp. Re.pr.l.	CRAIG	1775	52002012
L	Inf. L. Revel.	WARBURTON	1754	45018008
L	Infl.fut. L.	BRYSON	1778	65003003
L	Inhe. S.in L.	CAMPION	1700	54001012
L	Inord. L. W.	MASON	1758	46002015
L	John's l.life.	NEWTON	1782	46021022
L	Joy in the L.	WILKINSON	1660	34003018
L	K.& L.of G.	ROMAINE	1760	44012028
L	Kn. G.l.o. N.	WATTS	1753	47014015
L	Kn. Sin b. L.	CLARKE	1735	48007007
L	Kn. Sin b. L.	VENN	1759	48007009
L	L.& Equity.	PIERCE	1686	46013013
L	L.& Ob.t. Xt.	JENNINGS	1757	50005014
L	L.& P.ful. Xt.	BLACKALL	1723	43005017
L	L. D. G. Life.	ERSKINE	1764	51002019
L	L. G.& Man.	ECCLES	1755	43022037
L	L. G.& W.co.	DAWES	1733	62004004
L	L. G.& W.incon	GALE	1676	65002015
L	L. G.& W.incon	CLARKE	1734	65002015
L	L. G.& W.incon	DORMAN	1743	65002015
L	L. G.& W.incon	BALL	1756	65002015
L	L. G.& W.incon	CARR	1777	65002015
L	L. G.f.a. Xn.	ANONYMOUS	1770	47026023
L	L. G& W.incons	WAKE	1701	65002015
L	L. G& W.incons	ROGERS	1735	65002015
L	L. G& W.incons	SNAPE	1745	65002015
L	L. Xt. P. Xn.	RELLEY	1762	46014019
L	L.es.t.att. G.	HUNTER	1774	65004016
L	L.of G.& Br.	SMALRIDGE	1724	65004021
L	L.of G.& Br.	NEWTON	1736	65004021
L	L.of G.& Br.	HOWE	1744	65004020
L	L.of G.& M.	WARBURTON	1753	20017005
L	L.of G.& M.	WARBURTON	1753	65004020

Keyword	In its Context	Author	Year	BkChpVrs
L	L.of G.& N.	WILSON	1781	44012032
L	L.of G. Mot. O	PIERCE	1679	46014015
L	L.of G. Mot. O	READING	1724	46014015
L	L.of Moses	JORTIN	1774	19147019
L	L.our Right.	ROMAINE	1752	23045008
L	L.our Right.	WHITFIELD	1771	23060019
L	L.suit. Prof.	ADEY	1760	45012047
L	L's.l.suff.	DOOLITTLE	1682	49011026
L	Le. L.in for.	JONES	1775	03017008
L	Love fulf. L.	QUINCY	1750	51005014
L	M.d.o. Cl. L.	HARRISON	1730	48015029
L	M's. L.on E.	COLLETT	1774	01047009
L	Mat.of H. L.	SANDERSON	1722	20008015
L	Meaness. L.	DORRINGTON	1703	18014002
L	Mor.b. P. L.	HICKES	1726	45011042
L	Mor.l.of M.	BUESDSELL	1700	45010025
L	N. Desi.of L.	SMITH	1777	18042016
L	Negl. L. Sup.	ELSMERE	1767	45014018
L	No perf.in L.	WHITTY	1772	62003002
L	O. L.g.by Xt.	BRAILSFORD	1776	49015022
L	Ob.sign l. G.	SHERLOCK	1719	65005003
L	Obl. Hum. L.	THORP	1703	48013005
L	Obl. Hum. L.	SANDERSON	1722	48013005
L	Period of L.	E.	1679	18014005
L	Perp.mor. L.	HORNECK	1706	43005018
L	Perp.mor. L.	BLACKALL	1723	43005019
L	Perp.mor. L.	BLAIR	1740	43005018
L	Pleas.rel. L.	DORRINGTON	1703	20003017
L	Pleas.rel. L.	PEARSON	1718	20003017
L	Pleas.rel. L.	SOUTH	1727	20003017
L	Pleas.rel. L.	NEWLIN	1728	20003017
L	Pleas.rel. L.	WILDER	1729	20003017
L	Pleas.rel. L.	FORSTER	1732	20003017
L	Pleas.rel. L.	WESTLEY	1735	20003017
L	Pleas.rel. L.	WHEATLAND	1739	20003017
L	Pleas.rel. L.	FARRINGTON	1741	20003017
L	Pleas.rel. L.	OAKES	1747	20003017
L	Pleas.rel. L.	SEED	1750	20003017
L	Pleas.rel. L.	FOTHERGILL	1765	20003017
L	Pleas.rel. L.	STENNETT	1769	20003017
L	Pleas.rel. L.	JORTIN	1774	20003017
L	Prop. R.& L.	ACRES	1714	19078004
L	Purity of L.	SEATON	1720	01039010
L	R.con.w. L.	GERARD	1780	19116009
L	Rel.ch.bus.l.	BLACKALL	1723	43006033
L	Rel.ch.bus.l.	BEVERIDGE	1726	43006033
L	Rel.l.happy.	KILLINBECK	1717	21008012
L	Review of L.	DUCHAL	1765	19039005
L	Rew. L.of G.	PYLE	1776	49002009
L	Rich M.& L.	STEVENS	1697	45016019
L	Rich M.& L.	CRUSO	1698	45016019
L	Rich M.& L.	BRAGGE	1702	45016019
L	Rich M.& L.	WELCHMAN	1704	45016019
L	Rich M.& L.	ELLIS	1704	45016019
L	Rich M.& L.	HOLE	1716	45016019
L	Rich M.& L.	TILLOTSON	1735	45016019

Keyword	In its Context	Author	Year	BkChpVrs
L	Rich M.& L.	DODD	1757	45016019
L	Rich M.& L.	HUNTER	1774	45016019
L	Rule Pe.& L.	ELLIS	1684	53002003
L	S. S.rule of l	ELLIS	1704	45016029
L	Sanc. Xt's. L.	MACE	1751	44008035
L	Sanct. Xn. L.	SKELTON	1754	43025046
L	Sev.of G. L.	HOPKINS	1708	21008011
L	Shor.of H. L.	TIDCOMBE	1757	10019034
L	Short of L.	STEELE	1776	19014001
L	Short.of L.	WARREN	1748	19039004
L	Short.of L.	ADEY	1755	18014001
L	Short.of L.	STERNE	1760	18014002
L	Short.of L.	BRACKENRIDGE	1764	19039005
L	Sin.sh.&h.l.	PIERCE	1679	48006021
L	Sin.sh.&h.l.	TILLOTSON	1735	48006021
L	Sp.of G's. L.	HAWEIS	1762	51003010
L	Sund.b. L.	HOWARD	1742	43012041
L	Swear. L. M.	GRIFFYTH	1693	55004011
L	Swear. L. M.	SKERRET	1716	48013004
L	The L.good.	BROWNE	1749	48007019
L	To kee.l. G.	COOPER	1683	68000021
L	Un. Tr.& L.	PEARSE	1763	52004015
L	Use& End L.	MAYHEW	1755	19034012
L	Val.& L.o. S.	WELTON	1724	43016026
L	W.to L.& G.	TALBOT	1674	05005029
L	Way of L.	BRADY	1730	23040003
L	Whym.l. D.	MOSS	1732	46003019
L	X's.l.believ.	FARMER	1756	23040011
L	Xn. Lib.& L.	RICHARDSON	1752	51005013
L	Xn. Ob.& L.	WILTON	1724	48013001
L	Xn. Z.b. L.j.	SYNGE	1716	51004018
L	Xn.a. Jew. L.	WESTON	1747	43005020
L	Xn's C.to L.	BULKLEY	1771	51005013
L	Xnity per. L.	HICKES	1726	43005017
L	Xnity R.o. L.	ROBINSON	1739	46006068
L	Xr. L. Days.	FELL	1675	64003003
L	Xt. Bread. L.	CLARKE	1734	46006035
L	Xt. L.world.	SHERLOCK	1719	45002032
L	Xt. Res.& L.	BREKELL	1765	46011025
L	Xt.cam.f. L.	BROWNE	1749	43005017
L	Xt.per.m. L.	BLAIR	1740	43005017
L	Xt's. C. L. G.	CRAIG	1775	46011033
L	Xt's. L.to us.	HORTON	1679	69001005
L	Xt's.l.suffer.	BRAGGE	1706	43026036
L	Xt's.l.words	FLAVEL	1673	45023043
L	Xt's.l.words.	FLAVEL	1673	45023046
L	Xty. Com. L.	OUTRAM	1697	43005017
L	Xty. Com. L.	MUDGE	1739	43005017
L	Xty.perf. L.	TILLOTSON	1735	43005017
L	b. L. Just.	GOODWIN	1716	26017019
L	b. L. Justices.	WILLIS	1701	20012026
L	b. L. Justices.	FORSTER	1716	49001010
L	b. L. Mayor.	STANDISH	1684	05006011
L	b. Ld. L.	VESEY	1692	07017006
L'S	L's. Benevol.	WHITE	1757	46013034
L'S	L's. Exalt.	ELSMERE	1767	63003022

INDEXES TO THIRD VOLUME: E: KEYWORD-IN-CONTEXT INDEX OF OTHER SUBJECTS OR OCCASIONS

Keyword	In its Context	Author	Year	BkChpVrs
L'S	L's. Fortit.	WHITE	1757	61012001
L'S	L's. Humil.	WILDER	1741	43011029
L'S	L's. Humil.	WHITE	1757	43011029
L'S	L's. Patience	WHITE	1757	61012003
L'S	L's. Prayer.	JORTIN	1774	45011001
L'S	L's. S.n. Cov.	CHANDLER	1769	49011025
L'S	L's. Supper.	HARRIS	1736	49011024
L'S	L's. Supper.	KIPPIS	1758	49011029
L'S	L's. Supper.	OGDEN	1780	61010008
L'S	L's.l.suff.	DOOLITTLE	1682	49011026
L'S	L's.rebuke.	WEBB	1765	45009055
L'S	L's.supper.	STANHOPE	1715	45022001
L'S	L's.supper.	TOLLER	1769	49004007
L'S	L's.supper.	CASE	1774	47002042
L'S	L's Paths m.	CHANDLER	1769	19025010
L'S	L's Pro.true.	ECCLES	1755	11022021
L'S	L's Redeem.	WILLISON	1761	19107002
L'S	L's Redeem.	LAWSON	1764	19107008
L'S	L's Ur.& Th.	GILL	1773	05033008
L'S	Obl.to L's d.	ORTON	1769	02020008
LA	Gos. La. Nat.	BULLOCK	1728	43021033
LAB	Lab.in vain.	ANONYMOUS	1709	41008010
LABOUR	On Labour.	HORSEMANDEN	1766	01003019
LABOURERS	Labourers.	MANTON	1701	43019030
LABOURERS	Labourers.	BRAGGE	1704	43020001
LABOURERS	Labourers.	HOLE	1716	43020001
LABOURERS	Labourers.	HOADLY	1727	43020001
LABOURERS	Labourers.	WATERLAND	1742	43020016
LABOURERS	Labourers.	STEBBING	1760	43020016
LABOURERS	Labourers.	BOURN	1764	43019030
LADY	Lady-day.	GRIFFITH	1660	20024021
LAID	Axe laid t. R.	KEACH	1692	43003010
LAMB	Lamb of G.	WILLISON	1761	46001036
LAMB	Pasc. Lamb.	BUNDY	1740	46001029
LAMB	T. Lamb sla.	COLMAN	1728	69013008
LAMB	Wr.of Lamb	WATTS	1752	69016015
LAMB	Xt. Lamb.sl.	BRADBURY	1703	69005006
LAND	Land lux.	CARRINGTON	1776	23002007
LAST	Last. Judgm.	SHERIDAN	1720	47017031
LAST	Last. Judgm.	SHERIDAN	1720	68000014
LAST	Last. Judgm.	BOURDALOUE	1776	45021025
LAST	Last Judgm.	PARKHURST	1704	69020011
LAST	Last Judgm.	HEBDEN	1738	61009027
LAST	Last Judgm.	HORT	1738	61009027
LAST	Last Judgm.	COCKMAN	1750	61009027
LAST	Last Judgm.	ELSMERE	1767	50005010
LAST	Last Passover	WILCOX	1757	45022015
LAST	Roy.last.	LIMBORCH	1740	20031003
LAST	Xt's.last Dis.	DUCHAL	1753	46014001
LAST	3 Ev.last.t.	HILDROP	1711	43024021
LAST	3 Evil last T.	HILDROP	1711	44013019
LAT	Con.lat end.	HOLLAND	1753	05032029
LAT	Conc. Lat.	FOWNES	1660	56002003
LAT	Conc. Lat.	FELL	1667	54002008
LAT	Conc. Lat.	TURNER	1681	69019010
LAT	Conc. Lat.	BARROW	1687	43016019

Keyword	In its Context	Author	Year	BkChpVrs
LAT	Conc. Lat.	SHEPHEARD	1776	21007030
LAT	Conc.lat.	BARTON	1756	64001019
LATE	Late Cons.	ANONYMOUS	1723	19118001
LATE	Late Faith.	KILLINBECK	1717	46016030
LATE	Late Repent.	CLAGETT	1720	20001028
LATE	Late Repent.	BLACKALL	1723	46009003
LATE	On late Reb.	PETTER	1685	46021022
LATTER	Latter End.	BARROW	1716	19090012
LATTER	Latter End.	DUNLOP	1722	19090012
LATTER	Latter End.	TILLOTSON.	1735	19090012
LATTER	latter End	LUCAS	1722	21007002
LAUGHTER	Laughter.	GROVE	1702	21002001
LAUGHTER	Laughter.	MARKLAND	1729	21002001
LAW	At Law Lect.	LITTLETON	1680	45007033
LAW	Cerem. Law.	HEYLYN	1749	44002027
LAW	Cerem. Law.	HUTCHINSON	1740	51003019
LAW	Cerem. Law.	ROMAINE	1760	22004006
LAW	Go.to Law.	HORNECK	1706	43005040
LAW	Law est.b. F.	WESTLEY	1750	48003031
LAW	Law est.b. G.	TAYLOR	1704	48003031
LAW	Law i. Heart	LEIGHTON	1746	61008010
LAW	Law in X's h.	GILL	1773	05010005
LAW	Law o. G's h.	ERSKINE	1764	26043002
LAW	Law of laws.	ANONYMOUS	1719	57001005
LAW	Law of Faith	ROMAINE	1760	48003027
LAW	Law of Lib.	ZUBLY	1775	62002013
LAW	Law pre. G.	TRAIL	1696	61004016
LAW	Law.& P.	BUNDY	1740	43005017
LAW	Law.es. Gos.	LITTLETON	1680	43005017
LAW	Law.es. Gos.	HORNECK	1706	43005017
LAW	Law.es. Gos.	HOLE	1715	43005017
LAW	Law.es. Gos.	MOSS	1737	43005017
LAW	Law.of Xt.	BOURDALOUE	1776	43017005
LAW	Law& Gosp.	SMALRIDGE	1724	50003011
LAW	Law& Gosp.	ALTHAM	1732	50003009
LAW	Law& Gosp.	WATTS	1753	51003021
LAW	Law& Gosp.	BREKELL	1765	51003024
LAW	Law& Gosp.	DAVIES	1771	51003023
LAW	Law& Sin.	BERRIMAN	1751	65003004
LAW	Mor. Law.	BUERDSELL	1700	43006010
LAW	Mor. Law.	STENNETT	1732	43005008
LAW	Mor. Law.	WATTS	1753	48006023
LAW	Mor. Law.	WATTS	1753	65003004
LAW	Mor. Law.	ROMAINE	1760	48007012
LAW	Mor. Law.	PENTYCROSS	1781	48003019
LAW	R. Use Law	UNWIN	1773	48007009
LAW	Rig.of Law.	HUSSEY	1755	48008004
LAW	Royal law.	KIDDINGTON	1757	62002010
LAW	Sum.of Law.	LEIGHTON	1746	43022037
LAW	Use of Law.	REYNOLDS	1679	48007013
LAW	Usef. Law.	FLAVEL	1673	48007009
LAWF	Lawf.just w.	FOURESTIER	1758	43024006
LAWF	Lawf.things	WILKINSON	1677	45017027
LAWS	Law of laws.	ANONYMOUS	1719	57001005
LAWS	Laws of Dri.	CORNWALLIS	1705	52005019
LAWS	Penal Laws.	PASTON	1688	45009055

Keyword	In its Context	Author	Year	BkChpVrs
LAZ	Dives.& Laz.	TILLOTSON	1735	45016031
LAZ	Dives.& Laz.	STERNE	1766	45016031
LAZ	Dives.& Laz.	JORTIN	1774	45016031
LAZ	Dives& Laz.	STEVENS	1697	45016022
LAZ	Dives& Laz.	STEPHENS	1697	45016022
LAZ	Dives& Laz.	CRUSO	1697	45016027
LAZ	Dives& Laz.	STEVENT	1697	45016027
LAZ	Dives& Laz.	STEVENS	1697	45016030
LAZ	Dives& Laz.	CRUSO	1698	45016023
LAZ	Dives& Laz.	CRUSO	1698	45016030
LAZ	Dives& Laz.	WELCHMAN	1704	45016022
LAZ	Dives& Laz.	THEED	1710	45016027
LAZ	Dives& Laz.	BENNETT	1728	45016025
LAZ	Dives& Laz.	DODD	1757	45016025
LAZ	Dives& Laz.	BULKLEY	1771	45016031
LAZ	Dives& Laz.	BROUGHTON	1778	45016031
LAZ	Resur.o. Laz.	LANGHORNE	1764	45011044
LAZAR	Lazar. Rais.	BRAGGE	1702	46011001
LAZAR	Lazar. Rais.	WELCH	1752	46011003
LAZAR	Lazar. Rais.	DODD	1757	46011001
LAZAR	Resur. Lazar.	BENSON	1748	46011043
LAZAR	Resur. Lazar.	BULKLEY	1771	46011043
LD	Bap. Ld. Has.	JONES	1668	45003021
LD	Ld our Righ.	WOODWARD	1696	24013006
LD	Ld own.all.	CLARKSON	1696	13029011
LD	Ld rules all.	CLARKSON	1696	19103019
LD	Ld. Pres. Imp.	JAY	1682	61011033
LD	Ld. Right.	RUSSEN	1774	24023006
LD	Ld. Russel.	BURNET	1713	69014013
LD	Ld Gord.rel.	CLARKE	1781	19050015
LD	See the Ld.	GALE	1726	61012014
LD	Terr.of Ld.	STILLINGFLEET	1707	50005002
LD	Terr.of Ld.	PYLE	1777	50005010
LD	Xt. Ld Glory	RANDOLPH	1769	46012041
LD	Xt.our Ld.	BEVERIDGE	1720	46013013
LD	b. Ld. L.	VESEY	1692	07017006
LD	b. Ld Just.	KING	1685	23059006
LD'S	Exp. Ld's. Pr.	MANTON	1684	43006009
LD'S	Ld's redeem.	REYNOLDS	1679	49006019
LD'S	Ld's Prayer.	NEWTON	1782	43006009
LE	Le. L.in for.	JONES	1775	03017008
LEAD	Lead.of Sp.	JACOMB	1683	48008014
LEARN	Hum. Learn.	NEVILL	1681	20019002
LEARN	Learn.& Inf.	HAMMOND	1684	46007048
LEARN	Learn.& Mo.	MAINWARING	1780	53004012
LEARN	Learn.rec.	DODD	1772	20004007
LEAV	Leav. Phar.	BREKELL	1765	43016006
LEAV	Leav.the O.	FERNE	1721	46016028
LEAV	Xt.leav. Dis.	WILLISON	1761	46016007
LECT	At Law Lect.	LITTLETON	1680	45007033
LECT	Even. Lect.	BAINE	1758	48004006
LECT	Theo. Lect.	HENLEY	1729	45019022
LED	Led by Sp.	SOUTH	1724	48008014
LEG	Leg.& Ev. R.	SMITH	1673	48009031
LEG	Leg.of Dev.	BRAGGE	1702	45008026
LEG	Leg.of Dev.	DODD	1757	45008027

Keyword	In its Context	Author	Year	BkChpVrs
LEN	Len.o. Gosp.	TOTTIE	1775	46008010
LENT	Lent s.	ASHTON	1770	19119059
LENT	Lent.	LANEY	1668	55004011
LENT	Lent.	FRANK	1672	05032029
LENT	Lent.	ALLESTREE	1684	03016031
LENT	Lent.	WETENHALL	1691	19076010
LENT	Lent.	DORRINGTON	1703	50007010
LENT	Lent.	STANHOPE	1715	29002012
LENT	Lent.	TILLOTSON	1735	18033027
LENT	Lent.	SMITH	1740	43015028
LENT	Lent.	JEFFERY	1751	04023010
LENT	Lent.	FLETCHER	1772	19036006
LENT	Lent.	TUCKER	1776	62005016
LENT	Lent. F.	GUNNING	1662	45005035
LENT	Lent. F.	SYDALL	1713	45005034
LENT	Lent. F.	BAYLEY	1721	43009015
LENT	Lent. Fast.	MARSHAL	1706	43004002
LENT	Lent. Fast.	SMALRIDGE	1724	43004002
LENT	1 S. Lent.	FRANK	1672	50006002
LENT	1 S. Lent.	STANHOPE	1715	50006001
LENT	1 S. Lent.	HOLE	1716	50006001
LENT	1 S. Lent.	READING	1728	01019024
LENT	1 S. Lent.	READING	1730	01022011
LENT	1 S.in Lent.	PATE	1708	48001016
LENT	2 S. Lent.	STANHOPE	1715	43015021
LENT	2 S. Lent.	STANHOPE	1715	55004001
LENT	2 S. Lent.	HOLE	1716	55004001
LENT	2 S. Lent.	READING	1728	01027011
LENT	2 S. Lent.	READING	1730	01034030
LENT	3. S. Lent.	STANHOPE	1715	45011014
LENT	3. S. Lent.	HOLE	1716	45011014
LENT	3 S. Lent.	STANHOPE	1715	52005001
LENT	3 S. Lent.	HOLE	1716	52005001
LENT	3 S. Lent.	READING	1728	01039021
LENT	3 S. Lent.	READING	1730	01042021
LENT	4 S. Lent.	STANHOPE	1715	46006001
LENT	4 S. Lent.	HOLE	1716	46006001
LENT	4 S. Lent.	STANHOPE	1715	51004021
LENT	4 S. Lent.	HOLE	1716	51004021
LENT	4 S. Lent.	READING	1728	01043026
LENT	4 S. Lent.	READING	1730	01045005
LENT	5 S. Lent.	STANHOPE	1715	46008046
LENT	5 S. Lent.	HOLE	1716	46008046
LENT	5 S. Lent.	STANHOPE	1715	61009011
LENT	5 S. Lent.	HOLE	1716	61009011
LENT	5 S. Lent.	READING	1728	02003009
LENT	5 S. Lent.	READING	1730	02005001
LENT	6 S. Lent.	READING	1728	02009016
LENT	6 S. Lent.	READING	1730	02010001
LEP	Cure of Lep.	DODD	1757	43008001
LEP	Cure of Lep.	BULKLEY	1771	43008001
LEP	Ten Lep.&c.	BRAGGE	1702	45017012
LESS	Good Less.	STRYPE	1707	20014012
LESSON	Lesson on D.	CARRINGTON	1776	21011003
LESSON	Phar.lesson.	LONG	1677	43009013
LEV	Lev.& Conc.	STERNE	1766	07019003

Keyword	In its Context	Author	Year	BkChpVrs
LEV	Lev.o mind.	DOWNES	1761	52004014
LEX	Lex. Ignea.	SANCROFT	1666	24026009
LI	Gos.& L. Li.	ABERNETHY	1748	62002012
LI	Hid.li.o. Xn.	WATTS	1753	54003003
LI	Hid.li.o. Xn.	ERSKINE	1764	54003003
LI	Li.o. G.in M.	MOIR	1759	52004018
LI	Xt. Li.&life.	KELSEY	1721	46001004
LIA	G.m.lia.cor.	HICKMAN	1706	49015033
LIA	G.m.lia.cor.	TREBECK	1730	49015033
LIB	Ab. Xn. Lib.	LUCE	1672	63002016
LIB	Exh.pr. Lib.	SQUIRE	1716	51005001
LIB	Exh.to Lib.	SQUIRE	1714	51006010
LIB	Law of Lib.	ZUBLY	1775	62002013
LIB	Lib.hu.nat.	LAMBE	1681	49006012
LIB	Lib.m.&soc.	AGAR	1759	51005013
LIB	Lib.mor. Ag.	CLARKE	1734	46008032
LIB	Lib.of Belie.	FLAVEL	1673	46008036
LIB	Lib.of Cons.	HART	1726	48014010
LIB	On Lib.o. C.	SALKELD	1673	46011044
LIB	Xn. Lib.& L.	RICHARDSON	1752	51005013
LIB	Xn. Lib.stat.	ROE	1662	47015029
LIB	Xty true Lib.	NEWTON	1782	46008031
LIBER	Hum. Liber.	SKELTON	1754	46008031
LIBER	Liber.of M.	ORR	1739	46008032
LIBERAL	Xn. Liberal.	PAYNE	1763	43025040
LIBERALITY	Liberality.	HOLLAND	1753	45014012
LIBERTINISM	Libertinism.	SAURIN	1775	19094007
LIBERTY	Of Liberty.	SMITH	1740	63002016
LIBERTY	Real Liberty	SHERIDAN	1720	46008036
LIBERTY	Real Liberty	TILLOTSON	1735	46008036
LIBERTY	Real Liberty	SEAGRAVE	1737	46008036
LIBERTY	Real Liberty	HARTLEY	1754	46008036
LIBERTY	Real Liberty	SAURIN	1777	46008036
LIBERTY	Rel. Liberty.	BOURNE	1760	48014022
LIBERTY	Rel. Liberty.	BROWN	1764	51005001
LIBERTY	Rel. Liberty.	FAWCETT	1773	17004014
LIBERTY	Rel. Liberty.	RADCLIFFE	1771	47005029
LIBERTY	Rel. Liberty.	MAINWARING	1780	48014022
LIBERTY	Xn. Liberty.	HALL	1660	51005001
LIBERTY	Xn. Liberty.	BUTLER	1679	51005001
LIBERTY	Xn. Liberty.	OUTRAM	1697	51005013
LIBERTY	Xn. Liberty.	ANONYMOUS	1734	43006022
LIBERTY	Xn. Liberty.	ANONYMOUS	1734	45011052
LIBERTY	Xn. Liberty.	STEPHENS	1737	49006012
LIBERTY	Xn. Liberty.	BUNDY	1740	51005001
LIBERTY	Xn. Liberty.	FISHER	1741	64002019
LIBERTY	Xn. Liberty.	HAMMOND	1745	51003024
LIBERTY	Xn. Liberty.	ABERNETHY	1751	51005001
LIBERTY	Xn. Liberty.	BERRIMAN	1751	51005013
LIBERTY	Xn. Liberty.	DAVIES	1754	51005001
LICEN	Tong. Licen.	BRAILSFORD	1776	63003010
LICENT	Licent. Plea.	ORR	1749	57005006
LICENT	Licent. Thts.	BRADY	1704	50010005
LIES	Lies& Fals.	SOUTH	1727	20012022
LIEUT	Court. Lieut.	WELTON	1710	21008002
LIF	Go.lif.st. Er.	PEARSON	1718	46007017
LIF	Lif.& Im.&c.	DAVIES	1766	58001010
LIFE	Ang.life.	SHAW	1753	43022030
LIFE	Best G.et.life	AMORY	1766	46006068
LIFE	Bus.of life.	DORRINGTON	1705	46009004
LIFE	Busin.of life.	MAY	1757	21012013
LIFE	Call.of life.	SHARP	1734	49007017
LIFE	Cares of life.	DUCHAL	1765	21002023
LIFE	Country life.	STURMY	1712	23007011
LIFE	Dea.& Life.	MALBON	1715	48008013
LIFE	Decency life	WHICHCOTE	1703	48013013
LIFE	Diff. Xn.life.	CROFTON	1662	43007014
LIFE	Diff. Xn.life.	BARKER	1697	43007014
LIFE	Diff. Xn.life.	PARSONS	1711	43007013
LIFE	Diff. Xn.life.	GARDINER	1720	43007013
LIFE	Diff. Xn.life.	STEPHENS	1737	43007014
LIFE	Diff. Xn.life.	BUNDY	1740	43007014
LIFE	Diff. Xn.life.	WESTLEY	1750	43007013
LIFE	Divine life.	DAVIES	1771	51003020
LIFE	Duty of life.	MARRIOTT	1774	32006006
LIFE	Estim.of life.	BLAIR	1780	21012008
LIFE	Eter.life.	WILDER	1729	46017003
LIFE	Eter.life.	SHIRLEY	1762	46017003
LIFE	Eter.life&c.	GODDARD	1781	46006068
LIFE	Etern. Life.	WILKINSON	1660	44010017
LIFE	Etern. Life.	STRAIGHT	1741	46006068
LIFE	Etern.life.	REAY	1755	48006023
LIFE	Eternal.life.	TILLOTSON	1735	43016026
LIFE	Everl. Life.	BULL	1713	19103015
LIFE	Evil life co.	GLANVIL	1681	43022032
LIFE	Exem.life Xt	BAYLY	1721	46013015
LIFE	Far.to life.	LAMBERT	1779	45002029
LIFE	Farw.to life.	SHAW	1667	50005006
LIFE	Fou.life op.	FLAVEL	1673	49002002
LIFE	Fut. Life.	REAY	1755	46006068
LIFE	Fut. Life.	HODGE	1758	46006068
LIFE	Fut.life hap.	STRADLING	1692	49015019
LIFE	Fut.life.	BRYSON	1778	65003002
LIFE	Godly life.	CAWTON	1662	53001027
LIFE	Hol.of life.	CLARKE	1735	48012001
LIFE	Holy Life.	BOLDE	1675	63001015
LIFE	Hum.life.	FOSTER	1737	21007001
LIFE	Impr.of life.	WATTS	1753	49003022
LIFE	Improv.life.	BRODHURST	1733	19090012
LIFE	Improv.life.	SHIRLEY	1762	19090012
LIFE	Indiff.to life	MOSS	1732	49007029
LIFE	Indiff.to life	DAVIES	1766	49007029
LIFE	John's l.life.	NEWTON	1782	46021022
LIFE	L. D. G. Life.	ERSKINE	1764	51002019
LIFE	Life a Pilgr.	CONYBEARE	1759	61011013
LIFE	Life af. Flesh	CLARKE	1735	48008013
LIFE	Life everl.	NICOLSON	1661	43025046
LIFE	Life everl.	NEWCOME	1702	43025046
LIFE	Life everl.	OGDEN	1777	43025046
LIFE	Life everlast.	PIGOTT	1702	65005011
LIFE	Life fm. Xt.	TAYLOR	1719	46010010
LIFE	Life fm. Xt.	SHEPHERD	1748	65005012

Keyword	In its Context	Author	Year	BkChpVrs
LIFE	Life m.th. M.	BLAIR	1740	43006025
LIFE	Life of Dav.	CREYGHTON	1720	19119071
LIFE	Life of Fai.	MANTON	1689	62001006
LIFE	Life of Fai.	TOULMIN	1770	50005007
LIFE	Life of Faith	MANTON	1689	51002020
LIFE	Life of Faith	WELCH	1752	46005024
LIFE	Life of Faith.	BAXTER	1660	61011001
LIFE	Life of Faith.	WALLIS	1683	61010038
LIFE	Life of Faith.	MANTON	1689	61004002
LIFE	Life of Faith.	STUART	1753	61010038
LIFE	Life of Faith.	SAURIN	1777	34002014
LIFE	Life of Xt.	REYNOLDS	1679	53003010
LIFE	Life of Xt.	REYNOLDS	1679	65005012
LIFE	Life time.	ELLIS	1704	45016025
LIFE	Life time.	GILBERT	1724	45016025
LIFE	Life& D. R.	DUCHE	1779	19037037
LIFE	Life& Imm.	MOSS	1737	58001010
LIFE	Life& Imm.	KEDDINGTON	1757	58001010
LIFE	Life& Imm.	TIDCOMBE	1757	58001010
LIFE	Life& Imm.	LELAND	1769	58001010
LIFE	Life& Imm.	JORTIN	1774	58001010
LIFE	Life& Imm.	BRYSON	1778	58001010
LIFE	Life Pilgri.	WALKER	1764	19039012
LIFE	Life Pilgri.	DUCHE	1779	19039012
LIFE	Life Probat.	HORBERY	1774	43025028
LIFE	Life Steward	PYLE	1777	43025014
LIFE	Life Uncert.	MAY	1744	24028016
LIFE	Long life&c.	GERARD	1782	18007016
LIFE	Long Life.	ABERNETHY	1751	20003016
LIFE	Miser. Life.	DORRINGTON	1703	18005007
LIFE	Peace.life.	REEVES	1729	48012018
LIFE	Peace.life.	SOUTH	1744	48012018
LIFE	Period life.	FYSH	1738	20010027
LIFE	Plan of life.	DUCHAL	1765	52005015
LIFE	Predest.t.life	FIDDES	1720	48008029
LIFE	Predest.t.life	COOPER	1765	48008029
LIFE	R. Life t. Pl.	LAWSON	1764	19001002
LIFE	Relig. Life.	NORRIS	1728	19037038
LIFE	Relig. Life.	BOURN	1777	57004007
LIFE	Relig.life.	GALE	1726	45011028
LIFE	Relig.life.	GROVE	1742	20004018
LIFE	Relig.life.	JOHNSON	1740	55004001
LIFE	Relig.life.	ADEY	1755	23032017
LIFE	Riv.of Life.	ERSKINE	1764	69022001
LIFE	Rule of life.	MASON	1758	47020024
LIFE	Rule of life.	PETERS	1776	32006008
LIFE	Sav.priv.life	NEWTON	1782	45002051
LIFE	Short.h. Life	WARREN	1748	64001014
LIFE	Short.of life.	CONANT	1698	19090010
LIFE	Short.of life.	WHALEY	1695	62004014
LIFE	Spir. Life.	BEVERIDGE	1720	48008009
LIFE	Spir.life.	HORNE	1755	20020027
LIFE	Spir.life.	DAVIES	1766	52002004
LIFE	Tree of life.	BOLTON	1660	03010003
LIFE	Tree of life.	HOLLOWAY	1751	69002007
LIFE	Tree of life.	WILLISON	1761	69022002

Keyword	In its Context	Author	Year	BkChpVrs
LIFE	Tree of Life.	KENNICOTT	1747	01002008
LIFE	Uncert.of life	SHORTHOSE	1738	19090010
LIFE	V.life un.m.	BRYSON	1778	21001014
LIFE	Value of life.	MUNTON	1756	21011007
LIFE	Van.of life.	CREYGHTON	1720	19039007
LIFE	Van.of life.	NORRIS	1728	21011008
LIFE	Van.of life.	QUINCY	1750	19039005
LIFE	Van.of life.	KIMBER	1756	62004014
LIFE	Van.of life.	WARNEFORD	1776	01047009
LIFE	Ven. H.life.	HOWE	1702	19089047
LIFE	Way to life.	IBBOT	1726	43019017
LIFE	Xn. Life o. F.	TILLOTSON	1735	50005007
LIFE	Xn. Life.	TILLOTSON	1735	45013024
LIFE	Xt. Li.&life.	KELSEY	1721	46001004
LIFE	Xt. Xn's.life.	JACKSON	1756	53001021
LIFE	Xt.br.of life.	WILLISON	1761	20009005
LIFE	Xt's priv life	THEED	1712	45002051
LIFE	Xters.in life.	POWELL	1776	49013011
LIFE	Xtian.life.	SEED	1750	20004018
LIG	Dark.& Lig.	TAYLOR	1719	52005018
LIG	Div. Lig.&c.	STEELE	1776	19043003
LIG	Lig.m.shine.	BAXTER	1707	43005016
LIG	Mak.lig. Xt.	DAVIES	1766	43022005
LIG	Sp. Lig.& D.	SKELTON	1754	48013011
LIG	Xn.lig.cand.	HORNECK	1706	43005015
LIG	Xn.lig.cand.	BLAIR	1740	43005015
LIG	Xt. Lig.o. W.	WHARTON	1728	46008012
LIG	Xt. Lig.o. W.	KIMBER	1756	46008012
LIG	Xt. Lig.of w.	WATSON	1749	19019004
LIGHT	Fai.& Light.	BOSTON	1753	50005007
LIGHT	G.is Light.	COCK	1710	65001005
LIGHT	G.is Light.	STURMY	1716	65001005
LIGHT	Light o. Gos.	SHERLOCK	1722	55001009
LIGHT	Light of N.	CULVERWELL	1661	20020027
LIGHT	Light G.rej.	CONANT	1699	46003019
LIGHT	On Light.	SMITH	1717	45021026
LIGHT	Or.of Light.	MURRAY	1777	01001001
LIGHT	Sav. Light.	ERSKINE	1764	46014006
LIGHT	Xn. Light W.	HOLDEN	1755	43005014
LIGHT	Xn. Light W.	ORR	1772	43005014
LIGHT	Xt.light o. O.	BULKLEY	1771	46009005
LIKE	Xt.like Mos.	COLMAN	1728	05008015
LIKE	Xt.like Rain.	WILLISON	1761	19072006
LINC	b. Soc. Linc.	ANONYMOUS	1732	18034013
LINSW	Linsw. Gar.	CENNICK	1762	05022011
LIQ	Ag. Spi. Liq.	HALES	1754	23056012
LIQUORS	Sp. Liquors.	JACOMB	1736	24035008
LIT	Dan.lit. Sins.	HOPKINS	1710	43005019
LIT	Def.of Lit.	WARREN	1686	57002001
LIT	Exped. Lit.	HOLE	1725	19089007
LIT	Lit. Ch. Eng.	DURELL	1688	49011016
LITTLE	Little Child.	ALLESTRE	1684	44010015
LITTLE	Little Child.	HICKES	1726	44010014
LITTLE	Little Child.	LARDNER	1751	43019013
LITTLE	Little Piety.	HAMMOND	1684	24005002
LITTLE	Little Sins.	MAUDUIT	1710	43005019

INDEXES TO THIRD VOLUME: E: KEYWORD-IN-CONTEXT INDEX OF OTHER SUBJECTS OR OCCASIONS

Keyword	In its Context	Author	Year	BkChpVrs
LITUR	Def. Litur.	ATTERBURY	1734	25003041
LITUR	Def.of Litur.	PRIEST	1750	19096009
LITUR	Engl. Litur.	SNAPE	1745	48012012
LITURG	Liturg.usef.	SWINDEN	1713	45011002
LITURGY	Def. Liturgy.	ANNAND	1661	28014002
LITURGY	Ref. Liturgy.	GODDARD	1772	46017003
LIV	Dang.liv.&c.	WILSON	1781	49013011
LIV	Liv.& D. Fai.	NEWTON	1767	62002026
LIV	Liv. Peacea.	JORTIN	1774	48012018
LIV	Liv.by Faith.	SUTTON	1754	51003011
LIVE	Live everl.	EDWARDS	1713	43025046
LIVE	Live happy.	COTES	1721	21003012
LIVE	Live of Gos.	MEDE	1672	49009014
LIVERY	Caut. Livery	PENN	1767	20020001
LIVES	Soul lives.	WHEATLY	1746	21012007
LIVING	Way living.	ANONYMOUS	1732	21003001
LO	G's. Lo. Red.	CARMICHAEL	1757	65004011
LO	G's.lo.of ab.	TOWGOOD	1676	47007008
LO	Lo.& Ch.enf.	HOLE	1716	65004007
LO	Lo. Test. Xn.	SOUTHCOMBE	1752	46013034
LO	Lo.o. G.& M.	FARRINGTON	1741	57001005
LO	Lo.of G.& N.	HOLE	1716	43022034
LO	Lo.of G.&c.	BRAILSFORD	1776	19033026
LO	Lo.sup t.pr.	ROWLAND	1774	68000009
LO	Lo.t. G.& Xt.	<u>DAVIES</u>	1766	46021017
LO	Pe. Lo.g.bo.	BAYLY	1721	65004017
LO	Self-lo.& B.	WEBSTER	1748	58003001
LO	Vic.self-lo.	SHERLOCK	1702	58003001
LO	Xn. Co.&lo.	SMITH	1673	62004007
LO	Xt's.lo.to us.	<u>SHOWER</u>	1702	46015009
LOAV	Loav.& Fish.	DODD	1757	43014019
LOAV	Loav.& Fish.	<u>BULKLEY</u>	1771	46006012
LOAVES	Loaves& F.	HEYLIN	1761	43015036
LOGOLOGY	Logology.	COLLIER	1732	46001001
LOGOLOGY	Logology.	COLLIER	1732	46001003
LOND	F. F. Lond.	WOODWARD	1706	28006001
LOND	Fire Lond.	THORP	1677	43007012
LOND	Fire Lond.	STILLINGFLEET	1707	30004011
LOND	Fire Lond.	SALTER	1740	45013001
LOND	Fire Lond.	DOUGHTY	1744	19107034
LOND	Fire Lond.	<u>HOWE</u>	1744	27009025
LOND	Fire Lond.	CHAUNCEY	1747	49010011
LOND	Fire Lond.	APTHORPE	1770	34003002
LOND	Lond. Disp.	FRANKLIN	1774	44010014
LONG	G's long suff.	SAURIN	1775	21008011
LONG	Long life&c.	<u>GERARD</u>	1782	18007016
LONG	Long suff. G.	TILLOTSON	1735	21008011
LONG	Long Life.	<u>ABERNETHY</u>	1751	20003016
LOOK	Look to Xt.	<u>DAVIES</u>	1771	23045022
LORD	Joy in Lord.	REYNOLDS	1679	53004004
LORD	Lord sh.o. Xt	<u>WRIGHT</u>	1724	48014009
LORD	Our Lord.	BARROW	1716	52004005
LORD	Way of Lord.	MOSS	1733	45003004
LORD'S	Lord's chall.	<u>BRADBERRY</u>	1766	30004012
LORD'S	Lord's day.	BRYAN	1686	02020008
LORD'S	Lord's day.	BULKLY	1697	02020008
LORD'S	Lord's day.	VENN	1760	26020013
LORD'S	Lord's day.	<u>ORTON</u>	1769	03023003
LORD'S	Lord's supp.	<u>OGDEN</u>	1780	43026026
LORD'S	Lord's supp.	TEMPLE	1782	43026026
LORD'S	Lord's Day.	<u>ORTON</u>	1769	01002003
LORD'S	Lord's Pray.	<u>WITHERS</u>	1665	43006009
LORD'S	Lord's Pray.	FARINDON	1674	43006009
LORD'S	Lord's Pray.	STEPHENS	1699	43006009
LORD'S	Lord's Pray.	WHITBY	17--	43006009
LORD'S	Lord's Pray.	NEWCOME	1702	43006009
LORD'S	Lord's Pray.	<u>PIGGOTT</u>	1702	45011002
LORD'S	Lord's Pray.	HOPKINS	1710	43006009
LORD'S	Lord's Pray.	HOLE	1715	45011002
LORD'S	Lord's Pray.	TOPPING	1719	43006009
LORD'S	Lord's Pray.	HOLE	1719	45011002
LORD'S	Lord's Pray.	BLACKALL	1723	43006009
LORD'S	Lord's Pray.	MOSS	1732	45011002
LORD'S	Lord's Pray.	SYMPSON	1737	45011002
LORD'S	Lord's Pray.	BISSE	1740	43006009
LORD'S	Lord's Pray.	LEIGHTON	1746	43006009
LORD'S	Lord's Pray.	BALL	1756	43006009
LORD'S	Lord's Pray.	<u>WEST</u>	1758	43006009
LORD'S	Lord's Pray.	OGDEN	1770	43006009
LORD'S	Lord's Pray.	<u>WHITTY</u>	1772	43006009
LORD'S	Lord's Pray.	BURROUGH	1773	43006009
LORD'S	Lord's Supp.	MORICE	1660	03013015
LORD'S	Lord's Supp.	BERRIMAN	1751	43022004
LORD'S	Lord's Supp.	OGDEN	1780	69013008
LORD'S	Lord's-day.	WETENHALL	1697	69001003
LORD'S	Lord's-day.	<u>ORTON</u>	1769	23056002
LORD'S	Ob. Lord's d.	<u>ORTON</u>	1769	23058013
LORD'S	Ob. Lord's d.	D'COETLOGAN	1776	23058013
LORDS	b. Lords.	SMITH	1703	23066025
LOS	Salt los. Sav.	BLAIR	1740	43005012
LOSS	Gain&loss.	MOSS	1732	43016026
LOSS	Great.loss.	LIVESEY	1660	43016026
LOSS	Loss of Soul.	<u>WATSON</u>	1660	43016026
LOSS	Loss of Soul.	TAYLOR	1668	43016026
LOSS	Loss of Soul.	STILLINGFLEET	1707	43016026
LOSS	Loss of Soul.	<u>FOORD</u>	1719	43016026
LOSS	Loss of Soul.	SHOREY	1725	43016026
LOSS	Loss of Soul.	CLARKE	1735	43016026
LOSS	Loss of Soul.	<u>FAWCETT</u>	1749	43016026
LOSS	Loss of Soul.	DAVIS	1756	43016026
LOSS	Loss of Soul.	<u>MAY</u>	1757	43016026
LOSS	Loss of Soul.	<u>DUCHAL</u>	1765	43016026
LOSS	Loss of Soul.	EDWARDS	1775	43016026
LOSS	Loss.of Soul.	<u>BEVERLEY</u>	1694	43016026
LOSS	Souls& Loss.	SHEPHERD	1748	43016026
LOST	Lost Sheep.	BRAGGE	1704	45015004
LOST	Lost Sheep.	HOLE	1716	45015001
LOST	Lost Sheep.	DODD	1757	45015003
LOST	Lost Sheep.	STEBBING	1760	45015004
LOST	Lost Sheep.	<u>BULKLEY</u>	1771	45015007
LOST	Lost Sheep.	ROWLAND	1778	45015005
LOT	Mist.of Lot.	<u>WILCOX</u>	1757	01040036

Keyword	In its Context	Author	Year	BkChpVrs
LOT'S	Lot's wife.	HACKETT	1675	01019026
LOT'S	Lot's Destr.	ORTON	1776	45017032
LOT'S	Lot's Flight.	CENNICK	1762	01019017
LOT'S	Lot's Wife.	BRADY	1730	45017032
LOTS	Of Lots.	ATTERBURY	1743	20016033
LOV	Not.lov. Xt.	WILSON	1781	49016022
LOV	Things lov.	PYLE	1777	53004008
LOVE	Ag. Self-love	BUTLER	1716	53002021
LOVE	Broth. Love.	BRIDGE	1671	19133001
LOVE	Broth. Love.	BAYLY	1721	65003014
LOVE	Broth. Love.	WARREN	1748	65004011
LOVE	Broth. Love.	HUSSEY	1755	65004011
LOVE	Broth. Love.	DAVIS	1756	61013001
LOVE	Broth. Love.	MUSCOTT	1760	46013034
LOVE	Broth Love.	SWIFT	1754	61013001
LOVE	Conj. Love.	BRETT	1757	61013004
LOVE	Div. Love.	WELCH	1752	19062001
LOVE	Div. Love.	DAVIS	1756	43022036
LOVE	Div. Love.	WILLISON	1761	65003001
LOVE	Div. Love.	ELLIOTT	1764	65004010
LOVE	Divine Love.	ELLIOTT	1764	65005016
LOVE	Dom- Love.	HOLLAND	1753	19133001
LOVE	Filial Love.	DODD	1772	46019026
LOVE	Frat. Love.	DODD	1772	46011005
LOVE	G's love to us	BLAIR	1740	43007009
LOVE	G's. Love&c.	FLAVEL	1673	46003016
LOVE	G's. Love M's.	BEVERIDGE	1711	46003016
LOVE	G's Love&c.	KIMBER	1756	19146008
LOVE	God is Love.	RUST	1686	65004016
LOVE	God is Love.	BRADY	1704	65004008
LOVE	God is Love.	HUSSEY	1755	65004008
LOVE	God is Love.	DAVIES	1766	65004008
LOVE	God is Love.	LELAND	1769	65004008
LOVE	God's love.	HAMMOND	1684	26018031
LOVE	God's love.	SOUTH	1744	23027011
LOVE	God's Love.	DUNLOP	1722	48005008
LOVE	Love fulf. L.	QUINCY	1750	51005014
LOVE	Love in Red.	HUSSEY	1755	65004009
LOVE	Love in Red.	CARMICHAEL	1757	65004009
LOVE	Love in Red.	WITHERSPOON	1768	69001005
LOVE	Love o. God.	DUCHAL	1765	56003005
LOVE	Love o. God.	BOURDALOUE	1776	46007039
LOVE	Love o. Mon.	BARNES	1752	57006010
LOVE	Love o. Plea.	IBBOT	1726	57003004
LOVE	Love o. Plea.	SECKER	1770	57003004
LOVE	Love o.worl.	CREYGHTON	1720	54003002
LOVE	Love of plea.	BARKER	1748	23047008
LOVE	Love of Co.	WOODWARD	1693	19122008
LOVE	Love of Co.	STEPHENS	1721	19122006
LOVE	Love of Co.	JORTIN	1774	16005018
LOVE	Love of Cou.	BULKLEY	1761	19137005
LOVE	Love of G.	WHITAKER	1674	48008038
LOVE	Love of G.	CRUSO	1699	19026003
LOVE	Love of G.	DORRINGTON	1703	22001004
LOVE	Love of G.	SCOTT	1701	65005003
LOVE	Love of G.	COCK	1710	52003017

Keyword	In its Context	Author	Year	BkChpVrs
LOVE	Love of G.	SHARP	1729	43022037
LOVE	Love of G.	CROSSINGE	1732	19004006
LOVE	Love of G.	STENNETT	1732	44012030
LOVE	Love of G.	STENNETT	1732	65005003
LOVE	Love of G.	ATTERBURY	1743	44012029
LOVE	Love of G.	SEED	1743	44012030
LOVE	Love of G.	HUNT	1748	44012030
LOVE	Love of G.	WATTS	1753	44012030
LOVE	Love of G.	ROMAINE	1759	22001004
LOVE	Love of G.	WILLISON	1761	22001004
LOVE	Love of G.	JORTIN	1774	44012030
LOVE	Love of God	GELL	1676	43022037
LOVE	Love of God	ANNESLEY	1676	43022037
LOVE	Love of God	ELLIS	1686	43022037
LOVE	Love of God	NEWCOME	1702	43022037
LOVE	Love of God	BURNET	1713	43022035
LOVE	Love of God	EDWARDS	1713	43022037
LOVE	Love of God	HOLE	1715	43022037
LOVE	Love of God	BARROW	1716	43022037
LOVE	Love of God	KILLINBECK	1717	43022036
LOVE	Love of God	BEVERIDGE	1720	43022037
LOVE	Love of God	CREYGHTON	1720	43022037
LOVE	Love of God	BEVERIDGE	1720	43022037
LOVE	Love of God	READING	1724	43022037
LOVE	Love of God	BOYSE	1728	43022035
LOVE	Love of God	NORRIS	1728	43022037
LOVE	Love of God	SHARP	1729	43022035
LOVE	Love of God	SHARP	1729	43022037
LOVE	Love of God	ALTHAM	1732	43022037
LOVE	Love of God	CLARKE	1732	43022037
LOVE	Love of God	MUDGE	1739	43022037
LOVE	Love of God	ABERNETHY	1743	43022037
LOVE	Love of God	FOSTER	1744	43022037
LOVE	Love of God	BUTLER	1749	43022037
LOVE	Love of God	POTTER	1753	43022037
LOVE	Love of God	HUSSEY	1758	43022037
LOVE	Love of God	ADEY	1760	43022037
LOVE	Love of God	MASON	1761	43022037
LOVE	Love of God	SECKER	1770	43022037
LOVE	Love of God	LANGHORNE	1773	43022037
LOVE	Love of God	PETERS	1776	43022037
LOVE	Love of God.	WILLIAMS	1662	65004019
LOVE	Love of God.	SCOTT	1701	65004019
LOVE	Love of God.	DUNLOP	1722	19031023
LOVE	Love of God.	BOYSE	1728	65004010
LOVE	Love of God.	DAVIS	1756	19031023
LOVE	Love of Inte.	STENNETT	1732	53002021
LOVE	Love of Nov.	NEWTON	1782	47017021
LOVE	Love of Plea.	HOADLY	1754	58003004
LOVE	Love of Plea.	DALTON	1757	58003004
LOVE	Love of Plea.	COLE	1761	58003004
LOVE	Love of Plea.	WILLIAMS	1774	58003004
LOVE	Love of Pleas.	IBBOT	1726	58003004
LOVE	Love of Pleas.	OAKES	1747	58003004
LOVE	Love of Pleas.	PORTEUS	1772	58003004
LOVE	Love of Pleas.	PEARCE	1779	58003004

INDEXES TO THIRD VOLUME: E: KEYWORD-IN-CONTEXT INDEX OF OTHER SUBJECTS OR OCCASIONS

Keyword	In its Context	Author	Year	BkChpVrs
LOVE	Love of Vir.	MACE	1751	43005006
LOVE	Love of W.	RUSSEL	1746	43019016
LOVE	Love of Xt.	BRINSLEY	1667	46014028
LOVE	Love of Xt.	ERSKINE	1664	51002020
LOVE	Love of Xt.	NEST	1677	52006024
LOVE	Love of Xt.	PIERCE	1679	49016022
LOVE	Love of Xt.	EDWARDS	1692	49016022
LOVE	Love of Xt.	ADAMS	1716	49016022
LOVE	Love of Xt.	SHERLOCK	1719	50005014
LOVE	Love of Xt.	STEFFE	1743	50005010
LOVE	Love of Xt.	STEFFE	1743	50005014
LOVE	Love of Xt.	ROMAINE	1759	22001001
LOVE	Love of Xt.	ROMAINE	1759	22005016
LOVE	Love of Xt.	WILLISON	1761	52003019
LOVE	Love of Xt.	WILLISON	1761	65004019
LOVE	Love to Xt.	BOYSE	1728	63001008
LOVE	Love to Xt.	ORR	1739	43010037
LOVE	Love to Xt.	SOUTH	1744	43010037
LOVE	Love to Xt.	ABERNETHY	1748	43010037
LOVE	Love tow. G.	SKELTON	1754	45010027
LOVE	Love un. Sa.	HUBBARD	1729	63001008
LOVE	Love& Ch.	CLARKE	1734	65004021
LOVE	Love& Uni.	DAVIS	1756	50013011
LOVE	Love& Uni.	ANONYMOUS	1771	50013014
LOVE	Love& Unit.	SEED	1743	20015017
LOVE	Love&unity	CREED	1755	48015005
LOVE	Love Enem.	NEEDHAM	1679	43005044
LOVE	Love Enem.	ALLESTREE	1684	43005044
LOVE	Love Enem.	BURTON	1685	43005044
LOVE	Love Enem.	KIDDER	1697	43005043
LOVE	Love Enem.	HORNECK	1706	43005043
LOVE	Love Enem.	HORNECK	1706	43005044
LOVE	Love Enem.	HORNECK	1706	43005046
LOVE	Love Enem.	ANDERSON	1708	43005044
LOVE	Love Enem.	GARDINER	1720	43005043
LOVE	Love Enem.	KELSEY	1721	43005044
LOVE	Love Enem.	HAILES	1722	43005044
LOVE	Love Enem.	BLACKALL	1723	43005045
LOVE	Love Enem.	GALE	1726	43005048
LOVE	Love Enem.	SCOUGAL	1726	45006027
LOVE	Love Enem.	CARLETON	1736	43005044
LOVE	Love Enem.	PELIER	1737	43005044
LOVE	Love Enem.	BLAIR	1740	43005043
LOVE	Love Enem.	SMITH	1740	43005044
LOVE	Love Enem.	BLAIR	1740	43005045
LOVE	Love Enem.	BLAIR	1740	43005046
LOVE	Love Enem.	SEED	1743	43005044
LOVE	Love Enem.	EDWARDS	1745	43005044
LOVE	Love Enem.	BALGUY	1748	43005044
LOVE	Love Enem.	MACE	1751	43005043
LOVE	Love Enem.	WHITTY	1772	43005044
LOVE	Love Enem.	JORTIN	1774	43005044
LOVE	Love Enem.	PYLE	1777	45006027
LOVE	Love Enem.	BROUGHTON	1778	43005043
LOVE	Love Enem.	JORTIN	1774	48012020
LOVE	Love G.& N.	COCK	1710	43022035
LOVE	Love G.& N.	CARLETON	1736	45010027
LOVE	Love G.&c.	GUYSE	1757	65005003
LOVE	Love Glory.	SOUTH	1744	43023005
LOVE	Love Good.	BOURN	1777	19119015
LOVE	Love Neigh.	GELL	1676	43022039
LOVE	Love Neigh.	MILWARD	1676	43022039
LOVE	Love Neigh.	KILLIGREW	1685	43022040
LOVE	Love Neigh.	NEWCOME	1702	43022039
LOVE	Love Neigh.	EDWARDS	1713	43022039
LOVE	Love Neigh.	HOLE	1715	43022039
LOVE	Love Neigh.	BARROW	1716	43022039
LOVE	Love Neigh.	HOLE	1716	45010023
LOVE	Love Neigh.	KILLINBECK	1717	43022039
LOVE	Love Neigh.	BOYSE	1728	43022039
LOVE	Love Neigh.	ALTHAM	1732	43022037
LOVE	Love Neigh.	BLACKALL	1733	43005043
LOVE	Love Neigh.	EVANS	1737	43022039
LOVE	Love Neigh.	WATERLAND	1742	43022039
LOVE	Love Neigh.	BUTLER	1749	48013009
LOVE	Love Neigh.	NEAL	1757	46013034
LOVE	Love Neigh.	HUSSEY	1758	43022039
LOVE	Love Neigh.	MOTTERSHEAD	1759	43022039
LOVE	Love Neigh.	SECKER	1770	43022039
LOVE	Love Neigh.	PETERS	1776	43012036
LOVE	Love Neigh.	PETERS	1776	43022039
LOVE	Love Praise.	BLAIR	1780	46012043
LOVE	Love Wisd.	ABERNETHY	1751	20008017
LOVE	Mut. Love.	PIERCE	1679	46013035
LOVE	Mut. Love.	FRANKLYN	1724	48013008
LOVE	Mut. Love.	MORRIS	1743	46013035
LOVE	Mut. Love.	TIDCOMBE	1757	52005002
LOVE	Mutual Love	CLARKE	1727	65004007
LOVE	Mutual Love	WELCH	1752	65004007
LOVE	Peace& Love	JEKYLL	1675	61012014
LOVE	Pn. Love.	BOEHM	1717	49013004
LOVE	Prev. Love.	ERSKINE	1764	65004019
LOVE	Rede. Love.	BAINE	1778	69003020
LOVE	Rem.love G.	HICKES	1726	69002004
LOVE	Self-love.	BARROW	1716	58003002
LOVE	Self-love.	WATERLAND	1742	58003001
LOVE	Self-love.	COCKMAN	1750	58003002
LOVE	Self-love.	FREE	1750	65004019
LOVE	Self-love.	COWPER	1751	58003002
LOVE	Self-love.	WHITTY	1772	43022039
LOVE	Self-love.	JORTIN	1774	58003002
LOVE	Self-love&c.	CONANT	1703	49013005
LOVE	Signs of love.	BATES	1700	65005002
LOVE	Sinc.in Love	WHITE	1757	48012009
LOVE	Social Love.	BRADBURY	1749	61010024
LOVE	Visit.of Love	VENN	1759	19118018
LOVE	Xn. Love.	GOULD	1676	49013005
LOVE	Xn. Love.	MORE	1692	63001022
LOVE	Xn. Love.	WHICHCOTE	1698	52004031
LOVE	Xn. Love.	NOURSE	1708	49014001
LOVE	Xn. Love.	KENNET	1715	67000002
LOVE	Xn. Love.	BAYLY	1721	65003024

Keyword	In its Context	Author	Year	BkChpVrs
LOVE	Xn. Love.	WHITTY	1772	46013034
LOVE	Xn's. Love.	WORTHINGTON	1725	52005002
LOVE	Xn's Love.	WHITTY	1772	22008006
LOVE	Xt's. Love.	WELCH	1752	23042003
LOVE	Xt's. Love.	WILLISON	1761	69002005
LOVE	Xt's Love.	ROMAINE	1759	22008006
LOVERS	Lovers of G.	ERSKINE	1764	48008028
LOVING	Loving G.	BEVERIDGE	1720	48008028
LOW	Du.low con.	MARSHALL	1750	53004012
LOW	Low.believ.	WILLISON	1761	43008008
LOY	Count. Loy.	HUTCHINSON	1717	43023029
LOY	Loy.& Conf.	PLEYDELL	1682	48013004
LOY	Loy.& Peace	RAYMOND	1705	59003003
LOY	Loy. Peace.	ROLL	----	09025005
LOY	R. Loy.& Ch.	STUBBS	1704	63002017
LOY	Way to Loy.	OWEN	1684	59003001
LOY	Xn. Loy rev.	SPRINT	1694	63002017
LOYALISTS	b. Loyalists	BAXTER	1782	07015011
LOYALTY	Loyalty.	PHILIPS	1681	27010021
LOYALTY	Tr. Loyalty.	MYNORS	1716	23030010
LOYALTY	on Loyalty.	CURTOIS	1684	18034029
LUK	Zeal& Luk.	TAYLOR	1668	24048010
LUKE	St. Luke	TILLOTSON	1735	19112006
LUKE'S	St. Luke's d.	HACKETT	1675	47011026
LUKE'S	St. Luke's d.	JENNER	1676	58004011
LUKE'S	St. Luke's d.	FRANCIS	1773	50005020
LUKE'S	St. Luke's.d.	STANHOPE	1715	45010001
LUKE'S	St. Luke's.d.	HOLE	1716	45010001
LUKE'S	St. Luke's-d.	STANHOPE	1715	58004005
LUKE'S	St. Luke's-d.	HOLE	1716	58004005
LUKEW	Lukew.in R.	BRAMSTON	1713	69003015
LUKEWARM	Lukewarm.	SHERLOCK	1719	69003015
LUKEWARM	Lukewarm.	MILLER	1749	69003015
LUKEWARM	Lukewarm.	DAVIES	1766	69003015
LUKEWARMN	Lukewarmn.	SYLVESTER	1690	61010024
LUKEWARMN	Lukewarmn.	HARRIS	1732	69003015
LUST	Lust Ca.of S.	CLARKE	1735	62001014
LUST	Lust Ca.of S.	SOUTH	1744	62001014
LUST	Lust Ca.of S.	ABERNETHY	1751	62001014
LUST	Vag.lust&c.	OVINGTON	1712	49007002
LUSTS	Ag.sen. Lusts	WISE	1717	63002011
LUSTS	Ag.sen. Lusts	WESTON	1747	63002011
LUSTS	Cruc.t. Lusts.	SOUTH	1744	51005024
LUSTS	Cruc.t. Lusts.	BROWNE	1749	51005024
LUSTS	Flesh. Lusts.	SHERLOCK	1772	63002011
LUX	Avar.& Lux.	CONEY	1750	45012020
LUX	Land lux.	CARRINGTON	1776	23002007
LUX	Pri. Lux.&c.	CONANT	1708	26016049
LUX	Rich.& Lux.	MARRIOTT	1774	19059016
LUXURY	Luxury.	NEWTON	1782	45016019
LUXURY	Luxury&c.	ANONYMOUS	1747	57002009
LWG	G.on.o. Lwg.	MICHELL	1737	62004012
LY	Car.ly-in W.	LAWSON	1764	23049022
LY	Ly.to H. Gh.	NEWLIN	1728	47005003
LYING	Ag. Lying.	DRAKE	1760	52004025
LYING	Lying.	RAWLINS	1713	52004025

Keyword	In its Context	Author	Year	BkChpVrs
LYING	Lying.	SMALRIDGE	1724	52004025
LYING	Lying.	CLARKE	1735	52004025
LYING	Lying.	WILLIAMS	1774	52004025
LYING	Lying.	LAMONT	1780	54003009
M	A.f.m.f. G.a.	PARSONS	1774	50003006
M	A.m. Pr. Ir. S	SECKER	1766	20009006
M	Aff.m.o.joy.	HOWE	1744	62001002
M	Ag. F.of M.	WOOD	1775	20029025
M	Ag.m. Philo.	CRADDOCK	1739	49001023
M	Alm.g.& M.	HOLE	1725	49013003
M	An.&m. Id.	ANONYMOUS	1716	26008014
M	An. Co.m.	LANGHORNE	1777	47007026
M	An.m. Cl.	THANE	1706	51006009
M	An.m. Qua.	ANONYMOUS	1767	45016005
M	Analy.of M.	FREE	1764	01001026
M	At Quak.m.	ANONYMOUS	1771	49013014
M	B. R.n. M. S.	ANONYMOUS	1735	56002001
M	B.o. R. M.o. S	BENSON	17--	56002001
M	Bad M.rep.g.	SNAPE	1745	63004004
M	Blind M.cur.	BRAGGE	1706	44008022
M	Carn.&sp.m.	STILLINGFLEET	1707	48008006
M	Carn.&sp.m.	IBBOT	1726	48008006
M	Carn.&sp.m.	EVANS	1737	48008006
M	Cens. G's.m.	ALTHAM	1732	49004005
M	Ch.g.&b. M.	TILLOTSON	1735	65003010
M	Child.g. M.	ROSEWELL	1720	19116016
M	Coll.poor M.	MAULDEN	1738	20003006
M	Com.m.suff.	BRADY	1730	45016031
M	Conc.ad. M.	FULLWOOD	1673	20014034
M	Creat.of M.	BOSTON	1773	01001027
M	Creat.of M.	HORNE	1778	01001026
M	Cunning M.	SKELTON	1754	24009005
M	Cut.off M. E.	BULKLEY	1771	46018010
M	D. Inst.of M.	BETTY	1729	51001001
M	D. M.to pen.	DAVIES	1766	24031018
M	D. Virt.m. H.	WILLIAMS	1770	43005006
M	D.of P.& M.	SKELTON	1754	06024015
M	Du. Xs.& M.	WILSON	1781	46017004
M	Dut. M.& P.	WILSON	1781	49004001
M	Duty of M.	RALEIGH	1679	21012013
M	En.g.&b.m.	LUCAS	1722	20014032
M	En.g.&b.m.	TILLOTSON	1735	20014032
M	End& D. M.	SHERIDAN	1720	47017027
M	Ev.m.debtor	HUTCHINS	1782	49004007
M	Exc.div. M.	BEDFORD	1733	49014015
M	F. Hap.or M.	BUNDY	1740	45016025
M	Fear of M. S.	HUNT	1748	20029025
M	Fear G.& M.	DUNLOP	1722	45012004
M	G.dw.w. M.	FLEMING	1701	14006018
M	G.gov.m. A.	LELAND	1769	43010029
M	G.m.lia.cor.	HICKMAN	1706	49015033
M	G.m.lia.cor.	TREBECK	1730	49015033
M	G's just.& M.	ATTERBURY	1703	69004003
M	G's. L.to M.	PELLING	1694	46003016
M	G's.good. M.	SKEELER	1740	61002006
M	G's Im.in M.	FAWCETT	1749	01002026

Keyword	In its Context	Author	Year	BkChpVrs
M	Gen.&m. Z.	BULKLEY	1761	43016021
M	Good m. De.	WILCOX	1757	19027004
M	Good m. Du.	BURNETT	1774	09030006
M	Good m.exc.	BARKER	1763	19016003
M	Good.ho. M.	MOSS	1737	20004025
M	Good P.t.m.	AMORY	1766	43005045
M	Gr.&m. Gos.	CLAGETT	1720	43005019
M	H. Ign.& M.	BOURN	1777	18008009
M	Hap.hol. M.	PARKHURST	1706	43022030
M	Helps t.g. M.	STEELE	1683	49015002
M	Hon.stop. M.	TILLOTSON	1735	46007017
M	Hus.m. Em.	CORNWALLIS	1706	01026012
M	J.& M.of G.	ABERNETHY	1743	19089014
M	J.& M.of G.	KNOWLES	1750	19089014
M	Jes. Son o. M.	LARDNER	1760	45017022
M	Jes. Xt. G.m.	GUYSE	1719	48009005
M	Jes.m. Curse.	HURST	1678	51003010
M	Jes.m. Curse.	LARDNER	1769	51003013
M	Jud. G.& M.	HUNTER	1774	09016007
M	L.of G.& M.	WARBURTON	1753	20017005
M	L.of G.& M.	WARBURTON	1753	65004020
M	L's Paths m.	CHANDLER	1769	19025010
M	Li.o. G.in M.	MOIR	1759	52004018
M	Lib.m.&soc.	AGAR	1759	51005013
M	Liber.of M.	ORR	1739	46008032
M	Life m.th. M.	BLAIR	1740	43006025
M	Lig.m.shine.	BAXTER	1707	43005016
M	Lo.o. G.& M.	FARRINGTON	1741	57001005
M	M.& J. Gov.	BOURN	1760	19058010
M	M.& Xs.c. S.	SLADEN	1733	45014034
M	M. Anx.f.p.	DAVIES	1771	51004019
M	M. Or. Xn. R.	BOURN	1777	46006066
M	M.af. G.o. H.	EVANSON	1773	47013022
M	M.d.o. Cl. L.	HARRISON	1730	48015029
M	M.no.n.nec.	FIDDES	1720	64003003
M	M.pl.w.cri.	FARINDON	1672	51001010
M	M.reap.as s.	BOURN	1777	51006007
M	M.29.	LLOYD	1692	19118023
M	M.29.	ASPLIN	1715	10019011
M	M.29.	SKERRET	1717	19118023
M	Mir. Pr.d. M.	SKELTON	1754	46005036
M	Mir. Pr.d. M.	POWELL	1776	46005036
M	Mor.l.of M.	BUESDSELL	1700	45010025
M	Mortal.o. M.	HOPKINS	1710	61009027
M	Mortal.o. M.	FREE	1750	61009027
M	N. W.m.t. V.	ENFIELD	1772	43005014
M	Nat.&m. Inf.	SPARKE	1745	62001027
M	Nat.m.dead.	USHER	1678	25005016
M	Nat.m.dead.	USHER	1678	48006023
M	Nat.m.dead.	USHER	1678	51003022
M	No s. G.& M.	HOADLY	1754	45016013
M	No serv.t. M.	FAWCETT	1749	43006024
M	No M Mast.	BURTON	1685	43023008
M	O. G.f.& M.	FROST	1741	21005003
M	O.o. M.& Pe.	WILSON	1781	61013017
M	Ob. Xt's m.a.	CHANDLER	1769	47010040

Keyword	In its Context	Author	Year	BkChpVrs
M	Old&n. M.	BOSTON	1753	48006006
M	Old&n. M.	SECKER	1770	48006021
M	Old&n. M.	SHERLOCK	1772	48006021
M	Op. M.29.	FAWCONER	1763	19150004
M	P.& M. Duty.	WOOD	1773	49011001
M	Past. M.pr. S.	HILL	1755	07013023
M	Peace of M.	PAYNE	1698	43011029
M	Peace of M.	CARR	1777	19037038
M	Pers.in m. C.	STOCKDALE	1777	01049004
M	Pleas. G. M.	ANONYMOUS	1754	18036011
M	Pos.&m. Dut.	CARR	1777	43023009
M	Pr.' M.p.d.m.	CONYBEARE	1757	46020031
M	Pr.f. G's. M.	SMALRIDGE	1724	50001011
M	Pres.o.go.m.	WILCOX	1757	46017015
M	Pride&m. S.	STOCKDALE	1777	21010018
M	Prim. S.of M.	TAYLOR	1725	01001026
M	Pro. M.to A.	GERARD	1780	01022018
M	Prog.of M.	SKELTON	1754	19008005
M	R.ins.g.m. R	RANDOLPH	1738	50003005
M	R.ins.g.m. R.	JOHNSON	1731	50003005
M	R.perf.sy.m.	LAWSON	1764	43007020
M	Reas. Rel. M.	CALAMY	1670	48012001
M	Reas.in r.m.	PATTEN	1755	63003015
M	Reas.rel.m.	GRIFFITH	1763	53002013
M	Redem.o. M.	STURMY	1716	61002016
M	Rich M.& L.	STEVENS	1697	45016019
M	Rich M.& L.	CRUSO	1698	45016019
M	Rich M.& L.	BRAGGE	1702	45016019
M	Rich M.& L.	WELCHMAN	1704	45016019
M	Rich M.& L.	ELLIS	1704	45016019
M	Rich M.& L.	HOLE	1716	45016019
M	Rich M.& L.	TILLOTSON	1735	45016019
M	Rich M.& L.	DODD	1757	45016019
M	Rich M.& L.	HUNTER	1774	45016019
M	Right.m.	DUNLOP	1722	20012026
M	Rule m.act.	CLARKE	1734	45006044
M	Salv.f.div.m.	BOURN	1760	48007024
M	Self.de.r.m.	BRAILSFORD	1776	51006007
M	Self-den. M.	NEEDLER	1677	43005029
M	Self-den. M.	MOSS	1732	43005029
M	Self-den. M.	WESTON	1747	43005029
M	Ser.m.to Go.	FOTHERGILL	1765	57004008
M	Serv. G.& M.	BLACKALL	1723	43006024
M	Serv. G.& M.	BLAIR	1740	43006024
M	Si.& M.b. N.	ENGLAND	1700	52002001
M	Sinc.m.o. W.	ROWLAND	1774	63002002
M	So. H.or M.	SKELTON	1754	24013023
M	Soc.nat.o. M.	BUTLER	1749	48012004
M	Son m.judge	MARSH	1699	43024030
M	Soul of M.	FLAVEL	1673	01002007
M	St. Pa.c.&m.	BROUGHTON	1778	47009015
M	Subm.to M.	HORT	1738	63002013
M	Sure m.of D.	HEYWOOD	1672	23055005
M	Swear. L. M.	GRIFFYTH	1693	55004011
M	Swear. L. M.	SKERRET	1716	48013004
M	T.&eter.m.	FOTHERGILL	1765	43006033

Keyword	In its Context	Author	Year	BkChpVrs
M	Test.ne.f. M.	SKELTON	1754	58001013
M	Theory of m.	BROUGHTON	1778	41018008
M	Tr. D. Du. M.	BREVALL	1670	65005004
M	Tr.val.of M.	WHICHCOTE	1702	45016025
M	True g. M.	ORR	1773	21002003
M	Un. Pie.& M.	BLAIR	1777	47010004
M	Unw. G's M.	ORTON	1776	01032010
M	V.life un.m.	BRYSON	1778	21001014
M	Vess. M.& W.	DAVIES	1771	48009022
M	Vices of M.	MARRIOTT	1774	48001028
M	W.m pl. G.	WATERLAND	1742	20016004
M	Wd.m.flesh.	BRETT	1720	46001014
M	Weig.m. R.	ORR	1739	43023023
M	Weigh.m. R.	ORR	1739	45011042
M	Wh. D.of M.	HOOLE	1748	21012013
M	Who. Du. M.	BALL	1756	59002011
M	Wic. M.o. D.	CLARKE	1735	46008044
M	Wick. M. F.	HORTON	1679	45012020
M	Wick. M.de.	CLARKE	1736	56002011
M	Will.m.acc.	HICKES	1726	50008012
M	Wisd. Xt's. M.	TOTTIE	1775	45007035
M	Worldly M.	WILLIAMS	1770	45016008
M	Wrath of M.	MOSS	1733	62001020
M	Xcell. Xn. M.	GARDINER	1720	43005017
M	Xcell. Xn. M.	WESTLEY	1748	43005017
M	Xn. K.m. St.	FOTHERGILL	1765	53004001
M	Xn. M.& Re.	ROBINSON	1734	63001024
M	Xr.good M.	HUNTER	1774	45023050
M	Xt. G.& M.	HORBERY	1774	61001001
M	Xt. G.& M.	MEAD	1780	53002006
M	Xt. God- M.	EDWARDS	1749	46001014
M	Xt.draw. M.	WILLISON	1761	46012032
M	Xt.m. Sav.	VEAL	1703	19089019
M	Xt.per.m. L.	BLAIR	1740	43005017
M	Xt's. D.& M.	BURNET	1747	49001025
M	Xt's.auth. M.	FLAVEL	1673	46006027
M	Xt's.pers.m.	GUYSE	1757	46001018
M'	Part.of ot. M'	KITCHEN	1670	57005022
M'	Part.of ot. M'	MOSS	1737	57005022
M'S	Bad m's Imp.	FALLE	1694	21008011
M'S	C.to o.m's. S.	STOWE	1681	49003006
M'S	Err. M's.con.	GROVE	1747	48014016
M'S	G. M's Hope.	LACY	1720	19039008
M'S	G. M's Xrter.	WILCOX	1757	19084011
M'S	G.m's Del.	LELAND	1769	19037004
M'S	G.p. M's. F.	ANONYMOUS	1776	43006031
M'S	G's. Love M's.	BEVERIDGE	1711	46003016
M'S	Good m's p.	DAVIES	1679	19119057
M'S	Good m's Su.	HOLLAND	1753	19034019
M'S	M's co.w. G.	WILSON	1676	19073023
M'S	M's nat. St.	BOSTON	1773	19051005
M'S	M's nat. Sta.	WATKINS	1676	52002003
M'S	M's pre. St.	WEBB	1765	18005006
M'S	M's vileness.	WILLISON	1761	19008004
M'S	M's. Enm. G.	CHARNOCK	1699	48008007
M'S	M's. Fre.&c.	GODDARD	1781	62001014

Keyword	In its Context	Author	Year	BkChpVrs
M'S	M's. Impot.	MANTON	1676	48005006
M'S	M's. Insuffic.	CLARKSON	1696	46015005
M'S	M's. L.on E.	COLLETT	1774	01047009
M'S	M's. Redem.	OGDEN	1777	46014001
M'S	M's. Salvat.	LITTLETON	1680	57002004
M'S	M's. Sins n.c.	MACLAURIN	1772	62001013
M'S	M's. Soul sub.	BULL	1713	47001025
M'S	M's.con.&c.	TOULMIN	1770	51006007
M'S	M's.ina.k. S.	HURST	1660	48007007
M'S	M's.rel.to G.	FOSTER	1744	47017028
M'S	M's De.vain.	HORTON	1679	20019021
M'S	M's End&c.	BOSTON	1773	49010031
M'S	M's Inv.to H.	ORTON	1776	04010029
M'S	M's Sab.year.	CLARKE	1760	03025003
M'S	M's St.in P.	HUSSEY	1733	01002015
M'S	M's Temp.d.	GERARD	1780	20025008
M'S	M's Unders.	PYLE	1777	20017027
M'S	Rel.m's Dut.	HOLDEN	1755	20009012
M'S	Rich M's Ad.	WELCHMAN	1704	45016024
M'S	Rig.m's ref.	FLAVEL	1673	23026020
M'S	Seek.a.m's S.	WALLIS	1740	49010032
M'S	Unj.m's.d.	SMITH	1670	49006009
M'S	Virt.g.m's S.	CONEY	1730	20014014
M'S	Y. M's Mon.	H.	1673	21011009
MA	Ma. C.& E. S.	SIMONS	1743	64001010
MA	Ma. C.& E. S.	WARREN	1748	64001010
MA	Ma.b. Cr.&c.	ERSKINE	1764	23054005
MA	Ma.d.sup.p.	SLATER	1690	43013005
MA	Ma, C.& El.s.	SHARP	1734	64001010
MA	S.a.ador.ma.	PARRY	1666	43002009
MA	Xt.ma.of G.	STEVENS	1757	50005021
MADN	Madn. Sinn.	ORTON	1776	45015017
MAG	Beaut. Mag.	HALL	1660	19082001
MAG	Dut.of Mag.	WILSON	1781	05001017
MAG	F. Gr.mag.	LAMBERT	1779	24032008
MAG	Mag. Auth.	PASTON	1673	48013005
MAG	Mag. Duty.	SLATER	1690	48013003
MAGD	Mary Magd.	NEWLIN	1728	45007040
MAGI	Of Magi.	SOUTH	1744	43002003
MAGISTR	Magistr.&c.	BARNES	1752	48013001
MAGISTRACY	Magistracy.	CONEY	1750	19082006
MAGISTRATE	Magistrate.	JACKSON	1685	48013003
MAGISTRATES	Magistrates.	STOKES	1750	18029016
MAIN	Minist.main.	REES	1728	49009014
MAIN	Minist.main.	SPRY	1741	49009014
MAINT	Min. Maint.	SYMPSON	1661	13012032
MAINT	Mon. Maint.	BRUCE	1682	48013002
MAJESTY	G's. Majesty.	HUNT	1748	68000025
MAK	B. Pe.mak.	HORNECK	1706	43005009
MAK	B. Pe.mak.	NORRIS	1728	43005009
MAK	B. Pe.mak.	GROVE	1742	43005009
MAK	B. Pe.mak.	HALES	1766	43005009
MAK	B. Pe.mak.	ORR	1772	43005009
MAK	Mak. Heav.	BARROW	1716	47004024
MAK	Mak.lig. Xt.	DAVIES	1766	43022005
MAK	Peace mak.	EDWARDS	1726	43010010

INDEXES TO THIRD VOLUME: E: KEYWORD-IN-CONTEXT INDEX OF OTHER SUBJECTS OR OCCASIONS

Keyword	In its Context	Author	Year	BkChpVrs
MALEF	Cruc. Malef.	KEELING	1767	45023039
MALEV	Malev. Sent.	HEY	1774	52004031
MALICE	Malice&c.	BLAIR	1740	43005021
MAMM	Mamm. Unr.	THOMAS	1688	45016009
MAN	Creat.man.	HOWE	1676	21007029
MAN	Cure 1. Man.	BULKLEY	1771	47004008
MAN	Deprav.man	FELTON	1748	21007029
MAN	Duty of Man.	ANONYMOUS	1776	21012013
MAN	Exemp.man.	CARR	1777	55005022
MAN	Fall of Man.	WELLS	1676	48005012
MAN	Fall of Man.	ADAMS	1716	21007029
MAN	Fall of Man.	KING	1731	01002016
MAN	Fall of Man.	HUBBARD	1757	48005012
MAN	Fall of Man.	BARRINGTON	1770	01003001
MAN	Frail. Man.	CROWE	1744	19039004
MAN	Frame Man.	DAVIES	1720	19139014
MAN	Frame Man.	ATTERBURY	1743	19139014
MAN	G.man.flesh.	WEBB	1765	57003016
MAN	Good Man.	CLARKE	1734	01018019
MAN	Helpl. Man.	WALKER	1755	23063005
MAN	Ignor. Man.	BUTLER	1749	21008016
MAN	L. G.& Man.	ECCLES	1755	43022037
MAN	Man acc. Cr.	FARRINGTON	1769	48014012
MAN	Man b.blind.	BRAGGE	1702	46009001
MAN	Man b.blind.	DODD	1757	46009030
MAN	Man f. Virt.	GOUGH	1751	21012013
MAN	Man his o. E.	SKELTON	1754	51005017
MAN	Man.&eff. X's	BLACKALL	1723	43007028
MAN	Man.&eff. X's	BLAIR	1740	43007028
MAN	Man. Xt's. D.	FLAVEL	1673	37013007
MAN	Man. Xt's D.	FLAVEL	1673	23053007
MAN	Man.catch.	HICKERINGILL	1716	24005025
MAN	Man& Prov.	WEBB	1765	19008004
MAN	Man Vanity.	MILLER	1749	19039005
MAN	Misery Man.	GALLY	1723	18005007
MAN	Orig. St.man	GUYSE	1757	21007029
MAN	Orig.o. Man.	SHERIDAN	1720	47017026
MAN	P's man.o. S.	DUCHAL	1753	56002003
MAN	Pious Man.	COCK	1710	19024003
MAN	Pious Man.	SHARP	1729	19112004
MAN	Rich man.	BOURN	1764	45012016
MAN	Rig.&g.man	HICKMAN	1706	48005007
MAN	Rig.&g.man	FOSTER	1732	48005007
MAN	Rig.&g.man	HORBERY	1774	48005007
MAN	Soul of man.	FLAVEL	1673	69006009
MAN	Soul of Man.	FLAVEL	1673	52005029
MAN	Spirit man.	EDWARDS	1702	21003021
MAN	Spirit. Man.	BENSON	1748	49002014
MAN	T.&man. R.	LAW	1745	51004004
MAN	Van. Man.	NORRIS	1728	19039006
MAN	Van. Man.	REEVES	1729	19039006
MAN	Van. Man.	MASON	1742	19008004
MAN	W. Dut man.	WAPLE	1729	32006008
MAN	Way of Man.	LEIGHTON	1746	24010023
MAN	Wis.of Man.	GOUGH	1751	18028028
MAN	Xt.our Man.	WILLISON	1761	46006051
MAN'S	Man's End.	BOSTON	1773	19073024
MAN'S	Man's St. V.	WILSON	1676	19039005
MANIF	Xt's.manif.	CHANDLER	1769	65003008
MANIF	manif.of G.	WHICHCOTE	1703	48001019
MANK	Equal mank.	SAURIN	1777	20022001
MANNA	D.of Manna.	JENKINS	1779	02016018
MANNA	Hid. Manna.	HOLLOWAY	1751	69002017
MANNA	Manna in W.	BERRIMAN	1763	05008003
MANNA	Manna,type.	MEDE	1672	49010003
MANS	Many Mans.	HORTON	1679	46014002
MANS	Many Mans.	GRANT	1775	46014002
MANS	Many Mans.	HURD	1780	46014002
MANY	Many right.	HERVEY	1769	48005019
MANY	Many Mans.	HORTON	1679	46014002
MANY	Many Mans.	GRANT	1775	46014002
MANY	Many Mans.	HURD	1780	46014002
MAR	Dut.mar. St.	DELANY	1747	52005033
MAR	Xt.rep. Mar.	HORTON	1679	45010041
MAR'S	Mar's En. Xt.	HORTON	1679	45010038
MARCH	March.of Sl.	ANONYMOUS	1732	69018013
MARIN	Marin.mem.	REYNOLDS	1721	19107023
MARINER	Xn Mariner.	RUSSEN	1771	19046004
MARK	At N.mark.	ANONYMOUS	1774	19045005
MARK'S	St. Mark's d.	LITTLETON	1680	47015037
MARK'S	St. Mark's d.	PATRICK	1686	52004014
MARK'S	St. Mark's d.	STANHOPE	1715	46015001
MARK'S	St. Mark's d.	HOLE	1716	46015001
MARK'S	St. Mark's d.	BERRIMAN	1763	52004014
MARK'S	St. Mark's-d.	HOLE	1716	52004007
MARK'S	St. Mark's-d.	STANHOPE	1718	52004007
MARKS	Marks n.b.	WHITFIELD	1739	47019005
MARKS	Marks of R.	CARR	1777	06024014
MARLB	b. D. Marlb.	RICH	1685	48013002
MAROUM	Maroum.	RAMSAY	1680	23024021
MARR	Du.marr.st.	COCKBURN	1708	61013004
MARR	Marr. Hon.	SIMPSON	1774	61013004
MARR	Marr. Supp.	SHEPHERD	1748	43022005
MARR	Marr. Supp.	POTTER	1753	43022007
MARR	Marr. Supp.	DODD	1757	43022002
MARR	Marr. Supp.	ADEY	1760	43022002
MARR	Marr. Supp.	STEBBING	1760	43022002
MARR	Marr. Supp.	WILLISON	1761	43022002
MARR	Marr.in Can.	WHEATLY	1746	46002011
MARR	Marr.in Can.	DODD	1757	46002001
MARR	Marr.in Can.	BULKLEY	1771	46002001
MART	On Mart.&c.	MAINWARING	1780	58001008
MARTH	Marth. Mary	SCATTERGOOD	1723	45010041
MARTHA'S	Martha's C.	CONEY	1730	45010041
MARTYR	Martyr.con.	NICHOLS	1746	43005010
MARY	Marth. Mary	SCATTERGOOD	1723	45010041
MARY	Mary Magd.	NEWLIN	1728	45007040
MARY	Virgin Mary	MASTER	1710	45001026
MAS	Good Mas.	TERRY	1746	02018021
MAS	Obed.t. Mas.	SEATON	1720	54003022
MAS	2 S. X.mas.	READING	1730	23041001
MASS	Idol.of Mass.	ANONYMOUS	1680	45022019

Keyword	In its Context	Author	Year	BkChpVrs
MASS	No Mass&c.	SHARP	1735	49011023
MAST	Duty o. Mast.	FLEETWOOD	1737	54004001
MAST	Duty o. Mast.	BACON	1750	54004001
MAST	Duty o. Mast.	FRANKLIN	1765	54004001
MAST	Duty o. Mast.	ANONYMOUS	1776	54004005
MAST	Duty to Mast.	NICHOLS	1701	54003022
MAST	Duty to Mast.	FRANKLIN	1765	54003022
MAST	Duty Mast.	DELANY	1747	52006009
MAST	Mast.& Serv.	JANEWAY	1676	52006005
MAST	No M Mast.	BURTON	1685	43023008
MAST	Xt.our Mast.	BENNETT	1728	43023008
MAT	Auth.mat. F.	ANONYMOUS	1774	43023008
MAT	Mat.of H. L.	SANDERSON	1722	20008015
MAT	Rea.rel.mat.	RANDOLPH	1762	48001020
MAT	Subj mat. Pr.	FIDDES	1720	65005014
MATT	Matt.of Rel.	JEFFERY	1751	53001010
MATT	R. Rel.matt.	ANONYMOUS	1764	23046008
MATT	St. Matt.day.	LITTLETON	1680	43009009
MATT	St. Matt.day.	STANHOPE	1715	43009009
MATT	St. Matt.day.	HOLE	1716	43009009
MATT	St. Matt.day.	COOKE	1739	45012015
MATT	St. Matt.day.	WHEATLY	1746	43009009
MATTH	St. Matth.d.	COCK	1705	50004001
MATTH	St. Matth.d.	COCK	1705	50004005
MATTH	St. Matth.d.	STANHOPE	1715	50004001
MATTH	St. Matth.d.	HOLE	1716	50004001
MATTHIAS	St. Matthias.	STANHOPE	1715	43011025
MATTHIAS	St. Matthias.	HOLE	1716	43011025
MATTHIAS	St. Matthias.	STANHOPE	1715	47001015
MATTHIAS	St. Matthias.	HOLE	1716	47001015
MATTHIAS	St. Matthias.	COOKE	1739	47017022
MATTHIAS	St. Matthias.	WHEATLY	1746	47001023
MAY	May 14.	WISHEART	1719	19133001
MAY	May 24.	BARKSDALE	1660	10015025
MAYOR	b. L. Mayor.	STANDISH	1684	05006011
MD	Troub. Md.	NORRIS	1728	19094019
ME	Me.7 Com.	HORNECK	1706	43005027
ME	Me.7 Com.	BLACKALL	1723	43005027
ME	Me.7 Com.	BLAIR	1740	43005027
MEA	Mea. H. Nat.	BOURN	1777	19144003
MEA	Ord.mea.gr.	ADAMS	1690	45016031
MEANESS	Meaness. L.	DORRINGTON	1703	18014002
MEANS	Means o. Ho.	HAWEIS	1762	64001010
MEANS	Means o. Ho.	ELSMERE	1767	64001010
MEANS	Means of R.	FARRINGTON	1769	46004023
MEANS	Means of Sal.	BOURN	1777	52002008
MEANS	Means Gr.	WESTLEY	1749	38003007
MEAS	Meas.of Ch.	HORNECK	1706	43005042
MEAS	Meas.of Ch.	BLACKALL	1723	43005040
MEAS	Meas.of Ch.	BLAIR	1740	43005042
MEAT	Xt.sp.meat.	LE FRANK	1662	46004034
MED	Cons.o. Med.	FLAVEL	1673	46017019
MED	Fuln.o Med.	GILL	1773	54001019
MED	Med. Power.	ERSKINE	1764	43028018
MED	Med.of Xt.	WHICHCOTE	1703	54003017
MED	Relig. Med.	GOUGH	1709	01024063
MED	Winter med.	SHOWER	1709	19147015
MED	Xt. Med.& R.	LANGHORNE	1773	54001014
MED	Xt. Med.o. R.	STENNETT	1769	52002010
MEDIA	Media.expl.	DUCHAL	1765	57002005
MEDIAT	Xt. Mediat.	BRINSLEY	1667	61011024
MEDIAT	Xt's.mediat.	FLAVEL	1673	57002005
MEDIAT	Xt's.mediat.	BEVERIDGE	1720	57002005
MEDIAT	Xt's.mediat.	TILLOTSON	1735	57002005
MEDIAT	Xt's.mediat.	FOSTER	1744	57002005
MEDIAT	Xt's.mediat.	HUSSEY	1753	57002005
MEDIAT	Xt's.mediat.	PETERS	1776	57002005
MEDIATOR	Mediator.	WHITAKER	1676	57002005
MEDIATOR	Xt. Mediator	TAYLOR	1725	57002015
MEDIATORSH	Mediatorsh.	WARREN	1748	57002005
MEDIT	Dev. Medit.	WARNEFORD	1776	19004004
MEDIT	Div. Medit.	BRINSLEY	1667	19104034
MEDIT	Div. Medit.	BATES	1700	19119097
MEDIT	Div. Medit.	STEWARD	1734	19104034
MEDIT	Div. Medit.	PEARSE	1763	19104034
MEDITA	Div. Medita.	LEE	1751	19077012
MEDITAT	Rel. Meditat.	BRYSON	1778	19119015
MEDITATION	Meditation.	WAPLE	1720	19001002
MEDITATION	Meditation.	DAVIES	1720	19004004
MEDITATION	Meditation.	BURROUGHS	1733	19119011
MEDITATIONS	Meditations.	HUSSEY	1758	19019014
MEEK	Bless. Meek.	FARINDON	1674	43005005
MEEK	Bless. Meek.	LITTLETON	1680	43005005
MEEK	Bless. Meek.	HORNECK	1706	43005005
MEEK	Bless. Meek.	GARDINER	1720	43005005
MEEK	Bless. Meek.	BLACKALL	1723	43005004
MEEK	Bless. Meek.	EDWARDS	1726	43005005
MEEK	Bless. Meek.	COOKE	1739	43005005
MEEK	Bless. Meek.	BLAIR	1740	43005005
MEEK	Bless. Meek.	BUNDY	1740	43005005
MEEK	Bless. Meek.	GROVE	1742	43005005
MEEK	Bless. Meek.	WESTLEY	1748	43005005
MEEK	Bless. Meek.	COYTE	1761	43005005
MEEK	Bless. Meek.	ORR	1772	43005005
MEEK	Fem. Meek.	FORDYCE	1707	63003003
MEEK	H.& Meek.	ANONYMOUS	1776	43005003
MEEK	Meek.& Qui.	ORR	1749	63003004
MEEK	Wisd.meek.	BOSTON	1773	20014029
MEEKN	Xn. Meekn.	WHICHCOTE	1698	63003005
MEEKNESS	Meekness.	MEDE	1672	43011029
MEEKNESS	Meekness.	WILKINS	1682	20025015
MEEKNESS	Meekness.	HENRY	1726	63003004
MEEKNESS	Meekness.	HUNT	1748	43005005
MEEKNESS	Meekness.	JORTIN	1774	43005005
MEET	Mon.meet.	COCKRANE	1777	43010016
MEHOMETAN	Mehometan.	SCOTT	1743	65004001
MEL	Cure of mel.	BAXTER	1683	50002007
MEL	Relig. Mel.	NEWTON	1759	19042002
MELAN	Rel. Melan.	MOORE	1715	19042006
MELAN	Rel. Melan.	MOSS	1732	19042011
MELANC	Rel. Melanc.	CLARKE	1736	18006004
MELI	St. P.at Meli.	NEWTON	1782	47028001

INDEXES TO THIRD VOLUME: E: KEYWORD-IN-CONTEXT INDEX OF OTHER SUBJECTS OR OCCASIONS

Keyword	In its Context	Author	Year	BkChpVrs
MEM	Marin.mem.	REYNOLDS	1721	19107023
MEM	Sacr. Mem.	WILLISON	1761	02012014
MEN	Blast. Men.	WHICHCOTE	1702	19039011
MEN	Com.of Men	ROGERS	1736	43015009
MEN	Deg.of Men.	WHICHCOTE	1703	48001021
MEN	Degener.of Men	WHICHCOTE	1698	48001029
MEN	Degener.of Men	WHICHCOTE	1703	48001028
MEN	Excel. Men.	ROGERS	1735	20012026
MEN	Excel. Men.	ORR	1739	20012026
MEN	G. H. Men.	TILLOTSON	1735	19073025
MEN	Holy Men.	EMLYN	1742	45013029
MEN	Hon.all men	TRAPP	1752	63002017
MEN	Men offs. G.	HOLLAND	1753	47017028
MEN	Men G's.offs.	GOUGH	1751	47017028
MEN	Pleas. Men.	ADAMS	1716	51001010
MEN	Vicious Men	BRIGHT	1695	63004004
MEN	Wick. Men.	BRADY	1704	23057021
MEN	Y. Men.	WILCOX	1757	20023026
MEN	Y. Men.	WILCOX	1757	61003013
MENT	Ment. Indul.	GERARD	1782	24009003
MER	D.& H. Mer.	BRAILSFORD	1776	10024014
MER	Div.mer.ex.	CALAMY	1702	48009016
MER	G's pr. Mer.	HILL	1755	19059010
MER	G's.ch.mer.	MACLAURIN	1772	48008032
MER	Mer.f. X's E.	DEVEREL	1777	46008011
MER	Mer.of God.	TILLOTSON	1735	04014018
MER	Mer.of God.	HUNT	1748	04014019
MER	Mon.of Mer.	WHITAKER	1674	57001016
MER	Patt.of Mer.	CONYERS	1660	45006036
MER	Patt.of Mer.	CENNICK	1762	57001015
MER	Prer.of Mer.	ALLESTRE	1684	43009013
MER	Prov.of Mer.	PENTYCROSS	1781	23063005
MER	b. Brit. Mer.	GOLDWIN	1715	69018023
MERC	Bless.merc.	GARDINER	1720	43005007
MERC	Bless.merc.	BLACKALL	1723	43005007
MERC	Bless.merc.	EDWARDS	1726	43005007
MERC	Bless.merc.	COOKE	1739	43005007
MERC	Bless.merc.	BLAIR	1740	43005007
MERC	Bless.merc.	GROVE	1742	43005007
MERC	Merc. King.	BRAGGE	1702	43018023
MERC	Merc.of G.	SMITH	1762	02015001
MERCH	Spir. Merch.	JELINGER	1676	43013045
MERCH	Spir. Merch.	MEDLEY	1778	20003014
MERCH	b. Co.merch.	RAINSTORP	1684	10015021
MERCHANT	b. Merchant.	BRENT	1708	20003009
MERCIES	Brit. Mercies	WILLISON	1761	19147020
MERCIES	G's. Mercies	KIDDER	1697	47017028
MERCY	Abuse mercy	WILSON	1741	23005003
MERCY	G's mercy.	TAYLOR	1668	19086005
MERCY	G's mercy.	LEIGHTON	1746	23030015
MERCY	G's. Mercy.	TAYLOR	1668	48002004
MERCY	God's Mercy	HUSSEY	1758	45006036
MERCY	Mercy of G.	WHICHCOTE	1702	29002013
MERCY	Mercy of G.	GREGORY	1708	26033011
MERCY	Mercy of G.	WISHEART	1716	19062012
MERCY	Mercy of G.	NEWLIN	1720	19103004

Keyword	In its Context	Author	Year	BkChpVrs
MERCY	Mercy.	SEDGEWICK	1660	23055003
MERCY	Mercy.	DELANY	1754	45006036
MERCY	Pr.f. Mercy.	ERSKINE	1764	34003002
MERCY	Prev. Mercy.	BRINSLEY	1667	19021003
MERCY	Wor.mercy.	CATCOTT	1753	43025040
MERCY	of Mercy.	HORNECK	1706	43005007
MERCY	of Mercy.	NORRIS	1728	43005007
MERE	Mere Profes.	CLAGETT	1704	43007021
MERIT	Merit& Jus.	NEWMAN	1735	48004004
MERIT	Of Merit.	SOUTH	1727	18022002
MERITS	Merits of Xt.	HOADLY	1727	65002001
MES	Hum.st. Mes.	WEBB	1766	43002023
MES	N's mes.to D.	DE COURCY	1773	10012007
MESS	App.of Mess.	LAWSON	1764	45001078
MESS	Bapt. Mess.	STENNETT	1734	43011011
MESS	Bapt. Mess.	ECCLES	1755	43011002
MESS	Div. Mess.	DE COETLOGAN	1773	07003020
MESS	Gosp. Mess.	WARBURTON	1753	43010005
MESS	Gosp. Mess.	WARBURTON	1753	43010016
MESS	Jes. Mess.	TILLOTSON	1735	43011002
MESS	Mess. Xr.&c.	WARBURTON	1753	49001030
MESS	Mess.fm. D.	PAYNE	1698	45016031
MESS	Mess.foret.	BURTON	1764	23053001
MESS	Mess.foret.	FARQUAR	1772	23053003
MESS	Mess.of Cov.	HARRIS	1724	38003001
MESS	Off.of Mess.	CENNICK	1762	45004018
MESS	Pres. Mess.	TILLOTSON	1735	36002006
MESS	Prom. Mess.	WHICHCOTE	1698	47013023
MESS	Time Mess.	HARRIS	1724	27009026
MESS	Xt.tr. Mess.	FREE	1750	45007020
MESSIAH	Jes. Messiah.	BARROW	1716	46005037
MESSIAH	Jes. Messiah.	WEBB	1765	43027054
MESSIAS	Jes. Messias.	SHERLOCK	1719	45024025
MESSIAS	Jes. Messias.	BARROW	1716	47009022
METAM	Metam. Xna.	BEARE	1679	51006015
METH	Meth. Age.	PIGOTT	1762	01005027
METH	Meth.deceit	SMITH	1770	50004002
METH	Meth.do. A.	BLACKALL	1723	43006002
METH	Meth.do. A.	BLAIR	1740	43006002
METH	Meth.of Pre.	FIDDES	1720	43011005
METHOD	Ag. Method.	WILDER	1739	65004001
METHOD	Ag. Method.	BROWNSWORD	1749	43019020
METHOD	Ag. Method.	WHITE	1748	49014033
METHOD	Ag. Method.	POTTER	1758	46003005
METHOD	Ag. Method.	DODD	1759	52004003
METHOD	Ag. Method.	HELME	1762	61002003
METHOD	Ag Method.	LAND	1771	51005005
METHODISM	Methodism.	DOWNES	1761	47020028
METHODISM	Methodism.	DOWNES	1761	50004005
MI	Ab.of mi. G.	BULKLEY	1771	49011017
MI	Mi.f. D.o. G.	WILLIS	1720	53001017
MIC	Mic.&all- A.	MARSHALL	1731	61002005
MICH	Mich.d. Ang.	LITTLETON	1680	43018010
MICH	Mich.d. Ang.	PATRICK	1719	43018010
MICH	St. Mich.d.	MARSHALL	1731	49011010
MICH	St. Mich.day	PHILPOT	1663	46005007

Keyword	In its Context	Author	Year	BkChpVrs
MICH	St. Mich.day	STANHOPE	1715	43018001
MICH	St. Mich.day	HOLE	1716	43018001
MICH	St. Mich.day	STANHOPE	1715	69012007
MICH	St. Mich.day	HOLE	1716	69012007
MICH	St. Mich.day	LESTLEY	1721	69012007
MICHAELM	Michaelm.d.	STRADLING	1692	61001014
MID	Rel.mid. P.	BROWNE	1749	43011025
MIDD	Midd. Cond.	OAKEY	1683	20030008
MIDDL	Ag. Middl.	PARKER	1749	44016017
MIDDL	Ag. Middl.	JEPHSON	1750	44016017
MIDDLES	Middles. H.	YARDLEY	1749	45010037
MIDDLES	Middles. H.	FRANKLIN	1758	45010037
MIDDLES	Middles. H.	ASHTON	1770	58003004
MIDDLET	Ag. Middlet.	BAYLY	1751	61011004
MIL	Church mil.	NICOLSON	1661	22001005
MILLENIUM	Millenium.	HORT	1748	43006010
MILLENIUM	Millenium.	GREENHILL	1771	43009012
MILLENIUM	Millenium.	GREENHILL	1774	69020004
MIN	Coll.f. Min.	TRIMNELL	1711	48015013
MIN	Dig.of Min.	WALROND	1707	48011013
MIN	Dut.of Min.	HURRION	1721	61013017
MIN	Duty o. Min.	SCATTERGOOD	1723	57004016
MIN	Duty of Min.	GOODALL	1748	50006003
MIN	Duty of Min.	STUART	1753	50006003
MIN	Duty of Min.	WILSON	1781	50005010
MIN	Eff.fm. Min.	ST.	1757	43005015
MIN	Estab. Min.	BRADY	1713	48010014
MIN	Gosp. Min.	FLAVEL	1673	50005020
MIN	Gosp. Min.	BEVERIDGE	1720	50005020
MIN	Gosp. Min.	NEWTON	1780	52004015
MIN	Gosp. Min.d.	HARRIS	1710	45010016
MIN	Min. Angels.	WHEATLEY	1746	19091010
MIN	Min. Duty.	TAYLOR	1678	59002007
MIN	Min. Duty.	LOB.	1708	58002002
MIN	Min. Exhor.	GUYSE	1756	57004016
MIN	Min. Funct.	SCOUGAL	1726	50002016
MIN	Min. Funct.	ATTERBURY	1743	50002016
MIN	Min. Maint.	SYMPSON	1661	13012032
MIN	Min. Waters.	NICHOLS	1702	46005004
MIN	Min. Xrter.	CRAIG	1775	43005013
MIN	Min.be.est.	HICKES	1726	50003001
MIN	Min.n.g.off.	ERSKINE	1775	50006003
MIN	Min.o. Gosp.	CLAYTON	1776	49010033
MIN	Min.of Ang.	WILKINSON	1660	61001014
MIN	Min.pray.f.	EVANS	1723	55005025
MIN	Min.t.pr. G.	ANONYMOUS	1679	48001014
MIN	Res.to Min.	FRANCIS	1773	50004005
MIN	Settl. Min.	TOLLER	1772	45013030
MIN	Sobri. Min.	KENNET	1715	59002006
MIN	Stand. Min.	WILSON	1781	04006022
MIN	Success. Min.	SMITH	1716	48015029
MIN	Work o. Min.	ASH	1778	52004011
MIN	World-min.	HUNT	1748	65002015
MIN	World-min.	MASON	1758	65002015
MIN	World-min.	JORTIN	1774	65002015
MIN	Xt's. Min.	SAURIN	1775	48010021

Keyword	In its Context	Author	Year	BkChpVrs
MIND	A wor.mind.	DORRINGTON	1705	53003019
MIND	Cand.mind.	STURMY	1716	21007021
MIND	Carn.mind.	LEIGHTON	1746	48008007
MIND	Cult.o.mind	HUNT	1748	59002012
MIND	Dejec.mind.	WATERLAND	1742	20018014
MIND	Doub.mind.	SCOTT	1700	62001008
MIND	Doub.mind.	SMALRIDGE	1724	62004008
MIND	Hap.f.mind.	NEWMAN	1760	20014014
MIND	Heav.mind.	FARINGDON	1672	54003002
MIND	Heav.mind.	DORRINGTON	1703	54003002
MIND	Heav.mind.	FOORD	1719	54003002
MIND	Heav.mind.	BEVERIDGE	1720	54003002
MIND	Heav.mind.	NORRIS	1728	53003020
MIND	Heav.mind.	ALTHAM	1732	54003002
MIND	Heav.mind.	DORMAN	1743	54003002
MIND	Heav.mind.	FOTHERGILL	1765	54003002
MIND	Hon.mind.	WISHART	1733	46007017
MIND	Hon.mind.	WISHART	1733	46007013
MIND	Lev.o mind.	DOWNES	1761	52004014
MIND	Pea.of mind.	MACE	1751	48014022
MIND	Peace mind.	MACE	1751	48002012
MIND	Rel.fr.mind.	MARSHALL	1731	48002028
MIND	Sober-mind.	CALAMY	1717	59002006
MIND	Sober-mind.	DAVIS	1756	59002006
MIND	Spirit mind.	DAVIS	1756	48008006
MIND	Trou. Mind.	BINGHAM	1725	19103013
MIND	Virt.mind.	CLARKE	1734	27012010
MIND	Xt.mind. D.	COLMAN	1728	46013001
MINIS	Gosp. Minis.	DUCKINFIELD	1707	50002016
MINIS	Gosp. Minis.	KNOX	1768	48010005
MINIS	Minis. Office	GRIFFITH	1757	43010016
MINIS	Minis.office.	DUKE	1714	48010015
MINIS	Minis.virtue	TRAPP	1726	45006029
MINIS	Office Minis.	SIMPSON	1774	23062006
MINIST	Bapt. Minist.	HUNT	1748	43003001
MINIST	Con. Minist.	MAURICE	1719	59002015
MINIST	Dig. Minist.	SKELTON	1754	44010043
MINIST	Dut. Minist.	HODGES	1685	43005013
MINIST	Jos. Minist.	HUNTER	1774	01041046
MINIST	Minist. Duty	FULLWOOD	1673	57005017
MINIST	Minist. Joy.	MAY	1753	66000004
MINIST	Minist. Off.	ST.	1757	43005013
MINIST	Minist.duty.	NEWTON	1740	58002024
MINIST	Minist.instr.	LOBB	1712	47020026
MINIST	Minist.main.	REES	1728	49009014
MINIST	Minist.main.	SPRY	1741	49009014
MINIST	Minist.wt.	MEDE	1672	49004001
MINIST	Xn. Minist.	MOSS	1738	50004005
MINISTRY	Ministry.	CALAMY	1710	52004010
MINISTRY	Xn. Ministry	STILLINGFLEET	1760	49004001
MINISTRY	Xn. Ministry.	SUTTON	1718	49004001
MIR	Arg.fm. Mir.	JORTIN	1774	46011047
MIR	Credib. Mir.	RUTHERFORTH	1751	46020030
MIR	Mir. Cures.	STANHOPE	1715	43008001
MIR	Mir. Cures.	HOLE	1716	43008001
MIR	Mir. Pr.d. M.	SKELTON	1754	46005036

INDEXES TO THIRD VOLUME: E: KEYWORD-IN-CONTEXT INDEX OF OTHER SUBJECTS OR OCCASIONS

Keyword	In its Context	Author	Year	BkChpVrs
MIR	Mir. Pr.d. M.	POWELL	1776	46005036
MIR	Mir. Prop. G.	ATTERBURY	1730	23060022
MIR	Mir.consid.	MARKLAND	1729	43008027
MIR	Mir.or. Xt.r.	BOURN	1777	50002016
MIR	Mir.powers.	HIND	1755	49014023
MIR	Obj. Mir.ins.	POWELL	1776	47017032
MIR	Obser. Mir.	BULKLEY	1771	43004023
MIR	On Xt's. Mir.	CHANDLER	1769	46003002
MIR	Proof.b. Mir.	BULLOCK	1726	46015024
MIR	Vind. Mir.	BROOKES	1734	45007013
MIRACLES	Miracles.	GELL	1676	61002004
MIRACLES	Miracles.	BEVERLEY	1694	61002004
MIRACLES	Miracles.	ATTERBURY	1703	19072018
MIRACLES	Miracles.	BUERDSELL	1700	61002004
MIRACLES	Miracles.	ROGERS	1725	46010025
MIRACLES	Miracles.	BULLOCK	1726	46010037
MIRACLES	Miracles.	CONYBEARE	1721	61002004
MIRACLES	Miracles.	SUTTON	1730	45007021
MIRACLES	Miracles.	TILLOTSON	1735	61002004
MIRACLES	Miracles.	HODGE	1758	46005036
MIRACLES	Miracles.	HARVEST	1754	46018020
MIRACLES	Miracles.	SHERLOCK	1772	47002022
MIRACLES	On Miracles.	BRACKENRIDGE	1764	46003002
MIRACLES	Xt's Miracles	NEWTON	1782	46010024
MIS	Mis.of wick.	LANGHORNE	1773	23057020
MIS	Mis.of Sep.	STILLINGFLEET	1707	53003016
MIS	Mis.of Vice.	WEDDERSPOON	1733	24009005
MISAP	Misap. P. Ch.	WILSON	1768	41004001
MISAPP	Misapp. Cur.	GRIFFITH	1760	47017021
MISCH	Misch. Van.	FOSTER	1744	48001022
MISCHIEF	Mischief.	SYNGE	1720	21007017
MISER	Etern. Miser.	WISHEART	1716	19062012
MISER	Miser. Life.	DORRINGTON	1703	18005007
MISERY	Misery Man.	GALLY	1723	18005007
MISG	Misg. Zeal.	WAKE	1722	48010002
MISG	Misg. Zeal.	WARREN	1739	48010002
MISG	Misg. Zeal.	HOADLY	1754	48010002
MISL	Misl. Blindn.	JORTIN	1774	05027018
MISP	Misp.our aff.	REEVES	1713	58003004
MISS	Miss.of Past.	JOHNSON	1728	43009038
MISSION	Xt's.mission.	TOTTIE	1775	43011005
MIST	Mist.of Lot.	WILCOX	1757	01040036
MIST	Mist.princ.	WHALEY	1695	47026009
MISTAK	Mistak. Cens.	DOUGHTY	1761	47028004
MISTAK	Mistak. Cens.	DOWNES	1761	47028004
MITES	Wid.2 Mites.	WEBB	1772	45021001
MIX	Mix. Xter.	BOURN	1777	62001008
MN	Mn wout Xt.	BARNES	1752	53004013
MO	G's mo. Gov.	WARBURTON	1753	19144003
MO	Learn.& Mo.	MAINWARING	1780	53004012
MO	Mo.&pos. D.	CLARKE	1735	43022040
MO	Mo. Ag.o. G.	ABERNETHY	1743	69015004
MO	Reas. Mo.&c.	HARTE	1736	46014001
MO	Self. Den.& Mo	HORNECK	1706	43005029
MO	Self. Den.& Mo	BLACKALL	1723	43005029
MO	Self. Den.& Mo	BLAIR	1740	43005029

Keyword	In its Context	Author	Year	BkChpVrs
MO	Youth's mo.	D'COETLOGAN.	1777	21012001
MOCK	Fol mock.at Si	STILLINGFLEET	1707	20014009
MOCK	Fol mock.at Si	ROGERS	1730	20014009
MOCK	Fol mock.at Si	TRAPP	1752	20014009
MOCK	Fol.mock.at Si	DAVIES	1720	20014009
MOCK	Fol.mock.at Si	CLARKE	1734	20014009
MOCK	Mock.at Rel.	WARREN	1730	68000017
MOD	Mod. Fort.	FIDDES	1720	20030008
MOD	Mod. Passion.	FRANCIS	1773	20016032
MOD	Mod. Phar.	BISBIE	1683	43023015
MOD	Mod. Theo.	MARSH	1701	18038004
MOD	Vic. Mod.	COCKMAN	1750	44008038
MODER	Xn. Moder.	AUDLEY	1705	48012018
MODERATION	Moderation.	HOLMES	1661	53004005
MODERATION	Moderation.	HARWOOD	1662	53004005
MODERATION	Moderation.	PRICE	1663	53004005
MODERATION	Moderation.	SEIGNIOR	1670	53004005
MODERATION	Moderation.	HILL	1677	53004005
MODERATION	Moderation.	WILKINS	1682	53004005
MODERATION	Moderation.	BARKER	1697	53004005
MODERATION	Moderation.	BRADY	1704	53004005
MODERATION	Moderation.	KERSALL	1710	53004005
MODERATION	Moderation.	BRETT	1714	53004005
MODERATION	Moderation.	LENG	1715	53004005
MODERATION	Moderation.	SHERIDAN	1720	53004005
MODERATION	Moderation.	BAYLY	1721	53004005
MODERATION	Moderation.	HOLE	1725	53004005
MODERATION	Moderation.	STRAIGHT	1741	53004005
MODERATION	Moderation.	WATSON	1751	53004005
MODERATION	Moderation.	LARDNER	1769	53004009
MODERATION	Moderation.	SECKER	1771	53004005
MODESTY	Modesty&c.	HUNT	1748	53002003
MON	Love o. Mon.	BARNES	1752	57006010
MON	Mon. Maint.	BRUCE	1682	48013002
MON	Mon.b. East.	STANHOPE	1715	44014001
MON	Mon.essayed	BRENT	1728	21010019
MON	Mon.meet.	COCKRANE	1777	43010016
MON	Mon.of Mer.	WHITAKER	1674	57001016
MON	Y. M's Mon.	H.	1673	21011009
MON	Yout.mon.	GUYSE	1747	18013026
MOND	East. Mond.	STANHOPE	1715	45024013
MOND	East. Mond.	HOLE	1716	45024013
MOND	East. Mond.	STANHOPE	1715	47010034
MOND	East. Mond.	HOLE	1716	47010034
MOND	Mond.b. E.	STANHOPE	1715	23063001
MOND	Mond.b. E.	WARREN	1748	43011030
MOND	Whit. Mond.	STANHOPE	1714	47010034
MONEY	Use Money	WESTLEY	1771	45016009
MONM	Monm. Re.s.	WETENHAL	1686	63002017
MONOP	Monop. Cor.	DOWNES	1761	20011026
MONOP	Monop. Cor.	SAMPSON	1771	20011026
MOR	G's mor. Go.	BEARE	1710	19099001
MOR	G's mor. Go.	DUCHAL	1753	19098009
MOR	G's mor. Go.	DUCHAL	1765	19100003
MOR	Gos. Mor.	JONES	1741	53004008
MOR	Gos. Mor.	LARDNER	1751	53004008

Keyword	In its Context	Author	Year	BkChpVrs
MOR	Infl.sp. Mor.	FOSTER	1737	52005009
MOR	Lib.mor. Ag.	CLARKE	1734	46008032
MOR	Mor.&n. Ev.	FOSTER	1737	62001017
MOR	Mor.&p. D.	WHITBY	1720	43011030
MOR	Mor.&p. D.	MORRIS	1743	43012007
MOR	Mor.&p. D.	WESTON	1747	43012007
MOR	Mor.&pos.d.	WESTON	1747	43009013
MOR	Mor.&pos.d.	HUNT	1748	43009013
MOR	Mor. Cert.	SEED	1750	64001016
MOR	Mor. D.ab. P.	EMLYN	1742	43023023
MOR	Mor. Duties.	BURNET	1747	20015008
MOR	Mor. Evil.	AMORY	1766	19136001
MOR	Mor. Law.	BUERDSELL	1700	43006010
MOR	Mor. Law.	STENNETT	1732	43005008
MOR	Mor. Law.	WATTS	1753	48006023
MOR	Mor. Law.	WATTS	1753	65003004
MOR	Mor. Law.	ROMAINE	1760	48007012
MOR	Mor. Law.	PENTYCROSS	1781	48003019
MOR	Mor. Oblig.	HUNT	1748	23005020
MOR	Mor. Obliga.	HUNT	1748	32006008
MOR	Mor. P. Dut.	ROGERS	1736	43023023
MOR	Mor. Perf. G.	PRICE	1757	43005048
MOR	Mor. Perfec.	DUCHAL	1765	49003009
MOR	Mor. Qualif.	CLARKE	1734	47011024
MOR	Mor. Right.	LARDNER	1751	32006008
MOR	Mor. Virtue.	HALLYWELL	1692	53004008
MOR	Mor.b. P. L.	HICKES	1726	45011042
MOR	Mor.b. Rit.	MANTON	1708	43009013
MOR	Mor.1.of M.	BUESDSELL	1700	45010025
MOR	Mor.of Gos.	REAY	1755	44009040
MOR	Mor.p.o.rel.	WHICHCOTE	1703	59002012
MOR	Mor.subj.pr.	ENFIELD	1772	59003008
MOR	N. E.mor. G.	STEELE	1776	19126005
MOR	Perp.mor. L.	HORNECK	1706	43005018
MOR	Perp.mor. L.	BLACKALL	1723	43005019
MOR	Perp.mor. L.	BLAIR	1740	43005018
MOR	Pract.o.mor.	CLARKE	1734	46006044
MOR	Rel.& Mor.	HEYLYN	1749	32006008
MOR	Xt. Tea.mor.	DUCHAL	1753	43007025
MORAL	Moral Oblig.	HUNT	1748	59002012
MORAL	Xn. Moral.	FOSTER	1737	53004008
MORAL	Xn. Moral.	GOUGH	1751	53004008
MORALITY	Morality.	SEED	1743	54003023
MORALITY	Xn. Morality	WATTS	1753	53004008
MORD	H.& Mord.	THEED	1712	17005013
MORD	H.& Mord.	WHARTON	1728	17005013
MORE	More exc.w.	HUSSEY	1758	49012031
MORT	Inord. Mort.	BARNES	1752	54003005
MORT	Mort. Cattle.	BATES	1714	31004011
MORT	Mort.of Ch.	EATON	1764	18001018
MORT	Mort Sin&c.	HUBBARD	1757	52006013
MORT	Specu.mort.	TALBOT	1674	54003004
MORTAL	Mortal. Sins.	GREGORY	1708	65005016
MORTAL	Mortal.o. M.	HOPKINS	1710	61009027
MORTAL	Mortal.o. M.	FREE	1750	61009027
MORTALITY	Mortality.	CRUSO	1699	05034005

Keyword	In its Context	Author	Year	BkChpVrs
MORTALITY	Mortality.	WHITAKER	1712	47020032
MORTALITY	Mortality.	WILCOX	1757	19031004
MORTALITY	Mortality.	JORTIN	1774	19103015
MORTALITY	Mortality.	MARRIOTT	1771	48008010
MORTIF	Sens. Mortif.	ATKINSON	1775	54003005
MORTIFICAT	Mortificat.	FLAVEL	1673	51005024
MORTIFICAT	Mortificat.	CHARNOCK	1684	48008013
MORTIFICAT	Mortificat.	HOPKINS	1710	48008013
MOS	Mos.& Aar.	WOMOCK	1675	09024005
MOS	Mos. Prayer.	STERNE	1695	19090012
MOS	Xn.ab. Mos.	MICHELL	1737	61008006
MOS	Xt.like Mos.	COLMAN	1728	05008015
MOSES	L.of Moses	JORTIN	1774	19147019
MOSES	Xt.tr. Moses.	ERSKINE	1764	47007034
MOSES'	Moses' Petit.	KEELING	1767	02032031
MOSES'	Moses' Xter.	ENFIELD	1777	47007017
MOSES'S	Moses's self.	THEED	1712	61011024
MOT	Hagar's mot.	JENKINS	1779	01016013
MOT	L.of G. Mot. O	PIERCE	1679	46014015
MOT	L.of G. Mot. O	READING	1724	46014015
MOT	Mot.to Rep.	ELLIS	1704	45016031
MOT	Mot.to Virt.	BLAIR	1777	51006009
MOT	Tr. Mot. Ch.	ANONYMOUS	1688	47002041
MOTIVES	Xn. Motives.	WHICHCOTE	1698	53004008
MOUNT	Mount Ebal.	CULVERWELL	1661	07005023
MOUR	Mour.oth. S.	JENKINS	1683	64002007
MOUR	Tok.f.mour.	FLAVEL	1673	45007008
MOURN	Bless.mourn.	FARINDON	1672	43005004
MOURN	Bless.mourn.	ALLESTRE	1684	43005004
MOURN	Bless.mourn.	HORNECK	1706	43005004
MOURN	Bless.mourn.	BRAGGE	1713	43005004
MOURN	Bless.mourn.	LUCAS	1717	43005004
MOURN	Bless.mourn.	GARDINER	1720	43005004
MOURN	Bless.mourn.	BLACKALL	1723	43005004
MOURN	Bless.mourn.	EDWARDS	1726	43005004
MOURN	Bless.mourn.	NORRIS	1728	43005004
MOURN	Bless.mourn.	COOKE	1739	43005004
MOURN	Bless.mourn.	BLAIR	1740	43005004
MOURN	Bless.mourn.	GROVE	1742	43005004
MOURN	Bless.mourn.	ORR	1772	43005004
MP	Evil Co mp.	LAWSON	1764	20001015
MS	Peace of Ms	SCOTT	1700	46014027
MSELF	G.rev.mself.	CARR	1777	57002004
MU	Mu. Subject.	SWIFT	1744	63005005
MUCH	Talk.much.	DAWES	1733	20010019
MUR	Mur.repro.	HOPKINS	1689	49010010
MUR	Rape& Mur.	COLEIRE	1723	07019030
MURD	On a Murd.	FAWCETT	1764	10003034
MURDER	Murder.	BULKLEY	1761	65003015
MURDER	Of Murder.	LUPTON	1729	02020013
MURDER	Of Murder.	CLARKE	1736	02021014
MURDER	Of Murder.	STERNE	1769	02021014
MURMURING	Murmuring	FISHER	1741	21007010
MURMURING	Murmuring.	PATRICK	1689	49010010
MURMURING	Murmuring.	BRADFORD	1715	49010010
MUSTARD	Mustard seed	BRAGGE	1704	43013031

INDEXES TO THIRD VOLUME: E: KEYWORD-IN-CONTEXT INDEX OF OTHER SUBJECTS OR OCCASIONS

Keyword	In its Context	Author	Year	BkChpVrs
MUSTARD	Mustard seed	BOURN	1763	43013031
MUSTARD	Mustard seed	BULKLEY	1771	43013031
MUT	Mut. Edific.	ABERNETHY	1748	48015002
MUT	Mut. Eq.&h.	BOURN	1777	43007012
MUT	Mut. Exhor.	WAPLE	1718	61010025
MUT	Mut. Love.	PIERCE	1679	46013035
MUT	Mut. Love.	FRANKLYN	1724	48013008
MUT	Mut. Love.	MORRIS	1743	46013035
MUT	Mut. Love.	TIDCOMBE	1757	52005002
MUTINY	Mutiny.	RAMSEY	1781	04016012
MUTUAL	Mutual Love	CLARKE	1727	65004007
MUTUAL	Mutual Love	WELCH	1752	65004007
MYS	D. Prov.mys.	HOWE	1771	46013007
MYS	Mys o. Godl.	M'GEORGE	1727	57003016
MYS	Mys.o. Godl.	BRADBURY	1726	57003015
MYS	Mys.o. Godl.	LARDNER	1760	57003016
MYS	Mys.of Prov.	FLAVEL	1673	19057002
MYS	Xt.hid. Mys.	HARTLEY	1754	54001026
MYST	Gosp. Myst.	TAYLOR	1719	43013011
MYST	Myst.cred.	SMITH	1675	57003016
MYST	Myst.cred.	WHEATLY	1746	57003016
MYST	Myst.of Gos.	PACK	1691	48009005
MYST	Myst.of Rel.	CARR	1777	64003016
MYST	Myst.of Xty.	STILLINGFLEET	1707	57001015
MYST	Xt's.myst.c.	DODDERIDGE	1761	46008007
MYST	Xty a Myst.	BENSON	1748	52006019
MYSTER	Xn. Myster.	TERRY	1746	43013011
MYSTERIES	Mysteries.	WARD	1673	48001016
MYSTERIES	Mysteries.	EDWARDS	1698	57003016
MYSTERIES	Mysteries.	CONYBEARE	1723	49013012
MYSTERIES	Mysteries.	LITTLETON	1735	05029029
MYSTERIES	Mysteries.	HARVEST	1753	46003009
MYSTERIES	Mysteries.	REAY	1755	05029029
MYSTERIES	of Mysteries.	BAKER	1728	02033021
N	A. O.& N. T.	GILL	1773	47026022
N	Ag.n. Proph.	CALAMY	1708	24014004
N	All N.wine.	SPOONER	1771	43009017
N	At N.mark.	ANONYMOUS	1774	19045005
N	B. R.n. M. S.	ANONYMOUS	1735	56002001
N	Bapt.into N.o.	PIERCE	1718	49001013
N	Bapt.into N.o.	CLARKE	1734	49001013
N	Bel.n.to Bap.	CLARKE	1734	44016016
N	C.o. O.&n.t.	KNOX	1768	46005039
N	Conf.fash. N.	CARR	1777	48012002
N	Corr.o. H. N.	HAWEIS	1762	48005018
N	Cre.of N. T.	LARDNER	1769	64001015
N	D.all Xt's. N.	WILKINSON	1676	54003017
N	Draw.n. G.	EATON	1764	19073028
N	E.& N.o. Ch.	HOLE	1725	49013001
N	Ev.o. T.n.sc.	SMYTH	1717	58001010
N	Fai.&it's N.	FEUILLERADE	1717	51005006
N	Fai.n.to Sal.	CLAGETT	1704	61011006
N	Fai.n.to Sal.	HOPKINS	1708	47016031
N	Fear n.to Fai.	PIERCE	1679	49010012
N	Fu. St.n.t. H.	CONYBEARE	1757	49015019
N	G.n.arbitra.	FOSTER	1732	48009020

Keyword	In its Context	Author	Year	BkChpVrs
N	G.tempts n.	BERRIMAN	1763	62001013
N	G's. Co.n.gr.	DUNLOP	1722	65005003
N	G's. Co.n.gr.	BRADY	1730	65005003
N	Good wks.n.	TILLOTSON	1735	59003008
N	Gosp.n. Cre.	PALMER	1674	19025011
N	Gosp.n. Cre.	STRONG	1678	19025011
N	H. N.deprav.	MARRIOTT	1774	19051005
N	H.to G's N.	SKELTON	1754	03019030
N	Hea.n.in all.	BAINE	1778	49006009
N	In th.&n. W.	LITTLETON	1735	54003002
N	In. O.& N. T.	CALAMY	1710	64001021
N	Insuf.o. N. R.	TAYLOR	1732	49011014
N	Kn. G.l.o. N.	WATTS	1753	47014015
N	L.of G.& N.	WILSON	1781	44012032
N	L's. S.n. Cov.	CHANDLER	1769	49011025
N	Light of N.	CULVERWELL	1661	20020027
N	Lo.of G.& N.	HOLE	1716	43022034
N	Love G.& N.	COCK	1710	43022035
N	Love G.& N.	CARLETON	1736	45010027
N	M.no.n.nec.	FIDDES	1720	64003003
N	M's. Sins n.c.	MACLAURIN	1772	62001013
N	Marks n.b.	WHITFIELD	1739	47019005
N	Min.n.g.off.	ERSKINE	1775	50006003
N	Mor.&n. Ev.	FOSTER	1737	62001017
N	N.& D. Con.	CRAIG	1775	10012017
N	N.& P.of Ch.	CONANT	1703	49013004
N	N.& P.of Ch.	CROSSINGE	1722	49013004
N	N.& P.of Ch.	HOLE	1725	49013004
N	N.& R. Rel.	TUNSTALL	1759	03018004
N	N.& R. Rel.	UMFREVILLE	1759	47004012
N	N.& Use. Pr.	FOSTER	1744	43006006
N	N.&off.o. A.	TILLOTSON	1735	61001014
N	N.&off.o. A.	WHEATLY	1746	61001014
N	N. Desi.of L.	SMITH	1777	18042016
N	N. E.mor. G.	STEELE	1776	19126005
N	N. Eng. Dut.	NOYES	1698	24031023
N	N. Part.in S.	CLARKSON	1696	52005007
N	N. W.m.t. V.	ENFIELD	1772	43005014
N	N. Yr's. Gift.	DAVIES	1771	48013012
N	N.call.unc.	ANONYMOUS	1756	26033011
N	N.conf.t. W.	S.	1695	48012002
N	N.conf.t. W.	ERSKINE	1764	48012002
N	N.of Friend.	HORNE	1769	19055012
N	N.5.	REYNOLDS	1678	19129001
N	N.5.	PERSE	1689	19129001
N	N.5.	DAWES	1733	19129001
N	N.5.	MEADOWCOURT	1746	19129001
N	N.5.& Th.s.	WRIGHT	1710	46015012
N	N.5.b.	VENN	1778	62003017
N	Nat.& N.of Abs	HOLE	1716	46020023
N	Nat.& N.of Abs	BINGHAM	1726	46020023
N	O.& N. Test.	KNOX	1768	50004004
N	O.& N. Test.	KNOX	1768	64002001
N	O.& N. Test.	KNOX	1768	68000003
N	O. Rel.to N.	DUCHAL	1765	18038007
N	Old w.e.n. C.	PITTIS	1682	65002024

Keyword	In its Context	Author	Year	BkChpVrs
N	Old&n. M.	BOSTON	1753	48006006
N	Old&n. M.	SECKER	1770	48006021
N	Old&n. M.	SHERLOCK	1772	48006021
N	Pr. Xt's. N.	BEVERIDGE	1720	46014014
N	Pr.in Xt's. N.	KILLIGREW	1685	46016023
N	Pr.in Xt's. N.	SCOTT.	1743	46016023
N	Pr.in Xt's. N.	WESTON	1747	46016023
N	Pr.in Xt's. N.	LARDNER	1760	46016024
N	Pr.in Xt's. N.	BOSTON	1775	46016023
N	Pre. Xy.n.gr.	TILLOTSON	1735	65005003
N	Prof. G's N.	CARR	1777	03019012
N	Prot.p.n.sec.	FRANCIS	1773	48008031
N	R. N. G.& R.	COCKBURN	1708	61012012
N	R.due G's N.	SMALBROKE	1722	03019030
N	Rel.o.th.n.	HORTON	1679	45010042
N	Rel.o.th.n.	BEVERIDGE	1720	45010042
N	Rel.o.th.n.	GROVE	1742	45010042
N	Si.& M.b. N.	ENGLAND	1700	52002001
N	Sou. D.n.ce.	CASE	1774	58004003
N	Sp.&n.food.	BEVERIDGE	1720	46006027
N	Sup.f.our N.	WILLISON	1761	53004019
N	T.t. S.n.f. G.	SHARP	1734	62001013
N	T.t. S.n.f. G.	BURNET	1747	62001013
N	T.t. S.n.f. G.	ABERNETHY	1751	62001013
N	Tak. N.york.	OBERNE	1776	24013015
N	Tr. Xt.n.ne.	ERSKINE	1764	61013018
N	W. Xns.n. Ar.a	CLARKE	1736	51002017
N	W. Xns.n. Ar.a	GROVE	1741	51002017
N	Why n. Crea.	BARNES	1752	50005017
N	Xn.n.ash. G.	ENFIELD	1772	48002016
N	Xnty.n.incr.	SKELTON	1754	46017015
N	Xt.red.n. A.	COLMAN	1728	61002016
N	Xt's. R.& N.	PATTEN	1759	54002008
N	Xt's K.n.t.w.	GREENHILL	1768	46018036
N'S	N's mes.to D.	DE COURCY	1773	10012007
N'S	Wid. N's.son	BRAGGE	1702	45007011
N'S	Wid. N's.son	HOLE	1716	45007011
N'S	Wid. N's.son.	DODD	1757	45007012
N'S	Wid. N's.son.	CENNICK	1762	45007013
NA	Do all in Na.o	BARROW	1716	54003017
NA	Do all in Na.o	BEVERIDGE	1720	54003017
NA	Hum. Na. C.	WEBB	1772	05032005
NA	Imp. Xn. Na.	CROWE	1744	58002019
NA	Na. Jes.& Xt.	NEWTON	1782	45002021
NA	Na.of Hell.	MEDE	1672	20021016
NA	Pre.hum.na.	SNAPE	1745	61002007
NABAL	Nabal.	GOUGH	1751	09025025
NAME	G's g. Name.	ERSKINE	1764	19106008
NAME	God's name.	DAVIES	1766	02033018
NAME	Good Name.	MARKLAND	1729	21002016
NAME	Good Name.	CONEY	1750	20022001
NAME	Name in hea.	MANTON	1708	45009057
NAME	Name of G.	MEDE	1672	43006009
NAME	Name of G.	MEDE	1672	45011002
NAME	Name of G.	MOSS	1732	43006009
NAME	Name Jesus.	GROSVENOR	1724	43001021

Keyword	In its Context	Author	Year	BkChpVrs
NAME	Xn. Name.	GROSVENOR	1728	47011026
NAME	Xn. Name.	LITTLETON	1735	49001001
NAME	Xn. Name.	NEWTON	1760	47011026
NAME	Xn. Name.	BREKELL	1765	62002007
NAME	Xn. Name.	DAVIES	1766	47011026
NAME	Xt's. Name.	VINK	1675	45006022
NAMES	Names in H.	DAVIES	1771	45010020
NAMES	Names of Xt.	BOSTON	1753	23009006
NAT	Course Nat.	OGDEN	1770	47017027
NAT	Des.all Nat.	HARRIS	1724	36002006
NAT	Desp. L.nat.	HAMMOND	1684	48001026
NAT	Dign. H.nat.	BOURN	1777	19008005
NAT	G.&nat.per.	GUYSE	1757	46004024
NAT	Gos. La. Nat.	BULLOCK	1728	43021033
NAT	H. Nat.vind.	STERNE	1760	48014007
NAT	Hu.nat. Xt.	DAWSON	1765	57002005
NAT	Hum. Nat.	DORINGTON	1705	19100003
NAT	Inf. H. Nat.	CONYBEARE	1757	43025005
NAT	Integ.h.nat.	HOLDEN	1755	21007029
NAT	Lib.hu.nat.	LAMBE	1681	49006012
NAT	M's nat. St.	BOSTON	1773	19051005
NAT	M's nat. Sta.	WATKINS	1676	52002003
NAT	Mea. H. Nat.	BOURN	1777	19144003
NAT	Nat.& Grace	YOUNG	1706	43026035
NAT	Nat.& Grace	ANONYMOUS	1711	50005017
NAT	Nat.& In. R.	LAW	1768	32006008
NAT	Nat.& N.of Abs	HOLE	1716	46020023
NAT	Nat.& N.of Abs	BINGHAM	1726	46020023
NAT	Nat.& R. Rel.	TILLOTSON	1735	43009013
NAT	Nat.& R.rel.	BREKELL	1765	48002014
NAT	Nat.&m. Inf.	SPARKE	1745	62001027
NAT	Nat.&sp. P.	DRAKE	1677	48007023
NAT	Nat. Deliv.	BULKLEY	1761	19044001
NAT	Nat. Divis.	PORTER	1768	44003024
NAT	Nat. Evil.	AMORY	1766	62001013
NAT	Nat. G's. K.	CLARKE	1735	48014017
NAT	Nat. G's. K.	FOSTER	1737	48014017
NAT	Nat. G's. K.	ABERNETHY	1751	48014017
NAT	Nat. Iniq.	BRODBURST	1733	23001004
NAT	Nat. Judgm.	MOIR	1759	24009009
NAT	Nat. R.& Xn.	MARSHALL	1750	64001008
NAT	Nat. Relig.	SOUTH	1727	48001020
NAT	Nat. Relig.	TILLOTSON	1735	32006006
NAT	Nat. Relig.	SCOTT	1743	19051005
NAT	Nat. Relig.	SCOTT	1743	48002014
NAT	Nat. Relig.	DUCHAL	1765	47017028
NAT	Nat. Rep.	KNAGGS	1707	44006012
NAT	Nat. Rev. R.	HEYLIN	1749	18036002
NAT	Nat. Truth.	MEADOWCOURT	1724	46017017
NAT	Nat. Xt's. Bl.	HOADLY	1754	47003026
NAT	Nat.dis.b. Goo	STRADLING	1692	23005020
NAT	Nat.dis.b. Goo	SOUTH	1727	23005020
NAT	Nat.dis.b. Goo	MOSS	1732	23005020
NAT	Nat.dis.b. Goo	STEPHENS	1737	23005020
NAT	Nat.dis.b. Goo	ORR	1749	23005020
NAT	Nat.m.dead.	USHER	1678	25005016

Keyword	In its Context	Author	Year	BkChpVrs
NAT	Nat.m.dead.	USHER	1678	48006023
NAT	Nat.m.dead.	USHER	1678	51003022
NAT	Nat.o. Hope.	JOHNSON	1740	65003003
NAT	Nat.of truth.	STENNETT	1732	20023023
NAT	Nat.of Atte.	SMITH	1740	61002001
NAT	Nat.of Faith	CLARKE	1735	46020029
NAT	Nat.of Faith.	TRAPP	1722	48004003
NAT	Nat.of Faith.	HOLDEN	1755	43016015
NAT	Nat.of Faith.	WITHERSPOON	1768	65003023
NAT	Nat.of G.	JOHNSON	1728	46004024
NAT	Nat.of G.	JORTIN	1774	46004024
NAT	Nat.of Hol.	HAWEIS	1762	52002010
NAT	Nat.of Just.	WEBSTER	1754	43005006
NAT	Nat.of Oath.	BULLOCK	1723	43005033
NAT	Nat.of Rel.	WEST	1762	47019034
NAT	Nat.of Relig.	STENNETT	1769	49004020
NAT	Nat.of Sac.	CHANDLER	1769	49011023
NAT	Nat.of Sin.	BATTY	1739	65003004
NAT	Nat.of Sin.	BURNET	1747	48006012
NAT	Nat.of Tr.	PARKER	1754	46018038
NAT	Nat.of Tr.	PEARCE	1779	46018038
NAT	Nat.of Xy.	SECKER	1770	62001027
NAT	Nat.pr.p. Pr.	HUNTER	1774	49015041
NAT	Nat.wicked.	SEED	1750	23005004
NAT	R.& Nat. R.	MAYNARD	1722	19147020
NAT	Sin. St. Nat.	RILAND	1775	26033001
NAT	Soc.nat.o. M.	BUTLER	1749	48012004
NAT	True nat. E.	DOWNES	1761	06007012
NAT	True Nat. S.	CUDWORTH	1670	49015057
NAT	2 Nat.in Xt.	SALMON	1753	46001014
NATH	Nath. Par.	GOUGH	1751	10012007
NATH	Nath.repr.	TIDCOMBE	1757	10012007
NATIV	Xt's. Nativ.	ATKINSON	1775	65004010
NATIV	Xt's Nativ.	COWPER	1773	43001022
NATUR	Hum. Natur.	DUCHAL	1765	19034015
NATUR	Natur. Rel.	REAY	1755	49001021
NATURE	Div. Nature.	STURMY	1716	64001004
NATURE	Hum.nature	BUTLER	1749	48002014
NATURE	Nature of G.	ANONYMOUS	1776	18011007
NATURE	W.of Nature	TOTTIE	1775	43006028
NE	Ne.o Xt's. P.	FLAVEL	1673	61009023
NE	No ne. Com.	SECKER	1770	65002007
NE	Pos.& Ne. G.	ELSMERE	1767	23001016
NE	Test.ne.f. M.	SKELTON	1754	58001013
NE	Tr. Xt.n.ne.	ERSKINE	1764	61013018
NEB.'S	Neb.'s Dissr.	ORTON	1776	27004033
NEC	Ab.not nec.	ROE	1766	45012015
NEC	Go.wor.nec.	BULL	1713	28010012
NEC	Hol.nec.to S.	BENSON	1748	61012014
NEC	M.no.n.nec.	FIDDES	1720	64003003
NEC	Nec. Grace.	TILLOTSON	1735	46015005
NEC	Nec. Xn's w.	BOSTON	1773	21009010
NEC	Nec. Xt's. D.	DAVIS	1756	46011051
NEC	Nec.o. Righ.	IBBOT	1726	65003002
NEC	Nec.o. Righ.	MICHELL	1737	65003002
NEC	Nec.o. Righ.	SCOTT	1743	57006011

Keyword	In its Context	Author	Year	BkChpVrs
NEC	Nec.o. Subj.	WALKER	1684	48013001
NEC	Nec.o.tr. Re.	ELSMERE	1767	46009004
NEC	Nec.of D.t.	ROMAINE	1760	46006045
NEC	Nec.of Fai.	DELAUNE	1728	52004005
NEC	Nec.of Her.	ANONYMOUS	1688	49002009
NEC	Nec.of Her.	TAYLOR	1719	49011019
NEC	Nec.of Her.	WARREN	1739	49011019
NEC	Nec.of Her.	WHEATLY	1746	49011019
NEC	Nec.of Her.	TURTON	1749	49011019
NEC	Nec.of Her.	STEBBING	1760	49011019
NEC	Nec.of Her.	WARBURTON	1767	49011019
NEC	Nec.of Hol.	CLARKE	1735	61012014
NEC	Nec.of Pray.	HALES	1673	45018001
NEC	Nec.of Pray.	REEVES	1729	45018001
NEC	Nec.of Pray.	SHARP	1729	45018001
NEC	Nec.of Pray.	SKEELER	1772	45018001
NEC	Nec.of Pray.	GILL	1773	23054007
NEC	Nec.of Rel.	REEVES	1729	61012002
NEC	Nec.of Rep.	DAVIES	1771	47017030
NEC	Nec.of S.f. S.	GILL	1773	61002010
NEC	R.nec.to c. S.	SKELTON	1754	63002017
NEC	Xt's.suf.nec.	SHEPHERD	1748	45024046
NECES	Heres.neces.	BALLARD	1733	49011019
NECES	Neces. Obed.	ELSMERE	1767	43010022
NECES	Neces. R Pr.	BURNABY	1777	19111010
NECES	Neces.of O.	GARDINER	1720	43007021
NECES	Neces.of O.	WESTLEY	1750	43007021
NECES	Neces.of Ob.	HOLE	1717	43007021
NECES	Neces.of Ob.	FOORD	1719	43007021
NECES	Neces.of R.	DODDERIDGE	1742	46003003
NECES	Pract.neces.	TILLOTSON	1735	45012047
NECES	Revel.neces.	ROGERS	1729	61001001
NECESS	Bapt.necess.	BEVERIDGE	1720	46003005
NECESS	Bel.necess.	SNAPE	1745	46020031
NECESS	Necess. Bapt.	UMFREVILLE	1739	44016016
NECESS	Necess. Rep.	GREGORY	1708	47026020
NECESS	Necess. Rep.	WROUGHTON	1728	47020021
NECESS	Necess. Rep.	TILLOTSON	1735	47020021
NECESS	Necess. Rep.	BARNES	1752	23055007
NECESS	Necess. Rep.	SKELTON	1754	23055006
NECESS	Necess.of D.	BLACKLOCK	1776	12020001
NECESS	O.th.necess.	DELAUNE	1728	43006033
NECESS	Pract.necess.	PEARSON	1718	43007020
NECESS	Test.necess.	LOVE	1754	58002001
NEED	Need Revel.	CONYBEARE	1757	45001078
NEED	T.of Need.	ERSHINE	1764	26016008
NEEDF	O.th.needf.	WEBSTER	1753	45010042
NEEDF	O.th.needf.	MORRIS	1757	45010041
NEEDF	O.th.needf.	DODDERIDGE	1761	45010041
NEEDF	O.th.needf.	DAVIES	1766	45010041
NEEDF	O.th.needf.	HUNTER	1774	45010041
NEEDF	O.th.needf.	CRAIG	1775	45010041
NEEDL	Needl. Cur.	GODDARD	1781	46021022
NEG	Dan.neg. Sa.	QUINCY	1750	61002003
NEG	Dan.neg.rel.	STILLINGFLEET	1707	61002003
NEG	Neg. G's. Sal.	ROE	1766	61002003

Keyword	In its Context	Author	Year	BkChpVrs
NEG	Neg.of F. W.	ORTON	1769	24010025
NEG	Neg.of P. W.	TOULMIN	1770	16013011
NEGL	Negl. Gosp.	MARSH	1737	43022012
NEGL	Negl. L. Sup.	ELSMERE	1767	45014018
NEGL	Negl. R. Dut.	NEWCOME	1702	45014018
NEGL	Negl. R. Dut.	MARSH	1737	45014018
NEGL	Negl. R Dut.	DAVIES	1720	45014018
NEGL	Negl. Sal.da.	CONANT	1698	61002003
NEGL	Negl.of Xt.	WHITFIELD	1771	46005040
NEIG	Dut.to Neig.	BLAIR	1740	43007012
NEIGH	Duty Neigh.	ADEY	1760	43022039
NEIGH	Duty Neigh.	SHERLOCK	1772	43022040
NEIGH	G. E. Neigh.	ANONYMOUS	1776	43005016
NEIGH	Hom. Neigh.	BURNET	1713	43022039
NEIGH	Judg. Neigh.	PETERS	1776	62004012
NEIGH	Love Neigh.	GELL	1676	43022039
NEIGH	Love Neigh.	MILWARD	1676	43022039
NEIGH	Love Neigh.	KILLIGREW	1685	43022040
NEIGH	Love Neigh.	NEWCOME	1702	43022039
NEIGH	Love Neigh.	EDWARDS	1713	43022039
NEIGH	Love Neigh.	HOLE	1715	43022039
NEIGH	Love Neigh.	BARROW	1716	43022039
NEIGH	Love Neigh.	HOLE	1716	45010023
NEIGH	Love Neigh.	KILLINBECK	1717	43022039
NEIGH	Love Neigh.	BOYSE	1728	43022039
NEIGH	Love Neigh.	ALTHAM	1732	43022037
NEIGH	Love Neigh.	BLACKALL	1733	43005043
NEIGH	Love Neigh.	EVANS	1737	43022039
NEIGH	Love Neigh.	WATERLAND	1742	43022039
NEIGH	Love Neigh.	BUTLER	1749	48013009
NEIGH	Love Neigh.	NEAL	1757	46013034
NEIGH	Love Neigh.	HUSSEY	1758	43022039
NEIGH	Love Neigh.	MOTTERSHEAD	1759	43022039
NEIGH	Love Neigh.	SECKER	1770	43022039
NEIGH	Love Neigh.	PETERS	1776	43012036
NEIGH	Love Neigh.	PETERS	1776	43022039
NET	Net.	BOURN	1763	43013047
NEW	New Birth or R	BYAM	1675	46003005
NEW	New Birth or R	HOPKINS	1710	46003005
NEW	New Birth or R	HOLE	1715	46003005
NEW	New Birth or R	LAMBE	1717	46003005
NEW	New Birth or R	HOLE	1719	46003005
NEW	New Birth or R	FARINGTON	1741	46003005
NEW	New Birth or R	JONES	1756	46003005
NEW	New Birth.	BATTY	1739	46003008
NEW	New Birth.	STEPHENS	1737	65003009
NEW	New Birth.	SIMONS	1743	65003009
NEW	New Birth.	REAY	1755	46003007
NEW	New Birth.	WESTLEY	1771	46003007
NEW	New Birth.	WILSON	1781	46003007
NEW	New Chapl.	KENNET	1715	49003006
NEW	New Cr.or b.	HAMMOND	1684	51006015
NEW	New Cr.or b.	IBBOT	1726	51006015
NEW	New Cr.or b.	STEBBING	1739	51006015
NEW	New Creat.	FLAVEL	1673	50005017
NEW	New Creat.	CLARKSON	1696	51006015
NEW	New Creat.	BEVERIDGE	1720	52002010
NEW	New Creat.	GARNET	1739	51006015
NEW	New Creat.	SMITH	1753	51006015
NEW	New Creat.	STANTON	1758	50005017
NEW	New Style.	LLOYD	1753	01001014
NEW	T.new Song.	COLMAN	1728	69005009
NEWG	At Newg.ch.	FORSTER	1777	47009011
NEWS	G. News f. H	TOPLADY	1774	19089012
NEWS	G. News G.	ROWLAND	1774	43002008
NEWS	News.	HURST	1690	47017021
NIG	No Nig. Hea.	WATTS	1753	69021025
NIN	Nin.of Rec.	HERVEY	1759	50005018
NO	Ab.no Happ.	NEWMAN	1760	45012015
NO	G.no res. P.	MOORE	1716	47010034
NO	G.no res. P.	IBBOT	1726	47010034
NO	G.no res. P.	MUNTON	1756	47010034
NO	G.no res. P.	HUSSEY	1758	47010034
NO	G.no resp.of P	BARROW	1716	48002011
NO	G.no resp.of P	FOSTER	1744	48002011
NO	G.no R.o. P.	PYLE	1777	63001017
NO	Giv.no Off.	QUINCY	1750	49010032
NO	Godl.no fan.	ANONYMOUS	1683	63003015
NO	Godl.no Fan.	VEALE	1683	63003015
NO	Kgs.no.s. P.	HURST	1675	47026002
NO	M.no.n.nec.	FIDDES	1720	64003003
NO	No acc.by F.	ALLEN	1761	62002014
NO	No con.city.	STEBBING	1760	61013014
NO	No ne. Com.	SECKER	1770	65002007
NO	No per. H.h.	JOHNSON	1740	61011039
NO	No perf.in L.	WHITTY	1772	62003002
NO	No s. G.& M.	HOADLY	1754	45016013
NO	No serv.t. M.	FAWCETT	1749	43006024
NO	No ven. Sin.	JENKINS	1675	48006023
NO	No. Sins ven.	SMALRIDGE	1724	65003006
NO	No. Tr.in R.	WARNEFORD	1757	57006017
NO	No Ex.f.fall.	ROGERS	1735	49010012
NO	No Glorying	BULL	1713	24009023
NO	No Happ.h.	MASON	1758	32002010
NO	No M Mast.	BURTON	1685	43023008
NO	No Mass&c.	SHARP	1735	49011023
NO	No Nig. Hea.	WATTS	1753	69021025
NO	No Pain a bl.	WATTS	1753	69021004
NO	No Secrecy.	DELAUNE	1728	20005021
NO	No Tr.in R.	JONES	1690	57006017
NO	No Tr.in R.	GALE	1726	57006017
NO	No Tr.in R.	MARSHALL	1731	57006017
NO	No Transub.	LAWRENCE	1675	49011023
NO	Pleas.no H.	NEWMAN	1760	21002001
NO	Prof.no Sec.	BULKLEY	1752	43003009
NO	Rid.no f. Tr.	GODDARD	1781	21002002
NO	Spir.no resp.	CROOKE	1755	23029011
NO	no Peace to wic	HORTON	1679	23057021
NO	no Peace to wic	FOORD	1719	23057021
NOAH	Rev.o. Noah.	SCOTT	1743	61011007
NOAH	on Noah.	HACKET	1675	01008020
NOAH	on Noah.	HACKET	1675	01008021

INDEXES TO THIRD VOLUME: E: KEYWORD-IN-CONTEXT INDEX OF OTHER SUBJECTS OR OCCASIONS

Keyword	In its Context	Author	Year	BkChpVrs
NOAH'S	Noah's Ark.	WILLISON	1761	61011007
NOAH'S	Noah's Ark.	JENKINS	1779	01007016
NOAH'S	Noah's Xter.	MURRAY	1777	01008015
NOBIL	True Nobil.	WHISTON	1661	47017011
NOBLE	Noble Conv.	HORNE	1778	47008024
NOC	Noc.of Pur.	BROWNE	1749	62003017
NOMIN	Nomin. Xns.	WILCOX	1757	69003001
NOT	Ab.not nec.	ROE	1766	45012015
NOT	Cal.not Jud.	LLOYD	1765	46009001
NOT	Ev.th.not s.	SMITH	1717	45016019
NOT	G.not A.of S.	STEPHENS	1737	23045007
NOT	Immor. Not.	HOLDEN	1755	43015013
NOT	In Xt.or not.	FAWCETT	1757	50005017
NOT	Judge not.	HEYLIN	1761	43007001
NOT	Not ans.an.	SEATON	1720	59002009
NOT	Not as.o. G.	HARTLEY	1754	48001016
NOT	Not as.o. G.	SHIRLEY	1762	48001016
NOT	Not.lov. Xt.	WILSON	1781	49016022
NOT	Not.of Rep.	FARINGTON	1741	47003019
NOT	Not.t.b. Off.	HEYLYN	1749	43011004
NOT	R. Not.of G.	HUNT	1748	20009010
NOT	Rel.not sup.	ABERNETHY	1743	18028028
NOT	Temp. Ev.not G	BROWN	1722	45013004
NOT	Temp. Ev.not G	HOLLAND	1753	45013004
NOT	Xn.not asha.	MOIR	1759	63004016
NOT	Xnty not obj.	ENFIELD	1772	46006060
NOT	Xty.not sed.	SAURIN	1775	45023005
NOTES	Notes tr. Ch.	KIDDER	1697	47002042
NOTES	Notes tr. Ch.	KEITH	1704	47002041
NOTES	Notes tr. Ch.	CHANDLER	1735	57003014
NOV	Love of Nov.	NEWTON	1782	47017021
NOV	Nov.21.	DISNEY	1720	46015018
NUM	Num. Offspr.	ATTERBURY	1743	19127003
NUM	Num.of sav.	PYLE	1777	45013023
NUM	Num.of D.	CROWE	1744	19090012
NUM	Num.our D.	HAVETT	1703	19090012
NUM	On Num.7.	CLARKE	1759	01002002
O	A. O.& N. T.	GILL	1773	47026022
O	C.o. O.&n.t.	KNOX	1768	46005039
O	Confor.to O.	SMITH	1777	20029025
O	E. Tra. O. T.	WHITE	1778	16008007
O	Evid. O. T. P.	POWELL	1776	45024025
O	F.o. G.&c. O.	JONES	1778	63002017
O	Good earl. O.	MEAD	1683	25003027
O	Gosp.sin. O.	SUTTON	1718	43007021
O	Gosp.sin. O.	ABERNETHY	1748	43007021
O	In. O.& N. T.	CALAMY	1710	64001021
O	L.of G. Mot. O	PIERCE	1679	46014015
O	L.of G. Mot. O	READING	1724	46014015
O	Leav.the O.	FERNE	1721	46016028
O	Neces.of O.	GARDINER	1720	43007021
O	Neces.of O.	WESTLEY	1750	43007021
O	O.& N. Test.	KNOX	1768	50004004
O	O.& N. Test.	KNOX	1768	64002001
O	O.& N. Test.	KNOX	1768	68000003
O	O. G.f.& M.	FROST	1741	21005003

Keyword	In its Context	Author	Year	BkChpVrs
O	O. L.g.by Xt.	BRAILSFORD	1776	49015022
O	O. Rel.to N.	DUCHAL	1765	18038007
O	O. T. Proph.	POWELL	1776	43011002
O	O.o. M.& Pe.	WILSON	1781	61013017
O	O.th.necess.	DELAUNE	1728	43006033
O	O.th.needf.	WEBSTER	1753	45010042
O	O.th.needf.	MORRIS	1757	45010041
O	O.th.needf.	DODDERIDGE	1761	45010041
O	O.th.needf.	DAVIES	1766	45010041
O	O.th.needf.	HUNTER	1774	45010041
O	O.th.needf.	CRAIG	1775	45010041
O	O.30. J. Scot.	ANONYMOUS	1720	21003004
O	Xt.light o. O.	BULKLEY	1771	46009005
O	Xy.j.b. O. T.	BULLOCK	1726	61008007
OATH	Nat.of Oath.	BULLOCK	1723	43005033
OATH	Oath.	CATCOTT	1753	61006016
OATH	Rel.of Oath.	HORNECK	1706	43005033
OATH	Rel.of Oath.	NEWCOME	1715	43005033
OATHS	Oaths.	RALEIGH	1679	24004002
OATHS	Oaths.	DAVIES	1720	43014009
OATHS	Oaths.	PARRY	1722	02020007
OATHS	Oaths.	BURNET	1747	23065016
OATHS	Oaths& Sw.	ROST	1695	62005012
OATHS	Oaths& Sw.	ROBINSON	1710	62005012
OATHS	Oaths& Sw.	SHARP	1729	62005012
OATHS	Oaths& Sw.	LAMONT	1780	62005012
OATHS	Prom. Oaths.	SANDERSON	1722	04030002
OB	G's.cal.t.ob.	WARREN	1748	61003015
OB	Gosp. Ob. A.	BOURN	1760	46018036
OB	Gosp. Ob.an.	BOURN	1760	49001022
OB	Gui.ob. Fear	BRYSON	1778	49015056
OB	L.& Ob.t. Xt.	JENNINGS	1757	50005014
OB	Neces.of Ob.	HOLE	1717	43007021
OB	Neces.of Ob.	FOORD	1719	43007021
OB	Ob to sp. G.	SMALRIDGE	1724	61013017
OB	Ob. Lord's d.	ORTON	1769	23058013
OB	Ob. Lord's d.	D'COETLOGAN	1776	23058013
OB	Ob. Xt's m.a.	CHANDLER	1769	47010040
OB	Ob.of C.& A.	KENNICOTT	1747	01004001
OB	Ob.sign 1. G.	SHERLOCK	1719	65005003
OB	Ob.to sp. G.	BARROW	1716	61013017
OB	Ob.to D. W.	STEPHENS	1699	43006010
OB	Ob.to D. W.	NEWCOME	1702	43006010
OB	Ob.to D. W.	NORRIS	1728	43006010
OB	Ob.to D. W.	ROGERS	1736	43006010
OB	Ob.to Gov.	WATSON	1763	59003001
OB	Ob.to Rulers	AGAR	1759	48013001
OB	P.ob.of D. F.	DAVIES	1766	23066002
OB	T.ab.ob.&c.	MUNTON	1756	54003002
OB	Xn. Ob.& L.	WILTON	1724	48013001
OB	Xn's.ob.t. H.	TILLOTSON	1735	58002019
OB	Xt.auth. Ob.	HORT	1738	61005009
OBDUR	Jud. Obdur.	WILCOX	1757	26047011
OBE	Wors.& Obe.	JEFFERY	1751	46009031
OBED	Abso. Obed.	EMLYN	1742	19118009
OBED	Gosp. Obed.	HOPKINS	1708	43011025

Keyword	In its Context	Author	Year	BkChpVrs
OBED	Neces. Obed.	ELSMERE	1767	43010022
OBED	Obed.	HOLYDAY	1661	02020012
OBED	Obed.& Sac.	WITHERSPOON	1768	09015022
OBED	Obed. D. W.	SCATTERGOOD	1723	43007021
OBED	Obed. D. W.	SKEELER	1740	43007021
OBED	Obed. God.	EMLYN	1742	44010022
OBED	Obed.b. Rep.	PAYNE	1698	45015031
OBED	Obed.of Fai.	ROBOTHAM	1680	48016026
OBED	Obed.of Xt.	TATHAM	1780	48005018
OBED	Obed.spirit.	REEVES	1729	61013017
OBED	Obed.t. Gov.	SHERLOCK	1772	48013001
OBED	Obed.t. Mas.	SEATON	1720	54003022
OBED	Obed.to K.	GODDARD	1715	20029004
OBED	Obed.to Xt.	KIMBER	1756	43017005
OBED	Pass. Obed.	CALAMY	1683	48003008
OBED	Pass. Obed.	BERKELEY	1713	48013002
OBED	Perp. Obed.	SHEPHEARD	1748	51006009
OBED	Rel. Obed.	BOURN	1760	43006010
OBED	Relig. Obed.	ABERNETHY	1751	48014005
OBED	Rew. Obed.	ADEY	1760	43019017
OBED	Sin. Obed. G's	CLAGETT	1704	46007017
OBED	Sin. Obed. G's	ABERNETHY	1748	46007017
OBED	Sinc. Obed.	LORTIE	1720	19119106
OBED	Sinc. Obed.	JOHNSON	1740	46014023
OBED	Univ. Obed.	KEITH	1700	45001006
OBED	Univ. Obed.	WAPLE	1720	19119006
OBED	Univ. Obed.	WAPLE	1720	19119009
OBED	Univ. Obed.	BEVERIDGE	1720	45001006
OBED	Univ. Obed.	HICKES	1726	62002010
OBED	Univ. Obed.	IBBOTT	1726	62002010
OBED	Univ. Obed.	HICKES	1726	65003002
OBED	Univ. Obed.	HOADLY	1727	62002010
OBED	Univ. Obed.	MARSHALL	1731	45001006
OBED	Univ. Obed.	ROGERS	1735	62002010
OBED	Univ. Obed.	MOSS	1737	62002010
OBED	Univ. Obed.	WARREN	1739	62002010
OBED	Univ. Obed.	SHEPHERD	1748	45011042
OBED	Univ. Obed.	VENN	1740	62002010
OBED	Univ. Obed.	SEED	1743	62002010
OBED	Univ. Obed.	WEBSTER	1745	62002010
OBED	Univ. Obed.	DAVIS	1756	02030015
OBED	Univ. Obed.	GOUGH	1751	62002011
OBED	Univ. Obed.	CARR	1777	45001006
OBED	Univ. Obed.	SECKER	1771	62002010
OBED	Xn. Obed.	COCKBURN	1697	45006046
OBED	Xn. Obed.	STILLINGFLEET	1707	45006046
OBED	Xt's. Obed.	WILLIAMS	1750	48005019
OBED	Xt's. Obed.	MOIR	1759	48006001
OBED	Xt's Obed. P.	HEYLYN	1749	45002051
OBEDIE	Rel. Obedie.	WHICHCOTE	1703	48001017
OBEDIENCE	Obedience.	CHARNOCK	1684	46015014
OBEDIENCE	Obedience.	WILKINS	1682	61011026
OBEDIENCE	Obedience.	NOURSE	1708	48013001
OBEDIENCE	Obedience.	DUKE	1714	65002004
OBEDIENCE	Obedience.	BLAKEWAY	1716	48013001
OBEDIENCE	Obedience.	KETTLEWELL	1719	53004013

Keyword	In its Context	Author	Year	BkChpVrs
OBEDIENCE	Obedience.	STANHOPE	1727	43019017
OBEDIENCE	Obedience.	LEWIS	1735	46002011
OBEDIENCE	Obedience.	CLARKE	1735	69022014
OBEDIENCE	Obedience.	STEPHENS	1737	61012014
OBEDIENCE	Obedience.	DORMAN	1743	19119165
OBEDIENCE	Obedience.	LEIGHTON	1746	48013005
OBEDIENCE	Obedience.	TATHAM	1780	49012031
OBJ	G. Obj. Tr.	HOLLAND	1753	19118008
OBJ	G.o. Obj. F.	NEWLIN	1720	45012004
OBJ	G.o. Obj. F.	TILLOTSON	1735	45012004
OBJ	Obj. Mir.ins.	POWELL	1776	47017032
OBJ	Obj. Xt's.res.	WEBB	1772	43028011
OBJ	Obj.ag. Rev.	SEED	1750	49001025
OBJ	Obj.o.our af.	MILLER	1749	54003002
OBJ	Obj.of Faith	CHARNOCK	1684	46014001
OBJ	Obj.to Pr.a.	NEWMAN	1711	18021015
OBJ	Obj.to S.con.	AMORY	1775	49001025
OBJ	Xnty not obj.	ENFIELD	1772	46006060
OBJ	Xt.obj.o. Fai.	GOODWIN	16--	48008038
OBL	Obl. Hum. L.	THORP	1703	48013005
OBL	Obl. Hum. L.	SANDERSON	1722	48013005
OBL	Obl.of Bapt.	ALLESTREE	1684	48006003
OBL	Obl.to Hol.	WHITAKER	1674	58002019
OBL	Obl.to L's d.	ORTON	1769	02020008
OBLAT	Xt's. Oblat.	FLAVEL	1673	51004004
OBLIG	Mor. Oblig.	HUNT	1748	23005020
OBLIG	Moral Oblig.	HUNT	1748	59002012
OBLIG	Oblig. Godl.	SHARP	1734	52004001
OBLIG	Oblig. Xnity	ELSMERE	1767	23005004
OBLIGA	Mor. Obliga.	HUNT	1748	32006008
OBLIVION	Oblivion.	CULVERWELL	1661	23043025
OBS	Jer. Obs.&c.	ORTON	1776	24005004
OBS	Obs.of S. S.	WAPLE	1729	64003016
OBSER	Gen. Obser.	BLAIR	1740	43007024
OBSER	Obser. Mir.	BULKLEY	1771	43004023
OBSERV	Ag. Observ.	SMYTHIES	1684	51006002
OBSERV	Gen. Observ.	BLAIR	1740	43006009
OBST	Obst.in Rel.	CARMICHAEL	1757	61012001
OBSTRUCT	Obstruct.&c.	BOURN	1777	43007015
OBSTRUCT	Obstruct&c.	BOURN	1777	43007021
OBT	Rest.t.b.obt.	ALLESTREE	1684	43011028
OCC	Occ. Comm.	STUBBS	1702	11018021
OCCAS	Occas.of Par.	BOURN	1763	45015001
OCT	Oct.20.	BERWICK	1661	20014008
OECONOMY	Oeconomy.	WATKINSON	1763	46006012
OECONOMY	Oeconomy.	WATKINSON	1763	46020007
OF	Of a King.	BRAGGE	1702	43022002
OF	Of ag. Piety.	PEIRCE	1728	20016031
OF	Of the Ch.	SHARP	1735	49012013
OF	Of the Heart.	JONES	1678	54003023
OF	Of the Pass.	YOUNG	1728	54003002
OF	Of the Serp.	BURNET	1747	01003013
OF	Of.offences.	KINGSTON	1682	43018007
OF	Of.offences.	FOWLER	1683	43018007
OF	Of.offences.	CLAGETT	1704	43018007
OF	Of Angels.	SHEPHERD	1702	61001004

INDEXES TO THIRD VOLUME: E: KEYWORD-IN-CONTEXT INDEX OF OTHER SUBJECTS OR OCCASIONS

Keyword	In its Context	Author	Year	BkChpVrs
OF	Of Balaam.	THEED	1712	04023010
OF	Of Balaam.	WATERLAND	1742	04022010
OF	Of Blasph.	FORSTER	1744	02020007
OF	Of Charity.	BARROW	1716	52005002
OF	Of Churches	MEDE	1672	49011022
OF	Of Confid.	SOUTH	1744	52003012
OF	Of Counsel.	BALGUY	1748	20012015
OF	Of Death.	BATES	1700	61002015
OF	Of Dreams.	ATTERBURY	1703	18033014
OF	Of Establish.	CRUSO	1698	47011023
OF	Of Faith.	ALLESTRE	1684	44009024
OF	Of Faith.	WHALEY	1695	61011017
OF	Of Faith.	HOLE	1715	44009024
OF	Of Faith.	COOKE	1739	44009024
OF	Of Feasting.	SHERIDAN	1720	18001005
OF	Of Glory.	BUNDY	1750	51006014
OF	Of Goodn.	SMITH	1740	48002004
OF	Of Grace.	PELIERE	1737	40014003
OF	Of Heaven.	BOYSE	1728	52003014
OF	Of Hope.	SIMONS	1743	18008013
OF	Of Hypocr.	CLARKE	1736	18013016
OF	Of Justificat.	GIBBON	1676	48005001
OF	Of Liberty.	SMITH	1740	63002016
OF	Of Lots.	ATTERBURY	1743	20016033
OF	Of Magi.	SOUTH	1744	43002003
OF	Of Merit.	SOUTH	1727	18022002
OF	Of Murder.	LUPTON	1729	02020013
OF	Of Murder.	CLARKE	1736	02021014
OF	Of Murder.	STERNE	1769	02021014
OF	Of Offerings	MEDE	1672	19050014
OF	Of Peace.	BRETT	1720	65005007
OF	Of Prayer.	CLAGETT	1720	43006005
OF	Of Prayer.	GARDINER	1720	43006005
OF	Of Pride.	WHEATLAND	1739	20016005
OF	Of Rain.	HOLE	1716	09012017
OF	Of Reproof.	MOSS	1732	03019017
OF	Of Separat.	STANHOPE	1710	46006066
OF	Of Sin.	BATES	1690	01039009
OF	Of Sin.	WILSON	1781	04032023
OF	Of Slander.	FOSTER	1744	02020016
OF	Of Swear.	FLEETWOOD	1737	02020007
OF	Of Talents.	NEWTON	1782	43025014
OF	Of Tempta.	JEFFERY	1710	01003005
OF	Of Trouble.	LEIGHTONHOUSE	1697	19027013
OF	Of Tythes.	DELANY	1748	02020017
OF	Of Vanity.	COTES	1721	19144004
OF	Of Vanity.	COOKE	1739	19039005
OF	Of Vows	SHOWER	1702	07011035
OFF	Abr.off. Isaac	JENKINS	1779	01022012
OFF	Abr.off. Son.	SCOTT	1743	01022002
OFF	Abr.off. Son.	JORTIN	1774	01022001
OFF	Apostol. Off.	ST.	1757	43005013
OFF	Avoid. Off.	DAVIES	1754	44009047
OFF	Curse cut off.	TAYLOR	1679	01020005
OFF	Cut.off M. E.	BULKLEY	1771	46018010
OFF	Diff.off. Ch.	ROGERS	1730	49012028

Keyword	In its Context	Author	Year	BkChpVrs
OFF	Giv.no Off.	QUINCY	1750	49010032
OFF	Min.n:g.off.	ERSKINE	1775	50006003
OFF	Minist. Off.	ST.	1757	43005013
OFF	N.&off.o. A.	TILLOTSON	1735	61001014
OFF	N.&off.o. A.	WHEATLY	1746	61001014
OFF	Not.t.b. Off.	HEYLYN	1749	43011004
OFF	Off.& Succ.	HORTON	1679	49001024
OFF	Off. Op. H. S.	WARBURTON	1753	46014016
OFF	Off.ag. Gosp.	CLARKE	1735	45017001
OFF	Off.ag. Gosp.	HODGE	1758	43011006
OFF	Off.ag. Gosp.	SHERLOCK	1772	43011006
OFF	Off.ag. Xty.	ELSMERE	1767	43011006
OFF	Off.o. H. Gh.	CENNICK	1762	47002038
OFF	Off.o. H. Gh.	ELLIOTT	1764	63001012
OFF	Off.o. Spir.	HOWE	1726	51005025
OFF	Off.of Mess.	CENNICK	1762	45004018
OFF	R.&off.o. D.	COLMAN	1728	69022016
OFF	Resign. P.off.	PRIESTLEY	1773	63001013
OFF	Rock of off.	MARTIN	1771	48010003
OFF	Scand.&off.	BRADBURY	1723	43018007
OFF	Sinf.giv.off.	STEPHENS	1737	48014013
OFF	Xt's.pro.off.	FLAVEL	1673	45024045
OFF	Xt's.pro.off.	FLAVEL	1673	47003022
OFF	Xt's.pro.off.	BOSTON	1773	47003022
OFF	Xt's.req.off.	FLAVEL	1673	50010005
OFFENCE	Giv. Offence	PYLE	1777	45017001
OFFENCES	Giv.offences	BUNDY	1740	43018007
OFFENCES	Of.offences.	KINGSTON	1682	43018007
OFFENCES	Of.offences.	FOWLER	1683	43018007
OFFENCES	Of.offences.	CLAGETT	1704	43018007
OFFENCES	Offences.	BOYSE	1728	43018007
OFFENCES	Offences.	WISHART	1742	43018007
OFFERINGS	Of Offerings	MEDE	1672	19050014
OFFI	Offi.of Spir.	HOWE	1726	46003006
OFFI	Xt's reg.offi.	FLAVEL	1673	52001022
OFFICE	Ang.&office	BULL	1713	61001014
OFFICE	Ang.&office	BOYSE	1728	61001014
OFFICE	Ang.&office	HORT	1738	61001013
OFFICE	Ang.&office.	WHEATLY	1746	61001007
OFFICE	Bapt.office.	PIERS	1758	45001017
OFFICE	Minis. Office	GRIFFITH	1757	43010016
OFFICE	Minis.office.	DUKE	1714	48010015
OFFICE	Office of Bps.	LAWSON	1764	43010046
OFFICE	Office Minis.	SIMPSON	1774	23062006
OFFICE	Past. Office.	ALTHAM	1732	49004001
OFFICE	Past. Office.	BAINE	1778	38002006
OFFICE	Xt's. Office.	BOURN	1760	47005031
OFFICE	Xt's. Office.	WHITTY	1766	47005031
OFFICERS	b. Officers.	KENNET	1715	49014008
OFFICES	Offices of Sp.	HURRION	1734	50003008
OFFICES	Xt's Offices.	BOSTON	1773	37004013
OFFS	Men offs. G.	HOLLAND	1753	47017028
OFFS	Men G's.offs.	GOUGH	1751	47017028
OFFSP	Offsp. David	HARRIS	1724	23009006
OFFSPR	Num. Offspr.	ATTERBURY	1743	19127003
OLD	Old age.	EATON	1764	19071017

Keyword	In its Context	Author	Year	BkChpVrs
OLD	Old w.e.n. C.	PITTIS	1682	65002024
OLD	Old&n. M.	BOSTON	1753	48006006
OLD	Old&n. M.	SECKER	1770	48006021
OLD	Old&n. M.	SHERLOCK	1772	48006021
OLD	Old Age.	SMITH	1676	21012001
OLD	Old Paths.	STEFFE	1743	24006016
OMISS	Sins Omiss.	STILLINGFLEET	1707	62004017
OMISS	Sins Omiss.	MORRIS	1743	43025041
OMNI	God's Omni.	CLARKE	1732	18037016
OMNIP	Div. Omnip.	CHARNOCK	1684	24023024
OMNIP	Div. Omnip.	LUPTON	1726	24023024
OMNIP	Div. Omnip.	MOSS	1737	24023024
OMNIP	Div. Omnip.	BRACKENRIDGE	1764	24023024
OMNIP	Div. Omnip.	WESTON	1766	24023023
OMNIP	Div. Omnip.	JORTIN	1774	24023023
OMNIP	Div. Omnip.	AMORY	1775	24023023
OMNIP	Div. Omnip.	PETERS	1776	24023024
OMNIP	G's Omnip.	CLARKE	1732	11008027
OMNIP	Omnip.of G.	CHARNOCK	1684	18026014
OMNIP	Omnip.of G.	WHITBY	1710	01017001
OMNIP	Omnip.of G.	ABERNETHY	1743	01017001
OMNIP	Omnip.of G.	KNOWLES	1750	18026014
OMNIP	Xn. Omnip.	HALES	1673	53004013
OMNIP	Xn. Omnip.	HAMMOND	1684	53004013
OMNIP	Xn. Omnip.	BEVERIDGE	1720	53004013
OMNIPOT	Omnipot.	CLARKE	1732	19147005
OMNIPRE	G's Omnipre.	NEWTON	1759	19139007
OMNIPRE	Omnipre.	BENSON	1748	18022012
OMNIPRES	Omnipres.	TURNER	1683	19139007
OMNIPRES	Omnipres.	WHITBY	1710	19139007
OMNIPRES	Omnipres.	HOPKINS	1710	19139007
OMNIPRES	Omnipres.	BEVERIDGE	1720	19016008
OMNIPRES	Omnipres.	CREYGHTON	1720	19139006
OMNIPRES	Omnipres.	BRODHURST	1733	19016008
OMNIPRES	Omnipres.	TILLOTSON	1735	19139007
OMNIPRES	Omnipres.	SMITH	1740	19016008
OMNIPRES	Omnipres.	WILDER	1741	19139007
OMNIPRES	Omnipres.	ATTERBURY	1743	19139007
OMNIPRES	Omnipres.	ABERNETHY	1743	19139007
OMNIPRES	Omnipres.	GOUGH	1750	19139006
OMNIPRES	Omnipres.	FREE	1750	19139007
OMNIPRES	Omnipres.	ALLEN	1751	19139007
OMNIPRES	Omnipres.	LLOYD	1765	19139006
OMNIPRES	Omnipres.	LELAND	1769	19139007
OMNIPRES	Omnipres.	FRANCIS	1771	19139001
OMNIPRES	Omnipres.	SAURIN	1775	19139007
OMNIPRESEN	Omnipresen.	MARSHAL	1731	20015003
OMNIPRESEN	Omnipresen.	WALKER	1767	20015003
OMNIPRESEN	Omnipresen.	PEARCE	1779	20015003
OMNISC	G's. Omnisc.	WHITBY	1710	65003020
OMNISC	G's. Omnisc.	CARTER	1729	61004013
OMNISC	G's. Omnisc.	BATTY	1739	61004013
OMNISC	G's. Omnisc.	WILDER	1741	61004013
OMNISC	G's. Omnisc.	SOUTH	1744	65003020
OMNISC	G's. Omnisc.	STEELE	1776	61004013
OMNISC	Omnisc. Xt.	WOTTON	1720	44013032

Keyword	In its Context	Author	Year	BkChpVrs
OMNISCIEN	Omniscien.	SCOT	1743	14006030
OMNISCIENCE	Omniscience	LEIGHTONHOUSE	1697	19094009
OMNISCIENCE	Omniscience	CONANT	1703	19147005
OMNISCIENCE	Omniscience	ABERNETHY	1743	19147005
OMNISCIENCE	Omniscience	SOUTH	1744	19139003
OMNISCIENCE	Omniscience	MILLER	1749	19139002
OMNISCIENCE	Omniscience	KNOWLES	1750	19139003
OMNISCIENCE	Omniscience	BALL	1756	20015003
OMNISCIENCE	Omniscience	LELAND	1769	19139001
ON	On a Murd.	FAWCETT	1764	10003034
ON	On an Exec.	ROSEWELL	1716	04026010
ON	On an Exec.	DENHAM	1745	61008012
ON	On ap. Creed	BENNETT	1775	46020031
ON	On late Reb.	PETTER	1685	46021022
ON	On rob. Ch.	GREEN	1737	52004028
ON	On the Cate.	WALKER	1763	47016030
ON	On the Cate.	WALKER	1763	47016031
ON	On the Fall.	PARKER	1750	50011003
ON	On the Tim.	THOMSON	1757	03018025
ON	On the Trin.	WALLIS	1691	46017003
ON	On the Un.	ANONYMOUS	1706	41010027
ON	On the Un.	HUTCHINSON	1707	19068008
ON	On Bankrup.	CALAMY	1709	57006009
ON	On Baptism.	BROWNRIG	1661	47016033
ON	On Baptism.	MARTYN	1661	47016033
ON	On Baptism.	PATRICK	1670	47016033
ON	On Baptism.	HOLE	1715	47016033
ON	On Bigotry.	ENFIELD	1772	46004009
ON	On Board- S.	STOCKDALE	1777	63005008
ON	On C.& Exc.	ANONYMOUS	1779	02020001
ON	On Catechis.	BASSET	1684	63002013
ON	On Charity.	DODWELL	1749	49013013
ON	On Convers.	STEVENS	1760	50005021
ON	On Convict.	CASE	1774	47002037
ON	On Creed.	BYFIELD	1662	65005007
ON	On Death.	WHALEY	1708	50005005
ON	On Death.	SMALRIDGE	1724	53001021
ON	On Eternity.	HEYLYN	1761	05032029
ON	On Execu.	BROUGHTON	1713	10012005
ON	On Exercise.	ANONYMOUS	1772	20006009
ON	On Expedit.	PHILIPS	1725	05004007
ON	On Faith.	PARIS	1726	46014001
ON	On Faith.	BRACKENRIDGE	1764	47016031
ON	On Faith.	CARR	1777	61010038
ON	On Faith.	TATHAM	1780	46003036
ON	On Faithful.	WHICHCOTE	1702	61003012
ON	On Feasting.	WHEATLY	1746	18001004
ON	On Govern.	READING	1739	45019027
ON	On Honor.	MACQUEEN	1711	17006006
ON	On Labour.	HORSEMANDEN	1766	01003019
ON	On Lib.o. C.	SALKELD	1673	46011044
ON	On Light.	SMITH	1717	45021026
ON	On Mart.&c.	MAINWARING	1780	58001008
ON	On Miracles.	BRACKENRIDGE	1764	46003002
ON	On Num.7.	CLARKE	1759	01002002
ON	On Peace.	FRANCIS	1773	45002014

INDEXES TO THIRD VOLUME: E: KEYWORD-IN-CONTEXT INDEX OF OTHER SUBJECTS OR OCCASIONS

Keyword	In its Context	Author	Year	BkChpVrs
ON	On Prayer.	BRADBURY	1711	53004006
ON	On Revenge.	SMEDLEY	1719	48012021
ON	On Riots.	ROSEWELL	1715	47019040
ON	On S.a. D. S.	HOLE	1713	24026014
ON	On Time.	SHORTHOSE	1738	52005015
ON	On Transgr.	FELTON	1748	01003009
ON	On Travell.	BURNABY	1777	20001020
ON	On Xt's. Mir.	CHANDLER	1769	46003002
ONE	Bear one a B.	STRAIGHT	1741	62005011
ONE	One just o. A.	DORRINGTON	1683	49007031
ONE	One F.& F.	ROMAINE	1759	21001008
ONE'S	One's o. Bus.	ROSEWELL	1708	46021021
ONES	P's Pr.f. Ones	ORTON	1776	58001018
ONLY	G.only b.ser.	BEVERIDGE	1720	43004010
ONLY	Sal. Ch.only.	NEWCOME	1702	47002047
ONLY	Sal. Ch.only.	COCKBURN	1712	47002047
ONLY	Sal. Ch.only.	BOYS	1716	47002047
ONLY	Sal. Ch.only.	BEVERIDGE	1720	47002047
ONLY	Wor. G.only	GUYSE	1757	43015008
ONLY	Wor.only G.	COLLIER	1725	45004008
ONLY	Xt.only Found.	DAVIES	1766	23028016
OP	Door Sal.op.	F.	1667	69003020
OP	Fou.life op.	FLAVEL	1673	49002002
OP	Int.op.of Sp.	SECKER	1771	46014015
OP	Off. Op. H. S.	WARBURTON	1753	46014016
OP	Op. M.29.	FAWCONER	1763	19150004
OP	Op. Rebuke.	ANONYMOUS	1777	20027005
OPE	Ope.of Spir.	SECKER	1771	46015026
OPER	H. Sp. Oper.	WATERLAND	1742	48008014
OPER	Oper. H. G.	BADDELLEY	1752	46016008
OPERAT	Div. Operat.	DODDERIDGE	1742	49012006
OPIN	Opin.of Xt.	SAURIN	1775	43016013
OPP	Opp. Prot. F.	GIBBONS	1755	30006006
OPPRESSION	Oppression.	STEBBING	1760	21005008
OPPRESSION	Oppression.	KNOWLES	1769	20022016
OPPRESSION	Oppression.	ORTON	1776	21004001
OPTICKS	Sp. Opticks.	CULVERWELL	1661	49013012
OR	Bapt.or Reg.	ANONYMOUS	1708	59003004
OR	Death P. Or.	TRUSTLER	1759	20011016
OR	Death Pr. Or.	MACLAINE	1752	25003028
OR	Di Or.o. S. S.	SMITH	1769	51001011
OR	Diligence or I	BARROW	1716	48012011
OR	Diligence or I	BALGUY	1750	48012011
OR	Div. Or. Gos.	SWINDEN	1718	58003016
OR	Div. Or.o. R.	STENNETT	1769	62003017
OR	F. Hap.or M.	BUNDY	1740	45016025
OR	G.l.b.or. Xn.	WILKINS	1682	59002010
OR	G.l.b.or. Xn.	ROGERS	1735	59002010
OR	Imp.or.in C.	BLAIR	1780	49014040
OR	In Xt.or not.	FAWCETT	1757	50005017
OR	Invest. P. Or.	WILLEMSON	1747	37009016
OR	M. Or. Xn. R.	BOURN	1777	46006066
OR	Mir.or. Xt.r.	BOURN	1777	50002016
OR	New Birth or R	BYAM	1675	46003005
OR	New Birth or R	HOPKINS	1710	46003005
OR	New Birth or R	HOLE	1715	46003005
OR	New Birth or R	LAMBE	1717	46003005
OR	New Birth or R	HOLE	1719	46003005
OR	New Birth or R	FARINGTON	1741	46003005
OR	New Birth or R	JONES	1756	46003005
OR	New Cr.or b.	HAMMOND	1684	51006015
OR	New Cr.or b.	IBBOT	1726	51006015
OR	New Cr.or b.	STEBBING	1739	51006015
OR	Or.& C.o. S.	BATTY	1739	48005019
OR	Or. Civ. Gov.	HORNE	1778	48013004
OR	Or. H. H.sp.	WATSON	1660	63001022
OR	Or.civ. Auth.	PEARSON	1718	48013005
OR	Or.of Light.	MURRAY	1777	01001001
OR	Saint or Bru.	BAXTER	1707	45010041
OR	So. H.or M.	SKELTON	1754	24013023
OR	Spe.t. Or. G.	FENTON	1720	63004011
OR	b. Pr. Or.	PATRICK	1689	23011006
ORACLES	Oracles o. G.	BREKELL	1765	48003002
ORANGE	b. Pr. Orange	BURNET	1668	27012003
ORATORY	Xn. Oratory.	DAVIS	1756	47024025
ORATORY	Xn. Oratory.	PECKARD	1770	49001021
ORD	Dec.& Ord.	BISSE	1723	49014040
ORD	Eccles. Ord.	WAKEMAN	1664	47013004
ORD	Intro.to Ord.	HALL	1759	45010023
ORD	Ord.mea.gr.	ADAMS	1690	45016031
ORDER	Order Dut.	SLADE	1727	43023023
ORDER	Order Dut.	TRAPP	1752	43023023
ORIG	Orig. Guilt.	HAYWARD	1758	51003022
ORIG	Orig. Sin.	VINK	1676	48006006
ORIG	Orig. Sin.	CLARKSON	1696	19051005
ORIG	Orig. Sin.	BOEHM	1717	52004022
ORIG	Orig. Sin.	DELAUNE	1728	19051005
ORIG	Orig. Sin.	RIDGLEY	1725	48005018
ORIG	Orig. Sin.	TAYLOR	1725	52002001
ORIG	Orig. Sin.	CLARKE	1734	21007029
ORIG	Orig. Sin.	HEYLYN	1749	48005018
ORIG	Orig. Sin.	MILLER	1749	52002003
ORIG	Orig. Sin.	GREEN	1758	49015021
ORIG	Orig. Sin.	WESTLEY	1760	01006005
ORIG	Orig. Sin.	BOWMAN	1764	18014014
ORIG	Orig. Sin.	ELLIOTT	1764	48005019
ORIG	Orig. St.& F.	CHANDLER	1769	01002017
ORIG	Orig. St.man	GUYSE	1757	21007029
ORIG	Orig.o. Faith	ROTHERAM	1761	46010037
ORIG	Orig.o. Man.	SHERIDAN	1720	47017026
ORIG	Orig.o. Wars	RALEIGH	1679	62004001
ORIG	Orig.of Evil.	HENLEY	1731	23047007
ORIG	Orig.of Gri.	BEDFORD	1770	62004001
ORIG	Orig.thoug.	HUSSEY	1758	43015019
ORIGIN	Origin of W.	SHERIDAN	1720	47017024
ORIGIN	of Origin.	FELTON	1748	01004003
ORPH	Orph. Hope.	DODDERIDGE	1743	19027010
ORTH	St. Pl's.orth.	FLEMING	1759	59002015
OT	Part.of ot. M'	KITCHEN	1670	57005022
OT	Part.of ot. M'	MOSS	1737	57005022
OTH	Delight in oth	SWADLIN	1661	48001032
OTH	Delight in oth	SOUTH	1727	48001032

Keyword	In its Context	Author	Year	BkChpVrs
OTH	Mour.oth. S.	JENKINS	1683	64002007
OTHERS	Judg.others.	NEEDHAM	1679	49004005
OTHERS	Judg.others.	SMEDLEY	1719	62005012
OTHERS	Judg.others.	MAYNARD	1722	49004005
OUR	Comp.our P.	SNAPE	1745	45018011
OUR	Faith our S.	WILCOX	1757	19027014
OUR	G.our father	NICOLSON	1661	48008015
OUR	G.our Father	CLARKE	1732	43023009
OUR	G.our Friend	WALKER	1765	48008031
OUR	G.w.ab.our.	BARKER	1763	23055008
OUR	G's&our Th.	SHOWER	1699	23055007
OUR	God our Fai.	JONES	1741	23064008
OUR	God our Fat.	WILLISON	1761	24003019
OUR	God our Joy.	DUNLOP	1722	19043004
OUR	Jes.our Adv.	SUTTON	1718	65002001
OUR	Jes.our Ex.	VINCENT	1690	63002021
OUR	Jes.our Ex.	TILLOTSON	1735	63002021
OUR	L.our Right.	ROMAINE	1752	23045008
OUR	L.our Right.	WHITFIELD	1771	23060019
OUR	Ld our Righ.	WOODWARD	1696	24013006
OUR	Misp.our aff.	REEVES	1713	58003004
OUR	Num.our D.	HAVETT	1703	19090012
OUR	Obj.o.our af.	MILLER	1749	54003002
OUR	Our own Str.	BRADY	1730	43026033
OUR	Our Lord.	BARROW	1716	52004005
OUR	Our Right.	HARRIS	1724	24023006
OUR	Our Sins f.our	TILLOTSON	1735	62001013
OUR	Our Sins f.our	MOSS	1737	62001013
OUR	Prov.our Re.	ROGERS	1730	55005021
OUR	Quiet do.our o	FARINDON	1672	55004011
OUR	Quiet do.our o	BURTON	1685	55004011
OUR	Quiet do.our o	DUKE	1714	55004011
OUR	Quiet do.our o	BARROW	1716	55004011
OUR	Rel.our Busi.	WATSON	1677	45002049
OUR	Rel.our Int.	HOLDEN	1755	20011012
OUR	Sac.of our B.	HUSSEY	1758	48012001
OUR	Sup.f.our N.	WILLISON	1761	53004019
OUR	Xt our Safety	HARTLEY	1754	43014024
OUR	Xt our Surety	TAYLOR	1725	61006022
OUR	Xt.&our res.	ATTERBURY	1743	23026019
OUR	Xt.our Ark.	WILLISON	1761	01007001
OUR	Xt.our Com.	MOIR	1759	23032002
OUR	Xt.our Cov.	ERSKINE	1764	23042006
OUR	Xt.our Ld.	BEVERIDGE	1720	46013013
OUR	Xt.our Man.	WILLISON	1761	46006051
OUR	Xt.our Mast.	BENNETT	1728	43023008
OUR	Xt.our Patt.	SKELTON	1754	53002005
OUR	Xt.our Ref.	WILLISON	1761	61006018
OUR	Xt.our Rock.	WILLISON	1761	49010004
OUR	Xt.our Sav.	WELCH	1752	23062001
OUR	Xt.our Sav.	DAVIS	1756	61009026
OUR	Xt.our Shep.	DODDERIDGE	1736	23040011
OUR	Xt.our Shep.	HILL	1755	23040011
OUR	Xt.our Shep.	WILCOX	1757	23040011
OUR	Xt.our Supp.	ERSKINE	1757	22008005
OURSELV	Kno.ourselv.	NEWTON	1782	50013005

Keyword	In its Context	Author	Year	BkChpVrs
OUT	Work.out&c.o.	SHORTHOSE	1738	53002012
OUT	Work.out&c.o.	SNAPE	1745	53002012
OV	Con.ov. Evil.	ALTHAM	1732	48012021
OV	God.ov. Seas	STUBBS	1701	19135006
OV	Ov.right&c.	ALLEN	17--	21007016
OV	Ov.right&c.	ROMAINE	1760	21007016
OV	Xt's.tr.ov. D.	FANCH	1768	49015025
OVERCAREF	Overcaref.	STANHOPE	1727	43006034
OVERR	Da.being overr	STILLINGFLEET	1707	21007016
OVERR	Da.being overr	TRAPP	1739	21007016
OWN	H.own Fu.s.	ALEXANDER	1766	21009010
OWN	Ld own.all.	CLARKSON	1696	13029011
OWN	Our own Str.	BRADY	1730	43026033
OXF	Oxf.un.vind.	HENLEY	17--	23007004
OXF	Vind.of Oxf.	HENLEY	17--	63002012
P	A.& P.o. S. S.	NEAL	1757	58003016
P	Abim. P.sus.	ORTON	1776	01020011
P	Ap. S.p.o. Xy	LANGHORNE	1773	49015019
P	Bei.& P.o. G.	HOPKINS	1708	61011006
P	Ch p. F.& H.	HOLE	1725	49013013
P	Ch.d.to d. P.	BURNABY	1777	51006010
P	Comp.our P.	SNAPE	1745	45018011
P	Conf.pu.&p.	NICOLSON	1661	65001009
P	Conv.of P.	MARSHALL	1731	47017022
P	Conver. Y. P.	BURGESS	1690	21012001
P	D. P. Wales.	ATWOOD	1751	19146002
P	D.of P.& M.	SKELTON	1754	06024015
P	David's p. Xr	HARRIS	1755	45024044
P	Deac. P. Bps.	CRUCHY	1723	49012005
P	Death P. Or.	TRUSTLER	1759	20011016
P	Dis b. P.& B.	CONYBEARE	1757	47015039
P	Dut. M.& P.	WILSON	1781	49004001
P	Dut. Pas.& P.	HOWARD	1728	59002015
P	Evid. O. T. P.	POWELL	1776	45024025
P	F. Rew.& P.	CONANT	1708	48006023
P	F. Rew.& P.	CLARKE	1735	43025046
P	F.judg.c.& P.t	BRYAN	1685	50005010
P	F.judg.c.& P.t	BURNET	1747	50005010
P	Fai.p. Xn. L.	BOYSE	1728	51002020
P	Fut. Re.& P.	ROGERS	1736	51006007
P	G.no res. P.	MOORE	1716	47010034
P	G.no res. P.	IBBOT	1726	47010034
P	G.no res. P.	MUNTON	1756	47010034
P	G.no res. P.	HUSSEY	1758	47010034
P	G.no resp.of P	BARROW	1716	48002011
P	G.no resp.of P	FOSTER	1744	48002011
P	G.no R.o. P.	PYLE	1777	63001017
P	G.p. M's. F.	ANONYMOUS	1776	43006031
P	G's. For.& P.	MARSHALL	1731	64003009
P	G's. For.& P.	NEWSON	1781	64003009
P	G's.reg.to P.	WILCOX	1757	38003017
P	Good m's p.	DAVIES	1679	19119057
P	Good.sup. P.	BOURN	1777	45010017
P	Good P.t.m.	AMORY	1766	43005045
P	H. Gh.div. P.	LESTLEY	1720	46014016
P	Hap.early P.	GALLIMORE	1694	21012001

INDEXES TO THIRD VOLUME: E: KEYWORD-IN-CONTEXT INDEX OF OTHER SUBJECTS OR OCCASIONS

Keyword	In its Context	Author	Year	BkChpVrs
P	Happ.o.g. P.	ROWLAND	1775	48008028
P	Ig d.o. G's P.	RILAND	1764	28004006
P	Im.of G's. P.	HORNECK	1706	43005048
P	Im.of G's. P.	KELSEY	1721	43005048
P	Invest. P. Or.	WILLEMSON	1747	37009016
P	Jew.& Xn. P.	WESTON	1747	43023001
P	John's P.f. G.	ORTON	1776	67000002
P	Kgs.no.s. P.	HURST	1675	47026002
P	King. G.in P.	WILLIAMS	1738	49004020
P	Kno.wout P.	PRICE	1770	46013017
P	Know. Xn. P.	WAPLE	1718	46013015
P	Know. Xn. P.	TILLOTSON	1735	46013015
P	L.& P.ful. Xt.	BLACKALL	1723	43005017
P	L. Xt. P. Xn.	RELLEY	1762	46014019
P	Law.& P.	BUNDY	1740	43005017
P	M. Anx.f.p.	DAVIES	1771	51004019
P	M's St.in P.	HUSSEY	.1733	01002015
P	Ma.d.sup.p.	SLATER	1690	48013005
P	Misap. P. Ch.	WILSON	1768	41004001
P	Mor.&p. D.	WHITBY	1720	43011030
P	Mor.&p. D.	MORRIS	1743	43012007
P	Mor.&p. D.	WESTON	1747	43012007
P	Mor. D.ab. P.	EMLYN	1742	43023023
P	Mor. P. Dut.	ROGERS	1736	43023023
P	Mor.b. P. L.	HICKES	1726	45011042
P	Mor.p.o.rel.	WHICHCOTE	1703	59002012
P	N.& P.of Ch.	CONANT	1703	49013004
P	N.& P.of Ch.	CROSSINGE	1722	49013004
P	N.& P.of Ch.	HOLE	1725	49013004
P	Nat.&sp. P.	DRAKE	1677	48007023
P	Nat.pr.p. Pr.	HUNTER	1774	49015041
P	Ne.o Xt's. P.	FLAVEL	1673	61009023
P	Neg.of P. W.	TOULMIN	1770	16013011
P	P.& G. H. G.	PAYNE	1763	46014015
P	P.& M. Duty.	WOOD	1773	49011001
P	P.&c. X's. D.	LARDNER	1751	46015005
P	P. Fr. Bir.d.	SHAW	1729	13028009
P	P. Gosp.can.	FLEMING	1772	49002004
P	P. Kno.of G.	SUTTON	1754	24009024
P	P. Pil. Xrter.	CRAIG	1775	45023023
P	P.ob.of D. F.	DAVIES	1766	23066002
P	P.s.	LITTLETON	1680	43008025
P	P.s.	KILLIGREW	1685	37013006
P	P.s.	KENN	1713	32007008
P	P.s.	BEVERIDGE	1720	37012010
P	P.s.	CONEY	1750	37012010
P	P.s. E.s. As.s	BERRIMAN	1751	48008033
P	Pr. M.p.d.m.	CONYBEARE	1757	46020031
P	Pr. Xn.k.a.p.	JONES	1761	50005014
P	Prince of P.	HORNE	1778	37009009
P	Prot.p.n.sec.	FRANCIS	1773	48008031
P	Pub. P.of F.	BEVERIDGE	1720	43010032
P	Pub. W.b. P.	CLARKSON	1696	19087002
P	Qual.succ. P.	ELSMERE	1767	62004003
P	R.poor.p. C.	BRADY	1730	62002015
P	Rel.mid. P.	BROWNE	1749	43011025
P	Resign. P.off.	PRIESTLEY	1773	63001013
P	Sacra. P. S.	SHARP	1729	45022019
P	Sinc.acc.f. P.	SIMONS	1743	50008012
P	St. P.at Meli.	NEWTON	1782	47028001
P	St. P.b. Felix	NEWTON	1782	47024010
P	St. Step.d. P.	MAY	1757	47007058
P	To Young P.	WOODWARD	1697	45015018
P	Tr.time S. P.	TURNER	1684	49014020
P	W.to r.&p.	COLLINGES	1684	05008018
P	Ways Wis.p.	BARROW	1716	20003017
P	Ways Wis.p.	BEVERIDGE	1720	20003017
P	Xn. Hope p.	OUTRAM	1697	65003003
P	Xn.r.pr.sp p.	RANDOLPH	1777	47005038
P	Xt'cov.of P.	HILL	1755	23049008
P	Xt's. Div.p.fm	JOHNSON	1713	48001004
P	Xt's. Div.p.fm	BEVERIDGE	1720	48001004
P	Xt's. P.o. R.	LARDNER	1760	50007009
P	Xt's.p.rais.d.	MORRIS	1757	46005025
P	Xt's.warn. P.	HORTON	1679	45022031
P	Xt's.2 p.f. D.	FLAVEL	1673	49011023
P	Xt's Obed. P.	HEYLYN	1749	45002051
P	2 Arg.f. C. P.	BROOKS	1665	43006006
P'S	Ch.suf.f.p's c	BREKEL	1767	24031029
P'S	P's man.o. S.	DUCHAL	1753	56002003
P'S	P's. Ch. Tim.	NEWLIN	1728	58004005
P'S	P's. Thorn.	FANCH	1768	49012007
P'S	P's.wish exp.	WATERLAND	1742	48009003
P'S	P's.wish exp.	DODWELL	1752	48009003
P'S	P's.wish exp.	KEELING	1766	48009003
P'S	P's Pr.f. Ones	ORTON	1776	58001018
P'S	St. P's comm.	WATTS	1753	47025018
P'S	St. P's de. Xy	NEWTON	1782	49013001
P'S	St. P's preac.	BERRIMAN	1751	47024025
P'S	St. P's. Audit	SHERIDAN	1720	47017032
P'S	St. P's. C.i.	WILSON	1781	53001021
P'S	St. P's. Conf.	LEWIS	1729	47026026
P'S	St. P's. Def.	ATTERBURY	1734	47024025
P'S	St. P's. Def.	MOSS	1737	47024025
P'S	St. P's.choi.	ROGERS	1730	53001022
P'S	St. P's.d.to F	HOADLY	1754	47024024
P'S	St. P's.d.to F	CHANDLER	1769	47024025
P'S	St. P's.d.to F	HURD	1780	47024024
P'S	St. P's.strait	TRAPP	1752	53001023
PA	Dut.o. Pa.& Ch	ADAMS	1676	54003020
PA	Dut.o. Pa.& Ch	NICHOLS	1701	54003020
PA	St. Pa.c.&m.	BROUGHTON	1778	47009015
PA	Tem. Pa.&c.	ABERNETHY	1748	64001006
PAGG	Xty.& Pagg.	PENN	1756	47004012
PAIN	No Pain a bl.	WATTS	1753	69021004
PAINS	Pains o. Hell.	BOURDALOUE	1776	45016022
PAINT	Comp. Paint.	MORER	1708	50008018
PAINTING	on Painting.	ANONYMOUS	1752	19115005
PALM	Palm.s.	BADDELLEY	1766	46011035
PALM	Palm.s.	SECKER	1770	61012002
PALM	Palm- Sund.	GODDARD	1715	20024021
PAN	Pan.exp. Pe.	HENLEY	1729	61012007

Keyword	In its Context	Author	Year	BkChpVrs
PAP	Ant.ag. Pap.	OWEN	1683	63002003
PAP	Pap.& Phar.	BARTON	1766	43010014
PAP	Pap.& Phar.	BURTON	1766	43015001
PAP	Pap. Tyran.	DU MOULIN	1674	69018004
PAPISTS	Ag. Papists.	BAGSHAW	1680	48001018
PAR	Cl. Ad.t. Par.	STEDMAN	1776	58002006
PAR	Dut.to Par.	HOLLAND	1753	02020012
PAR	Duty of Par.	FLEETWOOD	1737	52006004
PAR	Duty of Par.	FLEETWOOD	1737	57005008
PAR	Duty of Par.	DELANY	1747	20022006
PAR	Duty to Par.	DAVIES	1754	02002002
PAR	G.cor.&par.	HOWE	1771	19099008
PAR	Gly.of Par.	BAYLYE	1710	49002009
PAR	Nath. Par.	GOUGH	1751	10012007
PAR	Occas.of Par.	BOURN	1763	45015001
PAR	Par. Counsil.	MAY	1744	20006020
PAR	Par. Instruct.	DYKES	1722	20031001
PAR	Par. Repent.	SHERLOCK	1772	19019012
PAR	Par. Sower.	WHEATLY	1746	45008005
PAR	Par. Sower.	ADEY	1755	45008004
PAR	Par. Talents.	CARR	1777	45019016
PAR	Par. Vin.&c.	MERRICK	1753	46015005
PAR	Par.explain.	CLARKE	1735	45016025
PAR	Par.interp.	ROMAINE	1756	26037004
PAR	Par.of Supp.	HOLE	1716	45014016
PAR	Par D.to Ch.	EATON	1764	20022006
PAR	Peace& Par.	CONANT	1698	49003011
PAR	b. Par. Cl.	MILBOURNE	1713	14029030
PAR	b. Par. Clerks	HILLIARD	1714	43006013
PARAB	Use of Parab.	BURNET	1747	45013006
PARAB	Xt's. Parab.	LELAND	1769	43013003
PARABLES	Parables.	BULKLEY	1771	43013013
PARABLES	Parables.	JORTIN	1774	43013013
PARABLES	of Parables.	MARKLAND	1729	43013003
PARABLES	of Parables.	WHEATLAND	1739	43013010
PARAC	Des.o. Parac.	FALLE	1695	46016007
PARAC	H. G. Parac.	LESTLEY	1720	46016007
PARAC	H. Gh. Parac.	BRETT	1720	46016007
PARALYT	Cure Paralyt.	BRAGGE	1702	45007001
PARALYTIC	Paralytic.	DODD	1757	45005018
PARALYTIC	Paralytic.	BULKLEY	1771	43009012
PARD	Believ.pard.	HILL	1755	19098008
PARD	Pard.& Salv.	BADDELLEY	1752	45007050
PARD	Pard.of Sin.	HOPKINS	1710	23043025
PARD	Pen.pard.	ECCLES	1755	45023043
PARDON	Pardon poss.	HOADLY	1727	61010026
PARE	Dut.of Pare.	LYE	1683	52006004
PAREN	Paren. Duty.	FRANKLIN	1765	52006004
PARENT	Reli Parent.	LARDNER	1751	58001005
PARENTAL	Parental Joy.	HOLLAND	1753	20023024
PARISH	Duty Parish.	NICHOLS	1701	55005013
PARL	Pray. Parl.	HOLE	1716	20011014
PAROCH	Paroch.com.	GRIFFITH	1711	49003005
PART	N. Part.in S.	CLARKSON	1696	52005007
PART	Part. Elect.	SLADEN	1732	56002013
PART	Part. Provid.	SEED	1743	19113005

Keyword	In its Context	Author	Year	BkChpVrs
PART	Part. Provid.	FOSTER	1744	69019006
PART	Part.of ot. M'	KITCHEN	1670	57005022
PART	Part.of ot. M'	MOSS	1737	57005022
PARTAK	Partak.&c.	SMALRIDGE	1724	57005022
PARTAK	Partak. Sin.	SMITH	1740	43027004
PARTAK	Partak. Sins.	FIDDES	1720	52005011
PARTIC	Partic. Prov.	ADAMS	1736	43010029
PARTIC	Partic. Prov.	DODWELL	1760	19033013
PARTIC	Partic. Prov.	CHANDLER	1769	19023006
PARTIC	Partic. Red.	HURRION	1732	59002014
PARTY	Party Zeal c.	RANDOLPH	1752	49003003
PAS	Dut. Pas.& P.	HOWARD	1728	59002015
PAS	Fas. W.pas.a.	DUNLOP	1722	49007031
PAS	Pas.& Peo. D.	ROE	1766	57004016
PAS	Us.& Ab. Pas.	HICKMAN	1706	47014015
PAS	Us.& Ab. Pas.	BATTY	1739	47014015
PASC	Pasc. Lamb.	BUNDY	1740	46001029
PASS	G.gov. Pass.	BLAIR	1780	19076010
PASS	Gov. Pass.	CLAGETT	1720	20025028
PASS	Govern. Pass.	HUSSEY	1755	47014015
PASS	Of the Pass.	YOUNG	1728	54003002
PASS	Pass. Obed.	CALAMY	1683	48003008
PASS	Pass. Obed.	BERKELEY	1713	48013002
PASS	Pass.disord.	BLAIR	1777	17005013
PASS	Pass.of Xt.	HALL	1661	46019030
PASS	Pass.of Xt.	SCOUGAL	1726	25001012
PASS	Pass.s.	ROYSE	1689	49006020
PASS	Pred. Pass.	ANONYMOUS	1708	46001019
PASS	Strait g.pass.	ANONYMOUS	1776	43007014
PASSI	Gov.of Passi.	CLARKE	1734	52004026
PASSI	Inord. Passi.	DAVIS	1756	65002016
PASSI	Reas.& Passi.	TOTTIE	1736	48007023
PASSION	Gov. Passion.	TRAPP	1751	45021019
PASSION	Mod. Passion.	FRANCIS	1773	20016032
PASSION	Passion.	BOURDALOUE	1776	49001022
PASSION	Xt's. Passion.	SPARKES	1663	43027001
PASSION	Xt's. Passion.	MUSCOTT	1760	53002008
PASSIONS	Gov. Passions	CARR	1777	20004023
PASSIONS	Passions.	BRAILSFORD	1776	43010036
PASSOVER	Last Passover	WILCOX	1757	45022015
PASSOVER	Xn. Passover.	RIDLEY	1736	49005007
PAST	Evang. Past.	FLAVEL	1673	43024045
PAST	Miss.of Past.	JOHNSON	1728	43009038
PAST	Past.& De. D.	WILSON	1736	24003015
PAST	Past. M.pr. S.	HILL	1755	07013023
PAST	Past. Office.	ALTHAM	1732	49004001
PAST	Past. Office.	BAINE	1778	38002006
PASTOR	Pastor. Adv.	SMITH	1775	51004016
PASTOR'S	Pastor's Duty	HENDLEY	1716	57006020
PASTOR'S	Pastor's Duty	HENDLEY	1716	58004002
PAT	Abu. G's Pat.	HOLLAND	1753	21008011
PAT	God's Pat.	SAURIN	1775	01015016
PAT	Hope& Pat.	STRAIGHT	1741	48012012
PAT	Pat.i.well-d.	MACE	1751	61010036
PAT	Xt. Pat.t. Xns	BEVERIDGE	1720	63001015
PATH	Path of Just.	ABERNETHY	1748	20004018

Keyword	In its Context	Author	Year	BkChpVrs
PATH	Path to Hon.	WHEATLAND	1739	20003016
PATHS	L's Paths m.	CHANDLER	1769	19025010
PATHS	Old Paths.	STEFFE	1743	24006016
PATI	Faith& Pati.	EMLYN	1742	61006012
PATI	Faith& Pati.	HARTLEY	1754	61006012
PATIEN	Div. Patien.	EMLYN	1742	69002021
PATIEN	Xn. Patien.	LORTIE	1720	62001002
PATIENCE	G's. Patience	WHITBY	1710	48002004
PATIENCE	G's. Patience	WISHEART	1716	48002004
PATIENCE	G's. Patience	HUNT	1748	48002004
PATIENCE	G's Patience	CLARKE	1732	21008011
PATIENCE	L's. Patience	WHITE	1757	61012003
PATIENCE	Patience.	GOODWIN	1666	62001001
PATIENCE	Patience.	DORRINGTON	1703	48012012
PATIENCE	Patience.	BARROW	1716	63002021
PATIENCE	Patience.	LORTIE	1720	62005008
PATIENCE	Patience.	SHORTHOSE	1738	45021019
PATIENCE	Patience.	HUNT	1748	54001011
PATIENCE	Patience.	CONYBEARE	1757	62001002
PATIENCE	Patience.	HEYLIN	1761	45021019
PATIENCE	Patience.	ADEY	1760	61012001
PATIENCE	Patience.	FARRINGTON	1769	58004005
PATIENCE	Patience.	SECKER	1771	45021019
PATIENCE	Patience.	HORNE	1778	57006011
PATIENCE	Xn. Patience	ANONYMOUS	1708	57001012
PATIENCE	Xn. Patience	EVANS	1737	61010036
PATR	Good Patr.	MACKQUEENE	1694	45007004
PATR	Rel.& Patr.	DAVIES	1755	10010012
PATRICK	St. Patrick.d.	HENRY	1756	45024005
PATRIOT	Dev. Patriot.	BULKLEY	1761	19018009
PATRIOT	Dev. Patriot.	BULKLEY	1761	19028009
PATRIOT	Gen. Patriot.	STEPHEN	1774	15009013
PATRIOT	Xn. Patriot.	MILNE	1780	45019041
PATRIOTISM	Patriotism.	MORGAN	1780	07005023
PATT	Heav. Patt.	YOUNG	1706	43006010
PATT	Patt.of Mer.	CONYERS	1660	45006036
PATT	Patt.of Mer.	CENNICK	1762	57001015
PATT	Xt.our Patt.	SKELTON	1754	53002005
PATTERN	Xn's. Pattern	SUTTON	1754	43011029
PAUL	Hum.in Paul	WATTS	1753	52002018
PAUL	Paul cap. Xt.	BREKELL	1765	50011014
PAUL	St. Paul.	FRANK	1672	16013014
PAUL'S	Paul's Conf.	HAMMOND	1684	57001015
PAUL'S	Paul's Conv.	GROVE	1741	51001015
PAUL'S	Paul's Conv.	WHITTY	1766	51001013
PAUL'S	Paul's Diffi.	CONYBEARE	1757	50011023
PAUL'S	Paul's Tem.	FANCH	1768	50012007
PAUL'S	Paul's Xrter.	WEST	1762	49009019
PAUL'S	Paul's Xrter.	ENFIELD	1777	49011001
PAUL'S	S. Paul's Sin.	SMITH	1740	46016002
PAUL'S	St. Paul's co.	STANHOPE	1715	43019027
PAUL'S	St. Paul's co.	HOLE	1716	43019027
PAUL'S	St. Paul's d.	NEEDHAM	1716	45014023
PAUL'S	St. Paul's d.	COBDEN	1757	47020024
PAUL'S	St. Paul's rel	SYNGE	1721	47024014
PAUL'S	St. Paul's.co.	HOLE	1716	47009001

Keyword	In its Context	Author	Year	BkChpVrs
PAUL'S	St. Paul's.co.	SHERIDAN	1720	47009003
PAUL'S	St. Paul's.co.	WATERLAND	1742	47009004
PAUL'S	St. Paul's.d.	STANHOPE	1715	47009001
PAUL'S	St. Paul's Co.	WILDER	1729	57001013
PAUL'S	St. Paul's Co.	FARMER	1756	57001013
PAUL'S	St. Paul's Fa.	SHERIDAN	1720	47024014
PAUL'S	St. Paul's Xr.	DUCHAL	1753	47020024
PAUL'S	St Paul's Co.	LUCAS	1717	49015009
PAY	Pay. Debts.	DELANY	1747	48013008
PAY	Pay. Debts.	BERRIMAN	1763	48013008
PE	B. Pe.mak.	HORNECK	1706	43005009
PE	B. Pe.mak.	NORRIS	1728	43005009
PE	B. Pe.mak.	GROVE	1742	43005009
PE	B. Pe.mak.	HALES	1766	43005009
PE	B. Pe.mak.	ORR	1772	43005009
PE	Bless.of b. Pe	COLLINGES	1684	43005010
PE	Bless.of b. Pe	BLACKBURNE	1708	43005010
PE	Bless.of b. Pe	BRAGGE	1713	43005010
PE	Bless.of b. Pe	GARDINER	1720	43005010
PE	Bless.of b. Pe	BLACKALL	1723	43005010
PE	Bless.of b. Pe	EDWARDS	1726	43005010
PE	Bless.of b. Pe	NORRIS	1728	43005010
PE	Bless.of b. Pe	BLAIR	1740	43005010
PE	Bless.of b. Pe	ORR	1772	43005010
PE	Har. Div. Pe.	WEST	1762	65001005
PE	O.o. M.& Pe.	WILSON	1781	61013017
PE	Pan.exp. Pe.	HENLEY	1729	61012007
PE	Pe.&imp. H.	MOORE	1716	50007001
PE	Pe.&imp. H.	LEIGHTON	1746	50007001
PE	Pe. Lo.g.bo.	BAYLY	1721	65004017
PE	Rule Pe.& L.	ELLIS	1684	53002003
PEA	Duty o. Pea.	GARDINER	1713	48014019
PEA	G.auth.pea.	COTES	1721	49014033
PEA	Joy Pea.& H.	LUCAS	1710	48015013
PEA	Pea wick. D.	HORTON	1679	55005003
PEA	Pea. Ch. Ch.	REYNOLDS	1679	48014009
PEA	Pea. Con.&c.	PRICE	1757	48015013
PEA	Pea.of mind.	MACE	1751	48014022
PEACE	Adv. Peace.	REGIS	1718	43005009
PEACE	Ch's Peace.	ADDERLEY	1679	19122006
PEACE	Cov.o. Peace.	SKELTON	1754	54001021
PEACE	Inw. Peace.	TILLOTSON	1735	19119165
PEACE	Loy.& Peace	RAYMOND	1705	59003003
PEACE	Loy. Peace.	ROLL	----	09025005
PEACE	Of Peace.	BRETT	1720	65005007
PEACE	On Peace.	FRANCIS	1773	45002014
PEACE	Peace mak.	EDWARDS	1726	43010010
PEACE	Peace mind.	MACE	1751	48002012
PEACE	Peace of G.	MOSS	1738	54003015
PEACE	Peace of Gr.	MAKENZIE	1779	18003017
PEACE	Peace of Jer.	REYNOLDS	1679	19122006
PEACE	Peace of M.	PAYNE	1698	43011029
PEACE	Peace of M.	CARR	1777	19037038
PEACE	Peace of Ms	SCOTT	1700	46014027
PEACE	Peace.	DALTON	1757	55005013
PEACE	Peace.	STERNE	1769	61012014

Keyword	In its Context	Author	Year	BkChpVrs
PEACE	Peace.	CARR	1777	48012018
PEACE	Peace. Tem.	SEATON	1720	01013008
PEACE	Peace.life.	REEVES	1729	48012018
PEACE	Peace.life.	SOUTH	1744	48012018
PEACE	Peace& Fri.	BRADY	1730	48012018
PEACE	Peace& Hol.	PIERCE	1679	61012014
PEACE	Peace& Hol.	UMFREVILLE	1739	61012014
PEACE	Peace& Joy.	CROSSINGE	1718	23032017
PEACE	Peace& Love	JEKYLL	1675	61012014
PEACE	Peace& Par.	CONANT	1698	49003011
PEACE	Peace& Qui.	HOWARD	1736	55004011
PEACE	Peace& Sub.	ROGERS	1730	55004011
PEACE	Peace& Un.	BURNET	1689	47007026
PEACE	Peace& Uni.	HOWELL	1712	54002015
PEACE	Peace& Uni.	ANONYMOUS	1712	54003015
PEACE	Peace& Uni.	HICKES	1726	53004007
PEACE	Peace Temp.	GARDINER	1720	43005009
PEACE	Peace Temp.	BLACKALL	1723	43005009
PEACE	Peace Temp.	EDWARDS	1726	43005009
PEACE	Peace Temp.	BLAIR	1740	43005009
PEACE	Peace Temp.	ABERNETHY	1751	43005009
PEACE	Peace Temp.	COBDEN	1757	43005009
PEACE	Rej.f. Peace.	PHILIPS	1775	23066010
PEACE	Relig. Peace.	TREBECK	1730	20016007
PEACE	Un.& Peace.	LUCAS	1710	52004002
PEACE	Uni.& Peace.	PIGGOTT	1714	48014019
PEACE	no Peace to wic	HORTON	1679	23057021
PEACE	no Peace to wic	FOORD	1719	23057021
PEACE	on the Peace.	ARMAND	1762	22002004
PEACEA	Liv. Peacea.	JORTIN	1774	48012018
PEACEAB	Peaceab. Xn.	ANONYMOUS	1678	48012018
PEACEABLEN	Peaceablen.	BARROW	1716	48012018
PEACEABLEN	Peaceablen.	BURNET	1747	48012018
PEACEABLEN	Peaceablen.	GROVE	1747	48012018
PEACEABLEN	Peaceablen.	WEBSTER	1748	48012018
PEACEABLEN	Peaceablen.	BALL	1756	48012018
PEARL	Pearl.	WILKINSON	1660	43013045
PEARL	Pearl.	BRAGGE	1702	43013045
PEARL	Pearl.	DOODD	1757	43013045
PEARL	Pearl.	STEBBING	1760	43013044
PEC	G's pec. Peo.	WEBBER	1738	05014002
PECUL	Pecul. Prov.	DAVIS	1756	19034008
PECUL	Pecul.dei.	HICKES	1713	48009004
PEN	D. M.to pen.	DAVIES	1766	24031018
PEN	G's.acc.pen.	BURNET	1747	65001009
PEN	Pen. Rake.	BOURN	1763	45015011
PEN	Pen. Rake.	POWELL	1776	45015011
PEN	Pen. Thief.	LIGHTFOOT	1684	45023042
PEN	Pen. Thief.	STANHOPE	1705	45023042
PEN	Pen. Thief.	WHISTON	1709	45023042
PEN	Pen. Thief.	HOADLY	1727	45023042
PEN	Pen. Thief.	BOYSE	1728	45023039
PEN	Pen. Thief.	BULKLEY	1752	45023043
PEN	Pen. Thief.	NEWMAN	1751	45023042
PEN	Pen. Thief.	JORTIN	1774	45023042
PEN	Pen. Thief.	EDWARDS	1775	45023042

Keyword	In its Context	Author	Year	BkChpVrs
PEN	Pen.pard.	ECCLES	1755	45023043
PEN	Pen.view. S.	WHITTY	1772	44014072
PEN	Thank. Pen.	BROME	1712	45007047
PEN	Thank. Pen.	DODD	1757	45007047
PEN	Thank. Pen.	DODD	1757	45008047
PENAL	Penal Laws.	PASTON	1688	45009055
PENAL	Penal Suffer.	REAY	1755	25003029
PENAN	Pub. Penan.	FORD	1696	51006001
PENANCE	Penance.	BOURDALOUE	1776	45003003
PENANCES	Penances.	STERNE	1769	65005003
PENIT	Penit.s.	BARLOW	1690	46008011
PENIT	Prod. Penit.	CREYGHTON	1720	45015018
PENIT	Prod. Penit.	ST.	1737	45015017
PENIT	Prod. Penit.	JORTIN	1774	45015018
PENIT	Sinc. Penit.	CREYGHTON	1720	45022062
PENIT	Sinc. Penit.	BRADY	1730	45022061
PENIT	True Penit.	BRADY	1730	45014023
PEO	G's pec. Peo.	WEBBER	1738	05014002
PEO	Jew. Peo.&c.	LARDNER	1743	48011011
PEO	Pas.& Peo. D.	ROE	1766	57004016
PEO	Peo. Rgt. S. S	SHARP	1735	64003016
PEOP	Peop.of W.	MURRAY	1777	01010001
PEOPLE	Y.people.	ABERNETHY	1751	19034011
PEOR	Baal Peor.	MORE	1692	19106028
PER	G.&nat.per.	GUYSE	1757	46004024
PER	No per. H.h.	JOHNSON	1740	61011039
PER	Per.& F. R.	SAUNDERS	1701	06024014
PER	Per.& F. R.	READER	1765	06024014
PER	Per.of Xn. K.	SAURIN	1775	61005012
PER	Per.to Union	SHUTTLEWORTH	1718	48015006
PER	Per.well-do.	DORMAN	1743	51006009
PER	Xnity per. L.	HICKES	1726	43005017
PER	Xt.per.m. L.	BLAIR	1740	43005017
PERF	D. Perf.in.	COYTE	1761	18011007
PERF	Exter. Perf.	HOADLY	1727	48010013
PERF	G's Pr.perf.	ERSKINE	1764	01028015
PERF	Hum. Perf.	MANTON	1685	53003015
PERF	Mor. Perf. G.	PRICE	1757	43005048
PERF	No perf.in L.	WHITTY	1772	62003002
PERF	Perf.& Unity	MANTON	1708	53003003
PERF	Perf. Gosp.	TRAPP	1752	58002011
PERF	Perf. Xter.	BOURN	1777	62001004
PERF	Perf.in hear.	WHITTY	1772	49015049
PERF	Perf.of Cha.	JEFFERY	1710	45014015
PERF	Perf.of Char.	HOLE	1725	49013009
PERF	Perf.unatt.	BALL	1756	43005048
PERF	R.perf.sy.m.	LAWSON	1764	43007020
PERF	Relig. Perf.	WILLIAMS	1774	19037037
PERF	Sinless Perf.	WATERLAND	1742	65003009
PERF	Xty.perf. L.	TILLOTSON	1735	43005017
PERFEC	Mor. Perfec.	DUCHAL	1765	49003009
PERFECT	Div. Perfect.	WEST	1762	46001005
PERFECT	G's. Perfect.	BOSTON	1773	46005024
PERFECT	Perfect. God.	ABERNETHY	1743	18011007
PERFECT	Rel. Perfect.	LUCAS	1697	61006001
PERFECT	Spir. Perfect.	BATES	1700	50007001

Keyword	In its Context	Author	Year	BkChpVrs
PERFECT	Xn. Perfect.	PARKER	1697	43005048
PERFECT	Xn. Perfect.	BLACKALL	1723	43005048
PERFECT	Xn. Perfect.	BLAIR	1740	43005048
PERFECT	Xn. Perfect.	JOHNSON	1740	50013011
PERFECT	Xn. Perfect.	SIMONS	1743	61006001
PERFECT	Xn. Perfect.	WESTLEY	1750	53003012
PERFECT	Xn. Perfect.	BRACKENRIDGE	1764	43005048
PERFECT	Xty.perfect.	GROVE	1741	54002010
PERFECTION	Perfection.	EDWARDS	1726	50013011
PERFECTION	Perfection.	ENFIELD	1772	50013011
PERIL	Peril.times.	BOSTON	1753	58003001
PERIOD	Period life.	FYSH	1738	20010027
PERIOD	Period of L.	E.	1679	18014005
PERJ	Perj.&c. Sw.	GARDINER	1720	43005033
PERJ	Perj.&c. Sw.	BLACKALL	1723	43005033
PERJ	Perj.&c. Sw.	BLAIR	1740	43005033
PERJ	Perj.&c. Sw.	LOVEDAY	1741	43005033
PERJURY	Ag. Perjury.	ROWLAND	1755	38003003
PERJURY	Perjury.	MOSS	1732	24004002
PERM	An. F.perm.	JENKINS	1779	01009003
PERP	Perp. Obed.	SHEPHEARD	1748	51006009
PERP	Perp. Xt's. K.	HUSSEY	1753	45001033
PERP	Perp.mor. L.	HORNECK	1706	43005018
PERP	Perp.mor. L.	BLACKALL	1723	43005019
PERP	Perp.mor. L.	BLAIR	1740	43005018
PERS	B.of Pers.for	FARINDON	1672	43005010
PERS	B.of Pers.for	HORNECK	1706	43005010
PERS	B.of Pers.for	GROVE	1742	43005010
PERS	Const.& Pers.	CREYGHTON	1720	49015058
PERS	Const.& Pers.	EVANS	1737	49015058
PERS	Pers. Duty.	CLARKE	1735	46021022
PERS	Pers. Holin.	HAWEIS	1762	61012014
PERS	Pers. Int. Xt.	CASE	1774	51002020
PERS	Pers. Prayer.	BOSTON	1753	45018001
PERS	Pers.in m. C.	STOCKDALE	1777	01049004
PERS	Pers.in Rel.	STENNET	1769	07008004
PERS	Pers.in Xty.	BATTY	1739	49009024
PERS	Pers.inc. Xy.	BRACKENRIDGE	1764	45009056
PERS	Pers.of H. G.	HARRISON	1734	46015026
PERS	Pers.of Xt.	NEWTON	1767	43011027
PERS	Pers.to Hol.	HARRISON	1710	50007001
PERS	Sp. Div. Pers.	BRETT	1720	46014016
PERS	To Y. Pers.	GROSVENOR	1714	19018023
PERS	To Y. Pers.	DAVIDSON	1772	21012001
PERS	Xt's.pers.m.	GUYSE	1757	46001018
PERS	Xt's.w.pers.	FLAVEL	1673	46001014
PERS	Young pers.	BOYSE	1728	44010021
PERSEC	Persec.unla.	JORTIN	1774	45014023
PERSECUT	Ag. Persecut.	BOURN	1777	43018007
PERSECUT	Ag. Persecut.	ROTHERAM	1780	45009055
PERSECUT	Persecut.foret	HORNECK	1706	43005011
PERSECUT	Persecut.foret	BLAIR	1740	43005010
PERSECUTION	Persecution.	HORNECK	1706	43005012
PERSECUTION	Persecution.	CLARKE	1735	45014023
PERSECUTION	Persecution.	DODDERIDGE	1736	45009055
PERSECUTION	Persecution.	BLAIR	1740	43005011

Keyword	In its Context	Author	Year	BkChpVrs
PERSECUTION	Persecution.	DODDERIDGE	1761	45011055
PERSEV	Fin. Persev.	PENTYCROSS	1781	48008038
PERSEV	Persev. Gra.	FARMER	1756	53001006
PERSEVER	Xn. Persever.	BRADY	1713	64003017
PERSEVERAN	Perseveran.	CLARKE	1736	69002007
PERSEVERANCE	Perseverance	HORTON	1679	46008030
PERSEVERANCE	Perseverance	STAFFORD	1701	19102028
PERSEVERANCE	Perseverance	EDWARDS	1726	69003011
PERSEVERANCE	Perseverance	HOLDEN	1755	43024013
PERSEVERANCE	Perseverance	WHITTY	1766	61003014
PERSON	Person of Xt.	HARWOOD	1772	54001015
PERSON	Xt's. Person.	NICHOLSON	1661	43016015
PERSONS	Y. Persons.	GREENE	1713	20023026
PERSUA	Persua.t. Ch.	DOUGHTY	1742	44012041
PESTILENCE	Pestilence.	HILDROP	1711	24009021
PET	Pet. Ignor.	HORTON	1679	46013007
PET	St. Pet.d. Xt.	GELL	1676	43010032
PET	St. Pet.d. Xt.	COOKE	1739	43010032
PET	St. Pet.d. Xt.	BUNDY	1740	43010033
PETER'S	Peter's deni.	ABERNETHY	1748	43026074
PETER'S	Peter's Conf.	ADAM	1776	43016016
PETER'S	Peter's Defect	LOVEDER	1756	44014071
PETER'S	Peter's Fall&r	STANHOPE	1705	44014072
PETER'S	Peter's Rep.	HART	1702	44014068
PETER'S	Peter's Rep.	SHERLOCK	1772	45022061
PETER'S	Peter's Xrter.	ENFIELD	1777	43026035
PETER'S	St. Peter's d.	GODDEN	1686	43016018
PETER'S	St. Peter's d.	PATRICK	1687	43016018
PETER'S	St. Peter's d.	STANHOPE	1715	47012001
PETER'S	St. Peter's d.	HOLE	1716	47012001
PETER'S	St. Peter's d.	MARSHALL	1731	44014029
PETER'S	St. Peter's d.	BERRIMAN	1763	43016018
PETER'S	St. Peter's.d.	MARSHALL	1731	47010034
PETER'S	St. Peter's Xr	STERNE	1769	47003012
PETERS	St. Peters d.	STANHOPE	1715	43016013
PETERS	St. Peters d.	HOLE	1716	43016013
PETIT	Cent. Petit.	ECCLES	1755	43008008
PETIT	Moses' Petit.	KEELING	1767	02032031
PH	St. Ph.& St. J	STANHOPE	1715	62001001
PH	St. Ph.& St. J	HOLE	1716	62001001
PHAR	Leav. Phar.	BREKELL	1765	43016006
PHAR	Mod. Phar.	BISBIE	1683	43023015
PHAR	Pap.& Phar.	BARTON	1766	43010014
PHAR	Pap.& Phar.	BURTON	1766	43015001
PHAR	Phar.& Pub.	CHARNOCK	1684	46001013
PHAR	Phar.& Pub.	BUNYAN	17--	46001013
PHAR	Phar.& Pub.	BRAGGE	1702	45018009
PHAR	Phar.& Pub.	HOLE	1716	45018009
PHAR	Phar.& Pub.	DODD	1757	45018009
PHAR	Phar.& Pub.	BARKER	1763	45018009
PHAR	Phar.& Pub.	BOURN	1764	45018009
PHAR	Phar.& Pub.	KNOWLES	1769	45018014
PHAR	Phar.& Pub.	BULKLEY	1771	45018009
PHAR	Phar.& Pub.	FRANCIS	1771	45018014
PHAR	Phar.& Pub.	JORTIN	1774	45018014
PHAR	Phar. Relig.	BURD	1759	43005020

Keyword	In its Context	Author	Year	BkChpVrs
PHAR	Phar. Right.	SMITH	1673	43019020
PHAR	Phar. Right.	HORTON	1679	44012034
PHAR	Phar. Right.	BLACKALL	1723	43005020
PHAR	Phar. Right.	SCATTERGOOD	1723	43005020
PHAR	Phar. Right.	BLAIR	1740	43005020
PHAR	Phar. Right.	SOUTH	1744	43005020
PHAR	Phar.lesson.	LONG	1677	43009013
PHAR	Pub.& Phar.	STRAIGHT	1741	45018014
PHAR	Pub.& Phar.	WATERLAND	1742	45018014
PHAR	Simon Phar.	VENN	1759	45007036
PHARIS	The Pharis.	HAMMOND	1684	45018011
PHIL	Ag. Phil.&c.	CASE	1774	54002008
PHIL	St. Phil.& J.	LITTLETON	1680	46001046
PHIL	St. Phil.& J.	STANHOPE	1715	46014001
PHIL	St. Phil.& J.	HOLE	1716	46014001
PHILANT	Div. Philant.	SHERLOCK	1772	46003016
PHILANTHOPY	Philanthopy	FRANK	1716	05033003
PHILANTHR	Philanthr.	STERNE	1760	45010036
PHILO	Ag.m. Philo.	CRADDOCK	1739	49001023
PHILOS	True Philos.	COLLIER	1730	01001001
PHILOS	Vain Philos.	SOUTH	1744	21001018
PHILOSP	Xn. Philosp.	DELANY	1766	54002008
PHINEAS	Phineas Z.	CATCOTT	1753	19106030
PHYS	Phys.of souls	SHEPHERD	1748	43009012
PI	Choi affl. Pi.	TILLOTSON	1735	61011024
PICT	Pict.of w.	EDWARDS	1726	18014001
PICT	Pict.of w.	ANONYMOUS	1754	18014001
PICT	Pict.of Tim.	WILLIAMS	1662	24014010
PICTURE	Picture o. Xt.	SYMPSON	1662	22005016
PIE	Faith pr. Pie.	BEVERIDGE	1720	47015009
PIE	Un. Pie.& M.	BLAIR	1777	47010004
PIERCED	Xt.pierced.	WILLISON	1761	37012010
PIETY	Adv.of Piety	BAINE	1778	69003004
PIETY	Comf. Piety.	SHERLOCK	1772	19119165
PIETY	Early Piety.	BUCK	1704	11018012
PIETY	Early Piety.	PARKHURST	1706	11018012
PIETY	Early Piety.	GOUGE	1706	21012001
PIETY	Early Piety.	BRAY	1714	21012001
PIETY	Early Piety.	SMYTHIES	1723	25003027
PIETY	Early Piety.	EVANS	1725	21012001
PIETY	Early Piety.	BRADY	1730	21012001
PIETY	Early Piety.	DICKSON	1731	21012001
PIETY	Early Piety.	JENNINGS	1743	24002002
PIETY	Early Piety.	ANONYMOUS	1745	11018001
PIETY	Early Piety.	LARDNER	1751	11018012
PIETY	Early Piety.	WILCOX	1757	48015007
PIETY	Early Piety.	GIBBONS	1763	11018012
PIETY	Early Piety.	BADDELLEY	1766	21012001
PIETY	Early Piety.	CHANDLER	1769	20008017
PIETY	Early Piety.	ROBINSON	1772	19144011
PIETY	Early Piety.	DODD	1772	20008017
PIETY	Early Piety.	WARNEFORD	1776	21012005
PIETY	Early Piety.	DEVERELL	1777	21012001
PIETY	False Piety.	WILLIAMS	1774	19050021
PIETY	Fem. Piety.	FORDYCE	1767	20031030
PIETY	Hab. Piety.	TOULMIN	1770	20023017

Keyword	In its Context	Author	Year	BkChpVrs
PIETY	Hap.of Piety	LANGHORNE	1773	19119001
PIETY	Infl.of Piety.	FOTHERGILL	1765	20003005
PIETY	Little Piety.	HAMMOND	1684	24005002
PIETY	Of ag. Piety.	PEIRCE	1728	20016031
PIETY	Piety secure.	BRADY	1730	20012021
PIETY	Piety to Xt.	WILLIAMS	1774	01001011
PIETY	Piety tow. G.	SEATON	1720	01024048
PIETY	Piety.	BOURDALOUE	1776	43005020
PIETY	Piety.	MILNE	1780	50007001
PIETY	Piety& Vir.	SYNGE	1733	19010004
PIETY	Profit. Piety.	FARRINGTON	1741	18021015
PIETY	Ruth's Piety.	JENKINS	1779	08001016
PIETY	Serious Piety	EVANS	1725	13028009
PIETY	Sing. Piety.	WRIGHT	1716	02023002
PIETY	True Piety.	BOURN	1777	19027004
PIETY	Xn. Piety.	FROYSELL	1678	58003012
PIL	P. Pil. Xrter.	CRAIG	1775	45023023
PIL	Pil.&c.o. Tr.	PATRICK	1687	57003015
PILATE	Pilate. Xrter.	WEST	1762	43027024
PILATE'S	Pilate's Ques.	WARBURTON	1753	46018038
PILATE'S	Pilate's Ques.	SANDWICH	1774	46018038
PILGR	Life a Pilgr.	CONYBEARE	1759	61011013
PILGRI	Life Pilgri.	WALKER	1764	19039012
PILGRI	Life Pilgri.	DUCHE	1779	19039012
PIOUS	Pious Man.	COCK	1710	19024003
PIOUS	Pious Man.	SHARP	1729	19112004
PITY	Pity& Cour.	MAINWARING	1760	64003008
PITY	Pity& Court.	MAINWARING	1780	63003008
PL	Adv.& Pl. R.	STOCKDALE	1777	55005016
PL	Imm. L.o. Pl.	CHANDLER	1769	58003004
PL	M.pl.w.cri.	FARINDON	1672	51001010
PL	Pl.best Rel.	DODSLEY	1745	20007017
PL	R. Life t. Pl.	LAWSON	1764	19001002
PL	Unlaw. Pl.	FORDYCE	1760	20007007
PL	W.m pl. G.	WATERLAND	1742	20016004
PL	Welcome Pl.	SHAW	1751	30004012
PL	Wis.r.t. Pl.	ANONYMOUS	1754	20003017
PL'S	St. Pl's.orth.	FLEMING	1759	59002015
PLAC	Plac.of wor.	BENNETT	1728	45006012
PLACE	Hiding place	ALLESTREE	1684	23026020
PLACES	Places of W.	DOWNES	1761	26034012
PLAG	Plag. Heart.	EDWARDS	1665	11008038
PLAIN	Plain Truth.	SMITH	1777	43002002
PLAN	Plan of life.	DUCHAL	1765	52005015
PLEA	Licent. Plea.	ORR	1749	57005006
PLEA	Love o. Plea.	IBBOT	1726	57003004
PLEA	Love o. Plea.	SECKER	1770	57003004
PLEA	Love of plea.	BARKER	1748	23047008
PLEA	Love of Plea.	HOADLY	1754	58003004
PLEA	Love of Plea.	DALTON	1757	58003004
PLEA	Love of Plea.	COLE	1761	58003004
PLEA	Love of Plea.	WILLIAMS	1774	58003004
PLEA	Plea for Tr.	WALKER	1710	11018021
PLEA	Plea.f. Ch. E.	HOLLINGWORTH	1676	46006068
PLEA	Plea.f.godly.	WATSON	1672	20012026
PLEA	Sensual Plea.	TOTTIE	1775	58003004

Keyword	In its Context	Author	Year	BkChpVrs
PLEAS	Fall.of Pleas.	AGAR	1759	19001001
PLEAS	Hon.& Pleas.	DODD	1772	20003013
PLEAS	Love of Pleas.	IBBOT	1726	58003004
PLEAS	Love of Pleas.	OAKES	1747	58003004
PLEAS	Love of Pleas.	PORTEUS	1772	58003004
PLEAS	Love of Pleas.	PEARCE	1779	58003004
PLEAS	Pleas. G. M.	ANONYMOUS	1754	18036011
PLEAS	Pleas. God.	BEVERIDGE	1720	55004001
PLEAS	Pleas. Men.	ADAMS	1716	51001010
PLEAS	Pleas.no H.	NEWMAN	1760	21002001
PLEAS	Pleas.rel. L.	DORRINGTON	1703	20003017
PLEAS	Pleas.rel. L.	PEARSON	1718	20003017
PLEAS	Pleas.rel. L.	SOUTH	1727	20003017
PLEAS	Pleas.rel. L.	NEWLIN	1728	20003017
PLEAS	Pleas.rel. L.	WILDER	1729	20003017
PLEAS	Pleas.rel. L.	FORSTER	1732	20003017
PLEAS	Pleas.rel. L.	WESTLEY	1735	20003017
PLEAS	Pleas.rel. L.	WHEATLAND	1739	20003017
PLEAS	Pleas.rel. L.	FARRINGTON	1741	20003017
PLEAS	Pleas.rel. L.	OAKES	1747	20003017
PLEAS	Pleas.rel. L.	SEED	1750	20003017
PLEAS	Pleas.rel. L.	FOTHERGILL	1765	20003017
PLEAS	Pleas.rel. L.	STENNETT	1769	20003017
PLEAS	Pleas.rel. L.	JORTIN	1774	20003017
PLEAS	Pre.pleas.&c	BOURN	1777	43025024
PLEAS	Reg.of Pleas.	LUCAS	1710	58003004
PLEAS	Reg.of Pleas.	HOOLE	1748	58003004
PLEASURE	Pleasure.	DODD	1772	21011009
PLOT	Disc. Plot.	LITTLETON	1680	19036005
PLOT	Disc. Plot.	LATHOM	1683	20008015
PLOT	Disc.of Plot.	BRADY	1706	02014013
PLOT	Discov. Plot.	ANONYMOUS	1683	28010002
PLOTT	Plott. Doom.	ANONYMOUS	1680	19037012
PLUCK	Pluck Eye.	BROWNE	1749	44009047
PLUR	Plur.worlds.	STURMY	1711	61011003
PN	Pn. Love.	BOEHM	1717	49013004
PO	Errors of Po.	TOWGOOD	1746	57004001
PO	F.& Po.o. G.	ATTERBURY	1699	58003005
PO	F.& Po.o. G.	BULL	1713	58003005
PO	Po.cor.o. Xy.	BARKER	1735	50011003
POL	Bl.pol.o. S.	FLAVEL	1673	50004003
POLI	Evang. Poli.	DUPORT	1661	53001027
POLIC	Eccles. Polic.	SOUTH	1727	11013033
POLICY	Craft Policy.	ELLIS	1704	45016003
POLICY	Sat. Policy.	GLANVILLE	1681	50002011
POLIG	Ag. Polig.	SHORTHOSE	1738	43019008
POLIT	Polit. Union.	SACHEVERELL	1702	20008015
POLIT	Univ. Polit.	BURTON	1764	55004011
POLL	Poll.of Sin.	REYNOLDS	1679	50007001
POLYG	Polyg.indef.	SMITH	1780	01002024
POMP	Pomp&c. W.	ANONYMOUS	1780	48012002
POOL	Pool Bethes.	DODD	1757	46005004
POOL	Pool Bethes.	BULKLEY	1771	46005002
POOR	Ch.to poor.	DYKES	1722	20031020
POOR	Ch.to poor.	STEBBING	1760	05015011
POOR	Ch.to Poor.	NORRIS	1728	65003017
POOR	Cha.to poor.	WILLIAMS	1774	45014012
POOR	Coll.f.poor.	SELLON	1763	20030008
POOR	Coll.poor M.	MAULDEN	1738	20003006
POOR	Dut. Poor.	SECKER	1770	43011005
POOR	Edu.poor G.	WILSON	1781	58001004
POOR	Emp. Poor.	JOHNSTON	1726	20013023
POOR	Hon.of poor.	MILNER	1750	45007022
POOR	Poor instr.	GREEN	1750	19068010
POOR	R.poor.p. C.	BRADY	1730	62002015
POOR	Rich&poor.	CONANT	1699	20022002
POOR	Rich&poor.	NEWTON	1736	20022002
POOR	Rich&poor.	GROVE	1742	20022002
POOR	Rich&poor.	CONYBEARE	1757	20022002
POOR	Rich&poor.	WHITE	1757	20022002
POOR	Rich&poor.	SKEELER	1772	20022002
POOR	Rich&poor.	JORTIN	1774	20022002
POOR	Rich&poor.	PYLE	1777	20022002
PORT	Ch. G's Port.	BLIGH	1765	05032009
POS	Mo.&pos. D.	CLARKE	1735	43022040
POS	Mor.&pos.d.	WESTON	1747	43009013
POS	Mor.&pos.d.	HUNT	1748	43009013
POS	Pos.& Ne. G.	ELSMERE	1767	23001016
POS	Pos.&m. Dut.	CARR	1777	43023009
POS	Pos. Inst.&c.	HUTCHINS	1782	12005012
POS	Pos. Instit.	GERARD	1780	45001016
POS	Pos.pr.o. Xy.	KNOX	1768	63001015
POS	Xn.pos.a.th.	IBBBOT	1726	50006010
POSS	Diab. Poss.	WHEATLY	1746	43017014
POSS	Pardon poss.	HOADLY	1727	61010026
POSS	Temp. Poss.	ABERNETHY	1751	45016008
POSSI	Assur.possi.	DOOLITTLE	1677	65005013
POSSIBLE	Rep.possible.	LUCAS	1717	24005003
POST	Xn's. Post.	PEMBERTON	1727	55004011
POV	Pov.of Spir.	LITTLETON	1680	43005003
POV	Pov.of Spir.	TURNER	1687	43005003
POV	Pov.of Spir.	HORNECK	1706	43005003
POV	Pov.of Spir.	YOUNG	1706	43005003
POV	Pov.of Spir.	GARDINER	1720	43005003
POV	Pov.of Spir.	EDWARDS	1726	43005003
POV	Pov.of Spir.	NORRIS	1728	43005003
POV	Pov.of Spir.	ALTHAM	1732	43005003
POV	Pov.of Spir.	DAWES	1733	43005003
POV	Pov.of Spir.	CLARKE	1734	43005003
POV	Pov.of Spir.	BLAIR	1740	43005003
POV	Pov.of Spir.	GROVE	1742	43005003
POV	Pov.of Spir.	SOUTH	1744	43005003
POV	Pov.of Spir.	KIMBER	1756	43005003
POV	Pov.of Spir.	ORR	1772	43005003
POVERTY	Poverty.	DYKES	1722	20031007
POVERTY	Poverty.	MARRIOTT	1774	45016020
POW	Frm. Pow. G.	TILLOTSON	1735	58003005
POW	Pow. Consc.	BLAIR	1777	01042021
POW	Pow. Gosp.	MARSH	1737	47019020
POW	Pow. Viol.	BARTLETT	1714	43011012
POW	Pow. Xt's D.	MAY	1757	46007046
POW	Pow.of Cha.	HOADLY	1727	63004008

Keyword	In its Context	Author	Year	BkChpVrs
POW	Pow.of Gos.	MONRO	1693	49002003
POW	Pow.of Pray.	KETTLEWELL	1719	43007007
POW	Pow.of Pray.	MOSS	1732	43007007
POW	Sat. Pow.b.	ERSKINE	1764	45022031
POW	Xt's.pow.h.	FOORD	1719	43008003
POWER	G's power.	HUNT	1748	19147005
POWER	G's Power	LEIGHTON	1746	19076010
POWER	G's Power.	NICHOLSON	1661	19078020
POWER	Med. Power.	ERSKINE	1764	43028018
POWER	Power of G.	WISHEART	1716	19062011
POWER	Power of G.	TILLOTSON	1735	19062011
POWER	Power of G.	BRACKENRIDGE	1764	19062011
POWER	Power Xnity	COOPER	1777	43005043
POWER	Regal Power	BERNARD	1661	48013002
POWERS	Mir.powers.	HIND	1755	49014023
POX	Small-pox.	WHITTY	1766	23026020
PR	A.m. Pr. Ir. S	SECKER	1766	20009006
PR	Ap.rul.o.pr.	WILLIAMS	1770	50004005
PR	Benef.of Pr.	IBBOT	1726	18021015
PR	Benef.of Pr.	LANGHORNE	1773	18021015
PR	Bir.of Pr.&c.	TURNER	1688	07017006
PR	Conc. En. Pr.	BROUGHTON	1778	46011047
PR	Conc. En. Pr.	MILNE	1780	46011047
PR	Dai.pub. Pr.	PEARSALL	1751	47002046
PR	Death Pr. Or.	MACLAINE	1752	25003028
PR	Def. Pr. Rel.	ATKINSON	1737	24006029
PR	Direct.to pr.	HORTON	1679	13004010
PR	Elijah's Pr.	MORRIS	1743	11017001
PR	Ete. Pr.o. Xt.	KELSEY	1691	61006020
PR	Ete. Pr.o. Xt.	STILLINGFLEET	1707	61006020
PR	Exh.pr. Lib.	SQUIRE	1716	51005001
PR	Exp. Ld's. Pr.	MANTON	1684	43006009
PR	Extemp. Pr.	SOUTH	1727	21005002
PR	Faith in Pr.	CLARKSON	1696	62001006
PR	Faith in Pr.	MATHER	1710	19072019
PR	Faith in Pr.	STUART	1753	03002013
PR	Faith pr. Pie.	BEVERIDGE	1720	47015009
PR	Fal Id.o. Pr.	SMITH	1673	64001021
PR	Forms of Pr.	PEARSON	1711	45011002
PR	Forms of Pr.	BULL	1713	57002001
PR	Forms of Pr.	CLAGETT	1720	43006009
PR	G's pr. Mer.	HILL	1755	19059010
PR	G's Pr.comf.	BAINE	1778	02033014
PR	G's Pr.perf.	ERSKINE	1764	01028015
PR	God's Pr.	COTES	1721	34002020
PR	Gos.how pr.	HAMOND	1690	54004005
PR	Grad. Pr. R.	SECKER	1770	23001016
PR	H.&pr.word	STUART	1773	46010025
PR	Hezek's Pr.	ORTON	1776	14030018
PR	Hon. Xn. Pr.	BRETT	1712	61005004
PR	Hyp.des. Pr.	ORTON	1776	24042020
PR	Imp. Re.pr.1.	CRAIG	1775	52002012
PR	.Import. Pr.	PENTYCROSS	1781	01032026
PR	Ineff.of pr.	MOIR	1776	48010021
PR	Inf. R.on Pr.	BLAIR	1777	19001003
PR	Jes.an. H. Pr.	WHEATLY	1746	61005009

Keyword	In its Context	Author	Year	BkChpVrs
PR	Jud. Pr. Rig.	SKELTON	1754	44014043
PR	Knowl.& Pr.	CHANDLER	1728	46013017
PR	Knowl.& Pr.	CONEY	1750	46013017
PR	Knowl.& Pr.	LANGHORNE	1773	46013017
PR	Lo.sup t.pr.	ROWLAND	1774	68000009
PR	Min.t.pr. G.	ANONYMOUS	1679	48001014
PR	Mir. Pr.d. M.	SKELTON	1754	46005036
PR	Mir. Pr.d. M.	POWELL	1776	46005036
PR	Mor.subj.pr.	ENFIELD	1772	59003008
PR	N.& Use. Pr.	FOSTER	1744	43006006
PR	Nat.pr.p. Pr.	HUNTER	1774	49015041
PR	Neces. R Pr.	BURNABY	1777	19111010
PR	Obj.to Pr.a.	NEWMAN	1711	18021015
PR	P's Pr.f. Ones	ORTON	1776	58001018
PR	Past. M.pr. S.	HILL	1755	07013023
PR	Pos.pr.o. Xy.	KNOX	1768	63001015
PR	Pr.& Almsg.	BEVERIDGE	1720	47010004
PR	Pr.& F.ineff.	WILLIAMS	1774	49015014
PR	Pr.& Preach.	CARPENDER	1708	47010033
PR	Pr.&f. State.	DUCHAL	1765	50004018
PR	Pr.&f. State.	ELSMERE	1767	50004018
PR	Pr.&fut.st. B.	COLLIER	1686	49015029
PR	Pr. Atheism.	BRAGGE	1713	59001016
PR	Pr. Atheism.	NORRIS	1728	59001016
PR	Pr. Atheism.	MILLER	1749	59001016
PR	Pr. Faith&c.	BEVERLEY	1683	19079006
PR	Pr. M.p.d.m.	CONYBEARE	1757	46020031
PR	Pr. Test. J. C	BRACKENRIDGE	1764	69019010
PR	Pr. W. Bth-d.	SMEDLEY	1716	63002017
PR	Pr. Xn.k.a.p.	JONES	1761	50005014
PR	Pr. Xt's. N.	BEVERIDGE	1720	46014014
PR	Pr.b.hinde.	PARKHURST	1707	63003007
PR	Pr.f. G's. M.	SMALRIDGE	1724	50001011
PR	Pr.f. Kings.	MOSS	1733	57002001
PR	Pr.f. Mercy.	ERSKINE	1764	34003002
PR	Pr.for You.	MAY	1753	13004010
PR	Pr.in kn. T.	VINCENT	1675	49014015
PR	Pr.in Xt's. N.	KILLIGREW	1685	46016023
PR	Pr.in Xt's. N.	SCOTT.	1743	46016023
PR	Pr.in Xt's. N.	WESTON	1747	46016023
PR	Pr.in Xt's. N.	LARDNER	1760	46016024
PR	Pr.in Xt's. N.	BOSTON	1775	46016023
PR	Pr.of Godl.	BYRDALL	1666	57004004
PR	Qual.of Pr.	BUERDSELL	1700	52006018
PR	Qual.of Pr.	FIDDES	1720	52006018
PR	R.& Pr.im.h.	WHEATLY	1746	61011039
PR	Right.pr. Ju.	ANONYMOUS	1721	49010015
PR	S.of G.pr. T.	CAMPBELL	1779	49001025
PR	Sins inf.&pr.	GODDARD	1781	19019012
PR	Sp. Help Pr.	STEVENS	1755	48008026
PR	Sp. Help Pr.	BOSTON	1775	48008026
PR	Stated F. Pr.	SMALRIDGE	1724	45011001
PR	Stated F. Pr.	MOSS	1732	45011001
PR	Subj mat. Pr.	FIDDES	1720	65005014
PR	Use& Int. Pr.	SHERLOCK	1740	64001019
PR	Van.of pr. R.	QUINCY	1750	59001016

Keyword	In its Context	Author	Year	BkChpVrs
PR	Van.of pr.st.	GROVE	1741	48008019
PR	Wand.in pr.	TENISON	1691	49007035
PR	Watch& Pr.	DYER	1666	44014038
PR	Watch& Pr.	CLAGETT	1707	43026041
PR	Watch& Pr.	STILLINGFLEET	1707	43026041
PR	Watch& Pr.	BROWNE	1749	43026041
PR	Wor.in pr. H	H.	1693	01034022
PR	Xn.r.pr.sp p.	RANDOLPH	1777	47005038
PR	Xn's.dut.pr.	FIDDES	1720	65005003
PR	Xt.pr.to Bel.	DAVIES	1766	63002007
PR	Xt Found Pr.	BEVERIDGE	1720	50001020
PR	Xt's. D.pr. A.	WITHERSPOON	1768	65002002
PR	Xt's.dy. Pr.	NEWMAN	1760	45023024
PR	Xt's.pr.af. R.	DELANY	1766	49015006
PR	Xt's.pr.to sp.	NEWSON	1781	63003019
PR	Xty pr. Hap.	BADDELLEY	1766	20003017
PR	Xy.pr.fm. Pr.	SKELTON	1754	69019010
PR	b. Pr. Or.	PATRICK	1689	23011006
PR	b. Pr. Orange	BURNET	1668	27012003
PR	1st pr.of R.	GERARD	1780	01003015
PRA	Ejac. Pra.	BENNETT	1735	16002010
PRA	Ejac. Pra.	OLDING	1767	16001004
PRA	Pra.& Th.	SCOUGAL	1726	19107015
PRAC	Prac. Atheist.	BATE	1748	48001020
PRAC	Prac.of Rel.	DUCHAL	1728	20008006
PRACT	Fai.& Pract.	WALKER	1763	65002003
PRACT	Pract. Athe.	OAKES	1747	52002012
PRACT	Pract. Good.	WOODCOCK	1690	48014001
PRACT	Pract. Xty.	HOPKINS	1710	53002012
PRACT	Pract.incons.	SEED	1743	48001018
PRACT	Pract.neces.	TILLOTSON	1735	45012047
PRACT	Pract.necess.	PEARSON	1718	43007020
PRACT	Pract.o. Rel.	WALLIS	1748	57004007
PRACT	Pract.o.mor.	CLARKE	1734	46006044
PRACT	Pract.of R.	DUCHAL	1728	19084010
PRACT	Pract.of Rel.	DUCHAL	1728	20012028
PRACTICE	Xn. Practice.	WHICHCOTE	1702	53003015
PRAD	Prad. Son.	SHARP	1734	45015017
PRAD	Prad. Son.	HOW	1761	45015017
PRAD	Prad. Son.	BADDELLEY	1766	45015017
PRAD	Prad. Son.	PYLE	1777	45015017
PRAIS	Prais. God.	BROWN	1722	55004001
PRAIS	Prais. God.	SAURIN	1775	19033001
PRAISE	Love Praise.	BLAIR	1780	46012043
PRAISE	Praise f. Rec,	LITTLETON	1680	23038017
PRAISE	Praise& Th.	GROVE	1741	19136001
PRAY	Abus.of Pray.	CARRINGTON	1776	62004003
PRAY	Agur's Pray.	BROWNRIG	1661	20030007
PRAY	Agur's Pray.	MEDE	1672	20030008
PRAY	Agur's Pray.	KIDDER	1697	20030007
PRAY	Agur's Pray.	FOSTER	1732	20030008
PRAY	Agur's Pray.	HORT	1738	20030007
PRAY	Agur's Pray.	HOADLY	1755	20030008
PRAY	Agur's Pray.	STEBBING	1760	20030008
PRAY	Agur's Pray.	SMITH	1777	20030008
PRAY	Alter. Pray.	HOLE	1716	19051015

Keyword	In its Context	Author	Year	BkChpVrs
PRAY	Anx.& Pray.	SHARP	1729	53004006
PRAY	Asa's Pray.	CUMMING	1739	14014011
PRAY	Belief. Pray.	WATTS	1753	18023003
PRAY	Ben.f. Pray.	OGDEN	1770	43007007
PRAY	Closet Pray.	SLATER	1691	43006006
PRAY	Closet Pray.	RESBURY	1693	43006006
PRAY	Com. Pray.	BISSE	1717	13016029
PRAY	Comm. Pray.	HEWERDINE	1717	47024014
PRAY	Comm Pray.	JONES	1750	57002001
PRAY	Conf.& Pray.	CONANT	1698	62005016
PRAY	Dut.of Pray.	CLARKE	1736	48012012
PRAY	Earn. Pray.	BAINE	1778	01032026
PRAY	Eff.of Pray.	STRAIGHT	1741	53004006
PRAY	Effic.o. Pray.	SCOTT	1711	45011013
PRAY	Effic.o. Pray.	TILLOTSON	1735	45011013
PRAY	Effic.o. Pray.	MOSS	1737	45011013
PRAY	Ex.of Pray.	GROSVENOR	1711	19073028
PRAY	Excell. Pray.	OGDEN	1770	45011008
PRAY	Fam. Pray.	DOOLITTLE	1676	06024015
PRAY	G.hear Pray.	BOSTON	1775	19065002
PRAY	House Pray.	MEDE	1672	44011017
PRAY	Lord's Pray.	WITHERS	1665	43006009
PRAY	Lord's Pray.	FARINDON	1674	43006009
PRAY	Lord's Pray.	STEPHENS	1699	43006009
PRAY	Lord's Pray.	WHITBY	17--	43006009
PRAY	Lord's Pray.	NEWCOME	1702	43006009
PRAY	Lord's Pray.	PIGGOTT	1702	45011002
PRAY	Lord's Pray.	HOPKINS	1710	43006009
PRAY	Lord's Pray.	HOLE	1715	45011002
PRAY	Lord's Pray.	TOPPING	1719	43006009
PRAY	Lord's Pray.	HOLE	1719	45011002
PRAY	Lord's Pray.	BLACKALL	1723	43006009
PRAY	Lord's Pray.	MOSS	1732	45011002
PRAY	Lord's Pray.	SYMPSON	1737	45011002
PRAY	Lord's Pray.	BISSE	1740	43006009
PRAY	Lord's Pray.	LEIGHTON	1746	43006009
PRAY	Lord's Pray.	BALL	1756	43006009
PRAY	Lord's Pray.	WEST	1758	43006009
PRAY	Lord's Pray.	OGDEN	1770	43006009
PRAY	Lord's Pray.	WHITTY	1772	43006009
PRAY	Lord's Pray.	BURROUGH	1773	43006009
PRAY	Min.pray.f.	EVANS	1723	55005025
PRAY	Nec.of Pray.	HALES	1673	45018001
PRAY	Nec.of Pray.	REEVES	1729	45018001
PRAY	Nec.of Pray.	SHARP	1729	45018001
PRAY	Nec.of Pray.	SKEELER	1772	45018001
PRAY	Nec.of Pray.	GILL	1773	23054007
PRAY	Pow.of Pray.	KETTLEWELL	1719	43007007
PRAY	Pow.of Pray.	MOSS	1732	43007007
PRAY	Pray.& Th.	CASE	1774	47002042
PRAY	Pray.&char.	HARTLEY	1737	13004010
PRAY	Pray. Parl.	HOLE	1716	20011014
PRAY	Pray.by Sp.	OUTRAM	1697	49014015
PRAY	Pray.f. Cou.	BARKER	1763	19122006
PRAY	Pray.in Fai.	WHITE	1677	62001006
PRAY	Prof.of Pray.	SMALRIDGE	1724	18021015

Keyword	In its Context	Author	Year	BkChpVrs
PRAY	Prof.of Pray.	SHARP	1729	18021015
PRAY	Pub. Pray.	DORRINGTON	1703	43021013
PRAY	Pub. Pray.	BEVERIDGE	1708	47003001
PRAY	Pub. Pray.	WARREN	1748	47003001
PRAY	Qualif. Pray.	GARDINER	1720	43007007
PRAY	Qualif. Pray.	HUNT	1748	43007007
PRAY	Reas.&c. Pray.	WESTON	1747	45011009
PRAY	Reas.of Pray.	SEED	1743	48012012
PRAY	Req.of Pray.	CARR	1777	62004003
PRAY	Sav.'s Pray.	MACGILL	1779	46017020
PRAY	Secret Pray.	LEE	1676	43006006
PRAY	Secret Pray.	BLACKALL	1723	43006005
PRAY	Secret Pray.	BLAIR	1740	43006005
PRAY	Secret Pray.	BLAIR	1740	43006006
PRAY	Secret Pray.	GROVE	1747	43006006
PRAY	Secret Pray.	MORRIS	1757	43006006
PRAY	Secret Pray.	ORTON	1769	43006006
PRAY	Succes. Pray.	BLACKALL	1723	43007009
PRAY	of Pray.&c.	BLACKALL	1723	43007007
PRAY	of Pray.&c.	SHARP	1729	43007007
PRAY	of Pray.&c.	BLAIR	1740	43007007
PRAY	of Pray.&c.	WARREN	1748	43007007
PRAYER	Fam. Prayer	WAPLE	1718	01018019
PRAYER	Fam. Prayer.	MORRIS	1757	63003007
PRAYER	Fam. Prayer.	WARNEFORD	1776	43018020
PRAYER	Freq. Prayer.	WAPLE	1718	45018001
PRAYER	Imp. Prayer.	BLAIR	1740	43007007
PRAYER	L's. Prayer.	JORTIN	1774	45011001
PRAYER	Ld's Prayer.	NEWTON	1782	43006009
PRAYER	Mos. Prayer.	STERNE	1695	19090012
PRAYER	Of Prayer.	CLAGETT	1720	43006005
PRAYER	Of Prayer.	GARDINER	1720	43006005
PRAYER	On Prayer.	BRADBURY	1711	53004006
PRAYER	Pers. Prayer.	BOSTON	1753	45018001
PRAYER	Prayer.	TAYLOR	1668	46009031
PRAYER	Prayer.	HOWE	1682	24014021
PRAYER	Prayer.	COMBER	1687	19055018
PRAYER	Prayer.	BUDGELL	1690	62004003
PRAYER	Prayer.	MANTON	1693	55005017
PRAYER	Prayer.	NEWCOME	1702	52006018
PRAYER	Prayer.	NOURSE	1708	52006018
PRAYER	Prayer.	MOORE	1716	19022025
PRAYER	Prayer.	WAPLE	1718	19092001
PRAYER	Prayer.	HOPKINS	1710	55005017
PRAYER	Prayer.	EARLE	1711	55005017
PRAYER	Prayer.	HARRIS	1711	57002001
PRAYER	Prayer.	BARROW	1716	55004017
PRAYER	Prayer.	BARROW	1716	55005017
PRAYER	Prayer.	WAPLE	1718	52006018
PRAYER	Prayer.	CROSSINGE	1720	55005017
PRAYER	Prayer.	WHARTON	1728	57002008
PRAYER	Prayer.	BURROUGHS	1733	55005017
PRAYER	Prayer.	COOKE	1739	53004006
PRAYER	Prayer.	LEACHMAN	1743	43026041
PRAYER	Prayer.	LEIGHTON	1746	24014007
PRAYER	Prayer.	ORR	1749	19065002

Keyword	In its Context	Author	Year	BkChpVrs
PRAYER	Prayer.	CONEY	1750	19066018
PRAYER	Prayer.	AMORY	1753	18021015
PRAYER	Prayer.	JONES	1756	14007014
PRAYER	Prayer.	MUNTON	1756	45011001
PRAYER	Prayer.	AGAR	1759	19103002
PRAYER	Prayer.	BUNDY	1750	55005017
PRAYER	Prayer.	MACE	1751	53004006
PRAYER	Prayer.	BALL	1756	55005017
PRAYER	Prayer.	KIMBER	1756	55005017
PRAYER	Prayer.	ELLIOTT	1764	52006018
PRAYER	Prayer.	CHURCHILL	1765	62005016
PRAYER	Prayer.	SIMS	1772	19066016
PRAYER	Prayer.	BOURDALOUE	1776	43015022
PRAYER	Prayer.	SMITH	1777	19005003
PRAYER	Prayer.	WALLIN	1770	55005017
PRAYER	Prayer.	SECKER	1771	49014015
PRAYER	Prayer.	ATKINSON	1775	55005017
PRAYER	Prayer.	BOSTON	1775	55005017
PRAYER	Prayer.	BOURN	1777	55005017
PRAYER	Prayer.	GODDARD	1781	55005017
PRAYER	Prayer&c.	REYNOLDS	1711	45011001
PRAYER	Prayer&c.	TATHAM	1780	45015013
PRAYER	Pub. Prayer.	MAPLETOST	1687	55005017
PRAYER	Pub. Prayer.	BENNETT	1728	49014016
PRAYER	Pub. Prayer.	EDWARDS	1731	47002046
PRAYER	of Prayer.	KING	1664	43006009
PRAYER	of Prayer.	JACKSON	1728	43006009
PRAYERS	Prayers.	STANHOPE	1727	43015028
PRE	Fal. Pre. Rel.	CLARKE	1735	43022011
PRE	Law pre. G.	TRAIL	1696	61004016
PRE	M's pre. St.	WEBB	1765	18005006
PRE	Meth.of Pre.	FIDDES	1720	43011005
PRE	Pre. Xy.n.gr.	TILLOTSON	1735	65005003
PRE	Pre.f. Death.	HOOK	1676	43025010
PRE	Pre.f. Death.	LUCAS	1722	23038001
PRE	Pre.f. Death.	WHEATLAND	1739	12020001
PRE	Pre.f. Death.	TIDCOMBE	1757	43024044
PRE	Pre.hum.na.	SNAPE	1745	61002007
PRE	Pre.pleas.&c	BOURN	1777	43025024
PRE	Soul pre.f. H.	WATTS	1753	50005005
PREA	Dut.of Prea.	LORTIE	1720	59002015
PREA	Duty o. Prea.	LORTIE	1720	58004002
PREA	Eff.of prea.	FLEMING	1701	50003005
PREA	Eff.of Prea.	STEWARD	1734	50002015
PREA	Prea.& H. D.	GODDARD	1781	05022002
PREA	Prea.precept	DODSON	1665	21007014
PREA	Wisest Prea.	WILKINSON	1712	20011030
PREAC	Du.of Preac.	MEADOWCOURT	1721	57001005
PREAC	Preac.tripar.	MOSSOM	1685	54001018
PREAC	Prim. Preac.	STAGDEN	1718	55002003
PREAC	St. P's preac.	BERRIMAN	1751	47024025
PREACH	Ben.preach.	SHERLOCK	1772	49001021
PREACH	Fem. Preach.	ERSKINE	1764	46004029
PREACH	Pr.& Preach.	CARPENDER	1708	47010033
PREACH	Preach. Prec.	ANONYMOUS	1665	21007014
PREACH	Preach. Xt.	JENNINGS	1722	49002002

Keyword	In its Context	Author	Year	BkChpVrs
PREACH	Preach. Xt.	STOKES	1759	49001023
PREACH	Preach.o. Xt.	WILLIAMS	1774	49001014
PREC	Preach. Prec.	ANONYMOUS	1665	21007014
PRECEPT	Prea.precept	DODSON	1665	21007014
PRED	Pred. Pass.	ANONYMOUS	1708	46001019
PREDEST	Predest.t.&c.	KING	1709	48008029
PREDEST	Predest.t.&c.	PARKER	1758	48008030
PREDEST	Predest.t.life	FIDDES	1720	48008029
PREDEST	Predest.t.life	COOPER	1765	48008029
PREDESTINAT	Predestinat.	ADAMS	1752	48008014
PREDESTINAT	Predestinat.	COWPER	1773	48008034
PREDESTINAT	Predestinat.	PENTYCROSS	1781	52001004
PREDICT	Xt's. Predict.	HODGE	1758	46013019
PREEXIS	Xt's. Preexis.	RUDD	1740	46017005
PREF	Pref.of Soul.	EVANS	1737	46006027
PREF	Sol.pref. W.	PICKARD	1752	11003009
PREFER	Rel. Prefer.	DYKES	1722	20031029
PREJ	Prej.ag. Xt.	TILLOTSON	1735	43011006
PREJUDICE	Prejudice.	MARSH	1737	43013057
PREP	Prep. Death.	BOURDALOUE	1776	45007012
PREP	Prep.f. Sacra.	SMITH	1740	63004007
PREP	Prep.for suff.	FLAVEL	1673	47021013
PREP	Prep.to.fast.	GREENHILL	1757	48010001
PREP	Sacra. Prep.	SOUTH	1727	43022012
PREPAR	Sacr.prepar.	RALEIGH	1679	49011028
PREPARATION	Preparation.	HAMMOND	1684	43003003
PRER	Prer.of Mer.	ALLESTRE	1684	43009013
PRES	Div. Pres.	NORRIS	1728	19016009
PRES	Episc.& Pres.	HICKES	1726	69013011
PRES	G.pres.of w.	LELAND	1769	16009006
PRES	G's pres. Sts.	S.	1695	56003016
PRES	G's pres.in C.	WHITTY	1772	19132014
PRES	G's Pres.	MEDE	1672	19132007
PRES	G's Pres.b. S.	BRADBURY	1772	19046005
PRES	God's Pres.	CARR	1777	20005021
PRES	Ld. Pres. Imp.	JAY	1682	61011033
PRES	Pres.&f. Ha.	ROBINSON	1736	62004017
PRES	Pres. Joy D.	WILCOX	1757	19097011
PRES	Pres. Mess.	TILLOTSON	1735	36002006
PRES	Pres. Prom.	WILCOX	1757	19034010
PRES	Pres. Schism.	WILLIAMS	1716	45018009
PRES	Pres.in Pros.	TAYLOR	1704	19030006
PRES	Pres.o.go.m.	WILCOX	1757	46017015
PRES	Pres.of Xt.	BEVERIDGE	1720	43018020
PRES	Real Pres.	SHARP	1735	46006053
PRES	Seam's pres.	FLAVEL	1673	19139009
PRES	Xt's. Pres.	BEVERIDGE	1720	43028020
PRES	Xt's. Pres.	REEVES	1729	43028020
PRES	Xt's. Pres.	MOSS	1733	43028020
PRES	Xt's. Pres.	HOOLE	1748	43028020
PRESENCE	G's presence	BARRINGTON	1770	01004016
PRESENCE	G's Presence	WELCH	1752	05012018
PRESERV	Div. Preserv.	HORBERY	1774	47017028
PRESERVATION	Preservation	WILCOX	1757	25003022
PRESU	Presu.&desp.	COLE	1676	45003004
PRESUM	Ag Presum.	ROGERS	1736	45017010

Keyword	In its Context	Author	Year	BkChpVrs
PRESUM	Presum. Sins	WATERLAND	1742	19019013
PRESUM	Presum. Sins	SOUTH	1744	19019013
PRESUM	Presum. Sins	MARSHAL	1750	19019013
PRESUM	Presum. Sins	ORR	1772	19019013
PRESUM	Presum. Sins.	SACHEVERELL	1708	04015030
PRESUM	Presum. Sins.	WARREN	1739	19019012
PRESUM	Presum. Sins.	SMITH	1740	19019012
PRESUM	Presum. Sins.	HOOLE	1748	19019013
PRET	Fal.pret.sal.	BLACKALL	1723	43007022
PREV	Prev. Interc.	HORNE	1778	04016047
PREV	Prev. Love.	ERSKINE	1764	65004019
PREV	Prev. Mercy.	BRINSLEY	1667	19021003
PREV	Prev. Robb.	ROMAINE	1757	43015019
PREV	Prev. Theft.	PENN	1757	52004028
PREV	Prev. Vices.	REYNER	1745	26016049
PREV	Prev. Wick.	FOSTER	1737	46009041
PREVARICAT	Prevaricat.	PYLE	1716	23005020
PREVENT	Prevent Sin.	SOUTH	1727	09025032
PRF	Int.prf o. Xy.	BOYSE	1728	65005010
PRI	Pri. Lux.&c.	CONANT	1708	26016049
PRI	Pri.incap.of W	ATTERBURY	1730	20014006
PRI	Pri.incap.of W	ABERNETHY	1751	20014006
PRIDE	Ag. Pride.	DELANY	1747	20026012
PRIDE	Of Pride.	WHEATLAND	1739	20016005
PRIDE	Pride.	PATRICK	1689	49004010
PRIDE	Pride.	CONANT	1703	49013004
PRIDE	Pride.	DORRINGTON	1703	65002016
PRIDE	Pride.	WATERLAND	1742	20016018
PRIDE	Pride.	SEED	1743	48012003
PRIDE	Pride.	STERNE	1766	45014010
PRIDE	Pride.	WARNEFORD	1776	49004007
PRIDE	Pride.	LAMONT	1780	20008013
PRIDE	Pride& Ang.	DEVEREL	1777	41010018
PRIDE	Pride& Hu.	BALGUY	1750	62004006
PRIDE	Pride&m. S.	STOCKDALE	1777	21010018
PRIDE	Pride Humb.	SKELTON	1754	20029023
PRIDE	Spir. Pride.	MAYO	1683	50012007
PRIDE	Spir. Pride.	TILLY	1737	45018009
PRIDE	Spir. Pride.	WATERLAND	1742	45017010
PRIDE	on Pride.	HOOKER	1705	34002004
PRIE	Xy.ho. Prie.	BEVERIDGE	1720	63002005
PRIEST	A Priest.	HARRIS	1724	19110004
PRIEST	Priest on Th.	HARRIS	1724	37004013
PRIEST	Priest.of Xt.	DODSON	1728	61005009
PRIESTCRA	Priestcra.&c.	ANONYMOUS	1715	65002018
PRIESTH	Xn. Priesth.	OCKLEY	1710	38002007
PRIESTH	Xn. Priesth.	ANONYMOUS	1718	46020021
PRIESTH	Xt's. Priesth.	HIBBERT	1662	61007026
PRIESTH	Xt's. Priesth.	WEST	1762	61007026
PRIESTH	Xt's. Priesth.	JOHNSON	1776	61008003
PRIM	Prim. Faith.	SOMMERS	1731	68000003
PRIM	Prim. Preac.	STAGDEN	1718	55002003
PRIM	Prim. Relig.	KEDDINGTON	1757	43019008
PRIM	Prim. S.of M.	TAYLOR	1725	01001026
PRIM	Prim. Xn.	GOULDE	1682	18036021
PRIN	Ex. Xn. Prin.	CHANDLER	1769	46015005

Keyword	In its Context	Author	Year	BkChpVrs
PRIN	Prin. Virtue.	FORSTER	1737	19119097
PRIN	Prin.o. Conf.	HAWKINS	1773	49001010
PRIN	Xn. Prin.sta.	SNAPE	1745	54002006
PRIN	b. Prin.of W.	HOWARD	1742	49013005
PRINC	False Princ.	OUTRAM	1697	43006023
PRINC	G.&b. Princ.	IBBOT	1726	43006022
PRINC	Gosp. Princ.	ERSKINE	1764	54002006
PRINC	Mist.princ.	WHALEY	1695	47026009
PRINC	Princ.of Xy.	CENNICK	1762	61005012
PRINC	Relig. Princ.	SNAPE	1745	43007024
PRINC	Rom. Princ.	BARNES	1752	48003008
PRINCE	Birth Prince.	CAESAR	1717	19127003
PRINCE	Prince of P.	HORNE	1778	37009009
PRIOR	Prior Xt's. R.	WELLS	1735	47026022
PRIS	Pris.convert.	WEBB	1765	47026033
PRIS	Pris.releas.	DENTON	1775	43025036
PRISON	Sp.in prison.	WHEATLAND	1739	63003018
PRISONERS	To Prisoners	DODD	1777	45007022
PRIV	Believ. Priv.	CENNICK	1762	46001012
PRIV	Ch. Priv.	DODSON	1728	24007004
PRIV	Priv. Discret.	KIDDER	1697	55005021
PRIV	Priv. Judgm.	SYNGE	1737	45012057
PRIV	Priv. Judgm.	FISHER	1741	47008031
PRIV	Priv. Reven.	BOSTON	1773	48012019
PRIV	Priv.o. Saints	DAVIS	1756	65003002
PRIV	Sav.priv.life	NEWTON	1782	45002051
PRIV	Sons G. Priv.	WHEATLAND	1739	65003001
PRIV	Xt's priv life	THEED	1712	45002051
PRIVI	Privi.of Cl.	DUDLEY	1731	64003016
PRIZE	Xn. Prize.	BEVERIDGE	1720	53003014
PRIZE	Xn's. Prize.	DUNLOP	1722	53003013
PRIZE	Xn's. Prize.	MASON	1758	53003013
PRO	Being G.pro.	BARROW	1716	46005017
PRO	C.pro. G. D.	RAWSON	1708	47015039
PRO	Ch.s. Fr. Pro.	HICKES	1713	50004009
PRO	G. Un.a Pro.	CHANDLER	1691	55005013
PRO	Jacob's Pro.	KEDDINGTON	1758	01050021
PRO	L's Pro.true.	ECCLES	1755	11022021
PRO	Pro.& Scept.	BARNES	1752	19097001
PRO	Pro. M.to A.	GERARD	1780	01022018
PRO	Pro.gr. Doct.	PALMER	1726	20014034
PRO	Pro.of Char.	FARINDON	1674	49013007
PRO	Pro.of Char.	HOWE	1681	49013006
PRO	Pro.of Char.	CONANT	1703	49013006
PRO	Pro.of Char.	CROSSINGE	1722	49013007
PRO	Pro.of Char.	HOLE	1725	49013005
PRO	Pro.of Char.	HOLE	1725	49013006
PRO	Pro.of Char.	HOLE	1725	49013007
PRO	Rew.pro.w.	CLARKE	1735	51006007
PRO	Su.w.of Pro.	NEWCOME	1724	64001019
PRO	Su.w.of Pro.	BRAY	1761	64001019
PRO	Swift pro. G.	MOSS	1732	47019020
PRO	Trust in Pro.	GARDINER	1720	43006019
PRO	Way try Pro.	BLACKALL	1723	65004001
PRO	Wisd.di.pro.	LELAND	1769	23028029
PRO	Wisd.of Pro.	ADAMS	1736	01045007

Keyword	In its Context	Author	Year	BkChpVrs
PRO	Xt's.pro.off.	FLAVEL	1673	45024045
PRO	Xt's.pro.off.	FLAVEL	1673	47003022
PRO	Xt's.pro.off.	BOSTON	1773	47003022
PROB	State Prob.	CLARKE	1734	45016012
PROBA	State Proba.	GOUGH	1751	23005003
PROBAT	Life Probat.	HORBERY	1774	43025028
PROCL	Procl. King.	WOMOCK	1660	19132018
PROCL	Procl. King.	HEYRICKE	1685	20021001
PROCL	Procl.s.	CAMFIELD	1685	14013005
PROCLA	Procla.s.	BARTHOLOMEW	1660	45011021
PROD	Prod. Penit.	CREYGHTON	1720	45015018
PROD	Prod. Penit.	ST.	1737	45015017
PROD	Prod. Penit.	JORTIN	1774	45015018
PROD	Prod. Son.	SEDGWICK	1660	45015011
PROD	Prod. Son.	ALLEINE	1674	45015023
PROD	Prod. Son.	BRAGGE	1702	45015011
PROD	Prod. Son.	GOODMAN	1707	45015011
PROD	Prod. Son.	WAPLE	1718	45015011
PROD	Prod. Son.	BOYSE	1728	45015011
PROD	Prod. Son.	ST.	1737	45015013
PROD	Prod. Son.	MUNTON	1756	45015010
PROD	Prod. Son.	DODD	1757	45015013
PROD	Prod. Son.	DODD	1757	45015018
PROD	Prod. Son.	DODD	1757	45015022
PROD	Prod. Son.	HEYLIN	1761	45015011
PROD	Prod. Son.	HOW	1761	45015011
PROD	Prod. Son.	HOW	1761	45015013
PROD	Prod. Son.	WILLISON	1761	45015018
PROD	Prod. Son.	HOW	1761	45015020
PROD	Prod. Son.	HOW	1761	45015021
PROD	Prod. Son.	HOW	1761	45015022
PROD	Prod. Son.	HOW	1761	45015023
PROD	Prod. Son.	STERNE	1766	45015013
PROD	Prod. Son.	HALES	1766	45015020
PROD	Prod. Son.	BADDELLY	1766	45015025
PROD	Prod. Son.	BULKLEY	1771	45015021
PROD	Prod. Son.	FARQUAR	1772	45015011
PROD	Prod. Son.	JORTIN	1774	45015031
PROD	Prod. Son.	ANONYMOUS	1776	45015018
PROD	Prod. Son.	WALLIN	1776	45015011
PROD	Prod. Xrter.	NEWTON	1782	45015011
PROF	Ag.prof.sw.	WRIGHT	1723	62005012
PROF	Extern. Prof.	LAWSON	1764	43007021
PROF	Form. Prof.	PORTER	1661	58003005
PROF	Imm.& Prof.	THANE	1700	46012026
PROF	L.suit. Prof.	ADEY	1760	45012047
PROF	Prof.& Infid.	BRAILSFORD	1776	23058001
PROF	Prof. G's N.	CARR	1777	03019012
PROF	Prof. Swear.	BRADBURY	1732	02020007
PROF	Prof. Swear.	CARRINGTON	1754	20018014
PROF	Prof. Swear.	CARRINGTON	1776	20018021
PROF	Prof.by Ser.	WILSON	1781	45008018
PROF	Prof.in K.	TAYLOR	1719	28006003
PROF	Prof.no Sec.	BULKLEY	1752	43003009
PROF	Prof.o. Godl.	HALES	1673	57004007
PROF	Prof.o. Godl.	SMITH	1740	57004007

Keyword	In its Context	Author	Year	BkChpVrs
PROF	Prof.o Godl.	BYRDALL	1666	57004007
PROF	Prof.of Pray.	SMALRIDGE	1724	18021015
PROF	Prof.of Pray.	SHARP	1729	18021015
PROF	Ra. Prof. Xy.	WILKINSON	1660	58002019
PROFANENESS	Profaneness.	CLARKE	1735	61012016
PROFES	Mere Profes.	CLAGETT	1704	43007021
PROFESSI	Xn. Professi.	MACE	1751	47026028
PROFIT	Godl.profit.	BARROW	1716	57004007
PROFIT	Godl.profit.	SCOTT	1718	57004007
PROFIT	Godl.profit.	ST.	1737	57004007
PROFIT	Godl.profit.	MILLER	1749	57004007
PROFIT	Profit. Piety.	FARRINGTON	1741	18021015
PROFUS	Ag. Profus.	BOURN	1777	45016009
PROG	Prog. Hell-f.	HENLEY	1730	11018024
PROG	Prog. Relig.	LAW	1745	21007010
PROG	Prog. Sin.	YOUNG	1706	19052007
PROG	Prog. V.& H.	ATTERBURY	1743	64003018
PROG	Prog. Vice.	NEWMAN	1738	19001001
PROG	Prog.of M.	SKELTON	1754	19008005
PROG	Prog.of Rel.	BOURN	1755	20004018
PROG	Prog.wick.	SHERLOCK	1719	23005020
PROGNOSTICS	Prognostics.	HOMES	1661	27012001
PROM	Chi.of Prom.	ERSKINE	1764	51004028
PROM	Div. Prom.	CRUSO	1698	50001020
PROM	Gosp. Prom.	TILLOTSON	1735	64001004
PROM	Pres. Prom.	WILCOX	1757	19034010
PROM	Prom. Faith.	WELCH	1752	46010024
PROM	Prom. Mess.	WHICHCOTE	1698	47013023
PROM	Prom. Oaths.	SANDERSON	1722	04030002
PROM	Prom.of G.	ROMAINE	1760	63003008
PROOF	Proof of G.	LATHAM	1678	48001020
PROOF	Proof.b. Mir.	BULLOCK	1726	46015024
PROOF	Proof.of Xy.	BATTY	1739	46001045
PROOF	S. S.proof. Xt	DAVIES	1720	46005039
PROP	+prop.+punish.	SMALRIDGE	1724	43011022
PROP	Disc.f. Prop.	BLACKALL	1723	43007016
PROP	Mir. Prop. G.	ATTERBURY	1730	23060022
PROP	Prop. R.& L.	ACRES	1714	19078004
PROP	Prop.of soul.	HILL	1667	21012007
PROP	Word. Prop.	CLAGETT	1704	64001019
PROP	Xt.gr. Prop.	WILSON	1746	65004010
PROP	Xt.prop. Sac.	SKELTON	1754	49015023
PROP	Zach's Prop.	VENN	1775	15005001
PROPH	Ag.fr. Proph.	CHISHULL	1707	62005008
PROPH	Ag.n. Proph.	CALAMY	1708	24014004
PROPH	Exp. Proph.	GARDINER	17--	23007014
PROPH	False Proph.	BLANCH	1708	51001007
PROPH	False Proph.	BLACKALL	1723	43007015
PROPH	False Proph.	ATTERBURY	1743	43007015
PROPH	Jac. Proph.	LAMBERT	1779	01032009
PROPH	Jes.t. Proph.	BULLOCK	1724	47003022
PROPH	Jew. Proph.	SCOTT	1743	55005020
PROPH	O. T. Proph.	POWELL	1776	43011002
PROPH	Proph. Writ.	SCOTT	1743	64001020
PROPH	Proph.of Xt.	HODGE	1758	46005039
PROPH	Scrip. Proph.	RAWLINS	1761	69019010

Keyword	In its Context	Author	Year	BkChpVrs
PROPH	Spi.o. Proph.	ANONYMOUS	1687	69019019
PROPH	Xt.a Proph.	DODSON	1728	61001001
PROPH	Xt.t. Proph.	BADDELLEY	1766	46006014
PROPH	on Proph.	TRAPP	1747	43016027
PROPHECIES	Prophecies.	HARDY	1770	45021028
PROPHECIES	Prophecies.	HARDY	1770	69005004
PROPHECIES	Prophecies.	HARDY	1770	69009006
PROPHECIES	Prophecies.	HARDY	1770	69010010
PROPHECIES	Prophecies.	HARDY	1770	69013001
PROPHECY	Prophecy.	BERRIMAN	1751	23041023
PROPHECY	Prophecy.	BAYLY	1751	46020031
PROPHECY	Prophecy.	HARDY	1770	23002008
PROPHECY	Prophecy.	GILL	1773	23010007
PROPHECYING	Prophecying	MEDE	1672	49011005
PROPHET	A Prophet.	HARRIS	1724	05018015
PROPITIA	Jes. Propitia.	COCKMAN	1750	65004010
PROS	Danger of Pros	BATES	1700	20001032
PROS	Danger of Pros	SOUTH	1727	20001032
PROS	Happ. Pros.	NEWMAN	1760	48012012
PROS	Pres.in Pros.	TAYLOR	1704	19030006
PROS	Pros. Ch. Ch.	CLAGETT	1720	23011009
PROS	Pros.of Jud.	CONEY	1750	19090008
PROS	Zion's Pros.	HILL	1755	23062006
PROSEC	Hon.prosec.	CONEY	1730	27006005
PROSELYTES	Proselytes.	MEDE	1672	47017004
PROSP	Abus. Prosp.	TREBECK	1730	20001032
PROSP	Adv.& Prosp.	BOURDALOUE	1776	43008023
PROSP	Prosp.& Aff.	DORRINGTON	1705	20013021
PROSP	Prosp.& Affl.	REYNER	1745	24049011
PROSP	Prosp. Wick.	HUSSEY	1758	24012001
PROSP	Prosp. Wick.	HUNTER	1774	24012001
PROSP	Prosp Adver.	BULL	1713	21007014
PROSP	Soul's Prosp.	BENN	1683	67000003
PROSP	Soul's Prosp.	WHITFIELD	1771	67000002
PROSP	Sudd. Prosp.	ASHTON	1770	05006010
PROSP	Wick. Prosp.	ROE	1766	18037007
PROSPERITY	Prosperity.	BURNET	1747	19037016
PROT	Adv.to Prot.	WILCOCKS	1709	55004001
PROT	Cath. Prot.	HARRISON	1781	43005022
PROT	Opp. Prot. F.	GIBBONS	1755	30006006
PROT	Prot. Char.	STILLINGFLEET	1707	51006009
PROT	Prot. R.vi. H.	COYTE	1761	47024014
PROT	Prot. Rule.	PYLE	1717	50013005
PROT	Prot. Truth.	BEVERLEY	1683	24010025
PROT	Prot.p.n.sec.	FRANCIS	1773	48008031
PROTES	Cath. Protes.	HARRISON	1781	45009056
PROTEST	Protest. Diss.	WILLIAMS	1738	44011029
PROV	D. Prov.mys.	HOWE	1771	46013007
PROV	Deny Prov.	BERRIMAN	1751	35001012
PROV	Dis.al.prov.	NEWMAN	1750	23005012
PROV	Div. Prov.	DEVEREL	1777	01045004
PROV	God's Prov.	UMFREVILLE	1739	19058011
PROV	Man& Prov.	WEBB	1765	19008004
PROV	Mys.of Prov.	FLAVEL	1673	19057002
PROV	Partic. Prov.	ADAMS	1736	43010029
PROV	Partic. Prov.	DODWELL	1760	19033013

Keyword	In its Context	Author	Year	BkChpVrs
PROV	Partic. Prov.	CHANDLER	1769	19023006
PROV	Pecul. Prov.	DAVIS	1756	19034008
PROV	Prov. G.aff.	LAWSON	1764	27004025
PROV	Prov. Relig.	COOKE	1739	55005021
PROV	Prov. Seas.	MOIR	1759	19065005
PROV	Prov.of Mer.	PENTYCROSS	1781	23063005
PROV	Prov.our Re.	ROGERS	1730	55005021
PROV	Prov.th.hon.	BARROW	1716	50008021
PROV	Prov.vin.	CRADOCK	1678	21009002
PROV	Prov.vin.	CARLETON	1736	21009002
PROV	Prov.vind.	CREYGHTON	1720	19058010
PROV	Prov.vind.	TREBECK	1730	19119137
PROV	Prov.vindic.	ALLEN	1751	43005045
PROV	S. S.prov. Xt.	LEIGHTONHOUSE	1697	46005039
PROV	Wis.prov.f.	BOURN	1777	43006019
PROV'D	G.prov'd.u.	SKELTON	1754	43011005
PROVI	Arg.f. Provi.	HUNTER	1774	18007020
PROVID	Div. Provid.	PINDAR	1679	19127001
PROVID	Div. Provid.	HERNE	1679	61004013
PROVID	Div. Provid.	OUTRAM	1680	43010029
PROVID	Div. Provid.	GOODMAN	1683	19017001
PROVID	Div. Provid.	DORRINGTON	1705	48011036
PROVID	Div. Provid.	HOPKINS	1710	43010029
PROVID	Div. Provid.	EDWARDS	1713	43010029
PROVID	Div. Provid.	BARKER	1748	43010029
PROVID	Div. Provid.	BOSTON	1753	23041014
PROVID	Div. Provid.	BOURN	1760	19036006
PROVID	Div. Provid.	DUCHAL	1765	23040015
PROVID	Div. Provid.	DAVIES	1766	19097001
PROVID	Div. Provid.	LELAND	1769	48011036
PROVID	Div. Provid.	CARR	1777	19097001
PROVID	G's. Provid.	EDWARDS	1713	63005007
PROVID	G's. Provid.	ATKINSON	1775	48011036
PROVID	G's Provid.	WILKINSON	1660	14016009
PROVID	Gen. Provid.	ADAMS	1736	13029011
PROVID	Part. Provid.	SEED	1743	19113005
PROVID	Part. Provid.	FOSTER	1744	69019006
PROVID	Provid.vindica	FARINDON	1674	24012001
PROVID	Provid.vindica	KILLINBECK	1717	24012001
PROVID	Provid.vindica	BALL	1756	24012001
PROVID	Rest. Provid.	ADAMS	1736	04024013
PROVID	Spec. Provid.	BENNETT	1728	20003005
PROVID	Sub. Provid.	ENFIELD	1772	43006010
PROVIDENCE	Providence vin	D'OYLY	1710	19073015
PROVIDENCE	Providence.	WILKINS	1677	21003011
PROVIDENCE	Providence.	COLLINGES	1678	11014001
PROVIDENCE	Providence.	COLLINGES	1678	18005006
PROVIDENCE	Providence.	COLLINGES	1678	19036006
PROVIDENCE	Providence.	COLLINGES	1678	19037001
PROVIDENCE	Providence.	COLLINGES	1678	19103019
PROVIDENCE	Providence.	COLLINGES	1678	19107043
PROVIDENCE	Providence.	COLLINGES	1678	23028029
PROVIDENCE	Providence.	COLLINGES	1678	28013009
PROVIDENCE	Providence.	COLLINGES	1678	34001013
PROVIDENCE	Providence.	COLLINGES	1678	47017030
PROVIDENCE	Providence.	COLLINGES	1678	48005020

Keyword	In its Context	Author	Year	BkChpVrs
PROVIDENCE	Providence.	COLLINGES	1678	48009015
PROVIDENCE	Providence.	COLLINGES	1678	48011033
PROVIDENCE	Providence.	COLLINGES	1678	49009009
PROVIDENCE	Providence.	COLLINGES	1678	51003022
PROVIDENCE	Providence.	COLLINGES	1678	52001011
PROVIDENCE	Providence.	COLLINGES	1678	56001009
PROVIDENCE	Providence.	COLLINGES	1678	61001003
PROVIDENCE	Providence.	COLLINGES	1678	61011003
PROVIDENCE	Providence.	COLLINGES	1687	19073012
PROVIDENCE	Providence.	RESBURY	1689	43006026
PROVIDENCE	Providence.	GOODMAN	1697	19097001
PROVIDENCE	Providence.	MARCH	1699	20016009
PROVIDENCE	Providence.	SCOTT	1701	19135006
PROVIDENCE	Providence.	ANONYMOUS	1711	19073015
PROVIDENCE	Providence.	MOORE	1715	20003006
PROVIDENCE	Providence.	WELTON	1724	21003011
PROVIDENCE	Providence.	SOUTH	1727	20016033
PROVIDENCE	Providence.	MARSHALL	1731	19073012
PROVIDENCE	Providence.	TALBOT	1731	34001013
PROVIDENCE	Providence.	STEWARD	1734	20003006
PROVIDENCE	Providence.	ADAMS	1736	21008014
PROVIDENCE	Providence.	TILLOTSON	1735	63005007
PROVIDENCE	Providence.	BALGUY	1748	19097001
PROVIDENCE	Providence.	HUNT	1748	19103019
PROVIDENCE	Providence.	MACE	1751	18011007
PROVIDENCE	Providence.	SUTTON	1754	20003006
PROVIDENCE	Providence.	HUSSEY	1755	19103019
PROVIDENCE	Providence.	WILCOX	1757	01031014
PROVIDENCE	Providence.	JENNINGS	1757	19103019
PROVIDENCE	Providence.	BOURN	1760	26018029
PROVIDENCE	Providence.	DODDERIDGE	1761	19107048
PROVIDENCE	Providence.	STERNE	1769	19073012
PROVIDENCE	Providence.	LELAND	1769	19103019
PROVIDENCE	Providence.	FARRINGTON	1769	34003017
PROVIDENCE	Providence.	BOSTON	1773	19107043
PROVIDENCE	Providence.	BOSTON	1773	43010029
PROVIDENCE	Providence.	HUNTER	1774	19024001
PROVIDENCE	Providence.	HUNTER	1774	47017028
PRUD	Hum. Prud.	CARLETON	1736	20003005
PRUD	Prud. Cond.	ROGERS	1735	48012017
PRUD	Prud.appar.	DYKES	1722	20031021
PRUD	Rel. Prud.	ABERNETHY	1748-	43007006
PRUD	Xn. Prud.	TAYLOR	1668	43009016
PRUD	Xn. Prud.	TAYLOR	1678	43010016
PRUD	Xn. Prud.	BRIGHT	1699	43007001
PRUD	Xn. Prud.	NOURSE	1705	43009015
PRUD	Xn. Prud.	EVANS	1737	43010016
PRUDEN	Rel. Pruden.	DYKES	1722	20031026
PRUDENCE	Prudence.	DODWELL	1749	20014015
PRUDENT	Rel.prudent	FIDDES	1720	21007016
PS	Ps.expl.	PETERS	1776	19109016
PSALMODY	Psalmody.	WELLS	1676	52005019
PSALMODY	Psalmody.	BURROUGHS	1712	19047007
PSALMODY	Psalmody.	BURNE	1774	19047001
PSALMODY	Psalmody.	ORTON	1775	19101004
PU	Conf.pu.&p.	NICOLSON	1661	65001009

Keyword	In its Context	Author	Year	BkChpVrs
PU	G's. D.of Pu.	CONYBEARE	1757	64003008
PU	Sin& Pu.o. S.	BOYSE	1728	68000006
PUB	Dai.pub. Pr.	PEARSALL	1751	47002046
PUB	Phar.& Pub.	CHARNOCK	1684	46001013
PUB	Phar.& Pub.	BUNYAN	17--	46001013
PUB	Phar.& Pub.	BRAGGE	1702	45018009
PUB	Phar.& Pub.	HOLE	1716	45018009
PUB	Phar.& Pub.	DODD	1757	45018009
PUB	Phar.& Pub.	BARKER	1763	45018009
PUB	Phar.& Pub.	BOURN	1764	45018009
PUB	Phar.& Pub.	KNOWLES	1769	45018014
PUB	Phar.& Pub.	BULKLEY	1771	45018009
PUB	Phar.& Pub.	FRANCIS	1771	45018014
PUB	Phar.& Pub.	JORTIN	1774	45018014
PUB	Pub.& Phar.	STRAIGHT	1741	45018014
PUB	Pub.& Phar.	WATERLAND	1742	45018014
PUB	Pub. Breach.	WEST	1716	19060002
PUB	Pub. Calam.	BOURN	1760	45013001
PUB	Pub. Instruc.	ABERNETHU	1751	20008034
PUB	Pub. P.of F.	BEVERIDGE	1720	43010032
PUB	Pub. Penan.	FORD	1696	51006001
PUB	Pub. Pray.	DORRINGTON	1703	43021013
PUB	Pub. Pray.	BEVERIDGE	1708	47003001
PUB	Pub. Pray.	WARREN	1748	47003001
PUB	Pub. Prayer.	MAPLETOST	1687	55005017
PUB	Pub. Prayer.	BENNETT	1728	49014016
PUB	Pub. Prayer.	EDWARDS	1731	47002046
PUB	Pub. Spirit.	PRATT	1700	49010024
PUB	Pub. Spirit.	GEREE	1706	49010023
PUB	Pub. Spirit.	TENISON	1711	49010024
PUB	Pub. Spirit.	CUMMING	1738	53002004
PUB	Pub. Virtue.	LANCASTER	1746	19137005
PUB	Pub. W.b. P.	CLARKSON	1696	19087002
PUB	Pub. Worsh.	ATTERBURY	1699	21005001
PUB	Pub. Worsh.	BAYLEY	1721	43018020
PUB	Pub. Worsh.	CLAYTON	1727	21005001
PUB	Pub. Worsh.	BENNETT	1728	01028017
PUB	Pub. Worsh.	ROGERS	1736	19084001
PUB	Pub. Worsh.	WOODS	1747	13016029
PUB	Pub. Worsh.	WISHART	1753	19122006
PUB	Pub. Worsh.	MUNTON	1756	19084001
PUB	Pub. Worsh.	DAVIS	1756	19121001
PUB	Pub. Worsh.	HOLLAND	1753	61010025
PUB	Pub. Worsh.	PRICE	1757	47002046
PUB	Pub. Worsh.	MORRIS	1757	61010025
PUB	Pub. Worsh.	MUSCOTT	1760	21005001
PUB	Pub. Worsh.	FOTHERGILL	1765	19089007
PUB	Pub. Worsh.	WEBB	1765	23002003
PUB	Pub. Worsh.	STERNE	1769	19095006
PUB	Pub. Worsh.	KNOX	1768	61010025
PUB	Pub. Worsh.	SMITH	1769	57002001
PUB	Pub. Worsh.	CRAIG	1775	19107031
PUB	Pub. Worsh.	CARR	1777	19095006
PUB	Pub. Worsh.	WILSON	1781	49014015
PUB	Pub.assemb.	BRIGGS	1675	61010025
PUB	Pub.rev.&c.	BRADBURY	1772	27002020
PUB	Sinc. Pub.w.	CLAYTON	1776	46004019
PUBL	Gosp. Publ.	ATTERBURY	1734	47026026
PUBL	Publ. Worsh.	PETRIE	1779	61013015
PUN	Fut. R.& Pun.	ADEY	1755	46005028
PUN	Fut Pun.ce.	PENTYCROSS	1781	19010013
PUN	Pun.annex.	SKELTON	1754	50005010
PUN	Pun.o. Apost.	BRETT	1720	61010028
PUN	Pun.of Hell.	LORTIE	1720	50005010
PUN	Pun.of Sinn.	WHICHCOTE	1698	48001026
PUN	Sin its Pun.	BOYSE	1728	24002019
PUNISH	+prop.+punish.	SMALRIDGE	1724	43011022
PUNISH	Cap. Punish.	DODD	1772	02020013
PUNISH	Fin. Punish.	LUCAS	1716	48002002
PUNISH	Fut. Punish.	FARRINGTON	1769	43025046
PUNISH	Fut. Punish.	BOURN	1760	56001009
PUNISH	Punish.of Diso	WHICHCOTE	1698	48001018
PUNISH	Tem.punish.	LANGHORNE	1773	21008011
PUR	Bless.pur in H	BEVERIDGE	1720	43005008
PUR	Bless.pur in H	BLACKALL	1723	43005008
PUR	Bless.pur in H	ABERNETHY	1751	43005008
PUR	Noc.of Pur.	BROWNE	1749	62003017
PUR	Pur. Heart.	CHEESEMAN	1663	43005008
PUR	Pur. Heart.	HORNECK	1706	43005008
PUR	Pur. Heart.	PERKINS	1707	43005008
PUR	Pur. Heart.	HOLE	1716	19051010
PUR	Pur. Heart.	GARDINER	1720	43005008
PUR	Pur. Heart.	EDWARDS	1726	43005008
PUR	Pur. Heart.	GALE	1726	43005008
PUR	Pur. Heart.	NORRIS	1728	43005008
PUR	Pur. Heart.	COOKE	1739	43005008
PUR	Pur. Heart.	BLAIR	1740	43005008
PUR	Pur. Heart.	GROVE	1742	43005008
PUR	Pur. Heart.	SOUTH	1744	43005008
PUR	Pur. Heart.	ORR	1772	43005008
PUR	Pur. Intent.	WESTLEY	1748	43006019
PUR	Pur.of H.	HILL	1755	20016001
PURCH	Purch.o. Rel.	MARKLAND	1729	43013045
PURE	Pure Rel.	MORE	1692	62001027
PURE	Pure Rel.	ELSMERE	1767	62001027
PURGAT	Ag. Purgat.	WEST	1675	49003015
PURGATORY	Purgatory.	EARLE	1735	65001007
PURIF	Purif. Tem.	SHERIDAN	1720	45019045
PURIF	Purif.s.	SPARKES	1666	45002022
PURIF	Purif.s.	FRANK	1672	45002027
PURIF	Purif.s.	FRANK	1672	45002028
PURIF	Purif.s.	HACKET	1675	45002027
PURIF	Purif.s.	STRADLING	1692	45002022
PURIF	Purif.s.	STANHOPE	1715	45002022
PURIF	Purif.s.	HOLE	1716	45002022
PURIF	Purif.s.	MARSHALL	1731	45002022
PURIF	Purif.s.	WHEATLY	1746	45002022
PURIF	Purif.s.	ERSKINE	1757	45002028
PURIFICAT	Purificat.	COCK	1705	38003003
PURIFICAT	Purificat.	STANHOPE	1715	38003001
PURIFICAT	Purificat.	HOLE	1716	38003001
PURIFICATION	Purification.	GALE	1704	45002029

Keyword	In its Context	Author	Year	BkChpVrs
PURIFICATION	Purification.	SHERLOCK	1719	19119009
PURIFICATION	Purification.	SOUTH	1724	65003003
PURITY	Purity of L.	SEATON	1720	01039010
PURITY	Purity& Ch.	BURTON	1684	62001027
PURITY	Xn. Purity.	HAMMOND	1684	50007001
PURITY	of Purity.	HOLE	1717	43008002
PURP	Purp.of Rel.	KETTLEWELL	1719	47011023
PUT	Put on Xt.	BRADY	1730	48013014
QU	Ter.& Qu. S.	CLARKE	1734	69002029
QUA	An.m. Qua.	ANONYMOUS	1767	45016005
QUAK	Ag. Quak.	KEITH	1707	61011006
QUAK	At Quak.m.	ANONYMOUS	1771	49013014
QUAK	Rec. Quak.	HASLEWOOD	1701	23055003
QUAKERI	Ag. Quakeri.	ANONYMOUS	1710	47002024
QUAKERS	Ag Quakers.	KEITH	1700	50005014
QUAL	Qual. Believ.	CLAGETT	1720	46006044
QUAL	Qual.f fu. H.	CLARKE	1734	69003004
QUAL	Qual.f.fu. H.	BULL	1713	69003004
QUAL	Qual.of Pr.	BUERDSELL	1700	52006018
QUAL	Qual.of Pr.	FIDDES	1720	52006018
QUAL	Qual.succ. P.	ELSMERE	1767	62004003
QUALIF	Mor. Qualif.	CLARKE	1734	47011024
QUALIF	Qualif. Pray.	GARDINER	1720	43007007
QUALIF	Qualif. Pray.	HUNT	1748	43007007
QUEB	Red. Queb.	MAYHEW	1759	19126003
QUEBEC	R.of Quebec	DAWSON	1760	19018049
QUEBEC	Sur. Quebec.	BULKLEY	1759	19102013
QUEEN'S	Queen's b.d.	MORER	1708	47010038
QUENCH	Quench Spi.	BOYSE	1728	55005019
QUENCH	Quench Spi.	MOSS	1733	55005019
QUES	Impor. Ques.	ANONYMOUS	1776	47016029
QUES	Pilate's Ques.	WARBURTON	1753	46018038
QUES	Pilate's Ques.	SANDWICH	1774	46018038
QUEST	Quest. G.cat.	ERSKINE	1764	43022043
QUI	Meek.& Qui.	ORR	1749	63003004
QUI	Peace& Qui.	HOWARD	1736	55004011
QUICK	Xt.quick. U.	COLMAN	1728	23011003
QUICK	Xt's.quick v.	ERSKINE	1764	46005025
QUIET	Du.of Quiet.	DAVIS	1756	55004011
QUIET	Quiet do.our o	FARINDON	1672	55004011
QUIET	Quiet do.our o	BURTON	1685	55004011
QUIET	Quiet do.our o	DUKE	1714	55004011
QUIET	Quiet do.our o	BARROW	1716	55004011.
QUIETNESS	Quietness.	KENNET	1715	55004011
QUINQUAG	Quinquag. S.	STANHOPE	1715	49013001
QUINQUAG	Quinquag. S.	HOLE	1716	49013001
QUINQUAG	Quinquag. S.	READING	1728	01009006
QUINQUAG	Quinquag. S.	READING	1730	01012001
QUINQUAG	Quinquag.s.	STANHOPE	1715	45018031
QUINQUAG	Quinquag.s.	HOLE	1716	45018031
R	Ade. R.of C.	SANDERSON	1722	62004012
R	Adv.& Pl. R.	STOCKDALE	1777	55005016
R	Ag. Ch.of R.	HILL	1680	69018004
R	Anc. Xn R.	REGIS	1753	01003015
R	Au.1.b. R. S.	ANDERSON	1720	68000003
R	Axe laid t. R.	KEACH	1692	43003010

Keyword	In its Context	Author	Year	BkChpVrs
R	B. R.n. M. S.	ANONYMOUS	1735	56002001
R	B.o. R. M.o. S	BENSON	17--	56002001
R	Boaz& R.	TURNER	1685	05025005
R	Bod. Ex.i. R.	SCOTT	1700	57004006
R	Caus.of R.	LONG	1684	62004001
R	Cen.in.w. R.	STEEL	1776	43007003
R	Ch. Ch.of R.	BAYLEY	1721	44007009
R	Ch.of R.im.	BENNETT	1714	43005019
R	Claim Ch. R.	BULKLEY	1761	43016018
R	Corr. Ch. R.	SKELTON	1754	65004001
R	Cruel R. Ch.	STEPHENS	1728	43005007
R	D.of R. R. In.	HORNECK	1706	43005023
R	Death b. R.	WHALEY	1695	43020009
R	Death-b. R.	SCAMLER	1685	19095008
R	Death-b. R.	WARREN	1748	47017030
R	Decay of R.	ATKINSON	1737	38003016
R	Decay of R.	ATKINSON	1737	38003017
R	Def. R. R.	HALLYWELL	1694	48001016
R	Diff. R.d. W.	SMALRIDGE	1724	49003008
R	Diff. R.d. W.	BOYSE	1728	49003008
R	Diff.st.tr. R.	JEFFERY	1751	58003015
R	Div. Or.o. R.	STENNETT	1769	62003017
R	Early R.	BOYSE	1728	13028009
R	Early R.	BOURN	1755	13028009
R	Eas.& Diff. R.	BRINGHURST	1689	43011030
R	Excel. Xn. R.	WHICHCOTE	1698	48001016
R	Extent.of R.	MARSHALL	1731	19119096
R	Extent.of R.	LEIGHTON	1746	19119096
R	F. St.of R.	DUCHE	1779	19001003
R	Fai.in the. R.	HILL	1755	61011013
R	Fut. R.& Pun.	ADEY	1755	46005028
R	G. A.of o. R.	BEVERIDGE	1720	50005018
R	G.no R.o. P.	PYLE	1777	63001017
R	G's. W.in R.	HUSSEY	1758	49002007
R	G's.right. R.	HUSSEY	1753	48003025
R	G's Glo.& R.	HUSSEY	1758	19008001
R	Grad. Pr. R.	SECKER	1770	23001016
R	Ho.o.r.at D.	STEPHENS	1699	53003013
R	How. R. S. S.	FOSTER	1732	46005039
R	Hypot.in R.	SCOTT	1743	20030006
R	Imp. Xn. R.	HOLDEN	1755	46007016
R	Import.of R.	FOTHERGILL	1765	19037031
R	Impro.in R.	STENNETT	1769	28014005
R	Incon.in R.	TIDCOMBE	1757	28006004
R	Incon.in R.	MASON	1758	28006004
R	Indiff.to R.	GRAY	1779	19085006
R	Inf. Ch.of R.	SMYTH	1735	50001024
R	Inf. R.in Ad.	BLAIR	1777	19027005
R	Inf. R.on Pr.	BLAIR	1777	19001003
R	Insuf.o. N. R.	TAYLOR	1732	49011014
R	Int.b.r.&w.	BOURDALOUE	1776	43013025
R	Joy& F.in R.	BLAIR	1777	19002011
R	Leg.& Ev. R.	SMITH	1673	48009031
R	Life& D. R.	DUCHE	1779	19037037
R	Lukew.in R.	BRAMSTON	1713	69003015
R	M. Or. Xn. R.	BOURN	1777	46006066

INDEXES TO THIRD VOLUME: E: KEYWORD-IN-CONTEXT INDEX OF OTHER SUBJECTS OR OCCASIONS

Keyword	In its Context	Author	Year	BkChpVrs
R	Marks of R.	CARR	1777	06024014
R	Means of R.	FARRINGTON	1769	46004023
R	Mir.or. Xt.r.	BOURN	1777	50002016
R	N.& R. Rel.	TUNSTALL	1759	03018004
R	N.& R. Rel.	UMFREVILLE	1759	47004012
R	Nat.& In. R.	LAW	1768	32006008
R	Nat.& R. Rel.	TILLOTSON	1735	43009013
R	Nat.& R.rel.	BREKELL	1765	48002014
R	Nat. R.& Xn.	MARSHALL	1750	64001008
R	Nat. Rev. R.	HEYLIN	1749	18036002
R	Neces. R Pr.	BURNABY	1777	19111010
R	Neces.of R.	DODDERIDGE	1742	46003003
R	Negl. R. Dut.	NEWCOME	1702	45014018
R	Negl. R. Dut.	MARSH	1737	45014018
R	Negl. R Dut.	DAVIES	1720	45014018
R	New Birth or R	BYAM	1675	46003005
R	New Birth or R	HOPKINS	1710	46003005
R	New Birth or R	HOLE	1715	46003005
R	New Birth or R	LAMBE	1717	46003005
R	New Birth or R	HOLE	1719	46003005
R	New Birth or R	FARINGTON	1741	46003005
R	New Birth or R	JONES	1756	46003005
R	No. Tr.in R.	WARNEFORD	1757	57006017
R	No Tr.in R.	JONES	1690	57006017
R	No Tr.in R.	GALE	1726	57006017
R	No Tr.in R.	MARSHALL	1731	57006017
R	Per.& F. R.	SAUNDERS	1701	06024014
R	Per.& F. R.	READER	1765	06024014
R	Peter's Fall&r	STANHOPE	1705	44014072
R	Pract.of R.	DUCHAL	1728	19084010
R	Prior Xt's. R.	WELLS	1735	47026022
R	Prop. R.& L.	ACRES	1714	19078004
R	Prot. R.vi. H.	COYTE	1761	47024014
R	R.& Nat. R.	MAYNARD	1722	19147020
R	R.& Pr.im.h.	WHEATLY	1746	61011039
R	R.&off.o. D.	COLMAN	1728	69022016
R	R. Care of F.	FORD	1770	01018019
R	R. Ed. Child.	DODDERIDGE	1743	20022006
R	R. G's.right.	DORRINGTON	1705	43005048
R	R. Gov.of F.	PICKARD	1762	01018019
R	R. Life t. Pl.	LAWSON	1764	19001002
R	R. Loy.& Ch.	STUBBS	1704	63002017
R	R. N. G.& R.	COCKBURN	1708	61012012
R	R. Not.of G.	HUNT	1748	20009010
R	R. Rel.matt.	ANONYMOUS	1764	23046008
R	R. Sea, X's bl	WILLISON	1761	02014015
R	R. Sold. J. R.	LARDNER	1760	43028012
R	R. U.& A. W.	PEARSON	1718	49007031
R	R. U.& A. W.	NORRIS	1728	49007031
R	R. U.& A. W.	MILLER	1749	49007031
R	R. U.& A. W.	ORR	1749	49007031
R	R. Use Law	UNWIN	1773	48007009
R	R. Xt's. Xter.	BREKELL	1765	43016018
R	R.ab. Busin.	BATTY	1739	45010041
R	R.con.w. L.	GERARD	1780	19116009
R	R.due G's N.	SMALBROKE	1722	03019030
R	R.imp. Soc.	CRAIG	1775	14015002
R	R.ins.g.m. R	RANDOLPH	1738	50003005
R	R.ins.g.m. R.	JOHNSON	1731	50003005
R	R.nec.to c. S.	SKELTON	1754	63002017
R	R.of Age H.	GERARD	1780	20016031
R	R.of Quebec	DAWSON	1760	19018049
R	R.perf.sy.m.	LAWSON	1764	43007020
R	R.poor.p. C.	BRADY	1730	62002015
R	R.to G.in Xt.	BRIGHT	1695	50005019
R	Rea.f. Xn's.r.	GALE	1726	55005016
R	Rea.f. Xn's.r.	MORRIS	1743	55005016
R	Rea.jud.r.ac.	CLARKE	1735	65003020
R	Reas.in r.m.	PATTEN	1755	63003015
R	Rec.& R.&c.	KILLINBECK	1717	43005023
R	Rec.& R.&c.	MOSS	1737	43005023
R	Req.of R.gr.	SPOONER	1771	19034015
R	S.& R. Wisd.	BADDERLEY	1752	20004005
R	Scope. Xn. R.	MONRO	1693	43005020
R	Self.de.r.m.	BRAILSFORD	1776	51006007
R	Spir. W.& R.	HUSSEY	1758	52001017
R	Spir. Xt's. R.	MICHELL	1737	45009054
R	Suff.for R.sa.	BRADBURY	1722	63003014
R	T.&man. R.	LAW	1745	51004004
R	Tem. Ad. R.	TAYLOR	1719	20003017
R	Tem. Ad. R.	STERNE	1769	20003017
R	Truth. Xn.r.	JORTIN	1730	45002032
R	Truth Xn. R.	JORTIN	1730	46010025
R	Truth Xn. R.	JORTIN	1730	46015024
R	U.of R.at D.	STENNETT	1769	19023004
R	Us.o. R.in R.	HOLDEN	1755	45012057
R	Van.of pr. R.	QUINCY	1750	59001016
R	W.to r.&p.	COLLINGES	1684	05008018
R	Weig.m. R.	ORR	1739	43023023
R	Weigh.m. R.	ORR	1739	45011042
R	Wind& S.r.	DODD	1757	44004039
R	Wind& S.r.	BULKLEY	1771	44004041
R	Wis.r.t. Pl.	ANONYMOUS	1754	20003017
R	Wisd.b. R.	CARR	1777	18027006
R	Xn. R.dem.	HUTCHINSON	1720	46015024
R	Xn.r.pr.sp p.	RANDOLPH	1777	47005038
R	Xnity R.o. L.	ROBINSON	1739	46006068
R	Xrticks tr. R.	QUINCY	1750	62003017
R	Xt. Med.& R.	LANGHORNE	1773	54001014
R	Xt. Med.o. R.	STENNETT	1769	52002010
R	Xt.at G's.r.h.	HURRION	1719	61012001
R	Xt.si.r.h. G.	FLAVEL	1673	61001003
R	Xt's. D. A.r.	HOADLY	1754	43020026
R	Xt's. P.o. R.	LARDNER	1760	50007009
R	Xt's. R.& N.	PATTEN	1759	54002008
R	Xt's.pr.af. R.	DELANY	1766	49015006
R	Zeal civ.& R.	WEBSTER	1776	19137005
R	1st pr.of R.	GERARD	1780	01003015
RA	Ra. Prof. Xy.	WILKINSON	1660	58002019
RACE	Celest. Race.	BUSH	1692	49009024
RACE	Xn. Race.	NEEDHAM	1679	61012001
RACE	Xn. Race.	SYLVESTER	1702	61012001

Keyword	In its Context	Author	Year	BkChpVrs
RACE	Xn. Race.	LUCAS	1710	61012001
RACE	Xn. Race.	JOHNSON	1713	61012001
RACE	Xn. Race.	BEVERIDGE	1720	49009024
RACE	Xn. Race.	DUNLOP	1722	61012001
RACE	Xn. Race.	CARTER	1729	49009024
RACE	Xn. Race.	HOADLY	1754	49009024
RACE	Xn. Race.	BADDELLEY	1766	61012001
RACHEL	Rachel comf.	HORNE	1778	24031015
RAILLERY	Raillery.	SHOREY	1725	68000017
RAIM	Anx.f.raim.	BLAIR	1740	43006028
RAIN	G.giv. Rain.	FOTHERGILL	1765	47014017
RAIN	Of Rain.	HOLE	1716	09012017
RAIN	Xt.like Rain.	WILLISON	1761	19072006
RAINB	Rainb. Cor.	ERSKINE	1757	69004003
RAIS	Lazar. Rais.	BRAGGE	1702	46011001
RAIS	Lazar. Rais.	WELCH	1752	46011003
RAIS	Lazar. Rais.	DODD	1757	46011001
RAIS	Xt's.p.rais.d.	MORRIS	1757	46005025
RAKE	Pen. Rake.	BOURN	1763	45015011
RAKE	Pen. Rake.	POWELL	1776	45015011
RANKS	Var. Ranks.	FOSTER	1737	63005005
RAPE	Rape& Mur.	COLEIRE	1723	07019030
RASH	Rash judgm.	SHOREY	1725	49004005
RASH	Rash.&v. S.	BERAULT	1698	62005012
RASH	Rash.&v. S.	BURNET	1713	62005012
RASH	Rash.&v. S.	BARROW	1716	62005012
RASH	Rash.&v. S.	GILBERT	1724	62005012
RASH	Rash.&v. S.	INNES	1726	62005012
RASH	Rash.&v. S.	BOSTON	1773	62005012
RASH	Rash. Swear.	BEVERIDGE	1720	43005033
RASH	Rash. Swear.	AGAR	1759	43005034
RASH	Rash.judg.	BLAIR	1740	43007004
RASH	Rash Cens.	MASON	1742	43007001
RASH	Rash Judg.	WATERLAND	1742	45013002
RASH	Rash Judg.	HOOLE	1748	45006037
RAT	Rat. Comm.	YARDLEY	1728	49014016
RAT	Xy.ca.rat. D.	ORR	1739	63003015
RATION	Ration. Rel.	BOURN	1760	49014020
RATION	Ration Faith	DODWELL	1745	63003015
RATIONAL	Xy.rational.	QUINCY	1750	49010015
RE	Dan.o.d. Re.	LANGHORNE	1773	46009004
RE	Ex. D.re. W.	ORR	1739	61010025
RE	Fai. Xt's. Re.	SKELTON	1754	47010040
RE	Fut. Re.& P.	ROGERS	1736	51006007
RE	Imp. Re.pr.l.	CRAIG	1775	52002012
RE	Monm. Re.s.	WETENHAL	1686	63002017
RE	Nec.o.tr. Re.	ELSMERE	1767	46009004
RE	Prov.our Re.	ROGERS	1730	55005021
RE	Re.of Right.	BRODHURST	1733	19012001
RE	Re.of Sains.	BOURDALOUE	1776	43005012
RE	Rew. Virt.& Re	DORRINGTON	1705	19019011
RE	Rew. Virt.& Re	BALGUY	1750	19019011
RE	Union in Re.	YOUNG	1706	46016031
RE	Xn. M.& Re.	ROBINSON	1734	63001024
REA	Insuf.of Rea.	ECCLES	1755	47017022
REA	Rea.f. Xn's.r.	GALE	1726	55005016
REA	Rea.f. Xn's.r.	MORRIS	1743	55005016
REA	Rea.jud.r.ac.	CLARKE	1735	65003020
REA	Rea.rel.mat.	RANDOLPH	1762	48001020
REA	Rel.rea.serv.	ASHTON	1770	32007006
READ	Read. H. S.	STRATFORD	1687	54003016
READ	Read. S. S.	CROFT	1697	46005039
READ	Read. S. S.	NOURSE	1708	46005039
READ	Read. S. S.	HARRIS	1717	43022029
READ	Read. S. S.	BRADBURY	1717	46005039
READ	Read. S. S.	NEWMAN	1717	46005039
READ	Read. S. S.	REYNOLDS	1717	47013015
READ	Read. S. S.	GROSVENOR	1717	62001021
READ	Read. S. S.	EARLE	1717	69001003
READ	Read. S. S.	BILLINGSLEY	1723	46005039
READ	Read. S. S.	DICKSON	1731	46005039
READ	Read. S. S.	ROGERS	1730	58003015
READ	Read. S. S.	STRAIGHT	1741	46005039
READ	Read. S. S.	WEBSTER	1745	45016008
READ	Read. S. S.	BUNDY	1750	43024015
READ	Read. S. S.	SKELTON	1754	46005039
READ	Read. S. S.	SMITH	1756	43022029
READ	Read. S. S.	WILCOX	1757	45024032
READ	Read. S. S.	MUNTON	1756	47017011
READ	Read. S. S.	NEWTON	1760	46005039
READ	Read. S. S.	STERNE	1769	46005039
READ	Read. S. S.	LANGHORNE	1773	47017011
READ	Read. S. S.	PETERS	1776	58003015
READ	Read.of S. S.	HARRIS	1717	43002023
READ	S. S.t.b.read.	FOWLER	1675	55005027
READ	T.read.of V.	HOPKINS	1771	16004023
READ	Xt's.read&c.	LEMAN	1749	43011028
REAL	Real.of Rel.	STENNETT	1769	58003005
REAL	Real Liberty	SHERIDAN	1720	46008036
REAL	Real Liberty	TILLOTSON	1735	46008036
REAL	Real Liberty	SEAGRAVE	1737	46008036
REAL	Real Liberty	HARTLEY	1754	46008036
REAL	Real Liberty	SAURIN	1777	46008036
REAL	Real Pres.	SHARP	1735	46006053
REAP	M.reap.as s.	BOURN	1777	51006007
REAS	Def. H. Reas.	BURNET	1747	49013012
REAS	H.reas.insuf.	SHUCKBURGH	1721	21001015
REAS	Hum. Reas.	NEWLIN	1720	27004031
REAS	Reas.& Passi.	TOTTIE	1736	48007023
REAS	Reas.& Rel.	ATTERBURY	1703	48012001
REAS	Reas.& Rel.	BALGUY	1748	49014020
REAS	Reas.& Rev.	FOSTER	1744	20020027
REAS	Reas.& Rev.	COWPER	1774	48001020
REAS	Reas.&c. Pray.	WESTON	1747	45011009
REAS	Reas. Mo.&c.	HARTE	1736	46014001
REAS	Reas. Rel.	GROVE	1741	18021015
REAS	Reas. Rel. M.	CALAMY	1670	48012001
REAS	Reas.bel. Xt.	HARRIS	1728	46011045
REAS	Reas.in r.m.	PATTEN	1755	63003015
REAS	Reas.in rel.	STONE	1771	23046008
REAS	Reas.in Rel.	BRADY	1713	47024025
REAS	Reas.in Rel.	BUNDY	1740	47018004

INDEXES TO THIRD VOLUME: E: KEYWORD-IN-CONTEXT INDEX OF OTHER SUBJECTS OR OCCASIONS

Keyword	In its Context	Author	Year	BkChpVrs
REAS	Reas.ins. G.	EDGCUMBE	1736	50003005
REAS	Reas.ins. G.	AGAR	1759	49002005
REAS	Reas.insuf.	BUNDY	1750	19019007
REAS	Reas.insuff.	JOHNSON	1740	46006066
REAS	Reas.judg.d.	JOHNSON	1733	46011026
REAS	Reas.of Fai.	WHARTON	1728	63003015
REAS	Reas.of Faith	SHERLOCK	1702	50004018
REAS	Reas.of Pray.	SEED	1743	48012012
REAS	Reas.rel.m.	GRIFFITH	1763	53002013
REAS	Reas.serv.	FAWCETT	1749	48012001
REAS	Use of Reas.	SMALRIDGE	1724	47017002
REASON	Reason.	WHITBY	1720	45012057
REASON	Xty.reason.	STEPHENS	1737	63003015
REASONA	Xty.reasona.	WISE	1717	65005003
REB	Def.of Reb.	BULKLEY	1761	19107001
REB	Flight Reb.	DODDRIDGE	1745	45001074
REB	On late Reb.	PETTER	1685	46021022
REB	Reb. Ch.	HOW	1731	45007005
REB	Reb. Ch.	CRANER	1749	16002020
REB	Reb.ag. G.	DUNLOP	1722	26016063
REB	Reb.for Sin.	T.	1667	23066015
REBUILD	Rebuild. Ch.	CONANT	1699	36002006
REBUKE	L's.rebuke.	WEBB	1765	45009055
REBUKE	Op. Rebuke.	ANONYMOUS	1777	20027005
REBUKE	Rebuke.	ANONYMOUS	1742	20027005
REC	Learn.rec.	DODD	1772	20004007
REC	Nin.of Rec.	HERVEY	1759	50005018
REC	Praise f. Rec,	LITTLETON	1680	23038017
REC	Rec.& R.&c.	KILLINBECK	1717	43005023
REC	Rec.& R.&c.	MOSS	1737	43005023
REC	Rec. Quak.	HASLEWOOD	1701	23055003
REC	Rec.f. Sick.	PETERS	1776	46005014
REC	Rec.of Gosp.	BADDELLEY	1752	46001012
REC	Rec.of Rew.	SOUTH	1727	61011024
REC	Rec.of Rew.	BADDELLEY	1752	61011026
REC	Rec.of Rew.	NEWTON	1782	61011033
REC	Rec.of Sin.	WHICHCOTE	1703	61002017
REC	Rec.s.	SALL	1675	43024015
REC	Rec.s.	MOTTE	1675	48005020
REC	Rec.s.	HUDLESTON	1729	11022021
REC	Sick.& Rec.	ROGERS	1691	19030003
REC	Sick.& Rec.	STANHOPE	1709	19030003
REC	Virt.rec.&c.	LARDNER	1760	69003018
RECANT	Recant.f.	DANVERS	1736	61009022
RECANT	Recant.s.	EGAN	1673	45022032
RECANT	Recant.s.	ADAMS	1700	19066016
RECANT	Recant.s.	AYLMER	1713	64002001
RECE	Unwo. Rece.	MEDE	1672	49010005
RECEI	Giv.&recei.	TILLOTSON	1735	47020035
RECEIV	Giv.&receiv.	COLLIER	1725	47020035
RECEIV	Receiv. Tr.	STRAIGHT	1741	52004015
RECEIV	Receiv.word	MAYHEW	1756	62001021
RECEIV	Receiv.word	BREKELL	1765	62001021
RECKONING	A reckoning.	ELLIS	1704	45016002
RECO	Broth. Reco.	REYNOLDS	1679	53003015
RECO	Reco.by Xt.	SHEPHERD	1748	52002013

Keyword	In its Context	Author	Year	BkChpVrs
RECON	D. Recon.& Rep	BLACKALL	1723	43005023
RECON	D. Recon.& Rep	BLAIR	1740	43005023
RECON	Recon.w. G.	BRADY	1713	50005020
RECON	Recon.w. G.	DAVIES	1766	50005020
RECON	Recon.w. G.	BOURN	1777	50005020
RECONC	Xn. Reconc.	WALL	1660	48005011
RECONCILIAT	Reconciliat.	WHICHCOTE	1703	50005020
RECTITUDE	Rectitude.	DUCHAL	1765	18013007
RED	Cov.of Red.	FLAVEL	1673	23053012
RED	G's. Lo. Red.	CARMICHAEL	1757	65004011
RED	Love in Red.	HUSSEY	1755	65004009
RED	Love in Red.	CARMICHAEL	1757	65004009
RED	Love in Red.	WITHERSPOON	1768	69001005
RED	Partic. Red.	HURRION	1732	59002014
RED	Red.& Sanct.	SHERLOCK	1772	52002018
RED	Red. Captive	BERRIMAN	1721	19102019
RED	Red. Queb.	MAYHEW	1759	19126003
RED	Red.b. Xt.	FLAVEL	1673	49001030
RED	Red.b. Xt.	USHER	1678	69021008
RED	Red.b. Xt.	ERSKINE	1764	49001030
RED	Red.b. Xt.	HALL	1777	48008003
RED	Red.by Xt.	USHER	1678	46001012
RED	Red.by Xt.	USHER	1678	53002006
RED	Red.by Xt.	ERSKINE	1764	69002009
RED	Xt.red.n. A.	COLMAN	1728	61002016
REDE	Rede. Love.	BAINE	1778	69003020
REDE	Rede. Time.	BURTON	1685	52005016
REDE	Rede. Time.	WADE	1692	52005016
REDE	Rede. Time.	BIRKWOOD	1693	52005016
REDE	Rede. Time.	SHEPPARD	17--	52005016
REDE	Rede. Time.	BRADY	1730	52005016
REDE	Rede. Time.	ROGERS	1735	52005016
REDE	Rede. Time.	SIMONS	1743	52005016
REDE	Rede. Time.	EVANS	1774	52005016
REDE	Rede. Time.	HORNECK	1774	52005016
REDE	Rede. Time.	HORNE	1778	52005016
REDE	Rede.by Xt.	USHER	1678	52001013
REDE	Rede.by Xt.	LOVEDER	1756	54001014
REDE	Univ. Rede.	BARROW	1716	57004010
REDE	Univ. Rede.	HUSSEY	1755	57002004
REDE	Xt.rede.&c.	BOSTON	1773	51004004
REDEE	Div. Redee.	DAWSON	1765	44001002
REDEE	Redee. Virt.	ROWLAND	1774	69003020
REDEEM	L's Redeem.	WILLISON	1761	19107002
REDEEM	L's Redeem.	LAWSON	1764	19107008
REDEEM	Ld's redeem.	REYNOLDS	1679	49006019
REDEEM	Redeem Bl.	WILLISON	1761	52001007
REDEEM	Xt. Redeem.	FARENDON	1672	49006020
REDEEM	Xt. Redeem.	COLE	1692	49006020
REDEM	C.& Redem.	EATON	1764	19071005
REDEM	M's. Redem.	OGDEN	1777	46014001
REDEM	Redem. Ref.	TERRY	1746	18019025
REDEM	Redem.b. Xt	DORRINGTON	1705	49006020
REDEM	Redem.o. M.	STURMY	1716	61002016
REDEM	Xn. Redem.	LANGHORNE	1773	59002014
REDEMPT	Redempt.	JACOMB	1676	23053010

Keyword	In its Context	Author	Year	BkChpVrs
REDEMPTION	Redemption	CRUSO	1699	19069004
REDEMPTION	Redemption	CLAYTON	1706	49001023
REDEMPTION	Redemption	HOPKINS	1712	51003010
REDEMPTION	Redemption	SCATTERGOOD	1723	49006020
REDEMPTION	Redemption	TILLOTSON	1735	49001024
REDEMPTION	Redemption	CATCOTT	1753	49001023
REDEMPTION	Redemption	HILL	1755	51003010
REDEMPTION	Redemption	HUSSEY	1758	52003010
REDEMPTION	Redemption	HAWEIS	1762	51003010
REDEMPTION	Redemption	FARRINGTON	1769	48005001
REDEMPTION	Redemption	BAINE	1778	61002010
REDUC	Reduc. Diss.	NADEN	1712	49012025
REECJ	Reecj. Xnity.	ROGERS	1727	46003019
REF	Artif. Ref.	MARRIOTT	1774	34002016
REF	G. Ref. Dist.	DUCHE	1779	19042011
REF	Redem. Ref.	TERRY	1746	18019025
REF	Ref. Liturgy.	GODDARD	1772	46017003
REF	Rig.m's ref.	FLAVEL	1673	23026020
REF	Xt.our Ref.	WILLISON	1761	61006018
REFL	Ser. Refl.s. D	WHITTY	1772	24008006
REFLECT	Rel. Reflect.	LANGHORNE	1773	36001007
REFLECT	Self-reflect.	CONANT	1699	25003040
REFLECTION	of Reflection	SMITH	1740	20004026
REFOR	Rule Refor.	PIERCE	1671	43019008
REFORM	Ch. Reform.	THOMAS	1661	21005001
REFORM	Reform.just.	STILLINGFLEET	1707	47024014
REFUGE	G. Refuge.	FARMER	1756	19142004
REFUGE	Sinn.refuge.	BAINE	1778	61006018
REFUGE	Xn's Refuge.	DELAUNE	1728	46016023
REFUGE	Xt. Refuge.	VENN	1759	23003002
REFUSED	Invi.refused.	BOURN	1764	45014016
REG	Add.to reg.	DODDERIDGE	1742	62001018
REG	Adop.& Reg.	DRAKE	1676	46001012
REG	Bapt.or Reg.	ANONYMOUS	1708	59003004
REG	G's.reg.to ri.	REYNER	1745	63003012
REG	G's.reg.to P.	WILCOX	1757	38003017
REG	Reg.of Pleas.	LUCAS	1710	58003004
REG	Reg.of Pleas.	HOOLE	1748	58003004
REG	Sins of Reg.	CHARNOCK	1684	65003009
REG	Xt's reg.offi.	FLAVEL	1673	52001022
REGAL	Regal Power	BERNARD	1661	48013002
REGAL	Xt's Regal.	REYNOLDS	1679	19110002
REGEN	Regen. Unr.	DUCHE	1779	19104029
REGENERAT	Regenerat.	WILKINSON	1660	46003010
REGENERAT	Regenerat.	FORD	1675	46003003
REGENERAT	Regenerat.	HORTON	1679	46003008
REGENERAT	Regenerat.	WALLIS	1682	46003003
REGENERAT	Regenerat.	CHARNOCK	1684	46003003
REGENERAT	Regenerat.	CHARNOCK	1684	50005017
REGENERAT	Regenerat.	CHARNOCK	1684	62001018
REGENERAT	Regenerat.	STANHOPE	1705	46003008
REGENERAT	Regenerat.	BAXTER	1707	46003009
REGENERAT	Regenerat.	BRADBURY	1703	69021005
REGENERAT	Regenerat.	BRADFORD	1709	59003004
REGENERAT	Regenerat.	BOEHM	1717	46003003
REGENERAT	Regenerat.	EDWARDS	1726	46003003

Keyword	In its Context	Author	Year	BkChpVrs
REGENERAT	Regenerat.	IBBOT	1726	46003003
REGENERAT	Regenerat.	WAPLE	1729	46003001
REGENERAT	Regenerat.	WAPLE	1729	46003003
REGENERAT	Regenerat.	WAPLE	1729	46003004
REGENERAT	Regenerat.	BEVERIDGE	1720	50005017
REGENERAT	Regenerat.	SHARP	1729	48012002
REGENERAT	Regenerat.	WAPLE	1729	50005017
REGENERAT	Regenerat.	SILVESTER	1738	46003005
REGENERAT	Regenerat.	ROGERS	1735	50005017
REGENERAT	Regenerat.	TILLOTSON	1735	51006015
REGENERAT	Regenerat.	ANONYMOUS	1739	50005007
REGENERAT	Regenerat.	WATERLAND	1742	46003009
REGENERAT	Regenerat.	BATEMAN	1747	46003005
REGENERAT	Regenerat.	WESTLEY	1748	46003008
REGENERAT	Regenerat.	WATERLAND	1740	59003004
REGENERAT	Regenerat.	DODDERIDGE	1742	50004017
REGENERAT	Regenerat.	DODDERIDGE	1742	50005017
REGENERAT	Regenerat.	HILL	1755	50005017
REGENERAT	Regenerat.	WALKER	1755	50005017
REGENERAT	Regenerat.	GREEN	1758	51006015
REGENERAT	Regenerat.	BREKELL	1761	46003003
REGENERAT	Regenerat.	SHIRLEY	1762	46003005
REGENERAT	Regenerat.	PEARSE	1763	46003008
REGENERAT	Regenerat.	BOWMAN	1764	46003005
REGENERAT	Regenerat.	ELLIOTT	1764	46003006
REGENERAT	Regenerat.	WHITTY	1768	69021005
REGENERAT	Regenerat.	BARBER	1770	46003003
REGENERAT	Regenerat.	DAVIES	1771	46003007
REGENERAT	Regenerat.	SIMPSON	1774	46003001
REGENERAT	Regenerat.	CRAIG	1775	46003003
REGENERAT	Regenerat.	PENTYCROSS	1781	46003003
REIGN	Reign of Sin.	REYNOLDS	1679	48006012
REIGN	Reign of Xt.	BAGSHAW	1669	37014005
REIGN	Reign.of Gr.	BAINE	1778	48005021
REIIG	Wis.b.reiig.	BARNES	1752	18028028
REJ	Duty of rej.	SCATTERGOOD	1723	21011009
REJ	Light G.rej.	CONANT	1699	46003019
REJ	Rej.everm.	BARROW	1716	55005016
REJ	Rej.f. Peace.	PHILIPS	1775	23066010
REJ	Rej.in God.	SMALRIDGE	1724	19097012
REJ	Rej.in Hope.	LELAND	1769	48005002
REJ	Rej.in Relig.	LANGHORNE	1773	53004004
REJ	Rej.of Gosp.	DAVIES	1771	46003019
REJ	Rule of Rej.	STRAIGHT	1671	53004004
REJECT	Heret.reject.	CONEY	1750	59003010
REJECT	Reject. Xt.	SOUTH	1744	43019022
REJECT	Reject.of Xt.	DAVIES	1771	44012006
REJOI	Rejoi.in H.	ANONYMOUS	1693	48012012
REJOICING	Xn.rejoicing	HERVEY	1770	53004004
REL	Adv.of Rel.	EDWARDS	1726	57004007
REL	Adv.of Rel.	DAVIES	1754	57004007
REL	Adv.of Rel.	FOTHERGILL	1765	57004007
REL	Adv.of Rel.	DELANY	1766	59002011
REL	Advant. Rel.	STERNE	1769	21012013
REL	Apol.f. Rel.	POOL	1673	43011019
REL	Ar.f. Xn. Rel.	KNOX	1768	63003015

INDEXES TO THIRD VOLUME: E: KEYWORD-IN-CONTEXT INDEX OF OTHER SUBJECTS OR OCCASIONS

Keyword	In its Context	Author	Year	BkChpVrs
REL	Barabb.rel.	ANONYMOUS	1711	46018020
REL	Beh.at rel.as.	ROBINSON	1776	58003014
REL	Civ.&rel. G.	MURRAY	1777	01003001
REL	Civ.&rel. L.	PECKARD	1754	63002016
REL	Conf.in Rel.	LANGHORNE	1773	49010012
REL	Const.in Rel.	COOKE	1689	44008038
REL	Curios.in Rel.	STANHOPE	1705	46021022
REL	Curios.in Rel.	SEED	1750	46021022
REL	D.rel.t. H. S.	GUYSE	1757	52004030
REL	Dan.neg.rel.	STILLINGFLEET	1707	61002003
REL	Dang.of Rel.	SMALRIDGE	1724	64002020
REL	Dang.of Rel.	ADEY	1760	64002022
REL	Decay o. Rel.	ATKINSON	1737	38003018
REL	Decl.in Rel.	BARKER	1748	69002004
REL	Decl.in Rel.	HOGG	1775	69002005
REL	Def. Pr. Rel.	ATKINSON	1737	24006029
REL	Defend. Rel.	DOUGHTY	1761	19139021
REL	Devot. Rel.	STEBBING	1760	45010039
REL	Diff. Rel.sur.	STENNETT	1769	43011030
REL	Diff.of Rel.	BALGUY	1748	46004009
REL	Diff.of Rel.	STENNETT	1769	43016024
REL	End&c. Rel.	TATHAM	1780	48006023
REL	Enq.in Rel.	HOADLY	1754	55005021
REL	Essen.of Rel.	WHICHCOTE	1703	52002022
REL	Ev.o. Xn.rel.	TATHAM	1780	61002003
REL	Exc. Xn. Rel.	TILLOTSON	1735	46003019
REL	Excell. Rel.	CORNWALL	1701	20008009
REL	Excell. Rel.	ABERNETHY	1751	20008006
REL	Exp.div. Rel.	CONYBEARE	1729	46006045
REL	Fal. Pre. Rel.	CLARKE	1735	43022011
REL	Form.in Rel.	LAKE	1705	58003005
REL	Form.in Rel.	DORMAN	1743	58003005
REL	Fruits of Rel.	STENNETT	1769	48006022
REL	G's.rel. Goo.	HUTCHINS	1771	65004016
REL	Glory in Rel.	WHICHCOTE	1707	24009023
REL	Glory in Rel.	WHICHCOTE	1707	24009024
REL	Habit. Rel.	AMORY	1775	19016008
REL	Hap.of Rel.	ATTERBURY	1699	57004007
REL	Hap.of Rel.	BEVERIDGE	1720	19144015
REL	Happ.rel. C.	REYNER	1745	20010029
REL	Heart of Rel.	ACTON	1714	24030021
REL	Idlen.in Rel.	BRAILSFORD	1776	43020006
REL	Igno.in Rel.	REYNER	1745	43015016
REL	Imp.in Rel.	STENNETT	1760	64003018
REL	Imp.of Rel.	STENNETT	1769	45010042
REL	Indif.in Rel.	LITTLETON	1684	47018017
REL	Indiff.in Rel.	WEBB	1765	69003017
REL	Ineq.rel.dis.	MAINWARING	1780	47010034
REL	Irres.in Rel.	CLARK	1742	47026028
REL	Know. Rel.	ORR	1739	48002014
REL	Ld Gord.rel.	CLARKE	1781	19050015
REL	M's.rel.to G.	FOSTER	1744	47017028
REL	Matt.of Rel.	JEFFERY	1751	53001010
REL	Mock.at Rel.	WARREN	1730	68000017
REL	Mor.p.o.rel.	WHICHCOTE	1703	59002012
REL	Myst.of Rel.	CARR	1777	64003016

Keyword	In its Context	Author	Year	BkChpVrs
REL	N.& R. Rel.	TUNSTALL	1759	03018004
REL	N.& R. Rel.	UMFREVILLE	1759	47004012
REL	Nat.& R. Rel.	TILLOTSON	1735	43009013
REL	Nat.& R.rel.	BREKELL	1765	48002014
REL	Nat.of Rel.	WEST	1762	47019034
REL	Natur. Rel.	REAY	1755	49001021
REL	Nec.of Rel.	REEVES	1729	61012002
REL	O. Rel.to N.	DUCHAL	1765	18038007
REL	Obst.in Rel.	CARMICHAEL	1757	61012001
REL	Pers.in Rel.	STENNET	1769	07008004
REL	Pl.best Rel.	DODSLEY	1745	20007017
REL	Pleas.rel. L.	DORRINGTON	1703	20003017
REL	Pleas.rel. L.	PEARSON	1718	20003017
REL	Pleas.rel. L.	SOUTH	1727	20003017
REL	Pleas.rel. L.	NEWLIN	1728	20003017
REL	Pleas.rel. L.	WILDER	1729	20003017
REL	Pleas.rel. L.	FORSTER	1732	20003017
REL	Pleas.rel. L.	WESTLEY	1735	20003017
REL	Pleas.rel. L.	WHEATLAND	1739	20003017
REL	Pleas.rel. L.	FARRINGTON	1741	20003017
REL	Pleas.rel. L.	OAKES	1747	20003017
REL	Pleas.rel. L.	SEED	1750	20003017
REL	Pleas.rel. L.	FOTHERGILL	1765	20003017
REL	Pleas.rel. L.	STENNETT	1769	20003017
REL	Pleas.rel. L.	JORTIN	1774	20003017
REL	Prac.of Rel.	DUCHAL	1728	20008006
REL	Pract.o. Rel.	WALLIS	1748	57004007
REL	Pract.of Rel.	DUCHAL	1728	20012028
REL	Prog.of Rel.	BOURN	1755	20004018
REL	Purch.o. Rel.	MARKLAND	1729	43013045
REL	Pure Rel.	MORE	1692	62001027
REL	Pure Rel.	ELSMERE	1767	62001027
REL	Purp.of Rel.	KETTLEWELL	1719	47011023
REL	R. Rel.matt.	ANONYMOUS	1764	23046008
REL	Ration. Rel.	BOURN	1760	49014020
REL	Rea.rel.mat.	RANDOLPH	1762	48001020
REL	Real.of Rel.	STENNETT	1769	58003005
REL	Reas.& Rel.	ATTERBURY	1703	48012001
REL	Reas.& Rel.	BALGUY	1748	49014020
REL	Reas. Rel.	GROVE	1741	18021015
REL	Reas. Rel. M.	CALAMY	1670	48012001
REL	Reas.in rel.	STONE	1771	23046008
REL	Reas.in Rel.	BRADY	1713	47024025
REL	Reas.in Rel.	BUNDY	1740	47018004
REL	Reas.rel.m.	GRIFFITH	1763	53002013
REL	Rel.& Gov.	HENLEY	1772	44012017
REL	Rel.& Kno.	ENFIELD	1780	43013033
REL	Rel.& Mor.	HEYLYN	1749	32006008
REL	Rel.& Patr.	DAVIES	1755	10010012
REL	Rel.& Vir.best	ROGERS	1730	63003013
REL	Rel.& Vir.best	WARREN	1739	63003013
REL	Rel.& Virt.c.	DOUGHTY	1761	20003007
REL	Rel.& Virtue	ANONYMOUS	1759	19016003
REL	Rel. Astron.	FAWCETT	1749	19008003
REL	Rel. Barabb.	ANONYMOUS	1771	46018040
REL	Rel. Comm.	BRUCE	1725	48015007

Keyword	In its Context	Author	Year	BkChpVrs
REL	Rel. Confid.	PYLE	1777	43003008
REL	Rel. Conver.	NEWMAN	1760	20010021
REL	Rel. Educat.	HOPKINS	1708	20022006
REL	Rel. Educat.	HOLLAND	1753	20022006
REL	Rel. Em.o. T.	CARR	1777	52005015
REL	Rel. Faith.	OUTRAM	1680	61010038
REL	Rel. Faith.	ORR	1749	61010038
REL	Rel. Fast.	BARKER	1676	44002020
REL	Rel. Fast.	BROME	1711	44002020
REL	Rel. Fear.	SHERLOCK	1772	19077009
REL	Rel. Hypoc.	CHEYNEY	1677	18027008
REL	Rel. Hypoc.	WELTON	1724	18027008
REL	Rel. Hypoc.	LITTLETON	1735	18027008
REL	Rel. Hypoc.	WILCOX	1751	18027008
REL	Rel. Hypoc.	WEEDON	1777	18027008
REL	Rel. Industry	COLMAN	1727	46009004
REL	Rel. Industry	FOTHERGILL	1757	46009004
REL	Rel. Industry	BOURN	1760	46006027
REL	Rel. Industry	FARRINGTON	1769	46006027
REL	Rel. Instruct.	SECKER	1770	43013016
REL	Rel. Know.	TERRY	1746	23011009
REL	Rel. Know.	BLAIR	1780	23011009
REL	Rel. Knowl.	BULKLEY	1752	46013017
REL	Rel. Liberty.	BOURNE	1760	48014022
REL	Rel. Liberty.	BROWN	1764	51005001
REL	Rel. Liberty.	FAWCETT	1773	17004014
REL	Rel. Liberty.	RADCLIFFE	1771	47005029
REL	Rel. Liberty.	MAINWARING	1780	48014022
REL	Rel. Meditat.	BRYSON	1778	19119015
REL	Rel. Melan.	MOORE	1715	19042006
REL	Rel. Melan.	MOSS	1732	19042011
REL	Rel. Melanc.	CLARKE	1736	18006004
REL	Rel. Obed.	BOURN	1760	43006010
REL	Rel. Obedie.	WHICHCOTE	1703	48001017
REL	Rel. Perfect.	LUCAS	1697	61006001
REL	Rel. Prefer.	DYKES	1722	20031029
REL	Rel. Prud.	ABERNETHY	1748	43007006
REL	Rel. Pruden.	DYKES	1722	20031026
REL	Rel. Reflect.	LANGHORNE	1773	36001007
REL	Rel. Resol.	BURROUGHS	1733	19119106
REL	Rel. Resol.	SHARP	1734	06024021
REL	Rel. Retre.	BLAIR	1777	19004004
REL	Rel. Scrup.	SHERLOCK	1772	19088015
REL	Rel. Singula.	NORRIS	1728	48012002
REL	Rel. Source.	COYTE	1761	20014014
REL	Rel. Stedfast.	BEVERIDGE	1720	49015058
REL	Rel. Trust.	TOULMIN	1770	19034008
REL	Rel. Truths.	CLARKE	1734	58002025
REL	Rel. Wisd.	ABERNETHY	1751	20001001
REL	Rel. Wisdom	LANGHORNE	1773	20004007
REL	Rel. Worsh.	WHARTON	1728	57001017
REL	Rel. Worship	BEVERIDGE	1720	46012029
REL	Rel. Xtian.	JEFFERY	1751	46017003
REL	Rel. Zeal.	PUGH	1710	51004018
REL	Rel.best ch.	NICOLSON	1661	45010041
REL	Rel.ch.bus.l.	BLACKALL	1723	43006033
REL	Rel.ch.bus.l.	BEVERIDGE	1726	43006033
REL	Rel.chief. C.	TRAPP	1752	43006023
REL	Rel.consist.	FOSTER	1744	43006024
REL	Rel.convers.	ABERNETHY	1748	38003016
REL	Rel.convers.	WOOD	1775	38003016
REL	Rel.easy.	LAMBE	1717	43011030
REL	Rel.easy.	NEWTON	1767	43011030
REL	Rel.excell.	SCOUGAL	1726	20012026
REL	Rel.first.con.	WILLIAMS	1665	43006033
REL	Rel.first.con.	TILLOTSON	1735	43006033
REL	Rel.for Soc.	TILLOTSON	1735	20014034
REL	Rel.fr.mind.	MARSHALL	1731	48002028
REL	Rel.indisp.	BRADY	1730	24005004
REL	Rel.l.happy.	KILLINBECK	1717	21008012
REL	Rel.m's Dut.	HOLDEN	1755	20009012
REL	Rel.mid. P.	BROWNE	1749	43011025
REL	Rel.not sup	ABERNETHY	1743	18028028
REL	Rel.o.th.n.	HORTON	1679	45010042
REL	Rel.o.th.n.	BEVERIDGE	1720	45010042
REL	Rel.o.th.n.	GROVE	1742	45010042
REL	Rel.of Oath.	HORNECK	1706	43005033
REL	Rel.of Oath.	NEWCOME	1715	43005033
REL	Rel.our Busi.	WATSON	1677	45002049
REL	Rel.our Int.	HOLDEN	1755	20011012
REL	Rel.prudent	FIDDES	1720	21007016
REL	Rel.rea.serv.	ASHTON	1770	32007006
REL	Rel.retirem.	ATTERBURY	1730	43014023
REL	Rel.retirem.	JORTIN	1774	43014023
REL	Rel.sec.f.w.	ROE	1766	43006033
REL	Rel.ser.aff.	DYER	1758	50005010
REL	Rev.of Rel.	SOME	1730	69003002
REL	Rew.of Rel.	REAY	1755	19019002
REL	Ridic.of Rel.	DELANY	1754	64003003
REL	S. S.of Rel.	HOLDEN	1755	45017021
REL	Sam.of Rel.	STENNETT	1769	49012013
REL	Sate of Rel.	LAW	1745	47017030
REL	Scoff.at Rel.	SUTTON	1754	64003003
REL	St. Paul's rel	SYNGE	1721	47024014
REL	State of Rel.	HESKETH	1679	26037003
REL	Stedf.in Rel.	WAKE	1701	49015058
REL	Stedf.in Rel.	WAKE	1716	64003017
REL	Stedf.in Rel.	WILDER	1741	49015058
REL	Sup. Xn. Rel.	OGDEN	1777	58002019
REL	Uud.in Rel.	ORR	1772	49014020
REL	Wisd.b. Rel.	DAVIES	1771	19111010
REL	Wisd.b. Rel.	HUNTER	1774	19111010
REL	Wisd.b. Rel.	ORTON	1776	19111010
REL	Wisd.of Rel.	STILLINGFLEET	1707	45007035
REL	Wisd.of Rel.	ADEY	1760	27012003
REL	Worth of rel.	WHICHCOTE	1702	53003007
REL	Xn. Rel.exc.	MOORE	1716	48015013
REL	Xn. Rel.vin.	SKEELER	1740	43011029
REL	Xt.& Xn.rel.	WILCOX	1757	22002016
RELAPSE	Relapse in S.	BOURDALOUE	1776	43009002
RELAPSE	Relapse.	SNAPE	1745	46005014
RELAPSE	Relapse Rep.	PYLE	1777	46005014

Keyword	In its Context	Author	Year	BkChpVrs
RELAPSES	Relapses.	SHEFFIELD	1677	61006004
RELAT	Relat. Duties	CLARKE	1734	54003020
RELATIONSHIP	Relationship	GOUGH	1751	43012049
RELEAS	Pris.releas.	DENTON	1775	43025036
RELI	Reli Parent.	LARDNER	1751	58001005
RELIANCE	Reliance.	JORTIN	1774	20003005
RELIEF	Gosp.relief.	MASON	1758	46006035
RELIG	Chus. Relig.	WATERLAND	1742	55005021
RELIG	Const. Relig.	GERARD	1780	49010013
RELIG	Desp. Relig.	SMITH	1777	55004008
RELIG	Early Relig.	ROGERS	1683	21012001
RELIG	Early Relig.	DORRINGTON	1703	21012001
RELIG	Early Relig.	WALKER	1720	21012001
RELIG	Early Relig.	SCATTERGOOD	1723	21012001
RELIG	Early Relig.	EDWARDS	1726	21012001
RELIG	Early Relig.	TILLOTSON	1735	21012001
RELIG	Early Relig.	WHITFIELD	1739	21012001
RELIG	Early Relig.	TRAPP	1752	21012001
RELIG	Early Relig.	WESTCOTT	1762	21012001
RELIG	Early Relig.	WESTON	1768	21012001
RELIG	Fam. Relig.	BELL	1672	06024015
RELIG	Fam. Relig.	PAYNE	1691	06024015
RELIG	Fam. Relig.	PARKHURST	1706	13016043
RELIG	Fam. Relig.	GIFFARD	1713	24010025
RELIG	Fam. Relig.	WHITFIELD	1739	06024015
RELIG	Fam. Relig.	BERRIMAM	1763	06024015
RELIG	Fam. Relig.	KNOX	1768	06024015
RELIG	Fam. Relig.	DAVIES	1766	57005008
RELIG	Fam. Relig.	SECKER	1770	06024015
RELIG	Fam. Relig.	WALLIN	1771	01018019
RELIG	Fam. Relig.	JORTIN	1774	06024015
RELIG	Fam. Relig.	HUNTER	1779	06024015
RELIG	Happ. Relig.	FIDDES	1720	21012013
RELIG	Nat. Relig.	SOUTH	1727	48001020
RELIG	Nat. Relig.	TILLOTSON	1735	32006006
RELIG	Nat. Relig.	SCOTT	1743	19051005
RELIG	Nat. Relig.	SCOTT	1743	48002014
RELIG	Nat. Relig.	DUCHAL	1765	47017028
RELIG	Nat.of Relig.	STENNETT	1769	49004020
RELIG	Phar. Relig.	BURD	1759	43005020
RELIG	Prim. Relig.	KEDDINGTON	1757	43019008
RELIG	Prog. Relig.	LAW	1745	21007010
RELIG	Prov. Relig.	COOKE	1739	55005021
RELIG	Rej.in Relig.	LANGHORNE	1773	53004004
RELIG	Relig. Abid.	STENNETT	1769	53001006
RELIG	Relig. Affec.	EDWARDS	1762	63001008
RELIG	Relig. Comf.	CARMICHAEL	1757	19094019
RELIG	Relig. Cont.	HOWE	1693	51005016
RELIG	Relig. Conv.	WARNEFORD	1776	52004029
RELIG	Relig. Death	DORRINGTON	1703	19037037
RELIG	Relig. Desc.	EVANS	1728	58001005
RELIG	Relig. Disc.	NORRIS	1728	19037030
RELIG	Relig. Disp.	IBBOT	1726	58002019
RELIG	Relig. Educ.	WROUGHTON	1728	01018019
RELIG	Relig. Fear.	BOURN	1760	45012004
RELIG	Relig. Fear.	LLOYD	1765	19002011

Keyword	In its Context	Author	Year	BkChpVrs
RELIG	Relig. Grat.	BOURN	1760	19103002
RELIG	Relig. Joy.	GROVE	1741	19097012
RELIG	Relig. Joy.	BOURN	1760	53004004
RELIG	Relig. Kn.	WEARE	1763	28004006
RELIG	Relig. Life.	NORRIS	1728	19037038
RELIG	Relig. Life.	BOURN	1777	57004007
RELIG	Relig. Med.	GOUGH	1709	01024063
RELIG	Relig. Mel.	NEWTON	1759	19042002
RELIG	Relig. Obed.	ABERNETHY	1751	48014005
RELIG	Relig. Peace.	TREBECK	1730	20016007
RELIG	Relig. Perf.	WILLIAMS	1774	19037037
RELIG	Relig. Princ.	SNAPE	1745	43007024
RELIG	Relig. Rest.	JONES	1741	43011028
RELIG	Relig. Rites.	SMALRIDGE	1724	49014040
RELIG	Relig. Sinc.	ATTERBURY	1734	50013005
RELIG	Relig. Super.	WILLIAMS	1774	23065005
RELIG	Relig. Vows.	DAVIS	1756	07011039
RELIG	Relig. Wisd.	MARKLAND	1729	21012013
RELIG	Relig. Wisd.	JORTIN	1774	48016019
RELIG	Relig. Wisd.	JORTIN	1774	62001005
RELIG	Relig. Zeal.	BIGGS	1774	68000003
RELIG	Relig. Zeal.	BURNABY	1780	51004018
RELIG	Relig.cons.	PYLE	1777	20004026
RELIG	Relig.easy.	HAMMON	1684	43011030
RELIG	Relig.easy.	DORRINGTOU	1703	43011029
RELIG	Relig.easy.	EDWARDS	1726	43011030
RELIG	Relig.in Affl.	STENNETT	1769	19046010
RELIG	Relig.life.	GALE	1726	45011028
RELIG	Relig.life.	GROVE	1742	20004018
RELIG	Relig.life.	JOHNSON	1740	55004001
RELIG	Relig.life.	ADEY	1755	23032017
RELIG	Relig.of Xt.	CHANDLER	1769	46008046
RELIG	Relig.tried.	SYNGE	1713	63003015
RELIG	Relig.urged.	DORRINGTON	1705	21012001
RELIG	Relig.urged;	DORRINGTON	1705	20003006
RELIG	Scoff. Relig.	GLANVILL	1681	64003003
RELIG	Scoff. Relig.	HAMMOND	1684	64003003
RELIG	Scoff. Relig.	ANONYMOUS	1716	64003003
RELIG	Scoff. Relig.	FOSTER	1732	64003003
RELIG	Scoff. Relig.	TILLOTSON	1735	64003003
RELIG	Scoff. Relig.	COYTE	1761	64003003
RELIG	Scoff. Relig.	CARR	1777	20014009
RELIG	Stead. Relig.	BRADBURY	1772	27006010
RELIG	Suff.f. Relig.	CLARKE	1735	54001024
RELIG	True Relig.	FRANK	1672	46003008
RELIG	True Relig.	SMITH	1673	20015024
RELIG	True Relig.	FOSTER	1744	46003008
RELIG	True Relig.	BURNET	1747	19130004
RELIG	True Relig.	WESTON	1747	20023023
RELIG	True Relig.	ROE	1766	43019017
RELIG	Vital Relig.	NEAL	1757	48007022
RELIG	Wis.b.relig.	BATTY	1739	18028028
RELIG	Wis.b.relig.	CARR	1777	18028028
RELIG	Wisd.relig.	CLARKE	1732	20009010
RELIG	Wisd.relig.	TILLOTSON	1735	19119096
RELIG	Xn. Relig.	DAVIES	1766	45016027

Keyword	In its Context	Author	Year	BkChpVrs
RELIG	Xn. Relig.	HARWOOD	1776	51005022
RELIG	Xt's. Relig.	BURNET	1747	43016025
RELIGION	Religion.	CASE	1676	58001013
RELIGION	Religion.	DORRINGTON	1705	19119073
RELIGION	Religion.	DORRINGTON	1705	32006006
RELIGION	Religion.	SOUTH	1727	20010009
RELIGION	Religion.	BUNDY	1740	19119034
RELIGION	Religion.	HOLDEN	1755	20014034
RELIGION	Religion.	FRANCIS	1766	20014034
RELIGION	Religion.	ASHTON	1770	61003012
RELIGION	Xn. Religion	CLIFFORD	1694	49011027
RELIGION	Xn. Religion	HEAD	1714	50005018
RELIGION	Xn. Religion	SYNGE	1720	23011006
RELIGION	Xn. Religion	BOURN	1760	48014007
RELIGION	Xn. Religion	SHARPE	1765	54001023
RELIGION	Xn. Religion	BOURDALOUE	1776	43012038
RELIGION	Xn. Religion	BOURN	1777	23009006
RELIGION	Xn. Religion.	OGILVIE	1766	52006010
RELIGION	Xn Religion.	HUNT	1748	46008012
RELURR	Xt's Relurr.	SAURIN	1775	19118015
RELY	Rely.on Fai.	HOADLY	1727	52002008
REM	Rem. Consc.	BOURDALOUE	1776	45019041
REM	Rem. Creat.	HORNECK	1686	21012001
REM	Rem. Creat.	HICKMAN	1708	21012001
REM	Rem. Creat.	DUNLOP	1722	21012001
REM	Rem.ag.+sin.	DORRINGTON	1703	19119106
REM	Rem.ag. An.	HOWE	1683	54002002
REM	Rem.f. Grie.	BURROUGHS	1662	19032009
REM	Rem.fm.&c.	READING	1724	56003004
REM	Rem.love G.	HICKES	1726	69002004
REM	Rem.of Tr.	TILLOTSON	1735	46014001
REMAI	Gold Remai.	STUART	1661	61010001
REMARKS	Remarks.	FLAVEL	1673	45023027
REME	Reme.of Xt.	ORTON	1776	58002008
REMEMB	D. Rememb.	GATAKER	1737	19013001
REMISS	Gosp.remiss.	BURROUGHS	1668	19032001
REMISS	Remiss. Sins.	PIGGOTT	1702	45024027
REMISS	Remiss. Sins.	PIGOTT	1702	45024047
REMISS	Remiss. Sins.	BRETT	1712	46020021
REMISS	Remiss. Sins.	WHITBY	1720	46020021
REMISS	Remiss.of S.	LANGHORNE	1773	19025011
REMN	G's. Remn.	ERSKINE	1741	69003004
REMOV	Remov. Gos.	CHARNOCK	1684	69002005
REN	Ren. Gosp.c.	ERSKINE	1764	22002013
REN	Ren.h.th. D.	RYVES	1715	50004002
RENEW	Cov.renew.	SKELTON	1754	49011028
RENEW	Renew.i. Sp.	HUSSEY	1758	52004023
RENT	Rent V.tem.	ERSKINE	1764	43027051
REP	Adv.& Rep.	HOLLAND	1753	20015032
REP	Bad M.rep.g.	SNAPE	1745	63004004
REP	Call to Rep.	CLARKE	1734	44002017
REP	Call to Rep.	WARREN	1748	44002017
REP	Call to Rep.	SUTTON	1754	61004007
REP	Caut.in Rep.	BLACKALL	1723	43007006
REP	Caut.in Rep.	BLAIR	1749	43007006
REP	Cens.& Rep.	GARDINER	1720	43007001

Keyword	In its Context	Author	Year	BkChpVrs
REP	D. B. Rep.	DORRINGTON	1703	04023010
REP	D. Recon.& Rep	BLACKALL	1723	43005023
REP	D. Reccn.& Rep	BLAIR	1740	43005023
REP	Dang. Rep.	CARR	1777	23055007
REP	Dea.b. Rep.	BEVERLEY	1670	45023039
REP	Dea.b. Rep.	VEAL	1690	45023042
REP	Dea.b. Rep.	MARCH	1699	45023039
REP	Dea.b. Rep.	LAKE	1705	45023043
REP	Dea.b. Rep.	FIDDES	1720	47026020
REP	Dea.b. Rep.	BURNET	1747	45023043
REP	Death b.rep.	SCOTT	1700	43025010
REP	Death b.rep.	SHERLOCK	1772	43027038
REP	Delay. Rep.	BLACKALL	1723	43005025
REP	Delay Rep.	SCOTT	1700	69002021
REP	Delay Rep.	LUCAS	1717	61003007
REP	Delay Rep.	CREYGHTON	1720	43024046
REP	Dut. Br. Rep.	CHANDLER	1769	45017003
REP	Duty of Rep.	HORTON	1679	51006004
REP	Elect.& Rep.	SCOTT	1743	48010019
REP	Evang. Rep.	HILL	1755	24031019
REP	Evang. Rep.	JOHNSON	1776	45024047
REP	Friend. Rep.	ATTERBURY	1699	20019025
REP	Friend. Rep.	FIDDES	1720	20019025
REP	Fruits Rep.	BURTON	1684	43003008
REP	Fruits Rep.	SCOTT	1700	43003008
REP	Gosp. Rep	HAMMOND	1684	43003002
REP	Gosp. Rep	HOLE	1716	43003002
REP	Gosp. Rep	SHIRLEY	1762	43003001
REP	Immed. Rep.	STEWARD	1734	23055006
REP	Immed. Rep.	FARRINGTON	1769	26018027
REP	Inno.b. Rep.	FIDDES	1720	45015007
REP	Joy on Rep.	TILLOTSON	1735	45015007
REP	Joy on Rep.	NALSON	1737	45015007
REP	Mot.to Rep.	ELLIS	1704	45016031
REP	Nat. Rep.	KNAGGS	1707	44006012
REP	Nec.of Rep.	DAVIES	1771	47017030
REP	Necess. Rep.	GREGORY	1708	47026020
REP	Necess. Rep.	WROUGHTON	1728	47020021
REP	Necess. Rep.	TILLOTSON	1735	47020021
REP	Necess. Rep.	BARNES	1752	23055007
REP	Necess. Rep.	SKELTON	1754	23055006
REP	Not.of Rep.	FARINGTON	1741	47003019
REP	Obed.b. Rep.	PAYNE	1698	45015031
REP	Peter's Rep.	HART	1702	44014068
REP	Peter's Rep.	SHERLOCK	1772	45022061
REP	Relapse Rep.	PYLE	1777	46005014
REP	Rep.& Faith.	HOLE	1715	44001015
REP	Rep.& Faith.	BEVERIDGE	1720	44001015
REP	Rep.& Faith.	JONES	1756	44001015
REP	Rep.& Faith.	ELLIOTT	1764	47020021
REP	Rep.& Faith.	CASE	1774	47002038
REP	Rep.& Un.	SHOWER	1688	23021011
REP	Rep. Sin. Joy	BROUGHTON	1778	45015007
REP	Rep. Stam.a.	MAYHEW	1767	19124007
REP	Rep.for.of F.	HORNE	1756	23040003
REP	Rep.possible.	LUCAS	1717	24005003

Keyword	In its Context	Author	Year	BkChpVrs
REP	Rep.stam. A.	CHAUNCY	1767	20025025
REP	Slight Rep.	USHER	1678	52002001
REP	Univ. Rep.	SHERIDAN	1720	47017030
REP	Xt.rep. Mar.	HORTON	1679	45010041
REPEN	Hab. Repen.	BENNETT	1728	23057015
REPEN	True Repen.	ALLEN	1751	45013003
REPENT	Da. Repent.	SECKER	1770	10012013
REPENT	Del. Repent.	BARROW	1716	19119060
REPENT	Del. Repent.	MARKLAND	1729	21012001
REPENT	Del. Repent.	SHARP	1734	19119059
REPENT	Del. Repent.	BURNET	1747	19119060
REPENT	Del. Repent.	WESTON	1747	19119060
REPENT	Del. Repent.	CLEMENT	1774	19119060
REPENT	Exh.repent.	MASON	1742	28010012
REPENT	Gos. Repent.	CHANDLER	1769	47011018
REPENT	Im. Repent.	WROUGHTON	1728	19119060
REPENT	Late Repent.	CLAGETT	1720	20001028
REPENT	Late Repent.	BLACKALL	1723	46009003
REPENT	Par. Repent.	SHERLOCK	1772	19019012
REPENT	Unf. Repent.	WALLIS	1692	24003010
REPENTANCE	Repentance.	TAYLOR	1668	24013016
REPENTANCE	Repentance.	BRIDGE	1671	30004012
REPENTANCE	Repentance.	MEDE	1672	44001015
REPENTANCE	Repentance.	CRAFTON	1676	47005031
REPENTANCE	Repentance.	BURTON	1684	43004017
REPENTANCE	Repentance.	HAMMOND	1684	47017030
REPENTANCE	Repentance.	CLARKSON	1696	45013003
REPENTANCE	Repentance.	SCOTT	1700	26018030
REPENTANCE	Repentance.	WHICHCOTE	1702	23001016
REPENTANCE	Repentance.	DORRINGTON	1703	43003001
REPENTANCE	Repentance.	ELLIS	1704	45016030
REPENTANCE	Repentance.	NOURSE	1705	29002012
REPENTANCE	Repentance.	HART	1702	47017030
REPENTANCE	Repentance.	BEVERIDGE	1720	23055007
REPENTANCE	Repentance.	BEVERIDGE	1720	45005032
REPENTANCE	Repentance.	BEVERIDGE	1720	45013003
REPENTANCE	Repentance.	SMALRIDGE	1724	61003007
REPENTANCE	Repentance.	WAPLE	1729	47003019
REPENTANCE	Repentance.	AGATE	1730	24005003
REPENTANCE	Repentance.	EARLE	1737	37007013
REPENTANCE	Repentance.	WILLIAMS	1738	28010012
REPENTANCE	Repentance.	BRODHURST	1733	69002005
REPENTANCE	Repentance.	STEPHENS	1737	61012017
REPENTANCE	Repentance.	STRAIGHT	1741	43003002
REPENTANCE	Repentance.	BURNET	1747	36001005
REPENTANCE	Repentance.	WESTON	1747	43003008
REPENTANCE	Repentance.	WESTON	1747	43004017
REPENTANCE	Repentance.	HUNT	1748	44001014
REPENTANCE	Repentance.	WARREN	1748	44001015
REPENTANCE	Repentance.	WESTLEY	1748	44001015
REPENTANCE	Repentance.	SOUTH	1744	69002016
REPENTANCE	Repentance.	HUNT	1748	47020021
REPENTANCE	Repentance.	PRIEST	1753	26018031
REPENTANCE	Repentance.	BALL	1756	44006012
REPENTANCE	Repentance.	BUNDY	1750	48013012
REPENTANCE	Repentance.	GOUGH	1751	61012017
REPENTANCE	Repentance.	WELCH	1752	69002002
REPENTANCE	Repentance.	ADEY	1760	44006011
REPENTANCE	Repentance.	DAVIS	1765	45015007
REPENTANCE	Repentance.	CHANDLER	1769	43009013
REPENTANCE	Repentance.	PENN	1769	45013003
REPENTANCE	Repentance.	CHANDLER	1769	47017030
REPENTANCE	Repentance.	LANGHORNE	1773	18011013
REPENTANCE	Repentance.	WHITFIELD	1771	47003019
REPENTANCE	Repentance.	SAURIN	1777	50007010
REPENTANCE	Repentance.	TATHAM	1780	47003019
REPET	Vain Repet.	BLACKALL	1723	43006007
REPET	Vain Repet.	BLAIR	1740	43006007
REPOS	Repos. Faith.	ERSKINE	1764	22002003
REPR	Adv.& Repr.	HOLLAND	1753	54003016
REPR	Ass' Repr.	JENKINS	1779	04022028
REPR	Broth. Repr.	BRADY	1713	55005014
REPR	Broth.repr.	SMALRIDGE	1724	48010001
REPR	Broth.repr.	ROWLAND	1774	43025018
REPR	Hab. Repr.	BENNETT	1723	19015002
REPR	Nath.repr.	TIDCOMBE	1757	10012007
REPR	Repr. Vanity	BOURN	1763	45017001
REPR	Repr.of Xt.	CENNICK	1762	61013013
REPRO	El.& Repro.	CLARKE	1734	48009023
REPRO	Mur.repro.	HOPKINS	1689	49010010
REPROOF	Of Reproof.	MOSS	1732	03019017
REPROOF	Reproof.	GALE	1726	43007003
REPROOF	Reproof.	HUNT	1748	20029001
REPROOF	Sp. Reproof.	WAPLE	1729	19050021
REPROOF	Spir.reproof.	WAPLE	1729	46016008
REPROOF	Xn. Reproof.	COCKMAN	1750	52005011
REPROOF	Xn. Reproof.	TRAPP	1752	51006001
REPROOFS	Reproofs.	OWEN	1676	19141005
REPUTATION	Reputation.	TRAPP	1752	53004008
REPUTATION	Reputation.	DALTON	1757	48014016
REQ	Agur's Req.	AGAR	1759	20030007
REQ	Agur's Req.	JORTIN	1774	20030007
REQ	Req.of Pray.	CARR	1777	62004003
REQ	Req.of R.gr.	SPOONER	1771	19034015
REQ	Xt's.req.off.	FLAVEL	1673	50010005
REQUEST	Ch.request.	BULL	1695	19122006
REQUEST	Sol. Request.	SMITH	1777	11003010
RES	Ev. Xt's. Res.	STEBBING	1760	47005032
RES	G.no res. P.	MOORE	1716	47010034
RES	G.no res. P.	IBBOT	1726	47010034
RES	G.no res. P.	MUNTON	1756	47010034
RES	G.no res. P.	HUSSEY	1758	47010034
RES	Josh. Res.	GOUGE	1663	06024015
RES	Obj. Xt's.res.	WEBB	1772	43028011
RES	Res. Body.	OGDEN	1777	49015035
RES	Res. Body.	BATEMAN	1780	49015035
RES	Res. Virtue.	BENNETT	1728	49015028
RES	Res.expla.	CHANDLER	1769	49015035
RES	Res.of B.&c.	PRICE	1757	61006002
RES	Res.of Body.	STILLINGFLEET	1707	47026008
RES	Res.of Xt.	TILLOTSON	1735	54003001
RES	Res.same B.	FELTON	1725	49015023

Keyword	In its Context	Author	Year	BkChpVrs
RES	Res.same B.	JOHNSON	1733	49015036
RES	Res.same B.	WHITFIELD	1751	49015035
RES	Res.the Dev.	COOKE	1739	63005008
RES	Res.to Min.	FRANCIS	1773	50004005
RES	Res.to Rew.	SCOTT	1743	58004007
RES	Res.univer.	FELTON	1733	49015023
RES	Test.of Res.	LANGHORNE	1773	49015023
RES	W. Hand res.	BRAGGE	1706	45006006
RES	Xt.&our res.	ATTERBURY	1743	23026019
RES	Xt. Res.& L.	BREKELL	1765	46011025
RES	Xt's. Res.&c.	JENNINGS	1757	47001002
RES	Xt's.d.&res.	JOHNSON	1728	47002031
RES	Xt's.res.imp.	WILSON	1781	47001021
RESENTMENT	Resentment.	BUTLER	1749	43005043
RESIGN	Resign. P.off.	PRIESTLEY	1773	63001013
RESIGN	Resign.to G.	CARR	1777	09003018
RESIGN	Xt's. Resign.	STANHOPE	1705	45022042
RESIGN	Xt's. Resign.	WILLISON	1761	46018004
RESIGNATION	Resignation.	SHOWER	1684	10015026
RESIGNATION	Resignation.	LUCAS	1722	43026039
RESIGNATION	Resignation.	SMALRIDGE	1724	43026039
RESIGNATION	Resignation.	DELAUNE	1728	43006010
RESIGNATION	Resignation.	STEWARD	1734	47021014
RESIGNATION	Resignation.	SEED	1743	18002010
RESIGNATION	Resignation.	MACE	1751	43026039
RESIGNATION	Resignation.	ADEY	1755	18014014
RESIGNATION	Resignation.	WILCOX	1757	03010003
RESIGNATION	Resignation.	MAY	1757	45023042
RESIGNATION	Resignation.	PAYNE	1763	32007007
RESIGNATION	Resignation.	JORTIN	1774	43026039
RESIGNATION	Resignation.	JOHNSON	1776	63001023
RESIST	Resist. Devil.	ST.	1737	62004007
RESIST	Resist.of Evil	PAYNE	1763	62004007
RESIST	Resist Devil.	ALLESTREE	1684	62004007
RESOL	Holy Resol.	TENISON	1695	19119106
RESOL	Holy Resol.	TILLOTSON	1735	18034031
RESOL	Holy Resol.	WARNEFORD	1776	19119106
RESOL	Keep Resol.	NEWSON	1781	43026035
RESOL	Rel. Resol.	BURROUGHS	1733	19119106
RESOL	Rel. Resol.	SHARP	1734	06024021
RESOL	Virt. Resol.	JANE	1692	19119106
RESOL	Virt. Resol.	MACE	1751	19119106
RESOL	Virt. Resol.	PYLE	1777	19119106
RESOL	Virt. Resol.	GERARD	1780	19119106
RESOLUT	Xn. Resolut.	WILDER	1741	19101004
RESOLUTION	Resolution.	LEIGHTON	1746	19119032
RESP	G.no resp.of P	BARROW	1716	48002011
RESP	G.no resp.of P	FOSTER	1744	48002011
RESP	Spir.no resp.	CROOKE	1755	23029011
REST	Ent.into rest.	BOSTON	1773	61004003
REST	Relig. Rest.	JONES	1741	43011028
REST	Rest. Episc.	LEIGHTON	1746	23028005
REST	Rest. Provid.	ADAMS	1736	04024013
REST	Rest.heav. S.	ELLIS	1685	43011028
REST	Rest.of Bel.	SHEPHEARD	1748	61004003
REST	Rest.t.b.obt.	ALLESTREE	1684	43011028

Keyword	In its Context	Author	Year	BkChpVrs
REST	Soul's rest. G	WILCOX	1757	19116007
REST	Xn. Rest.	WALKER	1764	43011028
REST	Xn. Rest.	BADDELLY	1766	43011028
RESTIT	Engl.restit.	REEVE	1661	20028002
RESTITUTION	Restitution.	WILLIAMS	1682	45019008
RESTITUTION	Restitution.	FORD	1711	45019008
RESTITUTION	Restitution.	BEVERIDGE	1720	45019008
RESTITUTION	Restitution.	TILLOTSON	1735	45019008
RESTITUTION	Restitution.	HUNT	1748	26033015
RESTITUTION	Restitution.	HEYLIN	1761	45019008
RESTITUTION	Restitution.	BURN	1774	09012003
RESTOR	Restor. Coin.	ANONYMOUS	1697	24006030
RESTORATION	Restoration.	PRICE	1660	19118023
RESULT	Result o. Vir.	DYKES	1722	20031031
RESUR	Resur. Body.	HORNE	1778	53003020
RESUR	Resur. Lazar.	BENSON	1748	46011043
RESUR	Resur. Lazar.	BULKLEY	1771	46011043
RESUR	Resur.expl.	WILSON	1781	43028011
RESUR	Resur.o. Laz.	LANGHORNE	1764	45011044
RESURR	Gen. Resurr.	DAVIES	1766	46005028
RESURR	Resurr.body	PIGGOTT	1702	46005028
RESURR	Resurr.body	HORT	1738	46005028
RESURR	Resurr.cert.	IBBOT	1726	49015021
RESURR	Resurr.cert.	IBBOT	1726	50011021
RESURR	Xt's. Resurr.	GARBUTT	1669	49015020
RESURR	Xt's. Resurr.	FLAVEL	1673	43026006
RESURR	Xt's. Resurr.	BRAGGE	1706	45024005
RESURR	Xt's. Resurr.	BARROW	1716	45024046
RESURR	Xt's. Resurr.	EDWARDS	1713	53003010
RESURR	Xt's. Resurr.	LACY	1720	45024005
RESURR	Xt's. Resurr.	CLARKE	1727	47002032
RESURR	Xt's. Resurr.	HORT	1738	45024005
RESURR	Xt's. Resurr.	MOSS	1732	49015058
RESURR	Xt's. Resurr.	WARREN	1739	49015020
RESURR	Xt's. Resurr.	WHITFIELD	1739	53003010
RESURR	Xt's. Resurr.	ADEY	1755	45024006
RESURR	Xt's. Resurr.	ECCLES	1755	47010040
RESURR	Xt's. Resurr.	ECCLES	1755	48006009
RESURR	Xt's. Resurr.	TIDCOMBE	1757	47004033
RESURR	Xt's. Resurr.	MORRIS	1757	48004024
RESURR	Xt's. Resurr.	HODGE	1758	47011024
RESURR	Xt's. Resurr.	SHIRLEY	1762	43028005
RESURR	Xt's. Resurr.	MUSCOTT	1760	47002032
RESURR	Xt's. Resurr.	CHANDLER	1769	47002032
RESURR	Xt's. Resurr.	BULKLEY	1771	46010017
RESURR	Xt's. Resurr.	BOURDALOUE	1776	44016006
RESURR	Xt's. Resurr.	SHERLOCK	1772	48004025
RESURR	Xt's. Resurr.	OGDEN	1777	47002031
RESURR	Xt's Resurr.	FOSTER	1720	47010040
RESURRECTION	Resurrection	NICOLSON	1661	53003021
RESURRECTION	Resurrection	GREGORY	1664	49015020
RESURRECTION	Resurrection	PARRY	1666	53003010
RESURRECTION	Resurrection	CALAMY	1676	47026008
RESURRECTION	Resurrection	ATTERBURY	1703	49015029
RESURRECTION	Resurrection	STURMY	1716	45020035
RESURRECTION	Resurrection	HOPKINS	1712	46020026

INDEXES TO THIRD VOLUME: E: KEYWORD-IN-CONTEXT INDEX OF OTHER SUBJECTS OR OCCASIONS

Keyword	In its Context	Author	Year	BkChpVrs
RESURRECTION	Resurrection	STUBBS	1713	47024021
RESURRECTION	Resurrection	SHERIDAN	1720	28006002
RESURRECTION	Resurrection	BEVERIDGE	1720	49015012
RESURRECTION	Resurrection	BEVERIDGE	1720	63001003
RESURRECTION	Resurrection	GALE	1726	49015058
RESURRECTION	Resurrection	FELTON	1730	43022029
RESURRECTION	Resurrection	GILL	1732	47026008
RESURRECTION	Resurrection	ADAMS	1732	49015020
RESURRECTION	Resurrection	TILLOTSON	1735	55004014
RESURRECTION	Resurrection	HEYLYN	1749	23011010
RESURRECTION	Resurrection	MASON	1742	47026008
RESURRECTION	Resurrection	BURNET	1747	58002007
RESURRECTION	Resurrection	DELANY	1754	49015051
RESURRECTION	Resurrection	ANONYMOUS	1761	18019025
RESURRECTION	Resurrection	HEYLYN	1761	46011021
RESURRECTION	Resurrection	TORRIANO	1767	43013049
RESURRECTION	Resurrection	MUSCOTT	1760	49015012
RESURRECTION	Resurrection	DOWNES	1761	49015020
RESURRECTION	Resurrection	BARKER	1763	49015020
RESURRECTION	Resurrection	ROE	1766	69020013
RESURRECTION	Resurrection	WARBURTON	1767	49015017
RESURRECTION	Resurrection	TOTTIE	1775	43022031
RESURRECTION	Resurrection	SIMS	1772	58002008
RESURRECTION	Resurrection	COWPER	1773	49015020
RESURRECTION	Resurrection	HORBERY	1774	47004023
RESURRECTION	Resurrection	ATKINSON	1775	49015020
RESURRECTION	Resurrection	CARR	1777	49006014
RESURRECTION	Resurrection	HOLMES	1777	53003021
RESURRECTION	Resurrection	WILSON	1781	45020034
RESURRECTION	Resurrection.	MORE	1692	54003001
RESURRECTION	Resurrection.	SHERIDAN	1720	52005014
RESURRECTION	Resurrection.	MUSCOTT	1760	54003001
RESURRECTION	Resurrection.	SHERLOCK	1772	54003001
RET	Child's ret.	CULVERWELL	1661	20023026
RET	Fut. Ret.just.	BARNES	1752	45016025
RET	Ret.flock Xt.	SPOONER	1751	63002015
RETALIATION	Retaliation.	MOSS	1737	43005038
RETALIATION	Retaliation.	HURD	1780	43005038
RETIREM	Rel.retirem.	ATTERBURY	1730	43014023
RETIREM	Rel.retirem.	JORTIN	1774	43014023
RETRE	Rel. Retre.	BLAIR	1777	19004004
RETRIB	Fin. Retrib.	MACE	1751	43013043
RETURN	G's Return.	BRINSLEY	1667	19090013
RETURN	Return to G.	READER	1765	24050005
RETURN	Seam.return.	FLAVEL	1673	05033019
REV	Adv.of Rev.	SAURIN	1775	49001021
REV	Def.of Rev.	SCOTT	1743	47002036
REV	Def.of Rev.	SCOTT.	1743	47015018
REV	Delig. Rev.	WILCOX	1757	19119092
REV	G.rev.mself.	CARR	1777	57002004
REV	Nat. Rev. R.	HEYLIN	1749	18036002
REV	Obj.ag. Rev.	SEED	1750	49001025
REV	Pub.rev.&c.	BRADBURY	1772	27002020
REV	Reas.& Rev.	FOSTER	1744	20020027
REV	Reas.& Rev.	COWPER	1774	48001020
REV	Rev.& Char.	BIRCH	1720	48012021

Keyword	In its Context	Author	Year	BkChpVrs
REV	Rev. Father.	HORTON	1679	46001018
REV	Rev. G's h.	MEDE	1672	21005001
REV	Rev. Know.	CRUSO	1699	43016017
REV	Rev.o. Noah.	SCOTT	1743	61011007
REV	Rev.of Rel.	SOME	1730	69003002
REV	Rev.to God.	CROWE	1744	24005024
REV	Sen. Rev.gr.	GREEN	1758	49010012
REV	Stand. Rev.	GROVE	1741	45016030
REV	Use of Rev.	RICHARDSON	1730	47017004
REV	Usef.of Rev.	ROBINSON	1733	46005030
REV	Util.of Rev.	CARR	1777	46012046
REV	Xn. Loy rev.	SPRINT	1694	63002017
REVEL	Div. Revel.	HENLEY	1729	54004014
REVEL	Gosp.revel.	LEECHMAN	1758	49001021
REVEL	Grad. Revel.	REAY	1755	61001001
REVEL	Inf. L. Revel.	WARBURTON	1754	45018008
REVEL	Need Revel.	CONYBEARE	1757	45001078
REVEL	Revel.neces.	ROGERS	1729	61001001
REVEL	Use of Revel.	STEBBING	1730	48008003
REVELAT	Div. Revelat.	BULLOCK	1726	65004006
REVELAT	Xn. Revelat.	ROBINSON	1733	46018037
REVELAT	Xn. Revelat.	LANGHORNE	1773	51004004
REVELATION	Revelation.	ROGERS	1729	63003015
REVELATION	Revelation.	RICHARDSON	1730	05018015
REVELATION	Revelation.	RICHARDSON	1730	53002011
REVELATION	Revelation.	RICHARDSON	1730	65002008
REVELATION	Revelation.	SAURIN	1775	45016027
REVEN	Priv. Reven.	BOSTON	1773	48012019
REVENG	Reveng. Ser.	STEBBING	1760	43018023
REVENGE	Ag. Revenge	STRATFORD	1684	48012017
REVENGE	Ag. Revenge	HORNECK	1697	43005021
REVENGE	Ag. Revenge.	LAMONT	1780	48012017
REVENGE	On Revenge.	SMEDLEY	1719	48012021
REVENGE	Revenge.	WILKINS	1682	48012019
REVENGE	Revenge.	PAYNE	1698	48012021
REVENGE	Revenge.	DELAUNE	1728	48012019
REVENGE	Revenge.	BALGUY	1750	48012019
REVENGE	Revenge.	STEBBING	1760	48012019
REVENGE	Revenge.	ANONYMOUS	1770	43006015
REVENGE	of Revenge.	HORNECK	1706	43005037
REVENGE	of Revenge.	BLACKALL	1723	43005038
REVER	Rever.to Ch.	BERRIMAN	1763	01028017
REVER	Self-rever.	DUCHAL	1765	49003017
REVIEW	Review of L.	DUCHAL	1765	19039005
REVILING	Ag.reviling.	SOUTH	1744	63002023
REVOLT	Ag. Revolt.	HAMMOND	1684	23001005
REVOLUT	on Revolut.	ROSEWELL	1712	19111009
REW	Cert. Rew.	MILLER	1749	49015058
REW	Ex.fut. Rew.	DORRINGTON	1705	54003001
REW	F. Rew.& P.	CONANT	1708	48006023
REW	F. Rew.& P.	CLARKE	1735	43025046
REW	Fu. Rew.cer.	DORRINGTON	1705	57004007
REW	Fut. Rew.	CLARKE	1736	69022011
REW	Fut. Rew.	BALGUY	1748	51006007
REW	Fut. Rew.	FARRINGTON	1769	49002009
REW	Fut.rew. Xn.	WILLIAMS	1774	69014025

Keyword	In its Context	Author	Year	BkChpVrs
REW	Fut.rew.un.	BULL	1713	61011026
REW	Rec.of Rew.	SOUTH	1727	61011024
REW	Rec.of Rew.	BADDELLEY	1752	61011026
REW	Rec.of Rew.	NEWTON	1782	61011033
REW	Res.to Rew.	SCOTT	1743	58004007
REW	Rew. Dilig.	SHARP	1674	43025029
REW	Rew. Fidel.	BOURN	1777	43025023
REW	Rew. L.of G.	PYLE	1776	49002009
REW	Rew. Obed.	ADEY	1760	43019017
REW	Rew. Right.	LUCAS	1710	46018036
REW	Rew. Virt.& Re	DORRINGTON	1705	19019011
REW	Rew. Virt.& Re	BALGUY	1750	19019011
REW	Rew.annex.	SKELTON	1754	54003002
REW	Rew.o Xn's.	ADEY	1760	58004007
REW	Rew.of Just.	CLARKE	1736	45014014
REW	Rew.of Rel.	REAY	1755	19019002
REW	Rew.of Xy.	MONRO	1693	53003014
REW	Rew.pro.w.	CLARKE	1735	51006007
REW	Xn's. Rew.	HUNT	1748	58002011
REWARD	Gd. Reward.	ATTERBURY	1743	61011006
REWARDS	Diff.rewards	MEDE	1672	43010041
REWARDS	Fut.rewards.	WHITBY	1720	48002006
RGT	Peo. Rgt. S. S	SHARP	1735	64003016
RI	Crown.o. Ri.	HAYWARD	1758	58004007
RI	G's.reg.to ri.	REYNER	1745	63003012
RI	Uns.ri.o. Xt.	FANCH	1768	52003008
RICH	Abuse Rich.	LANGHORNE	1773	21004006
RICH	Cha.to rich.	BOYSE	1728	57006017
RICH	Duty of rich.	SECKER	1770	57006017
RICH	Duty of rich.	ENFIELD	1772	53004012
RICH	Inh.rich Jew	BOURN	1763	45016019
RICH	Rich man.	BOURN	1764	45012016
RICH	Rich.& Lux.	MARRIOTT	1774	19059016
RICH	Rich&poor.	CONANT	1699	20022002
RICH	Rich&poor.	NEWTON	1736	20022002
RICH	Rich&poor.	GROVE	1742	20022002
RICH	Rich&poor.	CONYBEARE	1757	20022002
RICH	Rich&poor.	WHITE	1757	20022002
RICH	Rich&poor.	SKEELER	1772	20022002
RICH	Rich&poor.	JORTIN	1774	20022002
RICH	Rich&poor.	PYLE	1777	20022002
RICH	Rich Fool.	BRAGGE	1702	45012016
RICH	Rich Fool.	DODD	1757	45012021
RICH	Rich Fool.	DODD	1757	45012025
RICH	Rich Fool.	BULKLEY	1771	45012021
RICH	Rich Fool.	SHERLOCK	1772	45012021
RICH	Rich M.& L.	STEVENS	1697	45016019
RICH	Rich M.& L.	CRUSO	1698	45016019
RICH	Rich M.& L.	BRAGGE	1702	45016019
RICH	Rich M.& L.	WELCHMAN	1704	45016019
RICH	Rich M.& L.	ELLIS	1704	45016019
RICH	Rich M.& L.	HOLE	1716	45016019
RICH	Rich M.& L.	TILLOTSON	1735	45016019
RICH	Rich M.& L.	DODD	1757	45016019
RICH	Rich M.& L.	HUNTER	1774	45016019
RICH	Rich M's Ad.	WELCHMAN	1704	45016024

Keyword	In its Context	Author	Year	BkChpVrs
RICH	Snare Rich.	SHOREY	1725	43019024
RICHES	Dang.riches.	CARTWRIGHT	1662	43019024
RICHES	Folly Riches	MARKLAND	1729	21005010
RICHES	Hasty Riches	BERRIMAN	1751	20028020
RICHES	Trust Riches	BURNET	1747	45012020
RICHES	Use o. Riches	ELLIS	1704	45016009
RICHES	W.to Riches	WOOD	1698	43006033
RICHES	Xt's. Riches.	ADAM	1772	69003018
RID	Rid.no f. Tr.	GODDARD	1781	21002002
RIDIC	Ridic.of Rel.	DELANY	1754	64003003
RIDICULE	Ridicule.	DODD	1772	20014009
RIDICULE	Ridicule.	TOTTIE	1775	64003003
RIDICULE	on Ridicule.	ANONYMOUS	1716	21003004
RIG	Affl.of Rig.	HUNTER	1774	07006012
RIG	Death of rig.	CAWTON	1675	04023010
RIG	Death of rig.	LACY	1720	04023010
RIG	Death of rig.	BUNDY	1740	04023010
RIG	Death of rig.	ECCLES	1755	04023010
RIG	Death of rig.	FARMER	1756	04023010
RIG	Death of rig.	AGAR	1759	04023010
RIG	Death of rig.	BARCLAY	1777	04023010
RIG	Death Rig.	LUCAS	1722	21002015
RIG	Jud. Pr. Rig.	SKELTON	1754	44014043
RIG	Rig.&g.man	HICKMAN	1706	48005007
RIG	Rig.&g.man	FOSTER	1732	48005007
RIG	Rig.&g.man	HORBERY	1774	48005007
RIG	Rig. Intent.	CLAGETT	1720	43006022
RIG	Rig. Th.rig.	TATE	1666	20012005
RIG	Rig.civ. Go.	HOLE	1716	43022015
RIG	Rig.m's ref.	FLAVEL	1673	23026020
RIG	Rig.of Faith.	MILWAY	1751	53003009
RIG	Rig.of Judg.	MICHELL	1737	45012057
RIG	Rig.of Law.	HUSSEY	1755	48008004
RIG	Wick.& Rig.	LANGHORNE	1764	19118015
RIG	Wick.& Rig.	LANGHORNE	1764	20004018
RIG	Wick.&rig.	WEBB	1772	20028001
RIGH	Hap.of righ.	DUCHAL	1765	23060020
RIGH	Ld our Righ.	WOODWARD	1696	24013006
RIGH	Nec.o. Righ.	IBBOT	1726	65003002
RIGH	Nec.o. Righ.	MICHELL	1737	65003002
RIGH	Nec.o. Righ.	SCOTT	1743	57006011
RIGH	Righ.& Wic.	COCK	1710	38003018
RIGH	Robe of righ.	FARMER	1756	23061010
RIGH	Sun of Righ.	BRODBURST	1733	38004002
RIGHT	Bless.right.	HAWEIS	1762	20012028
RIGHT	Evan. Right.	TAYLOR	1673	43005020
RIGHT	Exem.right.	REEVES	1729	48012017
RIGHT	G's right.	HUNT	1748	19129004
RIGHT	G's right&c.	LELAND	1769	19145017
RIGHT	G's. Right.	MATHER	1701	48010003
RIGHT	G's. Right.	SEAGRAVE	1737	48010003
RIGHT	G's.right.	PAYNE	1698	48009014
RIGHT	G's.right. R.	HUSSEY	1753	48003025
RIGHT	G's Right.	HUSSEY	1753	27009007
RIGHT	Imp. Right.	VENN	1759	43019006
RIGHT	Imp. Right.	ROMAINE	1760	50005021

INDEXES TO THIRD VOLUME: E: KEYWORD-IN-CONTEXT INDEX OF OTHER SUBJECTS OR OCCASIONS

Keyword	In its Context	Author	Year	BkChpVrs
RIGHT	Imput.right.	COLE	1755	48009032
RIGHT	Joy of right.	WHICHCOTE	1702	19033001
RIGHT	Judg.right.	NORRIS	1728	46007024
RIGHT	Judg.right.	WILDER	1729	46007024
RIGHT	L.our Right.	ROMAINE	1752	23045008
RIGHT	L.our Right.	WHITFIELD	1771	23060019
RIGHT	Ld. Right.	RUSSEN	1774	24023006
RIGHT	Many right.	HERVEY	1769	48005019
RIGHT	Mor. Right.	LARDNER	1751	32006008
RIGHT	Our Right.	HARRIS	1724	24023006
RIGHT	Ov.right&c.	ALLEN	17--	21007016
RIGHT	Ov.right&c.	ROMAINE	1760	21007016
RIGHT	Phar. Right.	SMITH	1673	43019020
RIGHT	Phar. Right.	HORTON	1679	44012034
RIGHT	Phar. Right.	BLACKALL	1723	43005020
RIGHT	Phar. Right.	SCATTERGOOD	1723	43005020
RIGHT	Phar. Right.	BLAIR	1740	43005020
RIGHT	Phar. Right.	SOUTH	1744	43005020
RIGHT	R. G's.right.	DORRINGTON	1705	43005048
RIGHT	Re.of Right.	BRODHURST	1733	19012001
RIGHT	Rew. Right.	LUCAS	1710	46018036
RIGHT	Right hear.	SHIRLEY	1762	46008047
RIGHT	Right of G.	CLAGETT	1704	48001017
RIGHT	Right.&w.	CATCOTT	1753	20014032
RIGHT	Right. Def.	MOSS	1737	43005020
RIGHT	Right.deliv.	HORNE	1778	01019029
RIGHT	Right.happ.	ABERNETHY	1748	23003010
RIGHT	Right.m.	DUNLOP	1722	20012026
RIGHT	Right.of Fai.	WESTLEY	1746	48010005
RIGHT	Right.pr. Ju.	ANONYMOUS	1721	49010015
RIGHT	Rule right.	CAMFIELD	1671	43007012
RIGHT	Rule right.	CARTER	1738	43007012
RIGHT	Rule right.	CONYBEARE	1757	43007012
RIGHT	Rule right.	DAVIES	1766	43007012
RIGHT	Univ. Right.	DELANY	1747	62002010
RIGHT	Who Right.	OUTRAM	1697	65003002
RIGHT	Xt.o. Right.	RAWLIN	1741	24045024
RIGHTE	Xt's Righte.	BURTON	1763	24023006
RIGHTEO	Righteo.&c.	HOLDEN	1755	48014017
RIGHTEOUSN	Righteousn.	KIDDER	1697	43005020
RIGHTEOUSN	Righteousn.	GALE	1726	43003015
RIGHTEOUSN	Righteousn.	WHITE	1757	43005006
RIGHTEOUSN	Righteousn.	HUSSEY	1755	65003002
RIOTS	Ag. Riots.	KAGGS	1704	52005007
RIOTS	On Riots.	ROSEWELL	1715	47019040
RIOTS	Riots.	ROSEWELL	1715	47013040
RIS	Ris. Gener.	DODDERIDGE	1743	19022030
RISE	Jerus. Rise.	SHARP	1765	19028009
RISEN	Jesus risen.	HORNE	1778	45024034
RIT	Mor.b. Rit.	MANTON	1708	43009013
RITES	Relig. Rites.	SMALRIDGE	1724	49014040
RITES	Rites& Cer.	JEACOCKE	1702	43015009
RIV	Riv.of Life.	ERSKINE	1764	69022001
ROAD	Road to H.	YOUNG	1706	09002030
ROB	On rob. Ch.	GREEN	1737	52004028
ROB	Theft& Rob.	WILSON	1781	02020014

Keyword	In its Context	Author	Year	BkChpVrs
ROBB	Prev. Robb.	ROMAINE	1757	43015019
ROBE	Robe of righ.	FARMER	1756	23061010
ROCK	Rock of off.	MARTIN	1771	48010003
ROCK	Xt. Rock. Sal.	TAYLOR	1701	19061002
ROCK	Xt.our Rock.	WILLISON	1761	49010004
ROD	Sanct. Rod.	FARMER	1756	19094012
ROGAT	Rogat. S.	NOURSE	1708	48011036
ROGAT	Rogat. S.	STOCKWELL	1726	44004028
ROGAT	Rogat.week.	SMITH	1677	55005017
ROM	Rom. Princ.	BARNES	1752	48003008
ROM	Rom. Worsh.	STEPHENS	1728	43015009
ROME	Rome, Baby.	BARNARD	1759	69018004
ROMISH	Romish Acts.	BENNETT	1714	69017004
ROY	Roy. Sin.	CROXALL	1738	10012007
ROY	Roy. Sin.	TRAPP	1738	10012007
ROY	Roy. Sin.	ANONYMOUS	1753	10024012
ROY	Roy.last.	LIMBORCH	1740	20031003
ROYAL	Royal law.	KIDDINGTON	1757	62002010
ROYAL	Royal.o. Sai.	WELCH	1752	63002009
RUIN	Great Ruin.	ERSKINE	1764	27012009
RUINS	Creat.ruins.	MARRIOTT	1774	48008022
RUL	Ap.rul.o.pr.	WILLIAMS	1770	50004005
RUL	S. S. Rul. F.	MARSH	1737	45016031
RULE	Prot. Rule.	PYLE	1717	50013005
RULE	Rule m.act.	CLARKE	1734	45006044
RULE	Rule of life.	MASON	1758	47020024
RULE	Rule of life.	PETERS	1776	32006008
RULE	Rule of Rej.	STRAIGHT	1671	53004004
RULE	Rule right.	CAMFIELD	1671	43007012
RULE	Rule right.	CARTER	1738	43007012
RULE	Rule right.	CONYBEARE	1757	43007012
RULE	Rule right.	DAVIES	1766	43007012
RULE	Rule Behav.	MOGRIDGE	1766	43023001
RULE	Rule Equity.	ATTERBURY	1699	43007012
RULE	Rule Pe.& L.	ELLIS	1684	53002003
RULE	Rule Refor.	PIERCE	1671	43019008
RULE	S. S.rule of 1	ELLIS	1704	45016029
RULE	Wal.b. Rule.	HORTON	1679	51006016
RULE	Xn. Rule F.	MICHELL	1737	46005039
RULER'S	Ruler's S.c.	HALL	1661	46004046
RULERS	Duty Rulers.	DELANY	1747	48013003
RULERS	Ob.to Rulers	AGAR	1759	48013001
RULES	Ld rules all.	CLARKSON	1696	19103019
RULES	Rules f.judg.	BLACKALL	1723	43007003
RULES	Rules f.judg.	BLAIR	1740	43007003
RUN	Ag.b.run. G.	UNWIN	1773	48013007
RUN	Run.in debt.	NEWTON	1782	48013008
RUSSEL	Ld. Russel.	BURNET	1713	69014013
RUTH'S	Ruth's Piety.	JENKINS	1779	08001016
S	A.& P.o. S. S.	NEAL	1757	58003016
S	A.m. Pr. Ir. S	SECKER	1766	20009006
S	Adam's in. S.	GREEN	1758	19008003
S	Antiq.of S.	CATCOTT	1753	01002003
S	Ap. S.p.o. Xy	LANGHORNE	1773	49015019
S	Assist.o. H. S	BENNETT	1728	53001019
S	Au.1.b. R. S.	ANDERSON	1720	68000003

Keyword	In its Context	Author	Year	BkChpVrs
S	Auth.of S. S.	SCOTT	1700	46005039
S	Auth.of S. S.	GUYSE	1724	54003016
S	Author. S. S.	OWEN	1675	45016029
S	B. R.n. M. S.	ANONYMOUS	1735	56002001
S	B.o. R. M.o. S	BENSON	17--	56002001
S	Bel.of Fut. S.	ANONYMOUS	1776	45016025
S	Bl.pol.o. S.	FLAVEL	1673	50004003
S	Bosom S.	NEWCOMBE	1686	19018023
S	Buyers& S.	BRAGGE	1706	46002013
S	Buyers& S.	MARKLAND	1729	46002013
S	Buyers& S.	DODD	1757	43021012
S	Buyers& S.	BULKLEY	1771	46002013
S	C.to o.m's. S.	STOWE	1681	49003006
S	Change of S.	UMFREVILLE	1739	02020008
S	Chear.&w. S.	NEWTON	1759	20018014
S	Co.s.& W. S.	BERRIMAN	1751	47008014
S	Cov. S.h. Ha.	PEAD	1701	52002001
S	Cov. S.h. Ha.	WARREN	1748	52002001
S	D.rel.t. H. S.	GUYSE	1757	52004030
S	De. S.& H. G.	EVANS	1766	65005020
S	Den. S.a Dec.	NICOLSON	1661	65001008
S	Desires to S.	MOORE	1716	62001015
S	Di.au.o. S. S.	FAROM	1660	58003016
S	Di.au.o. S. S.	JACOMB	1660	58003016
S	Di Or.o. S. S.	SMITH	1769	51001011
S	Diff.of S. S.	ATTERBURY	1734	64003016
S	Div. Au. S. S.	HUMPHREYS	1712	55004008
S	Div. Au. S. S.	BELLAMY	1744	64002021
S	Dumb&d. S.	BRAGGE	1702	44009014
S	Epiph. S.	SNAPE	1745	49002007
S	Excel.of S. S.	SEED	1743	63003015
S	Excel.of S. S.	DAVIS	1756	19119092
S	Excell. S. S.	ANONYMOUS	1780	06001008
S	Excell.of S.	ZAMBRANA	1685	41010031
S	Faith our S.	WILCOX	1757	19027014
S	Faith w. S.	PEARSON	1718	46020029
S	Faith w. S.	SHERLOCK	1719	46020029
S	Fall&1st S.	BOSTON	1773	01003006
S	Fear of M. S.	HUNT	1748	20029025
S	G.not A.of S.	STEPHENS	1737	23045007
S	G's. J.in d. S	EDWARDS	1774	48003019
S	G's.dea.w. S.	STEPHENS	1737	48009017
S	G's Pres.b. S.	BRADBURY	1772	19046005
S	G's S.on Ad.	PYLE	1777	01003019
S	Gosp.w.o. S.	LARDNER	1751	47016031
S	H. S. S.	CROWNFIELD	1752	58003016
S	H. S. T.o. Xt.	JOHNSON	1776	46015026
S	Hear.of S.	BLAIR	1740	43005001
S	Her.& S.una.	MOSSOM	1685	49011019
S	Her.& S.una.	MARCH	1699	49011019
S	Her.& S.una.	CLAGETT	1704	49011019
S	Her.& S.una.	ROGERS	1736	49011019
S	Hol.nec.to S.	BENSON	1748	61012014
S	How. R. S. S.	FOSTER	1732	46005039
S	Immor.of S.	GALE	1726	43010028
S	Imp. Ad's. S.	TAYLOR	1725	48005019

Keyword	In its Context	Author	Year	BkChpVrs
S	Imp.of S.&c.	GAUNT	1769	62002024
S	Inhe. S.in L.	CAMPION	1700	54001012
S	Insp.of S. S.	HORBERY	1774	49007040
S	Insp.of S S.	SEED	1743	55002013
S	Inspi.of. S. S	BATTY	1739	58003016
S	Inspi.of S. S.	KIDDELL	1779	58003016
S	Inspir. S. S.	HORBERY	1774	55004008
S	Inspir.o. S. S	CALAMY	1710	48003002
S	Interp.o. S. S	JAMES	1729	47008030
S	Inv.t.thir. S.	DODDERIDGE	1761	46007037
S	Inv.t.thir. S.	PEARSE	1763	46007037
S	Jud. S.expl.	WILSON	1781	45022021
S	Kno.in F. S.	DODD	1767	10012023
S	Know.o. S. S.	TILLOTSON	1735	43023013
S	L's. S.n. Cov.	CHANDLER	1769	49011025
S	Lust Ca.of S.	CLARKE	1735	62001014
S	Lust Ca.of S.	SOUTH	1744	62001014
S	Lust Ca.of S.	ABERNETHY	1751	62001014
S	M.& Xs.c. S.	SLADEN	1733	45014034
S	M's.ina.k. S.	HURST	1660	48007007
S	Ma. C.& E. S.	SIMONS	1743	64001010
S	Ma. C.& E. S.	WARREN	1748	64001010
S	Mour.oth. S.	JENKINS	1683	64002007
S	N. Part.in S.	CLARKSON	1696	52005007
S	Nec.of S.f. S.	GILL	1773	61002010
S	Obj.to S.con.	AMORY	1775	49001025
S	Obs.of S. S.	WAPLE	1729	64003016
S	Off. Op. H. S.	WARBURTON	1753	46014016
S	On Board- S.	STOCKDALE	1777	63005008
S	On S.a. D. S.	HOLE	1713	24026014
S	Or.& C.o. S.	BATTY	1739	48005019
S	P's man.o. S.	DUCHAL	1753	56002003
S	Past. M.pr. S.	HILL	1755	07013023
S	Pen.view. S.	WHITTY	1772	44014072
S	Peo. Rgt. S. S	SHARP	1735	64003016
S	Pride&m. S.	STOCKDALE	1777	21010018
S	Prim. S.of M.	TAYLOR	1725	01001026
S	Quinquag. S.	STANHOPE	1715	49013001
S	Quinquag. S.	HOLE	1716	49013001
S	Quinquag. S.	READING	1728	01009006
S	Quinquag. S.	READING	1730	01012001
S	R.nec.to c. S.	SKELTON	1754	63002017
S	Rash.&v. S.	BERAULT	1698	62005012
S	Rash.&v. S.	BURNET	1713	62005012
S	Rash.&v. S.	BARROW	1716	62005012
S	Rash.&v. S.	GILBERT	1724	62005012
S	Rash.&v. S.	INNES	1726	62005012
S	Rash.&v. S.	BOSTON	1773	62005012
S	Read. H. S.	STRATFORD	1687	54003016
S	Read. S. S.	CROFT	1697	46005039
S	Read. S. S.	NOURSE	1708	46005039
S	Read. S. S.	HARRIS	1717	43022029
S	Read. S. S.	BRADBURY	1717	46005039
S	Read. S. S.	NEWMAN	1717	46005039
S	Read. S. S.	REYNOLDS	1717	47013015
S	Read. S. S.	GROSVENOR	1717	62001021

Keyword	In its Context	Author	Year	BkChpVrs
S	Read. S. S.	EARLE	1717	69001003
S	Read. S. S.	BILLINGSLEY	1723	46005039
S	Read. S. S.	DICKSON	1731	46005039
S	Read. S. S.	ROGERS	1730	58003015
S	Read. S. S.	STRAIGHT	1741	46005039
S	Read. S. S.	WEBSTER	1745	45016008
S	Read. S. S.	BUNDY	1750	43024015
S	Read. S. S.	SKELTON	1754	46005039
S	Read. S. S.	SMITH	1756	43022029
S	Read. S. S.	WILCOX	1757	45024032
S	Read. S. S.	MUNTON	1756	47017011
S	Read. S. S.	NEWTON	1760	46005039
S	Read. S. S.	STERNE	1769	46005039
S	Read. S. S.	LANGHORNE	1773	47017011
S	Read. S. S.	PETERS	1776	58003015
S	Read.of S. S.	HARRIS	1717	43002023
S	Relapse in S.	BOURDALOUE	1776	43009002
S	Remiss.of S.	LANGHORNE	1773	19025011
S	Rest.heav. S.	ELLIS	1685	43011028
S	Rogat. S.	NOURSE	1708	48011036
S	Rogat. S.	STOCKWELL	1726	44004028
S	Ruler's S.c.	HALL	1661	46004046
S	S.& R. Wisd.	BADDERLEY	1752	20004005
S	S.&ev. Eye.	BLAIR	1740	43006022
S	S. Paul's Sin.	SMITH	1740	46016002
S	S. S. G.f. Y.	BERRIMAN	1763	19119008
S	S. S. Rul. F.	MARSH	1737	45016031
S	S. S.of Rel.	HOLDEN	1755	45017021
S	S. S.on Auth.	GALE	1726	43023008
S	S. S.proof. Xt	DAVIES	1720	46005039
S	S. S.prov. Xt.	LEIGHTONHOUSE	1697	46005039
S	S. S.rule of 1	ELLIS	1704	45016029
S	S. S.suff.	MANTON	1675	56002015
S	S. S.t.b.read.	FOWLER	1675	55005027
S	S. S.wo.of G.	LUCAS	1710	55002013
S	S.a.ador.ma.	PARRY	1666	43002009
S	S.add to Gos.	TILLOTSON	1735	51001008
S	S.af. Induct.	BERRIMAN	1763	38002007
S	S.b. Easter.	STANHOPE	1715	43027001
S	S.b. Easter.	HOLE	1716	43027001
S	S.b. Easter.	ANONYMOUS	1776	69007014
S	S.b. Fair.	KEMP	1668	50002017
S	S.b. Xtmas.	WADE	1729	43011002
S	S.o. G.f.d. J.	DAVIES	1771	49003007
S	S.of G.pr. T.	CAMPBELL	1779	49001025
S	Sacra. P. S.	SHARP	1729	45022019
S	Scope of S. S.	BOSTON	1773	58001013
S	Seach. S. S.	CRAIG	1775	47017011
S	Search. S. S.	PATRICK	1685	64003016
S	Search. S. S.	WAPLE	1729	46005039
S	Search. S. S.	WHITFIELD	1739	46005039
S	Search. S. S.	AMORY	1775	46005039
S	Seek.a.m's S.	WALLIS	1740	49010032
S	Septuag. S.	STANHOPE	1715	49009024
S	Septuag. S.	HOLE	1716	49009024
S	Septuag. S.	READING	1728	01001001

Keyword	In its Context	Author	Year	BkChpVrs
S	Sexag. S.	READING	1724	01003022
S	Sexag. S.	READING	1728	01003001
S	Sexag. S.	READING	1730	01002015
S	Sexag. S.	READING	1730	01006001
S	Sexages. S.	STANHOPE	1715	50011019
S	Sexages. S.	HOLE	1716	50011019
S	Shep.of o. S.	WALKER	1765	63002025
S	Sin. D.of S.	DUNLOP	1722	23001005
S	Sin.worse. S.	VEAL	1703	43009012
S	Sin& Pu.o. S.	BOYSE	1728	68000006
S	South S. Cal.	SMITH	1721	50004018
S	St. S.	MONRO	1693	19026006
S	St. S.	VICKERS	1707	19094019
S	St. S.	LUCAS	1710	19026006
S	St. S.	FOORD	1719	19085008
S	St. S.	DICKSON	1731	19085008
S	Sta. F. Ch. S.	ERSKINE	1764	23030007
S	Stab.of S. S.	PARKHURST	1717	46010035
S	Study of S. S.	AMORY	1775	58003015
S	Sub.to S. B.	LANGHORNE	1773	62004007
S	Suf. T. S. Xy.	NALSON	1737	63002021
S	Suff.of. S. S.	BEVERIDGE	1720	58003016
S	Suff.of S. S.	ANONYMOUS	1771	48001016
S	T.a. T.b. S. S	GOAD	1664	55005021
S	T.t. S.n.f. G.	SHARP	1734	62001013
S	T.t. S.n.f. G.	BURNET	1747	62001013
S	T.t. S.n.f. G.	ABERNETHY	1751	62001013
S	Ter.& Qu. S.	CLARKE	1734	69002029
S	Tr.&c.o. S. S.	CALAMY	1710	58003016
S	Tr.&c.o. S. S.	BOYS	1716	58003016
S	Tr.&c.o. S. S.	CLARKE	1735	58003016
S	Tr.time S. P.	TURNER	1684	49014020
S	True Nat. S.	CUDWORTH	1670	49015057
S	Trump.of S.	SMITH	1660	21011009
S	Tues. W. S.	STANHOPE	1714	47008014
S	Use of S. S.	INGLIS	17--	58003016
S	Use of S. S.	GUYSE	1724	48015004
S	Use H. S. S.	HOPKINS	1710	54003016
S	Usef.of S. S.	ALLESTREE	1684	58003015
S	Val.& L.o. S.	WELTON	1724	43016026
S	Vice destr. S.	BUTLER	1719	43008022
S	Virt.g.m's S.	CONEY	1730	20014014
S	Walk.on S.	BRAGGE	1702	43014022
S	Way to et. S.	SYNGE	1734	55005021
S	Well-do. S.ag.	CLAGETT	1720	63003013
S	Well-do. S.ag.	CLARKE	1736	63003013
S	Well-do.a. S.	TILLOTSON	1735	63003013
S	Whole& S.	DAVIES	1771	43009012
S	Wind& S.r.	DODD	1757	44004039
S	Wind& S.r.	BULKLEY	1771	44004041
S	Worth.of S.	PARTRIDGE	1720	44008036
S	Xn's. Joy i. S	BOURN	1777	63001008
S	Xt. Sub.o. S.	SAURIN	1777	61010005
S	Xt.cru. G. S.	WADSWORTH	1675	61010012
S	Xt's. H.to S.	GOODWIN	16--	46013001
S	Xt's. S.& D.	COWPER	1773	49002002

Keyword	In its Context	Author	Year	BkChpVrs
S	Xt's. Suff.& S	CHARNOCK	1684	45024026
S	Xt's. Suff.& S	EDWARDS	1713	45024026
S	Xt's.comp. S.	DAVIES	1771	43023037
S	set forth S. S.	ROBINSON	1740	46006068
S	1 S. East.	STANHOPE	1714	46020019
S	1 S. East.	HOLE	1716	46020019
S	1 S. Easter.	READING	1728	04016007
S	1 S. Easter.	READING	1730	04022018
S	1 S. Epiph.	STANHOPE	1715	48012001
S	1 S. Epiph.	STANHOPE	1715	48013001
S	1 S. Epiph.	HOLE	1716	48012001
S	1 S. Epiph.	READING	1728	23044006
S	1 S. Epiph.	READING	1730	23046001
S	1 S. Lent.	FRANK	1672	50006002
S	1 S. Lent.	STANHOPE	1715	50006001
S	1 S. Lent.	HOLE	1716	50006001
S	1 S. Lent.	READING	1728	01019024
S	1 S. Lent.	READING	1730	01022011
S	1 S. Trin.	READING	1728	06010012
S	1 S. Trin.	READING	1730	06023011
S	1 S.af. East.	STANHOPE	1714	65005004
S	1 S.af. East.	HOLE	1716	65005004
S	1 S.af. Trin.	STANHOPE	1714	65004007
S	1 S.in Lent.	PATE	1708	48001016
S	1 S.in Year.	COCKBURN	1706	19090012
S	10 S. Trin.	STANHOPE	1714	45019041
S	10 S. Trin.	HOLE	1716	45019041
S	10 S. Trin.	STANHOPE	1714	49012001
S	10 S. Trin.	HOLE	1716	49012001
S	10 S. Trin.	READING	1728	11021028
S	10 S. Trin.	READING	1730	11022035
S	11 S. Trin.	STANHOPE	1714	45018009
S	11 S. Trin.	STANHOPE	1714	49015001
S	11 S. Trin.	HOLE	1716	49015001
S	11 S. Trin.	READING	1730	12009001
S	11 S. Trin.	QUINCY	1750	45018013
S	12 S. Trin.	STANHOPE	1714	43022001
S	12 S. Trin.	STANHOPE	1714	44007031
S	12 S. Trin.	HOLE	1716	44007031
S	12 S. Trin.	STANHOPE	1714	50003004
S	12 S. Trin.	HOLE	1716	50003004
S	12 S. Trin.	READING	1728	12010031
S	12 S. Trin.	READING	1730	12018004
S	13 S. Trin.	STANHOPE	1714	45010023
S	13 S. Trin.	STANHOPE	1714	51003016
S	13 S. Trin.	READING	1728	12019037
S	13 S. Trin.	READING	1730	12023025
S	14 S. Trin.	STANHOPE	1714	45017011
S	14 S. Trin.	STANHOPE	1714	51005016
S	14 S. Trin.	HOLE	1716	51005016
S	14 S. Trin.	READING	1728	24005001
S	14 S. Trin.	READING	1730	24022003
S	15 S. Trin.	STANHOPE	1714	51006011
S	15 S. Trin.	HOLE	1716	51006011
S	15 S. Trin.	READING	1728	24035018
S	15 S. Trin.	READING	1730	24036032
S	16 S. Trin.	STANHOPE	1714	45007011
S	16 S. Trin.	STANHOPE	1714	52003013
S	16 S. Trin.	HOLE	1716	52003013
S	16 S. Trin.	READING	1728	26002007
S	16 S. Trin.	READING	1730	26013004
S	17 S. Trin.	STANHOPE	1714	45014001
S	17 S. Trin.	STANHOPE	1713	52004001
S	17 S. Trin.	HOLE	1716	52004001
S	17 S. Trin.	READING	1728	26014007
S	17 S. Trin.	READING	1730	26018031
S	18 S. Trin.	STANHOPE	1714	43022034
S	18 S. Trin.	STANHOPE	1714	49001004
S	18 S. Trin.	HOLE	1716	49001004
S	18 S. Trin.	READING	1728	26020024
S	18 S. Trin.	READING	1730	26024024
S	19 S. Trin.	STANHOPE	1714	43009001
S	19 S. Trin.	STANHOPE	1715	43008023
S	19 S. Trin.	HOLE	1716	52004018
S	19 S. Trin.	READING	1728	27003016
S	19 S. Trin.	READING	1730	27006010
S	2 S. East.	STANHOPE	1714	46010011
S	2 S. East.	HOLE	1716	46010011
S	2 S. Easter.	H.	1686	26009005
S	2 S. Easter.	READING	1728	04023007
S	2 S. Easter.	READING	1730	04025010
S	2 S. Epiph.	STANHOPE	1715	46002001
S	2 S. Epiph.	HOLE	1716	46002001
S	2 S. Epiph.	STANHOPE	1715	48012006
S	2 S. Epiph.	HOLE	1716	48012006
S	2 S. Epiph.	READING	1728	23051012
S	2 S. Epiph.	READING	1730	23053001
S	2 S. Lent.	STANHOPE	1715	43015021
S	2 S. Lent.	STANHOPE	1715	55004001
S	2 S. Lent.	HOLE	1716	55004001
S	2 S. Lent.	READING	1728	01027011
S	2 S. Lent.	READING	1730	01034030
S	2 S. Trin.	STANHOPE	1714	45014016
S	2 S. Trin.	READING	1728	07004014
S	2 S. Trin.	READING	1730	07005001
S	2 S. X.mas.	READING	1730	23041001
S	2 S.af. East.	STANHOPE	1714	63002019
S	2 S.af. East.	HOLE	1716	63002019
S	2 S.af. Trin.	STANHOPE	1714	65003013
S	2 S.af. Trin.	HOLE	1716	65003013
S	2 S.un. S. D.	LEAKE	1773	49015033
S	20 S. Trin.	STANHOPE	1714	52005015
S	20 S. Trin.	HOLE	1716	52005015
S	20 S. Trin.	READING	1730	32006009
S	21 S. Trin.	STANHOPE	1714	46004046
S	21 S. Trin.	HOLE	1716	46004046
S	21 S. Trin.	STANHOPE	1714	52006010
S	21 S. Trin.	HOLE	1716	52006010
S	21 S. Trin.	READING	1728	34002004
S	22 S. Trin.	STANHOPE	1714	53001003
S	22 S. Trin.	HOLE	1716	53001003
S	22 S. Trin.	READING	1728	20002006

INDEXES TO THIRD VOLUME: E: KEYWORD-IN-CONTEXT INDEX OF OTHER SUBJECTS OR OCCASIONS

Keyword	In its Context	Author	Year	BkChpVrs
S	22 S. Trin.	READING	1728	29002012
S	22 S. Trin.	READING	1730	20001033
S	23 S. Trin.	STANHOPE	1714	53003017
S	23 S. Trin.	HOLE	1716	53003017
S	23 S. Trin.	READING	1728	20011011
S	23 S. Trin.	READING	1730	20012001
S	23 S. Trin.	READING	1730	20014013
S	24 S. Trin.	STANHOPE	1714	43009018
S	24 S. Trin.	STANHOPE	1714	43022015
S	24 S. Trin.	STANHOPE	1714	54001003
S	24 S. Trin.	HOLE	1716	54001003
S	24 S. Trin.	READING	1728	20013020
S	24 S. Trin.	READING	1728	20015001
S	24 S. Trin.	READING	1728	20017016
S	24 S. Trin.	READING	1730	20016021
S	25 S. Trin.	STANHOPE	1714	24023005
S	25 S. Trin.	STANHOPE	1714	46006005
S	25 S. Trin.	HOLE	1716	24023005
S	25 S. Trin.	HOLE	1716	46006005
S	26 S. Trin.	READING	1730	20019005
S	3. S. Lent.	STANHOPE	1715	45011014
S	3. S. Lent.	HOLE	1716	45011014
S	3 S. Easter.	STANHOPE	1714	46016016
S	3 S. Easter.	HOLE	1716	46016016
S	3 S. Easter.	READING	1728	05004001
S	3 S. Easter.	READING	1730	05005002
S	3 S. Epiph.	STANHOPE	1715	48012016
S	3 S. Epiph.	HOLE	1716	48012016
S	3 S. Epiph.	READING	1728	23055003
S	3 S. Epiph.	READING	1730	23056010
S	3 S. Lent.	STANHOPE	1715	52005001
S	3 S. Lent.	HOLE	1716	52005001
S	3 S. Lent.	READING	1728	01039021
S	3 S. Lent.	READING	1730	01042021
S	3 S. Trin.	STANHOPE	1714	45015001
S	3 S. Trin.	READING	1728	09002020
S	3 S. Trin.	READING	1730	09003012
S	3 S.af. East.	STANHOPE	1714	63002011
S	3 S.af. East.	HOLE	1716	63002011
S	3 S.af. Trin.	STANHOPE	1714	63005005
S	3 S.af. Trin.	HOLE	1716	63005005
S	4 S. East.	STANHOPE	1714	62001017
S	4 S. East.	HOLE	1716	62001017
S	4 S. Easter.	STANHOPE	1714	46016005
S	4 S. Easter.	READING	1728	05006006
S	4 S. Easter.	READING	1730	05007012
S	4 S. Epiph.	LITTLETON	1680	46003016
S	4 S. Epiph.	READING	1730	23057015
S	4 S. Epiph.	READING	1730	23058003
S	4 S. Lent.	STANHOPE	1715	46006001
S	4 S. Lent.	HOLE	1716	46006001
S	4 S. Lent.	STANHOPE	1715	51004021
S	4 S. Lent.	HOLE	1716	51004021
S	4 S. Lent.	READING	1728	01043026
S	4 S. Lent.	READING	1730	01045005
S	4 S. Trin.	GIFFARD	1681	09012017

Keyword	In its Context	Author	Year	BkChpVrs
S	4 S. Trin.	STANHOPE	1714	45006036
S	4 S. Trin.	STANHOPE	1714	48008018
S	4 S. Trin.	HOLE	1716	48008018
S	4 S. Trin.	READING	1728	09012016
S	4 S. Trin.	READING	1730	09013013
S	4 S. Xt.on C.	FLAVEL	1673	43027046
S	5 S. Easter.	STANHOPE	1714	46016023
S	5 S. Easter.	HOLE	1716	46016023
S	5 S. Easter.	READING	1728	05008003
S	5 S. Easter.	READING	1730	05009006
S	5 S. Epiph.	HOLE	1716	54003012
S	5 S. Epiph.	READING	1730	23059001
S	5 S. Epiph.	READING	1730	23064001
S	5 S. Lent.	STANHOPE	1715	46008046
S	5 S. Lent.	HOLE	1716	46008046
S	5 S. Lent.	STANHOPE	1715	61009011
S	5 S. Lent.	HOLE	1716	61009011
S	5 S. Lent.	READING	1728	02003009
S	5 S. Lent.	READING	1730	02005001
S	5 S. Trin.	STANHOPE	1714	45005001
S	5 S. Trin.	STANHOPE	1714	63003008
S	5 S. Trin.	HOLE	1716	63003008
S	5 S. Trin.	READING	1728	09015022
S	5 S. Trin.	READING	1730	09017056
S	5 S.af. East.	STANHOPE	1714	62001022
S	5 S.af. East.	HOLE	1716	62001022
S	6 S. Epiph.	STANHOPE	1715	43024023
S	6 S. Epiph.	HOLE	1716	43024023
S	6 S. Epiph.	READING	1730	23065001
S	6 S. Epiph.	READING	1730	23066001
S	6 S. Lent.	READING	1728	02009016
S	6 S. Lent.	READING	1730	02010001
S	6 S. Trin.	STANHOPE	1714	48006003
S	6 S. Trin.	READING	1730	10019001
S	7. S. Trin.	READING	1730	10024010
S	7 S. Trin.	STANHOPE	1714	44008001
S	7 S. Trin.	HOLE	1716	44008001
S	7 S. Trin.	STANHOPE	1714	48006019
S	7 S. Trin.	HOLE	1716	48006019
S	7 S. Trin.	READING	1728	10021001
S	8 S. Trin.	STANHOPE	1714	48008012
S	8 S. Trin.	HOLE	1716	48008012
S	8 S. Trin.	READING	1728	11013001
S	8 S. Trin.	READING	1730	11017024
S	9 S. Trin.	STANHOPE	1714	45016001
S	9 S. Trin.	STANHOPE	1714	49010001
S	9 S. Trin.	HOLE	1716	49010001
S	9 S. Trin.	READING	1728	11018017
S	9 S. Trin.	READING	1730	11019010
SA	Dan.neg. Sa.	QUINCY	1750	61002003
SA	Love un. Sa.	HUBBARD	1729	63001008
SA	Suff.for R.sa.	BRADBURY	1722	63003014
SA	Xns. H.& Sa.	WEBB	1765	63003005
SAB	M's Sab.year.	CLARKE	1760	03025003
SAB	Sanct.of Sab.	LAVINGTON	1743	05005012
SABB	End of Sabb.	ORR	1777	44002027

Keyword	In its Context	Author	Year	BkChpVrs
SABB	Keep. Sabb.	WROUGHTON	1716	02020008
SABBAT	Viol. Sabbat.	LAMONT	1780	05005012
SABBATH	Jew. Sabbath.	MEDE	1672	26020030
SABBATH	Sabbath.	CASE	1676	23058013
SABBATH	Sabbath.	SMITH	1675	61004009
SABBATH	Sabbath.	GREGORY	1681	02020009
SABBATH	Sabbath.	HOPKINS	1692	02020008
SABBATH	Sabbath.	DORRINGTON	1703	02020008
SABBATH	Sabbath.	PARKHURST	1707	26020012
SABBATH	Sabbath.	NOURSE	1708	02020008
SABBATH	Sabbath.	EDWARDS	1713	02020008
SABBATH	Sabbath.	HOLE	1715	02020008
SABBATH	Sabbath.	SHARP	1729	02020008
SABBATH	Sabbath.	WILDER	1729	02020009
SABBATH	Sabbath.	MARKLAND	1729	44002027
SABBATH	Sabbath.	HILL	1730	02020008
SABBATH	Sabbath.	SKEELER	1740	02020008
SABBATH	Sabbath.	FOSTER	1744	02020008
SABBATH	Sabbath.	CHANDLER	1760	01002002
SABBATH	Sabbath.	LLOYD	1765	26020030
SABBATH	Sabbath.	BRAILSFORD	1776	45006002
SABBATH	Sabbath.	KENNICOTT	1781	01002003
SABBATH	Sabbath.	GLASSE	1781	03019030
SABBATH	Sabbath&c.	MAYNARD	1724	21005001
SABBATH	Sabbath&c.	ORTON	1769	61004009
SABBATH	Xn. Sabbath.	BUNDY	1740	44002027
SABBATH	Xn. Sabbath.	PARRY	1753	44002027
SABBATH	Xn. Sabbath.	FLEMING	1777	44002027
SABBATH	of Sabbath.	COOKE	1739	43012008
SAC	Fals.ap. Sac.	WILLIAMS	1774	49011027
SAC	Nat.of Sac.	CHANDLER	1769	49011023
SAC	Obed.& Sac.	WITHERSPOON	1768	09015022
SAC	Sac.o.heart.	NALSON	1737	20023026
SAC	Sac.of our B.	HUSSEY	1758	48012001
SAC	Xt. Sac.f.us.	CHARNOCK	1684	49005007
SAC	Xt.prop. Sac.	SKELTON	1754	49015023
SACERD	Sacerd. Ben.	GIBSON	1709	14030018
SACR	Cr. Sacr. His.	POWELL	1776	46015021
SACR	Sacr. Almo.	FAWCETT	1757	49016002
SACR	Sacr. Almon.	FAWCETT	1757	23032008
SACR	Sacr. Friend.	DEVEREL	1777	09018003
SACR	Sacr. Mem.	WILLISON	1761	02012014
SACR	Sacr.prepar.	RALEIGH	1679	49011028
SACR	Sacr.s.	ALLEINE	1674	23009006
SACR	Sacr.s.	KENNET	1715	14029030
SACR	Sacr.worth.	OAKES	1739	49002027
SACRA	End of Sacra.	TATHAM	1780	47017030
SACRA	Gosp. Sacra.	EDWARDS	1702	22007002
SACRA	Prep.f. Sacra.	SMITH	1740	63004007
SACRA	Sacra.	MORICE	1660	14023019
SACRA	Sacra.	MORICE	1660	24015019
SACRA	Sacra.	MORICE	1660	29003013
SACRA	Sacra.	MORICE	1660	33001015
SACRA	Sacra.	MORICE	1660	37014021
SACRA	Sacra.	MORICE	1660	43007006
SACRA	Sacra.	MORICE	1660	43022001
SACRA	Sacra.	MAURICE	1660	48014001
SACRA	Sacra.	MAURICE	1660	49005011
SACRA	Sacra.	MAURICE	1660	49011027
SACRA	Sacra.	MAURICE	1660	49014040
SACRA	Sacra.	MORICE	1660	49015040
SACRA	Sacra.	MORRICE	1660	56003002
SACRA	Sacra.	MORICE	1660	57003009
SACRA	Sacra.	MORICE	1660	61013017
SACRA	Sacra.	MORICE	1660	63003015
SACRA	Sacra.	MORICE	1660	68000003
SACRA	Sacra.	FARINDON	1672	46006056
SACRA	Sacra.	FLAVEL	1673	46006055
SACRA	Sacra.	JACKSON	1673	46006056
SACRA	Sacra.	ALLEINE	1674	19040007
SACRA	Sacra.	ALLEINE	1674	43015028
SACRA	Sacra.	ALLEINE	1674	44001015
SACRA	Sacra.	ALLEINE	1674	45002010
SACRA	Sacra.	GELL	1676	46006055
SACRA	Sacra.	NEVILLE	1679	45022019
SACRA	Sacra.	FARINDON	1672	49011025
SACRA	Sacra.	FARINDON	1672	49011026
SACRA	Sacra.	FARINDON	1672	49011023
SACRA	Sacra.	ALLEINE	1674	52003019
SACRA	Sacra.	ALLEINE	1674	52005001
SACRA	Sacra.	WADSWORTH	1676	49011024
SACRA	Sacra.	GELL	1676	49011026
SACRA	Sacra.	VINES	1677	49005007
SACRA	Sacra.	USHER	1678	49011029
SACRA	Sacra.	SMITH	1679	49011026
SACRA	Sacra.	STANDFAST	1680	45009030
SACRA	Sacra.	SMYTH	1680	45022019
SACRA	Sacra.	MANTON	1688	14030018
SACRA	Sacra.	MANTON	1688	22001012
SACRA	Sacra.	MANTON	1688	43011007
SACRA	Sacra.	MANTON	1688	43022011
SACRA	Sacra.	MANTON	1688	45022020
SACRA	Sacra.	MANTON	1688	46013008
SACRA	Sacra.	CHARNOCK	1684	49011026
SACRA	Sacra.	HESKETH	1684	49011026
SACRA	Sacra.	CHARNOCK	1684	49011027
SACRA	Sacra.	HESKETH	1689	49011029
SACRA	Sacra.	LEIGHTONHOUSE	1697	45022019
SACRA	Sacra.	MANTON	1693	49011026
SACRA	Sacra.	P.	1693	49011029
SACRA	Sacra.	COCKBURN	1697	61010022
SACRA	Sacra.	CHARNOCK	1699	49011028
SACRA	Sacra.	HOWARD	17--	45023019
SACRA	Sacra.	HENWOOD	1701	46006053
SACRA	Sacra.	SHOWER	1702	22002004
SACRA	Sacra.	SHOWER	1702	45022015
SACRA	Sacra.	NEWCOME	1702	45022019
SACRA	Sacra.	SHOWER	1702	46010027
SACRA	Sacra.	MANTON	1703	23053001
SACRA	Sacra.	NOURSE	1705	45022019
SACRA	Sacra.	PARKHURST	1706	46006054
SACRA	Sacra.	GREGORY	1708	45022019

INDEXES TO THIRD VOLUME: E: KEYWORD-IN-CONTEXT INDEX OF OTHER SUBJECTS OR OCCASIONS

Keyword	In its Context	Author	Year	BkChpVrs
SACRA	Sacra.	COLBY	1709	43011028
SACRA	Sacra.	HENWOOD	1701	49011028
SACRA	Sacra.	SHOWER	1702	46018001
SACRA	Sacra.	SHOWER	1702	49006011
SACRA	Sacra.	SHOWER	1702	49010016
SACRA	Sacra.	NEWCOME	1702	49011024
SACRA	Sacra.	SHOWER	1702	49011028
SACRA	Sacra.	NEWCOME	1702	49011029
SACRA	Sacra.	SHOWER	1702	49011029
SACRA	Sacra.	SHOWER	1702	51006014
SACRA	Sacra.	DORRINGTON	1703	49011026
SACRA	Sacra.	ATTERBURY	1703	49011026
SACRA	Sacra.	WELTON	1708	49011025
SACRA	Sacra.	COLBY	1708	49011029
SACRA	Sacra.	SAYER	1708	49011029
SACRA	Sacra.	STRONG	1708	49011029
SACRA	Sacra.	HOPKINS	1712	20003017
SACRA	Sacra.	HOPKINS	1712	46006054
SACRA	Sacra.	PALMER	1710	49011029
SACRA	Sacra.	ROOTS	1711	47002042
SACRA	Sacra.	BUCHANAN	1712	49011027
SACRA	Sacra.	BOYS	1716	49010017
SACRA	Sacra.	WAKE	1716	49011024
SACRA	Sacra.	BOYS	1716	49011029
SACRA	Sacra.	ACTON	1717	46019005
SACRA	Sacra.	JACKSON	1728	43026026
SACRA	Sacra.	JOHNSON	1728	45022019
SACRA	Sacra.	JOHNSON	1728	46006027
SACRA	Sacra.	MARKLAND	1729	45022019
SACRA	Sacra.	BRETT	1720	49011029
SACRA	Sacra.	BAYLY	1721	49011026
SACRA	Sacra.	WELTON	1724	49011026
SACRA	Sacra.	CALAMY	1726	49011029
SACRA	Sacra.	WROUGHTON	1728	49011028
SACRA	Sacra.	JOHNSON	1728	61010008
SACRA	Sacra.	M'GEORGE	1729	49010016
SACRA	Sacra.	DICKSON	1731	43022002
SACRA	Sacra.	STENNETT	1732	46001029
SACRA	Sacra.	SHORTHOSE	1738	45022019
SACRA	Sacra.	UMFREVILLE	1739	43011028
SACRA	Sacra.	CLARKE	1734	49011025
SACRA	Sacra.	CLARKE	1734	49011027
SACRA	Sacra.	HARRIS	1735	49011024
SACRA	Sacra.	TILLOTSON	1735	49011026
SACRA	Sacra.	MOSS	1738	49010016
SACRA	Sacra.	UMFREVILLE	1739	49011028
SACRA	Sacra.	FARRINGTON	1741	43026026
SACRA	Sacra.	JOHNSON	1741	46006051
SACRA	Sacra.	RIDLEY	1742	46006051
SACRA	Sacra.	BURNET	1747	45022019
SACRA	Sacra.	BURNET	1747	46015014
SACRA	Sacra.	EMLYN	1742	49011025
SACRA	Sacra.	ATTERBURY	1743	49011028
SACRA	Sacra.	TERRY	1746	49010016
SACRA	Sacra.	WOODS	1747	49011025
SACRA	Sacra.	BURNET	1747	49011028

Keyword	In its Context	Author	Year	BkChpVrs
SACRA	Sacra.	WARREN	1748	49010021
SACRA	Sacra.	ALLEN	1751	45022019
SACRA	Sacra.	BARNES	1752	45022019
SACRA	Sacra.	DAVIS	1756	45022019
SACRA	Sacra.	ECCLES	1751	49011034
SACRA	Sacra.	BOSTON	1753	61011029
SACRA	Sacra.	PARRY	1755	49011026
SACRA	Sacra.	ADEY	1755	49011028
SACRA	Sacra.	BALL	1756	49011029
SACRA	Sacra.	DAVIS	1756	49011029
SACRA	Sacra.	MAY	1757	48011026
SACRA	Sacra.	NEAL	1757	49011023
SACRA	Sacra.	MAY	1757	49011026
SACRA	Sacra.	WILLISON	1761	06003005
SACRA	Sacra.	WHITTY	1766	45024032
SACRA	Sacra.	WHITTY	1768	43026041
SACRA	Sacra.	WHITTY	1768	46010015
SACRA	Sacra.	ALSOP	1769	43022011
SACRA	Sacra.	OWEN	1760	49011026
SACRA	Sacra.	WILLISON	1761	49011017
SACRA	Sacra.	SAVAGE	1763	49011024
SACRA	Sacra.	SHARP	1763	49011028
SACRA	Sacra.	WALSH	1764	49011028
SACRA	Sacra.	WHITTY	1766	46020020
SACRA	Sacra.	WESTON	1768	49011026
SACRA	Sacra.	CHANDLER	1769	49011022
SACRA	Sacra.	CHANDLER	1769	49011026
SACRA	Sacra.	WINCHESTER	1771	24002019
SACRA	Sacra.	WHITTY	1772	43005047
SACRA	Sacra.	WHITTY	1772	45022019
SACRA	Sacra.	BOSTON	1773	04023009
SACRA	Sacra.	WILLIAMS	1774	45022019
SACRA	Sacra.	IBBETSON	1775	45022019
SACRA	Sacra.	FARQUAR	1772	49011026
SACRA	Sacra.	WHITTY	1772	49011029
SACRA	Sacra.	BOSTON	1773	53001027
SACRA	Sacra.	WILSON	1781	45022019
SACRA	Sacra.	OGDEN	1780	49011026
SACRA	Sacra.	TATHAM	1780	49011026
SACRA	Sacra.	PENTYCROSS	1781	49011023
SACRA	Sacra.	WILSON	1781	49011026
SACRA	Sacra.	TEMPLE	1782	49011009
SACRA	Sacra. P. S.	SHARP	1729	45022019
SACRA	Sacra. Prep.	SOUTH	1727	43022012
SACRA	Sacra.s.	FULWOOD	1667	61012023
SACRA	Sacra.s.	VICKERS	1709	48012018
SACRA	Use of Sacra.	KEITH	1704	49012013
SACRA	of Sacra.	BUNDY	1740	43003015
SACRA	2 Sacra.	SILVESTER	1675	20030006
SACRA	2 Sacra.	LITTLETON	1680	65005008
SACRAMENT	Sacrament.	GOUGH	1709	45014022
SACRAMENTS	Sacraments.	NEWCOME	1702	43028019
SACRAMENTS	Sacraments.	LEIGHTON	1746	22001003
SACRIF	Abr. Sacrif.	MACE	1751	61011017
SACRIF	Sacrif.of Xt.	CLARKSON	1696	52005002
SACRIF	Sacrif.of Xt.	TILLOTSON	1735	61009026

Keyword	In its Context	Author	Year	BkChpVrs
SACRIF	Sacrif.of Xt.	SCOTT	1743	61010010
SACRIF	Sacrif.of Xt.	SCOTT	1743	61010011
SACRIF	Sacrif.of Xt.	WESTON	1747	61009012
SACRIF	Sacrif.of Xt.	SHERLOCK	1772	59002014
SACRIF	Xn. Sacrif.	MEDE	1672	38001011
SACRIF	Xt's. Sacrif.	WATERLAND	1742	52005001
SACRIFICE	Xn. Sacrifice.	YOUNG	1706	48012001
SACRIFICE	Xn. Sacrifice.	FIDDES	1720	48012001
SACRIFICE	Xn. Sacrifice.	HEYLYN	1749	48012001
SACRIFICE	of Sacrifice.	PEIRCE	1728	01004004
SACRIFICE	of Sacrifice.	RIDLEY	1736	01004003
SACRILEDGE	Sacriledge.	BASIRE	1668	48002022
SACRILEGE	Sacrilege.	MEDE	1672	47005003
SAD	Sad hand wr.	WILKINSON	1660	18013026
SADD	Sadd. Herod	STRAIGHT	1741	43022023
SAF	Believ. Saf.	GIBBES	1677	19004008
SAF	Saf.in Dang.	ERSKINE	1764	23026020
SAF	Saf.of Ch.	BAINE	1778	19087007
SAF	Saf.of Xn.	CENNICK	1762	26009006
SAFE	Safe in Xt.	WELCH	1752	48008002
SAFETY	Xt our Safety	HARTLEY	1754	43014024
SAGES	Sages Star	HALL	1661	43002002
SAI	Royal.o. Sai.	WELCH	1752	63002009
SAIL	Adv.to Sail.	HAYWARD	1746	19107031
SAINS	Re.of Sains.	BOURDALOUE	1776	43005012
SAINT	Saint or Bru.	BAXTER	1707	45010041
SAINT'S	Saint's com.	HAYDON	1770	48007024
SAINT'S	Saint's Eter.	RUSSEL	1746	55005017
SAINT'S	Saint's Exa.	ROE	1766	61012001
SAINTS	Dis.of Saints	WHITAKER	1674	09023005
SAINTS	Freed. Saints	WELCH	1752	45001074
SAINTS	Happ. Saints	WILLIAMS	16--	46020026
SAINTS	Inv o. Saints.	MAYO	1675	48010014
SAINTS	Priv.o. Saints	DAVIS	1756	65003002
SAINTS	Saints extr.	WILSON	1735	43008025
SAINTS	Saints imp.	WILSON	1735	49013010
SAINTS	Saints o. Ex.	BERRIMAN	1751	61006012
SAINTS	Saints Happ.	BEVERIDGE	1720	45012032
SAINTS	Saints Kings.	DUNLOP	1722	69001006
SAINTS	Saints Treas.	LAMBERT	1779	50003005
SAINTS	Tri.o. Saints.	BADDELLEY	1752	69007014
SAL	Assur.of Sal.	HAVETT	1703	63001009
SAL	Assur.of Sal.	HOPKINS	1710	61012028
SAL	Assur.of Sal.	KNIGHT	1728	61012028
SAL	Door Sal.op.	F.	1667	69003020
SAL	Fai.n.to Sal.	CLAGETT	1704	61011006
SAL	Fai.n.to Sal.	HOPKINS	1708	47016031
SAL	Fal.pret.sal.	BLACKALL	1723	43007022
SAL	Great.of Sal.	GREGORY	1696	61002003
SAL	Means of Sal.	BOURN	1777	52002008
SAL	Neg. G's. Sal.	ROE	1766	61002003
SAL	Negl. Sal.da.	CONANT	1698	61002003
SAL	Sal. Ch.only.	NEWCOME	1702	47002047
SAL	Sal. Ch.only.	COCKBURN	1712	47002047
SAL	Sal. Ch.only.	BOYS	1716	47002047
SAL	Sal. Ch.only.	BEVERIDGE	1720	47002047

Keyword	In its Context	Author	Year	BkChpVrs
SAL	Sal.by gr. G.	KIMBER	1756	59002011
SAL	Sal.in an. W.	SMITH	1696	47016030
SAL	Terms c. Sal.	SHARPE	1734	65003002
SAL	Xt. Rock. Sal.	TAYLOR	1701	19061002
SALT	Salt los. Sav.	BLAIR	1740	43005012
SALT	W.a. Salt.of t	GARDINER	1720	43005013
SALT	W.a. Salt.of t	BLAIR	1740	43005013
SALT	W.a. Salt.of t	WESTLEY	1748	43005013
SALT	Xns. Salt.	BLACKALL	1723	43005013
SALT	Xns. Salt. E.	HORNECK	1706	43005013
SALT	Xns. Salt. E.	ORR	1772	43005013
SALUTATION	Salutation.	KENNET	1715	54004015
SALV	Assu.of Salv.	SCOTT	1700	65003002
SALV	Con.of Salv.	TILLOTSON	1735	61005009
SALV	Diff.of Salv.	COOKE	1739	63004018
SALV	Diff.of Salv.	DAVIES	1766	63004018
SALV	Diffic. Salv.	STILLINGFLEET	1707	63004018
SALV	Diffic. Salv.	SCATTERGOOD	1723	63004018
SALV	Diffic. Salv.	WHARTON	1728	63004018
SALV	Diffic. Salv.	ROGERS	1735	63004018
SALV	Diffic. Salv.	WILCOX	1757	63004018
SALV	Faith c. Salv.	CHARNOCK	1684	46003036
SALV	Faith c. Salv.	MORRIS	1743	46003036
SALV	Gosp. Salv.	STILLINGFLEET	1707	48001016
SALV	Haz.of Salv.	TILLOTSON	1735	49003015
SALV	Pard.& Salv.	BADDELLEY	1752	45007050
SALV	Salv b. Faith	WESTLEY	1746	52002008
SALV	Salv b. Xt.al.	BEVERIDGE	1720	47004012
SALV	Salv.b. Faith.	ANONYMOUS	1768	52002008
SALV	Salv.b. Gra.	ACTON	1714	52002005
SALV	Salv.b. Gra.	DUNLOP	1722	52002008
SALV	Salv.b. Gra.	SUTTON	1754	52002008
SALV	Salv.b. Gra.	HAWEIS	1762	52002008
SALV	Salv.b. Xt.al.	STAYNOE	1700	47004012
SALV	Salv.b Faith	STRAIGHT	1741	52002008
SALV	Salv.b Grace	TAYLOR	1719	52002008
SALV	Salv.by Fai.	BEVERIDGE	1720	47016031
SALV	Salv.by Fai.	DUNLOP	1722	47016031
SALV	Salv.by Fai.	BARKER	1748	47016031
SALV	Salv.by Gra.	SPOONER	1771	59002011
SALV	Salv.by Xt.	WHICHCOTE	1702	58001009
SALV	Salv.by Xt.	SEAGRAVE	1737	46003016
SALV	Salv.by Xt.	BUNDY	1740	46004022
SALV	Salv.by Xt.	MALTUS	1762	43007021
SALV	Salv.by Xt.	CHANDLER	1769	47004012
SALV	Salv.by Xt.	WILSON	1781	57001015
SALV	Salv.f. J.& G.	SHIRLEY	1762	47010034
SALV	Salv.f.div.m.	BOURN	1760	48007024
SALV	Salv.faith al.	WARBURTON	1767	43022012
SALV	Salv.how att.	PAYNE	1698	47016030
SALV	Salv.how att.	HOPKINS	1708	47016030
SALV	Salv.how att.	JORTIN	1774	47016030
SALV	Salv.in Xt.	RELLY	1760	23042006
SALV	Salv.th. Jes.	DAVIES	1766	46003026
SALV	Salv.thr. Xt.	LORIMER	1713	47004012
SALV	Salv.thro' F.	BEVERIDGE	1720	53002012

INDEXES TO THIRD VOLUME: E: KEYWORD-IN-CONTEXT INDEX OF OTHER SUBJECTS OR OCCASIONS

Keyword	In its Context	Author	Year	BkChpVrs
SALV	Salv.to Sinn.	ERSKINE	1764	47014026
SALV	Terms Salv.	IBBOT	1726	48008018
SALV	Work. Salv.	CONANT	1698	53002012
SALV	Work. Salv.	SHERLOCK	1712	53002012
SALV	Work. Salv.	BREKELL	1765	53002012
SALV	Xt.gr. Salv.	BURNET	1747	61002003
SALVAT	Eter. Salvat.	SYNGE	1714	43019016
SALVAT	Eter. Salvat.	STEWARD	1734	57001015
SALVAT	Eter. Salvat.	HOLDEN	1755	57001015
SALVAT	Eter. Salvat.	LOVEDER	1756	57001016
SALVAT	Eter. Salvat.	PEARSE	1763	57001016
SALVAT	Free. Salvat.	PENTYCROSS	1781	48004005
SALVAT	Gosp. Salvat.	PARSON	1676	47016031
SALVAT	Gosp. Salvat.	PIERCE	1686	47016031
SALVAT	Gosp. Salvat.	MARCH	1699	61002003
SALVAT	Gosp. Salvat.	NEWCOME	1719	61002003
SALVAT	Gosp. Salvat.	SHARP	1729	47016031
SALVAT	Gosp. Salvat.	ROGERS	1735	61002003
SALVAT	Gosp. Salvat.	DAVIES	1754	53002012
SALVAT	Gosp. Salvat.	WALKER	1763	61002003
SALVAT	M's. Salvat.	LITTLETON	1680	57002004
SALVAT	Salvat.by Xt.	SHERLOCK	1772	57001015
SALVAT	Xn. Salvat.	LANGHORNE	1773	61002003
SALVAT	Xt's. Salvat.	NEWTON	1760	57001015
SALVATION	Salvation.	PARSONS	1770	47004012
SALVATION	Salvation.	SIMPSON	1774	48003023
SALVATION	Salvation.	HUTCHINS	1782	52002008
SAM	Sam. Vic.	JENKINS	1779	07015015
SAM	Sam.of Rel.	STENNETT	1769	49012013
SAM	Schism. Sam.	WARREN	1739	46004009
SAM	Wom. Sam.	LEWIS	1720	46004009
SAM	Wom. Sam.	CENNICK	1762	46004010
SAMAR	Good Samar.	BRAGGE	1702	45010030
SAMAR	Good Samar.	HOADLY	1755	45010037
SAMAR	Good Samar.	DODD	1757	45010037
SAMAR	Good Samar.	STEBBING	1760	45010037
SAMAR	Good Samar.	BOURN	1764	45010025
SAMAR	Good Samar.	BULKLEY	1771	45010036
SAMAR	Good Samar.	SHERLOCK	1772	45010029
SAMAR	Good Samar.	JORTIN	1774	45010030
SAMAR	Good Samar.	SANDWICH	1774	45010037
SAMAR	Good Samar.	PYLE	1777	45010029
SAMAR	Good Samar.	SMITH	1777	45010036
SAMAR	Good Samar.	BROUGHTON	1778	45010029
SAME	Ev.dut.same	CLAGETT	1704	21003015
SAME	Res.same B.	FELTON	1725	49015023
SAME	Res.same B.	JOHNSON	1733	49015036
SAME	Res.same B.	WHITFIELD	1751	49015035
SAME	Times same	SOUTH	1744	21007010
SANC	Sanc. Xt's. L.	MACE	1751	44008035
SANC	Sanc.of Gos.	HORBERRY	1774	43010028
SANCT	Gosp. Sanct.	CARDALE	1740	02020024
SANCT	H. Sp. Sanct.	FARMER	1756	46014026
SANCT	Red.& Sanct.	SHERLOCK	1772	52002018
SANCT	Sanct. Apost.	STERNE	1769	43011006
SANCT	Sanct. Rod.	FARMER	1756	19094012
SANCT	Sanct. Xn. L.	SKELTON	1754	43025046
SANCT	Sanct.of Sab.	LAVINGTON	1743	05005012
SANCT	Xn. Sanct.	BRAILSFORD	1776	05030015
SANCTIFICAT	Sanctificat.	EDWARDS	1726	55004003
SANCTIFICAT	Sanctificat.	BOWMAN	1764	52002010
SANCTIFICAT	Sanctificat.	ELLIOTT	1764	61010010
SANCTIFICAT	Sanctificat.	CLEMENT	1774	55005023
SANCTIFICAT	Sanctificat.	JOHNSON	1776	55005023
SAPH	Ann& Saph.	BULKLEY	1771	47005003
SAT	Sat. Policy.	GLANVILLE	1681	50002011
SAT	Sat. Pow.b.	ERSKINE	1764	45022031
SAT	Sat. Tempt.	FROYSELL	1678	50002011
SAT	Sat.transf.to	PARKHURST	1707	50011014
SAT	Sat.transf.to	SOUTH	1724	50011014
SATAN	Fall. Satan.	WARBURTON	1767	43004024
SATE	Fut. Sate.	RANDOLPH	1755	21012014
SATE	Sate of Rel.	LAW	1745	47017030
SATISF	Satisf.of Xt.	BUESDELL	1700	65002002
SATISF	Satisf.of Xt.	SHEPHEARD	1748	57002006
SATISF	Xt's. Satisf.	FLAVEL	1673	51003010
SATISF	Xt's. Satisf.	POOL	1676	54001020
SATISF	Xt's. Satisf.	MAUDUIT	1704	52005002
SATISF	Xt's. Satisf.	PEARSON	1718	54001014
SATISF	Xt's. Satisf.	LEEKE	1735	51002021
SATISF	Xt's. Satisf.	BROWNE	1749	47020028
SATISF	Xt's. Satisf.	BROWNE	1749	48003026
SATISF	Xt's Satisf.	NORRIS	1728	43003017
SATISFAC	Xt's. Satisfac	BEVERIDGE	1720	65002001
SATISFAC	Xt's Satisfac.	CREYGHTON	1720	52001007
SATYR	Satyr. Sland.	WILDER	1729	20010018
SATYR	Satyr. Sland.	TOTTIE	1775	20010018
SAV	A bleed. Sav.	DYER	1676	49005007
SAV	Div.of Sav.	SCOTT	1700	46001014
SAV	G.in Xt. Sav.	WATTS	1753	23045022
SAV	Num.of sav.	PYLE	1777	45013023
SAV	Salt los. Sav.	BLAIR	1740	43005012
SAV	Sav. Appear.	ERSKINE	1664	22002008
SAV	Sav. Bless.	ERSKINE	1764	36002019
SAV	Sav. Eloque.	NEWTON	1782	45002046
SAV	Sav. Fai.diff.	COLE	1690	52001019
SAV	Sav. Faith.	MANTON	1708	63001009
SAV	Sav. Faith.	GROVE	1747	48001016
SAV	Sav. Faith.	FAWCETT	1749	46020030
SAV	Sav. Faith.	WELCH	1752	61011001
SAV	Sav. Grace.	LORTIE	1720	52002005
SAV	Sav. Grace.	PIKE	1758	02033019
SAV	Sav. Interc.	OGDEN	1770	23054007
SAV	Sav. Know.	LEIGHTONHOUSE	1697	19086011
SAV	Sav. Know.	MARSHAL	1750	19086011
SAV	Sav. Knowl.	WARREN	1739	46017003
SAV	Sav. Knowl.	SNAPE	1745	46017003
SAV	Sav. Light.	ERSKINE	1764	46014006
SAV	Sav. Serpent.	WILLIAMS	1664	46003014
SAV	Sav.ex.teac.	LELAND	1769	46007046
SAV	Sav.priv.life	NEWTON	1782	45002051
SAV	Unseen Sav.	HAYWARD	1758	63001008

Keyword	In its Context	Author	Year	BkChpVrs	Keyword	In its Context	Author	Year	BkChpVrs
SAV	Xt.m. Sav.	VEAL	1703	19089019	SCORN	Ch.of Scorn.	STRAIGHT	1741	45006025
SAV	Xt.our Sav.	WELCH	1752	23062001	SCORNER	Scorner.	KEARNY	17--	20014006
SAV	Xt.our Sav.	DAVIS	1756	61009026	SCOT	O.30. J. Scot.	ANONYMOUS	1720	21003004
SAV	Xt.sav. Tem.	GILL	1773	43008025	SCOTCH	Scotch. Cov.	WREN	1662	19044018
SAV.'S	Sav.'s Doctr.	ORR	1739	46007046	SCOTL	Ch.of Scotl.	CARLYLE	1776	19048012
SAV.'S	Sav.'s Pray.	MACGILL	1779	46017020	SCRIBE	Scribe instr.	SOUTH	1727	43013052
SAV.'S	Sav.'s Xter.	DUCHAL	1753	46008046	SCRIBES	Scribes&c.	HORNECK	1706	43005020
SAVE	Xt.ab.to save	HOPKINS	1710	61007025	SCRIP	Diff.of Scrip.	NEWTON	1782	63003016
SAVED	Few saved.	SCOUGAL	1726	45013023	SCRIP	Div.of Scrip.	PINDAR	1728	53003016
SAVING	Saving Faith	MANTON	1708	61010039	SCRIP	Scrip.& Tra.	STILLINGFLEET	1707	54002006
SAVIOUR	G. Saviour.	KIMBER	1756	19050015	SCRIP	Scrip. Evid.	CLARKE	1735	45016031
SAVIOUR	Xt.a Saviour.	BEVERIDGE	1720	46006037	SCRIP	Scrip. Hist.	GIBSON	1761	64001016
SAVIOUR	Xt.a Saviour.	BEVERIDGE	1729	46005017	SCRIP	Scrip. Proph.	RAWLINS	1761	69019010
SAVIOUR	Xt.t. Saviour	COLE	1692	45001077	SCRIP	The Scrip.	HOPKINS	1708	64001019
SAVIOUR	Xt.t. Saviour	BOSTON	1753	65004014	SCRIPT	Dark Script.	PARKHURST	1706	47013027
SAVR	Exalt. Savr.	MARRYATT	1719	46020028	SCRIPT	Script.& Tr.	WRIGHT	1735	52002020
SAVR'S	Savr's.th.&c.	LARDNER	1760	46019028	SCRIPT	Script. Diff.	SHERLOCK	1772	47015001
SAVR'S	Savr's Disc.	NEWTON	1782	46004007	SCRIPT	Script. Xty.	WESTLEY	1746	47004031
SAY	2 Say.of Xt.	FLAVEL	1673	46019027	SCRIPT	Study script.	BOSTON	1773	23034016
SAY	5 Say.of Xt.	FLAVEL	1673	46019028	SCRIPTURES	Scriptures.	WATSON	1676	05017019
SAY	6 Say.of Xt.	FLAVEL	1673	46019030	SCRIPTURES	Scriptures.	DORRINGTON	1703	19019010
SC	Ev.o. T.n.sc.	SMYTH	1717	58001010	SCRIPTURES	Scriptures.	DUKE	1714	19019007
SC	Use o. Sc. Ex.	LLOYD	1765	53003017	SCRIPTURES	Scriptures.	BOSTON	1773	58003016
SCAND	Scand.&off.	BRADBURY	1723	43018007	SCRUP	Consc.scrup.	CALAMY	1683	45011041
SCANDAL	Giv. Scandal	WESTON	1747	44009042	SCRUP	Consc.scrup.	SOUTH	1727	45011035
SCANDAL	Scandal.	BOURDALOUE	1776	43011004	SCRUP	Rel. Scrup.	SHERLOCK	1772	19088015
SCANDAL	Tak. Scandal	WESTON	1747	44009043	SE	Se.sorts Xns.	WAPLE	1720	65002012
SCANDAL	Woe scandal	BEVERLEY	1683	43018007	SEA	R. Sea, X's bl	WILLISON	1761	02014015
SCEPT	Pro.& Scept.	BARNES	1752	19097001	SEA	Sea dan.& D.	RYTHER	1674	47027018
SCEPT	Scept. Comp.	COLE	1761	20019027	SEA	Sea.del.con.	BRADBURY	1772	05032036
SCEPT	Scept. Comp.	SHERLOCK	1772	20019027	SEACH	Seach. S. S.	CRAIG	1775	47017011
SCEPTICISM	Scepticism.	ACTON	1714	24008008	SEAL	Seal of Spir.	NICOLSON	1661	22008006
SCEPTICISM	Scepticism.	HORBERRY	1774	58003007	SEAL	Seal Adopt.	USHER	1678	48008015
SCH	Ben.of Sch.	ANONYMOUS	1780	45014014	SEAL	Seal Fo.o. G.	EVANSON	1773	58002019
SCH	Erect. Sch.	MARCH	1682	19034011	SEALED	Bel.sealed.	WILSON	1735	50001022
SCH	V. Sch.	THOMAS	1728	19034011	SEALED	Belie.sealed.	WILSON	1735	52001013
SCH	V.sch.& H.	COMBE	1708	20014034	SEAM	Disap. Seam.	FLAVEL	1673	45005005
SCH	Xn. Sch.con.	BOURN	1760	47010042	SEAM	Seam.farw.	FLAVEL	1673	47021005
SCHISM	Pres. Schism.	WILLIAMS	1716	45018009	SEAM	Seam.return.	FLAVEL	1673	05033019
SCHISM	Schism.	PIERCE	1679	56003006	SEAM	Succ. Seam.	FLAVEL	1673	05008017
SCHISM	Schism.	FOSTER	1732	49012025	SEAM'S	Seam's call.	BARNETT	1712	19107023
SCHISM	Schism. Sam.	WARREN	1739	46004009	SEAM'S	Seam's pres.	FLAVEL	1673	19139009
SCHISM	The Schism.	CULVERWELL	1661	49003004	SEAR	Xt.sear. H.	NEWLIN	1728	46002024
SCIENCE	Science.	DOWNES	1761	64001005	SEARCH	Search. S. S.	PATRICK	1685	64003016
SCOFF	Scoff. Relig.	GLANVILL	1681	64003003	SEARCH	Search. S. S.	WAPLE	1729	46005039
SCOFF	Scoff. Relig.	HAMMOND	1684	64003003	SEARCH	Search. S. S.	WHITFIELD	1739	46005039
SCOFF	Scoff. Relig.	ANONYMOUS	1716	64003003	SEARCH	Search. S. S.	AMORY	1775	46005039
SCOFF	Scoff. Relig.	FOSTER	1732	64003003	SEAS	God.ov. Seas	STUBBS	1701	19135006
SCOFF	Scoff. Relig.	TILLOTSON	1735	64003003	SEAS	Prov. Seas.	MOIR	1759	19065005
SCOFF	Scoff. Relig.	COYTE	1761	64003003	SEAS	Seas. Xn. Ex.	NICOLSON	1661	61003013
SCOFF	Scoff. Relig.	CARR	1777	20014009	SEAS	Tim.& Seas.	HORTON	1679	47001007
SCOFF	Scoff.at Rel.	SUTTON	1754	64003003	SEAS	Wor.in Seas.	CHEESE	1668	61011035
SCOPE	Scope of S. S.	BOSTON	1773	58001013	SEAS	Words seas.	CHEESE	1668	44014008
SCOPE	Scope of Ser.	HORNECK	1706	43005001	SEAS	Work& Seas.	TILLOTSON	1735	46009004
SCOPE	Scope of Ser.	BLAIR	1740	43005001	SEAS	Work& Seas.	SOUTH	1744	46009004
SCOPE	Scope. Xn. R.	MONRO	1693	43005020	SEC	Believ. Sec.	WELCH	1752	46010027

Keyword	In its Context	Author	Year	BkChpVrs
SEC	Fa.&sec. W.	JENNINGS	1757	52006018
SEC	Fa.&sec. W.	LANGHORNE	1773	52006018
SEC	Prof.no Sec.	BULKLEY	1752	43003009
SEC	Prot.p.n.sec.	FRANCIS	1773	48008031
SEC	Rel.sec.f.w.	ROE	1766	43006033
SEC	Sec.of w. Gr.	TAYLOR	1719	23065008
SEC	Van.of Sec.	NEWMAN	1760	19030006
SEC	Wick. Sec.g.	JORTIN	1774	45012020
SECOND	Second birth	STANHOPE	1705	46001012
SECR	Secr.things.	JORTIN	1774	05029029
SECRECY	No Secrecy.	DELAUNE	1728	20005021
SECRET	Secret Faults	SEDGEWICK	1660	19019012
SECRET	Secret Faults	REYNER	1745	19019012
SECRET	Secret Pray.	LEE	1676	43006006
SECRET	Secret Pray.	BLACKALL	1723	43006005
SECRET	Secret Pray.	BLAIR	1740	43006005
SECRET	Secret Pray.	BLAIR	1740	43006006
SECRET	Secret Pray.	GROVE	1747	43006006
SECRET	Secret Pray.	MORRIS	1757	43006006
SECRET	Secret Pray.	ORTON	1769	43006006
SECUL	Hier.secul.	PIERCE	1671	63002013
SECUR	Xn's. Secur.	NEWMAN	1760	46014019
SECURE	Piety secure.	BRADY	1730	20012021
SED	Cav.ag. Sed.	STANFAST	1660	43024004
SED	Xty.not sed.	SAURIN	1775	45023005
SEDUCERS	Ag. Seducers	HILLIARD	1717	54002004
SEDUCERS	Seducers.	HORTON	1679	51001008
SEE	Des.see. Xt.	WILCOX	1757	46012020
SEE	See the Ld.	GALE	1726	61012014
SEED	Mustard seed	BRAGGE	1704	43013031
SEED	Mustard seed	BOURN	1763	43013031
SEED	Mustard seed	BULKLEY	1771	43013031
SEED	Seed of Abr.	HARRIS	1724	01022018
SEED	Seed of Wo.	HARRIS	1724	01003015
SEEDSP	Seedsp.itself.	DODD	1757	44004026
SEEK	Seek. God.	BEVERIDGE	1720	23055006
SEEK	Seek. K.o. G.	FARINDON	1672	43006033
SEEK	Seek. K.o. G.	BURTON	1684	43006033
SEEK	Seek. K.o. G.	DUNLOP	1722	43006033
SEEK	Seek. K.o. G.	CLARKE	1732	43006033
SEEK	Seek. K.o. G.	JONES	1741	43006033
SEEK	Seek. Xt. D.	GUYSE	1729	20008017
SEEK	Seek.a.m's S.	WALLIS	1740	49010032
SEEK	Seek.th.abo.	SCATTERGOOD	1723	54003001
SEEK	Seek.th.abo.	SNAPE	1745	54003001
SEEK	Xt.seek. Fr.	CLARKSON	1696	45013006
SELF	Ag. Self-dec.	BOURN	1777	49003018
SELF	Ag. Self-love	BUTLER	1716	53002021
SELF	Dai. Self-ex.	WARREN	1710	19004004
SELF	Haz. Self- C.	JENKINS	1779	12008013
SELF	Moses's self.	THEED	1712	61011024
SELF	Self conceit.	ABERNETHY	1748	43006022
SELF	Self conceit.	BOURN	1777	20026012
SELF	Self ex.of G.	WHITAKER	1674	19018046
SELF	Self. Den.& Mo	HORNECK	1706	43005029
SELF	Self. Den.& Mo	BLACKALL	1723	43005029
SELF	Self. Den.& Mo	BLAIR	1740	43005029
SELF	Self. Govern.	IBBOT	1726	20016032
SELF	Self. Govern.	PIERCE	1731	20016032
SELF	Self.de.r.m.	BRAILSFORD	1776	51006007
SELF	Self Denial.	SMITH	1675	19131002
SELF	Self Govern.	ABERNETHY	1751	20025028
SELF	Self- Denial.	HAVETT	1703	43016024
SELF	Self- Denial.	WHITBY	1703	43016024
SELF	Self- Denial.	BRADY	1704	43016021
SELF	Self- Denial.	YOUNG	1706	43016024
SELF	Self- Denial.	EDWARDS	1726	43016024
SELF	Self- Denial.	TILLOTSON	1735	43016024
SELF	Self- Denial.	CARLETON	1736	43016026
SELF	Self- Denial.	STRAIGHT	1741	43016024
SELF	Self- Denial.	ABERNETHY	1748	43016021
SELF	Self- Denial.	WEST	1762	43016024
SELF	Self- Denial.	YOUNG	1764	43016024
SELF	Self- Denial.	WILLIAMS	1770	43016024
SELF	Self- Enq.	WHITFIELD	1771	04023023
SELF	Self- Know.	LANGHORNE	1773	19004004
SELF	Self-conceit.	CALAMY	1726	48012016
SELF	Self-conceit.	NEWTON	1736	48012016
SELF	Self-conceit.	ERSKINE	1764	20030012
SELF	Self-confid.	HENRY	1726	20015032
SELF	Self-confid.	MARTIN	1760	20028026
SELF	Self-confid.	ADEY	1760	49010012
SELF	Self-convict.	BURNET	1747	01042021
SELF	Self-de.t. G.	AMORY	1742	50004005
SELF	Self-deceit	BUTLER	1749	10012007
SELF	Self-deceit.	HORT	1738	62001022
SELF	Self-ded. G.	CHANDLER	1769	48012001
SELF	Self-den. M.	NEEDLER	1677	43005029
SELF	Self-den. M.	MOSS	1732	43005029
SELF	Self-den. M.	WESTON	1747	43005029
SELF	Self-denial	REYNOLDS	1679	43016024
SELF	Self-denial	MANTON	1689	43016024
SELF	Self-denial	SCOTT	1700	43016024
SELF	Self-denial	LACY	1720	43016024
SELF	Self-denial	JEPHSON	1742	43016024
SELF	Self-denial	SNAPE	1745	43016024
SELF	Self-denial	POTTER	1753	43016024
SELF	Self-denial	JORTIN	1774	43016024
SELF	Self-denial.	CHILLINGWORTH	1664	45009023
SELF	Self-denial.	GELL	1676	45009023
SELF	Self-denial.	BAXTER	1707	45009023
SELF	Self-denial.	COCK	1710	44008034
SELF	Self-denial.	WHITFIELD	1739	45009023
SELF	Self-denial.	ATTERBURY	1743	45009023
SELF	Self-denial.	HEYLYN	1749	45009023
SELF	Self-denial.	BOSTON	1753	45009023
SELF	Self-denial.	SECKER	1770	44008034
SELF	Self-denial.	WESTLEY	1771	45009023
SELF	Self-denial.	WILSON	1781	49015032
SELF	Self-denial& C	HOWARD	1710	43016024
SELF	Self-esteem.	STRAIGHT	1741	48012003
SELF	Self-exam.	LITTLETON	1680	49011028

Keyword	In its Context	Author	Year	BkChpVrs
SELF	Self-exam.	CHARNOCK	1684	50013005
SELF	Self-exam.	MATHER	1701	50013005
SELF	Self-exam.	HOLE	1717	50013005
SELF	Self-exam.	WAPLE	1718	50013005
SELF	Self-exam.	NEWLIN	1728	49011028
SELF	Self-exam.	M'GEORGE	1729	49011028
SELF	Self-exam.	WARREN	1748	50013005
SELF	Self-exam.	BALGUY	1750	50013005
SELF	Self-exam.	STERNE	1760	23001003
SELF	Self-exam.	BARKER	1763	50013005
SELF	Self-exam.	SECKER	1770	25003040
SELF	Self-exam.	ATKINSON	1775	51006004
SELF	Self-exam.	NEWSON	1781	25003040
SELF	Self-govern.	DUCHAL	1765	49006012
SELF	Self-inter.	STONE	1771	18001009
SELF	Self-know.	SWIFTH	1745	12008013
SELF	Self-know.	STERNE	1760	10012007
SELF	Self-know.	WILLIAMS	1774	19019012
SELF	Self-knowl.	WHARTON	1728	48012003
SELF	Self-lo.& B.	WEBSTER	1748	58003001
SELF	Self-love.	BARROW	1716	58003002
SELF	Self-love.	WATERLAND	1742	58003001
SELF	Self-love.	COCKMAN	1750	58003002
SELF	Self-love.	FREE	1750	65004019
SELF	Self-love.	COWPER	1751	58003002
SELF	Self-love.	WHITTY	1772	43022039
SELF	Self-love.	JORTIN	1774	58003002
SELF	Self-love&c.	CONANT	1703	49013005
SELF	Self-reflect.	CONANT	1699	25003040
SELF	Self-rever.	DUCHAL	1765	49003017
SELF	Self-suffic.	ECCLES	1755	43019022
SELF	Sin Self-con.	DODD	1755	45019022
SELF	Vic.self-lo.	SHERLOCK	1702	58003001
SELF	Xt's.self.exis	ROMAINE	1755	46001014
SELFISHN	Selfishn.&c.	WAPLE	1720	46015005
SEN	Ag.sen. Lusts	WISE	1717	63002011
SEN	Ag.sen. Lusts	WESTON	1747	63002011
SEN	Sen. Rev.gr.	GREEN	1758	49010012
SEN	Sen.af. Abs.	HOLE	1717	65002001
SENS	Sens. Mortif.	ATKINSON	1775	54003005
SENS	Sens.gr. Sep.	LONG	1677	68000019
SENSE	Sense of Suff.	HAVETT	1703	43026039
SENSUAL	Sensual Plea.	TOTTIE	1775	58003004
SENT	Delay Sent.	LENG	1699	21008011
SENT	Malev. Sent.	HEY	1774	52004031
SEP	Mis.of Sep.	STILLINGFLEET	1707	53003016
SEP	Sens.gr. Sep.	LONG	1677	68000019
SEP	Sep.st.happy	MARCH	1699	45023043
SEP	Soul's sep.st.	ADEY	1755	53001023
SEP	St.sep. Souls.	WHEATLY	1746	45016022
SEPAR	Separ. St.	ANONYMOUS	1660	21011009
SEPAR	Separ. St.	DORRINGTON	1703	69014013
SEPAR	Separ. St.	STURMY	1716	21011008
SEPAR	Separ. St.	GUYSE	1757	21012007
SEPAR	Separ. State.	LUCAS	1722	45016022
SEPARAT	Of Separat.	STANHOPE	1710	46006066

Keyword	In its Context	Author	Year	BkChpVrs
SEPT	Sept.27.	PELLING	1685	63003003
SEPTUAG	Septuag. S.	STANHOPE	1715	49009024
SEPTUAG	Septuag. S.	HOLE	1716	49009024
SEPTUAG	Septuag. S.	READING	1728	01001001
SER	Conf.w.ser.	MAY	1757	44012034
SER	G.only b.ser.	BEVERIDGE	1720	43004010
SER	G's.ser. Free.	DAVIS	1756	45001074
SER	Prof.by Ser.	WILSON	1781	45008018
SER	Rel.ser.aff.	DYER	1758	50005010
SER	Reveng. Ser.	STEBBING	1760	43018023
SER	Scope of Ser.	HORNECK	1706	43005001
SER	Scope of Ser.	BLAIR	1740	43005001
SER	Ser. Refl.s. D	WHITTY	1772	24008006
SER	Ser.con.o. D.	LOCKIER	1671	23057001
SER	Ser.exam.	BOURN	1764	43025014
SER	Ser.m.to Go.	FOTHERGILL	1765	57004008
SER	Unmer. Ser.	DODD	1757	43018035
SER	Xt. Fath.ser.	BRODHURST	1733	43012018
SERIOUS	Serious Piety	EVANS	1725	13028009
SERIOUSNESS	Seriousness.	HUNTER	1774	21002002
SERJ	At Serj. Inn.	PARKER	1750	45016031
SERM	Hear. Serm.	SMALRIDGE	1724	45008018
SERM	Hear. Serm.	WARREN	1739	45008018
SERM	Hear. Serm.	WHITFIELD	1739	45008018
SERM	Hear. Serm.	SECKER	1770	45008018
SERM	Hear Serm.	MOSS	1732	45008018
SERM	Hear Serm.	MARSHALL	1750	45008018
SERM	Xt's Serm.	HUNT	1748	43005001
SERP	Of the Serp.	BURNET	1747	01003013
SERP	Serp. Temp.	CHANDLER	1769	01003014
SERPENT	Sav. Serpent.	WILLIAMS	1664	46003014
SERV	Duty of Serv.	FLEETWOOD	1737	54003022
SERV	Duty of Serv.	DELANY	1747	52006005
SERV	Duty of Serv.	ANONYMOUS	1776	63002018
SERV	Good Serv.	EDWARDS	1726	45012043
SERV	Mast.& Serv.	JANEWAY	1676	52006005
SERV	No serv.t. M.	FAWCETT	1749	43006024
SERV	Reas.serv.	FAWCETT	1749	48012001
SERV	Rel.rea.serv.	ASHTON	1770	32007006
SERV	Serv. G.	ANONYMOUS	1754	06024024
SERV	Serv. G.& M.	BLACKALL	1723	43006024
SERV	Serv. G.& M.	BLAIR	1740	43006024
SERV	Unpr. Serv.	BRAGGE	1704	45017007
SERV	Unpr. Serv.	SCATTERGOOD	1723	45017010
SERV	Unpr. Serv.	HOADLY	1754	45017010
SERV	Unpr. Serv.	DODD	1757	45017010
SERV	Unpr. Serv.	BULKLEY	1771	45017010
SERV	Unpr. Serv.	TUCKER	1776	45017010
SERVANTS	G's. Servants	SHEPHEARD	1748	48006016
SET	set forth S. S.	ROBINSON	1740	46006068
SETT	Sett.aff.abo.	LLOYD	1765	54003002
SETTL	Settl. Min.	TOLLER	1772	45013030
SEV	Sev.of G. L.	HOPKINS	1708	21008011
SEV	Sev Dispen.	JEFFERY	1710	43008011
SEV	Sub.sev.s.	HARRISON	1691	23045024
SEVER	G's sever.&c.	S.	1695	26021013

Keyword	In its Context	Author	Year	BkChpVrs
SEVERITY	G's. Severity	SAURIN	1775	61012029
SEX	Fair Sex.	FOURDYCE	1776	46011005
SEX	Imp.of Sex.	FORDYCE	1767	57002008
SEXAG	Sexag. S.	READING	1724	01003022
SEXAG	Sexag. S.	READING	1728	01003001
SEXAG	Sexag. S.	READING	1730	01002015
SEXAG	Sexag. S.	READING	1730	01006001
SEXAGES	Sexages. S.	STANHOPE	1715	50011019
SEXAGES	Sexages. S.	HOLE	1716	50011019
SEXAGESIMA	Sexagesima.	STANHOPE	1715	45008004
SEXAGESIMA	Sexagesima.	HOLE	1716	45008004
SH	Fold Xt's Sh.	SMITH	1726	21001007
SH	H. Y.sh.o. H.	WATTS	1753	44010021
SH	Lord sh.o. Xt	WRIGHT	1724	48014009
SH	Sin.sh.&h.l.	PIERCE	1679	48006021
SH	Sin.sh.&h.l.	TILLOTSON	1735	48006021
SH	Xn's.sh.act.f.	CONANT	1699	67000005
SHAM	Sham. Sin.	BATTY	1739	48006021
SHAME	False Shame.	LAWSON	1764	45009026
SHAME	Shame wick.	DUNLOP	1722	27012002
SHAMEF	Sin.shamef.	DUKE	1714	48006021
SHAMELESSN	Shamelessn.	SOUTH	1727	24006015
SHEEP	Lost Sheep.	BRAGGE	1704	45015004
SHEEP	Lost Sheep.	HOLE	1716	45015001
SHEEP	Lost Sheep.	DODD	1757	45015003
SHEEP	Lost Sheep.	STEBBING	1760	45015004
SHEEP	Lost Sheep.	BULKLEY	1771	45015007
SHEEP	Lost Sheep.	ROWLAND	1778	45015005
SHEP	Shep.of o. S.	WALKER	1765	63002025
SHEP	T. Shep.b. K.	LANEY	1662	63002025
SHEP	Xt.our Shep.	DODDERIDGE	1736	23040011
SHEP	Xt.our Shep.	HILL	1755	23040011
SHEP	Xt.our Shep.	WILCOX	1757	23040011
SHEPH	Caref. Sheph.	BOURN	1763	45015003
SHEPH	Xt.g. Sheph.	PYLE	1777	46010010
SHEPHERD	G. Shepherd	BRODHURST	1733	19023003
SHILOH	The Shiloh.	HARRIS	1724	01049010
SHIMEI'S	Shimei's Xr.	STERNE	1760	10019021
SHINE	Lig.m.shine.	BAXTER	1707	43005016
SHIP	T. Jul. Ship.	RAMSAY	1681	47027015
SHIPWRECKS	Shipwrecks.	FRANKLIN	1751	47028001
SHOR	Shor.of time	FULLER	1700	49007029
SHOR	Shor.of H. L.	TIDCOMBE	1757	10019034
SHORT	G.short d.	ANONYMOUS	1745	19089045
SHORT	Short of L.	STEELE	1776	19014001
SHORT	Short.h. Life	WARREN	1748	64001014
SHORT	Short.of life.	CONANT	1698	19090010
SHORT	Short.of life.	WHALEY	1695	62004014
SHORT	Short.of L.	WARREN	1748	19039004
SHORT	Short.of L.	ADEY	1755	18014001
SHORT	Short.of L.	STERNE	1760	18014002
SHORT	Short.of L.	BRACKENRIDGE	1764	19039005
SHRO	Shro.& East.	HALES	1673	45016025
SHROVE	Shrove-sun.	SEPPENS	1679	49009027
SHUL	Call to Shul.	TANNER	1674	22006013
SI	Conc. Si.im.	HOLLAND	1753	18034022

Keyword	In its Context	Author	Year	BkChpVrs
SI	Fol mock.at Si	STILLINGFLEET	1707	20014009
SI	Fol mock.at Si	ROGERS	1730	20014009
SI	Fol mock.at Si	TRAPP	1752	20014009
SI	Fol.mock.at Si	DAVIES	1720	20014009
SI	Fol.mock.at Si	CLARKE	1734	20014009
SI	Si.& M.b. N.	ENGLAND	1700	52002001
SI	Si. H.groun.	ASHTON	1770	19119123
SI	Xt.si.r.h. G.	FLAVEL	1673	61001003
SIC	Vis.sic.	POLE	1677	18033023
SICK	A. Gen. Sick.	ANONYMOUS	1712	19091005
SICK	Dut.sick.	SECKER	1779	23038001
SICK	For sick.	BLADEN	1695	50005001
SICK	Rec.f. Sick.	PETERS	1776	46005014
SICK	Sick.& Rec.	ROGERS	1691	19030003
SICK	Sick.& Rec.	STANHOPE	1709	19030003
SICK	Sick Cattle.	WIND	1748	19136001
SIG	Strange Sig.	WILLISON	1761	45005026
SIGHT	Hear.& Sight	MARKLAND	1729	44007037
SIGN	A sign Wisd.	HORTON	1679	49001022
SIGN	Ob.sign l. G.	SHERLOCK	1719	65005003
SIGN	Sign of Jonas	JORTIN	1774	43012039
SIGN	Xt. Sign.s.ag.	BRACKENRIDGE	1764	45002034
SIGNS	Signs of love.	BATES	1700	65005002
SIM	Sim. Depart.	MOIR	1759	45002029
SIM	Sim. Speech.	HORNECK	1706	43005037
SIM	Sim. Speech.	BLAIR	1740	43005034
SIM	Sim. Speech.	GOUGH	1751	43005037
SIM	St. Sim.& J.	STANHOPE	1715	46015017
SIM	St. Sim.& J.	HOLE	1716	46015017
SIM	St. Sim.& Ju.	JACKSON	1673	68000004
SIM	St. Sim.& Ju.	TURNER	1678	58001007
SIM	St. Sim.& Ju.	ATTERBURY	1730	45016031
SIM	St. Sim.& St.	STANHOPE	1715	68000001
SIM	St. Sim.& St.	HOLE	1716	68000001
SIMON	Simon Phar.	VENN	1759	45007036
SIMONY	Simony.	MARSTON	1699	20020025
SIMP	Simp.of Xy.	TAYLOR	1719	50011013
SIMP	Xn. Simp.	BRAGGE	1713	50001012
SIMPLICITY	Simplicity.	HAMMOND	1684	20001022
SIMPLICITY	Simplicity.	STILLINGFLEET	1707	43010016
SIMPLICITY	Simplicity.	WATERLAND	1742	46001047
SIN	Aggr.of Sin.	CONYBEARE	1757	61010029
SIN	All und. Sin.	WITHERSPOON	1768	48003023
SIN	Cause of Sin.	JEFFERY	1710	21007029
SIN	Censur. Sin.	LUCAS	1710	46008007
SIN	Check. Sin.	GIBBON	1677	51005016
SIN	Conf.of Sin.	NEAL	1757	47003019
SIN	Cons.of Sin.	EVANS	1725	01039009
SIN	Cons.of Sin.	MUSCOTT	1760	48006021
SIN	Contem. Sin.	YOUNG	1706	45022048
SIN	Conv.of Sin.	CHARNOCK	1684	46016008
SIN	D.& D.o. Sin	PAYNE	1698	61003013
SIN	D.& D.o. Sin	WHICHCOTE	1702	61003013
SIN	D.& D.o. Sin	STILLINGFLEET	1707	61003013
SIN	D.& D.o. Sin	TILLOTSON	1735	61003013
SIN	Dan.kn. Sin	TILLOTSON	1735	48001018

Keyword	In its Context	Author	Year	BkChpVrs
SIN	Dea.wag. Sin	PEARSE	1763	48006023
SIN	Dead in Sin.	WAPLE	1720	52002004
SIN	Deceit. Sin.	LLOYD	1765	61003013
SIN	Deceit. Sin.	CRAIG	1775	19036002
SIN	Deceit.o. Sin	LUCAS	1716	52005006
SIN	Deceit.o. Sin.	CLARKE	1736	61003013
SIN	Defin.of Sin.	PYLE	1777	65003004
SIN	Delus.o. Sin.	SMITH	1769	51006007
SIN	Evil of Sin.	HORTON	1679	48006021
SIN	Evil of Sin.	CARLETON	1736	48006023
SIN	Foll.of Sin.	WAPLE	1729	20014024
SIN	Folly of Sin.	BRADY	1730	20001010
SIN	G.hates Sin.	DORRINGTON	1703	20015009
SIN	G's. L.to Sin.	CLARKE	1732	46003016
SIN	Gosp.sin. O.	SUTTON	1718	43007021
SIN	Gosp.sin. O.	ABERNETHY	1748	43007021
SIN	Guilt of Sin.	PYLE	1777	18007020
SIN	Infat.of Sin.	FIDDES	1720	61003013
SIN	Involun. Sin.	DORRINGTON	1703	48007019
SIN	Kn. Sin b. L.	CLARKE	1735	48007007
SIN	Kn. Sin b. L.	VENN	1759	48007009
SIN	Law& Sin.	BERRIMAN	1751	65003004
SIN	Mort Sin&c.	HUBBARD	1757	52006013
SIN	Nat.of Sin.	BATTY	1739	65003004
SIN	Nat.of Sin.	BURNET	1747	48006012
SIN	No ven. Sin.	JENKINS	1675	48006023
SIN	Of Sin.	BATES	1690	01039009
SIN	Of Sin.	WILSON	1781	04032023
SIN	Orig. Sin.	VINK	1676	48006006
SIN	Orig. Sin.	CLARKSON	1696	19051005
SIN	Orig. Sin.	BOEHM	1717	52004022
SIN	Orig. Sin.	DELAUNE	1728	19051005
SIN	Orig. Sin.	RIDGLEY	1725	48005018
SIN	Orig. Sin.	TAYLOR	1725	52002001
SIN	Orig. Sin.	CLARKE	1734	21007029
SIN	Orig. Sin.	HEYLYN	1749	48005018
SIN	Orig. Sin.	MILLER	1749	52002003
SIN	Orig. Sin.	GREEN	1758	49015021
SIN	Orig. Sin.	WESTLEY	1760	01006005
SIN	Orig. Sin.	BOWMAN	1764	18014014
SIN	Orig. Sin.	ELLIOTT	1764	48005019
SIN	Pard.of Sin.	HOPKINS	1710	23043025
SIN	Partak. Sin.	SMITH	1740	43027004
SIN	Poll.of Sin.	REYNOLDS	1679	50007001
SIN	Prevent Sin.	SOUTH	1727	09025032
SIN	Prog. Sin.	YOUNG	1706	19052007
SIN	Reb.for Sin.	T.	1667	23066015
SIN	Rec.of Sin.	WHICHCOTE	1703	61002017
SIN	Reign of Sin.	REYNOLDS	1679	48006012
SIN	Rem.ag.+sin.	DORRINGTON	1703	19119106
SIN	Rep. Sin. Joy	BROUGHTON	1778	45015007
SIN	Roy. Sin.	CROXALL	1738	10012007
SIN	Roy. Sin.	TRAPP	1738	10012007
SIN	Roy. Sin.	ANONYMOUS	1753	10024012
SIN	S. Paul's Sin.	SMITH	1740	46016002
SIN	Sham. Sin.	BATTY	1739	48006021

Keyword	In its Context	Author	Year	BkChpVrs
SIN	Sin ag. H. G.	HARRIS	1718	43012031
SIN	Sin ag. H. G.	SHARP	1729	43012031
SIN	Sin ag. H. G.	MARSHALL	1731	43012031
SIN	Sin ag. H. G.	TILLOTSON	1735	43012031
SIN	Sin ag. H. G.	STEPHENS	1737	43012031
SIN	Sin ag. H. G.	WATERLAND	1742	43012031
SIN	Sin ag. H. G.	GREEN	1747	43012031
SIN	Sin ag. H. G.	HOOLE	1748	43012031
SIN	Sin ag. H. G.	SECKER	1770	43012031
SIN	Sin ag. H. G.	JORTIN	1774	43012031
SIN	Sin ag. H. G.	PEARCE	1779	43012031
SIN	Sin deceitf.	PRIEST	1753	20011018
SIN	Sin dou.b.a.	ORTON	1776	48014023
SIN	Sin exc.sinf.	DUNLOP	1722	48008013
SIN	Sin fatal.	DUNLOP	1722	26018031
SIN	Sin hides G.	LEIGHTON	1746	23059001
SIN	Sin in Bel.	WESTLEY	1771	50005017
SIN	Sin its Pun.	BOYSE	1728	24002019
SIN	Sin of judg.	SIMONS	1743	49004005
SIN	Sin of Anger	STANHOPE	1714	43005020
SIN	Sin of Anger	HOLE	1716	43005020
SIN	Sin of Anger	FELTON	1748	01004005
SIN	Sin of Fraud.	CLARKE	1736	47005003
SIN	Sin un. Dea.	LAMBE	1717	65005016
SIN	Sin whence.	CLARKE	1736	24005004
SIN	Sin.	BOSTON	1773	65003004
SIN	Sin. D.of S.	DUNLOP	1722	23001005
SIN	Sin. Obed. G's	CLAGETT	1704	46007017
SIN	Sin. Obed. G's	ABERNETHY	1748	46007017
SIN	Sin. St. Nat.	RILAND	1775	26033001
SIN	Sin.account.	GLASSE	1781	48006021
SIN	Sin.ag. H. G.	ANONYMOUS	1740	44003028
SIN	Sin.ensl.&c.	NEWLIN	1718	64002019
SIN	Sin.exc.sinf.	DUNLOP	1722	48007013
SIN	Sin.gr. H. G.	WILSON	1781	52004030
SIN	Sin.inexcus.	WITHERSPOON	1768	19130003
SIN	Sin.of infid.	HAMMOND	1684	43010015
SIN	Sin.sh.&h.l.	PIERCE	1679	48006021
SIN	Sin.sh.&h.l.	TILLOTSON	1735	48006021
SIN	Sin.shamef.	DUKE	1714	48006021
SIN	Sin.temp. G.	ADAMS	1716	43004007
SIN	Sin.worse. S.	VEAL	1703	43009012
SIN	Sin& Death.	SOUTH	1744	48006023
SIN	Sin& Death.	CHANDLER	1769	48005012
SIN	Sin& Pu.o. S.	BOYSE	1728	68000006
SIN	Sin Apo. An.	WHEATLY	1746	68000006
SIN	Sin Folly.	MOORE	1716	23030010
SIN	Sin Self-con.	DODD	1755	45019022
SIN	Sinf. Sin.	WALKER	1755	19014002
SIN	Sinf.of Sin.	REYNOLDS	1679	48007009
SIN	Sinf.of Sin.	HILL	1755	48007013
SIN	Slav.of Sin.	WAPLE	1729	46008034
SIN	Slav.of Sin.	MOSS	1737	46008034
SIN	Slav.of Sin.	BATTY	1739	46008034
SIN	Slav.of Sin.	BALGUY	1748	46008034
SIN	Slav.of Sin.	CLEMENT	1774	46008034

Keyword	In its Context	Author	Year	BkChpVrs
SIN	Sorrow f. Sin	WARBURTON	1754	43026026
SIN	Sorrow f. Sin	WILLISON	1761	43026026
SIN	Sorrow f. Sin	CORNWALL	1773	43026026
SIN	Tak.aw. Sin.	SUTTON	1718	46001029
SIN	The Sin&c.	NEWTON	1782	61012001
SIN	Tou st.o. Sin.	FLAVEL	1673	69003017
SIN	Trag.of Sin.	JAY	1689	01011004
SIN	Unc. Sin Da.	CLARKSON	1696	52005008
SIN	Unpard. Sin.	RUSSEL	1746	65005016
SIN	Unprof. Sin.	DORRINGTON	1703	20022008
SIN	Veng.on Sin.	WHICHCOTE	1703	48001024
SIN	Veng.on Sin.	WHICHCOTE	1703	48001027
SIN	Veng.on Sin.	WHICHCOTE	1703	48001029
SIN	W.of Sin h.	DAVIES	1771	47009006
SIN	Wages of Sin	EDWARDS	1775	48006023
SIN	Xt.dy.f. Sin.	CLARKSON	1696	48005008
SINC	Relig. Sinc.	ATTERBURY	1734	50013005
SINC	Sinc. Obed.	LORTIE	1720	19119106
SINC	Sinc. Obed.	JOHNSON	1740	46014023
SINC	Sinc. Penit.	CREYGHTON	1720	45022062
SINC	Sinc. Penit.	BRADY	1730	45022061
SINC	Sinc. Pub.w.	CLAYTON	1776	46004019
SINC	Sinc.acc.f. P.	SIMONS	1743	50008012
SINC	Sinc.in Love	WHITE	1757	48012009
SINC	Sinc.m.o. W.	ROWLAND	1774	63002002
SINCER	Xn. Sincer.	CLAGETT	1720	53001010
SINCER	Xn. Sincer.	FIDDES	1720	53001010
SINCER	Xn. Sincer.	MILLER	1749	53001010
SINCERITY	Sincerity.	LITTLETON	1680	52006024
SINCERITY	Sincerity.	HALLYWELL	1692	46001047
SINCERITY	Sincerity.	HICKMAN	1706	46001047
SINCERITY	Sincerity.	BRADY	1713	48012009
SINCERITY	Sincerity.	SMITH	1719	55005021
SINCERITY	Sincerity.	NEWLIN	1720	19015002
SINCERITY	Sincerity.	PEIRCE	1728	46001046
SINCERITY	Sincerity.	WAPLE	1720	50001012
SINCERITY	Sincerity.	TILLOTSON	1735	46001047
SINCERITY	Sincerity.	FOSTER	1737	46001045
SINCERITY	Sincerity.	EVANS	1737	49005008
SINCERITY	Sincerity.	WHEATLY	1746	46001047
SINF	Sin exc.sinf.	DUNLOP	1722	48008013
SINF	Sin.exc.sinf.	DUNLOP	1722	48007013
SINF	Sinf. Compl.	GODDARD	1781	45009026
SINF	Sinf. Sin.	WALKER	1755	19014002
SINF	Sinf. Sleep.	BADDELLEY	1752	31001006
SINF	Sinf. Thoug.	TAYLOR	1725	01006005
SINF	Sinf.giv.off.	STEPHENS	1737	48014013
SINF	Sinf.of Sin.	REYNOLDS	1679	48007009
SINF	Sinf.of Sin.	HILL	1755	48007013
SINFUL	Sinful Com.	BACON	1760	02023002
SING	Sing. Piety.	WRIGHT	1716	02023002
SINGLE	Single Eye.	MORE	1692	43006022
SINGULA	Rel. Singula.	NORRIS	1728	48012002
SINLESS	Sinless Perf.	WATERLAND	1742	65003009
SINN	Call to Sinn.	DYER	1666	69003020
SINN	Chief Sinn.	CHARNOCK	1699	57001015

Keyword	In its Context	Author	Year	BkChpVrs
SINN	Conv. Sinn.	LITTLETON	1680	26018027
SINN	Conv. Sinn.	WHICHCOTE	1702	26018027
SINN	Destr. Sinn.	SOUTH	1766	19095011
SINN	Diff. Sinn.	CLARKE	1736	68000022
SINN	Dir.to Sinn.	DODDERIDGE	1742	47009006
SINN	Enc.f. Sinn.	ELLIOTT	1759	51002021
SINN	Folly Sinn.	DUNLOP	1722	24002005
SINN	Madn. Sinn.	ORTON	1776	45015017
SINN	Pun.of Sinn.	WHICHCOTE	1698	48001026
SINN	Salv.to Sinn.	ERSKINE	1764	47014026
SINN	Sinn. Arraig.	ANONYMOUS	1668	61010027
SINN	Sinn. Justif.	BRAGGE	1732	51002016
SINN	Sinn.call'd.	HORNE	1778	52005014
SINN	Sinn.disq.	WAPLE	1729	32006006
SINN	Sinn.refuge.	BAINE	1778	61006018
SINN	Sinn.und. C.	CLARKSON	1696	51003010
SINN'S	Sinn's doom.	DAVIES	1771	20029001
SINNER	Conv. Sinner	MEDE	1672	23055007
SINNER	Folly Sinner.	HOPKINS	1710	20014009
SINNER'S	Sinner's Tr.	LAMBERT	1779	19027009
SINS	Conf. Sins.	WADE	1697	65001009
SINS	Conf.of Sins.	BULKLEY	1752	65001009
SINS	Dan.lit. Sins.	HOPKINS	1710	43005019
SINS	Forg.of Sins.	KILLINBECK	1717	43009002
SINS	Forgiv. Sins.	BATES	1700	19130004
SINS	Forgiv. Sins.	MARSHALL	1750	19130004
SINS	Forgiv. Sins.	OGDEN	1777	45005020
SINS	Grief. Sins.	DORRINGTON	1703	19119158
SINS	Jer. Sins&c.	SMITH	1691	45019041
SINS	Little Sins.	MAUDUIT	1710	43005019
SINS	M's. Sins n.c.	MACLAURIN	1772	62001013
SINS	Mortal. Sins.	GREGORY	1708	65005016
SINS	No. Sins ven.	SMALRIDGE	1724	65003006
SINS	Our Sins f.our	TILLOTSON	1735	62001013
SINS	Our Sins f.our	MOSS	1737	62001013
SINS	Partak. Sins.	FIDDES	1720	52005011
SINS	Presum. Sins	WATERLAND	1742	19019013
SINS	Presum. Sins	SOUTH	1744	19019013
SINS	Presum. Sins	MARSHAL	1750	19019013
SINS	Presum. Sins	ORR	1772	19019013
SINS	Presum. Sins.	SACHEVERELL	1708	04015030
SINS	Presum. Sins.	WARREN	1739	19019012
SINS	Presum. Sins.	SMITH	1740	19019012
SINS	Presum. Sins.	HOOLE	1748	19019013
SINS	Remiss. Sins.	PIGGOTT	1702	45024027
SINS	Remiss. Sins.	PIGOTT	1702	45024047
SINS	Remiss. Sins.	BRETT	1712	46020021
SINS	Remiss. Sins.	WHITBY	1720	46020021
SINS	Sins inf.&pr.	GODDARD	1781	19019012
SINS	Sins of Igno.	HOOLE	1748	19019012
SINS	Sins of Reg.	CHARNOCK	1684	65003009
SINS	Sins Infirm.	WATERLAND	1742	43026041
SINS	Sins Infirm.	HOOLE	1748	43026041
SINS	Sins Omiss.	STILLINGFLEET	1707	62004017
SINS	Sins Omiss.	MORRIS	1743	43025041
SINS	Wilful Sins.	SCOTT	1700	65003009

Keyword	In its Context	Author	Year	BkChpVrs
SINS	Youth. Sins.	JENNINGS	1743	18013026
SINS	Youth Sins.	JENNINGS	1743	18011026
SIT	Ins. Sit. Brit	BONAR	1773	33003008
SKINNERS	Co. Skinners	CAWTHORNE	1748	23058012
SL	March.of Sl.	ANONYMOUS	1732	69018013
SL	Xt. Lamb.sl.	BRADBURY	1703	69005006
SL'S	Ag. Sl's.slee.	WHISTON	1709	53003008
SLA	T. Lamb sla.	COLMAN	1728	69013008
SLAN	Folly o. Slan.	BARROW	1716	20010018
SLAND	Satyr. Sland.	WILDER	1729	20010018
SLAND	Satyr. Sland.	TOTTIE	1775	20010018
SLAND	Sland. Tong.	MOSS	1737	19050020
SLANDER	Ag. Slander.	WEALES	1768	46008007
SLANDER	Of Slander.	FOSTER	1744	02020016
SLANDER	Slander.	FOWLER	1685	19101005
SLANDER	Slander.	WAKE	1701	19101005
SLANDER	Slander.	QUINCY	1750	19015001
SLANDER	Slander.	DOWNES	1761	19015003
SLANDER	Slander.	ANONYMOUS	1776	19015001
SLANDER	Slander&c.	HOPKINS	1692	02020016
SLAV	Slav.of Sin.	WAPLE	1729	46008034
SLAV	Slav.of Sin.	MOSS	1737	46008034
SLAV	Slav.of Sin.	BATTY	1739	46008034
SLAV	Slav.of Sin.	BALGUY	1748	46008034
SLAV	Slav.of Sin.	CLEMENT	1774	46008034
SLAVERY	Slavery.	MARRIOTT	1774	21004002
SLEE	Ag. Sl's.slee.	WHISTON	1709	53003008
SLEEP	Sinf. Sleep.	BADDELLEY	1752	31001006
SLEEPY	Sleepy s.	PENN	1769	47020009
SLIGHT	Slight Rep.	USHER	1678	52002001
SLOTH	Sloth.	HEYLYN	1749	48012011
SLOTH	Spir. Sloth.	SIMMONS	1677	19119037
SLOTHFULNESS	Slothfulness.	BERRIMAN	1751	20006006
SLUG	Warn. Slug.	MEADOWS	1768	20024030
SM	Diss.sm. Err.	BENTHAM	1669	62001016
SMALL	Small-pox.	WHITTY	1766	23026020
SNARE	Snare Rich.	SHOREY	1725	43019024
SO	So. H.or M.	SKELTON	1754	24013023
SOBER	Sober-mind.	CALAMY	1717	59002006
SOBER	Sober-mind.	DAVIS	1756	59002006
SOBR	Sobr.& Vig.	AGAR	1759	63005008
SOBRI	Sobri. Min.	KENNET	1715	59002006
SOBRIETY	Sobriety&c.	MOSS	1732	63004007
SOBRIETY	Sobriety&c.	PRICE	1757	59002011
SOBRIETY	Sobriety&c.	STEBBING	1760	63005008
SOC	Bible soc.	ROBINSON	1782	58003015
SOC	Lib.m.&soc.	AGAR	1759	51005013
SOC	R.imp. Soc.	CRAIG	1775	14015002
SOC	Rel.for Soc.	TILLOTSON	1735	20014034
SOC	Soc. Worship	BULKLEY	1752	46004023
SOC	Soc.nat.o. M.	BUTLER	1749	48012004
SOC	b. Soc. Linc.	ANONYMOUS	1732	18034013
SOCIAL	Social Love.	BRADBURY	1749	61010024
SOCIETY	b. Society.	BURROUGHS	1733	68000003
SOCIN	Ag. Socin.	SMITH	1696	65005007
SODOM	Sodom&c.	MURRAY	1777	01019001

Keyword	In its Context	Author	Year	BkChpVrs
SODOMY	Ag. Sodomy.	RUMLEY	1732	02023002
SODOMY	Ag. Sodomy.	LEWIS	1772	48001018
SOJ	Soj.on Earth.	HOADLY	1754	61013014
SOJ	Soj.on Earth.	CARR	1777	61013014
SOL	Dav.& Sol.	HARRINGTON	1714	19072001
SOL	Sol. Request.	SMITH	1777	11003010
SOL	Sol.pref. W.	PICKARD	1752	11003009
SOL'S	Sol's Judgm.	PENTYCROSS	1781	11003026
SOLD	Good Sold.	DAVIES	1758	01018019
SOLD	R. Sold. J. R.	LARDNER	1760	43028012
SOLDIER	Xn. Soldier.	KETTLEWELL	1719	43001021
SOLDIER	Xn. Soldier.	BROUGHTON	1737	47010001
SOLDIER	Xn. Soldier.	BADDELLEY	1752	52006011
SOLIC	Solic. Care.	SHERLOCK	1719	43006034
SOLIC	Solic. Care.	SMITH	1740	43006034
SOLIC	Solic. Care.	PRIEST	1753	43006034
SOLICIT	Virt. Solicit.	GERARD	1780	19119005
SOLITUDE	Solitude.	BLACKALL	1723	43006019
SON	Abr.off. Son.	SCOTT	1743	01022002
SON	Abr.off. Son.	JORTIN	1774	01022001
SON	Adv.to Son.	PEMBERTON	1727	13020010
SON	D.son&h.sp.	EVANS	1766	47005004
SON	F. Gl.by Son.	JOHNSON	1776	46016025
SON	Hav. Son.	PARKHURST	1707	65005012
SON	Jes. Son o. G.	LARDNER	1760	46020017
SON	Jes. Son o. M.	LARDNER	1760	45017022
SON	Prad. Son.	SHARP	1734	45015017
SON	Prad. Son.	HOW	1761	45015017
SON	Prad. Son.	BADDELLEY	1766	45015017
SON	Prad. Son.	PYLE	1777	45015017
SON	Prod. Son.	SEDGWICK	1660	45015011
SON	Prod. Son.	ALLEINE	1674	45015023
SON	Prod. Son.	BRAGGE	1702	45015011
SON	Prod. Son.	GOODMAN	1707	45015011
SON	Prod. Son.	WAPLE	1718	45015011
SON	Prod. Son.	BOYSE	1728	45015011
SON	Prod. Son.	ST.	1737	45015013
SON	Prod. Son.	MUNTON	1756	45015010
SON	Prod. Son.	DODD	1757	45015013
SON	Prod. Son.	DODD	1757	45015018
SON	Prod. Son.	DODD	1757	45015022
SON	Prod. Son.	HEYLIN	1761	45015011
SON	Prod. Son.	HOW	1761	45015011
SON	Prod. Son.	HOW	1761	45015013
SON	Prod. Son.	WILLISON	1761	45015018
SON	Prod. Son.	HOW	1761	45015020
SON	Prod. Son.	HOW	1761	45015021
SON	Prod. Son.	HOW	1761	45015022
SON	Prod. Son.	HOW	1761	45015023
SON	Prod. Son.	STERNE	1766	45015013
SON	Prod. Son.	HALES	1766	45015020
SON	Prod. Son.	BADDELLY	1766	45015025
SON	Prod. Son.	BULKLEY	1771	45015021
SON	Prod. Son.	FARQUAR	1772	45015011
SON	Prod. Son.	JORTIN	1774	45015031
SON	Prod. Son.	ANONYMOUS	1776	45015018

Keyword	In its Context	Author	Year	BkChpVrs
SON	Prod. Son.	WALLIN	1776	45015011
SON	Son m.judge	MARSH	1699	43024030
SON	Wid. N's.son	BRAGGE	1702	45007011
SON	Wid. N's.son	HOLE	1716	45007011
SON	Wid. N's.son.	DODD	1757	45007012
SON	Wid. N's.son.	CENNICK	1762	45007013
SON	Xt. Son of G.	GUYSE	1729	47009020
SONG	T.new Song.	COLMAN	1728	69005009
SONS	Cries sons G.	CENNICK	1762	44015037
SONS	Sons G. Priv.	WHEATLAND	1739	65003001
SONS	Two Sons.	BRAGGE	1704	43021028
SONS	Two Sons.	DODD	1757	43021032
SONS	Two Sons.	BOURN	1763	45021028
SONS	Two Sons.	BOURN	1764	43021028
SONS	Two Sons.	BULKLEY	1771	43021028
SONS	Xns. Sons G.	WILCOX	1757	65003001
SONSH	Sonsh.w. G.	DAVIES	1766	65003001
SONSHIP	Xt's. Sonship	WALLIN	1771	43022041
SONSHIP	Xt's. Sonship	WALLIN	1771	47009020
SONSHIP	Xt's. Sonship	WALLIN	1771	65005020
SONSHIP	Xt's Sonship.	WALLIN	1771	19002012
SOR	God's Sor.	STEWARD	1734	18033012
SORR	Godly Sorr.	LEIGHTON	1746	19119136
SORR	Godly Sorr.	SHERLOCK	1772	50007010
SORR	Joys& Sorr.	MARSHALL	1750	50004018
SORROW	Imp. Sorrow	ABERNETHY	1748	21007002
SORROW	Sorrow f. Sin	WARBURTON	1754	43026026
SORROW	Sorrow f. Sin	WILLISON	1761	43026026
SORROW	Sorrow f. Sin	CORNWALL	1773	43026026
SORTS	Se.sorts Xns.	WAPLE	1720	65002012
SOU	Frm.sou. W.	BEVERIDGE	1720	58001013
SOU	Sou. D.n.ce.	CASE	1774	58004003
SOUL	Care of Soul.	SUTTON	1754	05004009
SOUL	Dign.of Soul	WILKINSON	1660	44008036
SOUL	Exc.of Soul.	DORRINGTON	1703	37012001
SOUL	Exc.of Soul.	QUINCY	1750	43016026
SOUL	Exch.of Soul	JORTIN	1774	44008036
SOUL	Food of Soul.	DUCHAL	1765	46003034
SOUL	Imm. Soul.	BRYSON	1778	50005010
SOUL	Imm.o. Soul.	SMITH	1673	61011006
SOUL	Imm.o. Soul.	PARSONS	1721	58001010
SOUL	Immor. Soul.	MOORE	1715	43010028
SOUL	Immor. Soul.	STEPHENS	1728	43010028
SOUL	Immor. Soul.	WILDER	1729	43010028
SOUL	Immor. Soul.	PILLOK	1734	49010015
SOUL	Immor. Soul.	SOUTH	1744	43010028
SOUL	Int. St. Soul.	BATEMAN	1780	45023042
SOUL	Inter. Soul.	CARTER	1722	44008036
SOUL	Inter. Soul.	WHARTON	1728	44008036
SOUL	Inter. Soul.	DUPREE	1782	44008036
SOUL	Loss of Soul.	WATSON	1660	43016026
SOUL	Loss of Soul.	TAYLOR	1668	43016026
SOUL	Loss of Soul.	STILLINGFLEET	1707	43016026
SOUL	Loss of Soul.	FOORD	1719	43016026
SOUL	Loss of Soul.	SHOREY	1725	43016026
SOUL	Loss of Soul.	CLARKE	1735	43016026
SOUL	Loss of Soul.	FAWCETT	1749	43016026
SOUL	Loss of Soul.	DAVIS	1756	43016026
SOUL	Loss of Soul.	MAY	1757	43016026
SOUL	Loss of Soul.	DUCHAL	1765	43016026
SOUL	Loss of Soul.	EDWARDS	1775	43016026
SOUL	Loss.of Soul.	BEVERLEY	1694	43016026
SOUL	M's. Soul sub.	BULL	1713	47001025
SOUL	Pref.of Soul.	EVANS	1737	46006027
SOUL	Prop.of soul.	HILL	1667	21012007
SOUL	Soul dis.f. B.	HOLDEN	1755	45022043
SOUL	Soul immor.	TILLOTSON	1739	58001010
SOUL	Soul immor.	HOOLE	1748	21012007
SOUL	Soul immor.	WARREN	1748	57006012
SOUL	Soul lives.	WHEATLY	1746	21012007
SOUL	Soul of man.	FLAVEL	1673	69006009
SOUL	Soul of M.	FLAVEL	1673	01002007
SOUL	Soul of Man.	FLAVEL	1673	52005029
SOUL	Soul pre.f. H.	WATTS	1753	50005005
SOUL	Soul.	PRICE	1766	18032008
SOUL	Soul. Idolat.	CLARKSON	1696	52005009
SOUL	Soul.immor.	DELANY	1754	43010028
SOUL	Union Soul.	NORRIS	1728	19073028
SOUL	Val.of Soul.	ARMSTRONG	1704	43016026
SOUL	Val.of Soul.	BRADY	1706	43016026
SOUL	Val.of Soul.	KENNET	1715	43016026
SOUL	Val.of Soul.	BEVERIDGE	1720	43016026
SOUL	Val.of Soul.	MILLER	1749	43016026
SOUL	Wor.of Soul.	VINK	1683	43016026
SOUL	Wor.of Soul.	WAPLE	1720	43016026
SOUL	Worth of Scul	BARKER	1748	44008036
SOUL'S	Soul's rest. G	WILCOX	1757	19116007
SOUL'S	Soul's sep.st.	ADEY	1755	53001023
SOUL'S	Soul's Deje.	WHITFIELD	1771	19042005
SOUL'S	Soul's Prosp.	BENN	1683	67000003
SOUL'S	Soul's Prosp.	WHITFIELD	1771	67000002
SOULS	Care of souls.	DODDERIDGE	1761	20024011
SOULS	Hung.souls.	WILLISON	1761	45006021
SOULS	Imp.of Souls.	OAKES	1747	18032008
SOULS	Inj.to Souls.	CLAGETT	1720	20008036
SOULS	Phys.of souls	SHEPHERD	1748	43009012
SOULS	Souls ascens.	LOEFFS	1670	53001023
SOULS	Souls worth.	SCOTT	1700	43016026
SOULS	Souls worth.	SAURIN	1777	43016026
SOULS	Souls& Loss.	SHEPHERD	1748	43016026
SOULS	Souls Confl.	STURMY	1716	21008008
SOULS	St.sep. Souls.	WHEATLY	1746	45016022
SOUND	Sound Doct.	TAYLOR	1719	58004003
SOURCE	Rel. Source.	COYTE	1761	20014014
SOUTH	South S. Cal.	SMITH	1721	50004018
SOV	X's. Sov. Ch.	SAURIN	1777	48014007
SOVER	G's Sover.	HUSSEY	1755	05009017
SOW	Sow in T.	WILLISON	1761	19126005
SOWER	Par. Sower.	WHEATLY	1746	45008005
SOWER	Par. Sower.	ADEY	1755	45008004
SOWER	Sower.	BRAGGE	1702	43013003
SOWER	Sower.	BEVERIDGE	1720	43013018

Keyword	In its Context	Author	Year	BkChpVrs
SOWER	Sower.	LEIGHTON	1746	43013003
SOWER	Sower.	HOOLE	1748	43013003
SOWER	Sower.	HOOLE	1748	43013018
SOWER	Sower.	DODD	1757	43013018
SOWER	Sower.	HEYLIN	1761	43013003
SOWER	Sower.	BOURN	1763	43013001
SOWER	Sower.	BULKLEY	1771	43013003
SOWER	Sower.	HARWOOD	1776	43013003
SOWER	Sower.	BROUGHTON	1778	43013003
SOWER	The Sower.	CLARKE	1736	45008015
SOWER	The Sower.	DODD	1757	45008014
SP	Ass.of G's.sp.	HUSSEY	1758	46006045
SP	Carn.&sp.m.	STILLINGFLEET	1707	48008006
SP	Carn.&sp.m.	IBBOT	1726	48008006
SP	Carn.&sp.m.	EVANS	1737	48008006
SP	D.son&h.sp.	EVANS	1766	47005004
SP	Dif. Gifts sp.	CLARKE	1735	49012004
SP	Eff.of H. Sp.	SAURIN	1775	47002037
SP	Evil-sp.in g.	BARROW	1716	59003002
SP	Evil-sp.in g.	SCURLOCK	1733	59003002
SP	Evil-sp.in g.	SIMS	1772	59003002
SP	F. Sp. X's. D.	PEARSE	1763	48012011
SP	First Fr. Sp.	WESTLEY	1746	48008001
SP	Flesh& Sp.	BROWNE	1749	51005017
SP	Fruit of Sp.	HAWEIS	1762	52005009
SP	Fruit of Sp.	COWPER	1773	52005009
SP	Fruits of Sp.	ATTERBURY	1742	51005022
SP	Fruits of Sp.	KIMBER	1756	51005022
SP	Fruits of Sp.	SECKER	1771	51005022
SP	G.sp.&sp.w.	BAGSHAW	1662	46004024
SP	G.sp.&sp.w.	CHARNOCK	1684	46004024
SP	G.sp.&sp.w.	CLAGETT	1720	46004024
SP	G.sp.&sp.w.	ATTERBURY	1743	46004024
SP	G.sp.&sp.w.	BALGUY	1748	46004024
SP	G's. J.sp.&t.	LOCKIER	1671	48007025
SP	Gifts H. Sp.	TATHAM	1780	46014016
SP	Griev. H. Sp.	MOORE	1716	52004030
SP	Griev. H. Sp.	SCATTERGOOD	1723	52004030
SP	Griev. H. Sp.	SHARP	1734	52004030
SP	Griev. H. Sp.	TILLY	1737	52004030
SP	Griev. H. Sp.	ATTERBURY	1743	52004030
SP	H. Sp. Oper.	WATERLAND	1742	48008014
SP	H. Sp. Sanct.	FARMER	1756	46014026
SP	Infl.sp. Mor.	FOSTER	1737	52005009
SP	Int.op.of Sp.	SECKER	1771	46014015
SP	J.sp.&fut.st.	CARTER	1729	51006007
SP	Lead.of Sp.	JACOMB	1683	48008014
SP	Led by Sp.	SOUTH	1724	48008014
SP	Nat.&sp. P.	DRAKE	1677	48007023
SP	Ob to sp. G.	SMALRIDGE	1724	61013017
SP	Ob.to sp. G.	BARROW	1716	61013017
SP	Offices of Sp.	HURRION	1734	50003008
SP	Or. H. H.sp.	WATSON	1660	63001022
SP	Pray.by Sp.	OUTRAM	1697	49014015
SP	Renew.i. Sp.	HUSSEY	1758	52004023
SP	Sp.&n.food.	BEVERIDGE	1720	46006027

Keyword	In its Context	Author	Year	BkChpVrs
SP	Sp.&true W.	STILLINGFLEET	1707	46004024
SP	Sp.&true W.	ORR	1739	46004024
SP	Sp. Bon.& A.	WESTLEY	1746	48008015
SP	Sp. Div. Pers.	BRETT	1720	46014016
SP	Sp. Help Pr.	STEVENS	1755	48008026
SP	Sp. Help Pr.	BOSTON	1775	48008026
SP	Sp. Hous.de.	MASTERSON	1661	63002004
SP	Sp. Hung.&c	HORNECK	1706	43005006
SP	Sp. Hung.&c	GARDINER	1720	43005006
SP	Sp. Hung.&c	BLACKALL	1723	43005006
SP	Sp. Hung.&c	EDWARDS	1726	43005006
SP	Sp. Hung.&c	INNES	1726	43005006
SP	Sp. Hung.&c	NORRIS	1728	43005006
SP	Sp. Hung.&c	BLAIR	1740	43005006
SP	Sp. Hung.&c	GROVE	1742	43005006
SP	Sp. Lig.& D.	SKELTON	1754	48013011
SP	Sp. Liquors.	JACOMB	1736	24035008
SP	Sp. Opticks.	CULVERWELL	1661	49013012
SP	Sp. Reproof.	WAPLE	1729	19050021
SP	Sp.in prison.	WHEATLAND	1739	63003018
SP	Sp.kno.&ig.	MEDE	1672	65002003
SP	Sp.of Bond.	EVANS	1737	48008015
SP	Sp.of G's. L.	HAWEIS	1762	51003010
SP	Unclean Sp.	BRAGGE	1704	45011024
SP	Us.& Ab. Sp.	SHARP	1734	52004029
SP	Us.& Ab. Sp.	ROGERS	1735	52004029
SP	Us.& Ab. Sp.	TILLOTSON	1735	52004029
SP	Us.& Ab. Sp.	BATTY	1739	52004029
SP	Us.& Ab. Sp.	PEARCE	1779	52004029
SP	Vener. H. Sp.	BOURN	1777	52004030
SP	Walk.in Sp.	HORTON	1679	51005016
SP	Walk.in Sp.	ATTERBURY	1743	51005025
SP	Witn.o. Sp.	WESTLEY	1746	50001012
SP	Witn.of Sp.	SHARP	1734	48008016
SP	Witn.of Sp.	WESTLEY	1746	48008016
SP	Witn.of Sp.	WATTS	1753	48008016
SP	Witn.of Sp.	RANDOLPH	1768	48008016
SP	Witn.of Sp.	SHERLOCK	1772	48008016
SP	Witn.of Sp.	SECKER	1777	48008016
SP	Wor. Sp. Tr.	MEDE	1672	46004023
SP	Wor. Sp. Tr.	BUNDY	1750	46004023
SP	Work.of Sp.	FLAVEL	1673	46006044
SP	Xn.r.pr.sp p.	RANDOLPH	1777	47005038
SP	Xn's.sp.arm.	ANONYMOUS	1685	52006011
SP	Xt.sp.meat.	LE FRANK	1662	46004034
SP	Xt's.king.sp.	BRADBURY	1772	69011017
SP	Xt's.pr.to sp.	NEWSON	1781	63003019
SPE	Spe.t. Or. G.	FENTON	1720	63004011
SPEAK	Evil speak.	GORDON	1771	47023005
SPEAK	Evil.speak.	FIDDES	1720	19039001
SPEAK	Evil-speak.	LAMONT	1710	62001026
SPEAK	Evil-speak.	PEARSON	1718	62004010
SPEAK	Evil-speak.	SEED	1743	62004010
SPEAK	Evil-speak.	ADEY	1755	62004010
SPEAK	Evil-speak.	STERNE	1760	62001026
SPEAK	Evil-speak.	CARR	1777	62004010

INDEXES TO THIRD VOLUME: E: KEYWORD-IN-CONTEXT INDEX OF OTHER SUBJECTS OR OCCASIONS

Keyword	In its Context	Author	Year	BkChpVrs
SPEC	Spec. Com.	SHAW	1723	20028007
SPEC	Spec. Provid.	BENNETT	1728	20003005
SPECU	Specu.mort.	TALBOT	1674	54003004
SPECUL	Specul. Ath.	BATE	1748	48001020
SPEECH	Sim. Speech.	HORNECK	1706	43005037
SPEECH	Sim. Speech.	BLAIR	1740	43005034
SPEECH	Sim. Speech.	GOUGH	1751	43005037
SPEECH	Speech.	STEBBING	1739	43012037
SPI	Ag. Spi. Liq.	HALES	1754	23056012
SPI	Indwell. Spi.	FLAVEL	1673	65003024
SPI	Quench Spi.	BOYSE	1728	55005019
SPI	Quench Spi.	MOSS	1733	55005019
SPI	Spi.o. Proph.	ANONYMOUS	1687	69019019
SPI	Work of Spi.	FLAVEL	1673	52002001
SPIR	Beatif. Spir.	BOURN	1722	65003002
SPIR	Fill.w. Spir.	EVANS	1737	52005018
SPIR	Flesh& Spir.	TAYLOR	1668	43026041
SPIR	Flesh& Spir.	WATTS	1753	48008001
SPIR	G.&b. Spir.	WILSON	1781	44005013
SPIR	Gift of Spir.	JORTIN	1774	47001008
SPIR	Gifts of Spir.	BRADY	1713	51005022
SPIR	Gov.of Spir.	BARKER	1748	20025028
SPIR	Gov.of Spir.	BARKER	1748	20026028
SPIR	Inf. H. Spir.	ATTERBURY	1743	55005019
SPIR	Off.o. Spir.	HOWE	1726	51005025
SPIR	Offi.of Spir.	HOWE	1726	46003006
SPIR	Ope.of Spir.	SECKER	1771	46015026
SPIR	Pov.of Spir.	LITTLETON	1680	43005003
SPIR	Pov.of Spir.	TURNER	1687	43005003
SPIR	Pov.of Spir.	HORNECK	1706	43005003
SPIR	Pov.of Spir.	YOUNG	1706	43005003
SPIR	Pov.of Spir.	GARDINER	1720	43005003
SPIR	Pov.of Spir.	EDWARDS	1726	43005003
SPIR	Pov.of Spir.	NORRIS	1728	43005003
SPIR	Pov.of Spir.	ALTHAM	1732	43005003
SPIR	Pov.of Spir.	DAWES	1733	43005003
SPIR	Pov.of Spir.	CLARKE	1734	43005003
SPIR	Pov.of Spir.	BLAIR	1740	43005003
SPIR	Pov.of Spir.	GROVE	1742	43005003
SPIR	Pov.of Spir.	SOUTH	1744	43005003
SPIR	Pov.of Spir.	KIMBER	1756	43005003
SPIR	Pov.of Spir.	ORR	1772	43005003
SPIR	Seal of Spir.	NICOLSON	1661	22008006
SPIR	Spir. Advers.	ANONYMOUS	1731	63005008
SPIR	Spir. Advers.	ATTERBURY	1743	63005008
SPIR	Spir. Bapt.	WHITFIELD	1771	48006003
SPIR	Spir. Conv.	WAPLE	1729	52004030
SPIR	Spir. Death.	FLAVEL	1673	52005014
SPIR	Spir. Death.	DAVIES	1766	52002001
SPIR	Spir. Dilig.	BALGUY	1750	21009010
SPIR	Spir. Gifts.	COTES	1721	49014012
SPIR	Spir. Joy.	BRADY	1704	46016022
SPIR	Spir. Knowl.	TILLY	1737	49008002
SPIR	Spir. Life.	BEVERIDGE	1720	48008009
SPIR	Spir. Merch.	JELINGER	1676	43013045
SPIR	Spir. Merch.	MEDLEY	1778	20003014

Keyword	In its Context	Author	Year	BkChpVrs
SPIR	Spir. Perfect.	BATES	1700	50007001
SPIR	Spir. Pride.	MAYO	1683	50012007
SPIR	Spir. Pride.	TILLY	1737	45018009
SPIR	Spir. Pride.	WATERLAND	1742	45017010
SPIR	Spir. Sloth.	SIMMONS	1677	19119037
SPIR	Spir. Trans.	BEVERLEY	1687	43026026
SPIR	Spir. W.& R.	HUSSEY	1758	52001017
SPIR	Spir. Wisd.	VEAL	1676	23027011
SPIR	Spir. Worsh.	CREYGHTON	1720	46004024
SPIR	Spir. Xt's. R.	MICHELL	1737	45009054
SPIR	Spir.banq.	LAMBERT	1779	22002004
SPIR	Spir.life.	HORNE	1755	20020027
SPIR	Spir.life.	DAVIES	1766	52002004
SPIR	Spir.no resp.	CROOKE	1755	23029011
SPIR	Spir.of Xty.	LECHMAN	1779	58001007
SPIR	Spir.reproof.	WAPLE	1729	46016008
SPIR	Trial of Spir.	WATERLAND	1742	65004001
SPIR	Trial of Spir.	STEBBING	1760	65004001
SPIR	Trial of Spir.	RELLY	1762	65004001
SPIR	Trial of Spir.	PETERS	1776	65004001
SPIR	Un.of Spir.	LITTLETON	1680	52004003
SPIR	Woun. Spir.	SHERLOCK	1719	20018014
SPIR	Woun. Spir.	SOUTH	1744	20018014
SPIR	Woun. Spir.	SNAPE	1745	20018014
SPIR	Wt. Spir.&c.	EVANS	1737	45009055
SPIRIT	Cath. Spirit.	WESTLEY	1771	12010015
SPIRIT	Fiery Spirit.	HARRIS	1710	45009055
SPIRIT	Gift of Spirit	BENNETT	1728	45011013
SPIRIT	God a Spirit.	HAVETT	1703	46004024
SPIRIT	God's Spirit.	HUNT	1748	46004024
SPIRIT	Gosp. Spirit.	HAMMOND	1684	45009055
SPIRIT	Guid. Spirit.	HOLE	1716	46016005
SPIRIT	H. Spirit.	GUYSE	1721	49012011
SPIRIT	Husb.spirit.	FLAVEL	1673	49003009
SPIRIT	Obed.spirit.	REEVES	1729	61013017
SPIRIT	Pub. Spirit.	PRATT	1700	49010024
SPIRIT	Pub. Spirit.	GEREE	1706	49010023
SPIRIT	Pub. Spirit.	TENISON	1711	49010024
SPIRIT	Pub. Spirit.	CUMMING	1738	53002004
SPIRIT	Spirit man.	EDWARDS	1702	21003021
SPIRIT	Spirit mind.	DAVIS	1756	48008006
SPIRIT	Spirit of G.	WHITBY	1710	46004024
SPIRIT	Spirit of G.	CLARKE	1732	46004024
SPIRIT	Spirit of G.	TILLOTSON	1735	46004024
SPIRIT	Spirit of G.	WILDER	1741	46004024
SPIRIT	Spirit of G.	ABERNETHY	1743	46004024
SPIRIT	Spirit of G.	KNOWLES	1750	46004024
SPIRIT	Spirit. Man.	BENSON	1748	49002014
SPIRIT	Tend. Spirit	EVANS	1737	14034003
SPIRIT	Xn. Spirit.	EVANS	1737	52004023
SPIRIT	Xn. Spirit.	PYLE	1777	62003017
SPIRIT'S	Spirit's Infl.	ROMAINE	1759	22004016
SPIRITS	Beat. Spirits.	ROE	1766	65003002
SPIRITS	Evil Spirits.	GREGORY	1696	63005008
SPIRITS	Evil Spirits.	SEED	1750	63005008
SPITHEAD	At Spithead.	HOULTON	1740	09017037

Keyword	In its Context	Author	Year	BkChpVrs
SPOUSE	Xt.e. Spouse.	WHITLOCK	1698	28002015
SPRIN	Beaut. Sprin.	JONES	1763	22002010
ST	Ab.&c.o. St.	BEDFORD	1705	58002016
ST	Clear&st. Ju.	OUTRAM	1697	53001010
ST	Dep. St.&c.	SCOTT	1764	10011020
ST	Diff.st.tr. R.	JEFFERY	1751	58003015
ST	Du.marr.st.	COCKBURN	1708	61013004
ST	Dut.mar. St.	DELANY	1747	52005033
ST	Evid.fut.st.	AMORY	1766	43007011
ST	F. St.of R.	DUCHE	1779	19001003
ST	Fu. St.n.t. H.	CONYBEARE	1757	49015019
ST	Fut.st.its Ev.	FOSTER	1732	58001010
ST	Go.lif.st. Er.	PEARSON	1718	46007017
ST	Hap.o.fut.st.	BLAIR	1780	69007009
ST	Happ.fut. St.	WELTON	1724	49002009
ST	Happ.fut.st.	CARTER	1729	53003020
ST	Happ.fut.st.	BROWNE	1749	53003020
ST	Hum.st. Mes.	WEBB	1766	43002023
ST	Immed. St.	JORTIN	1774	43022032
ST	Int. St. Soul.	BATEMAN	1780	45023042
ST	Interm. St.	MARRIOTT	1775	49015014
ST	Interm. St.	MARRIOTT	1775	54003001
ST	J.sp.&fut.st.	CARTER	1729	51006007
ST	M's nat. St.	BOSTON	1773	19051005
ST	M's pre. St.	WEBB	1765	18005006
ST	M's St.in P.	HUSSEY	1733	01002015
ST	Man's St. V.	WILSON	1676	19039005
ST	Orig. St.& F.	CHANDLER	1769	01002017
ST	Orig. St.man	GUYSE	1757	21007029
ST	Pr.&fut.st. B.	COLLIER	1686	49015029
ST	Sep.st.happy	MARCH	1699	45023043
ST	Separ. St.	ANONYMOUS	1660	21011009
ST	Separ. St.	DORRINGTON	1703	69014013
ST	Separ. St.	STURMY	1716	21011008
ST	Separ. St.	GUYSE	1757	21012007
ST	Sin. St. Nat.	RILAND	1775	26033001
ST	Soul's sep.st.	ADEY	1755	53001023
ST	St. And. Day	FRANK	1672	43004020
ST	St. And. Day	LITTLETON	1680	43004018
ST	St. And. Day	STANHOPE	1715	43004018
ST	St. And. Day	HOLE	1716	43004018
ST	St. And.d.	HUNTER	1778	05015017
ST	St. Andr.d.	STRIPLING	1691	58002012
ST	St. Andr.day	STANHOPE	1715	48010009
ST	St. Andr.day	HOLE	1716	48010009
ST	St. Barn.day.	CRADOCK	1713	55005001
ST	St. Barn.day.	STANHOPE	1715	47011023
ST	St. Barn.day.	HOLE	1716	47011023
ST	St. Barnab.d.	STANHOPE	1715	46015012
ST	St. Barnab.d.	HOLE	1716	46015012
ST	St. Barth.day	SEIGNIOR	1670	47005012
ST	St. Barth.day	EDWARDS	1702	45022021
ST	St. Barth.day	COCK	1705	45022024
ST	St. Barth.day	BAXTER	1707	47020024
ST	St. Barth.day	STANHOPE	1715	45022023
ST	St. Barth.day	HOLE	1716	46001047

Keyword	In its Context	Author	Year	BkChpVrs
ST	St. Barth.day	STANHOPE	1715	47005012
ST	St. Barth.day	HOLE	1716	47005012
ST	St. Barth.day	MARSHALL	1731	46001047
ST	St. Barth.day	BARON	1742	47020023
ST	St. Cecil.day	BRADSHAW	1697	14005013
ST	St. David's d.	OWEN	1716	09012024
ST	St. J. Bapt.	LITTLETON	1680	43003002
ST	St. Jame's-d.	COOKE	1739	61010023
ST	St. James d.	STANHOPE	1715	43020020
ST	St. James d.	HOLE	1716	43020020
ST	St. James.	HOLE	1716	43016024
ST	St. John Bap.	STANHOPE	1715	45001057
ST	St. John Bap.	HOLE	1716	45001057
ST	St. John Bap.	NEWLIN	1720	44006020
ST	St. John Bap.	NEWLIN	1728	23057020
ST	St. John Bap.	MARSHALL	1731	43014008
ST	St. John Ev.	STANHOPE	1715	65001001
ST	St. John Ev.	HOLE	1716	65001001
ST	St. John's d.	PEGGE	1742	46001005
ST	St. John's Ev.	STANHOPE	1715	46021019
ST	St. John's Ev.	HOLE	1716	46021019
ST	St. Luke	TILLOTSON	1735	19112006
ST	St. Luke's d.	HACKETT	1675	47011026
ST	St. Luke's d.	JENNER	1676	58004011
ST	St. Luke's d.	FRANCIS	1773	50005020
ST	St. Luke's.d.	STANHOPE	1715	45010001
ST	St. Luke's.d.	HOLE	1716	45010001
ST	St. Luke's-d.	STANHOPE	1715	58004005
ST	St. Luke's-d.	HOLE	1716	58004005
ST	St. Mark's d.	LITTLETON	1680	47015037
ST	St. Mark's d.	PATRICK	1686	52004014
ST	St. Mark's d.	STANHOPE	1715	46015001
ST	St. Mark's d.	HOLE	1716	46015001
ST	St. Mark's d.	BERRIMAN	1763	52004014
ST	St. Mark's-d.	HOLE	1716	52004007
ST	St. Mark's-d.	STANHOPE	1718	52004007
ST	St. Matt.day.	LITTLETON	1680	43009009
ST	St. Matt.day.	STANHOPE	1715	43009009
ST	St. Matt.day.	HOLE	1716	43009009
ST	St. Matt.day.	COOKE	1739	45012015
ST	St. Matt.day.	WHEATLY	1746	43009009
ST	St. Matth.d.	COCK	1705	50004001
ST	St. Matth.d.	COCK	1705	50004005
ST	St. Matth.d.	STANHOPE	1715	50004001
ST	St. Matth.d.	HOLE	1716	50004001
ST	St. Matthias.	STANHOPE	1715	43011025
ST	St. Matthias.	HOLE	1716	43011025
ST	St. Matthias.	STANHOPE	1715	47001015
ST	St. Matthias.	HOLE	1716	47001015
ST	St. Matthias.	COOKE	1739	47017022
ST	St. Matthias.	WHEATLY	1746	47001023
ST	St. Mich.d.	MARSHALL	1731	49011010
ST	St. Mich.day	PHILPOT	1663	46005007
ST	St. Mich.day	STANHOPE	1715	43018001
ST	St. Mich.day	HOLE	1716	43018001
ST	St. Mich.day	STANHOPE	1715	69012007

Keyword	In its Context	Author	Year	BkChpVrs
ST	St. Mich.day	HOLE	1716	69012007
ST	St. Mich.day	LESTLEY	1721	69012007
ST	St. P.at Meli.	NEWTON	1782	47028001
ST	St. P.b. Felix	NEWTON	1782	47024010
ST	St. P's comm.	WATTS	1753	47025018
ST	St. P's de. Xy	NEWTON	1782	49013001
ST	St. P's preac.	BERRIMAN	1751	47024025
ST	St. P's. Audit	SHERIDAN	1720	47017032
ST	St. P's. C.i.	WILSON	1781	53001021
ST	St. P's. Conf.	LEWIS	1729	47026026
ST	St. P's. Def.	ATTERBURY	1734	47024025
ST	St. P's. Def.	MOSS	1737	47024025
ST	St. P's.choi.	ROGERS	1730	53001022
ST	St. P's.d.to F	HOADLY	1754	47024024
ST	St. P's.d.to F	CHANDLER	1769	47024025
ST	St. P's.d.to F	HURD	1780	47024024
ST	St. P's.strait	TRAPP	1752	53001023
ST	St. Pa.c.&m.	BROUGHTON	1778	47009015
ST	St. Patrick.d.	HENRY	1756	45024005
ST	St. Paul.	FRANK	1672	16013014
ST	St. Paul's co.	STANHOPE	1715	43019027
ST	St. Paul's co.	HOLE	1716	43019027
ST	St. Paul's d.	NEEDHAM	1716	45014023
ST	St. Paul's d.	COBDEN	1757	47020024
ST	St. Paul's rel	SYNGE	1721	47024014
ST	St. Paul's.co.	HOLE	1716	47009001
ST	St. Paul's.co.	SHERIDAN	1720	47009003
ST	St. Paul's.co.	WATERLAND	1742	47009004
ST	St. Paul's.d.	STANHOPE	1715	47009001
ST	St. Paul's Co.	WILDER	1729	57001013
ST	St. Paul's Co.	FARMER	1756	57001013
ST	St. Paul's Fa.	SHERIDAN	1720	47024014
ST	St. Paul's Xr.	DUCHAL	1753	47020024
ST	St. Pet.d. Xt.	GELL	1676	43010032
ST	St. Pet.d. Xt.	COOKE	1739	43010032
ST	St. Pet.d. Xt.	BUNDY	1740	43010033
ST	St. Peter's d.	GODDEN	1686	43016018
ST	St. Peter's d.	PATRICK	1687	43016018
ST	St. Peter's d.	STANHOPE	1715	47012001
ST	St. Peter's d.	HOLE	1716	47012001
ST	St. Peter's d.	MARSHALL	1731	44014029
ST	St. Peter's d.	BERRIMAN	1763	43016018
ST	St. Peter's.d.	MARSHALL	1731	47010034
ST	St. Peter's Xr	STERNE	1769	47003012
ST	St. Peters d.	STANHOPE	1715	43016013
ST	St. Peters d.	HOLE	1716	43016013
ST	St. Ph.& St. J	STANHOPE	1715	62001001
ST	St. Ph.& St. J	HOLE	1716	62001001
ST	St. Phil.& J.	LITTLETON	1680	46001046
ST	St. Phil.& J.	STANHOPE	1715	46014001
ST	St. Phil.& J.	HOLE	1716	46014001
ST	St. Pl's.orth.	FLEMING	1759	59002015
ST	St. S.	MONRO	1693	19026006
ST	St. S.	VICKERS	1707	19094019
ST	St. S.	LUCAS	1710	19026006
ST	St. S.	FOORD	1719	19085008

Keyword	In its Context	Author	Year	BkChpVrs
ST	St. S.	DICKSON	1731	19085008
ST	St. Sim.& J.	STANHOPE	1715	46015017
ST	St. Sim.& J.	HOLE	1716	46015017
ST	St. Sim.& Ju.	JACKSON	1673	68000004
ST	St. Sim.& Ju.	TURNER	1678	58001007
ST	St. Sim.& Ju.	ATTERBURY	1730	45016031
ST	St. Sim.& St.	STANHOPE	1715	68000001
ST	St. Sim.& St.	HOLE	1716	68000001
ST	St. Step.d. P.	MAY	1757	47007058
ST	St. Steph.d.	FRANK	1672	47007055
ST	St. Steph.d.	LITTLETON	1680	47007060
ST	St. Steph.d.	LIGHTFOOT	1684	47007053
ST	St. Steph.d.	WISE	1717	43013021
ST	St. Steph.d.	STANHOPE	1715	47007055
ST	St. Steph.d.	HOLE	1716	47007055
ST	St. Steph.d.	LEEKE	1727	47007037
ST	St. Steph.d.	ROBINSON	1730	58002022
ST	St. Steph.d.	SECKER	1771	47007059
ST	St. Steph.day	STANHOPE	1715	43023034
ST	St. Steph.day	HOLE	1716	43023034
ST	St. Steph.vis.	MAY	1757	47007056
ST	St. Tho.d.	STANHOPE	1715	52002019
ST	St. Tho.d.	HOLE	1716	52002019
ST	St. Tho.d.	WILDER	1741	46020027
ST	St. Tho.unb.	COCK	1710	46020027
ST	St. Tho.uub.	SHOWER	1702	46020027
ST	St. Thom.d.	HICKMAN	1713	50005007
ST	St. Thom.d.	STANHOPE	1715	46020024
ST	St. Thom.d.	HOLE	1716	46020024
ST	St. Thom.d.	ADAMS	1716	46020027
ST	St. Thom.d.	SCATTERGOOD	1723	46020027
ST	St. Thom.d.	LEEKE	1730	46014001
ST	St. Thom.d.	WHEATLY	1746	46020024
ST	St. Thom.d.	LARDNER	1760	46020029
ST	St.john bapt.	STANHOPE	1715	23040001
ST	St.john bapt.	HOLE	1716	23040001
ST	St.of Xns.	WAPLE	1720	52002021
ST	St.sep. Souls.	WHEATLY	1746	45016022
ST	St Paul's Co.	LUCAS	1717	49015009
ST	Tou st.o. Sin.	FLAVEL	1673	69003017
ST	Van.of pr.st.	GROVE	1741	48008019
ST	Wildern. St.	WESTLEY	1771	46016022
ST	Xn. Ev.o.f.st.	BOURN	1760	49015012
ST	Xn. K.m. St.	FOTHERGILL	1765	53004001
ST	Xn.st.suffer.	ATTERBURY	1734	63002021
STA	M's nat. Sta.	WATKINS	1676	52002003
STA	Sta. F. Ch. S.	ERSKINE	1764	23030007
STA	Xn. Prin.sta.	SNAPE	1745	54002006
STAB	Stab. Ch. Ch.	NICOLSON	1661	23002001
STAB	Stab.of time.	OUTRAM	1697	23033006
STAB	Stab.of S. S.	PARKHURST	1717	46010035
STABIL	Stabil.ch.ch.	NICOLSON	1661	23002003
STAM	Rep. Stam.a.	MAYHEW	1767	19124007
STAM	Rep.stam. A.	CHAUNCY	1767	20025025
STAND	Stand fast&c.	DUCHE	1775	51005001
STAND	Stand. Min.	WILSON	1781	04006022

Keyword	In its Context	Author	Year	BkChpVrs
STAND	Stand. Rev.	GROVE	1741	45016030
STAR	Sages Star	HALL	1661	43002002
STAR	Star in East.	DOWNES	1761	43002001
STAR	The star.	HARRIS	1724	04024017
STARS	Stars and C.	ANONYMOUS	1670	43002009
STAT	Xn. Lib.stat.	ROE	1662	47015029
STATE	Fnt. State.	CRAVEN	1775	61009027
STATE	Fut. State.	HART	1702	46014002
STATE	Fut. State.	ROMAINE	1739	44012024
STATE	Fut. State.	FOSTER	1744	21009002
STATE	Fut. State.	BURNET	1747	20014032
STATE	Fut. State.	BALGUY	1748	21012007
STATE	Fut. State.	BELLAMY	1744	47023008
STATE	Fut. State.	LARDNER	1751	19084011
STATE	Fut. State.	BOURN	1760	46014001
STATE	Fut. State.	BOURN	1760	47026008
STATE	Fut. State.	BOURN	1760	48002016
STATE	Fut. State.	DAVIES	1766	50004018
STATE	Fut. State.	CRAVEN	1775	21009002
STATE	Fut. State.	JORTIN	1774	61011013
STATE	Fut. State.	CRAVEN	1775	51006009
STATE	Fut. State.	CRAVEN	1775	61013008
STATE	Fut. State.	CRAVEN	1775	64003012
STATE	Fut. State.	BRAILSFORD	1776	48015004
STATE	Fut. State.	BLAIR	1777	49013012
STATE	Fut. State.	LAMONT	1780	63001003
STATE	Fut.state.	CALAMY	1726	58001010
STATE	Fut.state.	BOURN	1760	58001010
STATE	Fut.state.	TOTTIE	1775	58001010
STATE	Interm. State	SMALRIDGE	1724	23057002
STATE	Interm. State	HOLDEN	1755	45023043
STATE	Interm. State	GODDARD	1756	45023043
STATE	Interm. State	REGIS	1751	64002009
STATE	Interm. State	MARRIOTT	1775	46014001
STATE	Pr.&f. State.	DUCHAL	1765	50004018
STATE	Pr.&f. State.	ELSMERE	1767	50004018
STATE	Separ. State.	LUCAS	1722	45016022
STATE	State of G.	JORTIN	1774	43013043
STATE	State of Inn.	HAWEIS	1762	01001026
STATE	State of Rel.	HESKETH	1679	26037003
STATE	State world.	GIBBONS	1770	23021006
STATE	State Prob.	CLARKE	1734	45016012
STATE	State Proba.	GOUGH	1751	23005003
STATED	Ch.stated.	SEED	1750	20003027
STATED	Stated F. Pr.	SMALRIDGE	1724	45011001
STATED	Stated F. Pr.	MOSS	1732	45011001
STATES	States of An.	STURMY	1716	68000006
STE	Ste.in Xn. F.	STEVENS	1771	49016013
STEAD	Stead. Relig.	BRADBURY	1772	27006010
STEADY	Steady Virt.	DYKES	1722	20031025
STEAL	Steal. Tyth.	NEWTE	1711	20003009
STEAL	Tythe steal.	WAKE	1703	38003008
STEALING	Ag. Stealing.	WHITE	1747	52004028
STEDF	Stedf.in Fai.	BRADBURY	1749	61010023
STEDF	Stedf.in Rel.	WAKE	1701	49015058
STEDF	Stedf.in Rel.	WAKE	1716	64003017
STEDF	Stedf.in Rel.	WILDER	1741	49015058
STEDFAST	Rel. Stedfast.	BEVERIDGE	1720	49015058
STEP	St. Step.d. P.	MAY	1757	47007058
STEPH	St. Steph.d.	FRANK	1672	47007055
STEPH	St. Steph.d.	LITTLETON	1680	47007060
STEPH	St. Steph.d.	LIGHTFOOT	1684	47007053
STEPH	St. Steph.d.	WISE	1717	43013021
STEPH	St. Steph.d.	STANHOPE	1715	47007055
STEPH	St. Steph.d.	HOLE	1716	47007055
STEPH	St. Steph.d.	LEEKE	1727	47007037
STEPH	St. Steph.d.	ROBINSON	1730	58002022
STEPH	St. Steph.d.	SECKER	1771	47007059
STEPH	St. Steph.day	STANHOPE	1715	43023034
STEPH	St. Steph.day	HOLE	1716	43023034
STEPH	St. Steph.vis.	MAY	1757	47007056
STEW	Good Stew.	WESTLEY	1771	45016002
STEW	Stew.of Xt.	HILL	1755	45012042
STEW	Subtle Stew.	BOURN	1763	45016001
STEW	Unjust Stew.	BRAGGE	1704	45016001
STEW	Unjust Stew.	ELLIS	1704	45016001
STEW	Unjust Stew.	HOLE	1716	45016001
STEW	Unjust Stew.	WHEATLAND	1739	45016008
STEW	Unjust Stew.	DODD	1757	45016008
STEW	Unjust Stew.	ELSMERE	1767	45016008
STEW	Unjust Stew.	BULKLEY	1771	45016008
STEW	Unjust Stew.	JORTIN	1774	45016008
STEWARD	Life Steward	PYLE	1777	43025014
STEWARDSHIP	Stewardship	STURMY	1716	45016002
STOP	Hon.stop. M.	TILLOTSON	1735	46007017
STORY	Story of Jos.	LANGHORNE	1773	01045004
STR	Believ.str.h.	WALKER	1764	37009012
STR	Go.str.on Ea.	TILLOTSON	1735	61011013
STR	Gos.g.str.th.	WHITTY	1772	45005026
STR	Our own Str.	BRADY	1730	43026033
STR	Str.bet.two.	WILLISON	1761	53001023
STR	Str.for Faith.	STENNETT	1738	53001027
STR	Str.in Weak.	BOSTON	1753	50012009
STRA	Stra. Appar.	ALSOP	1683	35001008
STRAIT	St. P's.strait	TRAPP	1752	53001023
STRAIT	Strait g.pass.	ANONYMOUS	1776	43007014
STRAIT	Strait Gate.	IBBOT	1726	45013023
STRAIT	Strait Gate.	ATTERBURY	1743	44013021
STRAIT	Strait Gate.	ATTERBURY	1743	45013024
STRAIT	Strait Gate.	BOSTON	1753	43007013
STRAIT	Strait Gate.	SECKER	1770	45013023
STRAIT	Strait Gate.	SHERLOCK	1772	45013023
STRANGE	Strange Sig.	WILLISON	1761	45005026
STRENG	Streng.in Xt.	LAMBERT	1779	53004013
STRENG	Xn's. Streng.	JENKINS	1775	50012010
STRENG	Xn's Streng.	BENNETT	1728	49011010
STRIFE	Ag. Strife.	NOURSE	1708	58002024
STRIV	Folly of striv	BRAGGE	1713	23045009
STRIV	Folly of striv	BALGUY	1750	23045009
STS	Com.of Sts.	BEVERIDGE	1720	52002019
STS	Comm.o. Sts.	NICOLSON	1661	52004016
STS	G's pres. Sts.	S.	1695	56003016

INDEXES TO THIRD VOLUME: E: KEYWORD-IN-CONTEXT INDEX OF OTHER SUBJECTS OR OCCASIONS

Keyword	In its Context	Author	Year	BkChpVrs
STUD	Heav. Stud.	STEFFE	1743	63001012
STUDY	Study of S. S.	AMORY	1775	58003015
STUDY	Study script.	BOSTON	1773	23034016
STYLE	New Style.	LLOYD	1753	01001014
SU	Call.& El. Su.	BREKELL	1765	64001010
SU	Call.& El. Su.	SANDERCOCK	1776	64001010
SU	Ea. Tr.su.ac.	BLAIR	1740	43006019
SU	Good m's Su.	HOLLAND	1753	19034019
SU	Su.f.we&c.	ALTHAM	1732	63002020
SU	Su.sum.to ju.	VINCENT	1667	69022020
SU	Su.w.of Pro.	NEWCOME	1724	64001019
SU	Su.w.of Pro.	BRAY	1761	64001019
SUB	M's. Soul sub.	BULL	1713	47001025
SUB	Peace& Sub.	ROGERS	1730	55004011
SUB	Sub t. D. Ch.	SAVAGE	1732	61012009
SUB	Sub to Auth.	MOORE	1715	61010036
SUB	Sub. D. Will.	MEDE	1672	43007021
SUB	Sub. G's. W.	SCOTT	1700	45022042
SUB	Sub. G's. W.	BARROW	1716	45022042
SUB	Sub. Provid.	ENFIELD	1772	43006010
SUB	Sub.in Ch. E.	POWELL.	1776	49001010
SUB	Sub.sev.s.	HARRISON	1691	23045024
SUB	Sub.t. Di. W.	JONES	1741	46018011
SUB	Sub.t. G's w.	DU MOULIN	1684	43026039
SUB	Sub.t. G's w.	BATES	1700	43026039
SUB	Sub.t. G's w.	ATTERBURY	1743	43026039
SUB	Sub.to A.&c.	SHEPHEARD	1771	51005001
SUB	Sub.to S. B.	LANGHORNE	1773	62004007
SUB	Xt. Sub.o. S.	SAURIN	1777	61010005
SUBJ	Dut. Subj.	NICHOLS	1701	48013005
SUBJ	King& Subj.	BOURN	1764	43022001
SUBJ	Mor.subj.pr.	ENFIELD	1772	59003008
SUBJ	Nec.o. Subj.	WALKER	1684	48013001
SUBJ	Subj mat. Pr.	FIDDES	1720	65005014
SUBJ	Subj. Duty.	CLEAVER	1676	59003001
SUBJ	Subj. Duty.	CHISHULL	1716	59003001
SUBJ	Subj.to Gov.	BOURN	1777	59003001
SUBJECT	Dut. Subject	BURNET	1674	48013005
SUBJECT	Mu. Subject.	SWIFT	1744	63005005
SUBJECTION	Subjection.	HARE	1746	48013001
SUBJECTS	G's. Subjects	SHEPHEARD	1748	65003002
SUBLUN	Sublun. Enj.	DAVIS	1756	21008008
SUBM	Subm.to Aff.	D'COETLOGAN	1778	18001020
SUBM	Subm.to G.	ATTERBURY	1703	18002010
SUBM	Subm.to G.	JENKS	1700	48010003
SUBM	Subm.to M.	HORT	1738	63002013
SUBMISSION	Submission.	HUGHES	1694	19039009
SUBMISSION	Submission.	NORRIS	1728	46018011
SUBMISSION	Submission.	SOUTH	1744	19039009
SUBMISSION	Submission.	WARREN	1748	09003018
SUBMISSION	Submission.	SIMS	1772	19039010
SUBORDINAT	Subordinat.	MASON	1742	20020002
SUBSCRIPT	Subscript.	HALLIFAX	1772	50002017
SUBTLE	Subtle Stew.	BOURN	1763	45016001
SUC	Bab.& Suc.	COLMAN	1728	19008002
SUCC	Off.& Succ.	HORTON	1679	49001024
SUCC	Qual.succ. P.	ELSMERE	1767	62004003
SUCC	Succ. Gosp.	BOSTON	1753	23053001
SUCC	Succ. Seam.	FLAVEL	1673	05008017
SUCC	Succ.of Gos.	NEWTON	1767	43011025
SUCC	Succ.of Gos.	DAVIES	1771	50010004
SUCCES	Succes. Com.	DYKES	1722	20031018
SUCCES	Succes. Pray.	BLACKALL	1723	43007009
SUCCESS	Success. Min.	SMITH	1716	48015029
SUDD	Sudd. Prosp.	ASHTON	1770	05006010
SUF	Ch.suf.f.p's c	BREKEL	1767	24031029
SUF	G.sup.u.suf.	TILLOTSON	1735	63004019
SUF	Suf. T. S. Xy.	NALSON	1737	63002021
SUF	Suf.in Grave	WATTS	1753	18014013
SUF	Xt's. Suf.&c.	PRICE	1757	63003018
SUF	Xt's.suf.nec.	SHEPHERD	1748	45024046
SUFF	Com.m.suff.	BRADY	1730	45016031
SUFF	G's long suff.	SAURIN	1775	21008011
SUFF	Gos. Ev.suff.	WHARTON	1728	45016031
SUFF	Gos. Ev.suff.	WESTON	1747	45016031
SUFF	Gosp.suff.	NARSHALL	1731	50004003
SUFF	L's.l.suff.	DOOLITTLE	1682	49011026
SUFF	Long suff. G.	TILLOTSON	1735	21008011
SUFF	Prep.for suff.	FLAVEL	1673	47021013
SUFF	S. S.suff.	MANTON	1675	56002015
SUFF	Sense of Suff.	HAVETT	1703	43026039
SUFF	Suff.by Fire.	MILLS	1781	43025040
SUFF	Suff.f. Relig.	CLARKE	1735	54001024
SUFF	Suff.for R.sa.	BRADBURY	1722	63003014
SUFF	Suff.o. Grace	WILCOX	1757	50012009
SUFF	Suff.of d. Gr.	ATTERBURY	1699	50012009
SUFF	Suff.of d. Gr.	BEVERIDGE	1720	50012009
SUFF	Suff.of. S. S.	BEVERIDGE	1720	58003016
SUFF	Suff.of God.	BUNDY	1740	50003005
SUFF	Suff.of S. S.	ANONYMOUS	1771	48001016
SUFF	Suff.w.to Gl.	BRADY	1730	69007014
SUFF	Xn. Suff.&c.	ANONYMOUS	1733	63004012
SUFF	Xt's. Suff.& S	CHARNOCK	1684	45024026
SUFF	Xt's. Suff.& S	EDWARDS	1713	45024026
SUFFER	Penal Suffer.	REAY	1755	25003029
SUFFER	Suffer. Faith.	WILKINSON	1660	53001029
SUFFER	Suffer. Jesus.	FARMER	1757	63003018
SUFFER	Suffer.of X.	NEEDHAM	1679	61012002
SUFFER	Suffer.of Xt.	BROWNE	1749	61009026
SUFFER	Suffer.of Xt.	WILLISON	1761	45009022
SUFFER	Xn.st.suffer.	ATTERBURY	1734	63002021
SUFFER	Xt. Suffer.	PIGOTT	1702	23053005
SUFFER	Xt. Suffer.	ROGERS	1738	23053005
SUFFER	Xt's. Suffer.	STILLINGFLEET	1707	61012003
SUFFER	Xt's. Suffer.	MOSS	1732	61012003
SUFFER	Xt's. Suffer.	DAVIES	1771	46012027
SUFFER	Xt's. Suffer.	WHITTY	1772	45024026
SUFFER	Xt's. Suffer.	OGDEN	1777	49001018
SUFFER	Xt's.l.suffer.	BRAGGE	1706	43026036
SUFFER	Xt's Suffer.	DAVIS	1756	25001012
SUFFER	Xt's Suffer.	DAVIES	1766	23053010
SUFFERI	Xt's. Sufferi.	BRADBURY	1732	48008032

Keyword	In its Context	Author	Year	BkChpVrs
SUFFERI	Xt's. Sufferi.	CLARKE	1735	63003018
SUFFERING	Suffering.	HARRIS	1724	23053007
SUFFERING	Suffering.	NELSON	1737	61002010
SUFFERINGS	Sufferings.	HOWE	1744	63005010
SUFFIC	Self-suffic.	ECCLES	1755	43019022
SUFFICIENCY	Sufficiency.	COLLIER	1725	45012015
SUFFICIENCY	Sufficiency.	ROGERS	1735	20030008
SUHP	Xn's. Suhp.	HUNT	1748	46014001
SUIT	L.suit. Prof.	ADEY	1760	45012047
SUM	Su.sum.to ju.	VINCENT	1667	69022020
SUM	Sum.of Law.	LEIGHTON	1746	43022037
SUN	Shrove-sun.	SEPPENS	1679	49009027
SUN	Sun of Righ.	BRODBURST	1733	38004002
SUN	1 Sun. Trin.	STANHOPE	1714	45016019
SUN	15 Sun. Trin.	HOLE	1717	43006019
SUND	Palm- Sund.	GODDARD	1715	20024021
SUND	Sund.b. East.	KILLIGREW	1689	19110007
SUND	Sund.b. East.	STANHOPE	1715	53002005
SUND	Sund.b. East.	HOLE	1716	53002005
SUND	Sund.b. L.	HOWARD	1742	43012041
SUP	Dut.to Sup.	PRICE	1757	48013007
SUP	Elij. Sup.	THEAD	1712	11019004
SUP	G.sup.u.suf.	TILLOTSON	1735	63004019
SUP	Good.sup. P.	BOURN	1777	45010017
SUP	Lo.sup t.pr.	ROWLAND	1774	68000009
SUP	Ma.d.sup.p.	SLATER	1690	48013005
SUP	Negl. L. Sup.	ELSMERE	1767	45014018
SUP	Rel.not sup.	ABERNETHY	1743	18028028
SUP	Sup. K.in H.	PEARSE	1763	49013012
SUP	Sup. Xn. Rel.	OGDEN	1777	58002019
SUP	Sup.conc. Xt.	FLEMING	1772	23007013
SUP	Sup.f.our N.	WILLISON	1761	53004019
SUP	Sup.w. Ath.	WESTON	1739	53003006
SUPER	Relig. Super.	WILLIAMS	1774	23065005
SUPEREROGAT	Supererogat.	LYE	1675	45017010
SUPERST	Ag. Superst.	DODWELL	1754	19031007
SUPERST	Inc. Superst.	CHANDLER	1749	32004005
SUPERSTITION	Superstition.	PAYNE	1698	47017022
SUPERSTITION	Superstition.	ATTERBURY	1703	47017022
SUPERSTITION	Superstition.	STILLINGFLEET	1707	54002023
SUPERSTITION	Superstition.	IBBOT	1726	21007016
SUPERSTITION	Superstition.	IBBOT	1726	21008016
SUPERSTITION	Superstition.	SHERIDAN	1720	47017022
SUPERSTITION	Superstition.	ORR	1749	47017022
SUPERSTITION	Superstition.	HOLLAND	1753	19050021
SUPERSTITION	Superstition.	WHITE	1757	19054006
SUPERSTITION	Superstition.	HOADLY	1754	47017022
SUPERSTITION	Superstition.	DAVIS	1756	47017022
SUPERSTITION	Superstition.	WEST	1762	46016002
SUPP	Believ.supp.	BROUSTON	1699	23041014
SUPP	Lord's supp.	OGDEN	1780	43026026
SUPP	Lord's supp.	TEMPLE	1782	43026026
SUPP	Lord's Supp.	MORICE	1660	03013015
SUPP	Lord's Supp.	BERRIMAN	1751	43022004
SUPP	Lord's Supp.	OGDEN	1780	69013008
SUPP	Marr. Supp.	SHEPHERD	1748	43022005

Keyword	In its Context	Author	Year	BkChpVrs
SUPP	Marr. Supp.	POTTER	1753	43022007
SUPP	Marr. Supp.	DODD	1757	43022002
SUPP	Marr. Supp.	ADEY	1760	43022002
SUPP	Marr. Supp.	STEBBING	1760	43022002
SUPP	Marr. Supp.	WILLISON	1761	43022002
SUPP	Par.of Supp.	HOLE	1716	45014016
SUPP	Supp. Aged.	FARMER	1756	23044004
SUPP	Supp. Trou.	WILCOX	1757	43014027
SUPP	Xn. Supp. D.	COMBER	1691	19023004
SUPP	Xt.our Supp.	ERSKINE	1757	22008005
SUPPER	L's. Supper.	HARRIS	1736	49011024
SUPPER	L's. Supper.	KIPPIS	1758	49011029
SUPPER	L's. Supper.	OGDEN	1780	61010008
SUPPER	L's.supper.	STANHOPE	1715	45022001
SUPPER	L's.supper.	TOLLER	1769	49004007
SUPPER	L's.supper.	CASE	1774	47002042
SUPPORT	G. Support.	ADAMS	1736	19011003
SUPR	King's Supr.	CRAGGE	1661	48013001
SUPR	Supr. Crown.	RYE	1713	45020025
SUPRE	Supre. Good.	FARRINGTON	1741	19016011
SUR	Diff. Rel.sur.	STENNETT	1769	43011030
SUR	Sur. Quebec.	BULKLEY	1759	19102013
SURE	Sure m.of D.	HEYWOOD	1672	23055005
SURE	Sure walk.	DUKE	1714	20010009
SURE	Sure walk.	BARROW	1716	20010009
SURE	Sure walk.	CLARKE	1735	20010009
SURE	Sure Found.	ROMAINE	1756	23028016
SURE	T.sure Foun.	ROMAINE	1756	49003011
SURET	Chg.t. Suret.	HOLE	1719	52006004
SURETY	Xt our Surety	TAYLOR	1725	61006022
SURP	Surp.in D.	WATTS	1753	44013035
SURP	Surp.in D.	ADEY	1755	44013037
SURPL	Surpl.vind.	WESTFIELD	1660	19045007
SURPL	Surpl.vind.	WESTFIELD	1660	45024050
SURPL	Surpl.vind.	WESTFIELD	1660	47001009
SURPL	Surpl.vind.	WESTFIELD	1660	47001010
SUS	Abim. P.sus.	ORTON	1776	01020011
SW	Ag.prof.sw.	WRIGHT	1723	62005012
SW	F.&com. Sw.	SMALWOOD	1666	43005034
SW	F.&com. Sw.	WILSON	1700	43005034
SW	F.&com. Sw.	KINSMAN	1700	43005034
SW	F.&com. Sw.	HORNECK	1706	43005034
SW	F.&com. Sw.	GREGORY	1708	43005034
SW	F.&com. Sw.	CALAMY	1726	43005034
SW	F.&com. Sw.	LITTLETON	1735	43005034
SW	F.&com. Sw.	WHITFIELD	1739	43005034
SW	F.&com. Sw.	BOURN	1777	43005034
SW	Oaths& Sw.	ROST	1695	62005012
SW	Oaths& Sw.	ROBINSON	1710	62005012
SW	Oaths& Sw.	SHARP	1729	62005012
SW	Oaths& Sw.	LAMONT	1780	62005012
SW	Perj.&c. Sw.	GARDINER	1720	43005033
SW	Perj.&c. Sw.	BLACKALL	1723	43005033
SW	Perj.&c. Sw.	BLAIR	1740	43005033
SW	Perj.&c. Sw.	LOVEDAY	1741	43005033
SWEAR	Ag. Swear.	BOREMAN	1662	43005034

INDEXES TO THIRD VOLUME: E: KEYWORD-IN-CONTEXT INDEX OF OTHER SUBJECTS OR OCCASIONS

Keyword	In its Context	Author	Year	BkChpVrs
SWEAR	Ag. Swear.	NOURSE	1708	02020007
SWEAR	Ag. Swear.	PIERCE	1731	19111009
SWEAR	Ag. Swear.	SECKER	1770	62005012
SWEAR	Cur.&swear.	READING	1731	45016024
SWEAR	Of Swear.	FLEETWOOD	1737	02020007
SWEAR	Prof. Swear.	BRADBURY	1732	02020007
SWEAR	Prof. Swear.	CARRINGTON	1754	20018014
SWEAR	Prof. Swear.	CARRINGTON	1776	20018021
SWEAR	Rash. Swear.	BEVERIDGE	1720	43005033
SWEAR	Rash. Swear.	AGAR	1759	43005034
SWEAR	Swear. L. M.	GRIFFYTH	1693	55004011
SWEAR	Swear. L. M.	SKERRET	1716	48013004
SWEARING	Swearing.	WAKE	1722	43005033
SWEARING	Swearing.	NEWTON	1736	21009002
SWEARING	Swearing.	FRANCIS	1773	24023010
SWEARING	Swearing.	RAMSEY	1781	02020007
SWEARING	Swearing.	NEWTON	1782	43005034
SWIFT	Swift pro. G.	MOSS	1732	47019020
SWORD	The Sword.	HILDROP	1711	23034002
SY	Conc.ad Sy.	PIERCE	1661	47011028
SY	R.perf.sy.m.	LAWSON	1764	43007020
SYM	Ill bod. Sym.	PEMBERTON	1727	28007009
SYMP	Univ. Symp.	WOOD	1775	63003008
SYMPA	Sympa. Joy.	ENFIELD	1772	48012015
SYMPA	Sympa. Joy.	WOOD	1775	48012015
SYMPA	Xn. Sympa.	CONEY	1730	48012015
T	A. O.& N. T.	GILL	1773	47026022
T	A.d.t.s. X's.d	ORTON	1776	46008056
T	Axe laid t. R.	KEACH	1692	43003010
T	Barr. Fig- T.	LUCAS	1717	44011013
T	Barr. Fig- T.	BULKLEY	1771	44011021
T	Barr. Fig- T.	JORTIN	1774	44011021
T	C.o. O.&n.t.	KNOX	1768	46005039
T	Chg.t. Suret.	HOLE	1719	52006004
T	Cl. Ad.t. Par.	STEDMAN	1776	58002006
T	Cre.of N. T.	LARDNER	1769	64001015
T	Cruc.t. Lusts.	SOUTH	1744	51005024
T	Cruc.t. Lusts.	BROWNE	1749	51005024
T	D.rel.t. H. S.	GUYSE	1757	52004030
T	Deliv.fm. T.	FARINDON	1674	43006013
T	Deliv.fm. T.	EDWARDS	1713	43006013
T	Div. T.to Jes.	LARDNER	1760	43027052
T	E. Tra. O. T.	WHITE	1778	16008007
T	E.f. Xn.w. T.	HORNE	1671	68000020
T	Enmity to T.	TILLOTSON	1735	46003020
T	Eter. Hell T.	KILLINBECK	1717	45016023
T	Ev.o. T.n.sc.	SMYTH	1717	58001010
T	Evid. O. T. P.	POWELL	1776	45024025
T	Forg.t. Xt.a.	WHICHCOTE	1698	47013038
T	Forg.t. Xt.a.	HOOLE	1748	47013038
T	Forg.t. Xt.al.	SHERLOCK	1719	47013038
T	Fu. St.n.t. H.	CONYBEARE	1757	49015019
T	G.t. Father.	BARROW	1716	52004006
T	G's w.hid. T.	TAYLOR	1776	19112011
T	G's. J.sp.&t.	LOCKIER	1671	48007025
T	G's.cal.t.ob.	WARREN	1748	61003015
T	Good P.t.m.	AMORY	1766	43005045
T	Good T.in l.	DUCHAL	1765	53001010
T	H. S. T.o. Xt.	JOHNSON	1776	46015026
T	Hap. D.t. Xn.	LANGHORNE	1773	69014013
T	Helps t.g. M.	STEELE	1683	49015002
T	Ho.due t. G.	NORRIS	1728	58003003
T	Hol.w.t. Ha.	BROOKS	1662	61012014
T	Hope& T. G.	MARSHAL	1750	19042005
T	In. O.& N. T.	CALAMY	1710	64001021
T	Inv.t.thir. S.	DODDERIDGE	1761	46007037
T	Inv.t.thir. S.	PEARSE	1763	46007037
T	Jes.t. Proph.	BULLOCK	1724	47003022
T	Jos. T.of Xt.	WILLISON	1761	01045004
T	Jos. T.of Xt.	BLISS	1769	01045004
T	L.& Ob.t. Xt.	JENNINGS	1757	50005014
T	L.es.t.att. G.	HUNTER	1774	65004016
T	Lo.sup t.pr.	ROWLAND	1774	68000009
T	Lo.t. G.& Xt.	DAVIES	1766	46021017
T	Min.t.pr. G.	ANONYMOUS	1679	48001014
T	N. W.m.t. V.	ENFIELD	1772	43005014
T	N.conf.t. W.	S.	1695	48012002
T	N.conf.t. W.	ERSKINE	1764	48012002
T	Nec.of D.t.	ROMAINE	1760	46006045
T	No serv.t. M.	FAWCETT	1749	43006024
T	Not.t.b. Off.	HEYLYN	1749	43011004
T	O. T. Proph.	POWELL	1776	43011002
T	Obed.t. Gov.	SHERLOCK	1772	48013001
T	Obed.t. Mas.	SEATON	1720	54003022
T	Persua.t. Ch.	DOUGHTY	1742	44012041
T	Pr.in kn. T.	VINCENT	1675	49014015
T	Predest.t.&c.	KING	1709	48008029
T	Predest.t.&c.	PARKER	1758	48008030
T	Predest.t.life	FIDDES	1720	48008029
T	Predest.t.life	COOPER	1765	48008029
T	R. Life t. Pl.	LAWSON	1764	19001002
T	Rel. Em.o. T.	CARR	1777	52005015
T	Rest.t.b.obt.	ALLESTREE	1684	43011028
T	S. S.t.b.read.	FOWLER	1675	55005027
T	S.of G.pr. T.	CAMPBELL	1779	49001025
T	Self-de.t. G.	AMORY	1742	50004005
T	Sow in T.	WILLISON	1761	19126005
T	Spe.t. Or. G.	FENTON	1720	63004011
T	Sub t. D. Ch.	SAVAGE	1732	61012009
T	Sub.t. Di. W.	JONES	1741	46018011
T	Sub.t. G's w.	DU MOULIN	1684	43026039
T	Sub.t. G's w.	BATES	1700	43026039
T	Sub.t. G's w.	ATTERBURY	1743	43026039
T	Suf. T. S. Xy.	NALSON	1737	63002021
T	T.& Chance.	STERNE	1760	21009011
T	T.&eter.m.	FOTHERGILL	1765	43006033
T	T.&man. R.	LAW	1745	51004004
T	T. Hap.in G.	MASON	1758	24002013
T	T. Jul. Ship.	RAMSAY	1681	47027015
T	T. Lamb sla.	COLMAN	1728	69013008
T	T. Shep.b. K.	LANEY	1662	63002025
T	T. T. Xt's. B.	CATCOTT	1753	46001014

Keyword	In its Context	Author	Year	BkChpVrs
T	T. X's.c.fit.	FOSTER	1737	51004004
T	T. X's.c.fit.	CLEAVER	1743	51004004
T	T.a. T.b. S. S	GOAD	1664	55005021
T	T.ab.ob.&c.	MUNTON	1756	54003002
T	T.false Acc.	ANONYMOUS	1753	45016002
T	T.new Song.	COLMAN	1728	69005009
T	T.o.tr.&f.d.	ADAMS	1777	65004001
T	T.of Need.	ERSHINE	1764	26016008
T	T.read.of V.	HOPKINS	1771	16004023
T	T.s.	WARD	1746	19107002
T	T.sure Foun.	ROMAINE	1756	49003011
T	T.t. S.n.f. G.	SHARP	1734	62001013
T	T.t. S.n.f. G.	BURNET	1747	62001013
T	T.t. S.n.f. G.	ABERNETHY	1751	62001013
T	T.two Witn.	K.	1667	69011003
T	V.& Use of T.	ATTERBURY	1743	52005016
T	Van.wor. T.	LANGHORNE	1773	19039006
T	Wait.all T.	GREENHILL	1773	63004007
T	Warn.t. You.	TOULMIN	1770	45015012
T	Way t. Heav.	PHILIPS	1681	47002047
T	Wheat& T.	WHEATLY	1746	43013030
T	Wis.r.t. Pl.	ANONYMOUS	1754	20003017
T	Wo.ins.t. H.	CARR	1777	54003002
T	Worsh.u. T.	BOYS	1716	49014009
T	Worsh.u. T.	BAYES	1735	49014009
T	Xn's. G's. T.	BREKELL	1765	50006016
T	Xn's.des.t.d.	EDWARDS	1726	53001025
T	Xn's.ob.t. H.	TILLOTSON	1735	58002019
T	Xt. Gra.& T.	BEVERIDGE	1720	46001017
T	Xt. Pat.t. Xns	BEVERIDGE	1720	63001015
T	Xt.co.t.jud.	FLAVEL	1673	47010042
T	Xt.co.t.jud.	CARRINGTON	1750	47010042
T	Xt.do all t.w.	ORTON	1776	44007037
T	Xt.t. Head.	BAXTER	1675	49012027
T	Xt.t. Proph.	BADDELLEY	1766	46006014
T	Xt.t. Saviour	COLE	1692	45001077
T	Xt.t. Saviour	BOSTON	1753	65004014
T	Xt.t. Testat.	TAYLOR	1723	61009006
T	Xt.t. W.&c.	HORTON	1679	46014006
T	Xt.t. W.&c.	BEVERIDGE	1720	46014006
T	Xt's. F.t. Dis	LARDNER	1760	46014027
T	Xt's.auth. T.	LELAND	1769	43007028
T	Xt's.c.t. Xns.	MARTIN	1779	43005029
T	Xt's K.n.t.w.	GREENHILL	1768	46018036
T	Xy.j.b. O. T.	BULLOCK	1726	61008007
T	3 Ev.last.t.	HILDROP	1711	43024021
T	3 Evil last T.	HILDROP	1711	44013019
TA	Ta.up Cross.	CLARKSON	1696	45014027
TAK	Tak. Advice	MILNER	1751	20019020
TAK	Tak. N.york.	OBERNE	1776	24013015
TAK	Tak. Scandal	WESTON	1747	44009043
TAK	Tak. Xt's. Y.	MEDE	1672	43011028
TAK	Tak. Xt's. Y.	COCKBURE	1697	43011028
TAK	Tak. Xt's. Y.	BEVERIDGE	1720	43011029
TAK	Tak.aw. Sin.	SUTTON	1718	46001029
TAL	Improv. Tal.	GOUGH	1751	43025021

Keyword	In its Context	Author	Year	BkChpVrs
TAL	Improv. Tal.	WILSON	1781	45012048
TALEB	Ag. Taleb.	FROST	17--	03019016
TALENTS	Dif. Talents.	SHERLOCK	1772	45012048
TALENTS	Diff. Talents	MARKLAND	1729	43025014
TALENTS	Of Talents.	NEWTON	1782	43025014
TALENTS	Par. Talents.	CARR	1777	45019016
TALENTS	Talents.	DODD	1757	43025021
TALENTS	Talents.	DODD	1757	43025024
TALENTS	Talents.	STEBBING	1760	43025029
TALENTS	Talents.	BULKLEY	1771	43025029
TALENTS	The Talents.	BRAGGE	1702	43025014
TALK	Fool.talk.	BARROW	1716	52005004
TALK	Talk.much.	DAWES	1733	20010019
TARES	Tares.	BRAGGE	1702	43013024
TARES	Tares.	HOLE	1716	43013024
TARES	Tares.	ECCLES	1755	43013030
TARES	Tares.	DODD	1757	43013024
TARES	Tares.	STEBBING	1760	43013025
TARES	Tares.	BOURN	1763	43013024
TARES	Tares.	BULKLEY	1771	43013036
TARES	Tares.	SHERLOCK	1772	43013029
TEA	Tea. G.&c.	FLAVEL	1673	46006045
TEA	Un. Gos.tea.	FLEMING	1772	49001001
TEA	Xt. Tea.mor.	DUCHAL	1753	43007025
TEAC	Sav.ex.teac.	LELAND	1769	46007046
TEM	Carel. Tem.	CARTER	1729	20021029
TEM	Deliv.fm. Tem.	STEPHENS	1699	43006013
TEM	Deliv.fm. Tem.	BUCK	17--	43006013
TEM	Deliv.fm. Tem.	NEWCOME	1702	43006013
TEM	Deliv.fm. Tem.	HOLE	1715	43006013
TEM	Deliv.fm. Tem.	MANGEY	1717	43006013
TEM	Deliv.fm. Tem.	BLACKALL	1723	43006013
TEM	Deliv.fm. Tem.	JACKSON	1728	43006013
TEM	Deliv.fm. Tem.	MOSS	1732	43006013
TEM	Deliv.fm. Tem.	LITTLETON	1735	43006013
TEM	Deliv.fm. Tem.	BISSE	1740	43006013
TEM	Deliv.fm. Tem.	BLAIR	1740	43006013
TEM	Fast.& Tem.	BURNET	1747	45004012
TEM	Paul's Tem.	FANCH	1768	50012007
TEM	Peace. Tem.	SEATON	1720	01013008
TEM	Purif. Tem.	SHERIDAN	1720	45019045
TEM	Rent V.tem.	ERSKINE	1764	43027051
TEM	Tem. Ad. R.	TAYLOR	1719	20003017
TEM	Tem. Ad. R.	STERNE	1769	20003017
TEM	Tem. Bl.&c.	JENNINGS	1757	57004007
TEM	Tem. Bl.&c.	LARDNER	1769	57004007
TEM	Tem. Bl.&c.	JORTIN	1774	57004007
TEM	Tem. Pa.&c.	ABERNETHY	1748	64001006
TEM	Tem. Virtue	FORDYCE	1767	20004005
TEM	Tem.punish.	LANGHORNE	1773	21008011
TEM	Th.tem.&et.	BADLAND	1676	50004018
TEM	Th.tem.&et.	BEVERIDGE	1720	50004018
TEM	Xt.sav. Tem.	GILL	1773	43008025
TEM	Xt's.& Tem.	DAVIES	1720	45004013
TEMP	M's Temp.d.	GERARD	1780	20025008
TEMP	Peace Temp.	GARDINER	1720	43005009

INDEXES TO THIRD VOLUME: E: KEYWORD-IN-CONTEXT INDEX OF OTHER SUBJECTS OR OCCASIONS

Keyword	In its Context	Author	Year	BkChpVrs
TEMP	Peace Temp.	BLACKALL	1723	43005009
TEMP	Peace Temp.	EDWARDS	1726	43005009
TEMP	Peace Temp.	BLAIR	1740	43005009
TEMP	Peace Temp.	ABERNETHY	1751	43005009
TEMP	Peace Temp.	COBDEN	1757	43005009
TEMP	Serp. Temp.	CHANDLER	1769	01003014
TEMP	Sin.temp. G.	ADAMS	1716	43004007
TEMP	Temp.& Intempe	SMITH	1740	49009025
TEMP	Temp. Ev.not G	BROWN	1722	45013004
TEMP	Temp. Ev.not G	HOLLAND	1753	45013004
TEMP	Temp. Gosp.	WEST	1762	45009055
TEMP	Temp. Gosp.	JORTIN	1774	45009056
TEMP	Temp. Judg.	TREBECK	1730	45013001
TEMP	Temp. Poss.	ABERNETHY	1751	45016008
TEMP	Temp.o De.	WHARTON	1728	63005008
TEMPE	Xt's. Tempe.	EVANS	1737	53002005
TEMPE	Xt's. Tempe.	ENFIELD	1772	53002005
TEMPER	Jes. Temper.	GROSVENOR	1724	45024047
TEMPER	Temper.eat.	ANONYMOUS	1772	20023001
TEMPER	Xn. Temper.	EVANS	1737	64001004
TEMPERANCE	Temperance	BEVERIDGE	1720	45021034
TEMPERANCE	Temperance	DYKES	1722	20031004
TEMPERANCE	Temperance	EDWARDS	1726	45021034
TEMPERANCE	Temperance	EVANS	1737	45021034
TEMPERANCE	Temperance	COOKE	1739	49009025
TEMPERANCE	Temperance	DODWELL	1748	45021034
TEMPL	Templ. Des.	ERSKINE	1764	46002019
TEMPT	Dev. Tempt.	STAFFORD	1699	50002011
TEMPT	Dev. Tempt.	WAKE	1716	50002011
TEMPT	Dev. Tempt.	SHARP	1729	50002011
TEMPT	Dev. Tempt.	WHITFIELD	1739	50002011
TEMPT	Dev. Tempt.	WESTLEY	1750	50002011
TEMPT	G's Tempt.	FROYSELL	1678	01022001
TEMPT	Sat. Tempt.	FROYSELL	1678	50002011
TEMPT	Tempt. Bel.	FARMER	1756	56003005
TEMPT	Tempt. Xt.	SHOWER	1694	49010009
TEMPT	Xt's. Tempt.	SHERLOCK	1772	45004001
TEMPT	Xt's Tempt.	FLOWER	1669	43004009
TEMPT	Xt's Tempt.	FARINDON	1674	43004001
TEMPT	Xt's Tempt.	HACKET	1675	43004001
TEMPT	Xt's Tempt.	HACKET	1675	43004002
TEMPT	Xt's Tempt.	HACKET	1675	43004003
TEMPT	Xt's Tempt.	HACKET	1675	43004004
TEMPT	Xt's Tempt.	HACKET	1675	43004005
TEMPT	Xt's Tempt.	HACKET	1675	43004006
TEMPT	Xt's Tempt.	HACKET	1675	43004007
TEMPT	Xt's Tempt.	HACKET	1675	43004008
TEMPT	Xt's Tempt.	HACKET	1675	43004009
TEMPT	Xt's Tempt.	HACKET	1675	43004010
TEMPT	Xt's Tempt.	HACKET	1675	43004011
TEMPT	Xt's Tempt.	GELL	1676	43004004
TEMPT	Xt's Tempt.	PIERCE	1679	43004009
TEMPT	Xt's Tempt.	MANTON	1685	43004001
TEMPT	Xt's Tempt.	MANTON	1685	43004005
TEMPT	Xt's Tempt.	MANTON	1685	43004007
TEMPT	Xt's Tempt.	MANTON	1685	43004008

Keyword	In its Context	Author	Year	BkChpVrs
TEMPT	Xt's Tempt.	CONANT	1699	43004001
TEMPT	Xt's Tempt.	CONANT	1699	43004002
TEMPT	Xt's Tempt.	CONANT	1699	43004003
TEMPT	Xt's Tempt.	CONANT	1699	43004004
TEMPT	Xt's Tempt.	CONANT	1699	43004005
TEMPT	Xt's Tempt.	CONANT	1699	43004006
TEMPT	Xt's Tempt.	CONANT	1699	43004007
TEMPT	Xt's Tempt.	CONANT	1699	43004009
TEMPT	Xt's Tempt.	BRAGGE	1706	43004001
TEMPT	Xt's Tempt.	MANTON	1708	43004001
TEMPT	Xt's Tempt.	STANHOPE	1715	43004001
TEMPT	Xt's Tempt.	HOLE	1716	43004001
TEMPT	Xt's Tempt.	EYRE	1738	43004001
TEMPT	Xt's Tempt.	EYRE	1738	43004004
TEMPT	Xt's Tempt.	EYRE	1738	43004007
TEMPT	Xt's Tempt.	EYRE	1738	43004010
TEMPT	Xt's Tempt.	WHEATLY	1746	43004002
TEMPT	Xt's Tempt.	WHEATLY	1746	43004005
TEMPT	Xt's Tempt.	FARMER	1756	43004001
TEMPT	Xt's Tempt.	MUNTON	1756	43004001
TEMPT	Xt's Tempt.	WHITE	1757	43004001
TEMPT	Xt's Tempt.	CHANDLER	1769	43004001
TEMPT	Xt's Tempt.	BOURDALOUE	1776	43004001
TEMPTA	Ag. Tempta.	KILLINBECK	1717	18002009
TEMPTA	Of Tempta.	JEFFERY	1710	01003005
TEMPTAT	Temptat.	SCATTERGOOD	1723	62001012
TEMPTAT	Temptat.	SOUTH	1724	64002009
TEMPTAT	Temptat.	BALGUY	1750	61012001
TEMPTAT	Temptat.	WEBB	1765	24012005
TEMPTATION	Temptation.	ROSEWELL	1715	43026041
TEMPTATION	Temptation.	KILLINBECK	1717	50002011
TEMPTATION	Temptation.	WAPLE	1718	52006011
TEMPTATION	Temptation.	SOUTH	1724	43026041
TEMPTATION	Temptation.	SOUTH	1724	69003010
TEMPTATION	Temptation.	SKELTON	1754	20017003
TEMPTATION	Temptation.	SHERLOCK	1772	43026041
TEMPTATIONS	Temptations	CHILLINGWORTH	1664	49010013
TEMPTATIONS	Temptations	HICKES	1713	49010013
TEMPTATIONS	Temptations	SOUTH	1724	49010013
TEMPTATIONS	Temptations	MARSHALL	1731	62001012
TEMPTATIONS	Temptations	ATTERBURY	1734	49010013
TEMPTATIONS	Temptations	PETERS	1737	49010013
TEMPTATIONS	Temptations	CONEY	1750	49010013
TEMPTATIONS	Temptations	MARSHALL	1750	65002013
TEMPTATIONS	Temptations	TRAPP	1752	49010013
TEMPTATIONS	Temptations	LLOYD	1765	49010013
TEMPTS	G.tempts n.	BERRIMAN	1763	62001013
TEN	G. Ten. Gos.	BOTT	1724	45009056
TEN	G. Ten. Gos.	ORR	1739	45009056
TEN	G's ten. Ca.	BRADY	1730	23005003
TEN	Ten.of Virt.	TIDCOMBE	1757	19073003
TEN	Ten Lep.&c.	BRAGGE	1702	45017012
TEN	Ten Virgins.	GELL	1676	43025001
TEN	Ten Virgins.	BRAGGE	1702	43025001
TEN	Ten Virgins.	SHEPHERD	1702	43025001
TEN	Ten Virgins.	COLMAN	1707	43025001

Keyword	In its Context	Author	Year	BkChpVrs
TEN	Ten Virgins.	TILLOTSON	1735	43025001
TEN	Ten Virgins.	WHITFIELD	1740	43025013
TEN	Ten Virgins.	DODD	1757	43025001
TEN	Ten Virgins.	BOURN	1764	43025001
TEN	Ten Virgins.	BULKLEY	1771	43025001
TEN	Ten Virgins.	BROUGHTON	1778	43025013
TEND	Tend. Spirit	EVANS	1737	14034003
TEND	Tend.o. Xty.	GILBERT	1724	58001007
TEND	Tend.o. Xty.	HODGE	1758	46007018
TEND	Tend.of Xy.	SCOTT	1743	49001030
TER	Ter.& Qu. S.	CLARKE	1734	69002029
TERMS	Terms o. Sal.	SHARPE	1734	65003002
TERMS	Terms Acc.	HOADLY	1727	45010025
TERMS	Terms Com,	LORTIE	1720	43018007
TERMS	Terms Salv.	IBBOT	1726	48008018
TERR	Terr. Guilt.	CONEY	1730	47024025
TERR	Terr.of Ld.	STILLINGFLEET	1707	50005002
TERR	Terr.of Ld.	PYLE	1777	50005010
TERRIBLE	G.terrible.	ATTERBURY	1743	33001003
TEST	Lo. Test. Xn.	SOUTHCOMBE	1752	46013034
TEST	O.& N. Test.	KNOX	1768	50004004
TEST	O.& N. Test.	KNOX	1768	64002001
TEST	O.& N. Test.	KNOX	1768	68000003
TEST	Pr. Test. J. C	BRACKENRIDGE	1764	69019010
TEST	Test ag. Con.	SMITH	1719	50001012
TEST	Test.kno. Xt.	WHEATLY	1746	65002003
TEST	Test.ne.f. M.	SKELTON	1754	58001013
TEST	Test.necess.	LOVE	1754	58002001
TEST	Test.of Res.	LANGHORNE	1773	49015023
TESTAT	Xt.t. Testat.	TAYLOR	1723	61009006
TEXT	Text c.&ex.	MEDE	1672	61010005
TEXT	Text expl.	HORTON	1679	66000008
TEXT	Text expl.	ALLESTREE	1684	50006002
TEXT	Text expl.	ALLESTREE	1684	63004001
TEXT	Text expl.	MORE	1692	51006014
TEXT	Text expl.	CLAGETT	1704	48008028
TEXT	Text expl.	BULL	1713	50012007
TEXT	Text expl.	WAKE	1716	68000003
TEXT	Text expl.	DUNLOP	1722	56001001
TEXT	Text expl.	DUNLOP	1722	56001007
TEXT	Text expl.	SCATTERGOOD	1723	48013014
TEXT	Text expl.	SHARP	1734	43020016
TEXT	Text expl.	TILLOTSON	1734	45016008
TEXT	Text expl.	STEPHENS	1737	44013032
TEXT	Text expl.	ALTHAM	1732	65005011
TEXT	Text expl.	STEPHENS	1737	63003018
TEXT	Text expl.	STEPHENS	1737	63004007
TEXT	Text expl.	COOKE	1739	47024025
TEXT	Text expl.	GROVE	1741	43027046
TEXT	Text expl.	JOHNSON	1740	69014013
TEXT	Text expl.	GROVE	1741	49015019
TEXT	Text expl.	LEIGHTON	1746	48013011
TEXT	Text expl.	LEIGHTON	1746	49001030
TEXT	Text expl.	WESTLEY	1748	65003009
TEXT	Text expl.	WESTLEY	1771	52005014
TEXT	Text expla.	LEIGHTON	1746	45013001

Keyword	In its Context	Author	Year	BkChpVrs
TEXT	Text explai.	SHARP	1734	47013048
TEXT	Text.expl.	HORTON	1679	50013008
TEXT	Text.expl.	MORE	1692	46004031
TEXT	Text Expl.	KIDDER	1697	55005012
TH	Ab.free-th.	FOSTER	1732	51005013
TH	Const. Th.	BURROUGHS	1733	55005018
TH	Earthly Th.	SMITH	1740	45008014
TH	Ev.th.not s.	SMITH	1717	45016019
TH	Exp.fit.of th.	DOWARS	1775	21003002
TH	G's&our Th.	SHOWER	1699	23055007
TH	Gos.g.str.th.	WHITTY	1772	45005026
TH	Gos.un.th.u.	BEVERIDGE	1720	61004002
TH	Gos.un.th.u.	CLARKE	1727	61004002
TH	In th.&n. W.	LITTLETON	1735	54003002
TH	L's Ur.& Th.	GILL	1773	05033008
TH	Life m.th. M.	BLAIR	1740	43006025
TH	N.5.& Th.s.	WRIGHT	1710	46015012
TH	O.th.necess.	DELAUNE	1728	43006033
TH	O.th.needf.	WEBSTER	1753	45010042
TH	O.th.needf.	MORRIS	1757	45010041
TH	O.th.needf.	DODDERIDGE	1761	45010041
TH	O.th.needf.	DAVIES	1766	45010041
TH	O.th.needf.	HUNTER	1774	45010041
TH	O.th.needf.	CRAIG	1775	45010041
TH	Pra.& Th.	SCOUGAL	1726	19107015
TH	Praise& Th.	GROVE	1741	19136001
TH	Pray.& Th.	CASE	1774	47002042
TH	Priest on Th.	HARRIS	1724	37004013
TH	Prov.th.hon.	BARROW	1716	50008021
TH	Rel.o.th.n.	HORTON	1679	45010042
TH	Rel.o.th.n.	BEVERIDGE	1720	45010042
TH	Rel.o.th.n.	GROVE	1742	45010042
TH	Ren.h.th. D.	RYVES	1715	50004002
TH	Rig. Th.rig.	TATE	1666	20012005
TH	Salv.th. Jes.	DAVIES	1766	46003026
TH	Savr's.th.&c.	LARDNER	1760	46019028
TH	Seek.th.abo.	SCATTERGOOD	1723	54003001
TH	Seek.th.abo.	SNAPE	1745	54003001
TH	Th. Du. Xn's	GROVE	1741	55005018
TH	Th. Du. Xn's.	COOPER	1677	55005018
TH	Th. Du. Xn's.	DORRINGTON	1703	55005018
TH	Th. Du. Xn's.	BEVERIDGE	1720	55005018
TH	Th.tem.&et.	BADLAND	1676	50004018
TH	Th.tem.&et.	BEVERIDGE	1720	50004018
TH	Th.to G.&c.	PHILIPS	1775	19107043
TH	Vict.th. Xt.	WELCH	1752	48008037
TH	Xn.pos.a.th.	IBBBOT	1726	50006010
THANK	Thank. Pen.	BROME	1712	45007047
THANK	Thank. Pen.	DODD	1757	45007047
THANK	Thank. Pen.	DODD	1757	45008047
THE	The ac.time	RUSSEL	1746	50006002
THE	The bl.choi.	HART	1702	61011025
THE	The dark vis.	WILKINSON	1660	34002003
THE	The star.	HARRIS	1724	04024017
THE	The 3 Heav.	STURMY	1716	50012002
THE	The Adulte.	BRAGGE	1706	46008003

INDEXES TO THIRD VOLUME: E: KEYWORD-IN-CONTEXT INDEX OF OTHER SUBJECTS OR OCCASIONS

Keyword	In its Context	Author	Year	BkChpVrs
THE	The Almigh.	HOLE	1715	69001008
THE	The Angel.	HARRIS	1724	02023020
THE	The Creed.	WILSON	1781	46017003
THE	The Creed.	WILSON	1781	47002032
THE	The Creed.	WILSON	1781	59001016
THE	The Epis.expla	SMALRIDGE	1724	60000010
THE	The Epis.expla	MARSHALL	1731	60000010
THE	The Fall.	CRAIG	1775	01003001
THE	The Gospel.	TERRY	1746	49001021
THE	The Jailor c.	WEBB	1766	47016033
THE	The L.good.	BROWNE	1749	48007019
THE	The Pharis.	HAMMOND	1684	45018011
THE	The Schism.	CULVERWELL	1661	49003004
THE	The Scrip.	HOPKINS	1708	64001019
THE	The Shiloh.	HARRIS	1724	01049010
THE	The Sin&c.	NEWTON	1782	61012001
THE	The Sower.	CLARKE	1736	45008015
THE	The Sower.	DODD	1757	45008014
THE	The Sword.	HILDROP	1711	23034002
THE	The Talents.	BRAGGE	1702	43025014
THE	The Union.	COLLINS	1707	26037019
THE	The Vineya.	DODD	1757	43021033
THE	The Vineya.	BOURN	1764	43021033
THE	The Vineya.	BULKLEY	1771	43021037
THE	The Xn.	WHATLEY	1746	47026028
THEATRE	Div theatre.	WALL	1662	45003006
THEFT	Prev. Theft.	PENN	1757	52004028
THEFT	Theft.	HOPKINS	1692	02020015
THEFT	Theft.	FOSTER	1744	02020015
THEFT	Theft.	DELANY	1766	02020015
THEFT	Theft& Rob.	WILSON	1781	02020014
THEO	Mod. Theo.	MARSH	1701	18038004
THEO	Theo. Lect.	HENLEY	1729	45019022
THEOL	Xt's. Theol.	DERHAM	1730	47026028
THEORY	Theory of m.	BROUGHTON	1778	41018008
THHUGH	Evil.thhugh.	STEBBING	1760	43015019
THIEF	Pen. Thief.	LIGHTFOOT	1684	45023042
THIEF	Pen. Thief.	STANHOPE	1705	45023042
THIEF	Pen. Thief.	WHISTON	1709	45023042
THIEF	Pen. Thief.	HOADLY	1727	45023042
THIEF	Pen. Thief.	BOYSE	1728	45023039
THIEF	Pen. Thief.	BULKLEY	1752	45023043
THIEF	Pen. Thief.	NEWMAN	1751	45023042
THIEF	Pen. Thief.	JORTIN	1774	45023042
THIEF	Pen. Thief.	EDWARDS	1775	45023042
THINGS	Lawf.things	WILKINSON	1677	45017027
THINGS	Secr.things.	JORTIN	1774	05029029
THINGS	Things exc.	HUSSEY	1753	53001010
THINGS	Things exc.	WEBB	1772	53001010
THINGS	Things lov.	PYLE	1777	53004008
THINK	W.think&c.	WHITFIELD	1740	43022043
THIR	Inv.t.thir. S.	DODDERIDGE	1761	46007037
THIR	Inv.t.thir. S.	PEARSE	1763	46007037
THIS	Wis.o.this w.	CLARKE	1727	49001020
THO	St. Tho.d.	STANHOPE	1715	52002019
THO	St. Tho.d.	HOLE	1716	52002019

Keyword	In its Context	Author	Year	BkChpVrs
THO	St. Tho.d.	WILDER	1741	46020027
THO	St. Tho.unb.	COCK	1710	46020027
THO	St. Tho.uub.	SHOWER	1702	46020027
THO	Wandr. Tho.	WESTLEY	1771	50010004
THOM	St. Thom.d.	HICKMAN	1713	50005007
THOM	St. Thom.d.	STANHOPE	1715	46020024
THOM	St. Thom.d.	HOLE	1716	46020024
THOM	St. Thom.d.	ADAMS	1716	46020027
THOM	St. Thom.d.	SCATTERGOOD	1723	46020027
THOM	St. Thom.d.	LEEKE	1730	46014001
THOM	St. Thom.d.	WHEATLY	1746	46020024
THOM	St. Thom.d.	LARDNER	1760	46020029
THORN	P's. Thorn.	FANCH	1768	49012007
THORN	Thorn flesh.	JORTIN	1774	50012007
THOU	W.art thou	JENKINS	1779	01003009
THOUG	Evil Thoug.	FIDDES	1720	20024009
THOUG	Orig.thoug.	HUSSEY	1758	43015019
THOUG	Sinf. Thoug.	TAYLOR	1725	01006005
THOUGH	Evil.though.	CALAMY	1726	43015019
THOUGH	Evil.though.	CHILCOT	1734	43015019
THOUGH	Va. Though.	DORRINGTON	1703	19119113
THOUGHTS	Thoughts.	BOND	1711	43009004
THOUS	Five Thous.	BRAGGE	1702	46006005
THR	Hap.thr. Xt.	CLARKE	1736	59001002
THR	Salv.thr. Xt.	LORIMER	1713	47004012
THR	Thr.o Grace	WALKER	1765	61004016
THRIVE	W.to thrive.	GOUGE	1706	43010041
THRO'	Del.thro' Xt.	CLARKE	1735	48007024
THRO'	Salv.thro' F.	BEVERIDGE	1720	53002012
THTS	Licent. Thts.	BRADY	1704	50010005
THUR	Thur.b. East.	STANHOPE	1715	45023001
THURS	Thurs.b. E.	STANHOPE	1715	49011017
TI	Ti.of Dang.	HERVEY	1759	61011029
TID	Ag.ev. Tid.	ANONYMOUS	1710	19112007
TILLAGE	Tillage&c.	DYKES	1722	20031016
TIM	On the Tim.	THOMSON	1757	03018025
TIM	P's. Ch. Tim.	NEWLIN	1728	58004005
TIM	Pict.of Tim.	WILLIAMS	1662	24014010
TIM	Tim.& Seas.	HORTON	1679	47001007
TIM	Tim.in G.h.	AMORY	1775	19031015
TIME	Empl. Time.	DODD	1772	20006006
TIME	End of Time	RUSSELL	1746	69010005
TIME	End of Time	WATTS	1753	69010005
TIME	Husban time	LITTLETON	1735	19090012
TIME	Impr. Time.	GEE	1692	52005016
TIME	Impr. Time.	LARDNER	1769	52005016
TIME	Life time.	ELLIS	1704	45016025
TIME	Life time.	GILBERT	1724	45016025
TIME	On Time.	SHORTHOSE	1738	52005015
TIME	Rede. Time.	BURTON	1685	52005016
TIME	Rede. Time.	WADE	1692	52005016
TIME	Rede. Time.	BIRKWOOD	1693	52005016
TIME	Rede. Time.	SHEPPARD	17--	52005016
TIME	Rede. Time.	BRADY	1730	52005016
TIME	Rede. Time.	ROGERS	1735	52005016
TIME	Rede. Time.	SIMONS	1743	52005016

Keyword	In its Context	Author	Year	BkChpVrs
TIME	Rede. Time.	EVANS	1774	52005016
TIME	Rede. Time.	HORNECK	1774	52005016
TIME	Rede. Time.	HORNE	1778	52005016
TIME	Shor.of time	FULLER	1700	49007029
TIME	Stab.of time.	OUTRAM	1697	23033006
TIME	The ac.time	RUSSEL	1746	50006002
TIME	Time f.all.	HALL	1660	21003004
TIME	Time& Eter.	MANTON	1693	50004018
TIME	Time& Eter.	HOPKINS	1712	50004018
TIME	Time& Eter.	HORT	1738	50004018
TIME	Time& Eter.	JOHNSON	1740	50004018
TIME	Time& Eter.	HARWOOD	1767	50004018
TIME	Time Mess.	HARRIS	1724	27009026
TIME	Time Xt's. C.	PYLE	1777	69022012
TIME	Tr.time S. P.	TURNER	1684	49014020
TIME	Val.o. Time.	KENNET	1715	52005016
TIMES	Diff. Times.	WHICHCOTE	1702	19095007
TIMES	Peril.times.	BOSTON	1753	58003001
TIMES	Times same	SCUTH	1744	21007010
TIMOTH	Timoth. Xr.	OAKES	1747	58003015
TIMOTH	Timoth. Xr.	LOVEDER	1756	58003015
TIT	3d Tit.of Xt.	FLAVEL	1673	22005016
TITLE	Title on Cr.	FLAVEL	1673	45023038
TITLES	X's fam.titles	DYER	1666	23005016
TO	Ad.to Debt.	DREW	1725	05006012
TO	Add.to reg.	DODDERIDGE	1742	62001018
TO	Adm.to Att.	HORTON	1679	61002001
TO	Adm.to You.	EDWARDS	1775	58002022
TO	Adv.to appr.	DODD	1772	52006006
TO	Adv.to Prot.	WILCOCKS	1709	55004001
TO	Adv.to Sail.	HAYWARD	1746	19107031
TO	Adv.to Son.	PEMBERTON	1727	13020010
TO	Adv.to You.	ENFIELD	1772	11020011
TO	Advice to Y.	SHOWER	1699	19119009
TO	Appro.to G.	WATTS	1753	19065004
TO	Av.to Truth.	STRAIGHT	1741	46008045
TO	Bel. D.to L.	HALL	1777	51002019
TO	Bel.n.to Bap.	CLARKE	1734	44016016
TO	C.to o.m's. S.	STOWE	1681	49003006
TO	Call to unc.	BOURN	1754	26033002
TO	Call to Rep.	CLARKE	1734	44002017
TO	Call to Rep.	WARREN	1748	44002017
TO	Call to Rep.	SUTTON	1754	61004007
TO	Call to Shul.	TANNER	1674	22006013
TO	Call to Sinn.	DYER	1666	69003020
TO	Caution to Y.	MUNTON	1756	21011009
TO	Caution to Y.	STEBBING	1759	21011009
TO	Ch.d.to d. P.	BURNABY	1777	51006010
TO	Ch.to poor.	DYKES	1722	20031020
TO	Ch.to poor.	STEBBING	1760	05015011
TO	Ch.to Clergy	POTTER	1753	51004018
TO	Ch.to Poor.	NORRIS	1728	65003017
TO	Cha.to poor.	WILLIAMS	1774	45014012
TO	Cha.to rich.	BOYSE	1728	57006017
TO	Clem.to Br.	ANONYMOUS	1760	20012010
TO	Clem.to Br.	GRANGER	1772	20012010

Keyword	In its Context	Author	Year	BkChpVrs
TO	Com.to bapt.	BRETT	1712	43028019
TO	Com.to Xt.	HORTON	1679	46006037
TO	Com.to Xt.	CLARKSON	1696	46005040
TO	Com.to Xt.	BEVERIDGE	1720	46005040
TO	Com.to Xt.	COOKE	1739	46005040
TO	Com.to Xt.	HUNT	1748	46005040
TO	Com.to Xt.	NEWTON	1767	43011028
TO	Com.to Xt.	BARCLAY	1763	61007025
TO	Conf.to W.	SHARP	1734	48012002
TO	Conf.to W.	ROGER	1735	48012002
TO	Conf.to W.	NEWMAN	1760	48012002
TO	Conf.to W.	WEST	1762	48012002
TO	Conf.to W.	STENNETT	1771	48012002
TO	Confor.to O.	SMITH	1777	20029025
TO	Cup to all.	STEEL	1675	43026027
TO	D. M.to pen.	DAVIES	1766	24031018
TO	D.as done to.	BENNETT	1728	43007012
TO	Dedic.to G.	DAVIES	1766	49006019
TO	Desires to S.	MOORE	1716	62001015
TO	Dir.to Sinn.	DODDERIDGE	1742	47009006
TO	Dir.to Y.	NESBIT	1713	19119009
TO	Dir.to Y.	MAY	1744	19119009
TO	Direct.to pr.	HORTON	1679	13004010
TO	Div. T.to Jes.	LARDNER	1760	43027052
TO	Do go.to all.	BURTON	1685	51006010
TO	Do go.to all.	BILLINGSLEY	1712	51006010
TO	Du.to Equals	HUBBARD	1757	20018024
TO	Dut.to infer.	JENNINGS	1757	47010002
TO	Dut.to Neig.	BLAIR	1740	43007012
TO	Dut.to Par.	HOLLAND	1753	02020012
TO	Dut.to Sup.	PRICE	1757	48013007
TO	Duty to G.	HUNT	1748	18022021
TO	Duty to G.	JORTIN	1774	59002011
TO	Duty to Mast.	NICHOLS	1701	54003022
TO	Duty to Mast.	FRANKLIN	1765	54003022
TO	Duty to Par.	DAVIES	1754	02002002
TO	Eng.to Hol.	WILKINSON	1660	64003011
TO	Enmity to T.	TILLOTSON	1735	46003020
TO	Exh.to Lib.	SQUIRE	1714	51006010
TO	Fai.n.to Sal.	CLAGETT	1704	61011006
TO	Fai.n.to Sal.	HOPKINS	1708	47016031
TO	Far.to life.	LAMBERT	1779	45002029
TO	Farw.to life.	SHAW	1667	50005006
TO	Fear n.to Fai.	PIERCE	1679	49010012
TO	G.to be fear.	SMALRIDGE	1724	23051012
TO	G's love to us	BLAIR	1740	43007009
TO	G's. L.to M.	PELLING	1694	46003016
TO	G's. L.to Sin.	CLARKE	1732	46003016
TO	G's.reg.to ri.	REYNER	1745	63003012
TO	G's.reg.to P.	WILCOX	1757	38003017
TO	Glory to G.	HOLE	1717	45002024
TO	Go.to Law.	HORNECK	1706	43005040
TO	Grat.to G.	MAYNARD	1722	45017017
TO	Grat.to G.	BRADY	1730	45017017
TO	Grat.to G.	WHITE	1757	19086012
TO	Grat.to G.	EATON	1764	19116012

Keyword	In its Context	Author	Year	BkChpVrs
TO	Grat.to G.	DEVEREL	1777	19116012
TO	H.to G's N.	SKELTON	1754	03019030
TO	Hol.nec.to S.	BENSON	1748	61012014
TO	In.to w.o. G.	SNAPE	1745	49007029
TO	Indiff.to life	MOSS	1732	49007029
TO	Indiff.to life	DAVIES	1766	49007029
TO	Indiff.to R.	GRAY	1779	19085006
TO	Ingrat.to G.	DAVIES	1766	14032008
TO	Inj.to Souls.	CLAGETT	1720	20008036
TO	Intro.to Ord.	HALL	1759	45010023
TO	Introd.to Cr.	CARRINGTON	1750	50013005
TO	Inv.to Xt.	MAY	1757	69022003
TO	Inv.to Xt.	WHITTY	1766	69022017
TO	Kind.to Jew.	STEPHENS	1735	58001016
TO	Look to Xt.	DAVIES	1771	23045022
TO	Love to Xt.	BOYSE	1728	63001008
TO	Love to Xt.	ORR	1739	43010037
TO	Love to Xt.	SOUTH	1744	43010037
TO	Love to Xt.	ABERNETHY	1748	43010037
TO	Ly.to H. Gh.	NEWLIN	1728	47005003
TO	M's.rel.to G.	FOSTER	1744	47017028
TO	M's Inv.to H.	ORTON	1776	04010029
TO	Mot.to Rep.	ELLIS	1704	45016031
TO	Mot.to Virt.	BLAIR	1777	51006009
TO	N's mes.to D.	DE COURCY	1773	10012007
TO	O. Rel.to N.	DUCHAL	1765	18038007
TO	Ob to sp. G.	SMALRIDGE	1724	61013017
TO	Ob.to sp. G.	BARROW	1716	61013017
TO	Ob.to D. W.	STEPHENS	1699	43006010
TO	Ob.to D. W.	NEWCOME	1702	43006010
TO	Ob.to D. W.	NORRIS	1728	43006010
TO	Ob.to D. W.	ROGERS	1736	43006010
TO	Ob.to Gov.	WATSON	1763	59003001
TO	Ob.to Rulers	AGAR	1759	48013001
TO	Obed.to K.	GODDARD	1715	20029004
TO	Obed.to Xt.	KIMBER	1756	43017005
TO	Obj.to Pr.a.	NEWMAN	1711	18021015
TO	Obj.to S.con.	AMORY	1775	49001025
TO	Obl.to Hol.	WHITAKER	1674	58002019
TO	Obl.to L's d.	ORTON	1769	02020008
TO	Par D.to Ch.	EATON	1764	20022006
TO	Path to Hon.	WHEATLAND	1739	20003016
TO	Per.to Union	SHUTTLEWORTH	1718	48015006
TO	Pers.to Hol.	HARRISON	1710	50007001
TO	Piety to Xt.	WILLIAMS	1774	01001011
TO	Prep.to.fast.	GREENHILL	1757	48010001
TO	Pro. M.to A.	GERARD	1780	01022018
TO	R.nec.to c. S.	SKELTON	1754	63002017
TO	R.to G.in Xt.	BRIGHT	1695	50005019
TO	Res.to Min.	FRANCIS	1773	50004005
TO	Res.to Rew.	SCOTT	1743	58004007
TO	Resign.to G.	CARR	1777	09003018
TO	Return to G.	READER	1765	24050005
TO	Rev.to God.	CROWE	1744	24005024
TO	Rever.to Ch.	BERRIMAN	1763	01028017
TO	Road to H.	YOUNG	1706	09002030

Keyword	In its Context	Author	Year	BkChpVrs
TO	S.add to Gos.	TILLOTSON	1735	51001008
TO	Salv.to Sinn.	ERSKINE	1764	47014026
TO	Sat.transf.to	PARKHURST	1707	50011014
TO	Sat.transf.to	SOUTH	1724	50011014
TO	Ser.m.to Go.	FOTHERGILL	1765	57004008
TO	St. P's.d.to F	HOADLY	1754	47024024
TO	St. P's.d.to F	CHANDLER	1769	47024025
TO	St. P's.d.to F	HURD	1780	47024024
TO	Su.sum.to ju.	VINCENT	1667	69022020
TO	Sub to Auth.	MOORE	1715	61010036
TO	Sub.to A.&c.	SHEPHEARD	1771	51005001
TO	Sub.to S. B.	LANGHORNE	1773	62004007
TO	Subj.to Gov.	BOURN	1777	59003001
TO	Subm.to Aff.	D'COETLOGAN	1778	18001020
TO	Subm.to G.	ATTERBURY	1703	18002010
TO	Subm.to G.	JENKS	1700	48010003
TO	Subm.to M.	HORT	1738	63002013
TO	Suff.w.to Gl.	BRADY	1730	69007014
TO	Th.to G.&c.	PHILIPS	1775	19107043
TO	To aged.	STRYPE	1699	59002002
TO	To children.	PALMER	1777	46021015
TO	To do good.	GALE	1726	57006018
TO	To do o.duty	MILWARD	1683	48012021
TO	To kee.l. G.	COOPER	1683	68000021
TO	To Asses.	MURRAY	1772	07003022
TO	To Clergy.	BROWNRIG	1664	49014001
TO	To Prisoners	DODD	1777	45007022
TO	To Y. Pers.	GROSVENOR	1714	19018023
TO	To Y. Pers.	DAVIDSON	1772	21012001
TO	To Young P.	WOODWARD	1697	45015018
TO	To Youth.	STRYPE	1699	59002006
TO	Union to Xt.	SHOWER	1702	50005017
TO	Vir.& V. To.	PYLE	1777	43012036
TO	W.to r.&p.	COLLINGES	1684	05008018
TO	W.to thrive.	GOUGE	1706	43010041
TO	W.to L.& G.	TALBOT	1674	05005029
TO	W.to Riches	WOOD	1698	43006033
TO	Warn to Y.	ROSEWELL	1714	44010021
TO	Way to et. S.	SYNGE	1734	55005021
TO	Way to life.	IBBOT	1726	43019017
TO	Way to Glo.	HILL	1755	19107007
TO	Way to Hap.	RALEIGH	1679	43006033
TO	Way to Hap.	WHALEY	1695	61012013
TO	Way to Heav.	FERNE	1721	64001011
TO	Way to Loy.	OWEN	1684	59003001
TO	Wiv. D.to H.	FLEETWOOD	1737	63003001
TO	Wiv. D.to H.	FLEETWOOD	1737	63003003
TO	Wiv. D.to H.	FLEETWOOD	1737	63003004
TO	Word to Isr.	CHISHULL	1668	61003008
TO	Xn's C.to L.	BULKLEY	1771	51005013
TO	Xns.wa.to H.	ANONYMOUS	1726	47016030
TO	Xt.ab.to save	HOPKINS	1710	61007025
TO	Xt.hon.to F.	WILLIAMS	1770	63002007
TO	Xt.pr.to Bel.	DAVIES	1766	63002007
TO	Xt.to J.& G.	BROWNE	1722	45002032
TO	Xt's. H.to S.	GOODWIN	16--	46013001

Keyword	In its Context	Author	Year	BkChpVrs
TO	Xt's. L.to us.	HORTON	1679	69001005
TO	Xt's.c.to C.	WALLIN	1746	45023034
TO	Xt's.lo.to us.	SHOWER	1702	46015009
TO	Xt's.pr.to sp.	NEWSON	1781	63003019
TO	no Peace to wic	HORTON	1679	23057021
TO	no Peace to wic	FOORD	1719	23057021
TOK	Tok.f.mour.	FLAVEL	1673	45007008
TOLER	Univ. Toler.	SOWDEN	1780	48014004
TON	Brid.f. Ton.	HOOTTON	1709	62001026
TON	Gov.of Ton.	WEST	1676	52004029
TON	Gov.of Ton.	SHORTHOSE	1738	62001026
TON	Gov.of Ton.	BUTLER	1749	62001026
TONG	C.of Tong.	JENKINS	1779	01011006
TONG	Gov. Tong.	BARROW	1716	62003002
TONG	Gov. Tong.	FIDDES	1720	53001027
TONG	Gov. Tong.	LARDNER	1751	62003002
TONG	Sland. Tong.	MOSS	1737	19050020
TONG	Tong. Licen.	BRAILSFORD	1776	63003010
TONGUE	Go. Tongue.	TAYLOR	1668	52004029
TOR	Hell tor.ete.	JENKS	1707	48006023
TOR	Hell Tor.et.	MOSS	1732	43025046
TOR	Hell Tor.et.	TILLOTSON	1735	43025046
TOR	Hell Tor.et.	WARREN	1739	43025046
TOR	Hell Tor.et.	WHITFIELD	1739	43025046
TOR	Hell Tor.et.	VENN	1740	43025046
TOR	Hell Tor.et.	WATERHOUSE	1753	43025046
TOR	Tor.of wick.	ELLIS	1704	45016024
TORM	Hell torm.	DAWES	1733	43025041
TORM	Hell torm.	DAVIS	1756	43025041
TORM	Hell Torm.	DODWELL	1743	56001007
TORM	Hell- Torm.	DUNLOP	1722	44009046
TORM	Hell- Torm.	SCOTT	1743	48013013
TORM	Hell- Torm.	WATTS	1753	44009046
TORM	Hell-torm.	LAKE	1703	69021008
TOU	Tou st.o. Sin.	FLAVEL	1673	69003017
TOW	Conf.tow. G.	ABERNETHY	1751	65003012
TOW	Hu.tow. G.	WAPLE	1720	62004010
TOW	Love tow. G.	SKELTON	1754	45010027
TOW	Piety tow. G.	SEATON	1720	01024048
TR	Diff.st.tr. R.	JEFFERY	1751	58003015
TR	Ea. Tr.su.ac.	BLAIR	1740	43006019
TR	Enoch's Tr.	DODDERIDGE	1761	01005024
TR	Enoch's Tr.	BOSTON	1764	01005024
TR	Enoch's Tr.	MURRAY	1777	01005024
TR	F.in.j.tr.w.	BREVALL	1670	69002010
TR	G. Obj. Tr.	HOLLAND	1753	19118008
TR	Nat.of Tr.	PARKER	1754	46018038
TR	Nat.of Tr.	PEARCE	1779	46018038
TR	Nec.o.tr. Re.	ELSMERE	1767	46009004
TR	No. Tr.in R.	WARNEFORD	1757	57006017
TR	No Tr.in R.	JONES	1690	57006017
TR	No Tr.in R.	GALE	1726	57006017
TR	No Tr.in R.	MARSHALL	1731	57006017
TR	Notes tr. Ch.	KIDDER	1697	47002042
TR	Notes tr. Ch.	KEITH	1704	47002041
TR	Notes tr. Ch.	CHANDLER	1735	57003014

Keyword	In its Context	Author	Year	BkChpVrs
TR	Pil.&c.o. Tr.	PATRICK	1687	57003015
TR	Plea for Tr.	WALKER	1710	11018021
TR	Receiv. Tr.	STRAIGHT	1741	52004015
TR	Rem.of Tr.	TILLOTSON	1735	46014001
TR	Rid.no f. Tr.	GODDARD	1781	21002002
TR	Script.& Tr.	WRIGHT	1735	52002020
TR	Sinner's Tr.	LAMBERT	1779	19027009
TR	T.o.tr.&f.d.	ADAMS	1777	65004001
TR	Tr.& F. Co.	AGAR	1759	06023006
TR	Tr.&c.o. S. S.	CALAMY	1710	58003016
TR	Tr.&c.o. S. S.	BOYS	1716	58003016
TR	Tr.&c.o. S. S.	CLARKE	1735	58003016
TR	Tr.&f.wisd.	CARMICHAEL	1757	62003013
TR	Tr. Ch.of G.	CLARKE	1736	51004022
TR	Tr. D. Du. M.	BREVALL	1670	65005004
TR	Tr. Loyalty.	MYNORS	1716	23030010
TR	Tr. Mot. Ch.	ANONYMOUS	1688	47002041
TR	Tr. Xn.& W.	ORTON	1773	46017016
TR	Tr. Xn. Bapt.	RELLY	1762	52004005
TR	Tr. Xn. Fai.	CLARKE	1727	65005004
TR	Tr. Xn. Zeal.	CLARKE	1734	69003015
TR	Tr. Xn.b. Xr.	GODDARD	1781	47026029
TR	Tr. Xns.few.	CONEY	1730	69003004
TR	Tr. Xt.n.ne.	ERSKINE	1764	61013018
TR	Tr.of G.	WHITBY	1709	05032004
TR	Tr.of G.	TILLOTSON	1735	05032004
TR	Tr.s.	MANNINGHAM	1681	19103001
TR	Tr.s.	MORER	1717	46017021
TR	Tr.s.	CLARKE	1735	05029029
TR	Tr.time S. P.	TURNER	1684	49014020
TR	Tr.val.of M.	WHICHCOTE	1702	45016025
TR	Tri.tr.&f. D.	TILLOTSON	1735	65004001
TR	Un. G.& Tr.	TILLOTSON	1735	57002005
TR	Un. Tr.& L.	PEARSE	1763	52004015
TR	Ver.&tr. Co.	MICHELL	1737	57006004
TR	Wor. Sp. Tr.	MEDE	1672	46004023
TR	Wor. Sp. Tr.	BUNDY	1750	46004023
TR	Xrticks tr. R.	QUINCY	1750	62003017
TR	Xt.tr. Mess.	FREE	1750	45007020
TR	Xt.tr. Moses.	ERSKINE	1764	47007034
TR	Xt's.tr.ov. D.	FANCH	1768	49015025
TRA	E. Tra. O. T.	WHITE	1778	16008007
TRA	Enoch's Tra.	BOYSE	1728	61011005
TRA	Scrip.& Tra.	STILLINGFLEET	1707	54002006
TRA	Tra. Xt's. D.	HORTON	1679	66000009
TRADITIONS	Traditions.	CLAGETT	1704	43015001
TRAG	Trag.of Sin.	JAY	1689	01011004
TRANQUILITY	Tranquility.	STILLINGFLEET	1707	46016033
TRANS	Spir. Trans.	BEVERLEY	1687	43026026
TRANSF	Sat.transf.to	PARKHURST	1707	50011014
TRANSF	Sat.transf.to	SOUTH	1724	50011014
TRANSF	Transf.s.	BROWNRIG	1664	44009002
TRANSF	Xt's. Transf.	BROWNRIG	1664	43017002
TRANSF	Xt's. Transf.	BROWNRIG	1664	43017005
TRANSF	Xt's. Transf.	BROWNRIG	1664	43017006
TRANSF	Xt's. Transf.	MANTON	1685	43017001

INDEXES TO THIRD VOLUME: E: KEYWORD-IN-CONTEXT INDEX OF OTHER SUBJECTS OR OCCASIONS

Keyword	In its Context	Author	Year	BkChpVrs
TRANSF	Xt's. Transf.	MANTON	1685	43017002
TRANSF	Xt's. Transf.	MANTON	1685	43017003
TRANSF	Xt's. Transf.	MANTON	1685	43017004
TRANSF	Xt's. Transf.	GODDEN	1687	43017001
TRANSF	Xt's. Transf.	BRAGGE	1706	43017001
TRANSF	Xt's. Transf.	MANTON	1708	43017008
TRANSF	Xt's. Transf.	FARMER	1756	43017001
TRANSF	Xt's. Transf.	LELAND	1769	43017001
TRANSF	Xt's. Transf.	BULKLEY	1771	43017004
TRANSFIGUR	Transfigur.s.	BROWNRIG	1664	45009028
TRANSFIGUR	Transfigur.s.	BROWNRIG	1664	45009029
TRANSFIGUR	Transfigur.s.	BROWNRIG	1664	45009030
TRANSFIGUR	Transfigur.s.	BROWNRIG	1664	45009031
TRANSFIGUR	Transfigur.s.	BROWNRIG	1664	45009033
TRANSFIGUR	Transfigur.s.	FRANK	1672	45009033
TRANSFIGUR	Transfigur.s.	HACKET	1675	45009028
TRANSFIGUR	Transfigur.s.	HACKET	1675	45009029
TRANSFIGUR	Transfigur.s.	HACKET	1675	45009031
TRANSFIGUR	Transfigur.s.	HACKET	1675	45009033
TRANSFIGUR	Transfigur.s.	HACKET	1675	45009034
TRANSFIGUR	Transfigur.s.	HACKET	1675	45009035
TRANSFIGUR	Transfigur.s.	MANTON	1685	45009028
TRANSFIGUR	Transfigur.s.	MANTON	1685	45009029
TRANSFIGUR	Transfigur.s.	MANTON	1685	45009030
TRANSFIGUR	Transfigur.s.	MANTON	1685	45009032
TRANSGR	On Transgr.	FELTON	1748	01003009
TRANSL	Elij. Transl.	FARMER	1756	12002011
TRANSUB	Ag. Transub.	LE FRANK	1662	43026026
TRANSUB	Ag. Transub.	FOWLER	1699	45022019
TRANSUB	Ag. Transub.	DELANY	1766	43026026
TRANSUB	No Transub.	LAWRENCE	1675	49011023
TRANSUBS	Transubs.	CHANDLER	1769	49011024
TRANSUBST	Transubst.	TURNER	1679	49005007
TRANSUBST	Transubst.	BENSON	1748	49011024
TRANSUBSTA	Transubsta.	GRIFFITH	1701	46006060
TRAVELL	On Travell.	BURNABY	1777	20001020
TRAVELLER	Traveller.	BRAGGE	1704	44013034
TREA	Earth. Trea.	ADEY	1760	43006019
TREA	Judas Trea.	FLAVEL	1673	43026047
TREAS	Athal. Treas.	L.	1660	12011014
TREAS	Heav. Treas.	OUTRAM	1697	43006021
TREAS	Heav. Treas.	PAYNE	1698	43006019
TREAS	Heav. Treas.	HOPKINS	1710	43006020
TREAS	Heav. Treas.	CREYGHTON	1720	43006020
TREAS	Heav. Treas.	BROWN	1722	43006020
TREAS	Heav. Treas.	ADEY	1760	43006020
TREAS	Hid. Treas.	CENNICK	1762	43013044
TREAS	Saints Treas.	LAMBERT	1779	50003005
TREAS	Treas.field.	BULKLEY	1771	43013044
TREAS	True Treas.	WALLIS	1692	43006019
TREAS	Xn's. Treas.	WATTS	1753	49003021
TREAS	Xt's. Treas.	ERSKINE	1764	46016015
TREAT	Treat. Dist.	CLARKE	1727	19031011
TREE	Bar. Fig-tree	DODD	1757	43021018
TREE	Bar. Fig-tree.	BYRDALL	1667	45013006
TREE	Bar. Fig-tree.	BRAGGE	1702	45013006

Keyword	In its Context	Author	Year	BkChpVrs
TREE	Bar. Fig-tree.	BULKLEY	1771	45013007
TREE	Fig-tree.	BOURN	1764	45013006
TREE	Tree of life.	BOLTON	1660	03010003
TREE	Tree of life.	HOLLOWAY	1751	69002007
TREE	Tree of life.	WILLISON	1761	69022002
TREE	Tree of Life.	KENNICOTT	1747	01002008
TREES	Trees& Bra.	HOW	1723	07009014
TRI	Tri.o. Saints.	BADDELLEY	1752	69007014
TRI	Tri.of Fairh.	WILCOX	1757	43015021
TRI	Tri.of Faith.	FOORD	1719	65005004
TRI	Tri.of Faith.	FIDDES	1720	65005004
TRI	Tri.tr.&f. D.	TILLOTSON	1735	65004001
TRIAL	Trial of Spir.	WATERLAND	1742	65004001
TRIAL	Trial of Spir.	STEBBING	1760	65004001
TRIAL	Trial of Spir.	RELLY	1762	65004001
TRIAL	Trial of Spir.	PETERS	1776	65004001
TRIBE	Tribe Asher.	BEVERLEY	1693	05033025
TRIBULATION	Tribulation.	SCATTERGOOD	1723	45014026
TRID	Trid. Gosp	RAMSAY	1672	51001008
TRIED	Relig.tried.	SYNGE	1713	63003015
TRIN	Bapt.in Trin.	ANONYMOUS	1720	43028019
TRIN	On the Trin.	WALLIS	1691	46017003
TRIN	Trin.b.	JACOMB	1676	65005007
TRIN	Trin.b.	LITTLETON	1680	65005007
TRIN	Trin.b.	HOWELL	1711	65005007
TRIN	Trin.b.	LESTLEY	1720	65005007
TRIN	Trin.b.	MARSHALL	1731	65005007
TRIN	Trin.in Uni.	ATTERBURY	1743	65005007
TRIN	Trin.in Uni.	ADAMS	1752	65005007
TRIN	Trin.s.	FRANK	1672	69004008
TRIN	Trin.s.	JONES	1699	24023010
TRIN	Trin.s.	MAUDUIT	1694	50013014
TRIN	Trin.s.	BISSE	1708	61005004
TRIN	Trin.s.	CUMMINGS	1713	43003016
TRIN	Trin.s.	STANHOPE	1714	46003001
TRIN	Trin.s.	HOLE	1716	46003001
TRIN	Trin.s.	HICKMAN	1713	56002016
TRIN	Trin.s.	BARROW	1716	54003002
TRIN	Trin.s.	BEVERIDGE	1720	46010030
TRIN	Trin.s.	CALAMY	1722	43028019
TRIN	Trin.s.	NEWTON	1723	05029029
TRIN	Trin.s.	BEVERIDGE	1720	50013014
TRIN	Trin.s.	WATERLAND	1723	50013014
TRIN	Trin.s.	SOUTH	1727	54002002
TRIN	Trin.s.	WHARTON	1728	49002011
TRIN	Trin.s.	WAPLE	1729	49012006
TRIN	Trin.s.	NEWTON	1736	49002014
TRIN	Trin.s.	NEWTON	1736	49010014
TRIN	Trin.s.	WHEATLAND	1739	49008006
TRIN	Trin.s.	SMITH	1740	46003015
TRIN	Trin.s.	WESTON	1747	43004010
TRIN	Trin.s.	JOHNSON	1740	50013014
TRIN	Trin.s.	DODWELL	1745	50013014
TRIN	Trin.s.	HORBERY	1749	57003009
TRIN	Trin.s.	BERRIMAN	1751	43028019
TRIN	Trin.s.	UMFREVILLE	1759	05029029

Keyword	In its Context	Author	Year	BkChpVrs
TRIN	Trin.s.	BERRIMAN	1751	69004008
TRIN	Trin.s.	SECKER	1770	05029029
TRIN	Trin.s.	ANONYMOUS	1776	46003001
TRIN	Trin.s.	ORR	1772	52002018
TRIN	Trin- Xmas.	G.	1730	57003016
TRIN	1 S. Trin.	READING	1728	06010012
TRIN	1 S. Trin.	READING	1730	06023011
TRIN	1 S.af. Trin.	STANHOPE	1714	65004007
TRIN	1 Sun. Trin.	STANHOPE	1714	45016019
TRIN	10 S. Trin.	STANHOPE	1714	45019041
TRIN	10 S. Trin.	HOLE	1716	45019041
TRIN	10 S. Trin.	STANHOPE	1714	49012001
TRIN	10 S. Trin.	HOLE	1716	49012001
TRIN	10 S. Trin.	READING	1728	11021028
TRIN	10 S. Trin.	READING	1730	11022035
TRIN	11 S. Trin.	STANHOPE	1714	45018009
TRIN	11 S. Trin.	STANHOPE	1714	49015001
TRIN	11 S. Trin.	HOLE	1716	49015001
TRIN	11 S. Trin.	READING	1730	12009001
TRIN	11 S. Trin.	QUINCY	1750	45018013
TRIN	12 S. Trin.	STANHOPE	1714	43022001
TRIN	12 S. Trin.	STANHOPE	1714	44007031
TRIN	12 S. Trin.	HOLE	1716	44007031
TRIN	12 S. Trin.	STANHOPE	1714	50003004
TRIN	12 S. Trin.	HOLE	1716	50003004
TRIN	12 S. Trin.	READING	1728	12010031
TRIN	12 S. Trin.	READING	1730	12018004
TRIN	13 S. Trin.	STANHOPE	1714	45010023
TRIN	13 S. Trin.	STANHOPE	1714	51003016
TRIN	13 S. Trin.	READING	1728	12019037
TRIN	13 S. Trin.	READING	1730	12023025
TRIN	14 S. Trin.	STANHOPE	1714	45017011
TRIN	14 S. Trin.	STANHOPE	1714	51005016
TRIN	14 S. Trin.	HOLE	1716	51005016
TRIN	14 S. Trin.	READING	1728	24005001
TRIN	14 S. Trin.	READING	1730	24022003
TRIN	15 S. Trin.	STANHOPE	1714	51006011
TRIN	15 S. Trin.	HOLE	1716	51006011
TRIN	15 S. Trin.	READING	1728	24035018
TRIN	15 S. Trin.	READING	1730	24036032
TRIN	15 Sun. Trin.	HOLE	1717	43006019
TRIN	16 S. Trin.	STANHOPE	1714	45007011
TRIN	16 S. Trin.	STANHOPE	1714	52003013
TRIN	16 S. Trin.	HOLE	1716	52003013
TRIN	16 S. Trin.	READING	1728	26002007
TRIN	16 S. Trin.	READING	1730	26013004
TRIN	17 S. Trin.	STANHOPE	1714	45014001
TRIN	17 S. Trin.	STANHOPE	1713	52004001
TRIN	17 S. Trin.	HOLE	1716	52004001
TRIN	17 S. Trin.	READING	1728	26014007
TRIN	17 S. Trin.	READING	1730	26018031
TRIN	18 S. Trin.	STANHOPE	1714	43022034
TRIN	18 S. Trin.	STANHOPE	1714	49001004
TRIN	18 S. Trin.	HOLE	1716	49001004
TRIN	18 S. Trin.	READING	1728	26020024
TRIN	18 S. Trin.	READING	1730	26024024

Keyword	In its Context	Author	Year	BkChpVrs
TRIN	19 S. Trin.	STANHOPE	1714	43009001
TRIN	19 S. Trin.	STANHOPE	1715	43008023
TRIN	19 S. Trin.	HOLE	1716	52004018
TRIN	19 S. Trin.	READING	1728	27003016
TRIN	19 S. Trin.	READING	1730	27006010
TRIN	2 S. Trin.	STANHOPE	1714	45014016
TRIN	2 S. Trin.	READING	1728	07004014
TRIN	2 S. Trin.	READING	1730	07005001
TRIN	2 S.af. Trin.	STANHOPE	1714	65003013
TRIN	2 S.af. Trin.	HOLE	1716	65003013
TRIN	20 S. Trin.	STANHOPE	1714	52005015
TRIN	20 S. Trin.	HOLE	1716	52005015
TRIN	20 S. Trin.	READING	1730	32006009
TRIN	21 S. Trin.	STANHOPE	1714	46004046
TRIN	21 S. Trin.	HOLE	1716	46004046
TRIN	21 S. Trin.	STANHOPE	1714	52006010
TRIN	21 S. Trin.	HOLE	1716	52006010
TRIN	21 S. Trin.	READING	1728	34002004
TRIN	22 S. Trin.	STANHOPE	1714	53001003
TRIN	22 S. Trin.	HOLE	1716	53001003
TRIN	22 S. Trin.	READING	1728	20002006
TRIN	22 S. Trin.	READING	1728	29002012
TRIN	22 S. Trin.	READING	1730	20001033
TRIN	23 S. Trin.	STANHOPE	1714	53003017
TRIN	23 S. Trin.	HOLE	1716	53003017
TRIN	23 S. Trin.	READING	1728	20011011
TRIN	23 S. Trin.	READING	1730	20012001
TRIN	23 S. Trin.	READING	1730	20014013
TRIN	24 S. Trin.	STANHOPE	1714	43009018
TRIN	24 S. Trin.	STANHOPE	1714	43022015
TRIN	24 S. Trin.	STANHOPE	1714	54001003
TRIN	24 S. Trin.	HOLE	1716	54001003
TRIN	24 S. Trin.	READING	1728	20013020
TRIN	24 S. Trin.	READING	1728	20015001
TRIN	24 S. Trin.	READING	1728	20017016
TRIN	24 S. Trin.	READING	1730	20016021
TRIN	25 S. Trin.	STANHOPE	1714	24023005
TRIN	25 S. Trin.	STANHOPE	1714	46006005
TRIN	25 S. Trin.	HOLE	1716	24023005
TRIN	25 S. Trin.	HOLE	1716	46006005
TRIN	26 S. Trin.	READING	1730	20019005
TRIN	3 S. Trin.	STANHOPE	1714	45015001
TRIN	3 S. Trin.	READING	1728	09002020
TRIN	3 S. Trin.	READING	1730	09003012
TRIN	3 S.af. Trin.	STANHOPE	1714	63005005
TRIN	3 S.af. Trin.	HOLE	1716	63005005
TRIN	4 S. Trin.	GIFFARD	1681	09012017
TRIN	4 S. Trin.	STANHOPE	1714	45006036
TRIN	4 S. Trin.	STANHOPE	1714	48008018
TRIN	4 S. Trin.	HOLE	1716	48008018
TRIN	4 S. Trin.	READING	1728	09012016
TRIN	4 S. Trin.	READING	1730	09013013
TRIN	5 S. Trin.	STANHOPE	1714	45005001
TRIN	5 S. Trin.	STANHOPE	1714	63003008
TRIN	5 S. Trin.	HOLE	1716	63003008
TRIN	5 S. Trin.	READING	1728	09015022

Keyword	In its Context	Author	Year	BkChpVrs
TRIN	5 S. Trin.	READING	1730	09017056
TRIN	6 S. Trin.	STANHOPE	1714	48006003
TRIN	6 S. Trin.	READING	1730	10019001
TRIN	7. S. Trin.	READING	1730	10024010
TRIN	7 S. Trin.	STANHOPE	1714	44008001
TRIN	7 S. Trin.	HOLE	1716	44008001
TRIN	7 S. Trin.	STANHOPE	1714	48006019
TRIN	7 S. Trin.	HOLE	1716	48006019
TRIN	7 S. Trin.	READING	1728	10021001
TRIN	8 S. Trin.	STANHOPE	1714	48008012
TRIN	8 S. Trin.	HOLE	1716	48008012
TRIN	8 S. Trin.	READING	1728	11013001
TRIN	8 S. Trin.	READING	1730	11017024
TRIN	9 S. Trin.	STANHOPE	1714	45016001
TRIN	9 S. Trin.	STANHOPE	1714	49010001
TRIN	9 S. Trin.	HOLE	1716	49010001
TRIN	9 S. Trin.	READING	1728	11018017
TRIN	9 S. Trin.	READING	1730	11019010
TRINITY	Trinity.	HALL	1660	63001017
TRINITY	Trinity.	NEEDLER	1660	65005007
TRINITY	Trinity.	NICOLSON	1661	65005007
TRINITY	Trinity.	SPARKES	1663	65005007
TRINITY	Trinity.	PAYNE	1697	57003009
TRINITY	Trinity.	WISHEART	1716	65005007
TRINITY	Trinity.	CONINGESBY	1723	48001022
TRINITY	Trinity.	CLARKE	1735	65005008
TRINITY	Trinity.	SLOSS	1736	65005004
TRINITY	Trinity.	SWIFT	1744	65005007
TRINITY	Trinity.	ANONYMOUS	1750	01002001
TRINITY	Trinity.	FREE	1750	18036026
TRINITY	Trinity.	ADAMS	1752	46005007
TRINITY	Trinity.	SKELTON	1754	18011007
TRINITY	Trinity.	WATSON	1756	01018001
TRINITY	Trinity.	JENNINGS	1757	43028019
TRINITY	Trinity.	ALLEN	1751	65005007
TRINITY	Trinity.	WATTS	1753	52002010
TRINITY	Trinity.	ECCLES	1755	65005007
TRINITY	Trinity.	HAYWARD	1758	65005007
TRINITY	Trinity.	UMFREVILLE	1759	65005007
TRINITY	Trinity.	DAWSON	1765	18011007
TRINITY	Trinity.	PARSONS	1761	65005007
TRINITY	Trinity.	LAWSON	1764	49013009
TRINITY	Trinity.	DELANY	1766	65005007
TRINITY	Trinity.	ANONYMOUS	1771	43028018
TRINITY	Trinity.	BOSTON	1773	65005007
TRIPAR	Preac.tripar.	MOSSOM	1685	54001018
TRIUM	Xn. Trium.	MOSS	1732	49015055
TRIUM	Xn. Trium.	MOIR	1759	49005025
TRIUM	Xn's. Trium.	SACHEVERELL	1713	45023034
TRIUMP	Bel. Triump.	WILCOX	1757	18019025
TRIUMP	Fth.triump.	CONEY	1730	61011024
TRIUMPH	Fai.triumph.	DAVIES	1754	65005004
TROU	Supp. Trou.	WILCOX	1757	43014027
TROU	Trou. Mind.	BINGHAM	1725	19103013
TROUB	Troub. Md.	NORRIS	1728	19094019
TROUBLE	Ag. Trouble.	PATRICK	1707	46014001
TROUBLE	Of Trouble.	LEIGHTONHOUSE	1697	19027013
TROUBLES	Troubles.	NEWTON	1736	19038003
TRTH	Trth.b. Em.	PRICE	1661	51004016
TRU	Adv.of Tru.	TILLOTSON	1735	65004004
TRU	Tru.& Falsh.	MOSS	1732	52004025
TRUE	L's Pro.true.	ECCLES	1755	11022021
TRUE	Sp.&true W.	STILLINGFLEET	1707	46004024
TRUE	Sp.&true W.	ORR	1739	46004024
TRUE	True g. M.	ORR	1773	21002003
TRUE	True happ.	ORR	1749	23003010
TRUE	True nat. E.	DOWNES	1761	06007012
TRUE	True Circ.	MANTON	1685	53003003
TRUE	True Circ.	TILLY	1737	53003002
TRUE	True Devot.	BRAGGE	1713	45002025
TRUE	True Discip.	VEAL	1703	46008031
TRUE	True Freed.	ECCLES	1755	43002030
TRUE	True Gain.	REYNOLDS	1679	43016026
TRUE	True Happ.	DORRINGTON	1703	19004006
TRUE	True Happ.	STILLINGFLEET	1707	46006068
TRUE	True Happ.	HOPKINS	1710	69022014
TRUE	True Happ.	REYNER	1745	19004006
TRUE	True Nat. S.	CUDWORTH	1670	49015057
TRUE	True Nobil.	WHISTON	1661	47017011
TRUE	True Penit.	BRADY	1730	45014023
TRUE	True Philos.	COLLIER	1730	01001001
TRUE	True Piety.	BOURN	1777	19027004
TRUE	True Relig.	FRANK	1672	46003008
TRUE	True Relig.	SMITH	1673	20015024
TRUE	True Relig.	FOSTER	1744	46003008
TRUE	True Relig.	BURNET	1747	19130004
TRUE	True Relig.	WESTON	1747	20023023
TRUE	True Relig.	ROE	1766	43019017
TRUE	True Repen.	ALLEN	1751	45013003
TRUE	True Treas.	WALLIS	1692	43006019
TRUE	True Wisd.	MILLER	1749	20003021
TRUE	True Xnity.	WILLIAMS	1770	46018038
TRUE	True Xtian.	NICOLSON	1661	53003020
TRUE	True Xtians.	CLARKE	1736	65003009
TRUE	True Zeal.	HOLE	1725	51004018
TRUE	Xrter true C.	D'ASTOR	1700	04024005
TRUE	Xty true Lib.	NEWTON	1782	46008031
TRUMP	Trump.of G.	ERSKINE	1764	23027013
TRUMP	Trump.of S.	SMITH	1660	21011009
TRUST	Rel. Trust.	TOULMIN	1770	19034008
TRUST	Trust in G.	CONANT	1703	23026004
TRUST	Trust in G.	SPINCKES	1714	63003014
TRUST	Trust in G.	NEWLIN	1720	19037005
TRUST	Trust in G.	LUCAS	1722	19039007
TRUST	Trust in G.	SCATTERGOOD	1723	19028007
TRUST	Trust in G.	SMALRIDGE	1724	19042011
TRUST	Trust in G.	CLARKE	1727	19071001
TRUST	Trust in G.	WHARTON	1728	46014001
TRUST	Trust in G.	REEVES	1729	19034008
TRUST	Trust in G.	SHARP	1729	19042006
TRUST	Trust in G.	ROGERS	1738	24017007
TRUST	Trust in G.	SKEELER	1740	20016020

Keyword	In its Context	Author	Year	BkChpVrs
TRUST	Trust in G.	ABERNETHY	1743	19062008
TRUST	Trust in G.	ATTERBURY	1743	23049010
TRUST	Trust in G.	LEIGHTON	1746	19112007
TRUST	Trust in G.	LEIGHTON	1746	34003017
TRUST	Trust in G.	GIBSON	1749	19112007
TRUST	Trust in G.	CONEY	1750	20003005
TRUST	Trust in G.	BADDELLY	1752	23026004
TRUST	Trust in G.	WILCOX	1757	19083028
TRUST	Trust in G.	MOIR	1759	34003017
TRUST	Trust in G.	STEBBING	1760	20003005
TRUST	Trust in G.	WEARE	1767	43006011
TRUST	Trust in G.	STERNE	1769	19037003
TRUST	Trust in G.	LANGHORNE	1773	19118008
TRUST	Trust in G.	PHILIPS	1775	05004039
TRUST	Trust in G.	CARR	1777	24017007
TRUST	Trust in Pro.	GARDINER	1720	43006019
TRUST	Trust in Xt.	MAY	1757	52001012
TRUST	Trust Riches	BURNET	1747	45012020
TRUTH	Av.to Truth.	STRAIGHT	1741	46008045
TRUTH	Di. Truth ev.&	WHICHCOTE	1698	46007046
TRUTH	Diff. Truth.	CLARKE	1735	46004011
TRUTH	Div. Truth.	CROWE	1744	46003020
TRUTH	Div. Truth.	HUNTER	1774	46017017
TRUTH	Enq.a.truth.	SCOTT	1743	20002003
TRUTH	G's Truth.	LELAND	1769	19117002
TRUTH	G's Truth.	PENTYCROSS	1781	19031005
TRUTH	Nat. Truth.	MEADOWCOURT	1724	46017017
TRUTH	Nat.of truth.	STENNETT	1732	20023023
TRUTH	Plain Truth.	SMITH	1777	43002002
TRUTH	Prot. Truth.	BEVERLEY	1683	24010025
TRUTH	Truth diss.	SMITH	1777	43002005
TRUTH	Truth expl.	BRADY	1730	52004025
TRUTH	Truth expl.	BERRIMAN	1751	52004025
TRUTH	Truth o. Xty.	FAWCETT	1749	46006068
TRUTH	Truth of G.	WISHEART	1716	19108004
TRUTH	Truth of G.	HUNT	1748	69021015
TRUTH	Truth of Xy.	WAPLE	1729	65005007
TRUTH	Truth of Xy.	JORTIN	1730	46005033
TRUTH	Truth of Xy.	TILLOTSON.	1735	50004003
TRUTH	Truth of Xy.	WHEATLAND	1739	47019020
TRUTH	Truth of Xy.	BELLAMY	1744	47008001
TRUTH	Truth.	SOUTH	1744	59001001
TRUTH	Truth.	WARBURTON	1753	46013038
TRUTH	Truth.	BALL	1757	20023023
TRUTH	Truth.	HUSSEY	1753	46018038
TRUTH	Truth.	SAURIN	1775	20023023
TRUTH	Truth. Xn.r.	JORTIN	1730	45002032
TRUTH	Truth.what.	EDWARDS	1698	46018038
TRUTH	Truth& Cha.	MICHELL	1737	52004015
TRUTH	Truth& Fal.	REEVES	1712	52004025
TRUTH	Truth& Fal.	MAYHEW	1750	45012054
TRUTH	Truth&c.	WOOD	1775	43014009
TRUTH	Truth Xn. R.	JORTIN	1730	46010025
TRUTH	Truth Xn. R.	JORTIN	1730	46015024
TRUTHS	Rel. Truths.	CLARKE	1734	58002025
TRY	Way try Pro.	BLACKALL	1723	65004001

Keyword	In its Context	Author	Year	BkChpVrs
TUES	Tues. W. S.	STANHOPE	1714	47008014
TUES	Tues.b. East.	STANHOPE	1715	44015001
TUESD	East. Tuesd.	STANHOPE	1715	45024036
TUESD	East. Tuesd.	HOLE	1716	45024036
TUESD	East. Tuesd.	STANHOPE	1715	47013026
TUESD	East. Tuesd.	HOLE	1716	47013026
TUESD	East. Tuesd.	TRAPP	1730	62001021
TUESDAY	W. Tuesday.	STANHOPE	1714	46010001
TUESDAY	W. Tuesday.	HOLE	1716	46010001
TURN	Turn f.ev.w.	FOORD	1719	26033011
TUST	Tust in G.	ADEY	1755	19084013
TWO	Str.bet.two.	WILLISON	1761	53001023
TWO	T.two Witn.	K.	1667	69011003
TWO	Two Coven.	HARTLEY	1754	24031033
TWO	Two Coven.	TURNER	1771	24031033
TWO	Two Debt.	BULKLEY	1771	45007047
TWO	Two Sons.	BRAGGE	1704	43021028
TWO	Two Sons.	DODD	1757	43021032
TWO	Two Sons.	BOURN	1763	45021028
TWO	Two Sons.	BOURN	1764	43021028
TWO	Two Sons.	BULKLEY	1771	43021028
TYPE	Manna,type.	MEDE	1672	49010003
TYRAN	Pap. Tyran.	DU MOULIN	1674	69018004
TYTH	Steal. Tyth.	NEWTE	1711	20003009
TYTHE	Tythe steal.	WAKE	1703	38003008
TYTHES	Of Tythes.	DELANY	1748	02020017
TYTHES	of Tythes.	CROWTHER	1685	43023023
U	Bel. U.w. Xt.	LYE	1676	49006017
U	G.prov'd.u.	SKELTON	1754	43011005
U	G.sup.u.suf.	TILLOTSON	1735	63004019
U	Gos.un.th.u.	BEVERIDGE	1720	61004002
U	Gos.un.th.u.	CLARKE	1727	61004002
U	R. U.& A. W.	PEARSON	1718	49007031
U	R. U.& A. W.	NORRIS	1728	49007031
U	R. U.& A. W.	MILLER	1749	49007031
U	R. U.& A. W.	ORR	1749	49007031
U	U.& Ab.o.a.	EDWARDS	1698	57002008
U	U.& Ab.o.a.	NOURSE	1708	57002009
U	U.of R.at D.	STENNETT	1769	19023004
U	Worsh.u. T.	BOYS	1716	49014009
U	Worsh.u. T.	BAYES	1735	49014009
U	Xt.quick. U.	COLMAN	1728	23011003
U	Xt.u.w. Xns.	CLAGETT	1720	46015001
U	Xt's u.w. Ch.	NICOLSON	1661	50011002
U	Xt's. Adm.u.	CLARKE	1734	45017037
UN	B. Un.w. Xt.	FLAVEL	1673	46017023
UN	Church Un.	SHERLOCK	1719	19122006
UN	Disob.& Un.	SMALRIDGE	1724	65002004
UN	Fut.rew.un.	BULL	1713	61011026
UN	G. Un.a Pro.	CHANDLER	1691	55005013
UN	Gos.un.th.u.	BEVERIDGE	1720	61004002
UN	Gos.un.th.u.	CLARKE	1727	61004002
UN	Heart of Un.	PYLE	1777	61003012
UN	Idol.&v.un.	BARKER	1763	23046008
UN	Keep.un.&c.	THORNBY	1742	52004003
UN	Kn.& Ch.un.	WRIGHT	1732	49008001

INDEXES TO THIRD VOLUME: E: KEYWORD-IN-CONTEXT INDEX OF OTHER SUBJECTS OR OCCASIONS

Keyword	In its Context	Author	Year	BkChpVrs
UN	Love un. Sa.	HUBBARD	1729	63001008
UN	On the Un.	ANONYMOUS	1706	41010027
UN	On the Un.	HUTCHINSON	1707	19068008
UN	Oxf.un.vind.	HENLEY	17--	23007004
UN	Peace& Un.	BURNET	1689	47007026
UN	Rep.& Un.	SHOWER	1688	23021011
UN	Sin un. Dea.	LAMBE	1717	65005016
UN	Un.& Peace.	LUCAS	1710	52004002
UN	Un. C. Xn. C.	HOLBROOK	1727	55004007
UN	Un. G.& Tr.	TILLOTSON	1735	57002005
UN	Un. Gos.tea.	FLEMING	1772	49001001
UN	Un. Pie.& M.	BLAIR	1777	47010004
UN	Un. Tr.& L.	PEARSE	1763	52004015
UN	Un.o.worsh.	CLAYTON	1713	48012004
UN	Un.of God.	FORSTER	1744	02020001
UN	Un.of Spir.	LITTLETON	1680	52004003
UN	Un.of Xn. F.	SMITH	1682	52004005
UN	V.life un.m.	BRYSON	1778	21001014
UN	Virt.& V.un.	PECKARD	1775	23005020
UN	2 S.un. S. D.	LEAKE	1773	49015033
UNA	Her.& S.una.	MOSSOM	1685	49011019
UNA	Her.& S.una.	MARCH	1699	49011019
UNA	Her.& S.una.	CLAGETT	1704	49011019
UNA	Her.& S.una.	ROGERS	1736	49011019
UNANIM	Xn. Unanim.	WHICHCOTE	1703	53003015
UNANIM	Xn. Unanim.	DODDERIDGE	1761	53002001
UNANIMITY	Unanimity.	BRADBURY	1715	48014015
UNANIMITY	Unanimity.	HOLE	1725	50013011
UNANIMITY	Unanimity.	HOLDEN	1755	63003008
UNATT	Perf.unatt.	BALL	1756	43005048
UNB	Bel.& Unb.	IBBOT	1726	44016016
UNB	Caus.o. Unb.	TIDCOMBE	1757	46006066
UNB	Cond. Unb.	MORRIS	1743	46008024
UNB	Cond.o.unb.	FLAVEL	1673	46003018
UNB	Faith& Unb.	BURNET	1747	46020029
UNB	St. Tho.unb.	COCK	1710	46020027
UNB	Unb.o Jews.	CLAGETT	1720	46012037
UNB	Unb.unrea.	MORRIS	1743	44006001
UNBEL	Who Unbel.	CHARNOCK	1684	46006064
UNBELIEF	Unbelief.	CHARNOCK	1684	46016009
UNBELIEF	Unbelief.	ELLIS	1704	45016027
UNBELIEF	Unbelief.	BEVERIDGE	1720	45012046
UNBELIEF	Unbelief.	JENKINS	1779	12007002
UNC	Call to unc.	BOURN	1754	26033002
UNC	N.call.unc.	ANONYMOUS	1756	26033011
UNC	Unc. Sin Da.	CLARKSON	1696	52005008
UNCER	Death uncer.	FOTHERGILL	1765	44013032
UNCERT	Life Uncert.	MAY	1744	24028016
UNCERT	Uncert.of fut.	LEIGHTONHOUSE	1697	20027001
UNCERT	Uncert.of fut.	MOSS	1737	20027001
UNCERT	Uncert.of life	SHORTHOSE	1738	19090010
UNCH	Unch Cont.	STEEL	1690	51005015
UNCHANG	G.unchang.	TILLOTSON	1735	62001017
UNCHANG	Xt.unchang.	WILCOX	1757	61001012
UNCLEAN	Unclean Sp.	BRAGGE	1704	45011024
UNCT	Extre. Unct.	KILLINBECK	1717	62005014

Keyword	In its Context	Author	Year	BkChpVrs
UND	All und. Sin.	WITHERSPOON	1768	48003023
UND	Sinn.und. C.	CLARKSON	1696	51003010
UND	Und. Div.w.	BURTON	1685	52005017
UNDERS	M's Unders.	PYLE	1777	20017027
UNDISC	Undisc. Aff.	MARSHALL	1731	62004001
UNE	Une.distrib.	FRANCIS	1771	21008014
UNF	Gos.unf.&c.	ST.	1757	43005013
UNF	Unf. Repent.	WALLIS	1692	24003010
UNFR	Unfr.wks. D.	MOORE	1716	52005011
UNFUITFULN	Unfuitfuln.	WALKER	1682	45013006
UNI	Love& Uni.	DAVIS	1756	50013011
UNI	Love& Uni.	ANONYMOUS	1771	50013014
UNI	Peace& Uni.	HOWELL	1712	54002015
UNI	Peace& Uni.	ANONYMOUS	1712	54003015
UNI	Peace& Uni.	HICKES	1726	53004007
UNI	Trin.in Uni.	ATTERBURY	1743	65005007
UNI	Trin.in Uni.	ADAMS	1752	65005007
UNI	Uni.& Peace.	PIGGOTT	1714	48014019
UNION	Ch.& Union.	WAKE	1716	48015005
UNION	Per.to Union	SHUTTLEWORTH	1718	48015006
UNION	Polit. Union.	SACHEVERELL	1702	20008015
UNION	The Union.	COLLINS	1707	26037019
UNION	Union in Re.	YOUNG	1706	46016031
UNION	Union to Xt.	SHOWER	1702	50005017
UNION	Union w. G.	BARKER	1683	46017020
UNION	Union w. Xt.	FLOWER	1740	46014019
UNION	Union w. Xt.	ROMAINE	1759	22006001
UNION	Union.	SAUNDER	1744	19133001
UNION	Union Soul.	NORRIS	1728	19073028
UNIT	Love& Unit.	SEED	1743	20015017
UNITY	God's Unity	HUNT	1748	05004039
UNITY	Love&unity	CREED	1755	48015005
UNITY	Perf.& Unity	MANTON	1708	53003003
UNITY	Unity of Ch.	CLAGETT	1704	49012013
UNITY	Unity of Ch.	BARROW	1716	52004004
UNITY	Unity of Ch.	SHERIDAN	1720	46010016
UNITY	Unity of Ch.	BENNETT	1728	49012013
UNITY	Unity of G.	WHITBY	1710	44012029
UNITY	Unity of G.	CLARKE	1732	43004010
UNITY	Unity of G.	ABERNETHY	1743	05006004
UNITY	Unity of G.	ATTERBURY	1743	23045005
UNITY	Unity of G.	KNOWLES	1750	05006004
UNITY	Unity of G.	SKELTON	1754	23045008
UNITY	Unity of G.	COCKMAN	1750	49008004
UNITY	Unity of G.	BOSTON	1773	05006004
UNITY	Unity of G.	BOSTON	1773	49008004
UNITY	Unity.	WROE	1682	19133001
UNITY	Unity.	PHILIPS	1710	19133001
UNITY	Unity.	WARTER	1767	19133001
UNITY	Unity&c.	STILLINGFLEET	1781	19122006
UNITY	Xn. Unity	WARREN	1692	52004003
UNITY	Xn. Unity	THORNBY	1742	46017001
UNITY	Xn. Unity.	BERRIMAN	1763	52004003
UNIV	Flood univ.	EDWARDS	1702	01007019
UNIV	Univ. Benev.	TUTTY	1741	45010037
UNIV	Univ. Benev.	STONE	1771	49013003

Keyword	In its Context	Author	Year	BkChpVrs
UNIV	Univ. Benev.	ORR	1772	49013013
UNIV	Univ. Benev.	STOCKDALE	1773	49013013
UNIV	Univ. Char.	FOSTER	1737	49013003
UNIV	Univ. Guilt.	WALKER	1764	48003019
UNIV	Univ. Judg.	SMALBROOKE	1706	46005028
UNIV	Univ. Judg.	BOURN	1764	43025031
UNIV	Univ. Judg.	DAVIES	1766	47017030
UNIV	Univ. Obed.	KEITH	1700	45001006
UNIV	Univ. Obed.	WAPLE	1720	19119006
UNIV	Univ. Obed.	WAPLE	1720	19119009
UNIV	Univ. Obed.	BEVERIDGE	1720	45001006
UNIV	Univ. Obed.	HICKES	1726	62002010
UNIV	Univ. Obed.	IBBOTT	1726	62002010
UNIV	Univ. Obed.	HICKES	1726	65003002
UNIV	Univ. Obed.	HOADLY	1727	62002010
UNIV	Univ. Obed.	MARSHALL	1731	45001006
UNIV	Univ. Obed.	ROGERS	1735	62002010
UNIV	Univ. Obed.	MOSS	1737	62002010
UNIV	Univ. Obed.	WARREN	1739	62002010
UNIV	Univ. Obed.	SHEPHERD	1748	45011042
UNIV	Univ. Obed.	VENN	1740	62002010
UNIV	Univ. Obed.	SEED	1743	62002010
UNIV	Univ. Obed.	WEBSTER	1745	62002010
UNIV	Univ. Obed.	DAVIS	1756	02030015
UNIV	Univ. Obed.	GOUGH	1751	62002011
UNIV	Univ. Obed.	CARR	1777	45001006
UNIV	Univ. Obed.	SECKER	1771	62002010
UNIV	Univ. Polit.	BURTON	1764	55004011
UNIV	Univ. Rede.	BARROW	1716	57004010
UNIV	Univ. Rede.	HUSSEY	1755	57002004
UNIV	Univ. Rep.	SHERIDAN	1720	47017030
UNIV	Univ. Right.	DELANY	1747	62002010
UNIV	Univ. Symp.	WOOD	1775	63003008
UNIV	Univ. Toler.	SOWDEN	1780	48014004
UNIV	b. Univ.	LIGHTFOOT	1684	49014026
UNIV	b. Univ.	LIGHTFOOT	1684	63005013
UNIV	b. Univ.	STUBBS	1722	20003005
UNIV	b. Univ.	HOLE	1720	47014017
UNIV	b. Univ.	WYNNE	1724	55004011
UNIVER	Res.univer.	FELTON	1733	49015023
UNIVER	b. Univer.	BELLAS	1779	10024011
UNIVERSITY	b. University	LIGHTFOOT	1684	45011002
UNIVERSITY	b. University	LIGHTFOOT	1684	48008023
UNIVERSITY	b University	WESTLEY	1742	52005014
UNJ	Unj.m's.d.	SMITH	1670	49006009
UNJUST	Unjust Stew.	BRAGGE	1704	45016001
UNJUST	Unjust Stew.	ELLIS	1704	45016001
UNJUST	Unjust Stew.	HOLE	1716	45016001
UNJUST	Unjust Stew.	WHEATLAND	1739	45016008
UNJUST	Unjust Stew.	DODD	1757	45016008
UNJUST	Unjust Stew.	ELSMERE	1767	45016008
UNJUST	Unjust Stew.	BULKLEY	1771	45016008
UNJUST	Unjust Stew.	JORTIN	1774	45016008
UNLA	Persec.unla.	JORTIN	1774	45014023
UNLAW	Unlaw. Pl.	FORDYCE	1760	20007007
UNMER	Unmer. Ser.	DODD	1757	43018035

Keyword	In its Context	Author	Year	BkChpVrs
UNPARD	Unpard. Sin.	RUSSEL	1746	65005016
UNPR	Unpr. Serv.	BRAGGE	1704	45017007
UNPR	Unpr. Serv.	SCATTERGOOD	1723	45017010
UNPR	Unpr. Serv.	HOADLY	1754	45017010
UNPR	Unpr. Serv.	DODD	1757	45017010
UNPR	Unpr. Serv.	BULKLEY	1771	45017010
UNPR	Unpr. Serv.	TUCKER	1776	45017010
UNPROF	Unprof. Sin.	DORRINGTON	1703	20022008
UNR	Mamm. Unr.	THOMAS	1688	45016009
UNR	Regen. Unr.	DUCHE	1779	19104029
UNREA	Unb.unrea.	MORRIS	1743	44006001
UNREA	Unrea. Anx.	FOORD	1719	43006034
UNREA	Unrea. Anx.	BLACKALL	1723	43006034
UNREA	Unrea. Anx.	BLAIR	1740	43006034
UNREA	Unrea. Anx.	BUNDY	1740	43006034
UNREAS	Del.unreas.	LARDNER	1751	19119060
UNREG	Xrter unreg.	DODDERIDGE	1742	52002001
UNS	G's.w.uns.	MOIR	1759	48011033
UNS	Uns.ri.o. Xt.	FANCH	1768	52003008
UNS	Ways H.uns.	DAVIS	1756	19077019
UNSEEN	Unseen Sav.	HAYWARD	1758	63001008
UNSP	Unsp. Gift.	HORNE	1778	52004007
UNW	Bel.unw. W.	ERSKINE	1764	65005010
UNW	Unw. Faith.	SMITH	1751	62002018
UNW	Unw. G's M.	ORTON	1776	01032010
UNWO	Unwo. Rece.	MEDE	1672	49010005
UP	Ta.up Cross.	CLARKSON	1696	45014027
UPRIGHTNESS	Uprightness.	JORTIN	1774	20010009
UPRIGHTNESS	Uprightness.	CRAIG	1775	23026007
UR	L's Ur.& Th.	GILL	1773	05033008
URGED	Relig.urged.	DORRINGTON	1705	21012001
URGED	Relig.urged;	DORRINGTON	1705	20003006
US	G's love to us	BLAIR	1740	43007009
US	God w.us.	BRADBURY	1772	23008009
US	Us.& Ab. Pas.	HICKMAN	1706	47014015
US	Us.& Ab. Pas.	BATTY	1739	47014015
US	Us.& Ab. Sp.	SHARP	1734	52004029
US	Us.& Ab. Sp.	ROGERS	1735	52004029
US	Us.& Ab. Sp.	TILLOTSON	1735	52004029
US	Us.& Ab. Sp.	BATTY	1739	52004029
US	Us.& Ab. Sp.	PEARCE	1779	52004029
US	Us.o. R.in R.	HOLDEN	1755	45012057
US	Xt. Sac.f.us.	CHARNOCK	1684	49005007
US	Xt's. L.to us.	HORTON	1679	69001005
US	Xt's.lo.to us.	SHOWER	1702	46015009
USE	N.& Use. Pr.	FOSTER	1744	43006006
USE	R. Use Law	UNWIN	1773	48007009
USE	Use o. Clergy	ROBINSON	1735	57006020
USE	Use o. Riches	ELLIS	1704	45016009
USE	Use o. Sc. Ex.	LLOYD	1765	53003017
USE	Use of Law.	REYNOLDS	1679	48007013
USE	Use of Parab.	BURNET	1747	45013006
USE	Use of Reas.	SMALRIDGE	1724	47017002
USE	Use of Rev.	RICHARDSON	1730	47017004
USE	Use of Revel.	STEBBING	1730	48008003
USE	Use of S. S.	INGLIS	17--	58003016

Keyword	In its Context	Author	Year	BkChpVrs
USE	Use of S. S.	GUYSE	1724	48015004
USE	Use of Sacra.	KEITH	1704	49012013
USE	Use.o. Creed	BAYLY	1721	58001013
USE	Use& A. W.	ANONYMOUS	1772	20031006
USE	Use& Ab. W.	CARTER	1729	49007031
USE	Use& End L.	MAYHEW	1755	19034012
USE	Use& Int. Pr.	SHERLOCK	1740	64001019
USE	Use H. S. S.	HOPKINS	1710	54003016
USE	Use Money	WESTLEY	1771	45016009
USE	V.& Use of T.	ATTERBURY	1743	52005016
USE	Xn. Use o. W.	BISSE	1717	49007031
USEF	Liturg.usef.	SWINDEN	1713	45011002
USEF	Usef. Indust.	DYKES	1722	20031024
USEF	Usef. Law.	FLAVEL	1673	48007009
USEF	Usef.of Rev.	ROBINSON	1733	46005030
USEF	Usef.of S. S.	ALLESTREE	1684	58003015
USUR	Usur.cast.	JELLINGER	1676	19015005
USUR	Usur.cast.	JELINGER	1676	43016026
USURP	Ins. Usurp.	T.	1669	11021019
USURPER	Ins. Usurper.	T.	1660	45004006
UTIL	Util.of Rev.	CARR	1777	46012046
UUB	St. Tho.uub.	SHOWER	1702	46020027
UUBEC	Uubec. Con.	SMITH	1740	53001027
UUD	Uud.in Rel.	ORR	1772	49014020
V	Ch. Cens. V.	NICOLSON	1661	49004021
V	Ch.of Eng.v.	LE FRANK	1662	49011018
V	Cl V. Xt's bl.	CHARNOCK	1684	65001007
V	Idol.&v.un.	BARKER	1763	23046008
V	Man's St. V.	WILSON	1676	19039005
V	N. W.m.t. V.	ENFIELD	1772	43005014
V	Prog. V.& H.	ATTERBURY	1743	64003018
V	Rash.&v. S.	BERAULT	1698	62005012
V	Rash.&v. S.	BURNET	1713	62005012
V	Rash.&v. S.	BARROW	1716	62005012
V	Rash.&v. S.	GILBERT	1724	62005012
V	Rash.&v. S.	INNES	1726	62005012
V	Rash.&v. S.	BOSTON	1773	62005012
V	Rent V.tem.	ERSKINE	1764	43027051
V	T.read.of V.	HOPKINS	1771	16004023
V	V.& Use of T.	ATTERBURY	1743	52005016
V	V. Sch.	THOMAS	1728	19034011
V	V. World.	HOPKINS	1710	21001002
V	V. World.	MARKLAND	1729	21001002
V	V. World.	BESTON	1739	21001002
V	V. World.	RICH	1750	21001002
V	V. World.	CONYBEARE	1757	21001002
V	V. World.	ERSKINE	1764	21001002
V	V.disp. Gos.	PRICE	1757	45001072
V	V.dry Bones.	CENNICK	1762	26037014
V	V.life un.m.	BRYSON	1778	21001014
V	V.sch.& H.	COMBE	1708	20014034
V	Vir.& V. To.	PYLE	1777	43012036
V	Virt.& V.un.	PECKARD	1775	23005020
V	Virtue& V.	BALGUY	1748	20003035
V	Watchm.v.	BULL	1695	29002001
V	World.v. Xt.	ERSKINE	1764	23008018

Keyword	In its Context	Author	Year	BkChpVrs
V	Xt's.quick v.	ERSKINE	1764	46005025
VA	Va. Though.	DORRINGTON	1703	19119113
VA	Va.of C.& Y.	WILLIAMS	1750	21011010
VAG	Vag.lust&c.	OVINGTON	1712	49007002
VAIN	Lab.in vain.	ANONYMOUS	1709	41008010
VAIN	M's De.vain.	HORTON	1679	20019021
VAIN	Vain Gl. Ben.o	CARLETON	1736	51005026
VAIN	Vain Gl. Ben.o	MILLER	1749	51005026
VAIN	Vain Glory.	BLACKALL	1723	43006001
VAIN	Vain Glory.	BLAIR	1740	43006001
VAIN	Vain Philos.	SOUTH	1744	21001018
VAIN	Vain Repet.	BLACKALL	1723	43006007
VAIN	Vain Repet.	BLAIR	1740	43006007
VAIN	Wisd.vain.	WILKINS	1682	21001018
VAL	Tr.val.of M.	WHICHCOTE	1702	45016025
VAL	Val.& L.o. S.	WELTON	1724	43016026
VAL	Val.o. Time.	KENNET	1715	52005016
VAL	Val.of Soul.	ARMSTRONG	1704	43016026
VAL	Val.of Soul.	BRADY	1706	43016026
VAL	Val.of Soul.	KENNET	1715	43016026
VAL	Val.of Soul.	BEVERIDGE	1720	43016026
VAL	Val.of Soul.	MILLER	1749	43016026
VALLEYO	Valleyo. Vis.	ERSKINE	1741	26037009
VALUE	Value of life.	MUNTON	1756	21011007
VALUE	Value of Gr.	WILCOX	1757	22001012
VAN	Hum. Van.	BALGUY	1750	19094011
VAN	Misch. Van.	FOSTER	1744	48001022
VAN	Van. Creat.	REYNOLDS	1679	21001014
VAN	Van. Creat.	PIERCE	1731	19119096
VAN	Van. Di. Des.	HODGES	1676	45016030
VAN	Van. Man.	NORRIS	1728	19039006
VAN	Van. Man.	REEVES	1729	19039006
VAN	Van. Man.	MASON	1742	19008004
VAN	Van. Youth.	HICKMAN	1706	21011009
VAN	Van.h.judg.	ABERNETHY	1748	49004003
VAN	Van.hu. Enj.	OGILVIE	1766	49007031
VAN	Van.of h. W.	DELAUNE	1728	48012016
VAN	Van.of life.	CREYGHTON	1720	19039007
VAN	Van.of life.	NORRIS	1728	21011008
VAN	Van.of life.	QUINCY	1750	19039005
VAN	Van.of life.	KIMBER	1756	62004014
VAN	Van.of life.	WARNEFORD	1776	01047009
VAN	Van.of pr. R.	QUINCY	1750	59001016
VAN	Van.of pr.st.	GROVE	1741	48008019
VAN	Van.of Sec.	NEWMAN	1760	19030006
VAN	Van.wor. T.	LANGHORNE	1773	19039006
VANITY	Man Vanity.	MILLER	1749	19039005
VANITY	Of Vanity.	COTES	1721	19144004
VANITY	Of Vanity.	COOKE	1739	19039005
VANITY	Repr. Vanity	BOURN	1763	45017001
VAR	Var. Ranks.	FOSTER	1737	63005005
VEN	No ven. Sin.	JENKINS	1675	48006023
VEN	No. Sins ven.	SMALRIDGE	1724	65003006
VEN	Ven. H.life.	HOWE	1702	19089047
VENER	Vener. H. Sp.	BOURN	1777	52004030
VENG	Veng.on Sin.	WHICHCOTE	1703	48001024

Keyword	In its Context	Author	Year	BkChpVrs
VENG	Veng.on Sin.	WHICHCOTE	1703	48001027
VENG	Veng.on Sin.	WHICHCOTE	1703	48001029
VENGEANCE	Vengeance.	GLOVER	1664	48012019
VER	Ver.&tr. Co.	MICHELL	1737	57006004
VERACITY	G's veracity.	LOVEDER	1756	04023019
VERACITY	Veracity.	EVANS	1737	52004025
VERACITY	Veracity.	DODWELL	1748	52004025
VERY	Xt.very G.	HORNE	1775	48010013
VESS	Vess. M.& W.	DAVIES	1771	48009022
VI	Gen.judg.vi.	COCKMAN	1750	65003003
VI	Prot. R.vi. H.	COYTE	1761	47024014
VI	Vi. Cau. Evil.	QUINCY	1750	20019003
VIC	Sam. Vic.	JENKINS	1779	07015015
VIC	Vic. Mod.	COCKMAN	1750	44008038
VIC	Vic.of Ac. E.	POWELL	1776	61012001
VIC	Vic.self-lo.	SHERLOCK	1702	58003001
VICAR	Aug. Vicar.	COOKE	1723	45001046
VICE	Dang. Vice.	BAINE	1778	48001018
VICE	Mis.of Vice.	WEDDERSPOON	1733	24009005
VICE	Prog. Vice.	NEWMAN	1738	19001001
VICE	Vice ca. Inf.	PYLE	1777	46007017
VICE	Vice destr. S.	BUTLER	1719	43008022
VICES	Caus.o Vices	CARR	1777	61012001
VICES	Prev. Vices.	REYNER	1745	26016049
VICES	Vices of M.	MARRIOTT	1774	48001028
VICIOUS	Vicious Hab.	HORTON	1679	24013023
VICIOUS	Vicious Hab.	CONANT	1699	24013023
VICIOUS	Vicious Hab.	HAVETT	1703	24013023
VICIOUS	Vicious Hab.	CARTER	1729	24013023
VICIOUS	Vicious Hab.	CARR	1777	24013023
VICIOUS	Vicious Men	BRIGHT	1695	63004004
VICT	Faith's Vict.	BATTELY	1694	65005004
VICT	Faith's Vict.	BRADY	1730	65005004
VICT	Happy Vict.	ERSKINE	1764	48008037
VICT	Vict.of Faith	ALLESTREE	1684	65005004
VICT	Vict.of Faith	MONRO	1693	65005004
VICT	Vict.of Faith	STRATFORD	1700	65005005
VICT	Vict.of Faith	BEVERIDGE	1720	65005005
VICT	Vict.of Faith	DAWES	1733	65005004
VICT	Vict.of Faith	MOSS	1737	65005004
VICT	Vict.of Faith	PEARCE	1770	65005005
VICT	Vict.th. Xt.	WELCH	1752	48008037
VICT	Xn's. Vict.	BAINE	1778	65005004
VICTOR	Victor. Viol.	BYRDALL	1666	43011012
VIEW	Pen.view. S.	WHITTY	1772	44014072
VIEW	View X's. D.	BOURN	1777	43007024
VIG	Sobr.& Vig.	AGAR	1759	63005008
VILENESS	M's vileness.	WILLISON	1761	19008004
VIN	Par. Vin.&c.	MERRICK	1753	46015005
VIN	Prov.vin.	CRADOCK	1678	21009002
VIN	Prov.vin.	CARLETON	1736	21009002
VIN	Providence vin	D'OYLY	1710	19073015
VIN	Vin.o.hims.	JOHNSON	1730	46007024
VIN	Xn. Rel.vin.	SKEELER	1740	43011029
VIND	Clergy vind.	LEWIS	1710	49004013
VIND	Comm.vind.	CAMFIELD	1680	05027015

Keyword	In its Context	Author	Year	BkChpVrs
VIND	Comm.vind.	CLARKE	1736	05027026
VIND	Episc. Vind.	NICOLSON	1661	61013017
VIND	H. Nat.vind.	STERNE	1760	48014007
VIND	Oxf.un.vind.	HENLEY	17--	23007004
VIND	Prov.vind.	CREYGHTON	1720	19058010
VIND	Prov.vind.	TREBECK	1730	19119137
VIND	Surpl.vind.	WESTFIELD	1660	19045007
VIND	Surpl.vind.	WESTFIELD	1660	45024050
VIND	Surpl.vind.	WESTFIELD	1660	47001009
VIND	Surpl.vind.	WESTFIELD	1660	47001010
VIND	Vind. Mir.	BROOKES	1734	45007013
VIND	Vind.of Oxf.	HENLEY	17--	63002012
VIND	Xnity vind.	BALGUY	1750	45007035
VINDIC	Prov.vindic.	ALLEN	1751	43005045
VINDICA	Provid.vindica	FARINDON	1674	24012001
VINDICA	Provid.vindica	KILLINBECK	1717	24012001
VINDICA	Provid.vindica	BALL	1756	24012001
VINE	British Vine.	BULKLEY	1764	19080008
VINEYA	The Vineya.	DODD	1757	43021033
VINEYA	The Vineya.	BOURN	1764	43021033
VINEYA	The Vineya.	BULKLEY	1771	43021037
VIOL	Pow. Viol.	BARTLETT	1714	43011012
VIOL	Victor. Viol.	BYRDALL	1666	43011012
VIOL	Viol. Floods.	FARRER	1768	19090004
VIOL	Viol. Sabbat.	LAMONT	1780	05005012
VIR	Fem. Vir.&c.	FORDYCE	1767	54004006
VIR	Foun.of Vir.	MOLE	1732	19011007
VIR	Love of Vir.	MACE	1751	43005006
VIR	Piety& Vir.	SYNGE	1733	19010004
VIR	Rel.& Vir.best	ROGERS	1730	63003013
VIR	Rel.& Vir.best	WARREN	1739	63003013
VIR	Result o. Vir.	DYKES	1722	20031031
VIR	Vir.& V. To.	PYLE	1777	43012036
VIRG	Xt b.of virg.	KENNICOTT	1765	23007013
VIRGIN	Virgin Mary	MASTER	1710	45001026
VIRGINS	Fool. Virgins	FOORD	1719	43025010
VIRGINS	Ten Virgins.	GELL	1676	43025001
VIRGINS	Ten Virgins.	BRAGGE	1702	43025001
VIRGINS	Ten Virgins.	SHEPHERD	1702	43025001
VIRGINS	Ten Virgins.	COLMAN	1707	43025001
VIRGINS	Ten Virgins.	TILLOTSON	1735	43025001
VIRGINS	Ten Virgins.	WHITFIELD	1740	43025013
VIRGINS	Ten Virgins.	DODD	1757	43025001
VIRGINS	Ten Virgins.	BOURN	1764	43025001
VIRGINS	Ten Virgins.	BULKLEY	1771	43025001
VIRGINS	Ten Virgins.	BROUGHTON	1778	43025013
VIRT	Advant.virt.	GERARD	1780	19037016
VIRT	D. Virt.m. H.	WILLIAMS	1770	43005006
VIRT	Fai.& Virt.	MARSHALL	1750	57001018
VIRT	Man f. Virt.	GOUGH	1751	21012013
VIRT	Mot.to Virt.	BLAIR	1777	51006009
VIRT	Redee. Virt.	ROWLAND	1774	69003020
VIRT	Rel.& Virt.c.	DOUGHTY	1761	20003007
VIRT	Rew. Virt.& Re	DORRINGTON	1705	19019011
VIRT	Rew. Virt.& Re	BALGUY	1750	19019011
VIRT	Steady Virt.	DYKES	1722	20031025

Keyword	In its Context	Author	Year	BkChpVrs
VIRT	Ten.of Virt.	TIDCOMBE	1757	19073003
VIRT	Virt.& Bel.	BEVERIDGE	1720	46020029
VIRT	Virt.& Bel.	BATTY	1739	46020029
VIRT	Virt.& Bel.	BERRIMAN	1751	46020029
VIRT	Virt.& V.un.	PECKARD	1775	23005020
VIRT	Virt. Child.	TAYLOR	----	20010001
VIRT	Virt. Resol.	JANE	1692	19119106
VIRT	Virt. Resol.	MACE	1751	19119106
VIRT	Virt. Resol.	PYLE	1777	19119106
VIRT	Virt. Resol.	GERARD	1780	19119106
VIRT	Virt. Solicit.	GERARD	1780	19119005
VIRT	Virt. Wife.	BRAY	1754	20031010
VIRT	Virt. Youth.	EATON	1764	19119009
VIRT	Virt.g.m's S.	CONEY	1730	20014014
VIRT	Virt.mind.	CLARKE	1734	27012010
VIRT	Virt.rec.&c.	LARDNER	1760	69003018
VIRTUE	Fa.& Virtue.	MOSS	1732	64001005
VIRTUE	Fem. Virtue.	DYKES	1722	20031010
VIRTUE	Fem. Virtue.	FORDYCE	1767	20031010
VIRTUE	Minis.virtue	TRAPP	1726	45006029
VIRTUE	Mor. Virtue.	HALLYWELL	1692	53004008
VIRTUE	Prin. Virtue.	FORSTER	1737	19119097
VIRTUE	Pub. Virtue.	LANCASTER	1746	19137005
VIRTUE	Rel.& Virtue	ANONYMOUS	1759	19016003
VIRTUE	Res. Virtue.	BENNETT	1728	49015028
VIRTUE	Tem. Virtue	FORDYCE	1767	20004005
VIRTUE	Virtue.	HOLLAND	1753	53004008
VIRTUE	Virtue& V.	BALGUY	1748	20003035
VIRTUE	Xn. Virtue.	DELANY	1754	43011030
VIS	St. Steph.vis.	MAY	1757	47007056
VIS	The dark vis.	WILKINSON	1660	34002003
VIS	Valleyo. Vis.	ERSKINE	1741	26037009
VIS	Vis.&inv. W.	ORR	1772	50004018
VIS	Vis. Judgm.	BRODBURST	1733	14028010
VIS	Vis. Wheels.	MEAD	1689	26010013
VIS	Vis.sic.	POLE	1677	18033023
VISION	Beat. Vision.	REEVES	1729	65003002
VISION	Beat. Vision.	CENNICK	1762	46001029
VISION	Isai's Vision.	JENKINS	1779	23006001
VISION	Vision.	COOKE	1739	45016030
VISIT	Friend. Visit.	HENRY	1704	47015036
VISIT	Visit.of Love	VENN	1759	19118018
VITAL	Vital Relig.	NEAL	1757	48007022
VOLUN	Volun.exile.	FREE	1763	49009013
VOLUNT	b. Volunt.	CHAMBRE	1759	52006010
VOLUNT	b. Volunt.	ROBERTSON	1780	13019013
VOLUPTUOUS	Voluptuous.	DORRINGTON	1703	58003004
VOTAR	Dev. Votar.	CORNWALLIS	1705	19116009
VOW	Jacob's Vow.	HALES	1673	01028020
VOW	Jepth. Vow.	HOLBROOK	1731	07011030
VOW	Jepth. Vow.	ROMAINE	1744	07011030
VOW	Jepth. Vow.	RANDOLPH	1766	07011030
VOW	Jepth. Vow.	SMITH	1777	07011030
VOWS	Of Vows	SHOWER	1702	07011035
VOWS	Relig. Vows.	DAVIS	1756	07011039
VOWS	Vows.	HURST	1677	19116012
VOWS	Vows.	SHOWER	1702	61006017
VOX	Vox Corvi.	CLOGIE	1694	54003008
W	Ab.h. G's w.	PIDDLE	1777	26033030
W	Abid.w. G.	CHANDLER	1769	49007024
W	Af.high. W.	MARKLAND	1729	46002011
W	Ag.conf. W.	LARDNER	1739	48012002
W	Agr.w. Adv.	HORNECK	1706	43005025
W	Agr.w. Adv.	BLAIR	1740	43005025
W	B. Un.w. Xt.	FLAVEL	1673	46017023
W	Balaam's W.	PYLE	1777	04023010
W	Bel. U.w. Xt.	LYE	1676	49006017
W	Bel.unw. W.	ERSKINE	1764	65005010
W	Bp's Co.w. C.	LUZANEY	1697	58001013
W	Car.ly-in W.	LAWSON	1764	23049022
W	Cen.in.w. R.	STEEL	1776	43007003
W	Chear.&w. S.	NEWTON	1759	20018014
W	Co. Ch.be.w.	ADAMS	1683	57002015
W	Co. King. W.	EARL	1725	20010007
W	Co.s.& W. S.	BERRIMAN	1751	47008014
W	Com. Xt's.w.	DAVIS	1756	46017004
W	Com.w. G.	HENRY	1713	19025005
W	Con.in w.d.	DUCHAL	1765	48002007
W	Con.in w.d.	CHANDLER	1769	48002007
W	Con.in w.d.	PYLE	1777	48002007
W	Conf.div. W.	AICKIN	1705	47009006
W	Conf.to W.	SHARP	1734	48012002
W	Conf.to W.	ROGER	1735	48012002
W	Conf.to W.	NEWMAN	1760	48012002
W	Conf.to W.	WEST	1762	48012002
W	Conf.to W.	STENNETT	1771	48012002
W	Conf.w.ser.	MAY	1757	44012034
W	Conv.w. G.	CRUSO	1698	24003032
W	Corrp. G.w.	GIPPS	1697	20030006
W	Cov.of W.	BOSTON	1773	01002016
W	Dan.70 W.	MARKWICK	1728	27009024
W	Dan.70 W.	BLAYNEY	1775	27009020
W	Delig. G's w.	LELAND	1769	19111002
W	Di. W.in Cr.	DAVIS	1756	19104015
W	Diff. R.d. W.	SMALRIDGE	1724	49003008
W	Diff. R.d. W.	BOYSE	1728	49003008
W	Do&h. G's w.	DORMAN	1743	62001022
W	Do&h. W.	BROWNRIG	1664	62001022
W	Do&h. W.	BEVERIDGE	1720	62001022
W	Do&h. W.	ALTHAM	1732	62001022
W	Do&h. W.	ATTERBURY	1743	62001022
W	Dut. H.& W.	NICHOLS	1701	54003018
W	Dut. H.& W.	FLEETWOOD	1737	54003019
W	E.f. Xn.w. T.	HORNE	1671	68000020
W	E.walk.w. G	MACE	1751	01005024
W	E.walk.w. G.	FANCH	1768	01005024
W	E.walk.w. G.	BRACKENRIDGE	1775	01005024
W	Ember W.	HOLE	1716	48010014
W	Ex. D.re. W.	ORR	1739	61010025
W	F.&good W.	DUKE	1714	52002008
W	F.in.j.tr.w.	BREVALL	1670	69002010
W	Fa.&sec. W.	JENNINGS	1757	52006018

Keyword	In its Context	Author	Year	BkChpVrs
W	Fa.&sec. W.	LANGHORNE	1773	52006018
W	Fai.w.b. L.	GROVE	1742	51005006
W	Faith ab W.	JOHNSON	1740	43008010
W	Faith w. S.	PEARSON	1718	46020029
W	Faith w. S.	SHERLOCK	1719	46020029
W	Faith.ins.w. W	BEVERIDGE	1720	43007021
W	Faith.ins.w. W	BLACKALL	1723	43007021
W	Fas. W.pas.a.	DUNLOP	1722	49007031
W	Fashi.of W.	BREKELL	1765	49007031
W	Fill.w. Spir.	EVANS	1737	52005018
W	Fol.gain W.	PYLE	1777	45009025
W	Fool.&w. B.	SOUTH	1727	43007026
W	Fool.&w. B.	BLAIR	1740	43007026
W	Friend w. G.	COOKE	1739	46015014
W	Frm.sou. W.	BEVERIDGE	1720	58001013
W	Fth&w.b. L.	TAYLOR	1678	62002024
W	G.dw.w. M.	FLEMING	1701	14006018
W	G.pres.of w.	LELAND	1769	16009006
W	G.sp.&sp.w.	BAGSHAW	1662	46004024
W	G.sp.&sp.w.	CHARNOCK	1684	46004024
W	G.sp.&sp.w.	CLAGETT	1720	46004024
W	G.sp.&sp.w.	ATTERBURY	1743	46004024
W	G.sp.&sp.w.	BALGUY	1748	46004024
W	G.w.ab.our.	BARKER	1763	23055008
W	G.w.incom.	SAURIN	1775	23055008
W	G.wond. W.	WILLISON	1761	18037014
W	G's w.beaut.	HUSSEY	1755	21003011
W	G's w.hid. T.	TAYLOR	1776	19112011
W	G's w.in D.	HOWE	1771	19107023
W	G's. Gov. W.	DUCHAL	1765	46014011
W	G's. W.in R.	HUSSEY	1758	49002007
W	G's.dea.w. S.	STEPHENS	1737	48009017
W	G's.w.uns.	MOIR	1759	48011033
W	God w.us.	BRADBURY	1772	23008009
W	Gos. W.o G.	BAINE	1778	49002007
W	Gosp h.f w.	BARKER	1763	43011025
W	Gosp.w.o. S.	LARDNER	1751	47016031
W	H. W. Xr. Xs.	POWELL	1776	43005011
W	Hear G's.w.	DORRINGTON	1703	49001021
W	Hear G's.w.	WAKE	1716	45008008
W	Hol.w.t. Ha.	BROOKS	1662	61012014
W	Imp.of w.	LARDNER	1751	43012036
W	Imp.of w.&c	FOTHERGILL	1765	24005003
W	In th.&n. W.	LITTLETON	1735	54003002
W	In.to w.o. G.	SNAPE	1745	49007029
W	Inord. L. W.	MASON	1758	46002015
W	Int.b.r.&w.	BOURDALOUE	1776	43013025
W	Interc.w. G.	NALSON	1737	18022021
W	Interc.w. G.	REAY	1755	18022021
W	Interc.w. G.	RICHMOND	1764	18022021
W	Interc.w. G.	LANGHORNE	1773	18022021
W	Joh. Xr.& W.	DUCHAL	1753	46021024
W	Kno. G's W.	NEEDHAM	1679	46007017
W	L. G.& W.co.	DAWES	1733	62004004
W	L. G.& W.incon	GALE	1676	65002015
W	L. G.& W.incon	CLARKE	1734	65002015

Keyword	In its Context	Author	Year	BkChpVrs
W	L. G.& W.incon	DORMAN	1743	65002015
W	L. G.& W.incon	BALL	1756	65002015
W	L. G.& W.incon	CARR	1777	65002015
W	L. G& W.incons	WAKE	1701	65002015
W	L. G& W.incons	ROGERS	1735	65002015
W	L. G& W.incons	SNAPE	1745	65002015
W	Lawf.just w.	FOURESTIER	1758	43024006
W	Love of W.	RUSSEL	1746	43019016
W	M.pl.w.cri.	FARINDON	1672	51001010
W	M's co.w. G.	WILSON	1676	19073023
W	Manna in W.	BERRIMAN	1763	05008003
W	More exc.w.	HUSSEY	1758	49012031
W	N. W.m.t. V.	ENFIELD	1772	43005014
W	N.conf.t. W.	S.	1695	48012002
W	N.conf.t. W.	ERSKINE	1764	48012002
W	Nec. Xn's w.	BOSTON	1773	21009010
W	Neg.of F. W.	ORTON	1769	24010025
W	Neg.of P. W.	TOULMIN	1770	16013011
W	Ob.to D. W.	STEPHENS	1699	43006010
W	Ob.to D. W.	NEWCOME	1702	43006010
W	Ob.to D. W.	NORRIS	1728	43006010
W	Ob.to D. W.	ROGERS	1736	43006010
W	Obed. D. W.	SCATTERGOOD	1723	43007021
W	Obed. D. W.	SKEELER	1740	43007021
W	Old w.e.n. C.	PITTIS	1682	65002024
W	Origin of W.	SHERIDAN	1720	47017024
W	Peop.of W.	MURRAY	1777	01010001
W	Pict.of w.	EDWARDS	1726	18014001
W	Pict.of w.	ANONYMOUS	1754	18014001
W	Places of W.	DOWNES	1761	26034012
W	Pomp&c. W.	ANONYMOUS	1780	48012002
W	Pr. W. Bth-d.	SMEDLEY	1716	63002017
W	Pri.incap.of W	ATTERBURY	1730	20014006
W	Pri.incap.of W	ABERNETHY	1751	20014005
W	Pub. W.b. P.	CLARKSON	1696	19087002
W	R. U.& A. W.	PEARSON	1718	49007031
W	R. U & A. W.	NORRIS	1728	49007031
W	R. U.& A. W.	MILLER	1749	49007031
W	R. U.& A. W.	ORR	1749	49007031
W	R.con.w. L.	GERARD	1780	19116009
W	Recon.w. G.	BRADY	1713	50005020
W	Recon.w. G.	DAVIES	1766	50005020
W	Recon.w. G.	BOURN	1777	50005020
W	Rel.sec.f.w.	ROE	1766	43006033
W	Rew.pro.w.	CLARKE	1735	51006007
W	Right.&w.	CATCOTT	1753	20014032
W	Sal.in an. W.	SMITH	1696	47016030
W	Sec.of w. Gr.	TAYLOR	1719	23065008
W	Sinc. Pub.w.	CLAYTON	1776	46004019
W	Sinc.m.o. W.	ROWLAND	1774	63002002
W	Sol.pref. W.	PICKARD	1752	11003009
W	Sonsh.w. G.	DAVIES	1766	65003001
W	Sp.&true W.	STILLINGFLEET	1707	46004024
W	Sp.&true W.	ORR	1739	46004024
W	Spir. W.& R.	HUSSEY	1758	52001017
W	Su.w.of Pro.	NEWCOME	1724	64001019

Keyword	In its Context	Author	Year	BkChpVrs
W	Su.w.of Pro.	BRAY	1761	64001019
W	Sub. G's. W.	SCOTT	1700	45022042
W	Sub. G's. W.	BARROW	1716	45022042
W	Sub.t. Di. W.	JONES	1741	46018011
W	Sub.t. G's w.	DU MOULIN	1684	43026039
W	Sub.t. G's w.	BATES	1700	43026039
W	Sub.t. G's w.	ATTERBURY	1743	43026039
W	Suff.w.to Gl.	BRADY	1730	69007014
W	Sup.w. Ath.	WESTON	1739	53003006
W	Tr. Xn.& W.	ORTON	1773	46017016
W	Tues. W. S.	STANHOPE	1714	47008014
W	Turn f.ev.w.	FOORD	1719	26033011
W	Und. Div.w.	BURTON	1685	52005017
W	Union w. G.	BARKER	1683	46017020
W	Union w. Xt.	FLOWER	1740	46014019
W	Union w. Xt.	ROMAINE	1759	22006001
W	Use& A. W.	ANONYMOUS	1772	20031006
W	Use& Ab. W.	CARTER	1729	49007031
W	Van.of h. W.	DELAUNE	1728	48012016
W	Vess. M.& W.	DAVIES	1771	48009022
W	Vis.&inv. W.	ORR	1772	50004018
W	W.& D. Wis.	OUTRAM	1697	45016008
W	W.& D. Wis.	NORRIS	1728	45016008
W	W.& D. Wis.	SMITH	1740	45016008
W	W.& G.o. G.	KNOWLES	1750	48011033
W	W.&f. Buil.	BRAGGE	1704	43007024
W	W. Dut man.	WAPLE	1729	32006008
W	W. Hand res.	BRAGGE	1706	45006006
W	W. Tuesday.	STANHOPE	1714	46010001
W	W. Tuesday.	HOLE	1716	46010001
W	W. Xns.n. Ar.a	CLARKE	1736	51002017
W	W. Xns.n. Ar.a	GROVE	1741	51002017
W	W.a. Salt.of t	GARDINER	1720	43005013
W	W.a. Salt.of t	BLAIR	1740	43005013
W	W.a. Salt.of t	WESTLEY	1748	43005013
W	W.art thou	JENKINS	1779	01003009
W	W.exc. Folly	ANONYMOUS	1776	21002013
W	W.m pl. G.	WATERLAND	1742	20016004
W	W.of Nature	TOTTIE	1775	43006028
W	W.of Sin h.	DAVIES	1771	47009006
W	W.think&c.	WHITFIELD	1740	43022043
W	W.to r.&p.	COLLINGES	1684	05008018
W	W.to thrive.	GOUGE	1706	43010041
W	W.to L.& G.	TALBOT	1674	05005029
W	W.to Riches	WOOD	1698	43006033
W	W.w. F.c. J.	HORNE	1761	62002014
W	Walk.w.o. G	GROVE	1741	55002012
W	Wat.into W.	BRAGGE	1702	46002001
W	Wis.o.this w.	CLARKE	1727	49001020
W	Wor.w.fool.	SOUTH	1727	49003019
W	Wor.w.imp.	ELLIS	1704	45016008
W	Wor.w.imp.	KETTLEWELL	1719	45016008
W	X's Good w.	HILL	1755	05033016
W	Xn. Light W.	HOLDEN	1755	43005014
W	Xn. Light W.	ORR	1772	43005014
W	Xn. Use o. W.	BISSE	1717	49007031

Keyword	In its Context	Author	Year	BkChpVrs
W	Xt. Lig.o. W.	WHARTON	1728	46008012
W	Xt. Lig.o. W.	KIMBER	1756	46008012
W	Xt. Lig.of w.	WATSON	1749	19019004
W	Xt.do all t.w.	ORTON	1776	44007037
W	Xt.eq.w. G.	LESTLEY	1720	53002006
W	Xt.eq.w. G.	SHERLOCK	1772	53002006
W	Xt.faith. W.	HORTON	1679	69001005
W	Xt.t. W.&c.	HORTON	1679	46014006
W	Xt.t. W.&c.	BEVERIDGE	1720	46014006
W	Xt.u.w. Xns.	CLAGETT	1720	46015001
W	Xt's u.w. Ch.	NICOLSON	1661	50011002
W	Xt's.good W.	BOSTON	1773	45019005
W	Xt's.w.pers.	FLAVEL	1673	46001014
W	Xt's K.n.t.w.	GREENHILL	1768	46018036
W	b. Prin.of W.	HOWARD	1742	49013005
W'S	W's Ans.im.	GILL	1752	13012032
WA	Xns.wa.to H.	ANONYMOUS	1726	47016030
WAG	Dea.wag. Sin	PEARSE	1763	48006023
WAGES	Wages of Sin	EDWARDS	1775	48006023
WAIT	Wait f. Cha.	COBDEN	1757	18014014
WAIT	Wait on G.	PEARSE	1763	23040031
WAIT	Wait.all T.	GREENHILL	1773	63004007
WAL	Wal.b. Rule.	HORTON	1679	51006016
WALES	D. P. Wales.	ATWOOD	1751	19146002
WALK	E.walk.w. G	MACE	1751	01005024
WALK	E.walk.w. G.	FANCH	1768	01005024
WALK	E.walk.w. G.	BRACKENRIDGE	1775	01005024
WALK	Josh.walk.	ORTON	1776	37003006
WALK	Sure walk.	DUKE	1714	20010009
WALK	Sure walk.	BARROW	1716	20010009
WALK	Sure walk.	CLARKE	1735	20010009
WALK	Walk.b. Fai.	NORRIS	1728	50005007
WALK	Walk.b. Fai.	MILLER	1749	50005007
WALK	Walk.b. Fai.	ABERNETHY	1751	50005007
WALK	Walk.exalt.	BURTON	1685	52005015
WALK	Walk.in Sp.	HORTON	1679	51005016
WALK	Walk.in Sp.	ATTERBURY	1743	51005025
WALK	Walk.in Xt.	HILL	1755	54002006
WALK	Walk.on S.	BRAGGE	1702	43014022
WALK	Walk.w.o. G	GROVE	1741	55002012
WAND	Wand.in pr.	TENISON	1691	49007035
WANDR	Wandr. Tho.	WESTLEY	1771	50010004
WANT	Want Faith.	CLAGETT	1704	45018008
WARF	Xn's. Warf.	HAYWARD	1758	58004007
WARN	Engl.warn.	OWEN	1694	26005008
WARN	Warn to Y.	ROSEWELL	1714	44010021
WARN	Warn. Slug.	MEADOWS	1768	20024030
WARN	Warn.t. You.	TOULMIN	1770	45015012
WARN	Xt's.warn. P.	HORTON	1679	45022031
WARS	Orig.o. Wars	RALEIGH	1679	62004001
WASH	Wash. Feet.	BRAGGE	1706	46013004
WAT	Glast- Wat.	RAWLINS	1771	46005002
WAT	Wat.into W.	BRAGGE	1702	46002001
WATCH	Cont.watch.	LITTLETON	1735	44013037
WATCH	Watch& Pr.	DYER	1666	44014038
WATCH	Watch& Pr.	CLAGETT	1707	43026041

Keyword	In its Context	Author	Year	BkChpVrs
WATCH	Watch& Pr.	STILLINGFLEET	1707	43026041
WATCH	Watch& Pr.	BROWNE	1749	43026041
WATCH	Watch-an.i.	GILL	1773	14020020
WATCH	Weak watch.	SKELTON	1754	49010012
WATCHF	Xn. Watchf.	CARTER	1729	44013037
WATCHFULN	Watchfuln.	DUNLOP	1722	43025013
WATCHFULN	Watchfuln.	EDWARDS	1726	43025013
WATCHFULN	Watchfuln.	BENNETT	1728	69016015
WATCHFULN	Watchfuln.	BRADY	1730	43024042
WATCHFULN	Watchfuln.	COCKMAN	1750	43025013
WATCHFULN	Watchfuln.	WELCH	1752	43026048
WATCHFULN	Watchfuln.	ROMAINE	1756	43025013
WATCHFULN	Watchfuln.	DODD	1757	43025013
WATCHFULN	Watchfuln.	STEBBING	1760	43025013
WATCHFULN	Watchfuln.	MUSCOTT	1760	44013037
WATCHFULN	Watchfuln.	WALKER	1764	45012035
WATCHFULN	Watchfuln.	FOTHERGILL	1765	43025013
WATCHFULN	Watchfuln.	WHITTY	1772	43026040
WATCHM	Watchm.v.	BULL	1695	29002001
WATCHM'S	Watchm's a.	GILL	1773	23021011
WATER	Clean Water.	ERSKINE	1764	26036025
WATER	Water Bapt.	COLLINGES	1680	48006003
WATER	Water-bapt.	ANONYMOUS	1715	43028019
WATERS	Bath Waters.	JACKSON	1707	19103003
WATERS	Min. Waters.	NICHOLS	1702	46005004
WAY	Way living.	ANONYMOUS	1732	21003001
WAY	Way of Hap.	GLANVIL	1681	45013024
WAY	Way of Kno.	TAYLOR	1678	46007017
WAY	Way of L.	BRADY	1730	23040003
WAY	Way of Lord.	MOSS	1733	45003004
WAY	Way of Man.	LEIGHTON	1746	24010023
WAY	Way t. Heav.	PHILIPS	1681	47002047
WAY	Way to et. S.	SYNGE	1734	55005021
WAY	Way to life.	IBBOT	1726	43019017
WAY	Way to Glo.	HILL	1755	19107007
WAY	Way to Hap.	RALEIGH	1679	43006033
WAY	Way to Hap.	WHALEY	1695	61012013
WAY	Way to Heav.	FERNE	1721	64001011
WAY	Way to Loy.	OWEN	1684	59003001
WAY	Way try Pro.	BLACKALL	1723	65004001
WAYS	Ways of Wis.	ABERNETHY	1751	20003017
WAYS	Ways H.uns.	DAVIS	1756	19077019
WAYS	Ways Wis.p.	BARROW	1716	20003017
WAYS	Ways Wis.p.	BEVERIDGE	1720	20003017
WD	Bib.wd.o. G.	SKELTON	1754	58003014
WD	Wd.m.flesh.	BRETT	1720	46001014
WE	Su.f.we&c.	ALTHAM	1732	63002020
WEAK	Str.in Weak.	BOSTON	1753	50012009
WEAK	Weak consc.	SOUTH	1727	49008012
WEAK	Weak watch.	SKELTON	1754	49010012
WEAK	Weak. Faith.	STANHOPE	1705	44009024
WEAK	Weak.of F.	PAYNE	1763	23042003
WEALTH	Get. Wealth.	BRADFORD	1720	20013011
WEALTH	Get. Wealth.	HUTCHINS	1782	20013011
WEATH	Cold Weath.	STEWARD	1734	19147015
WED	Wed.b. East.	STANHOPE	1715	61009016

Keyword	In its Context	Author	Year	BkChpVrs
WEEK	Emb. Week.	HOLE	1716	52004011
WEEK	Rogat.week.	SMITH	1677	55005017
WEEKS	70 Weeks.	WOODROFFE	1702	27009024
WEEKS	70 Weeks.	WINTER	1777	27009024
WEEPING	Jes.weeping.	LOTHIAN	1776	46011035
WEIG	Weig.m. R.	ORR	1739	43023023
WEIGH	Weigh.m. R.	ORR	1739	45011042
WEIGHTS	Fal. Weights	DRAKE	1697	20016011
WEIGHTS	Fal. Weights	DICKINSON	1779	20020010
WELCH	Welch. F.	WILLIAMS	1731	19033012
WELCH	Welch F.	SCURLOCK	1736	19118024
WELCOME	Welcome Pl.	SHAW	1751	30004012
WELL	Pat.i.well-d.	MACE	1751	61010036
WELL	Per.well-do.	DORMAN	1743	51006009
WELL	Well-do. S.ag.	CLAGETT	1720	63003013
WELL	Well-do. S.ag.	CLARKE	1736	63003013
WELL	Well-do.a. S.	TILLOTSON	1735	63003013
WELL	Well-doing.	DAVIES	1754	51006009
WELL	Well-doing.	SHERLOCK	1772	51006009
WEST	West. Inf.	BRUCE	1752	45010037
WESTM	Westm. Disp.	SOWDEN	1766	63003008
WESTM	Westm. Jub.	PEARCE	1760	20031031
WH	Fuln. G.wh.	ALSOP	1690	52003019
WH	Wh. D.of M.	HOOLE	1748	21012013
WHAT	Truth.what.	EDWARDS	1698	46018038
WHEAT	Wheat& T.	WHEATLY	1746	43013030
WHEELS	Vis. Wheels.	MEAD	1689	26010013
WHENCE	Sin whence.	CLARKE	1736	24005004
WHIT	Whit. Mond.	STANHOPE	1714	47010034
WHITEH	At Whiteh.	HACKET	1675	46006011
WHITEH	at Whiteh.	HACKET	1675	46004013
WHITEH	at Whiteh.	HACKET	1675	46004014
WHO	Who. Du. M.	BALL	1756	59002011
WHO	Who Right.	OUTRAM	1697	65003002
WHO	Who Unbel.	CHARNOCK	1684	46006064
WHOLE	Whole& S.	DAVIES	1771	43009012
WHOR	Whor.wom.	HAMMOND	1684	26016030
WHOREDOM	Whoredom.	NOURSE	1708	02020014
WHORING	Ag.whoring	ANONYMOUS	1743	50007009
WHY	Why n. Crea.	BARNES	1752	50005017
WHYM	Whym.l. D.	MOSS	1732	46003019
WIC	Folly of wic.	LANGHORNE	1773	23057021
WIC	Righ.& Wic.	COCK	1710	38003018
WIC	Wic. M.o. D.	CLARKE	1735	46008044
WIC	no Peace to wic	HORTON	1679	23057021
WIC	no Peace to wic	FOORD	1719	23057021
WICK	Cond.wick.	WELCH	1752	46003018
WICK	Fear.wick.	DUKE	1714	20010024
WICK	Gr.wick.&c.	STUART	1753	48003010
WICK	Mis.of wick.	LANGHORNE	1773	23057020
WICK	Pea wick. D.	HORTON	1679	55005003
WICK	Prev. Wick.	FOSTER	1737	46009041
WICK	Prog.wick.	SHERLOCK	1719	23005020
WICK	Prosp. Wick.	HUSSEY	1758	24012001
WICK	Prosp. Wick.	HUNTER	1774	24012001
WICK	Shame wick.	DUNLOP	1722	27012002

INDEXES TO THIRD VOLUME: E: KEYWORD-IN-CONTEXT INDEX OF OTHER SUBJECTS OR OCCASIONS

Keyword	In its Context	Author	Year	BkChpVrs
WICK	Tor.of wick.	ELLIS	1704	45016024
WICK	Wick.& Rig.	LANGHORNE	1764	19118015
WICK	Wick.& Rig.	LANGHORNE	1764	20004018
WICK	Wick.&rig.	WEBB	1772	20028001
WICK	Wick. M. F.	HORTON	1679	45012020
WICK	Wick. M.de.	CLARKE	1736	56002011
WICK	Wick. Men.	BRADY	1704	23057021
WICK	Wick. Prosp.	ROE	1766	18037007
WICK	Wick. Sec.g.	JORTIN	1774	45012020
WICK	Wick.husb.	ANONYMOUS	1703	43021033
WICK	Wick.husb.	BRAGGE	1704	43021033
WICKED	Nat.wicked.	SEED	1750	23005004
WICKED	Wicked. Xns	ATTERBURY	1734	57006001
WID	Ch.s.f. Wid.	CHANDLER	1748	50009012
WID	Import. Wid.	BRAGGE	1702	45018001
WID	Import. Wid.	DODD	1757	45018001
WID	Import. Wid.	BULKLEY	1771	45018006
WID	Wid. N's.son	BRAGGE	1702	45007011
WID	Wid. N's.son	HOLE	1716	45007011
WID	Wid. N's.son.	DODD	1757	45007012
WID	Wid. N's.son.	CENNICK	1762	45007013
WID	Wid.of Zar.	WEBB	1772	11017012
WID	Wid.2 Mites.	WEBB	1772	45021001
WID'S	Wid's. Assid.	BOURN	1763	45018001
WIFE	Lot's wife.	HACKETT	1675	01019026
WIFE	Lot's Wife.	BRADY	1730	45017032
WIFE	Virt. Wife.	BRAY	1754	20031010
WILD	God in wild.	PEARSE	1763	28013005
WILDERN	Wildern. St.	WESTLEY	1771	46016022
WILF	Ignor.wilf.	SECKER	1770	45012057
WILF	Wilf. Darkn.	WEST	1762	46003019
WILF	Wilf. Darkn.	SHERLOCK	1772	46003019
WILF	Wilf. Ignor.	SCOTT	1743	64003005
WILFUL	Wilful Sins.	SCOTT	1700	65003009
WILL	Co. G's.will.	NALSON	1737	61010006
WILL	Co. G's.will.	NALSON	1737	61010009
WILL	Fre.of Will.	MARRIOTT	1774	19073011
WILL	Free Will.	TOPLADY	1774	19115001
WILL	King.& Will of	BLACKALL	1723	43006010
WILL	King.& Will of	BISSE	1740	43006010
WILL	King.& Will of	BLAIR	1740	43006010
WILL	Sub. D. Will.	MEDE	1672	43007021
WILL	Will.m.acc.	HICKES	1726	50008012
WILL	Will-worsh.	STEPHENS	1737	54002023
WIND	Wind& S.r.	DODD	1757	44004039
WIND	Wind& S.r.	BULKLEY	1771	44004041
WINE	All N.wine.	SPOONER	1771	43009017
WINTER	Winter med.	SHOWER	1709	19147015
WIS	Anal. D.wis.	BARTON	1737	45006038
WIS	Div. Wis. Cr.	TILLOTSON	1735	19104024
WIS	Div. Wis. Cr.	BOURN	1760	19104024
WIS	Div. Wis. Cr.	WEST	1762	19104024
WIS	Div. Wis. Cr.	STONE	1771	19104024
WIS	W.& D. Wis.	OUTRAM	1697	45016008
WIS	W.& D. Wis.	NORRIS	1728	45016008
WIS	W.& D. Wis.	SMITH	1740	45016008

Keyword	In its Context	Author	Year	BkChpVrs
WIS	Ways of Wis.	ABERNETHY	1751	20003017
WIS	Ways Wis.p.	BARROW	1716	20003017
WIS	Ways Wis.p.	BEVERIDGE	1720	20003017
WIS	Wis.b.reiig.	BARNES	1752	18028028
WIS	Wis.b.relig.	BATTY	1739	18028028
WIS	Wis.b.relig.	CARR	1777	18028028
WIS	Wis.o.this w.	CLARKE	1727	49001020
WIS	Wis.of Man.	GOUGH	1751	18028028
WIS	Wis.prov.f.	BOURN	1777	43006019
WIS	Wis.r.t. Pl.	ANONYMOUS	1754	20003017
WIS	World. Wis.	FIDDES	1720	43016026
WIS	Xt's. D. Wis.	PARKHURST	1707	65003008
WISD	A sign Wisd.	HORTON	1679	49001022
WISD	Best. Wisd.	BRUNNING	1660	62003017
WISD	Def. H.wisd.	FIDDES	1720	21001018
WISD	Def. H.wisd.	MARKLAND	1729	21001018
WISD	Def. Wisd.	BOURN	1777	18028028
WISD	Div. Wisd.	BARTON	1737	46003012
WISD	G's wisd.&c.	SAURIN	1775	24032019
WISD	G's. Wisd.	HUNT	1748	57001017
WISD	Godly Wisd.	LEIGHTON	1746	19107043
WISD	Heav. Wisd.	MOSS	1737	62003017
WISD	Heav. Wisd.	LEIGHTON	1746	62003017
WISD	Heav. Wisd.	SHERLOCK	1772	62003017
WISD	Hon. Wisd.	BAYLY	1721	20014008
WISD	Love Wisd.	ABERNETHY	1751	20008017
WISD	Rel. Wisd.	ABERNETHY	1751	20001001
WISD	Relig. Wisd.	MARKLAND	1729	21012013
WISD	Relig. Wisd.	JORTIN	1774	48016019
WISD	Relig. Wisd.	JORTIN	1774	62001005
WISD	S.& R. Wisd.	BADDERLEY	1752	20004005
WISD	Spir. Wisd.	VEAL	1676	23027011
WISD	Tr.&f.wisd.	CARMICHAEL	1757	62003013
WISD	True Wisd.	MILLER	1749	20003021
WISD	Wisd.& Inn.	BAGNOLD	1709	43010016
WISD	Wisd. Creat.	BOURN	1760	47017026
WISD	Wisd. Gl. G.	TILLOTSON	1735	68000025
WISD	Wisd. Holin.	BEVERIDGE	1720	19111010
WISD	Wisd. Justif.	H.	1699	45007035
WISD	Wisd. Xt's. M.	TOTTIE	1775	45007035
WISD	Wisd.attain.	LARDNER	1751	20008017
WISD	Wisd.b. R.	CARR	1777	18027006
WISD	Wisd.b. Rel.	DAVIES	1771	19111010
WISD	Wisd.b. Rel.	HUNTER	1774	19111010
WISD	Wisd.b. Rel.	ORTON	1776	19111010
WISD	Wisd.believ.	YOUNG	1706	48001022
WISD	Wisd.di.pro.	LELAND	1769	23028029
WISD	Wisd.in Cre.	BOURN	1760	18035010
WISD	Wisd.justif.	MANTON	1708	43011018
WISD	Wisd.meek.	BOSTON	1773	20014029
WISD	Wisd.of G.	HORTON	1679	49001021
WISD	Wisd.of G.	CHARNOCK	1684	48016027
WISD	Wisd.of G.	WHITBY	1710	48016027
WISD	Wisd.of G.	WISHEART	1716	68000025
WISD	Wisd.of G.	ABERNETHY	1743	57001017
WISD	Wisd.of Pro.	ADAMS	1736	01045007

Keyword	In its Context	Author	Year	BkChpVrs
WISD	Wisd.of Rel.	STILLINGFLEET	1707	45007035
WISD	Wisd.of Rel.	ADEY	1760	27012003
WISD	Wisd.relig.	CLARKE	1732	20009010
WISD	Wisd.relig.	TILLOTSON	1735	19119096
WISD	Wisd.vain.	WILKINS	1682	21001018
WISD	Worl. Wisd.	ALLESTREE	1684	45016008
WISD	Worl. Wisd.	BARKER	1748	45016008
WISDOM	Rel. Wisdom	LANGHORNE	1773	20004007
WISDOM	Wisdom.	ABERNETHY	1751	20024005
WISEST	Wisest Prea.	WILKINSON	1712	20011030
WISH	Agur's wish.	NEWTON	1759	20030007
WISH	P's.wish exp.	WATERLAND	1742	48009003
WISH	P's.wish exp.	DODWELL	1752	48009003
WISH	P's.wish exp.	KEELING	1766	48009003
WISL	Divine Wisl.	CREYGHTON	1720	43006010
WIT	In.wit.o. Xy.	WATTS	1753	65005010
WITCHCRAFT	Witchcraft.	JUXON	1736	02022018
WITH	Acc.with G.	BOSTON	1775	50008012
WITH	Com.with G.	SYLVESTER	1683	65001007
WITH	Com.with G.	HUNT	1748	65001006
WITH	Fell.with G.	CLARKSON	1696	65001003
WITH	Fell.with G.	MACE	1751	65001003
WITH	With.hand.	DODD	1757	43012013
WITN	T.two Witn.	K.	1667	69011003
WITN	Witn.& Eart.	C.	1692	69011013
WITN	Witn.o. Sp.	WESTLEY	1746	50001012
WITN	Witn.of Sp.	SHARP	1734	48008016
WITN	Witn.of Sp.	WESTLEY	1746	48008016
WITN	Witn.of Sp.	WATTS	1753	48008016
WITN	Witn.of Sp.	RANDOLPH	1768	48008016
WITN	Witn.of Sp.	SHERLOCK	1772	48008016
WITN	Witn.of Sp.	SECKER	1777	48008016
WITNES	Witnes.f. G.	ERSKINE	1764	23043012
WITNESS	Fal. Witness.	CLARKE	1736	20024028
WIV	Wiv.& H. D.	STEELE	1676	52005033
WIV	Wiv.& H. D.	HOLE	1719	52005033
WIV	Wiv.& H. D.	ANONYMOUS	1754	52006002
WIV	Wiv.& H. D.	ANONYMOUS	1754	52006004
WIV	Wiv.& H. D.	FRANKLIN	1765	52005033
WIV	Wiv. D.to H.	FLEETWOOD	1737	63003001
WIV	Wiv. D.to H.	FLEETWOOD	1737	63003003
WIV	Wiv. D.to H.	FLEETWOOD	1737	63003004
WIVE'S	Wive's& Hus. D	ANONYMOUS	1776	52005033
WK'S	G's Wk's g.	DUCHAL	1765	01001031
WKS	Good wks.n.	TILLOTSON	1735	59003008
WKS	Unfr.wks. D.	MOORE	1716	52005011
WKS	Wks. Dark.	ALTHAM	1732	48013012
WLK	Wlk.as Xt.d.	BARROW	1716	65002006
WO	Ang.wo. Xt.	BRETT	1720	61001006
WO	S. S.wo.of G.	LUCAS	1710	55002013
WO	Seed of Wo.	HARRIS	1724	01003015
WO	Wo.anoin. J.	LARDNER	1760	43026013
WO	Wo.ins.t. H.	CARR	1777	54003002
WOE	Woe scandal	BEVERLEY	1683	43018007
WOM	Whor.wom.	HAMMOND	1684	26016030
WOM	Wom. Sam.	LEWIS	1720	46004009

Keyword	In its Context	Author	Year	BkChpVrs
WOM	Wom. Sam.	CENNICK	1762	46004010
WOM	Wom.blo. Is.	DODD	1757	45009042
WOMAN	Woman Can.	GODDARD	1781	43005028
WON	Won.& Fear.	CREYGHTON	1720	44010032
WOND	G.wond. W.	WILLISON	1761	18037014
WOR	A wor.mind.	DORRINGTON	1705	53003019
WOR	Cathe. Wor.	BISSE	1720	13016004
WOR	Cor.of Wor.	MONRO	1693	64001004
WOR	Cov.of Wor.	TATHAM	1780	48005012
WOR	Dec.in Wor.	SUTTON	1717	49014040
WOR	Desc.o. Wor.	STERNE	1769	64003011
WOR	Diss.of Wor.	DAVIES	1720	64003011
WOR	Diss.of Wor.	WEBB	1772	64003011
WOR	Fr.wor. Enj.	KIMBER	1756	65002017
WOR	G's wor.&c.	JOHNSON	1776	58002009
WOR	Go.wor.nec.	BULL	1713	28010012
WOR	Just.by Wor.	GALE	1726	53003009
WOR	Just.by Wor.	BRADBURY	1772	48004003
WOR	Plac.of wor.	BENNETT	1728	45006012
WOR	Van.wor. T.	LANGHORNE	1773	19039006
WOR	Wor. Conq.	ALLEINE	1676	65005004
WOR	Wor. Darkn.	SECKER	1770	52005011
WOR	Wor. G.only	GUYSE	1757	43015008
WOR	Wor. Great.	REYNER	1745	27005027
WOR	Wor. Sp. Tr.	MEDE	1672	46004023
WOR	Wor. Sp. Tr.	BUNDY	1750	46004023
WOR	Wor.in pr. H	H.	1693	01034022
WOR	Wor.in Seas.	CHEESE	1668	61011035
WOR	Wor.mercy.	CATCOTT	1753	43025040
WOR	Wor.of Soul.	VINK	1683	43016026
WOR	Wor.of Soul.	WAPLE	1720	43016026
WOR	Wor.only G.	COLLIER	1725	45004008
WOR	Wor.w.fool.	SOUTH	1727	49003019
WOR	Wor.w.imp.	ELLIS	1704	45016008
WOR	Wor.w.imp.	KETTLEWELL	1719	45016008
WOR	Xt. Wor. Car.	ORTON	1776	44006003
WORD	H.&do word	FIDDES	1720	62001022
WORD	H.&do word	SNAPE	1745	62001023
WORD	H.&pr.word	STUART	1773	46010025
WORD	H&do word	MORE	1692	62001022
WORD	Hear word.	BRADBURY	1713	23052007
WORD	Hear word.	REYNOLDS	1713	61003007
WORD	Hear. Word.	NEWMAN	1713	20028009
WORD	Hear.word.	CLARKSON	1696	45008018
WORD	Hear.word.	HARRIS	1713	45008018
WORD	Hear.word.	EARLE	1711	55005020
WORD	Hear.word.	BROWN	1722	55002013
WORD	Hear.word.	RICHMOND	1764	45008018
WORD	Hear.word.	HURD	1780	45008018
WORD	Hear.word.	NEWSON	1781	45008018
WORD	Heard word	SEIGNIOR	1676	62001021
WORD	Heart word.	GROSVENOR	1713	62001019
WORD	Receiv.word	MAYHEW	1756	62001021
WORD	Receiv.word	BREKELL	1765	62001021
WORD	Word ev. G.	BRETT	1720	46001001
WORD	Word ev. G.	LESTLEY	1720	46001001

Keyword	In its Context	Author	Year	BkChpVrs
WORD	Word of G.	SCATTERGOOD	1723	47017011
WORD	Word of G.	HART	1767	24002004
WORD	Word of G.	BOURDALOUE	1776	46008047
WORD	Word of G.	JOHNSON	1776	55002013
WORD	Word to Isr.	CHISHULL	1668	61003008
WORD	Word. Prop.	CLAGETT	1704	64001019
WORD	Word Idol.	WALKER	1755	62004004
WORD	Writt.word.	TEMPLE	1772	43010034
WORD	Writt.word.	TEMPLE	1772	47008030
WORDS	Force words.	SOUTH	1727	23005020
WORDS	Idle words.	GALE	1726	43012036
WORDS	Idle words.	SECKER	1770	43012036
WORDS	Idle words.	SHERLOCK	1772	43012036
WORDS	Words judg.	LITTLETON	1735	43012036
WORDS	Words seas.	CHEESE	1668	44014008
WORDS	Xt's.l.words	FLAVEL	1673	45023043
WORDS	Xt's.l.words.	FLAVEL	1673	45023046
WORK	Work o. Min.	ASH	1778	52004011
WORK	Work of Spi.	FLAVEL	1673	52002001
WORK	Work. Salv.	CONANT	1698	53002012
WORK	Work. Salv.	SHERLOCK	1712	53002012
WORK	Work. Salv.	BREKELL	1765	53002012
WORK	Work.of Sp.	FLAVEL	1673	46006044
WORK	Work.out&c.o.	SHORTHOSE	1738	53002012
WORK	Work.out&c.o.	SNAPE	1745	53002012
WORK	Work& Seas.	TILLOTSON	1735	46009004
WORK	Work& Seas.	SOUTH	1744	46009004
WORKS	Fth&works.	MOORE	1716	62002022
WORKS	Fth&works.	NEWLIN	1720	62002010
WORKS	Fth&works.	WARREN	1748	62002010
WORKS	Good works.	EDWARDS	1726	52002010
WORKS	Good works.	JONES	1756	46014015
WORKS	Good works.	BALGUY	1750	49015058
WORKS	Good Works	BEVERIDGE	1720	19037027
WORKS	Good Works	SMALRIDGE	1724	61006010
WORKS	Good Works	GALE	1726	57006019
WORKS	Good Works.	PENTYCROSS	1781	45017009
WORKS	Just by works	HOOKER	1705	34001004
WORKS	Works of Fl.	MOSS	1733	51005019
WORL	G's go.worl.	LELAND	1769	19135006
WORL	Love o.worl.	CREYGHTON	1720	54003002
WORL	Worl. Busin.	WHITFIELD	1739	43008022
WORL	Worl. Gain.	BYRDALL	1666	44008036
WORL	Worl. Wisd.	ALLESTREE	1684	45016008
WORL	Worl. Wisd.	BARKER	1748	45016008
WORLD	Burn. World	JOHNSON	1740	64003011
WORLD	G.go.world.	HUNT	1748	19022028
WORLD	G.go.world.	BRACKENRIDGE	1764	19022028
WORLD	G.go.world.	LELAND	1769	19022028
WORLD	State world.	GIBBONS	1770	23021006
WORLD	V. World.	HOPKINS	1710	21001002
WORLD	V. World.	MARKLAND	1729	21001002
WORLD	V. World.	BESTON	1739	21001002
WORLD	V. World.	RICH	1750	21001002
WORLD	V. World.	CONYBEARE	1757	21001002
WORLD	V. World.	ERSKINE	1764	21001002

Keyword	In its Context	Author	Year	BkChpVrs
WORLD	World. Cares	BLACKALL	1723	43006025
WORLD	World. Div.	BOURDALOUE	1776	46016020
WORLD	World. Gr.	WEBB	1772	27004030
WORLD	World. Wis.	FIDDES	1720	43016026
WORLD	World.happ.	SHARP	1734	21002011
WORLD	World.kind.	STANHOPE	1700	45014023
WORLD	World.v. Xt.	ERSKINE	1764	23008018
WORLD	World Amb.	BAYLY	1721	46005044
WORLD	World Amb.	STRAIGHT	1741	46005044
WORLD	World-min.	HUNT	1748	65002015
WORLD	World-min.	MASON	1758	65002015
WORLD	World-min.	JORTIN	1774	65002015
WORLD	Xt. L.world.	SHERLOCK	1719	45002032
WORLDLY	Worldly Ca.	MARSHALL	1731	58004013
WORLDLY	Worldly M.	WILLIAMS	1770	45016008
WORLDS	Plur.worlds.	STURMY	1711	61011003
WORS	Angel.wors.	SCATTERGOOD	1723	54002018
WORS	Wors.& Obe.	JEFFERY	1751	46009031
WORSE	Sin.worse. S.	VEAL	1703	43009012
WORSH	Celes.worsh.	FERNE	1721	23006003
WORSH	Dev. Worsh.	BAINE	1778	19005007
WORSH	Div. Worsh.	HALL	1661	46004024
WORSH	Div. Worsh.	MUDGE	1739	19096009
WORSH	Extr. Worsh.	ATTERBURY	1734	19095006
WORSH	Fam. Worsh.	SLATER	1694	06024015
WORSH	Fam. Worsh.	YOUNG	1746	06024015
WORSH	Fam. Worsh.	WESTON	1766	06024015
WORSH	Fam. Worsh.	ORTON	1769	10006020
WORSH	Fam. Worsh.	ORTON	1769	18021015
WORSH	Fam. Worsh.	ORTON	1769	19101002
WORSH	Fam. Worsh.	ORTON	1769	20003033
WORSH	Fam. Worsh.	ORTON	1760	47010002
WORSH	Freq. Worsh.	LOVELL	1774	23002002
WORSH	Hyp.worsh.	BENNETT	1714	44007006
WORSH	Idol. Worsh.	BENNETT	1714	47017016
WORSH	Imag.worsh.	TULLIE	1686	02020004
WORSH	Imag.worsh.	WELCH	1752	02020004
WORSH	Pub. Worsh.	ATTERBURY	1699	21005001
WORSH	Pub. Worsh.	BAYLEY	1721	43018020
WORSH	Pub. Worsh.	CLAYTON	1727	21005001
WORSH	Pub. Worsh.	BENNETT	1728	01028017
WORSH	Pub. Worsh.	ROGERS	1736	19084001
WORSH	Pub. Worsh.	WOODS	1747	13016029
WORSH	Pub. Worsh.	WISHART	1753	19122006
WORSH	Pub. Worsh.	MUNTON	1756	19084001
WORSH	Pub. Worsh.	DAVIS	1756	19121001
WORSH	Pub. Worsh.	HOLLAND	1753	61010025
WORSH	Pub. Worsh.	PRICE	1757	47002046
WORSH	Pub. Worsh.	MORRIS	1757	61010025
WORSH	Pub. Worsh.	MUSCOTT	1760	21005001
WORSH	Pub. Worsh.	FOTHERGILL	1765	19089007
WORSH	Pub. Worsh.	WEBB	1765	23002003
WORSH	Pub. Worsh.	STERNE	1769	19095006
WORSH	Pub. Worsh.	KNOX	1768	61010025
WORSH	Pub. Worsh.	SMITH	1769	57002001
WORSH	Pub. Worsh.	CRAIG	1775	19107031

Keyword	In its Context	Author	Year	BkChpVrs
WORSH	Pub. Worsh.	CARR	1777	19095006
WORSH	Pub. Worsh.	WILSON	1781	49014015
WORSH	Publ. Worsh.	PETRIE	1779	61013015
WORSH	Rel. Worsh.	WHARTON	1728	57001017
WORSH	Rom. Worsh.	STEPHENS	1728	43015009
WORSH	Spir. Worsh.	CREYGHTON	1720	46004024
WORSH	Un.o.worsh.	CLAYTON	1713	48012004
WORSH	Will-worsh.	STEPHENS	1737	54002023
WORSH	Worsh. God.	PHILIPS	1717	21005001
WORSH	Worsh. God.	WAPLE	1720	21005001
WORSH	Worsh. God.	DORMAN	1743	19100002
WORSH	Worsh. God.	ABERNETHY	1751	21005001
WORSH	Worsh. God.	WILSON	1781	69005010
WORSH	Worsh.o. Xt.	LESTLEY	1720	61001006
WORSH	Worsh.of G.	CLARKE	1727	19096009
WORSH	Worsh.of G.	BURNET	1747	19096008
WORSH	Worsh.of G.	EMLYN	1742	47017025
WORSH	Worsh.of G.	LANGHORNE	1773	46004024
WORSH	Worsh.u. T.	BOYS	1716	49014009
WORSH	Worsh.u. T.	BAYES	1735	49014009
WORSH	Xn. Worsh.	CRUSO	1734	47024014
WORSH	Xn. Worsh.	BUNDY	1740	19116018
WORSHIP	Rel. Worship	BEVERIDGE	1720	46012029
WORSHIP	Soc. Worship	BULKLEY	1752	46004023
WORSHIP	Xn. Worship	WILLIAMS	1778	46004024
WORTH	Gosp.worth.	CARKEET	1719	43010011
WORTH	Sacr.worth.	OAKES	1739	49002027
WORTH	Souls worth.	SCOTT	1700	43016026
WORTH	Souls worth.	SAURIN	1777	43016026
WORTH	Worth of rel.	WHICHCOTE	1702	53003007
WORTH	Worth of Soul	BARKER	1748	44008036
WORTH	Worth. Co.	DYKE	1667	13015013
WORTH	Worth.com.	BEVERIDGE	1720	49011029
WORTH	Worth.of S.	PARTRIDGE	1720	44008036
WOSD	Wosd.of G.	CLARKE	1732	54002003
WOUN	Woun. Cons.	DAWES	1733	20018010
WOUN	Woun. Cons.	WILCOX	1757	20018014
WOUN	Woun. Cons.	ELSMERE	1767	20018014
WOUN	Woun. Cons.	PYLE	1777	20018014
WOUN	Woun. Spir.	SHERLOCK	1719	20018014
WOUN	Woun. Spir.	SOUTH	1744	20018014
WOUN	Woun. Spir.	SNAPE	1745	20018014
WOUT	Kno.wout P.	PRICE	1770	46013017
WOUT	Mn wout Xt.	BARNES	1752	53004013
WP	Image wp.	NEEDLER	1675	43004010
WP	Wp.inw.&o.	WAPLE	1720	48012001
WP	Wp.of God.	CLAGETT	1704	43004010
WP	Wp.of God.	DORRINGTON	1712	43004010
WR	Sad hand wr.	WILKINSON	1660	18013026
WR	Wr.of Lamb	WATTS	1752	69016015
WRA	D.o. G's wra.	GODDARD	1781	45019041
WRATH	Wrath of M.	MOSS	1733	62001020
WRIT	Proph. Writ.	SCOTT	1743	64001020
WRITT	Writt.word.	TEMPLE	1772	43010034
WRITT	Writt.word.	TEMPLE	1772	47008030
WRONG	Wrong Cons.	BOURDALOUE	1776	46001022

Keyword	In its Context	Author	Year	BkChpVrs
WRTH	G's wrth.dr.	HOPKINS	1710	61010030
WT	Minist.wt.	MEDE	1672	49004001
WT	Wt. Spir.&c.	EVANS	1737	45009055
X	E.dr. X. F. B.	SUTTON	1754	46006053
X	Kn.o. X.in G.	COLE	1692	46008054
X	Suffer.of X.	NEEDHAM	1679	61012002
X	2 S. X.mas.	READING	1730	23041001
X'S	A.d.t.s. X's.d	ORTON	1776	46008056
X'S	F. Sp. X's. D.	PEARSE	1763	48012011
X'S	Law in X's h.	GILL	1773	05010005
X'S	Man.&eff. X's	BLACKALL	1723	43007028
X'S	Man.&eff. X's	BLAIR	1740	43007028
X'S	Mer.f. X's E.	DEVEREL	1777	46008011
X'S	P.&c. X's. D.	LARDNER	1751	46015005
X'S	R. Sea, X's bl	WILLISON	1761	02014015
X'S	T. X's.c.fit.	FOSTER	1737	51004004
X'S	T. X's.c.fit.	CLEAVER	1743	51004004
X'S	View X's. D.	BOURN	1777	43007024
X'S	X's fam.titles	DYER	1666	23005016
X'S	X's. Ch.&c.	WHITTY	1772	52003014
X'S	X's. Sov. Ch.	SAURIN	1777	48014007
X'S	X's.d.b.cup.	BRINSLEY	1660	46018011
X'S	X's.l.believ.	FARMER	1756	23040011
X'S	X's Good w.	HILL	1755	05033016
XCELL	Xcell. Xn. M.	GARDINER	1720	43005017
XCELL	Xcell. Xn. M	WESTLEY	1748	43005017
XENCY	Xency of Ch.	ELSMERE	1767	45014014
XMAS	Trin- Xmas.	G.	1730	57003016
XN	Ab. Xn. Lib.	LUCE	1672	63002016
XN	Agr.alm. Xn.	BREKELL	1765	47026028
XN	Almost. Xn.	WHITFIELD	1739	47026028
XN	Almost Xn.	MEAD	1666	47026028
XN	Almost Xn.	HOPKINS	1710	47026028
XN	Almost Xn.	WESTLEY	1746	47026028
XN	Anc. Xn R.	REGIS	1753	01003015
XN	Ar.f. Xn. Rel.	KNOX	1768	63003015
XN	Decr. Xn. F.	GREENHILL	1756	45018008
XN	Diff. Xn.life.	CROFTON	1662	43007014
XN	Diff. Xn.life.	BARKER	1697	43007014
XN	Diff. Xn.life.	PARSONS	1711	43007013
XN	Diff. Xn.life.	GARDINER	1720	43007013
XN	Diff. Xn.life.	STEPHENS	1737	43007014
XN	Diff. Xn.life.	BUNDY	1740	43007014
XN	Diff. Xn.life.	WESTLEY	1750	43007013
XN	E.f. Xn.w. T.	HORNE	1671	68000020
XN	Eas. Xn. Dut.	STILEMAN	1733	43011030
XN	Elect. Xn.	STANHOPE	1705	43022014
XN	Ev.o. Xn.rel.	TATHAM	1780	61002003
XN	Ex. Xn. Prin.	CHANDLER	1769	46015005
XN	Exc. Xn. Rel.	TILLOTSON	1735	46003019
XN	Excel. Xn. R.	WHICHCOTE	1698	48001016
XN	Exer.of Xn.	WHICHCOTE	1702	53003012
XN	Fai.p. Xn. L.	BOYSE	1728	51002020
XN	Faithf. Xn.	ADEY	1755	69002010
XN	Fut.rew. Xn.	WILLIAMS	1774	69014025
XN	G.l.b.or. Xn.	WILKINS	1682	59002010

Keyword	In its Context	Author	Year	BkChpVrs
XN	G.l.b.or. Xn.	ROGERS	1735	59002010
XN	Hap. D.t. Xn.	LANGHORNE	1773	69014013
XN	Hid.li.o. Xn.	WATTS	1753	54003003
XN	Hid.li.o. Xn.	ERSKINE	1764	54003003
XN	Hon. Xn. Pr.	BRETT	1712	61005004
XN	Hope of Xn.	FARRINGTON	1741	65003003
XN	Imp. Xn. Na.	CROWE	1744	58002019
XN	Imp. Xn. R.	HOLDEN	1755	46007016
XN	Jew.& Xn. P.	WESTON	1747	43023001
XN	Joy of g. Xn.	BATTY	1739	53004004
XN	Know. Xn. P.	WAPLE	1718	46013015
XN	Know. Xn. P.	TILLOTSON	1735	46013015
XN	L. G.f.a. Xn.	ANONYMOUS	1770	47026023
XN	L. Xt. P. Xn.	RELLEY	1762	46014019
XN	Lo. Test. Xn.	SOUTHCOMBE	1752	46013034
XN	M. Or. Xn. R.	BOURN	1777	46006066
XN	Nat. R.& Xn.	MARSHALL	1750	64001008
XN	Peaceab. Xn.	ANONYMOUS	1678	48012018
XN	Per.of Xn. K.	SAURIN	1775	61005012
XN	Pr. Xn.k.a.p.	JONES	1761	50005014
XN	Prim. Xn.	GOULDE	1682	18036021
XN	Saf.of Xn.	CENNICK	1762	26009006
XN	Sanct. Xn. L.	SKELTON	1754	43025046
XN	Scope. Xn. R.	MONRO	1693	43005020
XN	Seas. Xn. Ex.	NICOLSON	1661	61003013
XN	Ste.in Xn. F.	STEVENS	1771	49016013
XN	Sup. Xn. Rel.	OGDEN	1777	58002019
XN	The Xn.	WHATLEY	1746	47026028
XN	Tr. Xn.& W.	ORTON	1773	46017016
XN	Tr. Xn. Bapt.	RELLY	1762	52004005
XN	Tr. Xn. Fai.	CLARKE	1727	65005004
XN	Tr. Xn. Zeal.	CLARKE	1734	69003015
XN	Tr. Xn.b. Xr.	GODDARD	1781	47026029
XN	Truth. Xn.r.	JORTIN	1730	45002032
XN	Truth Xn. R.	JORTIN	1730	46010025
XN	Truth Xn. R.	JORTIN	1730	46015024
XN	Un. C. Xn. C.	HOLBROOK	1727	55004007
XN	Un.of Xn. F.	SMITH	1682	52004005
XN	Xcell. Xn. M.	GARDINER	1720	43005017
XN	Xcell. Xn. M.	WESTLEY	1748	43005017
XN	Xn. Abstin.	BRADY	1713	49009025
XN	Xn. Altar&c.	BRETT	1713	61013010
XN	Xn. Assert.	ECCLES	1755	43010034
XN	Xn. Baptism.	WATTS	1753	43028019
XN	Xn. Baptism.	FLEMING	1771	63003015
XN	Xn. Belief.	CLELAND	1660	48010011
XN	Xn. Benefic.	FIDDES	1720	61013016
XN	Xn. Benefic.	HUTCHINS	1782	20003009
XN	Xn. Benevol.	MOSS	1737	48012009
XN	Xn. Benevol.	STRAIGHT	1741	48012009
XN	Xn. Benevol.	HEYLYN	1749	48012009
XN	Xn. Benevol.	COCKMAN	1750	61013016
XN	Xn. Call.& E.	BERRIMAN	1751	64001010
XN	Xn. Caution.	SCATTERGOOD	1723	49010012
XN	Xn. Charity.	LLOYD	1705	61012014
XN	Xn. Charity.	COTES	1721	46013034
XN	Xn. Charity.	IBBOT	1726	49013013
XN	Xn. Charity.	WESTON	1747	57001005
XN	Xn. Charity.	COCKMAN	1750	57001005
XN	Xn. Charity.	HOLDEN	1757	49016014
XN	Xn. Charity.	MILNE	1780	54003014
XN	Xn. Church.	KEDDINGTON	1757	61013008
XN	Xn. Circums.	ALTHAM	1732	52005015
XN	Xn. Circums.	OGILVIE	1766	52005015
XN	Xn. Circums.	ORR	1772	52005015
XN	Xn. Co.&lo.	SMITH	1673	62004007
XN	Xn. Con.&c.	WALLIN	1764	49009027
XN	Xn. Confid.	LEIGHTON	1746	19042008
XN	Xn. Conq.	MOSS	1738	48012021
XN	Xn. Convers.	CHAMBRE	1711	53001027
XN	Xn. Convers.	KELSEY	1721	53001027
XN	Xn. Convers.	DAWES	1733	53001027
XN	Xn. Convers.	HOLLAND	1753	52004001
XN	Xn. Convers.	BRACKENRIDGE	1764	53001027
XN	Xn. Convers.	ELSMERE	1767	53001027
XN	Xn. Courage.	LLOYD	1765	20028001
XN	Xn. Course.	OLDISWORTH	1666	49009024
XN	Xn. Course.	LUCAS	1710	49009024
XN	Xn. Course.	EVANS	1725	45014028
XN	Xn. Course.	WALKER	1765	49009024
XN	Xn. Course.	WEBB	1765	49009024
XN	Xn. Course.	NEWTON	1767	49009024
XN	Xn. Coven.	WHISTON	1709	61008006
XN	Xn. Crown.	HAYWARD	1758	58004008
XN	Xn. D.& Ho.	WEBB	1772	54001009
XN	Xn. Diligen.	GROVE	1741	46009004
XN	Xn. Diligen.	WATTS	1753	20013004
XN	Xn. Dispens.	FIDDES	1720	57001015
XN	Xn. Dispens.	WATTS	1753	61008006
XN	Xn. Educat.	HARRIS	1715	20022006
XN	Xn. Educat.	BUNDY	1740	52006004
XN	Xn. Educat.	ANONYMOUS	1742	52006004
XN	Xn. Equity.	TALBOT	1706	43007012
XN	Xn. Equity.	EVANS	1737	43007012
XN	Xn. Equity.	WATTS	1753	43007012
XN	Xn. Ev.o.f.st.	BOURN	1760	49015012
XN	Xn. Faith	TILLOTSON	1735	46020031
XN	Xn. Faith.	ROGERS	1736	48010010
XN	Xn. Faith.	EVANS	1737	50005007
XN	Xn. Faith.	BUNDY	1740	50005007
XN	Xn. Faith.	ALLEN	1751	65005004
XN	Xn. Faith.	BADDELLEY	1752	47016030
XN	Xn. Faith.	SECKER	1770	48010010
XN	Xn. Faith.	ATKINSON	1775	49013013
XN	Xn. Fasting.	BROME	1711	43006016
XN	Xn. Fasting.	CLAGETT	1720	43006016
XN	Xn. Fellows.	WATTS	1753	48015006
XN	Xn. Forbear.	COCK	1710	52004002
XN	Xn. Forgiven.	TILLY	1737	45006037
XN	Xn. Fortit.	EVANS	1737	64001005
XN	Xn. Fortitu.	ABERNETHY	1748	64001005
XN	Xn. Fortitu.	KENNICOTT	1757	48008035

Keyword	In its Context	Author	Year	BkChpVrs
XN	Xn. Fortitu.	BADDELLEY	1766	27003016
XN	Xn. Happin.	VENN	1759	50013014
XN	Xn. Hear.	ELLIS	1694	49003007
XN	Xn. Holiness	HAMMOND	1745	44005036
XN	Xn. Holiness	HAMMOND	1745	46001029
XN	Xn. Holiness	HAMMOND	1745	61013014
XN	Xn. Hope p.	OUTRAM	1697	65003003
XN	Xn. Hope.	NICOLSON	1661	53003020
XN	Xn. Hope.	MOSS	1737	48015013
XN	Xn. Hope.	TILLY	1737	61006019
XN	Xn. Hope.	SKEELER	1740	65003003
XN	Xn. Hope.	HOWE	1744	48005005
XN	Xn. Hu.	KING	1705	53002003
XN	Xn. Hum.&c	EVANS	1737	54003012
XN	Xn. Humil.	COCKMAN	1750	63005005
XN	Xn. Indeed.	POWELL	1730	47011026
XN	Xn. Joy.	BURROUGHS	1733	55005016
XN	Xn. Joy.	COCKMAN	1750	53004004
XN	Xn. Joy.	FARQUAR	1772	55005016
XN	Xn. K.m. St.	FOTHERGILL	1765	53004001
XN	Xn. Knowl.	REYNOLDS	1679	53003008
XN	Xn. Knowl.	TILLOTSON	1735	53003008
XN	Xn. Knowl.	SMITH	1740	45018040
XN	Xn. Knowl.	JORTIN	1774	20015014
XN	Xn. Lib.& L.	RICHARDSON	1752	51005013
XN	Xn. Lib.stat.	ROE	1662	47015029
XN	Xn. Liberal.	PAYNE	1763	43025040
XN	Xn. Liberty.	HALL	1660	51005001
XN	Xn. Liberty.	BUTLER	1679	51005001
XN	Xn. Liberty.	OUTRAM	1697	51005013
XN	Xn. Liberty.	ANONYMOUS	1734	43006022
XN	Xn. Liberty.	ANONYMOUS	1734	45011052
XN	Xn. Liberty.	STEPHENS	1737	49006012
XN	Xn. Liberty.	BUNDY	1740	51005001
XN	Xn. Liberty.	FISHER	1741	64002019
XN	Xn. Liberty.	HAMMOND	1745	51003024
XN	Xn. Liberty.	ABERNETHY	1751	51005001
XN	Xn. Liberty.	BERRIMAN	1751	51005013
XN	Xn. Liberty.	DAVIES	1754	51005001
XN	Xn. Life o. F.	TILLOTSON	1735	50005007
XN	Xn. Life.	TILLOTSON	1735	45013024
XN	Xn. Light W.	HOLDEN	1755	43005014
XN	Xn. Light W.	ORR	1772	43005014
XN	Xn. Love.	GOULD	1676	49013005
XN	Xn. Love.	MORE	1692	63001022
XN	Xn. Love.	WHICHCOTE	1698	52004031
XN	Xn. Love.	NOURSE	1708	49014001
XN	Xn. Love.	KENNET	1715	67000002
XN	Xn. Love.	BAYLY	1721	65003024
XN	Xn. Love.	WHITTY	1772	46013034
XN	Xn. Loy rev.	SPRINT	1694	63002017
XN	Xn. M.& Re.	ROBINSON	1734	63001024
XN	Xn. Meekn.	WHICHCOTE	1698	63003005
XN	Xn. Minist.	MOSS	1738	50004005
XN	Xn. Ministry	STILLINGFLEET	1760	49004001
XN	Xn. Ministry.	SUTTON	1718	49004001

Keyword	In its Context	Author	Year	BkChpVrs
XN	Xn. Moder.	AUDLEY	1705	48012018
XN	Xn. Moral.	FOSTER	1737	53004008
XN	Xn. Moral.	GOUGH	1751	53004008
XN	Xn. Morality	WATTS	1753	53004008
XN	Xn. Motives.	WHICHCOTE	1698	53004008
XN	Xn. Myster.	TERRY	1746	43013011
XN	Xn. Name.	GROSVENOR	1728	47011026
XN	Xn. Name.	LITTLETON	1735	49001001
XN	Xn. Name.	NEWTON	1760	47011026
XN	Xn. Name.	BREKELL	1765	62002007
XN	Xn. Name.	DAVIES	1766	47011026
XN	Xn. Ob.& L.	WILTON	1724	48013001
XN	Xn. Obed.	COCKBURN	1697	45006046
XN	Xn. Obed.	STILLINGFLEET	1707	45006046
XN	Xn. Omnip.	HALES	1673	53004013
XN	Xn. Omnip.	HAMMOND	1684	53004013
XN	Xn. Omnip.	BEVERIDGE	1720	53004013
XN	Xn. Oratory.	DAVIS	1756	47024025
XN	Xn. Oratory.	PECKARD	1770	49001021
XN	Xn. Passover.	RIDLEY	1736	49005007
XN	Xn. Patien.	LORTIE	1720	62001002
XN	Xn. Patience	ANONYMOUS	1708	57001012
XN	Xn. Patience	EVANS	1737	61010036
XN	Xn. Patriot.	MILNE	1780	45019041
XN	Xn. Perfect.	PARKER	1697	43005048
XN	Xn. Perfect.	BLACKALL	1723	43005048
XN	Xn. Perfect.	BLAIR	1740	43005048
XN	Xn. Perfect.	JOHNSON	1740	50013011
XN	Xn. Perfect.	SIMONS	1743	61006001
XN	Xn. Perfect.	WESTLEY	1750	53003012
XN	Xn. Perfect.	BRACKENRIDGE	1764	43005048
XN	Xn. Persever.	BRADY	1713	64003017
XN	Xn. Philosp.	DELANY	1766	54002008
XN	Xn. Piety.	FROYSELL	1678	58003012
XN	Xn. Practice.	WHICHCOTE	1702	53003015
XN	Xn. Priesth.	OCKLEY	1710	38002007
XN	Xn. Priesth.	ANONYMOUS	1718	46020021
XN	Xn. Prin.sta.	SNAPE	1745	54002006
XN	Xn. Prize.	BEVERIDGE	1720	53003014
XN	Xn. Professi.	MACE	1751	47026028
XN	Xn. Prud.	TAYLOR	1668	43009016
XN	Xn. Prud.	TAYLOR	1678	43010016
XN	Xn. Prud.	BRIGHT	1699	43007001
XN	Xn. Prud.	NOURSE	1705	43009015
XN	Xn. Prud.	EVANS	1737	43010016
XN	Xn. Purity.	HAMMOND	1684	50007001
XN	Xn. R.dem.	HUTCHINSON	1720	46015024
XN	Xn. Race.	NEEDHAM	1679	61012001
XN	Xn. Race.	SYLVESTER	1702	61012001
XN	Xn. Race.	LUCAS	1710	61012001
XN	Xn. Race.	JOHNSON	1713	61012001
XN	Xn. Race.	BEVERIDGE	1720	49009024
XN	Xn. Race.	DUNLOP	1722	61012001
XN	Xn. Race.	CARTER	1729	49009024
XN	Xn. Race.	HOADLY	1754	49009024
XN	Xn. Race.	BADDELLEY	1766	61012001

INDEXES TO THIRD VOLUME: E: KEYWORD-IN-CONTEXT INDEX OF OTHER SUBJECTS OR OCCASIONS

Keyword	In its Context	Author	Year	BkChpVrs
XN	Xn. Reconc.	WALL	1660	48005011
XN	Xn. Redem.	LANGHORNE	1773	59002014
XN	Xn. Rel.exc.	MOORE	1716	48015013
XN	Xn. Rel.vin.	SKEELER	1740	43011029
XN	Xn. Relig.	DAVIES	1766	45016027
XN	Xn. Relig.	HARWOOD	1776	51005022
XN	Xn. Religion	CLIFFORD	1694	49011027
XN	Xn. Religion	HEAD	1714	50005018
XN	Xn. Religion	SYNGE	1720	23011006
XN	Xn. Religion	BOURN	1760	48014007
XN	Xn. Religion	SHARPE	1765	54001023
XN	Xn. Religion	BOURDALOUE	1776	43012038
XN	Xn. Religion	BOURN	1777	23009006
XN	Xn. Religion.	OGILVIE	1766	52006010
XN	Xn. Reproof.	COCKMAN	1750	52005011
XN	Xn. Reproof.	TRAPP	1752	51006001
XN	Xn. Resolut.	WILDER	1741	19101004
XN	Xn. Rest.	WALKER	1764	43011028
XN	Xn. Rest.	BADDELLY	1766	43011028
XN	Xn. Revelat.	ROBINSON	1733	46018037
XN	Xn. Revelat.	LANGHORNE	1773	51004004
XN	Xn. Rule F.	MICHELL	1737	46005039
XN	Xn. Sabbath.	BUNDY	1740	44002027
XN	Xn. Sabbath.	PARRY	1753	44002027
XN	Xn. Sabbath.	FLEMING	1777	44002027
XN	Xn. Sacrif.	MEDE	1672	38001011
XN	Xn. Sacrifice.	YOUNG	1706	48012001
XN	Xn. Sacrifice.	FIDDES	1720	48012001
XN	Xn. Sacrifice.	HEYLYN	1749	48012001
XN	Xn. Salvat.	LANGHORNE	1773	61002003
XN	Xn. Sanct.	BRAILSFORD	1776	05030015
XN	Xn. Sch.con.	BOURN	1760	47010042
XN	Xn. Simp.	BRAGGE	1713	50001012
XN	Xn. Sincer.	CLAGETT	1720	53001010
XN	Xn. Sincer.	FIDDES	1720	53001010
XN	Xn. Sincer.	MILLER	1749	53001010
XN	Xn. Soldier.	KETTLEWELL	1719	43001021
XN	Xn. Soldier.	BROUGHTON	1737	47010001
XN	Xn. Soldier.	BADDELLEY	1752	52006011
XN	Xn. Spirit.	EVANS	1737	52004023
XN	Xn. Spirit.	PYLE	1777	62003017
XN	Xn. Suff.&c.	ANONYMOUS	1733	63004012
XN	Xn. Supp. D.	COMBER	1691	19023004
XN	Xn. Sympa.	CONEY	1730	48012015
XN	Xn. Temper.	EVANS	1737	64001004
XN	Xn. Trium.	MOSS	1732	49015055
XN	Xn. Trium.	MOIR	1759	49005025
XN	Xn. Unanim.	WHICHCOTE	1703	53003015
XN	Xn. Unanim.	DODDERIDGE	1761	53002001
XN	Xn. Unity.	WARREN	1692	52004003
XN	Xn. Unity.	THORNBY	1742	46017001
XN	Xn. Unity.	BERRIMAN	1763	52004003
XN	Xn. Use o. W.	BISSE	1717	49007031
XN	Xn. Virtue.	DELANY	1754	43011030
XN	Xn. Watchf.	CARTER	1729	44013037
XN	Xn. Worsh.	CRUSO	1734	47024014
XN	Xn. Worsh.	BUNDY	1740	19116018
XN	Xn. Worship	WILLIAMS	1778	46004024
XN	Xn. Z.b. L.j.	SYNGE	1716	51004018
XN	Xn. Zeal.	CRUSO	1699	51004006
XN	Xn. Zeal.	SHERLOCK	1727	68000003
XN	Xn. Zeal.	EVANS	1737	69003019
XN	Xn. Zeal.	SCOTT	1739	68000003
XN	Xn. Zeal.	CARMICHAEL	1757	51004018
XN	Xn. Zeal.	BILSTONE	1761	51004017
XN	Xn. Zeal.	WEBB	1765	51004018
XN	Xn. Zeal.	ORTON	1773	53002021
XN	Xn.a. Jew. L.	WESTON	1747	43005020
XN	Xn.ab. Mos.	MICHELL	1737	61008006
XN	Xn.comp. A.	GURNALL	1662	52006017
XN	Xn.lig.cand.	HORNECK	1706	43005015
XN	Xn.lig.cand.	BLAIR	1740	43005015
XN	Xn.n.ash. G.	ENFIELD	1772	48002016
XN	Xn.not asha.	MOIR	1759	63004016
XN	Xn.pos.a.th.	IBBBOT	1726	50006010
XN	Xn.r.pr.sp p.	RANDOLPH	1777	47005038
XN	Xn.rejoicing	HERVEY	1770	53004004
XN	Xn.st.suffer.	ATTERBURY	1734	63002021
XN	Xn Charity.	ROLLS	1672	49001010
XN	Xn Mariner.	RUSSEN	1771	19046004
XN	Xn Religion.	HUNT	1748	46008012
XN	Xt.& Xn.rel.	WILCOX	1757	22002016
XN'S	Nec. Xn's w.	BOSTON	1773	21009010
XN'S	Rea.f. Xn's.r.	GALE	1726	55005016
XN'S	Rea.f. Xn's.r.	MORRIS	1743	55005016
XN'S	Rew.o Xn's.	ADEY	1760	58004007
XN'S	Th. Du. Xn's	GROVE	1741	55005018
XN'S	Th. Du. Xn's.	COOPER	1677	55005018
XN'S	Th. Du. Xn's.	DORRINGTON	1703	55005018
XN'S	Th. Du. Xn's.	BEVERIDGE	1720	55005018
XN'S	Xn's. Arm.	WILSON	1781	52006010
XN'S	Xn's. Conq.	TAYLOR	1678	48007019
XN'S	Xn's. D.easy.	SMITH	1740	51004031
XN'S	Xn's. G's. T.	BREKELL	1765	50006016
XN'S	Xn's. Gl.& J.	BUNDY	1740	55002020
XN'S	Xn's. Hope.	WALKER	1765	48008032
XN'S	Xn's. Joy i. S	BOURN	1777	63001008
XN'S	Xn's. Joy.	BRADBURY	1713	46020024
XN'S	Xn's. Joy&c.	BRADBURY	1772	47020024
XN'S	Xn's. Love.	WORTHINGTON	1725	52005002
XN'S	Xn's. Pattern	SUTTON	1754	43011029
XN'S	Xn's. Post.	PEMBERTON	1727	55004011
XN'S	Xn's. Prize.	DUNLOP	1722	53003013
XN'S	Xn's. Prize.	MASON	1758	53003013
XN'S	Xn's. Rew.	HUNT	1748	58002011
XN'S	Xn's. Secur.	NEWMAN	1760	46014019
XN'S	Xn's. Streng.	JENKINS	1775	50012010
XN'S	Xn's. Suhp.	HUNT	1748	46014001
XN'S	Xn's. Treas.	WATTS	1753	49003021
XN'S	Xn's. Trium.	SACHEVERELL	1713	45023034
XN'S	Xn's. Vict.	BAINE	1778	65005004
XN'S	Xn's. Warf.	HAYWARD	1758	58004007

Keyword	In its Context	Author	Year	BkChpVrs
XN'S	Xn's. Xrter.	BOURDALOUE	1776	43022041
XN'S	Xn's.des.t.d.	EDWARDS	1726	53001025
XN'S	Xn's.dut.pr.	FIDDES	1720	65005003
XN'S	Xn's.growth	GOODWIN	16--	46015002
XN'S	Xn's.ob.t. H.	TILLOTSON	1735	58002019
XN'S	Xn's.sh.act.f.	CONANT	1699	67000005
XN'S	Xn's.sp.arm.	ANONYMOUS	1685	52006011
XN'S	Xn's& H. H.	BARNES	1752	20010028
XN'S	Xn's C.to L.	BULKLEY	1771	51005013
XN'S	Xn's Duty.	WALLIN	1756	19046008
XN'S	Xn's Duty.	BAINES	1778	47011023
XN'S	Xn's Guide.	FULWOOD	1673	54001010
XN'S	Xn's Love.	WHITTY	1772	22008006
XN'S	Xn's Refuge.	DELAUNE	1728	46016023
XN'S	Xn's Streng.	BENNETT	1728	49011010
XN'S	Xn's Xter.	VENN	1759	19121001
XN'S	Xt. Xn's.life.	JACKSON	1756	53001021
XNA	Metam. Xna.	BEARE	1679	51006015
XNITY	Arg.f. Xnity.	POWELL	1776	46005037
XNITY	Conif. Xnity	MOSS	1737	43011028
XNITY	Def.of Xnity	SCOTT	1743	46014001
XNITY	Excel. Xnity	WILDER	1741	49001018
XNITY	Oblig. Xnity	ELSMERE	1767	23005004
XNITY	Power Xnity	COOPER	1777	43005043
XNITY	Reecj. Xnity.	ROGERS	1727	46003019
XNITY	True Xnity.	WILLIAMS	1770	46018038
XNITY	Xnity per. L.	HICKES	1726	43005017
XNITY	Xnity vind.	BALGUY	1750	45007035
XNITY	Xnity.	ADEY	1755	55005021
XNITY	Xnity.	SAURIN	1775	65004004
XNITY	Xnity.justif.	BULLOCK	1726	45024025
XNITY	Xnity.justif.	BULLOCK	1726	47003025
XNITY	Xnity R.o. L.	ROBINSON	1739	46006068
XNS	Adv.of Xns.	HODGE	1758	43005047
XNS	Doubt. Xns.	FARMER	1756	43014031
XNS	Nomin. Xns.	WILCOX	1757	69003001
XNS	Se.sorts Xns.	WAPLE	1720	65002012
XNS	St.of Xns.	WAPLE	1720	52002021
XNS	Tr. Xns.few.	CONEY	1730	69003004
XNS	W. Xns.n. Ar.a	CLARKE	1736	51002017
XNS	W. Xns.n. Ar.a	GROVE	1741	51002017
XNS	Wicked. Xns	ATTERBURY	1734	57006001
XNS	Xns fors.all.	SUTTON	1754	45014033
XNS	Xns. H.& Sa.	WEBB	1765	63003005
XNS	Xns. Salt.	BLACKALL	1723	43005013
XNS	Xns. Salt. E.	HORNECK	1706	43005013
XNS	Xns. Salt. E.	ORR	1772	43005013
XNS	Xns. Sons G.	WILCOX	1757	65003001
XNS	Xns.conspic.	BLAIR	1740	43005014
XNS	Xns.excel.	PRICE	1661	43005047
XNS	Xns.wa.to H.	ANONYMOUS	1726	47016030
XNS	Xt. Pat.t. Xns	BEVERIDGE	1720	63001015
XNS	Xt.u.w. Xns.	CLAGETT	1720	46015001
XNS	Xt's.c.t. Xns.	MARTIN	1779	43005029
XNS'	Joy D. Xns'.	BEVERIDGE	1720	53004004
XNTY	Bel.of Xnty.	HAWKINS	1756	45012057

Keyword	In its Context	Author	Year	BkChpVrs
XNTY	Xnty not obj.	ENFIELD	1772	46006060
XNTY	Xnty.n.incr.	SKELTON	1754	46017015
XR	Ad.& Ev. Xr.	MURRAY	1777	01002015
XR	Balaam's Xr.	JORTIN	1755	04022012
XR	David's p. Xr	HARRIS	1755	45024044
XR	David's Xr.	PORTEUS	1761	09013013
XR	David's Xr.	CLEAVER	1762	09013013
XR	David's Xr.	ENFIELD	1777	10007008
XR	H. W. Xr. Xs.	POWELL	1776	43005011
XR	Joh. Xr.& W.	DUCHAL	1753	46021024
XR	Mess. Xr.&c.	WARBURTON	1753	49001030
XR	Shimei's Xr.	STERNE	1760	10019021
XR	St. Paul's Xr.	DUCHAL	1753	47020024
XR	St. Peter's Xr	STERNE	1769	47003012
XR	Timoth. Xr.	OAKES	1747	58003015
XR	Timoth. Xr.	LOVEDER	1756	58003015
XR	Tr. Xn.b. Xr.	GODDARD	1781	47026029
XR	Xr. L. Days.	FELL	1675	64003003
XR	Xr. Xt's. Dis.	MAY	1757	47004013
XR	Xr.good M.	HUNTER	1774	45023050
XR	Xr.of Abram	ENFIELD	1777	62002023
XR	Xr.of Friend	LOCKIER	1761	20017017
XRTER	Abr's Xrter.	MURRAY	1777	01025019
XRTER	Barna. Xrter.	BARTLETT	1716	47011024
XRTER	Cath. Xrter.	GLANVILL	1681	63001022
XRTER	Cent. Xrter.	WILKINS	1682	45007005
XRTER	Dav. Xrter.	PEMBERTON	1727	47013036
XRTER	G. M's Xrter.	WILCOX	1757	19084011
XRTER	G. Xrter.b. F.	WORTHINGTON	1775	20022001
XRTER	Haz. Xrter.	BLAIR	1780	12008012
XRTER	Hd's. Xrter.	CRAIG	1775	44006020
XRTER	Jacob's Xrter	ENFIELD	1777	01025027
XRTER	Jacob's Xrter.	MURRAY	1777	01028001
XRTER	Job's Xrter.	ENFIELD	1777	18001001
XRTER	Jon. Xrter.	CRAIG	1775	31004004
XRTER	Jos. Xrter.	ENFIELD	1777	01045004
XRTER	Jos. Xrter.	MURRAY	1777	01037003
XRTER	Josep. Xrter.	ENFIELD	1777	01037034
XRTER	Josi. Xrter.	CLARIDGE	1692	12023025
XRTER	Josi. Xrter.	MAY	1744	14034003
XRTER	Judas Xrter.	CRAIG	1775	43026014
XRTER	Min. Xrter.	CRAIG	1775	43005013
XRTER	P. Pil. Xrter.	CRAIG	1775	45023023
XRTER	Paul's Xrter.	WEST	1762	49009019
XRTER	Paul's Xrter.	ENFIELD	1777	49011001
XRTER	Peter's Xrter.	ENFIELD	1777	43026035
XRTER	Pilate. Xrter.	WEST	1762	43027024
XRTER	Prod. Xrter.	NEWTON	1782	45015011
XRTER	Xn's. Xrter.	BOURDALOUE	1776	43022041
XRTER	Xrter of Diss.	WRIGHT	1712	47028022
XRTER	Xrter true C.	D'ASTOR	1700	04024005
XRTER	Xrter unreg.	DODDERIDGE	1742	52002001
XRTER	Xrter. Gosp.	ROBINSON	1738	43020026
XRTER	Xrter.of Xt.	MUTTER	1776	46001014
XRTER	Xt's. Xrter.	HIBBERT	1662	49011003
XRTER	Xt's. Xrter.	SEAGRAVE	1737	43022043

INDEXES TO THIRD VOLUME: E: KEYWORD-IN-CONTEXT INDEX OF OTHER SUBJECTS OR OCCASIONS

Keyword	In its Context	Author	Year	BkChpVrs
XRTER	Xt's. Xrter.	ENFIELD	1777	43011029
XRTER	Xt's. Xrter.	ENFIELD	1777	46013015
XRTICKS	Xrticks tr. R.	QUINCY	1750	62003017
XS	Du. Xs.& M.	WILSON	1781	46017004
XS	H. W. Xr. Xs.	POWELL	1776	43005011
XS	M.& Xs.c. S.	SLADEN	1733	45014034
XT	A.d. A.a. Xt.	DOUGHTY	1761	49015022
XT	Abid.in Xt.	PEARSON	1718	65002028
XT	Abid.in Xt.	BEVERIDGE	1720	46015007
XT	Ad's L.b. Xt.	MASON	1758	48005015
XT	Agony of Xt.	BROWNE	1749	43026038
XT	Ang.wo. Xt.	BRETT	1720	61001006
XT	Asha.of Xt.	WEST	1762	44008038
XT	Asha.of Xt.	SHERLOCK	1772	44008038
XT	B. Un.w. Xt.	FLAVEL	1673	46017023
XT	Bel. U.w. Xt.	LYE	1676	49006017
XT	Belief in Xt.	OUTRAM	1697	46014001
XT	Belief in Xt.	CRAIG	1775	46006019
XT	Believ. J. Xt.	ABERNETHY	1751	65003023
XT	Benef.of Xt.	STAFFORD	1699	61002015
XT	Birth of Xt.	COLMAN	1728	19022009
XT	Birth of Xt.	SAURIN	1775	23010006
XT	Birth of Xt.	BOURDALOUE	1776	45002010
XT	Cath. Ch. Xt.	CLARKE	1734	61012022
XT	Ch.del.by Xt	ERSKINE	1764	21009014
XT	Ch.of Xt.	MARCH	1689	69002005
XT	Ch.of Xt.	HILLIARD	1717	43006010
XT	Circu.of Xt.	WARREN	1748	61002016
XT	Citship.o. Xt.	WHICHCOTE	1702	53003020
XT	Com.of Xt.	MANTON	1679	56002001
XT	Com.of Xt.	LEIGHTON	1746	23060001
XT	Com.to Xt.	HORTON	1679	46006037
XT	Com.to Xt.	CLARKSON	1696	46005040
XT	Com.to Xt.	BEVERIDGE	1720	46005040
XT	Com.to Xt.	COOKE	1739	46005040
XT	Com.to Xt.	HUNT	1748	46005040
XT	Com.to Xt.	NEWTON	1767	43011028
XT	Com.to Xt.	BARCLAY	1763	61007025
XT	Comp.i. Xt.	WHITAKER	1667	54003011
XT	Comp.of Xt.	BLAIR	1780	61004015
XT	Consp.ag. Xt	SHERIDAN	1720	44012014
XT	Cross of Xt.	BEVERIDGE	1720	51006014
XT	Cross of Xt.	MOIR	1759	51004014
XT	Crucif. Xt.	WILKINSON	1660	51005024
XT	Death of Xt.	BARROW	1716	49015003
XT	Death of Xt.	SOMERVILLE	1779	43027054
XT	Death of Xt.	LANGHORNE	1773	46019030
XT	Death of Xt.	BLAIR	1777	46017001
XT	Death of Xt.	SAURIN	1777	50005014
XT	Deity of Xt.	RUSSEL	1719	59002013
XT	Del.thro' Xt.	CLARKE	1735	48007024
XT	Des.see. Xt.	WILCOX	1757	46012020
XT	Di.&inc. Xt.	WISE	1717	51004004
XT	Dig.& H. Xt.	CLARKE	1727	65004009
XT	Divin.of Xt.	WHITAKER	1674	59002010
XT	Divin.of Xt.	SKELTON	1692	46014009
XT	Divin.of Xt.	PAYNE	1697	46010036
XT	Divin.of Xt.	LA MOTHE	1693	53002006
XT	Divin.of Xt.	JEFFERY	1726	46001001
XT	Divin.of Xt.	HURRION	1734	49003016
XT	Divin.of Xt.	SCOTT	1743	23043010
XT	Divin.of Xt.	RANDOLPH	1753	44013023
XT	Divin.of Xt.	REGIS	1753	46001001
XT	Divin.of Xt.	HAYWARD	1758	48009005
XT	Divin.of Xt.	WHITTY	1766	69022002
XT	Ete. Pr.o. Xt.	KELSEY	1691	61006020
XT	Ete. Pr.o. Xt.	STILLINGFLEET	1707	61006020
XT	Ev. K.of Xt.	BOURN	1777	49015021
XT	Exam.of Xt.	MOSS	1732	49011001
XT	Exam.of Xt.	MILLER	1749	43011029
XT	Excell.in Xt.	FLAVEL	1673	49002008
XT	Exem.life Xt	BAYLY	1721	46013015
XT	Faith in Xt.	BEVERIDGE	1720	46001012
XT	Faith in Xt.	SCATTERGOOD	1723	43009021
XT	Faith in Xt.	EVANS	1737	63001008
XT	Faith in Xt.	JOHNSON	1740	47010043
XT	Faith in Xt.	WALKER	1755	46006037
XT	Faith in Xt.	WILLIAMS	1770	46003036
XT	Faith in Xt.	SHERLOCK	1772	46006067
XT	Forg.t. Xt.a.	WHICHCOTE	1698	47013038
XT	Forg.t. Xt.a.	HOOLE	1748	47013038
XT	Forg.t. Xt.al.	SHERLOCK	1719	47013038
XT	Form. Xt.	HORTON	1679	51004019
XT	G.in Xt. Sav.	WATTS	1753	23045022
XT	G's. L.in Xt.	WILKINSON	1660	48005008
XT	G's. L.in Xt.	LELAND	1769	48005011
XT	G's. L.in Xt.	WALKER	1775	48005010
XT	Gl.in C.o. Xt.	MACLAURIN	1772	51006014
XT	Glory in Xt.	WITHERSPOON	1768	51006014
XT	God in Xt.	KIMBER	1756	49001030
XT	Grace of Xt.	DUNLOP	1722	50008009
XT	Grow. K. Xt.	VINCENT	1683	64003018
XT	H. S. T.o. Xt.	JOHNSON	1776	46015026
XT	Hap.thr. Xt.	CLARKE	1736	59001002
XT	Heath.b. Xt.	SHERLOCK	1719	52002012
XT	Hope in Xt.	BROUGHTON	1778	49015019
XT	Hu.nat. Xt.	DAWSON	1765	57002005
XT	Imit.of Xt.	FLAVEL	1673	64002006
XT	Imit.of Xt.	DUKE	1703	65002006
XT	Imit.of Xt.	BARROW	1716	49004016
XT	Imit.of Xt.	EDWARDS	1726	46012015
XT	Imit.of Xt.	SHARP	1734	63002021
XT	Imit.of Xt.	HUBBARD	1757	65002006
XT	Imit.of Xt.	CARR	1777	63002021
XT	In Xt.or not.	FAWCETT	1757	50005017
XT	Inc.o. Xt.&c.	NEAL	1757	51004004
XT	Interc.of Xt.	BROWNE	1749	61009024
XT	Inv.to Xt.	MAY	1757	69022003
XT	Inv.to Xt.	WHITTY	1766	69022017
XT	J. Xt. Im. G.	BRETT	1720	54001015
XT	J. Xt. Im. G.	LESTLEY	1720	54001015
XT	Jes. Xt. G.m.	GUYSE	1719	48009005

Keyword	In its Context	Author	Year	BkChpVrs
XT	Jes.the Xt.	GROVE	1741	47004027
XT	Jesus Xt.	BARROW	1716	52001013
XT	Jos. T.of Xt.	WILLISON	1761	01045004
XT	Jos. T.of Xt.	BLISS	1769	01045004
XT	Joy in Xt. J.	DODSON	1728	53003003
XT	Judg.by Xt.	HURRION	1712	58004001
XT	Judg.of Xt.	NEWTON	1736	50005010
XT	Just.by Xt.	WHITFIELD	1739	49006011
XT	Ki.o. Xt.& A.	K.	1667	69016001
XT	Kn. Xt.cruc.	CHARNOCK	1684	49002002
XT	Kn. Xt.cruc.	BEVERIDGE	1720	49002002
XT	Kn. Xt.cruc.	FIDDES	1720	49002002
XT	Kn. Xt.cruc.	WHITFIELD	1739	49002002
XT	Kn. Xt.cruc.	SHEPHEARD	1748	49002002
XT	Kn. Xt.cruc.	BUNDY	1750	49002002
XT	Kno. G.& Xt.	WOOD	1674	48001019
XT	Know. J. Xt.	BOLDE	1697	53003008
XT	Know. J. Xt.	NEWMAN	1728	49002002
XT	Know.o. Xt.	CLARKSON	1696	53003008
XT	Know.o. Xt.	FARRINGTON	1741	53003008
XT	Know.o. Xt.	HAYDON	1772	53003008
XT	Knowl. J. Xt.	STEBBING	1721	53003007
XT	Knowl.o. Xt.	CHANDLER	1753	53003007
XT	L.& Ob.t. Xt.	JENNINGS	1757	50005014
XT	L.& P.ful. Xt.	BLACKALL	1723	43005017
XT	L. Xt. P. Xn.	RELLEY	1762	46014019
XT	Law.of Xt.	BOURDALOUE	1776	43017005
XT	Life fm. Xt.	TAYLOR	1719	46010010
XT	Life fm. Xt.	SHEPHERD	1748	65005012
XT	Life of Xt.	REYNOLDS	1679	53003010
XT	Life of Xt.	REYNOLDS	1679	65005012
XT	Lo.t. G.& Xt.	DAVIES	1766	46021017
XT	Look to Xt.	DAVIES	1771	23045022
XT	Lord sh.o. Xt	WRIGHT	1724	48014009
XT	Love of Xt.	BRINSLEY	1667	46014028
XT	Love of Xt.	ERSKINE	1664	51002020
XT	Love of Xt.	NEST	1677	52006024
XT	Love of Xt.	PIERCE	1679	49016022
XT	Love of Xt.	EDWARDS	1692	49016022
XT	Love of Xt.	ADAMS	1716	49016022
XT	Love of Xt.	SHERLOCK	1719	50005014
XT	Love of Xt.	STEFFE	1743	50005010
XT	Love of Xt.	STEFFE	1743	50005014
XT	Love of Xt.	ROMAINE	1759	22001001
XT	Love of Xt.	ROMAINE	1759	22005016
XT	Love of Xt.	WILLISON	1761	52003019
XT	Love of Xt.	WILLISON	1761	65004019
XT	Love to Xt.	BOYSE	1728	63001008
XT	Love to Xt.	ORR	1739	43010037
XT	Love to Xt.	SOUTH	1744	43010037
XT	Love to Xt.	ABERNETHY	1748	43010037
XT	Mak.lig. Xt.	DAVIES	1766	43022005
XT	Mar's En. Xt.	HORTON	1679	45010038
XT	Med.of Xt.	WHICHCOTE	1703	54003017
XT	Merits of Xt.	HOADLY	1727	65002001
XT	Mir.or. Xt.r.	BOURN	1777	50002016
XT	Mn wout Xt.	BARNES	1752	53004013
XT	Na. Jes.& Xt.	NEWTON	1782	45002021
XT	Names of Xt.	BOSTON	1753	23009006
XT	Negl.of Xt.	WHITFIELD	1771	46005040
XT	Not.lov. Xt.	WILSON	1781	49016022
XT	O. L.g.by Xt.	BRAILSFORD	1776	49015022
XT	Obed.of Xt.	TATHAM	1780	48005018
XT	Obed.to Xt.	KIMBER	1756	43017005
XT	Omnisc. Xt.	WOTTON	1720	44013032
XT	Opin.of Xt.	SAURIN	1775	43016013
XT	Pass.of Xt.	HALL	1661	46019030
XT	Pass.of Xt.	SCOUGAL	1726	25001012
XT	Paul cap. Xt.	BREKELL	1765	50011014
XT	Pers. Int. Xt.	CASE	1774	51002020
XT	Pers.of Xt.	NEWTON	1767	43011027
XT	Person of Xt.	HARWOOD	1772	54001015
XT	Picture o. Xt.	SYMPSON	1662	22005016
XT	Piety to Xt.	WILLIAMS	1774	01001011
XT	Preach. Xt.	JENNINGS	1722	49002002
XT	Preach. Xt.	STOKES	1759	49001023
XT	Preach.o. Xt.	WILLIAMS	1774	49001014
XT	Prej.ag. Xt.	TILLOTSON	1735	43011006
XT	Pres.of Xt.	BEVERIDGE	1720	43018020
XT	Priest.of Xt.	DODSON	1728	61005009
XT	Proph.of Xt.	HODGE	1758	46005039
XT	Put on Xt.	BRADY	1730	48013014
XT	R.to G.in Xt.	BRIGHT	1695	50005019
XT	Reas.bel. Xt.	HARRIS	1728	46011045
XT	Reco.by Xt.	SHEPHERD	1748	52002013
XT	Red.b. Xt.	FLAVEL	1673	49001030
XT	Red.b. Xt.	USHER	1678	69021008
XT	Red.b. Xt.	ERSKINE	1764	49001030
XT	Red.b. Xt.	HALL	1777	48008003
XT	Red.by Xt.	USHER	1678	46001012
XT	Red.by Xt.	USHER	1678	53002006
XT	Red.by Xt.	ERSKINE	1764	69002009
XT	Rede.by Xt.	USHER	1678	52001013
XT	Rede.by Xt.	LOVEDER	1756	54001014
XT	Redem.b. Xt	DORRINGTON	1705	49006020
XT	Reign of Xt.	BAGSHAW	1669	37014005
XT	Reject. Xt.	SOUTH	1744	43019022
XT	Reject.of Xt.	DAVIES	1771	44012006
XT	Relig.of Xt.	CHANDLER	1769	46008046
XT	Reme.of Xt.	ORTON	1776	58002008
XT	Repr.of Xt.	CENNICK	1762	61013013
XT	Res.of Xt.	TILLOTSON	1735	54003001
XT	Ret.flock Xt.	SPOONER	1751	63002015
XT	S. S.proof. Xt	DAVIES	1720	46005039
XT	S. S.prov. Xt.	LEIGHTONHOUSE	1697	46005039
XT	Sacrif.of Xt.	CLARKSON	1696	52005002
XT	Sacrif.of Xt.	TILLOTSON	1735	61009026
XT	Sacrif.of Xt.	SCOTT	1743	61010010
XT	Sacrif.of Xt.	SCOTT	1743	61010011
XT	Sacrif.of Xt.	WESTON	1747	61009012
XT	Sacrif.of Xt.	SHERLOCK	1772	59002014
XT	Safe in Xt.	WELCH	1752	48008002

INDEXES TO THIRD VOLUME: E: KEYWORD-IN-CONTEXT INDEX OF OTHER SUBJECTS OR OCCASIONS

Keyword	In its Context	Author	Year	BkChpVrs
XT	Salv b. Xt.al.	BEVERIDGE	1720	47004012
XT	Salv.b. Xt.al.	STAYNOE	1700	47004012
XT	Salv.by Xt.	WHICHCOTE	1702	58001009
XT	Salv.by Xt.	SEAGRAVE	1737	46003016
XT	Salv.by Xt.	BUNDY	1740	46004022
XT	Salv.by Xt.	MALTUS	1762	43007021
XT	Salv.by Xt.	CHANDLER	1769	47004012
XT	Salv.by Xt.	WILSON	1781	57001015
XT	Salv.in Xt.	RELLY	1760	23042006
XT	Salv.thr. Xt.	LORIMER	1713	47004012
XT	Salvat.by Xt.	SHERLOCK	1772	57001015
XT	Satisf.of Xt.	BUESDELL	1700	65002002
XT	Satisf.of Xt.	SHEPHEARD	1748	57002006
XT	Seek. Xt. D.	GUYSE	1729	20008017
XT	St. Pet.d. Xt.	GELL	1676	43010032
XT	St. Pet.d. Xt.	COOKE	1739	43010032
XT	St. Pet.d. Xt.	BUNDY	1740	43010033
XT	Stew.of Xt.	HILL	1755	45012042
XT	Streng.in Xt.	LAMBERT	1779	53004013
XT	Suffer.of Xt.	BROWNE	1749	61009026
XT	Suffer.of Xt.	WILLISON	1761	45009022
XT	Sup.conc. Xt.	FLEMING	1772	23007013
XT	Tempt. Xt.	SHOWER	1694	49010009
XT	Test.kno. Xt.	WHEATLY	1746	65002003
XT	Tr. Xt.n.ne.	ERSKINE	1764	61013018
XT	Trust in Xt.	MAY	1757	52001012
XT	Union to Xt.	SHOWER	1702	50005017
XT	Union w. Xt.	FLOWER	1740	46014019
XT	Union w. Xt.	ROMAINE	1759	22006001
XT	Uns.ri.o. Xt.	FANCH	1768	52003008
XT	Vict.th. Xt.	WELCH	1752	48008037
XT	Walk.in Xt.	HILL	1755	54002006
XT	Wlk.as Xt.d.	BARROW	1716	65002006
XT	World.v. Xt.	ERSKINE	1764	23008018
XT	Worsh.o. Xt.	LESTLEY	1720	61001006
XT	Xrter.of Xt.	MUTTER	1776	46001014
XT	Xt b.of virg.	KENNICOTT	1765	23007013
XT	Xt our Safety	HARTLEY	1754	43014024
XT	Xt our Surety	TAYLOR	1725	61006022
XT	Xt.& Bapt.	CONEY	1730	45007033
XT	Xt.& Bapt.	HOADLY	1754	45007033
XT	Xt.& Believ.	M'GEORGE	1729	19045011
XT	Xt.& Xn.rel.	WILCOX	1757	22002016
XT	Xt.&c.	DODDERIDGE	1743	51004019
XT	Xt.&our res.	ATTERBURY	1743	23026019
XT	Xt. Bread. L.	CLARKE	1734	46006035
XT	Xt. Crucified	KELSEY	1691	49001023
XT	Xt. Fath.ser.	BRODHURST	1733	43012018
XT	Xt. Friend.	CASE	1774	20018024
XT	Xt. G.& M.	HORBERY	1774	61001001
XT	Xt. G.& M.	MEAD	1780	53002006
XT	Xt. G. Exem.	BUNDY	1740	63002021
XT	Xt. G. Exem.	FOSTER	1744	63002021
XT	Xt. G. Exem.	COCKMAN	1750	63002021
XT	Xt. G. Exem.	HOLLAND	1753	63002021
XT	Xt. G.of Isr.	BRADBURY	1752	01032030

Keyword	In its Context	Author	Year	BkChpVrs
XT	Xt. G's. Ima.	MASON	1758	50003006
XT	Xt. God- M.	EDWARDS	1749	46001014
XT	Xt. Gra.& T.	BEVERIDGE	1720	46001017
XT	Xt. Ima.o. G.	MASON	1758	50004006
XT	Xt. King.of.	SAURIN	1775	46018036
XT	Xt. L.world.	SHERLOCK	1719	45002032
XT	Xt. Lamb.sl.	BRADBURY	1703	69005006
XT	Xt. Ld Glory	RANDOLPH	1769	46012041
XT	Xt. Li.&life.	KELSEY	1721	46001004
XT	Xt. Lig.o. W.	WHARTON	1728	46008012
XT	Xt. Lig.o. W.	KIMBER	1756	46008012
XT	Xt. Lig.of w.	WATSON	1749	19019004
XT	Xt. Med.& R.	LANGHORNE	1773	54001014
XT	Xt. Med.o. R.	STENNETT	1769	52002010
XT	Xt. Mediat.	BRINSLEY	1667	61011024
XT	Xt. Mediator	TAYLOR	1725	57002015
XT	Xt. Pat.t. Xns	BEVERIDGE	1720	63001015
XT	Xt. Redeem.	FARENDON	1672	49006020
XT	Xt. Redeem.	COLE	1692	49006020
XT	Xt. Refuge.	VENN	1759	23003002
XT	Xt. Res.& L.	BREKELL	1765	46011025
XT	Xt. Rock. Sal.	TAYLOR	1701	19061002
XT	Xt. Sac.f.us.	CHARNOCK	1684	49005007
XT	Xt. Sign.s.ag.	BRACKENRIDGE	1764	45002034
XT	Xt. Son of G.	GUYSE	1729	47009020
XT	Xt. Sub.o. S.	SAURIN	1777	61010005
XT	Xt. Suffer.	PIGOTT	1702	23053005
XT	Xt. Suffer.	ROGERS	1738	23053005
XT	Xt. Tea.mor.	DUCHAL	1753	43007025
XT	Xt. Wor. Car.	ORTON	1776	44006003
XT	Xt. Xn's.life.	JACKSON	1756	53001021
XT	Xt.a Gift.	WILLISON	1761	50009015
XT	Xt.a Proph.	DODSON	1728	61001001
XT	Xt.a Saviour.	BEVERIDGE	1720	46006037
XT	Xt.a Saviour.	BEVERIDGE	1729	46005017
XT	Xt.ab.to save	HOPKINS	1710	61007025
XT	Xt.all in all.	ROWLAND	1774	61001009
XT	Xt.all in all.	JOHNSON	1776	49001030
XT	Xt.at G's.r.h.	HURRION	1719	61012001
XT	Xt.auth. Ob.	HORT	1738	61005009
XT	Xt.belov.&c.	BOSTON	1775	52001006
XT	Xt.br.of life.	WILLISON	1761	20009005
XT	Xt.c.charity	CONYBEARE	1757	49013013
XT	Xt.cam.f. L.	BROWNE	1749	43005017
XT	Xt.co. Apost.	SECKER	1771	43028019
XT	Xt.co.t.jud.	FLAVEL	1673	47010042
XT	Xt.co.t.jud.	CARRINGTON	1750	47010042
XT	Xt.com. Jud.	MALBON	1673	43016027
XT	Xt.com. Jud.	RALEIGH	1679	43016027
XT	Xt.cru. G. S.	WADSWORTH	1675	61010012
XT	Xt.cru.daily.	SKELTON	1754	44015021
XT	Xt.crucified.	LATHOM	1666	52004014
XT	Xt.crucified.	LATHOM	1666	62003017
XT	Xt.crucified.	COLMAN	1728	51003001
XT	Xt.dest. Dea.	BREKELL	1765	61011015
XT	Xt.do all t.w.	ORTON	1776	44007037

Keyword	In its Context	Author	Year	BkChpVrs
XT	Xt.draw. M.	WILLISON	1761	46012032
XT	Xt.dy.f. Sin.	CLARKSON	1696	48005008
XT	Xt.e. Spouse.	WHITLOCK	1698	28002015
XT	Xt.eq.w. G.	LESTLEY	1720	53002006
XT	Xt.eq.w. G.	SHERLOCK	1772	53002006
XT	Xt.exalted.	TREBELL	1703	23045004
XT	Xt.exalted.	TREBELL	1703	23055004
XT	Xt.faith. W.	HORTON	1679	69001005
XT	Xt.first F.&c.	BREKELL	1765	49015020
XT	Xt.g. Sheph.	PYLE	1777	46010010
XT	Xt.glorified.	MAY	1757	56001010
XT	Xt.gr. Prop.	WILSON	1746	65004010
XT	Xt.gr. Salv.	BURNET	1747	61002003
XT	Xt.hid. Mys.	HARTLEY	1754	54001026
XT	Xt.ho.of Gl.	BALL	1692	54001027
XT	Xt.hon.to F.	WILLIAMS	1770	63002007
XT	Xt.humiliat.	WILLISON	1761	23055005
XT	Xt.humiliat.	SHERLOCK	1772	23055003
XT	Xt.in Gard.	MAY	1757	46018001
XT	Xt.in Glory.	FLAVEL	1673	20008030
XT	Xt.key Hell.	DUNLOP	1722	69001018
XT	Xt.knocking	WILLISON	1761	69003020
XT	Xt.leav. Dis.	WILLISON	1761	46016007
XT	Xt.light o. O.	BULKLEY	1771	46009005
XT	Xt.like Mos.	COLMAN	1728	05008015
XT	Xt.like Rain.	WILLISON	1761	19072006
XT	Xt.m. Sav.	VEAL	1703	19089019
XT	Xt.ma.of G.	STEVENS	1757	50005021
XT	Xt.mind. D.	COLMAN	1728	46013001
XT	Xt.o. Right.	RAWLIN	1741	24045024
XT	Xt.obj.o. Fai.	GOODWIN	16--	48008038
XT	Xt.on Cross.	WILLISON	1761	46003014
XT	Xt.on Judg.	JOHNSON	1776	43025031
XT	Xt.only Found.	DAVIES	1766	23028016
XT	Xt.our Ark.	WILLISON	1761	01007001
XT	Xt.our Com.	MOIR	1759	23032002
XT	Xt.our Cov.	ERSKINE	1764	23042006
XT	Xt.our Ld.	BEVERIDGE	1720	46013013
XT	Xt.our Man.	WILLISON	1761	46006051
XT	Xt.our Mast.	BENNETT	1728	43023008
XT	Xt.our Patt.	SKELTON	1754	53002005
XT	Xt.our Ref.	WILLISON	1761	61006018
XT	Xt.our Rock.	WILLISON	1761	49010004
XT	Xt.our Sav.	WELCH	1752	23062001
XT	Xt.our Sav.	DAVIS	1756	61009026
XT	Xt.our Shep.	DODDERIDGE	1736	23040011
XT	Xt.our Shep.	HILL	1755	23040011
XT	Xt.our Shep.	WILCOX	1757	23040011
XT	Xt.our Supp.	ERSKINE	1757	22008005
XT	Xt.per.m. L.	BLAIR	1740	43005017
XT	Xt.pierced.	WILLISON	1761	37012010
XT	Xt.pr.to Bel.	DAVIES	1766	63002007
XT	Xt.prop. Sac.	SKELTON	1754	49015023
XT	Xt.quick. U.	COLMAN	1728	23011003
XT	Xt.red.n. A.	COLMAN	1728	61002016
XT	Xt.rede.&c.	BOSTON	1773	51004004
XT	Xt.rep. Mar.	HORTON	1679	45010041
XT	Xt.sav. Tem.	GILL	1773	43008025
XT	Xt.sear. H.	NEWLIN	1728	46002024
XT	Xt.seek. Fr.	CLARKSON	1696	45013006
XT	Xt.si.r.h. G.	FLAVEL	1673	61001003
XT	Xt.sp.meat.	LE FRANK	1662	46004034
XT	Xt.t. Head.	BAXTER	1675	49012027
XT	Xt.t. Proph.	BADDELLEY	1766	46006014
XT	Xt.t. Saviour	COLE	1692	45001077
XT	Xt.t. Saviour	BOSTON	1753	65004014
XT	Xt.t. Testat.	TAYLOR	1723	61009006
XT	Xt.t. W.&c.	HORTON	1679	46014006
XT	Xt.t. W.&c.	BEVERIDGE	1720	46014006
XT	Xt.the judge	DUNLOP	1722	48002016
XT	Xt.the Des.	NICOLSON	1661	22001001
XT	Xt.to J.& G.	BROWNE	1722	45002032
XT	Xt.tr. Mess.	FREE	1750	45007020
XT	Xt.tr. Moses.	ERSKINE	1764	47007034
XT	Xt.u.w. Xns.	CLAGETT	1720	46015001
XT	Xt.unchang.	WILCOX	1757	61001012
XT	Xt.very G.	HORNE	1775	48010013
XT	Xt.2 Adam.	PENTYCROSS	1781	48005014
XT	Xt Found Pr.	BEVERIDGE	1720	50001020
XT	Yoke of Xt.	WHARTON	1728	43011030
XT	2 Nat.in Xt.	SALMON	1753	46001014
XT	2 Say.of Xt.	FLAVEL	1673	46019027
XT	3d Tit.of Xt.	FLAVEL	1673	22005016
XT	4 S. Xt.on C.	FLAVEL	1673	43027046
XT	5 Say.of Xt.	FLAVEL	1673	46019028
XT	6 Say.of Xt.	FLAVEL	1673	46019030
XT'	Exc.o. Xt'.o.	FLAVEL	1673	61010014
XT'	Xt'. Divin.	SMITH	1777	46001001
XT'COV	Xt'cov.of P.	HILL	1755	23049008
XT'S	Adv. Xt's.as.	BEVERIDGE	1720	46014002
XT'S	Adv. Xt's.as.	WARREN	1748	46014002
XT'S	Bel. Xt's. Fr.	BOSTON	1773	46015014
XT'S	Bless. Xt's. Y	PETERS	1776	43011028
XT'S	Cl V. Xt's bl.	CHARNOCK	1684	65001007
XT'S	Com. Xt's.b.	JONES	1756	49010016
XT'S	Com. Xt's.w.	DAVIS	1756	46017004
XT'S	D.all Xt's. N.	WILKINSON	1676	54003017
XT'S	Des. Xt's.co.	PAYNE	1763	69022020
XT'S	Eas. Xt's. Y.	DODD	1757	43011028
XT'S	End Xt's.g.h.	JOHNSON	1740	59002014
XT'S	Ev. Xt's. Res.	STEBBING	1760	47005032
XT'S	Fai. Xt's. Re.	SKELTON	1754	47010040
XT'S	Fold Xt's Sh.	SMITH	1726	21001007
XT'S	Gov. Xt's.ch.	BAINE	1778	49005012
XT'S	Instr. Xt's. D	FLAVEL	1673	45023034
XT'S	Man. Xt's. D.	FLAVEL	1673	37013007
XT'S	Man. Xt's D.	FLAVEL	1673	23053007
XT'S	Nat. Xt's. Bl.	HOADLY	1754	47003026
XT'S	Ne.o Xt's. P.	FLAVEL	1673	61009023
XT'S	Nec. Xt's. D.	DAVIS	1756	46011051
XT'S	Ob. Xt's m.a.	CHANDLER	1769	47010040
XT'S	Obj. Xt's.res.	WEBB	1772	43028011

Keyword	In its Context	Author	Year	BkChpVrs
XT'S	On Xt's. Mir.	CHANDLER	1769	46003002
XT'S	Perp. Xt's. K.	HUSSEY	1753	45001033
XT'S	Pow. Xt's D.	MAY	1757	46007046
XT'S	Pr. Xt's. N.	BEVERIDGE	1720	46014014
XT'S	Pr.in Xt's. N.	KILLIGREW	1685	46016023
XT'S	Pr.in Xt's. N.	SCOTT.	1743	46016023
XT'S	Pr.in Xt's. N.	WESTON	1747	46016023
XT'S	Pr.in Xt's. N.	LARDNER	1760	46016024
XT'S	Pr.in Xt's. N.	BOSTON	1775	46016023
XT'S	Prior Xt's. R.	WELLS	1735	47026022
XT'S	R. Xt's. Xter.	BREKELL	1765	43016018
XT'S	Sanc. Xt's. L.	MACE	1751	44008035
XT'S	Spir. Xt's. R.	MICHELL	1737	45009054
XT'S	T. T. Xt's. B.	CATCOTT	1753	46001014
XT'S	Tak. Xt's. Y.	MEDE	1672	43011028
XT'S	Tak. Xt's. Y.	COCKBURE	1697	43011028
XT'S	Tak. Xt's. Y.	BEVERIDGE	1720	43011029
XT'S	Time Xt's. C.	PYLE	1777	69022012
XT'S	Tra. Xt's. D.	HORTON	1679	66000009
XT'S	Wisd. Xt's. M.	TOTTIE	1775	45007035
XT'S	Xr. Xt's. Dis.	MAY	1757	47004013
XT'S	Xt's apol.f.d.	ORTON	1776	43026004
XT'S	Xt's appear.	FIDDES	1720	23053002
XT'S	Xt's humil.	FLAVEL	1673	23053002
XT'S	Xt's priv life	THEED	1712	45002051
XT'S	Xt's reg.offi.	FLAVEL	1673	52001022
XT'S	Xt's u.w. Ch.	NICOLSON	1661	50011002
XT'S	Xt's.& Tem.	DAVIES	1720	45004013
XT'S	Xt's. A.expl.	WATERLAND	1742	45020037
XT'S	Xt's. Adm.u.	CLARKE	1734	45017037
XT'S	Xt's. Advent.	BURNET	1747	48015008
XT'S	Xt's. Agony.	WILLISON	1761	45022044
XT'S	Xt's. Appear.	ERSKINE	1764	19040007
XT'S	Xt's. Atone.	WATTS	1753	69013008
XT'S	Xt's. Author.	GARDINER	1720	43007028
XT'S	Xt's. Author.	CLARKE	1735	43028018
XT'S	Xt's. Author.	TILLOTSON	1735	43028018
XT'S	Xt's. Blood.	BROWNE	1749	61009014
XT'S	Xt's. C. L. G.	CRAIG	1775	46011033
XT'S	Xt's. Calling.	BENSON	1748	45005031
XT'S	Xt's. Co.&c.	HORTON	1679	69022017
XT'S	Xt's. Comf.	HORTON	1679	46014018
XT'S	Xt's. Crucif.	BRINSLEY	1667	49001023
XT'S	Xt's. Crucif.	HORTON	1679	49001023
XT'S	Xt's. Crucif.	COLE	1692	49001023
XT'S	Xt's. Crucif.	HUSSEY	1753	49001002
XT'S	Xt's. Crucif.	LOVEDER	1756	49001023
XT'S	Xt's. Crucif.	VENN	1759	49001023
XT'S	Xt's. D.& M.	BURNET	1747	49001025
XT'S	Xt's. D. A.r.	HOADLY	1754	43020026
XT'S	Xt's. D. Hell.	ROBINSON	1660	47002027
XT'S	Xt's. D. Hell.	PIGOTT	1702	47002026
XT'S	Xt's. D. Hell.	HOLE	1715	47002027
XT'S	Xt's. D. Hell.	BARROW	1716	47002027
XT'S	Xt's. D. Hell.	BOYS	1716	47002027
XT'S	Xt's. D. Hell.	FISHER	1741	47002027

Keyword	In its Context	Author	Year	BkChpVrs
XT'S	Xt's. D. Hell.	TERRY	1746	47002027
XT'S	Xt's. D. Wis.	PARKHURST	1707	65003008
XT'S	Xt's. D.foret.	MEDE	1672	45024045
XT'S	Xt's. D.in. H.	NICOLSON	1661	52004009
XT'S	Xt's. D.in. H.	HURRION	1719	52004010
XT'S	Xt's. D.on C.	FLAVEL	1673	47002023
XT'S	Xt's. D.pr. A.	WITHERSPOON	1768	65002002
XT'S	Xt's. Death.	CHARNOCK	1684	52005002
XT'S	Xt's. Div.&c.	TILLOTSON	1735	48001004
XT'S	Xt's. Div.p.fm	JOHNSON	1713	48001004
XT'S	Xt's. Div.p.fm	BEVERIDGE	1720	48001004
XT'S	Xt's. Divin.	BUERDSELL	1700	46001001
XT'S	Xt's. Divin.	PALKE	1719	46020028
XT'S	Xt's. Divin.	CONANT	1722	48009005
XT'S	Xt's. Divin.	SKELTON	1754	46005022
XT'S	Xt's. Divin.	SKELTON	1754	53003008
XT'S	Xt's. Divin.	SAURIN	1777	69005011
XT'S	Xt's. Eloqu.	BROUGHTON	1778	46007046
XT'S	Xt's. En.ill.t	FLAVEL	1673	45023023
XT'S	Xt's. Exalt.	TAYLOR	1676	53002009
XT'S	Xt's. Exalt.	LITTLETON	1680	53002009
XT'S	Xt's. Exalt.	CLARKE	1727	47002033
XT'S	Xt's. Exalt.	BENNETT	1735	53002009
XT'S	Xt's. Exalt.	TERRY	1746	53002009
XT'S	Xt's. Exalt.	WATTS	1753	47002033
XT'S	Xt's. Exalt.	CATCOTT	1753	53002009
XT'S	Xt's. Exalt.	WARNEFORD	1757	53002009
XT'S	Xt's. Exam.	JOHNSON	1740	43011029
XT'S	Xt's. Examp.	CALAMY	1726	47010038
XT'S	Xt's. Examp.	TILLOTSON	1735	47010038
XT'S	Xt's. Examp.	WILDER	1741	47010038
XT'S	Xt's. Examp.	SCOTT	1743	64001021
XT'S	Xt's. Examp.	LELAND	1769	46013015
XT'S	Xt's. Examp.	LELAND	1769	46018029
XT'S	Xt's. Examp.	LELAND	1769	52005002
XT'S	Xt's. Examp.	LELAND	1769	53002005
XT'S	Xt's. F.t. Dis	LARDNER	1760	46014027
XT'S	Xt's. Friends.	ALLESTREE	1684	46015014
XT'S	Xt's. Friends.	HAVETT	1703	46015014
XT'S	Xt's. Friends.	HICKES	1713	46015014
XT'S	Xt's. Friends.	BEESTON	1739	46015014
XT'S	Xt's. Gl. H.	FANCH	1768	49015028
XT'S	Xt's. H.tc S.	GOODWIN	16--	46013001
XT'S	Xt's. Humil.	FLAVEL	1673	46017011
XT'S	Xt's. Humil.	MERITON	1676	53002008
XT'S	Xt's. Humil.	COLLIER	1725	50008009
XT'S	Xt's. Humil.	M'GEORGE	1727	53002007
XT'S	Xt's. Humil.	CLARKE	1735	43016021
XT'S	Xt's. Humil.	MOSS	1738	53002005
XT'S	Xt's. Humil.	COWPER	1773	53002005
XT'S	Xt's. Incarn.	PIGOTT	1702	45001035
XT'S	Xt's. Incarn.	SOUTH	1744	61002016
XT'S	Xt's. Incarn.	HOOLE	1748	57003016
XT'S	Xt's. Incarn.	FAWCETT	1749	61002017
XT'S	Xt's. Incarn.	BOSTON	1773	45001035
XT'S	Xt's. Incarn.	OGDEN	1777	45001034

Keyword	In its Context	Author	Year	BkChpVrs
XT'S	Xt's. Incarn.	COWPER	1773	61002016
XT'S	Xt's. Incense	ORTON	1776	69008003
XT'S	Xt's. Inst.gr.	TOTTIE	1775	46016012
XT'S	Xt's. Interc.	FLAVEL	1673	61006023
XT'S	Xt's. Interc.	CHARNOCK	1684	65002001
XT'S	Xt's. Interc.	CRUSO	1699	61007025
XT'S	Xt's. Interc.	HURRION	1719	61007025
XT'S	Xt's. Interc.	STENNETT	1732	61007025
XT'S	Xt's. Interc.	DODDERIDGE	1736	61007025
XT'S	Xt's. Interc.	HUBBARD	1757	48008034
XT'S	Xt's. Interc.	FANCH	1768	46017024
XT'S	Xt's. Inv. Ch.	DAVIES	1758	44010014
XT'S	Xt's. Invit.	GREGORY	1696	43011028
XT'S	Xt's. Invit.	SCATTERGOOD	1723	43011028
XT'S	Xt's. Invit.	NEWTON	1736	43011028
XT'S	Xt's. Invitat.	CLARKSON	1696	69003020
XT'S	Xt's. Kingd.	HALES	1673	46018036
XT'S	Xt's. Kingd.	BARNE	1682	46018036
XT'S	Xt's. Kingd.	C.	1717	46018036
XT'S	Xt's. Kingd.	LOVELING	1717	46018036
XT'S	Xt's. Kingd.	TRAPP	1717	46018036
XT'S	Xt's. Kingd.	GROVE	1747	46018036
XT'S	Xt's. Kingd.	HUSSEY	1753	61001008
XT'S	Xt's. Kingd.	HOADLY	1754	46018036
XT'S	Xt's. Kingd.	RADCLIFF	1763	46018036
XT'S	Xt's. Kingd.	BREKELL	1765	46018036
XT'S	Xt's. Kingd.	DAVIES	1766	46018037
XT'S	Xt's. Kingd.	ANONYMOUS	1776	43006010
XT'S	Xt's. Kingd.	HARWOOD	1772	49015024
XT'S	Xt's. Kingd.	PYLE	1777	46018036
XT'S	Xt's. L.to us.	HORTON	1679	69001005
XT'S	Xt's. Love.	WELCH	1752	23042003
XT'S	Xt's. Love.	WILLISON	1761	69002005
XT'S	Xt's. Min.	SAURIN	1775	48010021
XT'S	Xt's. Name.	VINK	1675	45006022
XT'S	Xt's. Nativ.	ATKINSON	1775	65004010
XT'S	Xt's. Obed.	WILLIAMS	1750	48005019
XT'S	Xt's. Obed.	MOIR	1759	48006001
XT'S	Xt's. Oblat.	FLAVEL	1673	51004004
XT'S	Xt's. Office.	BOURN	1760	47005031
XT'S	Xt's. Office.	WHITTY	1766	47005031
XT'S	Xt's. P.o. R.	LARDNER	1760	50007009
XT'S	Xt's. Parab.	LELAND	1769	43013003
XT'S	Xt's. Passion.	SPARKES	1663	43027001
XT'S	Xt's. Passion.	MUSCOTT	1760	53002008
XT'S	Xt's. Person.	NICHOLSON	1661	43016015
XT'S	Xt's. Predict.	HODGE	1758	46013019
XT'S	Xt's. Preexis.	RUDD	1740	46017005
XT'S	Xt's. Pres.	BEVERIDGE	1720	43028020
XT'S	Xt's. Pres.	REEVES	1729	43028020
XT'S	Xt's. Pres.	MOSS	1733	43028020
XT'S	Xt's. Pres.	HOOLE	1748	43028020
XT'S	Xt's. Priesth.	HIBBERT	1662	61007026
XT'S	Xt's. Priesth.	WEST	1762	61007026
XT'S	Xt's. Priesth.	JOHNSON	1776	61008003
XT'S	Xt's. R.& N.	PATTEN	1759	54002008
XT'S	Xt's. Relig.	BURNET	1747	43016025
XT'S	Xt's. Res.&c.	JENNINGS	1757	47001002
XT'S	Xt's. Resign.	STANHOPE	1705	45022042
XT'S	Xt's. Resign.	WILLISON	1761	46018004
XT'S	Xt's. Resurr.	GARBUTT	1669	49015020
XT'S	Xt's. Resurr.	FLAVEL	1673	43028006
XT'S	Xt's. Resurr.	BRAGGE	1706	45024005
XT'S	Xt's. Resurr.	BARROW	1716	45024046
XT'S	Xt's. Resurr.	EDWARDS	1713	53003010
XT'S	Xt's. Resurr.	LACY	1720	45024005
XT'S	Xt's. Resurr.	CLARKE	1727	47002032
XT'S	Xt's. Resurr.	HORT	1738	45024005
XT'S	Xt's. Resurr.	MOSS	1732	49015058
XT'S	Xt's. Resurr.	WARREN	1739	49015020
XT'S	Xt's. Resurr.	WHITFIELD	1739	53003010
XT'S	Xt's. Resurr.	ADEY	1755	45024006
XT'S	Xt's. Resurr.	ECCLES	1755	47010040
XT'S	Xt's. Resurr.	ECCLES	1755	48006009
XT'S	Xt's. Resurr.	TIDCOMBE	1757	47004033
XT'S	Xt's. Resurr.	MORRIS	1757	48004024
XT'S	Xt's. Resurr.	HODGE	1758	47011024
XT'S	Xt's. Resurr.	SHIRLEY	1762	43028005
XT'S	Xt's. Resurr.	MUSCOTT	1760	47002032
XT'S	Xt's. Resurr.	CHANDLER	1769	47002032
XT'S	Xt's. Resurr.	BULKLEY	1771	46010017
XT'S	Xt's. Resurr.	BOURDALOUE	1776	44016006
XT'S	Xt's. Resurr.	SHERLOCK	1772	48004025
XT'S	Xt's. Resurr.	OGDEN	1777	47002031
XT'S	Xt's. Riches.	ADAM	1772	69003018
XT'S	Xt's. S.& D.	COWPER	1773	49002002
XT'S	Xt's. Sacrif.	WATERLAND	1742	52005001
XT'S	Xt's. Salvat.	NEWTON	1760	57001015
XT'S	Xt's. Satisf.	FLAVEL	1673	51003010
XT'S	Xt's. Satisf.	POOL	1676	54001020
XT'S	Xt's. Satisf.	MAUDUIT	1704	52005002
XT'S	Xt's. Satisf.	PEARSON	1718	54001014
XT'S	Xt's. Satisf.	LEEKE	1735	51002021
XT'S	Xt's. Satisf.	BROWNE	1749	47020028
XT'S	Xt's. Satisf.	BROWNE	1749	48003026
XT'S	Xt's. Satisfac	BEVERIDGE	1720	65002001
XT'S	Xt's. Sonship	WALLIN	1771	43022041
XT'S	Xt's. Sonship	WALLIN	1771	47009020
XT'S	Xt's. Sonship	WALLIN	1771	65005020
XT'S	Xt's. Suf.&c.	PRICE	1757	63003018
XT'S	Xt's. Suff.& S	CHARNOCK	1684	45024026
XT'S	Xt's. Suff.& S	EDWARDS	1713	45024026
XT'S	Xt's. Suffer.	STILLINGFLEET	1707	61012003
XT'S	Xt's. Suffer.	MOSS	1732	61012003
XT'S	Xt's. Suffer.	DAVIES	1771	46012027
XT'S	Xt's. Suffer.	WHITTY	1772	45024026
XT'S	Xt's. Suffer.	OGDEN	1777	49001018
XT'S	Xt's. Sufferi.	BRADBURY	1732	48008032
XT'S	Xt's. Sufferi.	CLARKE	1735	63003018
XT'S	Xt's. Tempe.	EVANS	1737	53002005
XT'S	Xt's. Tempe.	ENFIELD	1772	53002005
XT'S	Xt's. Tempt.	SHERLOCK	1772	45004001

Keyword	In its Context	Author	Year	BkChpVrs
XT'S	Xt's. Theol.	DERHAM	1730	47026028
XT'S	Xt's. Transf.	BROWNRIG	1664	43017002
XT'S	Xt's. Transf.	BROWNRIG	1664	43017005
XT'S	Xt's. Transf.	BROWNRIG	1664	43017006
XT'S	Xt's. Transf.	MANTON	1685	43017001
XT'S	Xt's. Transf.	MANTON	1685	43017002
XT'S	Xt's. Transf.	MANTON	1685	43017003
XT'S	Xt's. Transf.	MANTON	1685	43017004
XT'S	Xt's. Transf.	GODDEN	1687	43017001
XT'S	Xt's. Transf.	BRAGGE	1706	43017001
XT'S	Xt's. Transf.	MANTON	1708	43017008
XT'S	Xt's. Transf.	FARMER	1756	43017001
XT'S	Xt's. Transf.	LELAND	1769	43017001
XT'S	Xt's. Transf.	BULKLEY	1771	43017004
XT'S	Xt's. Treas.	ERSKINE	1764	46016015
XT'S	Xt's. Xrter.	HIBBERT	1662	49011003
XT'S	Xt's. Xrter.	SEAGRAVE	1737	43022043
XT'S	Xt's. Xrter.	ENFIELD	1777	43011029
XT'S	Xt's. Xrter.	ENFIELD	1777	46013015
XT'S	Xt's.addit.	MOSS	1737	43005021
XT'S	Xt's.app.&c.	CATCOTT	1753	53002006
XT'S	Xt's.app.b. I.	CATCOTT	1753	53002006
XT'S	Xt's.auth. M.	FLAVEL	1673	46006027
XT'S	Xt's.auth. T.	LELAND	1769	43007028
XT'S	Xt's.blood	ROMAINE	1760	37013001
XT'S	Xt's.blood.	ERSKINE	1764	37013007
XT'S	Xt's.c.t. Xns.	MARTIN	1779	43005029
XT'S	Xt's.c.to C.	WALLIN	1746	45023034
XT'S	Xt's.coming	MEDE	1672	44001014
XT'S	Xt's.coming.	WARREN	1748	64001016
XT'S	Xt's.coming.	CHANDLER	1769	57001015
XT'S	Xt's.comp. S.	DAVIES	1771	43023037
XT'S	Xt's.compas.	MUNTON	1756	45019041
XT'S	Xt's.compas.	DAVIES	1766	43012020
XT'S	Xt's.crucif.	HURRION	1727	49002002
XT'S	Xt's.crucif.	ATKINSON	1775	49002002
XT'S	Xt's.crucifix.	HUSSEY	1753	47002023
XT'S	Xt's.d.&res.	JOHNSON	1728	47002031
XT'S	Xt's.dy. Ch.	WILLISON	1761	49002024
XT'S	Xt's.dy. Pr.	NEWMAN	1760	45023024
XT'S	Xt's.easy Y.	HOADLEY	1754	43011030
XT'S	Xt's.easy Y.	JORTIN	1774	43011030
XT'S	Xt's.ent.i. H.	EMLYN	1742	61006020
XT'S	Xt's.fin.app.	WHITAKER	1773	43025044
XT'S	Xt's.good W.	BOSTON	1773	45019005
XT'S	Xt's.gr. Int.	PARR	1661	45019041
XT'S	Xt's.king.sp.	BRADBURY	1772	69011017
XT'S	Xt's.l.suffer.	BRAGGE	1706	43026036
XT'S	Xt's.l.words	FLAVEL	1673	45023043
XT'S	Xt's.l.words.	FLAVEL	1673	45023046
XT'S	Xt's.last Dis.	DUCHAL	1753	46014001
XT'S	Xt's.lo.to us.	SHOWER	1702	46015009
XT'S	Xt's.manif.	CHANDLER	1769	65003008
XT'S	Xt's.mediat.	FLAVEL	1673	57002005
XT'S	Xt's.mediat.	BEVERIDGE	1720	57002005
XT'S	Xt's.mediat.	TILLOTSON	1735	57002005

Keyword	In its Context	Author	Year	BkChpVrs
XT'S	Xt's.mediat.	FOSTER	1744	57002005
XT'S	Xt's.mediat.	HUSSEY	1753	57002005
XT'S	Xt's.mediat.	PETERS	1776	57002005
XT'S	Xt's.mission.	TOTTIE	1775	43011005
XT'S	Xt's.myst.c.	DODDERIDGE	1761	46008007
XT'S	Xt's.p.rais.d.	MORRIS	1757	46005025
XT'S	Xt's.pers.m.	GUYSE	1757	46001018
XT'S	Xt's.pow.h.	FOORD	1719	43008003
XT'S	Xt's.pr.af. R.	DELANY	1766	49015006
XT'S	Xt's.pr.to sp.	NEWSON	1781	63003019
XT'S	Xt's.pro.off.	FLAVEL	1673	45024045
XT'S	Xt's.pro.off.	FLAVEL	1673	47003022
XT'S	Xt's.pro.off.	BOSTON	1773	47003022
XT'S	Xt's.quick v.	ERSKINE	1764	46005025
XT'S	Xt's.read&c.	LEMAN	1749	43011028
XT'S	Xt's.req.off.	FLAVEL	1673	50010005
XT'S	Xt's.res.imp.	WILSON	1781	47001021
XT'S	Xt's.self.exis	ROMAINE	1755	46001014
XT'S	Xt's.suf.nec.	SHEPHERD	1748	45024046
XT'S	Xt's.tr.ov. D.	FANCH	1768	49015025
XT'S	Xt's.w.pers.	FLAVEL	1673	46001014
XT'S	Xt's.warn. P.	HORTON	1679	45022031
XT'S	Xt's.2 p.f. D.	FLAVEL	1673	49011023
XT'S	Xt's.2 Com.	WILSON	1781	69022012
XT'S	Xt's.2d.com.	NEWMAN	1760	61009028
XT'S	Xt's.2d.com.	TOTTIE	1775	43024037
XT'S	Xt's Baptism	HALL	1661	43003015
XT'S	Xt's Baptism	HACKET	1675	43003013
XT'S	Xt's Baptism	HACKET	1675	43003014
XT'S	Xt's Baptism	HACKET	1675	43003015
XT'S	Xt's Baptism	HACKET	1675	43003016
XT'S	Xt's Baptism	HACKET	1675	43003017
XT'S	Xt's Com.	ROMAINE	1759	22008014
XT'S	Xt's Delight.	COLMAN	1728	20008031
XT'S	Xt's Exam.	STEBBING	1760	63002021
XT'S	Xt's Fast.	WILLIAMS	1667	43004002
XT'S	Xt's Fast.	THEED	1712	43004002
XT'S	Xt's K.n.t.w.	GREENHILL	1768	46018036
XT'S	Xt's Kingd.	REYNOLDS	1679	19110001
XT'S	Xt's Kingd.	GROVE	1735	46018016
XT'S	Xt's Love.	ROMAINE	1759	22008006
XT'S	Xt's Miracles	NEWTON	1782	46010024
XT'S	Xt's Nativ.	COWPER	1773	43001022
XT'S	Xt's Obed. P.	HEYLYN	1749	45002051
XT'S	Xt's Offices.	BOSTON	1773	37004013
XT'S	Xt's Regal.	REYNOLDS	1679	19110002
XT'S	Xt's Relurr.	SAURIN	1775	19118015
XT'S	Xt's Resurr.	FOSTER	1720	47010040
XT'S	Xt's Righte.	BURTON	1763	24023006
XT'S	Xt's Satisf.	NORRIS	1728	43003017
XT'S	Xt's Satisfac.	CREYGHTON	1720	52001007
XT'S	Xt's Serm.	HUNT	1748	43005001
XT'S	Xt's Sonship.	WALLIN	1771	19002012
XT'S	Xt's Suffer.	DAVIS	1756	25001012
XT'S	Xt's Suffer.	DAVIES	1766	23053010
XT'S	Xt's Tempt.	FLOWER	1669	43004009

Keyword	In its Context	Author	Year	BkChpVrs
XT'S	Xt's Tempt.	FARINDON	1674	43004001
XT'S	Xt's Tempt.	HACKET	1675	43004001
XT'S	Xt's Tempt.	HACKET	1675	43004002
XT'S	Xt's Tempt.	HACKET	1675	43004003
XT'S	Xt's Tempt.	HACKET	1675	43004004
XT'S	Xt's Tempt.	HACKET	1675	43004005
XT'S	Xt's Tempt.	HACKET	1675	43004006
XT'S	Xt's Tempt.	HACKET	1675	43004007
XT'S	Xt's Tempt.	HACKET	1675	43004008
XT'S	Xt's Tempt.	HACKET	1675	43004009
XT'S	Xt's Tempt.	HACKET	1675	43004010
XT'S	Xt's Tempt.	HACKET	1675	43004011
XT'S	Xt's Tempt.	GELL	1676	43004004
XT'S	Xt's Tempt.	PIERCE	1679	43004009
XT'S	Xt's Tempt.	MANTON	1685	43004001
XT'S	Xt's Tempt.	MANTON	1685	43004005
XT'S	Xt's Tempt.	MANTON	1685	43004007
XT'S	Xt's Tempt.	MANTON	1685	43004008
XT'S	Xt's Tempt.	CONANT	1699	43004001
XT'S	Xt's Tempt.	CONANT	1699	43004002
XT'S	Xt's Tempt.	CONANT	1699	43004003
XT'S	Xt's Tempt.	CONANT	1699	43004004
XT'S	Xt's Tempt.	CONANT	1699	43004005
XT'S	Xt's Tempt.	CONANT	1699	43004006
XT'S	Xt's Tempt.	CONANT	1699	43004007
XT'S	Xt's Tempt.	CONANT	1699	43004009
XT'S	Xt's Tempt.	BRAGGE	1706	43004001
XT'S	Xt's Tempt.	MANTON	1708	43004001
XT'S	Xt's Tempt.	STANHOPE	1715	43004001
XT'S	Xt's Tempt.	HOLE	1716	43004001
XT'S	Xt's Tempt.	EYRE	1738	43004001
XT'S	Xt's Tempt.	EYRE	1738	43004004
XT'S	Xt's Tempt.	EYRE	1738	43004007
XT'S	Xt's Tempt.	EYRE	1738	43004010
XT'S	Xt's Tempt.	WHEATLY	1746	43004002
XT'S	Xt's Tempt.	WHEATLY	1746	43004005
XT'S	Xt's Tempt.	FARMER	1756	43004001
XT'S	Xt's Tempt.	MUNTON	1756	43004001
XT'S	Xt's Tempt.	WHITE	1757	43004001
XT'S	Xt's Tempt.	CHANDLER	1769	43004001
XT'S	Xt's Tempt.	BOURDALOUE	1776	43004001
XTE	Integ.of Xte.	DUCHAL	1765	21010001
XTER	Dan's. Xter.	ENFIELD	1777	27006005
XTER	Mix. Xter.	BOURN	1777	62001008
XTER	Moses' Xter.	ENFIELD	1777	47007017
XTER	Noah's Xter.	MURRAY	1777	01008015
XTER	Perf. Xter.	BOURN	1777	62001004
XTER	R. Xt's. Xter.	BREKELL	1765	43016018
XTER	Sav.'s Xter.	DUCHAL	1753	46008046
XTER	Xn's Xter.	VENN	1759	19121001
XTERS	Xters.in life.	POWELL	1776	49013011
XTIAN	Rel. Xtian.	JEFFERY	1751	46017003
XTIAN	True Xtian.	NICOLSON	1661	53003020
XTIAN	Xtian.life.	SEED	1750	20004018
XTIANITY	Xtianity.	WILKINS	1682	48014017
XTIANS	True Xtians.	CLARKE	1736	65003009

Keyword	In its Context	Author	Year	BkChpVrs
XTMAS	S.b. Xtmas.	WADE	1729	43011002
XTMAS	Xtmas d.	DELANY	1754	48013013
XTMAS	Xtmas d.	ORR	1772	46006045
XTMAS	Xtmas s.	SIBS	16--	45002013
XTMAS	Xtmas s.	BURROUGHS	1660	23009006
XTMAS	Xtmas s.	NICOLSON	1661	23053008
XTMAS	Xtmas s.	BROWNRIG	1661	36002007
XTMAS	Xtmas s.	MARTYN	1661	36002007
XTMAS	Xtmas s.	BROWNRIG	1661	46003019
XTMAS	Xtmas s.	MARTYN	1661	46003019
XTMAS	Xtmas s.	FRANK	1672	19008004
XTMAS	Xtmas s.	FRANK	1672	19045003
XTMAS	Xtmas s.	FRANK	1672	23011010
XTMAS	Xtmas s.	MEDE	1672	45002013
XTMAS	Xtmas s.	FRANK	1672	46001016
XTMAS	Xtmas s.	FARINDON	1674	19072006
XTMAS	Xtmas s.	BYAM	1675	43001018
XTMAS	Xtmas s.	HACKET	1675	45002013
XTMAS	Xtmas s.	HACKET	1675	45011027
XTMAS	Xtmas s.	RALEIGH	1679	23053008
XTMAS	Xtmas s.	FRANK	1672	50008009
XTMAS	Xtmas s.	GIBBES	1677	63003013
XTMAS	Xtmas s.	LITTLETON	1680	23009006
XTMAS	Xtmas s.	LITTLETON	1680	46001014
XTMAS	Xtmas s.	BOYS	1687	46001016
XTMAS	Xtmas s.	STRADLING	1692	59002014
XTMAS	Xtmas s.	NEWCOME	1702	46001014
XTMAS	Xtmas s.	DORRINGTON	1703	46003016
XTMAS	Xtmas s.	GALE	1704	23007014
XTMAS	Xtmas s.	GALE	1704	46001014
XTMAS	Xtmas s.	PERKINS	1707	46001014
XTMAS	Xtmas s.	BROME	1709	46001014
XTMAS	Xtmas s.	ROBINSON	1707	48014006
XTMAS	Xtmas s.	HOPKINS	1710	45002013
XTMAS	Xtmas s.	HICKMAN	1713	46001014
XTMAS	Xtmas s.	HOLE	1715	46001014
XTMAS	Xtmas s.	BOYS	1716	46001014
XTMAS	Xtmas s.	MOORE	1716	46003016
XTMAS	Xtmas s.	HOLE	1717	46003016
XTMAS	Xtmas s.	SHERIDAN	1720	23009006
XTMAS	Xtmas s.	LESTLEY	1720	46001014
XTMAS	Xtmas s.	FIDDES	1720	46003016
XTMAS	Xtmas s.	BROWN	1722	46001014
XTMAS	Xtmas s.	BLACKALL	1723	23005011
XTMAS	Xtmas s.	NEWLIN	1720	57001015
XTMAS	Xtmas s.	SHARP	1729	61009026
XTMAS	Xtmas s.	READING	1730	23007014
XTMAS	Xtmas s.	BRADY	1730	23009006
XTMAS	Xtmas s.	READING	1730	23009006
XTMAS	Xtmas s.	TREBECK	1730	45001046
XTMAS	Xtmas s.	MARSHAL	1731	23005004
XTMAS	Xtmas s.	PEERS	1731	43005017
XTMAS	Xtmas s.	COLLIER	1732	46001014
XTMAS	Xtmas s.	ATTERBURY	1734	43011006
XTMAS	Xtmas s.	CLARKE	1735	23009006
XTMAS	Xtmas s.	TILLOTSON	1735	46001014

INDEXES TO THIRD VOLUME: E: KEYWORD-IN-CONTEXT INDEX OF OTHER SUBJECTS OR OCCASIONS

Keyword	In its Context	Author	Year	BkChpVrs
XTMAS	Xtmas s.	NEWTON	1736	23060001
XTMAS	Xtmas s.	NEWTON	1736	32005002
XTMAS	Xtmas s.	VENN	1740	23009006
XTMAS	Xtmas s.	PIERS	1743	23007014
XTMAS	Xtmas s.	CROWE	1744	43001018
XTMAS	Xtmas s.	WESTON	1747	43011030
XTMAS	Xtmas s.	WARREN	1748	23009006
XTMAS	Xtmas s.	WESTON	1747	46018037
XTMAS	Xtmas s.	CARRINGTON	1750	43001018
XTMAS	Xtmas s.	MAXWELL	1757	23061001
XTMAS	Xtmas s.	WHITE	1757	45002013
XTMAS	Xtmas s.	CONYBEARE	1757	45002014
XTMAS	Xtmas s.	HUSSEY	1755	65003008
XTMAS	Xtmas s.	SIMS	1772	46003016
XTMAS	Xtmas s.	HORNE	1778	46001014
XTMAS	Xtmas-day.	PIETY	1737	52002004
XTMAS	Xtmas-day.	TOULMIN	1770	54002016
XTNING	Xtning.	CORNWALLIS	1705	05004023
XTS	Eas. Xts. Y.	COCKBURN	1697	43011028
XTS	Eas. Xts. Y.	CLAGETT	1704	43011028
XTS	Eas. Xts. Y.	BEVERIDGE	1720	43011028
XTY	Abus.of Xty.	FISHER	1741	43010034
XTY	Adv.of Xty.	BURTON	1685	52003006
XTY	Adv.of Xty.	STERNE	1766	48001022
XTY	Bless.of Xty.	CARMICHAEL	1757	54001012
XTY	Def.of Xty.	SHARPE	1755	47002022
XTY	Des.& H. Xty	WILSON	1781	57004015
XTY	Duty of Xty.	HORT	1738	59002011
XTY	Duty of Xty.	KIMBER	1756	68000020
XTY	End of Xty.	BOURN	1755	49001030
XTY	Excell. Xty.	WHISTON	1709	53001023
XTY	Excell. Xty.	BARROW	1716	49002006
XTY	Fruits o. Xty.	HORBERRY	1774	43007006
XTY	Myst.of Xty.	STILLINGFLEET	1707	57001015
XTY	Off.ag. Xty.	ELSMERE	1767	43011006
XTY	Pers.in Xty.	BATTY	1739	49009024
XTY	Pract. Xty.	HOPKINS	1710	53002012
XTY	Script. Xty.	WESTLEY	1746	47004031
XTY	Spir.of Xty.	LECHMAN	1779	58001007
XTY	Tend.o. Xty.	GILBERT	1724	58001007
XTY	Tend.o. Xty.	HODGE	1758	46007018
XTY	Truth o. Xty.	FAWCETT	1749	46006068
XTY	Xty a Myst.	BENSON	1748	52006019
XTY	Xty pr. Hap.	BADDELLEY	1766	20003017
XTY	Xty true Lib.	NEWTON	1782	46008031
XTY	Xty.& Pagg.	PENN	1756	47004012
XTY	Xty. Com. L.	OUTRAM	1697	43005017
XTY	Xty. Com. L.	MUDGE	1739	43005017
XTY	Xty.b. Juda.	ROBOTHAM	1756	51003021
XTY	Xty.demons.	BELLAMY	1744	47026026
XTY	Xty.easy Y.	BRAGGE	1713	43011030
XTY	Xty.easy Y.	BEVERIDGE	1720	43011030
XTY	Xty.easy Y.	BARNES	1752	43011030
XTY	Xty.not sed.	SAURIN	1775	45023005
XTY	Xty.perf. L.	TILLOTSON	1735	43005017
XTY	Xty.perfect.	GROVE	1741	54002010

Keyword	In its Context	Author	Year	BkChpVrs
XTY	Xty.reason.	STEPHENS	1737	63003015
XTY	Xty.reasona.	WISE	1717	65005003
XTY	Zeal f. Xty.	THEED	1712	68000003
XTY	Zeal f. Xty.	TILLY	1729	68000003
XY	Ap. S.p.o. Xy	LANGHORNE	1773	49015019
XY	Belief.of Xy.	GOUGH	1751	65001004
XY	Des.& H. Xy.	WILSON	1781	57004001
XY	Design of Xy	ANONYMOUS	1739	48008006
XY	Design of Xy	HUNT	1748	48008005
XY	Enq.into Xy.	DUCHAL	1753	50004002
XY	Evid.of Xy.	DODDERIDGE	1736	64001016
XY	Evid.of Xy.	CAMPLIN	1777	50004007
XY	Fund.of Xy.	SKELTON	1754	61010038
XY	In.wit.o. Xy.	WATTS	1753	65005010
XY	Int.ex.o. Xy.	BULLOCK	1726	46008046
XY	Int.prf o. Xy.	BOYSE	1728	65005010
XY	Nat.of Xy.	SECKER	1770	62001027
XY	Pers.inc. Xy.	BRACKENRIDGE	1764	45009056
XY	Po.cor.o. Xy.	BARKER	1735	50011003
XY	Pos.pr.o. Xy.	KNOX	1768	63001015
XY	Pre. Xy.n.gr.	TILLOTSON	1735	65005003
XY	Princ.of Xy.	CENNICK	1762	61005012
XY	Proof.of Xy.	BATTY	1739	46001045
XY	Ra. Prof. Xy.	WILKINSON	1660	58002019
XY	Rew.of Xy.	MONRO	1693	53003014
XY	Simp.of Xy.	TAYLOR	1719	50011013
XY	St. P's de. Xy	NEWTON	1782	49013001
XY	Suf. T. S. Xy.	NALSON	1737	63002021
XY	Tend.of Xy.	SCOTT	1743	49001030
XY	Truth of Xy.	WAPLE	1729	65005007
XY	Truth of Xy.	JORTIN	1730	46005033
XY	Truth of Xy.	TILLOTSON.	1735	50004003
XY	Truth of Xy.	WHEATLAND	1739	47019020
XY	Truth of Xy.	BELLAMY	1744	47008001
XY	Xy.ca.rat. D.	ORR	1739	63003015
XY	Xy.demons.	BREKELL	1765	49002004
XY	Xy.fo.on Ar.	COOKSEY	1743	63003015
XY	Xy.ho. Prie.	BEVERIDGE	1720	63002005
XY	Xy.j.b. O. T.	BULLOCK	1726	61008007
XY	Xy.pr.fm. Pr.	SKELTON	1754	69019010
XY	Xy.rational.	QUINCY	1750	49010015
Y	Advice to Y.	SHOWER	1699	19119009
Y	Beg.& E.o. Y.	CLEMENT	1774	61009027
Y	Bless. Xt's. Y	PETERS	1776	43011028
Y	Caution to Y.	MUNTON	1756	21011009
Y	Caution to Y.	STEBBING	1759	21011009
Y	Conver. Y. P.	BURGESS	1690	21012001
Y	Del.d. Y& A.	BENSON	1725	21012001
Y	Dir.to Y.	NESBIT	1713	19119009
Y	Dir.to Y.	MAY	1744	19119009
Y	Duty of Y.	SECKER	1770	59002006
Y	Eas. Xt's. Y.	DODD	1757	43011028
Y	Eas. Xts. Y.	COCKBURN	1697	43011028
Y	Eas. Xts. Y.	CLAGETT	1704	43011028
Y	Eas. Xts. Y.	BEVERIDGE	1720	43011028
Y	Educ.of Y.	KIDDER	17--	52006004

Keyword	In its Context	Author	Year	BkChpVrs
Y	H. Y.sh.o. H.	WATTS	1753	44010021
Y	S. S. G.f. Y.	BERRIMAN	1763	19119008
Y	Tak. Xt's. Y.	MEDE	1672	43011028
Y	Tak. Xt's. Y.	COCKBURE	1697	43011028
Y	Tak. Xt's. Y.	BEVERIDGE	1720	43011029
Y	To Y. Pers.	GROSVENOR	1714	19018023
Y	To Y. Pers.	DAVIDSON	1772	21012001
Y	Va.of C.& Y.	WILLIAMS	1750	21011010
Y	Warn to Y.	ROSEWELL	1714	44010021
Y	Xt's.easy Y.	HOADLEY	1754	43011030
Y	Xt's.easy Y.	JORTIN	1774	43011030
Y	Xty.easy Y.	BRAGGE	1713	43011030
Y	Xty.easy Y.	BEVERIDGE	1720	43011030
Y	Xty.easy Y.	BARNES	1752	43011030
Y	Y. M's Mon.	H.	1673	21011009
Y	Y. Men.	WILCOX	1757	20023026
Y	Y. Men.	WILCOX	1757	61003013
Y	Y. Persons.	GREENE	1713	20023026
Y	Y.people.	ABERNETHY	1751	19034011
YEAR	M's Sab.year.	CLARKE	1760	03025003
YEAR	Year Audit.	ANONYMOUS	1735	19090009
YEAR	1 S.in Year.	COCKBURN	1706	19090012
YO	Duty of Yo.	BLAIR	1777	58002006
YOKE	Yoke of Xt.	WHARTON	1728	43011030
YORK	Tak. N.york.	OBERNE	1776	24013015
YOU	Adm.to You.	EDWARDS	1775	58002022
YOU	Adv.to You.	ENFIELD	1772	11020011
YOU	Pr.for You.	MAY	1753	13004010
YOU	Warn.t. You.	TOULMIN	1770	45015012
YOUNG	To Young P.	WOODWARD	1697	45015018
YOUNG	Young pers.	BOYSE	1728	44010021
YOUT	Yout.mon.	GUYSE	1747	18013026
YOUTH	Death Youth	TOULMIN	1770	45007012
YOUTH	To Youth.	STRYPE	1699	59002006
YOUTH	Van. Youth.	HICKMAN	1706	21011009
YOUTH	Virt. Youth.	EATON	1764	19119009
YOUTH	Youth f. G.	POWELL	1676	21012001
YOUTH	Youth. Sins.	JENNINGS	1743	18013026
YOUTH	Youth& A.	DUCHAL	1765	18032006
YOUTH	Youth Sins.	JENNINGS	1743	18011026
YOUTH'S	Youth's mo.	D'COETLOGAN.	1777	21012001
YR'S	N. Yr's. Gift.	DAVIES	1771	48013012
Z	Gen.&m. Z.	BULKLEY	1761	43016021
Z	Good&b. Z.	SEIGNIOR	1670	51004017
Z	Phineas Z.	CATCOTT	1753	19106030
Z	Xn. Z.b. L.j.	SYNGE	1716	51004018
ZACH'S	Zach's Prop.	VENN	1775	15005001
ZACHEUS'S	Zacheus's C.	SHEPHERD	1703	45019001
ZACHEUS'S	Zacheus's C.	BRAGGE	1706	45019002
ZAR	Wid.of Zar.	WEBB	1772	11017012
ZEAL	Excess. Zeal.	JORTIN	1774	21007016
ZEAL	Excess. Zeal.	ANONYMOUS	1776	21007016
ZEAL	Misg. Zeal.	WAKE	1722	48010002
ZEAL	Misg. Zeal.	WARREN	1739	48010002
ZEAL	Misg. Zeal.	HOADLY	1754	48010002
ZEAL	Party Zeal c.	RANDOLPH	1752	49003003
ZEAL	Rel. Zeal.	PUGH	1710	51004018
ZEAL	Relig. Zeal.	BIGGS	1774	68000003
ZEAL	Relig. Zeal.	BURNABY	1780	51004018
ZEAL	Tr. Xn. Zeal.	CLARKE	1734	69003015
ZEAL	True Zeal.	HOLE	1725	51004018
ZEAL	Xn. Zeal.	CRUSO	1699	51004006
ZEAL	Xn. Zeal.	SHERLOCK	1727	68000003
ZEAL	Xn. Zeal.	EVANS	1737	69003019
ZEAL	Xn. Zeal.	SCOTT	1739	68000003
ZEAL	Xn. Zeal.	CARMICHAEL	1757	51004018
ZEAL	Xn. Zeal.	BILSTONE	1761	51004017
ZEAL	Xn. Zeal.	WEBB	1765	51004018
ZEAL	Xn. Zeal.	ORTON	1773	53002021
ZEAL	Zeal ag. En.	STELLING	1755	51004018
ZEAL	Zeal civ.& R.	WEBSTER	1776	19137005
ZEAL	Zeal f. Ar. F.	OGDEN	1777	68000003
ZEAL	Zeal f. Ch.	PRIEST	1753	19122006
ZEAL	Zeal f. Faith.	REEVES	1729	68000003
ZEAL	Zeal f. G's H.	CLARKE	1727	16010039
ZEAL	Zeal f. Xty.	THFED	1712	68000003
ZEAL	Zeal f. Xty.	TILLY	1729	68000003
ZEAL	Zeal.	BRADY	1704	51004018
ZEAL	Zeal.	EDWARDS	1726	51004018
ZEAL	Zeal.	SMITH	1729	48010002
ZEAL	Zeal.	COOKE	1739	48010002
ZEAL	Zeal.	CARMICHAEL	1757	51004016
ZEAL	Zeal.	DELANY	1766	51004018
ZEAL	Zeal& Luk.	TAYLOR	1668	24048010
ZEB	Zeb.& Iss.bl.	ORTON	1776	05033018
ZION	Cit.of Zion.	BOSTON	1773	19015001
ZION'S	Zion's Pros.	HILL	1755	23062006
1	Au.1.b. R. S.	ANDERSON	1720	68000003
1	Aug.1.	BOLDE	1715	19136023
1	Aug.1.	ANONYMOUS	1726	27004017
1	Aug.1.	BENSON	1758	19044001
1	Aug.1.	LANGFORD	1759	04023023
1	Aug.1.	PRIOR	1750	69018004
1	Aug.1.	HODGE	1751	19078003
1	Aug.1.	PICKARD	1761	19147001
1	G.1 Ca.1. E.	TILLOTSON	1735	48011036
1	1 Art. Creed.	CARRINGTON	1750	46014026
1	1 Art. Creed.	CARRINGTON	1750	49008006
1	1 S. East.	STANHOPE	1714	46020019
1	1 S. East.	HOLE	1716	46020019
1	1 S. Easter.	READING	1728	04016007
1	1 S. Easter.	READING	1730	04022018
1	1 S. Epiph.	STANHOPE	1715	48012001
1	1 S. Epiph.	STANHOPE	1715	48013001
1	1 S. Epiph.	HOLE	1716	48012001
1	1 S. Epiph.	READING	1728	23044006
1	1 S. Epiph.	READING	1730	23046001
1	1 S. Lent.	FRANK	1672	50006002
1	1 S. Lent.	STANHOPE	1715	50006001
1	1 S. Lent.	HOLE	1716	50006001
1	1 S. Lent.	READING	1728	01019024
1	1 S. Lent.	READING	1730	01022011

INDEXES TO THIRD VOLUME: E: KEYWORD-IN-CONTEXT INDEX OF OTHER SUBJECTS OR OCCASIONS

Keyword	In its Context	Author	Year	BkChpVrs
1	1 S. Trin.	READING	1728	06010012
1	1 S. Trin.	READING	1730	06023011
1	1 S.af. East.	STANHOPE	1714	65005004
1	1 S.af. East.	HOLE	1716	65005004
1	1 S.af. Trin.	STANHOPE	1714	65004007
1	1 S.in Lent.	PATE	1708	48001016
1	1 S.in Year.	COCKBURN	1706	19090012
1	1 Sun. Trin.	STANHOPE	1714	45016019
1ST	Fall&1st S.	BOSTON	1773	01003006
1ST	1st pr.of R.	GERARD	1780	01003015
10	June 10.	KNAGGS	1716	46005014
10	10 Art. Creed	EDWARDS	1713	47010043
10	10 Art. Creed	CARRINGTON	1750	47010043
10	10 S. Trin.	STANHOPE	1714	45019041
10	10 S. Trin.	HOLE	1716	45019041
10	10 S. Trin.	STANHOPE	1714	49012001
10	10 S. Trin.	HOLE	1716	49012001
10	10 S. Trin.	READING	1728	11021028
10	10 S. Trin.	READING	1730	11022035
11	June 11.	ERSKINE	1710	52004003
11	11 Art. Creed	CARRINGTON	1750	49015023
11	11 Art Creed.	NEWCOME	1702	47024015
11	11 Art Creed.	EDWARDS	1713	47024015
11	11 S. Trin.	STANHOPE	1714	45018009
11	11 S. Trin.	STANHOPE	1714	49015001
11	11 S. Trin.	HOLE	1716	49015001
11	11 S. Trin.	READING	1730	12009001
11	11 S. Trin.	QUINCY	1750	45018013
12	June 12.	KNAGGS	1715	20013010
12	12 Article.	CARRINGTON	1750	43025046
12	12 S. Trin.	STANHOPE	1714	43022001
12	12 S. Trin.	STANHOPE	1714	44007031
12	12 S. Trin.	HOLE	1716	44007031
12	12 S. Trin.	STANHOPE	1714	50003004
12	12 S. Trin.	HOLE	1716	50003004
12	12 S. Trin.	READING	1728	12010031
12	12 S. Trin.	READING	1730	12018004
13	13 S. Trin.	STANHOPE	1714	45010023
13	13 S. Trin.	STANHOPE	1714	51003016
13	13 S. Trin.	READING	1728	12019037
13	13 S. Trin.	READING	1730	12023025
14	May 14.	WISHEART	1719	19133001
14	14 S. Trin.	STANHOPE	1714	45017011
14	14 S. Trin.	STANHOPE	1714	51005016
14	14 S. Trin.	HOLE	1716	51005016
14	14 S. Trin.	READING	1728	24005001
14	14 S. Trin.	READING	1730	24022003
15	15 S. Trin.	STANHOPE	1714	51006011
15	15 S. Trin.	HOLE	1716	51006011
15	15 S. Trin.	READING	1728	24035018
15	15 S. Trin.	READING	1730	24036032
15	15 Sun. Trin.	HOLE	1717	43006019
16	16 S. Trin.	STANHOPE	1714	45007011
16	16 S. Trin.	STANHOPE	1714	52003013
16	16 S. Trin.	HOLE	1716	52003013
16	16 S. Trin.	READING	1728	26002007

Keyword	In its Context	Author	Year	BkChpVrs
16	16 S. Trin.	READING	1730	26013004
17	17 S. Trin.	STANHOPE	1714	45014001
17	17 S. Trin.	STANHOPE	1713	52004001
17	17 S. Trin.	HOLE	1716	52004001
17	17 S. Trin.	READING	1728	26014007
17	17 S. Trin.	READING	1730	26018031
18	18 S. Trin.	STANHOPE	1714	43022034
18	18 S. Trin.	STANHOPE	1714	49001004
18	18 S. Trin.	HOLE	1716	49001004
18	18 S. Trin.	READING	1728	26020024
18	18 S. Trin.	READING	1730	26024024
187	Diss.187	WARD	1761	48001011
19	Aug.19.	STANLEY	1662	19014007
19	19 S. Trin.	STANHOPE	1714	43009001
19	19 S. Trin.	STANHOPE	1715	43008023
19	19 S. Trin.	HOLE	1716	52004018
19	19 S. Trin.	READING	1728	27003016
19	19 S. Trin.	READING	1730	27006010
2	Art.2 Creed.	EDWARDS	1713	46001014
2	July 2.	STERNE	1699	18036024
2	Wid.2 Mites.	WEBB	1772	45021001
2	Xt.2 Adam.	PENTYCROSS	1781	48005014
2	Xt's.2 p.f. D.	FLAVEL	1673	49011023
2	Xt's.2 Com.	WILSON	1781	69022012
2	2 Arg.f. C. P.	BROOKS	1665	43006006
2	2 Art. Creed.	HOLE	1715	47008037
2	2 Art. Creed.	CARRINGTON	1750	47008037
2	2 Nat.in Xt.	SALMON	1753	46001014
2	2 S. East.	STANHOPE	1714	46010011
2	2 S. East.	HOLE	1716	46010011
2	2 S. Easter.	H.	1686	26009005
2	2 S. Easter.	READING	1728	04023007
2	2 S. Easter.	READING	1730	04025010
2	2 S. Epiph.	STANHOPE	1715	46002001
2	2 S. Epiph.	HOLE	1716	46002001
2	2 S. Epiph.	STANHOPE	1715	48012006
2	2 S. Epiph.	HOLE	1716	48012006
2	2 S. Epiph.	READING	1728	23051012
2	2 S. Epiph.	READING	1730	23053001
2	2 S. Lent.	STANHOPE	1715	43015021
2	2 S. Lent.	STANHOPE	1715	55004001
2	2 S. Lent.	HOLE	1716	55004001
2	2 S. Lent.	READING	1728	01027011
2	2 S. Lent.	READING	1730	01034030
2	2 S. Trin.	STANHOPE	1714	45014016
2	2 S. Trin.	READING	1728	07004014
2	2 S. Trin.	READING	1730	07005001
2	2 S. X.mas.	READING	1730	23041001
2	2 S.af. East.	STANHOPE	1714	63002019
2	2 S.af. East.	HOLE	1716	63002019
2	2 S.af. Trin.	STANHOPE	1714	65003013
2	2 S.af. Trin.	HOLE	1716	65003013
2	2 S.un. S. D.	LEAKE	1773	49015033
2	2 Sacra.	SILVESTER	1675	20030006
2	2 Sacra.	LITTLETON	1680	65005008
2	2 Say.of Xt.	FLAVEL	1673	46019027

Keyword	In its Context	Author	Year	BkChpVrs
2D	Xt's.2d.com.	NEWMAN	1760	61009028
2D	Xt's.2d.com.	TOTTIE	1775	43024037
20	Oct.20.	BERWICK	1661	20014008
20	20 S. Trin.	STANHOPE	1714	52005015
20	20 S. Trin.	HOLE	1716	52005015
20	20 S. Trin.	READING	1730	32006009
21	April 21.	SCLATER	1681	19106016
21	June 21.	THOMPSON	1685	59003001
21	Nov.21.	DISNEY	1720	46015018
21	21 S. Trin.	STANHOPE	1714	46004046
21	21 S. Trin.	HOLE	1716	46004046
21	21 S. Trin.	STANHOPE	1714	52006010
21	21 S. Trin.	HOLE	1716	52006010
21	21 S. Trin.	READING	1728	34002004
22	22 S. Trin.	STANHOPE	1714	53001003
22	22 S. Trin.	HOLE	1716	53001003
22	22 S. Trin.	READING	1728	20002006
22	22 S. Trin.	READING	1728	29002012
22	22 S. Trin.	READING	1730	20001033
23	23 S. Trin.	STANHOPE	1714	53003017
23	23 S. Trin.	HOLE	1716	53003017
23	23 S. Trin.	READING	1728	20011011
23	23 S. Trin.	READING	1730	20012001
23	23 S. Trin.	READING	1730	20014013
24	May 24.	BARKSDALE	1660	10015025
24	24 S. Trin.	STANHOPE	1714	43009018
24	24 S. Trin.	STANHOPE	1714	43022015
24	24 S. Trin.	STANHOPE	1714	54001003
24	24 S. Trin.	HOLE	1716	54001003
24	24 S. Trin.	READING	1728	20013020
24	24 S. Trin.	READING	1728	20015001
24	24 S. Trin.	READING	1728	20017016
24	24 S. Trin.	READING	1730	20016021
25	25 S. Trin.	STANHOPE	1714	24023005
25	25 S. Trin.	STANHOPE	1714	46006005
25	25 S. Trin.	HOLE	1716	24023005
25	25 S. Trin.	HOLE	1716	46006005
26	26 S. Trin.	READING	1730	20019005
27	Sept.27.	PELLING	1685	63003003
29	M.29.	LLOYD	1692	19118023
29	M.29.	ASPLIN	1715	10019011
29	M.29.	SKERRET	1717	19118023
29	Op. M.29.	FAWCONER	1763	19150004
3	The 3 Heav.	STURMY	1716	50012002
3	3. S. Lent.	STANHOPE	1715	45011014
3	3. S. Lent.	HOLE	1716	45011014
3	3 Ev.last.t.	HILDROP	1711	43024021
3	3 Evil last T.	HILDROP	1711	44013019
3	3 S. Easter.	STANHOPE	1714	46016016
3	3 S. Easter.	HOLE	1716	46016016
3	3 S. Easter.	READING	1728	05004001
3	3 S. Easter.	READING	1730	05005002
3	3 S. Epiph.	STANHOPE	1715	48012016
3	3 S. Epiph.	HOLE	1716	48012016
3	3 S. Epiph.	READING	1728	23055003
3	3 S. Epiph.	READING	1730	23056010

Keyword	In its Context	Author	Year	BkChpVrs
3	3 S. Lent.	STANHOPE	1715	52005001
3	3 S. Lent.	HOLE	1716	52005001
3	3 S. Lent.	READING	1728	01039021
3	3 S. Lent.	READING	1730	01042021
3	3 S. Trin.	STANHOPE	1714	45015001
3	3 S. Trin.	READING	1728	09002020
3	3 S. Trin.	READING	1730	09003012
3	3 S.af. East.	STANHOPE	1714	63002011
3	3 S.af. East.	HOLE	1716	63002011
3	3 S.af. Trin.	STANHOPE	1714	63005005
3	3 S.af. Trin.	HOLE	1716	63005005
3D	3d Tit.of Xt.	FLAVEL	1673	22005016
30	O.30. J. Scot.	ANONYMOUS	1720	21003004
31	Dec.31.	STEPHENS	1707	46008032
4	4 Article.	CARRINGTON	1750	43027026
4	4 S. East.	STANHOPE	1714	62001017
4	4 S. East.	HOLE	1716	62001017
4	4 S. Easter.	STANHOPE	1714	46016005
4	4 S. Easter.	READING	1728	05006006
4	4 S. Easter.	READING	1730	05007012
4	4 S. Epiph.	LITTLETON	1680	46003016
4	4 S. Epiph.	READING	1730	23057015
4	4 S. Epiph.	READING	1730	23058003
4	4 S. Lent.	STANHOPE	1715	46006001
4	4 S. Lent.	HOLE	1716	46006001
4	4 S. Lent.	STANHOPE	1715	51004021
4	4 S. Lent.	HOLE	1716	51004021
4	4 S. Lent.	READING	1728	01043026
4	4 S. Lent.	READING	1730	01045005
4	4 S. Trin.	GIFFARD	1681	09012017
4	4 S. Trin.	STANHOPE	1714	45006036
4	4 S. Trin.	STANHOPE	1714	48008018
4	4 S. Trin.	HOLE	1716	48008018
4	4 S. Trin.	READING	1728	09012016
4	4 S. Trin.	READING	1730	09013013
4	4 S. Xt.on C.	FLAVEL	1673	43027046
5	N.5.	REYNOLDS	1678	19129001
5	N.5.	PERSE	1689	19129001
5	N.5.	DAWES	1733	19129001
5	N.5.	MEADOWCOURT	1746	19129001
5	N.5.& Th.s.	WRIGHT	1710	46015012
5	N.5.b.	VENN	1778	62003017
5	5 Art. Creed.	HOLE	1715	49015003
5	5 Art. Creed.	CARRINGTON	1750	49015003
5	5 S. Easter.	STANHOPE	1714	46016023
5	5 S. Easter.	HOLE	1716	46016023
5	5 S. Easter.	READING	1728	05008003
5	5 S. Easter.	READING	1730	05009006
5	5 S. Epiph.	HOLE	1716	54003012
5	5 S. Epiph.	READING	1730	23059001
5	5 S. Epiph.	READING	1730	23064001
5	5 S. Lent.	STANHOPE	1715	46008046
5	5 S. Lent.	HOLE	1716	46008046
5	5 S. Lent.	STANHOPE	1715	61009011
5	5 S. Lent.	HOLE	1716	61009011
5	5 S. Lent.	READING	1728	02003009

INDEXES TO THIRD VOLUME: E: KEYWORD-IN-CONTEXT INDEX OF OTHER SUBJECTS OR OCCASIONS

Keyword	In its Context	Author	Year	BkChpVrs
5	5 S. Lent.	READING	1730	02005001
5	5 S. Trin.	STANHOPE	1714	45005001
5	5 S. Trin.	STANHOPE	1714	63003008
5	5 S. Trin.	HOLE	1716	63003008
5	5 S. Trin.	READING	1728	09015022
5	5 S. Trin.	READING	1730	09017056
5	5 S.af. East.	STANHOPE	1714	62001022
5	5 S.af. East.	HOLE	1716	62001022
5	5 Say.of Xt.	FLAVEL	1673	46019028
5TH	Art.5th.	NEWCOME	1702	44016019
5TH	Art.5th.	EDWARDS	1713	44016019
5TH	Art.5th.	HOLE	1715	44016019
6	Art.6.	CARRINGTON	1750	63003022
6	6 S. Epiph.	STANHOPE	1715	43024023
6	6 S. Epiph.	HOLE	1716	43024023
6	6 S. Epiph.	READING	1730	23065001
6	6 S. Epiph.	READING	1730	23066001
6	6 S. Lent.	READING	1728	02009016
6	6 S. Lent.	READING	1730	02010001
6	6 S. Trin.	STANHOPE	1714	48006003
6	6 S. Trin.	READING	1730	10019001
6	6 Say.of Xt.	FLAVEL	1673	46019030
7	Me.7 Com.	HORNECK	1706	43005027
7	Me.7 Com.	BLACKALL	1723	43005027
7	Me.7 Com.	BLAIR	1740	43005027
7	On Num.7.	CLARKE	1759	01002002
7	7. S. Trin.	READING	1730	10024010
7	7 Archang.	MEDE	1672	37004010
7	7 S. Trin.	STANHOPE	1714	44008001
7	7 S. Trin.	HOLE	1716	44008001
7	7 S. Trin.	STANHOPE	1714	48006019
7	7 S. Trin.	HOLE	1716	48006019
7	7 S. Trin.	READING	1728	10021001
70	Dan.70 W.	MARKWICK	1728	27009024
70	Dan.70 W.	BLAYNEY	1775	27009020
70	70 Weeks.	WOODROFFE	1702	27009024
70	70 Weeks.	WINTER	1777	27009024
8	Aug.8.	SMITH	1714	14009008
8	8 Art. Creed.	EDWARDS	1713	48008009
8	8 S. Trin.	STANHOPE	1714	48008012
8	8 S. Trin.	HOLE	1716	48008012
8	8 S. Trin.	READING	1728	11013001
8	8 S. Trin.	READING	1730	11017024
9	9 Art. Creed.	CARRINGTON	1750	43016018
9	9 S. Trin.	STANHOPE	1714	45016001
9	9 S. Trin.	STANHOPE	1714	49010001
9	9 S. Trin.	HOLE	1716	49010001
9	9 S. Trin.	READING	1728	11018017
9	9 S. Trin.	READING	1730	11019010

(INDEXES TO FIFTH VOLUME)

INDEX A: SOME NOTABLE SERIES OF LECTURES

Notes:

(1) Relation between this index and Index A to Third Volume. Their contents: The following Index A to the Fifth Volume supplements Index A to the Third Volume. Both indexes relate to sermons printed after delivery in one of the lecture series that were prominent within Cooke's period. Index A to the Third Volume notes every sermon that Cooke in his first volume and hence we in our Third Volume have recorded as belonging to such a series. It does not, however, make note of various editions in which the sermons were published. The present Index A to the Fifth Volume makes such note so far as relevant publications are listed in Cooke's second volume and hence in our Fifth Volume, where each edition that is listed in Cooke's second volume is recorded under the year of printing that Cooke has given for it. Thus in effect the present index affords for each series a chronological conspectus of publications containing sermons in the series but not of the sermons in these publications; and the other index affords a conspectus of the sermons (and their biblical texts) but not of the publications in which they appeared.

In using the present index, however, a reader should not assume that its chronological conspectus will in respect to every lecture series include every publication; for although Cooke often listed alternative editions where he thought it useful to do so, he worked under constraints of space in his second volume and of time in his research for it. In his first volume, on the other hand, Cooke attempted to list every sermon printed within his period and to note in his record of it any sermon that belonged to a prominent lecture series. He had excellent success in regard to the most eminent series; some success in regard to sermons in less eminent series.

Cooke of course considered any lecture to be outside the scope of his lists if it was not printed after its oral delivery, as also any lecture that did not develop or apply some biblical text stated as theme at its beginning. For the first of these reasons he omitted from his lists certain lectures that were delivered, under auspices of the Royal Society, in the Boyle series; for the second reason he omitted others of that series. Some of the lecture series (including the Boyle) are described in the introductory pages of the present volume. All of the series named below were established by private endowment or were financially supported by lay groups.

(2) Special symbols: Dates and formats of publications are indicated by obvious means. The underlining of an author's name means that John Cooke italicized the name to indicate that the author was Nonconformist rather than Anglican. The abbreviation "ss." stands for "single sermon", and "coll." indicates that a publication was probably a collection of sermons or of materials including a sermon (e.g., a biography containing a sermon by or a funeral sermon about its subject figure.)

INDEXES TO FIFTH VOLUME: A: SERIES OF LECTURES

Bampton's Lecture <"Bamp.L.">

1780
BANDINELL James 8° coll.

1781
NEVE Timothy 8° coll.

1782
HOLMES Robert. MA. 8° coll.

Berry - Street Sermons : See the heading in Index B

Bishop Warburton's Lecture : See Warburton's Lecture

Boyle's Lecture <"B.L.">

BURNETT Tho. DD. -° coll. BUTLER Joseph -° coll. CLARKE John -° coll.
IBBOT Benj. DD. -° coll. WILLIAMS John -° coll. WOODWARD Josiah -° coll.
<Most Boyle Lectures recorded at end of our Fifth Volume under "Publications of Year ----" were published in the 1739 collective edition, edited by Sampson Letsome, which was so well known in Cooke's day that, in cataloguing an author's contributions to it, Cooke's sources of information for his second volume apparently often omitted date of its publication.>

1692
BENTLEY Richard 4° coll.

1700
BRADFORD Samuel 4° coll.

1701
ANONYMOUS 4° coll. STANHOPE George 4° coll.

1702
STANHOPE George 4° coll.

1703
GASTRELL Francis 8° coll.

1708
BLACKALL Offspring 8° coll. TURNER John 8° coll. WHISTON Will. M.A. 8° coll.
WILLIAMS John 8° coll.

1709
BUTLER Lilly 8° coll.

1717
LENG John 8° coll.

1721,1722
GURDON Brampton 8° coll.

<1727>
<DERHAM Will. 8° coll> <"Physico-Theology": Although neither Cooke nor his predecessor Letsome notes this work as Derham's Boyle Lectures, both record it, citing Derham's biblical text incorrectly as Psalms iii. 2 instead of Psalms 111. 2.>

1733
BERRIMAN William 8° coll. BERRIMAN William 8° coll.

1739
ANONYMOUS fo. coll. BENTLEY Richard fo. coll. BERRIMAN William fo coll.
BRADFORD Samuel fo. coll. BUTLER Lilly fo. coll. GASTRELL Francis fo. coll.
GURDON Brampton fo. coll. HANCOCK John fo. coll. HARRIS John fo. coll.
LENG John fo. coll. STANHOPE George fo. coll. TURNER John fo. coll.
WHISTON Will. M.A. fo. coll. WILLIAMS John fo. coll.

(List of the printed Boyle lectures is continued on following page.)

1742
BISCOE Rich 8° coll.
1743
TWELLS Leonard 8° coll.
1763
HEATHCOTE Ralph 4° 2s.
1769
WORTHINGTON William 8° coll.
1773
OWEN Hen. DD. 8° coll.

Busby's Lecture < Also see Joseph Parsons, "30 Lect. in 8° 1761. On the Principles of the Christian Religion According To Dr. Busby's Plan" >
1775
BENNETT Thomas 8° coll.

Butcher's Lecture <"Butch.L.">
1729
HENLEY John 8° ss.

Coward's Lecture : <"Cow.L."> See the heading in Index B

Eastcheap Lectures <"East.C.L."> (Or "Weigh House Lectures": See comment after that heading in present index.)
1724
ANONYMOUS 12° coll. <For contents see note attached to the entry in our Fifth Volume>

Fairchild's Lecture <"Fairch.L.">
1730
DENNE John 4° ss.
1733
DENNE John 4° ss.
1745
DENNE John 8° ss.
1760
STUKELEY William 4° 3s.
1763
STUKELEY William 4° 3s.

Hutchin's Lecture <"H.L." or "Hutch.">
1729
MANGEY Thomas 8° ss.
1731
WATSON Joseph 8° ss.
1732
STEBBING Henry 8° ss.
1745
NEWTON Thomas 8° 2s. <A booklet of 2s., of which apparently only 1s. was a Hutchin's Lecture.>
1752
SHUCKFORD Samuel 8° ss.
1755
RIDLEY Glocester 4° ss.
1760
STEBBING Hen. DD.jun. 4° ss.
1763
BUTLER John 4° ss.

INDEXES TO FIFTH VOLUME: A: SERIES OF LECTURES

Lady Moyer's Lecture : See Moyer's Lecture

Lime Street Lectures : <"L.S.s."> See the heading in Index B to Fifth Volume.

Merchant's Lecture <"Merch.L."> (Also see Pinners Hall, Lectures at)

Year	Author	Format	Author	Format	Author	Format
1701	MATHER Nathaniel	8° coll.				
1777	WINTER Richard	8° coll.				

Moyer's Lecture <"M.L.">

Year	Author	Format	Author	Format	Author	Format
1720	WATERLAND Daniel	8° coll.				
1721	KNIGHT James	8° coll.				
1725	BERRIMAN William	8° coll.				
1726	BISHOP Thomas	8° coll.				
1729	TRAPP Joseph	8° coll.				
1731	TRAPP Joseph	8° coll.				
1732	BROWNE John	8° coll.	FELTON Henry	8° coll.		
1738	WHEATLY Charles	8° coll.				
1741	BEDFORD Arthur	8° coll.	BERRIMAN John	8° coll.	BERRIMAN William	8° ss.
1742	RIDLEY Glocester	8° coll.				
1743	SEED Jeremiah	8° coll.	TWELLS Leonard	8° coll.		
1765	DAWSON Benj. LL.D.	8° coll.				
1774	MORELL Thomas	4° ss.				

Pinners <or Pinmakers> Hall, Lectures at (Also see Merchant's Lecture.)

Year	Author	Format
1701	MATHER Nathaniel	8° coll.
1704	ROW Benjamin	8° ss.
1741	RAWLIN Richard	8° coll.
1777	WINTER Richard	8° coll.

Warburton's Lecture <"Bp.W.L.">

1776

HALLIFAX Samuel 8° coll. HURD Richard 8° coll.

1780

BAGOTT Lewis 8° coll.

Weigh House Lectures: Cooke does not give the name "Weigh House" to any lectures, but the lectures so entitled by some later bibliographers were delivered in Little Eastcheap and include, or are included among, those in the two-volume publication that Cooke names "Eastcheap Lectures," q.v. above in the present index.

(INDEXES TO FIFTH VOLUME)

INDEX B: SOME COLLECTIONS OF SERMONS BY ANONYMOUS OR SEVERAL AUTHORS

Notes:

(1) Relation between this index and Index B to the Third Volume: The following Index B to the Fifth Volume supplements Index B to the Third Volume, which also relates to collective editions each containing sermons by more than one author. The relation between the two indexes regarding collective editions of several authorship is analogous to the relation between the two indexes regarding lecture series that is described in note (1) on the title page of the index immediately preceding this one. It should be noted, however, that Cooke did not usually record a sermon as published in an edition of several authorship if he had already found it in a better or more convenient edition; and therefore many sermons within certain of these editions go unmarked as such in Cooke's first volume and hence in our Third Volume -- *e.g.*, the sermons published in "The Protestant System," as is explained below that heading in the present index.

(2) Special symbols: Dates and formats of publications are indicated by obvious means. The underlining of an author's name means that John Cooke italicized the name to indicate that the author was Nonconformist rather than Anglican.

(3) Alternative forms of issue [or of preservation]: "coll.", "ss.", fascicle: As stated in parenthetic comments after certain headings below, some sermons published in some collective editions of several authorship were apparently issued [or at least preserved] not only in collected sets but also in the form of single sermons or of fascicles containing the sermons of single authors, these often being printed in the same year and perhaps from the same type-settings as the sermons within the more inclusive volumes. [Or in some cases librarians or other collectors may have retained or catalogued only those portions of a large unbound volume that were relevant to their special concerns.] Where the record in our Fifth Volume suggests an alternative form of issue [or preservation] of a sermon published in a collective edition, this fact has been indicated in the present Index B by entry of "ss." or (*e.g.*) "4s." in place of "coll." within the relevant item.

INDEXES TO FIFTH VOLUME: B: COLLECTIONS OF SEVERAL AUTHORSHIP

Bellamy's Family Preacher	<Cooke's records indicate a 1-vol. collective ed. 1754 and a 2-vol. ed. 1776 of sermons, some of which apparently were, or had been, issued also as ss.>							
1754	BELLAMY Daniel	8°	coll.	BRAY Thomas	8° ss.	HALES Stephen		8° coll.
	WEBSTER William	8°	coll.	WEBSTER William	8° coll.			
1756	WEBSTER William	8°	ss.					
1776	BELLAMY Daniel	4°	coll	CARRINGTON James, jun.	4° coll.	CARRINGTON James, sen.		4° coll.
Berrystreet (or Bury Street) Sermons	<Records in Cooke's first volume indicate ss. issues apart from and in addition to the inclusive publication.>							
1757	ANONYMOUS	8°	coll.	GUYSE John	8° 7 ss.	JENNINGS Dav.		8° 7 ss.
	HUBBARD John	8°	9 ss.	NEALE Daniel	8° 7 ss.	PRICE Samuel		8° 8 ss.
Collection of Farewell Sermons	<For bibliographical discussion, see introductory pages of the present volume.>							
1662	CALAMY Edmund	4°	ss.	LYE Thomas	4° ss.			
	MEAD Matthew	4°	ss.	WATSON Thomas	4° ss.			
1663	ANONYM.	4°	coll.	ANONYMOUS	4° coll.	BATES Will.	2s.	4° coll.
	BULL	4°	coll.	CALAMY Benjamin	4° coll.	CALAMY Edmund		4° coll.
	COLLINS	4°	coll.	COOPER Will.	2s. 4° coll.	CRODACOTT John		4° ss.
	EVANKE George	4°	coll.	GASPINE John	4° coll.	GREW Obadiah		4° coll.
	HORTON Thomas	4°	ss.	JACOMB	2s. 4° coll.	JENKINS Will.	2t., 2s.	4° coll.
	LAMB P.	4°	coll.	LYE Thomas	4° coll.	MANTON Thomas		4° coll.
	N. - - - - G.	4°	coll.	NEWCOMEN Matthew	4° coll.	PLEDGER		4° coll.
	SCLATER	4°	coll.	SEAMAN	4° coll.	THORN George		4° coll.
	VENNING Ralph	4°	coll.	WADSWORTH	4° coll.	WATSON Tho.	3t., 3s.	4° coll.
Conjugal Duty, Discourses on	<Coll. ed. published in 4 parts 1732, 1736, 1740 republishing sermons earlier available in other eds.: Wilkinson's as early as 1607, Latimer's perhaps even earlier.>							
16--	SECKER Will.	12°	ss.					
1607	WILKINSON Robert	4°	ss.					
1641	MASTER Thomas	-°	ss.					
1681	GRANTHAM Tho. M.A.	4°	ss.					
1682	WILKINSON Robert	4°	ss.					
1698	ANONYMOUS	4°	ss.					
1699	SPRINT John	8°	ss.					
17--	HACKET Roger	12°	ss.	TAYLOR Thomas	12° ss.	WHATLEY William		12° ss.
1706	CORNWALLIS Henry	12°	ss.					
1708	MOXON Mordecai	12°	ss.					
1709	GRANTHAM Tho. M.A.	8°	ss.					

1710

MASTER Thomas	-°	ss.						

1732

COLBY John	12°	ss.	CORNWALLIS Henry	12°	coll.	CROMPTON William	12°	ss.
LATIMER Bp.	12°	ss.	MEAD Matthew	12°	ss.	PARSONS Bartholomew	12°	ss.

1735

FORD John	8°	2s.						

1740

ANONYMOUS	12°	coll.	ANONYMOUS	12°	ss.	BRADSHAW William	12°	ss.
FORD John	12°	coll.	GATAKER Thomas	12°	ss.	GRANTHAM Tho. M.A.	12°	coll.
HACKET Roger	12°	ss.	HARDY Nathaniel	12°	ss.	KING John	12°	ss.
MASTER Thomas	12°	coll.	MEAD Matthew	8°	coll.	MEGGOT Richard	12°	ss.
PARSONS Bartholomew	12°	ss.	SECKER Will.	12°	ss.	SNAWSEL Robert	12°	ss.
TAYLOR Thomas	12°	ss.	WILKINSON Robert	12°	coll.			

Coward's Lecture <Hubbard, John, ed., "Christ's Loveliness and Glory ... at Coward's Lecture." London, 1729.>

1729

ANONYMOUS	8°	coll.	GODWIN Edward	8°	coll.

Discourses against Popery <Apparently issued both in pamphlet ("ss.") form and in an inclusive volume>

1735

ANONYMOUS	-°	coll.	BARKER John	8°	ss.	BAYES Joshua	8°	ss.
BURROUGHS Joseph	8°	ss.	CHANDLER Samuel	8°	ss.	EARL Jabez	8°	ss.
GROSVENOR Benjamin	8°	ss.	HARRIS William	8°	ss.	HARRIS William	8°	ss.
HUGHES Obadiah	8°	ss.	HUNT Jerem.	8°	ss.			
LEAVESLY Thomas	8°	ss.	LOWMAN Moses	8°	ss.	NEALE Daniel	8°	ss.
NEWMAN John	8°	ss.	SMYTH George	8°	ss.	WRIGHT Samuel	8°	ss.

Enfield's English Preacher <"Sermons ... selected, revised, and abridged from Various Authors." 9 vv. London 1773-74>
(For comment, see note below heading "Protestant System" in present Index B.)

LEECHMAN William	-°	coll.	MACKEWEN Robert	-°	coll.

17--

RADCLIFFE E.	8°	ss.	TAYLOR Philip	8°	ss.

1734

MACKEWEN Robert	8°	ss.

1743

LEECHMAN William	8°	ss.

1765

OWEN E.	8°	ss.

Farewell Sermons, Collection of : See Collection of Farewell Sermons

House of Mourning <Featly, Daniel, et al. "Θρηνοικος [Threnoikos]. The House of Mourning.">

1660

ANONYMOUS	fo.	coll.

Limestreet Sermons <Apparently issued both in an inclusive volume and in fascicle or pamphlet ("ss.") form>

1731

HURRION John	8°	4s.

1732

ANONYMOUS	8°	coll.	BRADBURY Thomas	8°	3s.	BRAGGE Robert	8°	ss.&4s.
GILL John	8°	ss.	GOODWIN Peter	8°	ss.	HALL Thomas	8°	2s.
HURRION John	8°	ss.	SLADEN John	8°	ss.	TAYLOR Abraham	8°	ss.
TAYLOR Abraham	8°	ss.	TAYLOR Abraham	8°	ss.	TAYLOR Abraham	8°	ss.
WILSON Samuel	8°	2s.						

INDEXES TO FIFTH VOLUME: B: COLLECTIONS OF SEVERAL AUTHORSHIP

Mercurius Theologicus, containing Mr. Harris's 8 S. & Dr. Blackall's 8 S. at Boyle's Lecture

1701
ANONYMOUS 4° coll.

Morning Exercise — Seven titles of collective editions of Morning Exercises are listed below in a logical, but not alphabetical, order. In Cooke's first volume there occur abbreviations of two further titles. One of these is simply "Morning Exercise"; the other is "Continuation of Morning Exercise at Cripplegate." They do not appear below because they do not occur in Cooke's second volume, upon which our Fifth Volume depends for information about collective editions. Possible causes and bibliographical significances of this and other differences between Cooke's first and second volumes in their records concerning the various Morning Exercises are stated in the introduction to the present volume of indexes.

Morning Exercise at Cripplegate <"m.e.C."> (Note: See parenthsis following "Morning Exercise at Cripplegate, Supplement to.")

1661
TILLOTSON John 4° coll.
WILKINSON Henry 4° coll.

1667
ANNESLEY Samuel 4° coll.
WHITAKER William 4° coll.

1675
VINCENT Nathaniel 4° coll.

1676
GIBBON 4° coll.

1677
BRUMHALL 4° coll.
DOOLITTLE Thomas 4° coll.
GREENHILL William 4° coll.
KITCHIN John 4° coll.
MALLERY Thomas 4° coll.
NEEDLER Benjamin 4° coll.
POOL Matthew 4° coll.
TILLOTSON John 4° coll.
WILKINSON Henry 4° coll.
CLARKSON David 4° coll.
DRAKE Roger 4° coll.
HILL 4° coll.
LEE Samuel 4° coll.
MANTON Thomas 4° coll.
NEST 4° coll.
SHEFFIELD John 4° coll.
WATSON Thomas 4° coll.
COOPER William 4° coll.
GOUGE Thomas 4° coll.
HURST Henry 4° coll.
LYE Thomas 4° coll.
NEAST Thomas 4° coll.
PLEDGER Elias 4° coll.
SIMMONS John 4° coll.
WHITE 4° coll.

Morning Exercise at Cripplegate, Supplement to <"s.m.e.C."> (The critical apparatus in our Fifth Volume discloses that five of the items recorded in Cooke II as "s.m.e.C." were recorded in Cooke I as "s.m.e." and another four as "m.e.C." Relevant items in the set here below have been marked, respectively, with "sme" or "meC.")

1673
WEST Edward 4° coll. <Cooke II date "1673" for WEST "s.m.e.C." probably a misprint of "1676">

1674
ANNESLEY Samuel 4° coll.
CASE Thomas "meC" 4° coll.
ANNESLEY Samuel 4° coll.

1676
ADAMS Richard 4° coll.
COLE Thomas 4° coll.
JANEWAY James "sme" 4° coll.
LYE Thomas "meC" 4° coll.
POOL Matthew "meC" 4° coll.
VEAL Edward 4° coll.
BARKER Matthew 4° coll.
GALE Theophilus 4° coll.
JENKINS William "sme" 4° coll.
MANTON Thomas 4° coll.
STEEL Richard 4° coll.
WATSON Thomas "meC" 4° coll.
BAXTER Richard 4° coll.
JACOMB Thomas "sme" 4° coll.
LEE Samuel "sme" 4° coll.
MILWARD John 4° coll.
SYLVESTER Matthew 4° coll.
WILKINSON Henry "sme" 4° coll.

Morning Exercise, Supplement to <"s.m.e."> (Note: See parenthesis following "Morning Exercise at Cripplegate, Supplement to.")

Year	Author		Format	Author		Format	Author		Format
1674									
	FOWLER Edward		4° coll.	SEIGNOR George		4° coll.			
1676									
	DOOLITTLE Thomas		4° coll.	HOOK		4° coll.	OWEN John		4° coll.
	VINCENT Thomas		4° coll.	WADSWORTH Thomas		4° coll.	WELLS Edward		4° coll.

Morning Exercise, Casuistical <"C.m.e."> (Note: The critical apparatus in our Fifth Volume discloses that most of the items recorded in Cooke II as "C.m.e" are recorded in Cooke I as "c.m.e." All relevant items in the set below have been marked with "cme.")

Year	Author		Format	Author		Format	Author		Format
1673									
	CRAIL	"cme"	4° coll.						
1683									
	BARKER John	"cme"	4° coll.	COLE Thomas	"cme"	4° coll.	HOW John	"cme"	4° coll.
	HURST Henry	"cme"	4° coll.	JACOMB Thomas	"cme"	4° coll.	JENKINS William	"cme"	4° coll.
	LOBB Stephen	"cme"	4° coll.	LYE Thomas	"cme"	4° coll.	MAYO Richard	"cme"	4° coll.
	MILWARD John	"cme"	4° coll.	OAKEY		4° coll.	SINGLETON	"cme"	4° coll.
	SLATER Samuel		4° coll.	STEEL Richard	"cme"	4° coll.			
1690									
	ANNESLEY Samuel		4° coll.	BARKER Matthew		4° coll.	COLE Thomas	"cme"	4° coll.
	HAMMOND George	"cme"	4° coll.	HURST Henry	"cme"	4° coll.	MAYO Richard	"cme"	4° coll.
	SLATER Samuel	"cme"	4° coll.	STEEL Richard	"cme"	4° coll.			

Morning Exercise, Continuation of <"c.m.e."> (Note: See parenthesis following "Morning Exercise, Casuistical.")

Year	Author	Format	Author	Format	Author	Format
1683						
	ADAMS Richard	4° coll.	ALSOP Nathaniel	4° coll.	ANNESLEY Samuel	4° coll.
	ANNESLEY Samuel	4° coll.	ANONYMOUS	4° coll.	ANONYMOUS	4° coll.
	ANONYMOUS	4° coll.	ANONYMOUS	4° coll.	BAXTER Richard	4° coll.
	DOOLITTLE Thomas	4° coll.	OWEN John	4° coll.	VINCENT Nathaniel	4° coll.
	VINK Peter	4° coll.	WOODCOCK Francis	4° coll.		
1690						
	ADAMS Richard	4° coll.	ALSOP Nathaniel	4° coll.	BURGESS Daniel	4° coll.
	SYLVESTER Matthew	4° coll.	VEAL Edward	4° coll.	VINCENT Nathaniel	4° coll.
	WILLIAMS Daniel	4° coll.	WOODCOCK Francis	4° coll.		

Morning Exercise against Popery <"m.e.P."> (Cooke I and Cooke II both record as "m.e.P." all the items below.)

Year	Author	Format	Author	Format	Author	Format
1675						
	ANNESLEY Samuel	4° coll.	BAXTER Richard	4° coll.	CLARKSON David	4° coll.
	DOOLITTLE Thomas	4° coll.	FAIRCLOUGH Samuel	4° coll.	FOWLER Christopher	4° coll.
	HURST Henry	4° coll.	JENKINS William	4° coll.	LAWRENCE George	4° coll.
	LEE Samuel	4° coll.	LYE Thomas	4° coll.	MANTON Thomas	4° coll.
	MAYO Richard	4° coll.	NEEDLER Benjamin	4° coll.	OWEN John	4° coll.
	POOL Matthew	4° coll.	STEEL Richard	4° coll.	SYLVESTER Matthew	4° coll.
	VEAL Edward	4° coll.	VINCENT Thomas	4° coll.	VINK Peter	4° coll.
	WADSWORTH Thomas	4° coll.	WEST Edward	4° coll.	WILKINSON Henry	4° coll.

INDEXES TO FIFTH VOLUME: B: COLLECTIONS OF SEVERAL AUTHORSHIP

Morning Exercise at St. Giles <"m.e.G."> (Cooke I agrees with Cooke II in recording as "m.e.G." all items below.)
1676

ADAMS Richard	4° coll.	ANNESLEY Samuel	4° coll.	CALAMY Edmund	4° coll.
CASE Thomas	4° coll.	COOPER William	4° coll.	CRAFTON	4° coll.
DRAKE Roger	4° coll.	GIBBON	4° coll.	HOW John	4° coll.
JACOMB Samuel	4° coll.	JACOMB Samuel	4° coll.	JACOMB Thomas	4° coll.
LYE Thomas	4° coll.	MANTON Thomas	4° coll.	MERITON John	4° coll.
NEEDLER Benjamin	4° coll.	PARSON Thomas	4° coll.	POOL Matthew	4° coll.
SHEFFIELD John	4° coll.	TAYLOR Thomas	4° coll.	VINK Peter	4° coll.
WATKINS	4° coll.	WATSON Thomas	4° coll.	WELLS Edward	4° coll.
WHITAKER William	4° coll.	WHITE	4° coll.	WOODCOCK Francis	4° coll.

Popery, against: For "Sermons against Popery," see "Discourses against Popery."
For "Morning Exercises against Popery," see the heading under "Morning Exercises."

Protestant System <"The Protestant System: containing Discourses on the Principal Doctrines of Natural and Revealed Religion." 2 vols., London, 1758>

Note regarding "The Protestant System," The English Preacher," and "The Scotch Preacher":

In the 2-vol. "Protestant System" (London, 1758) and in Enfield's later 9-vol. "English Preacher" (London, 1773-74) Cooke apparently found few sermons that he had not already recorded as published in editions better than these because less abbreviated or more exact in text or more convenient for his readers to obtain -- e.g., in collective editions of the individual authors' works. Indeed, although in his list of authors' publications (his second volume) Cooke makes some references to these two collections, in his list of sermons per se he makes no reference whatever to one of them: Enfield's "The English Preacher." Hence the title does not appear in Index B to our Third Volume but only (supra) in the present Index B to our Fifth Volume.

In contrast to the small number of listings that Cooke obtained from the two London collections stands the much larger number that he obtained from a collection published in Edinburgh: "The Scotch Preacher" (q.v. below in the present index). The first volume of this collection was printed one year after the last volume of Enfield's "The English Preacher," and the choice of titles suggests that the two collections were intended to complement each other in some way. It is worthy of note that in logical union the areas denoted by these two titles comprise the characteristics of pulpit utterance within the universe of discourse denoted by the title of the earlier collection "The Protestant System" -- or at least would so so for most writers and readers of the English language in Cooke's day.

A coherence of editorial purpose for all three collections is indicated, though slightly, by the fact that Cooke records one sermon as published in them all. This he records as by William Leechman (in Cooke I also "Leachman" and "Lechman"), "Principal of the University in Glascow," (sic.) and as printed first in a single-sermon edition at "Glascow." Cooke records a sermon by a different author as published in two of the collections: in both "The Protestant System" and "The English Preacher." He lists it as by William Robertson, "Principal of the University in Edinburgh," as delivered to the Society for the Propagation of Christian Knowledge, and as first printed (presumably in London) in a single-sermon edition of 1755. Robertson is shown as Anglican in Cooke's second volume, as Nonconformist in his first. Perhaps the record showing Robertson as Anglican was affected by scribal or printing error, or perhaps Robertson moved from the Presbyterian fold into the Anglican. Leechman is shown as Nonconformist in both of Cooke's volumes.

Almost all authors to whom Cooke attributes publication in "The Scotch Preacher" he shows as Nonconformist; we should expect this. The few authors to whom he attributes publication in "The English Preacher" or "The Protestant System" he likewise shows mostly as Nonconformist. This may or may not be because he has found the sermons of Anglican preachers in preferable editions editions and has recorded them so.

All records in our Fifth Volume that contain some reference to "The Protestant System" are noted below.

LEECHMAN William -° coll.
17--
BARKER John 8° coll.
1743
LEECHMAN William 8° ss.
1754
FORDYCE James 8° ss.
1755
ROBERTSON Will. DD. 8° ss.
177-
GRIGG 8° ss.
1775
ROBERTSON Will. DD. 12° ss.

Scotch Preacher <"The Scotch Preacher: or, A Collection of Sermons. By Some of the Most Eminent Clergymen of the Church of Scotland." 4 vols., Edinburgh, 1775-1789.>
(Apparently many sermons in the three volumes of 1775, 76, 79, were published also or earlier as ss.)

1743
LEECHMAN William 8° ss.
1746
WISHART George 8° ss.
1750
BLAIR Hugh 8° ss.
1755
ROBERTSON Will. DD. 8° ss.
1758
LEECHMAN William 12° ss.
1760
CUMING Patrick 8° ss.
1762
DICK Robert 8° ss.
1765
ERSKINE John 8° ss.
1768
LEECHMAN William 12° ss.
1775
ANONYMOUS 12° coll. ERSKINE John 12° ss. FORDYCE James 12° coll.
LEECHMAN William 12° coll. ROBERTSON Will. DD. 12° ss. WISHART George 12° coll.
1776
ANONYMOUS 12° coll. DICK Robert 8° ss. GERARD Alex. DD. 12° coll.
LEECHMAN William 12° coll. LOTHIAN William 12° ss. LOTHIAN William 12° ss.
MUTTER Thomas 12° ss. SCOTLAND John 12° ss. SOMERVILLE Thomas 12° ss.
WEBSTER Alexander 12° ss.

INDEXES TO FIFTH VOLUME: B: COLLECTIONS OF SEVERAL AUTHORSHIP

1779

ANONYMOUS	12°	coll.	BONAR John	12°	coll.	CAMPBELL George	12°	coll.
CARLYLE Alexander	12°	coll.	GRAY Andrew	12°	ss.	HUNTER Andrew	12°	coll.
LEECHMAN William	-°	coll.	M'FARLAN John	12°	ss.	MACGILL William	12°	ss.
MACKENZIE John	12°	ss.	OGILVIE John	12°	ss.	PETRIE Robert	12°	ss.
SOMERVILLE Thomas	12°	ss.						

Shower's Mourner's Companion <Shower, John (ed.), "The Mourner's Companion ...." London, 1692; 2nd ed. 1699>

1699

SPADEMAN John	8°	ss.

(I N D E X E S T O F I F T H V O L U M E)

I N D E X C : R E F E R E N C E S T O P E O P L E

Notes:

(1) Format of This Index: On each page of the index below there are two columns of entries. On the left of each entry is the name of the person to whom reference is made in John Cooke's description of the publication that is identified on the right of the entry by means of format, date, and author's name. The context of the reference is summarized after the name of the person to whom reference is made.

(2) Special Symbols: The underlining of an author's name means that John Cooke italicized it to indicate that the author was a Nonconformist rather than an Anglican. The abbreviation "ss." stands for "single sermon", and "coll." indicates that a publication was probably a collection of sermons or a miscellany of some kind.

(3) King or Queen: For a list of sermons delivered before King or Queen, see, among the preceding INDEXES TO THIRD VOLUME, the relevant heading in INDEX C: SOME SPECIAL AUDIENCES TO WHOM SERMONS WERE ADDRESSED. For a list of Funerals of Royalty, see the relevant heading within INDEX D: OCCASIONS OR CAUSES, also among the preceding INDEXES TO THIRD VOLUME.

INDEXES TO FIFTH VOLUME: C: REFERENCES TO PEOPLE

Reference	Format	Date	Type	Author
A. C., anon.author	8°	1667	ss.	ANONYMOUS
A. C., translator	12°	1776	coll	BOURDALOUE
Abbott,Mord., death of	8°	1700	ss.	PIGGOTT John
Abbott,Mord., fun.of	8°	1700	ss.	HARRISON Thomas
Abney,Mary, fun.of	8°	1749	ss.	PRICE Samuel
Abney,Sir Tho., fun.of	8°	1722	ss.	SMITH Jeremiah
Adams,Peter, fun.of	4°	1676	ss.	LATHAM Paul
Adams,Rev. Rich., fun.of	-°	----	ss.	HOW John
Adams,Sir Thomas, fun.of	4°	1663	ss.	HARDY Nathaniel
Aikin,John, fun.of	4°	1780	ss.	ENFIELD William
Airey,Joseph, fun.of	8°	1739	ss.	WILSON William
Albermarle,Duke of, fun.	4°	1670	ss.	WARD Seth
Allen,Mr., fun.of	4°	1686	ss.	KIDDER Richard
Allen,Mr., murder of	8°	1768	ss.	FREE John
Alleyne,Joseph, fun.of	8°	1673	ss.	NEWTON George
Alston,Lady Eliz., fun.of	4°	1678	ss.	DILLINGHAM William
Amory,T., fun.of	8°	1774	ss.	FLEXMAN R. DD
Amory,T., published by	8°	1769	coll	CHANDLER Samuel
Anderson,Mr., fun.of	8°	1767	ss.	GILL John
Andrew,K., anon.author	8°	1768	coll	ANONYMOUS
Andrews,Rev. Mord., fun.	8°	1750	ss.	GUYSE John
Ann,Queen, death of	8°	1714	ss.	NOONE George
Ann,Queen, death of	8°	1714	ss.	SHAW Ferdinando
Ann,Queen, fun.of	8°	1714	coll	BLOWER John
Anne,Queen, death of	8°	1714	ss.	CHARLTON Samuel
Anthony,Earl of Harold	4°	1724	ss.	PARNE Thomas
Armyne,Lady, fun.of	8°	1678	ss.	ANONYMOUS
Ash,J., fun.of	8°	1779	ss.	EVANS Caleb
Ashburnham,Bp., cons.of	4°	1754	ss.	TREVEGAR Luke
Ashhurst,Henry, fun.of	4°	1680	ss.	BAXTER Richard
Ashursh,Lady Dianna, fun.	4°	1708	ss.	MAYO Richard
Ashurst,Benj., fun.of	8°	1678	ss.	BATES William
Ashworth,Caleb, fun.of	8°	1775	ss.	PALMER Samuel
Aske,Rev. Mr., fun.of	4°	1676	ss.	CLARK John
Asty,Rev. J., fun.of	8°	1730	ss.	GUYSE John
Atfield,Dr., fun.of	4°	1684	ss.	PEARSON Richard
Atherton,Bp., fun.of	8°	1709	ss.	BARNARD Nicholas
Atherton,John, fun.of	8°	1660	ss.	LIVESEY James
Atterbury's imprisonment	8°	1722	ss.	CHAMBRES Charles
Bagott,Bp., cons.of	4°	1782	ss.	RANDOLPH John
Baker,Bp., cons.of	4°	1723	ss.	LISLE Samuel
Baker,Will., fun.of	4°	1692	ss.	DENT Edward
Ball,Thomas, fun.of	4°	1660	ss.	HOW John
Bamfield,F., fun.of	4°	1684	ss.	COLLINS Hercules
Bampton's Lecture	8°	1780	coll	BANDINELL James
Banks,Eliz., fun.of	12°	1711	ss.	RIDGLEY Thomas
Barbauld,Rev., ordination	8°	1775	ss.	WHITESIDE John
Barker,Mrs., fun.of	8°	1705	ss.	PINSENT John
Barnardiston,Ann, fun.of	3°	1682	ss.	SHOWER John
Barrington. Viscount, fun.	-°	----	ss.	MACKEWEN Robert
Barrington,Bp., cons.of	4°	1769	ss.	STINTON George
Barrington,Viscount, fun.	8°	1734	ss.	MACKEWEN Robert
Barton,Rob., fun.of	4°	1703	ss.	DAGGE Jonathan
Bates,Dr., fun.of	F.O.	1700	ss.	HOW John
Bates,Dr., fun.of	8°	1699	ss.	HOW John
Baxter,Mrs., fun.of	4°	1681	ss.	HOW John
Baynard,Mrs., fun.of	4°	1697	ss.	PRUDE John
Beauclerk,Bp., cons.of	4°	1746	ss.	BALLARD Edward
Bedford,Duke of, fun.of	4°	1700	ss.	FREEMAN Samuel
Bell,Mrs. Eliz., fun.of	4°	1686	ss.	PECK John
Bennet,Rev. J., fun.of	8°	1726	ss.	CALAMY Edmund
Bennett,B., fun.of	8°	1725	ss.	WORTHINGTON John
Benson,Rev. Geo., fun.of	8°	1762	ss.	PICKARD Edward
Berriman,Dr., fun.of	4°	1750	ss.	RIDLEY Glocester
Best,Francis, murder of	8°	1771	ss.	FAWCETT Benjamin
Billingsley,J., an.author	12°	1712	ss.	ANONYMOUS
Bisse,Bp., cons.of	4°	1710	ss.	ADAMS John
Blackall,Bp., cons.of	4°	1708	ss.	BRADFORD Samuel
Blackall's Boyle Lectures	4°	1701	coll	ANONYMOUS
Blackburne,Bp., cons.of	8°	1717	ss.	RAYNER William
Bland,Dr., fun.of	8°	1768	ss.	LAW Edmund
Bludworth,Sir Tho., fun.	4°	1682	ss.	FREEMAN Samuel
Blundell,Mr., fun.of	4°	1718	ss.	MARSHALL Nathaniel
Bolde,Sam., anon.author	8°	1715	ss.	ANONYMOUS
Bolingbroke., against	4°	1753	ss.	LEMOINE Abraham
Bolingbroke,Ld., against	8°	1755	ss.	RANDOLPH Thomas
Bolton,Dean, fun.of	8°	1764	ss.	WRAY U. W. M.A.
Bond,Mr., fun.of	4°	1686	ss.	N. - - - - T.
Bonnell,James	8°	1699	ss.	WETENHALL Edward
Boulter,Bp., cons.of	8°	1719	ss.	STEPHENS Henry
Bourn,Rev. Mr., fun.of	8°	1754	ss.	BLYTH S.
Bourn,Sam., fun.of	8°	1722	ss.	BOURN Samuel
Bowers,Bp., cons.of	4°	1722	ss.	WILKINS David
Bowman, against	4°	1731	ss.	SMITH Joseph
Boyle,Mr., fun.of	4°	1692	ss.	BURNET Gilbert
Boyse,Joseph, Fun.of	FO.	1728	ss.	CHOPPIN R.
Bradbury,Rev. Tho., fun.	8°	1759	ss.	WINTER Richard
Bradford,Bp., cons.of	4°	1720	ss.	DENNE John
Bradley,John, anon.author	4°	1706	ss.	ANONYMOUS
Bradley,T., own fun.s.	4°	1670	ss.	BRADLEY Thomas
Bradshaigh,Lady, fun.of	4°	1695	ss.	TAYLOR Zachary
Bradshaigh,Sir Roger, fun	4°	1684	ss.	WROE Christopher
Bradshaw,Matt., fun.of	8°	1743	ss.	LATHAM Ebenezer
Brady,Dr., fun.of	8°	1726	ss.	STACKHOUSE Thomas
Bragge,Rev. Mr., fun.of	8°	1738	ss.	BRADBURY Thomas
Brattle,Rev. Mr., fun.of	8°	1717	ss.	COLEMAN Benjamin
Bretton,Dr. Rob., fun.of	4°	1672	ss.	PARR Richard
Bridgman,Lady, fun.of	4°	1702	ss.	FOX Joseph
Britain,Mrs. Susan, fun.	8°	1773	ss.	STENNETT Samuel
Broderick,Sir Alan, fun.	4°	1681	ss.	RESBURY Nathaniel
Brome,Edm., anon.author	8°	1712	ss.	ANONYMOUS
Bromley,Mrs., fun.of	4°	1706	ss.	WALLS George
Brook,Lady, fun.of	4°	1691	ss.	BURNET Gilbert
Brookes,Lady Eliz., fun.	12°	1684	ss.	PARKHURST Nathaniel
Brooks,Mrs. Joanna, fun.	8°	1712	ss.	JONES William
Browne,Bp., cons.of	8°	1710	ss.	SYNGE Edward
Browne,S., fun.of	8°	1732	ss.	ATKEY Anthony
Brownrig,Bp., fun.of	12°	1660	ss.	GAUDEN John
Brownsword,Henry, fun.of	4°	1688	ss.	CRUSO Timothy
Brumley,Jos., fun.of	4°	1698	ss.	WIGHT Thomas
Bryars, anon.author	8°	1712	ss.	ANONYMOUS
Buckler,Ben., anon,author	8°	1759	ss.	ANONYMOUS

Subject	Size	Year	Type	Author
Buckman,Henry, fun.of	4°	1765	ss.	SCHWAB Christ. E.
Bulkeley,Edw., fun.of	4°	1715	ss.	STEVANSON William
Bull,Bp., cons.of	4°	1705	ss.	WAUGH John
Bullivant,Mrs., murdered	4°	1698	ss.	CROOKE B. M.A.
Burch,S., fun.of	8°	1741	ss.	STENNETT Joseph
Burford,S., ordination	8°	1769	ss.	STENNETT Samuel
Burgoigne,Lady, fun.of	4°	1694	ss.	WHYYLE Humphrey
Burkitt,Rev., fun.of	8°	1704	ss.	PARKHURST Nathaniel
Burnet,Bp., cons.of	4°	1689	ss.	HORNECK Anthony
Burroughs,Rev. Jos., fun.	8°	1761	ss.	NOBLE Daniel
Busby's (Dr.) Plan	8°	1761	coll	PARSONS Joseph
Busby's(Dr.) Lecture	8°	1775	coll	BENNETT Thomas
Butler,Bp., cons.of	4°	1777	ss.	STURGES John
Butt,Jer., fun.of	4°	1694	ss.	VEAL Edward
C. H., anon.author	8°	1709	ss.	ANONYMOUS
C. W., anon.author	4°	1692	ss.	ANONYMOUS
Cade,Will., fun.of	4°	1671	ss.	LAKE John
Calamy,Rev. Benj., fun.of	4°	1686	ss.	SHERLOCK William
Calamy,Rev. Edm., fun.of	8°	1732	ss.	MAYO Daniel
Capel,Lady, fun.of	4°	1661	ss.	BARKER Edmund
Carlisle,Earl, fun.of	4°	1661	ss.	REEVE Thomas
Carmichael,Mr., baptism	8°	1765	ss.	GILL John
Caroline,Queen, death of	8°	1737	ss.	BYRCH William
Castell,Mr., fun.of	4°	1698	ss.	STANHOPE George
Cave,John, anon.author	4°	1679	ss.	ANONYMOUS
Cavendish,Hon., commem.of	4°	1675	ss.	NAILOUR William
Cawley,Rev. Mr., fun.of	4°	1748	ss.	CHURCH Tho. DD.
Cawton,Rev. Tho., fun.of	4°	1677	ss.	VINCENT Nathaniel
Chamberlain,W., fun.of	4°	1698	ss.	KING John
Chandler,Bp., cons.of	8°	1717	ss.	BYRCHE William
Chandler,Dr. Sam., fun.of	8°	1766	ss.	AMORY Thomas
Charles I and King David	4°	1660	ss.	ANONYMOUS
Charles Ist, fun.of	12°	1670	ss.	CARRE Thomas
Charles,King, murder of	4°	1686	ss.	ANONYMOUS
Charnock,Stephen, fun.of	4°	1680	ss.	JOHNSON John
Chatham,Earl of, death	4°	1778	ss.	BULKELEY Charles
Chesterfield,Ld., against	8°	1775	ss.	PECKARD Peter
Cholmondeley,Lady, fun.of	4°	1692	ss.	CATHERALL Samuel
Clapham,J., anon.author	4°	1684	ss.	ANONYMOUS
Clark,Dr., fun.of	8°	1750	ss.	DODDRIDGE Philip
Clark,Rev. Mr., fun.of	8°	1770	ss.	ASHWORTH Caleb
Clark,Samuel, ord.of	8°	1712	ss.	SMITH Jeremiah
Clarke,Mrs., fun.of	8°	1730	ss.	RUDD Sayer
Clarke,Rev. Joseph, fun.	4°	1751	ss.	WOODDESON Richard
Clarke,Rev. Matt., fun.of	8°	1726	ss.	NEALE Daniel
Clarke,Rev. Sam., fun.of	8°	1701	ss.	COX Samuel
Clavering,Bp., cons.of	4°	1724	ss.	MAYO Richard
Clements,Hen., fun.of	8°	1720	ss.	ALLET Thomas
Clericus, anon.author	8°	1780	ss.	ANONYMOUS
Clinton,Lady, fun.of	8°	1708	ss.	ROSEWELL Samuel
Coad,Rev. Tho., fun.of	8°	1750	ss.	MILNER John
Cocks,Sir Rich., anon.	8°	1722	ss.	ANONYMOUS
Codrington,Col., fun.of	4°	1710	ss.	GORDON Will. M.A.
Collett,Dr., fun.of	8°	1780	ss.	JAMES David
Collett,Jos., fun.of	8°	1742	ss.	STENNETT Joseph
Collier,Jer., anon.author	4°	1695	ss.	ANONYMOUS

Subject	Size	Year	Type	Author
Collingwood,Col. F., fun.	4°	1699	ss.	HESKITH Thomas
Collins,Tho., anon.author	8°	1725	ss.	ANONYMOUS
Colston,Mr., death of	4°	1721	ss.	HARCOURT James
Colston,Mr., fun.of	8°	1721	ss.	BRENT Charles
Colston's birthday	4°	1755	ss.	HAWKINS William
Compton,Bp., cons.of	4°	1675	ss.	JANE Will. DD.
Compton,Bp., fun.of	4°	1713	ss.	COCKBURN John
Compton,Bp., fun.of	4°	1713	ss.	GOOCH Thomas Sir
Compton,Bp., fun.of	4°	1713	ss.	WHITFELD Will. DD.
Compton,Lady, fun.of	4°	1687	ss.	ATTERBURY Lewis
Conder,J., fun.of	8°	1781	ss.	WEBB James
Conelly,W., M. P.,death	8°	1754	ss.	WEATE William
Connor,Dr., fun.of	4°	1699	ss.	HAYLEY William
Conybeare,Bp., cons.of	8°	1750	ss.	WEBBER Francis
Cook,Col. Edw., fun.of	4°	1684	ss.	THORNE Edmund
Cook,Tho., fun.of	8°	1703	ss.	LORRAIN Paul
Cooke,Lady Mary, fun.of	4°	1709	ss.	COOKE Thomas
Cooke,Shadrach	4°	1691	ss.	ANONYMOUS
Cooper,John, murder of	8°	1702	ss.	WOODWARD Josiah
Copping,Rev., fun.of	4°	1704	ss.	MILBOURNE Luke
Corbert,J., fun.of	4°	16--	ss.	BAXTER Richard
Cornbury,Lady, fun.of	8°	1706	ss.	SHARP J. M.A.
Cornish,Hen., fun.of	4°	1699	ss.	OLLYFFE John
Cornish,J., fun.	8°	1728	ss.	BAYES Joshua
Cornwallis,Bp., cons.of	4°	1750	ss.	THOMAS H. M.A.
Cosin,Bp., before	8°	1707	ss.	COCK John
Cosin,Bp., fun.of	8°	1673	ss.	BASIRE Isaac
Costivel,Mrs., fun.of	4°	1695	ss.	WEBB Jessop
Cotton,Rev., fun.of	8°	1730	ss.	WRIGHT Samuel
Country Clergyman, by a	8°	1719	ss.	ANONYMOUS
Country Clergyman, by a	8°	1715	ss.	ANONYMOUS
Country- Gentleman, by a	12°	1768	coll	ANONYMOUS
Cox,Mrs. Rebecca, fun.of	8°	1769	ss.	WALLIN Benjamin
Cox,Thomas, fun.of	8°	1769	ss.	WALLIN Benjamin
Coxe,Mary, fun.of	12°	1680	ss.	BAXTER Richard
Creed,Mrs., fun.of	4°	1728	ss.	LEE Henry
Creyk,Rev. J., fun.of	4°	1757	ss.	GREEN John
Croft,Bp., cons.of	4°	1662	ss.	MAYNE Jasper
Cromwell,Will., fun.of	8°	1772	ss.	GIBBONS Thomas
Crown,Mrs., fun.of	4°	1685	ss.	SCOTT John
Cruso,Rev. Tim., fun.of	4°	1698	ss.	MEAD Matthew
Culme,Rev., fun.of	4°	1692	ss.	SOUTHCOMB Lewis
Cumberland,Duke of, death	8°	1765	ss.	CORBYN Benjamin
Cumberland,Duke, death of	8°	1765	ss.	WALLIN Benjamin
Cumberland,Duke, thanks.	8°	1746	ss.	PIETY Thomas
Cunningham,Rev. J., fun.	8°	1716	ss.	WRIGHT Samuel
Cutts,Lady, fun.of	4°	1698	ss.	PROVOSTE John
Cutts,Lady, fun.of	4°	1697	ss.	WIGAN William
Czar, fun.of the	4°	1725	ss.	CONSERT Thomas
D. P., anon.author	8°	1703	ss.	ANONYMOUS
Dalkeith,Earl of, fun.of	8°	1750	ss.	ROBERTS Charles
Darracott,Rev., fun.of	12°	1759	ss.	FAWCETT Benjamin
Davey,Tho., translator	8°	1762	ss.	ARMAND James
Davies,J., translator	12°	1778	coll	ROWLAND Daniel
Davies,Rev. S., fun.of	8°	1771	coll	DAVIES Samuel
Davies,Rev. S., fun.of	8°	1766	coll	DAVIES Samuel

Reference	Format	Year	Type	Author
Davies,Rev. Sam., fun.of	8°	1761	ss.	FINLEY Sam. DD.
Davies,Rev., fun.of	8°	1761	ss.	GIBBONS Thomas
Davis,Dr. John, fun.of	8°	1718	ss.	WARD Richard
Dawes,Bp., cons.of	8°	1708	ss.	MILNER William
Dawes,Mrs., fun.of	4°	1693	ss.	PRITCHARD Thomas
Dawes,Sir, death of	8°	1724	ss.	WARREN Robert
Dawson,J., fun.of	8°	1757	ss.	WORTHINGTON Hugh
Day-labourer, fun.of	8°	1712	ss.	BRYARS John
Dealtry,J., death of	4°	1773	ss.	COOPER William
Delamere,Lord, fun.of	4°	1684	ss.	CAWDREY Zachary
Dent,Mr., fun.of	4°	1709	ss.	BRAY Thomas
Derby,Countess, fun.of	4°	1703	ss.	HUNTER Richard
Devon,Duke of, fun.of	8°	1707	ss.	GRIFFITH John
Devonshire,Duke, fun.of	8°	1708	ss.	KENNET White
Digby,Lady, fun.of	FO.	1719	coll	KETTLEWELL John
Digby,Lady, fun.of	4°	1684	ss.	KETTLEWELL John
Digby,Lord, fun.of	FO.	1719	coll	KETTLEWELL John
Digby,Lord, fun.of	4°	1685	ss.	KETTLEWELL John
Disney,Mrs. Cath., death	12°	1692	ss.	SCOFFIN William
Dobell,Mr., murder of	8°	1714	ss.	WOODFORD Matthew
Dodderidge,Dr., fun.of	8°	1752	ss.	ORTON Job
Dodderidge,P., fun.of	8°	1752	ss.	FROST Richard
Donn,Abraham, fun.of	12°	1775	ss.	HERVEY James
Doolittle,Rev., fun.of	12°	1707	ss.	WILLIAMS Daniel
Doughty,Rev., fun.of	4°	1768	ss.	NICOLLS Christ.
Doughty, anon.author	8°	1742	ss.	ANONYMOUS
Drew,W., fun.of	8°	1727	ss.	BALL Jacob
Droghede,Countess, fun.of	8°	1756	ss.	BOOKER More
du Moulin, translator	4°	1670	ss.	BREVAL Frank Durant
Dublin,Abp., fun.of	4°	1694	ss.	DOPPING Anthony
Dubois,S., fun.of	8°	1726	ss.	WAGENER Peter
Duckfield,Nath., fun.of	12°	1682	ss.	WALKER Anthony
Dudley,Dutchess of, fun.	4°	1669	ss.	BOREMAN Rich. DD.
Dunster,Mrs. Ann, fun.of	4°	1754	ss.	TOTTON William
Dunwell,Anth., death of	8°	1692	ss.	ROGERS Thomas
Duppa,Bp., fun.of	4°	1662	ss.	KING Henry
Durley,Mrs., fun.of	4°	1717	ss.	JAMES Ptolemy
E., of Yarmouth,fun.of	4°	1683	ss.	HILDEYARD John
Egerton,Bp., cons.of	4°	1724	ss.	CROXALL Sam. DD.
Eglin,Earl of, fun.of	4°	1664	ss.	PEARSON Richard
Eglington,Earl of, fun.of	8°	1770	ss.	CUNYNGHAM Alexander
Eldridge,Mr., fun.of	8°	1773	ss.	HOWE Thomas
Eldridge,Persis, fun.of	8°	1770	ss.	HOWE Thomas
Elliot,Sarah, fun.of	8°	1763	ss.	ELLIOTT John
Ellys,Bp., cons.of	4°	1753	ss.	JENNER Char. DD.
Emlyn,Mr., fun.of	8°	1741	ss.	FOSTER James
Estlin,J. P., ord.of	8°	1778	ss.	ENFIELD William
Eustace,Sir, fun.of	4°	1665	ss.	SHERIDAN William
Evans,Bp., cons.of	4°	1702	ss.	HAYLEY William
Evans,Rev. Hugh, fun.of	8°	1781	ss.	EVANS Caleb
F. D.,(or John Higgins)	4°	1688	ss.	ANONYMOUS
F. S., translator	FO.	1672	coll	DAILLE John
Fairclough,Richard, fun.	-°	----	ss.	HOW John
Fairclough,S., fun.of	4°	1692	ss.	PARKHURST Nathaniel
Fanshaw,Sir J., fun.of	4°	1667	ss.	BAGSHAW Henry
Farindon	FO.	1674	ss.	M. - - - - R.

Reference	Format	Year	Type	Author
Farmor,Lady Mary, fun.of	4°	1670	ss.	DOBSON John
Fenn,Mrs., fun.of	4°	1679	ss.	SPARKE Robert
Finley,Sam., printed in	8°	1771	coll	DAVIES Samuel
Finley,Sam., printed in	8°	1766	coll	DAVIES Samuel
Firmin,Tho., fun.of	12°	1698	ss.	ANONYMOUS
Fisher,Mrs. Eliz., fun.of	4°	1698	ss.	MILNER William
Fleetwood,Bp., anon.auth.	8°	1710	ss.	ANONYMOUS
Fleetwood,Bp., cons.of	4°	1708	ss.	ADAMS John
Fleming,Dr. Caleb, fun.of	8°	1779	ss.	PALMER John
Floyd,James, fun.of	8°	1759	ss.	ASHWORTH Caleb
Ford,Elizabeth, fun.of	8°	1781	ss.	FORD William,jun
Fordwich,Lady, fun.of	4°	1669	ss.	MOULIN DU Peter
Foster,Dr. James, death	8°	1753	ss.	BULKELEY Charles
Foster,J., fun.of	1°	1753	ss.	FLEMING Caleb
Fothergill,Dr., an.author	12°	1772	coll	ANONYMOUS
Fox,Charles, fun.of	8°	1713	ss.	EYRE Rich. M.A.
Fox,Sir Steph., fun.of	4°	1716	ss.	EYRE Rich. M.A.
Foxon,J., fun.of	8°	1723	ss.	CLARKE Matthew
Frederick's(Pr.)birthday	8°	1729	ss.	SHAW Ferdinando
Frost,Rev. B., fun.of	8°	1764	ss.	FRANCIS John
Frost,Rev. Mr., fun.of	8°	1778	ss.	HOWE Thomas
Fryer,John, fun.of	8°	1725	ss.	BALL Jacob
Fullerton,Mrs., fun.of	4°	1735	ss.	BARNARD Francis
G. T., anon.author	8°	1693	ss.	ANONYMOUS
Gainsborough,Earl of, fun	8°	1714	ss.	ROGERS Samuel
Gainsborough,Earl of, fun	4°	1751	ss.	SKYNNER John
Gale,Rev. J., fun.of	8°	1722	ss.	KINCH John
Galway,John, interment of	8°	1777	ss.	ENFIELD William
Gaspine,Rev. John, fun.of	8°	1741	ss.	MILLS William
George,King, accession	8°	1714	ss.	SHAW Ferdinando
Geree,Rev. J., fun.of	4°	1774	ss.	PENROSE Thomas,jun
Gething,Lady, fun.of	4°	1700	ss.	BIRCH Peter
Gibbons,T., printed in	8°	1771	coll	DAVIES Samuel
Gibbons,T., printed in	8°	1766	coll	DAVIES Samuel
Gibson,Bp., cons.of	8°	1716	ss.	BOULTER Hugh
Gibson,Eliz., fun.of	4°	1692	ss.	ANONYMOUS
Gilbert,Bp., cons.of	4°	1740	ss.	ALLEN John
Gill,Dr. J., fun.of	-°	1771	ss.	STENNETT Samuel
Gill,Dr. J., fun.of	8°	1771	ss.	WALLIN Benjamin
Gilson,Daniel, fun.of	8°	1728	ss.	TREN John
Glanvill,J., anon.author	4°	1670	ss.	ANONYMOUS
Glanville,Mr., fun.of	4°	1681	ss.	PLEYDELL Josias
Glascock,Mr., fun.of	4°	1690	ss.	SHELTON William
Gledhill,J., fun.of	8°	1728	ss.	BARKER John
Gloucester,Duke of, fun.	4°	1700	ss.	GARDINER James
Godfrey,Sir E., fun.of	4°	1678	ss.	LLOYD William
Godwin,Edw., fun.of	8°	1764	ss.	LANGFORD William
Gooch,Bp., cons.of	4°	1737	ss.	SHUCKFORD Samuel
Gordon, anon.author	8°	1732	ss.	ANONYMOUS
Gordon's,Lord, release of	12°	1781	ss.	CLARKE Augustus
Gould,Lady, fun.of	4°	1713	ss.	ATTERBURY Lewis
Gowart,Godfrey, fun.of	8°	1750	ss.	LILIENTHAL William
Grandorge,Dr., fun.of	8°	1730	ss.	BLOMER Ralph
Gray,Mrs. Susanna, fun.	4°	1672	ss.	WARING Robert
Green,Bp., cons.of	4°	1721	ss.	STURGES John
Green,Thomas, fun.of	4°	1763	ss.	HOOPER William

Reference	Format	Year	Type	Author
Gregory,Rev. Tho., fun.of	4°	1692	ss.	POWELL Jos. M.A.
Greswold,Ann, fun.of	4°	1691	ss.	WRIGHT John
Grew, fun.of	8°	1712	ss.	SHOWER John
Grigg,Rev. Mr., fun.of	4°	1670	ss.	PATRICK Simon
Grimshaw,Rev., fun.of	8°	1763	ss.	VENN H. M.A.
Grosvenor,B., fun.of	8°	1758	ss.	BARKER John
Grosvenor,B., ordination	12°	1709	ss.	WILLIAMS Daniel
Grove,Rev. Henry, fun.of	8°	1738	ss.	STRONG James
Grundy,Eliz., Mrs.,fun.	8°	1777	ss.	FENNER Ludd John
Guerden, shorthand?scribe	4°	1680	ss.	CROMWELL Oliver
Guilford,Lady, fun.of	4°	1699	ss.	HORNECK Philip
Guilford,Lady, fun.of	4°	1700	ss.	KNIGHT John
Gunning,Bp., fun.of	4°	1685	ss.	GOWER Humphrey
Guyse,Dr., fun.of	8°	1762	ss.	CONDER John
H. H.,S. J., anon.author	4°	1686	ss.	ANONYMOUS
Hadfield,T., fun.of	8°	1741	ss.	CHANDLER Samuel
Hale,Sir Matthew, fun.of	4°	1677	ss.	GRIFFITH Evan
Hall,Mr., fun.of	8°	1716	ss.	CLARK John
Hall,Rev. Tho., fun.of	8°	1762	ss.	WINTER Richard
Hall,T., fun.of	8°	1675	coll	MOORE Richard
Hallam, before,for murder	8°	1732	ss.	GUTHRIE James
Haman, wicked life,&death	8°	1740	ss.	WEBSTER
Hammond,Mrs. Jud., fun.of	-°	----	ss.	HOW John
Harcourt,Mrs. Ellen, fun.	4°	1661	ss.	HENCHMAN Richard
Hardy,Dean, fun.of	4°	1663	ss.	MEGGOT Richard
Hardy,Dr., fun.of	4°	1670	ss.	PATRICK Simon
Hare,Bp., cons.of	8°	1727	ss.	KILBOURN Robert
Harman,James, fun.of	4°	1711	ss.	MILLECHAMP Richard
Harold,Earl of, fun.of	4°	1724	ss.	PARNE Thomas
Harris,Bp., cons.of	4°	1729	ss.	THOMAS John
Harris,Philip, fun.of	4°	1681	ss.	QUICKE John
Harris,Rev. Will., fun.of	8°	1740	ss.	LARDNER Nathaniel
Harris,Will., fun.of	8°	1740	ss.	GROSVENOR Benjamin
Harris's Boyle Lectures	4°	1701	coll	ANONYMOUS
Harrison,Rev. J., fun.of	8°	1749	ss.	DAVIDSON Thomas
Harrison, horrible suicide	8°	1703	ss.	HOWSON Robert
Hart,Rev. Mr., fun.of	8°	1768	ss.	HUGHES John
Harvey,Rev. Mr., fun.of	8°	1729	ss.	HARRIS William
Hastings,Ld. T., baptism	4°	1668	ss.	JONES John
Havers,Clopton, fun.of	4°	1702	ss.	BUTLER Lilly
Hay,Dr., fun.of	4°	1753	ss.	KING Arnold
Haylett,Rev. Mr., fun.of	8°	1720	ss.	GRAILLE John
Hayter,Bp., fun.of	8°	1762	ss.	STAINSBY Richard
Henley,Rev. Phocion, fun.	8°	1764	ss.	SMITH James
Henry,Matt., fun.of	8°	1714	ss.	BATES John
Henry,Mrs., fun.of	8°	1712	ss.	HENRY Matthew
Henry,Rev. Matt., fun.of	8°	1714	ss.	REYNOLDS John
Henry,Rev. Matt., fun.of	8°	1704	ss.	TONG William
Henry,Rev. Matt., fun.of	8°	1714	ss.	WILLIAMS Daniel
Herring,Bp., cons.of	4°	1738	ss.	DENNE John
Hervey,Rev., death of	8°	1759	ss.	ROMAINE William
Hickeringill,Edm., author	4°	1700	ss.	ANONYMOUS
Higgins,John, anon.author	4°	1688	ss.	ANONYMOUS
Hildrop,J., anon.author	8°	1711	coll	ANONYMOUS
Hill,Miss, a gift serm.by	8°	1755	ss.	ROMAINE William
Hinchliffe,Bp., cons.of	4°	1769	ss.	LORT Michael
Hind,John, fun.of	4°	1704	ss.	TAYLOR Christopher
Hoadly,Bp. Ben., cons.of	8°	1716	ss.	HOADLY John
Hoadly,Bp., against	8°	1717	ss.	INNES Alexander
Hocker,Rev. William, fun.	8°	1722	ss.	REYNOLDS Thomas
Holcroft,Francis, fun.of	4°	1692	ss.	MILWAY Thomas
Holden,S., fun.of	8°	1740	ss.	COLMAN Benjamin
Holle,John, fun.of	4°	1680	ss.	REYNER Samuel
Holles,Lady, fun.of	4°	1682	ss.	WATERS James
Hollis,Mrs., fun.of	8°	1724	ss.	HUNT Jerem. DD.
Hollis,T., fun.of	8°	1731	ss.	HUNT Jerem. DD.
Hooper,Bp., cons.of	4°	1704	ss.	ISHAM Zach. DD.
Hopkins,Bp., fun.of	4°	1690	ss.	TENNISON Richard
Houblon,Mr., fun.of	4°	1682	ss.	BURNET Gilbert
Houghton,John, fun.of	-°	----	ss.	HOW John
Houghton,Sir H., fun.of	4°	1678	ss.	BUSHEL Seth
How,John, fun.of	8°	1767	ss.	ELLIOTT John
Howard,John, anon.author	8°	1728	ss.	ANONYMOUS
Howard,John, anon.author	12°	1710	ss.	ANONYMOUS
Howland,Mrs. Mary, fun.of	8°	1719	ss.	HOADLY Benjamin
Hubbard,Rev. J., fun.of	8°	1743	ss.	GUYSE John
Hughes,Mrs. Eliz., fun.of	8°	1736	ss.	WRIGHT Samuel
Hughes,Rev. John, fun.of	8°	1711	ss.	CROFT Thomas
Hughes,Rev. Obad., fun.of	8°	1752	ss.	ALLEN John
Hunt,J., fun.of	8°	1748	coll	LARDNER Nathaniel
Ibbot (Dr.), against	4°	1721	ss.	SLADE Joseph
Ives,Will., fun.of	8°	1719	ss.	COOKE Edward
J. C.,Rev., fun.of	4°	1758	ss.	WOODDESON Richard
J. C., anon.author	8°	1708	ss.	ANONYMOUS
J. W., anon.author	8°	1761	ss.	ANONYMOUS
Jackson,Tho., fun.of	8°	1775	ss.	MIDDLETON Erasmus
Jacomb,Mr., fun.of	4°	1660	ss.	PATRICK Simon
Jacomb,R., ordination of	8°	1782	ss.	KIPPIS Andrew
James,King, proclaiming	4°	1685	ss.	CAMFIELD Benjamin
James,Rev. S., fun.of	8°	1773	ss.	WALLIN Benjamin
Jeffery,Dr., fun.of	-°	1720	ss.	JONES Samuel
Jekyll,Dr. Tho., fun.of	4°	1698	ss.	WILLIAMS John
Jenk,B., anon.author	4°	1689	ss.	ANONYMOUS
Jennings,Rev. Dr. D., fun	8°	1762	ss.	SAVAGE Morton Sam.
Johnson,Bp., cons.of	4°	1752	ss.	MARKHAM William
Johnson,Bp., fun.of	4°	1776	ss.	BUTT George
Johnson,George, fun.of	4°	1683	ss.	WERGE Richard
Johnson,Rev., fun.of	8°	1768	ss.	PEACOCK John
Johnson,Sarah, fun.of	8°	1774	ss.	JENNINGS Nathaniel
Johnson,Sir Henry, fun.of	4°	1684	ss.	PECK Samuel
Jollie,J., fun.of	8°	1704	ss.	JOLLIE Timothy
Jollie,Tim., fun.of	8°	1715	ss.	DE LA ROSE John
Jollie,Tim., fun.of	8°	1757	ss.	JENNINGS David
Jones,Rev. G., fun.of	8°	1705	ss.	PARKHURST Nathaniel
Jones,Rev., fun.of	8°	1762	ss.	ROMAINE William
K. H., anon.author	8°	1667	ss.	ANONYMOUS
Keene,Bp., cons.of	4°	1752	ss.	GREEN John
Keene,Martha, fun.of	8°	1767	ss.	WALLIN Benjamin
Keith,Sir Basil(Jamaica)	8°	1777	ss.	LINDSAY John
Kelley,Mrs., fun.of	8°	1724	ss.	WOOD James
Kennet,Bp., cons.of	8°	1718	ss.	WADDINGTON Edward
Kennet,Bp., cons.of	8°	1723	ss.	WHITE Thomas

Reference	Format	Date	Type	Author
Kennet,Dr., fun.of	4°	1717	ss.	TAUBMAN Nathaniel
Kenrick,Dr., fun.of	4°	1753	ss.	BUTLER John
Kimber,Rev., fun.of	-°	1754	ss.	BURROUGHS Joseph
Kinch,Dr., fun.of	8°	1731	ss.	HUNT Jerem. DD.
King,Abp., fun.of	8°	1729	ss.	D. - - - - R.
King,Dr. Will., fun.of	8°	1769	ss.	WATSON J.
King,Mrs., fun.of	8°	1726	ss.	EVANS John
Kipping,Tho., fun.of	4°	1713	ss.	REYNER Kirby
Kirby,Rev. Tho., fun.of	8°	1728	ss.	MORRIS Joseph
Knatchbull,Rev., fun.of	8°	1773	ss.	FELTON William
la Fite,Dan, translator	4°	1694	ss.	MORUS Monsieur
Lady, by a	12°	1770	coll	ANONYMOUS
Lady, by a	8°	1716	ss.	ANONYMOUS
Lady, by a	8°	1780	ss.	ANONYMOUS
Lambert,Bp., cons.of	4°	1717	ss.	TYREL Duke
Lane,Lady, fun.of	4°	1699	ss.	TAYLOR Nathaniel
Langford,Rev. Will., fun.	8°	1775	ss.	GIBBONS Thomas
Langham,Rt. Hon. Mrs.	8°	1665	ss.	FORD Simon
Lauderdale,Duke of, fun.	4°	1683	ss.	GASKARTH John
Laugher,Rev. Tim., fun.of	8°	1769	ss.	KIPPIS Andrew
Law,Bp., cons.of	4°	1782	ss.	PALEY William
Law,Will., anon.author	8°	1718	ss.	ANONYMOUS
Lawrence,Mr., fun.of	8°	1712	ss.	HENRY Matthew
Lawrence,Rev. Dr., fun.of	8°	1760	ss.	FORDYCE James
Layman,Loyal, anon.author	8°	1708	ss.	ANONYMOUS
Layman, by a	8°	1732	ss.	ANONYMOUS
Layman, by a (Gordon)	8°	1732	ss.	ANONYMOUS
Lee,John, Esq.,fun.of	4°	1704	ss.	WERNDLY J. C.
Leicester,Sir Robt., fun.	4°	1684	ss.	FORENESS E.
Leland,T., fun.of	8°	1766	ss.	WELD Isaac
Leng,Bp., cons.of	4°	1723	ss.	GURDON Brampton
Lethieullier,Sir, fun.of	4°	1690	ss.	MERITON Thomas
Levett (a merchant), fun.	8°	1724	ss.	RAINSFORD Giles
Lewis,Francis, fun.of	8°	1708	ss.	CALAMY Edmund
Lewis, translator	8°	1722	coll	SANDERSON Robert
Lexington,Lady, fun.of	4°	1676	ss.	HOLDEN Samuel
Lexington,Lord, fun.of	4°	1676	ss.	HOLDEN Samuel
Lexington,Lord, fun.of	4°	1723	ss.	NAISH James
Ligoe,Tho., fun.of	4°	1707	ss.	OLLYFFE William
Linager,Robt., fun.of	4°	1683	ss.	ROGERS Thomas
Lloyd,Tho., fun.of	4°	1669	ss.	WOOLNOUGH Thomas
Lob,Stephen, fun.of	4°	1699	ss.	GOODWIN Thomas
Loftus,Rev. Barth., fun.	8°	1751	ss.	SOWDEN Benjamin
Longhurst,Jos., fun.of	8°	1769	ss.	WILTON Samuel
Lorrain,Mrs., fun.of	4°	1705	ss.	SHUTE Henry
Lovelace,Lord, fun.of	4°	1709	ss.	VESEY William
Lowman,Rev. Moses, fun.of	8°	1752	ss.	CHANDLER Samuel
Lowth,Bp., cons.of	4°	1766	ss.	BARTON Phi. B.D.
Lumley,Lady, fun.of	4°	1704	ss.	COOKE Henry M.
Lumley,Lady, fun.of	4°	1693	ss.	PRITCHARD Thomas
Lythgoe,Mr., fun.of	8°	1758	ss.	OWEN Charles
Lyttleton,Bp., cons.of	4°	1762	ss.	PARKER William
Macgowan,Rev., fun.of	8°	1780	ss.	WALLIN Benjamin
Madan's work, against	8°	1780	ss.	SMITH John
Madock,Dan., fun.of	8°	1745	ss.	LATHAM Ebenezer
Maisters,Rev. J., fun.of	8°	1717	ss.	HUNT Jerem. DD.
Majesty's assass.attempt	4°	1696	ss.	ALSOP Vincent
Malborough,Duke, before	8°	1746	ss.	HARE Francis
Malborough,Duke, before	8°	1711	ss.	HARE Francis
Malborough,Duke, thanks.	8°	1746	ss.	HARE Francis
Malborough,Duke, thanks.	4°	1709	ss.	HARE Francis
Malborough,Duke, thanks.	4°	1704	ss.	TRIMNEL Charles
Manningham,Bp., cons.of	4°	1709	ss.	STONESTREET William
Manton,T., fun.of	8°	1678	ss.	BATES William
Margetson,J., fun.of	4°	1679	ss.	JONES Henry
Margetson,Mrs. Ann, fun.	4°	1693	ss.	LAMBERT Ralph
Marketman,J., executed	12°	1720	ss.	ANONYMOUS
Marrow,Lady, fun.of	4°	1715	ss.	HOUGH John
Marryatt,Dr., fun.of	-°	1754	ss.	HALL Thomas
Marsh,Abp. N., fun.of	4°	1714	ss.	KING William
Mary,Lady, fun.of	4°	1679	ss.	WILLES Samuel
Masillon, translated from	8°	1769	coll	DODD W. LLD.
Mason,Rev. J., fun.of	8°	1780	ss.	EVANS Caleb
Mason,Rev. John, fun.of	8°	1763	ss.	HODGE John
Matty,Matthew, fun.of	4°	1776	ss.	LAYARD Peter Chas.
Mawson,Bp., cons.of	4°	1739	ss.	CHAPMAN John
May,Ld., before	4°	1692	ss.	FORD Simon
Maynard,James, fun.of	8°	1781	ss.	TOULMIN Joshua
Maynard,Lady, fun.of	4°	1682	ss.	KEN Thomas
Mayo,Rev. Dan., fun.of	8°	1733	ss.	HARRIS William
Mead,Rev. Matt., fun.of	-°	----	ss.	HOW John
Meggott,Rev. Rich., fun.	4°	1693	ss.	SHERLOCK William
Merrill,Rev. J., fun.of	8°	1716	ss.	WARREN John
Methodist, by a	8°	1739	ss.	ANONYMOUS
Middleton,Dr., against	8°	1750	ss.	JEPHSON Alexander
Miles,Henry, fun.of	8°	1763	ss.	FURNEAUX Philip
Milford,John, fun.of	4°	1692	ss.	EASTON Thomas
Miller,Rev. Mr., fun.of	8°	1718	ss.	FORSTER Thomas
Mills,J., fun.of	8°	1717	ss.	WRIGHT Samuel
Minister, by a	4°	1697	ss.	ANONYMOUS
Missenden,Mr., fun.of	4°	1727	ss.	LEWIS George
Mitchel,Mr., fun.of	4°	1671	ss.	LLOYD William
Montrose,Marquiss, fun.of	4°	1673	ss.	BURNET Alexander
Morris,Rev., fun.of	8°	1755	ss.	BURROUGHS Joseph
Morton,Bp., fun.of	4°	1660	ss.	BARWICK John
Mottershead,Mary, fun.of	8°	1732	ss.	TIDCOMBE Jerem.
Mount- Alexander,Earl of	4°	1663	ss.	RUST George
Mount,Richard, fun.of	8°	1722	ss.	NEWMAN John
Mowsley,Tho., fun.of	12°	1669	ss.	JANEWAY James
Munn,Mrs. Hannah, fun.of	8°	1779	ss.	WALLIN Benjamin
Murdin,Eleanor, fun.of	8°	1713	ss.	REYNOLDS Thomas
Myonnett, fun.own mother	8°	1725	ss.	MYONNETT John
Neale,David, fun.of	8°	1743	ss.	JENNINGS David
Neale,Thomas, fun.of	8°	1705	ss.	PARKHURST Nathaniel
Nelson,Mr., fun.of	8°	1714	ss.	MARSHALL John
Neville,Grey, fun.of	8°	1723	ss.	HUNT Jerem. DD.
Neville,Lady C., fun.of	4°	1715	ss.	MALTON William
Neville,Mrs., fun.of	8°	1715	ss.	ISAAC John
Newcastle,Lady Jane, fun.	4°	1669	ss.	LITTLETON Adam
Newman,Rev. J., fun.of	8°	1738	ss.	BARKER John
Newman,Rev. T., fun.of	8°	1758	ss.	PICKARD Edward
Newman,Sam., fun.of	8°	1735	ss.	BARKER John

Reference	Size	Year	Type	Author
Nicholas,John, fun.of	8°	1744	ss.	ALLEN John
Nichols,Rev. Dr., fun.of	8°	1774	ss.	SMITH James
Nicholson,Bp., cons.of	4°	1702	ss.	GIBSON Edmund
Nightingale,Mrs., fun.of	8°	1711	ss.	HEWERDINE Thomas
Noble,Mr., execution of	8°	1713	ss.	BROUGHTON John
Non-juror, by a	4°	1695	ss.	ANONYMOUS
Norbane,Walter, fun.of	4°	1660	ss.	HAYWOOD William
North,Bp., cons.of	8°	1775	ss.	BALGUY Thomas
Northam,Earl of, baptism	8°	1660	ss.	TOWERS John
Northampton,Earl of, fun.	8°	1660	ss.	TOWERS John
Norton,Lady D., fun.of	4°	1703	ss.	MANNINGHAM Thomas
Norton,Mrs. Anne, fun.of	-°	----	ss.	FULLER Ignatius
Norton,Sir John, fun.of	4°	1687	ss.	MANNINGHAM Thomas
Norwich,Lady Anna., fun.	8°	1705	ss.	BLACKWELL Samuel
Notcutt,John, ord.of	8°	1735	ss.	FORD William,sen
Oldfield,Dr., fun.of	8°	1730	ss.	HUGHES Obadiah
Onslow,Lady, fun.of	8°	1731	ss.	STEPHENS George
Orford,Countess of, fun.	4°	1702	ss.	BARKER Samuel
Orrery,Earl of, fun.of	4°	1681	ss.	MORRIS Thomas
Osbaldeston,Bp., cons.of	-°	----	ss.	WILLS John
Owen, fun.of	8°	1706	ss.	HENRY Matthew
P. E.,Benedictine author	4°	1686	ss.	ANONYMOUS
P. T.,Sir, preached at	4°	1680	ss.	CROMWELL Oliver
Page,Mary, fun.of	8°	1728	ss.	HARRISON Thomas
Page,Mrs., fun.of	8°	1729	ss.	RICHARDSON Thomas
Paget,Lady, fun.of	4°	1673	ss.	JENNY Jehu
Papillon,Jane, fun.of	8°	1698	ss.	WOODHOUSE John
Parkhurst,Nath., fun.of	12°	1708	ss.	S. - - - - - J.
Parr,Mrs., fun.of	4°	1688	ss.	HIGDON William
Parry,J., fun.of	8°	1725	ss.	BENSON George
Parsons,Rev. John, death	4°	1778	ss.	YOUNG Toy William
Patrick,Bp., anon.author	4°	1678	ss.	ANONYMOUS
Patrick,Bp., anon.author	4°	1687	ss.	ANONYMOUS
Payne,George, fun.of	4°	1700	ss.	OLIVER Richard
Pearce,Bp. Z., an.author	12°	1736	ss.	ANONYMOUS
Pearce,Bp., cons.of	8°	1748	ss.	JORTIN John
Peirce,Rev. J., fun.of	8°	1726	ss.	HALLET Joseph
Pelling,Dr., fun.of	4°	1750	ss.	CHURCH Tho. DD.
Pemberton,Eben., fun.of	8°	1717	ss.	COLEMAN Benjamin
Pembroke,Countess, fun.of	4°	1677	ss.	RAINBOW Edward
Peyton,Lady C., fun.of	4°	1661	ss.	EVES George
Phene,N., ordination	8°	1770	ss.	TOWLE Thomas
Phillibrowne,Mrs., fun.of	8°	1727	ss.	NEALE Daniel
Pickard,Rev. Edw., fun.of	8°	1778	ss.	TAYLOR Thomas
Pickering,Capt. G., fun.	4°	1704	ss.	W. - - - - - J.
Pomfret,Rev., fun.of	8°	1722	ss.	REYNOLDS Thomas
Pomfret,T., fun.of	4°	1706	ss.	HUMPHREYS A.
Postlewait,J., fun.of	4°	1713	ss.	HANCOCK John
Potter,Bp., cons.of	4°	1715	ss.	RYE George
Presbyter,Anglican, anon.	4°	1683	ss.	ANONYMOUS
Presbyter,Anglican, by a	8°	1708	ss.	ANONYMOUS
Presbyter,Anglican, by a	12°	1713	ss.	ANONYMOUS
Preston dead by own bear	8°	1709	ss.	PEAD Deuel
Price,Lady, fun.of	8°	1732	ss.	RICHARDS Thomas
Prince of Wales, death of	4°	1751	ss.	ATWOOD George
Prince of Wales, marriage	8°	1736	ss.	ATKINSON B. Andrew
Prince,Rev. Edw., fun.of	8°	1708	ss.	FERNE Robert
Protestant, by a	4°	1680	ss.	ANONYMOUS
Prussia,King of, fun.of	4°	1713	ss.	CAESAR J. James
Prussia,King, victory of	4°	1758	ss.	CAPPE Newcome
Prussia,Queen of, fun.of	4°	1705	ss.	CAESAR J. James
Pye,Esq., fun.of	4°	1759	ss.	TAYLOR John
Quaker, by a	4°	1768	ss.	ANONYMOUS
Quaker, by a	4°	1771	ss.	ANONYMOUS
R. A., anon.author	8°	1664	ss.	ANONYMOUS
R. J., anon.author	4°	1677	ss.	ANONYMOUS
R. J., anon.author	4°	1663	ss.	ANONYMOUS
Rainbow,Bp., fun.of	8°	1688	ss.	TULLY Thomas
Ralphson,R., fun.of	4°	1684	ss.	COLLINS Hercules
Ratcliffe,Mr., fun.of	8°	1728	ss.	EVANS John
Rawson, anon.author	4°	1704	ss.	ANONYMOUS
Reed,Rev. Mr., fun.of	8°	1755	ss.	BENSON George
Rees,Rev. D., fun.of	8°	1748	ss.	STENNETT Joseph
Reeve,Mary, fun.of	4°	1685	ss.	HILL Joseph
Reyner,Joshua, fun.of	8°	1762	ss.	ELLIOTT John
Reyner,Rev. Will., fun.of	4°	1764	ss.	RIDER William
Reynolds,Bp., cons.of	8°	1721	ss.	RUSSELL John
Reynolds,Bp., fun.of	4°	1677	ss.	RIVELY Benedict
Reynolds,Edward, fun.of	4°	1699	ss.	GIBBS William
Reynolds,Mr., ordination	8°	1766	ss.	WALLIN Benjamin
Rich,Lord, fun.of	4°	1664	ss.	WALKER Anthony
Richards,Mr., ordination	-°	1763	ss.	WALLIN Benjamin
Richardson,Sir A., fun.of	4°	1661	ss.	SMALWOOD George
Richmond,Countess, fun.of	8°	1708	ss.	FISHER John
Richmond,Duke of, death	4°	1752	ss.	AUDLEY Matthew
Richmond,Duke of, to	4°	1778	ss.	ANONYMOUS
Richmond,Duke of, to	4°	1778	ss.	ANONYMOUS
Ritchbell,Rev.g., fun.of	4°	1684	ss.	ALGOOD Major
Robarts,Mrs. Ann, fun.of	8°	1771	ss.	EVANS Caleb
Robinson,Ben., fun.of	8°	1724	ss.	CUMMING John
Robinson,Bp., cons.of	4°	1710	ss.	ADAMS John
Robinson,R., transl.&pub.	8°	1775	coll	SAURIN James
Robinson,R., transl.&pub.	8°	1775	coll	SAURIN James
Robinson,R., transl.&pub.	8°	1777	coll	SAURIN James
Rochester,Earl of, fun.of	4°	1680	ss.	PARSONS Robert
Rodney,Admiral, thanks.	4°	1781	ss.	BRADSHAW Tho.
Rogers,Dr. John, fun.of	8°	1729	ss.	MARSHALL Nathaniel
Rogers,Lady, fun.of	8°	1663	ss.	HOOKE Richard
Rogerson,Rev., fun.of	8°	1760	ss.	LOWTHIAN S.
Rose,Mr., fun.of	8°	1765	ss.	KAY Matthew
Rosewell,Tho., fun.of	4°	1691	ss.	MEAD Matthew
Rotheram,Cal., fun.of	4°	1752	ss.	DAYE James
Rouquet,Rev. Mr., fun.of	8°	1776	ss.	EVANS Caleb
Rowney,Thomas, fun.of	8°	1759	ss.	BILSTONE John
Russel,Lady, fun.of	8°	1721	ss.	KNIGHT Samuel
Russel,Mr., fun.of	8°	1714	ss.	NESBITT John
Russel,Sir Fran., fun.of	4°	1706	ss.	BROOKE James
Rutland,Duke of, fun.of	4°	1711	ss.	FELTON Henry
Rutland,Dutchess, fun.of	8°	1711	ss.	BURSCOUGH William
Rutter,Mrs. Dor., fun.of	4°	1663	ss.	OLDISWORTH Giles
S. S., anon.author	8°	1703	ss.	ANONYMOUS
S. S., anon.author	8°	1666	ss.	ANONYMOUS

Reference	Size	Date	Type	Author
S. S., anon.author	8°	1666	ss.	ANONYMOUS
S. S., anon.author	8°	1666	ss.	ANONYMOUS
S. S., anon.author	8°	1667	ss.	ANONYMOUS
S. T., anon.author	-°	1675	ss.	ANONYMOUS
Sacheverell,Dr., fun.of	4°	1711	ss.	SAINT John Pawlet
Sachiverell, sentence ag.	4°	1713	ss.	HOLE Matthew
Sampson,Mrs. E., fun.of	4°	1690	ss.	HOW John
Sandercock,Rev. E., fun.	8°	1770	ss.	CAPPE Newcome
Sanderson,Rev. S., fun.of	8°	1766	ss.	PALMER Samuel
Sare,Mr., fun.of	4°	1724	ss.	STANHOPE George
Sarum,Bp.of, cons.of	4°	1757	ss.	DODWELL William
Saunders,Thomas, fun.of	8°	1736	ss.	SOME David
Saurin,J.	8°	1781	ss.	ROBINSON Robert
Scott,Dr., fun.of	4°	1695	ss.	ISHAM Zach. DD.
Scott,Wm., published by	4°	1750	ss.	CHURCH Tho. DD.
Scougal,Dr., fun.of	8°	1726	coll	GAIRDEN George
Scougal,Henry, fun.of	8°	1726	coll	SCOUGAL Henry
Seaman,Laz., fun.of	4°	1675	ss.	JENKYN William
Shadwell, fun.of	4°	1693	ss.	BRADY Nich. DD.
Sharp,Abp., fun.of	8°	1714	coll	BLOWER John
Sharp,Arch., fun.of	8°	1714	ss.	KNAGGS Thomas
Shaw,Rev. Jeffery, fun.of	4°	1696	ss.	OFFLEY William
Shepherd,Tim., fun.of	8°	1733	ss.	FORD William,sen
Sherard,Christ., fun.of	4°	1682	ss.	LAXTON Thomas
Sherlock,Bp., cons.of	4°	1728	ss.	WAITE Tho. M.A.
Sherlock,Bp., death of	4°	1762	ss.	NICOLLS Samuel
Sherlock,Dr. R., fun.of	4°	1690	ss.	CRANE Thomas
Shipley,Bp., cons.of	4°	1769	ss.	BALGUY Thomas
Shovel,Sir Cloud., fun.of	8°	1707	ss.	BUTLER D.
Sidney,Alger., beheading	8°	1683	ss.	ANONYMOUS
Simson,Rev. P., fun.of	8°	1773	ss.	DALTON J.
Smith,George, fun.of	8°	1746	ss.	CHANDLER Samuel
Smith,Isaac, ordination	8°	1778	ss.	WRIGHT Thomas
Smith,Jer., fun.of	8°	1723	ss.	CLARKE Matthew
Smith,R., murdered wife	8°	1732	ss.	ANONYMOUS
Smith,Rev. John, fun.of	4°	1673	ss.	PATRICK Simon
Smythe,Sir S., fun.of	8°	1778	ss.	D'COETLOGAN Char.
Snape's (Dr.) Character	8°	1742	ss.	MORELL Thomas
Soame,Mrs. S., fun.of	8°	1692	ss.	WRIGHT Timothy
Soame,Mrs. Sus., fun.of	8°	1692	ss.	FLEMING Robert
Spoile,Mrs., murder of	8°	1763	ss.	PARSONS Joseph
St. Chrysostom, translated	4°	1776	ss.	LEWIS Edward
Stagden,H., fun.of	8°	1727	ss.	BILLINGSLEY John
Staynoe,Rev. Mr., fun.of	4°	1708	ss.	ADAMS John
Steel,Rev. Rich., fun.of	8°	1693	ss.	HAMMOND George
Stennett,Jos., fun.of	8°	1758	ss.	GILL John
Stennett,Mrs. R., fun.	8°	1744	ss.	WILSON Samuel
Stennett,Rev. J., fun.of	4°	1769	ss.	TURNER Daniel
Stephens,Mr., fun.of	4°	1694	ss.	CALAMY Edmund
Stratford,Will., fun.of	4°	1754	ss.	HUNTER Thomas
Sturges,Rev. Mr., fun.of	8°	1756	ss.	FRANKLIN Thomas
Styleman's gift to parish	4°	1761	ss.	PIERS Henry
Superville, translated	-°	1739	ss.	ANONYMOUS
Superville, translated	4°	1739	ss.	PAGET Thomas
Swynfen,John, anon.author	8°	1712	ss.	ANONYMOUS
Sylvester,Rev., fun.of	8°	1708	ss.	CALAMY Edmund
Symmons,John, fun.of	4°	1693	ss.	BROOKE John
Symonds, ordination of	-°	1767	ss.	KING Samuel
Symson,Dr., fun.of	4°	1704	ss.	MILBOURNE Luke
T. D., anon.author	8°	1667	ss.	ANONYMOUS
T. D., anon.author	8°	1678	ss.	ANONYMOUS
T. G.,D. D., anon.author	4°	1690	ss.	ANONYMOUS
T. G.,Published by	FO.	1681	coll	GOODWIN Thomas
T. P., anon.author	4°	1689	ss.	ANONYMOUS
Tate,Martha, fun.of	8°	1751	ss.	HITCHIN Edward
Tavistock,Marquess, fun.	4°	1667	ss.	BEDFORD Thomas
Taylor,Bp., fun.of	4°	1668	ss.	RUST George
Taylor,J., fun.of	8°	1761	ss.	HARWOOD Edward
Tenison,Bp., cons.of	4°	1692	ss.	STANLEY William
Thomas,Bp., cons.of	4°	1774	ss.	BELL William
Thomas,Bp., cons.of	4°	1744	ss.	TAYLOR John
Thomas,Bp., cons.of	-°	----	ss.	WILLS John
Thurlow,Bp., cons.of	4°	1779	ss.	WESTON Phipps
Tilling,R., conversion of	8°	1760	ss.	STEVENS John
Tillotson,Abp., cons.of	4°	1691	ss.	BARKER Ralph
Tillotson,Abp., fun.of	4°	1694	ss.	BURNET Gilbert
Tindal,A Letter To	8°	1731	ss.	HOLBROOK Anthony
Tindal,A Letter To	8°	1731	ss.	HOLBROOK Anthony
Tindal's work, against	8°	1730	ss.	PEERS Richard
Tomkins,Benj., fun.of	8°	1732	ss.	BELBIN Peter
Tompkins,Mrs., fun.of	8°	1761	ss.	TURNER Daniel
Tongue,Rev. Ez., fun.of	4°	1681	ss.	JONES Thomas
Toplady,Rev., publ.by	-°	1770	ss.	MAYHEW Jonathan
Towerson,Dr., fun.of	4°	1697	ss.	STANHOPE George
Trapp,Jos., anon.author	12°	1737	ss.	ANONYMOUS
Travers,Rev. Mr., fun.of	4°	1705	ss.	BOYSE Joseph
Treacher,Rev. B., death	8°	1766	ss.	BULKELEY Charles
Trimnel,Bp., cons.of	4°	1708	ss.	BRADFORD Samuel
Trimnell,Bp., fun.of	4°	1723	ss.	STEPHENS Lewis
Tristram,Mrs., fun.of	8°	1758	ss.	PEARSHALL Richard
Trosse's (G.) Life	8°	1714	ss.	HALLET Joseph
Turenne,Marshall, fun.of	4°	1677	ss.	CLAUDE Francis
Turner,Dr. Tho., fun.of	4°	1672	ss.	MOULIN DU Peter
Tyler,Bp., cons.of	4°	1706	ss.	SYDALL Elias
Tyte,Susan, fun.of	4°	1692	ss.	SPRINT John
Umphreville,Dr., fun.of	4°	1706	ss.	MANNINGHAM Thomas
Upton,Dr., fun.of	8°	1711	ss.	WRIGHT Samuel
Vane,Hon. John, Fun.of	4°	1724	ss.	CURTEIS Thomas
Vere,Lady Mary, fun.of	8°	1672	ss.	GURNALL William
Vincent,Rev. Tho., fun.of	4°	1679	ss.	SLATER Samuel
Vink,Rev. Mr., fun.of	-°	----	ss.	HOW John
Vinor,Sir Tho., fun.of	4°	1683	ss.	HESKETH Henry
Voyce,Will., fun.of	8°	1728	ss.	GODWIN Edward
W. L., anon.author	12°	1740	coll	ANONYMOUS
W. R., anon.author	4°	1694	ss.	ANONYMOUS
W. W., anon.author	4°	1681	ss.	ANONYMOUS
Wake,Abp., enthroned	4°	1716	ss.	BLOMER Ralph
Wake,Bp., cons.of	4°	1706	ss.	KENNET White
Walburgh,A., fun.of	8°	1749	ss.	HUGHES Obadiah
Walcott,Mrs. Ann, fun.of	4°	1782	ss.	PENTYCROSS Thomas
Walker,Dr. Anth., fun.of	4°	1692	ss.	WOODWARD Josiah
Walter,Rich., fun.of	4°	1692	ss.	SHOWER John

Walton,Isaac, printed in	8°	1678	ss.	HOOKER Richard
Warburton,Bp., cons.of	8°	1760	ss.	NEWTON Thomas
Warburton's (Bp.) Lect.	8°	1780	coll	BAGOTT Lewis
Warren,Bp., cons.of	4°	1779	ss.	NEWTON Benjamin
Warren,Mrs., fun.of	4°	1680	ss.	PYKE William
Warrington,Countess, fun.	4°	1691	ss.	WROE Christopher
Warrington,Earl of, fun.	4°	1694	ss.	WROE Christopher
Warwick,Countess, fun.of	8°	1678	ss.	WALKER Anthony
Warwick,Earl of, fun.of	4°	1673	ss.	WALKER Anthony
Watts,Dr. Isaac, fun.of	8°	1749	ss.	MILNER John
Watts,Mich., fun.of	8°	1708	ss.	CALAMY Edmund
Watts,Mrs. Mary, fun.of	4°	1705	ss.	WOODWARD Josiah
Watts,Rev. Isaac, fun.of	8°	1749	ss.	ASHWORTH Caleb
Weatherly,Rev., fun.of	8°	1752	ss.	BURROUGHS Joseph
Webb,Robert, fun.of	8°	1728	ss.	LUCAS Thomas
West's Charity, anniv.of	8°	1774	ss.	HALWARD John
West's Charity, on	4°	1781	ss.	NICOLLS John
Weston,Bp., cons.of	4°	1724	ss.	GILBERT John
Wharton,Lady Mary, fun.	4°	1674	ss.	WATKINSON P.
Whillington,Isaac, fun.of	8°	1773	ss.	WRIGHT Paul
Whitby. Dan., anon.author	8°	1720	ss.	ANONYMOUS
Whitby. Dan., anon.author	8°	1714	ss.	ANONYMOUS
Whitchcote,Lady, fun.of	4°	1726	ss.	MASON John
Whitchurch,Mr., fun.of	4°	1692	ss.	PARSLEY Henry
White,Bp., cons.of	4°	1718	ss.	CLAGETT Nicholas
Whitfield,Rev. G., death	8°	1770	ss.	EDWARDS David
Whitfield,Rev. G., fun.of	8°	1770	ss.	ELLINGTON Edward
Whitfield,Rev., death of	8°	1770	ss.	LANGFORD John
Whitfield,Rev., death of	8°	1770	ss.	PARSONS Jonathan

Whitfield,Rev., death of	8°	1770	ss.	PEMBERTON Ebenezer
Whitfield,Rev., death of	8°	1770	ss.	VENN H. M.A.
Whitfield,Rev.g., fun.of	8°	1770	ss.	ELLIOTT John
Whitworth,Lord, fun.of	4°	1725	ss.	LEWIS George
Wilcocks,Bp., cons.of	8°	1721	ss.	RUSSELL John
Wild,Tim, fun.of	8°	1758	ss.	PICKARD Edward
Wildman,Thomas, fun.of	8°	1754	ss.	WALLIN Benjamin
Wilkins,Bp., fun.of	4°	1673	ss.	LLOYD William
Wilkinson,J., fun.of	8°	1763	ss.	LOWTHIAN S.
Wilks,Mrs. Mary, death of	8°	1732	ss.	FOSTER James
WILLIAM III,King, mem. of	8°	1725	ss.	EARL Jabez
Williams,Bp. John	4°	1678	ss.	ANONYMOUS
Williams,Rev. Dan., fun.	8°	1716	ss.	EVANS John
Wilson,Bp., fun.of	4°	1781	ss.	MOORE Philip
Wilson,Bp, fun.of	-°	17--	ss.	MOORE Philip
Wilton,Rev., sam.,fun.of	8°	1778	ss.	PALMER Samuel
Wilton,Thomas, fun.of	8°	1776	ss.	GIBBONS Thomas
Winter,Richard, fun.of	-°	1776	ss.	WINTER Richard
Wiseman,Edm., fun.of	4°	1694	ss.	SEVILL William
Wollatson,F., fun.of	4°	1685	ss.	CAVE John
Wood,Mrs., fun.of	8°	1737	ss.	LANGFORD William
Wood,Rev. S., fun.of	8°	1767	ss.	HOWE Thomas
Woolston,2 s.against	8°	1728	ss.	HARRIS William
Woolston, against	8°	1726	ss.	REYNELL Carew
Woolston, against	8°	1730	ss.	SUTTON Prideaux
Worthington,Hugh, ord.of	8°	1782	ss.	KIPPIS Andrew
Wright,Rev. T., ord.of	8°	1759	ss.	CHANDLER Samuel
Wright,S., ordination	12°	1709	ss.	WILLIAMS Daniel
Yeates,Susan, fun.of	12°	1688	ss.	WOORDEN Thomas
Yonge,Bp., cons.of	4°	1758	ss.	BACKHOUSE James

(INDEXES TO FIFTH VOLUME)

INDEX D: PLACES OF PUBLICATION OR DELIVERY OTHER THAN LONDON

Note 1: The following index is divided into two parts --

Part One: Places of Publication Other than London, and in the Case of Sermons in Pamphlet Editions ["ss."] Presumably Also the Places of Their Oral Delivery

Part Two: Places of Delivery (but Presumarly Not Also of Publication)

Note 2: Limitations of the data here indexed, and degree of accuracy in the distribution of items into Parts One and Two of the index --

Users of the following index of places of publication or delivery other than London should be aware of the degree of accuracy to be expected in it. In the Preface to his work, John Cooke stated that he and his friends had put themselves to much expense and labor in consulting title pages and library catalogues to make accurate note of places of publication. His word should be accepted on this point. However, Cooke did not present his information without ambiguity or error.

In the first place, like his predecessor Sampson Letsome, Cooke saved space by omitting to name London where London was the place of publication or delivery. But since (again like Letsome) he did not mark in any special way those entries for which he could obtain no information about place of publication, it should not be assumed that every item not indexed in this list was published in London, although certainly the great majority of such items were published there.

In the second place, Cooke did not in every case succeed in distinguishing unequivocally between place of publication and place of delivery. Careful study of the format of his entries discloses that, in general, if a name was used to designate place of publication, Cooke italicized it and printed it before his description of the occasion or subject matter of the publication. On the other hand, if he used the name to designate the place where a sermon was delivered but not published, he printed it after his description of the occasion, put some such preposition as "at" in front of it, and left it in roman type. But his intention is not clear (1) where the italic type is omitted in a place name put before the description of occasion, (2) where an italicized place name is put immediately before the word "Infirmary" or "Hospital" in front of the description of occasion, and (3) where a place name is italicized after an "at."

In the indexes below, every publication concerning which Cooke (or his printer) left his intention equivocally expressed in one of the three ways described above has been classified as printed at the place named in italics, even although in some instances the classification seems obviously wrong. This practice has been followed for three reasons: the rule seems to result in more right than wrong classifications; it brings oddities to attention instead of obscuring them and so may stimulate further bibliographical investigations; and a clearly stated and exactly followed rule in treatment of ambiguities seems better than escape from what appear to be obvious errors by means of silent correction of these few and random treatment of the other ambiguous entries. The rule that has been adopted expresses the judgment of the editor after comparison of seventy-four ambiguous entries with the British Museum Catalogue of Printed Books. The seventy-four included all or almost all the ambiguous entries except those concerning publications by anonymous authors or by authors so prolific that identification of a publication would consume more time than the purpose of the search would justify. For thirty-two of the seventy-four entries no matching entry of any kind was to be found in the Catalogue -- a result to be expected in view of the fact that most of them concerned ephemeral pamphlets printed outside the usual centers of publication. For the remaining forty-two, the Catalogue listed works by the same author on the same subject and with the same date of publication (or a date one year later). For twenty-three of these forty-two, the Catalogue entry confirmed the rule that has been adopted here, and for nineteen it did not. Even in these cases, of course, lack of confirmation does not always mean that the rule is in error. Hence in conclusion we may judge that less than fifty percent of the ambiguous entries are classified wrongly below. The number of ambiguous entries is around ten per cent of the total number (nine hundred forty) of entries that are indexed in the two major parts of the present index. Thus the number of entries that have been mistakenly assigned to one instead of the other of the two parts of Index D is probably less than five percent of the number of entries in Index D taken as a whole.

Note 3: Form of Index D and symbols used within it

Within the following index, names of places of publication or delivery as given in Cooke's records are listed in alphabetical order, without regard to classification as English, Scottish, Irish, colonial, or foreign. Indented below each place name are dates; and indented below each date are listed in alphabetical order the names of authors whom Cooke's records indicate to have published or delivered a sermon or set of sermons on that date at the place named. If Cooke's records show an author to have published or delivered more than one sermon or set of sermons within that year at that place, the author's name appears more than once under the date. Following each author's name on each of its appearances below a date come symbols to indicate format and type of edition in which the sermon or set of sermons was printed. Formats are represented by the conventional symbols for them. Types of edition are represented by "ss.", for single-sermon (pamphlet or booklet) edition, and by "coll.", for collective edition. Underlining of an author's name indicates that in Cooke's record the author is shown as Nonconformist rather than Anglican.

PART ONE OF INDEX D TO FIFTH VOLUME

PLACES OF PUBLICATION OTHER THAN LONDON

AND, IN THE CASE OF SERMONS IN PAMPHLET EDITIONS, PRESUMABLY ALSO THE PLACES OF THEIR ORAL DELIVERY

<u>N.B.</u> Before using Part One of Index D to the Fifth Volume, see notes 1 and 2, above, concerning the two parts of Index D.

Place / Year	Author	Format	Author	Format
Aberdeen				
1660	DOWGLASS Robert	12° ss.		
1701	<u>CALDER</u> <u>R.</u>	8° ss.		
Abingdon				
1727	STOCKWELL Joseph	8° ss.		
1771	<u>TURNER</u> <u>Daniel</u>	12° coll.		
Amsterdam				
1703	COCKBURN John	4° ss.	COCKBURN John	4° ss.
Anapolis				
1755	STERLING James	8° ss.		
Ashford				
1782	WHITFELD Francis	4° ss.		

INDEXES TO FIFTH VOLUME: D: PLACES OF PUBLICATION OTHER THAN LONDON

Place / Year	Author	Format	Author	Format
Bath				
1742	WARBURTON William	8° ss.		
1750	BROWN John	8° ss.		
1757	WAINHOUSE Richard	4° ss.		
1759	OLIVE R.	4° ss.		
1770	VENN H. M.A.	8° ss.		
1772	WINTER Cornelius	8° ss.		
1774	COLLETT J.	8° coll.		
1778	HAWEIS Tho. LL.B.	8° ss.		
Belfast				
1724	ABERNETHY John	4° ss.		
1725	BRUCE Michael	8° ss.		
1778	BRYSON James	8° coll.		
Birmingham				
1716	SOUTHALL Thomas	8° ss.		
1769	GAUNT John	8° ss.		
1770	BROMWICH	8° ss.	PARSONS John	8° ss.
1771	ADAMTHWAITE John	4° ss.		
1778	ADAMTHWAITE John	4° ss.		
Berlin				
1758	SACK A. W. F.	4° ss.		
Blackbourn				
1775	HEWERTSON	8° ss.		
Boston				
1712	MATHER Cotton	8° ss.		
1717	COLEMAN Benjamin	8° ss.		
1722	WILLARD S.	8° ss.		
1727	FOXCROFT Thomas	8° ss.		

1728	PRINCE Tho. M.A.	8° ss.	SEWELL Joseph	8° ss.
1732	HARWARD	8° ss.		
1745	PRINCE Tho. M.A.	8° ss.		
1747	PRINCE Tho. M.A.	8° ss.		
Boveytracy	Church, Devon			
1698	STOOKE Francis	4° ss.		
Bristol				
1699	WATERMAN Hugh	4° ss.		
1708	HOLE Matthew	8° ss.		
1710	HOLE Matthew	4° ss.	HOLE Matthew	8° ss.
1711	HOLE Matthew	8° ss.		
1713	ABBOT Henry	8° ss.	HOLE Matthew	8° ss.
1715	GOLDWIN William	4° ss.		
1721	GIBB John	4° ss.		
1722	BURNETT Tho. DD.	8° ss.		
1738	REYNELL Carew	4° ss.		
1745	CATCOTT Alex. Stopford	4° ss.		
1746	PIERS Henry	8° ss.		
1750	HORLER Joseph	8° ss.		
1752	BROUGHTON Thomas	4° ss.	CONYBEARE John	4° ss.
176-	NEWTON Thomas	4° ss.		
1771	WESLEY John	12° coll.		
1779	DAY Robert	8° ss.		
Cambridge				
1660	SPENCER John	4° ss.		
1661	DUPORT James	4° ss.		
1665	EDWARDS John	4° ss.		
1668				

INDEXES TO FIFTH VOLUME: D: PLACES OF PUBLICATION OTHER THAN LONDON (Camb.)

	KEMP Edward	4° ss.	STARKEY William	4° ss.		
1669	DAVENPORT John	4° ss.	SPENCER John	8° ss.		
1670	BARNE Miles	4° ss.	HUME John	4° ss.	JOHNSON James	4° ss.
	JOHNSON James	8° ss.	SEIGNIOR George	4° ss.		
1671	NORTH John	4° ss.				
1675	JACKSON William	4° ss.				
1676	SCATTERGOOD Samuel	4° ss.	TEMPLER John	4° ss.		
1682	BARNE Miles	4° ss.				
1683	BARNE Miles	4° ss.	BURRELL John	4° ss.		
1684	ASPIN William	4° ss.				
1685	GOSTWYKE William	4° ss.	GOWER Humphrey	4° ss.		
1686	RUST George	4° coll.	THURLIN Thomas	4° ss.		
1693	RUSSEL John	4° ss.	WALKER Thomas	4° ss.		
1695	FOWLER Edward	-° ss.				
1698	HUTCHINSON Francis	4° ss.	NOURSE Peter	4° ss.		
1699	LENG John	4° ss.				
1700	GASKARTH John	4° ss.	HARE Francis	4° ss.		
1701	ALLEYNE John	4° ss.	MARSH Richard	4° ss.		
1704	COOKE Henry M.	4° ss.	LENG John	4° ss.	SAVAGE John	4° ss.
	SAVAGE John	4° ss.	SHERWILL Thomas	4° ss.	SHERWILL Thomas	4° ss.
1707	ALLEYNE John	4° ss.	CANNON Robert	4° ss.		
1709	SHERWILL Thomas	8° ss.				
1711	BROME Edmond	8° coll.	GREEN John	8° ss.	GREEN John	8° ss.
1713	OLDHAM George	4° ss.				
1714	WALLER John	4° ss.				
1715	BENTLEY Richard	8° ss.				
1716	NEEDHAM Peter	8° ss.	STURMY Daniel	8° coll.	WATERLAND Daniel	8° ss.
	WATERLAND Theodoric	8° ss.				
1717	LAUGHTON Richard	4° ss.				
1718	COLBATCH John	4° ss.	WHITFIELD John	8° ss.		

1720	CREYGHTON Robert	8° coll.				
1722	WHITFIELD John	8° ss.				
1723	SHUCKFORD Samuel	4° ss.				
1724	DOUGHTY Gregory WHITFIELD John	4° ss. 8° ss.	NEWCOME John	8° ss.	PARNE Thomas	4° ss.
1726	PARIS John	8° coll.				
1728	BAKER William LONG Roger	8° ss. 8° ss.	HOUGH Thomas NICHOLS Nathaniel	4° ss. 8° ss.	LEEKE Robert	8° ss.
1729	STEBBING Henry	8° ss.				
1731	JOHNSON Thomas	8° ss.				
1732	GRETTON Phillips	8° ss.				
1736	PIGG Thomas	4° ss.				
1738	WILLIAMS Philip	4° ss.				
1739	CRADOCK John	4° ss.				
1741	GARNET John	4° ss.				
1743	LAW Edmund	8° ss.				
1744	NEWCOME John	4° ss.	PARNE Thomas	8° ss.		
1745	GARNET John WILLIAMS Philip	4° ss. 4° ss.	LAW Edmund	8° coll.	MASTERS Robert	8° ss.
1746	MAYS Christopher WARREN Richard	8° ss. 4° ss.	RUTHERFORTH Thomas WESTON William	4° ss. 8° ss.	WESTON William	8° ss.
1748	POWELL Matthew	8° ss.				
1749	GREEN John	4° ss.	TAYLOR John	4° ss.		
1750	HUBBARD Henry	4° ss.				
1752	GREEN John	4° ss.	HURD Richard	4° ss.		
1753	HURD Richard	8° ss.				
1756	ROSS John	4° ss.				
1758	NEWTON Benjamin	4° ss.				
1762	DELAP John	4° ss.				

INDEXES TO FIFTH VOLUME: D: PLACES OF PUBLICATION OTHER THAN LONDON (Camb./Cant.)

1766	WALTON W.	4° ss.				
1767	GORDON John	4° ss.	PORTEUS Beilby	4° ss.	POWELL William Samuel	4° ss.
1768	MARTYN Thomas	4° ss.				
1769	HALLIFAX Samuel	4° ss.	HALLIFAX Samuel	4° ss.		
1770	HALLIFAX Samuel	4° ss.				
1771	HEY John	8° ss.	RUTHERFORTH Thomas	4° ss.		
1772	HALLIFAX Samuel	8° ss.				
1773	CHURCHILL F.F.	4° ss.	EDWARDS Thomas	8° ss.	HEY John	8° ss.
1774	HEY John	8° ss.	HEY John	8° ss.		
1777	COOPER Samuel	4° ss.	HEY John	4° ss.	WARREN John	4° ss.
1780	COOKE William	4° ss.	MAINWARING John. B.D.	8° coll.	<u>ROBINSON</u> <u>Robert</u>	8° ss.
1781	COOKE William	4° ss.	POSTLEWAITE T. B.D.	4° ss.		
Canterbury						
1688	BROWNE Thomas	4° ss.	BROWNE Thomas	4° ss.		
1700	EDWARDS John	8° ss.	GASKARTH John	4° ss.		
1701	MARSDEN Robert	4° ss.				
1712	BLOMER Ralph	4° ss.				
1719	DRAKE Samuel	8° ss.				
1724	DRAKE Samuel	4° ss.				
1732	GRETTON Phillips	8° ss.				
1746	TERRY Isaac	8° coll.				
1749	MOODY Samuel	8° ss.				
1780	CORNWALLIS James	4° ss.				
Carmarthen						
1748	SCURLOCK David	8° ss.				
Cheltenham						
1750	RICH Edward Pickering	4° ss.				

Cherbury
1697
SWANNE John 4° ss.

Chester
1710
OLIVER John. M.A. 4° ss.
1711
COWPER John 8° ss. OLIVER John. M.A. 8° ss.

Colchester
1778
LEAKE Martin William 8° ss.

Corke
1691
WETENHALL Edward 8° ss.

Coventry
1744
VAUGHAN Thomas 8° ss.

Crewkerne, Somerset
1773
COKE Thomas 8° ss.

Devon (Also see Exeter)
1739
WEBBER Francis. DD. 8° ss.
1748
MILLES Jeremiah 8° ss.
1765
WIGHT Robert 4° ss.
1770
MOORE George 4° ss.
1780
MARSHALL John 8° ss.

Dublin
1660
HACKET Thomas 8° ss.
1663
RUST George 4° ss.
1666
TATE Faithful 12° ss.
1670
TEATE Joseph 4° ss.
1672
BERRY Richard 4° ss.
1673
WOLLEY Edward 4° ss.
1674
SALL Andrew 8° ss.
1676
JONES Henry 4° ss.

INDEXES TO FIFTH VOLUME: D: PLACES OF PUBLICATION OTHER THAN LONDON (Dublin)

1682	MANBY Peter	4° ss.		
1683	VESEY John	4° ss.		
1685	KING William	4° ss.		
1689	SMITH Edward	4° ss.		
1691	STERNE John	4° ss.		
1692	WALKINGTON Edward	4° ss.	WETENHALL Edward	4° ss.
1694	ASH St. George	4° ss.		
1695	STERNE John	4° ss.		
1697	BULKLY John	4° ss.	WETENHALL Edward	12° ss.
1698	ARWAKER Edmund	4° ss.	BROWNE Peter	8° ss.
1699	STERNE John	4° ss.		
1700	HAMILTON William	4° ss.		
1704	STERNE John	4° ss.		
1705	AICKIN Joseph	12° ss.		
1707	SYNGE Samuel	4° ss.		
1708	STOUGHTON William	4° ss.		
1712	ECHLIN John	8° ss.		
1714	BOULTER Hugh	4° ss.		
1715	NICHOLSON Edward	12° ss.		
1716	FORSTER Nicholas	4° ss.		
1717	DAVIES Rowland	8° ss.		
1719	SYNGE Edward	4° ss.		
1721	DOWNES Henry	4° ss.		
1722	HOWARD Robert	4° ss.		
1723	HUTCHINSON Francis	4° ss.		
1724	GODWIN Timothy	4° ss.		
1725	DOWNES Henry	4° ss.		
1727	CLAYTON Robert.	4° ss.		

1733	MAULE Henry	4° ss.	SYNGE Edward	12° ss.	SYNGE Edward	12° ss.
	TENNISON Edward	4° ss.				
1735	RUNDLE Thomas	4° ss.				
1736	RUNDLE Thomas	4° ss.				
1738	HORT Josiah	8° coll.	HOWARD Robert	4° ss.		
1739	COPPING John	4° ss.				
1740	CLAYTON Robert.	4° ss.				
1742	STONE George	4° ss.				
1744	CARY Mordecai	4° ss.				
1745	FLETCHER Thomas	4° ss.				
1747	KEARNY John	4° ss.				
1748	COX Michael	4° ss.	HORT Rob. M.A.	8° ss.		
1752	BARNARD William	4° ss.				
1756	HENRY William	8° ss.				
1759	STONE George	4° ss.				
1764	WOODWARD Richard	4° ss.				
1765	CUMBERLAND Denison	4° ss.				
1772	FLETCHER William	8° coll.				
1775	WOODWARD Richard	4° ss.				
1780	CAMPBELL Thomas	4° ss.				
Durham						
1781	PYLE Benjamin	8° ss.				
Edinburgh						
1661	PATERSON John	4° ss.				
1681	MENZIES John.	4° ss.				
1682	CARTWRIGHT Thomas	4° ss.				
1694	BOSTON Thomas	8° ss.	MACKQUEEN John	4° ss.		
1716	RANKEN David	8° coll.	RANKEN David	8° coll.	WISHEART William	8° coll.

1717	RANKEN David	8° ss.		
1719	FOORD Joseph	8° coll.	WISHEART William	4° ss.
1722	DUNLOP William	8° coll.		
1723	WEBSTER James	12° coll.		
1728	COCKBURN Patrick	8° ss.		
1731	DICKSON James	8° coll.		
1734	PILLOK Thomas	8° ss.	DONALDSON Thomas	8° ss.
1738	STEWART John	12° ss.		
1740	WEBSTER	8° ss.		
1743	HUNTER John	8° ss.	HUNTER John	12° ss.
1746	LEIGHTON Robert	8° coll.	WEBSTER Alexander	8° ss.
1748	IMRIE David	8° ss.		
1750	ROBERTS Charles	8° ss.		
1752	WISHART George	8° ss.		
1762	DICK Robert	8° ss.		
1776	DICK Robert	8° ss.		
1779	ERSKINE John	8° ss.		

Eton

1682	PERSE Will. M.A.	4° ss.
1683	TAYLOR Zachary	4° ss.
1700	CHETWOOD Knightly	7° ss.
1702	ADAMS John	4° ss.

Exeter (Also see Devon)

1698	GILBERT John	4° ss.
1699	GILBERT John	4° ss.
1708	SMITH Humphrey	4° ss.
1709	ROBERTS William	4° ss.
1710	MULES Walter	8° ss.

Place/Year	Author	Format	Author	Format	Author	Format
1712	ATKINS Robert	12° coll.	WOLCOMBE Robert	8° ss.	WOLCOMBE Robert	8° ss.
1715	ATKINS Robert	8° ss.	JENKINSON Richard	8° ss.		
1716	SQUIRE Fran. M.A.	8° ss.				
1717	NEWCOME Daniel	8° ss.	RAYNER William	8° ss.		
1718	RAYNER William	8° ss.	MANSTON Joseph	8° ss.		
1722	FARTHING Ralph	8° ss.				
1723	FOULKES Peter	4° ss.				
1724	PAUL William	4° ss.				
1725	NEWTE Samuel	8° ss.				
1730	BLACKALL Theophilus	4° ss.				
1731	NATION William	8° ss.				
1735	STEPHENS Lewis	4° ss.				
1740	TREVANNION Hugh	4° ss.	TREVANNION Hugh	4° ss.		
1741	CLARKE Alured	4° ss.				
1743	SIMONS William	8° coll.	SLEECH John	4° ss.		
1756	LAVINGTON George	8° ss.				
Felsted						
1763	ABDY Stotherd	4° ss.				
Glasgow						
1673	BURNET Alexander	4° ss.				
1741	LEECHMAN William	8° ss.				
1743	LEECHMAN William	8° ss.				
Gloucester						
17--	SALTER Samuel	8° ss.				
1720	JAMES John	8° ss.				
1724	ABBOT Henry	8° ss.				
1750	MOSELEY John	8° ss.				

1755
TALBOT George 4° ss.

Hague
1752
MACLAINE Archibald 8° ss.

Hereford
1741
CROXALL Sam. DD. 8° ss.
1742
CONINGESBY George 8° ss.
1778
HORNE Thomas 4° ss.
1781
RUDD A. M.A. 8° ss.

Honiton, Devon
1765
HARRISON R. 8° ss.

Hull
1746
NICHOLS Nicholas 8° ss.
1749
WHATLEY Robert 8° ss.

Ipswich
1717
HARRISON John 4° ss.
1727
CURTIS William 8° ss. GIBSON John 8° ss.
1746
CANNING Richard 8° ss.
1747
CANNING Richard 8° ss.
1751
CLUBB John 4° ss.
1759
SCOTT Thomas 8° ss.

Jamaica
1722
GALPINE Calvin 4° ss.

Kendal
1740
RUDD James 8° ss.

Kingston, Jamaica
1718
JOHNSTON William 4° ss.

Kingston, Surrey
1769
VENN H. M.A. 8° ss.

Place / Year	Name	Format	Name	Format
Lancaster				
1773	ANONYMOUS	8° ss.		
Leeds				
1739	STORY T.	-° ss.		
1769	SCOTT James	4° ss.	SCOTT James	4° ss.
1773	PRIESTLEY Joseph	8° ss.		
Leicester				
1726	ARNALD Richard	4° ss.		
1737	ARNALD Richard	4° ss.		
1756	HEATHCOTE Ralph	8° ss.		
Lincoln				
1680	HINDMARSH Thomas	4° ss.		
1699	HESKETH Henry	4° ss.		
1712	GARMSTON John	4° ss.		
1746	BARR John	8° ss.	BENET Gilbert	8° ss.
1752	GEORGE William	4° ss.		
1754	MORTON Thomas	4° ss.		
1769	STINTON George	4° ss.		
1771	GREEN John	4° ss.		
1777	YORKE James	4° ss.		
1779	WHITCOMBE John	4° ss.		
Liverpool				
1719	HORROBIN Robert	8° ss.		
1722	WOLSTENHOLME Henry	8° ss.		
1723	ALANSON. Edward	4° ss.		
1745	WOLSTENHOLME Henry	4° ss.		
1765	OWEN E.	8° ss.		

INDEXES TO FIFTH VOLUME: D: PLACES OF PUBLICATION OTHER THAN LONDON

Place / Year	Author	Format	Author	Format
Maidstone				
1735	HANCOCK Thomas Saul	8° ss.		
Malborough				
1780	JAMES David	8° ss.		
Manchester				
----	BROOKE Henry	-° ss.		
1750	WARD Abel	8° ss.		
1751	WATSON John	8° ss.		
Middlesex				
1749	YARDLEY Edward	4° ss.		
1750	THOMAS John	4° ss.		
Monmouth				
1747	EUSTANCE Evans	4° ss.		
Newcastle				
1712	SMITH John	4° ss.		
1731	TURNOR Thomas	8° ss.		
1737	TEW Edm. DD.	4° ss.		
1750	TEW Edm. DD.	4° ss.		
1752	COOKE	8° ss.		
1754	DOCKWRAY Thomas	4° ss.		
1755	LAMBE William	4° ss.	WOOD Andrew	8° ss.
1756	NOWELL William. M.A.	4° ss.	TEW Edm. DD.	4° ss.
1757	LOWTH Robert	4° ss.		
1766	DARCH John	4° ss.		
1768	FAWCETT Richard	4° ss.		
1771	ROTHERAM John	4° ss.		
1777	SCOTT James	4° ss.		

INDEXES TO FIFTH VOLUME: D: PLACES OF PUBLICATION OTHER THAN LONDON

New York

1709

VESEY William 4° ss.

1728

PINDAR Thomas 8° ss.

1759

BOSTWICK David 8° ss.

Norfolk

1709

ANONYMOUS 8° ss.

1772

YONGE Philip 4° ss.

Northampton

1721

GILLMAN John 8° ss.

1722

BOLDERO John 8° ss.

1741

BOWLES Thomas 4° ss.

1743

DODDRIDGE Philip 8° ss.

1744

GREY Richard 8° ss.

1745

HOLME Thomas 8° ss.

1746

LAYNG Henry 8° ss.

1747

BISHOP Hawley 8° ss.

1748

THOMAS John 8° ss.

1749

NIXON John 8° ss.

1750

HARTLEY Thomas 8° ss.

Norwich

1701

JONES Samuel 4° ss.

1702

GRAILLE John 4° ss. GROVE Edward 4° ss.

1704

BRETT Joseph 4° ss. HOADLY John 4° ss. ROBINSON John 4° ss.

1705

RAYMOND George 4° ss.

1706

PYLE Tho. M.A. 4° ss.

1707

JEGON William 4° ss.

1708

BROWNE Theophilus 4° ss. RAYMOND George 4° ss. TRIMNEL Charles 8° ss.

1710

BUCHANAN Charles 4° ss.

INDEXES TO FIFTH VOLUME: D: PLACES OF PUBLICATION OTHER THAN LONDON

Year	Author	Format	Author	Format	Author	Format
1712	BUCHANAN Charles	8° ss.	BUTTS Robert	4° ss.		
1715	LOVE Barry	4° ss.				
1716	CLARK John	8° ss.	RUSSEL John	8° ss.		
1718	BALDWIN James	8° ss.				
1719	POSTLEWAITE Matthew	4° ss.				
1720	ANONYMOUS	12° ss.				
1725	SUTTON William	8° ss.				
1729	KENWRICK George	8° ss.	FROST Richard	4° ss.		
1734	SHUCKFORD Samuel	8° ss.				
1738	BOTT Thomas	8° ss.				
1739	BOOKEY Sacheverell	4° ss.	LEEKE Robert	4° ss.		
1746	KERRICK Charles	8° ss.				
1752	CROWNFIELD Henry	8° ss.				
1753	ANONYMOUS	8° ss.	RIDLEY Glocester	4° ss.		
1756	TAYLOR John	8° ss.				
1764	GREEN John	4° ss.				
1767	TORRIANO Nathaniel	8° coll.				
1780	PARR Samuel	4° ss.				
Nottingham						
1717	HUTCHINSON Michael	8° ss.	KILLINBECK John	8° coll.		
1719	PROUDMAN John	8° ss.				
1722	DISNEY John	8° ss.				
1723	NAISH James	4° ss.				
1724	BRALESFORD Humphry	8° ss.	DISNEY John	8° ss.	STANHOPE Michael	8° ss.
Oxford						
———	FOTHERGILL Thomas	-° ss.				
1660	GREGORY Fran. DD.	4° ss.	MARTIN John	4° ss.	WILKINSON Henry	4° ss.

1661						
	ELLIS Clement	4° ss.	HOLYDAY Barton	8° coll.	PRICE John	8° ss.
	PRICE John	8° ss.	PRICE John	8° ss.	PRICE John	8° ss.
1662						
	SHERLEY William	4° ss.	WALL John	8° ss.		
	CALAMY Edmund	4° ss.				
1664						
	HALL Edmund	8° ss.	MAYNE Jasper	4° ss.		
1665						
	FORD Simon	4° ss.				
1666						
	OLDISWORTH Giles	4° ss.	WILLIAMS Griffith	4° ss.		
1667						
	STOKES David	4° ss.	STOKES David	4° ss.		
1669						
	SHERLOCK Richard	4° ss.				
1671						
	PIERCE Tho. DD.	4° coll.				
1673						
	SHARROCK Robert	4° coll.				
1674						
	WOOD A. Edward	8° coll.				
1677						
	OLDISWORTH Giles	4° ss.				
1678						
	USHER James	fo.coll.				
1679						
	WALLIS John	4° ss.				
1680						
	GREENWOOD Daniel	4° ss.				
1681						
	BENNION John	4° ss.				
1683						
	JEMMAT Samuel	4° ss.				
1684						
	ANONYMOUS	8° ss.				
1685						
	IRONSIDE Gilbert	4° ss.	NORRIS John	4° ss.		
1688						
	CUDWORTH John	4° ss.	HELLIER Henry	4° ss.		
1691						
	JANE Will. DD.	4° ss.	SPARK Tho. DD.	4° ss.		
1692						
	JANE Will. DD.	4° ss.	WHITING Charles	4° ss.		
1694						
	CAMPION Abraham	4° ss.	SYKES Thomas	4° ss.	WHITEHALL Rob. M.A.	4° ss.
	MATHER Nathaniel	4° ss.				
1697						
	BECONSALL Thomas	4° ss.				
1698						
	JONES David	4° ss.				
1699						
	BARON John	4° ss.				
17--						
	ROOTES Richard	8° ss.				
1700						
	WOODROFFE Benjamin	4° ss.				

INDEXES TO FIFTH VOLUME: D: PLACES OF PUBLICATION OTHER THAN LONDON (Oxford)

Year						
1701	MILLES Thomas	8° ss.				
1702	PALMER Charles	4° ss.	SACHEVERELL Henry	4° ss.	SACHEVERELL Henry	4° ss.
1703	CHAPMAN Stephen	4° ss.	DAGGE Jonathan	4° ss.	WOODROFFE Benjamin	4° ss.
1704	ADDISON Anthony	4° ss.	COOKE Thomas	4° ss.	SACHEVERELL Henry	4° ss.
1705	MATHER John	4° ss.	RENNELL Thomas	4° ss.	ROYSE Geor. DD.	4° ss.
	TILLY William	4° ss.				
1706	GEREE John	4° ss.	MATTHEWS John	4° ss.	SACHEVERELL Henry	4° ss.
	SMALBROKE Richard	4° ss.	SMITH Joshua	4° ss.	WILDER John	4° ss.
	WOODROFFE Benjamin	4° ss.				
1707	MILLES Thomas	4° ss.				
1708	DOWNES Henry	8° ss.	SACHEVERELL Henry	4° ss.	STEPHENS Henry	4° ss.
	WILLET John	4° ss.				
1710	LEWIS Henry	8° ss.	WHALEY Nathanael	8° ss.		
1711	BISSE Thomas	8° ss.	HOWELL Will. M.A.	8° ss.	ROOTES Richard	8° ss.
1712	ARCHER Edmund	8° ss.	BISSE Thomas	4° ss.	DORRINGTON Theophilus	8° ss.
	HOWELL Will. M.A.	8° ss.	HUMPHREYS Thomas	8° ss.	IBBETSON Richard	8° ss.
1713	AYLMER William	8° ss.	BISSE Thomas	8° ss.	DINGLEY William	8° ss.
	EYRE Rich. M.A.	8° ss.	EYRE Rich. M.A.	8° ss.	GARDINER James	4° ss.
	REEVES William	4° ss.				
1714	DUKE Rich. M.A.	8° coll.	GODDARD Philip	8° ss.	LOMBARD Daniel	8° ss.
	ROWDEN John	8° ss.	RYE George	8° ss.		
1715	EYRE Rich. M.A.	8° ss.				
1716	HOLE Matthew	8° ss.	NEWTON Richard	4° ss.	PEARSE Robert	8° ss.
1717	DOD Thomas	8° ss.	HANNES William	8° ss.	HIND Thomas	8° ss.
	PEARSE Robert	8° ss.	SMALRIDGE George	8° coll.	STOCKWELL Joseph	8° ss.
1718	NEWLIN Thomas	8° ss.	NEWLIN Thomas	8° ss.	TILLY William	8° ss.
1719	GIBSON John	8° ss.	HOLDSWORTH Winch. DD.	8° ss.		
1720	NEWLIN Thomas	8° coll.	WILDER John	8° coll.		
1721	COTES Digby	8° coll.	HOLE Matthew	8° ss.	PARSONS Thomas	8° ss.
	PARSONS Thomas	8° ss.	PEARSE Robert	8° ss.		
1722	BERRIMAN William	4° ss.	CONYBEARE John	8° ss.		
1723	CONINGESBY George	8° ss.	CONYBEARE John	8° ss.	NORRIS John	12° ss.
1724	REYNELL Carew	4° ss.	SMALRIDGE George	fo. coll.		

1725	HOLE Matthew	8° coll.	KING John	8° ss.		
1726	CONYBEARE John	8° ss.	EYRE Rich. M.A.	4° ss.	NEWLIN Thomas	8° coll.
1727	CONYBEARE John	8° ss.				
1728	JONES John	8° ss.	NEWLIN Thomas	8° coll.		
1729	BETTY Joseph	8° ss.	BURTON John	4° ss.	BURTON John	4° ss.
	JAMES William	8° ss.	NEWLIN Thomas	8° ss.		
1730	GREY Richard	8° ss.	ROBINSON Thomas	8° ss.		
1731	BULKELEY Benj. DD.	8° ss.				
1732	GATTON Benjamin	8° coll.	PANTING Matthew	4° ss.	SILVESTER Tipping	4° ss.
	SILVESTER Tipping	4° ss.				
1733	COCKMAN Thomas	8° ss.	CONINGESBY George	8° ss.	CONYBEARE John	8° ss.
	RANDOLPH Thomas	8° ss.	TROUGHEAR Thomas	8° ss.		
1734	BURTON John	8° ss.				
1735	FELTON Henry	8° ss.	PATTEN Thomas	8° ss.		
1736	FELTON Henry	8° ss.	FELTON Henry	8° ss.	HOLLOWAY Benjamin	8° ss.
1737	DUBOIS Peter	8° ss.	HARTE Walter	8° ss.	STEPHENS William	8° coll.
1738	HUTCHINSON Thomas	8° ss.	PAYNE Thomas	8° ss.	PERROT Humphrey	8° ss.
	WEBBER Francis. DD.	8° ss.				
1739	CLEAVER Will. M.A.	8° ss.	HOLLOWAY Benjamin	8° ss.	RANDOLPH Thomas	8° ss.
	WILDER John	8° ss.				
1740	BISSE Thomas	8° coll.	HUTCHINSON Thomas	8° ss.		
1741	BURTON John	8° ss.	GAMBOLD John	8° ss.	SPRY John	8° ss.
	WILDER John	8° coll.				
1742	CONINGESBY George	8° ss.	WEBBER Francis. DD.	8° ss.		
1743	CLEAVER Will. M.A.	8° ss.	DODWELL William	8° ss.	EDWARDS Joseph	8° ss.
	HUNT Thomas	4° ss.				
1744	BENTHAM Edward	8° ss.	BURTON John	8° ss.	DODWELL William	8° ss.
	MERRICK James	4° ss.	SPRY John	8° ss.		
1745	DALTON John	4° ss.	DODWELL William	8° ss.	DODWELL William	8° ss.
	GARDNER William	8° ss.	HORBERY Matt. DD.	8° ss.	SPRY John	8° ss.
1746	BURTON John	8° ss.	BURTON John	8° ss.	FORSTER Nathaniel	8° ss.
	HURLY James	8° ss.	PARKER William	8° ss.		
1747	BROWN Richard	8° ss.	NEVE Timothy	8° ss.		

INDEXES TO FIFTH VOLUME: D: PLACES OF PUBLICATION OTHER THAN LONDON (Oxford)

1748	BEAR John	8° ss.	IBBETSON James	8° ss.	PARKER William	8° ss.
	WHITING Charles	8° ss.				
1749	FOTHERGILL Thomas	8° ss.	HORBERY Matt. DD.	8° ss.	PARKER William	8° ss.
	WATSON George	4° ss.				
1750	BROWN Richard	8° ss.	CLEAVER Will. M.A.	8° ss.	DODWELL William	8° ss.
	PARKER William	8° ss.	WEBBER Francis. DD.	8° ss.		
1751	WHITFIELD Henry	8° ss.				
1752	CONYBEARE John	4° ss.	DODWELL William	8° ss.	HAWKINS William	8° ss.
	JENNER Thomas	8° ss.	RANDOLPH Thomas	8° ss.		
1753	FOTHERGILL Thomas	8° ss.				
1754	SHARP William	8° ss.				
1755	RANDOLPH Thomas	8° ss.	SHARP William	4° ss.		
1756	HORNE Geo. DD.	8° ss.	HORNE Geo. DD.	8° ss.	HORNE Geo. DD.	8° ss.
1757	GRIFFITH Thomas	8° ss.				
1758	WEBBER Francis. DD.	4° ss.				
1759	BURTON John	8° coll.	NEVE Timothy	8° ss.		
1760	BURTON John	8° ss.	GRIFFITH Thomas	8° ss.		
1761	HITCHCOCK Thomas	8° ss.	HORNE Geo. DD.	8° ss.	HORNE Geo. DD.	8° ss.
	ROTHERAM John	8° ss.	SIMPSON Joseph	8° ss.		
1762	FOTHERGILL Thomas	8° ss.	HORNE Geo. DD.	8° ss.	RANDOLPH Thomas	8° ss.
	ROTHERAM John	8° ss.				
1763	GRIFFITH Thomas	8° ss.				
1765	FOTHERGILL Geo. DD.	8° coll.				
1766	ROTHERAM John	8° ss.				
1767	RANDOLPH Thomas	8° ss.				
1768	KENNICOTT Benjamin	8° ss.	RANDOLPH Thomas	8° ss.	RANDOLPH Thomas	8° ss.
1769	FRAMPTON Matt. LLD.	4° ss.	HAWKINS William	8° ss.	RANDOLPH Thomas	8° ss.
	WHITFIELD Henry	4° ss.				
1771	LOWTH Robert	4° ss.	STONE Edward	8° coll.		
1773	COOKE John	8° ss.	GRIFFITH Thomas	8° ss.		
1774	HORNE Geo. DD.	4° ss.				

1775
HORNE Geo. DD. 8° ss. HORNE Geo. DD. 8° ss. NICOLL Richard 8° ss.
1776
BAGOTT Lewis 4° ss.
1777
CHELSUM James 4° ss. COOPER Miles 4° ss. HOLMES Robert. MA. 4° ss.
STONE Edward 8° coll.
1778
BUTLER John 4° ss.
1779
RANDOLPH John 4° ss. WILLIAMSON James 8° ss.
1781
CROWE William 4° ss. NEVE Timothy 8° coll.
1782
DUPREE Edward 4° ss. RANDOLPH John 4° ss.

Paris
1684
WAKE William 4° ss.

Philadelphia
1737
PETERS Richard 4° coll.

Preston
1728
WHITE George 8° ss.

Reading
1727
SLADE Joseph 4° ss.
1740
WALLIS John 8° ss.
1766
POWYS Thomas 8° ss.
1777
COCHRANE James 4° ss.
1780
COCHRANE James 4° ss.

Revel, Russia
1725
CONSERT Thomas 4° ss.

Richmond
1747
COMER William 8° ss.

Rotterdam
1685
HILL Joseph 4° ss.

Rouen
1689
GRENVILLE Denis 4° ss.

INDEXES TO FIFTH VOLUME: D: PLACES OF PUBLICATION OTHER THAN LONDON

Salisbury (Also see Sarum)

1768

DODWELL William 8° ss.

1769

MOSS Charles 8° ss.

1770

OGLE N. DD. 8° ss. WILLIAMS Benjamin 8° coll.

1773

CORNWALL M. P. 12° coll.

Salop (Also see Shrewsbury and Shropshire)

1726

JONES Samuel 8° ss.

1727

HUMPHREYS John 8° ss.

1747

HORBERY Matt. DD. 8° ss.

1749

ADAMS William 4° ss.

1759

REYNOLDS M.A. 8° ss.

1761

DOVE Richard 8° ss.

1771

HUMPHRIES Thomas 8° ss.

1779

WARTER Thomas 8° ss.

1780

HILL Bryam 8° ss.

Sarum (Also see Salisbury)

1734

FANCOURT Samuel 8° ss.

1746

GILBERT John 8° ss.

1767

GREEN Thomas 8° ss.

1771

STONEHOUSE James 8° ss.

Sherborne

1741

FISHER John 8° coll.

1746

DAGGE Robert 8° ss.

1747

HARE Tho. M.A. 4° ss.

1748

SHEPHEARD Will. M.A. 8° coll.

Shrewsbury (Also see Salop and Shropshire)

1715

FELTON George 8° ss.

1716

POWELL William 12° ss.

INDEXES TO FIFTH VOLUME: D: PLACES OF PUBLICATION OTHER THAN LONDON

Stafford
1756
CREWE Joseph 4° ss.

Stamford
1720
PECK Fran. M.A. 8° ss.
1725
HANNES William 4° ss.

Tiverton
1753
FORT Francis 8° ss.

Truro, Cornwall
1779
FURLY Samuel 4° ss.

Tunbridge
1684
WALKER Anthony 12° ss.
1694
CORNWALLIS Henry 12° ss.
1715
SYDALL Elias 4° ss. TRIMNEL Charles 4° ss.
1735
CURTEIS Thomas 8° ss.
1754
TOWERS Johnstone 4° ss.

Warrington
1711
NEWCOME Henry 8° ss.
1754
HUNTER Thomas 8° coll.
1769
FARRINGTON William 8° coll.

Winchester
1736
CLARKE Alured 4° ss.
1777
BURLEIGH Richard 4° ss.

Winton
1732
BUDWORTH William 8° ss.

Worcester
1711
PARSONS Thomas 8° ss.
1715
GOOD Thomas 4° ss.

Place	Year	Author	Format	Author	Format	Author	Format
	1720	COMBE Edward	4° ss.				
	1736	STAPYLTON Miles	8° coll.				
	1748	MORELL Thomas	8° ss.				
	1749	SMALRIDGE Philip	4° ss.				
	1750	WILMOT George	4° ss.				
	1751	TOTTIE John	8° ss.				
	1752	WAUGH John	8° ss.				
	1753	MEADOWCOURT Richard	8° ss.				
	1756	WILSON Bernard	4° ss.				
	1770	RAWLINS John	8° ss.				
	1773	RAWLINS John	8° ss.				
	1779	MOSS Thomas	4° ss.				
York							
	1661	BRADLEY Thomas	4° ss.				
	1663	BRADLEY Thomas	4° ss.	BRADLEY Thomas	4° ss.	BRADLEY Thomas	4° ss.
		BRADLEY Thomas	4° ss.				
	1666	BRADLEY Christopher	4° ss.				
	1679	BARKER George	8° ss.				
	1691	HALLEY George	4° ss.	TULLIE George	4° ss.		
	1696	HESLEDEN Thomas	4° ss.				
	1697	BARKER George	8° ss.				
	1704	PEARSON William	4° ss.				
	1706	ANONYMOUS	4° ss.	BRADLEY John	4° ss.	PERSE Will. M.A.	4° ss.
		TERRICK Samuel	4° ss.				
	1710	SCOTT Thomas	8° ss.				
	1716	BROWNE W. M.A.	8° ss.				
	1717	COATES James	8° ss.				
	1718	BARNARD Tho. M.A.	8° ss.	DANNYE Robert	4° ss.		

Year	Name	Format	Name	Format	Name	Format
1722						
	BELL George	8° ss.	HITCHMOUGH Richard	8° ss.	HITCHMOUGH Richard	8° ss.
	MARSH George	8° ss.				
1724						
	CLARKE Thomas	8° ss.				
1726						
	JOHNSTON Samuel	8° ss.				
1730						
	CLARKE Stephen	8° ss.				
1732						
	HEBER John	-° ss.				
1735						
	DRAKE W. M.A.	8° ss.	MOSELEY Richard	8° ss.		
1736						
	MAWER John	8° ss.				
1737						
	TOPHAM Edward	8° ss.				
1740						
	HOGGART Will.	8° ss.				
1742						
	BLACKBURNE Francis	8° ss.				
1744						
	WILLATTS Charles	4° ss.				
1745						
	DAVILLE John	8° ss.	DUPONT John	8° ss.	HARGREAVES Robert	8° ss.
	HARGREAVES Robert	8° ss.	HILL J. S. DD.	8° ss.	HOWDELL William	8° ss.
	SUGER Zachariah	8° ss.				
1746						
	DUPONT John	8° ss.	HOLMES William	8° ss.	IBBETSON James	8° ss.
	PENDLEBURY William	8° coll.	PLAXTON John	8° ss.		
1748						
	WIND J.	8° ss.				
1749						
	COLLINS Thomas	8° ss.				
1770						
	ALLANSON	8° ss.				
1780						
	SCOTT James	4° ss.	TORRE Nicholas	4° ss.	<u>CAPPE</u> <u>Newcome</u>	8° ss.
1781						
	BEILBY Samuel	4° ss.	TILLARD Richard M.A.	4° ss.	<u>HARRISON</u> <u>R.</u>	8° coll.
1782						
	DEALTRY R. B. M.A.	4° ss.				

(INDEXES TO FIFTH VOLUME)

PART TWO OF INDEX D: PLACES OF DELIVERY
(BUT PRESUMABLY NOT ALSO OF PUBLICATION)

Abingdon
1683
BARON William 4° ss.

Bath
1749
BAYLY Edward 8° ss.
1782
PENTYCROSS Thomas 4° ss.

Biddeford
1775
HERVEY James 12° ss.

Bengal, Fort Will.
1708
ANDERSON William 8° coll.

Boston
1770
LATHROP John 4° ss.

Bradfield
1703
HOWSON Robert 8° ss.

INDEXES TO FIFTH VOLUME: D: PART TWO: PLACES OF DELIVERY (BUT PRESUMABLY NOT ALSO OF PUBLICATION)

Bristol

1744
CASTLEMAN John 4° ss.

1766
CAMPLIN John 4° ss.

1767
ANONYMOUS 8° ss.

1768
ANONYMOUS 4° ss.

Brussels

1744
TAYLOR John 8° ss.

Cambridge

1753
BATE James 4° ss.

Castle Ashby

1660
TOWERS John 8° ss.

Chelmsford

1710
BERNARD Thomas 4° ss.

Chesham

1771
SPOONER Thomas 8° coll.

Colchester

1706
SMITHIES William, jun 8° ss.

Crediton

1743
TOWGOOD Micaiah 8° ss.

Deptford

1695
FINGLASS John 4° ss.

Devon

1760
BLACKETT Bridges Edw. 4° ss.

Dublin

1769
MANN Isaac 12° ss.

1779
TRAIL Jacob 4° ss.

Dumfries
- 1731
  - WALLACE Robert — 8° ss.

Ghent, camp near
- 1696
  - WILLIAMS William — 4° ss.

Gravesend
- 1728
  - HOW James — 8° ss.

Greenwich
- 1748
  - BUTLEY John — 4° ss.

Hammersmith
- 1726
  - BEARNE Edward — 4° ss.

Hertford
- 1740
  - BROWNE Charles — 4° ss.

Isleworth
- 1719
  - COLEIRE Richard — 4° ss.
- 1723
  - COLEIRE Richard — 8° ss.
- 1729
  - COLEIRE Richard — 4° ss.
- 1738
  - COLEIRE Richard — 4° ss.

Kingston <Surrey?>
- 1721
  - COLEIRE Richard — 4° ss.
- 1726
  - COLEIRE Richard — 4° ss.
- 1727
  - COLEIRE Richard — 4° ss.
- 1743
  - ALLEN William — 8° ss.

Leeds
- 1745
  - CROWTHER John — 8° ss.

INDEXES TO FIFTH VOLUME: D: PART TWO: PLACES OF DELIVERY (BUT PRESUMABLY NOT ALSO OF PUBLICATION)

Lincoln's - Inn - Fields <London>
1680
CROMWELL Oliver 4° ss.

Lisbon
1709
WILCOCKS Joseph 4° ss.
1746
PARKER Stavely 8° ss.

Liverpool
1766
BREKELL John 8° ss.
1769
BREKELL John 8° ss.

Maldon
1697
BRAMSTON William 4° ss.

Manchester
1755
FOXLEY Thomas 8° ss.

Newcastle
1688
MITCALFE Phil. 4° ss.
1748
KEENE Edmund 8° ss.
1752
WIBBERSLEY John 8° ss.

Newgate Prison
1695
CROOKE B. M.A. 4° coll.
1744
ALLEN Thomas 8° ss.

Newhaven
1760
BEACH John 8° ss.

New York
1776
O'BEIRNE 4° ss.

Norfolk
1671
SMYTHIES William 4° ss.

Oxford
1662
ANONYMOUS 4° ss.
1742
COLEIRE Richard 4° ss.
1749
BILSTONE John 8° coll.

Plymouth
1771
BLACKETT Bridges Edwar 4° ss.

Richmond
1715
BRADY Nich. DD. 4° ss.

Salop
1751
BINNELL Robert 8° ss.

Sarum (Also see Salisbury)
1726
WHITBY Daniel 8° coll.

Shropshire (Also see Salop and Shrewsbury)
1715
ANONYMOUS 8° ss.

Symsbury, Connecticut
1782
BAXTER Simeon 8° ss.

(the) Temple, London
1714
BRAMSTON William 4° ss.

Tunbridge
1714
ASH St. George 4° ss.

Warrington
1777
ENFIELD William 8° ss.

West Acre, Norfolk
1703
HILDYARD Francis 8° ss.

Williamburgh <*sic*. in Cooke's record. The place is Williamsburg, Virginia.>
1746
STITH John 4° ss.

INDEXES TO FIFTH VOLUME: D: PART TWO: PLACES OF DELIVERY (BUT PRESUMABLY NOT ALSO OF PUBLICATION)

Winchester
1729
MARKLAND Abraham 8° coll.

Windsor
1686
ANONYMOUS 4° ss.

Worcester
1737
BANNER Richard 8° ss.
1743
BROOKER Daniel 4° ss.
1747
MORELL Thomas 8° ss.

Yarmouth
1683
HILDEYARD John 4° ss.

York
1704
C. - - - - T. 4° ss.

(I N D E X E S T O F I F T H V O L U M E)

I N D E X E : L I B R A R I E S N A M E D I N C O O K E ' S L I S T S

Contents and Arrangement of This Index:

Among the sources of Cooke's information, as Cooke states in his Preface, were the libraries at Oxford and Cambridge, the library at Eton College, and in London the collections at the British Museum, at the Dr. Williams's Library, and at Sion College. He seems also to have consulted the collection at St. Paul's on occasion. The present index names the libraries in which, according to his listings, he found pulpit publications; and it identifies the items that his listings assign to each of them. Part One of the index concerns libraries at Oxford, Part Two the libraries at Cambridge, and Part Three the libraries elsewhere. Under the name of each library indexed, the items are arranged in order of the year of publication; then within the group for each year, they are arranged in two sets according to Cooke's classification of the authors as Anglican or Nonconformist; and within each of these classifications, they are arranged alphabetically by authors' surnames. This grouping enables the reader to characterize the holdings of each library as of the year 1783 of Cooke's work. In this index, as in the lists to which it refers, the underlining of an author's name represents the italic type which Cooke used to indicate that an author was a Nonconformist rather than an Anglican.

P A R T O N E O F I N D E X E : O X F O R D L I B R A R I E S

All Souls College ("All S.")

Year	Author	Format	Author	Format	Author	Format
1662	WREN Matthew	4° ss.				
1668	RUST George	4° ss.				
1670	CUDWORTH Ralph	8° ss.	WARD Seth	4° ss.		
1672	FARINDON Anth. B.D.	fo.coll.	HASCARD Gregory	4° ss.	WARD Seth	8°coll.
1673	PATRICK Simon	4° ss.	SMITH John	4°coll.	WARD Seth	4° ss.
1674	JAMES Henry	4° ss.	WARD Seth	4° ss.	WARD Seth	8°coll.
1676	DUPORT James	4°coll.	PATRICK Simon	4° ss.	TEMPLER John	4° ss.

Year	Name	Format	Name	Format	Name	Format
1677	CRADOCK Zechary	4° ss.	PITTIS Thomas	4° ss.	RIVELY Benedict	4° ss.
	SUDBURY John	4° ss.	THORP George	4° ss.		
1678	BATTIE William	4° ss.	LLEWELIN David	4° ss.		
1679	FARINDON Anth. B.D.	fo.coll.	HORNE Thomas	4° ss.	HORTON Thomas	fo.coll.
	LYNFORD Thomas	4° ss.	NEEDHAM Robert	8° coll.	THOMAS John	4° ss.
	WALLIS John	4° ss.	WILLIAMS John	4° ss.		
1680	BATTIE William	4° ss.	DOVE Heb. DD.	4° ss.	HASCARD Gregory	4° ss.
	HICHMAN Charles	4° ss.	PARSONS Robert	4° ss.		
1681	FOWLER Edward	4° ss.	MAURICE Henry	4° ss.	SILL William	4° ss.
	STRATFORD Nicholas	4° ss.				
1682	CUTLORE Joseph	4° ss.	FREEMAN Samuel	4° ss.	INETT John	4° ss.
	KIDDER Richard	4° ss.	LAMBE John	4° ss.	PAYNE William	4° ss.
	WILKINS John	8° coll.				
1683	BISBIE Nathaniel	4° ss.	FOWLER Edward	4° ss.	GASKARTH John	4° ss.
	PAYNE William	4° ss.	PAYNE William	4° ss.		
1684	ALLESTREE Richard	fo.coll.	BRIDGE Francis	4° ss.	BURTON Hezekiah	8° coll.
	CAVE Will. DD.	4° ss.	LAMBE John	4° ss.	LEIGH Thomas	4° ss.
	SMYTHIES William	4° ss.	WAKE William	4° ss.		
1685	BURNET Gilbert	4° ss.	BURTON Hezekiah	8° coll.	FOWLER Edward	4° ss.
	GRAILLE John	8° ss.	GRAILLE John	8° coll.	HODGES Thomas	4° ss.
	SHERLOCK William	4° ss.	TURNER Francis	4° ss.	TURNER Tho. DD.	4° ss.
	WAGSTAFFE Thomas	4° ss.				
1686	ANONYMOUS	4° ss.				
1687	ANONYMOUS	4° ss.				
1688	BURNET Gilbert	8° ss.	DUREL John	4° ss.		
1689	BURNET Gilbert	4° ss.	BURNET Gilbert	4° ss.	BURNET Gilbert	4° ss.
	PATRICK Simon	4° ss.				
1690	BURNET Gilbert	4° ss.	BURNET Gilbert	4° ss.	BURNET Gilbert	4° ss.
	FOWLER Edward	4° ss.	FREEMAN Samuel	4° ss.	FREEMAN Samuel	4° ss.
	HICHMAN Charles	4° ss.	MASTERS Samuel	4° ss.	SHELTON William	4° ss.
	SMITH Humphrey	4° ss.	SMITH Humphrey	4° ss.	WILLES John	4° ss.
1691	BLAGRAVE Jonathan	4° ss.	HOOPER George	4° ss.	JANE Will. DD.	4° ss.
	KING William	4° ss.	NORRIS John	8° coll.	SPARK Tho. DD.	4° ss.
1692	BENTLEY Richard	4° coll.	BRADFORD Samuel	4° ss.	BURNET Gilbert	4° ss.
	JONES David	4° ss.	JONES David	4° ss.	STRADLING Geor. DD.	8° coll.
1694	BURNET Gilbert	4° ss.	BURNET Gilbert	4° ss.	HALLYWELL Henry	8° ss.
	NORRIS John	8° coll.				
1695	ADAMS John	4° ss.	ANONYMOUS	4° ss.	FISHER Joseph	4° ss.
	HOOPER George	4° ss.	ISHAM Zach. DD.	4° ss.	TENISON Thomas	4° ss.

Year	Name	Format	Name	Format	Name	Format
	WHALEY Nathanael	8° coll.				
1696						
	BENTLEY Richard	4° ss.				
1697						
	GOODMAN John	8° coll.	LANGFORD Emanuel	4° ss.	OWTRAM William	8° coll.
1698						
	NOURSE Peter	4° ss.	WHALEY Nathanael	8° coll.	WHITFELD Will. DD.	4° ss.
	WHITFELD Will. DD.	4° ss.	WHITFELD Will. DD.	4° ss.		
1699						
	EDWARDS John	4° ss.	JONES David	4° ss.		
1700						
	CAMPION Abraham	4° ss.	EDWARDS John	8° ss.	ELLISON Nath. DD.	8° ss.
	GASKARTH John	4° ss.	GASKARTH John	4° ss.	KEITH George	4° ss.
1701						
	CORNWALL John	4° ss.	ISHAM Zach. DD.	4° ss.	MARSDEN Robert	4° ss.
	SHERLOCK William	4° ss.				
1702						
	BRAGGE Francis	8° coll.	BRAGGE Francis	8° coll.	DELAUNE William	4° ss.
	SACHEVERELL Henry	4° ss.	TRELAWNEY Jonathan Sir	4° ss.		
1703						
	FULLER Thomas	4° ss.	WOODROFFE Benjamin	4° ss.		
1704						
	BRAGGE Francis	8° coll.	BUTLER Lilly	4° ss.	CLAGETT William	8° coll.
	CLAGETT William	8° coll.	GASTRELL Francis	4° ss.	LENG John	4° ss.
	SAVAGE John	4° ss.	WHALEY Nathanael	12° coll.	WHALEY Nathanael	12° coll.
	HUSSEY Joseph	4° ss.				
1706						
	ALTHAM Roger	4° ss.	HICHMAN Charles	8° coll.	WOTTON William	4° ss.
1707						
	ALLEYNE John	4° ss.	SAVAGE William	4° ss.	STILLINGFLEET Edward	fo. coll.
1708						
	LITTELL Tho. DD.	4° ss.	STANLEY William	8° ss.	WILLIAMS John	8° coll.
1709						
	BROME Edmond	8° coll.	COX Thomas	4° ss.	LYNFORD Thomas	8° ss.
	PELLING John	4° ss.	SHERWILL Thomas	8° ss.		
1710						
	SPRAT Thomas	8° coll.	WALKER John	8° ss.	WEST Richard	8° ss.
	WHITBY Daniel	8° coll.				
1711						
	GREEN Robert	8° ss.				
1712						
	BRETT Thomas	8° coll.				
1713						
	BRAGGE Francis	8° coll.	BRETT Thomas	8° coll.	SACHEVERELL Henry	4° ss.
1714						
	BRETT Thomas	8° coll.				
1715						
	BRETT Joseph	8° coll.	LENG John	4° ss.	MARSH Richard	8° ss.
	SAVAGE William	4° ss.				
1716						
	BARROW Isaac	fo. coll.	BISSE Thomas	8° ss.		
1717						
	SMALRIDGE George	8° coll.				
1719						
	SHERLOCK William	8° coll.				
1720						

Year	Name	Format	Name	Format	Name	Format
	FIDDES Rich. DD.	fo. ss.	FIDDES Rich. DD.	fo. ss.	MANGEY Thomas	4° ss.
	NEWLIN Thomas	8° coll.				
1721	SAUNDERS Erasmus	8° ss.				
1722	SUTTON William	8° ss.				
1723	ANONYMOUS	8° ss.	BLACKALL Offspring	fo.coll.	GIBSON Edmund	4° ss.
1724	HOUGH Nathaniel	4° ss.	SMALRIDGE George	fo.coll.	SOUTH Robert	8° coll.
1725	BISSE Thomas	8° ss.				
1726	BAKER William	4° ss.	BRAGGE Francis	8° coll.	CONYBEARE John	8° ss.
	NEWLIN Thomas	8° coll.	OLIVER Edward	4° ss.		
1727	BISSE Thomas	8° ss.	LENG John	4° ss.	ROGERS John	8° coll.
	SOUTH Robert	8° coll.	WATSON Joseph	4° ss.		
1728	BULLOCK Thomas	8° ss.	FIDDES Rich. DD.	fo.coll.	LONG Roger	8° ss.
	NEWLIN Thomas	8° coll.	NORRIS John	8° coll.	NORRIS John	9° coll.
	READING Will. M.A.	8° coll.				
1729	BISSE Thomas	8° ss.				
1730	ATTERBURY Francis	8° coll.	BRADSHAW William	4° ss.	CLARKE Samuel	8° coll.
	LITTLETON Edward	4° ss.	READING Will. M.A.	8° coll.	ROGERS John	8° coll.
1731	MARSHALL Nathaniel	8° coll.				
1732	FERREBEE Michael	4° ss.				
1733	MAULE Henry	4° ss.	RANDOLPH Thomas	8° ss.	<u>GIFFORD A.</u>	8° ss.
1735	LYNCH John	4° ss.	ROGERS John	8° coll.	SHARP John	8° coll.
	TILLOTSON John	fo.coll.				
1736	CLAGETT Nicholas	4° ss.	ROGERS John	8° coll.	WATTS George	4° ss.
1737	DUBOIS Peter	8° ss.	MORELL Thomas	8° ss.	STEPHENS William	8° coll.
	WARREN Robert	4° ss.				
1738	CONYBEARE John	4° ss.	EYRE Robert	8° ss.	HOWARD Robert	4° ss.
	HUTCHINSON Thomas	8° ss.	ROGERS John	8° coll.	WARBURTON William	8° ss.
	WEBBER Francis. DD.	8° ss.	WILLIAMS Philip	4° ss.		
1739	BALGUY John	8° coll.	BATTY Adam	8° coll.	BENTLEY Richard	fo.coll.
	HARRIS John	fo.coll.	MORELL Thomas	8° ss.	STEBBING Henry	8° ss.
	THOMAS John	4° ss.	WILCOCKS Joseph	4° ss.	WILLIAMS John	fo.coll.
1740	BENSON Martin	4° ss.	BISSE Thomas	8° coll.	BUNDY Richard	8° coll.
1741	BATEMAN Edmund	4° ss.	BOLTON Robert	8° ss.	CROXALL Sam. DD.	8° ss.
	STRAIGHT John	8° coll.				
1742	BEST William	4° ss.	STEBBING Henry	4° ss.	TRAPP Joseph	4° ss.

Year	Name	Format	Name	Format	Name	Format
	WEBBER Francis. DD.	8° ss.				
1743						
	BRUCE Lew. DD.	4° ss.	MAWSON Matthias	4° ss.	THOMAS John	4° ss.
	TWELLS Leonard	8° coll.				
1744						
	CARY Mordecai	4° ss.	DELANY Patrick	4° ss.	GILBERT John	4° ss.
	HUTTON Matthew	4° ss.				
1745						
	BEARCROFT Philip	4° ss.	DALTON John	4° ss.	FLETCHER Thomas	4° ss.
	GARDNER William	8° ss.	HOLME Thomas	8° ss.	HUTTON Matthew	4° ss.
	THOMAS John	4° ss.	TREVOR Richard	4° ss.	WEBSTER William	8° coll.
	<u>PRINCE</u> <u>Tho.</u> <u>M.A.</u>	8° ss.				
1746						
	FORSTER Nathaniel	8° ss.	HARE Francis	8° coll.	HUTTON Matthew	4° ss.
	LAVINGTON George	4° ss.	NICOLLS Samuel	8° ss.	THOMAS John	4° ss.
	WARBURTON William	8° ss.				
1747						
	CHAUNCY Angel	4° ss.	COSTARD George	8° ss.	GIBBON Will. M.A.	4° ss.
	TREVOR Richard	4° ss.	WEBSTER William	8° ss.	<u>STEVENSON</u> <u>B.</u>	8° ss.
1748						
	BEARCROFT Philip	4° ss.	WARBURTON William	-° ss.		
1749						
	BILSTONE John	8° coll.	BUTLER Joseph	8° coll.	ELLYS Anthony	4° ss.
	GEORGE William	4° ss.	NICOLLS Samuel	4° ss.	SQUIRE Samuel	4° ss.
1750						
	COCKMAN Thomas	8° coll.	MADDOX Isaac	4° ss.	MOSS Charles	4° ss.
	SEED Jeremiah	-° coll.	<u>ERSKINE</u> <u>John</u>	8° ss.		
1751						
	ALLEN Fifield	4° ss.	BERRIMAN William	8° coll.	MONOUX Lewis	4° ss.
1752						
	TOWNLEY James	4° ss.				
1753						
	ANONYMOUS	8° ss.	HAYTER Thomas	4° ss.	<u>WATTS</u> <u>Isaac</u>	4° coll.
1754						
	HOADLY Benjamin	8° coll.	SHARP William	8° ss.	WEBSTER William	8° coll.
1755						
	SHARP William	4° ss.	SHARP William	8° ss.		
1756						
	BLAKE Edward	8° ss.	CORNWALLIS Frederick	8° ss.	HALL Charles	4° ss.
	HORNE Geo. DD.	8° ss.	HORNE Geo. DD.	8° ss.	LOVEDER Thomas	8° coll.
	MOSS Charles	4° ss.	ROSS John	4° ss.	ROSS John	4° ss.
	STEBBING Hen. DD. jun.	8° ss.	TERRICK Richard	4° ss.		
1757						
	CONYBEARE John	8° coll.	DODWELL William	4° ss.	HOOPER George	fo. coll.
1758						
	DODWELL William	4° ss.	GREEN John	8° coll.	HUME John	4° ss.
	OGDEN Samuel	4° ss.	OGDEN Samuel	4° ss.	TERRICK Richard	4° ss.
	TERRICK Richard	4° ss.	THOMAS John	4° ss.		
1759						
	ANONYMOUS	8° ss.	BUCKLER Benjamin	8° ss.	FLETCHER Philip	4° ss.
1760						
	MUSCUTT James	8° coll.				
1761						
	HORNE Geo. DD.	8° ss.	ROTHERAM John	8° ss.		
1763						
	DELANY Patrick	4° ss.	RICHARDSON Robert	4° ss.		

Year	Name	Format	Name	Format	Name	Format
1764	MAURICE Henry	8° ss.				
1765	FRANKLIN Thomas	8° coll.				
1766	DELANY Patrick	8° coll.	ROE James	8° coll.	SECKER William	8° coll.
1770	BARRINGTON Lord	8° coll.	SECKER William	8° coll.		
1771	HALLIFAX James	4° ss.	SECKER William	8° coll.	SECKER William	8° coll.
1772	MARSTON William	8° ss.	SHERLOCK Thomas	8° coll.		
1773	HORNE Geo. DD.	8° ss.				
1774	JORTIN John	8° coll.	SHERLOCK Thomas	8° coll.		
1776	BRAILSFORD J. M.A.	8° coll.				
1777	RANDOLPH Thomas	8° ss.				
1778	WHITE Joseph	4° ss.				
1790	TENISON Thomas	4° ss.				

Balliol College ("Bal.")

Year	Name	Format	Name	Format	Name	Format
1624	LUSHINGTON Thomas	12° ss.				
1644	PEARSON John	4° ss.				
1660	GRIFFITH Matthew	12° ss.	SUDBURY John	4° ss.	WALSALL Francis	4° ss.
1661	COLET John	4° ss.	MORLEY George	4° ss.	WALSALL Francis	4° ss.
1662	BURY Arthur RILAND John	4° ss. 4° ss.	LANEY Benjamin RILAND John	4° ss. 4° ss.	MAYNE Jasper <u>CALAMY</u> <u>Edmund</u>	4° ss. 4° ss.
1665	KERSWEL John. B.D.	4° ss.	LANEY Benjamin	4° ss.		
1670	MERITON John	4° ss.	<u>CALAMY</u> <u>Edmund</u>	4° ss.		
1673	HALES John	4° coll.	JACKSON Thomas	fo.coll.	SMITH John	4° coll.
1674	GOULDE William	4° ss.				
1675	CONOLD Robert WOOLLEY John	4° ss. 4° ss.	GREGORY Fran. DD.	4° ss.	SMITH Thomas	4° ss.
1677	BRAMHALL John	fo.coll.				
1678	LLEWELIN David	4° ss.	ROLLS Samuel	8° coll.	TAYLOR Jeremy	fo.coll.
1679	HORTON Thomas	fo.coll.	WYATT Will. M.A.	4° ss.		
1680	HICKERINGILL Edmond	4° coll.	HICKERINGILL Edmond.	4° ss.	LONG Thomas	4° ss.

Year	Name	Format	Name	Format	Name	Format
1681	CAVE John	8° ss.	HOW John	12° ss.		
1682	KNIGHT John	4° ss.	SMITH Thomas	4° ss.	WILKINS John	8° coll.
1683	CALAMY Benjamin	4° ss.	SHERLOCK William	4° ss.		
1684	CURTOIS John	4° ss.	HAMMOND Henry	fo.coll.	LIGHTFOOT J. DD.	fo.coll.
1685	ELLIS Ph.	4° ss.	ELLIS Ph.	4° ss.	GODWYN Morgan	4° ss.
1686	ANONYMOUS	4° ss.	NEWCOME Peter	4° ss.	THURLIN Thomas	4° ss.
1687	PATRICK Simon	4° ss.	BEVERLEY Thomas	4° ss.		
1688	BROWNE Thomas	4° ss.	BROWNE Thomas	4° ss.		
1689	OLLYFFE John	4° ss.				
1691	LLOYD William	4° ss.	WALLIS John	4° ss.	WALLIS John	4° coll.
1692	BENTLEY Richard	4° coll.	WALLIS John	4° coll.		
1693	MONRO Alexander	4° coll.				
1694	SANCROFT William	8° coll.				
1695	TENISON Thomas	4° ss.				
1696	MEGGOT Richard	8° coll.				
1697	BURNET Gilbert	4° ss.	GOODMAN John	4° ss.	GOODMAN John	8° coll.
	OWTRAM William	8° coll.				
1699	BARON John	4° ss.	CONANT John	8° coll.		
1700	ELLISON Nath. DD.	8° ss.				
1701	COLET John	-° ss.	PEARSON John	8° ss.		
1702	SACHEVERELL Henry	4° ss.	SACHEVERELL Henry	4° ss.		
1704	SACHEVERELL Henry	4° ss.				
1705	LAKE Edward	8° coll.				
1706	TALBOT James	12° ss.				
1707	GOODMAN John	8° ss.	STILLINGFLEET Edward	fo.coll.		
1708	KENNET White	8° ss.				
1709	KING William	8° ss.				
1710	BINCKES William	8° ss.	BURNET Gilbert	8° ss.	CORNEWALL Fred. M.A.	8° ss.
	HOWARD John	12° ss.	LEWIS Henry	8° ss.		

Year	Name	Format	Name	Format	Name	Format
1711	ANONYMOUS	8° ss.	BURSCOUGH William	8° ss.	CHISHULL Edmund	4° ss.
	GOOCH Thomas Sir	4° ss.	HOWELL Will. M.A.	8° ss.	SAINT John Pawlet	4° ss.
1712	ASH St. George	8° ss.	BISSE Thomas	4° ss.	CHISHULL Edmund	8° ss.
	IBBETSON Richard	8° ss.	NEWTON Richard	4° ss.	PICKERING Robert	8° ss.
1713	BISSE Thomas	8° ss.	BULL George	8° coll.	HICKES George	8° coll.
	HUSBANDS Thomas	8° ss.	NEWTON Richard	4° ss.	SACHEVERELL Henry	4° ss.
	SACHEVERELL Henry	4° ss.	TRAPP Joseph	4° ss.		
1714	RYE George	8° ss.				
1715	BENTLEY Richard	8° ss.	RAWLINS Gershom	8° ss.		
1716	BURSCOUGH William	4° ss.	PEARSE Robert	8° ss.		
1717	SMALRIDGE George	8° coll.	SOUTH Robert	8° ss.		
1718	SCOTT John	fo.coll.				
1719	KETTLEWELL John	fo.coll.	MARTIN David	8° ss.		
1720	FIDDES Rich. DD.	fo. ss.	FIDDES Rich. DD.	fo. ss.		
1721	KNIGHT James	8° coll.	LESTLEY Charles	fo.coll.		
1723	CONINGESBY George	8° ss.				
1724	SMALRIDGE George	fo.coll.				
1725	COLLIER Jeremy	8° coll.				
1726	BISSE Thomas	8° ss.	CALAMY Benjamin	8° coll.	HICKES George	8° coll.
1727	DERHAM Will. DD.	8° ss.	WHITBY Daniel	8° coll.		
1728	DELAUNE William	8° coll.	FIDDES Rich. DD.	fo.coll.	JONES John	8° ss.
	WHARTON Henry	8° coll.	WHARTON Henry	8° coll.	WHITBY Daniel	8° coll.
1729	LUPTON William	8° coll.				
1730	ATTERBURY Francis	8° coll.	COX Chamberlain Tho. M	8° ss.	DERHAM Will. DD.	8° ss.
	SUTTON Prideaux	8° ss.				
1733	CONINGESBY George	8° ss.	MOSS Robert	8° coll.		
1735	SHARP John	8° coll.				
1737	MOSS Robert	8° coll.				
1738	CROXALL Sam. DD.	8° ss.	MOSS Robert	8° coll.	PAYNE Thomas	8° ss.
1739	BENTLEY Richard	fo.coll.	TRAPP Joseph	8° ss.		
1741	BERRIMAN William	8° ss.	LUSHINGTON Thomas	8° ss.	STRAIGHT John	8° coll.

Year	Name	Format	Name	Format	Name	Format
1742	WATERLAND Daniel	8° coll.				
1743	HUNT Thomas	4° ss.	TWELLS Leonard	8° coll.	ABERNETHY John	8° coll.
1746	BEST William	8° ss.				
1748	ABERNETHY John	8° coll.				
1751	ABERNETHY John	8° coll.				
1752	HAWKINS William	8° ss.	HAYTER Thomas	4° ss.		
1755	JORTIN John	8° coll.				
1757	CONYBEARE John	8° coll.	HOOPER George	fo. coll.		
1759	ANONYMOUS	8° ss.	BUCKLER Benjamin	4° ss.		
1765	KENNICOTT Benjamin	8° ss.				
1766	DELANY Patrick	8° coll.				
1772	SHERLOCK Thomas	8° coll.				

Bodleian Library ("Bod.")

Year	Name	Format	Name	Format	Name	Format
----	FULLER Ignatius	-° ss.	HOOK Christopher	8° ss.	WILLIAMS John	-° coll.
1605	MASON Francis	-° ss.				
1607	WILKINSON Robert	4° ss.				
1660	BARWICK John	4° ss.	BRUNSELL Samuel	4° ss.	CREED William	4° ss.
	DOWGLASS Robert	12° ss.	GAUDEN John	4° ss.	GAUDEN John	4° ss.
	GAUDEN John	4° ss.	GAUDEN John	12° ss.	HODGES Thomas	4° ss.
	LESTLEY Henry	4° ss.	LIVESEY James	8° ss.	LIVESEY James	8° ss.
	LIVESEY John	8° ss.	STANLEY Edward	-° ss.	SUDBURY John	4° ss.
	WALL John	8° ss.	WALL John	8° ss.	BROOKS Thomas	8° ss.
	POOL Matthew	4° ss.	SECKER Will.	8° ss.	VENNING Ralph	8° ss.
	WILKINSON Henry	4° ss.	WILKINSON Henry	4° coll.		
1661	BERNARD Nicholas	4° ss.	CADE Anthony	4° ss.	COLET John	4° ss.
	CRAGGE John	8° ss.	DUPORT James	4° ss.	ELLIS Clement	4° ss.
	GAUDEN John	4° ss.	MASTERSON George	12° ss.	STANLEY Edward	-° ss.
	SYMPSON Matthias	4° ss.	THOMAS Michael	4° ss.	TILLOTSON John	4° coll.
	BROOKS Thomas	8° ss.				
1662	AYLEWORTH William.	8° ss.	BOREMAN Rich. DD.	8° ss.	GUNNING Peter	4° ss.
	GURNALL William	4° ss.	LANEY Benjamin	4° ss.	PRIAULX John	4° ss.
	STANLEY Edward	8° ss.	WALL John	8° ss.	WREN Matthew	4° ss.
	CAWTON Thomas	8° ss.	CROFTON Zechariah	4° ss.	LYE Thomas	4° ss.
	WATSON Thomas	4° ss.				
1663	CARPENTER Richard	4° ss.	HINDE Samuel	4° ss.	LANEY Benjamin	4° ss.
	PHILPOT Thomas	4° ss.	RILAND John	4° ss.	WETENHALL Edward	4° ss.

Year	Name	Format	Name	Format	Name	Format
1664	BROWNRIG Ralph	fo.coll.	CHILLINGWORTH William	fo.coll.	GLOVER Henry	4° ss.
	GREGORY John	4° ss.	HALL Edmund	8° ss.	HOWE Obadiah	4° ss.
	JOHNSON Will. DD.	12° ss.	MAYNE Jasper	4° ss.	SCATTERGOOD Anthonie	4° ss.
1665	DOLBEN John	4° ss.	DOLBEN John	4° ss.	FORD Simon	4° ss.
	LANEY Benjamin	4° ss.	LANEY Benjamin	4° ss.	SMITH Samuel	-° ss.
	BROOKS Thomas	8° ss.				
1666	OLDISWORTH Giles	4° ss.	WILLIAMS Griffith	4° ss.	BYRDALL Thomas	12° ss.
	BYRDALL Thomas	12° ss.	BYRDALL Thomas	12° ss.	BYRDALL Thomas	12° ss.
1667	BARKSDALE Clement	8° ss.	FULLWOOD Francis	4° ss.	STOKES David	4° ss.
	STOKES David	4° ss.				
1668	ARROWSMITH John	8° coll.	BASIRE Isaac	8° ss.	LINGARD Ric. DD.	4° ss.
	SMITH Thomas	4° ss.	BROOKS Thomas	8° ss.	CHISHUL John	8° ss.
1669	CONANT Malachi	4° ss.	H. - - - - G.	8° ss.	SHERLOCK Richard	4° ss.
	SPENCER John	8° ss.				
1670	ANONYMOUS	-° ss.	ANONYMOUS	4° ss.	ANONYMOUS	4° ss.
	ANONYMOUS	8° ss.	BASSET Will.	4° ss.	BREVAL Frank Durant de	4° ss.
	BREVAL Frank Durant de	4° ss.	CUDWORTH Ralph	8° ss.	DOBSON John	4° ss.
	GLANVIL Joseph	4° ss.	JOHNSON James	4° ss.	JOHNSON James	8° ss.
	LOEFFS Isaac	8° ss.	MERITON John	4° ss.	PARRY John	4° ss.
	PATRICK Simon	4° ss.	PATRICK Simon	8° ss.	SEIGNIOR George	8° coll.
	SMITH William	8° ss.	STRAIGHT John	4° ss.	WARD Seth	4° ss.
	BROOKS Thomas	4° ss.	STEEL Richard	8° coll.		
1671	DURHAM William	4° ss.	HORNE John	8° ss.	PIERCE Tho. DD.	4° coll.
	SCLATER William	4° ss.	STRAIGHT John	4° ss.	GREENHILL William	8° coll.
1672	ANONYMOUS	8° ss.	ANONYMOUS	8° ss.	BERRY Richard	4° ss.
	FARINDON Anth. B.D.	fo.coll.	FRANK Mark	fo.coll.	FULLER Ignatius	8° ss.
	FULLER Ignatius	8° ss.	GURNALL William	8° ss.	HACKET Thomas	4° ss.
	HARRISON Robert	4° ss.	HARRISON Robert	4° ss.	HASCARD Gregory	4° ss.
	HEYWOOD Oliver	8° ss.	HORTON Thomas	4° ss.	MEDE Joseph	fo.coll.
	WARING Robert	4° ss.	WATSON Thomas	8° ss.		
1673	ANONYMOUS	8° ss.	ASHETON William	4° ss.	BASIRE Isaac	8° ss.
	EGAN Anthony	4° ss.	GREGORY Fran. DD.	4° ss.	HALES John	4° coll.
	HAYWARD Roger	4° ss.	JACKSON Thomas	fo.coll.	LAMBE John	4° ss.
	LLOYD William	4° ss.	NEVILLE Robert	4° ss.	NEWTON George	8° ss.
	PASTON James	4° ss.	PATRICK Simon	4° ss.	SAYER Joseph	4° ss.
	SHARROCK Robert	4° coll.	SMITH John	4° coll.	WALKER Anthony	4° ss.
	WILKINS John	4° ss.	MALBON Samuel	8° ss.	PALMER Anthony	8° ss.
	POOL Matthew	4° ss.	WEST Edward	4° coll.		
1674	CROFT Herbert	4° ss.	FOWLER Edward	4° coll.	GREGORY Fran. DD.	4° ss.
	HARDCASTLE Thomas	8° coll.	KELSEY Joseph	4° ss.	LIVESEY James	8° ss.
	LLOYD William	4° ss.	LODINGTON Thomas	4° ss.	LODINGTON Thomas	4° ss.
	MOULIN DU Peter	4° ss.	PRINCE John	4° ss.	SALL Andrew	8° ss.
	SEIGNIOR George	4° coll.	SHARPE Lewis	12° ss.	SMITH William	8° ss.
	SMITH William	8° ss.	TANNER Thomas	4° ss.	TAYLOR Jeremy	8° ss.
	WARD Hamnett	4° ss.	WATKINSON P.	4° ss.	WOOD A. Edward	8° coll.

Year	Name	Format	Name	Format	Name	Format
	ALLEINE Richard	8° ss.	ANNESLEY Samuel	4° coll.	ANNESLEY Samuel	4° coll.
	BRAGGE Robert	4° ss.	CASE Thomas	4° coll.	MATHER Increase	12° coll.
	PALMER Anthony	8° ss.	RYTHER John	8° ss.		
1675						
	BARNE Miles	4° ss.	BOLDE Samuel	4° ss.	BURNET Gilbert	4° ss.
	BURNET Gilbert	4° ss.	BYAM Henry	8° coll.	FELL John	4° ss.
	FORD Stephen	8° ss.	GARBUTT Richard	8° ss.	GREGORY Fran. DD.	4° ss.
	GREGORY Fran. DD.	4° ss.	HACKET John	fo.coll.	HIGHAM John	8° ss.
	HOTCHKIS Thomas	8° ss.	JACKSON William	4° ss.	JANE Will. DD.	4° ss.
	MEGGOT Richard	4° ss.	MOTTE DE LA Francis	4° ss.	NAILOUR William	4° ss.
	PATRICK Simon	8° ss.	POPE James	8° ss.	SMITH Thomas	4° ss.
	SMITH Thomas	4° ss.	STANDISH John	4° ss.	STOPFORD Joshua	8° ss.
	STRADLING Geor. DD.	4° ss.	STRONG James	8° ss.	STUBBE Henry	8° ss.
	SUDBURY John	4° ss.	TAYLOR Jeremy	8° ss.	TAYLOR Jeremy	8° ss.
	WOMOCK Lawrence	4° coll.	VINCENT Nathaniel	4° coll.	WILKINSON Henry	4° coll.
1676						
	ALLINGTON John	4° ss.	BAGSHAW Henry	4° ss.	CARTWRIGHT Thomas	4° ss.
	CAVE Will. DD.	4° ss.	COOK John	4° ss.	DUPORT James	4° coll.
	DYER Richard	8° ss.	GOULDE William	4° ss.	HALSEY James	8° ss.
	HAYWARD Roger	4° ss.	HOLLINGWORTH Richard	12° ss.	HORDEN John	4° ss.
	HOWELL William	4° ss.	JENNER Dav. B.D.	4° ss.	JONES Henry	4° ss.
	LATHAM Paul	4° ss.	LUZANCY Hippolytus Du	4° ss.	PARKER Timothy	4° ss.
	PATRICK Simon	4° ss.	PIGOTT Henry	4° ss.	ROSSINGTON James	4° ss.
	SPANHEIM Frederick	4° ss.	STAINFORTH William	4° ss.	STANDFAST Richard	4° ss.
	STRONG James	8° ss.	SUDBURY John	4° ss.	TEMPLER John	4° ss.
	TOWGOOD Richard	4° ss.	WILLIS Thomas	4° ss.	WYLLYS J. M.A.	4° ss.
	ADAMS Richard	4° coll.	ALLEINE Richard	8° ss.	BARKER Matthew	4° coll.
	BAXTER Richard	4° coll.	COLE Thomas	4° coll.	COOPER William	4° coll.
	HOOK	4° coll.	JENKINS William	4° coll.	MILWARD John	4° coll.
	NEEDLER Benjamin	4° coll.	PARSON Thomas	4° coll.	SHEFFIELD John	4° coll.
	STEEL Richard	4° coll.	SYLVESTER Matthew	4° coll.	TUCKNEY Anthony	4° coll.
	VEAL Edward	4° coll.	VINCENT Thomas	4° coll.	WELLS Edward	4° coll.
	WILKINSON Henry	4° coll.	WILSON John	8° ss.	WOODCOCK Francis	4° coll.
1677						
	ARDERNE James	4° ss.	B. - - - - R.	4° ss.	BRAMHALL John	fo.coll.
	CLAUDE Francis	4° ss.	CRADOCK Zechary	4° ss.	GIBBES Charles	4° coll.
	GRIFFITH Evan	4° ss.	HORNECK Anthony	4° ss.	MITCHELL Jonathan	4° coll.
	PATRICK Simon	8° ss.	PINDAR William	4° ss.	RAINBOW Edward	4° ss.
	TANNER Thomas	4° ss.	THORP George	4° ss.	TILLOTSON John	4° coll.
	TURNER Bryan	4° ss.	WILKINS John	12° coll.		
1678						
	ANONYMOUS	4° ss.	BAKER Aaron	4° ss.	BATTIE William	4° ss.
	BUTLER John	4° ss.	CADE William	4° ss.	CAMFIELD Benjamin	4° ss.
	CAMFIELD Benjamin	8° ss.	CAVE John	4° ss.	CROFT Herbert	4° ss.
	DILLINGHAM William	4° ss.	FORD Simon	8° ss.	HOOKER Richard	8° ss.
	LAMPLUGH Thomas	4° ss.	PATRICK Simon	4° ss.	REYNOLDS John	4° ss.
	ROLLS Samuel	8° coll.	USHER James	fo.coll.	WALKER Anthony	8° ss.
	WALKER Anthony	8° ss.	WILLIAMS John	4° ss.	COLLINGES John	4° coll.
	FROYSELL Thomas	8° coll.	HURST Henry	8° ss.		
1679						
	ALSOP George	4° ss.	ANONYMOUS	8° ss.	BEARE Nicholas	4° ss.
	BEDLE Joseph	4° ss.	CROFT Herbert	4° ss.	DAVIES James	4° ss.
	DURHAM William	4° ss.	E. - - - - E.	8° ss.	FARINDON Anth. B.D.	fo.coll.
	HEYWOOD Oliver	8° ss.	HORTON Thomas	fo.coll.	JANE Will. DD.	4° ss.
	JONES Henry	4° ss.	LLOYD William	4° ss.	LLOYD William	4° ss.
	NEEDHAM Robert	8° coll.	NEVILLE Robert	4° ss.	OATES Titus	4° ss.

Year	Name	Format	Name	Format	Name	Format
	PELLING Edward	4° ss.	PIERCE Tho. DD.	4° coll.	PIERCE Tho. DD.	4° coll.
	RALEIGH Walter	4° coll.	REYNOLDS Edward	fo. coll.	SMITH Thomas	4° ss.
	SPARKE Robert	4° ss.	THOMAS John	4° ss.	WALLIS John	4° ss.
	WHITBY Daniel	4° ss.	WILLIAMS John	4° ss.	WILSON Thomas	4° ss.
	WYATT Will. M.A.	4° ss.	GRAY Andrew	8° coll.		
1680	BURNET Gilbert	4° ss.	FELL John	4° ss.	HANCOCKE Robert	4° ss.
	HICKERINGILL Edmond	4° coll.	HICKERINGILL Edmond.	4° ss.	PARSONS Robert	4° ss.
	REYNER Samuel	4° ss.	COLLINGES John	4° ss.		
1681	BENNION John	4° ss.	BURNET Gilbert	4° ss.	C. - - - - N.	4° ss.
	GREGORY John	12° ss.	HICKERINGILL Edmond	4° coll.	HICKERINGILL Edmond.	4° ss.
	HOOPER George	4° ss.	HOOPER George	4° ss.	MAURICE Henry	4° ss.
	STRIPLING Thomas	4° ss.	TENISON Thomas	4° ss.	TURNER Francis	4° ss.
1682	BISBIE Nathaniel	4° ss.	BOLDE Samuel	4° ss.	CAMFIELD Benjamin	4° coll.
	CAVE John	4° ss.	CLIFFORD Will. M.A.	4° ss.	COMBER Thomas	4° ss.
	FREEMAN Samuel	4° ss.	KINGSTON Richard	4° ss.	WALLIS John	4° ss.
	WETENHALL Edward	4° ss.	WETENHALL Edward	4° ss.	WILKINSON Robert	4° ss.
	WRAY William	4° ss.				
1683	CALAMY Benjamin	4° ss.	FOWLER Edward	4° ss.	FOX Francis	4° ss.
	POWELL Charles	4° ss.	STRATFORD Nicholas	4° ss.	TURNER John	8° ss.
	WILLIAMS John	4° ss.	ANNESLEY Samuel	4° coll.	COLE Thomas	4° coll.
	MAYO Richard	4° coll.	SLATER Samuel	4° coll.	VINCENT Nathaniel	4° coll.
	WOODCOCK Francis	4° coll.				
1684	ALLESTREE Richard	fo. coll.	ANONYMOUS	4° ss.	ANONYMOUS	8° ss.
	CAMFIELD Benjamin	4° ss.	CURTOIS John	4° ss.	FALKNER Will. DD.	4° coll.
	GRENVILLE Denis	4° ss.	HAMMOND Henry	fo. coll.	HESKETH Henry	4° ss.
	HICKES George	4° ss.	HUGHES William	4° ss.	KETTLEWELL John	4° ss.
	KETTLEWELL John	4° ss.	LIGHTFOOT J. DD.	fo. coll.	STRATFORD Nicholas	8° ss.
	TURNER John	8° ss.	CHARNOCK Stephen	fo. coll.		
1685	BURNET Gilbert	4° ss.	COOKE Shadrach	4° ss.	FOWLER Edward	4° ss.
	GOWER Humphrey	4° ss.	GOWER Humphrey	4° ss.	GRENVILLE Denis	4° ss.
	HUTTON Charles	4° ss.	IRONSIDE Gilbert	4° ss.	PELLING Edward	4° ss.
	SHERLOCK William	4° ss.	TURNER Francis	4° ss.	TURNER John	8° ss.
	TURNER Tho. DD.	4° ss.	WAGSTAFFE Thomas	4° ss.	WILLOUGHBY Stephen	4° ss.
1686	CARTWRIGHT Thomas	4° ss.	CRISPE Samuel	4° ss.	HICHMAN Charles	4° ss.
	KIDDER Richard	4° ss.	PATRICK Simon	4° ss.	PIERCE Tho. DD.	4° ss.
	THURLIN Thomas	4° ss.	TULLIE George	4° ss.	TURNER John	4° ss.
	WYVILL Christopher	4° ss.				
1687	BARROW Isaac	fo. coll.	BARROW Isaac	fo. coll.	BOLDE Samuel	12° ss.
	CLUTTERBUCK Tho. DD.	4° ss.	MANNINGHAM Thomas	4° ss.	MAPLETOFT John	4° ss.
	PATRICK Simon	4° ss.	PATRICK Simon	4° ss.	STRATFORD Nicholas	4° ss.
1688	ANONYMOUS	4° ss.	BROWNE Thomas	4° ss.	BROWNE Thomas	4° ss.
	BURNET Gilbert	8° ss.	CUDWORTH John	4° ss.	DUREL John	4° ss.
	FOWLER Edward	4° ss.	GOLTY Richard	4° ss.	HELLIER Henry	4° ss.
	PASTON James	4° ss.	TULLY Thomas	8° ss.	WAGSTAFFE Thomas	4° ss.
	SCARISBRIKE Edward	4° ss.	SYLVESTER Matthew	8° ss.	WOORDEN Thomas	12° ss.
1689	BEVERIDGE William	4° ss.	BRINGHURST Isaac	4° ss.	BURNET Gilbert	4° ss.

Year	Author	Format	Author	Format	Author	Format
	BURNET Gilbert	4° ss.	BURNET Gilbert	4° ss.	BURNET Gilbert	4° ss.
	HORNECK Anthony	4° ss.	JAY Stephen	4° ss.	KILLIGREW Henry. DD.	4° ss.
	LLOYD William	4° ss.	MARIOTT Thomas	4° ss.	NEWCOME Henry	4° ss.
	PATRICK Simon	4° ss.	PATRICK Simon	4° ss.	PATRICK Simon	4° ss.
	PATRICK Simon	4° ss.	RESBURY Nathaniel	4° ss.	ROYSE Geor. DD.	4° ss.
	SANDERSON Robert	fo.coll.	SHERLOCK William	8° ss.	STAINFORTH William	4° ss.
	STRYPE John	4° ss.				
169-						
	ANONYMOUS	8° ss.				
1690						
	ANONYMOUS	8° ss.	BARLOW William	8° ss.	BARLOW William	8° ss.
	BUDGELL Gilbert	4° ss.	BURNET Gilbert	4° ss.	BURNET Gilbert	4° ss.
	BURNET Gilbert	8° ss.	FOWLER Edward	4° ss.	FREEMAN Samuel	4° ss.
	FREEMAN Samuel	4° ss.	HAMMOND George	4° coll.	HICHMAN Charles	4° ss.
	IRONSIDE Gilbert	4° ss.	IRONSIDE Gilbert	4° ss.	JONES David	4° ss.
	KIDDER Richard	4° ss.	LLOYD William	4° ss.	PATRICK Simon	4° ss.
	ROYSE Geor. DD.	4° ss.	SMITH Humphrey	4° ss.	SMITH Humphrey	4° ss.
	TENISON Thomas	4° ss.	WHITTLE Seth	4° ss.	ALSOP Nathaniel	4° coll.
	BARKER Matthew	4° coll.	BURGESS Daniel	4° coll.	COLE Thomas	4° coll.
	HURST Henry	4° coll.	MATHER Increase	8° ss.	MAYO Richard	4° coll.
	SLATER Samuel	4° ss.	SLATER Samuel	4° coll.	STEEL Richard	4° coll.
	SYLVESTER Matthew	4° coll.	VEAL Edward	4° coll.	VINCENT Nathaniel	4° coll.
	WILLIAMS Daniel	4° coll.	WOODCOCK Francis	4° coll.		
1691						
	ANONYMOUS	4° ss.	BARKER Ralph	4° ss.	BURNET Gilbert	4° ss.
	BURNET Gilbert	4° ss.	CLARKE Joshua	4° ss.	COMBER Thomas	4° ss.
	COOKE Shadrach	4° ss.	CROSLEY David	4° ss.	DOVE Heb. DD.	4° ss.
	FOWLER Edward	4° ss.	HALLEY George	4° ss.	HARRISON Michael	8° ss.
	HARRISON Michael	8° ss.	HARRISON Michael	8° ss.	HOOPER George	4° ss.
	IRONSIDE Gilbert	4° ss.	IRONSIDE Gilbert	4° ss.	JANE Will. DD.	4° ss.
	KELSEY Joseph	4° ss.	KELSEY Joseph	4° ss.	KING William	4° ss.
	LAMBE John	4° ss.	LLOYD William	4° ss.	LLOYD William	4° ss.
	LYNFORD Thomas	4° ss.	MASON John	4° ss.	NORRIS John	8° coll.
	NORRIS John	8° coll.	PATRICK Simon	4° ss.	RESBURY Nathaniel	4° ss.
	SHERLOCK William	8° ss.	TALBOT William	4° ss.	TAYLOR Nathaniel	4° ss.
	TENISON Thomas	4° ss.	TULLIE George	4° ss.	WALKER Anthony	4° ss.
	WALLIS John	4° coll.	WRIGHT John	4° ss.	WROE Christopher	4° ss.
	CHANDLER Samuel	8° coll.	SLATER Samuel	8° ss.		
1692						
	ANONYMOUS	4° ss.	ANONYMOUS	8° ss.	BARTON Samuel	4° ss.
	BOWCHIER Richard	4° ss.	BURNET Gilbert	4° ss.	BURY Arthur	4° ss.
	BUSH William	8° ss.	CATHERALL Samuel	4° ss.	CLARIDGE Richard	4° ss.
	EASTON Thomas	4° ss.	EDWARDS John	8° coll.	FALLE Philip	4° ss.
	FLEMING Robert	8° ss.	FORD Simon	4° ss.	FOWLER Edward	4° ss.
	GEE Edward	4° ss.	HALLYWELL Henry	8° ss.	HALLYWELL Henry	8° ss.
	HOPKINS Ezekiel	4° coll.	HOWARD John	4° ss.	JANE Will. DD.	4° ss.
	JONES David	4° ss.	KIDDER Richard	4° ss.	MILWAY Thomas	4° ss.
	MORE Henry	8° coll.	PARKHURST Nathaniel	4° ss.	PARSLEY Henry	4° ss.
	PATRICK Simon	4° ss.	PELLING Edward	4° ss.	POWELL Jos. M.A.	4° ss.
	RESBURY Nathaniel	4° ss.	SHERLOCK William	4° ss.	SHERLOCK William	4° ss.
	SKELTON Bernard	4° ss.	SOUTHCOMB Lewis	4° ss.	STANLEY William	4° ss.
	STRADLING Geor. DD.	8° coll.	WALLIS John	4° coll.	WETENHALL Edward	4° ss.
	WOODWARD Josiah	4° ss.	DENT Edward	4° ss.	KEACH Benjamin	4° ss.
	MARSHALL Walter	8° ss.	SPRINT John	4° ss.	TAYLOR Thomas	8° ss.
	WRIGHT Timothy	8° ss.				
1693						

Year	Name	Format	Name	Format	Name	Format
	ANONYMOUS	4° ss.	ANONYMOUS	8° ss.	ANONYMOUS	12° ss.
	BRADY Nich. DD.	4° ss.	BYNNS Richard	4° ss.	ELLESBY James	4° ss.
	EYRE Robert	4° ss.	HAMMOND George	8° ss.	HICHMAN Charles	4° ss.
	HOLLINGWORTH Richard	4° ss.	LAMBE John	4° ss.	LAMBE John	4° ss.
	MANNINGHAM Thomas	4° ss.	MONRO Alexander	4° coll.	NORRIS John	8° coll.
	PELLING Edward	4° ss.	PRITCHARD Thomas	4° ss.	PRITCHARD Thomas	4° ss.
	STRENGFELLOW William	4° ss.	STUBBS Philip	4° ss.	STUBBS Philip	4° ss.
	WARLY Jonas	4° ss.	WHITAKER Thomas	8° ss.	WOODWARD Josiah	4° ss.
	DOOLITTLE Samuel	4° ss.	SLATER Samuel	8° ss.	T. - - - - G.	8° ss.
1694						
	BATTELY John	4° ss.	BOWATER John	8° ss.	BURNET Gilbert	4° ss.
	BURNET Gilbert	4° ss.	CAMPION Abraham	4° ss.	CLOGIE Alex.	12° ss.
	HALLYWELL Henry	8° ss.	HOOPER George	4° ss.	HUGHES William	8° ss.
	KEACK Elias	4° ss.	KIDDER Richard	4° ss.	KIDDER Richard	4° ss.
	MANNINGHAM Thomas	4° ss.	NEWMAN Richard	4° ss.	NORRIS John	8° coll.
	OWEN Jonathan	4° ss.	PEAD Deuel	8° ss.	SANCROFT William	8° coll.
	STAMPER Francis	8° ss.	STEPHENS William	4° ss.	SYKES Thomas	4° ss.
	TENISON Thomas	4° ss.	TENISON Thomas	4° ss.	TYLER John	4° ss.
	WIGAN William	4° ss.	BEVERLEY Thomas	4° ss.	CALAMY Edmund	4° ss.
	MAUDUIT Isaac	8° ss.	SHOWER John	8° ss.	SHOWER John	8° ss.
	SLATER Samuel	8° ss.	SPRINT John	-° ss.	STAFFORD Richard	8° coll.
1695						
	BLADEN Thomas	4° coll.	COLLIER Jeremy	4° ss.	GRIFFYTH John	4° ss.
	HOOPER George	4° ss.	ISHAM Zach. DD.	4° ss.	STENNETT Joseph	8° ss.
1696						
	HASCARD Gregory	4° ss.	KETTLEWELL John	8° coll.	LANCASTER William	4° ss.
	STAFFORD Richard	8° coll.				
1697						
	BUTLER Lilly	8° ss.	GOODMAN John	4° ss.		
1698						
	JEKYLL Thomas	8° ss.	LESTLEY Charles	4° ss.	STAFFORD Richard	8° coll.
1699						
	ATTERBURY Lewis	8° coll.	BARON John	4° ss.	CONANT John	8° coll.
	HANCOCK John	8° ss.	SHERLOCK William	8° ss.	CHARNOCK Stephen	8° coll.
	STAFFORD Richard	8° ss.				
17--						
	WILSON William	8° ss.				
1700						
	ANONYMOUS	8° ss.	ASHETON William	4° ss.	BIRCH Peter	4° ss.
	BRADFORD Samuel	4° coll.	EDWARDS John	8° ss.	EYRE Robert	4° ss.
	KEITH George	4° ss.	KEITH George	4° ss.	SCATTERGOOD Samuel	8° coll.
	WOODWARD Josiah	4° ss.				
1701						
	COLET John	-° ss.	ELLIS John	8° ss.	HOOPER George	4° ss.
	JENNINGS John	4° ss.	MILLES Thomas	8° ss.	SHERLOCK William	4° ss.
	STUBBS Philip	4° ss.	WHINCOP Thomas	4° ss.		
1702						
	BRAGGE Francis	8° coll.	MICHEL Humph. M.A.	4° ss.	MICHEL Humph. M.A.	4° ss.
	MICHEL Humph. M.A.	4° ss.	SACHEVERELL Henry	4° ss.	SACHEVERELL Henry	4° ss.
	TALBOT William	8° ss.	WAKE William	8° coll.		
1703						
	BARNES Joshua	4° ss.	CHAPMAN Richard	4° ss.	CHAPMAN Richard	4° ss.
	CHAPMAN Stephen	4° ss.	DORRINGTON Theophilus	8° coll.	KEITH George	4° ss.
	LORRAIN Paul	8° ss.	WHITBY Daniel	fo. ss.	WHITING Charles	4° ss.
	WOODROFFE Benjamin	4° ss.				
1704						

Year	Name	Format	Name	Format	Name	Format
	ADDISON Anthony	4° ss.	BRAGGE Francis	8° coll.	BURNET Gilbert	4° ss.
	CLAGETT William	8° coll.	CLAGETT William	8° coll.	ELSTOB Will. M.A.	4° ss.
	ELSTOB Will. M.A.	4° ss.	FINCH Will. Lepold	4° ss.	GASTRELL Francis	4° ss.
	GRANT John	4° ss.	HOOPER George	4° ss.	SACHEVERELL Henry	4° ss.
	STUBBS Philip	4° ss.	WILLIS Richard	4° ss.		
1705						
	DORRINGTON Theophilus	8° coll.	HOADLY Benjamin	4° ss.	LAKE Edward	8° coll.
	MASON Francis	4° ss.	MATHER John	4° ss.	RENNELL Thomas	4° ss.
	ROYSE Geor. DD.	4° ss.	SAYER Fr. M.A.	4° ss.	SHERLOCK William	-° ss.
	STANHOPE George	4° ss.	TILLY William	4° ss.		
1706						
	GEREE John	4° ss.	HICHMAN Charles	8° coll.	MATTHEWS John	4° ss.
	SACHEVERELL Henry	4° ss.	SMALBROKE Richard	4° ss.	STANHOPE George	4° ss.
	STANHOPE George	4° ss.	TRAPP Joseph	4° ss.	WILDER John	4° ss.
	WOODROFFE Benjamin	4° ss.				
1707						
	BEAN Charles	4° ss.	BROUGHTON John	4° ss.	GOODMAN John	8° ss.
	SMITH Thomas	8° ss.	STILLINGFLEET Edward	fo.coll.		
1708						
	BISSE Thomas	4° ss.	CLAVERING Robert	4° ss.	DONGWORTH Richard	4° ss.
	DOWNES Henry	8° ss.	FISHER John	8° ss.	HOPKINS William	8° coll.
	KENNET White	8° ss.	KENNET White	8° ss.	MAYO Richard	4° ss.
	SACHEVERELL Henry	4° ss.	STEPHENS Henry	4° ss.	TRIMNEL Charles	4° ss.
	WILLET John	4° ss.	WILLIAMS John	8° ss.	WILLIAMS John	8° ss.
	WILLIAMS John	8° coll.				
1709						
	BAYLY Thomas	8° ss.	HOARD Samuel	8° ss.	LESTLEY Henry	8° ss.
	LYNFORD Thomas	8° ss.				
1710						
	ADAMS John	4° ss.	ARCHER Edmond	8° ss.	BERDMORE	4° ss.
	CORNEWALL Fred. M.A.	8° ss.	DANE John	4° ss.	FOX Francis	8° ss.
	GATTON Benjamin	4° ss.	GODDARD Thomas	4° ss.	GODDARD Thomas	8° ss.
	HIGDEN Will. DD.	4° ss.	JOHNSON Samuel	-° coll.	LEWIS Henry	8° ss.
	NEEDHAM John	8° ss.	RIVERS Tho. LL.D.	4° ss.	SPRAT Thomas	8° coll.
	STANHOPE Michael	8° ss.	SWIFT Thomas	8° ss.	SYNGE Edward	8° ss.
	TRIMNEL Charles	4° ss.	WELLS Edward	8° ss.	WHALEY Nathanael	8° ss.
	WHITEAR William	4° ss.				
1711						
	BEVERIDGE William	8° coll.	BISSE Thomas	8° ss.	BURSCOUGH William	8° ss.
	HARE Francis	8° ss.	HOADLY Benjamin	8° coll.	HOWELL Will. M.A.	8° ss.
	RICHARDSON William	4° ss.	ROOTES Richard	8° ss.	SAINT John Pawlet	4° ss.
	STUBBS Philip	8° ss.	TODD Hugh	4° ss.	TRAPP Joseph	4° ss.
	WATTS Robert	8° ss.	WILLIS Richard	4° ss.	<u>WRIGHT</u> <u>Samuel</u>	8° ss.
1712						
	ALTHAM Roger	4° ss.	BISSE Thomas	4° ss.	BISSE Thomas	8° ss.
	BRETT Thomas	8° coll.	DOBOURDIEU Jean Armand	8° ss.	DORRINGTON Theophilus	8° ss.
	HAYLEY Tho. DD.	8° ss.	HOPKINS Ezekiel	8° coll.	HOWELL Will. M.A.	8° ss.
	HUMPHREYS Thomas	8° ss.	IBBETSON Richard	8° ss.	LORRAIN Paul	8° ss.
	REEVES William	4° ss.	SHUTTLEWOOD John	8° ss.	STEPHENS William	4° ss.
	STUBBS Philip	4° ss.	SYNGE Edward	8° ss.	TILLY William	8° coll.
	WHITAKER Thomas	8° coll.	<u>WRIGHT</u> <u>Samuel</u>	8° ss.		
1713						
	AYLMER William	8° ss.	BRAMSTON William	4° ss.	BRETT Thomas	8° coll.
	BULL George	8° coll.	BURNET Gilbert	8° coll.	DINGLEY William	8° ss.
	GARDINER James	4° ss.	HICHMAN Charles	8° coll.	HOOPER George	4° ss.
	JOHNSON Samuel	fo.coll.	KEN Thomas	8° coll.	NEWTON Richard	4° ss.

Year	Name	Format	Name	Format	Name	Format
	SACHEVERELL Henry	4° ss.				
1714	BINGHAM Joseph	8° ss.	BLACKBURNE Lancelot.	4° ss.	BRADSHAW William	8° ss.
	BRETT Thomas	8° coll.	BURNET Gilbert	4° ss.	BURNET Gilbert	8° ss.
	DUKE Rich. M.A.	8° coll.	KENNET White	8° ss.	LOMBARD Daniel	8° ss.
	RAMSAY John	4° ss.	RYE George	8° ss.	SPINCKES Nathaniel	8° ss.
	WOODFORD Matthew	8° ss.				
1715	ACRES Joseph	8° ss.	BRETT Joseph	8° coll.	WILLIS Richard	4° ss.
1716	BARROW Isaac	fo.coll.	BOYS James	fo.coll.	GARMSTON Shadrach	8° ss.
	GARMSTON Shadrach	8° ss.	HOADLY Benjamin	8° ss.	WAKE William	8° coll.
	WILLIS Richard	4° ss.				
1717	BISSE Thomas	8° ss.	DOD Thomas	8° ss.	HOADLY Benjamin	4° ss.
	HOLE Matthew	8° coll.	LENG John	8° coll.	SMALRIDGE George	8° coll.
	STEPHENS William	8° ss.	SUTTON Gibbon	8° ss.		
1718	CHANDLER Edward	4° ss.	CHANDLER Edward	8° ss.	CLARK N.	8° coll.
	HAYLEY Tho. DD.	8° ss.	HENDLEY William	8° ss.	NEWLIN Thomas	8° ss.
	PEARSON William	8° coll.	SCOTT John	fo.coll.	TILLY William	8° ss.
1719	HARE Francis	4° ss.	MARTIN David	8° ss.	CUMMING John	8° ss.
1720	BEVERIDGE William	fo.coll.	BISSE Thomas	8° ss.	BLAIR James	8° coll.
	DISNEY John	8° ss.	FIDDES Rich. DD.	fo. ss.	NEWLIN Thomas	8° coll.
	SHERIDAN William	8° coll.	WATERLAND Daniel	8° coll.	WHITBY Daniel	8° coll.
	WILDER John	8° coll.	WILLS Benjamin	8° ss.		
1721	BERRIMAN William	4° ss.	BERRIMAN William	4° ss.	COTES Digby	8° coll.
	HOADLY Benjamin	4° ss.	KNIGHT James	8° coll.	LESTLEY Charles	fo. ss.
	LESTLEY Charles	fo.coll.	WRIGHT Samuel	8° ss.		
1722	BERRIMAN William	4° ss.	BERRIMAN William	4° ss.	CHAMBRES Charles	8° ss.
	CONYBEARE John	8° ss.	MASSEY Edmund	8° ss.	PARNE Thomas	8° ss.
	RANDOLPH Herbert	4° ss.	SANDERSON Robert	8° coll.	TRAPP Joseph	8° coll.
	WAKE William	8° coll.				
1723	BLAIR James	8° coll.				
1724	READING Will. M.A.	8° coll.	SMALRIDGE George	fo.coll.	SOUTH Robert	8° coll.
1725	BERRIMAN William	4° ss.	BERRIMAN William	8° coll.	BINGHAM Joseph	fo. ss.
	COLLIER Jeremy	8° coll.	HOLE Matthew	8° coll.		
1726	ANONYMOUS	12° ss.	BERRIMAN William	4° ss.	BINGHAM Joseph	fo.coll.
	BISHOP Thomas	8° coll.	CALAMY Benjamin	8° coll.	NEWLIN Thomas	8° coll.
	PARIS John	8° coll.				
1727	BRIDGES Ralph	4° ss.	DERHAM Will. DD.	8° ss.	ROGERS John	8° coll.
	SOUTH Robert	8° coll.				
1728	DELAUNE William	8° coll.	FIDDES Rich. DD.	fo.coll.	HENLEY John	8° ss.
	MAURICE Peter	8° ss.	NEWLIN Thomas	8° coll.	NORRIS John	8° coll.
	READING Will. M.A.	8° coll.	SYKES Arthur Ashley	8° ss.	WHARTON Henry	8° coll.
	WHARTON Henry	8° coll.	COLEMAN Benjamin	8° coll.		

Year	Name	Format	Name	Format	Name	Format
1729						
	HENLEY John	8° ss.	HENLEY John	8° ss.	LUPTON William	8° coll.
	REEVES William	8° coll.	THOMAS John	4° ss.	TRAPP Joseph	4° ss.
1730						
	ATTERBURY Francis	8° coll.	BRADSHAW William	4° ss.	BRADY Nich. DD.	8° coll.
	CLARKE Samuel	8° coll.	CROXALL Sam. DD.	8° ss.	HENLEY John	8° ss.
	READING Will. M.A.	8° coll.	ROGERS John	8° coll.		
1731						
	MARSHALL Nathaniel	8° coll.	WALLACE Robert	8° ss.	WISHART William	8° ss.
1732						
	FELTON Henry	8° coll.	MOSS Robert	8° coll.	FOSTER James	8° ss.
	FOSTER James	8° coll.				
1733						
	MOSS Robert	8° coll.				
1734						
	RINGER Thomas	8° coll.				
1735						
	LITTLETON Edward	8° coll.	ROGERS John	8° coll.	SHARP John	8° coll.
	STILLINGFLEET Edward	8° ss.	TILLOTSON John	fo.coll.		
1736						
	CARLETON George	8° coll.	ROGERS John	8° coll.		
1737						
	HARTE Walter	8° ss.	MOSS Robert	8° coll.	TILLY William	-° coll.
	FOSTER James	8° coll.				
1738						
	HUTCHINSON Thomas	8° ss.	MOSS Robert	8° coll.	ROGERS John	8° coll.
	WHEATLY Charles	8° coll.				
1739						
	LENG John	fo.coll.	WILLIAMS John	fo.coll.		
1740						
	HUTCHINSON Thomas	8° ss.	VENN Richard	8° coll.		
1741						
	BEDFORD Arthur	8° ss.	FOSTER James	8° ss.		
1742						
	WATERLAND Daniel	8° coll.				
1743						
	TWELLS Leonard	8° coll.	ABERNETHY John	8° coll.		
1744						
	BELLAMY Daniel	8° coll.	FOSTER James	8° coll.		
1746						
	LEIGHTON Robert	8° coll.				
1747						
	KENNICOTT Benjamin	8° ss.	KENNICOTT Benjamin	8° ss.		
1748						
	DODWELL William	8° coll.	ABERNETHY John	8° coll.		
1749						
	BILSTONE John	8° coll.	BUTLER Joseph	8° coll.	DODWELL William	8° coll.
	HEYLYN John	4° coll.	KENNICOTT Benjamin	8° ss.	PARKER William	8° ss.
1750						
	ANONYMOUS	8° ss.	PARKER William	8° ss.	RICH Edward Pickering	4° ss.
	STUKELEY William	4° ss.				
1751						
	BERRIMAN William	8° coll.	CONYBEARE John	4° ss.	CONYBEARE John	8° ss.
	ABERNETHY John	8° coll.				
1752						
	CONYBEARE John	4° ss.	COSTARD George	8° coll.	HAWKINS William	8° ss.

Year	Name	Format	Name	Format	Name	Format
	MARKHAM William	4° ss.				
1753	HURD Richard	8° ss.	KENNICOTT Benjamin	8° ss.	STUART John	4° ss.
	STUART John	4° ss.	STUART John	4° ss.	STUART John	4° ss.
	STUART John	4° ss.	STUART John	4° ss.		
1754	BARTON Philip	8° ss.	BELLAMY Daniel	8° coll.	SUTTON William	8° coll.
1755	PARKER William	8° ss.				
1756	ALCOCK Thomas	8° ss.				
1757	BARTON Philip	8° ss.	COBDEN Edward	4° coll.	KENNICOTT Benjamin	8° ss.
1759	AGAR William	8° coll.	STEBBING Hen. DD. jun.	8° coll.		
1760	PARSONS Joseph	4° ss.	SCROPE John	8° ss.	STERNE Lawrence	12° coll.
1763	BERRIMAN William	8° coll.	BOURN Samuel	8° coll.		
1764	BURTON John	8° coll.	MAURICE Henry	8° ss.	BOURN Samuel	8° coll.
	ERSKINE Ralph	fo. coll.				
1765	BREKELL John	8° coll.	FOTHERGILL Geo. DD.	8° coll.	KENNICOTT Benjamin	8° ss.
	WALKER Robert	8° coll.				
1766	BURTON John	8° coll.	SECKER William	8° coll.	STERNE Lawrence	12° coll.
1767	ELSMERE Sloane	1° coll.	PARSONS Joseph	4° ss.	WEARE Thomas	8° ss.
	MAYHEW Jonathan	8° coll.				
1769	WORTHINGTON William	8° coll.				
1770	SECKER William	8° coll.				
1771	PARKER William	4° ss.	SECKER William	8° coll.	SECKER William	8° coll.
	WHITFIELD George	8° coll.				
1772	DODD W. LLD.	12° coll.	SCOTT William	8° ss.	SHERLOCK Thomas	8° coll.
	ENFIELD William	12° coll.				
1773	BOSTON Thomas	8° coll.	BOSTON Thomas	8° coll.	BOSTON Thomas	8° coll.
	BOSTON Thomas	8° coll.				
1774	MORELL Thomas	4° ss.	SHERLOCK Thomas	8° coll.		
1775	BOSTON Thomas	8° coll.	BOSTON Thomas	8° coll.		
1776	BELLAMY Daniel	4° coll.	HALLIFAX Samuel	8° coll.	HURD Richard	8° coll.
	WARNEFORD John	8° coll.	MOIR John	12° coll.		
1777	BLAIR Hugh	8° coll.	BOURN Samuel	8° coll.	ENFIELD William	12° coll.
1778	HORNE Geo. DD.	8° coll.	TOWNSON Thomas	4° coll.		
1780	BANDINELL James	8° coll.	HOWELL James	4° ss.	BLAIR Hugh	8° coll.

Year	Name	Format	Name	Format	Name	Format
	GERARD Alex. DD.	8° coll.				
1781						
	WILSON Thomas	4° coll.				
Brasenose College ("Braz.N.")						
17--						
	TUNSTALL James	8° coll.				
1721						
	COKER Thomas	8° ss.				
1724						
	HARRIS William	8° coll.				
1730						
	GREY Richard	8° ss.				
1735						
	ANONYMOUS	-° coll.	BARKER John	8° ss.	BAYES Joshua	8° ss.
	BURROUGHS Joseph	8° ss.	CHANDLER Samuel	8° ss.	EARL Jabez	8° ss.
	GROSVENOR Benjamin	8° ss.	HARRIS William	8° ss.	HARRIS William	8° ss.
	HUGHES Obadiah	8° ss.	HUNT Jerem. DD.	8° ss.	LEAVESLY Thomas	8° ss.
	LOWMAN Moses	8° ss.	NEALE Daniel	8° ss.	NEWMAN John	8° ss.
	SMYTH George	8° ss.	WRIGHT Samuel	8° ss.		
1740						
	WATERLAND Daniel	8° ss.				
1747						
	DELANY Patrick	8° coll.				
1748						
	DODWELL William	8° coll.				
1749						
	DODWELL William	8° coll.	BRADBURY Thomas	8° coll.		
1750						
	ASHTON Thomas	8° ss.	WILLIAMS Richard	8° ss.	YARDLEY Edward	4° ss.
1751						
	RUTHERFORTH Thomas	4° ss.				
1752						
	CHAPMAN John	4° ss.	CHURCH Tho. DD.	4° ss.	CONYBEARE John	4° ss.
	HAWKINS William	8° ss.	PARKER William	8° ss.		
1753						
	CHURCH Tho. DD.	4° ss.	CRESSET Edward	8° ss.	DRUMMOND Robert	4° ss.
	HAYTER Thomas	4° ss.	PARKER William	8° ss.	POTTER John	8° coll.
	DUCHAL James	8° coll.				
1754						
	CHURCH Tho. DD.	4° ss.	DELANY Patrick	8° coll.	DRUMMOND Robert	4° ss.
	SKELTON Philip	8° coll.				
1755						
	EDEN Robert	4° ss.	FRIEND William	4° ss.	JAGO Richard	8° ss.
	KEENE Edmund	4° ss.	SALTER Samuel	4° ss.		
1756						
	CORNWALLIS Frederick	8° ss.	GREEN Richard	4° ss.	HALL Charles	4° ss.
	HERRING Thomas	4° ss.	NICOLLS Samuel	4° ss.	ROSS John	4° ss.
	SPRY John	8° ss.	STEBBING Hen. DD. jun.	8° ss.	WATKINS Richard	8° ss.
	WESTON Stephen	4° ss.				
1757						
	CONYBEARE John	8° coll.	KEENE Edmund	4° ss.	PARKER William	4° ss.
	RIDLEY Glocester	4° ss.				
1758						
	DODWELL William	4° ss.	PARKER William	8° ss.	STOPFORD James	4° ss.
	TERRICK Richard	4° ss.	WEBBER Francis. DD.	4° ss.		

Year	Name	Format	Name	Format	Name	Format
1759	BURTON John	8° coll.	ELLYS Anthony	4° ss.	ROSS John	4° ss.
1760	DODWELL William	8° ss.	HALL Charles	8° ss.	HALLIFAX Samuel	8° ss.
	NEWTON Thomas	8° ss.	PARSONS Joseph	4° ss.	STEBBING Hen. DD. jun.	4° ss.
	STERNE Lawrence	12° coll.	STILLINGFLEET James	8° ss.	FORDYCE James	12° ss.
1761	NEGUS Thomas	4° ss.	PORTEUS Beilby	8° ss.	ROTHERAM John	8° ss.
	SIMPSON Joseph	8° ss.	TERRICK Richard	4° ss.	YONGE Philip	4° ss.
1762	CLEAVER Will. M.A.	8° ss.	CORNWALLIS Frederick	4° ss.	HUME John	4° ss.
	PARKER William	4° ss.	RANDOLPH Thomas	8° ss.	ROTHERAM John	8° ss.
1763	BERRIMAN William	8° coll.	BRAY Tho. DD.	4° ss.	DELANY Patrick	4° ss.
	EGERTON John	4° ss.	GREEN John	4° ss.	NOWELL William. M.A.	4° ss.
	ROTHERAM John	8° ss.				
1764	BURTON John	8° coll.	FREE John	8° ss.	FREE John	8° ss.
	RIVERS Sir Peter	4° ss.	TERRICK Richard	4° ss.		
1765	NEWTON Thomas	4° ss.	RUTHERFORTH Thomas	4° ss.	SHARP Gregory	8° ss.
	YONGE Philip	4° ss.				
1766	BURTON John	8° coll.	SHARP Gregory	8° ss.	STERNE Lawrence	12° coll.
	WARBURTON William	4° ss.				
1767	EWER John	4° ss.	LOWTH Robert	4° ss.	PARSONS Joseph	4° ss.
	PORTEUS Beilby	4° ss.	FORDYCE James	12° coll.		
1768	FINCH Robert Pool	4° ss.	WORTHINGTON William	8° ss.		
1769	MARKHAM William	4° ss.	NEWTON Thomas	4° ss.	YONGE Philip	4° ss.

Christ Church College ("Ch.Ch.")

Year	Name	Format	Name	Format	Name	Format
----	ANONYMOUS	-° ss.	WILLIAMS John	-° coll.		
16--	FORD Simon	-° ss.				
1660	BARWICK John	4° ss.	HACKET John	4° ss.	HARDY Nathaniel	4° ss.
	PATRICK Simon	4° ss.	PRICE John	4° ss.	SHELDON Gilbert	4° ss.
	SUDBURY John	4° ss.	BAXTER Richard	4° ss.		
1661	BROWNRIG Ralph	fo. coll.	COLET John	4° ss.	FORD Simon	4° ss.
	STEPHENS Thomas	8° coll.				
1662	HARDY Nathaniel	4° ss.	LANEY Benjamin	4° ss.	CALAMY Edmund	4° ss.
1663	HARDY Nathaniel	4° ss.	LANEY Benjamin	4° ss.		
1665	DOLBEN John	4° ss.	DOLBEN John	4° ss.	FORD Simon	4° ss.
	LANEY Benjamin	4° ss.	LANEY Benjamin	4° ss.		
1666	ALLESTREE Richard	4° ss.	DOLBEN John	4° ss.	HARDY Nathaniel	4° ss.

Year	Name	Format	Name	Format	Name	Format
	HARDY Nathaniel	4° ss.	KILLIGREW Henry. DD.	4° ss.	PERRINCHIEF Richard	4° ss.
1667	BAGSHAW Henry	4° ss.	FULLWOOD Francis	4° ss.	ANNESLEY Samuel	4° coll.
1668	ANONYMOUS	8° ss.	LLOYD William	4° ss.		
1669	BOREMAN Rich. DD.	4° ss.	HOWES John	4° ss.		
1670	GLANVIL Joseph	4° ss.	PATRICK Simon	4° ss.	WARD Seth	4° ss.
1671	DUNCOMB Thomas	4° ss.	LAKE John	4° ss.	NORTH John	4° ss.
1672	DAILLE John	fo.coll.	FARINDON Anth. B.D.	fo.coll.	HASCARD Gregory	4° ss.
	MOULIN DU Peter	4° ss.	WARD Seth	8° coll.	WARING Robert	4° ss.
1673	ANONYMOUS	12° ss.	ASHETON William	4° ss.	BAGSHAW Henry	4° ss.
	HAYWARD Roger	4° ss.	JACKSON Thomas	fo.coll.	LLOYD William	4° ss.
	SAYER Joseph	4° ss.	SMITH John	4° coll.	WOLLEY Edward	4° ss.
1674	JAMES Henry	4° ss.	LLOYD William	4° ss.	LODINGTON Thomas	4° ss.
	LODINGTON Thomas	4° ss.	SALL Andrew	8° ss.	TAYLOR Jeremy	8° ss.
	WARD Hamnett	4° ss.	WARD Seth	4° ss.	WARD Seth	8° coll.
	ANNESLEY Samuel	4° coll.				
1675	ANONYMOUS	4° ss.	BARNE Miles	4° ss.	BONHOME Joshua	4° ss.
	BURNET Gilbert	4° ss.	FELL John	4° ss.	HACKET John	fo.coll.
	JANE Will. DD.	4° ss.	JEKYLL Thomas	4° coll.	LANEY Benjamin	4° ss.
	SMITH Henry	4° coll.	SMITH Thomas	4° ss.	STRADLING Geor. DD.	4° ss.
	SUDBURY John	4° ss.	WOOLLEY John	4° ss.		
1676	CARTWRIGHT Thomas	4° ss.	CAVE Will. DD.	4° ss.	HOWELL William	4° ss.
	JENNER Dav. B.D.	4° ss.	JONES Henry	4° ss.	LUZANCY Hippolytus Du	4° ss.
	STAINFORTH William	4° ss.	TEMPLER John	4° ss.		
1677	ARDERNE James	4° ss.	CRADOCK Zechary	4° ss.	PINDAR William	4° ss.
	SUDBURY John	4° ss.	WILKINS John	12° coll.		
1678	ANONYMOUS	4° ss.	BUTLER John	4° ss.	CROFT Herbert	4° ss.
	FORD Simon	8° ss.	LAMPLUGH Thomas	4° ss.	LLOYD William	4° ss.
	PATRICK Simon	4° ss.	REYNOLDS John	4° ss.	TAYLOR Jeremy	fo.coll.
	THOMAS William	4° ss.				
1679	ANONYMOUS	4° ss.	DURHAM William	4° ss.	FARINDON Anth. B.D.	fo.coll.
	HESKETH Henry	4° ss.	HORTON Thomas	fo.coll.	JANE Will. DD.	4° ss.
	LLOYD William	4° ss.	LLOYD William	4° ss.	OATES Titus	4° ss.
	PELLING Edward	4° ss.	PELLING Edward	4° ss.	PINDAR William	4° ss.
	RALEIGH Walter	4° coll.	REYNOLDS Edward	fo.coll.	SMITH Thomas	4° ss.
	WHITBY Daniel	4° ss.	WOODROFFE Benjamin	4° ss.	WYATT Will. M.A.	4° ss.
1680	BURNET Gilbert	4° ss.	DOVE Heb. DD.	4° ss.	FELL John	4° ss.
	HASCARD Gregory	4° ss.	HICHMAN Charles	4° ss.	HICKERINGILL Edmond	4° coll.
	HICKERINGILL Edmond.	4° ss.	PARSONS Robert	4° ss.	PATRICK Simon	4° ss.
	RAMSAY William	4° ss.	RAMSAY William	4° ss.	BAXTER Richard	4° ss.
	CROMWELL Oliver	4° ss.				
1681	BURNET Gilbert	4° ss.	HICHMAN Charles	4° ss.	JEKYLL Thomas	4° ss.

Year	Name	Format	Name	Format	Name	Format
	LLOYD William	4° ss.	MAURICE Henry	4° ss.	PATRICK Simon	4° ss.
	PATRICK Simon	4° ss.	STRATFORD Nicholas	4° ss.	TURNER Francis	4° ss.
	WALLS George	4° ss.				
1682						
	BARNE Miles	4° ss.	CALAMY Benjamin	4° ss.	COMBER Thomas	4° ss.
	DOVE Heb. DD.	4° ss.	EVANS John	4° ss.	FULLER Samuel	4° ss.
	FULLER Samuel	4° ss.	JEKYLL Thomas	4° ss.	KNIGHT John	4° ss.
	MARCH John	4° ss.	PELLING Edward	4° ss.	RICHARDSON Joshua	4° ss.
	WILKINS John	8° coll.				
1683						
	BARON William	4° ss.	BARROW John	4° ss.	CALAMY Benjamin	4° ss.
	FOWLER Edward	4° ss.	GIPPS Tho.	4° coll.	HESKETH Henry	4° ss.
	HICKES George	4° ss.	PAYNE William	4° ss.	PAYNE William	4° ss.
	PELLING Edward	4° ss.	POMFRET Tho. M.A.	4° ss.	PRICE John	4° ss.
	RODERICK Richard	4° ss.	RUST George	4° ss.	TURNER Francis	5° ss.
	TURNER John	8° ss.	WAGSTAFFE Thomas	4° ss.		
1684						
	ALLESTREE Richard	fo. coll.	ALLESTREE Richard	fo. coll.	ATTERBURY Lewis	4° ss.
	BRIDGE Francis	4° ss.	BURTON Hezekiah	8° coll.	BUTLER John	4° ss.
	CALAMY Benjamin	4° ss.	CALAMY Benjamin	4° ss.	CAMFIELD Benjamin	4° ss.
	CARTWRIGHT Thomas	4° ss.	CAVE Will. DD.	4° ss.	ELLESBY James	4° ss.
	FALKNER Will. DD.	4° coll.	HAMMOND Henry	fo. coll.	HESKETH Henry	4° ss.
	KETTLEWELL John	4° ss.	KETTLEWELL John	4° ss.	LAKE Edward	4° ss.
	LEIGH Thomas	4° ss.	LIGHTFOOT J. DD.	fo. coll.	PEARSON Richard	4° ss.
	PEARSON Richard	4° ss.	PITTIS Thomas	4° ss.	SMYTHIES William	4° ss.
	TURNER Francis	4° ss.	TURNER Francis	4° ss.		
1685						
	BURNET Gilbert	4° ss.	BURTON Hezekiah	8° coll.	ELLIS Ph.	4° ss.
	ELLIS Ph.	4° ss.	FOWLER Edward	4° ss.	GASKARTH John	4° ss.
	HOLLAND Richard	4° ss.	HUTTON Charles	4° ss.	IRONSIDE Gilbert	4° ss.
	KETTLEWELL John	4° ss.	KETTLEWELL John	4° ss.	PELLING Edward	4° ss.
	PELLING Edward	4° ss.	ROBERTS Richard	4° ss.	SHERLOCK William	4° ss.
	TURNER Francis	4° ss.	TURNER Francis	4° ss.	TURNER Francis	4° ss.
	TURNER Tho. DD.	4° ss.	WAGSTAFFE Thomas	4° ss.		
1686						
	ANONYMOUS	4° ss.	ANONYMOUS	4° ss.	ATTERBURY Lewis	4° ss.
	BEAULIEU Luke	4° ss.	CARTWRIGHT Thomas	4° ss.	ELLIS Ph.	4° ss.
	KIDDER Richard	4° ss.	KING William	4° ss.	NEWCOME Peter	4° ss.
	PATRICK Simon	4° ss.	STAYNOE Thomas	4° ss.	TULLIE George	4° ss.
	YOUNG Edward	12° ss.				
1687						
	ANONYMOUS	4° ss.	ATTERBURY Lewis	4° ss.	COMBER Thomas	4° ss.
	PATRICK Simon	4° ss.	STRATFORD Nicholas	4° ss.		
1688						
	BURNET Gilbert	8° ss.	CUDWORTH John	4° ss.	FOWLER Edward	4° ss.
	HELLIER Henry	4° ss.	WAGSTAFFE Thomas	4° ss.		
1689						
	ANONYMOUS	4° ss.	BEVERIDGE William	4° ss.	BIRCH Peter	4° ss.
	BROGRAVE Robert	4° ss.	BURNET Gilbert	4° ss.	BURNET Gilbert	4° ss.
	CARSWELL Francis	4° ss.	HORNECK Anthony	4° ss.	LLOYD William	4° ss.
	LYNFORD Thomas	4° ss.	PATRICK Simon	4° ss.	PATRICK Simon	4° ss.
	PATRICK Simon	4° ss.	PATRICK Simon	4° ss.	PATRICK Simon	4° ss.
	RESBURY Nathaniel	4° ss.	SANDERSON Robert	fo. coll.	TENISON Thomas	4° ss.
	TULLIE George	4° ss.	VESEY John	4° ss.	MEAD Matthew	4° ss.
1690						
	ANONYMOUS	4° ss.	BUDGELL Gilbert	4° ss.	BURNET Gilbert	4° ss.

Year	Name	Format	Name	Format	Name	Format
	FOWLER Edward	4° ss.	FREEMAN Samuel	4° ss.	GROVE Robert	4° ss.
	HICHMAN Charles	4° ss.	KIDDER Richard	4° ss.	MASTERS Samuel	4° ss.
	PATRICK Simon	4° ss.	PELLING Edward	4° ss.	SMITH Humphrey	4° ss.
	TENISON Thomas	4° ss.	WILLES John	4° ss.		
1691						
	BUTLER Lilly	4° ss.	CLARKE Joshua	4° ss.	FOWLER Edward	4° ss.
	JANE Will. DD.	4° ss.	KELSEY Joseph	4° ss.	KING William	4° ss.
	LLOYD William	4° ss.	LYNFORD Thomas	4° ss.	PATRICK Simon	4° ss.
	PAYNE William	4° ss.	RESBURY Nathaniel	4° ss.	TALBOT William	4° ss.
	TENISON Thomas	4° ss.	TENISON Thomas	4° ss.	WROE Christopher	4° ss.
1692						
	BENTLEY Richard	4° coll.	BURNET Gilbert	4° ss.	GEE Edward	4° ss.
	HICHMAN Charles	4° ss.	JANE Will. DD.	4° ss.	MANNINGHAM Thomas	4° ss.
	MANNINGHAM Thomas	4° ss.	MORE Henry	8° coll.	PELLING Edward	4° ss.
	SHERLOCK William	4° ss.	SHERLOCK William	4° ss.	SMYTHIES William	4° ss.
	STANLEY William	4° ss.	STRADLING Geor. DD.	8° coll.		
1693						
	FREEMAN Samuel	4° ss.	HOLLINGWORTH Richard	4° ss.	LAKE Edward	4° ss.
	MANNINGHAM Thomas	4° ss.	STUBBS Philip	4° ss.	VESEY John	4° ss.
1694						
	BIRCH Peter	4° ss.	BURNET Gilbert	4° ss.	CAMPION Abraham	4° ss.
	COMBER Thomas	4° ss.	FREEMAN Samuel	4° ss.	KIDDER Richard	4° ss.
	MANNINGHAM Thomas	4° ss.	MANNINGHAM Thomas	4° ss.	NORRIS John	8° coll.
	PROWDE Francis	4° ss.	SANCROFT William	8° coll.	SYKES Thomas	4° ss.
	TENISON Thomas	4° ss.	TENISON Thomas	4° ss.	WHITEHALL Rob. M.A.	4° ss.
	WROE Christopher	4° ss.				
1695						
	ALLESTREE Charles	4° ss.	ANONYMOUS	4° ss.	FISHER Joseph	4° ss.
	HARTCLIFFE John	4° ss.	HAYLEY William	4° ss.	HICHMAN Charles	4° ss.
	ISHAM Zach. DD.	4° ss.	KENNET White	4° ss.	LAMBE John	4° ss.
	MANNINGHAM Thomas	4° ss.	MAPLETOFT John	4° ss.	PAYNE William	4° ss.
	TENISON Thomas	4° ss.	WILLIAMS John	4° ss.	WILLIAMS John	4° ss.
	<u>STENNETT</u> <u>Joseph</u>	8° ss.				
1696						
	BENTLEY Richard	4° ss.	BORFET Abiel	4° ss.	BUTLER Lilly	4° ss.
	BUTLER Lilly	4° ss.	FORD Simon	4° ss.	GREGORY Thomas	8° coll.
	ISHAM Zach. DD.	4° ss.	KETTLEWELL John	8° coll.	LANCASTER William	4° ss.
	MEGGOT Richard	8° coll.	MERITON Henry	4° ss.	<u>STAFFORD</u> <u>Richard</u>	8° ss.
1697						
	BECONSALL Thomas	4° ss.	BRADFORD Samuel	8° ss.	BUTLER Lilly	8° ss.
	ENTWISLE Edmund	4° ss.	GIPPS Tho.	4° ss.	GOODMAN John	4° ss.
	GOODMAN John	8° coll.	HANCOCK John	4° ss.	HORNECK Anthony	8° ss.
	JEKYLL Thomas	4° ss.	LUZANCY Hippolytus Du	4° ss.	WETENHALL Edward	12° ss.
1698						
	BEDFORD William	4° ss.	BUTLER Lilly	4° ss.	EDWARDS John	8° coll.
	FREEMAN Samuel	4° ss.	LYNFORD Thomas	4° ss.	PROVOSTE John	4° ss.
	WHICHCOTE Benj. DD.	8° coll.	WILLIAMS John	4° ss.		
1699						
	ATTERBURY Lewis	8° coll.	BRAY Thomas	4° ss.	FOWLER Edward	4° ss.
	HANCOCK John	8° ss.	HAYLEY William	4° ss.	HAYLEY William	12° ss.
	MORER Thomas	4° ss.				
17--						
	TALBOT William	8° ss.				
1700						
	BRADFORD Samuel	4° coll.	D'ASTOR DE Laussac A.	4° ss.	FREEMAN Samuel	4° ss.
	HOLLAND Rich. M.A.	4° ss.	KEITH George	4° ss.	KEITH George	4° ss.

Year	Name	Format	Name	Format	Name	Format
	SHELLEY Peter	4° ss.	STRATFORD Nicholas	4° ss.	BATES William	fo. coll.
1701	ANONYMOUS	4° coll.	BISSE Philip	4° ss.	BRYDGES Henry	4° ss.
	BURGHOPE M	4° ss.	BUTLER Lilly	4° ss.	COLET John	-° ss.
	HAYLEY William	4° ss.	HOUGH John	4° ss.	HOWARD John	4° ss.
	ISHAM Zach. DD.	4° ss.	MILLES Thomas	8° ss.	STANHOPE George	4° coll.
	STUBBS Philip	4° ss.	STUBBS Philip	4° ss.		
1702	BINCKES William	4° ss.	BRAGGE Francis	8° coll.	BRAGGE Francis	8° coll.
	BUTLER Lilly	4° ss.	DELAUNE William	4° ss.	GIBSON Edmund	4° ss.
	HAYLEY William	4° ss.	HILL Anthony	8° ss.	HOUGH John	4° ss.
	KIMBERLEY Jonathan	4° ss.	LESTLEY Charles	8° ss.	NEEDHAM William	4° ss.
	NICHOLS Will. DD.	4° ss.	SACHEVERELL Henry	4° ss.	SACHEVERELL Henry	4° ss.
	SPRAT Thomas	4° ss.	STANHOPE George	4° coll.	STUBBS Philip	4° ss.
	STUBBS Philip	4° ss.	TRELAWNEY Jonathan Sir	4° ss.	WAKE William	8° coll.
	WHICHCOTE Benj. DD.	8° coll.	WILLIS Richard	4° ss.	WILLIS Richard	4° ss.
1703	ALTHAM Roger	4° ss.	ATTERBURY Lewis	8° coll.	CHAPMAN Richard	4° ss.
	COCKBURN John	4° ss.	COCKBURN John	4° ss.	DORRINGTON Theophilus	8° coll.
	DUKE Rich. M.A.	4° ss.	FULLER Thomas	4° ss.	GASTRELL Francis	8° ss.
	HUNTER Richard	4° ss.	MANNINGHAM Thomas	4° ss.	NICOLSON William	4° ss.
	STANHOPE George	4° ss.	STANHOPE George	4° ss.	WHICHCOTE Benj. DD.	8° coll.
	WHITBY Daniel	fo. ss.	WHITFELD Will. DD.	4° ss.	WHITING Charles	4° ss.
	WOODROFFE Benjamin	4° ss.				
1704	BINCKES William	4° ss.	BRAGGE Francis	8° coll.	BURNET Gilbert	4° ss.
	BURNET Gilbert	4° ss.	BUTLER Lilly	4° ss.	CLAGETT Nicholas	4° ss.
	CLAGETT William	8° coll.	CLAGETT William	8° coll.	DUKE Rich. M.A.	4° ss.
	DUKE Rich. M.A.	4° ss.	FINCH Will. Lepold	4° ss.	FOWLER Edward	4° ss.
	GASTRELL Francis	4° ss.	GASTRELL Francis	4° ss.	HOOPER George	4° ss.
	HOUGH John	4° ss.	ISHAM Zach. DD.	4° ss.	KENNET White	4° ss.
	KENNET White	4° ss.	KING William	4° ss.	LENG John	4° ss.
	MANNINGHAM Thomas	4° ss.	NORRIS Richard	4° ss.	SAVAGE John	4° ss.
	SHERWILL Thomas	4° ss.	STUBBS Philip	4° ss.	WALLS George	4° ss.
	WILLIAMS John	4° ss.	WILLIS Richard	4° ss.	WROE Christopher	4° ss.
	WYNNE Robert	4° ss.				
1705	ALTHAM Roger	4° ss.	ATTERBURY Lewis	4° ss.	BLACKBURNE Lancelot.	4° ss.
	CARTE Sam. M.A.	4° ss.	COCK John	12° coll.	HARRIS John	4° ss.
	HOUGH John	4° ss.	HOUGH John	4° ss.	ISHAM Zach. DD.	4° ss.
	JONES Charles	4° ss.	KEITH George	4° ss.	KENNET White	4° ss.
	KING William	4° ss.	KING William	4° ss.	LAKE Edward	8° coll.
	OVINGTON John	4° ss.	POOLEY Giles	4° ss.	RENNELL Thomas	4° ss.
	SPRAT Thomas	4° ss.	TALBOT William	4° ss.	TILLY William	4° ss.
	VERNEY Geo.	4° ss.	WAUGH John	4° ss.	WELLS Zachary	4° ss.
	WILLIS Richard	4° ss.	WILLIS Richard	4° ss.		
1706	ALTHAM Roger	4° ss.	BEAULIEU Luke	4° ss.	BURNET Gilbert	4° ss.
	BURNET Gilbert	4° ss.	DORRINGTON Theophilus	4° ss.	GEREE John	4° ss.
	HORNECK Anthony	8° coll.	KENNET White	4° ss.	KENNET White	4° ss.
	KENNET White	4° ss.	MANNINGHAM Thomas	4° ss.	SMALBROKE Richard	4° ss.
	STUBBS Philip	4° ss.	SYDALL Elias	4° ss.	TORRIANO Alexander	4° ss.
	WALLS George	4° ss.	WALLS George	4° ss.	WEST Richard	4° ss.
	WILLIAMS John	4° ss.	WOTTON William	4° ss.	YOUNG Edward	8° coll.
1707	BROUGHTON John	4° ss.	CHANDLER Edward	4° ss.	GOODMAN John	8° ss.

Year	Name	Format	Name	Format	Name	Format
	HORT Josiah	4° ss.	MILLES Thomas	4° ss.	OLDFIELD Joshua	8° ss.
	PATRICK Simon	12° ss.	STILLINGFLEET Edward	fo.coll.	TRIMNEL Charles	4° ss.
	WHICHCOTE Benj. DD.	8° coll.	WILLIAMS Charles	4° ss.	WILLIS Richard	4° ss.
	WISE Thomas	4° ss.				
1708						
	BISSE Thomas	4° ss.	BLACKBURNE Lancelot.	4° ss.	BRADFORD Samuel	4° ss.
	BRAY Thomas	8° ss.	DOWNES Henry	8° ss.	FISHER John	8° ss.
	KENNET White	8° ss.	RAWSON Jos. DD.	4° ss.	SMITH Humphrey	4° ss.
	STANHOPE George	4° coll.	TRIMNEL Charles	4° ss.	WHISTON Will. M.A.	8° ss.
	WILLIAMS John	8° ss.	WILLIAMS John	8° ss.	WILLIAMS John	8° coll.
	WOODCOCK Josiah	8° ss.				
1709						
	BRAY Thomas	4° ss.	BRYDGES Henry	8° ss.	CHAPMAN Richard	4° ss.
	HARE Francis	4° ss.	KING William	8° ss.	MANNINGHAM Thomas	4° ss.
	PELLING John	4° ss.	RAWSON Jos. DD.	4° ss.	SACHEVERELL Henry	4° ss.
	SACHEVERELL Henry	4° ss.	SMITH John	4° ss.	STUBBS Philip	4° ss.
	TRIMNEL Charles	4° ss.	TRIMNEL Charles	4° ss.	WILLIS Richard	8° ss.
1710						
	BINCKES William	8° ss.	BRADFORD Samuel	4° ss.	GODDARD Thomas	4° ss.
	HOPKINS Ezekiel	fo.coll.	KELSAL Edward	8° ss.	ROBINSON John	4° ss.
	SPRAT Thomas	8° coll.	TILLY William	4° ss.	TRIMNEL Charles	4° ss.
	WHALEY Nathanael	8° ss.	WHITBY Daniel	8° coll.		
1711						
	ANONYMOUS	8° ss.	BISSE Philip	4° ss.	BOWTELL John	8° ss.
	COLNET William	8° ss.	DIBBEN Thomas	8° ss.	FRIEND Robert	4° ss.
	HAYLEY Tho. DD.	4° ss.	HOADLY Benjamin	8° coll.	KENNET White	4° ss.
	RICHARDSON William	4° ss.	TENNISON Edward	4° ss.	TRAPP Joseph	4° ss.
	TRIMNEL Charles	4° ss.	WEST Richard	4° ss.	WILLIS Richard	4° ss.
1712						
	ANONYMOUS	8° ss.	BRETT Thomas	8° coll.	BROWNE Francis	4° ss.
	DORRINGTON Theophilus	8° ss.	HOUGH John	4° ss.	JENNINGS John	4° ss.
	KENNET White	4° ss.	KENNET White	4° ss.	LYNFORD Thomas	4° ss.
	NADEN Thomas	8° ss.	NEWTON Richard	4° ss.	REEVES William	4° ss.
	SHUTTLEWOOD John	8° ss.	STUBBS Philip	4° ss.	TRIMNEL Charles	4° ss.
	WILLOUGHBY Lord De Bro	4° ss.				
1713						
	AYLMER William	8° ss.	BELL George	8° ss.	BISSE Thomas	8° ss.
	BRETT Thomas	8° coll.	BULL George	8° coll.	BURNET Gilbert	8° coll.
	COCKBURN John	4° ss.	DINGLEY William	8° ss.	HICKES George	8° coll.
	NEWTON Richard	4° ss.	STANHOPE George	4° ss.	WAUGH John	4° ss.
	WHITFELD Will. DD.	4° ss.				
1714						
	ANONYMOUS	8° ss.	BLACKBURNE Lancelot.	4° ss.	BRETT Thomas	8° coll.
	BURNET Gilbert	4° ss.	CHANDLER Edward	8° ss.	CLAGETT Nicholas	4° ss.
	DUKE Rich. M.A.	8° coll.	FORSTER William	8° ss.	GASTRELL Francis	4° ss.
	HAWTAYNE Will. M.A.	8° ss.	HILLIARD Samuel	8° ss.	KENNET White	8° ss.
	REEVES William	4° ss.	REEVES William	4° ss.	ROBINSON John	4° ss.
	STANHOPE George	4° ss.	TRIMNEL David	8° ss.	BENNET Benjamin	8° coll.
	STINTON Benjamin	8° ss.				
1715						
	ASH St. George	4° ss.	BENTLEY Richard	8° ss.	BLACKBURNE Lancelot.	4° ss.
	BRETT Joseph	8° coll.	BURSCOUGH William	4° ss.	COLEIRE Richard	8° ss.
	GIBSON Edmund	4° ss.	KENNET Basil	8° coll.	LENG John	4° ss.
	LENG John	8° ss.	LOVE Barry	4° ss.	LYNFORD Thomas	4° ss.
	LYNFORD Thomas	4° ss.	PHILIPPS Philip	8° ss.	SHOREY William	8° ss.
	SHUCKBURGH George	4° ss.	SKERRET Ralph	8° ss.	STANHOPE George	4° coll.

Year	Name	Format	Name	Format	Name	Format
	TRIMNEL Charles	4° ss.	TRIMNEL Charles	4° ss.	TURNER John	4° ss.
	WILLIS Richard	4° ss.	WYNNE John	4° ss.		
1716	ASH St. George	4° ss.	BARROW Isaac	fo.coll.	BOULTER Hugh	4° ss.
	BOULTER Hugh	8° ss.	BOULTER Hugh	8° ss.	BURSCOUGH William	4° ss.
	COLEIRE Richard	4° ss.	GIBSON Edmund	4° ss.	GODWIN Timothy	4° ss.
	GODWIN Timothy	4° ss.	GREENE Thomas	4° ss.	HARE Francis	8° ss.
	KENNET White	4° ss.	KENNET White	8° ss.	LENG John	8° ss.
	NICOLSON William	4° ss.	RAWSON Jos. DD.	8° ss.	SKERRET Ralph	4° ss.
	SKERRET Ralph	4° ss.	SKERRET Ralph	8° ss.	STANHOPE George	4° coll.
	STURMY Daniel	8° coll.	SYNGE Edward	8° ss.	SYNGE Edward	8° ss.
	TURNER John	8° ss.	WAKE William	8° coll.	WEST Richard	4° ss.
	WILLIS Richard	4° ss.				
1717	BENNET Thomas	4° ss.	BENTLEY Richard	4° ss.	BISSE Philip	4° ss.
	BISSE Thomas	8° ss.	CAESAR J. James	4° ss.	LAMBE Charles	8° coll.
	LENG John	8° coll.	LORTIE Andrew	12° ss.	LOVELING Benjamin	8° ss.
	OFFLEY Walter	4° ss.	PYLE Tho. M.A.	8° ss.	RAYNER William	8° ss.
	SKERRET Ralph	8° ss.	SMALRIDGE George	8° coll.	SMITH Henry	4° ss.
	STUART William	8° ss.	SYKES Arthur Ashley	8° ss.	TALBOT William	4° ss.
	TAUBMAN Nathaniel	4° ss.	WAUGH John	4° ss.	WAUGH John	4° ss.
	WISE Thomas	8° coll.	WRIGHT John	4° ss.		
1718	BRADFORD Samuel	8° ss.	CHANDLER Edward	4° ss.	CHANDLER Edward	8° ss.
	CLAGETT Nicholas	4° ss.	CLARK N.	8° coll.	COLBATCH John	4° ss.
	HAYLEY Tho. DD.	4° ss.	HAYLEY Tho. DD.	8° ss.	PEARSON William	8° coll.
	SCOTT John	fo.coll.				
1719	BRADFORD Samuel	4° ss.	CHANDLER Edward	4° ss.	HARE Francis	4° ss.
	JENNINGS John	8° ss.	KETTLEWELL John	fo.coll.	SHERLOCK William	8° coll.
	SMITH Joseph	4° ss.	STEPHENS Henry	8° ss.	WAUGH John	4° ss.
1720	BEVERIDGE William	fo.coll.	BLAIR James	8° coll.	BOULTER Hugh	4° ss.
	BRADFORD Samuel	4° ss.	CLAGETT William	8° coll.	DOWNES Henry	4° ss.
	FIDDES Rich. DD.	fo. ss.	FIDDES Rich. DD.	fo. ss.	GARDINER James	8° coll.
	SMALBROKE Richard	8° ss.	WATERLAND Daniel	8° coll.	WHITBY Daniel	8° coll.
	WILCOCKS Joseph	4° ss.				
1721	BOULTER Hugh	4° ss.	BROWNE John	8° coll.	KNIGHT James	8° coll.
	LESTLEY Charles	fo. ss.	LESTLEY Charles	fo.coll.	SAUNDERS Erasmus	8° ss.
	STEBBING Henry	8° ss.	STEPHENS Lewis	4° ss.	WADDINGTON Edward	8° ss.
1722	BOULTER Hugh	4° ss.	CONYBEARE John	8° ss.	IBBETSON Richard	4° ss.
	MARSHALL Nathaniel	8° ss.	MAYNARD Edward	8° coll.	WAKE William	8° coll.
	WAUGH John	4° ss.	CALAMY Edmund	8° coll.		
1723	BLACKALL Offspring	fo.coll.	CONYBEARE John	8° ss.	GIBSON Edmund	4° ss.
	HARE Francis	4° ss.	STEPHENS Lewis	4° ss.	BRADBURY Thomas	8° coll.
1724	GILBERT John	8° coll.	GREENE Thomas	4° ss.	MAYNARD Edward	8° coll.
	SMALRIDGE George	fo.coll.	SOUTH Robert	8° coll.	WYNNE John	4° ss.
1725	SYNGE Edward	8° ss.				
1726	BISHOP Thomas	8° coll.	BRAGGE Francis	8° coll.	BULLOCK Thomas	8° coll.
	CALAMY Benjamin	8° coll.	CONYBEARE John	8° ss.	IBBOT Benj. DD.	8° coll.

Year	Name	Format	Name	Format	Name	Format
	SCOUGAL Henry	8° coll.	STACKHOUSE Thomas	8° ss.	WILCOCKS Joseph	4° ss.
1727	CLAYTON Thomas	8° ss.	CONYBEARE John	8° ss.	DERHAM Will. DD.	8° ss.
	LENG John	4° ss.	REYNOLDS Richard	4° ss.	ROGERS John	8° coll.
	SMALBROKE Richard	8° ss.	SOUTH Robert	8° coll.	STANHOPE George	8° coll.
1728	DELAUNE William	8° coll.	FIDDES Rich. DD.	fo.coll.	NORRIS John	8° coll.
	READING Will. M.A.	8° coll.	WHARTON Henry	8° coll.	WHARTON Henry	8° coll.
1729	CARTER Benjamin	8° coll.	CONYBEARE John	8° ss.	EGERTON Henry	4° ss.
	GIBSON Edmund	8° coll.	REEVES William	8° coll.		
1730	ATTERBURY Francis	8° coll.	CLARKE Samuel	8° coll.	DERHAM Will. DD.	8° ss.
	READING Will. M.A.	8° coll.	ROGERS John	8° coll.		
1732	FELTON Henry	8° coll.				
1733	CONYBEARE John	8° ss.	TREBECK Andr. DD.	8° ss.		
1734	CLARKE Samuel	8° coll.				
1735	HARE Francis	4° ss.	ROGERS John	8° coll.	STILLINGFLEET Edward	8° ss.
	TILLOTSON John	fo.coll.				
1736	ROGERS John	8° coll.				
1737	FLEETWOOD William	fo.coll.				
1738	CONYBEARE John	4° ss.	ROGERS John	8° coll.		
1739	BENTLEY Richard	fo.coll.	GASTRELL Francis	fo. ss.	GURDON Brampton	8° coll.
	GURDON Brampton	fo.coll.	HANCOCK John	fo. ss.	HARRIS John	fo.coll.
	LENG John	fo.coll.	STANHOPE George	fo.coll.	WHISTON Will. M.A.	fo. ss.
	WILLIAMS John	fo.coll.				
1744	CARY Mordecai	4° ss.				
1748	HUNT Jerem. DD.	8° coll.				
1749	CONYBEARE John	8° ss.				
1751	BERRIMAN William	8° coll.	CONYBEARE John	4° ss.	CONYBEARE John	8° ss.
1752	CONYBEARE John	4° ss.	CONYBEARE John	4° ss.		
1753	POTTER John	8° coll.	WARBURTON William	8° coll.		
1754	HOADLY Benjamin	8° coll.	WARBURTON William	8° coll.		
1757	CONYBEARE John	8° coll.	HOOPER George	fo.coll.		
1764	MAURICE Henry	8° ss.				
1771	SECKER William	8° coll.				
1772	SHERLOCK Thomas	8° coll.				

Year	Name	Format	Name	Format	Name	Format
1775	HUNT Thomas	4° coll.				
1776	IBBOT Benj. DD.	-° coll.				
1778	TOWNSON Thomas	4° coll.				
1780	BAGOTT Lewis	8° coll.				
1784	BEAULIEU Luke	4° ss.				
1790	TENISON Thomas	4° ss.				

Corpus Christi College ("C.C.C.")

Year	Name	Format	Name	Format	Name	Format
1660	PATRICK Simon	4° ss.	WARRE Richard	4° ss.		
1661	BERNARD Nicholas	4° ss.	DUPORT James	4° ss.	MORLEY George	4° ss.
1662	KING Henry	4° ss.				
1663	READING John	4° ss.				
1664	BROWNRIG Ralph	fo.coll.	GOAD John	4° ss.	JOHNSON Will. DD.	12° ss.
1665	FORD Simon	8° ss.				
1668	LLOYD William	4° ss.				
1669	BOREMAN Rich. DD.	4° ss.				
1670	CUDWORTH Ralph	8° ss.				
1671	NORTH John	4° ss.				
1672	GARDINER Samuel	4° ss.	MOULIN DU Peter	4° ss.	WARD Seth	8° coll.
1673	LLOYD William	4° ss.	WARD Seth	4° ss.		
1674	FORD Simon WARD Seth	8° ss. 8° coll.	KELSEY Joseph	4° ss.	WARD Seth	4° ss.
1675	LANEY Benjamin	4° ss.	SUDBURY John	4° ss.		
1677	PINDAR William	4° ss.	TURNER Bryan	4° ss.		
1678	ANONYMOUS	4° ss.	HOOKER Richard	8° ss.	LLOYD William	4° ss.
1679	JANE Will. DD. MANNINGHAM Thomas	4° ss. 8° ss.	LLOYD William PINDAR William	4° ss. 4° ss.	MANNINGHAM Thomas	8° ss.
1680	DOVE Heb. DD. SMITH Samuel	4° ss. 4° ss.	HOLLINGWORTH Richard	4° ss.	PARSONS Robert	4° ss.
1681	FOWLER Edward MANNINGHAM Thomas	4° ss. 4° ss.	HOOPER George RESBURY Nathaniel	4° ss. 4° ss.	LLOYD William TURNER Bryan	4° ss. 4° ss.

Year	Name	Format	Name	Format	Name	Format
1682						
	EVANS John	4° ss.	FREEMAN Samuel	4° ss.	KEN Thomas	4° ss.
	TURNER Francis	4° ss.	WILKINS John	8° coll.		
1683						
	FOWLER Edward	4° ss.	MEGGOT Richard	4° ss.	PAYNE William	4° ss.
	PAYNE William	4° ss.	PELLING Edward	4° ss.	TURNER Francis	5° ss.
	TURNER John	8° ss.				
1684						
	BROWNE Philip	4° ss.	BURTON Hezekiah	8° coll.	CAVE Will. DD.	4° ss.
	FALKNER Will. DD.	4° coll.	KETTLEWELL John	4° ss.	MANNINGHAM Thomas	4° ss.
	PEARSON Richard	4° ss.	TURNER Francis	4° ss.	TURNER Francis	4° ss.
	TURNER Francis	4° ss.				
1685						
	BURTON Hezekiah	8° coll.	CAVE John	4° ss.	DOVE Heb. DD.	4° ss.
	ELLIS Ph.	4° ss.	FOWLER Edward	4° ss.	FOWLER Edward	4° ss.
	GOWER Humphrey	4° ss.	GOWER Humphrey	4° ss.	HORNE Thomas	4° ss.
	IRONSIDE Gilbert	4° ss.	KETTLEWELL John	4° ss.	MANNINGHAM Thomas	4° ss.
	MASTERS Samuel	4° ss.	TURNER Francis	4° ss.	TURNER Francis	4° ss.
	TURNER John	8° ss.	TURNER Tho. DD.	4° ss.	WAGSTAFFE Thomas	4° ss.
1686						
	BRYAN Matt. LLD.	4° ss.	MANNINGHAM Thomas	4° ss.		
1687						
	HAYLEY William	4° ss.	MANNINGHAM Thomas	4° ss.		
1688						
	BROWNE Thomas	4° ss.	FOWLER Edward	4° ss.		
1689						
	BURNET Gilbert	4° ss.	PATRICK Simon	4° ss.		
1692						
	BENTLEY Richard	4° coll.	JANE Will. DD.	4° ss.	STANLEY William	4° ss.
1693						
	MONRO Alexander	4° coll.	STUBBS Philip	4° ss.		
1694						
	BATTELY John	4° ss.	HALLYWELL Henry	8° ss.	SANCROFT William	8° coll.
	SEVILL William	4° ss.	SYKES Thomas	4° ss.		
1695						
	ISHAM Zach. DD.	4° ss.	WHALEY Nathanael	8° coll.		
1696						
	BARTON Samuel	4° ss.	ISHAM Zach. DD.	4° ss.		
1697						
	COCKBURN John	8° coll.	GOODMAN John	8° coll.	OWTRAM William	8° coll.
1698						
	BARTON Samuel	4° ss.	CHISHULL Edmund	4° ss.	PAYNE William	8° coll.
	WHITFELD Will. DD.	4° ss.				
1699						
	BRAY Thomas	4° ss.	CONANT John	8° coll.		
1700						
	ISHAM Zach. DD.	4° ss.	PRAT Samuel	4° ss.		
1701						
	BARTON Samuel	4° ss.	BISSE Philip	4° ss.	GARDINER James	4° ss.
	HALLIFAX Will. DD.	4° ss.	HOOPER George	4° ss.	HOUGH John	4° ss.
	TISSER John	4° ss.				
1702						
	GIBSON Edmund	4° ss.	HOUGH John	4° ss.		
1703						
	GASTRELL Francis	8° ss.	WHITING Charles	4° ss.	WOODROFFE Benjamin	4° ss.
1704						

INDEXES TO FIFTH VOLUME: E: LIBRARIES: PART ONE: OXFORD (Corpus)

Year	Name	Format	Name	Format	Name	Format
	BINCKES William	4° ss.	CLAGETT William	8° coll.	CLAGETT William	8° coll.
	FINCH Will. Lepold	4° ss.	GASTRELL Francis	4° ss.	HOOPER George	4° ss.
	HOUGH John	4° ss.	ISHAM Zach. DD.	4° ss.	PRAT Samuel	4° ss.
	SACHEVERELL Henry	4° ss.	WHALEY Nathanael	12° coll.	WILLIS Richard	4° ss.
1705	HOUGH John	4° ss.	HOUGH John	4° ss.	ISHAM Zach. DD.	4° ss.
	MATHER John	4° ss.				
1706	GEREE John	4° ss.	HICHMAN Charles	8° coll.	KENNET White	4° ss.
	KENNET White	4° ss.	SMALBROKE Richard	4° ss.	SMITH Joshua	4° ss.
	YOUNG Edward	8° coll.				
1707	CHISHULL Edmund	4° ss.	MILLES Thomas	4° ss.		
1708	SACHEVERELL Henry	4° ss.	STANHOPE George	4° coll.	STEPHENS Henry	4° ss.
	WILLIAMS John	8° coll.				
1709	GIBSON Sam.	8° ss.	PELLING John	4° ss.		
1710	BISSE Philip	4° ss.	ELLISON Nath. DD.	4° ss.	KENNET White	4° ss.
	RIVERS Tho. LL.D.	4° ss.	SAINT John Pawlet	4° ss.	WHITBY Daniel	8° coll.
1711	BISSE Philip	4° ss.	BISSE Thomas	8° ss.	RICHARDSON William	4° ss.
	SAINT John Pawlet	4° ss.				
1712	BISSE Thomas	4° ss.	BISSE Thomas	8° ss.	CHISHULL Edmund	1° ss.
	CHISHULL Edmund	8° ss.	GASTRELL Francis	4° ss.	KENNET White	4° ss.
	NEWTON Richard	4° ss.	TILLY William	8° coll.	WILLOUGHBY Lord De Bro	4° ss.
1713	BISSE Thomas	8° ss.	BULL George	8° coll.	COCKBURN John	4° ss.
	HICHMAN Charles	8° coll.	HICKES George	8° coll.	HOOPER George	4° ss.
	SACHEVERELL Henry	4° ss.	TILLY William	8° ss.		
1714	CHISHULL Edmund	4° ss.	WAPLE Edward	8° coll.		
1715	KENNET Basil	8° coll.	STANHOPE George	4° coll.		
1716	BISSE Thomas	8° ss.	STANHOPE George	4° coll.		
1717	BISSE Philip	4° ss.	BISSE Thomas	8° ss.	BISSE Thomas	8° ss.
	MANGEY Thomas	8° coll.				
1718	CHISHULL Edmund	8° coll.	SCOTT John	fo.coll.	TILLY William	8° ss.
	WAPLE Edward	8° coll.				
1719	SHERLOCK William	8° coll.				
1720	CLAGETT William	8° coll.	WAPLE Edward	8° coll.	WATERLAND Daniel	8° coll.
1722	TRAPP Joseph	8° coll.				
1723	BLACKALL Offspring	fo.coll.				
1724	SOUTH Robert	8° coll.				
1726	CALAMY Benjamin	8° coll.				

Year	Name	Format	Name	Format	Name	Format
1727	ROGERS John	8° coll.	SOUTH Robert	8° coll.		
1729	WAPLE Edward	8° coll.				
1730	ROGERS John	8° coll.				
1735	ROGERS John	8° coll.	SHARP John	8° coll.		
1736	ROGERS John	8° coll.				
1737	STEPHENS William	8° coll.	TILLY William	-° coll.		
1738	ROGERS John	8° coll.				
1739	BENTLEY Richard	fo.coll.	GASTRELL Francis	fo. ss.	HARRIS John	fo.coll.
	WILLIAMS John	fo.coll.				
1741	BEDFORD Arthur	8° ss.	SPRY John	8° ss.		
1743	TWELLS Leonard	8° coll.				
1744	SPRY John	8° ss.				
1746	FORSTER Nathaniel	8° ss.				
1757	CONYBEARE John	8° coll.	HOOPER George	fo.coll.		
1760	MUSCUTT James	8° coll.				
1764	BURTON John	8° coll.				
1766	BURTON John	8° coll.				

Exeter College ("Ex.C.")

Year	Name	Format	Name	Format
----	ALCOCK Thomas	-° ss.		
1681	MAURICE Henry	4° ss.		
1713	CALAMY Edmund	8° ss.		
1737	PEIRCE James	4° coll.		
1741	CLARKE Alured	4° ss.		
1752	MARKHAM William	4° ss.		
1753	HAYTER Thomas	4° ss.		
1755	HAYTER Thomas	4° ss.	HAYTER Thomas	4° ss.
1756	ALCOCK Thomas	8° ss.		
1758	BILSTONE John	8° ss.		
1759				

Year	Name	Format	Name	Format	Name	Format
	HAYTER Thomas	4° ss.				
1763	BILSTONE John	8° ss.				
1764	LOWTH Robert	4° ss.	MAURICE Henry	8° ss.		
1766	DARCH John	4° ss.				
1767	LOWTH Robert	4° ss.				
1769	STINTON George	4° ss.				
1772	LOVE Samuel	8° ss.	PORTEUS Beilby	4° ss.		
1773	COWPER Spencer	8° coll.				

Hertford College ("Hert.")

Year	Name	Format	Name	Format	Name	Format
1689	SHERLOCK William	8° ss.				
17--	ROOTES Richard	8° ss.				
1705	SHERLOCK William	-° ss.				
1706	BURNET Gilbert	4° ss.	MANNINGHAM Thomas	4° ss.	STANHOPE George	4° ss.
1707	BRADY Nich. DD. TYLER John	8° ss. 4° ss.	MANNINGHAM Thomas	8° ss.	MILBOURNE Luke	8° ss.
1708	MILNER William	8° ss.				
1709	BRYDGES Henry SACHEVERELL Henry	8° ss. 4° ss.	MANNINGHAM Thomas	4° ss.	PELLING John	4° ss.
1710	ARCHER Edmond	8° ss.				
1711	BOND Henry TRAPP Joseph	8° coll. 4° ss.	BURSCOUGH William TRAPP Joseph	8° ss. 4° ss.	GOOCH Thomas Sir	4° ss.
1713	GOOCH Thomas Sir	4° ss.	SACHEVERELL Henry	4° ss.		
1720	GARDINER James	8° coll.	WATERLAND Daniel	8° coll.		
1721	KNIGHT James	8° coll.				
1727	DERHAM Will. DD.	8° ss.				
1729	GIBSON Edmund	8° coll.				
1730	CLARKE Samuel	8° coll.	DERHAM Will. DD.	8° ss.	JORTIN John	12° coll.
1735	TILLOTSON John	fo. coll.				
1740	ZINZENDORF Count	12° coll.				
1747	BURNET Gilbert	8° coll.				

Year	Name	Format	Name	Format	Name	Format
1749						
	HEYLYN John	4° coll.				

Jesus College ("Jes.")

Year	Name	Format	Name	Format	Name	Format

	CLARKE John	-° coll.	WOODWARD Josiah	-° coll.		
1605						
	MASON Francis	-° ss.				
1610						
	STAYNOE Thomas	4° ss.				
1663						
	ANONYMOUS	4° ss.				
1668						
	LLOYD William	4° ss.				
1671						
	NORTH John	4° ss.				
1673						
	WARD Seth	4° ss.				
1677						
	CRADOCK Zechary	4° ss.	MARCH John	4° ss.		
1678						
	TAYLOR Jeremy	fo.coll.				
1679						
	PELLING Edward	4° ss.				
1680						
	BURNET Gilbert	4° ss.	CAVE Will. DD.	4° ss.	FELL John	4° ss.
1681						
	TENISON Thomas	4° ss.				
1682						
	WILKINS John	8° coll.				
1683						
	RODERICK Richard	4° ss.				
1684						
	HAMMOND Henry	fo.coll.	TURNER Francis	4° ss.		
1685						
	NORRIS John	4° ss.	SCOTT John	4° ss.		
1686						
	CARTWRIGHT Thomas	4° ss.	GODDEN Thomas	4° ss.	PATRICK Simon	4° ss.
1687						
	ANONYMOUS	4° ss.				
1689						
	BURNET Gilbert	4° ss.	PATRICK Simon	4° ss.	TENISON Thomas	4° ss.
	TULLIE George	4° ss.				
1690						
	BURNET Gilbert	4° ss.	FOWLER Edward	4° ss.	FREEMAN Samuel	4° ss.
	GROVE Robert	4° ss.	HICHMAN Charles	4° ss.	HICHMAN Charles	4° ss.
	WILLES John	4° ss.				
1691						
	BURNET Gilbert	4° ss.	SPARK Tho. DD.	4° ss.		
1692						
	GEE Edward	4° ss.	HICHMAN Charles	4° ss.	SHERLOCK William	4° ss.
	STANLEY William	4° ss.	STRADLING Geor. DD.	8° coll.	WHITING Charles	4° ss.
1693						
	HICHMAN Charles	4° ss.	STUBBS Philip	4° ss.		
1694						
	BIRCH Peter	4° ss.	SYKES Thomas	4° ss.		

Year	Name	Format	Name	Format	Name	Format
1695	BULL Digby	4° ss.	BULL Digby	4° ss.	HUMPHREYS Humphrey	4° ss.
1696	ADAMS John	4° ss.	ISHAM Zach. DD.	4° ss.	LANCASTER William	4° ss.
1697	BECONSALL Thomas	4° ss.	PAYNE William	12° ss.		
1698	ANONYMOUS	12° ss.				
1700	ISHAM Zach. DD.	4° ss.	MAURICE David	4° ss.	BATES William	fo.coll.
1701	ISHAM Zach. DD. STUBBS Philip	4° ss. 4° ss.	MILLES Thomas	8° ss.	SCOTT William	8° coll.
1702	HOUGH John SACHEVERELL Henry	4° ss. 4° ss.	KIMBERLEY Jonathan	4° ss.	NEEDHAM William	4° ss.
1703	DUKE Rich. M.A.	4° ss.	WHITING Charles	4° ss.		
1704	BINCKES William GASTRELL Francis SACHEVERELL Henry	4° ss. 4° ss. 4° ss.	FINCH Will. Lepold ISHAM Zach. DD. WYNNE Robert	4° ss. 4° ss. 4° ss.	GASTRELL Francis KENNET White	4° ss. 4° ss.
1705	ADAMS John TILLY William	4° ss. 4° ss.	ISHAM Zach. DD.	4° ss.	MASON Francis	4° ss.
1706	CRADOCK Zechary SMALBROKE Richard WOTTON William	4° ss. 4° ss. 4° ss.	GEREE John WILLIAMS John	4° ss. 4° ss.	HIGGINS Francis WOODROFFE Benjamin	4° ss. 4° ss.
1707	MILLES Thomas	4° ss.				
1708	SAUNDERS Erasmus WILLIAMS John	8° ss. 8° coll.	TURNER John	8° coll.	WHITFELD Will. DD.	4° ss.
1709	PELLING John	4° ss.				
1710	ADAMS John	4° ss.	D'OYLY Robert	4° ss.	RIVERS Tho. LL.D.	4° ss.
1711	SAINT John Pawlet	4° ss.				
1712	BRETT Thomas	8° coll.				
1713	BRETT Thomas	8° coll.				
1714	BRETT Thomas	8° coll.				
1718	SCOTT John	fo.coll.				
1719	KETTLEWELL John	fo.coll.				
1723	NORRIS John	12° ss.				
1727	WHITBY Daniel	8° coll.				
1728	WHITBY Daniel	8° coll.				

Year	Author	Format	Author	Format	Author	Format
1730	CLARKE Samuel	8° coll.				
1735	HARE Francis	4° ss.				
1739	ANONYMOUS	fo.coll.	GURDON Brampton	8° coll.	GURDON Brampton	fo.coll.
	TURNER John	fo.coll.	WILLIAMS John	fo.coll.		
1743	THOMAS John	4° ss.				
1745	HUTTON Matthew	4° ss.				
1751	BERRIMAN William	8° coll.				
1757	CONYBEARE John	8° coll.	GRIFFITH Thomas	8° ss.		
1758	PARKER William	8° ss.				
1760	GRIFFITH Thomas	8° ss.				

Lincoln College ("Linc.")

Year	Author	Format	Author	Format	Author	Format
----	WILLIAMS John	-° coll.				
1618	PARSONS Bartholomew	4° ss.				
1660	HACKET John	4° ss.				
1669	MOULIN DU Peter	4° ss.				
1670	DOBSON John	4° ss.				
1675	BURNET Gilbert	4° ss.				
1677	CRADOCK Zechary	4° ss.				
1679	WALLIS John	4° ss.				
1680	PARSONS Robert	4° ss.				
1683	BARNE Miles	4° ss.	CALAMY Benjamin	4° ss.		
1689	BURNET Gilbert	4° ss.				
1691	KELSEY Joseph	4° ss.				
1692	BOWCHIER Richard	4° ss.				
1693	PRITCHARD Thomas	4° ss.	STUBBS Philip	4° ss.	STUBBS Philip	4° ss.
1694	CORNWALLIS Henry	12° ss.	TENISON Thomas	4° ss.	WHITEHALL Rob. M.A.	4° ss.
	WIGAN William	4° ss.				
17--	PARSONS Bartholomew	8° ss.				
1701	HAYLEY William	4° ss.				

Year	Name	Format	Name	Format	Name	Format
1706						
	BURNET Gilbert	4° ss.				
1707						
	ADAMSON John	8° ss.	COCK John	8° ss.		
1708						
	ADAMS Rice	8° ss.	COCKBURN John	8° ss.	FEATLY Daniel	8° ss.
	MOXON Mordecai	12° ss.	WILLIAMS John	8° ss.	WILLIAMS John	8° ss.
	WILLIAMS John	8° coll.	WOODCOCK Josiah	8° ss.		
1709						
	ADAMS John	4° ss.	ANONYMOUS	8° ss.	ANONYMOUS	8° ss.
	BAGNOLD Joseph	8° ss.	CHAPMAN Richard	4° ss.	EDWARDS John	8° ss.
	HILLIARD Samuel	8° ss.	PALMER Samuel	8° ss.	ROBERTS William	4° ss.
	SACHEVERELL Henry	4° ss.				
1710						
	ADAMS John	4° ss.	ANONYMOUS	8° ss.	ARCHER Edmond	8° ss.
	BEARE Nicholas	8° ss.	BENNET Thomas	8° ss.	BINCKES William	8° ss.
	BISSE Philip	4° ss.	BLOMER Ralph	8° ss.	BRADFORD Samuel	4° ss.
	BRADFORD Samuel	8° ss.	BURNET Gilbert	8° ss.	BUTLER Lilly	4° ss.
	CORNEWALL Fred. M.A.	8° ss.	FARMERIE William	8° ss.	GODDARD Thomas	8° ss.
	HARRIS Higgins	4° ss.	HARRISON John	8° ss.	HIGDEN Will. DD.	4° ss.
	KENNET White	8° ss.	KNAGGS Thomas	8° ss.	MILBOURNE Luke	8° ss.
	MULES Walter	8° ss.	NEEDHAM John	8° ss.	NEWCOME Peter	8° ss.
	PUGH Hugh	8° ss.	RICHMOND Henry	8° coll.	ROBINSON John	4° ss.
	SWIFT Thomas	8° ss.	SYNGE Edward	8° ss.	TRIMNEL Charles	4° ss.
	TROUTBECK John	8° ss.	WALKER John	8° ss.	WALKER John	8° ss.
	WELLS Edward	8° ss.	WELTON Richard	4° ss.	WEST Richard	8° ss.
	WHALEY Nathanael	8° ss.				
1711						
	BISSE Philip	4° ss.	BOWTELL John	8° ss.	BURNET Gilbert	4° ss.
	BURSCOUGH William	8° ss.	CHISHULL Edmund	4° ss.	FELTON Henry	4° ss.
	FRIEND Robert	4° ss.	GOOCH Thomas Sir	4° ss.	HOWELL Will. M.A.	8° ss.
	JENNINGS John	8° ss.	JENNINGS John	8° ss.	MILBOURNE Luke	8° ss.
	RICHARDSON William	4° ss.	SCOTT Alexander	8° coll.	TRAPP Joseph	4° ss.
	TRAPP Joseph	4° ss.	WILLIS Richard	4° ss.		
1712						
	ADAMS John	4° ss.	ALTHAM Roger	4° ss.	ANONYMOUS	8° ss.
	BISSE Thomas	4° ss.	BRETT Thomas	8° coll.	BYNNS Richard	8° ss.
	CHISHULL Edmund	8° ss.	DORRINGTON Theophilus	8° ss.	FINCH Henry	4° ss.
	GASTRELL Francis	4° ss.	HAYLEY Tho. DD.	8° ss.	HOWELL Will. M.A.	8° ss.
	HUMPHREYS Thomas	8° ss.	LECHE Thomas	8° ss.	LOVELING Benjamin	8° ss.
	NEWTON Richard	4° ss.	POTTER John	8° ss.	TASWELL William	4° ss.
1713						
	AYLMER William	8° ss.	BRAMSTON William	4° ss.	BRETT Thomas	8° coll.
	DINGLEY William	8° ss.	GARDINER James	8° ss.	GOOCH Thomas Sir	4° ss.
	HARRISON Joseph	8° ss.	HORNE Thomas	8° ss.	NEWTON Robert	4° ss.
	REEVES William	4° ss.	SACHEVERELL Henry	4° ss.	SACHEVERELL Henry	4° ss.
	TILLY William	8° ss.	TRAPP Joseph	4° ss.	WAUGH John	4° ss.
	WAUGH John	4° ss.				
1714						
	BISSE Thomas	4° ss.	BRETT Thomas	8° coll.	GASTRELL Francis	4° ss.
	HEAD Henry	8° ss.	MARSHALL John	8° ss.	REEVES William	4° ss.
	ROWDEN John	8° ss.	SMITH Joseph	4° ss.	WILLIAMS John	8° ss.
	WOODFORD Matthew	8° ss.				
1715						
	BRETT Joseph	8° coll.	LYNFORD Thomas	4° ss.		
1716						

Year	Name	Format	Name	Format	Name	Format
	ADAMS William	8° coll.	ANONYMOUS	8° ss.	BENNET Thomas	8° ss.
	BURSCOUGH William	4° ss.				
1717						
	BISSE Thomas	8° ss.	DOD Thomas	8° ss.	HIND Thomas	8° ss.
	STEPHENS William	8° ss.	TRAPP Joseph	8° ss.		
1718						
	NEWLIN Thomas	8° ss.				
1719						
	HARE Francis	4° ss.	HOLDSWORTH Winch. DD.	8° ss.	KNIGHT James	4° ss.
	RUSSELL John	8° ss.	STEPHENS William	8° ss.		
1720						
	BOULTER Hugh	4° ss.	MANGEY Thomas	4° ss.	WILCOCKS Joseph	4° ss.
1721						
	HARCOURT James	4° ss.				
1722						
	CONYBEARE John	8° ss.	STEPHENS William	8° ss.		
1723						
	CONYBEARE John	8° ss.				
1727						
	CLAYTON Thomas	8° ss.				
1730						
	ATTERBURY Francis	8° coll.	GREY Richard	8° ss.		
1731						
	BULKELEY Benj. DD.	8° ss.				
1732						
	TRAPP Joseph	8° ss.				
1733						
	COCKMAN Thomas	8° ss.	CONINGESBY George	8° ss.	CONYBEARE John	8° ss.
	TROUGHEAR Thomas	8° ss.				
1737						
	HARTE Walter	8° ss.	STEPHENS William	8° coll.		
1738						
	CROXALL Sam. DD.	8° ss.	HUTCHINSON Thomas	8° ss.	WEBBER Francis. DD.	8° ss.
1739						
	STEBBING Henry	8° ss.	TRAPP Joseph	8° ss.	WILLIAMS John	fo. coll.
1740						
	BISSE Thomas	8° coll.	HUTCHINSON Thomas	8° ss.	NEWTON Richard	8° ss.
	WATERLAND Daniel	8° ss.				
1758						
	WEBBER Francis. DD.	4° ss.				
1773						
	HORNE Geo. DD.	8° ss.				
1790						
	TENISON Thomas	4° ss.				

Magdalen College ("Magd.")

Year	Name	Format	Name	Format

	WOODWARD Josiah	-° coll.		
1605				
	MASON Francis	-° ss.		
1627				
	MAYNWARING Roger	4° ss.		
1641				
	MASTER Thomas	-° ss.		
1660				
	GREGORY Fran. DD.	4° ss.	SHELDON Gilbert	4° ss.

Year	Name	Format	Name	Format	Name	Format
1661	FORD Simon	4° ss.	GREEFFIELD Thomas	4° ss.	LLOYD William	4° ss.
	MORLEY George	4° ss.				
1662	LANEY Benjamin	4° ss.	MAYNE Jasper	4° ss.	WREN Matthew	4° ss.
1663	LANEY Benjamin	4° ss.				
1664	BROWNRIG Ralph	fo.coll.	PEARSON Richard	4° ss.		
1665	DOLBEN John	4° ss.	FORD Simon	4° ss.	LANEY Benjamin	4° ss.
	LANEY Benjamin	4° ss.				
1666	KILLIGREW Henry. DD.	4° ss.	PERRINCHIEF Richard	4° ss.		
1668	LINGARD Ric. DD.	4° ss.				
1670	BREVAL Frank Durant de	4° ss.	DOBSON John	4° ss.	WARD Seth	4° ss.
	STEEL Richard	8° coll.				
1671	LAKE John	4° ss.	PIERCE Tho. DD.	4° coll.		
1672	FULLWOOD Francis	4° ss.	WARD Seth	8° coll.		
1673	HAYWARD Roger	4° ss.	LLOYD William	4° ss.		
1674	CROFT Herbert	4° ss.	JAMES Henry	4° ss.	LLOYD William	4° ss.
	TANNER Thomas	4° ss.	WARD Seth	4° ss.	WARD Seth	8° coll.
	ANNESLEY Samuel	4° coll.				
1675	BARNE Miles	4° ss.	BURNET Gilbert	4° ss.	BURNET Gilbert	4° ss.
	FELL John	4° ss.	JANE Will. DD.	4° ss.	LANEY Benjamin	4° ss.
	NAILOUR William	4° ss.	SMITH Thomas	4° ss.	SMITH Thomas	4° ss.
1676	HAYWARD Roger	4° ss.	JONES Henry	4° ss.	LUZANCY Hippolytus Du	4° ss.
	TEMPLER John	4° ss.				
1677	CRADOCK Zechary	4° ss.	PINDAR William	4° ss.		
1678	BURNET Gilbert	4° ss.	BUTLER John	4° ss.	CROFT Herbert	4° ss.
	LAMPLUGH Thomas	4° ss.	LATHAM Paul	4° ss.	LLOYD William	4° ss.
	PATRICK Simon	4° ss.	PATRICK Simon	4° ss.	THOMAS William	4° ss.
	USHER James	fo.coll.				
1679	CROFT Herbert	4° ss.	HERNE Samuel	4° ss.	JANE Will. DD.	4° ss.
	LLOYD William	4° ss.	LLOYD William	4° ss.	MANNINGHAM Thomas	8° ss.
	MANNINGHAM Thomas	8° ss.	NEEDHAM Robert	8° coll.	PIERCE Tho. DD.	4° coll.
	PINDAR William	4° ss.	SMITH Thomas	4° ss.	WYATT Will. M.A.	4° ss.
1680	BURNET Gilbert	4° ss.	CAVE Will. DD.	4° ss.	DOVE Heb. DD.	4° ss.
	FELL John	4° ss.	HICHMAN Charles	4° ss.	HICKERINGILL Edmond	4° coll.
	HICKERINGILL Edmond.	4° ss.	JEKYLL Thomas	4° ss.	LITTLETON Adam	fo.coll.
1681	BURNET Gilbert	4° ss.	BURNET Gilbert	4° ss.	GIFFARD Francis	4° ss.
	GLANVIL Joseph	4° coll.	HICHMAN Charles	4° ss.	HOOPER George	4° ss.
	HOOPER George	4° ss.	LLOYD William	4° ss.	PATRICK Simon	4° ss.

Year	Name	Format	Name	Format	Name	Format
	PATRICK Simon	4° ss.	RESBURY Nathaniel	4° ss.	STRATFORD Nicholas	4° ss.
	TURNER Francis	4° ss.				
1682						
	ALLEN John	4° ss.	BURNET Gilbert	4° ss.	CALAMY Benjamin	4° ss.
	COMBER Thomas	4° ss.	EVANS John	4° ss.	FULLER Samuel	4° ss.
	FULLER Samuel	4° ss.	JAMES John	4° ss.	JEKYLL Thomas	4° ss.
	KEN Thomas	4° ss.	SMITH Thomas	4° ss.	WETENHALL Edward	4° ss.
	WETENHALL Edward	4° ss.				
1683						
	CALAMY Benjamin	4° ss.	CALAMY Benjamin	4° ss.	CLAGETT Nich. M.A.	4° ss.
	FOLEY Samuel	4° ss.	FOLEY Samuel	4° ss.	HICKES George	4° ss.
	PELLING Edward	4° ss.	PELLING Edward	4° ss.	PELLING Edward	4° ss.
	PELLING Edward	4° ss.	SHERLOCK William	4° ss.		
1684						
	BASSET Will.	4° ss.	BRIDGE Francis	4° ss.	CALAMY Benjamin	4° ss.
	CAVE Will. DD.	4° ss.	FALKNER Will. DD.	4° coll.	GRENVILLE Denis	4° ss.
	HAMMOND Henry	fo.coll.	KETTLEWELL John	4° ss.	KETTLEWELL John	4° ss.
	LAKE Edward	4° ss.	LOWDE James	4° ss.	MOULIN DU Peter	8° coll.
	VESEY John	4° ss.				
1685						
	ALLESTREE Charles	4° ss.	DOVE Heb. DD.	4° ss.	GASKARTH John	4° ss.
	GOWER Humphrey	4° ss.	GRENVILLE Denis	4° ss.	HESKETH Henry	8° ss.
	PELLING Edward	4° ss.	SHERLOCK William	4° ss.	TURNER Francis	4° ss.
	TURNER Francis	4° ss.	WAGSTAFFE Thomas	4° ss.	ZAMBRANA De Barzia Jos	4° ss.
1686						
	BEAULIEU Luke	4° ss.	BOSSUET Benigne James	4° ss.	CARTWRIGHT Thomas	4° ss.
	COLLIER Jeremy	4° ss.	DOVE Heb. DD.	4° ss.	HICHMAN Charles	4° ss.
	LAMBE John	4° ss.	TULLIE George	4° ss.	YOUNG Edward	12° ss.
1687						
	ANONYMOUS	4° ss.	MANNINGHAM Thomas	4° ss.	PATRICK Simon	4° ss.
1688						
	BURNET Gilbert	8° ss.	CUDWORTH John	4° ss.	KENRICK Daniel	4° ss.
1689						
	BEVERIDGE William	4° ss.	BIRCH Peter	4° ss.	BURNET Gilbert	4° ss.
	BURNET Gilbert	4° ss.	BURNET Gilbert	4° ss.	CARSWELL Francis	4° ss.
	HORNECK Anthony	4° ss.	PATRICK Simon	4° ss.	PATRICK Simon	4° ss.
	PATRICK Simon	4° ss.	PATRICK Simon	4° ss.	PATRICK Simon	4° ss.
	RESBURY Nathaniel	4° ss.	SANDERSON Robert	fo.coll.	SHERLOCK William	8° ss.
	TENISON Thomas	4° ss.	VESEY John	4° ss.	WATTS Tho. M.A.	4° ss.
1690						
	BURNET Gilbert	4° ss.	BURNET Gilbert	4° ss.	GROVE Robert	4° ss.
	HICHMAN Charles	4° ss.	PATRICK Simon	4° ss.	PELLING Edward	4° ss.
	TENISON Thomas	4° ss.	WICHART John	4° ss.		
1691						
	ASTON Thomas	4° ss.	BARKER Ralph	4° ss.	BURNET Gilbert	4° ss.
	BURNET Gilbert	4° ss.	DOVE Heb. DD.	4° ss.	ELLIS Clement	4° ss.
	HOOPER George	4° ss.	JANE Will. DD.	4° ss.	PATRICK Simon	4° ss.
	RESBURY Nathaniel	4° ss.	SHERLOCK William	8° ss.	TENISON Thomas	4° ss.
	WALLIS John	4° coll.	WRIGHT John	4° ss.		
1692						
	BARTON Samuel	4° ss.	BURNET Gilbert	4° ss.	FOWLER Edward	4° ss.
	HALLYWELL Henry	8° ss.	HICHMAN Charles	4° ss.	HOWARD John	4° ss.
	JANE Will. DD.	4° ss.	JONES David	4° ss.	KIDDER Richard	4° ss.
	MANNINGHAM Thomas	4° ss.	MORSE Robert	4° ss.	PELLING Edward	4° ss.
	RESBURY Nathaniel	4° ss.	SHERLOCK William	4° ss.	SHERLOCK William	4° ss.
	SKELTON Bernard	4° ss.	STANLEY William	4° ss.	WALLIS John	4° coll.

Year	Name	Format	Name	Format	Name	Format
1693	HICHMAN Charles	4° ss.	MANNINGHAM Thomas	4° ss.	STUBBS Philip	4° ss.
	STUBBS Philip	4° ss.				
1694	ASH St. George	4° ss.	BATTELY John	4° ss.	BIRCH Peter	4° ss.
	BURNET Gilbert	4° ss.	BURNET Gilbert	4° ss.	CAMPION Abraham	4° ss.
	FREEMAN Samuel	4° ss.	SANCROFT William	8° coll.	STRATFORD Nicholas	4° ss.
	SYKES Thomas	4° ss.	TENISON Thomas	4° ss.	TENISON Thomas	4° ss.
	WIGAN William	4° ss.				
1695	ADAMS John	4° ss.	BRIGHT George	8° coll.	BURNET Gilbert	4° ss.
	GARDINER James	4° ss.	HARTCLIFFE John	4° ss.	HAYLEY William	4° ss.
	HOOPER George	4° ss.	ISHAM Zach. DD.	4° ss.	LAMBE John	4° ss.
	MANNINGHAM Thomas	4° ss.	PAYNE William	4° ss.	WHALEY Nathanael	8° coll.
	WILLIAMS John	4° ss.				
1696	ADAMS John	4° ss.	BENTLEY Richard	4° ss.	FITZWILLIAM John	12° ss.
	HASCARD Gregory	4° ss.	HASCARD Gregory	4° ss.		
1697	BECONSALL Thomas	4° ss.	BURNET Gilbert	4° ss.	BURNET Gilbert	4° ss.
	BURNET Gilbert	4° ss.	ENTWISLE Edmund	4° ss.	LLOYD William	4° ss.
	TRIMNEL Charles	4° ss.				
1698	BURNET Gilbert	4° ss.	GILBERT John	4° ss.	WHICHCOTE Benj. DD.	8° coll.
1699	BRAY Thomas	4° ss.	SHERLOCK William	8° ss.		
1700	HARE Francis	4° ss.	STEPHENS William	4° ss.		
1701	BISSE Philip	4° ss.	HAYLEY William	4° ss.	HOOPER George	4° ss.
	HOUGH John	4° ss.	LAMBE John	4° ss.	MANNINGHAM Thomas	4° ss.
	MILLES Thomas	8° ss.				
1702	BINCKES William	4° ss.	HOUGH John	4° ss.	KIMBERLEY Jonathan	4° ss.
	NEEDHAM William	4° ss.	NEWCOME Peter	8° coll.	SACHEVERELL Henry	4° ss.
	SACHEVERELL Henry	4° ss.	STUBBS Philip	4° ss.	STUBBS Philip	4° ss.
	TRELAWNEY Jonathan Sir	4° ss.	WAKE William	8° coll.	WHICHCOTE Benj. DD.	8° coll.
1703	GASTRELL Francis	8° ss.	KEITH George	4° ss.	STANHOPE George	4° ss.
	WHICHCOTE Benj. DD.	8° coll.				
1704	BINCKES William	4° ss.	GASTRELL Francis	4° ss.	ISHAM Zach. DD.	4° ss.
	MANNINGHAM Thomas	4° ss.	SACHEVERELL Henry	4° ss.	SHERLOCK William	4° ss.
	WHALEY Nathanael	12° coll.	WILLIS Richard	4° ss.		
1705	HOUGH John	4° ss.	ISHAM Zach. DD.	4° ss.	LAKE Edward	8° coll.
	MASON Francis	4° ss.	RENNELL Thomas	4° ss.	SHERLOCK William	-° ss.
	STANHOPE George	4° ss.	TILLY William	4° ss.	WILLIS Richard	4° ss.
1706	BURNET Gilbert	4° ss.	CRADOCK Zechary	4° ss.	HICHMAN Charles	8° coll.
	KENNET White	4° ss.	KENNET White	4° ss.	KNAGGS Thomas	4° ss.
	MANNINGHAM Thomas	4° ss.	SACHEVERELL Henry	4° ss.	SMALBROKE Richard	4° ss.
	STANHOPE George	4° ss.	STANHOPE George	4° ss.	WOTTON William	4° ss.
	YOUNG Edward	8° coll.				
1707	ADAMS John	4° ss.	ADAMS John	4° ss.	BEAN Charles	4° ss.

Year	Name	Format	Name	Format	Name	Format
	BROUGHTON John	4° ss.	CHANDLER Edward	4° ss.	EDWARDS John	8° ss.
	GRANT John	4° ss.	HACKET Lawrence	4° ss.	SMITH Thomas	8° ss.
	WHICHCOTE Benj. DD.	8° coll.				
1708	ADAMS John	4° ss.	ADAMS John	4° ss.	BISSE Thomas	4° ss.
	COCKBURN John	8° ss.	EYRE Robert	4° ss.	FEATLY Daniel	8° ss.
	MILNER William	8° ss.	RAWSON Jos. DD.	4° coll.	STANHOPE Michael	8° ss.
	TRIMNEL Charles	4° ss.	TURNER John	8° coll.	WHALEY Nathanael	8° ss.
	WHISTON Will. M.A.	8° ss.				
1709	HOUGH John	4° ss.	KING William	8° ss.	LYNFORD Thomas	8° ss.
	MANNINGHAM Thomas	4° ss.	MAYNWARING Roger	8° ss.	SACHEVERELL Henry	4° ss.
	TRIMNEL Charles	4° ss.	TRIMNEL Charles	4° ss.	TRIMNEL Charles	8° ss.
	TURNER John	8° ss.				
1710	ADAMS John	4° ss.	ARCHER Edmond	8° ss.	BINCKES William	8° ss.
	BURNET Gilbert	8° ss.	CHANDLER Edward	8° ss.	HOPKINS Ezekiel	fo.coll.
	KNAGGS Thomas	8° ss.	LEWIS Henry	8° ss.	MASTER Thomas	-° ss.
	ROBINSON John	4° ss.	SPRAT Thomas	8° coll.	SYNGE Edward	8° ss.
	TRIMNEL Charles	4° ss.	WEST Richard	8° ss.		
1711	BISSE Thomas	8° ss.	CROFT Thomas	8° ss.	FRIEND Robert	4° ss.
	SAINT John Pawlet	4° ss.				
1712	ASH St. George	8° ss.	BISSE Thomas	4° ss.	BISSE Thomas	8° ss.
	LOVELING Benjamin	8° ss.	NEWTON Richard	4° ss.	TRIMNEL Charles	4° ss.
	WILLOUGHBY Lord De Bro	4° ss.				
1713	AYLMER William	8° ss.	BISSE Thomas	8° ss.	GOOCH Thomas Sir	4° ss.
	HICHMAN Charles	8° coll.	HICKES George	8° coll.	HOOPER George	4° ss.
	SACHEVERELL Henry	4° ss.				
1714	BISSE Thomas	4° ss.	MARSHALL John	8° ss.	READING Will. M.A.	8° ss.
	REEVES William	4° ss.	REEVES William	4° ss.		
1715	BENTLEY Richard	8° ss.	EYRE Rich. M.A.	8° ss.	HOLE Matthew	8° coll.
	ISAAC John	8° ss.	WILLIS Richard	4° ss.	WISE Thomas	8° ss.
1716	ADAMS William	8° coll.	BAKER William	8° ss.	BURSCOUGH William	4° ss.
	CROSSE Richard	8° ss.	CROSSE Richard	8° ss.	EYRE Rich. M.A.	4° ss.
	GIBSON Edmund	4° ss.	HICKERINGILL Edmond.	8° coll.	HOADLY Benjamin	4° ss.
	HOLE Matthew	8° ss.	HOLE Matthew	8° coll.	NEWTON Richard	4° ss.
	PEARSE Robert	8° ss.	WAKE William	8° coll.	WATERLAND Daniel	8° ss.
1717	BENTLEY Richard	4° ss.	BISSE Philip	4° ss.	BISSE Thomas	8° ss.
	DOD Thomas	8° ss.	HANNES William	8° ss.	HIND Thomas	8° ss.
	HOLE Matthew	8° coll.	LENG John	8° coll.	MANGEY Thomas	8° coll.
	MORER Thomas	8° coll.	WELCHMAN Edward	8° ss.		
1718	NEWLIN Thomas	8° ss.	NEWLIN Thomas	8° ss.	SCOTT John	fo.coll.
1719	GIBSON John	8° ss.	HARE Francis	4° ss.	HOLE Matthew	8° coll.
	STEPHENS William	8° ss.				
1720	BEVERIDGE William	fo.coll.	FIDDES Rich. DD.	fo. ss.	KENNET White	4° ss.
	MANGEY Thomas	4° ss.	NEWLIN Thomas	8° coll.	WATERLAND Daniel	8° coll.

Year	Name	Format	Name	Format	Name	Format
1721	COTES Digby	8° coll.				
1722	BENTHAM Edward	4° ss.	MAYNARD Edward	8° coll.	TRAPP Joseph	8° coll.
	WAKE William	8° coll.				
1723	WATERLAND Daniel	8° ss.				
1724	HOUGH Nathaniel	4° ss.	MAYNARD Edward	8° coll.	SOUTH Robert	8° coll.
1726	IBBOT Benj. DD.	8° coll.	NEWLIN Thomas	8° coll.		
1727	CLAYTON Thomas	8° ss.	SOUTH Robert	8° coll.		
1728	FIDDES Rich. DD.	fo.coll.	NEWLIN Thomas	8° coll.		
1730	ATTERBURY Francis	8° coll.				
1735	TILLOTSON John	fo.coll.				
1739	ANONYMOUS	fo.coll.	GASTRELL Francis	fo. ss.	HANCOCK John	fo. ss.
	HARRIS John	fo.coll.	LENG John	fo.coll.	TURNER John	fo.coll.
	WARREN John	8° coll.	WHISTON Will. M.A.	fo. ss.		
1742	WATERLAND Daniel	8° coll.				
1749	HEYLYN John	4° coll.				
1751	BERRIMAN William	8° coll.				
1752	TRAPP Joseph	8° coll.				
1757	CONYBEARE John	8° coll.				
1764	KENNET White	4° ss.				
1766	DELANY Patrick	8° coll.				
1769	<u>LELAND</u> <u>Thomas</u>	8° coll.				
1771	LOWTH Robert	4° ss.				
1776	IBBOT Benj. DD.	-° coll.				
1790	TENISON Thomas	4° ss.				
1797	KIDDER Richard	8° coll.				
Merton College ("Mert.")						
1664	BROWNRIG Ralph	fo.coll.				
1672	FARINDON Anth. B.D.	fo.coll.				
1673	HALES John	4° coll.	JACKSON Thomas	fo.coll.		
1674						

Year	Name	Format	Name	Format	Name	Format
	TAYLOR Jeremy	8° ss.				
1677						
	BRAMHALL John	fo.coll.				
1679						
	FARINDON Anth. B.D.	fo.coll.				
1680						
	LITTLETON Adam	fo.coll.				
1684						
	HAMMOND Henry	fo.coll.	LIGHTFOOT J. DD.	fo.coll.		
1702						
	NEWCOME Peter	8° coll.				
1704						
	CLAGETT William	8° coll.	CLAGETT William	8° coll.		
1707						
	STILLINGFLEET Edward	fo.coll.				
1713						
	BULL George	8° coll.				
1716						
	ADAMS William	8° coll.	BARROW Isaac	fo.coll.		
1718						
	SCOTT John	fo.coll.				
1719						
	KETTLEWELL John	fo.coll.				
1720						
	BEVERIDGE William	fo.coll.	FIDDES Rich. DD.	fo. ss.	FIDDES Rich. DD.	fo. ss.
	WATERLAND Daniel	8° coll.				
1726						
	CALAMY Benjamin	8° coll.				
1728						
	FIDDES Rich. DD.	fo.coll.	NORRIS John	9° coll.		
1734						
	CLARKE Samuel	8° coll.				
1735						
	TILLOTSON John	fo.coll.				
1737						
	FLEETWOOD William	fo.coll.				
New College	("New")					
1671						
	PIERCE Tho. DD.	4° coll.				
1673						
	JACKSON Thomas	fo.coll.	LLOYD William	4° ss.	SMITH John	4° coll.
1674						
	<u>ANNESLEY</u> <u>Samuel</u>	4° coll.				
1682						
	WILKINS John	8° coll.				
1684						
	ALLESTREE Richard	fo.coll.	HAMMOND Henry	fo.coll.	LIGHTFOOT J. DD.	fo.coll.
	<u>CHARNOCK</u> <u>Stephen</u>	fo.coll.				
1689						
	SHERLOCK William	8° ss.				
1691						
	NORRIS John	8° coll.				
1692						
	BENTLEY Richard	4° coll.	STRADLING Geor. DD.	8° coll.		
1693						

Year	Name	Format	Name	Format	Name	Format
	MONRO Alexander	4°coll.				
1694						
	NORRIS John	8°coll.				
1699						
	CONANT John	8°coll.	CHARNOCK Stephen	8°coll.	HOW John	8° ss.
1700						
	HOW John	fo. ss.				
1701						
	STANHOPE George	4°coll.				
1702						
	STANHOPE George	4°coll.				
1705						
	SHERLOCK William	-° ss.				
1706						
	YOUNG Edward	8°coll.				
1707						
	STILLINGFLEET Edward	fo.coll.				
1708						
	STANHOPE George	4°coll.	WILLIAMS John	8°coll.		
1710						
	HOPKINS Ezekiel	fo.coll.				
1713						
	BULL George HICKES George	8°coll. 8°coll.	BURNET Gilbert	8°coll.	HICHMAN Charles	8°coll.
1715						
	KENNET Basil	8°coll.	STANHOPE George	4°coll.		
1716						
	BARROW Isaac	fo.coll.	STANHOPE George	4°coll.		
1717						
	LENG John	8°coll.	SMALRIDGE George	8°coll.	STEPHENS William	8° ss.
1719						
	KETTLEWELL John	fo.coll.	STEPHENS William	8° ss.		
1720						
	CLAGETT William	8°coll.	NEWCOME John	8° ss.	WATERLAND Daniel	8°coll.
1722						
	CONYBEARE John	8° ss.	STEPHENS William	8° ss.		
1723						
	BLACKALL Offspring	fo.coll.	CONYBEARE John	8° ss.		
1724						
	NEWCOME John STEPHENS William	8° ss. 8° ss.	SMALRIDGE George	fo.coll.	SOUTH Robert	8°coll.
1726						
	BISHOP Thomas IBBOT Benj. DD.	8°coll. 8°coll.	BULLOCK Thomas	8°coll.	CONYBEARE John	8° ss.
1727						
	DERHAM Will. DD.	8° ss.	ROGERS John	8°coll.	SOUTH Robert	8°coll.
1728						
	NORRIS John	8°coll.	NORRIS John	9°coll.		
1730						
	ATTERBURY Francis DERHAM Will. DD.	8°coll. 8° ss.	BRADY Nich. DD. JORTIN John	8°coll. 12°coll.	CLARKE Samuel ROGERS John	8°coll. 8°coll.
1731						
	MARSHALL Nathaniel	8°coll.				
1732						
	BROWNE John	8°coll.	FELTON Henry	8°coll.		
1733						

Year	Name	Format	Name	Format	Name	Format
1735	MOSS Robert	8°coll.				
1736	ROGERS John	8°coll.	SHARP John	8°coll.	TILLOTSON John	fo.coll.
1737	ROGERS John	8°coll.				
1738	FLEETWOOD William	fo.coll.	MOSS Robert	8°coll.		
1739	MOSS Robert	8°coll.	ROGERS John	8°coll.		
1741	ANONYMOUS GURDON Brampton WILLIAMS John	fo.coll. fo.coll. fo.coll.	BENTLEY Richard LENG John	fo.coll. fo.coll.	GURDON Brampton STANHOPE George	8°coll. fo.coll.
1742	BEDFORD Arthur	8° ss.				
1743	BISCOE Rich	8°coll.	RIDLEY Glocester	8°coll.	WATERLAND Daniel	8°coll.
1745	STACKHOUSE Thomas	fo. ss.	TWELLS Leonard	8°coll.		
1746	SNAPE Andrew	8°coll.	WEBSTER William	8°coll.		
1747	LEIGHTON Robert	8°coll.	WHEATLY Charles	8°coll.		
1749	DELANY Patrick	8°coll.				
1750	BUTLER Joseph	8°coll.	HEYLYN John	4°coll.		
1751	COCKMAN Thomas	8°coll.	MARSHALL Nathaniel	8°coll.	SEED Jeremiah	-°coll.
1752	BERRIMAN William	8°coll.				
1757	TRAPP Joseph	8°coll.				
1765	CONYBEARE John	8°coll.				
1770	FOTHERGILL Geo. DD.	8°coll.				
1771	SECKER William	8°coll.				
1772	SECKER William	8°coll.				
1776	SHERLOCK Thomas	8°coll.				
1797	IBBOT Benj. DD.	-°coll.				
	KIDDER Richard	8°coll.				

Oriel College ("Or.")

Year	Name	Format
1660	SOUTH Robert	-°coll.
1661	BARTHOLOMEW William	4° ss.
1662	COPLESTONE John	4° ss.

Year	Name	Format	Name	Format	Name	Format
	BURY Arthur	4° ss.	MAYNE Jasper	4° ss.	WALWYN William	4° ss.
1663	STILEMAN John	4° ss.				
1664	KING Henry	4° ss.				
1665	FORD Simon	4° ss.				
1672	LUCE Richard	4° ss.	MEDE Joseph	fo.coll.		
1673	ANONYMOUS WARD Seth	12° ss. 4° ss.	JACKSON Thomas	fo.coll.	PEARSON John	4° ss.
1675	JANE Will. DD.	4° ss.				
1676	SUDBURY John	4° ss.				
1677	BRAMHALL John	fo.coll.	RIVELY Benedict	4° ss.		
1678	LAMPLUGH Thomas	4° ss.	LLOYD William	4° ss.	TAYLOR Jeremy	fo.coll.
1679	RALEIGH Walter	4° coll.	REYNOLDS Edward	fo.coll.	WALLIS John	4° ss.
1680	BURNET Gilbert PARSONS Robert	4° ss. 4° ss.	BURNET Gilbert	4° ss.	OWTRAM William	8° coll.
1681	BURNET Gilbert	4° ss.	BURNET Gilbert	4° ss.	JONES Thomas	4° ss.
1682	BURNET Gilbert	4° ss.	KNIGHT John	4° ss.	WILKINS John	8° coll.
1683	ANONYMOUS	4° ss.	CALAMY Benjamin	4° ss.	SHERLOCK William	4° ss.
1684	CALAMY Benjamin	4° ss.	HAMMOND Henry	fo.coll.		
1685	BURNET Gilbert	4° ss.	SHERLOCK William	4° ss.	TURNER Francis	4° ss.
1686	CARTWRIGHT Thomas	4° ss.	DOVE Heb. DD.	4° ss.		
1688	BROWNE Thomas	4° ss.	BURNET Gilbert	8° ss.		
1689	BURNET Gilbert	4° ss.	PATRICK Simon	4° ss.		
1690	BURNET Gilbert FREEMAN Samuel	4° ss. 4° ss.	BURNET Gilbert	4° ss.	BURNET Gilbert	4° ss.
1691	BURNET Gilbert HOOPER George	4° ss. 4° ss.	BURNET Gilbert WALLIS John	4° ss. 4° coll.	BURNET Gilbert	4° ss.
1692	BURNET Gilbert WALLIS John	4° ss. 4° coll.	MORE Henry	8° coll.	SHERLOCK William	4° ss.
1693	FREEMAN Samuel	4° ss.	STUBBS Philip	4° ss.	VESEY John	4° ss.
1694	BATTELY John BURNET Gilbert SANCROFT William	4° ss. 4° ss. 8° coll.	BURNET Gilbert MANSELL John	4° ss. 4° ss.	BURNET Gilbert MANSELL John	4° ss. 4° ss.

Year	Name	Size	Name	Size	Name	Size
1695	ALLESTREE Charles	4° ss.	BURNET Gilbert	4° ss.		
1696	BENTLEY Richard	4° ss.	KETTLEWELL John	8° coll.	MEGGOT Richard	8° coll.
	PATRICK Simon	4° ss.				
1697	BURNET Gilbert	4° ss.	BURNET Gilbert	4° ss.	BURNET Gilbert	4° ss.
	GOODMAN John	4° ss.	HEYRICK Thomas	4° ss.		
1698	BURNET Gilbert	4° ss.	WHALEY Nathanael	8° coll.	WHICHCOTE Benj. DD.	8° coll.
1699	GIBBS William	4° ss.				
1700	BURNET Gilbert	4° ss.				
1701	MARSDEN Robert	4° ss.	SHERLOCK William	4° ss.		
1702	SACHEVERELL Henry	4° ss.	TRELAWNEY Jonathan Sir	4° ss.	WAKE William	8° coll.
	WHICHCOTE Benj. DD.	8° coll.				
1703	WHICHCOTE Benj. DD.	8° coll.				
1704	BISSET Will.	8° ss.	BURNET Gilbert	4° ss.	BURNET Gilbert	4° ss.
	CLAGETT William	8° coll.	GASTRELL Francis	4° ss.	ISHAM Zach. DD.	4° ss.
	SACHEVERELL Henry	4° ss.	WHALEY Nathanael	12° coll.		
1705	ROYSE Geor. DD.	4° ss.				
1706	BURNET Gilbert	4° ss.	NICOLSON William	4° ss.	SACHEVERELL Henry	4° ss.
	YOUNG Edward	8° coll.				
1707	ADAMS John	4° ss.	ADAMS John	4° ss.	GOODMAN John	8° ss.
	HASLEWOOD John	4° ss.	NICOLSON William	4° ss.	TRIMNEL Charles	4° ss.
	WHICHCOTE Benj. DD.	8° coll.				
1708	ADAMS John	4° ss.	BISSE Thomas	4° ss.	DOWNES Henry	8° ss.
	EYRE Robert	4° ss.	SACHEVERELL Henry	4° ss.	STOUGHTON William	4° ss.
	TRIMNEL Charles	4° ss.	WHITFELD Will. DD.	4° ss.	WILLET John	4° ss.
1709	HARE Francis	4° ss.	HOUGH John	4° ss.	PELLING John	4° ss.
	RENNELL Thomas	4° ss.	SACHEVERELL Henry	4° ss.	SACHEVERELL Henry	4° ss.
1710	BURNET Gilbert	8° ss.	BURNET Gilbert	8° ss.	HARRISON John	8° ss.
	LEWIS Henry	8° ss.	SPRAT Thomas	8° coll.	TILLY William	4° ss.
	WEST Richard	8° ss.	WHALEY Nathanael	8° ss.		
1711	BURNET Gilbert	4° ss.	SAINT John Pawlet	4° ss.		
1712	HUMPHREYS Thomas	8° ss.	TILLY William	8° coll.	TRIMNEL Charles	4° ss.
1713	BISSE Thomas	8° ss.	NEWTON Richard	4° ss.	SACHEVERELL Henry	4° ss.
	SAUNDERS Erasmus	8° ss.	TILLY William	8° ss.		
1714	BURNET Gilbert	4° ss.	DUKE Rich. M.A.	8° coll.		
1715	RYE George	4° ss.	TRIMNEL Charles	4° ss.		

Year	Name	Format	Name	Format	Name	Format
1716	BARROW Isaac	fo.coll.	NEWTON Richard	4° ss.	WAKE William	8° coll.
1717	SMALRIDGE George	8° coll.				
1719	SHERLOCK William	8° coll.				
1720	FIDDES Rich. DD.	fo. ss.				
1721	WADDINGTON Edward	8° ss.				
1722	WAKE William	8° coll.	WILCOCKS Joseph	4° ss.	WILKINS David	4° ss.
1723	LISLE Samuel	4° ss.				
1724	DRAKE Samuel	4° ss.	GILBERT John	4° ss.	MAYO Richard	4° ss.
	MEADOWCOURT Richard	8° ss.	REYNELL Carew	4° ss.	SMALRIDGE George	fo.coll.
	STANHOPE George	4° ss.	WILCOCKS Joseph	4° ss.		
1725	LOCKIER Francis	4° ss.				
1726	BULLOCK Thomas	8° coll.	NEWLIN Thomas	8° coll.		
1727	GREENE Thomas	4° ss.	LENG John	4° ss.	WHITBY Daniel	8° coll.
1728	FIDDES Rich. DD.	fo.coll.	NEWLIN Thomas	8° coll.	WHITBY Daniel	8° coll.
1729	GIBSON Edmund	8° coll.				
1730	ATTERBURY Francis	8° coll.				
1735	SHARP John	8° coll.	TILLOTSON John	fo.coll.		
1737	TILLY William	-° coll.				
1739	HARRIS John	fo.coll.				
1749	BUTLER Joseph	8° coll.				
1757	CONYBEARE John	8° coll.				
1763	BERRIMAN William	8° coll.				
1766	DELANY Patrick	8° coll.				
1772	SHERLOCK Thomas	8° coll.				

Pembroke College ("Pemb.")

Year	Name	Format	Name	Format	Name	Format
----	FULLER Ignatius	-° ss.				
1672	FRANK Mark	fo.coll.	FULLER Ignatius	8° ss.	FULLER Ignatius	8° ss.
1673	JACKSON Thomas	fo.coll.				
1677	GIBBES Charles	4° coll.	WILKINS John	12° coll.		

Year	Name	Format	Name	Format	Name	Format
1678	TAYLOR Jeremy	fo.coll.				
1679	NEEDHAM Robert	8° coll.				
1680	LITTLETON Adam	fo.coll.				
1682	CAMFIELD Benjamin	4° coll.				
1684	ALLESTREE Richard	fo.coll.	BURTON Hezekiah	8° coll.		
1685	BURTON Hezekiah	8° coll.	KILLIGREW Henry. DD.	4° coll.		
1693	BATES William	8° coll.				
1694	HALLYWELL Henry	8° ss.				
1695	WHALEY Nathanael	8° coll.				
1696	KETTLEWELL John	8° coll.				
1697	GOODMAN John	8° coll.	LEIGHTONHOUSE Walter	8° coll.		
1702	BRAGGE Francis SHOWER John	8° coll. 8° coll.	BRAGGE Francis	8° coll.	NEWCOME Peter	8° coll.
1704	BRAGGE Francis WHALEY Nathanael	8° coll. 12° coll.	CLAGETT William	8° coll.	CLAGETT William	8° coll.
1706	HICHMAN Charles	8° coll.	HORNECK Anthony	8° coll.	YOUNG Edward	8° coll.
1707	STILLINGFLEET Edward	fo.coll.				
1710	LUCAS Richard	8° coll.				
1713	BULL George	8° coll.				
1717	BOEHM Anthony William	8° coll.				
1719	SHERLOCK William	8° coll.				
1720	WATERLAND Daniel	8° coll.				
1723	BLACKALL Offspring	fo.coll.				
1724	SOUTH Robert	8° coll.				
1726	BRAGGE Francis	8° coll.				
1727	ROGERS John	8° coll.	SOUTH Robert	8° coll.		
1728	NORRIS John	9° coll.	WHARTON Henry	8° coll.	WHARTON Henry	8° coll.
1730	ATTERBURY Francis	8° coll.	CLARKE Samuel	8° coll.	ROGERS John	8° coll.
1731	MARSHALL Nathaniel	8° coll.				

Year	Name	Format	Name	Format	Name	Format
1735	ROGERS John	8° coll.	SHARP John	8° coll.	TILLOTSON John	fo.coll.
1736	ROGERS John	8° coll.				
1738	ROGERS John	8° coll.				
1751	BERRIMAN William	8° coll.				
1757	GRIFFITH Thomas	8° ss.	HOOPER George	fo.coll.		
1760	GRIFFITH Thomas	8° ss.				
1763	GRIFFITH Thomas	8° ss.				
1766	DELANY Patrick	8° coll.	SECKER William	8° coll.		
1773	GRIFFITH Thomas	8° ss.				
1777	ADAMS William	8° coll.				
1797	KIDDER Richard	8° coll.				

Queen's College ("Queen's")

Year	Name	Format	Name	Format	Name	Format
----	FULLER Ignatius	-° ss.	SCOTT Thomas	-° ss.		
1605	MASON Francis	-° ss.				
1660	BARWICK John	4° ss.				
1661	BROWNRIG Ralph	fo.coll.	HENCHMAN Richard	4° ss.	MORLEY George	4° ss.
	STRODE William	4° ss.				
1662	WATSON Thomas	4° ss.				
1663	BOREMAN Rich. DD.	4° ss.	LEE Richard	4° ss.		
1667	ANONYMOUS	4° ss.				
1668	LINGARD Ric. DD.	4° ss.	LLOYD William	4° ss.		
1670	BREVAL Frank Durant de	4° ss.	BREVAL Frank Durant de	4° ss.	PARRY John	4° ss.
	PATRICK Simon	8° ss.				
1671	PIERCE Tho. DD.	4° coll.				
1672	BERRY Richard	4° ss.	FARINDON Anth. B.D.	fo.coll.	FULLER Ignatius	8° ss.
	FULLER Ignatius	8° ss.	FULLWOOD Francis	4° ss.	WARD Seth	8° coll.
1673	EGAN Anthony	4° ss.	LAMBE John	4° ss.	LLOYD William	4° ss.
	NEVILLE Robert	4° ss.	PEARSON John	4° ss.	SMITH John	4° coll.
1674	CROFT Herbert	4° ss.	LLOYD William	4° ss.	LODINGTON Thomas	4° ss.
	MEGGOT Richard	4° ss.	TAYLOR Jeremy	8° ss.	WARD Seth	4° ss.
	WARD Seth	8° coll.				

Year	Name	Format	Name	Format	Name	Format
1675	BARNE Miles	4° ss.	FELL John	4° ss.	GREGORY Fran. DD.	4° ss.
	HACKET John	fo.coll.	JANE Will. DD.	4° ss.	JEKYLL Thomas	4° coll.
	NAILOUR William	4° ss.	SMITH Thomas	4° ss.	SMITH Thomas	4° ss.
	STANDISH John	4° ss.	STRADLING Geor. DD.	4° ss.		
1676	CARTWRIGHT Thomas	4° ss.	CAVE Will. DD.	4° ss.	LUZANCY Hippolytus Du	4° ss.
	MILL John	4° ss.	PATRICK Simon	4° ss.	SCATTERGOOD Samuel	4° ss.
	SUDBURY John	4° ss.				
1677	ARDERNE James	4° ss.	INGELO Nathaniel	8° ss.	PITTIS Thomas	4° ss.
	RIVELY Benedict	4° ss.	SUDBURY John	4° ss.	WILKINS John	12° coll.
	CHEYNEY John	12° ss.				
1678	BUTLER John	4° ss.	CAMFIELD Benjamin	4° ss.	HOOKER Richard	8° ss.
	LAMPLUGH Thomas	4° ss.	PATRICK Simon	4° ss.	TAYLOR Jeremy	fo.coll.
	USHER James	fo.coll.				
1679	FARINDON Anth. B.D.	fo.coll.	LLOYD William	4° ss.	OATES Titus	4° ss.
1680	BURNET Gilbert	4° ss.	HICKERINGILL Edmond	4° coll.	HICKERINGILL Edmond.	4° ss.
	PATRICK Simon	4° ss.	CROMWELL Oliver	4° ss.		
1681	BENNION John	4° ss.				
1682	SMITH Thomas	4° ss.				
1683	BARNE Miles	4° ss.	GASKARTH John	4° ss.	TURNER Francis	5° ss.
1684	ALLESTREE Richard	fo.coll.	BURTON Hezekiah	8° coll.	FALKNER Will. DD.	4° coll.
	HAMMOND Henry	fo.coll.	LIGHTFOOT J. DD.	fo.coll.	MOULIN DU Peter	8° coll.
	SMYTHIES William	4° ss.	TURNER Francis	4° ss.	VINCENT Nathaniel	4° ss.
1685	BURTON Hezekiah	8° coll.	IRONSIDE Gilbert	4° ss.	KILLIGREW Henry. DD.	4° coll.
	TURNER Francis	4° ss.	TURNER Francis	4° ss.		
1686	PIERCE Tho. DD.	4° ss.				
1687	COMBER Thomas	4° ss.				
1688	HELLIER Henry	4° ss.				
1694	SANCROFT William	8° coll.				
1696	MEGGOT Richard	8° coll.				
1698	EDWARDS John	8° coll.	HUTCHINSON Francis	4° ss.		
1700	BATES William	fo.coll.				
1701	ISHAM Zach. DD.	4° ss.				
1704	CLAGETT William	8° coll.	CLAGETT William	8° coll.	ISHAM Zach. DD.	4° ss.
	LENG John	4° ss.	PEARSON William	4° ss.	WILLIS Richard	4° ss.
1705	ISHAM Zach. DD.	4° ss.	MASON Francis	4° ss.	WAUGH John	4° ss.

1706	WOTTON William	4° ss.				
1707	BARKER Richard	4° ss.	SMITH Thomas	8° ss.	STILLINGFLEET Edward	fo.coll.
1710	HOPKINS Ezekiel	fo.coll.				
1711	HARE Francis	8° ss.				
1713	BELL George	4° ss.	WAUGH John	4° ss.		
1714	SMITH Joseph	4° ss.				
1717	SMALRIDGE George	8° coll.				
1720	FIDDES Rich. DD.	fo. ss.	FIDDES Rich. DD.	fo. ss.		
1721	LESTLEY Charles	fo.coll.				
1724	SMALRIDGE George	fo.coll.	SOUTH Robert	8° coll.		
1727	SOUTH Robert	8° coll.				
1728	FIDDES Rich. DD.	fo.coll.				
1730	CLARKE Samuel	8° coll.				
1735	TILLOTSON John	fo.coll.				
1739	ANONYMOUS	fo.coll.				
1749	BIRCH Thomas	4° ss.				
1757	WAINHOUSE Richard	4° ss.				
1765	FOTHERGILL Geo. DD.	8° coll.				

St. John's College ("St.John's")

----	CLARKE John	-° coll.	SOUTH Robert	-° coll.	WOODWARD Josiah	-° coll.
1660	BARWICK John	4° ss.	GAUDEN John	12° ss.		
1668	RUST George	4° ss.				
1673	HALES John	4° coll.				
1675	PATRICK Simon	8° ss.				
1677	BRAMHALL John	fo.coll.				
1678	TAYLOR Jeremy	fo.coll.				
1684	LIGHTFOOT J. DD.	fo.coll.				
1686	H. - - - - H.	4° ss.	KIDDER Richard	4° ss.		

1689	BEVERIDGE William	4° ss.				
1691	KELSEY Joseph	4° ss.	WALLIS John	4° ss.	WALLIS John	4°coll.
1692	WALLIS John	4°coll.				
1697	GOODMAN John	4° ss.				
1698	EDWARDS John	8°coll.				
1700	BRADFORD Samuel	4°coll.	<u>BATES William</u>	fo.coll.		
1701	STANHOPE George	4°coll.				
1702	STANHOPE George	4°coll.				
1703	ALTHAM Roger	4° ss.				
1706	HICHMAN Charles	8°coll.				
1707	GOODMAN John	8° ss.				
1708	STANHOPE George WILLIAMS John	4°coll. 8°coll.	TURNER John	8°coll.	WHISTON Will. M.A.	8° ss.
1709	KING William	8° ss.	ROBERTS William	4° ss.		
1710	SPRAT Thomas	8°coll.				
1713	BURNET Gilbert	8°coll.	HICHMAN Charles	8°coll.		
1714	BINGHAM Joseph	8° ss.	WAPLE Edward	8°coll.		
1715	KENNET Basil	8°coll.	STANHOPE George	4°coll.		
1716	BARROW Isaac	fo.coll.	STANHOPE George	4°coll.		
1717	LENG John	8°coll.	SMALRIDGE George	8°coll.		
1718	SCOTT John	fo.coll.	WAPLE Edward	8°coll.		
1719	SHERLOCK William	8°coll.				
1720	CLAGETT William	8°coll.	FIDDES Rich. DD.	fo. ss.	WAPLE Edward	8°coll.
1721	LESTLEY Charles	fo.coll.				
1723	BLACKALL Offspring	fo.coll.				
1724	SMALRIDGE George	fo.coll.				
1725	BINGHAM Joseph	fo. ss.	COLLIER Jeremy	8°coll.		
1726	BINGHAM Joseph	fo.coll.	CALAMY Benjamin	8°coll.		
1727						

	DERHAM Will. DD.	8° ss.	ROGERS John	8° coll.	STANHOPE George	8° coll.
1728						
	DELAUNE William	8° coll.	FIDDES Rich. DD.	fo.coll.	WHARTON Henry	8° coll.
	WHARTON Henry	8° coll.				
1729						
	LUPTON William	8° coll.	WAPLE Edward	8° coll.		
1730						
	BRADY Nich. DD.	8° coll.	BRADY Nich. DD.	8° coll.	CLARKE Samuel	8° coll.
	DERHAM Will. DD.	8° ss.	ROGERS John	8° coll.		
1731						
	KING William	4° coll.	MARSHALL Nathaniel	8° coll.		
1733						
	BERRIMAN William	8° coll.				
1735						
	LITTLETON Edward	8° coll.	ROGERS John	8° coll.	SHARP John	8° coll.
	TILLOTSON John	fo.coll.				
1736						
	ROGERS John	8° coll.				
1737						
	FLEETWOOD William	fo.coll.				
1738						
	ROGERS John	8° coll.				
1739						
	ANONYMOUS	fo.coll.	BERRIMAN William	fo.coll.	GURDON Brampton	8° coll.
	GURDON Brampton	fo.coll.	HANCOCK John	fo. ss.	LENG John	fo.coll.
	STANHOPE George	fo.coll.	TURNER John	fo.coll.	WHISTON Will. M.A.	fo. ss.
	WILLIAMS John	fo.coll.				
1741						
	BERRIMAN William	8° ss.	TOWNLEY James	4° ss.	TOWNLEY James	4° ss.
1743						
	STACKHOUSE Thomas	fo. ss.				
1752						
	CATCOTT Alex. Stopford	8° coll.	TOWNLEY James	4° ss.		
1753						
	ANONYMOUS	8° ss.				
1766						
	DELANY Patrick	8° coll.				
1772						
	SHERLOCK Thomas	8° coll.				
1776						
	WARNEFORD John	8° coll.				

Trinity College ("Trin.")

1672				
	FARINDON Anth. B.D.	fo.coll.		
1673				
	LLOYD William	4° ss.		
1675				
	BURNET Gilbert	4° ss.	BURNET Gilbert	4° ss.
1677				
	BRAMHALL John	fo.coll.		
1679				
	DAVIES James	4° ss.	FARINDON Anth. B.D.	fo.coll.
1680				
	FELL John	4° ss.		
1684				

	HAMMOND Henry	fo.coll.	CHARNOCK Stephen	fo.coll.
1695				
	FISHER Joseph	4° ss.		
1696				
	DAY Henry	4° ss.		
1699				
	CHARNOCK Stephen	8° coll.		
1702				
	SACHEVERELL Henry	4° ss.		
1712				
	WILLOUGHBY Lord De Bro	4° ss.		
1716				
	BARROW Isaac	fo.coll.		
1717				
	SMALRIDGE George	8° coll.		
1718				
	SCOTT John	fo.coll.		
1720				
	WATERLAND Daniel	8° coll.		
1721				
	LESTLEY Charles	fo.coll.		
1722				
	CALAMY Edmund	8° coll.		
1723				
	BLACKALL Offspring	fo.coll.		
1724				
	SMALRIDGE George	fo.coll.		
1725				
	BERRIMAN William	8° coll.		
1727				
	DERHAM Will. DD.	8° ss.		
1730				
	DERHAM Will. DD.	8° ss.		
1735				
	TILLOTSON John	fo.coll.		
1741				
	BERRIMAN William	8° ss.		
1742				
	STEBBING Henry	4° ss.		
1751				
	BERRIMAN William	8° coll.		
1766				
	DELANY Patrick	8° coll.		
1774				
	JORTIN John	8° coll.		

University College ("Univ.")

	FLEETWOOD William	-° coll.		
1607				
	WILKINSON Robert	4° ss.		
1641				
	MASTER Thomas	-° ss.		
1660				
	GAUDEN John	4° ss.	GAUDEN John	12° ss.
1661				

	BROWNRIG Ralph	fo.coll.	GAUDEN John	4° ss.	GREEFFIELD Thomas	4° ss.
	HEYLYN Pet. DD.	4° ss.	NICOLSON William	fo.coll.	PHILIPS John	4° ss.
	HIBBERT Hen	4° ss.				
1662						
	BERIDGE John	4° ss.	HARDY Nathaniel	4° ss.	MAYNE Jasper	4° ss.
	WALWYN William	4° ss.	WINTER John	4° ss.		
1663						
	BRADLEY Thomas	4° ss.	PARKER John	4° ss.		
1664						
	MAYNE Jasper	4° ss.	PEARSON Richard	4° ss.		
1666						
	HARDY Nathaniel	4° ss.	HUNTER Josiah	4° ss.		
1667						
	BRADLEY Thomas	4° ss.				
1668						
	LLOYD William	4° ss.	RUST George	4° ss.		
1669						
	MOULIN DU Peter	4° ss.				
1670						
	BARNE Miles	4° ss.	BARTON David	4° ss.	BRADLEY Thomas	4° ss.
	CUDWORTH Ralph	8° ss.	PATRICK Simon	4° ss.	WARD Seth	4° ss.
1671						
	NORTH John	4° ss.	PIERCE Tho. DD.	4° coll.		
1672						
	FULLWOOD Francis	4° ss.				
1673						
	HALES John	4° coll.	JACKSON Thomas	fo.coll.	LLOYD William	4° ss.
	PATRICK Simon	4° ss.	SMITH John	4° coll.		
1674						
	JAMES Henry	4° ss.	LLOYD William	4° ss.	LODINGTON Thomas	4° ss.
	MOULIN DU Peter	4° ss.	PRINCE John	4° ss.	SALL Andrew	8° ss.
1675						
	BARNE Miles	4° ss.	BURNET Gilbert	4° ss.	FELL John	4° ss.
	JACKSON William	4° ss.	JANE Will. DD.	4° ss.	LANEY Benjamin	4° ss.
	MEGGOT Richard	4° ss.	STANDISH John	4° ss.	STRADLING Geor. DD.	4° ss.
1676						
	CARTWRIGHT Thomas	4° ss.	CAVE Will. DD.	4° ss.	HORDEN John	4° ss.
	MILL John	4° ss.	STAINFORTH William	-° ss.	TEMPLER John	4° ss.
1677						
	BRAMHALL John	fo.coll.	CRADOCK Zechary	4° ss.	PINDAR William	4° ss.
	PITTIS Thomas	4° ss.	THORP George	4° ss.	TURNER Bryan	4° ss.
	WILKINS John	12° coll.				
1679						
	HESKETH Henry	4° ss.	LLOYD William	4° ss.	PINDAR William	4° ss.
	REYNOLDS Edward	fo.coll.				
1680						
	PARSONS Robert	4° ss.				
1682						
	WILKINSON Robert	4° ss.				
1683						
	BARNE Miles	4° ss.	STANDISH John	4° ss.	STRATFORD Nicholas	4° ss.
1684						
	ALLESTREE Richard	fo.coll.	BURTON Hezekiah	8° coll.	HAMMOND Henry	fo.coll.
	HESKETH Henry	4° ss.	LIGHTFOOT J. DD.	fo.coll.	STRATFORD Nicholas	8° ss.
	TURNER John	8° ss.				
1685						

	BURTON Hezekiah	8° coll.	GODWYN Morgan	4° ss.		
1686	PATRICK Simon	4° ss.				
1687	HORNECK Anthony	8° ss.	PATRICK Simon	4° ss.		
1689	SHERLOCK William	8° ss.	STAINFORTH William	4° ss.		
1690	FOWLER Edward	4° ss.	HICHMAN Charles	4° ss.	PATRICK Simon	4° ss.
1691	KELSEY Joseph	4° ss.	PAYNE William	4° ss.	SHERLOCK William	8° ss.
1692	BENTLEY Richard	4° coll.	BOWCHIER Richard	4° ss.	BURNET Gilbert	4° ss.
	EDWARDS John	8° coll.	GEE Edward	4° ss.	HICHMAN Charles	4° ss.
	MANNINGHAM Thomas	4° ss.	RESBURY Nathaniel	4° ss.	SHERLOCK William	4° ss.
	STANHOPE George	4° ss.	STRADLING Geor. DD.	8° coll.		
1693	LAMBE John	4° ss.	PRITCHARD Thomas	4° ss.	STUBBS Philip	4° ss.
1694	BURNET Gilbert	4° ss.	CORNWALLIS Henry	12° ss.	NORRIS John	8° coll.
1695	TENISON Thomas	4° ss.				
1696	KETTLEWELL John	8° coll.				
1697	BECONSALL Thomas	4° ss.	BURNET Gilbert	4° ss.		
1699	SHERLOCK William	8° ss.	<u>SPRINT John</u>	8° ss.		
1700	HARE Francis	4° ss.	KNAGGS Thomas	4° ss.		
1702	BRAGGE Francis	8° coll.	BRAGGE Francis	8° coll.	EDWARDS John	8° coll.
	SACHEVERELL Henry	4° ss.				
1703	BUCK Maximilian	8° ss.	LAKE Edward	4° ss.		
1704	BRAGGE Francis	8° coll.	DUKE Rich. M.A.	4° ss.	GASTRELL Francis	4° ss.
	KENNET White	4° ss.	SACHEVERELL Henry	4° ss.		
1705	LAKE Edward	8° coll.	ROYSE Geor. DD.	4° ss.	SHERLOCK William	-° ss.
	STANHOPE George	4° ss.	STANHOPE George	4° ss.	TILLY William	4° ss.
	WILLIS Richard	4° ss.				
1706	HIGGINS Francis	4° ss.	KENNET White	4° ss.	NICOLSON William	4° ss.
	SHARP J. M.A.	8° ss.	SMALBROKE Richard	4° ss.	WOTTON William	4° ss.
	YOUNG Edward	8° coll.	<u>EVANS John</u>	8° ss.		
1707	ADAMS John	4° ss.	ADAMS John	4° ss.	BRADY Nich. DD.	8° ss.
	CHISHULL Edmund	4° ss.	KING James	4° ss.	KNAGGS Thomas	8° ss.
	LIGHTFOOT Robert	8° ss.	NELSON Hen.	8° ss.	PATRICK Simon	4° ss.
	STILEMAN John	8° ss.	STILLINGFLEET Edward	fo. coll.	WILLIS Richard	4° ss.
1708	ADAMS John	4° ss.	ADAMS Rice	8° ss.	BLACKBURNE Lancelot.	4° ss.
	CANNELL Joseph	4° ss.	COLBY Samuel	8° ss.	DOWNES Henry	8° ss.
	DUNSTER Sam. DD.	8° ss.	EYRE Robert	4° ss.	FEATLY Daniel	8° ss.
	KNAGGS Thomas	8° ss.	KNAGGS Thomas	8° ss.	LAMBERT Ralph	4° ss.

	MANNINGHAM Thomas	6° ss.	MILNER William	8° ss.	STANHOPE George	4° coll.
	STEPHENS Henry	4° ss.	TRAPP Joseph	4° ss.	TRIMNEL Charles	4° ss.
	WHITFELD Will. DD.	4° ss.				
1709						
	ANONYMOUS	8° ss.	BRAY Thomas	4° ss.	BRYDGES Henry	8° ss.
	COLBY Samuel	8° ss.	HILLIARD Samuel	8° ss.	KENNET White	8° ss.
	PELLING John	4° ss.	RENNELL Thomas	4° ss.	SACHEVERELL Henry	4° ss.
	WILLIS Richard	8° ss.				
1710						
	ANONYMOUS	8° ss.	ARCHER Edmond	8° ss.	HARRISON John	8° ss.
	HIGDEN Will. DD.	4° ss.	JACKSON John	8° ss.	MASTER Thomas	-° ss.
	RIVERS Tho. LL.D.	4° ss.	TILLY William	4° ss.	<u>BROWN</u> <u>Simon</u>	8° ss.
1711						
	BEVERIDGE William	8° coll.	FRIEND Robert	4° ss.	GOOCH Thomas Sir	4° ss.
	HOADLY Benjamin	8° coll.				
1712						
	GASTRELL Francis	4° ss.				
1713						
	BULL George	8° coll.				
1715						
	STANHOPE George	4° coll.				
1716						
	BARROW Isaac	fo.coll.	STANHOPE George	4° coll.		
1717						
	BISSE Thomas	8° ss.	MANGEY Thomas	8° coll.	SMALRIDGE George	8° coll.
1718						
	SCOTT John	fo.coll.				
1719						
	SHERLOCK William	8° coll.				
1720						
	FIDDES Rich. DD.	fo. ss.	FIDDES Rich. DD.	fo. ss.	WATERLAND Daniel	8° coll.
1721						
	KNIGHT James	8° coll.				
1724						
	SMALRIDGE George	fo.coll.	SOUTH Robert	8° coll.		
1726						
	BRAGGE Francis	8° coll.	BULLOCK Thomas	4° ss.	BULLOCK Thomas	8° coll.
	CALAMY Benjamin	8° coll.				
1727						
	DERHAM Will. DD.	8° ss.	ROGERS John	8° coll.	SOUTH Robert	8° coll.
	STANHOPE George	8° coll.				
1728						
	FIDDES Rich. DD.	fo.coll.	NORRIS John	8° coll.	NORRIS John	9° coll.
	READING Will. M.A.	8° coll.				
1729						
	GIBSON Edmund	8° coll.				
1730						
	ATTERBURY Francis	8° coll.	CLARKE Samuel	8° coll.	DERHAM Will. DD.	8° ss.
	READING Will. M.A.	8° coll.	ROGERS John	8° coll.		
1734						
	CLARKE Samuel	8° coll.				
1735						
	ROGERS John	8° coll.	TILLOTSON John	fo.coll.		
1736						
	ROGERS John	8° coll.				
1738						

Year						
	ROGERS John	8°coll.				
1739	BENTLEY Richard	fo.coll.				
1749	BUTLER Joseph	8°coll.				
1750	SEED Jeremiah	-°coll.				
1756	MUNTON Anthony	8°coll.				
1757	CONYBEARE John	8°coll.				
1762	SMITH Will. DD.	8°coll.				
1766	DELANY Patrick	8°coll.				
1775	HUNT Thomas	4°coll.				

Wadham College ("Wadh.")

Year						
1664	BROWNRIG Ralph	fo.coll.				
1670	CUDWORTH Ralph	8° ss.				
1673	JACKSON Thomas	fo.coll.				
1679	LLOYD William	4° ss.				
1680	BURNET Gilbert	4° ss.	BURNET Gilbert	4° ss.		
1681	BURNET Gilbert	4° ss.				
1682	BURNET Gilbert	4° ss.	BURY Arthur	8° ss.		
1684	SHOWER John	4° ss.				
1685	BURNET Gilbert	4° ss.	TURNER Francis	4° ss.		
1686	DOVE Heb. DD.	4° ss.				
1688	BURNET Gilbert	8° ss.				
1689	BURNET Gilbert	4° ss.	BURNET Gilbert	4° ss.	BURNET Gilbert	4° ss.
1690	BURNET Gilbert	4° ss.	BURNET Gilbert	4° ss.	BURNET Gilbert	8° ss.
1691	BURNET Gilbert	4° ss.	BURNET Gilbert	4° ss.	BURNET Gilbert	4° ss.
	SHERLOCK William	8° ss.	TENISON Thomas	4° ss.		
1692	BENTLEY Richard	4°coll.	BURNET Gilbert	4° ss.	FOWLER Edward	4° ss.
1693	LAKE Edward	4° ss.				
1694	BURNET Gilbert	4° ss.	BURNET Gilbert	4° ss.	BURNET Gilbert	4° ss.
1695	BURNET Gilbert	4° ss.	WHINCOP Thomas	4° ss.		

1696	ISHAM Zach. DD.	4° ss.				
1697	BURNET Gilbert	4° ss.	BURNET Gilbert	4° ss.	BURNET Gilbert	4° ss.
1698	BURNET Gilbert	4° ss.	WHICHCOTE Benj. DD.	8° coll.		
1699	SHERLOCK William	8° ss.				
1700	ASHETON William	8° ss.	BURNET Gilbert	4° ss.		
1701	BISSE Philip	4° ss.	MARSHALL Nathaniel	4° ss.		
1702	WHICHCOTE Benj. DD.	8° coll.				
1703	KENNET White	4° ss.	WHICHCOTE Benj. DD.	8° coll.		
1704	BURNET Gilbert	4° ss.	BURNET Gilbert	4° ss.	BUTLER Lilly	4° ss.
1706	ALTHAM Roger	4° ss.				
1707	TRIMNEL Charles	4° ss.	WHICHCOTE Benj. DD.	8° coll.		
1709	BAKER William	4° ss.				
1710	KNAGGS Thomas	8° ss.				
1711	LLOYD Robert Lumley	8° ss.				
1712	ANONYMOUS	8° ss.				
1713	BELL George	4° ss.	BRADFORD Samuel	4° ss.	BURNET Gilbert	8° coll.
1714	BOULTER Hugh BURNET Gilbert SACHEVERELL Henry	4° ss. 8° ss. 4° ss.	BURNET Gilbert CHISHULL Edmund	4° ss. 4° ss.	BURNET Gilbert FARMERIE William	4° ss. 8° ss.
1715	SAVAGE William	4° ss.				
1716	BARROW Isaac BRADBURY Thomas	fo. coll. 8° ss.	BISSE Thomas	8° ss.	STURMY Daniel	8° coll.
1717	TALBOT William	4° ss.				
1720	SHERIDAN William	8° coll.				
1721	MEADOWCOURT Richard	8° ss.	WATERLAND Daniel	8° ss.		
1722	BURSCOUGH William	4° ss.	MEADOWCOURT Richard	8° ss.		
1724	EDGLEY Samuel	4° ss.	SOUTH Robert	8° coll.		
1725	ROPER Joseph. DD.	4° ss.				
1727	BLACKALL Offspring SOUTH Robert	8° coll. 8° coll.	DERHAM Will. DD.	8° ss.	HUTCHINSON Michael	4° ss.

Year						
1728						
MAURICE Peter	8° ss.	READING Will. M.A.	8° coll.			
1729						
KILBOURN Robert	4° ss.	LUPTON William	8° coll.	REEVES William	8° coll.	
1730						
BRIDEOAKE Ralph READING Will. M.A.	4° ss. 8° coll.	CLARKE Samuel	8° coll.	DERHAM Will. DD.	8° ss.	
1731						
BOWMAN William	8° ss.					
1732						
ALTHAM Roger	8° coll.	FOSTER James	8° coll.			
1735						
LITTLETON Edward	8° coll.	TILLOTSON John	fo.coll.			
1737						
FLEETWOOD William	fo.coll.	FOSTER James	8° coll.			
1738						
BOURN Samuel	8° ss.					
1739						
BENTLEY Richard	fo.coll.					
1741						
STRAIGHT John	8° coll.	SYMONDS Edward	8° ss.	GROVE Henry	8° coll.	
1742						
AUDLEY Matthew	4° ss.					
1743						
MADDOX Isaac	4° ss.	ABERNETHY John	8° coll.			
1744						
MADDOX Isaac	4° ss.	FOSTER James	8° coll.			
1745						
GILBERT John	4° ss.					
1746						
HUTTON Matthew	4° ss.					
1747						
BURNET Gilbert	8° coll.					
1749						
HEYLYN John	4° coll.	MILLER James	8° coll.	THOMAS John	4° ss.	
1750						
COCKMAN Thomas	8° coll.	MAWSON Matthias	4° ss.	SEED Jeremiah	-° coll.	
1751						
TREVOR Richard	4° ss.					
1752						
CORNWALLIS Frederick	4° ss.					
1753						
WISHART William	12° coll.					
1754						
HOADLY Benjamin	8° coll.					
1755						
JORTIN John	8° coll.					
1756						
BLAKE Edward	8° ss.					
1757						
AUDLEY Matthew	4° ss.	CONYBEARE John	8° coll.	HOOPER George	fo.coll.	
1759						
HAYTER Thomas	4° ss.					
1760						
YONGE Philip	4° ss.	NEWMAN Thomas	8° coll.			
1761						

Year	Name	Format	Name	Format	Name	Format
	DOUGHTY John	8°coll.	TERRICK Richard	4° ss.		
1764	BURTON John	8°coll.	NEWCOME Richard	4° ss.		
1765	LLOYD Peirson	8°coll.	SQUIRE Samuel	4° ss.		
1766	BURTON John	8°coll.	EWER John	4° ss.		
1770	ASHTON Thomas	8°coll.				
1771	SECKER William	8°coll.				
1772	SHERLOCK Thomas	8°coll.				
1774	GOULD Will.	4° ss.	SHERLOCK Thomas	8°coll.		
1778	WHITE Joseph	4° ss.				

Worcester College ("Worc.")

Year	Name	Format	Name	Format	Name	Format
----	FOTHERGILL Thomas	-° ss.				
16--	BAXTER Richard	4° ss.				
1624	LUSHINGTON Thomas	12° ss.				
1627	MAYNWARING Roger	4° ss.				
1660	BRUNSELL Samuel	4° ss.	BUCK James	4° ss.	CONYERS Tobias	4° ss.
	CREED William	4° ss.	GAUDEN John	4° ss.	HACKET John	4° ss.
	PRICE John	4° ss.	SHELDON Gilbert	4° ss.	SUDBURY John	4° ss.
	TOWERS Samuel	4° ss.	WOMOCK Lawrence	4° ss.	PATERSON John	4° ss.
1661	FORD Simon	4° ss.	HEYLYN Pet. DD.	4° ss.	KING Henry	4° ss.
	MORLEY George	4° ss.	TILLOTSON John	4°coll.		
1662	MAYNE Jasper	4° ss.				
1666	DOLBEN John	4° ss.				
1672	FARINDON Anth. B.D.	fo.coll.	FULLWOOD Francis	4° ss.		
1673	GREGORY Fran. DD.	4° ss.				
1675	BURNET Gilbert	4° ss.	FELL John	4° ss.	HACKET John	fo.coll.
	LANEY Benjamin	4° ss.				
1677	CRADOCK Zechary	4° ss.	HORNECK Anthony	4° ss.	PINDAR William	4° ss.
	TILLOTSON John	4°coll.				
1678	LLOYD William	4° ss.	PATRICK Simon	4° ss.		
1679	FARINDON Anth. B.D.	fo.coll.	JANE Will. DD.	4° ss.	OATES Titus	4° ss.
	WYATT Will. M.A.	4° ss.				
1680	FELL John	4° ss.	PARSONS Robert	4° ss.		

1681						
	BURNET Gilbert	4° ss.	GLANVIL Joseph	4° coll.	HOOPER George	4° ss.
	MAURICE Henry	4° ss.	SCLATER Edward	4° ss.		
1682						
	ALSOP Nathaniel	4° ss.				
1683						
	ANONYMOUS	4° ss.	BARNE Miles	4° ss.	CALAMY Benjamin	4° ss.
	CHAPMAN John	4° ss.	PELLING Edward	4° ss.		
1684						
	BOLTON William	4° ss.	CALAMY Benjamin	4° ss.		
1685						
	ELLIS Ph.	4° ss.	MANNINGHAM Thomas	4° ss.	NORRIS John	4° ss.
	SHERLOCK William	4° ss.	TURNER Francis	4° ss.		
1688						
	BURNET Gilbert	8° ss.	HELLIER Henry	4° ss.		
1689						
	BIRCH Peter	4° ss.	PATRICK Simon	4° ss.	SHERLOCK William	8° ss.
1691						
	JANE Will. DD.	4° ss.				
1692						
	BENTLEY Richard	4° coll.	MORE Henry	8° coll.		
1693						
	STUBBS Philip	4° ss.				
1694						
	WHITEHALL Rob. M.A.	4° ss.				
1695						
	HOOPER George	4° ss.				
1696						
	BORFET Abiel	4° ss.				
1699						
	JONES David	4° ss.				
17--						
	CASTLE Abraham	8° ss.	TUNSTALL James	8° coll.		
1700						
	EYRE Robert	4° ss.	KNAGGS Thomas	4° ss.	STEPHENS William	4° ss.
	WEST Richard	4° ss.				
1701						
	HOOPER George	4° ss.	HOUGH John	4° ss.	ISHAM Zach. DD.	4° ss.
	STANHOPE George	4° coll.	STUBBS Philip	4° ss.		
1702						
	SPRAT Thomas	4° ss.	STANHOPE George	4° coll.	STUBBS Philip	4° ss.
	STUBBS Philip	4° ss.	STUBBS Philip	4° ss.	WILLIS Richard	4° ss.
1703						
	DUKE Rich. M.A.	4° ss.	RESBURY Nathaniel	4° ss.		
1704						
	BINCKES William	4° ss.	FINCH Will. Lepold	4° ss.	HOOPER George	4° ss.
	KENNET White	4° ss.	STUBBS Philip	4° ss.	STUBBS Philip	4° ss.
1705						
	ADAMS John	4° ss.	AUDLEY Matthew	4° ss.	SHERLOCK William	-° ss.
	STANHOPE George	4° ss.	STANHOPE George	4° ss.	WILLIS Richard	4° ss.
	WILLIS Richard	4° ss.				
1706						
	BRADY Nich. DD.	8° coll.	BURNET Gilbert	4° ss.	CRADOCK Zechary	4° ss.
	HIGGINS Francis	4° ss.	LENG John	8° ss.	PEAD Deuel	8° ss.
	SACHEVERELL Henry	4° ss.	STANHOPE George	4° ss.	STUBBS Philip	4° ss.
1707						

	CHISHULL Edmund	4° ss.	KNAGGS Thomas	8° ss.	NICOLSON William	4° ss.
	PAUL William	8° ss.				
1708	ADAMS John	4° ss.	ADAMS John	4° ss.	ANONYMOUS	8° ss.
	CHETWOOD Knightly	4° ss.	EYRE Robert	4° ss.	KENNET White	8° ss.
	MANNINGHAM Thomas	1° ss.	SACHEVERELL Henry	4° ss.	TRIMNEL Charles	4° ss.
1709	BRYDGES Henry	8° ss.	HARE Francis	4° ss.	HILLIARD Samuel	8° ss.
	KING William	8° ss.	MAYNWARING Roger	8° ss.	ROBERTS William	4° ss.
	SACHEVERELL Henry	4° ss.	SACHEVERELL Henry	4° ss.	STUBBS Philip	4° ss.
	TRIMNEL Charles	4° ss.	WILLIS Richard	8° ss.		
1710	BURNET Gilbert	8° ss.	BURNET Gilbert	8° ss.	D'OYLY Robert	4° ss.
	GODDARD Thomas	4° ss.	HOPKINS Ezekiel	fo.coll.	NEEDHAM John	8° ss.
	RIVERS Tho. LL.D.	4° ss.	SPRAT Thomas	8° coll.	SWIFT Thomas	8° ss.
	TILLY William	4° ss.	TROUTBECK John	8° ss.		
1711	BISSE Philip	4° ss.	GOOCH Thomas Sir	4° ss.	HARE Francis	8° ss.
	RICHARDSON William	4° ss.				
1712	ASH St. George	8° ss.	BRETT Thomas	8° coll.	FINCH Henry	4° ss.
	HUMPHREYS Thomas	8° ss.	IBBETSON Richard	8° ss.	NEWTON Richard	4° ss.
	STEPHENS William	4° ss.	TRIMNEL Charles	4° ss.		
1713	BISSE Thomas	8° ss.	BRETT Thomas	8° coll.	COLEIRE Richard	4° ss.
	DINGLEY William	8° ss.	HICHMAN Charles	8° coll.	HOOPER George	4° ss.
	NEWTON Richard	4° ss.	SACHEVERELL Henry	4° ss.	STUBBS Philip	3° ss.
	STUBBS Philip	4° ss.				
1714	BRETT Thomas	8° coll.	BURNET Gilbert	4° ss.	BURNET Gilbert	8° ss.
	CHISHULL Edmund	4° ss.	COCKS Sir Robert	8° ss.	DUKE Rich. M.A.	8° coll.
	LOMBARD Daniel	8° ss.	MARSHALL John	8° ss.	MARSHALL Nathaniel	8° ss.
	REEVES William	4° ss.	RYE George	8° ss.	SMITH Joseph	4° ss.
1715	BRETT Joseph	8° coll.	COCKS Sir Robert	8° ss.		
1716	ADAMS William	8° coll.	ANONYMOUS	8° ss.	BARROW Isaac	fo.coll.
	BENNET Thomas	8° ss.	EYRE Rich. M.A.	4° ss.	HAYLEY Tho. DD.	8° ss.
	HOLE Matthew	8° ss.	NEWTON Richard	4° ss.		
1717	BISSE Philip	4° ss.	DOD Thomas	8° ss.	LENG John	8° coll.
	STEPHENS William	8° ss.	TRAPP Joseph	8° ss.		
1718	MARSHALL Nathaniel	4° ss.	NEWLIN Thomas	8° ss.	SCOTT John	fo.coll.
	STUBBS Philip	8° ss.				
1719	BRADFORD Samuel	4° ss.	GIBSON John	8° ss.	HARE Francis	4° ss.
	HOLDSWORTH Winch. DD.	8° ss.	MANGEY Thomas	4° ss.	MANGEY Thomas	8° ss.
	STEPHENS William	8° ss.				
1720	ALLET Thomas	8° ss.	BEVERIDGE William	fo.coll.	BOULTER Hugh	4° ss.
	CROSSINGE Richard	8° ss.	FIDDES Rich. DD.	fo. ss.	FIDDES Rich. DD.	fo. ss.
	MANGEY Thomas	4° ss.	WILCOCKS Joseph	4° ss.	WILDER John	8° coll.
1721	COTES Digby	8° coll.	GREENE Thomas	4° ss.	HARCOURT James	4° ss.
	KNIGHT James	8° coll.	MARSHALL Nathaniel	4° ss.	WATERLAND Daniel	8° ss.

1722						
	BENTHAM Edward	4° ss.	BERRIMAN William	4° ss.	CONYBEARE John	8° ss.
	MEADOWCOURT Richard	8° ss.	STEPHENS William	8° ss.		
1723						
	ALDRICH Charles	4° ss.	BLACKALL Offspring	fo.coll.	CONINGESBY George	8° ss.
	CONYBEARE John	8° ss.	GIBSON Edmund	4° ss.	NORRIS John	12° ss.
	STANHOPE Michael	4° ss.				
1724						
	DOUGHTY Gregory	4° ss.	HOUGH Nathaniel	4° ss.	LAVINGTON George	8° ss.
	REYNELL Carew	4° ss.	SOUTH Robert	8° coll.	STEPHENS William	8° ss.
	WAUGH John	4° ss.	WILCOCKS Joseph	4° ss.		
1725						
	ANONYMOUS	8° ss.	COLLIER Jeremy	8° coll.	FELTON Henry	8° ss.
	KING John	8° ss.	LAVINGTON George	8° ss.	LOCKIER Francis	4° ss.
	PHILIPS John	4° ss.				
1726						
	BAKER William	4° ss.	BEARCROFT Philip	8° ss.	BULLOCK Thomas	8° coll.
	CALAMY Benjamin	8° coll.	CONYBEARE John	8° ss.	DOLBEN Sir John	4° ss.
	TRAPP Joseph	8° ss.	WILCOCKS Joseph	4° ss.	WYNNE John	8° ss.
1727						
	CONYBEARE John	8° ss.	DERHAM Will. DD.	8° ss.	PEARCE Zachary	4° ss.
	ROGERS John	8° coll.	SOUTH Robert	8° coll.	STANHOPE George	8° coll.
	STOCKWELL Joseph	8° ss.				
1728						
	BROOKE James	8° ss.	DELAUNE William	8° coll.	FIDDES Rich. DD.	fo.coll.
	JONES John	8° ss.	LEEKE Robert	8° ss.	WILCOCKS Joseph	4° ss.
	YOUNG Edward	4° ss.				
1729						
	BETTY Joseph	8° ss.	BURTON John	4° ss.	BURTON John	4° ss.
	CONYBEARE John	8° ss.	GIBSON Edmund	8° coll.	KILBOURN Robert	4° ss.
	LUPTON William	8° coll.	REEVES William	8° coll.	THOMAS John	4° ss.
	TRAPP Joseph	4° ss.	YOUNG Edward	8° ss.		
1730						
	ATTERBURY Francis	8° coll.	CLARKE Samuel	8° coll.	CROXALL Sam. DD.	8° ss.
	DERHAM Will. DD.	8° ss.	LITTLETON Edward	4° ss.	MIDDLETON John	4° ss.
	ROBINSON Thomas	8° ss.	ROGERS John	8° coll.	SPATEMAN Thomas	4° ss.
1731						
	BOWMAN William	8° ss.	CLARKE Alured	4° ss.	HARE Francis	4° ss.
	JOHNSON Thomas	8° ss.	MARSHALL Nathaniel	8° coll.		
1732						
	BERKELEY George	4° ss.	FELTON Henry	8° coll.	MIDDLETON John	4° ss.
	MOSS Robert	8° coll.	PANTING Matthew	4° ss.	SILVESTER Tipping	4° ss.
	STEBBING Henry	8° ss.	TRAPP Joseph	8° ss.	<u>FOSTER</u> <u>James</u>	8° coll.
1733						
	BURTON John	4° ss.	COCKMAN Thomas	8° ss.	CONYBEARE John	8° ss.
	FELTON Henry	8° ss.	FELTON Henry	8° ss.	MAULE Henry	4° ss.
	MAWSON Matthias	4° ss.	MOSS Robert	8° coll.	RANDOLPH Thomas	8° ss.
1734						
	BALLARD Edward	8° ss.	BEST William	8° ss.	BURTON John	8° ss.
	RINGER Thomas	8° coll.				
1735						
	BARTON Philip	4° ss.	EYRE Robert	8° ss.	FELTON Henry	8° ss.
	HARE Francis	4° ss.	ROGERS John	8° coll.	SHARP John	8° coll.
	TILLOTSON John	fo.coll.				
1736						
	AYSCOUGH Francis	4° ss.	DENNIS Samuel	4° ss.	EDWARDS Joseph	8° ss.

	FELTON Henry	8° ss.	HOLLOWAY Benjamin	8° ss.	KNIGHT James	8° ss.
	ROGERS John	8° coll.	STACKHOUSE Thomas	8° ss.	TOTTIE John	8° ss.
	WATTS George	4° ss.				
1737	BANNER Richard	8° ss.	HARTE Walter	8° ss.	MOSS Robert	8° coll.
	STEPHENS William	8° coll.	<u>FOSTER James</u>	8° coll.		
1738	CONYBEARE John	4° ss.	HOWARD Robert	4° ss.	HUTCHINSON Thomas	8° ss.
	MOSS Robert	8° coll.	PERROT Humphrey	8° ss.	ROGERS John	8° coll.
	WARBURTON William	8° ss.	WEBBER Francis. DD.	8° ss.		
1739	BENTLEY Richard	fo.coll.	CLEAVER Will. M.A.	8° ss.	CRADOCK John	4° ss.
	LENG John	fo.coll.	MUDGE Zechary	8° coll.	RANDOLPH Thomas	8° ss.
	STANHOPE George	fo.coll.	WILCOCKS Joseph	4° ss.		
1740	BARTON Philip	4° ss.	BISSE Thomas	8° coll.	CLAYTON Robert.	4° ss.
	HUTCHINSON Thomas	8° ss.	MIDDLETON P	8° ss.	NEWTON Richard	8° ss.
1741	BURTON John	8° ss.	GAMBOLD John	8° ss.	LUSHINGTON Thomas	8° ss.
	PEARCE Zachary	4° ss.	SMITH William	4° ss.	SPRY John	8° ss.
1742	BERRIMAN William	4° ss.	BEST William	4° ss.	CONINGESBY George	8° ss.
	GILBERT John	4° ss.	STONE George	4° ss.	WARBURTON William	8° ss.
	WEBBER Francis. DD.	8° ss.				
1743	CLEAVER Will. M.A.	8° ss.	DODWELL William	8° ss.	EDEN Robert	4° ss.
	EDEN Robert	4° ss.	EDWARDS Joseph	8° ss.	GILBERT John	4° ss.
	THOMAS John	4° ss.	TWELLS Leonard	8° coll.	<u>ABERNETHY John</u>	8° coll.
1744	BENTHAM Edward	8° ss.	BURTON John	8° ss.	CARY Mordecai	4° ss.
	DELANY Patrick	4° ss.	DODWELL William	8° ss.	GILBERT John	4° ss.
	HUTTON Matthew	4° ss.	SPRY John	8° ss.	SWIFT Jonathan	4° coll.
	<u>FOSTER James</u>	8° coll.				
1745	DALTON John	4° ss.	DODWELL William	8° ss.	DODWELL William	8° ss.
	FLETCHER Thomas	4° ss.	GARDNER William	8° ss.	GILBERT John	4° ss.
	HORBERY Matt. DD.	8° ss.	HUTTON Matthew	4° ss.	SPRY John	8° ss.
	TERRICK Richard	4° ss.	TREVOR Richard	4° ss.	WARBURTON William	8° ss.
	WARBURTON William	8° ss.	WILSON Thomas	8° ss.		
1746	BURTON John	8° ss.	BURTON John	8° ss.	FORSTER Nathaniel	8° ss.
	LAVINGTON George	4° ss.	LEIGHTON Robert	8° coll.	MADDOX Isaac	4° ss.
	OLIVER R.	8° ss.	PARKER William	8° ss.	RUTHERFORTH Thomas	4° ss.
	WARBURTON William	8° ss.				
1747	BROWN Richard	8° ss.	DALTON John	4° ss.	TREVOR Richard	4° ss.
	TREVOR Richard	4° ss.				
1748	BEARCROFT Philip	4° ss.	WARBURTON William	-° ss.		
1749	BUTLER Joseph	8° coll.	CONYBEARE John	8° ss.	FOTHERGILL Thomas	8° ss.
	HORBERY Matt. DD.	8° ss.	MADDOX Isaac	4° ss.		
1750	BARTON Philip	4° ss.	BENTHAM Edward	8° ss.	BROWN Richard	8° ss.
	CLEAVER Will. M.A.	8° ss.	COKAYNE Will. B.D.	4° ss.	DODWELL William	8° ss.
	MARSHALL Nathaniel	8° coll.	PICKERING Thomas	4° ss.	TREVOR Richard	4° ss.

	WEBBER Francis. DD.	8° ss.	WILMOT George	4° ss.		
1751						
	CONYBEARE John	4° ss.	CONYBEARE John	8° ss.	HALES Stephen	4° ss.
	RUTHERFORTH Thomas	4° ss.	TOTTIE John	8° ss.	WHITFIELD Henry	8° ss.
1752						
	BEAUCLERE James	4° ss.	CONYBEARE John	4° ss.	DODWELL William	8° ss.
	GREY Richard	4° ss.	JENNER Thomas	8° ss.	RANDOLPH Thomas	8° ss.
1753						
	WARBURTON William	8° coll.	DUCHAL James	8° coll.		
1754						
	BARTON Philip	8° ss.	DODWELL William	8° ss.	EDEN Robert	4° ss.
	HOADLY Benjamin	8° coll.	WARBURTON William	8° coll.		
1755						
	DODWELL William	8° ss.	EDEN Robert	4° ss.	HIND Richard	4° ss.
	RANDOLPH Thomas	8° ss.				
1756						
	GREEN Richard	4° ss.	NETTO Isaac	4° ss.		
1757						
	CONYBEARE John	8° coll.	GRIFFITH Thomas	8° ss.	SNOWDEN James	8° ss.
1758						
	DODWELL William	8° ss.	KEDDINGTON R. DD.	8° ss.	PARKER William	8° ss.
	SNOWDEN James	8° ss.	WEBBER Francis. DD.	4° ss.		
1759						
	ANONYMOUS	8° ss.	BILSTONE John	8° ss.	BUCKLER Benjamin	4° ss.
	FLETCHER Philip	4° ss.	NEVE Timothy	8° ss.		
1760						
	DODWELL William	8° ss.	GRIFFITH Thomas	8° ss.	PEARCE Zachary	4° ss.
	STILLINGFLEET James	8° ss.	SWANN Gilbert	8° ss.		
1761						
	BRAY Tho. DD.	8° ss.	HITCHCOCK Thomas	8° ss.	HORNE Geo. DD.	8° ss.
	PARSONS Joseph	8° coll.	ROTHERAM John	8° ss.	SIMPSON Joseph	8° ss.
	TERRICK Richard	4° ss.				
1762						
	BARTON Henry	4° ss.	CLEAVER Will. M.A.	8° ss.	CORNWALLIS Frederick	4° ss.
	RANDOLPH Thomas	8° ss.	ROTHERAM John	8° ss.		
1763						
	BRAY Tho. DD.	4° ss.	DELANY Patrick	4° ss.	GRIFFITH Thomas	8° ss.
	JEFFERSON Jacob	8° ss.	ROTHERAM John	8° ss.		
1764						
	MAURICE Henry	8° ss.				
1765						
	FOTHERGILL Geo. DD.	8° coll.	KENNICOTT Benjamin	8° ss.	NEWTON Thomas	4° ss.
	SHARP Gregory	8° ss.				
1766						
	BARTON Phi. B.D.	4° ss.	SHARP Gregory	8° ss.	TUCKER Josiah	4° ss.
1767						
	RANDOLPH Thomas	8° ss.				
1768						
	RANDOLPH Thomas	8° ss.	RANDOLPH Thomas	8° ss.		
1769						
	FRAMPTON Matt. LLD.	4° ss.	MARKHAM William	4° ss.	RANDOLPH Thomas	8° ss.
	WHITFIELD Henry	4° ss.	WORTHINGTON William	8° coll.	YONGE Philip	4° ss.
1770						
	BARRINGTON Lord	8° coll.	EYRE Richard	4° ss.		
1771						
	HALLIFAX James	4° ss.	LOWTH Robert	4° ss.	SECKER William	8° coll.

1772	SHERLOCK Thomas	8° coll.				
1773	HORNE Geo. DD.	8° ss.	LOWTH Robert	4° ss.	RYMER Thomas	4° ss.
1774	FINCH Robert Pool	4° ss.	MARKHAM William	4° ss.	SHERLOCK Thomas	8° coll.
1775	HORNE Geo. DD.	8° ss.	NICOLL Richard	8° ss.	OGLE N. DD.	4° ss.
1776	HURD Richard	8° coll.				
1777	COOPER Miles	4° ss.	RANDOLPH Thomas	8° ss.		
1790	TENISON Thomas	4° ss.				

(INDEXES TO FIFTH VOLUME)

PART TWO OF INDEX E : CAMBRIDGE LIBRARIES

Clare Hall	("Cl.H.")					
1661						
	HALL Joseph	fo.coll.				
1668						
	LINGARD Ric. DD.	4° ss.				
1672						
	MEDE Joseph	fo.coll.	WARD Seth	8° coll.		
1673						
	CALAMY Benjamin	4° ss.				
1674						
	WARD Seth	8° coll.				
1682						
	CALAMY Benjamin	4° ss.	KEN Thomas	4° ss.	WILKINS John	8° coll.
1683						
	CALAMY Benjamin	4° ss.	CALAMY Benjamin	4° ss.	CALAMY Benjamin	4° ss.
1684						
	CALAMY Benjamin	4° ss.	CALAMY Benjamin	4° ss.	HAMMOND Henry	fo.coll.
	VINCENT Nathaniel	4° ss.				
1688						
	BURNET Gilbert	8° ss.				
1689						
	ANONYMOUS	4° ss.	BURNET Gilbert	4° ss.	HORNECK Anthony	4° ss.
	PATRICK Simon	4° ss.	PATRICK Simon	4° ss.	SANDERSON Robert	fo.coll.
	STAINFORTH William	4° ss.				
1690						
	BURNET Gilbert	4° ss.	BURNET Gilbert	4° ss.	FREEMAN Samuel	4° ss.
	FREEMAN Samuel	4° ss.				
1691						
	JANE Will. DD.	4° ss.	KELSEY Joseph	4° ss.	PATRICK Simon	4° ss.
1692						
	BENTLEY Richard	4° coll.	KIDDER Richard	4° ss.	STANHOPE George	4° ss.

INDEXES TO FIFTH VOLUME: E: LIBRARIES: PART TWO: CAMBRIDGE (Clare Hall)

Year	Name	Format	Name	Format	Name	Format
1694	BIRCH Peter	4° ss.	TENISON Thomas	4° ss.		
1695	HARTCLIFFE John TENISON Thomas	4° ss. 4° ss.	HAYLEY William	4° ss.	MANNINGHAM Thomas	4° ss.
1696	ALSOP Vincent	4° ss.				
1697	WIGAN William	4° ss.				
1698	PROVOSTE John	4° ss.				
1699	BROUSTON. M.	4° ss.	HAYLEY William	4° ss.		
1700	FREEMAN Samuel	4° ss.	HARE Francis	4° ss.	KEITH George	4° ss.
1701	HOWARD John	4° ss.	JOHNSON John	8° ss.		
1702	STUBBS Philip	4° ss.	STUBBS Philip	4° ss.	TRELAWNEY Jonathan Sir	4° ss.
1703	NICOLSON William	4° ss.	PRIDEAUX Humphrey	4° ss.		
1704	SHERWILL Thomas	4° ss.	TRIMNEL Charles	4° ss.		
1705	BROUGHTON John	4° ss.	STANHOPE George	4° ss.		
1706	KENNET White	4° ss.				
1707	CANNON Robert STILLINGFLEET Edward	4° ss. fo.coll.	CHISHULL Edmund WISE Thomas	4° ss. 4° ss.	HUTCHINSON Francis	8° ss.
1708	BLACKALL Offspring	8° coll.	MILNER William	8° ss.	TRIMNEL Charles	4° ss.
1709	KING William	8° ss.				
1710	LAMBE Henry	8° ss.	SPRAT Thomas	8° coll.		
1711	HOADLY Benjamin	8° coll.				
1712	HAYLEY Tho. DD.	8° ss.				
1714	BURNET Gilbert MAPLETOFT John	4° ss. 4° ss.	CLAGETT Nicholas	4° ss.	DOD Samuel	4° ss.
1715	BENTLEY Richard	8° ss.	GIBSON Edmund	4° ss.	SYDALL Elias	4° ss.
1716	BARROW Isaac WATERLAND Daniel	fo.coll. 8° ss.	HARE Francis WATERLAND Theodoric	8° ss. 8° ss.	NEEDHAM Peter	8° ss.
1717	BENTLEY Richard PYLE Tho. M.A.	4° ss. 8° ss.	LAUGHTON Richard	4° ss.	LENG John	8° coll.
1718	BRADFORD Samuel	8° ss.	CLAGETT Nicholas	4° ss.	SCOTT John	fo.coll.
1719	BRADFORD Samuel	4° ss.	WAUGH John	4° ss.		
1721						

Year	Author	Format	Author	Format	Author	Format
	GREENE Thomas	4° ss.	HARVEY Francis	4° ss.	MARSHALL Nathaniel	4° ss.
	WATERLAND Daniel	8° ss.	WRENCH Jonathan	8° ss.		
1723	HARGRAVES James	4° ss.				
1724	HARGRAVES James	4° ss.	NEWCOME John	8° ss.		
1726	BULLOCK Thomas	8° coll.	CLAGETT Nicholas	4° ss.	IBBOT Benj. DD.	8° coll.
1727	DERHAM Will. DD.	8° ss.	ROGERS John	8° coll.		
1728	BULLOCK Thomas	8° ss.	HARRIS William	8° ss.		
1729	GIBSON Edmund	8° coll.				
1730	ATTERBURY Francis	8° coll.	ROGERS John	8° coll.	STEBBING Henry	8° ss.
1733	ROBINSON Christopher	8° coll.				
1734	CLARKE Samuel	8° coll.				
1735	ROGERS John	8° coll.	TILLOTSON John	fo.coll.		
1736	ROGERS John	8° coll.				
1737	FLEETWOOD William	fo.coll.	PEIRCE James	4° coll.		
1738	HOWARD Robert	4° ss.	ROGERS John	8° coll.	WEBBER Francis. DD.	8° ss.
1739	ANONYMOUS	fo.coll.	BENTLEY Richard	fo.coll.	LENG John	fo.coll.
	WILCOCKS Joseph	4° ss.				
1740	CLAYTON Robert	4° ss.				
1746	LEIGHTON Robert	8° coll.				
1749	MADDOX Isaac	4° ss.				
1751	BERRIMAN William	8° coll.	RUTHERFORTH Thomas	4° ss.		
1755	RANDOLPH Thomas	8° ss.				
1757	HOOPER George	fo.coll.				
1761	NEGUS Thomas	4° ss.				
1766	DELANY Patrick	8° coll.				
1772	SHERLOCK Thomas	8° coll.				
1776	IBBOT Benj. DD.	-° coll.				
1790	TENISON Thomas	4° ss.				

Corpus Christi College ("C.C.C.")

1674

Year	Author	Format	Author	Format
	SMITH William	8° ss.	SMITH William	8° ss.

Jesus College ("Jes.")

Year	Author	Format	Author	Format
1680	FELL John	4° ss.		
1701	ALLEYNE John	4° ss.		
1702	ALTHAM Roger	4° ss.	SACHEVERELL Henry	4° ss.
1703	ALTHAM Roger	4° ss.		
1712	ARCHER Edmund	8° ss.		
1716	ANONYMOUS	8° ss.		

King's College ("Kings's" or "K.")

1672	MEDE Joseph	fo.coll.
1675	HACKET John	fo.coll.
1676	GELL Robert	fo.coll.
1678	TAYLOR Jeremy	fo.coll.
1684	ALLESTREE Richard	fo.coll.
1689	SANDERSON Robert	fo.coll.
1708	FEATLY Daniel	8° ss.
1716	BARROW Isaac	fo.coll.
1717	SMALRIDGE George	8° coll.
1718	SCOTT John	fo.coll.
1720	FIDDES Rich. DD.	fo. ss.
1724	SMALRIDGE George	fo.coll.
1734	CLARKE Samuel	8° coll.
1737	FLEETWOOD William	fo.coll.
1739	ANONYMOUS	fo.coll.
1741	FARRINGTON Richard	8° coll.
1743	TWELLS Leonard	8° coll.
1747	WESTON Stephen	8° coll.
1757	HOOPER George	fo.coll.
1766		

Year	Author	Format	Author	Format	Author	Format
	DELANY Patrick	8° coll.				
Magdalene College ("Magd.")						
1662	CARYL Joseph	4° ss.	LYE Thomas	4° ss.		
1663	CALAMY Benjamin	4° coll.	JENKINS William	4° coll.	LAMB P.	4° coll.
	NEWCOMEN Matthew	4° coll.	SEAMAN	4° coll.	VENNING Ralph	4° coll.
1674	LLOYD William	4° ss.				
1676	BARKER Matthew	4° coll.				
1677	WILKINS John	12° coll.				
1678	LAMPLUGH Thomas	4° ss.	LLOYD William	4° ss.		
1680	HICKERINGILL Edmond	4° coll.	HICKERINGILL Edmond.	4° ss.		
1686	GODDEN Thomas	4° ss.				
1691	PELLING Edward	4° ss.				
1694	HOOPER George	4° ss.				
1700	BATES William	fo. coll.				
1715	ISAAC John	8° ss.				
Pembroke College ("Pemb.")						
1684	ALLESTREE Richard	fo. coll.				
1697	GOODMAN John	8° coll.				
Public Library ("Pub.L")						
----	FLEETWOOD William	-° coll.	SOUTH Robert	-° coll.	WOODWARD Josiah	-° coll.
1660	BARWICK John	4° ss.	GAUDEN John	4° ss.	GAUDEN John	12° ss.
	SUDBURY John	4° ss.	T. - - - - A.	8° coll.	BAXTER Richard	4° ss.
	BURGESS Cornelius	8° ss.				
1661	BAGSHAW Edward	4° ss.	FORD Simon	4° ss.	MORLEY George	4° ss.
	PHILIPS John	4° ss.	SHUTE Christopher	4° ss.	STEPHENS Thomas	8° coll.
	STUART Richard	12° coll.				
1662	LANEY Benjamin	4° ss.	CALAMY Edmund	4° ss.		
1663	HARDY Nathaniel	4° ss.	HAYWOOD William	4° ss.		
1664	BROWNRIG Ralph	fo. coll.	JOHNSON Will. DD.	12° ss.	SCATTERGOOD Anthonie	4° ss.
1665	KING Henry	4° ss.	LANEY Benjamin	4° ss.		
1666	PERRINCHIEF Richard	4° ss.				

Year	Name	Format	Name	Format	Name	Format
1667	BAGSHAW Henry	4° ss.				
1668	LLOYD William	4° ss.	SMITH Thomas	4° ss.		
1669	JANEWAY James	12° ss.				
1670	DOBSON John	4° ss.	PATRICK Simon	8° ss.	WARD Seth	4° ss.
	STEEL Richard	8° coll.				
1671	NORTH John	4° ss.	LOCKIER Nicholas	12° coll.		
1672	BOYS Edward	8° coll.	DAILLE John	fo. coll.	FARINDON Anth. B.D.	fo. coll.
	GARDINER Samuel	4° ss.	WARD Seth	8° coll.	RYTHER John	8° coll.
1673	EGAN Anthony	4° ss.	HALES John	4° coll.	HOLLINGWORTH Richard	4° ss.
	JENNY Jehu	4° ss.	LAMBE John	4° ss.	SMITH John	4° coll.
1674	GOULDE William	4° ss.	LLOYD William	4° ss.	SMITH William	8° ss.
	SMITH William	8° ss.	WARD Seth	4° ss.	WARD Seth	8° coll.
	RYTHER John	8° ss.				
1675	BARNE Miles	4° ss.	BURNET Gilbert	4° ss.	BURNET Gilbert	4° ss.
	FELL John	4° ss.	JANE Will. DD.	4° ss.	LANEY Benjamin	4° ss.
	NAILOUR William	4° ss.	STUBBE Henry	8° ss.	TAYLOR Jeremy	8° ss.
	TAYLOR Jeremy	8° ss.	WOOLLEY John	4° ss.		
1676	ALLINGTON John	4° ss.	HOWELL William	4° ss.	PARKER Timothy	4° ss.
	PATRICK Simon	4° ss.	ROSSINGTON James	4° ss.	SPANHEIM Frederick	4° ss.
	STRONG James	8° ss.	PHELPES Charles	12° ss.	POWELL Thomas	12° ss.
	TUCKNEY Anthony	4° coll.				
1677	CLAUDE Francis	4° ss.	MITCHELL Jonathan	4° coll.	PINDAR William	4° ss.
	PITTIS Thomas	4° ss.	RAINBOW Edward	4° ss.	SMITH William	4° ss.
	SMITH William	4° ss.	SUDBURY John	4° ss.	THORP George	4° ss.
	TURNER Bryan	4° ss.				
1678	BUTLER John	4° ss.	DILLINGHAM William	4° ss.	HESKETH Henry	4° ss.
	JAMES John	4° ss.	LAMPLUGH Thomas	4° ss.	LLEWELIN David	4° ss.
	LLOYD William	4° ss.	PATRICK Simon	4° ss.	PATRICK Simon	4° ss.
	ROLLS Samuel	8° coll.	USHER James	fo. coll.		
1679	BASSET Will.	4° ss.	FARINDON Anth. B.D.	fo. coll.	HORNE Thomas	4° ss.
	HORTON Thomas	fo. coll.	JANE Will. DD.	4° ss.	LLOYD William	4° ss.
	MANNINGHAM Thomas	8° ss.	NEEDHAM Robert	8° coll.	PELLING Edward	4° ss.
	PIERCE Tho. DD.	4° coll.	PINDAR William	4° ss.	SMITH Thomas	4° ss.
	TURNER John	4° ss.	WALLIS John	4° ss.	WILLES Samuel	4° ss.
	WYATT Will. M.A.	4° ss.	GRAY Andrew	8° coll.		
1680	CAMFIELD Benjamin	4° ss.	FYLER Samuel	4° ss.	HANCOCKE Robert	4° ss.
	HINDMARSH Thomas	4° ss.	LAMBE John	4° ss.	PATRICK Simon	4° ss.
	ROWLEY John	4° ss.	BAXTER Richard	4° ss.		
1681	BURNET Gilbert	4° ss.	FOWLER Edward	4° ss.	GIFFARD Francis	4° ss.
	HICHMAN Charles	4° ss.	JEKYLL Thomas	4° ss.	LLOYD William	4° ss.
	MANNINGHAM Thomas	4° ss.	NEVILLE Robert	4° ss.	NICOLS Daniel	4° ss.

Year	Name	Format	Name	Format	Name	Format
	OKES John	4° ss.	PATRICK Simon	4° ss.	PATRICK Simon	4° ss.
	RESBURY Nathaniel	4° ss.	RESBURY Nathaniel	4° ss.	SILL William	4° ss.
	TENISON Thomas	4° ss.	TURNER Bryan	4° ss.	TURNER Francis	4° ss.
1682						
	BALL Richard	4° ss.	BISBIE Nathaniel	4° ss.	CALAMY Benjamin	4° ss.
	CHETWYND John	4° ss.	CUTLORE Joseph	4° ss.	DOVE Heb. DD.	4° ss.
	EVANS John	4° ss.	FREEMAN Samuel	4° ss.	GOULDE William	4° ss.
	HOLLINGWORTH Richard	4° ss.	INETT John	4° ss.	LAMBE John	4° ss.
	MARKLAND Abraham	4° ss.	NEVILLE Robert	4° ss.	ORME William	4° ss.
	PELLING Edward	4° ss.	PITTIS Thomas	4° ss.	SMITH Thomas	4° ss.
	WALLIS John	4° ss.	WENSLEY Robert	4° ss.	WHITFELD John	4° ss.
	WILKINS John	8° coll.	WRAY William	4° ss.	WROE Christopher	4° ss.
1683						
	CALAMY Benjamin	4° ss.	CALAMY Benjamin	4° ss.	CLAGETT Nich. M.A.	4° ss.
	FITZWILLIAM John	4° ss.	FOWLER Edward	4° ss.	FOX Francis	4° ss.
	GASKARTH John	4° ss.	HOFFMAN Benjamin	4° ss.	HOPKINS William	4° ss.
	KINGSTON Richard	4° ss.	NEVILLE Robert	4° ss.	PAYNE William	4° ss.
	PAYNE William	4° ss.	PELLING Edward	4° ss.	PELLING Edward	4° ss.
	SHERLOCK William	4° ss.	SMITH William	4° ss.	STANDISH John	4° ss.
	STRATFORD Nicholas	4° ss.	TURNER Francis	5° ss.	TURNER John	4° ss.
	TURNER John	8° ss.	JENKINS William	4° coll.	MAYO Richard	4° coll.
	SLATER Samuel	4° coll.				
1684						
	BISBIE Nathaniel	4° ss.	CALAMY Benjamin	4° ss.	HAMMOND Henry	fo.coll.
	HESKETH Henry	4° ss.	KETTLEWELL John	4° ss.	LAMBE John	4° ss.
	LOWDE James	4° ss.	MANNINGHAM Thomas	4° ss.	PEARSON Richard	4° ss.
	PEARSON Richard	4° ss.	RODERICK Richard	4° ss.	TURNER Francis	4° ss.
	TURNER Francis	4° ss.	CHARNOCK Stephen	fo.coll.		
1685						
	BULKELEY Richard	4° ss.	CAMFIELD Benjamin	4° ss.	DOVE Heb. DD.	4° ss.
	FOWLER Edward	4° ss.	FOWLER Edward	4° ss.	GASKARTH John	4° ss.
	GOSTWYKE William	4° ss.	MANNINGHAM Thomas	4° ss.	PETTER John	4° ss.
	RICH Samuel	4° ss.	SHERLOCK William	4° ss.	TURNER Francis	4° ss.
	TURNER Francis	4° ss.	TURNER Tho. DD.	4° ss.		
1686						
	DOVE Heb. DD.	4° ss.	KIDDER Richard	4° ss.	PATRICK Simon	4° ss.
	PIERCE Tho. DD.	4° ss.	STAYNOE Thomas	4° ss.		
1687						
	CLUTTERBUCK Tho. DD.	4° ss.	MANNINGHAM Thomas	4° ss.	MAPLETOFT John	4° ss.
1688						
	BROWNE Thomas	4° ss.	BROWNE Thomas	4° ss.	CUDWORTH John	4° ss.
	FOWLER Edward	4° ss.	MITCALFE Phil.	4° ss.	TULLY Thomas	8° ss.
	WAGSTAFFE Thomas	4° ss.	SYLVESTER Matthew	8° ss.		
1689						
	BURNET Gilbert	4° ss.	BURNET Gilbert	4° ss.	BURNET Gilbert	4° ss.
	BURNET Gilbert	4° ss.	HORNECK Anthony	4° ss.	LLOYD William	4° ss.
	MARIOTT Thomas	4° ss.	PATRICK Simon	4° ss.	PATRICK Simon	4° ss.
	PATRICK Simon	4° ss.	SANDERSON Robert	fo.coll.	SHERLOCK William	8° ss.
	TENISON Thomas	4° ss.	TULLIE George	4° ss.	CRUSO Timothy	4° ss.
1690						
	BURNET Gilbert	4° ss.	FOWLER Edward	4° ss.	FREEMAN Samuel	4° ss.
	FREEMAN Samuel	4° ss.	HAMMOND George	4° coll.	HICHMAN Charles	4° ss.
	KIDDER Richard	4° ss.	LLOYD William	4° ss.	TENISON Thomas	4° ss.
	TENNISON Richard	4° ss.	WHITTLE Seth	4° ss.	MAYO Richard	4° coll.
	SLATER Samuel	4° coll.	STEEL Richard	4° coll.	SYLVESTER Matthew	4° coll.
	WILLIAMS Daniel	4° coll.				

Year	Name	Format	Name	Format	Name	Format
1691	BURNET Gilbert	4° ss.	BURNET Gilbert	4° ss.	BURNET Gilbert	4° ss.
	CLARK Joshua	4° ss.	DOVE Heb. DD.	4° ss.	FOWLER Edward	4° ss.
	LAMBE John	4° ss.	LLOYD William	4° ss.	PATRICK Simon	4° ss.
	PELLING Edward	4° ss.	SHERLOCK William	8° ss.	TALBOT William	4° ss.
	TENISON Thomas	4° ss.				
1692	BENTLEY Richard	4° coll.	BURNET Gilbert	4° ss.	CATHERALL Samuel	4° ss.
	HICKERINGILL Edmond	4° coll.	HICKERINGILL Edmond.	4° ss.	JONES David	4° ss.
	LLOYD William	4° ss.	MANNINGHAM Thomas	4° ss.	MORE Henry	8° coll.
	SHERLOCK William	4° ss.	SHERLOCK William	4° ss.	STANLEY William	4° ss.
	WETENHALL Edward	4° ss.	WHITTELL John	4° ss.	ROGERS Thomas	8° ss.
	WRIGHT Timothy	8° ss.				
1693	ANONYMOUS	4° ss.	ANONYMOUS	8° ss.	BLAGRAVE Jonathan	4° ss.
	BRADY Nich. DD.	4° ss.	EYRE Robert	4° ss.	FREEMAN Samuel	4° ss.
	HAMMOND George	8° ss.	HICHMAN Charles	4° ss.	HOLLINGWORTH Richard	4° ss.
	KNAGGS Thomas	4° ss.	LAKE Edward	4° ss.	LAMBE John	4° ss.
	LAMBE John	4° ss.	MANNINGHAM Thomas	4° ss.	MONRO Alexander	4° coll.
	RUSSEL John	4° ss.	STUBBS Philip	4° ss.	WALKER Thomas	4° ss.
	WHITAKER Thomas	8° ss.	SLATER Samuel	8° ss.		
1694	BATTELL Ralph	4° ss.	BURNET Gilbert	4° ss.	BURNET Gilbert	4° ss.
	COMBER Thomas	4° ss.	CORNWALLIS Henry	12° ss.	HUGHES William	8° ss.
	KEACK Elias	4° ss.	MANNINGHAM Thomas	4° ss.	MANSELL John	4° ss.
	MANSELL John	4° ss.	PELLING Edward	8° ss.	PETTER John	4° ss.
	SANCROFT William	8° coll.	STEPHENS William	4° ss.	SWYNFEN John	4° ss.
	TENISON Thomas	4° ss.	TENISON Thomas	4° ss.	TYLER John	4° ss.
	WROE Christopher	4° ss.	BEVERLEY Thomas	4° ss.	CALAMY Edmund	4° ss.
	SLATER Samuel	8° ss.	STAFFORD Richard	8° coll.		
1695	BRAMSTON William	4° ss.	BRIGHT George	8° coll.	BURNET Gilbert	4° ss.
	FALLE Philip	4° ss.	ISHAM Zach. DD.	4° ss.	MANNINGHAM Thomas	4° ss.
	MAPLETOFT John	4° ss.	PAYNE William	4° ss.	POWELL Jos. M.A.	4° ss.
	WHALEY Nathanael	8° coll.	GOODWIN Thomas	4° ss.	HOW John	4° ss.
1696	MEGGOT Richard	8° coll.	PATRICK Simon	4° ss.		
1697	BRAMSTON William	4° ss.	BURNET Gilbert	4° ss.	BURNET Gilbert	4° ss.
	GOODMAN John	8° coll.	HEYRICK Thomas	4° ss.	OWTRAM William	8° coll.
	PAYNE William	12° ss.	PRAT Samuel	4° ss.	WATTS Tho. M.A.	4° ss.
1698	CLARK Joshua	4° ss.	HOWARD John	4° ss.	HUTCHINSON Francis	4° ss.
	WHITFELD Will. DD.	4° ss.	BEVERLEY Thomas	4° ss.		
1699	LENG John	4° ss.	MARSTON Edward	4° ss.	SHERLOCK William	8° ss.
	CHARNOCK Stephen	8° coll.	SHOWER John	12° coll.		
1700	ELLISON Nath. DD.	8° ss.	GASKARTH John	4° ss.	HAYLEY William	4° ss.
	STRATFORD Nicholas	4° ss.				
1701	CORNWALL John	4° ss.	HOWARD John	4° ss.	MANNINGHAM Thomas	4° ss.
	MARSDEN Robert	4° ss.	MILLES Thomas	8° ss.	POMFRET Samuel	12° ss.
	STANHOPE George	4° ss.	STANHOPE George	4° coll.	STUBBS Philip	4° ss.
	STUBBS Philip	4° ss.	WILSON Thomas	8° coll.	POPE Michael	8° coll.
1702						

Year	Name	Size	Name	Size	Name	Size
	BINCKES William	4° ss.	BRAGGE Francis	8° coll.	BUTLER Lilly	4° ss.
	GIBSON Edmund	4° ss.	KENNET White	12° ss.	SPRAT Thomas	4° ss.
	STANHOPE George	4° ss.	STANHOPE George	4° coll.	STUBBS Philip	4° ss.
	STUBBS Philip	4° ss.	STUBBS Philip	4° ss.	TALBOT William	8° ss.
	WAKE William	8° coll.	WILLIS Richard	4° ss.	ROBINSON Benjamin	4° ss.
1703						
	LYNG William	4° ss.	NICOLSON William	4° ss.	STANHOPE George	4° ss.
	STANHOPE George	4° ss.				
1704						
	BRADFORD Samuel	4° ss.	BRAGGE Francis	8° coll.	BURNET Gilbert	4° ss.
	BURNET Gilbert	4° ss.	CLAGETT Nicholas	4° ss.	CLAGETT William	8° coll.
	CLAGETT William	8° coll.	DOBOURDIEU Jean Armand	4° ss.	ELSTOB Will. M.A.	4° ss.
	FINA Ferdinand	4° ss.	GALE Thomas	8° coll.	HOADLY John	4° ss.
	HOUGH Nathaniel	4° ss.	KENNET White	4° ss.	KENNET White	4° ss.
	LLOYD Robert Lumley	4° ss.	NORRIS Richard	4° ss.	OFFLEY William. M.A.	4° ss.
	SHERWILL Thomas	4° ss.	TRIMNEL Charles	4° ss.	WAKE Robert	4° ss.
	WHALEY Nathanael	12° coll.				
1705						
	BOWBER Thomas	4° ss.	HARRIS John	4° ss.	HOADLY Benjamin	4° ss.
	HOUGH John	4° ss.	HOUGH John	4° ss.	KENNET White	4° ss.
	KING William	4° ss.	LLOYD Robert Lumley	4° ss.	SHERLOCK William	-° ss.
	STANHOPE George	4° ss.	WAUGH John	4° ss.	WILLIS Richard	4° ss.
1706						
	BURNET Gilbert	4° ss.	HICHMAN Charles	8° coll.	KENNET White	8° ss.
	KNAGGS Thomas	4° ss.	STANHOPE George	4° ss.	TORRIANO Alexander	4° ss.
	WOTTON William	4° ss.	YOUNG Edward	8° coll.		
1707						
	BROUGHTON John	4° ss.	GRANT John	4° ss.	HUTCHINSON Francis	8° ss.
	HUTCHINSON Francis	8° ss.	MILLES Thomas	4° ss.	PATRICK Simon	12° ss.
	STILEMAN John	8° ss.	STILLINGFLEET Edward	fo.coll.	STRYPE John	4° ss.
	THEYER Charles	4° ss.	WILLIS Richard	4° ss.	DENT Giles	4° ss.
1708						
	BEVERIDGE William	8° ss.	BEVERIDGE William	8° ss.	BRAY Thomas	8° ss.
	HOADLY Benjamin	4° ss.	HOADLY John	4° ss.	KENNET White	8° ss.
	LAMBERT Ralph	4° ss.	MAYO Richard	4° ss.	MORER Thomas	8° coll.
	S. - - - - J.	12° ss.	STEPHENS Henry	4° ss.	WILLIAMS John	8° coll.
	DENT Giles	4° ss.				
1709						
	BROME Edmond	8° coll.	HOUGH John	4° ss.	KENNET White	8° ss.
	KING William	8° ss.	MANNINGHAM Thomas	4° ss.	PEAD Deuel	8° ss.
	PEAKE William	4° ss.	RENNELL Thomas	4° ss.	SMITH John	4° ss.
	TRIMNEL Charles	4° ss.	SHOWER John	8° ss.		
1710						
	BINCKES William	8° ss.	BISSE Philip	4° ss.	BURNET Gilbert	8° ss.
	CHANDLER Edward	8° ss.	CORNEWALL Fred. M.A.	8° ss.	FOX Francis	8° ss.
	GODDARD Thomas	4° ss.	GODDARD Thomas	8° ss.	JEFFERY John	8° coll.
	KENNET White	4° ss.	KENNET White	8° ss.	OAKELY Simon	8° ss.
	SPRAT Thomas	8° coll.	SYNGE Edward	8° ss.	TRIMNEL Charles	4° ss.
	WELTON Richard	4° ss.	WHITEAR William	4° ss.		
1711						
	BISSE Philip	4° ss.	BURSCOUGH William	8° ss.	CHAMBRE Richard	4° ss.
	CHISHULL Edmund	4° ss.	HOADLY Benjamin	8° coll.	JENNINGS John	8° ss.
	JENNINGS John	8° ss.	KENNET White	4° ss.	SAINT John Pawlet	4° ss.
	TENNISON Edward	4° ss.	TRIMNEL Charles	4° ss.	WEST Richard	4° ss.
	WRIGHT Samuel	8° ss.				
1712						

Year	Name	Format	Name	Format	Name	Format
	BRETT Thomas	8° coll.	FINCH Henry	4° ss.	HAYLEY Tho. DD.	8° ss.
	IBBETSON Richard	8° ss.	KENNET White	4° ss.	KENNET White	4° ss.
	LORRAIN Paul	8° ss.	SHUTTLEWOOD John	8° ss.	STUBBS Philip	4° ss.
	SYNGE Edward	8° ss.	TRIMNEL Charles	4° ss.	WHITAKER Thomas	8° coll.
	DENT Giles	8° ss.	HENRY Matthew	8° ss.	WRIGHT Samuel	8° ss.
1713	BRETT Thomas	8° coll.	BULL George	8° coll.	BURNET Gilbert	8° coll.
	GASKARTH John	4° ss.	MANNINGHAM Thomas	8° ss.	WAUGH John	4° ss.
1714	BISSE Thomas	4° ss.	BOULTER Hugh	4° ss.	BRETT Thomas	8° coll.
	BURNET Gilbert	4° ss.	BURNET Gilbert	8° ss.	RAMSAY John	4° ss.
	SMITH Elisha	8° ss.	STANHOPE George	4° ss.		
1715	BRETT Joseph	8° coll.				
1716	BARROW Isaac	fo. coll.	BISSE Thomas	8° ss.	LUCAS Richard	8° coll.
	WAKE William	8° coll.	WISHEART William	8° coll.		
1717	BISSE Philip	4° ss.	BISSE Thomas	8° ss.	LUCAS Richard	8° coll.
	SMALRIDGE George	8° coll.	SOUTH Robert	8° ss.		
1718	CHANDLER Edward	4° ss.	SCOTT John	fo. coll.		
1719	SHERLOCK William	8° coll.				
1720	BEVERIDGE William	fo. coll.	FIDDES Rich. DD.	fo. ss.	WHITBY Daniel	8° coll.
1721	WRIGHT Samuel	8° ss.				
1722	LUCAS Richard	8° coll.	WAKE William	8° coll.	WAUGH John	4° ss.
	DUNLOP William	8° coll.				
1723	BLACKALL Offspring	fo. coll.				
1724	READING Will. M.A.	8° coll.	SMALRIDGE George	fo. coll.	SOUTH Robert	8° coll.
1725	COLLIER Jeremy	8° coll.	WORTHINGTON John	8° coll.		
1726	CALAMY Benjamin	8° coll.	WILCOCKS Joseph	4° ss.		
1727	LENG John	4° ss.	REYNOLDS Richard	4° ss.	SOUTH Robert	8° coll.
	STOCKWELL Joseph	8° ss.				
1728	DELAUNE William	8° coll.	DOUGHTY Thomas	8° coll.	FIDDES Rich. DD.	fo. coll.
1729	LUPTON William	8° coll.				
1730	BRADY Nich. DD.	8° coll.	CLARKE Samuel	8° coll.	JORTIN John	12° coll.
1732	MOSS Robert	8° coll.				
1733	DAWES Sir William	8° coll.	MAULE Henry	4° ss.	FORD William, sen	8° ss.
1734	CLARKE Samuel	8° coll.				
1735	TILLOTSON John	fo. coll.				

Year	Author	Format	Author	Format	Author	Format
1736	RUNDLE Thomas	4° ss.				
1737	FLEETWOOD William	fo.coll.				
1738	MILES Henry	8° ss.				
1739	BENTLEY Richard	fo.coll.	STANHOPE George	fo.coll.	WILLIAMS John	fo.coll.
1743	ABERNETHY John	8° coll.				
1746	HARE Francis	8° coll.				
1748	ABERNETHY John	8° coll.				
1749	HEYLYN John	4° coll.	DAVIDSON Thomas	8° ss.		
1751	BERRIMAN William	8° coll.	JEFFERY John	8° coll.	ABERNETHY John	8° coll.
1752	RICHARDSON John	8° ss.				
1753	POTTER John	8° coll.	BOSTON Thomas	8° coll.	DUCHAL James	8° coll.
1754	BELLAMY Daniel	8° coll.	HOADLY Benjamin	8° coll.		
1755	JORTIN John	8° coll.				
1757	HOOPER George	fo.coll.				
1760	STERNE Lawrence	12° coll.				
1764	BROOKE Z. DD.	8° coll.	LAWSON John	8° coll.	ERSKINE Ralph	fo.coll.
1765	BREKELL John	8° coll.				
1766	SECKER William	8° coll.	STERNE Lawrence	12° coll.		
1767	ELSMERE Sloane	1° coll.	MAYHEW Jonathan	8° coll.		
1769	STERNE Lawrence	12° coll.	WORTHINGTON William	8° coll.		
1770	OGDEN Samuel	8° coll.				
1771	WHITFIELD George	8° coll.				
1772	DODD W. LLD.	12° coll.				
1776	BELLAMY Daniel	4° coll.	HALLIFAX Samuel	8° coll.		
1777	HURD Richard	8° coll.	ENFIELD William	12° coll.		
1780	GERARD Alex. DD.	8° coll.				
1790	TENISON Thomas	4° ss.				

Queen's College ("Queen's")

Year	Name	Format	Name	Format	Name	Format
----	LARDNER Nathaniel	-° ss.	MACKEWEN Robert	-° ss.		
1641	MASTER Thomas	-° ss.				
1660	BAXTER Richard	4° ss.				
1661	BROWNRIG Ralph	fo.coll.	HALL Joseph	fo.coll.		
1663	MASON Charles	4° ss.				
1664	CHILLINGWORTH William	fo.coll.				
1668	BURNET Gilbert	4° ss.	LINGARD Ric. DD.	4° ss.		
1669	MOULIN DU Peter	4° ss.				
1672	HASCARD Gregory	4° ss.	MEDE Joseph	fo.coll.	WARD Seth	8° coll.
1673	HALES John	4° coll.	JACKSON Thomas	fo.coll.	SMITH John	4° coll.
1674	JAMES Henry WARD Seth	4° ss. 8° coll.	LLOYD William	4° ss.	SALL Andrew	8° ss.
1675	HACKET John	fo.coll.	SMITH Thomas	4° ss.		
1676	HOLDEN Samuel	4° ss.	HOLDEN Samuel	4° ss.	PIGOTT Henry	4° ss.
1677	BRAMHALL John	fo.coll.	CRADOCK Zechary	4° ss.		
1678	JAMES John	4° ss.				
1679	HORTON Thomas NEEDHAM Robert	fo.coll. 8° coll.	LYNFORD Thomas NEVILLE Robert	4° ss. 4° ss.	MANNINGHAM Thomas	8° ss.
1680	LITTLETON Adam	fo.coll.	PARSONS Robert	4° ss.		
1681	MANNINGHAM Thomas	4° ss.	RESBURY Nathaniel	4° ss.	TENISON Thomas	4° ss.
1682	ALLEN John WILKINS John	4° ss. 8° coll.	BOLDE Samuel	4° ss.	CALAMY Benjamin	4° ss.
1683	BARNE Miles SMITH William	4° ss. 4° ss.	CALAMY Benjamin WILLES Samuel	4° ss. 4° ss.	HOPKINS William	4° ss.
1684	ALLESTREE Richard CALAMY Benjamin MANNINGHAM Thomas	fo.coll. 4° ss. 4° ss.	BRYAN Matt. LLD. CAMFIELD Benjamin WROE Christopher	4° ss. 4° ss. 4° ss.	BURTON Hezekiah HAMMOND Henry	8° coll. fo.coll.
1685	BURTON Hezekiah	8° coll.	ELLIS Clement	12° ss.	MANNINGHAM Thomas	4° ss.
1686	MANNINGHAM Thomas	4° ss.				
1687	HORNECK Anthony	8° ss.	MANNINGHAM Thomas	4° ss.		
1688	BROWNE Thomas	4° ss.	BROWNE Thomas	4° ss.		

Year	Name	Format	Name	Format	Name	Format
1689	BURNET Gilbert	4° ss.	SHERLOCK William	8° ss.		
1690	BURNET Gilbert	4° ss.	MAUNDRELL Henry	4° ss.		
1691	BLAGRAVE Jonathan	4° ss.	JANE Will. DD.	4° ss.	SHERLOCK William	8° ss.
1692	EDWARDS John	8° coll.				
1693	MARCH John	4° coll.	PRITCHARD Thomas	4° ss.	STUBBS Philip	4° ss.
1694	BURNET Gilbert	4° ss.	COMBER Thomas	4° ss.	MANSELL John	4° ss.
	MANSELL John	4° ss.	NORRIS John	8° coll.	SANCROFT William	8° coll.
1695	BURNET Gilbert	4° ss.	FISHER Joseph	4° ss.	GARDINER James	4° ss.
	GROVE Robert	4° ss.	ISHAM Zach. DD.	4° ss.	MAPLETOFT John	4° ss.
	TAYLOR Zachary	4° ss.	WHINCOP Thomas	4° ss.	WILLIAMS John	4° ss.
1696	BARTON Samuel	4° ss.	GREGORY Thomas	8° coll.	<u>CLARKSON</u> <u>David</u>	fo.coll.
1697	BOLDE Samuel	8° ss.	TRIMNEL Charles	4° ss.		
1698	WHICHCOTE Benj. DD.	8° coll.				
1699	BRAY Thomas	4° ss.	CONANT John	8° coll.	HAYLEY William	4° ss.
	LENG John	4° ss.	MARCH John	8° coll.	MARSTON Edward	4° ss.
	SHERLOCK William	8° ss.				
17--	TUNSTALL James	8° coll.				
1700	ASHETON William	4° ss.	BRADFORD Samuel	4° coll.	GASKARTH John	4° ss.
	GASKARTH John	4° ss.	HARE Francis	4° ss.	KNAGGS Thomas	4° ss.
	SHELLEY Peter	4° ss.	STANHOPE George	8° coll.		
1701	BISSE Philip	4° ss.	ISHAM Zach. DD.	4° ss.	JENNINGS John	4° ss.
	MANNINGHAM Thomas	4° ss.	MARSDEN Robert	4° ss.	MARSH Richard	4° ss.
	SHERLOCK William	4° ss.				
1702	BRAGGE Francis	8° coll.	BRAGGE Francis	8° coll.	NEEDHAM William	4° ss.
	NEWCOME Peter	8° coll.	SACHEVERELL Henry	4° ss.	TRELAWNEY Jonathan Sir	4° ss.
	WHICHCOTE Benj. DD.	8° coll.	WILLIS Richard	4° ss.		
1703	BUCK Maximilian	8° ss.	KENNET White	4° ss.	LAKE Edward	4° ss.
	RESBURY Nathaniel	4° ss.	WHICHCOTE Benj. DD.	8° coll.		
1704	BISSET Will.	8° ss.	BRAGGE Francis	8° coll.	BURNET Gilbert	4° ss.
	BURNET Gilbert	4° ss.	BUTLER Lilly	4° ss.	CLAGETT William	8° coll.
	CLAGETT William	8° coll.	COOKE Thomas	4° ss.	ELLIS Clement	8° coll.
	FOWLER Edward	4° ss.	GASTRELL Francis	4° ss.	LENG John	4° ss.
	PARKHURST Nathaniel	8° ss.	PARKHURST Nathaniel	8° ss.	SACHEVERELL Henry	4° ss.
	SAVAGE John	4° ss.	SAVAGE John	4° ss.	SHERLOCK William	4° ss.
	SHERWILL Thomas	4° ss.	SHERWILL Thomas	4° ss.	WILLIAMS John	4° ss.
	WILLIS Richard	4° ss.	WROE Christopher	4° ss.	WYNNE Robert	4° ss.
1705	ADAMS John	4° ss.	HARRIS John	4° ss.	HOUGH John	4° ss.
	KENNET White	4° ss.	POOLEY Giles	4° ss.	REEVES William	4° ss.

Year	Name	Size	Name	Size	Name	Size
	SHERLOCK William	-° ss.	STANHOPE George	4° ss.	TILLY William	4° ss.
	WAUGH John	4° ss.	WILLIS Richard	4° ss.		
1706	BRAMSTON William	4° ss.	BURNET Gilbert	4° ss.	BURNET Gilbert	4° ss.
	CRADOCK Zechary	4° ss.	HIGGINS Francis	4° ss.	KENNET White	4° ss.
	KENNET White	4° ss.	KENNET White	8° ss.	STANHOPE George	4° ss.
	STANHOPE George	4° ss.	THANE John	4° ss.	TORRIANO Alexander	4° ss.
	WILLIAMS John	4° ss.	WOTTON William	4° ss.		
1707	ADAMS John	4° ss.	ADAMS John	4° ss.	CHISHULL Edmund	4° ss.
	HOADLY John	4° ss.	KING James	4° ss.	KNAGGS Thomas	8° ss.
	NELSON Hen.	8° ss.	PERKINS Joseph	8° ss.	SAVAGE William	4° ss.
	TRIMNEL Charles	4° ss.	WHICHCOTE Benj. DD.	8° coll.	WILLIS Richard	4° ss.
1708	ADAMS John	4° ss.	BISSE Thomas	4° ss.	BRADFORD Samuel	4° ss.
	BRAY Thomas	8° ss.	CANNELL Joseph	4° ss.	DUNSTER Sam. DD.	8° ss.
	EYRE Robert	4° ss.	KNAGGS Thomas	8° ss.	LAMBERT Ralph	4° ss.
	LITTELL Tho. DD.	4° ss.	MANNINGHAM Thomas	6° ss.	MILNER William	8° ss.
	RAWSON Jos. DD.	4° ss.	RAWSON Jos. DD.	4° coll.	STEPHENS Henry	4° ss.
	TRIMNEL Charles	4° ss.	TRIMNEL Charles	8° ss.	WILLET John	4° ss.
	WILLIAMS John	8° coll.	FERNE Robert	8° ss.	HARRIS William	8° ss.
1709	BRAY Thomas	4° ss.	HARE Francis	4° ss.	KENNET White	8° ss.
	KING William	8° ss.	MANNINGHAM Thomas	4° ss.	PELLING John	4° ss.
	RAWSON Jos. DD.	4° ss.	RENNELL Thomas	4° ss.	ROBERTS William	4° ss.
	SACHEVERELL Henry	4° ss.	SHERWILL Thomas	8° ss.	STANHOPE George	8° ss.
	TRIMNEL Charles	8° ss.	TURNER John	8° ss.	WILCOCKS Joseph	4° ss.
	WILLIS Richard	8° ss.	STENNETT Joseph	8° ss.		
1710	ANONYMOUS	8° ss.	ARCHER Edmond	8° ss.	BINCKES William	8° ss.
	BRADFORD Samuel	8° ss.	CORNEWALL Fred. M.A.	8° ss.	HIGDEN Will. DD.	4° ss.
	HOPKINS Ezekiel	fo. coll.	JACKSON John	8° ss.	KELSAL Edward	8° ss.
	KENNET White	4° ss.	LUNN William	4° ss.	MASTER Thomas	-° ss.
	PUGH Hugh	8° ss.	RICHMOND Henry	8° coll.	SPRAT Thomas	8° coll.
	WEST Richard	8° ss.	WHALEY Nathanael	8° ss.	WRIGHT Samuel	8° ss.
1711	ANONYMOUS	8° ss.	BOWTELL John	8° ss.	CHISHULL Edmund	4° ss.
	FRIEND Robert	4° ss.	GOOCH Thomas Sir	4° ss.	HARE Francis	8° ss.
	HAYLEY Tho. DD.	4° ss.	JENNINGS John	8° ss.	KENNET White	4° ss.
	TENNISON Edward	4° ss.				
1712	ASH St. George	8° ss.	AYERST William	8° ss.	BRETT Thomas	8° coll.
	CHISHULL Edmund	1° ss.	CHISHULL Edmund	8° ss.	GARMSTON John	4° ss.
	HUMPHREYS Thomas	8° ss.	KENNET White	4° ss.	LYNFORD Thomas	4° ss.
	NEWTON Richard	4° ss.	POTTER John	8° ss.	REEVES William	4° ss.
	SMITH John	8° ss.	TILLY William	8° coll.	TRIMNEL Charles	4° ss.
	WILLOUGHBY Lord De Bro	4° ss.				
1713	BRADFORD Samuel	4° ss.	BRAMSTON William	4° ss.	BRETT Thomas	8° coll.
	BULL George	8° coll.	CLAYTON Thomas	4° ss.	COLEIRE Richard	4° ss.
	COWPER John	8° ss.	EDWARDS John	8° coll.	LAW William	8° ss.
	LENG John	4° ss.	MANNINGHAM Thomas	8° ss.	REEVES William	4° ss.
	SACHEVERELL Henry	4° ss.	SACHEVERELL Henry	4° ss.	WYVILL John	8° ss.
	CALAMY Edmund	8° ss.	REYNOLDS Thomas	8° ss.		
1714	ANONYMOUS	8° ss.	BLACKBURNE Lancelot.	4° ss.	BRAMSTON William	4° ss.

Year	Name	Format	Name	Format	Name	Format
	BRETT Thomas	8° coll.	BURNET Gilbert	4° ss.	BURNET Gilbert	4° ss.
	BURNET Gilbert	8° ss.	CHISHULL Edmund	4° ss.	CLAGETT Nicholas	4° ss.
	DUKE Rich. M.A.	8° coll.	FORSTER William	8° ss.	FORSTER William	8° ss.
	GASTRELL Francis	4° ss.	KENNET White	8° ss.	LOMBARD Daniel	8° ss.
	MARSHALL Nathaniel	8° ss.	ROBINSON John	4° ss.	RYE George	8° ss.
	SMEDLEY Jonathan	8° ss.	SMITH Elisha	8° ss.	SQUIRE Fran. M.A.	8° ss.
	STANHOPE George	4° ss.	WALLER John	4° ss.	BATES John	8° ss.
	CALAMY Edmund	8° ss.	HARRINGTON J.	8° ss.		
1715						
	AWBREY Timothy	4° ss.	BLENNERHAYSETT Thomas	8° ss.	BRETT Joseph	8° coll.
	BULL Michael	8° ss.	BURSCOUGH William	4° ss.	CARTER Nicholas	8° ss.
	DE LA ROSE John	8° ss.	EYRE Rich. M.A.	8° ss.	FORSTER Nicholas	8° ss.
	HOLE Matthew	8° coll.	KENNET Basil	8° coll.	KENNET White	4° ss.
	KENNET White	4° ss.	LENG John	4° ss.	LOVELL Edw. DD.	4° ss.
	LYNFORD Thomas	4° ss.	RYE George	4° ss.	SMEDLEY Jonathan	4° ss.
	SMITH Elisha	8° ss.	SYDALL Elias	4° ss.	SYDALL Elias	4° ss.
	TOPPING Henry	8° ss.	TRIMNEL Charles	4° ss.	TRIMNEL Charles	4° ss.
	WRIGHT John	4° ss.				
1716						
	BARROW Isaac	fo.coll.	BRADFORD Samuel	4° ss.	CHANDLER Edward	4° ss.
	CURTEIS Thomas	8° ss.	GIBSON Edmund	4° ss.	HARE Francis	8° ss.
	KNAGGS Thomas	8° ss.	LENG John	4° ss.	LUCAS Richard	8° coll.
	MYNORS Willoughby	8° ss.	NEEDHAM Peter	8° ss.	PEARSE Robert	8° ss.
	SMEDLEY Jonathan	4° ss.	SMEDLEY Jonathan	8° ss.	SYDALL Elias	8° ss.
	WATERLAND Daniel	8° ss.	WEST Richard	4° ss.	WILLIS Richard	4° ss.
	EVANS John	8° ss.				
1717						
	BENTLEY Richard	4° ss.	BISSE Philip	4° ss.	HIND Thomas	8° ss.
	HOADLY John	8° ss.	LAUGHTON Richard	4° ss.	LENG John	8° coll.
	MANGEY Thomas	8° coll.	STANHOPE Michael	4° ss.	STEPHENS William	8° ss.
	SYKES Arthur Ashley	8° ss.	HUNT Jerem. DD.	8° ss.		
1718						
	BRADFORD Samuel	8° ss.	CHANDLER Edward	4° ss.	CHANDLER Edward	8° ss.
	CLAGETT Nicholas	4° ss.	COLBATCH John	4° ss.	CROSSINGE Richard	8° ss.
	SCOTT John	fo.coll.	WHITFIELD John	8° ss.		
1719						
	BRADFORD Samuel	4° ss.	BRADFORD Samuel	4° ss.	HARE Francis	4° ss.
	HORROBIN Robert	8° ss.	JACOMB Willium	8° ss.	MANGEY Thomas	4° ss.
	MANGEY Thomas	4° ss.	MANGEY Thomas	8° ss.	MARSHALL Nathaniel	8° ss.
	SMEDLEY Jonathan	8° coll.	STEPHENS William	8° ss.		
1720						
	ANONYMOUS	8° ss.	BRADFORD Samuel	4° ss.	MANGEY Thomas	4° ss.
	SMALBROKE Richard	8° ss.	WATERLAND Daniel	8° coll.	WHITBY Daniel	8° coll.
	SMYTH George	8° ss.				
1721						
	MEADOWCOURT Richard	8° ss.	PATERSON James	8° ss.	REYNOLDS Richard	4° ss.
	STURGES John	4° ss.	WADDINGTON Edward	8° ss.	WATERLAND Daniel	8° ss.
	NEALE Daniel	8° ss.				
1722						
	BERRIMAN William	4° ss.	BOWERS Thomas	8° ss.	BURSCOUGH William	4° ss.
	CONYBEARE John	8° ss.	HARRIS Daniel	8° ss.	MASSEY Edmund	8° ss.
	MEADOWCOURT Richard	8° ss.	PARNE Thomas	8° ss.	SMALBROKE Richard	8° ss.
	STEPHENS William	8° ss.	SYKES Arthur Ashley	8° ss.	TEMPLE A. M.A.	8° ss.
	WAUGH John	4° ss.	WHITFIELD John	8° ss.	WILKINS David	4° ss.
	WOTTON William	8° ss.	NEALE Daniel	8° ss.	NEWMAN John	8° ss.
	REYNOLDS Thomas	8° ss.				

Year	Name	Format	Name	Format	Name	Format
1723	BULL Rob.	8° ss.	BULLOCK Thomas	4° ss.	COLEIRE Richard	8° ss.
	CONYBEARE John	8° ss.	DENNE John	4° ss.	GIBSON Edmund	4° ss.
	GURDON Brampton	4° ss.	HARE Francis	4° ss.	LISLE Samuel	4° ss.
	MEADOWCOURT Richard	4° ss.	SHUCKFORD Samuel	4° ss.	HUNT Jerem. DD.	8° ss.
	WRIGHT Samuel	8° ss.				
1724	ARROWSMITH Edward	4° ss.	BOTT Thomas	8° ss.	BRADFORD Samuel	8° ss.
	BRAMSTON John	8° ss.	BULLOCK Thomas	8° ss.	CHANDLER Edward	4° ss.
	CROXALL Sam. DD.	4° ss.	DOUGHTY Gregory	4° ss.	DRAKE Samuel	4° ss.
	EDGLEY Samuel	4° ss.	LAVINGTON George	8° ss.	MANNINGHAM Thomas	4° ss.
	MEADOWCOURT Richard	8° ss.	NEWCOME John	8° ss.	PARNE Thomas	4° ss.
	PAUL William	4° ss.	REYNELL Carew	4° ss.	SHUCKFORD Samuel	4° ss.
	STEPHENS William	8° ss.	WHITFIELD John	8° ss.	WYNNE John	4° ss.
1725	BERRIMAN William	8° coll.	BISSE Thomas	8° ss.	BURNET Gilbert	8° ss.
	DENNE John	4° ss.	FELTON Henry	8° ss.	HARRIS John	4° ss.
	KNIGHT Samuel	8° ss.	MASSEY Edmund	8° ss.	MASSEY Edmund	8° ss.
	SYKES Arthur Ashley	4° ss.	RIDGLEY Thomas	8° ss.		
1726	BAKER William	4° ss.	BERRIMAN William	4° ss.	BISHOP Thomas	8° coll.
	BRAGGE Francis	8° coll.	BURNETT Tho. DD.	8° ss.	CALAMY Benjamin	8° coll.
	CONYBEARE John	8° ss.	DENNE John	4° ss.	GREENE Thomas	8° ss.
	INNES Alexander	4° ss.	LAVINGTON George	-° ss.	MANGEY Thomas	8° ss.
	MEADOWCOURT Richard	8° ss.	OLIVER Edward	4° ss.	SMALBROKE Richard	4° ss.
	STEPHENS Lewis	4° ss.	WHITBY Daniel	8° coll.	WYNNE John	8° ss.
	NEALE Daniel	8° ss.				
1727	BISSE Thomas	8° ss.	BISSET Will.	8° ss.	CONYBEARE John	8° ss.
	DERHAM Will. DD.	8° ss.	EGERTON Henry	4° ss.	GARMSTON John	8° ss.
	HENLEY John	8° ss.	HOLBROOK Anthony	8° ss.	HOLBROOK Anthony	8° ss.
	LENG John	4° ss.	PEARCE Zachary	4° ss.	ROGERS John	8° coll.
	SMALBROKE Richard	8° ss.	TILLY William	4° ss.	TRIMNELL William	4° ss.
	WATSON Joseph	4° ss.	WHITBY Daniel	8° coll.	NEALE Daniel	8° ss.
1728	BULLOCK Thomas	8° ss.	HEYLYN John	8° ss.	LEEKE Robert	8° ss.
	MAURICE Peter	8° ss.	NEWCOME Richard	8° ss.	NORRIS John	8° coll.
	SMALBROKE Richard	4° ss.	WHARTON Henry	8° coll.	WHARTON Henry	8° coll.
	WHITBY Daniel	8° coll.	YOUNG Edward	4° ss.	CHOPPIN R.	fo. ss.
	EVANS John	8° ss.	HARRISON Thomas	8° ss.	PEIRCE James	1° coll.
	TREN John	8° ss.				
1729	BETTY Joseph	8° ss.	BISSE Thomas	8° ss.	CARTER Benjamin	8° coll.
	CONYBEARE John	8° ss.	DENNE John	4° ss.	EGERTON Henry	4° ss.
	GIBSON Edmund	8° coll.	HENLEY John	8° ss.	HUDDLESTON Will.	8° ss.
	JAMES William	8° ss.	KNIGHT Samuel	8° ss.	LEEKE Robert	8° ss.
	LEWIS George	8° ss.	MANGEY Thomas	8° ss.	MARSHALL Nathaniel	8° ss.
	RICHARDSON Thomas	8° ss.	SHERMAN T.	8° ss.	STEBBING Henry	8° ss.
	THOMAS John	4° ss.	TRAPP Joseph	4° ss.	WADDINGTON Edward	4° ss.
	WADE George. DD.	8° coll.	YOUNG Edward	8° ss.	EARL Jabez	8° ss.
	FROST Richard	8° ss.	GUYSE John	8° ss.	HARRIS William	8° ss.
	WOOD James	8° ss.				
1730	BOTT Thomas	8° ss.	BRADY Nich. DD.	8° coll.	CROXALL Sam. DD.	8° ss.
	DENNE John	4° ss.	DENNE John	4° ss.	DERHAM Will. DD.	8° ss.
	HARE Francis	4° ss.	JORTIN John	12° coll.	LITTLETON Edward	4° ss.

Year	Name	Format	Name	Format	Name	Format
	MIDDLETON John	4° ss.	NICOLS John	8° ss.	PEARCE Zachary	4° ss.
	ROBINSON Thomas	8° ss.	ROGERS John	8° coll.	STEBBING Henry	8° ss.
	TRAPP Joseph	4° ss.	TRAPP Joseph	8° ss.	GUYSE John	8° ss.
	HUGHES Obadiah	8° ss.				
1731						
	ANDREW Tho	8° ss.	ANONYMOUS	8° ss.	BOWMAN William	8° ss.
	CLARKE Alured	4° ss.	CURTEIS Thomas	4° ss.	HARE Francis	4° ss.
	KNIGHT Samuel	8° ss.	READING Will. M.A.	8° ss.	WATSON Joseph	8° ss.
	BURROUGHS Joseph	8° ss.	CLEGG James	8° ss.	NATION William	8° ss.
1732						
	BERKELEY George	4° ss.	BROOKE Thomas	8° ss.	GORDON	8° ss.
	SMALBROKE Richard	4° ss.	STEBBING Henry	8° ss.	ATKEY Anthony	8° ss.
	FOSTER James	8° ss.	FOSTER James	8° coll.	MAYO Daniel	8° ss.
	WILLS Benjamin	8° ss.				
1733						
	COCKMAN Thomas	8° ss.	CONYBEARE John	8° ss.	DENNE John	4° ss.
	GOUGH Strickland.	4° ss.	MANGEY Thomas	4° ss.	MAULE Henry	4° ss.
	MONOUX Lewis	8° ss.	MOODY Samuel	4° ss.	PILKINGTON Matthew	4° ss.
	SCURLOCK David	8° ss.	STEBBING Henry	4° ss.	TENNISON Edward	4° ss.
	TREBECK Andr. DD.	8° ss.	BURROUGHS James	8° coll.	PARTINGTON John	8° ss.
1734						
	BATE James	4° ss.	MACRO Thomas	8° ss.	MADDOX Isaac	4° ss.
	RUNDLE Thomas	4° ss.	SILVESTER Tipping	4° ss.	BENSON George	8° ss.
	FANCOURT Samuel	8° ss.	MACKEWEN Robert	8° ss.		
1735						
	ANONYMOUS	-° coll.	BARTON Philip	4° ss.	DREW Robert	8° ss.
	HALES Stephen	4° ss.	HARE Francis	4° ss.	KERRICK Samuel	8° ss.
	LAVINGTON George	4° ss.	LISLE Samuel	4° ss.	LYNCH John	4° ss.
	PATTEN Thomas	8° ss.	PEARCE Zachary	4° ss.	ROGERS John	8° coll.
	RUNDLE Thomas	4° ss.	SHARP John	8° coll.	STILLINGFLEET Edward	8° ss.
	TILLOTSON John	fo.coll.				
1736						
	BENSON Martin	4° ss.	CLAGETT Nicholas	4° ss.	CLAGETT Nicholas	4° ss.
	CLARKE Alured	4° ss.	GREY Richard	8° ss.	KNIGHT James	8° ss.
	MADDOX Isaac	4° ss.	NEWTON Benjamin	8° coll.	ROGERS John	8° coll.
	STACKHOUSE Thomas	8° ss.	WATTS George	4° ss.	SAY Samuel	8° ss.
	SOME David	8° ss.				
1737						
	ARROWSMITH Edward	4° ss.	BERRIMAN William	8° ss.	CROWE William	4° ss.
	DENNE John	4° ss.	FLEETWOOD William	fo.coll.	HARTE Walter	8° ss.
	ROPER Joseph. DD.	4° ss.	SHUCKFORD Samuel	4° ss.	TILLY William	-° coll.
	WARREN Robert	4° ss.	WEBSTER William	8° ss.	FOSTER James	8° coll.
	PEIRCE James	4° coll.				
1738						
	BATEMAN Edmund	4° ss.	BEARCROFT Philip	4° ss.	BEDFORD Arthur	8° ss.
	BENSON Martin	4° ss.	CARTER Nicholas	8° coll.	CONYBEARE John	4° ss.
	DELANY Patrick	8° ss.	DENNE John	4° ss.	FYSH Henry	8° ss.
	HOWARD Robert	4° ss.	HUTCHINSON Thomas	8° ss.	MARTEN Edmond	8° ss.
	ROGERS John	8° coll.	SIMPSON Will. DD.	8° ss.	STRONG James	8° ss.
	WARBURTON William	8° ss.	WEBSTER William	8° ss.	WILLIAMS Philip	4° ss.
	CHANDLER Samuel	8° ss.				
1739						
	ALLEN Fifield	4° ss.	BANYER Edward	4° ss.	BERRIMAN William	4° ss.
	CHAPMAN John	4° ss.	CLAGETT Nicholas	4° ss.	COPPING John	4° ss.
	GURDON Brampton	8° coll.	GURDON Brampton	fo.coll.	HANCOCK John	fo. ss.
	HARRIS John	fo.coll.	LENG John	fo.coll.	WESTON William	8° ss.

Year	Name	Format	Name	Format	Name	Format
	WILCOCKS Joseph	4° ss.	WILLIAMS John	fo.coll.	SCOTT Thomas	8° ss.
1740	ALLEN John	4° ss.	BARTON Philip	4° ss.	BATEMAN Edmund	4° ss.
	BENSON Martin	4° ss.	BUNDY Richard	8° coll.	CLAYTON Robert	4° ss.
	CROWE William	4° ss.	GARNET John	4° ss.	GOOCH Thomas Sir	4° ss.
	HUTCHINSON Thomas	8° ss.	MAWSON Matthias	4° ss.	MEADOWCOURT Richard	8° ss.
	NEWTON Richard	8° ss.	PARKER Robert	4° ss.	VENN Richard	8° coll.
	WATERLAND Daniel	8° ss.	WHALLEY John	4° ss.	STENNETT Joseph	8° ss.
1741	BERRIMAN William	8° ss.	CLARKE Alured	4° ss.	CLARKE Reuben	4° ss.
	CROXALL Sam. DD.	8° ss.	GOODALL Henry	4° ss.	HUTTON Matthew	4° ss.
	MADDOX Isaac	4° ss.	MAWSON Matthias	4° ss.	NICHOLL John	8° ss.
	PEARCE Zachary	4° ss.	SPRY John	8° ss.	SYMONDS Edward	8° ss.
	BARKER John	8° ss.	FOSTER James	8° ss.	GROVE Henry	8° coll.
	LEECHMAN William	8° ss.	WRIGHT Samuel	8° coll.		
1742	BERRIMAN William	4° ss.	BERRIMAN William	4° ss.	BEST William	4° ss.
	CLAGETT Nicholas	4° ss.	JEPHSON Alexander	8° ss.	MADDOX Isaac	4° ss.
	MORELL Thomas	8° ss.	PEGGE Samuel	8° ss.	POWELL William	8° ss.
	RIDLEY Glocester	8° coll.	RIDLEY Glocester	8° coll.	STEBBING Henry	4° ss.
	STONE George	4° ss.	WARBURTON William	8° ss.	WATERLAND Daniel	8° coll.
	WEBSTER William	8° ss.	DODDRIDGE Philip	8° ss.	EMLYN Thomas	8° coll.
	GROVE Henry	8° coll.	JENNINGS David	8° ss.	STENNETT Joseph	8° ss.
1743	BATEMAN Edmund	4° ss.	BEARCROFT Philip	4° ss.	EDEN Robert	4° ss.
	EDWARDS Joseph	8° ss.	GIBSON Edmund	8° ss.	LAW Edmund	8° ss.
	MADDOX Isaac	4° ss.	MAWSON Matthias	4° ss.	PEARCE Zachary	4° ss.
	PIERS Henry	8° ss.	SLEECH John	4° ss.	STACKHOUSE Thomas	fo. ss.
	THOMAS John	4° ss.	TRAPP Joseph	4° ss.	DODDRIDGE Philip	8° ss.
	DODDRIDGE Philip	8° coll.	GUYSE John	8° ss.	JENNINGS David	8° ss.
	LATHAM Ebenezer	8° ss.	LEECHMAN William	8° ss.	MORRIS Joseph	8° coll.
	STEFFE Thomas	12° coll.				
1744	BENTHAM Edward	8° ss.	CROWE William	8° coll.	DELANY Patrick	4° ss.
	DENNE John	4° ss.	MADDOX Isaac	4° ss.	NEWCOME John	4° ss.
	PARNE Thomas	8° ss.	SIMPSON Bolton	4° ss.	WILLATTS Charles	4° ss.
	FOSTER James	8° coll.				
1745	BEARCROFT Philip	4° ss.	DENNE John	4° ss.	DENNE John	8° ss.
	DOWNES John	4° ss.	FLETCHER Thomas	4° ss.	GARNET John	4° ss.
	GILBERT John	4° ss.	HOLME Thomas	8° ss.	HORBERY Matt. DD.	8° ss.
	HUTTON Matthew	4° ss.	LISLE Samuel	4° ss.	SQUIRE Samuel	4° ss.
	STEBBING Henry	4° ss.	THOMAS John	4° ss.	TREVOR Richard	4° ss.
	WEBSTER William	8° coll.	LATHAM Ebenezer	8° ss.	PRINCE Tho. M.A.	8° ss.
	SMYTH George	8° ss.				
1746	BALLARD Edward	4° ss.	BATEMAN Wynne	4° ss.	BEST William	8° ss.
	FORSTER Nathaniel	8° ss.	HARVEST George	4° ss.	HAYTER Thomas	4° ss.
	HILDROP John	8° ss.	HUTTON Matthew	4° ss.	LAVINGTON George	4° ss.
	LEIGHTON Robert	8° coll.	MADDOX Isaac	4° ss.	MAWSON Matthias	4° ss.
	PARKER William	8° ss.	RIDLEY Glocester	4° ss.	RUTHERFORTH Thomas	4° ss.
	SYKES Arthur Ashley	4° ss.	TUNSTALL James	4° ss.	WILLIAMS Philip	8° ss.
	GROVE Henry	1° coll.	LATHAM Ebenezer	8° ss.		
1747	BISHOP Hawley	8° ss.	DELANY Patrick	8° coll.	HORBERY Matt. DD.	8° ss.
	KENNICOTT Benjamin	8° ss.	KENNICOTT Benjamin	8° ss.	LAVINGTON George	4° ss.

Year	Name	Size	Name	Size	Name	Size
	NEVE Timothy	8° ss.	KNIGHT Henry	8° coll.	PRINCE Tho. M.A.	8° ss.
	PRINCE Tho. M.A.	8° ss.				
1748	CHAPMAN John	4° ss.	HORT Rob. M.A.	8° ss.	MUDGE Zechary	4° ss.
	PARKER William	8° ss.	POWELL Matthew	8° ss.	WARBURTON William	-° ss.
	ABERNETHY John	8° coll.	AMORY Thomas	8° coll.	BENSON George	8° ss.
	BENSON George	8° coll.	CHANDLER Samuel	4° ss.	LARDNER Nathaniel	8° coll.
	STENNETT Joseph	8° ss.				
1749	BRINGHURST J. M.A.	4° ss.	BUTLER Joseph	8° coll.	CONYBEARE John	8° ss.
	ELLYS Anthony	4° ss.	GEORGE William	4° ss.	GREEN John	4° ss.
	HEYLYN John	4° coll.	HORBERY Matt. DD.	8° ss.	KENNICOTT Benjamin	8° ss.
	MADDOX Isaac	4° ss.	ORR John	8° coll.	PEARCE Zachary	4° ss.
	TAYLOR John	4° ss.	TUCKER Josiah	8° coll.	WHATLEY Robert	4° ss.
	CHANDLER Samuel	8° ss.	MILNER John	8° ss.		
1750	ANONYMOUS	8° ss.	BALGUY John	8° coll.	BARTON Philip	4° ss.
	BENTHAM Edward	8° ss.	BUNDY Richard	8° coll.	COOKE Will. DD.	8° ss.
	DOWNES Robert	4° ss.	HAYTER Thomas	4° ss.	HUBBARD Henry	4° ss.
	KNOWLES Thomas	8° coll.	MADDOX Isaac	4° ss.	RIDLEY Glocester	4° ss.
	YARDLEY Edward	4° ss.	HOLLAND John	8° ss.	MASON John	8° ss.
1751	ALLEN Fifield	4° ss.	CHURCH Tho. DD.	4° ss.	CORNWALLIS Frederick	4° ss.
	EVANS John	8° ss.	GOODALL Henry	4° ss.	GOUGH Strickland.	8° coll.
	HALES Stephen	4° ss.	JEFFERY John	8° coll.	MICKLEBOURGH John	8° ss.
	RUTHERFORTH Thomas	4° ss.	SMITH William	8° ss.	TOTTIE John	8° ss.
	WEBSTER William	8° ss.	ABERNETHY John	8° coll.	ABERNETHY John	8° coll.
	LARDNER Nathaniel	8° coll.				
1752	BROUGHTON Thomas	4° ss.	CONYBEARE John	4° ss.	COSTARD George	8° coll.
	DODWELL William	8° ss.	GREEN John	4° ss.	GREY Richard	4° ss.
	HAYTER Thomas	4° ss.	HURD Richard	4° ss.	MADDOX Isaac	4° ss.
	MARKHAM William	4° ss.	SHUCKFORD Samuel	8° ss.	SMITH William	8° ss.
	TRAPP Joseph	8° coll.	WILLIAM George	4° ss.	BULKELEY Charles	8° coll.
	CHANDLER Samuel	8° ss.	DAYE James	4° ss.	ORTON Job	8° ss.
1753	BLACKBURNE Francis	8° ss.	BLACKBURNE Francis	8° ss.	BUTLER John	4° ss.
	CRESSET Edward	8° ss.	DRUMMOND Robert	4° ss.	ELWORTHY John	8° ss.
	JENNER Char. DD.	4° ss.	JOHNSON James	4° ss.	KEENE Edmund	4° ss.
	KENNICOTT Benjamin	8° ss.	MADDOX Isaac	4° ss.	SMITH William	8° ss.
	AMORY Thomas	8° coll.	BULKELEY Charles	8° ss.	CHANDLER Samuel	8° ss.
	STENNETT Samuel	8° ss.				
1754	ELLYS Anthony	4° ss.	HOADLY Benjamin	8° coll.	PLUMPTREE Charles	4° ss.
	WEBSTER William	8° ss.	BLYTH S.	8° ss.		
1755	HAYTER Thomas	4° ss.	HAYTER Thomas	4° ss.	KEENE Edmund	4° ss.
	PILKINGTON Matthew	8° ss.	ROBERTSON Will. DD.	8° ss.	SALTER Samuel	4° ss.
	SHARP Gregory	8° ss.	TAOALBOB	8° ss.	BENSON George	8° ss.
	BURROUGHS Joseph	8° ss.	CONDER John	8° ss.	FURNEAUX Philip	8° ss.
	MILNER John	8° ss.				
1756	GODDARD Peter Stephen	8° ss.	HALL Charles	4° ss.	HEATHCOTE Ralph	8° ss.
	KIDGELL John	8° ss.	LAVINGTON George	8° ss.	NICOLLS Samuel	4° ss.
	PENNINGTON John	8° ss.	PENNINGTON John	8° ss.	ROSS John	4° ss.
	SEWARD Thomas	8° ss.	STEBBING Hen. DD. jun.	8° ss.	WEBSTER William	8° ss.

INDEXES TO FIFTH VOLUME: E: LIBRARIES: PART TWO: CAMBRIDGE (Queen's)

Year						
	BULKELEY Charles	8° ss.	BULKELEY Charles	8° ss.	ERSKINE John	8° ss.
	KIMBER Isaac	8° coll.	MASON John	8° ss.	MILNER John	8° ss.
1757						
	CONYBEARE John	8° coll.	GRIFFITH Thomas	8° ss.	KEENE Edmund	4° ss.
	KENNICOTT Benjamin	8° ss.	LOWTH Robert	4° ss.	RIDLEY Glocester	4° ss.
	TAYLOR John	4° ss.				
1758						
	BACKHOUSE James	4° ss.	DODWELL William	4° ss.	HUSSEY Christopher	8° coll.
	KEDDINGTON R. DD.	8° ss.	LOWTH Robert	4° ss.	OGDEN Samuel	4° ss.
	OGDEN Samuel	4° ss.	STOPFORD James	4° ss.	TERRICK Richard	4° ss.
	THOMAS John	4° ss.	VENN H. M.A.	4° ss.	WEBBER Francis. DD.	4° ss.
	BENSON George	8° ss.	DICK Robert	8° ss.	LEECHMAN William	12° ss.
	PICKARD Edward	8° ss.	TOWGOOD Micaiah	8° ss.		
1759						
	ANONYMOUS	8° ss.	BUCKLER Benjamin	4° ss.	BURTON John	8° coll.
	DAWSON Benj. LL.D.	4° ss.	FLETCHER Philip	4° ss.	GODDARD Peter Stephen	8° ss.
	GREEN John	4° ss.	HAYTER Thomas	4° ss.	IBBETSON James	4° ss.
	NEVE Timothy	8° ss.	PATTEN Thomas	8° ss.	ROSS John	4° ss.
	STEBBING Hen. DD. jun.	8° coll.	ASHWORTH Caleb	8° ss.	BULKELEY Charles	8° ss.
	CHANDLER Samuel	8° ss.	CHANDLER Samuel	8° ss.	FLEMING Caleb	8° ss.
	GERARD Alex. DD.	8° ss.	MAYHEW Jonathan	8° ss.		
1760						
	COURTAIL John	4° ss.	CUMING Patrick	8° ss.	DODWELL William	8° ss.
	GRIFFITH Thomas	8° ss.	PEARCE Zachary	4° ss.	PEARCE Zachary	4° ss.
	SQUIRE Samuel	4° ss.	STEBBING Hen. DD. jun.	4° ss.	STERNE Lawrence	12° coll.
	BOURN Samuel	8° coll.	CHANDLER Samuel	8° ss.	CHANDLER Samuel	8° ss.
	FLEMING Caleb	8° ss.				
1761						
	ALLEN John	8° ss.	DRUMMOND Robert	4° ss.	FRIEND William	4° ss.
	GREENWOOD William	8° ss.	PORTEUS Beilby	8° ss.	ROTHERAM John	8° ss.
	YONGE Philip	4° ss.	GIBBONS Thomas	8° ss.	GIBSON John	8° ss.
	HARWOOD Edward	8° ss.	NOBLE Daniel	8° ss.		
1762						
	BARTON Henry	4° ss.	NICOLLS Samuel	4° ss.	ROTHERAM John	8° ss.
	SALTER Samuel	4° ss.	STAINSBY Richard	8° ss.	ARMAND James	8° ss.
	DUCHAL James	8° coll.	MAULDEN J.	8° ss.	PICKARD Edward	8° ss.
	SAVAGE Morton Samuel	8° ss.				
1763						
	BACKHOUSE William	4° ss.	BUTLER John	4° ss.	DELANY Patrick	4° ss.
	EGERTON John	4° ss.	GREEN John	4° ss.	GREEN John	4° ss.
	GRIFFITH Thomas	8° ss.	HEATHCOTE Ralph	4° ss.	HERRING Thomas	8° coll.
	LORT Michael	4° ss.	ROTHERAM John	8° ss.	BOURN Samuel	8° coll.
	FURNEAUX Philip	8° ss.	HODGE John	8° ss.		
1764						
	BURTON John	8° coll.	LOWTH Robert	4° ss.	NEWTON Thomas	4° ss.
	RICHARDSON William	4° ss.	BOURN Samuel	8° coll.	DUCHAL James	8° coll.
	DUCHAL James	8° coll.	LANGFORD William	8° ss.	PRIESTLEY Joseph	8° ss.
1765						
	DAWSON Benj. LL.D.	8° coll.	KENNICOTT Benjamin	8° ss.	OWEN E.	8° ss.
	RUTHERFORTH Thomas	4° ss.	SHARP Gregory	8° ss.	YONGE Philip	4° ss.
1766						
	BARTON Phi. B.D.	4° ss.	BURTON John	8° ss.	BURTON John	8° coll.
	KEELING Barthol. M.A.	8° ss.	ROTHERAM John	8° ss.	SECKER William	8° coll.
	SHARP Gregory	8° ss.	STERNE Lawrence	12° coll.	WARBURTON William	4° ss.
	AMORY Thomas	8° ss.	AMORY Thomas	8° coll.	OSWALD James	8° ss.
	PRICE Richard	8° ss.	WELD Isaac	8° ss.		

Year	Name	Size	Name	Size	Name	Size
1767						
	BREKELL John	8° ss.	DODD W. LLD.	8° ss.	EWER John	4° ss.
	FORSTER Nathaniel	8° ss.	GORDON John	4° ss.	PORTEUS Beilby	4° ss.
	PORTEUS Beilby	4° ss.	FORDYCE James	12° coll.	MAYHEW Jonathan	8° ss.
1768						
	GREEN John	4° ss.	LAW Edmund	8° ss.	MARTYN Thomas	4° ss.
	RANDOLPH Thomas	8° ss.	SUMNER Robert	8° ss.	LEECHMAN William	12° ss.
1769						
	BALGUY Thomas	4° ss.	GODDARD Peter Stephen	4° ss.	HALLIFAX Samuel	4° ss.
	HALLIFAX Samuel	4° ss.	LORT Michael	4° ss.	NEWTON Thomas	4° ss.
	SCOTT James	4° ss.	STEBBING Hen. DD. jun.	8° ss.	STERNE Lawrence	12° coll.
	STINTON George	4° ss.	STINTON George	4° ss.	WATSON Richard	4° ss.
	CHANDLER Samuel	8° coll.	FURNEAUX Philip	8° ss.	KIPPIS Andrew	8° ss.
	LELAND Thomas	8° coll.				
1770						
	KEPPEL Frederick	4° ss.	OGDEN Samuel	8° coll.	PECKARD Peter	8° ss.
	SECKER William	8° coll.	SHIPLEY Jonathan	4° ss.	SMITH Haddon	8° ss.
	VENN H. M.A.	8° ss.	ASHWORTH Caleb	8° ss.	ENFIELD William	8° ss.
1771						
	FRANCIS	12° coll.	PYLE Tho. M.A.	1° coll.	SECKER William	8° coll.
	SECKER William	8° coll.	CAMPBELL George	8° ss.	FLEMING Caleb	8° ss.
	FLEMING Caleb	8° ss.	FLEMING Caleb	8° ss.	GRAHAM W. M.A.	8° ss.
	ORTON Job	12° coll.	STENNETT Samuel	-° ss.	TOULMIN Joshua	8° ss.
1772						
	ADAM Thomas	8° ss.	GODDARD Thomas	8° ss.	HALLIFAX Samuel	8° ss.
	HAMILTON Hugh	4° ss.	SHARP Gregory	8° coll.	SHERLOCK Thomas	8° coll.
	TEMPLE A. M.A.	8° ss.	FLEMING Caleb	8° ss.	FLEMING Caleb	8° coll.
	GIBBONS Thomas	8° ss.				
1773						
	ALLEN John	8° ss.	BURROUGH Henry	8° coll.	EDWARDS Thomas	8° ss.
	GRIFFITH Thomas	8° ss.	HEY John	8° ss.	JEBB John	8° ss.
	LANGHORNE John	12° coll.	OWEN Hen. DD.	8° coll.	RYMER Thomas	4° ss.
	SALISBURY William	8° ss.	WHELDON John	8° ss.	WILLIAMS David	12° ss.
1774						
	HEY John	8° ss.	HEY John	8° ss.	JORTIN John	8° coll.
	FLEXMAN R. DD	8° ss.	LATHAM Ebenezer	8° coll.		
1775						
	BLAYNEY Benjamin	4° ss.	MARRIOTT George	8° ss.	MARRIOTT George	8° coll.
	PECKARD Peter	8° ss.	ROBERTSON Will. DD.	12° ss.	AMORY Thomas	8° coll.
	PALMER Samuel	8° ss.	WOOD William	12° coll.		
1776						
	HALLIFAX Samuel	8° coll.	HENLEY S.	4° ss.	POWELL William Samuel	8° coll.
	TUCKER Josiah	8° coll.	HARWOOD Edward	12° coll.		
1777						
	CRAVEN William	8° coll.	HURD Richard	8° coll.	RANDOLPH Thomas	8° ss.
1779						
	BONAR John	12° coll.	LEECHMAN William	-° ss.		

St. John's College ("St.John's")

Year	Name	Size	Name	Size	Name	Size
1610						
	STAYNOE Thomas	4° ss.				
1624						
	LUSHINGTON Thomas	12° ss.				
1660						
	BARWICK John	4° ss.	HACKET John	4° ss.	HODGES Thomas	4° ss.
	SHELDON Gilbert	4° ss.	SPENCER John	4° ss.	SUDBURY John	4° ss.

Year	Name	Format	Name	Format	Name	Format
	POOL Matthew	4° ss.				
1661	KING Henry	4° ss.	MORLEY George	4° ss.	STRODE William	4° ss.
1662	LANEY Benjamin	4° ss.				
1663	LANEY Benjamin	4° ss.	LANEY Benjamin	4° ss.	LEE Richard	4° ss.
1666	HALL George	4° ss.				
1667	BAGSHAW Henry	4° ss.				
1668	LLOYD William	4° ss.	STARKEY William	4° ss.		
1670	HOLE Matthew	4° ss.	SEIGNIOR George	4° ss.	WEST Rich. DD.	4° ss.
1671	DUNCOMB Thomas	4° ss.	NORTH John	4° ss.		
1672	ALLINGTON John	4° ss.	MOULIN DU Peter	4° ss.		
1673	BUSHEL Seth	4° ss.	GREGORY Fran. DD.	4° ss.	LAMBE John	4° ss.
	LLOYD William	4° ss.	MASON Charles	4° ss.	NEVILLE Robert	4° ss.
	WARD Seth	4° ss.	ANNESLEY Samuel	4° ss.		
1674	GOULDE William	4° ss.	JAMES Henry	4° ss.	LLOYD William	4° ss.
	PRINCE John	4° ss.				
1675	FELL John	4° ss.	GREGORY Fran. DD.	4° ss.	JACKSON William	4° ss.
	JANE Will. DD.	4° ss.	LANEY Benjamin	4° ss.	MOTTE DE LA Francis	4° ss.
	NAILOUR William	4° ss.	STANDISH John	4° ss.	STRADLING Geor. DD.	4° ss.
	SUDBURY John	4° ss.				
1676	GOULDE William	4° ss.	HAYWARD Roger	4° ss.	HODGES Thomas	4° ss.
	HOWELL William	4° ss.	JENNER Dav. B.D.	4° ss.	JONES Henry	4° ss.
	LUZANCY Hippolytus Du	4° ss.	PATRICK Simon	4° ss.	SUDBURY John	4° ss.
	TEMPLER John	4° ss.				
1677	PITTIS Thomas	4° ss.	RAINBOW Edward	4° ss.	THORP George	4° ss.
	TURNER Bryan	4° ss.	VINCENT Nathaniel	4° ss.		
1678	BABINGTON Humfrey	4° ss.	BUTLER John	4° ss.	CADE William	4° ss.
	CAVE John	4° ss.	JAMES John	4° ss.	LATHAM Paul	4° ss.
	LLOYD William	4° ss.				
1679	CROFT Herbert	4° ss.	JANE Will. DD.	4° ss.	LLOYD William	4° ss.
	OATES Titus	4° ss.	PELLING Edward	4° ss.	PELLING Edward	4° ss.
	PINDAR William	4° ss.	WOODROFFE Benjamin	4° ss.		
1680	BURNET Gilbert	4° ss.	FELL John	4° ss.	HASCARD Gregory	4° ss.
	HICKERINGILL Edmond	4° coll.	HICKERINGILL Edmond.	4° ss.	CROMWELL Oliver	4° ss.
1681	BURNET Gilbert	4° ss.	BURNET Gilbert	4° ss.	CAVE John	8° ss.
	FOWLER Edward	4° ss.	LLOYD William	4° ss.	MAURICE Henry	4° ss.
	TURNER Francis	4° ss.				
1682	BARNE Miles	4° ss.	BISBIE Nathaniel	4° ss.	CALAMY Benjamin	4° ss.

Year	Name	Format	Name	Format	Name	Format
	DOVE Heb. DD.	4° ss.	FULLER Samuel	4° ss.	GOULDE William	4° ss.
	HOLLINGWORTH Richard	4° ss.	KEN Thomas	4° ss.	KNIGHT John	4° ss.
	PERSE Will. M.A.	4° ss.	SMITH Thomas	4° ss.	TURNER Francis	4° ss.
	WRAY William	4° ss.	WRAY William	4° ss.		
1683						
	BARNE Miles	4° ss.	BARROW John	4° ss.	BOLTON William	4° ss.
	BURRELL John	4° ss.	CALAMY Benjamin	4° ss.	FITZWILLIAM John	4° ss.
	GIPPS Tho.	4° coll.	HARRISON John	4° ss.	HESKETH Henry	4° ss.
	HILDEYARD John	4° ss.	MILBOURNE Luke	4° ss.	PAYNE William	4° ss.
	PAYNE William	4° ss.	POMFRET Tho. M.A.	4° ss.	SMITH William	4° ss.
	STANDISH John	4° ss.	TURNER Francis	5° ss.	TURNER John	4° ss.
1684						
	BARNE Miles	4° ss.	BOLTON William	4° ss.	BORASTON George	4° ss.
	BRIDGE Francis	4° ss.	CALAMY Benjamin	4° ss.	CARTWRIGHT Thomas	4° ss.
	STANDISH John	4° ss.	TURNER Francis	4° ss.	TURNER Francis	4° ss.
	TURNER Francis	4° ss.				
1685						
	ASTON Thomas	4° ss.	BURNET Gilbert	4° ss.	FYSH Thomas	4° ss.
	GOWER Humphrey	4° ss.	GOWER Humphrey	4° ss.	HODGES Thomas	4° ss.
	STAINFORTH William	4° ss.	THOMPSON Richard	4° ss.	TURNER Francis	4° ss.
	TURNER Francis	4° ss.	TURNER Francis	4° ss.	TURNER Tho. DD.	4° ss.
	WAGSTAFFE Thomas	4° ss.	WENSLEY Robert	4° ss.		
1686						
	BETHAM John	4° ss.	STAINFORTH William	4° ss.	THURLIN Thomas	4° ss.
1687						
	MANNINGHAM Thomas	4° ss.				
1688						
	BROWNE Thomas	4° ss.	BROWNE Thomas	4° ss.	BURNET Gilbert	8° ss.
	HELLIER Henry	4° ss.				
1689						
	BURNET Gilbert	4° ss.	BURNET Gilbert	4° ss.	HORNECK Anthony	4° ss.
	MARIOTT Thomas	4° ss.	MARIOTT Thomas	4° ss.	PATRICK Simon	4° ss.
	TENISON Thomas	4° ss.				
1690						
	BURNET Gilbert	4° ss.	BURNET Gilbert	4° ss.	BURNET Gilbert	4° ss.
	KIDDER Richard	4° ss.	LLOYD William	4° ss.	PELLING Edward	4° ss.
1691						
	BURNET Gilbert	4° ss.	BURNET Gilbert	4° ss.	KELSEY Joseph	4° ss.
	LYNFORD Thomas	4° ss.	THORNTON Stephen	4° ss.		
1692						
	BENTLEY Richard	4° coll.	BURNET Gilbert	4° ss.	MANNINGHAM Thomas	4° ss.
	SKELTON Bernard	4° ss.				
1693						
	LAKE Edward	4° ss.	RUSSEL John	4° ss.	STUBBS Philip	4° ss.
	STUBBS Philip	4° ss.	WALKER Thomas	4° ss.		
1694						
	BIRCH Peter	4° ss.	BURNET Gilbert	4° ss.	BURNET Gilbert	4° ss.
	CORNWALLIS Henry	12° ss.	PROWDE Francis	4° ss.	TENISON Thomas	4° ss.
	WIGAN William	4° ss.	WROE Christopher	4° ss.		
1695						
	BURNET Gilbert	4° ss.	FISHER Joseph	4° ss.	HUMPHREYS Humphrey	4° ss.
	ISHAM Zach. DD.	4° ss.	KENNET White	4° ss.	MANNINGHAM Thomas	4° ss.
	PAYNE William	4° ss.	SHORE John	4° ss.	TALBOT William	4° ss.
	TENISON Thomas	4° ss.	GOODWIN Thomas	4° ss.		
1696						
	KETTLEWELL John	8° coll.	LANCASTER William	4° ss.	NEWTE John	4° ss.

Year	Name	Format	Name	Format	Name	Format
	PATRICK Simon	4° ss.	SAYWELL Samuel	4° ss.		
1697	BURNET Gilbert	4° ss.	COMBER Thomas	4° ss.	GREGORY Fran. DD.	4° ss.
	LANGFORD Emanuel	4° ss.	LLOYD William	4° ss.	PRAT Samuel	4° ss.
	STANHOPE George	4° ss.	TRIMNEL Charles	4° ss.	WILLIAMS John	4° ss.
	HOW John	4° ss.				
1698	CHISHULL Edmund	4° ss.	GILBERT John	4° ss.	HUTCHINSON Francis	4° ss.
	MILBOURNE Luke	4° ss.	MILNER William	4° ss.	NOURSE Peter	4° ss.
	OLIVER Edward	4° ss.	WHITFELD Will. DD.	4° ss.	WIGHT Thomas	4° ss.
1699	EDWARDS John	4° ss.	HAYLEY William	4° ss.	HAYLEY William	12° ss.
	LENG John	4° ss.	MARSTON Edward	4° ss.	PULLEYN John	4° ss.
	WETENHALL Edward	8° ss.	HOW John	8° ss.		
1700	ASHETON William	4° ss.	BURNET Gilbert	4° ss.	CHETWOOD Knightly	7° ss.
	ELLISON Nath. DD.	8° ss.	EYRE Robert	4° ss.	FALLE Philip	4° ss.
	GASKARTH John	4° ss.	GASKARTH John	4° ss.	HESKITH Thomas	4° ss.
	ISHAM Zach. DD.	4° ss.	KNIGHT John	4° ss.	NAISH Thomas	4° ss.
	SHUTTLEWORTH John	4° ss.	HOW John	fo. ss.		
1701	BRYDGES Henry	4° ss.	HAYLEY William	4° ss.	HOUGH John	4° ss.
	ISHAM Zach. DD.	4° ss.	MANNINGHAM Thomas	4° ss.	MARSDEN Robert	4° ss.
	MARSH Richard	4° ss.	MILLES Thomas	8° ss.	WILLIS Richard	4° ss.
1702	ADAMS John	4° ss.	BURD Richard	4° ss.	DELAUNE William	4° ss.
	GIBSON Edmund	4° ss.	GRAILLE John	4° ss.	HAYLEY William	4° ss.
	HOUGH John	4° ss.	KIMBERLEY Jonathan	4° ss.	NEEDHAM William	4° ss.
	NEWTON Robert	4° ss.	NICHOLS Will. DD.	4° ss.	SACHEVERELL Henry	4° ss.
	SACHEVERELL Henry	4° ss.	STANHOPE George	4° ss.	STUBBS Philip	4° ss.
	TRELAWNEY Jonathan Sir	4° ss.	WHINCOP Thomas	4° ss.	WILLIS Richard	4° ss.
1703	BARNES Joshua	4° ss.	CLARKE Edward	4° ss.	CLIFTON Jo.	4° ss.
	FULLER Thomas	4° ss.	LAKE Edward	4° ss.	LYNG William	4° ss.
	NEWTON Robert	4° ss.	NICOLSON William	4° ss.	PRIDEAUX Humphrey	4° ss.
	RESBURY Nathaniel	4° ss.	STANHOPE George	4° ss.	WHITFELD Will. DD.	4° ss.
	WHITING Charles	4° ss.	WOODROFFE Benjamin	4° ss.		
1704	BINCKES William	4° ss.	BLACKALL Anthony	4° ss.	BRETT Joseph	4° ss.
	BURGHOPE George	4° ss.	BURNET Gilbert	4° ss.	BURNET Gilbert	4° ss.
	COCK John	8° ss.	FINCH Will. Lepold	4° ss.	GASTRELL Francis	4° ss.
	GRANT John	4° ss.	ISHAM Zach. DD.	4° ss.	KENNET White	4° ss.
	KING William	4° ss.	LENG John	4° ss.	MANNINGHAM Thomas	4° ss.
	MILBOURNE Luke	4° ss.	PEARSON William	4° ss.	SAVAGE John	4° ss.
	SMEATON Samuel	4° ss.	TUCKER William	4° ss.	WHITFELD Will. DD.	4° ss.
	WILLIAMS John	4° ss.	WILLIS Richard	4° ss.	HUSSEY Joseph	4° ss.
1705	BOWBER Thomas	4° ss.	HOUGH John	4° ss.	ISHAM Zach. DD.	4° ss.
	KENNET White	4° ss.	OVINGTON John	4° ss.	POOLEY Giles	4° ss.
	REEVES William	4° ss.	ROYSE Geor. DD.	4° ss.	TALBOT William	4° ss.
	WAUGH John	4° ss.	WOODWARD Josiah	4° ss.	SPADEMAN John	4° ss.
1706	SACHEVERELL Henry	4° ss.	STUBBS Philip	4° ss.	WOTTON William	4° ss.
1707	ADAMS John	4° ss.	ADAMS John	4° ss.	BARKER Richard	4° ss.
	HASLEWOOD John	4° ss.	JENKS Richard	4° ss.	NELSON Hen.	8° ss.

Year	Name	Size	Type	Name	Size	Type	Name	Size	Type
	NICOLSON William	4°	ss.	TRIMNEL Charles	4°	ss.			
1708	ADAMS John	4°	ss.	ADAMS John	4°	ss.	BISSE Thomas	4°	ss.
	BRADFORD Samuel	4°	ss.	CHETWOOD Knightly	4°	ss.	EYRE Robert	4°	ss.
	HOADLY John	4°	ss.	KENNET White	8°	ss.	LITTELL Tho. DD.	4°	ss.
	MILBOURNE Luke	8°	ss.	MILNER William	8°	ss.	STOUGHTON William	4°	ss.
	TRAPP Joseph	4°	ss.	WILLET John	4°	ss.	WILLIAMS John	8°	coll.
	CALAMY Edmund	8°	ss.						
1709	ADAMS John	4°	ss.	CHAPMAN Richard	4°	ss.	EDWARDS John	8°	ss.
	HOUGH John	4°	ss.	KING William	8°	ss.	MILBOURNE Luke	8°	ss.
	ROBERTS William	4°	ss.	SACHEVERELL Henry	4°	ss.	SMITH John	4°	ss.
	SHOWER John	8°	ss.						
1710	BENNET Thomas	8°	ss.	BISSE Philip	4°	ss.	BLOMER Ralph	8°	ss.
	BRADFORD Samuel	8°	ss.	BURNET Gilbert	8°	ss.	COLLINS Richard	8°	ss.
	HIGDEN Will. DD.	4°	ss.	KENNET White	4°	ss.	KENNET White	8°	ss.
	LEWIS Henry	8°	ss.	LEWIS John	8°	ss.	OLDHAM George	8°	ss.
	ROBINSON John	4°	ss.	SAINT John Pawlet	4°	ss.	SPRAT Thomas	8°	coll.
	SWIFT Thomas	8°	ss.	THOMAS John	4°	ss.	WEST Richard	8°	ss.
1711	BISSE Thomas	8°	ss.	BOWTELL John	8°	ss.	COOKE Shadrach	8°	ss.
	DIBBEN Thomas	8°	ss.	FRIEND Robert	4°	ss.	LLOYD Robert Lumley	8°	ss.
	TRAPP Joseph	4°	ss.	TRAPP Joseph	4°	ss.			
1712	ALTHAM Roger	4°	ss.	ANONYMOUS	8°	ss.	BISSE Thomas	4°	ss.
	BRETT Thomas	8°	coll.	BRIDGEN Will. DD	8°	ss.	BROWNE Francis	4°	ss.
	CHISHULL Edmund	1°	ss.	CHISHULL Edmund	8°	ss.	CHISHULL Edmund	8°	ss.
	DORRINGTON Theophilus	8°	ss.	HOUGH Nathaniel	4°	ss.	NEWTON Richard	4°	ss.
	POTTER John	8°	ss.	SMITH John	4°	ss.	TASWELL William	4°	ss.
	TILLY William	8°	coll.	WOLCOMBE Robert	8°	ss.			
1713	BELL George	8°	ss.	BERKELEY George	8°	ss.	BRAMSTON William	4°	ss.
	BRETT Thomas	8°	coll.	COWPER John	8°	ss.	CRADOCK William	8°	ss.
	CUMMINGS George	4°	ss.	DINGLEY William	8°	ss.	GARDINER James	8°	ss.
	HICHMAN Charles	8°	coll.	HILLIARD Samuel	8°	ss.	HOLE Matthew	4°	ss.
	HOLE Matthew	8°	ss.	LAW William	8°	ss.	OAKELY Simon	8°	ss.
	OLDHAM George	4°	ss.	PERCIVALE William	4°	ss.	SACHEVERELL Henry	4°	ss.
	STANHOPE George	4°	ss.	STUBBS Philip	4°	ss.	TRAPP Joseph	4°	ss.
	WAUGH John	4°	ss.						
1714	BLOWER John	8°	coll.	BRAMSTON William	4°	ss.	BRETT Thomas	8°	coll.
	BURNET Gilbert	4°	ss.	CHISHULL Edmund	4°	ss.	MILBOURNE Luke	8°	ss.
	NOONE George	8°	ss.	READING Will. M.A.	8°	ss.	WALLER John	4°	ss.
	WILLIAMS John	8°	ss.						
1715	BENTLEY Richard	8°	ss.	BRETT Joseph	8°	coll.	BURSCOUGH William	8°	ss.
	EYRE Rich. M.A.	8°	ss.	GREENE Thomas	8°	ss.	HOLE Matthew	8°	ss.
	HOLE Matthew	8°	ss.	JENKINSON Richard	8°	ss.	KENNET Basil	8°	coll.
	LACY James	8°	ss.	MILBOURNE Luke	8°	ss.			
1716	BAKER William	8°	ss.	BISSE Thomas	8°	ss.	FORSTER Nicholas	4°	ss.
	RUSSEL John	8°	ss.	CALAMY Edmund	8°	ss.	ENTY John	4°	ss.
1717	BISSE Thomas	8°	ss.	BISSE Thomas	8°	ss.	BYRCHE William	8°	ss.
	DOD Thomas	8°	ss.	HOADLY John	8°	ss.	MANGEY Thomas	8°	coll.

Year	Name	Size	Name	Size	Name	Size
	STEWARD William	8° ss.	STUART William	8° ss.		
1718						
	BARNARD Tho. M.A.	8° ss.	CHANDLER Edward	4° ss.	CHANDLER Edward	8° ss.
	COLBATCH John	4° ss.	CRADOCK William	8° ss.	LEWIS John	8° ss.
	MANSTON Joseph	8° ss.	WRIGHT Samuel	8° ss.		
1719						
	HOLDSWORTH Winch. DD.	8° ss.	KNIGHT James	4° ss.	SMITH Roger	8° ss.
	TOPPING Henry	8° ss.	ROBINSON Benjamin	8° ss.	WRIGHT Samuel	8° ss.
1720						
	GRAILLE John	8° ss.	HINTON Edward	4° ss.	KENNET White	4° ss.
	NEWCOME John	8° ss.	WATERLAND Daniel	8° coll.	CALAMY Edmund	8° ss.
1721						
	CLARKE Joseph	4° ss.				
1722						
	IBBETSON Richard	4° ss.	TRAPP Joseph	8° coll.		
1724						
	NEWCOME John	8° ss.				
1727						
	DERHAM Will. DD.	8° ss.				
1728						
	BLOMFIELD Barrington	8° ss.	LONG Roger	8° ss.	ROPER Joseph. DD.	4° ss.
1729						
	GIBSON Edmund	8° coll.				
1733						
	DAWES Sir William	8° coll.				
1737						
	TILLY William	-° coll.				
1739						
	BENTLEY Richard	fo. coll.	BOLTON Robert	4° ss.	HANCOCK John	fo. ss.
	HARRIS John	fo. coll.	WILLIAMS John	fo. coll.		
1741						
	LUSHINGTON Thomas	8° ss.				
1745						
	HUTTON Matthew	4° ss.				
1752						
	CONYBEARE John	4° ss.	OSBALDESTON Richard	4° ss.		
1763						
	DELANY Patrick	4° ss.	DELANY Patrick	4° ss.		
1764						
	MAURICE Henry	8° ss.	TERRICK Richard	4° ss.		
1784						
	BEAULIEU Luke	4° ss.				

Trinity College ("Trin.")

Year	Name	Size	Name	Size	Name	Size

	HOADLY Benjamin	-° coll.				
16--						
	JANEWAY James	12° ss.				
1644						
	PEARSON John	4° ss.				
1660						
	ALLINGTON John	12° ss.	ALLINGTON John	12° ss.	BARKER Edmund	4° ss.
	BARWICK John	4° ss.	DOWGLASS Robert	12° ss.	GODMAN William	4° ss.
	MERITON John	4° ss.	BAXTER Richard	4° ss.	BAXTER Richard	4° ss.
	MEAD Matthew	4° ss.				
1661						

Year	Name	Format	Name	Format	Name	Format
	BARKER Edmund	4° ss.	GREEFFIELD Thomas	4° ss.	MORLEY George	4° ss.
1662	LE FRANK James	8° coll.	MAYNE Jasper	4° ss.	RILAND John	4° ss.
	RILAND John	4° ss.				
1663	WETENHALL Edward	4° ss.				
1664	BROWNRIG Ralph	fo. coll.	CHILLINGWORTH William	fo. coll.	LUKE John	4° ss.
1665	DOLBEN John	4° ss.	DOLBEN John	4° ss.	KING Henry	4° ss.
	LANEY Benjamin	4° ss.				
1666	BOTELER Edward	12° ss.	KILLIGREW Henry. DD.	4° ss.		
1667	ANNESLEY Samuel	4° coll.				
1668	KEMP Edward	4° ss.	WETENHALL Edward	4° ss.		
1669	BOREMAN Rich. DD.	4° ss.	WINTER John	12° ss.	WINTER John	12° ss.
1670	BARNE Miles	4° ss.	BASSET Will.	4° ss.	CUDWORTH Ralph	8° ss.
	DOBSON John	4° ss.	HUME John	4° ss.	PARRY John	4° ss.
	BRYAN John	8° ss.				
1671	DURHAM William	4° ss.	NORTH John	4° ss.		
1672	ALLINGTON John	4° ss.	FARINDON Anth. B.D.	fo. coll.	GURNALL William	8° ss.
	LUCE Richard	4° ss.				
1673	ASHETON William	4° ss.	JACKSON Thomas	fo. coll.	LAMBE John	4° ss.
	PEARSON John	4° ss.				
1674	JAMES Henry	4° ss.	LLOYD William	4° ss.	LODINGTON Thomas	4° ss.
	LODINGTON Thomas	4° ss.	ANNESLEY Samuel	4° coll.		
1675	BONHOME Joshua	4° ss.	FELL John	4° ss.	HACKET John	fo. coll.
	LANEY Benjamin	4° ss.	NAILOUR William	4° ss.		
1676	ADDERLEY Thomas	4° ss.	ALLINGTON John	4° ss.	CARTWRIGHT Thomas	4° ss.
	COOK John	4° ss.	HOLDEN Samuel	4° ss.	HOLDEN Samuel	4° ss.
	JENNER Dav. B.D.	4° ss.				
1677	BRAMHALL John	fo. coll.	CRADOCK Zechary	4° ss.	RIVELY Benedict	4° ss.
	WILKINS John	12° coll.	NALTON James	8° coll.		
1678	BABINGTON Humfrey	4° ss.	CADE William	4° ss.	JAMES John	4° ss.
	LAMPLUGH Thomas	4° ss.	LLOYD William	4° ss.	PATRICK Simon	4° ss.
1679	BASSET Will.	4° ss.	FARINDON Anth. B.D.	fo. coll.	HERNE Samuel	4° ss.
	HORTON Thomas	fo. coll.	LLOYD William	4° ss.	LLOYD William	4° ss.
	LYNFORD Thomas	4° ss.	OATES Titus	4° ss.	PELLING Edward	4° ss.
	PELLING Edward	4° ss.				
1680	ANONYMOUS	4° ss.	BAGSHAW Henry	8° coll.	BURNET Gilbert	4° ss.
	DOVE Heb. DD.	4° ss.	FELL John	4° ss.	HICKERINGILL Edmond	4° coll.
	HICKERINGILL Edmond.	4° ss.	LITTLETON Adam	fo. coll.	PARSONS Robert	4° ss.

Year	Name	Format	Name	Format	Name	Format
	RAMSAY William	4° ss.	RAMSAY William	4° ss.	RAMSAY William	4° ss.
	CROMWELL Oliver	4° ss.				
1681	BURNET Gilbert	4° ss.	BURNET Gilbert	4° ss.	FOWLER Edward	4° ss.
	FREEMAN Samuel	4° ss.	GIFFARD Francis	4° ss.	PATRICK Simon	4° ss.
	PATRICK Simon	4° ss.	RAMSAY William	4° ss.	RESBURY Nathaniel	4° ss.
	GOODWIN Thomas	fo.coll.				
1682	BARNE Miles	4° ss.	BISBIE Nathaniel	4° ss.	COMBER Thomas	4° ss.
	CUTLORE Joseph	4° ss.	FOWLER Matthew	4° ss.	FULLER Samuel	4° ss.
	KEN Thomas	4° ss.	KIDDER Richard	4° ss.	KNIGHT John	4° ss.
	PELLING Edward	4° ss.	PERSE Will. M.A.	4° ss.	POMFRET Tho. M.A.	4° ss.
	WETENHALL Edward	4° ss.	WETENHALL Edward	4° ss.	WILKINS John	8° coll.
	WRAY William	4° ss.	BRUCE Titus	4° ss.		
1683	BARNE Miles	4° ss.	CALAMY Benjamin	4° ss.	CALAMY Benjamin	4° ss.
	HILDEYARD John	4° ss.	HOPKINS William	4° ss.	JEMMAT Samuel	4° ss.
	MILBOURNE Luke	4° ss.	POMFRET Tho. M.A.	4° ss.		
1684	BARNE Miles	4° ss.	BRIDGE Francis	4° ss.	GRENVILLE Denis	4° ss.
	HAMMOND Henry	fo.coll.	HESKETH Henry	4° ss.	LAYTON Joseph	4° ss.
	PARKHURST Nathaniel	12° ss.	WROE Christopher	4° ss.	CHARNOCK Stephen	fo.coll.
1685	CAVE John	4° ss.	DOVE Heb. DD.	4° ss.	ELLIS Ph.	4° ss.
	GOSTWYKE William	4° ss.	GOWER Humphrey	4° ss.	IRONSIDE Gilbert	4° ss.
	MANNINGHAM Thomas	4° ss.	PELLING Edward	4° ss.	SHERLOCK William	4° ss.
	WYVILL Christopher	4° ss.				
1686	BETHAM John	4° ss.	DOVE Heb. DD.	4° ss.	HORNECK Anthony	12° ss.
	WETENHALL Edward	12° coll.				
1687	BOLDE Samuel	12° ss.	HORNECK Anthony	8° ss.		
1689	BIRCH Peter	4° ss.	BURNET Gilbert	4° ss.	BURNET Gilbert	4° ss.
	BURNET Gilbert	4° ss.	CARSWELL Francis	4° ss.	LYNFORD Thomas	4° ss.
	PATRICK Simon	4° ss.	PATRICK Simon	4° ss.	PERSE Will. M.A.	4° ss.
	SANDERSON Robert	fo.coll.				
1690	BURNET Gilbert	4° ss.	BURNET Gilbert	4° ss.	FREEMAN Samuel	4° ss.
	HICHMAN Charles	4° ss.	JONES David	4° ss.	PATRICK Simon	4° ss.
	PELLING Edward	4° ss.	ROYSE Geor. DD.	4° ss.	WHITTLE Seth	4° ss.
	WILLES John	4° ss.				
1691	ALLESTREE Thomas	8° coll.	BARKER Ralph	4° ss.	BLAGRAVE Jonathan	4° ss.
	BURNET Gilbert	4° ss.	BURNET Gilbert	4° ss.	BURNET Gilbert	4° ss.
	ELLIS Clement	4° ss.	NORRIS John	8° coll.	CHANDLER Samuel	8° coll.
1692	BENTLEY Richard	4° coll.	BRADFORD Samuel	4° ss.	BURNET Gilbert	4° ss.
	HOPKINS Ezekiel	4° coll.	JONES David	4° ss.	MANNINGHAM Thomas	4° ss.
	PELLING Edward	4° ss.				
1693	FREEMAN Samuel	4° ss.	LAMBE John	4° ss.	LAMBE John	4° ss.
	MANNINGHAM Thomas	4° ss.	MARCH John	4° coll.	RESBURY Nathaniel	4° ss.
1694	BIRCH Peter	4° ss.	BURNET Gilbert	4° ss.	BURNET Gilbert	4° ss.
	BURNET Gilbert	4° ss.	COMBER Thomas	4° ss.	CORNWALLIS Henry	12° ss.

Year	Name	Format	Name	Format	Name	Format
	FREEMAN Samuel	4° ss.	HOOPER George	4° ss.	MORUS Monsieur	4° ss.
	NORRIS John	8° coll.	PETTER John	4° ss.	SANCROFT William	8° coll.
	WHYYLE Humphrey	4° ss.				
1695	ADAMS John	4° ss.	BULL Digby	4° ss.	CORBIN W.	4° ss.
	FALLE Philip	4° ss.	FISHER Joseph	4° ss.	GARDINER James	4° ss.
	HARTCLIFFE John	4° ss.	HAYLEY William	4° ss.	HICHMAN Charles	4° ss.
	HOOPER George	4° ss.	HORNECK Anthony	4° ss.	ISHAM Zach. DD.	4° ss.
	MANNINGHAM Thomas	4° ss.	PAYNE William	4° ss.	POWELL Jos. M.A.	4° ss.
	RUE DE LA	4° ss.	BEVERLEY Thomas	4° ss.	GOODWIN Thomas	4° ss.
1696	BARTON Samuel	4° ss.	BENTLEY Richard	4° ss.	DAY Henry	4° ss.
	EDZARD J. E.	4° ss.	FORD Simon	4° ss.	GREGORY Fran. DD.	4° ss.
	HASCARD Gregory	4° ss.	KEITH George	4° ss.	KETTLEWELL John	8° coll.
	LANCASTER William	4° ss.	PATRICK Simon	4° ss.	PEAD Deuel	4° ss.
	PEAD Deuel	4° ss.	WILLIAMS John	4° ss.		
1697	BECONSALL Thomas	4° ss.	BRAMSTON William	4° ss.	BURNET Gilbert	4° ss.
	BURNET Gilbert	4° ss.	COCKBURN John	8° coll.	COMBER Thomas	4° ss.
	GOODMAN John	4° ss.	GOODMAN John	8° coll.	HITCHCOCK John	4° ss.
	LANGFORD Emanuel	4° ss.	LLOYD William	4° ss.	PRAT Samuel	4° ss.
	PRAT Samuel	4° ss.	WIGAN William	4° ss.	WILLIAMS John	4° ss.
	WILLIAMS John	4° ss.				
1698	BURNET Gilbert	4° ss.	CHISHULL Edmund	4° ss.	COLLINS S. M.A.	4° ss.
	HUTCHINSON Francis	4° ss.	LYNFORD Thomas	4° ss.	NICHOLS Will. DD.	4° ss.
	NOURSE Peter	4° ss.	PAGET Simon	4° ss.	PAYNE William	8° coll.
	PROVOSTE John	4° ss.	BEVERLEY Thomas	4° ss.		
1699	BRAY Thomas	4° ss.	CONANT John	8° coll.	EDWARDS John	4° ss.
	GIBBS William	4° ss.	HESKETH Henry	4° ss.	JONES David	4° ss.
	LENG John	4° ss.	MARCH John	8° coll.	CHARNOCK Stephen	8° coll.
1700	BRADFORD Samuel	4° coll.	GASKARTH John	4° ss.	GASKARTH John	4° ss.
	HARE Francis	4° ss.	NAISH Thomas	4° ss.	BATES William	fo. coll.
1701	BISSE Philip	4° ss.	CORNWALL John	4° ss.	HAYLEY William	4° ss.
	ISHAM Zach. DD.	4° ss.	MANNINGHAM Thomas	4° ss.	MARSDEN Robert	4° ss.
	MARSH Richard	4° ss.	PEARSON John	8° ss.		
1702	BARKER Samuel	4° ss.	BRAGGE Francis	8° coll.	HAYLEY William	4° ss.
	SACHEVERELL Henry	4° ss.	SACHEVERELL Henry	4° ss.	WILLIS Richard	4° ss.
1703	BUCK Maximilian	8° ss.	DORRINGTON Theophilus	8° coll.	DUKE Rich. M.A.	4° ss.
	HAVETT John	8° coll.	KENNET White	4° ss.	RESBURY Nathaniel	4° ss.
1704	BRADY Nich. DD.	8° coll.	BRAGGE Francis	8° coll.	BUTLER Lilly	4° ss.
	DUKE Rich. M.A.	4° ss.	FOWLER Edward	4° ss.	GASTRELL Francis	4° ss.
	LENG John	4° ss.	SACHEVERELL Henry	4° ss.	SHERWILL Thomas	4° ss.
	SHERWILL Thomas	4° ss.	WILLIS Richard	4° ss.	WOTTON James	4° ss.
	WYNNE Robert	4° ss.				
1705	ADAMS John	4° ss.	ALTHAM Roger	4° ss.	BLACKBURNE Lancelot.	4° ss.
	HIGGINS Francis	8° ss.	WILLIS Richard	4° ss.		
1706	BRADY Nich. DD.	8° coll.	BURNET Gilbert	4° ss.	CRADOCK Zechary	4° ss.

Year	Name	Format	Name	Format	Name	Format
	DORRINGTON Theophilus	4° ss.	GERY Robert	4° ss.	HORNECK Anthony	8° coll.
	HOUGH Nathaniel	4° ss.	KENNET White	4° ss.	KENNET White	4° ss.
	MANNINGHAM Thomas	4° ss.	MANNINGHAM Thomas	4° ss.	NICOLSON William	4° ss.
	PEAD Deuel	8° ss.	SHARP J. M.A.	8° ss.	WOTTON William	4° ss.
	EVANS John	8° ss.				
1707						
	ADAMS John	4° ss.	ADAMS John	4° ss.	ALLEYNE John	4° ss.
	BRADY Nich. DD.	8° ss.	BROUGHTON John	4° ss.	COCK John	8° ss.
	FOWLER Edward	8° ss.	GOODMAN John	8° ss.	HASLEWOOD John	4° ss.
	HOADLY John	4° ss.	HUTCHINSON Francis	8° ss.	KING James	4° ss.
	KNAGGS Thomas	8° ss.	LIGHTFOOT Robert	8° ss.	MILBOURNE Luke	8° ss.
	NELSON Hen.	8° ss.	OLLYFFE John	8° ss.	PERKINS Joseph	8° ss.
	SAVAGE William	4° ss.	WILLIS Richard	4° ss.		
1708						
	ADAMS John	4° ss.	ADAMS John	4° ss.	ANONYMOUS	8° ss.
	BISSE Thomas	4° ss.	BLACKBURNE Lancelot.	4° ss.	BRADFORD Samuel	4° ss.
	COCKBURN John	8° ss.	DUNSTER Sam. DD.	8° ss.	EYRE Robert	4° ss.
	HOADLY John	4° ss.	KENNET White	8° ss.	KNAGGS Thomas	8° ss.
	LAMBERT Ralph	4° ss.	MANNINGHAM Thomas	1° ss.	MANNINGHAM Thomas	6° ss.
	MILBOURNE Luke	8° ss.	RAWSON Jos. DD.	4° coll.	WILLIAMS John	8° coll.
1709						
	ADAMS John	4° ss.	BRADFORD Samuel	8° ss.	BRAY Thomas	4° ss.
	BRYDGES Henry	8° ss.	HARE Francis	4° ss.	HILLIARD Samuel	8° ss.
	HOUGH John	4° ss.	KING William	8° ss.	LYNFORD Thomas	8° ss.
	LYNFORD Thomas	8° ss.	NICHOLS Will. DD.	8° ss.	PELLING John	4° ss.
	RENNELL Thomas	4° ss.	ROBERTS William	4° ss.	SACHEVERELL Henry	4° ss.
	SACHEVERELL Henry	4° ss.	SHERWILL Thomas	8° ss.	WILLIS Richard	8° ss.
	WOODWARD Josiah	8° ss.				
1710						
	BENNET Thomas	8° ss.	BINCKES William	8° ss.	BISSE Philip	4° ss.
	BLOMER Ralph	8° ss.	BRADFORD Samuel	8° ss.	BURNET Gilbert	8° ss.
	BYNNS Richard	8° ss.	COLLINS Richard	8° ss.	HARRISON John	8° ss.
	JACKSON John	8° ss.	KENNET White	4° ss.	WEST Richard	8° ss.
1711						
	GOOCH Thomas Sir	4° ss.	HOADLY Benjamin	8° coll.		
1712						
	ALTHAM Roger	4° ss.	AYERST William	8° ss.	BYNNS Richard	8° ss.
	DORRINGTON Theophilus	8° ss.	FINCH Henry	4° ss.		
1713						
	BULL George	8° coll.	CLAYTON Thomas	4° ss.	SACHEVERELL Henry	4° ss.
1714						
	BRAMSTON William	4° ss.	BURNET Gilbert	4° ss.	BURNET Gilbert	8° ss.
	CLAGETT Nicholas	4° ss.				
1715						
	BENTLEY Richard	8° ss.	HOADLY Benjamin	8° ss.	HOUGH Nathaniel	8° ss.
	WILLIS Richard	4° ss.				
1716						
	ASTRY Francis	4° ss.	BARROW Isaac	fo.coll.	BRADFORD Samuel	4° ss.
	CHANDLER Edward	4° ss.	HOADLY Benjamin	8° ss.	LUCAS Richard	8° coll.
	WATERLAND Daniel	8° ss.				
1717						
	ANDREWS Thomas	8° ss.				
1718						
	BRADFORD Samuel	8° ss.	CHANDLER Edward	4° ss.	CLAGETT Nicholas	4° ss.
	SCOTT John	fo.coll.	WHITFIELD John	8° ss.		
1719						

	BOULTER Hugh	8° ss.	HARE Francis	4° ss.		
1720	FIDDES Rich. DD.	fo. ss.	WATERLAND Daniel	8° coll.	WOTTON William	8° ss.
1721	HARCOURT James	4° ss.	HOADLY Benjamin	4° ss.	KELSEY Joseph	8° coll.
1722	WHITFIELD John	8° ss.				
1723	BLACKALL Offspring	fo.coll.	WATERLAND Daniel	4° ss.		
1724	WHITFIELD John	8° ss.				
1725	KNIGHT Samuel	8° ss.				
1726	CALAMY Benjamin	8° coll.				
1727	DERHAM Will. DD.	8° ss.				
1728	FIDDES Rich. DD. WHARTON Henry	fo.coll. 8° coll.	NORRIS John	8° coll.	WHARTON Henry	8° coll.
1729	GIBSON Edmund	8° coll.				
1730	ATTERBURY Francis	8° coll.	CLARKE Samuel	8° coll.		
1731	HARE Francis	4° ss.				
1732	<u>FOSTER</u> <u>James</u>	8° coll.				
1733	DAWES Sir William	8° coll.	MOSS Robert	8° coll.		
1734	CLARKE Samuel	8° coll.				
1735	SHARP John	8° coll.				
1737	FLEETWOOD William	fo.coll.	MOSS Robert	8° coll.	<u>FOSTER</u> <u>James</u>	8° coll.
1738	MOSS Robert	8° coll.				
1739	ANONYMOUS	fo.coll.	BENTLEY Richard	fo.coll.	WILLIAMS John	fo.coll.
1740	GARNET John	4° ss.				
1741	<u>FOSTER</u> <u>James</u>	8° ss.				
1744	BELLAMY Daniel	8° coll.	<u>FOSTER</u> <u>James</u>	8° coll.		
1745	NICOLLS Samuel	8° ss.	WEBSTER William	8° coll.		
1746	NICOLLS Samuel	8° ss.	RUTHERFORTH Thomas	4° ss.		
1748	BEARCROFT Philip	4° ss.				
1749	GEORGE William	4° ss.	NICOLLS Samuel	4° ss.	ORR John	8° coll.
1750	HUBBARD Henry	4° ss.				

Year	Author	Format	Author	Format	Author	Format
1751	BERRIMAN William	8° coll.	RUTHERFORTH Thomas	4° ss.		
1753	DUCHAL James	8° coll.				
1756	YONGE Philip	4° ss.				
1757	CONYBEARE John	8° coll.				
1764	KENNET White	4° ss.				
1765	LLOYD Peirson	8° coll.				
1766	DELANY Patrick	8° coll.	SECKER William	8° coll.		
1770	BARRINGTON Lord	8° coll.	OGDEN Samuel	8° coll.		
1771	PYLE Tho. M.A.	1° coll.				
1772	ORR John	8° coll.	SHERLOCK Thomas	8° coll.		
1774	JORTIN John	8° coll.				
1775	WOOD William	12° coll.				
1776	HALLIFAX Samuel	8° coll.				
1777	OGDEN Samuel	8° coll.				
1778	HORNE Geo. DD.	8° coll.				
1780	BAGOTT Lewis	8° coll.	BANDINELL James	8° coll.	HURD Richard	8° coll.
	OGDEN Samuel	12° coll.				

(INDEXES TO FIFTH VOLUME)

PART THREE OF INDEX E : LIBRARIES AT LONDON AND ETON

British Museum ("Brit.M.")

Year	Author	Format	Author	Format	Author	Format
16--	FLEETWOOD William	-° coll.	RUSSEL J.	8° ss.		
1660	ANONYMOUS	8° ss.	BAXTER Richard	4° ss.		
1661	BARWICK John SHELDON Gilbert BAXTER Richard	4° ss. 4° ss. 4° ss.	FEATLY Daniel SPENCER John CALVERT Thomas	4° ss. 4° ss. 12° ss.	KNELL Paul ADIS Henry	8° coll. 4° ss.
1662	HEYLYN Pet. DD.	4° ss.	REEVE Thomas	4° ss.	TILLOTSON John	4° coll.
1663	MAYNE Jasper	4° ss.				
1664	MEGGOT Richard	4° ss.				
1666	GREGORY John	4° ss.				
1668	HARDY Nathaniel	4° ss.	MEAD Matthew	8° ss.		
1669	RUST George	4° ss.	STARKEY William	4° ss.		
1670	LITTLETON Adam	4° ss.				
1672	SEIGNIOR George	4° ss.				
1674	GURNALL William	8° ss.	LONG Thomas	8° ss.	PARR Richard	4° ss.
1675	ANONYMOUS	4° ss.				

INDEXES TO FIFTH VOLUME: E: LIBRARIES: PART THREE: LONDON AND ETON (British Museum)

Year	Name	Format	Name	Format	Name	Format
	MOORE Richard	8° coll.				
1677	TILLOTSON John	4° coll.				
1678	BUSHEL Seth	4° ss.	LAMPLUGH Thomas	4° ss.	THOMAS William	4° ss.
1679	BASSET Will.	4° ss.	PELLING Edward	4° ss.		
1680	BURNET Gilbert	4° ss.	DOVE Heb. DD.	4° ss.	HASCARD Gregory	4° ss.
1681	FOWLER Edward	4° ss.	HOOPER George	4° ss.	JEKYLL Thomas	4° ss.
	JONES Thomas	4° ss.	NEVILLE Robert	4° ss.	NICOLS Daniel	4° ss.
	PLEYDELL Josias	4° ss.				
1682	ALSOP Nathaniel	4° ss.	BURNET Gilbert	4° ss.	CARTWRIGHT Thomas	4° ss.
	CREYGHTON Robert	4° ss.	FREEMAN Samuel	4° ss.	HESKETH Henry	4° ss.
	INETT John	4° ss.	PITTIS Thomas	4° ss.	PLEYDELL Josias	4° coll.
	RICHARDSON Joshua	4° ss.	WENSLEY Robert	4° ss.	WROE Christopher	4° ss.
	SHOWER John	3° ss.				
1683	BISBIE Nathaniel	4° ss.	HOFFMAN Benjamin	4° ss.	PELLING Edward	4° ss.
	VESEY John	4° ss.	WILLES Samuel	4° ss.	MATHER Samuel	4° coll.
	ROGERS Thomas	4° ss.				
1684	ALLESTREE Richard	fo. coll.	COLLINS Hercules	4° ss.	HESKETH Henry	4° ss.
1685	BURNET Gilbert	4° ss.	DOVE Heb. DD.	4° ss.	HASCARD Gregory	4° ss.
	NORRIS John	4° ss.	HILL Joseph	4° ss.		
1686	PECK John	4° ss.	SHERLOCK William	4° ss.		
1687	ANONYMOUS	4° ss.	CLAGETT William	4° ss.	NICHOLETS Charles	4° ss.
	PERSAL	4° ss.				
1688	CRUSO Timothy	4° ss.	TAYLOR Nathaniel	4° ss.		
1689	BOLDE Samuel	4° ss.	HOPKINS Mar. M.A.	4° ss.	HORNECK Anthony	-° ss.
	LLOYD William	4° ss.	WALKER	4° ss.	AYRAY James	8° ss.
	CRUSO Timothy	4° ss.				
1690	MASTERS Samuel	4° ss.	MERITON Thomas	4° ss.	TOPHAM George	4° ss.
	WHITTLE Seth	4° ss.				
1691	BURNET Gilbert	4° ss.	SPARK Tho. DD.	4° ss.	WALLIS John	4° ss.
	ROGERS Thomas	8° coll.				
1692	ANONYMOUS	4° ss.	EASTON Thomas	4° ss.	HUTCHINSON Francis	4° ss.
	LEIGHTONHOUSE Walter	4° ss.	MILWAY Thomas	4° ss.	POWELL Jos. M.A.	4° ss.
	RAYMOND George	4° ss.	DENT Edward	4° ss.	SPRINT John	4° ss.
1693	BRADY Nich. DD.	4° ss.	CLERKE Samuel	4° ss.	HAMMOND George	8° ss.
	HILL John. M.A.	4° ss.	KIDDER Richard	4° ss.	LAKE Edward	4° ss.
	NORTON Joseph	4° ss.	SHERLOCK William	4° ss.	WALKER Thomas	4° ss.
	WARREN Erasmus	1° ss.	MAYNE Zachariah	4° ss.		
1694	HARTCLIFFE John	4° ss.	PROWDE Francis	4° ss.	SHANK John	4° ss.

Year	Name	Format	Name	Format	Name	Format
	WROE Christopher	4° ss.	BOSTON Thomas	8° ss.	MATHER Nathaniel	4° ss.
	VEAL Edward	4° ss.				
1695						
	ADAMS John	4° ss.	BRADY Nich. DD.	4° ss.	BRIGHT George	8° coll.
	BURNET Gilbert	4° ss.	MAPLETOFT John	4° ss.	STRYPE John	4° ss.
	TALBOT William	4° ss.				
1696						
	OFFLEY William. M.A.	4° ss.	TALBOT William	4° ss.		
1697						
	ANONYMOUS	4° ss.	BRADY Nich. DD.	4° ss.	BURNET Gilbert	4° ss.
	BURNET Gilbert	4° ss.	GOODMAN John	8° coll.	OWTRAM William	8° coll.
	PRUDE John	4° ss.	WIGAN William	4° ss.	WOODWARD Josiah	4° ss.
1698						
	HUTCHINSON Francis	4° ss.	MILNER William	4° ss.	NICHOLS Will. DD.	4° ss.
	OLIVER Edward	4° ss.	PROVOSTE John	4° ss.	WOODHOUSE John	8° ss.
1699						
	HAYLEY William	4° ss.	HAYLEY William	12° ss.	LENG John	4° ss.
	SHOWER John	12° coll.	TAYLOR Nathaniel	4° ss.		
17--						
	BROOME William	8° ss.	HARRISON Thomas	8° ss.	HARRISON Thomas	8° ss.
1700						
	PRAT Samuel	4° ss.				
1701						
	HARRIS John	4° ss.	HAYLEY William	4° ss.	HOUGH John	4° ss.
	JENNINGS John	4° ss.	MARSHALL Nathaniel	4° ss.	SALMON Thomas	4° ss.
	SCOTT William	8° coll.	CALDER R.	8° ss.		
1702						
	BUTLER Lilly	4° ss.	COLLINS Hercules	8° ss.	HOLLAND Rich. M.A.	4° ss.
	SPRAT Thomas	4° ss.	BENTLEY William	8° ss.	HOW John	8° ss.
1703						
	HUNTER Richard	4° ss.	KENNET White	4° ss.	PRIDEAUX Humphrey	4° ss.
1704						
	BISSET Will.	8° ss.	BURNET Gilbert	4° ss.	DUKE Rich. M.A.	4° ss.
	GASTRELL Francis	4° ss.	HOUGH John	4° ss.	HOUGH Nathaniel	4° ss.
	KENNET White	4° ss.	MANNINGHAM Thomas	4° ss.	TAYLOR Christopher	4° ss.
	FREKE Thomas	4° ss.				
1705						
	CAESAR J. James	4° ss.	SPRAT Thomas	4° ss.		
1706						
	GREY Thomas	12° ss.	HUMPHREYS A.	4° ss.	WALLS George	4° ss.
1707						
	ANONYMOUS	8° ss.	CANNON Robert	4° ss.	EDWARDS John	8° ss.
	EDWARDS John	8° ss.	GLEN A. M.A.	4° ss.	HORT Josiah	4° ss.
	STANDEN Jos.	4° ss.	WALROND John	8° ss.	WISE Thomas	4° ss.
	STENNETT Joseph	4° ss.				
1708						
	ANDERSON William	8° coll.	COCKBURN John	8° ss.	GREGORY Thomas	8° coll.
	HOADLY Benjamin	4° ss.	HOADLY Benjamin	4° ss.	LAMBERT Ralph	4° ss.
	MANNINGHAM Thomas	6° ss.	MILBOURNE Luke	8° ss.	STANLEY William	8° ss.
	WHISTON Will. M.A.	8° ss.	CALAMY Edmund	8° ss.	CALAMY Edmund	8° ss.
	CALAMY Edmund	8° ss.				
1709						
	COOKE Thomas	4° ss.	HARE Francis	4° ss.	HOUGH John	4° ss.
	MANNINGHAM Thomas	4° ss.	VESEY William	4° ss.	WILCOCKS Joseph	4° ss.
	WILLIS Richard	8° ss.	STENNETT Joseph	8° ss.		
1710						

Year	Name	Format	Name	Format	Name	Format
	GORDON Will. M.A.	4° ss.	HARRIS John	8° ss.	JEFFERY John	8° coll.
	KENNET White	4° ss.	WELTON Richard	4° ss.	WISE Thomas	8° ss.
	EARL Jabez	8° ss.				
1711	ASPLIN Samuel	8° ss.	JENNINGS John	8° ss.	KENNET White	4° ss.
	SAINT John Pawlet	4° ss.	TRIMNEL Charles	4° ss.		
1712	ASH St. George	8° ss.	BLOMER Ralph	4° ss.	BROWNE Francis	4° ss.
	CHISHULL Edmund	8° ss.	HOUGH John	4° ss.	TRIMNEL Charles	4° ss.
	MATHER Cotton	8° ss.				
1713	HANCOCK John	4° ss.	TRAPP Joseph	4° ss.	WEBSTER R.	8° ss.
	SMITH Jeremiah	8° ss.				
1714	ASH St. George	4° ss.	BURNET Gilbert	4° ss.	DOBOURDIEU Jean Armand	8° ss.
	DOD Samuel	4° ss.	WALLER John	4° ss.	WHITFELD Will. DD.	4° ss.
	WHITFELD Will. DD.	4° ss.	ANDERSON James	8° ss.		
1715	BURSCOUGH William	4° ss.	DAVY J.	8° coll.	KENNET White	4° ss.
	KENNET White	4° ss.	RAWLINS Gershom	8° ss.	STEVANSON William	4° ss.
	SYDALL Elias	4° ss.	TRIMNEL Charles	4° ss.	WRIGHT Samuel	8° ss.
1716	ANONYMOUS	8° ss.	ANONYMOUS	8° ss.	ANONYMOUS	8° ss.
	CARTER Nicholas	8° ss.	CARTER Nicholas	8° ss.	GIBSON Edmund	4° ss.
	HARE Francis	8° ss.	HOADLY Benjamin	4° ss.	LENG John	8° ss.
	LUCAS Richard	8° coll.	NEEDHAM Peter	8° ss.	SMEDLEY Jonathan	8° ss.
	SYDALL Elias	8° ss.	WEST Richard	4° ss.	GROSVENOR Benjamin	8° ss.
1717	MOULD Bernard	8° ss.	SMITH Elisha	8° ss.	BRADBURY Thomas	8° ss.
	COLEMAN Benjamin	8° ss.				
1718	CARTER Benjamin	4° ss.	TAYLOR Abdias	8° ss.	WARD Richard	8° ss.
1719	BUTLER William	4° ss.	BRADBURY Thomas	8° ss.	PEIRCE James	8° ss.
	ROSEWELL Samuel	8° ss.	WISHEART William	4° ss.		
1720	ANONYMOUS	8° ss.	BOULTER Hugh	4° ss.	HEYLYN John	8° ss.
	JONES Walter	8° ss.	WILCOCKS Joseph	4° ss.	LOWMAN Moses	8° ss.
	PEIRCE James	8° ss.	SMYTH George	8° ss.		
1721	BROWNE John	8° coll.	KELSEY Joseph	8° coll.	KNAGGS Thomas	4° ss.
	MASSEY Edmund	8° ss.	PARSONS Thomas	8° ss.	HARRIS William	8° ss.
1722	BURSCOUGH William	4° ss.	CARTER Benjamin	4° ss.	SALWEY John	8° ss.
	SYKES Arthur Ashley	8° ss.	WOTTON William	8° ss.	BROWN Simon	8° coll.
	CALAMY Edmund	8° coll.	KINCH John	8° ss.	WILLARD S.	8° ss.
1723	BULLOCK Thomas	4° ss.	BURROW Robert	8° ss.	DENNE John	4° ss.
	LISLE Samuel	4° ss.	NORRIS John	12° ss.	CLARKE Matthew	8° ss.
	CLARKE Matthew	8° ss.				
1724	BOTT Thomas	8° ss.	BULLOCK Thomas	8° ss.	CUMMING John	8° ss.
	MAYO Richard	4° ss.	MEADOWCOURT Richard	8° ss.	NAYLOR Quintus	8° ss.
	WOOD James	8° ss.				
1725	FELTON Henry	8° ss.	LOCKIER Francis	4° ss.	SYKES Arthur Ashley	4° ss.

Year	Name	Size	Name	Size	Name	Size
	BALL Jacob	8° ss.				
1726						
	CALAMY Benjamin	8° coll.	CLARKE Alured	4° ss.	COLLIER Jeremy	8° ss.
	IBBOT Benj. DD.	8° coll.	LENG John	4° ss.	SCOUGAL Henry	8° coll.
	WHITBY Daniel	8° coll.	WYNNE John	4° ss.	EVANS John	8° ss.
	MANTON Thomas	8° ss.				
1727						
	BOYDELL John	8° ss.	CONYBEARE John	8° ss.	KILBOURN Robert	8° ss.
	MARSHALL Nathaniel	8° ss.	PARKER Henry	4° ss.	PEARCE Zachary	4° ss.
	SMALBROKE Richard	8° ss.	BILLINGSLEY John	8° ss.	EVANS John	8° ss.
	SMYTH George	8° ss.				
1728						
	BATTY Adam	4° ss.	BULLOCK Thomas	8° ss.	HOUGH Thomas	4° ss.
	MAURICE Peter	8° ss.	ROPER Joseph. DD.	4° ss.	STEPHENS Henry	8° coll.
	STEVENSON William	8° ss.	WATSON Joseph	4° ss.	CHANDLER Samuel	8° ss.
	DUCHAL James	8° coll.	PINDAR Thomas	8° ss.	PRINCE Tho. M.A.	8° ss.
	SEWELL Joseph	8° ss.				
1729						
	BURROW Robert	8° ss.	CONYBEARE John	8° ss.	GIBSON Edmund	8° coll.
	JONES David	4° ss.	KILBOURN Robert	4° ss.	LUPTON William	8° coll.
1730						
	DENNE John	4° ss.	LITTLETON Edward	4° ss.	BURROUGHS Joseph	8° ss.
	EVANS John	8° ss.				
1731						
	BOWMAN William	8° ss.	CLARKE Alured	4° ss.	CURTEIS Thomas	4° ss.
	MARSHALL Nathaniel	8° coll.				
1732						
	CROSSINGE Richard	8° ss.	FERREBEE Michael	4° ss.	HARWARD	8° ss.
	MIDDLETON John	4° ss.	MOSS Robert	8° coll.	STEBBING Henry	8° ss.
	TIDCOMBE Jerem.	8° ss.	WARREN Robert	4° ss.	MOLE Thomas	-° ss.
1733						
	COCKMAN Thomas	8° ss.	DENNE John	4° ss.	FELTON Henry	8° ss.
	FELTON Henry	8° ss.	JOHNSTON George	8° ss.	MAULE Henry	4° ss.
	TREBECK Andr. DD.	8° ss.	WATTS George	4° ss.	BURROUGHS Joseph	8° ss.
	PARTINGTON John	8° ss.	SANDERCOCK Edward	8° ss.	WEDDERSPOON Patrick	8° coll.
1734						
	BALLARD Edward	8° ss.	CROWE William	4° ss.	PILLOK Thomas	8° ss.
	RINGER Thomas	8° coll.	RUNDLE Thomas	4° ss.	SHUCKFORD Samuel	8° ss.
	SYNGE Edward	12° ss.				
1735						
	ANONYMOUS	8° ss.	ARROWSMITH Edward	4° ss.	CROWE William	8° ss.
	DREW Robert	8° ss.	HALES Stephen	4° ss.	KERRICK Samuel	8° ss.
	RUNDLE Thomas	4° ss.	STILLINGFLEET Edward	8° ss.	BURROUGHS Joseph	8° ss.
	GROSVENOR Benjamin	8° ss.	NEALE Daniel	8° ss.	SMYTH George	8° ss.
	WRIGHT Samuel	8° ss.				
1736						
	CATCOTT Alex. Stopford	4° ss.	CLARKE Alured	4° ss.	MYONNETT John	8° ss.
	TOTTIE John	8° ss.	WATTS George	4° ss.	SAY Samuel	8° ss.
	SOME David	8° ss.				
1737						
	ANONYMOUS	8° ss.	BROOME William	4° ss.	BUTTS Robert	4° ss.
	DENNE John	8° ss.	HARTE Walter	8° ss.	SHUCKFORD Samuel	4° ss.
	THOMAS John	4° ss.	LANGFORD William	8° ss.		
1738						
	BATEMAN Edmund	4° ss.	DELANY Patrick	8° ss.	HUTCHINSON Thomas	8° ss.
	KNIGHT Samuel	4° ss.	MARTEN Edmond	8° ss.	SHORTHOSE Hugh	8° coll.

Year	Name	Format	Name	Format	Name	Format
	SYNGE Edward	12° ss.	SYNGE Edward	12° ss.	WARNER Ferdinand	4° ss.
	WEBBER Francis. DD.	8° ss.	WILLIAMS Philip	4° ss.	CHANDLER Samuel	8° ss.
	STEWART John	12° ss.				
1739	ANONYMOUS	8° ss.	BOLTON Robert	4° ss.	CHAPMAN John	4° ss.
	CLAGETT Nicholas	4° ss.	COPPING John	4° ss.	CRADOCK John	4° ss.
	STEBBING Henry	8° ss.	WESTON William	8° ss.	WHEATLAND Tho. M.A.	8° coll.
	WHISTON Will. M.A.	fo. ss.	STORY T.	-° ss.	WILSON William	8° ss.
1740	CARTER Nicholas	8° ss.	CLAYTON Robert.	4° ss.	NEWTON Richard	8° ss.
	PARKER Robert	4° ss.	SALTER Samuel	4° ss.	SKEELER Thomas	8° coll.
	WHALLEY John	4° ss.				
1741	GOODALL Henry	4° ss.	LEECHMAN William	8° ss.		
1742	BISCOE Rich	8° coll.	DOWNES John	8° ss.	HUMPHREYS Thomas	8° ss.
	PEGGE Samuel	8° ss.	STUKELEY William	4° ss.	TERRICK Richard	4° ss.
	WATTS George	4° ss.	GUYSE John	8° coll.		
1743	BRUCE Lew. DD.	4° ss.	CLEAVER Will. M.A.	8° ss.	COOKSEY John	8° ss.
	DODWELL William	8° ss.	EDWARDS Joseph	8° ss.	GILBERT John	4° ss.
	SEED Jeremiah	8° coll.	THOMAS John	4° ss.	HUNTER John	8° ss.
	HUNTER John	12° ss.	JENNINGS David	8° ss.	LARDNER Nathaniel	8° ss.
	LEECHMAN William	8° ss.	MILNER John	8° ss.	MORRIS Joseph	8° coll.
1744	BURTON John	8° ss.	CARY Mordecai	4° ss.	DENNE John	4° ss.
	LISLE Samuel	4° ss.	SPRY John	8° ss.	SWIFT Jonathan	4° coll.
	TREBECK Andr. DD.	4° ss.				
1745	CUMING Patrick	8° ss.	DALTON John	4° ss.	DENNE John	8° ss.
	GARNET John	4° ss.	HILL J. S. DD.	8° ss.	LIPTROTT B.	8° ss.
	MEADOWCOURT Richard	8° ss.	SIMS Joseph	4° ss.	SPARKE John	8° ss.
	STEBBING Henry	4° ss.	WHITE John	8° ss.	LATHAM Ebenezer	8° ss.
	ROBERTS Samuel	8° ss.				
1746	BUTLER John	8° ss.	HAYTER Thomas	4° ss.	HUTTON Matthew	4° ss.
	MADDOX Isaac	4° ss.	SYKES Arthur Ashley	4° ss.	THOMAS John	4° ss.
	TUNSTALL James	4° ss.	CHANDLER Samuel	8° ss.	HUGHES Obadiah	8° ss.
	NEWMAN Thomas	8° ss.	WALLACE Robert	8° ss.	WISHART George	8° ss.
1747	BURNET Gilbert	8° coll.	WILSON William	8° ss.		
1748	COX Michael	4° ss.	DRUMMOND Robert	4° ss.	JORTIN John	8° ss.
	KEENE Edmund	8° ss.	MILLES Jeremiah	8° ss.	NICOLLS Samuel	4° ss.
	BARKER John	8° coll.	LARDNER Nathaniel	8° coll.		
1749	BIRCH Thomas	4° ss.	BUTLER Joseph	8° coll.	DRUMMOND Robert	4° ss.
	GREEN John	4° ss.	ORR John	8° coll.	SQUIRE Samuel	4° ss.
	TAYLOR John	4° ss.	WATSON Thomas	4° ss.	WHATLEY Robert	4° ss.
	WHATLEY Robert	8° ss.				
1750	FRANKLIN Thomas	4° ss.	MOSS Charles	4° ss.	SEED Jeremiah	-° coll.
	TREVOR Richard	4° ss.	PRIOR William	8° ss.	WILLIAMS Daniel	8° coll.
1751	CHURCH Tho. DD.	4° ss.	HALES Stephen	4° ss.	LEMOINE Abraham	4° ss.
	MICKLEBOURGH John	8° ss.	SQUIRE Samuel	4° ss.	THOMAS John	4° ss.

Year	Name	Format	Name	Format	Name	Format
1752						
	BRUCE Lew. DD.	4° ss.	CHAPMAN John	4° ss.	CHURCH Tho. DD.	4° ss.
	CRADOCK John	4° ss.	GREEN John	4° ss.	HAYTER Thomas	4° ss.
	MARKHAM William	4° ss.	PARKER William	8° ss.	RANDOLPH Herbert	8° ss.
	THOMAS John	4° ss.	BURROUGHS Joseph	8° ss.	RICHARDSON John	8° ss.
	WISHART George	8° ss.				
1753						
	BUTLER John	4° ss.	HOWARD Leonard	4° ss.	KING Arnold	4° ss.
	LEMOINE Abraham	4° ss.	LLOYD P. M.A.	8° ss.	PARKER William	8° ss.
	WINSTANLEY	8° ss.	AMORY Thomas	8° coll.	DUCHAL James	8° coll.
	FLEMING Caleb	1° ss.				
1754	PRIOR William	8° ss.				
1755	PARKER William	8° ss.				
1756	MOSS Charles	4° ss.				
1758	WEBBER Francis. DD.	4° ss.				
1762	DICK Robert	8° ss.				
1763	LOWTHIAN S.	8° ss.				
1775	WISHART George	12° ss.				
1776	IBBOT Benj. DD.	-° coll.	DICK Robert	8° ss.		
1781	FORD William, jun	8° ss.				

Dr. Williams's Library ("Dr.Ws's")

Year	Name	Format	Name	Format	Name	Format
1660	WILKINSON Henry	4° coll.				
1665	TWISSE Robert	4° ss.				
1667	VINES Richard	8° coll.				
1679	NEEDHAM Robert	8° coll.				
1684	BURTON Hezekiah	8° coll.				
1685	BURTON Hezekiah	8° coll.				
1693	MONRO Alexander	4° coll.				
1694	NORRIS John	8° coll.	SANCROFT William	8° coll.		
1695	S. - - - - H.	12° ss.	WHALEY Nathanael	8° coll.		
1696	MEGGOT Richard	8° coll.				
1697	COCKBURN John	8° coll.				
1698	EDWARDS John	8° coll.	PAYNE William	8° coll.	WHALEY Nathanael	8° coll.
	WHICHCOTE Benj. DD.	8° coll.				

INDEXES TO FIFTH VOLUME: E: LIBRARIES: PART THREE: LONDON AND ETON (Dr. Williams's)

Year	Author	Format	Author	Format	Author	Format
1699						
	CONANT John	8° coll.				
1700						
	STANHOPE George	8° coll.				
1701						
	COX Samuel	8° ss.				
1702						
	EDWARDS John	8° coll.	WAKE William	8° coll.		
1703						
	DORRINGTON Theophilus	8° coll.				
1704						
	WHALEY Nathanael	12° coll.	WHALEY Nathanael	12° coll.		
1705						
	DORRINGTON Theophilus	8° coll.	LAKE Edward	8° coll.		
1707						
	STILLINGFLEET Edward	fo.coll.	BAXTER Richard	fo.coll.	COLMAN Benjamin	8° coll.
1710						
	JEFFERY John	8° coll.				
1711						
	BEVERIDGE William	8° coll.				
1714						
	PIGGOTT John	8° coll.				
1716						
	BARROW Isaac	fo.coll.	WAKE William	8° coll.		
1718						
	SCOTT John	fo.coll.				
1719						
	SHERLOCK William	8° coll.				
1720						
	SHERIDAN William	8° coll.				
1721						
	KNIGHT James	8° coll.				
1722						
	WAKE William	8° coll.	CALAMY Edmund	8° coll.		
1724						
	SOUTH Robert	8° coll.	HARRIS William	8° coll.		
1726						
	HICKES George	8° coll.				
1727						
	SOUTH Robert	8° coll.				
1728						
	NORRIS John PEIRCE James	8° coll. 1° coll.	WHARTON Henry	8° coll.	WHARTON Henry	8° coll.
1732						
	FOSTER James	8° coll.	STENNETT Joseph	8° coll.		
1734						
	CLARKE Samuel	8° coll.				
1735						
	SHARP John	8° coll.				
1736						
	DODDRIDGE Philip	12° coll.				
1737						
	FLEETWOOD William	fo.coll.	FOSTER James	8° coll.		
1742						
	RIDLEY Glocester	8° coll.	EMLYN Thomas	8° coll.		
1743						

Year	Name	Format	Name	Format	Name	Format
1744	DODDRIDGE Philip	8° coll.	JENNINGS David	12° coll.	MORRIS Joseph	8° coll.
1746	FOSTER James	8° coll.				
1747	LEIGHTON Robert	8° coll.				
1748	KNIGHT Henry	8° coll.				
1750	ABERNETHY John	8° coll.				
1751	MAYHEW Jonathan	8° coll.	WILLIAMS Daniel	8° coll.		
1752	JEFFERY John	8° coll.	ABERNETHY John	8° coll.		
1754	CATCOTT Alex. Stopford	8° coll.				
1758	HOADLY Benjamin	8° coll.				
1760	HODGE John	8° coll.				
1763	LARDNER Nathaniel	8° coll.				
1765	HERRING Thomas	8° coll.	SHARP Tho. DD.	8° coll.		
1766	CHURCHILL Charles	8° coll.				
1769	AMORY Thomas	8° coll.				
1772	FREE John	8° ss.				
1775	FLEMING Caleb	8° coll.				
1781	AMORY Thomas	8° coll.				
1797	WILSON Thomas	4° coll.				
	KIDDER Richard	8° coll.				

Eton College ("Eton")

Year	Name	Format	Name	Format	Name	Format
	ANONYMOUS	-° ss.				
1660	BURNEY Richard	4° ss.				
1676	PARKER Timothy	4° ss.				
1679	MANNINGHAM Thomas	8° ss.	MANNINGHAM Thomas	8° ss.	WALLIS John	4° ss.
1680	ANONYMOUS	4° ss.				
1682	CUTLORE Joseph	4° ss.	LAMBE John	4° ss.	PERSE Will. M.A.	4° ss.
1683	MEGGOT Richard	4° ss.	WAGSTAFFE Thomas	4° ss.		
1684	WALKER John	8° ss.				
1685						

INDEXES TO FIFTH VOLUME: E: LIBRARIES: PART THREE: LONDON AND ETON (Eton College)

Year	Name	Format	Name	Format	Name	Format
	HODGES Thomas	4° ss.				
1687	GIFFORD Bonaventura	4° ss.				
1688	BROWNE Thomas	4° ss.	BROWNE Thomas	4° ss.		
1689	BROGRAVE Robert	4° ss.	OLLYFFE John	4° ss.	RESBURY Nathaniel	4° ss.
1690	MAUNDRELL Henry	4° ss.				
1691	IRONSIDE Gilbert	4° ss.	RESBURY Nathaniel	4° ss.		
1693	PRITCHARD Thomas	4° ss.				
1695	CROSSE Walter	4° ss.	HARTCLIFFE John	4° ss.	WILLIAMS John	4° ss.
1696	BRADY Nich. DD.	4° ss.	NEWTE John	4° ss.	TOWERSON Gabriel	4° ss.
1697	BURNET Gilbert	4° ss.	BUTLER Lilly	8° ss.		
1698	ECHÁRD Lawr. M.A.	4° ss.	WESLEY Samuel	8° ss.	SPADEMAN John	8° ss.
1699	CALAMY Edmund	8° ss.				
1700	BRADFORD Samuel	4° ss.	NYE Stephen	8° ss.		
1701	ALLEYNE John SHERLOCK William	4° ss. 4° ss.	ANONYMOUS	8° ss.	BYNNS Richard	4° ss.
1702	HESKITH Thomas	4° ss.	TALBOT William	8° ss.	SHOWER John	4° ss.
1703	STANHOPE George	4° ss.				
1704	GASTRELL Francis FLEMING Robert	4° ss. 8° ss.	WERNDLY J. C.	4° ss.	WILLIS Richard	12° ss.
1705	MILLECHAMP Richard STANHOPE George	4° ss. 4° ss.	NEWCOME Peter	4° ss.	REEVES William	4° ss.
1706	STEPHENS William WILLIAMS John	8° coll. 4° ss.	SYDALL Elias STENNETT Joseph	4° ss. 4° ss.	WELCHMAN Edward	4° ss.
1707	ANONYMOUS OLLYFFE George DENT Giles	8° ss. 8° ss. 4° ss.	BRADY Nich. DD. SAVAGE William	8° ss. 4° ss.	MILBOURNE Luke STRYPE John	8° ss. 4° ss.
1708	ANONYMOUS KNAGGS Thomas	8° ss. 8° ss.	ANONYMOUS	8° ss.	DOWNES Henry	8° ss.
1709	ADAMS John NICHOLS Will. DD. TURNER John	4° ss. 8° ss. 8° ss.	COX Thomas RAWSON Jos. DD.	4° ss. 4° ss.	EDWARDS John TRIMNEL Charles	8° ss. 8° ss.
1710	LURANCY Hippol de	8° ss.	TRIMNEL Charles	4° ss.	WELLS Edward	8° ss.
1711	ANONYMOUS	12° ss.	CANHAM P. L L B.	8° ss.	COOKE Shadrach	8° ss.

Year	Name		Name		Name	
	STRYPE John	8° ss.	<u>DENT Giles</u>	4° ss.		
1712						
	BRETT Thomas	8° coll.	DOBOURDIEU Jean Armand	8° ss.	LYNFORD Thomas	4° ss.
	NEWCOME Henry	8° ss.	SMITH John	8° ss.	STEPHENS William	4° ss.
1713						
	BERKELEY George	8° ss.	BRETT Thomas	8° coll.	MILBOURNE Luke	8° ss.
	WAUGH John	4° ss.	<u>DENT Giles</u>	8° ss.		
1714						
	BOULTER Hugh	4° ss.	BRETT Thomas	8° coll.	BULL Rob.	8° ss.
	BUTLER Lilly	4° ss.	HILLIARD Samuel	8° ss.	RAWSON Jos. DD.	8° ss.
	<u>REYNOLDS John</u>	8° ss.				
1715						
	BOULTER Hugh	8° ss.	BRETT Joseph	8° coll.	EYRE Rich. M.A.	8° ss.
	FURSMAN John	8° ss.	GREENE Thomas	8° ss.	HOUGH Nathaniel	8° ss.
	LLOYD William	8° ss.	NEWCOME Peter	8° ss.	RYE George	4° ss.
	SKERRET Ralph	8° ss.	SMALBROKE Richard	8° ss.	SMEDLEY Jonathan	4° ss.
	SYDALL Elias	4° ss.				
1716						
	ANONYMOUS	8° ss.	BLOMER Ralph	4° ss.	BOULTER Hugh	8° ss.
	BRADFORD Samuel	8° ss.	EYRE Rich. M.A.	4° ss.	GREENE Thomas	4° ss.
	HAYLEY Tho. DD.	8° ss.	NEWTON Richard	4° ss.	SKERRET Ralph	4° ss.
	SKERRET Ralph	4° ss.	SKERRET Ralph	8° ss.	TURNER John	8° ss.
	<u>CALAMY Edmund</u>	8° ss.				
1717						
	BEDFORD Arthur	8° ss.	BENTLEY Richard	4° ss.	CARTER Benjamin	4° ss.
	MARSHALL Nathaniel	8° ss.	STANHOPE Michael	4° ss.	SYKES Arthur Ashley	8° ss.
	TAUBMAN Nathaniel	4° ss.	<u>CUMMING John</u>	8° ss.		
1718						
	BURROUGH John	8° ss.	COLBATCH John	4° ss.	CRADOCK William	8° ss.
	MARSHALL Nathaniel	4° ss.	PAYNE Thomas	4° ss.	RUNDLE Thomas	8° ss.
	STUBBS Philip	8° ss.	WADDINGTON Edward	8° ss.		
1719						
	DOWNES Henry	4° ss.	LENG John	8° ss.	<u>EARL Jabez</u>	8° ss.
	<u>PALKE William</u>	8° ss.				
1720						
	CLAGETT Nicholas	4° ss.	DISNEY John	8° ss.	DOWNES Henry	4° ss.
	JOHNSTON Henry	8° ss.	SMALBROKE Richard	8° ss.	<u>CALAMY Edmund</u>	8° ss.
1721						
	BERRIMAN John	8° ss.	CARTER Benjamin	4° ss.	DOWNES Henry	4° ss.
	HAYLEY Tho. DD.	4° ss.	MEADOWCOURT Richard	8° ss.	RUSSELL John	8° ss.
	SAUNDERS Erasmus	8° ss.	SLADE Joseph	4° ss.		
1722						
	BERRIMAN William	4° ss.	CLERKE Francis	8° ss.	IBBETSON Richard	4° ss.
1723						
	BULL Rob.	8° ss.	BUTLER William	4° ss.	COOKE Shadrach	8° ss.
	GURDON Brampton	4° ss.	HUTCHINSON Francis	4° ss.	MAWSON Matthias	4° ss.
	SKERRET Ralph	4° ss.	WATERLAND Daniel	8° ss.		
1724						
	BRAMSTON John	8° ss.	CHANDLER Edward	4° ss.	DOBOURDIEU Jean Armand	8° ss.
	EDGLEY Samuel	4° ss.	KNIGHT Samuel	8° ss.	SMALBROKE Richard	8° ss.
	SMITH Elisha	8° ss.				
1726						
	MEADOWCOURT Richard	8° ss.	STEPHENS Lewis	4° ss.	<u>CUMMING Patrick</u>	8° ss.
1727						
	BISSET Will.	8° ss.	TILLY William	4° ss.		
1728						

Year	Name	Format	Name	Format	Name	Format
	HEYLYN John	8° ss.	SMALBROKE Richard	4° ss.	WILCOCKS Joseph	4° ss.
1729	ANONYMOUS	8° ss.	JAMES William	8° ss.	THOMAS John	4° ss.
	WADDINGTON Edward	4° ss.	WADE George. DD.	8° coll.	BRADBURY Thomas	8° ss.
1730	STEBBING Henry	8° ss.				
1733	BURTON John	4° ss.				
1736	PEARCE Zachary	12° ss.				
1739	WILCOCKS Joseph	4° ss.				
1741	CLARKE Alured	4° ss.				
1743	HOLE William	4° ss.	SLEECH John	4° ss.		
1744	BEARCROFT Philip	4° ss.	BENTHAM Edward	8° ss.	SPRY John	8° ss.
	WILLATTS Charles	4° ss.				
1746	BALLARD Edward	4° ss.				
1747	HUME John	4° ss.	KENNICOTT Benjamin	8° ss.	KENNICOTT Benjamin	8° ss.
	MORELL Thomas	8° ss.	WESTON Stephen	8° coll.		
1748	CHAPMAN John	4° ss.	MILLES Jeremiah	8° ss.		
1749	SQUIRE Samuel	4° ss.				
1750	BENTHAM Edward	8° ss.	COOKE Will. DD.	8° ss.	WEBBER Francis. DD.	8° ss.
1752	AYSCOUGH Francis	4° ss.	MADDOX Isaac	4° ss.	OSBALDESTON Richard	4° ss.
1753	KENNICOTT Benjamin	8° ss.				
1763	BERRIMAN William	8° coll.				
1764	BURTON John	8° coll.				
1766	BURTON John	8° ss.	BURTON John	8° coll.		
1779	ANONYMOUS	8° ss.				
1781	GOLDWIN William	4° ss.				

Sion College ("Sion")

Year	Name	Format	Name	Format	Name	Format
----	HARDY Nathaniel	-° coll.				
1607	WILKINSON Robert	4° ss.				
1610	STAYNOE Thomas	4° ss.				
1627	MAYNWARING Roger	4° ss.				
1660	BARKER Edmund	4° ss.	CLELAND Thomas	4° ss.	DUNCH John	4° ss.

Year	Name	Format	Name	Format	Name	Format
	GAUDEN John	4° ss.	LIVESEY James	8° ss.	LIVESEY James	8° ss.
	LIVESEY John	8° ss.	PATRICK Simon	4° ss.	STANDFAST Richard	8° ss.
	TOWERS John	8° ss.	TOWERS John	8° ss.	TOWERS John	8° ss.
	BROOKS Thomas	8° ss.	POOL Matthew	4° ss.	WILKINSON Henry	4° coll.
1661	BROWNRIG Ralph	fo.coll.	COLET John	4° ss.	COPLESTONE John	4° ss.
	CRAGGE John	8° ss.	HEYRICK Richard	4° ss.	MASTERSON George	12° ss.
	WILLAN Edward	4° ss.	BROOKS Thomas	8° ss.		
1662	BOREMAN Rich. DD.	8° ss.	LANEY Benjamin	4° ss.	WINTER John	4° ss.
	WINTER John	4° ss.	WREN Matthew	4° ss.	BROOKS Thomas	8° ss.
	BROOKS Thomas	8° ss.	HIBBERT Hen	fo.coll.		
1663	LANEY Benjamin	4° ss.	LEE Richard	4° ss.	MASON Charles	4° ss.
	WOMOCK Lawrence	4° ss.				
1664	BROWNRIG Ralph	fo.coll.	MARTIN John	4° ss.	PEARSON Richard	4° ss.
1665	DOLBEN John	4° ss.	DOLBEN John	4° ss.	EDWARDS John	4° ss.
	KINGSTON Richard	4° ss.	LANEY Benjamin	4° ss.	LANEY Benjamin	4° ss.
	WILLIAMS Griffith	4° coll.				
1666	HALL George	4° ss.	PERRINCHIEF Richard	4° ss.		
1667	BAGSHAW Henry	4° ss.	BRADLEY Thomas	4° ss.		
1668	BASIRE Isaac	8° ss.	GEARING William	4° ss.	LINGARD Ric. DD.	4° ss.
1669	CONANT Malachi	4° ss.	DAVENPORT John	4° ss.	SPARROW Anthony	4° ss.
1670	DOBSON John	4° ss.	PATRICK Simon	4° ss.	PATRICK Simon	8° ss.
	SEIGNIOR George	8° coll.	WARD Seth	4° ss.	WEST Rich. DD.	4° ss.
	BEVERLEY Thomas	4° ss.	BRYAN John	8° ss.		
1671	DURHAM William	4° ss.	NORTH John	4° ss.	PIERCE Tho. DD.	4° coll.
	GREENHILL William	8° coll.	WILKINSON Henry	8° ss.		
1672	BELL William	4° ss.	BOYS Edward	8° coll.	FARINDON Anth. B.D.	fo.coll.
	FRANK Mark	fo.coll.	GARDINER Samuel	4° ss.	HORTON Thomas	4° ss.
	MEDE Joseph	fo.coll.	MOULIN DU Peter	4° ss.	WARD Seth	8° coll.
1673	BAGSHAW Henry	4° ss.	CALAMY Benjamin	4° ss.	EGAN Anthony	4° ss.
	HALES John	4° coll.	HAYWARD Roger	4° ss.	HOLLINGWORTH Richard	4° ss.
	JACKSON Thomas	fo.coll.	LAMBE John	4° ss.	LLOYD William	4° ss.
	PASTON James	4° ss.	PATRICK Simon	4° ss.	PEARSON John	4° ss.
	SHARROCK Robert	4° coll.	WARD Seth	4° ss.		
1674	CROFT Herbert	4° ss.	JAMES Henry	4° ss.	KELSEY Joseph	4° ss.
	LIVESEY James	8° ss.	WARD Hamnett	4° ss.	WARD Seth	8° coll.
1675	BARNE Miles	4° ss.	BONHOME Joshua	4° ss.	BURNET Gilbert	4° ss.
	DURHAM William	4° ss.	FELL John	4° ss.	GREGORY Fran. DD.	4° ss.
	JANE Will. DD.	4° ss.	JEKYLL Thomas	4° coll.	LANEY Benjamin	4° ss.
	MEGGOT Richard	4° ss.	MOTTE DE LA Francis	4° ss.	NAILOUR William	4° ss.
	SMITH Henry	4° coll.	SMITH Thomas	4° ss.	SUDBURY John	4° ss.
	WOOLLEY John	4° ss.				

Year	Name	Format	Name	Format	Name	Format
1676	CARTWRIGHT Thomas	4° ss.	CAVE Will. DD.	4° ss.	CLEAVER John	4° ss.
	HORDEN John	4° ss.	JENNER Dav. B.D.	4° ss.	MILL John	4° ss.
	SCATTERGOOD Samuel	4° ss.	SUDBURY John	4° ss.	TEMPLER John	4° ss.
	TUCKNEY Anthony	4° coll.				
1677	BRAMHALL John	fo. coll.	CRADOCK Zechary	4° ss.	GIBBES Charles	4° coll.
	MARCH John	4° ss.	PINDAR William	4° ss.	PITTIS Thomas	4° ss.
	RAINBOW Edward	4° ss.	SUDBURY John	4° ss.	TURNER Bryan	4° ss.
	WILKINS John	12° coll.				
1678	BATTIE William	4° ss.	BELL William	4° ss.	BROME James	4° ss.
	CADE William	4° ss.	CAVE John	4° ss.	CROFT Herbert	4° ss.
	DILLINGHAM William	4° ss.	FORD Simon	8° ss.	JAMES John	4° ss.
	LATHAM Paul	4° ss.	PATRICK Simon	4° ss.	PATRICK Simon	4° ss.
	REYNOLDS John	4° ss.	ROLLS Samuel	8° coll.	WALKER Anthony	8° ss.
	FROYSELL Thomas	8° coll.				
1679	BARKSDALE Clement	4° ss.	BROME James	4° ss.	FARINDON Anth. B.D.	fo. coll.
	HERNE Samuel	4° ss.	HORNE Thomas	4° ss.	JANE Will. DD.	4° ss.
	LLOYD William	4° ss.	LYNFORD Thomas	4° ss.	MANNINGHAM Thomas	8° ss.
	MANNINGHAM Thomas	8° ss.	OATES Titus	4° ss.	PIERCE Tho. DD.	4° coll.
	PIERCE Tho. DD.	4° coll.	PIERCE Tho. DD.	4° coll.	RALEIGH Walter	4° coll.
	REYNOLDS Edward	fo. coll.	TURNER John	4° ss.	WILLIAMS John	4° ss.
1680	BAGSHAW Henry	8° coll.	BATTIE William	4° ss.	CAMFIELD Benjamin	4° ss.
	CAVE Will. DD.	4° ss.	FELL John	4° ss.	HOLDEN Richard	4° ss.
	LAMBE John	4° ss.	LITTLETON Adam	4° ss.	LITTLETON Adam	fo. coll.
	NANFAN Bridges	8° ss.	OWTRAM William	8° coll.	PATRICK Simon	4° ss.
	ROBOTHAM Charles	12° ss.	ROBOTHAM Charles	12° ss.	JOHNSON John	4° ss.
1681	BURNET Gilbert	4° ss.	C. - - - - N.	4° ss.	CAVE John	8° ss.
	FREEMAN Samuel	4° ss.	HICHMAN Charles	4° ss.	HOOPER George	4° ss.
	MANNINGHAM Thomas	4° ss.	PATRICK Simon	4° ss.	PATRICK Simon	4° ss.
	RESBURY Nathaniel	4° ss.	RESBURY Nathaniel	4° ss.	ROGERS John	4° ss.
	TURNER Francis	4° ss.	WALLS George	4° ss.	WILSON Thomas	4° ss.
1682	BARNE Miles	4° ss.	CAMFIELD Benjamin	4° coll.	CAVE John	4° ss.
	COMBER Thomas	4° ss.	DOVE Heb. DD.	4° ss.	EVANS John	4° ss.
	FULLER Samuel	4° ss.	HUGHES William	8° ss.	JAMES John	4° ss.
	KIDDER Richard	4° ss.	KINGSTON Richard	4° ss.	MILBOURNE Luke	4° ss.
	PAYNE William	4° ss.	PELLING Edward	4° ss.	PERSE Will. M.A.	4° ss.
	TURNER Francis	4° ss.	WALKER Anthony	4° ss.	WALLIS John	4° ss.
	WETENHALL Edward	4° ss.	WETENHALL Edward	4° ss.	WILKINSON Robert	4° ss.
	WRAY William	4° ss.	BRUCE Titus	4° ss.		
1683	BARROW John	4° ss.	BASSET Will.	4° ss.	BOLTON William	4° ss.
	CALAMY Benjamin	4° ss.	CAVE John	4° coll.	CLAGETT Nich. M.A.	4° ss.
	FOWLER Edward	4° ss.	HOPKINS William	4° ss.	KIMBERLEY Jonathan	4° ss.
	MEGGOT Richard	4° ss.	MORLEY George	4° ss.	PELLING Edward	4° ss.
	POWELL Charles	4° ss.	RODERICK Richard	4° ss.	RUST George	4° ss.
	TURNER Francis	5° ss.	TURNER John	4° ss.	COLLINGES John	4° ss.
1684	BROWNE Philip	4° ss.	BRYAN Matt. LLD.	4° ss.	BURTON Hezekiah	8° coll.
	CAMFIELD Benjamin	4° ss.	FORENESS E.	4° ss.	HALL Timothy	4° ss.
	HESKETH Henry	4° ss.	KETTLEWELL John	4° ss.	LAKE Edward	4° ss.

Year	Name	Format	Name	Format	Name	Format
	LAMBE John	4° ss.	LEIGH Thomas	4° ss.	MANNINGHAM Thomas	4° ss.
	NEWTON John	4° ss.	PEARSON Richard	4° ss.	RODERICK Richard	4° ss.
	SMYTHIES William	4° ss.	STRATFORD Nicholas	8° ss.	TURNER Francis	4° ss.
	TURNER John	8° ss.	VINCENT Nathaniel	4° ss.	WAKE William	4° ss.
1685						
	ADEE Nicholas	4° ss.	ALLESTREE Charles	4° ss.	ANDERSON Henry	4° ss.
	BURTON Hezekiah	8° coll.	CAVE John	4° ss.	COOKE Shadrach	4° ss.
	FOWLER Edward	4° ss.	FYSH Thomas	4° ss.	GASKARTH John	4° ss.
	HUTTON Charles	4° ss.	MANNINGHAM Thomas	4° ss.	MOSSOM Robert	fo. coll.
	PELLING Edward	4° ss.	SHERLOCK William	4° ss.	SION Alexander	4° ss.
	TURNER Tho. DD.	4° ss.	WHITBY Daniel	4° ss.	WHITBY Daniel	4° ss.
	WHITBY Daniel	4° ss.	WILLIAMS John	4° ss.		
1686						
	CARTWRIGHT Thomas	4° ss.	COLLIER Jeremy	4° ss.	FEN James	4° ss.
	HICHMAN Charles	4° ss.	KIDDER Richard	4° ss.	KING William	4° ss.
	MANNINGHAM Thomas	4° ss.	PATRICK Simon	4° ss.	PIERCE Tho. DD.	4° ss.
	TULLIE George	4° ss.	TURNER John	4° ss.		
1687						
	COMBER Thomas	4° ss.	HAYLEY William	4° ss.	MANNINGHAM Thomas	4° ss.
	MAPLETOFT John	4° ss.	PATRICK Simon	4° ss.	STRATFORD Nicholas	4° ss.
	TURNER John	4° ss.	BEVERLEY Thomas	4° ss.		
1688						
	BROWNE Thomas	4° ss.	BROWNE Thomas	4° ss.	BURNET Gilbert	8° ss.
	DUREL John	4° ss.	HELLIER Henry	4° ss.	SCARISBRIKE Edward	4° ss.
	SCARISBRIKE Edward	4° ss.				
1689						
	BEVERIDGE William	4° ss.	BRINGHURST Isaac	4° ss.	CARSWELL Francis	4° ss.
	HALL Timothy	4° ss.	JAY Stephen	4° ss.	LLOYD William	4° ss.
	MARIOTT Thomas	4° ss.	OLLYFFE John	4° ss.	PATRICK Simon	4° ss.
	PATRICK Simon	4° ss.	PATRICK Simon	4° ss.	RESBURY Nathaniel	4° ss.
	ROYSE Geor. DD.	4° ss.	STRYPE John	4° ss.	TENISON Thomas	4° ss.
	TULLIE George	4° ss.	VESEY John	4° ss.	WILSON William	4° ss.
1690						
	BURNET Gilbert	4° ss.	FREEMAN Samuel	4° ss.	FREEMAN Samuel	4° ss.
	HICHMAN Charles	4° ss.	HICHMAN Charles	4° ss.	KIDDER Richard	4° ss.
	LLOYD William	4° ss.	PATRICK Simon	4° ss.	PELLING Edward	4° ss.
	ROYSE Geor. DD.	4° ss.	TENISON Thomas	4° ss.	TENNISON Richard	4° ss.
	WICHART John	4° ss.				
1691						
	BARKER Ralph	4° ss.	BURNET Gilbert	4° ss.	CLARKE Joshua	4° ss.
	COOKE Shadrach	4° ss.	DOVE Heb. DD.	4° ss.	FOWLER Edward	4° ss.
	JANE Will. DD.	4° ss.	KELSEY Joseph	4° ss.	KING William	4° ss.
	LLOYD William	4° ss.	PATRICK Simon	4° ss.	PELLING Edward	4° ss.
	TENISON Thomas	4° ss.	TENISON Thomas	4° ss.	WALLIS John	4° coll.
	MEAD Matthew	4° ss.				
1692						
	BENTLEY Richard	4° coll.	FOWLER Edward	4° ss.	GEE Edward	4° ss.
	HICKERINGILL Edmond	4° coll.	HICKERINGILL Edmond.	4° ss.	JANE Will. DD.	4° ss.
	JONES David	4° ss.	KIDDER Richard	4° ss.	LINDESAY Thomas	4° ss.
	MANNINGHAM Thomas	4° ss.	MANNINGHAM Thomas	4° ss.	PATRICK Simon	4° ss.
	POWELL Jos. M.A.	4° ss.	SHERLOCK William	4° ss.	SMYTHIES William	4° ss.
	STANLEY William	4° ss.	WALLIS John	4° coll.	WETENHALL Edward	4° ss.
	WHITING Charles	4° ss.	ROGERS Thomas	8° ss.		
1693						
	CROSS Walter	4° ss.	FREEMAN Samuel	4° ss.	HICHMAN Charles	4° ss.
	HOLLINGWORTH Richard	4° ss.	KNAGGS Thomas	4° ss.	MANNINGHAM Thomas	4° ss.

Year	Name	Format	Name	Format	Name	Format
	MONRO Alexander	4° coll.	PRITCHARD Thomas	4° ss.	RESBURY Nathaniel	4° ss.
	ROBERTS Edward	4° ss.	STRENGFELLOW William	4° ss.	WARLY Jonas	4° ss.
	BEVERLEY Thomas	4° ss.				
1694	BATTELL Ralph	4° ss.	CAMPION Abraham	4° ss.	FREEMAN Samuel	4° ss.
	HOOPER George	4° ss.	KIDDER Richard	4° ss.	KIDDER Richard	4° ss.
	MANNINGHAM Thomas	4° ss.	MANNINGHAM Thomas	4° ss.	SANCROFT William	8° coll.
	STEPHENS William	4° ss.	STRATFORD Nicholas	4° ss.	SYKES Thomas	4° ss.
	TENISON Thomas	4° ss.	TENISON Thomas	4° ss.	BEVERLEY Thomas	4° ss.
1695	ADAMS John	4° ss.	CORBIN W.	4° ss.	FISHER Joseph	4° ss.
	GARDINER James	4° ss.	GROVE Robert	4° ss.	HAYLEY William	4° ss.
	HICHMAN Charles	4° ss.	LAMBE John	4° ss.	MANNINGHAM Thomas	4° ss.
	MANNINGHAM Thomas	4° ss.	RUE DE LA	4° ss.	TENISON Thomas	4° ss.
	WHINCOP Thomas	4° ss.	WILLIAMS John	4° ss.	WILLIAMS John	4° ss.
	BEVERLEY Thomas	4° ss.	BEVERLEY Thomas	4° ss.	HOW John	4° ss.
1696	ADAMS John	4° ss.	BRADFORD Samuel	4° ss.	GARDINER James	4° ss.
	ISHAM Zach. DD.	4° ss.	KEITH George	4° ss.	LAMBE John	4° ss.
	LANCASTER William	4° ss.	MERITON Henry	4° ss.	NEWTE John	4° ss.
	PATRICK Simon	4° ss.	SMITH William	4° ss.	STAFFORD Richard	8° ss.
1697	BRAMSTON William	4° ss.	COCKBURN John	8° coll.	COMBER Thomas	4° ss.
	LLOYD William	4° ss.	LUZANCY Hippolytus Du	4° ss.	SEWELL Thomas	4° ss.
	STANHOPE George	4° ss.	STAFFORD Richard	8° ss.	STAFFORD Richard	12° ss.
1698	LYNFORD Thomas	4° ss.	MILBOURNE Luke	4° ss.		
1699	CONANT John	8° coll.	EDWARDS John	4° ss.	HESKETH Henry	4° ss.
	SMALWOOD James	4° ss.	GOODWIN Thomas	4° ss.		
1700	ADAMS John	4° ss.	CHETWOOD Knightly	7° ss.	ELLISON Nath. DD.	8° ss.
	FREEMAN Samuel	4° ss.	HARE Francis	4° ss.	HOLLAND Rich. M.A.	4° ss.
	KEITH George	4° ss.	KNAGGS Thomas	4° ss.	MAURICE David	4° ss.
	SHUTTLEWORTH John	4° ss.	STEPHENS William	4° ss.		
1701	BISSE Philip	4° ss.	COLET John	-° ss.	HASLEWOOD John	4° ss.
	HEYWOOD Oliver	8° ss.	HOOPER George	4° ss.	ISHAM Zach. DD.	4° ss.
	MARSH Richard	4° ss.	PEAD Deuel	4° ss.	SHERLOCK William	4° ss.
	STUBBS Philip	4° ss.	WHINCOP Thomas	4° ss.	STAFFORD Richard	8° ss.
1702	BRAGGE Francis	8° coll.	HILL Anthony	8° ss.	HOLLAND Rich. M.A.	4° ss.
	NEEDHAM William	4° ss.	NICHOLS Will. DD.	4° ss.	SACHEVERELL Henry	4° ss.
	TRELAWNEY Jonathan Sir	4° ss.	WAKE William	8° coll.	WILLIAMS John	4° ss.
1703	RESBURY Nathaniel	4° ss.	WHITBY Daniel	4° ss.		
1704	BRAGGE Francis	8° coll.	BURNET Gilbert	4° ss.	COOKE Thomas	4° ss.
	ELSTOB Will. M.A.	4° ss.	ELSTOB Will. M.A.	4° ss.	FINA Ferdinand	4° ss.
	GALE Thomas	8° coll.	GASTRELL Francis	4° ss.	HOOPER George	4° ss.
	ISHAM Zach. DD.	4° ss.	KING William	4° ss.	LENG John	4° ss.
	MILBOURNE Luke	4° ss.	SACHEVERELL Henry	4° ss.	SAVAGE John	4° ss.
	SHERLOCK William	4° ss.	SHERWILL Thomas	4° ss.	SHERWILL Thomas	4° ss.
	SMEATON Samuel	4° ss.	SPARROW Anthony	4° ss.	WILLIS Richard	4° ss.
1705	ADAMS John	4° ss.	ALTHAM Roger	4° ss.	GASKARTH John	4° ss.

Year	Name	Size	Name	Size	Name	Size
	HIGGINS Francis	8° ss.	HOADLY Benjamin	4° ss.	JEPHSON Alexander	4° ss.
	KING William	4° ss.	MATHER John	4° ss.	REEVES William	4° ss.
	STANHOPE George	4° ss.	STANHOPE George	4° ss.	WILLIS Richard	4° ss.
	WILLIS Richard	4° ss.				
1706	BURNET Gilbert	4° ss.	BURNET Gilbert	4° ss.	DORRINGTON Theophilus	4° ss.
	GARDINER James	4° ss.	GERY Robert	4° ss.	HOUGH Nathaniel	4° ss.
	KENNET White	4° ss.	KENNET White	4° ss.	KENNET White	4° ss.
	KING William	4° ss.	KNAGGS Thomas	4° ss.	MANNINGHAM Thomas	4° ss.
	NICHOLSON William	4° ss.	OWEN Thomas	4° ss.	SACHEVERELL Henry	4° ss.
	SHARP J. M.A.	8° ss.	SMALBROKE Richard	4° ss.	STANHOPE George	4° ss.
	STANHOPE George	4° ss.	TRAPP Joseph	4° ss.	WELTON Richard	4° ss.
	WOTTON William	4° ss.	STENNETT Joseph	4° ss.		
1707	BRADY Nich. DD.	8° ss.	BRADY Nich. DD.	8° ss.	BROUGHTON John	4° ss.
	CHISHULL Edmund	4° ss.	HACKET Lawrence	4° ss.	HASLEWOOD John	4° ss.
	HOADLY John	4° ss.	JENKS Richard	4° ss.	LIGHTFOOT Robert	8° ss.
	MANNINGHAM Thomas	8° ss.	MILBOURNE Luke	8° ss.	NELSON Hen.	8° ss.
	NICOLSON William	4° ss.	PATRICK Simon	4° ss.	RODERICK Richard	4° ss.
	STRYPE John	4° ss.	TYLER John	4° ss.	WILLIAMS Charles	4° ss.
	WILLIAMS Charles	4° ss.	WILLIS Richard	4° ss.	DENT Giles	4° ss.
1708	ADAMS John	4° ss.	ADAMS John	4° ss.	ADAMS Rice	8° ss.
	CANNELL Joseph	4° ss.	CHETWOOD Knightly	4° ss.	DOWNES Henry	8° ss.
	EYRE Robert	4° ss.	KENNET White	8° ss.	KNAGGS Thomas	8° ss.
	MANNINGHAM Thomas	1° ss.	MILNER William	8° ss.	SACHEVERELL Henry	4° ss.
	STEPHENS Henry	4° ss.	STOUGHTON William	4° ss.		
1709	BRYDGES Henry	8° ss.	EDWARDS John	8° ss.	GIBSON Sam.	8° ss.
	HOARD Samuel	8° ss.	KENNET White	8° ss.	LYNFORD Thomas	8° ss.
	MAYNWARING Roger	8° ss.	PALMER Samuel	8° ss.	PELLING John	4° ss.
	RAWSON Jos. DD.	4° ss.	SACHEVERELL Henry	4° ss.	SACHEVERELL Henry	4° ss.
	TRIMNEL Charles	4° ss.	TRIMNEL Charles	4° ss.		
1710	ADAMS John	4° ss.	ARCHER Edmund	8° ss.	BENNET Thomas	8° ss.
	BERDMORE	4° ss.	BINCKES William	8° ss.	BRADFORD Samuel	4° ss.
	BRADFORD Samuel	8° ss.	BURNET Gilbert	8° ss.	BUTLER Lilly	4° ss.
	CORNEWALL Fred. M.A.	8° ss.	DANE John	4° ss.	GATTON Benjamin	4° ss.
	GODDARD Thomas	4° ss.	GODDARD Thomas	8° ss.	HIGDEN Will. DD.	4° ss.
	JOHNSON Samuel	-° coll.	KENNET White	4° ss.	LAMBE Henry	8° ss.
	LEWIS Henry	8° ss.	LUCAS Richard	8° coll.	LUNN William	4° ss.
	NEEDHAM John	8° ss.	PHILIPS David	8° ss.	PRIEST Simon	8° ss.
	STANHOPE Michael	8° ss.	SWIFT Thomas	8° ss.	SYNGE Edward	8° ss.
	WELLS Edward	8° ss.	WELTON Richard	4° ss.	WEST Richard	8° ss.
	WHALEY Nathanael	8° ss.				
1711	BISSE Thomas	8° ss.	BISSE Thomas	8° ss.	COLNET William	8° ss.
	CROFT Thomas	8° ss.	FRIEND Robert	4° ss.	GOOCH Thomas Sir	4° ss.
	GRIFFITH Robert	4° ss.	HARE Francis	8° ss.	HOWELL Will. M.A.	8° ss.
	JENNINGS John	8° ss.	RICHARDSON William	4° ss.	SAINT John Pawlet	4° ss.
	STUBBS Philip	8° ss.	TRAPP Joseph	4° ss.	WATTS Robert	8° ss.
	WRIGHT Samuel	8° ss.				
1712	ALTHAM Roger	4° ss.	ARCHER Edmund	8° ss.	BISSE Thomas	4° ss.
	BRETT Thomas	8° coll.	CHISHULL Edmund	1° ss.	CHISHULL Edmund	8° ss.
	DOBOURDIEU Jean Armand	8° ss.	DORRINGTON Theophilus	8° ss.	HAYLEY Tho. DD.	8° ss.

Year	Name	Format	Name	Format	Name	Format
	HOWELL Will. M.A.	8° ss.	IBBETSON Richard	8° ss.	KENNET White	4° ss.
	LORRAIN Paul	8° ss.	REEVES William	4° ss.	SHUTTLEWOOD John	8° ss.
	STEPHENS William	4° ss.	STUBBS Philip	4° ss.	SYNGE Edward	8° ss.
	TASWELL William	4° ss.	TILLY William	8° coll.	TRIMNEL Charles	4° ss.
	WHITAKER Thomas	8° coll.	WRIGHT Samuel	8° ss.		
1713	BRADFORD Samuel	4° ss.	BRETT Thomas	8° coll.	BROUGHTON John	8° ss.
	BULL George	8° coll.	BURNET Gilbert	8° coll.	COLLIER Arthur	8° ss.
	CUMMINGS George	8° ss.	EYRE Rich. M.A.	8° ss.	GARDINER James	4° ss.
	GOOCH Thomas Sir	4° ss.	HOOPER George	4° ss.	JOHNSON Samuel	fo. coll.
	MILBOURNE Luke	4° ss.	NEWTON Richard	4° ss.	NEWTON Robert	4° ss.
	REEVES William	4° ss.	SACHEVERELL Henry	4° ss.	GREENE John	8° ss.
1714	BISSE Thomas	4° ss.	BRAMSTON William	4° ss.	BRETT Thomas	8° coll.
	BURNET Gilbert	4° ss.	CHISHULL Edmund	4° ss.	LOMBARD Daniel	8° ss.
	MARSHALL John	8° ss.	MARSHALL Nathaniel	8° ss.	RAMSAY John	4° ss.
	READING Will. M.A.	8° ss.	ROBINSON John	4° ss.	RYE George	8° ss.
	SACHEVERELL Henry	4° ss.	SMEDLEY Jonathan	8° ss.	SPINCKES Nathaniel	8° ss.
	STANHOPE George	4° ss.	WILLIAMS John	8° ss.	WOODFORD Matthew	8° ss.
	ANDERSON James	8° ss.	BATES John	8° ss.		
1715	ACRES Joseph	8° ss.	BENTLEY Richard	8° ss.	BRETT Joseph	8° coll.
	HOADLY Benjamin	8° ss.	HOLE Matthew	8° ss.	LACY James	8° ss.
	MILBOURNE Luke	8° ss.	RAWLINS Gershom	8° ss.	SAVAGE William	4° ss.
	SHOREY William	8° ss.	SKERRET Ralph	8° ss.	TOPPING Henry	8° ss.
	WAUGH John	8° ss.	WHATELEY Josiah	8° ss.	WHATELEY Josiah	8° ss.
	WILLIS Richard	4° ss.				
1716	BARROW Isaac	fo. coll.	BENNET Thomas	8° ss.	BISSE Thomas	8° ss.
	BLACKBURNE Lancelot.	4° ss.	BLENNERHAYSETT Thomas	4° ss.	BOYS James	fo. coll.
	CHANDLER Edward	4° ss.	EYRE Rich. M.A.	4° ss.	HOADLY Benjamin	8° ss.
	MANGEY Thomas	8° ss.	MYNORS Willoughby	8° ss.	NEWTON Richard	4° ss.
	PEPLOE Samuel	8° ss.	PEPLOE Samuel	8° ss.	STURMY Daniel	8° coll.
	WILLIS Richard	4° ss.	ENTY John	4° ss.	WISHEART William	8° coll.
1717	BYRCHE William	8° ss.	HANNES William	8° ss.	HOADLY Benjamin	4° ss.
	SMALRIDGE George	8° coll.	STUART William	8° ss.	SUTTON Gibbon	8° ss.
1718	BRYAN Augustine	8° ss.	HAYLEY Tho. DD.	8° ss.	KINNERSLEY Thomas	8° ss.
	MARSHALL Nathaniel	4° ss.	SUTTON Gibbon	8° coll.		
1719	BRADFORD Samuel	4° ss.	CHANDLER Edward	4° ss.	DRAKE Samuel	8° ss.
	HOLDSWORTH Winch. DD.	8° ss.	KETTLEWELL John	fo. coll.	KNIGHT James	4° ss.
	MANGEY Thomas	4° ss.	MANGEY Thomas	4° ss.	MARSHALL Nathaniel	8° ss.
	SOLEY Joseph	4° ss.	TOPPING Henry	8° ss.	PALKE William	8° ss.
1720	ALLET Thomas	8° ss.	BLAIR James	8° coll.	FIDDES Rich. DD.	fo. ss.
	HASLEWOOD Francis	4° ss.	KNIGHT James	4° ss.	NEWCOME John	8° ss.
	WOTTON William	8° ss.				
1721	BAYLY Benjamin	8° coll.	BERRIMAN John	8° ss.	BERRIMAN William	4° ss.
	BERRIMAN William	4° ss.	BOULTER Hugh	4° ss.	GILLMAN John	8° ss.
	HOADLY Benjamin	4° ss.	HOLE Matthew	8° ss.	MARSHALL Nathaniel	4° ss.
	MARSHALL Nathaniel	4° ss.	STEBBING Henry	8° ss.	WATERLAND Daniel	8° ss.
1722	BERRIMAN William	4° ss.	BERRIMAN William	4° ss.	CONYBEARE John	8° ss.

Year	Name	Format	Name	Format	Name	Format
	IBBETSON Richard	4° ss.	LOWTH Will. DD.	8° ss.	MARSHALL Nathaniel	4° ss.
	MASSEY Edmund	8° ss.	WAUGH John	4° ss.		
1723						
	RODERICK Richard	4° ss.	WALKER John	8° ss.	WATERLAND Daniel	4° ss.
	WATERLAND Daniel	4° ss.	WATERLAND Daniel	8° ss.	WEBSTER James	12° coll.
1724						
	CROWE William	8° ss.	READING Will. M.A.	8° coll.	SMALRIDGE George	fo. coll.
	WILCOCKS Joseph	4° ss.				
1725						
	BERRIMAN William	4° ss.	BERRIMAN William	8° coll.	COLLIER Jeremy	8° coll.
	DREW Robert	8° ss.	MASSEY Edmund	8° ss.	ROPER Joseph. DD.	4° ss.
	SHOREY William	8° coll.				
1726						
	BERRIMAN William	4° ss.	BINGHAM Joseph	fo. coll.	BISHOP Thomas	8° coll.
	BULLOCK Thomas	4° ss.	BULLOCK Thomas	8° coll.	CONYBEARE John	8° ss.
1727						
	TILLY William	4° ss.				
1728						
	DELAUNE William	8° coll.	READING Will. M.A.	8° coll.	WHARTON Henry	8° coll.
	WHARTON Henry	8° coll.	YOUNG Edward	4° ss.	COLEMAN Benjamin	8° coll.
1729						
	HUDDLESTON Will.	8° ss.	JOHNSON Sam. M.A.	8° ss.	LUPTON William	8° coll.
	MARSHALL Nathaniel	8° ss.	YOUNG Edward	8° ss.		
1730						
	BERRIMAN William	8° ss.	BRADY Nich. DD.	8° coll.	CROXALL Sam. DD.	8° ss.
	JORTIN John	12° coll.	READING Will. M.A.	8° coll.	STEBBING Henry	8° ss.
1731						
	READING Will. M.A.	8° ss.	TURNOR Thomas	8° ss.	WISHART William	8° ss.
1732						
	BERKELEY George	4° ss.	CONWAY George	8° ss.	FELTON Henry	8° coll.
	GRETTON Phillips	8° ss.	FOSTER James	8° coll.		
1733						
	ASTRY Francis	4° ss.	BERRIMAN William	4° ss.	BERRIMAN William	8° coll.
	COCKMAN Thomas	8° ss.	DAWES Sir William	8° coll.	FELTON Henry	8° ss.
	MOSS Robert	8° coll.	TENNISON Edward	4° ss.		
1735						
	EYRE Robert	8° ss.	SHARP John	8° coll.	TILLOTSON John	fo. coll.
1736						
	CLAGETT Nicholas	4° ss.	KNIGHT James	8° ss.		
1737						
	BERRIMAN William	8° ss.	MOSS Robert	8° coll.	TILLY William	-° coll.
	FOSTER James	8° coll.				
1738						
	BEDFORD Arthur	8° ss.	MOSS Robert	8° coll.	WARBURTON William	8° ss.
1739						
	BENTLEY Richard	fo. coll.	BERRIMAN William	4° ss.	BERRIMAN William	fo. coll.
	COPPING John	4° ss.	THOMAS John	4° ss.		
1740						
	BATEMAN Edmund	4° ss.	THOMAS John	4° ss.		
1741						
	BEDFORD Arthur	8° ss.	BERRIMAN John	8° coll.	SYMONDS Edward	8° ss.
1742						
	BERRIMAN William	4° ss.	DORMAN William	8° coll.	GUYSE John	8° coll.
1743						
	STACKHOUSE Thomas	fo. ss.	TRAPP Joseph	4° ss.		
1744						

INDEXES TO FIFTH VOLUME: E: LIBRARIES: PART THREE: LONDON AND ETON (Sion/St.Paul's)

Year	Name	Format	Name	Format	Name	Format
	GILBERT John	4° ss.	FOSTER James	8° coll.		
1745	BEARCROFT Philip GOUGH Strickland.	4° ss. 8° ss.	DENNE John LAVINGTON George	4° ss. 8° ss.	DUBORDIEU John	4° ss.
1746	HUTTON Matthew	4° ss.	LAVINGTON George	4° ss.		
1747	TRAPP Joseph	8° coll.				
1748	WARBURTON William	-° ss.				
1749	HEYLYN John	4° coll.				
1751	BERRIMAN William	8° coll.	GOUGH Strickland.	8° coll.	JEFFERY John	8° coll.
1754	SUTTON William	8° coll.				
1759	AGAR William	8° coll.				
1763	SHARP Tho. DD.	8° coll.				
1764	BRACKENRIDGE William	8° coll.	LAWSON John	8° coll.	ERSKINE Ralph	fo.coll.
1765	BREKELL John	8° coll.	WALKER Robert	8° coll.		
1767	ELSMERE Sloane MAYHEW Jonathan	1° coll. 8° coll.	NEWTON John	8° coll.	FORDYCE James	12° coll.
1772	DODD W. LLD.	12° coll.	ENFIELD William	12° coll.		
1774	JORTIN John	8° coll.				
1776	HALLIFAX Samuel MOIR John	8° coll. 12° coll.	HURD Richard	8° coll.	FORDYCE James	8° ss.
1777	BLAIR Hugh	8° coll.	ENFIELD William	12° coll.		
1790	TENISON Thomas	4° ss.				
St. Paul's	("St.Paul's")					
1669	GARBUTT Richard	12° ss.				
1699	GARBUTT Richard	12° ss.				
1704	MAUDUIT Isaac	8° ss.				
1706	FOWLER Edward	8° ss.				

BIBLICAL BOOKS TO WHICH REFERENCE IS MADE IN THIS EDITION OF COOKE'S WORK

Code No.	Book of Bible	Cooke's Abbrev.
01	Genesis	Gen.
02	Exodus	Exod.
03	Leviticus	Levit. or Lev.
04	Numbers	Numb. or Num.
05	Deuteronomy	Deut.
06	Joshua	Josh.
07	Judges	Judg.
08	Ruth	
09	I Samuel	1 Sam.
10	II Samuel	2 Sam.
11	I Kings	1 Kings
12	II Kings	2 Kings
13	I Chronicles	1 Chron.
14	II Chronicles	2 Chron.
15	Ezra	
16	Nehemiah	Nehem. or Neh.
17	Esther	Esth.
18	Job	
19	Psalms	Ps.
20	Proverbs	Prov.
21	Ecclesiastes	Eccles.
22	Song of Solomon or Canticles	Cantic. or Cant.
23	Isaiah	Isai.

Code No.	Book of Bible	Cooke's Abbrev.
24	Jeremiah	Jerem. or Jer.
25	Lamentations	Lament. or Lam.
26	Ezekiel	Ezek.
27	Daniel	Dan.
28	Hosea	Hos.
29	Joel	
30	Amos	
31	Jonah	Jon.
32	Micah	Mic.
33	Nahum	
34	Habakkuk	Hab.
35	Zephaniah	Zeph.
36	Haggai	Hag.
37	Zechariah	Zech. or Zach.
38	Malachi	Mal.
39	Tobit	
40	Wisdom of Solomon	Wisdom or Wisd.
41	Ecclesiasticus	Ecclusus. or Ecclus.
42	II Maccabees	2 Maccab.
43	St. Matthew	Matth. or Matt.
44	St. Mark	Mark
45	St. Luke	Luke
46	St. John	John

Code No.	Book of Bible	Cooke's Abbrev.
47	Acts	
48	Romans	Rom.
49	I Corinthians	1 Cor.
50	II Corinthians	2 Cor.
51	Galatians	Gal.
52	Ephesians	Ephes.
53	Philippians	Phil.
54	Colossians	Col.
55	I Thessalonians	1 Thess.
56	II Thessalonians	2 Thess.
57	I Timothy	1 Tim.
58	II Timothy	2 Tim.
59	Titus	Tit.
60	Philemon	
61	Hebrews	Heb.
62	James	
63	I Peter	1 Pet.
64	II Peter	2 Pet.
65	I John	1 John
66	II John	2 John
67	III John	3 John
68	Jude	
69	Revelations	Rev.
70	Bib. Text Unknown	

DATE DUE
